CALIFORNIA WITH KIDS

CAREY SIMON
and
CHARLENE MARMER SOLOMON

□

1989–1990

Published by Prentice Hall Trade Division
A Division of Simon & Schuster Inc.
Gulf + Western Building
One Gulf + Western Plaza
New York, NY 10023

ISBN 0-13-332057-X

ISSN 1040-9386

Manufactured in the United States of America

Text design: Levavi & Levavi, Inc.

*Although every effort was made to ensure the accuracy
of price information appearing in this book,
it should be kept in mind that prices
can and do fluctuate in the course of time.*

CONTENTS

MAPS

Acknowledgments

When we began this book, we never knew how much we would rely on our friends, family, and colleagues. This book has been an effort of love, and there are a few special people who traveled the roads with us, giving us encouragement all the way. My hugs and kisses go to Louise Weiss and Helen Stewart for being there for me, to Laura Siemans for making it possible for me to finish this, to Magdalena Diaz Velásquez for loving Janey so much—and to Charlene for not disowning me during the rough parts.

—C.S.

No book is written by the authors alone, but a travel book about parents and kids requires the support of lots of people. The glamour and fun of traveling around the state of California with children quickly pales when a working mother faces up to the stark realities of research and writing on the road—with children in tow. Tape recorder, transcriber, and steno pads lay side-by-side in hotel rooms with sandpails and water wings. Work must go on even when one child is carsick; plans can't be scrapped when a child sprains his toe. Such research couldn't have been accomplished without the help of some very special people. I had such people in my corner: Shirley Solomon and Melinda Marmer, two caring human beings whose insight and enthusiasm were boundless, and who always kept laughter as part of the work; Lynn Allen and Terry Paule, who always knew just the right thing to say; and finally Irving and Barbara Marmer, who taught me firsthand that traveling with kids—no matter how many and how far—is a glorious way to create treasured memories. Thank you also to Carey, who has always taught me a lot about other people, and taught me about myself.

—C.M.S.

OUR THANKS GO TO: While working on this book, we met scores of gracious people whose excitement about this project made it special. We would especially like to thank our agent, Jeanne Drewsen, for her enthusiasm and support, Marilyn Wood for believing in the project, and Judith de Rubini, whose wit and expertise made this a delightful first book experience. Special thanks go also to Judith Backover, Debra Lee Baldwin, Rosalia Escalante, Julie Getzelman, Marlene Goland, Linda Goldstein, David Groves, Marcia Morgan, Clark Norton, Sharon Odegaard, Jeff Paule, Misaray Torres, Louise Weiss, and Jody Welborn for their excellent professional help.

We won't forget the assistance and generosity of Fred Sater of the California Office of Tourism and the special help of many other people in convention and visitors bureaus around the state: Charlie Aldinger (Monterey Peninsula), Laurie De Selms (San Diego), Jonnie Eylar (San Luis Obispo County), Elaine Martin-Cali and Vicki Morris (Anaheim), John Poimiroo (Yosemite National Park), Lynda Rahbar and Lucy Steffens (Sacramento), John Reginato (Shasta-Cascade Wonderland), and Sandi Sable (Mammoth Lakes Resort).

To my traveling buddies who made the trips so much fun: Danny, whose love and patience know no bounds; and Janey, who, I hope, will someday thank me for putting her through this!

—Carey

To my family who travel with me on all my journeys: Alan, who loves me enough to go through the creative process again and again; and Andrew and Elizabeth, who know the secrets of life without even trying. You made this book a real trip!

—Charlene

Inflation Alert

It is hardly a secret that inflation continues to batter the United States as it does everywhere else. The authors of this book have spent laborious hours attempting to ensure the accuracy of prices appearing in this guide. As we go to press, we believe we have obtained the most reliable data possible. Nonetheless, in the lifetime of this edition—particularly its second year (1990)—the wise traveler will add 15% to 20% to the prices quoted throughout these pages.

INTRODUCTION

A FAMILY GUIDE TO CALIFORNIA

□ □ □

Family vacations mean different things to different people. Some parents take their children with them whenever and wherever they go. Others believe that children do well only in certain places—Grandma's cabin in the country or Disneyland. Whichever you choose, or if you're somewhere in the middle, we're here to share with you what we've learned—through experience—about traveling with children.

For the best-humored, adventurous, flexible parent, family travel is a kick. For the faint-of-heart or those who like complete predictability, we warn you— hold onto your hat! You're about to embark on a wonderful adventure.

1. CALIFORNIA WITH KIDS

A BEGINNING: How did this book start? It began when one of us, Carey Simon, took (then) 1-year-old Jane to Paris and found herself ordering pâté (it was closest to chopped liver) and consommé ("It's chicken soup, honey") off the room-service menu because she didn't know where to buy baby food at 9 p.m. It continued when the other, Charlene Solomon, wrestled with changing baby Elizabeth's dirty diapers in an airplane seat while trying to enjoy 7-year-old Andrew's exuberance about being 30,000 feet above the ground.

It crystallized when we agreed that in spite of all the apparatus we had to carry, all the advance planning required, all the early mornings in hotel rooms when we worried about whether the television cartoons were too loud for the people next door, we still loved traveling with our children—and intended to keep enjoying it as they grew.

We weren't alone.

We shared long, funny stories with friends about which child did the "best" in first-class restaurants and which toddler was carried the most on hikes. We watched frustrated parents on airline flights trying to get food to their child before the designated mealtime. We shared experiences about rude hotel desk clerks who eyed our kids as if they were fleas, and about restaurant personnel who made us feel like lepers when we arrived with young children.

That's how the book began.

We were constantly asked by new parents what they should take on weekend trips with their baby. We were asked which fine restaurants and hotels were cordial to children, and which moderately priced and inexpensive places adults would enjoy too. It became clear that there were lots of people just like us who wanted to take their kids with them to places not always considered "family" establishments. It became apparent that this book had to be written.

There is no other comprehensive travel guide like this one, which has activities, accommodations, and restaurants tested by parents and their children. That's not to say that our three little wayfarers tried everything you find in this book. But their perspectives (and those of their friends, older cousins, and acquaintances) have always been the guidelines we've followed.

For example, restaurant and hotel staffs had to be friendly to children to be included. In the cases where we feel a restaurant or hotel would be a good experience for older kids, we state that. Our descriptions of sightseeing attractions are also written with children in mind. You'll notice we don't catalog a museum's collection. Instead, we often tell you which exhibits excite the kids. We don't give a step-by-step guide to the theme parks, but we do tell you if you can buy diapers there, or if you should bring along your own apple juice.

WHY CALIFORNIA?: We chose California because it's the perfect family travel destination. It presents so many opportunities for different vacations. You can take ocean, desert, mountain, and city trips. There are scores of children's activities and all sorts of places to stay, from resorts and first-class hotels to houseboats, cabins, condos, and campgrounds.

2. HOW TO TRAVEL WITH KIDS

When you travel with your children, the whole world opens up. Everyday events become adventures—wanted and unwanted. It's a chance to share activities in a way that makes them lifelong memories. You can't duplicate the astonishment in children's eyes when they catch their first glimpse of the Golden Gate Bridge. You can't anticipate the joy they'll have playing tag with the ocean waves. And you'll never believe the excitement they feel the first time they see Disneyland.

And then there's the unexpected: for us, an evening swim with the kids in a hotel pool on a warm California night; a flight attendant who had 7-year-old Andrew help pass out candies at the end of the flight; a hike in Yosemite that brought us face-to-face with a coyote; a powerful friendship that sprouted up between two 4-year-olds in a Palm Springs resort; two 10-year-olds racing their remote-control cars in the airport lounge. Or your daughter holding her first starfish or climbing her first "mountain." And there are the delightful adult experiences—like the people you meet because their kids and your kids are playing in the hotel swimming pool together; the fellow parents who travel by air with their entourage of diapers, formula, and baby toys, with whom you commiserate while walking a fussy baby.

And of course there are the experiences that at the time you're sure will ruin your vacation, but that make you laugh later when you reminisce—like the baby who couldn't get used to the new crib and cried for the first four nights of a seven-day vacation; or the toddler who became carsick every time you got in the car to continue your trip; the hotel reservations that weren't honored, and the room-service menus that served only spinach quiche and medallions of veal.

Lifetime travelers ourselves, and now with our families, it is our hope to open the world of travel and fun to other families. Prepare to laugh and be surprised, and be sure to get out the scrapbooks because there will be lots to remember!

SOME ADVICE: The best advice we can give you is threefold: First, plan ahead. Most children want to know how long it takes to get where you're going and what they'll be doing once they arrive. With kids, it's not much fun to just arrive in town without knowing what there is to do as a family. That's not to say that you can't have spontaneity, but be sure to have some game plan in mind, even if it changes as you go along.

Second, don't expect too much from your kids. On a short holiday you can't cover every sightseeing attraction, every historical monument, and every activity with children. You'll just end up with cranky, unhappy kids and a horrible vacation. So either plan a longer trip or a second visit another time. But whatever you do, make lots of rest stops and take lots of energy breaks.

Third, and possibly most important, be sure to approach your family vacation with a grand sense of humor. It won't all be perfect, but some of it will be fabulous. In any event, you'll be spending treasured time together as a family.

PREPARATION: It may be that you used to be the kind of people who took spontaneous weekend trips, threw a bathing suit in the car and just went. Obviously you can't do that anymore. Although some spontaneity is still possible, now you have to plan ahead—where to go, when to go, what forms of transportation to use, and what to pack.

Planning Your Trip

When you conjure up visions of a perfect family vacation, what do you see? Are you enjoying the outdoors—hiking, boating, waterskiing—or are you visiting museums, art galleries, and cultural attractions? Do you want a city sightseeing vacation, or a seaside, mountain, or desert excursion? Are you planning to camp, stay in a hotel, or rent a condo or home?

Consider it all. Then take into account the age of your children, what they're capable of doing, and what they enjoy most. If you love museums but your kids can barely tolerate them, it's fruitless to plan a vacation filled with gallery-hopping. The kids will be restless and frustrated—and so will you, in the end.

Good family vacations balance everyone's likes. We like to include our kids in part of the planning. Experienced travelers advise that after you, as adults, have determined the expense and length of the vacation, you discuss with the kids the options that are available. Take them with you to get travel brochures and maps. Write the visitors' bureaus or chambers of commerce of the places you intend to visit for details of current happenings. Get a good guidebook for further source material. Everyone will get excited about some aspect of the trip.

A Few Tips

Be realistic about your expectations. Remember that when your kids are at home, they follow a routine and know what to expect. Consider how your children will react when they're taken out of that routine, and plan accordingly. Remember, too, that travel requires a lot of waiting around. The relief you may feel when you finally reach your hotel room may not be felt by a youngster who has just experienced a wait in the hotel lobby, preceded by waits at the airport, on the plane, and in the taxi. Remember that *you* can anticipate the great thrills you'll have on the special rides and attractions at theme parks—even when you're standing in a 20-minute-long line. Most children, even very sophisticated ones, have trouble with that.

Many child-development experts will tell you that brothers and sisters may bicker even more than usual when they're traveling. Of course, it depends on the kind of traveling you do, but the discomfort of an eight-hour car trip is felt by all, especially those little munchkins in the back seat who are tucked in with the extra luggage.

Also, remember that kids can get homesick for familiar surroundings. We've always been amazed how happy our children are to get home to their own rooms —even when they enjoyed their trip and continually talk fondly about the vacation. To help with that, be sure to bring favorite cuddlies, blankets, and even familiar music cassette tapes for evening relaxation and bedtime.

Toddlers seem to be the ones who have the toughest time adapting to the changes inherent in traveling. If you're on a five-hour coast-to-coast flight, your infant will often sleep through much of it, and your school-age kids and teens may occupy themselves with movies, games, books, and thoughts. Your toddler, however, is a different breed. He or she may sleep for a while, but then wake up disoriented and cranky; may love visiting with people or become shy and clingy. And in the hotel room, you never know what awaits at nap and sleep time, especially if you've made a big jump in clock time.

We always think about traveling from our toddler's point of view because she can make or break the trip. We divide up long sightseeing days with lots of activity breaks where she can run around. It's surprising how we forget that children, even those as young as kindergarten age, get absorbed in many of the joys of traveling—as we do—but a 2-, 3-, or 4-year-old just doesn't appreciate the same things. Take this into consideration.

Some people suggest that a way to help your young child prepare for a time change is to start before you leave on your trip. Slightly shift your schedule to start altering the child's internal clock.

We request that the crib be in the hotel room *before* we arrive. (By the way, most hotel cribs do not come with bumper guards—we use towels in their place.) We recommend spending some time in the room and having the little one take a nap in the new surroundings before it's time to go to sleep for the night. In fact, we spend time in the room so that all the kids get used to it. Our 7-year-old takes out his toys and arranges them, just so, in a place he wants as his play area. Yours may also.

Also, plan to go at a slower pace than you might do without kids. And always have extra snacks and juice along with you, no matter where you travel—in a car, airplane, or train. We keep a stash in the hotel room and, for emergencies, in Mom's purse.

Packing

Before we had children, packing for a trip was a simple exercise. We could pack at the last minute, take several different outfits, depending on the length of stay, and not think too much beyond packing a warm enough sweater, several books, and a hairdryer. Sometimes, of course, we'd end up buying something on the trip because we forgot that important item. But it was all fairly painless.

Packing when you travel with kids is an entirely different matter—that is, if you want to stay sane. First of all, you can forget the magazines and novels for yourselves (unless you have children who are older or remarkably self-sufficient), and your own wardrobe becomes considerably less important than it ever was. (But remember that teething infants can soil almost as many of your shirts as their own.)

Sure, you can wait until the last minute and throw things into several suitcases, but you'll pay for it over and over again. And remember, too, that the younger the child, the greater the need for a plan.

We know now that when we travel with our kids, packing is an experiment in wizardry. How do you pack the contents of half a home into a tiny suitcase? We allow each child one suitcase for clothes and a backpack for toys and books. No matter how we limit the number of things each child can take, there's always the extra stuffed animal and favorite game that has to be included at the last minute.

Before we pack, we first decide whether we're going to use coin-operated laundries or hotel cleaning services, or whether we're going to bring all the soiled laundry home. Once this is decided, we still try to take as little as we think we can get away with, and then think about it again to see if we can cut back. Naturally, this requires advance planning, actually laying out clothes a few days ahead and writing things down. Depending on the vacation—time of year and length—we start thinking about the kids' clothes at least a week or two in advance. We make a list for each child, including the type of clothing and the amount we'll need.

Need we tell you that kids get dirty, wet, and messy? We've learned that we need an extra outfit per day for most children over the age of 3 (excluding teens, of course). For children under 3, we pack at least three outfits, or plan ahead which ones can be hand-washed and used again. The key is to plan on the children needing many changes of clothing.

We also pack a set of clothes that we keep in a carry-on bag for the plane or a car bag, in case we can't get to the suitcases right away (or in case the luggage gets lost). If you're going to a different climate, don't forget to put that coat or sundress where you can get to it easily.

Consider in advance how many diapers you'll need before you have to get to a market again, and what kind of toys you'll want with you, and which cassette tapes to bring.

And don't forget to write down the names of the medications your kids will need. This is a good time to check on the quantity of such items as prescription cough medicine, Tylenol, and other potential middle-of-the-night necessities. Be sure to pack a thermometer, and if you have a tot in diapers, pack lots of baby wipes and diaper-rash medications. We always include towelettes for all our kids.

For younger children, it doesn't hurt to bring flexible straws and a small plastic cup also. We found too often that glasses in restaurants were too tall and cups on airlines too fat, or that only bottled drinks were available. We also bring a cheap nightlight to ease little ones' fears at night. If you have curious toddlers, you'll find outlet covers handy to bring along too. And we pack a box of plastic bags, which come in handy for loose toys, wet bathing suits, horribly soiled clothes, and crackers from demolished boxes (the new stain-remover sticks are invaluable for those of you who have elected to take soiled clothes back home).

Toys

People have different opinions about the number of toys you should take on a trip. We bring some new toys and some old favorites. The kids each get his or her own backpack (or small toy box in the back seat of the car) in which they pack the toys and books they especially want. We stash new playthings in our suitcase or bag and dole them out when the kids tire of what they've brought. When the trip is a long one, we actually wrap the new toys and distribute them to the kids at key moments—timed to hold their interest. We'll alternate creative-type toys, such as crayons, with toys and games that require some concentration and thinking. We always include items that we enjoy playing with too, since we'll be doing lots of that. Most toy stores have a large variety of travel games and toys.

Once your child is old enough to enjoy cassette tape stories and songs, you've found a real treasure. These kept Andrew occupied for hours at a time, long enough so that he endured very long car trips as well as his parents did.

When you're traveling, be sure to leave the messy, noisy toys and projects at home. Puzzles and games with little pieces can also give you grief. Our least-favorite words on a cross-country flight were, "Oh, I dropped some again!" Picture yourself picking up little game pieces in a crowded, baggage-filled row of airline seats. There are better ways to have fun and meet your neighbors.

Here are some ideas of what to take along: packages of stickers and sticker books, magnetic drawing boards and alphabet boards, magnetic games, hand puppets, write-and-wipe boards, Colorforms™, crayons that don't melt, coloring books, tracing paper and things to trace, self-inking stamps and paper. For older kids, you might want to bring small cars, decks of cards, and a journal or a cassette recorder in which they can describe their experiences. (Check the earphones before you purchase the recorder. After surprising 4-year-old Jane with one on the plane, we spent the next hour trying to make them fit her small head.) We often put together a craft box with lots of goodies that the kids can use to create artistic treasures. Try it! If your child will need scissors, purchase safety scissors at a specialty shop. On car trips, you can bring song books and music cassettes. (If you're renting a car, check ahead as to whether there's a tape deck.)

For tips on removing crayon, marker, and glue spots, you can get a booklet from **Binney & Smith,** Consumer Affairs, Department P., P.O. Box 431, Easton, PA 18044. Send a self-addressed, stamped no. 10 envelope.

Precautions

When visiting crowded sightseeing attractions, dress kids in bright clothing so it's easy for you to keep an eye on them, but also decide what your children should do if you should get separated while sightseeing—and talk with them about it.

Every time you check into a new hotel room, it's a good idea to consider what you would do if there is a fire. Where are the exits? Which adult is responsible for which child or children?

In medical matters, be prepared. Be sure to pack all the medications your children may need, and take along your doctors' phone numbers. (Call your personal physician if you have a serious problem—even if it's long distance.) If you're flying, be sure that any signs of congestion or a cold are seen by your doctor. He or she can tell you what to do to prevent inner-ear injury. You might also ask about nasal sprays and oral decongestants for your kids for takeoff and landing.

Be prepared for motion sickness. Kids who never get motion sickness in a car can get it on a boat, in a stuffy airplane, or on a train. Those of you who have tried to get a pill down the throat of an uncooperative child will appreciate the joys of liquid Dramamine, which you can give to kids over 2 (we mixed it with soda before getting on the boat from Catalina). Ask your pediatrician about other remedies.

You'll want a first-aid kit. The Red Cross Kit has all you'll need in an emergency; it is only 10 by 12 inches and weighs under two pounds. Write to **American Red Cross Auto First Aid Kit,** Box D, Haworth, NJ 07641.

And on a less threatening note, we always have all reservation confirmations sent to us in writing. Whenever possible, it's best to have something written down—and with you—to show in the event of a problem.

If you are planning to register your kids for some of the children's programs at the hotels we talk about, or in the day-care or ski schools we list, be sure to find out whether you need to make your reservations for those things in advance. Policies change, and you don't want to make big vacation plans which include children's programs only to get there and find out your kids can't get in.

AIR TRAVEL: Flying is always an adventure. Too bad you can't predict if it's going to be a good one or a bad one.

The kids, especially young ones who need to be confined to a small area, get very antsy. You don't have the control you do in a car where you can stop when you want to let the kids run around. And some young children may become frightened.

To ward off negative experiences, we talk with our young children before the trip about what will happen. If your children are flying for the first time, some people think it helps if you take them to an airport to look at the planes before your trip. Bringing a favorite blanket or stuffed animal will help a lot too.

Once on board, remember that cabin temperature can vary. Bring extra clothes for each child (always a change of clothes) and make sure that what they wear is layered, loose, and comfortable.

Waiting in airports can be the torment of many a parent. Although we try to time our arrival so we won't be too early but won't have to run for the plane, it's impossible to predict when a plane will leave late. In the event of a delayed departure, we take our children for walks, try to find video arcades, and look for other kids their age in the waiting area for them to play with. When all else fails, we attempt to find a corner area where we can spread out and play on the floor (ugh!).

Warning: Whatever you do, don't leave the terminal. We were once assured by airline officials that we had a three-hour delay, so we took a long walk. When we returned (an hour ahead of time), the plane had already departed. The airline officials said they had paged and paged, but all passengers who didn't return to the flight had to rebook.

Some airline personnel suggest that you bring along your young child's car seat. It helps to protect the youngster, and in some cases it's useful for keeping the child where you want him or her. Your child may be more likely to sit for a longer period of time in a familiar car seat than in a large seat with a lap belt. For a seat that will really help restrain your infant in an accident, look on the back of the seat for this statement: "This child-restraint system conforms to all applicable federal motor vehicle safety conditions." If the seat has been manufactured after 1985, the note will add: "This is certified for aircraft."

Rexanne Forbes, manager of airport service for Alaska Airlines, suggests that if your child is a lap child (kids under 2 years old), the airline will let you use the car seat if there are empty seats on the flight. For those of you who've never flown with your children before, you might be interested to know that if yours is a lap child, you should never belt the child in with you. Belt yourself in, then hold the child in your lap in a chest-to-chest position. If rocking the child in your arms, cradle him. This position should be used on takeoff and landing.

Although kids need to move around, don't let them crawl around on the floors or in aisles where they could get their fingers pinched or stepped on. Don't let them loose, especially in galleys where there are hot liquids and all kinds of things that are dangerous in little hands.

Request special seating if necessary. Seats facing the bulkhead, with no seat in front, can be comfortable, but because of the fold-in trays, they don't have retractable armrests. Parents should know that kids can't sit in Exit rows, so it's important to tell the reservationist when you book seats that you are bringing children so they don't inadvertently put you there. Some airlines have cardboard infant beds with tiny pads that you can put at your feet if you're in the bulkhead seats. Ask in advance.

There's nothing worse than trying to change a baby in an airplane rest room. Some international carriers have pull-down diaper-changing tables; most domestic airlines don't. (In the past, we've taken the airline blanket and a plastic changing pad into the bathroom and spread the blanket on the toilet seat and put the pad on top.) Some flight attendants will offer to let you use the jump seat—ask. If there's an area not occupied, you can go there. In the cabin, you can fold up the armrest and use the seats, but some nonparents are offended and complain. Remember to be discreet and considerate. Take the diaper and dispose of it in the rest room in an in-flight sick bag or plastic bag.

If babies are on bottles, most airlines do warm bottles and baby food—ask when booking flights—and all airlines carry milk and a selection of juices. Alaska Airlines even carries emergency diapers.

Most airlines serve special kids' meals upon request—usually hamburgers or hot dogs, and sometimes spaghetti. But believe us, you don't want to order spaghetti for your young child on an airplane! Place your meal requests with the reservationist at least 24 hours in advance.

Another helpful hint is to carry on a small umbrella stroller that will fit in an overhead bin. This is good for layovers or delays, and is especially helpful for a parent who is carrying many things and is traveling alone with a child.

And always, always bring along snacks and beverages in a carry-on bag. The kids may not always be able to wait for the scheduled meals and you don't even know if they will actually eat the airline food. (Goodness knows, many adults don't.) We pack a full goodie bag, complete with fresh fruit, bread, raisins, crackers and cheese, pretzels, and lots of individual boxes of juice. Kids get very thirsty on flights. In that goodie bag, we also include several flexible straws (and for little ones, drinking cups with lids).

Finally, airlines will allow you to board in advance with children. This is wonderful if you're carrying on tons of things and/or have more than one child to settle. If you feel your kid needs to expend that last bit of energy, try talking the flight attendant into letting one adult get on board with all the paraphernalia and the other one stay with the child until the last minutes of boarding.

As we mentioned in the "Precautions" section, call your physician if your child has the slightest cold, as there can be long-term damage to ears because of changes in cabin pressurization. You might also want to find out about nose drops for kids who don't have cold symptoms. Swallowing is what helps to equalize the pressure in one's head, so small children should always have something to drink or suck on during ascent or descent—a bottle or pacifier—and older kids can chew gum or suck on a hard candy.

If you need other suggestions, you might want to contact special services desk of **Alaska Airlines** (tel. toll free 800/426-0333) to ask for the brochure "Tips for Young Travelers."

CAR TRAVEL : Traveling in a car with children is unlike any other experience. It's one that cannot be adequately described. You have to experience it to understand it. Remember that you'll all be enclosed in a very small space for an extended period of time. Good humor, lots to do—and eat and drink—are the order of the day.

The main rule is plan to stop every few hours to break up the monotony and allow the kids time to get out and move around. Your stops don't always have to be at restaurants to eat. You can stop when you see a lovely park or where you know there's a special attraction.

Seating arrangements in the car are important too. One parent might get into the back seat along with the kids to ward off trouble. This helps especially if one child is having a hard time, or if your kids tend to bicker or get rowdy when you're on the road. It's better than constantly having to turn around and lean over the front seat, getting nauseous as you look backward. It also protects you from running the risk of being ticketed for not wearing a seatbelt (a law in California).

Also, be sure to bring along an adequate supply of pacifiers, bottles, and snacks. If you want kids to fall asleep, sometimes stroking their heads, along with soft music and the motion of the car, will do the trick. If you're in the back seat with them, it helps if you prevent their heads from flopping around. Prop little kids' heads up with pillows in the car seat. Pack enough pillows and blankets for everyone.

To deal with "When will we get there?" we get a roadmap and a yellow marking pen before we leave on the trip and plot out the route, circling different points of interest or particular milestones. When we pass those points (or a few minutes before we approach them), we talk about them. This not only gives children a sense of accomplishing the miles, but also tends to make them take a more active interest in the landmarks of the trip. Of course, this takes a little preparation on your part. But the game plan can be as simple as calculating where you'll stop for gas and roadside stretches and letting the kids know these details.

When driving during the day, anticipate where the sun will be. If you can't keep the kids out of the sun, use a visor. Children really get uncomfortable with sun in their eyes, and they may complain unmercifully if they're hot and sweaty. Driving through the California desert can be a grueling experience. Without our knowing it until later, one of our children actually got sunburnt from it. You can get a dark cellophane-like material that sticks to the window and can be moved around depending where the sun is.

To combat motion sickness, experts suggest eating lemon drops, lemon cookies, or peppermint; also foods high in carbohydrates, and salt-covered foods such as crackers or pretzels, which cut down the production of what causes nausea. Again, ask your pediatrician for advice. Also, remember not to allow kids to read while the car is in motion.

Now for the problem of preventing boredom. Some of the games we play are especially well suited for automobile travel. For kids over 6, try the geography game, where one person chooses a place (country, city, region, etc.) and the next person has to name a place whose first letter begins with the last letter of the previous place name.

Another fun way to pass the time is to make up a game using the license plates of passing vehicles. Young kids can look for the letters of the alphabet in sequence. Older children can try to spell words or find cars from every state in the union. Very little children can name the colors of passing cars or look for particular colors.

And an all-time favorite is a group sing.

RENTAL CARS: One of your first decisions will be whether or not you need to rent a car. If you are renting, be sure the agency has car seats for children 4 years old and younger (it's required by law in California). Be sure to specify that you need one—and reserve it.

Often you'll get better rates from smaller companies. Check around and ask about discounts. If you're in a large city, you might consider renting from a company that is located near your hotel, since some rates are higher if you rent at airports. Always ask about discounts.

If you're used to the ease of getting kids in and out of a four-door car at home, be sure to request such a model. And if you're accustomed to electric windows so you're not always reaching back to open the window for your toddler (usually they demand it when you're on the freeway!), ask for a car with that feature. Air conditioning, too, is important during the summer in California. All this sounds elementary, but if you've ever arrived in a town ready to use a rental car for a week only to find you hadn't requested the conveniences you—and the kids—are used to, you'll realize how important it is to ask for these things in advance.

TRAINS AND BOATS: Traveling on trains and boats requires different considerations and arrangements.

Trains

Train travel, although not the luxurious form of transportation it used to be, is still one way to see the scenery without having to constantly stop for gas, or find a restaurant or hotel. Kids can move around, play easier than in a car, and often learn a lot about this mode of transportation.

For overnight travelers, **Amtrak** (tel. toll free 800/USA-RAIL) offers family bedrooms on some of its trains. You'll have to check your individual route for information on what accommodations are available.

Short trips, such as those from Los Angeles to San Diego or Santa Barbara, can be fun experiences for children, and the journey itself can be the adventure rather than the destination. You can take a morning train from L.A. to San Diego, for instance, take a trolley to the Embarcadero, have lunch, and then return that evening.

Boats

There are boats—and then there are ships. Cruising with kids has become big business, and many cruise lines are getting in on the act. Most family cruises offer children's programs (often all-day activities), babysitting, children's meals, and family-style accommodations. Many lines offer these cruises during summer or holidays. Some have programs year round. Check with individual cruise lines, depending on where you plan to embark.

Boating, especially in California, is a very common activity. As a visitor, you'll more than likely take a harbor cruise of some sort, or a whale-watching or fishing trip. Note the time of year and water conditions if you have a child prone to motion sickness. Even in California you can get cold on the high seas, so wear layers of clothing. Rubber-soled shoes will help you—and the children—keep your balance. Short trips are best with young children. If you're going on a longer journey, check whether the boat has food and rest-room facilities. You might even ask if one of the boats has stabilizers for a smoother ride. (To get to Catalina, for instance, you have a choice of one line with and one without stabilizers.)

PREPARING CHILDREN FOR THE OUTDOORS: You may have exceptional children, but ours need to be prepared in advance to enjoy outdoor vacationing. Many city kids do. They need to be told how much fun they're going to have without video games nearby. In fact, the first time 7-year-old Andrew entered a forest, he noticed there were no TV antennas and was convinced his vacation was ruined.

While parents who have hiked with their youngsters at an early age probably won't have this problem, most kids need a little advance help from you so they can really enjoy what's in store for them. The first, and most important, way to help your kids love the outdoors is to let them feel your excitement and enjoyment. Even the most jaded, citified child looks in wonder when parents convey their awe at towering peaks or their pleasure at walking on soft pine needles in a dense forest.

We start talking to our group early about the animals we might see, the wildlife in the forest, the environment, and the weather. We use books about the area and about wildlife in general to illustrate some of the wonders we might encounter. Kids relate easily to animals—from Bambi to butterflies—so use that awareness as a bridge to help them become sensitive to the wooded, wild environment. Let little children know that they'll be seeing some big things and hearing some loud noises—huge trees, surging waterfalls, mammoth mountains and cliffs. A case in point: when 3-year-old Janey got her first look at the colossal Redwood trees, she was so terrified of "the giants" we had to cut the trip short. We hadn't prepared her for what she was about to see, never dreaming that the size of those trees could be overwhelming to a little person.

We also find it helpful to mention before we leave home that television won't be an important part of the vacation (of course, unless that isn't true). We encourage the kids to take board games, books, and coloring books and crayons to keep them occupied on quiet evenings.

You know your children and what sparks their imaginations. Maybe it's the idea of collecting autumn leaves for a school project or anticipating how many different kinds of animals they'll encounter. You might want to play a game with them, like trying to find camouflaged insects and other creatures. If you're planning special activities, such as horseback riding or bicycling, talk about them. Share your natural enthusiasm. Some children just need a little encouragement when Disneyland isn't the destination.

Remember two more important things about the mountain areas. First, there's lots of dust and pollen and "interesting" blooming foliage around. Be sure to bring medication for children who suffer from such allergies. Second, the altitude is higher. Be conscious of changes in children's behavior because of possible reactions to the change in altitude. Ask your pediatrician for advice.

Cautions

Park rangers are the "wise men" of the national park system. They are fully aware of the dangers for kids within these pristine areas, and they've shared their wisdom with us. Their suggestions are as follows:

SCRAMBLING. Kids are natural scramblers. They love to scurry up one rock and scramble to the next one above it. Scrambling can be dangerous, say the rangers, and parents must be responsible for where their kids scramble. Teach them about safe climbing. Only let your kids scramble if the area is completely safe—no perched rock, no slick or wet areas on which they can slip and fall.

WILDLIFE. Don't attempt to feed the wild animals. Wild animals that become too tame because of feeding by humans are in grave danger during the winter months when there's no one to feed them and they no longer know how to forage for food. Heed all bear warnings, and follow advice about where to store food.

Remember that wild animals are just that—wild. Deer can be more dangerous to little children than bears. Parents, who would never dream of putting their child within reach of a bear, have been known to put their toddlers too close to the "cute" little fawn to grab a great photo, only to have an angry male deer (antlers and all) charge the child.

SWIMMING AND WATER ACTIVITIES. Rivers and lakes are especially enticing. We'll make suggestions as we go along for good watering holes, but in general, avoid wading into water that is rushing and swirling. Generally the spring and early summer pose the greatest threat because melting snow swells rivers and streams, creating unsafe places to play. If signs aren't posted for swimming (and they usually aren't), ask a passing ranger or stop at a visitors center to inquire about the conditions. Most important, *avoid rocks that are near misty, foggy, and wet areas.* Don't rely on your visual senses to determine if they are safe or not. Rocks near the water have been made slick by years of water agitation that has smoothed them down. A beckoning large rock that is too close to a waterfall or is receiving mist from fast-running water is a treacherous place to be—for you or your kids —and can turn into disaster. Always avoid ledges near waterfalls, no matter how enticing and safe they look.

Speaking about water, it's probably safest not to drink water unless you know that it's pure. Unfortunately, the wilderness is not always blessed with clean water, so be sure to ask a park ranger about which places have pure water before letting the kids drink from streams and little pools.

HIKING. Remind your kids to stay on trails, to stay with the group, and to be careful when they pick up rocks. It's best for them to move a big rock with their feet first to be sure it isn't protecting a snake's home. Also, caution young children not to put their hands down holes in the ground. Try to find out if there is poison oak or poison ivy in the area, and show your children what it looks like. Finally, always stay *close* to your toddler or preschooler on the trail.

CLOTHING. Typically, mountain areas have a range of climates and temperatures because of the terrain. During the summer it can reach the mid-90s, and during the winter it can fall below 30°. It varies throughout Yosemite, for instance, because the elevation ranges from 2,000 to over 12,000 feet. During the summer months, thunderstorms occur with great frequency.

As a general rule, the best way to pack for the mountains and the rugged northern California coast is to bring layers of clothing. The air trapped between the layers acts as an insulator. A lot of people bring just one heavy jacket and a sweater. You can't do much with this gear—you either have it on or off. It's much wiser to wear several light layers, so you can remove clothes layer by layer and still not have too much to carry. Many people have found that jogging gear is good hiking gear.

During the summer, wear shorts and a light shirt with a jogging outfit on top of that, and carry a rain jacket that you can roll up and keep in your daypack. That's usually more than adequate for summer hiking, even if a sudden storm hits. You also might want a hat or sun visor.

In fall and winter, add a heavier jacket, a turtleneck, a sweater, and a water-repellent parka. It is critical to wear a hat because you lose a lot of heat through an exposed head.

Small children might insist on taking their favorite backpack. If you want to let them, have them practice carrying it *packed* before you leave home. Be sure they can handle it all the way, or guess who'll end up carrying the extra gear!

CAMPING. Avid adult campers agree that you can take children of almost any age camping. Infants certainly aren't a problem. If there's any questionable age group, it's the toddlers, because this group is more apt to walk away from a campsite or stick their hands in a bright, inviting campfire. If there's a perfect age, it's over 5. This seems to be the time children are more willing to help at camp chores and are genuinely curious about what they are seeing and doing. Remember, no matter what the age, always keep an eye on your child. If she's old enough, have her wear a whistle every day and establish a code so you'll know it's her. If there is a problem—she's hurt, lost, or confused—the whistle will help you find her.

Any camping-equipment store will have lists of items you should take. Add to it a potty chair to put outside your tent—even for older kids—so you don't have to forage in the woods in the middle of the night. If there's room in the car, bring along a playpen or corral for crawlers and even toddlers. Then you can relax at your campsite without always having to run after them.

Don't take lots of toys. *Do* take lots of clothes. Don't make this the trip you attempt to cook food the kids have never eaten before. Do think about making your first trip a short one if you're not an experienced camper, and consider renting camping equipment rather than buying it. Be sure to take a first-aid kit that includes any necessary medications (like children's Tylenol), insect repellent, sunscreen, and a snakebite kit. Include lots of diapers, and take books and indoor games, in case you're rained in.

If you're unsure of how you'll feel about sleeping in a tent, try renting a camper the first time. No matter what you decide—tent or vehicle—be sure to make reservations if you're traveling during prime season or on holiday weekends. Ask whether the campground is next to a river (if you have curious toddlers), in a hilly area (how perfect for them to get hurt rolling down hills!), and for the less rugged among you, ask whether there are showers—and of course, flush toilets.

For reservations within the California State Park System, you can call the **Department of Parks and Recreation** (tel. toll free 800/444-PARK). Or write **Mistix** for a family camping reservation application: P.O. Box 85705, San Diego, CA 92138.

HOUSEBOATING: Houseboating is like a rich man's form of camping.

Where else can you sit on the prow of a boat watching exquisite scenery, while you have (if you want) a microwave, television, video-cassette player, barbecue, and all the comforts of home while you are outdoors? (Remember, though, that they don't have phones.)

Houseboating gives you the opportunity to fall asleep with the water lapping against your boat. Even when a lake is crowded you can find a secluded spot where you don't hear anyone else's noise. Often, you can pull up and dock somewhere and hike in beautiful countryside. The kids can run around and collect shells, or they can fish, climb rocks, swim, snorkel, or laze on a raft.

Think of it as camping out in terms of what you are going to carry on. While your accommodations can be very luxurious and your food can be of any variety (you can even cook gourmet meals), remember that you will be using lake water to shower and your fresh water will be somewhat limited, although you can always restock.

Keep in mind that you will not need a lot of different kinds of clothes on your houseboat. However, bring lots of sunscreen, zories, and extra pairs of beat-up tennis shoes.

When you consider houseboating, check ahead for what you'll need to bring. You will usually need your own linens, but that varies. (We roll them up into the sleeping bags so they don't take any additional space in our luggage.)

Depending on the operation, checking into a houseboat can require a lot of patience. There may be ten people coming in at around the same time, and they all have to be taken to their boat and shown how to use it, which is called giving a "shakedown." The boat is checked out, similar to a rental car, so that if something is not working or is damaged when you are shown the boat, you will not be responsible for it upon your return.

While we've been lucky with a check-in that only took an hour, others have taken as long as six hours to check in. Delays can be caused by arriving before you are scheduled, having many people arrive at the same time, or because others are checking out simultaneously.

The size of the operation can determine the ease of checking in. The larger ones have amenities that make it easier. For example, you pull your car up to a parking lot, just as you would in a hotel, check in, wait in line as you would in a hotel if there were several people in front of you. Soon they will tell you which boat is yours. Then you take your car down a ramp—depending on how low the lake is will determine how far you need to go. Ask about the procedure before you rent the boat so you know what you're getting into.

BED-AND-BREAKFASTS WITH KIDS: B&Bs are unique places to stay on a vacation. Some are cozy and make you feel as if you're truly staying in someone's home. Some have historical significance or are architecturally interesting. Some are decorated whimsically; some are stuffed to the rafters with antiques and collectibles.

No matter what their décor, B&Bs are usually smaller than hotels, with paper-thin walls. They are geared to people who want to meet other people on an informal basis, such as over breakfast or an evening glass of sherry, and for those who don't want the impersonal feeling of a hotel.

If you have a child who sits politely through breakfast, is not prone to tantrums, and is willing to live without TV in the room (in most cases), then a bed-and-breakfast establishment will be a fun place to stay. We don't recommend these places for families with infants or very young children. And in fact, many B&Bs won't accept children under a certain age.

Some parents are immune to the noise their kids make. A 3-year-old throwing a temper tantrum in the lobby of any hotel is going to be difficult for everyone to deal with. But in a bed-and-breakfast establishment, it's impossible. When you're sitting at the same table with a number of strangers and your child becomes difficult, you'll feel very uncomfortable. Bring only children who respect the privacy of others.

RENTING CONDOS AND CABINS: When you book a hotel room, you

usually don't have much choice about your room configuration. When renting a condo (or even a cabin), you often do, and this becomes an important item when you're staying for at least a week.

When you're planning to rent such an accommodation with kids, it's especially important to ask in advance about certain things. Is the unit one or two stories? (We once inadvertently rented a two-story condo when Janey was crawling. Without a safety gate, we were in constant fear that she'd fall down the steps.) What comes with the unit? Be sure to ask if the unit has linens, towels, dishes, a toaster, pots, silverware, and a coffee pot. Does it open up right to a pool or to mountains, streams, or the street? Can you get cribs and a highchair? Are there twin beds, bunk beds, etc.? How many bathrooms are there? (This becomes important if you're sharing the condo with another family.) Is there a working TV? Can you get a VCR? Is there daily maid service, or is it up to you to make your beds and wash the dishes every day?

Can you park close to your unit? (Who wants to carry gobs of stuff—and the baby—a distance to the car for every day's outing.) Are there places outdoors for the kids to play? (Unless you ask, you never know whether your condo faces a freeway and opens up to concrete, or whether there are great play areas.) Are there markets nearby? Is there a phone in the unit, and if not, can installation be arranged? (You don't want to be without a phone in the event of an emergency.)

If you're staying in a winter resort, how far are you from the slopes? (Stay toward the bottom of the mountain, not the top—it will be easier to get to the lifts, and you won't have to face slick winter roads uphill with a car full of kids.) Is there a covered garage? Is wood provided for the fireplace?

And finally, try to use a rental service with a lenient cancellation policy. Sometimes you can find a service that will allow you to cancel as late as 48 hours in advance. Unlike a hotel, you are giving a substantial deposit for a condo (it could be $500 to $1,000 for a week's rental). There's nothing worse than having your kids come down with the flu right before you are due to leave and be faced with losing that deposit.

3. THE DOLLARWISE TRAVEL CLUB—HOW TO SAVE MONEY ON ALL YOUR TRAVELS

In this book we'll be looking at how to get your money's worth traveling with kids in California, but there is a "device" for saving money and determining value on *all* your trips. It's the popular, international Frommer's Dollarwise Travel Club, now in its 28th successful year of operation. The club was formed at the urging of numerous readers of the Frommer Guides, who felt that such an organization could provide continuing travel information and a sense of community to value-minded travelers in all parts of the world. And so it does!

In keeping with the budget concept, the annual membership fee is low and is immediately exceeded by the value of your benefits. Upon receipt of $18 (U.S. residents), or $20 U.S. by check drawn on a U.S. bank or via international postal money order in U.S. funds (Canadian, Mexican, and other foreign residents) to cover one year's membership, we will send all new members the following items.

(1) Any *two* of the following books

Please designate in your letter which two you wish to receive:

Frommer™ $-A-Day® Guides
    Europe on $40 a Day
    Australia on $30 a Day
    Eastern Europe on $25 a Day
    England on $40 a Day

Greece on $30 a Day
Hawaii on $50 a Day
India on $25 a Day
Ireland on $35 a Day
Israel on $30 & $35 a Day
Mexico (plus Belize and Guatemala) on $25 a Day
New York on $50 a Day
New Zealand on $40 a Day
Scandinavia on $60 a Day
Scotland and Wales on $40 a Day
South America on $35 a Day
Spain and Morocco (plus the Canary Is.) on $40 a Day
Turkey on $30 a Day
Washington, D.C., & Historic Virginia on $40 a Day

($-A-Day Guides document hundreds of budget accommodations and facilities, helping you get the most for your travel dollars.)

Frommer Guides

Australia
Austria and Hungary
Belgium, Holland, & Luxembourg
Bermuda and The Bahamas
Brazil
Canada
Caribbean
Egypt
England and Scotland
France
Germany
Italy
Japan and Hong Kong
Portugal, Madeira, and the Azores
South Pacific
Switzerland and Liechtenstein
Alaska
California and Las Vegas
Florida
Mid-Atlantic States
New England
New York State
Northwest
Skiing USA—East
Skiing USA—West
Southeast and New Orleans
Southeast Asia
Southwest
Texas
USA

(Frommer Guides discuss accommodations and facilities in all price ranges, with emphasis on the medium-priced.)

Frommer™ Touring Guides

Australia
Egypt
Florence

London
Paris
Scotland
Thailand
Venice

(These new, color illustrated guides include walking tours, cultural and historic sites, and other vital travel information.)

Gault Millau
Chicago
France
Italy
London
Los Angeles
New England
New York
San Francisco
Washington, D.C.

(Irreverent, savvy, and comprehensive, each of these renowned guides candidly reviews over 1,000 restaurants, hotels, shops, nightspots, museums, and sights.)

Serious Shopper's Guides
Italy
London
Los Angeles
Paris

(Practical and comprehensive, each of these handsomely illustrated guides lists hundreds of stores, selling everything from antiques to wine, conveniently organized alphabetically by category.)

A Shopper's Guide to the Caribbean
(Two experienced Caribbean hands guide you through this shopper's paradise, offering witty insights and helpful tips on the wares and emporia of more than 25 islands.)

Beat the High Cost of Travel
(This practical guide details how to save money on absolutely all travel items—accommodations, transportation, dining, sightseeing, shopping, taxes, and more. Includes special budget information for seniors, students, singles, and families.)

Bed & Breakfast—North America
(This guide contains a directory of over 150 organizations that offer bed & breakfast referrals and reservations throughout North America. The scenic attractions, and major schools and universities near the homes of each are also listed.)

California with Kids
(A must for parents traveling in California, providing key information on selecting the best accommodations, restaurants, and sightseeing attractions for the particular needs of the family, whether the kids are toddlers, school-age, preteens, or teens.)

Dollarwise Cruises
(This complete guide covers all the basics of cruising—ports of call, costs, fly-

cruise package bargains, cabin selection booking, embarkation and debarkation and describes in detail over 60 or so ships cruising the waters of Alaska, the Caribbean, Mexico, Hawaii, Panama, Canada, and the United States.)

Dollarwise Skiing Europe
(Describes top ski resorts in Austria, France, Italy, and Switzerland. Illustrated with maps of each resort area. Includes supplement on Argentinian resorts.)

Frommer's Belgium
(Arthur Frommer unlocks the treasures of a country overlooked by most travelers to Europe. Discover the medieval charm, modern sophistication, and natural beauty of this quintessentially European country.)

Guide to Honeymoon Destinations
(A special guide for that most romantic trip of your life, with full details on planning and choosing the destination that will be just right in the U.S. [California, New England, Hawaii, Florida, New York, South Carolina, etc.], Canada, Mexico, and the Caribbean.)

Marilyn Wood's Wonderful Weekends
(This very selective guide covers the best mini-vacation destinations within a 200-mile radius of New York City. It describes special country inns and other accommodations, restaurants, picnic spots, sights, and activities—all the information needed for a two- or three-day stay.)

Manhattan's Outdoor Sculpture
(A total guide, fully illustrated with black-and-white photos, to more than 300 sculptures and monuments that grace Manhattan's plazas, parks, and other public spaces.)

Motorist's Phrase Book
(A practical phrase book in French, German, and Spanish designed specifically for the English-speaking motorist touring abroad.)

Paris Rendez-Vous
(An amusing and *au courant guide* to the best meeting places in Paris, organized for hour-to-hour use: from power breakfasts and fun brunches, through tea at four or cocktails at five, to romantic dinners and dancing 'til dawn.)

Swap and Go—Home Exchanging Made Easy
(Two veteran home exchangers explain in detail all the money-saving benefits of a home exchange, and then describe precisely how to do it. Also includes information on home rentals and many tips on low-cost travel.)

The Candy Apple: New York for Kids
(A spirited guide to the wonders of the Big Apple by a savvy New York grandmother with a kid's-eye view to fun. Indispensable for visitors and residents alike.)

The New World of Travel
(From America's #1 travel expert, Arthur Frommer, an annual sourcebook with the hottest news and latest trends that's guaranteed to change the way you travel—and save you hundreds of dollars. Jam-packed with alternative new modes of travel that will lead you to vacations that cater to the mind, the spirit, and a sense of thrift.)

Travel Diary and Record Book
(A 96-page diary for personal travel notes plus a section for such vital data as passport and traveler's check numbers, itinerary, postcard list, special people and places to visit, and a reference section with temperature and conversion charts, and world maps with distance zones.)

Where to Stay USA
(By the Council on International Educational Exchange, this extraordinary guide is the first to list accommodations in all 50 states that cost anywhere from $3 to $30 per night.)

(2) Any *one* of the Frommer™ City Guides

Amsterdam
Athens
Atlantic City and Cape May
Boston
Cancún, Cozumel, and the Yucatán
Chicago
Dublin and Ireland
Hawaii
Las Vegas
Lisbon, Madrid, and Costa del Sol
London
Los Angeles
Mexico City and Acapulco
Minneapolis and St. Paul
Montréal and Québec City
New Orleans
New York
Orlando, Disney World, and EPCOT
Paris
Philadelphia
Rio
Rome
San Francisco
Santa Fe and Taos
Sydney
Washington, D.C.

(Pocket-size guides to hotels, restaurants, nightspots, and sightseeing attractions covering all price ranges.)

(3) A one-year subscription to *The Dollarwise® Traveler*

This quarterly eight-page tabloid newspaper keeps you up to date on fastbreaking developments in low-cost travel in all parts of the world bringing you the latest money-saving information—the kind of information you'd have to pay $35 a year to obtain elsewhere. This consumer-conscious publication also features columns of special interest to readers: **Hospitality Exchange** (members all over the world who are willing to provide hospitality to other members as they pass through their home cities); **Share-a-Trip** (offers and requests from members for travel companions who can share costs and help avoid the burdensome single supplement); and **Readers Ask . . . Readers Reply** (travel questions from members to which other members reply with authentic firsthand information).

(4) Your personal membership card

Membership entitles you to purchase through the club all Frommer publications for a third to a half off their regular prices during the term of your membership.

So why not join this hardy band of international budgeteers and participate in its exchange of travel information and hospitality? Simply send your name and address, together with your annual membership fee of $18 (U.S. residents) or $20 U.S. (Canadian, Mexican, and other foreign residents), by check drawn on a U.S. bank or via international postal money order in U.S. funds to: Frommer's Dollarwise Travel Club, Inc., Gulf + Western Building, One Gulf + Western Plaza, New York, NY 10023. And please remember to specify which *two* of the books in section (1) and which *one* in section (2) you wish to receive in your initial package of members' benefits. Or, if you prefer, use the order form at the end of the book and enclose $18 or $20 in U.S. currency.

Once you are a member, there is no obligation to buy additional books. No books will be mailed to you without your specific order.

CHAPTER I

GETTING THERE

□ □ □

1. TRAVELING TO CALIFORNIA
2. TRAVELING WITHIN CALIFORNIA

When you travel with children, transportation is a major consideration. In the previous chapter you found ideas and suggestions to make your family travel as pleasant as possible. This chapter presents some travel options.

Before you start on your journey, you might want to contact the **California Office of Tourism,** P.O. Box 9278, Dept. T-72, Van Nuys, CA 91409 (tel. toll free 800/TO-CALIF [ext.] 72). They'll provide you with plenty of information about the state. If you have specific questions they can't answer, they'll tell you who can.

1. TRAVELING TO CALIFORNIA

BY AIR: Most major airlines fly into Los Angeles International (LAX) and San Francisco International (SFO). You might be surprised to learn that many carriers also fly directly to several smaller airports within California.

Consider your vacation destinations first, then see if you can fly to the city closest to your destination. For example, don't assume that LAX is the best place to arrive. You might be better off flying into one of the Los Angeles area's other airports, such as Burbank-Glendale-Pasadena or Ontario International, or to Orange County's John Wayne Airport. The same applies to northern California. Oakland and Sacramento airports are easy to navigate and are served by many major carriers.

Talk with a travel agent to check out the best fares. Especially when traveling with children, costs can mount, and in many cases, lower children's fares are available.

BY TRAIN: You'll find that **Amtrak** (tel. toll free 800/USA-RAIL) offers transportation to California from many cities. The *California Zephyr* runs from Chicago to San Francisco via Denver and Salt Lake City. The *Southwest Chief* offers service between Los Angeles and Chicago via Albuquerque. The *Desert Wind* services Los Angeles, Denver, and Chicago. The *Sunset Limited* services Los Angeles and New Orleans via San Antonio. And if you're coming from the Northeast, the *Cardinal* runs from New York to Chicago, where you can connect with either the *Southwest Chief* or the *California Zephyr.* Round-trip adult fare for any of these routes is $239. Children ages 2 to 11 pay half fare.

Some of the trains have complete dining cars with full-service restaurants; others have snackbars. Some have bedrooms with sleeping berths; others have family bedrooms—rooms that are the full width of the train, with windows on both sides.

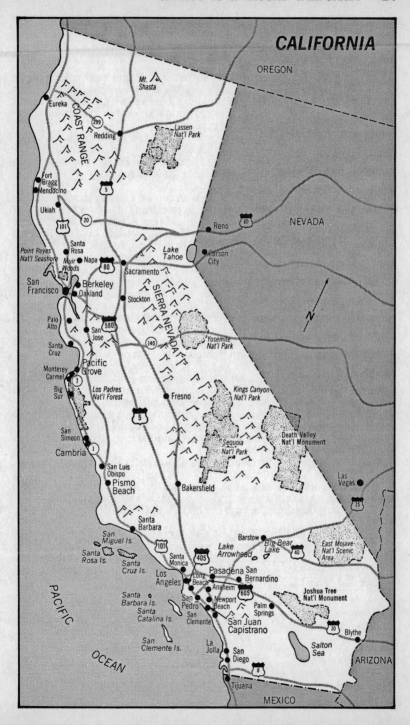

CALIFORNIA

OREGON

Mt. Shasta

Eureka

COAST RANGE

Redding

Lassen Nat'l Park

Fort Bragg
Mendocino

Ukiah

299

5

20

101

Santa Rosa

Point Reyes Nat'l Seashore

Muir Woods

Napa

80

Reno

80

NEVADA

Lake Tahoe

Carson City

Sacramento

San Francisco

Berkeley
Oakland

Stockton

SIERRA NEVADA

Palo Alto

580

San Jose

Santa Cruz

140

Yosemite Nat'l Park

Monterey
Carmel

Pacific Grove

1

Big Sur

Los Padres Nat'l Forest

Fresno

Kings Canyon Nat'l Park

5

San Simeon

1

Cambria

Sequoia Nat'l Park

Death Valley Nat'l Monument

San Luis Obispo

Pismo Beach

Bakersfield

Las Vegas

15

Santa Barbara

San Miguel Is.

101

Barstow

Big Bear Lake

East Mojave Nat'l Scenic Area

Santa Rosa Is.

Santa Cruz Is.

Lake Arrowhead

40

Santa Monica

405

Pasadena

San Bernardino

Los Angeles

Long Beach

Anaheim

Joshua Tree Nat'l Monument

Santa Barbara Is.

San Pedro

Newport Beach

605

Santa Catalina Is.

San Clemente

Palm Springs

San Juan Capistrano

PACIFIC

San Clemente Is.

La Jolla

San Diego

Salton Sea

10

Blythe

ARIZONA

OCEAN

8

Tijuana

MEXICO

When you consider train travel, ask about family fares and package tours. They make such options considerably more affordable.

2. TRAVELING WITHIN CALIFORNIA

BY CAR: Although California is over 350 miles wide, and has over 1,200 miles of coastline, driving through the state is one of the lovelier ways to vacation as a family. The countryside, the ocean, and the mountains are spectacular, and certainly the way to see them is to be able to drive at your own pace, stopping whenever you and the kids feel the urge to explore.

Be sure to get a good map before you start. If you're a member of the American Automobile Association, you can get all kinds of wonderful, detailed information from your nearest office. Each chapter of this book will also give you specific driving instructions to get you where you want to go.

BY AIR: Many national and international carriers have service between Los Angeles and San Francisco. Don't automatically rule them out in favor of the smaller airlines; they sometimes offer better fares. In addition: **Alaska Air** has convenient service from Los Angeles area airports to San Francisco and Oakland (call toll free 800/555-1212 to find your local toll-free number); **American Airlines** (tel. toll free 800/433-7300) services many of the smaller airports such as Fresno, Monterey, Palm Springs, Redding, San Jose, and San Luis Obispo, as well as the larger Bay Area (San Francisco/Oakland) and southern California (LAX, Burbank, Ontario, Long Beach, and Orange County–John Wayne, San Diego) airports; **America West** (tel. toll free 800/247-5692) has over 100 daily flights between nine state airports; and **USAir** (formerly PSA) services many smaller cities, such as Burbank, Concord, Fresno, Long Beach, Monterey, Ontario, Anaheim (Orange County–John Wayne), as well as the major airports in the state (call toll free 800/555-1212 to find your local toll-free number.)

BY TRAIN: There are several **Amtrak** routes within California. Its *Coast Starlight* runs the length of California. Originating in Los Angeles, it stops in Santa Barbara, San Luis Obispo, Salinas, San Jose, Oakland (with a shuttle to San Francisco), Sacramento, and Redding (among other cities), and continues north to Seattle. The *San Diegan* connects San Diego to Los Angeles via Orange County. This very popular line is a fun way to travel, and the trips are so short that it's pleasant with almost any child.

Did you know you can take the train to Yosemite? Well, most of the way, anyway. The *San Joaquin* runs the length of the San Joaquin Valley, connecting Bakersfield, Fresno, Merced, and Stockton with San Francisco/Oakland. With bus connections, you can really get off the beaten path without a car.

For more information, call toll free 800/USA-RAIL.

BUSES AND TOURS: Within California, you might want to consider **Greyhound/Trailway Bus Lines** (tel. toll free 800/237-8211). And be sure to check out touring bus companies, such as **California Parlor Car Tours** (call toll free 800/555-1212 for your local toll-free number) and the **Gray Line, Inc.** (call toll free 800/555-1212 for your local toll-free number).

CHAPTER II

SAN FRANCISCO

□ □ □

1. GETTING THERE

2. GETTING YOUR BEARINGS

3. GETTING AROUND

4. WHERE TO STAY

5. WHERE TO EAT

6. WHAT TO DO AND SEE

One of the most breathtakingly beautiful cities in the world, San Francisco is at once quaint and cosmopolitan. It is a city of contrasts. Shiny, stunning steel bridges and pinnacle-like skyscrapers sit within minutes of Victorian dwellings and classic cathedrals. Authentic Chinese herb shops with their ancient remedies are found within blocks of bawdy strip joints. You might see an old Chinese woman who carries her groceries tied in a cloth sack sitting on a bus next to a punk rocker with spiked-hair who is plugged into a Walkman. And of course there's the weather. The city can be thick with fog or crystalline bright. Or it can be both—in different parts of town.

While San Francisco is known as a sophisticated international city, it also has the largest man-made park in the world, it sits within part of the most popular national park in the country, and it is minutes away from spectacular ocean scenery.

It's no wonder that San Francisco charms almost 2.75 million visitors a year. It will charm you too, and delight your kids. And unless you're very unusual, there are so many sights to see and things to do that your family will never be bored.

Known as one of the great cities of the world, it is surprisingly small. With only 750,000 people (although the entire Bay Area has 5.9 million), it's located at the very tip of a 32-mile-long peninsula. You can think of it like the nail of your thumb—with Fisherman's Wharf at the end. In this area of less than 47 square miles, there are over 40 hills, 11 islands, 200 parks and playgrounds, 47 museums, 182 buildings that have been designated historical landmarks, 14,000 Victorian homes, and 4,200 restaurants. The city offers 54 foreign-language newspapers.

Many people think of San Francisco as an adult city, and indeed it is . . . but not exclusively. It's a cosmopolitan city that offers abundant things to do for both parents and children together. It is a chance for children to experience the excitement of an urban community like New York, London, and Tokyo, with the advantage of easy escape to the beautiful outdoors when they're tired of the intellectual and sophisticated.

San Francisco's rich history is a mixture of cultures—Spanish and American Old West. A Spanish settlement called Yerba Buena was established here in 1776 by Juan Bautista de Anza; in 1847, under the United States flag, its name was changed to San Francisco. The discovery of gold in the California foothills some 140 miles away brought tens of thousands of people to the area, so that by the height of the Gold Rush in 1849 and 1850, the little town had become quite a city. By 1869 the transcontinental railroad had completed its link to San Francisco, and with it came even more people.

Possibly the one event that everyone knows in San Francisco's history is the Great Earthquake and Fire of 1906. The quake was 8.25 on the Richter scale, and destroyed over 25,000 buildings! Surprisingly, the quake only did part of the damage; the greatest part of the disaster is attributable to the fire.

The city began to rebuild immediately, and by 1915 San Francisco rejoiced and celebrated at the Panama-Pacific International Exposition.

1. GETTING THERE

IF YOU'RE DRIVING: There are several routes to San Francisco. From Los Angeles, take I-405 north to I-5 north through the San Joaquin Valley. (Check a map first, since you may be located close enough to I-5 to link up with it and avoid I-405 altogether.) Hook up with I-580 west to I-80 west (San Francisco–Oakland Bay Bridge) into the city. (This is the fastest but most boring route.) Or you can take I-405 north to U.S. 101 west (and north) to San Luis Obispo. At San Luis, take either U.S. 101 or Calif. 1 north to San Francisco. (These routes, especially Calif. 1, are slower but very picturesque and interesting.) From Sacramento, take I-80 west.

A Stop Along the Way

I-5 is the fastest way to get north and south, but it's probably one of the most boring highways you'll ever take. There are very few towns (or even gas stations) on this stretch of road. On our treks north, we stop for a stretch and run-around at the junction of Calif. 58 and I-5, near Buttonwillow (about 110 miles north of Los Angeles). There's a Carl's Jr. with a playground. Then we have a real rest and activity break at Harris Ranch, and finally we stop at one of the towns in the north end of the valley.

Harris Ranch (tel. 209/935-0717, or toll free 800/942-2333) is midway between Los Angeles and San Francisco on I-5 in the small town of Coalinga. Harris Ranch is actually a full-service rest area that includes a restaurant, bakery, country store, gas station, hotel—and even a private airstrip. The early-California–style buildings have large rooms and open hallways; the ranch is an inviting place to stop for a meal and run-around. Allow about 1½ hours.

Clearly a family-oriented spot, Harris Ranch even has a ladies' rest room with a little girl's stall, as well as a vanity area that is good for changing diapers. "Sesame Street" dolls and Disney toys are available for youngsters who may be in need of diversions after the long stretch of nonstop driving.

Even though this is basically a highway rest stop, the food is good and the service attentive. Busboys offer boosters and highchairs even before you ask. Breakfasts range from waffles to huevos rancheros (prices from $5 to $9). Lunch and dinner are served from 11 a.m. to 11 p.m., and include salads, sandwiches, burgers, Mexican specialties, and steaks (prices from $7.25 to $14.50). Harris Ranch also serves special complete dinners in their Fountain Court room (starting at 5 p.m.) that include roast lamb, sweetbreads, and prime rib among the entrees (prices from $12 to $19). The children's menu (for kids 10 and under)

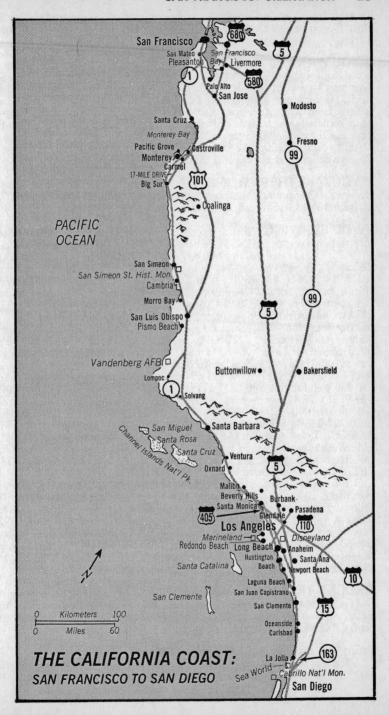

THE CALIFORNIA COAST:
SAN FRANCISCO TO SAN DIEGO

features hamburgers, grilled cheese sandwiches, and barbecued beef ribs for $3. Open from 6 a.m. to 11 p.m. No reservations. Most major credit cards are honored.

IF YOU WANT TO TAKE THE TRAIN: The train is an especially fun way to get to San Francisco, and **Amtrak**, with its San Francisco office in the Transbay Terminal, 1st and Mission Streets (tel. 415/957-9525, or toll free 800/USA-RAIL), is the way to go. Amtrak's *Coast Starlight*, originating in Los Angeles, runs the length of the California coast and goes inland up to Portland and Seattle. More accurately, the train disembarks in Oakland and a shuttle takes you to the Transbay Terminal in San Francisco.

The *California Zephyr* comes into Oakland from parts east, originating in Chicago and stopping in Omaha, Denver, and other major cities.

IF YOU TAKE THE BUS: The major transcontinental bus line that services the Bay Area is **Greyhound/Trailways Bus Lines,** with its main terminal at 50 7th St. (tel. 415/433-1500, or toll free 800/531-5332).

IF YOU'RE FLYING: These are some of the airlines that fly into **San Francisco International Airport** (tel. 415/761-0800), located 14 miles south of San Francisco: Air Canada (tel. toll free 800/422-6232), Air France (tel. toll free 800/237-2747), Alaska Airlines (tel. toll free 800/426-0333), American Airlines (tel. toll free 800/433-7300), Braniff Airways (tel. toll free 800/272-6433), British Airways (tel. toll free 800/247-9297), Canadian Airlines International (tel. toll free 800/426-7000), Cathay Pacific Airways (tel. toll free 800/233-2742), China Airlines (tel. toll free 800/227-5118), Continental Airlines (tel. toll free 800/435-0040), Delta Airlines (tel. toll free 800/221-1212), Eastern Airlines (tel. toll free 800/327-8376), Hawaiian Airlines (tel. toll free 800/367-5320), Japan Air Lines (tel. toll free 800/525-3663), Korean Airlines (tel. toll free 800/531-2626), Lufthansa (tel. toll free 800/645-3880), Mexicana Airlines (tel. toll free 800/531-7921), Northwest (tel. toll free 800/225-2525), Pan Am (tel. toll free 800/221-1111), Philippine Airlines (tel. toll free 800/435-9725), Piedmont Airlines (tel. toll free 800/251-5720), Quantas Airlines (tel. toll free 800/227-4500), Scandinavian Airlines System (SAS) (tel. toll free 800/221-2350), Singapore Airlines (tel. toll free 800/742-3333), Southwest Airlines (tel. toll free 800/531-5601), TWA (tel. toll free 800/221-2000), United Airlines and United Express (tel. toll free 800/241-6522), USAir (tel. toll free 800/428-4322), and UTA French Airlines (tel. toll free 800/237-2623). There are also charters that fly into San Francisco.

You might choose to fly into **Oakland International Airport,** a smaller airport that is easier to navigate. It's easy to get into San Francisco from there. The following airlines service Oakland International Airport: Alaska Airlines (tel. toll free 800/426-0333), America West Airlines (tel. toll free 800/247-5692), American Airlines (tel. toll free 800/433-7300), Continental Airlines (tel. toll free 800/435-0040), Delta Airlines (tel. toll free 800/221-1212), Frontier Airlines (tel. toll free 800/255-5050), USAir (tel. toll free 800/428-4322), and United Airlines and United Express (tel. toll free 800/241-6522).

GROUND TRANSPORTATION TO THE CITY: You can do quite well in San Francisco without a car; in fact, in many ways it's preferable not to have one. Because of this, there are many companies that take you from the airport to a central location in the city or directly to your hotel.

From San Francisco International Airport

The **Bay Area SuperShuttle,** 700 16th St. (tel. 415/558-8500, or toll free 800/554-5543), takes you door to door, 24 hours a day. When you land at SFO and have gathered your bags, go upstairs to the departure level and to the outer curb where you'll find the city-bound shuttles. Reservations are strongly advised when you're heading toward the airport. Fare: $8 for adults and children over 4, $4 for children ages 2 to 4, free for children under 2.

The **SFO Airporter Bus,** 301 Ellis St. (tel. 415/673-2433 or 415/495-8404), offers transportation between SFO and its terminal in Union Square. It also has regular stops at certain hotels on Fisherman's Wharf and in the financial district. It runs every 20 to 30 minutes. Fare: $4 for adults, $2 for children 5 to 11, free for children under 5.

Associated Limousines of San Francisco, 1398 Bryant St. (tel. 415/431-7000, or toll free 800/255-2660). Door-to-door transportation. Fare: $8 per person, $4 for children under 5. Two bags per person, then extra charges apply.

Lorrie's Travel and Tours, Inc., 1800 3rd St. (tel. 415/626-2113), offers door-to-door service. Fare: $7 for adults, $4 for children 2 to 12; children under 2 (on a parent's lap) are free.

Taxis are plentiful in this city. A trip from the airport to downtown will cost approximately $25. Taxi fares in San Francisco are approximately $2.90 for the first mile, $1.50 for each additional mile. You can pick up a cab anywhere, but if you need to call, here are few to choose from: **Allied Taxi Service** (tel. 415/826-9494), **DeSoto Cab Company** (tel. 415/673-0333), **Luxor Cab** (tel. 415/282-4141), and **Veteran's Taxicab Company** (tel. 415/552-1300).

All the major car-rental agencies are represented in San Francisco. Among them, you'll find: **Avis Rent-A-Car** (tel. 415/885-5011, or toll free 800/331-1212), **Budget Rent-A-Car** (tel. 415/875-6850, or toll free 800/527-0700), **Dollar Rent-A-Car** (tel. 415/692-1205 or 415/952-6200), **Hertz Rent-A-Car** (tel. 415/771-2200, or toll free 800/654-3131), and **Thrifty Rent-A-Car** (tel. 415/673-6675, or toll free 800/367-2277).

From Oakland International Airport

If you're flying into Oakland International Airport, you can get into San Francisco, Oakland, and Berkeley using a variety of transportation methods. **AC Transit** (tel. 415/839-2882) will take you to different locations in Oakland. You can then transfer and take a bus to the San Francisco Transbay Terminal, where BART (Bay Area Rapid Transit; tel. 415/465-BART) will take you directly under the bay and into the city. An **AIR BART van** (tel. 415/444-4200) will take you from the airport to the nearest BART station. Ask at the airport information booth for directions.

Possibly the easiest way for you and your family (although the most expensive of the three) is to take a limousine. **569-LIMO, Inc.,** is a good choice. It will take you door to door—from the airport to your destination. It's best to call ahead, but if you can't, just call from an airport phone and you'll have a short wait.

There are major **car-rental agencies** at Oakland International Airport.

You may wish to contact the **Oakland Convention and Visitors Bureau,** 1000 Broadway, Suite 200, Oakland, CA 94607 (tel. 415/839-9000, or toll free 800/444-7270).

2. GETTING YOUR BEARINGS

San Francisco is located at the tip of a peninsula, with Fisherman's Wharf at the northernmost tip and the Golden Gate Bridge on the northwest side.

Created in a traditional grid-like pattern (although it's sometimes hard to tell because the grid is laid over some steep terrain), the city's major sightseeing spots are easy to find. Market Street and Van Ness Avenue are the major thoroughfares. With a good map, you can easily find your way almost anywhere you want to go.

One of your first moves should be to contact the **San Francisco Convention**

and Visitors Bureau Information Center at Hallidie Plaza, 900 Market St. at Powell Street (tel. 415/391-2000). There is a multilingual staff to help you. Hours are 9 a.m. to 5:30 p.m. Monday through Friday, 9 a.m. to 3 p.m. on Saturday, and 10 a.m. to 2 p.m. on Sunday. If you want to plan your trip in advance, you can write to the San Francisco Convention and Visitors Bureau, P.O. Box 6979, San Francisco, CA 94101, and they will send you a packet of invaluable information, including maps. Request the Visitor's Kit and send $1 for postage and handling.

Another good place is the **Visitors Information Center** of the Redwood Empire Association, One Market Plaza, Spear Street Tower, Suite 1000, San Francisco, CA 94105 (tel. 415/543-8334). There are loads of brochures and maps here, covering San Francisco and parts north. Ask for the Redwood Empire Visitor's Guide. It's free if you stop by, but if you write ahead, send $1 for postage and handling. The center is open Monday through Friday from 9 a.m. to 4:30 p.m.

Once you're in town, you can get **recorded tourist information** by dialing 415/391-2001. Look for the small weekly publications that give you up-to-date information about many of the current happenings in the city.

GOLDEN GATE BRIDGE:
The Golden Gate Bridge is one of the most famous—and beautiful—landmarks in the world. Painted bright red-orange, it towers vibrantly above the white-flecked, brilliant aquamarine waters where the Pacific Ocean meets San Francisco Bay. It looms up, almost as if it comes out of nowhere, and is framed by dark-green rolling hills and crystal waters.

Because of the enormous engineering challenges involved in constructing a bridge of this nature over water 318 feet deep in some places, the project was originally nicknamed "The Bridge That Couldn't Be Built." But on May 27, 1937, at a cost of $35 million, the Golden Gate Bridge was completed.

It's majestic from any angle, and you can enjoy the bridge by sailing under it, driving across it, viewing it from distant points in the city . . . even walking on it. Like millions of other people, you'll find yourself looking for views of it as you roam the city, and finding reasons to cross it. Breathtaking when it stands there bathed in full sunlight, it is also wondrous to see shrouded in the mist or partially covered by cumulus clouds.

The 1.7-mile-long bridge also serves as a commuter passageway between San Francisco and Marin Counties. There's a toll booth for southbound traffic; the pedestrian walkway is free.

SAN FRANCISCO–OAKLAND BAY BRIDGE:
Linking San Francisco with the East Bay cities of Oakland and Berkeley, the Bay Bridge is 8½ miles long, one of the world's longest steel bridges. Attractive in its own right, the silver, double-decker bridge is a major commuter route, with five lanes in either direction. There is no pedestrian walkway, and a toll is collected westbound.

PARTS OF TOWN:
San Francisco, like many other large metropolitan areas, is a cluster of diverse neighborhoods. Here are some brief descriptions of the ones you're most likely to frequent on your visit.

Union Square is a lovely shopping district whose heart (the Square) is bordered by Powell, Stockton, Post, and Geary Streets. This bustling, colorful neighborhood of fashionable shops and luxury hotels is in many ways the "hub" of the city, and there are hundreds of restaurants in the streets adjoining Union Square. Note, however, that during peak hours this delightful area becomes a bit difficult with strollers and children in tow. Nearby is famous **Nob Hill**, the area around California and Mason Streets that was once called "the hill of palaces" by Robert Louis Stevenson. Today it is home to magnificent hotels, beautiful Grace Cathedral, and charming Huntington Park. **Chinatown** is the 24-square-block area that surrounds Grant Avenue between Bush and Columbus, home to the largest Chinese community outside Asia. Adjacent to Chinatown is **North Beach,** the northeastern area of the city whose main street is Columbus Avenue. Although not really a tourist section for children (especially in the evening when its bars, jazz clubs, and topless cabarets come alive), it is home to some of the city's best family restaurants.

San Francisco features 24 miles of waterfront, with more than 40 deep-water piers for commercial and passenger ships. The area of interest is the **Embar-cadero,** which starts at the Ferry Building (at the foot of Market Street; you'll spot it immediately—it's the charming clock tower) and continues toward the Northern Waterfront. The **Northern Waterfront** is roughly the area from Pier 39 to Ghirardelli Square, which also includes Fisherman's Wharf, The Cannery, and the Hyde Street Pier. Nearby are the Marina District and Union Street. The **Marina District** offers many moderately priced accommodations and has some of the best small parks in the city. Union Street between the 1600 and 2200 blocks is the area known as **Cow Hollow,** a trendy, upscale shopping and restaurant area with restored Victorian buildings and quaint little courtyards.

Japantown (or "Nihonmachi") is San Francisco's Tokyo-like quarter for things Japanese; Post and Buchanan Streets border the five-acre complex called Japan Center. Some 3½ miles from downtown, the **Richmond District and Clement Street** offer a wonderful international mixture of ethnic groups and their shopping, restaurants, and cultural buildings. Chinese, Indonesian, Thai, Korean, Vietnamese, Russian, Greek, Jewish, and other nationalities are represented here; be sure to go for a delightful—and educational—stroll before you partake in one of the area's good restaurants. Nearby, **Golden Gate Park,** the largest man-made park in the world, encompasses well over 1,000 acres. There are band concerts on Sunday (weather permitting), as well as museums, an aquarium, a planetarium, gardens, lakes, and other recreational features. And finally, we go back again to the center—this time, the **Civic Center,** an area comprised of government buildings and performing arts centers, all of which are quite lovely. While the area doesn't offer much in the way of family sightseeing, a brief walk around affords an opportunity to look at some wonderful architecture: for example, San Francisco City Hall is a spectacular French Renaissance structure with a dome taller than the Capitol building in Washington, D.C.

If you're driving, one of the best ways to orient yourself is to take the **49-Mile Drive,** which takes you through the city's main areas of interest. Pick up a free *San Francisco Visitor Map* at the Visitor Information Center, and follow the blue-and-white seagull signs as the route takes you past most of the places you'll want to visit, as well as other scenic and historical points. Plan to spend several hours.

3. GETTING AROUND

Once you're settled in, you'll find that this compact city is easy to navigate. For starters, pick up a good map. You'll find that it's most fun to walk, and you can walk almost anywhere (especially if you've brought comfortable shoes). Leave your car behind and when you get tired of walking, there's convenient—and affordable—public and private transportation.

PUBLIC TRANSPORTATION: San Francisco provides wonderful transportation facilities at bargain prices.

MUNI (San Francisco Municipal Railway)

Headquartered at 949 Presidio Ave. (tel. 415/673-MUNI), MUNI is the general name of San Francisco's 700-mile public transportation system. It includes more than 1,000 buses (on some 70 lines), cable cars (see below), trolleys, and light rail vehicles (these operate underground downtown and on the streets

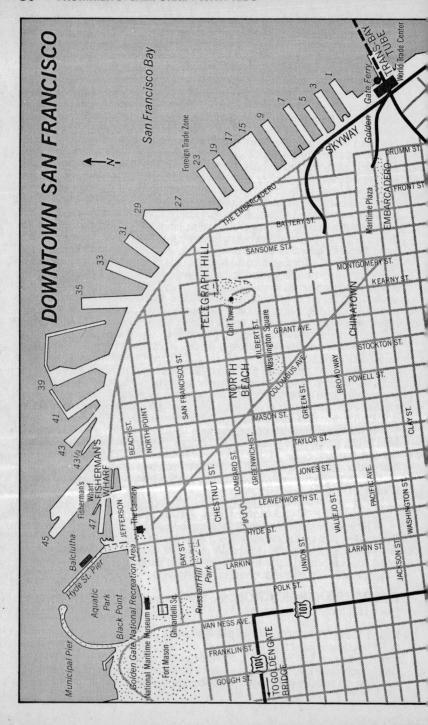

DOWNTOWN SAN FRANCISCO

in the outer areas of town). And it's a deal, with fares at 85¢ for adults and 25¢ for children 5 to 17 (except on cable cars, where it's $2 for adults and $1 for children 5 to 17), and 15¢ for seniors; children under 5 ride free. Free transfers are good for two changes of vehicle within 90 minutes. *Note:* Exact change is required on all MUNI vehicles.

You might want to get *The Official San Francisco Street and Transit Guide,* a map of the MUNI routes and transit connections, available at most bookstores for $1.25. You can also get information by writing MUNI, Muni Map, 949 Presidio Ave., Room 222, San Francisco, CA 94115. Enclose a check or money order for $1.75 (includes 50¢ postage) payable to "MUNI Map."

There are self-service ticket machines at all major stops and terminals. (These are located at Powell and Market Streets, California and Drumm Streets, California Street and Van Ness Avenue, Bay and Taylor Streets, Beach and Hyde Streets, and California and Grant Streets.) At these machines, for $6 adults can purchase a 24-hour pass that entitles you to ride the cable cars, underground, and buses for a whole day. If you prefer to talk with someone on the phone about your exact destination, the MUNI people are extremely helpful. Just be prepared to hold on the phone for a while.

CABLE CARS. There are three cable-car routes. The Powell-Hyde Line starts at Powell and Market Streets, runs by Union Square down to Victorian Park at the Maritime Museum and Aquatic Park, and ends near Ghirardelli Square. The Powell-Mason Line also starts at Powell and Market Streets and runs by Union Square, but its route takes it to Bay Street, near Pier 39 and Fisherman's Wharf. The California Street Line runs from the foot of Market Street at Drumm Street (in front of the Hyatt Regency) up over Nob Hill to Van Ness Avenue.

For more on the cable cars, see the "What to Do and See" section in this chapter.

BART (Bay Area Rapid Transit)

BART, headquartered at 800 Madison St., Oakland (tel. 415/788-BART), is the 71-mile underground transportation system that links San Francisco with Daly City and the East Bay cities of Oakland and Berkeley. BART is clean, space age in design, and a treat for kids. We found ourselves riding around the city just so our children could experience the exhilarating sensation of subway travel. The fast trains speeding through their underground tunnels are an activity in themselves, and BART stations are conveniently located throughout the city so you can plan your sightseeing with that in mind. BART operates from 6 a.m. to midnight Monday through Saturday and 9 a.m. to midnight on Sunday.

Each person over 4 years old must have a ticket, and ticket prices depend on your destination. Your kids will love the automated ticket machines (which accept nickles, dimes, quarters, and $1 and $5 bills) and the automatic ticket takers at the fare gate. Be sure to save your tickets because you'll need them when you exit. Some people even purchase a round-trip excursion ticket—for $2.60 you can ride anywhere in the system for three hours (note that you must enter and exit at the same station).

AC Transit

This is the way to get to the East Bay via the San Francisco–Oakland Bay Bridge. AC Transit is located in the Transbay Terminal, 1st and Mission Streets (tel. 415/839-2882).

Golden Gate Transit

This is the system that gets you to Marin County via the Golden Gate Bridge. Golden Gate Transit's home base is also in the Transbay Terminal, 1st and Mission Streets (tel. 415/332-6600).

SAM Trans (San Mateo County Transit District)

This system connects you to the peninsula cities, and is also located in the Transbay Terminal, 1st and Mission Streets (tel. 415/761-7000).

OTHER WAYS TO GO: There are taxis and private limousines and van services that will take you door to door. Limousines can be chartered for a group or for an individual (see the "Getting There" section, above, for details).

When You're Driving

San Francisco is a unique city when it comes to driving. Nowhere else do you find such steep hills in such densely crowded neighborhoods. Possibly the most important tip for driving the hills may have to do with parking on them. Always use your parking brake and curb your wheels. This means, when you are parking uphill, turn the tires toward the street, and when facing downhill, turn the tires toward the curb. In San Francisco, this is the law. Another rule is that cable cars and streetcars *always* have the right-of-way, as do pedestrians.

Finally, don't be embarrassed to use your parking brake if you have to stop in the middle of a steep hill.

Tours

Although we rarely take our kids on tour buses (because of their limited attention spans and their need to get up and move around), we know people who've taken their older children and have found it enjoyable. We like the **Gray Line, Inc.,** 151 Fremont St. (tel. 415/896-1515), which offers a wide array of tours in comfortable buses. Currently, Gray Line offers many tours of San Francisco and the Bay Area that range from a few hours to a full day. Prices for a half-day tour are $19.50 for adults and $9.75 for children 5 to 11; children under 5 are free. Full-day tours vary in price. Reservations recommended.

Ferry Service

The **Red-and-White Fleet** (tel. 415/546-2896, or toll free 800/445-8880 in California) leaves for Sausalito, Tiburon, and Angel Island from Pier 43. Ferries for Alcatraz, Angel Island, and Marine World Africa USA operate from Pier 41. Commuter service to Tiburon and Vallejo is available from the Ferry Building. Tickets can be purchased in advance. Schedules vary depending on the time of year; call for specific information.

Golden Gate Ferries, leaving from the Ferry Building at the foot of Market Street (tel. 415/332-6600), has service to Sausalito and Larkspur. The crossing to Sausalito takes approximately 30 minutes.

4. WHERE TO STAY

San Francisco is the visitor's and conventioneer's mecca, which means it has more hotels—and excellent ones too—than you can imagine. Many warmly welcome children. We've divided the hotels first by area, because when you travel with kids, you're concerned about location as much as amenities and price. Then we've listed hotels within neighborhoods by price—deluxe, upper bracket, moderate, and budget. San Francisco hotels tend to be more expensive than those in other cities, so what we term "moderate" might be considered expensive elsewhere; you must judge by the listed prices.

Tip: Check the parking situation if you've brought a car. It can add substantially to your hotel bill.

UNION SQUARE: Many families like staying in the Union Square area. It is quintessential San Francisco—clanging cable cars, elegant shopping, bustling crowds. Centrally located, it's an easy bus ride, cable-car jaunt, or taxi getaway to almost everything the city has to offer. It is one of our favorite places in the city, and offers a simply fabulous array of choice hotel accommodations. If you have a car, however, the above advice about hotel parking fees certainly applies: they can be astronomical.

There are two little parks in this area for children to expend energy. One is the Square at Union Square. It's pleasant, but can be very crowded. The other is Huntington Park, a beautiful pocket park at the top of Nob Hill. There are several small markets in this area, and a 24-hour Walgreen's Drugstore (which stocks milk, diapers, formula, etc.) at 500 Geary St. (tel. 415/673-8411 or 415/673-8413).

Deluxe

The crème de la crème is the **Four Seasons Clift Hotel,** 495 Geary St. (at Taylor Street), San Francisco, CA 94102 (tel. 415/775-4700, or toll free 800/268-6282). Imagine this: you want to stay in a first-class hotel. You call to make a reservation. Not only does the reservationist take your name, but the names and ages of your kids—and information about their interests!

One of San Francisco's landmarks, the Clift Hotel is known for its luxurious rooms and superb service. The staff treats you like you're an honored guest; nothing is too much trouble for them. They even learn your name! Because the hotel lobby is rather small, you feel as though you're visiting a beautiful mansion, with people there to serve you but not intrude. Although it has 329 rooms spread over 17 floors, its feel is a far cry from the usual commercial hotel.

When you go out for dinner and come back in the evening, the room is straightened up, the bed covers are turned down, a terrycloth robe is laid out on your bed, as is a flower and a shoeshine bag (for complimentary overnight shoeshine service). As if 24-hour room service isn't enough, the room-service trays are always adorned with a perfect rose. There is also 24-hour valet and twice-daily maid service.

The Clift also boasts a concierge who knows almost everything there is to know about San Francisco, and who honors all requests with ease. Not only has the concierge been known to meet guests at the airport and have their bags delivered and unpacked, but he also offers parents a list of activities and restaurants that cater to children.

Formerly strictly a businessperson's hotel, the Clift now caters to traveling families too. The hotel is gracious and wonderful to children, providing for their every need. Parents will be happy to know that in addition to cribs and refrigerators (available upon request), the hotel can provide bibs, diapers, bottles, strollers, humidifiers, and baby bathtubs. There's even a pediatrician on call—24 hours a day. There are magazines for teenagers, toys for tots, and even bedtime snacks of cookies (either Oreos or Mrs. Fields) and milk. In fact, parents can arrive empty-handed and within a short time have the basic necessities to make their stay a pleasant one. Other special things the hotel does for children: sends up a packet of baseball cards and comic books, provides the kids with their own plush terrycloth mini-robes, and sends up popcorn in a basket with balloons flying.

Those unfamiliar with the Clift's two world-famous dining and drinking rooms—the French Room and the Redwood Room—are in for a treat (you should make a point of seeing the hotel even if you can't stay there). Even the French Room (with its wine list of over 20,000 bottles of fine wine) serves breakfast, lunch, and dinner and has its share of highchairs and a children's menu. (See the "Where to Eat" section, below, for details.)

The Redwood Room is acclaimed as one of San Francisco's cultural and architectural traditions. It is entirely paneled in aged redwood burl polished to a shining luster, and the 20-foot ceilings make you feel as if you're sitting in the middle of a redwood forest. Designed in classic art deco style, it is an experience not to be missed.

A San Francisco tradition is high tea in the lobby of the Clift. Served Monday through Saturday, full high tea costs $10.75 per person. Reservations are suggested. One special treat is the Children's Christmas Tea, held in conjunction with the American Conservatory Theater presentation of *A Christmas Carol* (call ahead for details).

The 329 rooms of the Clift are elegantly furnished in quiet, understated tones with fine fabrics and Georgian reproduction furniture, some with satinwood inlays. Oversize rooms are standard. There are telephones in each room and each bath—some phones even have two lines and a hold button. In addition, there's a dataport for computer access. We had a small television in the armoire; other rooms have large-console TVs—all have remote control. Several rooms feature two bathrooms.

Superior and deluxe rooms (with queen- or king-size beds) range from $175 to $190 single and $195 to $210 double. We like the Four Seasons rooms the best. These are bedroom-sitting room combinations that range in price from $220 to $240. Executive Suites have French doors separating the sitting area from the bedroom, as well as two baths, and cost $275, single or double. Suites run $575 to $750.

The Family Plan at the Clift (for children 18 and under) offers two rooms with connecting doors, each room charged at the single-occupancy rate. Children sleep free. Rates are lower on some weekends, so ask about specials. Cribs and rollaways are free. Parking costs $14 per day, with in-and-out privileges.

The **Hyatt on Union Square,** 345 Stockton St. (at Post Street), San Francisco, CA 94108 (tel. 415/398-1234, or toll free 800/228-9000), surprised us. Though it's perfectly situated in the heart of Union Square, and generally thought to cater to businesspeople, the hotel's staff and management go out of their way to encourage families to stay here.

Complete with all the usual Hyatt touches (24-hour room service—here it even includes pizza—full concierge service, nightly turndown, and complimentary fruit at the front desk), this one has an added benefit if you're taking youngsters. The lovely lobby—done in warm tones of caramel and shrimp with exquisite Mozambique wood—is much smaller than you'd expect for such a large hotel, and you can keep track of your children more easily than in the enormous (though breathtaking) sister hotel, the Hyatt Regency. Standing in the lobby, it's hard to believe that the hotel has 36 floors with 693 rooms (all have views). This is a friendly place where the staff smile and talk with children. The emphasis here is on personalized care. Adults have access to the San Francisco Tennis Club: pay court fees and get use of Jacuzzi, sauna, steam, weight room, aerobics, and Nautilus equipment.

The hotel has special touches for children, and the Plaza Restaurant is a great place to take the kids. Its high ceilings, stained-glass dome, and giant picture windows that look out onto Union Square provide an open feeling for dining. The children's menu offers great kid-meals from $1.50 to $3.50, accompanied by coloring book, crayons, and helium balloons. All regular menu items (which range from $3.75 to $12.75) are available for children in half portions for half price. It's open from 7 a.m. to 10:30 p.m. every day.

Napper's, Too is another moderately priced restaurant good for families. Napper Valley, which is open in the summer, is an outdoor restaurant that overlooks the square. For elegant evening dining, recommended for teens and adults, the One-Up Restaurant is located at the rooftop level. It offers sensational views of the Transamerica Pyramid, Alcatraz, and the Golden Gate Bridge.

The hotel has just undergone a multi-million-dollar renovation. Earth tones and woods predominate in these spacious rooms, which have mini-bars, televisions with remote control, two phones (one in the bathroom), and small game tables perfect for eating or for children's games. And surprise—the bathrooms have tiny televisions.

Rates for singles are $218; for doubles, $248 (with a king-size bed or two double beds). Cribs and rollaways are free. Adjoining rooms are available. Children under 12 are free in their parents' room. The fee for indoor valet parking (with no in-and-out charges) is $14.

If you want to stay at one of the truly grand old hotels, the **Westin St. Francis,** located at 335 Powell St. (on Union Square, between Post and Geary Streets), San Francisco, CA 94102 (tel. 415/397-7000, or toll free 800/228-3000), is one that treats families nicely. The enormous 6,000-square-foot lobby is done in stunning rosewood; with ceilings several stories high, set off with huge crystal chandeliers, it is a stunning picture of old-world opulence. This huge hotel boasts 1,200 rooms (600 of which were added with the new 32-story tower), five outdoor glass elevators (the kids love them), distinctive shops, and one of the busiest lobbies you'll see. You have to keep a close eye on the little ones—this is a place where kids are just absorbed into the tumult. During Christmas and Easter holidays there are decorations all around, and many schoolchildren come here on class outings.

Other amenities include concierge service, 24-hour room service, airport transportation, business services, doctor on-call, and laundry service. Babysitting can be arranged through the concierge.

The St. Francis is known for several of its restaurants. The Dutch Kitchen is surprisingly pleasant to children. Open daily from 6 a.m. to 11:30 p.m., it has a wonderfully complete menu for adults, as well as highchairs, boosters, a children's menu, coloring book and crayons, and very friendly waitresses. (See the "Where to Eat" section, below, for details.) The Compass Rose restaurant is like an English drawing room that opens onto the lobby. It serves lunch and high tea: lunch entrees cost $7.75 to $10.50; high tea, $10.

If you stand in Victor's, the restaurant on the 32nd floor, it's like having all of San Francisco at your feet. Although Victor's is open daily for dinner, it's probably best to take the kids here for Sunday brunch. (The brunch costs $23.50 for adults, $9 for kids under 12, and if you need either a highchair or booster, just say so when you make reservations.)

We suggest that you ask for rooms in the main building (unless you prefer ultramodern rooms); they are large and very quiet. Hallways of the original building are wide-corridored spaces with beautiful rugs, and the rooms are high-ceilinged and elegant. Some of them are enormous, with love seats and plenty of room for cribs and rollaways. Bathrooms have large sink and counter areas. Suites are two rooms with a connecting door, each with love seat or couch and loads of space. Tower rooms, all of which have bay windows, are large with small entry halls. In-room amenities for all rooms include bathroom scales, turndown service upon request, and SpectraVision; tower rooms have remote-control TV.

Rates are as follows: in the main building, standard rooms are $135 single and $165 double, medium-size rooms are $170 single and $200 double, and deluxe rooms are $215 single and $235 double; in the tower, medium-size rooms are $200 single and $230 double, and deluxe rooms are $230 single and $260 double. Children under 18 are free if additional beds are not needed. Ask about weekend specials, as they can offer quite a savings. Family Plan means that when two rooms are booked, each room is billed at the single-occupancy rate. Cribs are free; rollaways cost $30 (per stay). There's garage parking on premises for $17 per 24 hours, with in-and-out privileges.

We always feel comfortable taking our offspring to a Hilton hotel since we know that the chain has a welcome policy toward kids. The **San Francisco Hilton and Towers,** 333 O'Farrell St. (at Mason Street), San Francisco, CA 94102 (tel. 415/771-1400, or toll free 800/HILTONS), offers the chain's usual high level of service and amenities, and the $210-million renovation has added some beautiful, unusual touches. Also called Hilton Square, the hotel is comprised of three towers of differing heights, over 1,900 rooms (1,600 have been renovated; 300 are new), a large swimming pool area, a health center, a promenade of shops, and four restaurants.

The main lobby is grand indeed, completely done in marble with accents of beige and light-rose hues that accentuate the color of the stone. Two giant crystal chandeliers and enormously high ceilings make for a spectacular entry into the hotel.

The hotel has two very attractive features for traveling families: the large, heated outdoor pool (open from 7 a.m. to 7 p.m.), which is protected on all sides to block the wind; and indoor self-parking ($14 per day) on the same floor as your room, so that you have immediate access to your car. (Tell the reservationist you're interested when you book your room, since only certain floors in certain buildings have this feature.) We found this helpful on a number of occasions when we didn't need to bring every toy into the room at once, but could exchange items as we used the car to go sightseeing.

Other hotel amenities include 24-hour room service, laundry and dry cleaning, 24-hour café, business center, concierge service, and car-rental agencies located within the hotel complex. The concierge will arrange babysitting.

For a charming place to eat breakfast, lunch, or dinner, you might want to try the Café on the Square. It's open 24 hours a day, and re-creates the ambience of a sidewalk café. Prices are typical for hotel coffeeshops. In addition to regular menu items, the Café on the Square offers tempting buffets for breakfast, lunch, and dinner. Kiku restaurant serves authentic Japanese food for lunch and dinner. Phil Lehr's Steakery is a dinner place specializing in steaks and chops. Finally, Henri's (open for lunch and dinner), the rooftop restaurant, has a fabulous panoramic view, and during the holidays they have special activities for the kids here.

The Hilton offers king-, queen-, and double-bedded rooms, all tastefully decorated, many with views of the city. All rooms have tub/shower combinations, mini-bars, remote-control color TVs, and SpectraVision. Each has a desk and chair. Rooms with two queen-size beds are very large, and the suites are huge.

Rates are $130 to $210 single (depending on location and type of room), and $150 to $230 double; suites start at $250. Children sleep free in the same room as adults. No charge for cribs.

The Upper Bracket

If you're looking for a charming bed-and-breakfast–style accommodation, the **White Swan Inn** is just the place. Located on the Nob Hill slope of Union Square at 845 Bush St., San Francisco, CA 94108 (tel. 415/775-6698 or 415/775-1755), this delightful 40-room inn welcomes families.

This traditional English-style hotel has lots of period antique pieces and English accents—hunting prints, black-and-white granite sinks and tabletops—set off by mahogany woods and beautiful hunter-green and burgundy wallpaper. Beveled glass doors open to the lobby in which many little teddy bears greet you; some sit on the stairs, others are on the floor next to the restored carousel horse. There are wood-burning fireplaces in three public areas—the upstairs lobby (where you enter from the street), the library, and the lounge—as well as a fireplace and bathroom in every guest room.

While the White Swan is bed-and-breakfast style, it is a little easier than a traditional bed-and-breakfast if you're traveling with kids. This isn't someone's home, so rather than worry about inconveniencing your host, you can feel assured that the 24-hour front-desk staff caters to guests' needs. There is also a concierge.

The White Swan (and the hotels Petite Auberge and Marina Inn) is owned by Four Sisters, Inc. Kimberly Post, one of the four sisters, suggests that when you book your reservation at any bed-and-breakfast, you tell the clerk the ages of your children. Ask if there are extra charges. Ask which are the best rooms. If you worry that your kids might have problems at mealtime, ask if special arrangements can be made for them; for example, at the White Swan they'll bring breakfast to your room or to the library. If it's available, the small conference room can be set up so the kids will have more space. During the day the children can bring toys and games into the library to play. When kids are staying at the inn you may see blocks set up in a corner, coloring books laid out on the table, and tots curled up on the floor with a teddy bear.

At the White Swan, there are two rooms on each floor that have a walk-in closet big enough for a portacrib in the bathroom. And of course a suite is great for people with kids because there are two rooms.

Amenities include terrycloth robes, a wonderful breakfast (croissants, cereal, juices, eggs, potatoes, fruit, and choice of teas or coffee), full afternoon tea (which includes breads, cakes, vegetables and dips, sweets), and wine or sherry service. Breakfast is served in the dining room from 7 a.m. to 10:30 a.m.— boosters and highchairs are available—or it can be brought to your room. For an extra fee, there is room service for a light evening meal (6 to 11 p.m.), and the kitchen will heat anything on request.

If you'll require babysitting services during your stay, mention this to the receptionist when you reserve your room.

Rates are $145 for a room with a queen-size bed, $160 for a king-size bed, and $250 for suites (which consist of a sitting room with a sofa bed, a bedroom, two baths, and an adjoining hallway). There is a $15-per-day additional charge for children over 4 years old to cover the cost of food. Rollways are $15. Valet parking is available from 7 a.m. to 11 p.m. for $15 per day, with in-and-out privileges.

Just a few doors away is the sister **Petite Auberge,** 863 Bush St., San Francisco, CA 94108 (tel. 415/928-6000), a cozy inn. This lovely little place with 26 rooms is probably better for small families with older children. Decorated like a French country inn, with straw hats, bouquets of fresh flowers, and colored baskets all around, it is done in subtle tones of peach and French country blues. This inn also has a small eating area for breakfast—on a smaller scale than at the White Swan—and a fireplace in the lobby. Concierge service is available. The staff will arrange babysitting, but they ask you to request it when you reserve your room.

Eighteen of the 26 delightful rooms have fireplaces. Other amenities include a full breakfast (available from 7 to 10:30 a.m.), English tea in the afternoon (with crûdités, breads, and sweets), and wine or sherry. Room service is available for light evening meals from 6 to 11 p.m. You'll also be given fluffy terry robes.

While cribs are available at no charge, the small rooms and ambience of the inn are more apropos to an older child. If you are bringing young children, let the reservation clerk know when you book.

Rates range from $105 to $195, but the only rooms appropriate for families are those in the upper range, from $155. There is a $15-per-day additional charge for children over 4 years old to cover the cost of food. Rollaways are $15. Valet parking is available from 7 a.m. to 11 p.m. for $15 per day, with in-and-out privileges.

Moderately Priced

There's a new kind of hotel in San Francisco. Called "boutique hotels," they are generally small, European-style accommodations that have recently been renovated. We think they have lots of advantages for traveling families. The first is obviously price: these hotels cost 40% less than the majors, and the savings are even greater when compared with many of the new hotels. Some guests also like staying in smaller hotels because of the increased interaction with the staff: they get to know the kids, and help the parents keep them happy. However, there are two drawbacks. Many small hotels have very small bathrooms—some with virtually no counter space. Most have dressing areas with space, but they may not be near the bath. The second drawback is the street noise, which can be a problem in this city in all but the largest, most modern hotels.

It may seem surprising that one of the small European-style hotels that clearly caters to businesspeople also welcomes families. The **Hotel Bedford,** 761 Post St. (between Jones and Leavenworth Streets), San Francisco, CA 94109 (tel. 415/673-6040, or toll free 800/227-5642, 800/652-1889 in California), not only has a staff that is friendly and warm to children, but because of the size of the hotel (144 rooms) and the philosophy of manager Mark Allen, it even makes grownups feel like special guests.

This newly renovated 1933-vintage hotel is three blocks from Union Square, near many restaurants and shopping. A charming place, its standard rooms are beautifully decorated, and many of them have panoramic views of the city. Our kids were particularly enchanted with the VCRs in every room (you can rent movies in the lobby), and adults love the complimentary wine served every evening in the lovely English-style lobby. Parlor suites consist of a bedroom (with a double or queen-size bed) and an adjoining parlor that has two over-stuffed chairs and a sleeper sofa. The family suites consist of two bedrooms, one with twin beds; there is one small bathroom with bath and shower, but little storage space. There are refrigerators (honor bars) in every room, and room service is available from 4 p.m. until midnight. There is same-day laundry service, and valet parking available at $10.50 per day, with in-and-out privileges.

Rates at the Hotel Bedford are $95, single or double; $145 to $155 for parlor suites; and $155 to $160 for family suites. There is no charge for children under 12 in their parents' room; cribs are free, but there is a $10 charge for roll-aways.

If you want a hotel where the manager really understands families and kids, **Villa Florence** may be just the place for you. It's located right on Union Square at 225 Powell St. (near Geary Street), San Francisco, CA 94102 (tel. 415/397-7700, or toll free 800/553-4411, 800/243-5700 in California), on the Powell Street cable-car line (which goes to Fisherman's Wharf). General manager Michael Shure has a real appreciation for parents traveling with their kids: "We've seen it all," he says. He tells the story of a 4-year-old who got separated from his parents; the child was found within minutes. How? Shure ordered the front door closed, with instructions not to let out any children until the youngster was found. He's the kind of guy who commiserates with you as you're chasing your children around the lobby.

The lobby will fool you, though. It's 16th-century Italian Renaissance style with a wood-burning fireplace and colonnaded entrance. At first you might not think that it's a place for children. However, the lobby is spacious and the rooms are inviting. Most important, the staff knows how to handle families, and will be glad to help you in whatever ways they can. Babysitting can be arranged through the front-desk staff.

While the hotel doesn't have a restaurant of its own, Kuleto's Italian Restaurant (tel. 415/397-7720) opens into the lobby. Open from 7 a.m. to 11 p.m., it was rated the best new restaurant in 1986 by *San Francisco Focus* magazine. The restaurant has an antipasto bar, serves full breakfasts, lunches, and dinners, and offers highchairs and boosters.

The 177 guest rooms, decorated with pastels and floral prints, are sound-proof. They have honor-bar/refrigerators, color televisions with remote control, and VCRs. Room service is available from 6:30 to 10:30 a.m. and 4 p.m. to midnight.

There are many different kinds of rooms here, so be sure to specify what you want when you make your reservations. As a sample, rates are $102, single or double (could have a king-size or queen-size bed, but might have a double); $119 for one of the 30 junior suites (one bedroom, all with king-size beds); and $159 for a deluxe suite (two bedrooms). Children stay free in their parents' room; cribs are free, but rollaways cost $15.

Another delightful European-style inn is the **Hotel Juliana,** 590 Bush St. (at Stockton Street), San Francisco, CA 94108 (tel. 415/392-2540, or toll free 800/382-8800, 800/372-8800 in California). This lovely little hotel is meticulously kept and delightful to look at. Amenities include honor-bar/refrigerator and remote-control color television in each room, and VCR service available. Babysitting can be arranged through the front desk. You can also request use of a hairdryer, ironing board, and even a lint roller.

The 107 guest rooms range in price from $104 for regular size to $125 for junior suites to $135 for executive suites. Rates are per room, not per guest, and include complimentary tea and coffee throughout the day and complimentary wines served in the evening. Cribs are free; rollaways cost $10.

Hotel Diva, 440 Geary St., San Francisco, CA 94102 (tel. 415/885-0200, or toll free 800/553-1900), between Mason and Taylor Streets in the heart of the theater district, across the street from the A.C.T. and Curran Theaters, is a kick—and a delight to the teens we know who adore it. Architecturally and design wise, it's as far from the traditional European-style hotel as you can get—and a surprise find in San Francisco. Hi-tech, Italian style, and futuristic (you feel like you're entering another age), the Diva has its own little gallery of celebrity handprints on the sidewalk in front of the hotel (including those of Gina Lolobrigida, Carol Channing, Leontyne Price, and Talia Shire) and a small art gallery with rotating exhibits. As you enter the lobby via the large chrome doors, you'll be struck by the circular chrome reception desk, the floor-to-ceiling mirrors, and the four large video-playing televisions suspended high on the wall behind the front desk.

This hotel is a deceiver—the staff likes children. An unusual convenience is that each floor has a small room (with a few tables) set up for the complimentary breakfast. These rooms can be used as playrooms or reading rooms for youngsters—or parents trying to flee the din of television or bickering brothers and sisters. There is room service (cold sandwiches) from 11 a.m. to 11 p.m., and the Salamagundi restaurant is two doors away (see the "Where to Eat" section for details).

Each guest room has a videocassette player, and there is a library of 300 tapes to choose from at $5.75 each. Highly polished lacquer furniture, down comforters, and contemporary-style pillow shams adorn the rooms. Each of the 107 rooms has an honor-bar/refrigerator, two telephones, and luxury toiletries. Other touches include free newspapers, overnight shoeshine, and use of IBM personal computers (this might be the place to take families when you're on business).

Rates are $95 to $105, single or double, depending on the size of the room; suites cost up to $275. The $95 rooms are large enough to include a crib but would be cramped with a rollaway. For families, we recommend the $105 rooms, called "executive kings" (really mini-suites)—ask for the ones that have two rooms. These consist of a bedroom with a queen-size bed (and VCR unit), a little hall (actually part of the vanity area), and a sitting area that is more like a small living room. The sitting room also has a VCR, a closet, and a Sico bed (a Murphy bed) that pulls out of the wall. There is also a table and chairs, and room for a crib and an additional rollaway. It might be crowded for a family of more than five, but it can accommodate them. No charge for cribs or for children under 12 in their parents' room, but rollaways cost $10. Maximum of two children per room at no charge; for each additional child there is a $10 charge. Additional adults also pay $10 each. Complimentary continental breakfast includes croissants, coffee, and tea. There's 24-hour valet parking for $10.50 per day.

The **Kensington Park Hotel,** 450 Post St. (near Powell Street), San Francisco, CA 94102 (tel. 415/788-6400, or toll free 800/553-1900), is another small (82 rooms), recently renovated hotel in Union Square. European in flavor, this hotel has a small lobby area in which a pianist plays every evening while complimentary tea and sherry are served. The décor and Spanish Gothic architecture in the lobby fix the attention.

The rooms are fairly good size. They have television, radio, and such extra touches as pillow shams, terrycloth robes (in rooms on upper floors), and toiletries. Bathrooms have phones, and refrigerators are available. Each floor has three or four connecting rooms available, which are good for families. They are corner rooms, which we especially liked since it allowed us peace of mind when the kids were a little noisy.

Room service is available from 6:30 to 9:30 a.m. and 4 p.m. to midnight. Complimentary continental breakfast (coffee, croissants, and juice) is served daily. Every floor has a small eating area or serving area in which coffee and tea are available.

While there is no restaurant on the premises, there is a deli next door, and the Dutch Kitchen (part of the Westin St. Francis) is across the street. Room service is available from 11 a.m. to 11 p.m., and includes cold sandwiches.

(Interesting tidbit: The lobby for the hotel is on the first floor, hotel rooms are on the 5th through 12th floors, Theater on the Square is on the second floor, and the Elks Club is on the third and fourth floors. In other words, this is a multiuse building.)

Rooms cost $95 on lower floors and $105 on upper floors. No charge for cribs. Children under 12 (maximum of two) are free if additional beds are not needed. Children 12 and older are charged $10, as is each additional younger child. Valet parking is available for $14 per day.

The **Monticello Inn,** 80 Cyril Magnin St. (near Ellis Street two blocks from Union Square), San Francisco, CA 94102 (tel. 415/392-8800, or toll free 800/669-7777), is like taking a step back to colonial days. Another hostelry we recommend for older children and teens, this is a delight for anyone who likes Federal-period furniture (Chippendale reproductions, plus a grandfather clock with a brass face in the lobby) and history.

The gracious lobby (with wood-burning fireplace) beckons you to sit and relax, and the separate parlor (where wine is served) has a game table and writing desk. It's a find but only for those parents with quiet, well-behaved children. The prices are great, the location is good, and the ambience is like stepping into Thomas Jefferson's sitting room.

While there is no restaurant in the hotel, the Corona Bar and Grill (tel. 415/392-5500) is adjacent, and serves lunch and dinner.

With only 91 rooms, there is a personal hospitality to the place. This feeling is carried out in the guest-room décor with canopied beds and pine furniture. Services and amenities include a stocked honor-bar/refrigerator and remote-control color television, with VCRs available. There is an on-site garage that charges $10 per day, with in-and-out privileges.

Rates include complimentary continental breakfast, complimentary tea and coffee served throughout the day, plus wine service in the evening. There is a health club across the street that guests can use for an additional fee.

Guest rooms cost $99 for rooms with either twin beds or a queen-size bed (ask for rooms with bath and shower), junior suites (one bedroom with either a king-size or queen-size bed) are $119, and executive suites (two bedrooms with either a king-size or queen-size bed) rent for $129. There is a grand suite with a fireplace for $149. No charge for children sleeping in their parents' room; cribs are free, but rollaways cost $15.

Hotel Vintage Court, 650 Bush St., San Francisco, CA 94108 (tel. 415/392-4666, or toll free 800/654-1100, 800/654-7266 in California), between Powell and Stockton Streets on the Nob Hill side of Union Square, has a lovely, warm ambience that we think is charming for families with older children. Step down into a cozy lobby with a wood-burning fireplace.

Room service is available from 4 p.m. to midnight. Other amenities include complimentary coffee and tea available in the lobby throughout the day and served on each floor in the morning, and complimentary wine every evening in the lobby. The concierge service can arrange babysitting. The desk clerks boast a thorough knowledge of the Napa Valley area and will be delighted to map out a great trip to the vineyards for you.

There is no hotel dining room, which can be a problem with youngsters. However, Masa's Restaurant (a nationally acclaimed French restaurant) is adjacent to the hotel, with an entrance in the lobby. Hotel guests may partake in a continental breakfast buffet ($5.50 per person) that includes fresh fruit, fresh-squeezed juices, croissants, muffins, and coffee.

The hotel is smallish—only 106 rooms—and cozy. The wine-country theme is carried throughout. Not only is the décor in burgundy, but many guest rooms and suites are named for individual California wineries. This is a very attractive hotel. Rooms have refrigerators with honor bar, color televisions, and VCRs. First-run movies are available at $6 ($1 for a second movie). Some rooms have window seats (covered with floral-print pillows that coordinate with country chintz bedspreads).

Rates are $99 for all rooms. Ask for the larger rooms that have bath/shower combinations. Cribs are free; rollaways cost $10. Some adjoining rooms are available.

Located in the financial district near Union Square is the **Galleria Park Hotel,** 191 Sutter St., San Francisco, CA 94104 (tel. 415/781-3060, or toll free 800/792-9639, 800/792-9855 in California), a historic 1911 building that was completely renovated in 1985. The atrium lobby has a working fireplace and a fabulous restored 1907 skylight. Although the hotel bills itself as a businessman's hotel, it's one of the few hotels that has an outside area in which kids can play.

One of the best things about this hotel is the marvelous outdoor jogging track with wood benches and trees. In this downtown area with little space for children, this is a wonderful, safe haven where kids can play and really run around. The track is located next to the Crocker Galleria shopping area.

The 177 bright and smartly decorated rooms look less like a commercial hotel than many, are good sized, and come with stocked honor-bar/refrigerator, color television with remote control, air conditioning (unusual here), and a writing desk. One of the most important features in a downtown hotel, the rooms are thoroughly soundproofed, helping to keep out the noise and keep you relaxed about the noise your youngsters might make. Some bathrooms have showers only, so request a tub if you desire one. Junior suites have a small wet bar and refrigerator, plus a king-size bed and sofa; others have queen-size beds with stereo units.

There is an on-site garage, which charges $10 per day. Room service is provided by restaurant on the premises, the Brasserie Chambord, from 6:30 a.m. to 9 p.m. Monday through Saturday, to 11 p.m. on Sunday.

All rates are per room, regardless of the number of people in them. Guest rooms rent for $119; suites for $135 to $325. Connecting rooms are available. No charge for cribs; rollaways cost $15.

The **Handlery Union Square Hotel,** 351 Geary St. (between Mason and Powell Streets), San Francisco, CA 94102 (tel. 415/781-7800, or toll free 800/223-0888, 800/522-5455 in New York), is another moderately priced accommodation in Union Square, and used to be known as the Handlery Motor Inn. In fact, this is a completely renovated 1988 version of two hotels: the Handlery Motor Inn and the Hotel Stewart. Both these hotels were owned by the Handlery family, who decided to put $5 million into a renovation project—

then gave it a new name. What used to be the Handlery has been completely upgraded and is now called the Handlery Club, which features rooms that are a little bigger, decorated more elegantly, and have a few more amenities than the rooms in the old Hotel Stewart.

The guest rooms and common rooms are bright and tastefully decorated in mauve and mint green with complementary print fabrics. Polished wood banisters adorn the hallways. Endearing acquisitions in the main lobby are the commissioned oil paintings that depict the scene in front of the Hotel Stewart in old San Francisco.

But the real surprise is the heated outdoor swimming pool. It's a good-sized one too, with plenty of lounge chairs.

If you need babysitting, it can be arranged by the front-desk staff. Another surprise is the parking. At $7.50 a day, with in-and-out privileges, it represents a real bargain in downtown San Francisco.

The Handlery is serviced by New Joe's restaurant, which opens into the lobby. Serving breakfast, lunch, and dinner in the restaurant, New Joe's also provides room service from 7 a.m. to 10:30 p.m. Highchairs and boosters are available.

All 378 good-sized rooms open to an inner hallway. They have color TV and in-room movies, little makeup mirrors in the bathrooms, and Vidal Sassoon amenities. A "deluxe king" is a very large room—some have bay windows that look out toward Union Square. A standard double room can be small though, so you should request a large room when you reserve. Also request a tub/shower combination if you prefer.

Rates are $69 to $85 single and $79 to $95 double. Suites (two large rooms with a king-size bed and a sofa sleeper that opens to a double bed) range from $95 to $220. The upgraded rooms in the Handlery Club (those renovated rooms from the Handlery Motor Inn) cost $115 to $130. Children 14 and under are free in same room with their parents. Cribs are free, but there are no rollaways. Connecting rooms are available.

Budget

Hotel Union Square, 114 Powell St. (at Ellis Street), San Francisco, CA 94102 (tel. 415/397-3000, or toll free 800/553-1900), standing in the midst of tourist shops and traffic, was built in 1913 and was known as the Golden State Hotel. In this art deco hotel, Dashiell Hammett wrote *The Maltese Falcon*. The Powell Street cable car runs right in front of the hotel.

The Union Square's 131 rooms all have color TV in addition to such room amenities as bath gels, shampoos, and soaps. Turndown service and complimentary continental breakfast are also offered. Rates range from $72 to $98. Some rooms have two queen-size beds; these rooms are large, with plenty of room for a rollaway or crib. There is parking in a lot on the premises for $14 a day.

THE EMBARCADERO: Many people like this area, located at the foot of Market Street, because it is extremely convenient.

When you need diapers and sundries, you can try Russell's, at Four Embarcadero Center (tel. 415/397-9565). Want to let the kids run off some of their energy? The plaza area at the Embarcadero Center is one place. Another, a nice little grassy park, is located between Davis, Front, Jackson, and Pacific Streets.

The **Hyatt Regency San Francisco,** 5 Embarcadero Center, San Francisco, CA 94111 (tel. 415/788-1234, or toll free 800/228-9000), has one of the most dramatic—and popular—lobbies in all of San Francisco (maybe California). Designed by architect John Portman, who originated the atrium-court lobby, the 20-story, pyramid-like building has seven sides and a 300-foot-long skylight in the roof.

You'll catch your breath as you enter the lobby—even if you're not a big fan of contemporary architecture. This is the center of activity in the hotel (and, we suspect, the neighborhood). There's no shh, shh, here. Instead there's movement, life, sounds. Regularly scheduled musicians perform in the atrium lobby. (You'll even see groups of children on field trips with their teachers.)

There are full size trees, thousands of plants and shrubs, a running stream, and the wonderful *Eclipse* sculpture fountain. As the water drapes down around the fountain's sides, it looks like plastic wrap. Kids stand at the edge of the fountain, carefully running their fingers around the edge to be sure it *is* water and not plastic wrap. This is a fun place for kids, who enjoy exploring the park-like atmosphere. During holiday season they might spot the Easter Bunny or Santa's helpers. And make sure they see the gingerbread house display (made of real gingerbread).

Then there are the five glass elevators that are edged with tiny lights, a real treat to children who oooh! and ahhh! as they glide up and down. Probably the only drawback here is that your children can get so caught up in everything they see that they wander off.

The hotel's location is another plus, with a BART station next door, the Ferry Building across the street, and the California Street cable-car line originating outside the hotel's doorsteps. The hotel is adjacent to the Embarcadero Center (the enormous shopping complex of 135 shops and 40 restaurants) and opens onto the Embarcadero Plaza. The huge plaza is host to lots of skateboarders, who love to ride on the smooth cement—great for watching.

There is full concierge service (the staff will be glad to arrange for babysitting), 24-hour room service, doctor and dentist on-call, valet parking with in-and-out privileges, same-day dry cleaning and laundry, retail shops (gift shop, beauty salon, jewelry and women's clothes boutiques), and guest privileges at a nearby health club.

The Market Place Bar and Restaurant has an outdoor and indoor eating area, and offers a nice selection of lighter fare. It is open daily for lunch ($8 to $12.50) and dinner (average dinner is $21). Mrs. Candy's is a café located in the atrium lobby, serving breakfast, lunch, and dinner as well as light pastries and snacks. Breakfasts cost $3.50 to $11; lunches are $4.75 to $11; dinners are $8 to $19. The Equinox is the hotel's expensive rooftop restaurant and lounge that makes a 360° rotation every 45 minutes. It's open for lunch and dinner daily. Highchairs and boosters are available in all restaurants, and children's plates are half price. Sunday brunch (with more than 100 different dishes) is served in the atrium lobby from 10 a.m. to 2 p.m.

Each of the 803 guest rooms has a view of either the bay or the city, and has sliding glass doors. Many of the rooms have balconies with little tables and chairs. There are a number of one- and two-bedroom suites, as well as the regular rooms that have king- or queen-size beds with small sitting areas. All have mini-honor bars, SpectraVision TV, and tub/shower combinations as well as in-room amenities.

Room rates are $175 to $218 single and $205 to $248 double (depending on location). Suites start at $350. Kids under 18 are free when they occupy the same room as their parents. Cribs are free. The Family Plan means that if two rooms are occupied, the single rate is charged for each. Additional adults pay $25 per night. Connecting rooms are available.

NOB HILL AREA: Nob Hill is the crossroads for the Powell, California, and Hyde Street cable cars. It is a beautiful location with charming Huntington Park at its crest.

You'll find several neighborhood markets if you head down toward Union Square. Walgreen's Drugstore, 500 Geary St. (tel. 415/673-8411 or 415/673-8413), is open 24 hours a day and stocks milk, diapers, formula, and other necessities.

The **Fairmont Hotel,** 950 Mason St. (at California Street, atop Nob Hill), San Francisco, CA 94106 (tel. 415/772-5000), is as ornate a hotel as you'll find. The 80-year-old grand dame has an enormous lobby done in red velvets with black accents. The formal carriage entrance leads you into the huge room with crystal chandeliers, where massive Corinthian columns support the lavishly carved gilt ceiling. Today most kids know the hotel as the one on the television series "Hotel," and will ask you to wander inside it.

The Fairmont, with more than 600 rooms, has been called a city within a city. It has nine restaurants, a barbershop, beauty shop, drugstore, florist, gift shop, even a bank. In addition to 24-hour room service, it offers concierge service, parking, babysitting, and a doctor on-call. The concierge will make arrangements for you if you want to use tennis courts, a gym, or a swimming pool.

Many of the spacious rooms have high ceilings and huge picture windows. All rooms are air-conditioned and have cable color TVs with free HBO. The baths have shower/tub combinations and the amenity baskets we've come to rely on. You have a choice of king-size, queen-size, double, or single beds.

Rates in the main building are $140 to $170 single and $170 to $200 double for interior rooms, $165 to $190 single and $195 to $220 double for exterior rooms. Rates in the tower are $175 to $230 single and $205 to $260 double. Suites start at $450 (in the main building). Connecting rooms are available, and cribs are free. Each additional person (including children) is charged $30 per night. Parking is $15.75 per day.

FISHERMAN'S WHARF: Many traveling families love to stay at Fisherman's Wharf—and there are several advantages to staying here when you're with the kids. The Wharf abounds with things for children to do—Pier 39, the attractions on the Wharf itself, boat rides, the Cannery, the Hyde Street Pier, and Ghirardelli Square (see the "What to Do" section for details). It's a tourist area, so kids are just part of the general scene. In addition, there is a little more open space than downtown, making it a little easier to meander and stroll and let the children run around. In fact, you'd be hard-pressed to find a restaurant in the area that isn't well prepared for kids, regardless of the price bracket.

Like other parts of the city, parking is a problem here too. But many hotels at the Wharf anticipate the family vacationer and offer free or lower-cost parking (always ask if you have in-and-out-privileges). You can leave your car at the hotel for the vast majority of excursions you take. In fact, it will be much easier if you don't have the car to worry about.

Waterfront Park (near Pier 39) and Aquatic Park (across from Ghirardelli Square) are wonderful places where you can let the kids play. If you need a 24-hour pharmacy, there's a Walgreen's at 3201 Divisidero St., near Lombard (tel. 415/931-6415).

Deluxe

If you prefer to stay in elegantly appointed accommodations, you might choose the **San Francisco Marriott Fisherman's Wharf,** 1250 Columbus Ave., San Francisco, CA 94133 (tel. 415/775-7555, or toll free 800/228-9290). Polished brass, overstuffed chairs, and chandeliers grace the spacious lobby, which is decorated like a large living room with lots of small conversation areas. Wellington's Restaurant and the Lobby Lounge open into it.

Amenities include twice-daily housekeeping service, complimentary morning newspaper, and nightly turndown service with a little sweet just for fun. Room service is available from 6:30 a.m. to 11 p.m. The front desk will give you referrals to a babysitting agency. Other amenities include complimentary limo service to the financial district on weekday mornings, valet parking, 24-hour movies, and free HBO, ESPN, and CNN.

Wellington's Restaurant is open daily for breakfast, lunch, and dinner. Breakfasts average $6, lunches average $7, and dinners range from $6 to $23. It has boosters, highchairs, and a varied children's menu (prices from $3 to $5). The lobby lounge has complimentary hors d'oeuvres from 5 to 7 p.m. and features a piano player every evening.

The 256 handsomely decorated rooms have beautiful wood furniture. All rooms have two telephones, shower and bath, and such amenities as complimentary shampoo, bubblebath, and lotions. Refrigerators are available upon request for $10 per day. Suites consist of a parlor (with a sofabed), kitchen area (with refrigerator, dining table, and bath), plus the one or two bedrooms that connect. Each bedroom has its own bath, so the two-bedroom suite has three baths. Each floor has an inviting little sitting area lobby off the elevator.

Rates are $150 single and $165 double; junior suites are $195 single and $210 double. One-bedroom suites rent for $350 and two-bedroom suites start at $475. Be sure to ask about special packages and seasonal rates. Connecting rooms are available. Cribs are free; rollaways cost $10. Children under 18 stay free in their parents' room. Parking is $12 a day, with in-and-out privileges.

Upper Bracket

The entrance to the **Sheraton at Fisherman's Wharf,** 2500 Mason St., San Francisco, CA 94133 (tel. 415/362-5500, or toll free 800/325-3535), is wide and open, bringing the outdoor wharf motif into the hotel style. Grayed wood, nautical rope, and greenery are used. This isn't a high-rise hotel, but rather one with only four floors that takes up an entire city block, giving the hostelry a resort ambience. There are three buildings, but you never have to go outside to cross to another building.

The outdoor swimming pool has a large, shallow area that is good for kids. Lots of families stay at this hotel, as it's conveniently situated—just a few blocks from Pier 39 and Ghirardelli Square. Babysitting can be arranged by the guest services people through a referral service. Guest services will also arrange for tours and sightseeing needs. There's 24-hour room service, and also an express checkout that can be done with your credit card using the television monitor so you can avoid the crowd at the front desk.

For food, the Mason Beach Grill serves breakfast, lunch, and dinner in a contemporary eatery, with varied menus for all meals. In the evening there's also an all-you-can-eat seafood buffet at $15.50 for adults and $13 for children under 12. Breakfast ranges from $5 to $10; lunch, from $5 to $13; dinners run $6.50 to $16. A children's menu is available. For a drink, try Chanen's Lounge, an old San Francisco–style saloon.

The 525 attractive, newly decorated rooms are done in muted tones of gray and peach. Each has a TV with free HBO and Sports Channel, and in-room movies are available for $6.75. The large rooms (with two double beds) have enough space for a crib. Bathrooms feature tubs and showers and lots of counter space. Complete in-room amenities are provided. Refrigerators can be requested for the length of your stay for a flat charge of $20. Rooms open onto large, airy hallways decorated with plants and small trees.

Rooms rent for $120 to $160 single and $140 to $180 double (depending on location). Ask if there are any special packages available; they can be significantly less expensive. Children under 17 stay free in their parents' room if a rollaway bed is not needed. Cribs are free; rollaways cost $20. Connecting rooms are available. Parking costs $8 per day, with in-and-out privileges.

One block up from Fisherman's Wharf, but still in the midst of all the activity is the **Holiday Inn Fisherman's Wharf,** 1300 Columbus Ave., San Francisco, CA 94133 (tel. 415/771-9000, or toll free 800/HOLIDAY). It's located across the street from the Cannery and Anchorage Shopping Centers near the cable-car turnaround. Traditionally a family place, this contemporary-style hotel consists of two buildings across the street from each other (the Columbus building and the Beach building). There is a little van to shuttle people from one to the other when it's raining.

The swimming pool area is nice and large, and is surrounded by little umbrella-shaded tables. There is a coin-operated laundry (washer and dryer) in each of the two buildings for guest use. Babysitting may be arranged by guests through an agency. Room service is available from 6 a.m. to 10 p.m.

The Columbus building houses Charley's Restaurant and Lounge, which specializes in sumptuous buffets for breakfast, lunch, and dinner. The breakfast and lunch buffets cost $8 for adults and $4.50 for children, and the dinner buffet runs $15 for adults and $11 for kids. Regular menu items are also offered. Boosters and highchairs are available.

All 580 comfortable rooms are decorated in soft, muted tones and have bath/shower combinations, table and chairs, and televisions offering free Showtime as well as pay channels. The large one- and two-bedroom suites have a living room with a sofa bed, television, eating area, kitchen, and large dining table and chairs, with plenty of room for a crib or rollaway.

Room rates vary seasonally (the highest prices are in the summer): $110 to $127 single, $126 to $143 double. Add $11 per night if you want a king-size bed. A one-bedroom suite rents for $250; a two-bedroom suite is $350. Connecting rooms are available. Cribs are free; rollaways cost $9 per night. Children under 17 are free when sharing a room with a parent. Additional adults are charged $15 per night. Free parking.

Located just off the Wharf, the **Ramada Hotel at Fisherman's Wharf,** 590 Bay St. (at Jones Street), San Francisco, CA 94133 (tel. 415/885-4700, or toll free 800/2-RAMADA), gives good value for the money and has a great location. But we think the nicest features are the sundeck, jogging track (ten times around is a mile), and par-course. Moms and dads can lounge in the sun while little ones play nearby. Kids need to be supervised, but only hotel guests can use the area, so it is secure. Guests may arrange babysitting through a referral service. Room service is available from 6 a.m. to 10 p.m. (the kitchen is closed from 2 to 5 p.m.). Soft-drink and ice machines are located on each floor.

The Conch Pearl Restaurant on premises serves breakfast ($4 to $9.25), lunch ($6.50 to $10), and dinner ($6.50 to $15). A very reasonably priced children's breakfast menu is provided. Highchairs and boosters are available. There's a lobby bar called the Pelican's Lounge.

The 231 spacious, bright rooms, renovated in 1985, have either a king-size bed or two double beds, plus small game tables, and can accommodate even two children, including a baby crib or rollaway. All bathrooms have vanity areas, showers, and tubs. Pay movies are available. Rooms, decorated in light mauve and brown or burgundy and blues, face either an open courtyard or the street.

"Superior" rooms with king-size beds have sofa beds and coffee tables—and can sleep four or five people. Master suites are huge, and also have refrigerators.

Rooms with two double beds cost $98 to $120 single and $113 to $135 double; "deluxe" rooms (with one king-size bed) are $105 to $125 single and $120 to $140 double; "superior" rooms (with one king-size bed and a sofa bed) rent for $140 to $155 single and $155 to $170 double. A master suite (with a king-size bed, a sofa bed, and a wet bar) is priced at $200 to $240 single and $240 to $270 double. Cribs are free; rollaways cost $15. Children under 18 stay free in their parents' room if an extra bed is not needed. Connecting rooms are available. There's free parking in an adjacent garage.

The only bayfront hotel at Fisherman's Wharf is the **San Francisco Travelodge Viscount Club at the Wharf,** 250 Beach St., San Francisco, CA 94133 (tel. 415/392-6700, or toll free 800/255-3050). This nicely landscaped hotel has a swimming pool with a large three-foot wading area. Some rooms have outdoor balconies with views of the *Balclutha* (see the "What to Do and See" section, below) and the swimming pool.

Early morning, you might want to get the family together and have breakfast at Angellina's, where you can see Alcatraz Island. Angellina's is a family-style restaurant, open daily from 7 a.m. to 8 p.m. during summers and holidays (for winter hours, ask at the front desk). Angellina's has a children's menu for breakfast, lunch, and dinner, priced from $2.75 to $4. Adult meals average $6 at breakfast, $6.50 at lunch, and $10 at dinner.

The 250 rooms are done in pleasing tones of blue and beige, with tie-back drapes and coordinated headboards. Each has a view—either of the bay or of the city (Coit Tower and the Pyramid). You can choose from two double beds or one king-size bed. The bathrooms have been completely redecorated and modernized. Not all bathrooms have tubs, so request one in advance if it is important to you. Refrigerators are free upon request. The concierge will arrange for babysitting.

Family rooms have two double beds and a sofa bed that opens into a double bed. In theory, you could sleep six people in one of these large rooms.

Rates change seasonally and vary according to location in the hotel: singles range from $105 to $150 and doubles range from $115 to $160. Suites cost $200 to $300 per night. Connecting rooms and no-smoking rooms are available. Cribs are free; rollaways cost $10 per night. Children 18 and under are free when sharing their parents' room. The hotel will try to upgrade whenever possible, so be sure to tell the clerk at the time you make your reservations that you're bringing your family.

Moderately Priced

Located on the Hyde Street cable-car line, just a little off the main area of the Wharf (near Ghirardelli Square and the Cannery) is **Hyde Park Suites,** 2655 Hyde St. (at North Point Street), San Francisco, CA 94109 (tel. 415/771-0200, or toll free 800/227-3608).

The hotel itself is pretty and only four floors high (unusual in this high-rise city). The guest suites are built around a contemporary, early California–style atrium, which gives the hotel an open feeling. The courtyard, with its terracotta tiles, wicker furniture, fountain, lots of plants, and small trees that reach up to the skylight, give it an out-of-doors feel. Children love playing in the atrium, and are welcome to do so as long as a parent is with them. A complimentary glass of wine is served every evening in the courtyard.

Each room has a stocked honor bar. Babysitting can be arranged through the concierge. A coin-operated washer/dryer is available. Other touches include 24-hour concierge service, free limo service to downtown, nightly turndown service, free coffee and tea in your room, and complimentary morning newspaper.

Free continental breakfast is served every morning in the lobby, and a fruit basket is filled at all times with apples and oranges for guests. Grocery delivery service is available, and a limited-menu room service is offered from 4 p.m. till midnight (light sandwiches, salads).

More like a home away from home, these suites come with fully equipped kitchens, including microwave and dishwasher. Although they tend to be a bit on the small side, the suites can function like an apartment and have enough space in the living room for a crib and rollaway. Some have private patios. Each suite has two televisions, tub/shower combinations, and a small dining table. The bedroom is completely separate. Guests also receive such amenities as shampoo, conditioner, and body lotion, as well as terrycloth bathrobes.

Rates range from $125 to $200. Sunday through Thursday a limited number of $125 (one-bedroom) suites are available; these otherwise rent for $150. Third-floor suites with a view of the bay or with a balcony cost $175. Two-bedroom suites that sleep up to six people are available for $200. Children under 12 stay free, and those 12 and over are charged $10 each per night. Cribs are free, as are rollaways for children under 12. Parking or valet parking is available at $10 per day, with in-and-out privileges.

Budget

A budget-priced alternative is the **Columbus Motor Inn,** 1075 Columbus Ave., San Francisco, CA 94133 (tel. 415/885-1492), located between Fisherman's Wharf and North Beach. The 45 rooms have king-size, queen-size, or extra-long double beds, separate vanity areas, color televisions, and in-room coffee. Family suites have separate sitting rooms.

This is a simple place—no lobby, just a front desk. But it is pleasant and less expensive than hostelries with more elaborate facilities. Free parking is available on the premises, and babysitting may be arranged by guests through a bonded babysitting service.

Rooms with a king-size bed rent for $67 single, $72 double. Rooms with two double beds cost $72, single or double, plus $5 each for a third or fourth person. Rooms with two queen-size beds and a sofa bed are $80, single or double, plus $5 for each additional person (up to a total of six). A two-room suite with king- and queen-size beds (accommodating one to four people) costs $94. A two-room suite with two double beds and a queen-size bed (accommodating up to six) rents for $98 for one to four people, plus $5 for each additional person (up to six). Cribs are free; rollaways cost $5 per night. Children under 5 stay free in their parents' room.

Six blocks from Fisherman's Wharf at Union Street is the **Vagabond Inn,** 2550 Van Ness Ave., San Francisco, CA 94109 (tel. 415/776-7500, or toll free 800/522-1555), a place so centrally located that it's claimed you can get anywhere in the city without ever using your car. But the biggest draw here is price. These nice rooms come with complimentary continental breakfast (orange juice, doughnuts, and coffee), all-day coffee and tea, and apples in the lobby.

Management here is extremely accommodating to families and will give you referrals for babysitters. The nice-sized pool area has a little patio and gazebo. Continental breakfast is served from 7 to 9 a.m. The inn is adjacent to the City Café, which is open 24 hours and has a full coffeeshop menu. Boosters only available.

Since the 132 rooms vary considerably in size, be sure to tell the reservationist that you're bringing a couple of kids and you want a larger room. Some accommodations are large enough to sleep six people and even have room for a crib. These layouts have large sitting areas in addition to a small game table and chair. Request a bathtub if you have a preference.

Room rates are seasonal. In high season (July 1 to September 30), singles cost $80; doubles, $85. The rest of the year the prices range from $60 to $70 single and $65 to $75 double. Family rooms are available and cost $125 to $150. Children under 18 are free in the same room as their parents. No charge for cribs. Free parking.

LOMBARD STREET/MARINA AREA: The Marina area is a good choice for families because you can find more moderately priced accommodations here. In fact, if you're looking for budget lodgings, this is the area we recommend. Conveniently located near Fisherman's Wharf (and surrounding Ghirardelli Square, the Cannery, Pier 39, Maritime Museum), Union Street, and not too far from downtown, it is less congested here than in most of the other areas of town —certainly less than Fisherman's Wharf and the Union Square area.

There is a neighborhood park at Chestnut and Laguna, which features playground equipment, a community center, and tennis courts—and you're close to

Aquatic Park as well. There is a 24-hour pharmacy, Walgreen's, at 3201 Divisidero St. (tel. 415/931-6415), and a market at 15 Marina Blvd. (tel. 415/563-4946).

Best Bet for the Money

A wonderful bed-and-breakfast–style place, the **Marina Inn,** 3110 Octavia St. (at Lombard Street), San Francisco, CA 94123 (tel. 415/928-1000), is definitely the best buy in this area if you don't mind a small space. This budget-priced accommodation, owned by the same management as the White Swan and Petite Auberge, was designed for the "price-sensitive traveler." Created to feel like an English country-style inn, you enter the four-story Victorian hotel and walk into a small foyer that has vaulted ceilings and is light with color. The inn is bright and fresh, with lots of pink marble, brass fixtures, and simple pine furniture.

Manager Suzie Baum says that people are so happy to have comfortable rooms at this price that many take a second room for their kids—exactly what we would suggest (if you can afford it), given that many of the rooms are very small. There are no adjoining rooms, but you can get two next door to each other. Since some of the rooms are very small, be sure to indicate that you're bringing your family when you make reservations. Suzie wants to accommodate families and encourages people to ask her if they need special arrangements. Ask if there are special rates because they will upgrade your room at certain times.

Tastefully decorated, the English country-inn theme is carried on throughout. If you're lucky, you'll get a room with a charming bay window and seat. All 40 rooms have pine furniture, queen-size poster beds, and quilts that are set off by the pretty pastel-flowered wallpaper and forest-green carpet. Rooms have private baths with showers and tubs, plus phones and TV.

There is a small common room that has a microwave, a small refrigerator, and all-day coffee and tea service. This is where complimentary continental breakfast (juice, fresh muffins, choice of hot beverage) is served. Guests are encouraged to take their breakfast back to their rooms, however, since this room is quite small. When breakfast is not being served, you're welcome to let the kids play their board games here. Other amenities include turndown service, one-day laundry service (or take your own to a laundromat one block away), fresh flowers, and a huge basket of apples available at all times at the front desk. The front desk will help you make babysitting and sightseeing reservations.

Rates range from $55 to $85, single or double (depending on size and location of room), and include a free continental breakfast and afternoon sherry. Cribs are provided free, but there is a $15 daily charge for children over 4.

Budget

Cow Hollow Motor Inn, 2190 Lombard St. (at Steiner Street), San Francisco, CA 94123 (tel. 415/921-5800 or 415/922-8500), has 117 spacious, newly decorated and some newly constructed rooms. While some of the inside rooms are dark, the décor—light pink and blue pastels with flowered wallpaper—makes even these rooms acceptable. Ask for an outside room. They're bright and quite lovely.

Rooms are tastefully decorated, and some are so large that even with a king-size bed, there's a space for a crib and a rollaway and you'll still have plenty of room to move around. Most of the rooms have two extra-long double beds, however, and are quite nice. Rooms have tubs and showers, large sink areas in the bathroom, and a vanity area with a mirror. Each room has a coffee maker.

While the motor inn doesn't have room service or a restaurant, Mel's Drive-in (see the "Where to Eat" section for details) is directly across the street.

Rooms with a king-size bed rent for $67 single and $72 double. Those with two double beds cost $72, single or double, plus $5 for each additional occupant up to four. Rooms with two double beds and a sofa bed rent for $77, single or double, plus $5 for each additional occupant up to four. Connecting rooms are available. There's no charge for cribs, but rollaways cost $5 per night. Children under 5 stay free in their parents' room. Free parking.

Owned by the same folks as Cow Hollow, the **Chelsea Motor Inn,** 2095 Lombard St. (at Fillmore Street), San Francisco, CA 94123 (tel. 415/563-5600), is another attractive budget-priced alternative. Somewhat surprising are the extra touches here: a no-smoking floor, a security elevator that opens only with a room key, king- and queen-size beds or extra-long double beds, queen-size sofa beds, and coffee and tea in the room.

These are large, comfortable rooms (60 of them) done up in earth tones—beige, brown, cinnamon—and set off with touches of blue. Each is equipped with shower and cast-iron tub, and a vanity area with mirror. Some third-floor rooms have a view.

Rooms with a king-size bed cost $65 single, $70 double. Rooms with two double beds are $70, single or double, plus $5 each for a third or fourth occupant. Rooms with two queen-size beds and a sofa bed rent for $78, single or double; additional occupants (to a total of four) are charged $5 each. Connecting rooms are available. No charge for cribs; rollaways cost $5. Children under 5 stay free in their parents' room. Free parking.

The **Coventry Motor Inn,** 1901 Lombard St. (at Buchanan Street), San Francisco, CA 94123 (tel. 415/567-1200), is another small (69 rooms) motor inn that offers families good value and pleasant surroundings. Also owned by the same people who own Cow Hollow Motor Inn, this hostelry opened in 1984. The simple rooms are attractively furnished and have either king-size or extra-long double beds, small game tables with chairs, and a convenient bath/vanity area. There is in-room coffee and indoor parking.

Rates are $65 single and $70 double in rooms with king-size beds; those with two double beds are $70, single or double; $75 triple; and $80 quad. Family rooms consisting of two queen-size beds and a sofa bed cost $78, single or double; additional occupants (up to a total of five) pay $5 each per night. Cribs are free; rollaways cost $5. Children 5 and under stay free in their parents' room; children over 5 are charged $5 per night.

The **Quality Inn,** 2775 Van Ness Ave. (at Lombard Street), San Francisco, CA 94109 (tel. 415/928-5000, or toll free 800/228-5151), is an excellent choice in the budget-price bracket. The rooms are clean and attractive, there's a good little restaurant on the premises, and you can't beat the location—seven blocks to Ghirardelli Square.

The hotel's 140 guest rooms are divided into two types. On one side of the hotel are average-sized rooms with one queen-size bed, a table and chairs, and a desk. The bathrooms are small, but do have tub/shower combinations. These rooms can accommodate a crib or rollaway, but may seem cramped.

On the other side are larger rooms, which have a beautiful view of the bay and the Golden Gate Bridge. These have two double beds, a game table and chairs, and a desk, as well as a good-size bathroom.

All rooms have color television, in-room movies, and complimentary coffee service. One surprise for such a budget-bracket hostelry is the fine coffeeshop, called Brandi's, which is open for breakfast, lunch, and dinner. The food is quite good, and is also available through room service.

Rates change seasonally. From May to November singles cost $79 to $94 and doubles are $89 to $114; the rest of the year, singles run $69 to $91 and doubles rent for $79 to $101. Adjoining rooms are available. No charge for cribs; rollaways cost $10. Children under 16 stay free when occupying the same room as a parent. Each additional person pays $10. Free parking.

The best thing about the **Lombard Motor Inn,** 1475 Lombard St. (at Franklin Street, near Van Ness Avenue), San Francisco, CA 94123 (tel. 415/441-6000), is its convenient location. Don't expect anything fancy here, but rates are very reasonable and you'll find it clean and pleasant.

Standard rooms include in-room coffee and a king-size or extra-long double bed. If you want a bath with a tub/shower, you need to request it at the time you make your reservations. There's no charge for local telephone calls. Free indoor parking on the premises.

Rooms with a king-size bed rent for $54 single and $60 double. Rooms with two double beds cost $64, single or double; additional guests pay $4 each per night. Connecting rooms are available. No charge for cribs; rollaways cost $5. Children under 10 stay free in their parents' room.

JAPANTOWN: This area of the city is a bit off the beaten hotel path, but many people like the unusual ambience of Japantown. The Plaza area is a good one for energetic children, and there is a 24-hour Safeway market at 1335 Webster St. (tel. 415/921-4557), near Japan Center.

Moderate

The **Queen Anne Hotel,** 1590 Sutter St., San Francisco, CA 94109 (tel. 415/441-2828), is a stately Victorian building of the 1890s that has been elegantly restored to make guests feel as if they are stepping into another era. Dark, traditional woods set off the other antique pieces—some of polished brass, others of shining silver. And the restored Victorian grand staircase is exquisite. The lobby has a large parlor area separated from the registration desk and has several conversation groups. There is another small room, called the library (which can be closed off), where there is a fireplace, card table and chairs, and upholstered chairs that offer a comfortable place for reading.

What about children? Manager George Wright encourages families to visit . . . and loves children. He says they get lots of them here. The atmosphere of the hotel is somewhat quiet, even hushed, without being stuffy, so if your children fit that description, it's a great place to experience the beauty of the city in a lovely setting. Older, more reserved children will do best here. Or more aptly stated, parents of older, more reserved children will do best because they won't have to worry about the kids.

This graceful, handsome hotel also sends a free continental breakfast to each room and offers tea, coffee, and sherry service in the parlor in the afternoon.

Each of the 49 guest rooms and suites is unique and decorated in antiques. Some rooms have beautiful bay windows, fireplaces, wet bars, and parlors. Most have tall windows set off by sheers behind richly colored side drapes and other authentic Victorian detailings. Armoires are found in some of the rooms instead of closets, and most rooms are large enough to comfortably accommodate a rollaway or crib. You can request a small refrigerator for use during your stay. All rooms have remote-control color TV, AM/FM radio, and phones in bedroom and bathroom. All the bathrooms have been completely modernized and include a tub/shower combination.

Rates quoted are for single or double occupancy and range from $89 to $139, including the complimentary continental breakfast and afternoon sherry. There are three one-bedroom suites in which the parlor has a queen-size sofa bed and these cost $139 per night. Children under 13 are free when sharing a room with an adult, and there is a $20 charge for each additional person.

Budget

If you'd like to stay in Japantown, **Best Western Kyoto Inn,** 1800 Sutter St. (at Buchanan Street), San Francisco, CA 94115 (tel. 415/921-4000, or toll free 800/528-1234), is a small, quiet hotel with 125 accommodations. Although the rooms are Western style, this small urban hotel has an air of Japan. It's located in a quiet neighborhood, with public transportation to downtown and other areas available every five or ten minutes. Step down into the sunken lobby with its polished brass doors and feel the suggestion of Japan with wood-framed, shoji-style windows.

Café Mums, located on the first floor, is open from 7 a.m. to 10 p.m. Breakfasts cost $4 to $9.50, lunches are $3.50 to $7, and dinners run $5.50 to $11. Japanese specialties available.

As for the accommodations, the rooms with two double beds are fair-sized and open onto interior hallways. The one- and two-bedroom suites have a parlor with a couch that turns into a double bed, a small eating table and chairs, a refrigerator, television, coffee table, and rattan chairs. Each suite bedroom comes with two double beds and has its own bathroom with steambath. There's plenty of room for a crib in the parlor. A one-bedroom suite could comfortably sleep a family of five or six.

Rooms rent for $67 single ($73 with steambath) and $77 double ($83 with steambath). One- and two-bedroom suites range from $130 to $200 per night. Connecting rooms are available. No charge for cribs; rollaways cost $10. Children 18 and under are free when sharing their parents' room. If a family needs more than one room, each room will be charged at the single rate regardless of the number of occupants. Parking is $4 per night.

5. WHERE TO EAT

It's been said that San Francisco has so many restaurants that if you ate in a different one for every meal, it would take you four years to try them all. And new ones open all the time!

San Francisco is an epicurean's dream—even if that food lover has kids and wants to dine with them. Hundreds of restaurants welcome families. We've chosen many of them, listed them by neighborhood first and price second. And we've limited cuisine to the types that children are most likely to eat. Enjoy.

UNION SQUARE: One of the great things about the Union Square area is that it's packed with restaurants, many of them in hotels. You can walk down almost any block and find at least three restaurants. These are the ones we liked best.

Remember, though, that parking in this area can be a major headache. Unless we so specify, parking is on the street. There's one main parking lot under Union Square and others on side streets, but the rates are high. If at all possible, take a taxi or use public transportation. And, remember that distances are short, so walking is often the best way to get from one place to another.

Expensive

The **French Room,** in the Four Seasons Clift Hotel, 495 Geary St. (tel. 415/775-4700), is a spectacularly ornate restaurant. The 18th-century French décor (complete with relief-style paneled walls) is set off by tall tapestry-framed windows and elegant crystal chandeliers. There are Louis XV petit-point chairs, Queen Anne–style love seats, and mahogany console servers. But this award-winning French-continental restaurant features more than just beautiful surroundings. And to our delight, it welcomes children!

Open for breakfast, lunch, and dinner, the restaurant is famous for its evening meals and its collection of over 20,000 bottles of fine French and California wines. Prime rib, fresh lamb sausage with wild mushrooms, medallions of veal, and fresh seafood are just a few of the dinner specialties. There is also an alternative menu that offers entrees low in calories, sodium, and cholesterol. Samples from this menu include linguine with clams in chablis sauce, grilled fish (with garlic and roasted peppers), and delicacies such as breast of partridge or warm eggplant salad. The average check per person, including beverage, is $12 at breakfast, $20 at lunch, and $40 at dinner.

The children's menu features macaroni and cheese, junior beef or cheese-burgers, chicken fingers, and jumbo hot dogs, with prices from $2.50 to $5.25. The restaurant is also willing to serve children smaller portions of most items on the regular menu.

Highchairs and boosters are available, and the staff greets children with a smile and a small trinket—a coloring book, a comic book, or the like. Ours especially loved the baseball trading cards.

The French Room is open daily. Breakfast is served from 7 to 11 a.m.; lunch hours are noon to 2 p.m. (Monday through Saturday); and dinner is available from 6 to 10:30 p.m. daily. Sunday brunch is offered from 11 a.m. to 2 p.m. and costs $25 for adults, $17.50 for children. Reservations are suggested. All major credit cards accepted. Valet parking.

Tucked away behind the chic shops of Union Square at 19 Maiden Lane, the **Iron Horse Restaurant** (tel. 415/362-8133) is like stepping into an old San Francisco establishment. The restaurant has a British air about it—dimly lit, sconces on the wall, white linen cloths. It's a lovely place to enjoy an out-of-the-ordinary Italian dinner.

When we were there, the staff was exceptionally nice to kids (several of whom dined there at 9 p.m.), bringing bread and three cherries in the Shirley Temple, but the wait for dinner was quite long, so be prepared. By the time Andrew's entree came, he was very impatient and hungry. The dim light makes it difficult for kids to read; the tablecloths make bringing crayons questionable. While we saw a toddler there, we'd suggest this place for well-behaved youngsters or older kids. These folks welcome children, and will warm baby bottles and baby food, and make a wide array of children's drinks. We'd suggest that you go early to avoid the romantic diners and businesspeople.

The food is good and the menu is printed daily to feature all the specials. The lunch menu is extensive, offering the likes of 15 different salads, sandwiches, omelets, pasta, seafood, and hot entrees. Prices range from $3 for mixed garden greens to $16 for New York Angus sirloin steak.

For dinner, we loved the marinated rack of lamb ($19) and the cannelloni della casa ($11). The artichoke-and-seafood salad was a special treat ($6.75), and the above-mentioned steak was tender and large. You might split an order of luscious, rich gnocchi.

Request a highchair when you make your reservation. Boosters are also available. No children's menu here, but the staff is extremely helpful in offering ideas to kids about what to eat and will prepare half orders whenever possible (for half price). Reservations are accepted.

Open Monday through Saturday for lunch from 11:30 a.m. to 4 p.m., and daily for dinner from 5:30 to 10:30 p.m. Major credit cards accepted.

Not actually at Union Square, but at the top of Nob Hill in the Fairmont Hotel, the **Tonga Room** (tel. 415/772-5278) is a tropical paradise. If you don't want to eat pricey Polynesian food with the kids, be sure at least to come for drinks and a look-around.

Housed in the Fairmont Hotel, the Tonga Room is built around the hotel's transformed Olympic swimming pool. The décor is totally South Seas, with grass thatched huts and masts of large sailing vessels. There is a large boat floating on the pool, and it "rains" about every 30 minutes! Flowers and plants surround the pool and the dining tables. You can imagine what a thrill the kids get from this place.

The Tonga Special dinner (for two or more people) is a special recommendation. For $15.50 per person, you can dine on Imperial eggroll, soup, Manchurian beef, almond chicken, sweet-and-sour pork, rice, and dessert. The Imperial Banquet (for three or more) is $35 per person and includes winter-melon soup, Flower Drum duck, Seven Seas lobster, stir-fried filet mignon, and six appetizers. À la carte entrees are available too, at $4.25 to $30.25.

There are highchairs and boosters available. Open for dinner only, seven nights a week from 5 p.m. to midnight. Reservations are strongly advised. Most major credit cards are accepted, and there is valet parking for $3 per hour.

Moderate

The **Dutch Kitchen** is located in the Westin St. Francis Hotel, 335 Powell St. (tel. 415/397-7000). We were surprised that this café in the ultra-luxurious St. Francis would be as gracious to children as they are. Andrew thinks of this place as one of the truly great breakfast spots in the world. Crayons and the "Kids' Kruise" menu (which doubles as a coloring page) are handed to each child as quickly as steaming coffee is brought to the table for the grownups. While the adults fill up on fresh berries, melons, and croissants at the Continental Breakfast Buffet ($7.50), the children delight in French toast with fruit and pancakes with sausage or bacon ($4). Other adult breakfast items include buttermilk pancakes ($5.75) and full egg breakfasts that range from $5.75 to $11.50.

Lunch and dinner run the gamut from salads, sandwiches, and pastas (starting at $4.25, averaging about $7.50) to more elaborate entrees (salmon at $13.50, prime rib for $13.75) and early-bird complete dinners ($11, featuring London broil, chicken, or linguine with clam-and-herb sauce). These dinner specials are served Monday through Saturday from 5 to 7 p.m. Kids can have grilled cheese, chicken, or cheeseburgers, with fries, beverage, and dessert, for $5.

Breakfast is served daily from 6 to 11:30 a.m., lunch is from 11:30 a.m. to 5 p.m., and dinner, from 5 to 11:30 p.m. You can park in the hotel lot—but it's costly. *Note:* If you have a stroller, don't enter the restaurant via Post Street—the stairs will do you in. Enter through the hotel lobby, which is located on Powell Street. Major credit cards are accepted.

Looking for a great place for your teens and preteens? **Lori's Diner,** 336 Mason St., near Geary Street (tel. 415/392-8646), a fun, trendy eatery, may just be the place. There's lots of polished chrome and 1950s memorabilia (Elvis and James Dean posters everywhere), but what really grabs the kids is the '50s jukebox filled with Sha-Na-Na music.

While there are no highchairs, booster seats fit easily in the high-gloss red booths. Our kids loved the place. They watched the cook make the burgers and shakes—always a treat. This place is so trendy they even sell Lori's Diner T-shirts for $12.

The staff is friendly, and the food is good American fare—a palate pleaser for youngsters of all ages. While there's no children's menu, two children (or an adult and one child) can split one of the enormous burgers, which the cook will cut in half in the kitchen. The staff will be glad to warm bottles and baby food as well.

This restaurant is a real treat at any time. It's open 24 hours a day, seven days a week. That's unusual, even in San Francisco. Breakfasts are priced from $3.75 (pancakes) to $9 (steak and eggs). Hot dogs run from $4 to $6, and terrific burgers start at $4.50 (with fries). No credit cards or reservations.

Mama's of San Francisco, 398 Geary St., near Mason Street (tel. 415/788-1004), is another great eatery at Union Square—and an excellent alternative to pricey hotel coffeeshops. Good American fare for breakfast and lunch, and Italian food for dinner. Mama's has a reputation for originality and quality food among the locals.

For breakfast (served all day), munch on fresh-baked muffins, sweet rolls, or croissants for $1.25, while you wait for a truly original omelet. We had the Californian omelet (fresh vegetables and herbs, for $7 with home fries and sourdough toast) and Swedish cinnamon French toast ($4). Another great egg dish is the eggs Union Square (scrambled eggs with tomato, green onion, and ham at $5). If you're in the mood for something different, try the three-berry omelet (strawberry, raspberry, and blueberry plus yogurt and sour cream) or the apple pan doré (thin slices of French toast topped with Granny Smith and Red Delicious apples, butter, and cinnamon, at $7).

Lunch (served from 11 a.m. to 5 p.m.) consists of an array of salads (Nob Hill Salad is chicken, avocado, and fresh fruit with mixed greens at $8.50) and Mama's original sandwiches (Slim Joe is ground chuck with grilled onion and jack cheese on a French bread baguette, at $6.50).

The dinner menu is quite extensive. Good sandwiches and hamburgers are available for $5 to $7. Prime rib, veal, and pasta dinners range from $8 to $19. All include fresh vegetable and pasta or potatoes.

The children's menu features pasta, chicken, and sandwiches, and ranges in price from $4.50 to $6.50. For breakfast, the kids may have smaller portions or adult orders may be split in the kitchen for two children. Your server will warm bottles and baby food. The service here is very fast, and highchairs and boosters are available. Open from 7 a.m. to 12:30 a.m. Sunday through Thursday, and on Friday and Saturday till 1 a.m., every day except Christmas. All major credit cards accepted. Full bar. Another branch is **Mama's on Washington Square,** at 1701 Stockton St., near Filbert Street (tel. 415/362-6421). No credit cards. Hours are 7 a.m. to 3 p.m. daily.

Inexpensive

Salamagundi, 442 Geary St., near Mason Street (tel. 415/441-0894), is across the street from the A.C.T. and Curran Theaters. This soup-and-sandwich place is probably the best casual, inexpensive place to take kids before or after an outing—the theater, cable-car rides, walking through Union Square. The food is very good and the prices are reasonable.

There are 50 different homemade soups, three of them offered daily (favorites include lentil, country chicken with biscuits, and burgundy beef with noodles). For the price of a bowl ($3) you get a refill, and believe me you'll want it because it's delicious. Salads, quiche, and unusual sandwiches round out the bill of fare in this buffet-style restaurant. Prices range from $2.50 for a slice of quiche to $5 for soup, salad, roll, and drink. Boosters and highchairs are available. Children can easily split adult orders.

Hours are 11 a.m. to midnight daily.

There are other Salamagundi branches at Two Embarcadero Center (tel. 415/982-5603), open Monday through Friday from 11 a.m. to 9 p.m., on Saturday from 11:30 a.m. to 5:30 p.m. (closed Sunday); and 39 Grove St., Civic Center (tel. 415/431-7337), open Monday through Saturday from 11 a.m. to 9 p.m. and on Sunday from 11:30 a.m. to 8 p.m.

Sears Fine Food, 439 Powell St., on Union Square (tel. 415/986-1160), is about as famous as any coffeeshop can get. World renown for its sourdough French toast ($4.75), dollar-sized Swedish pancakes—you get 18 of them per serving, for $3.50—and crisp waffles (from $3.50 to $4.75), this family-oriented restaurant is as popular with the locals as with the tourists. We loved the apple dumpling ($4), and the turkey sandwich is always a big winner ($6) with our family.

There's often a line out the door because the food is scrumptious—but we were assured that it always moves quickly, only a ten-minute wait. And with Union Square and all the fascinating shops nearby, Dad could wait in line while Mom and the kids browse.

Open from 7 a.m. to 2:30 p.m. Wednesday through Sunday. There are booster seats but no highchairs. There is no children's menu, but they'll split adult portions and warm baby bottles and food. No credit cards or reservations.

If your family is into baseball, **Lefty O' Doul's,** 333 Geary St. (tel. 415/982-8900), is a legendary oldtime sports bar, and is known for serving good family-style fare. Baseball memorabilia surrounds you, and it's a fun place (once your eyes get used to the dim light) for children, who can spend lots of time looking at the mementos. The televisions at either end of the bar are always tuned to "the game," and the back dining room has a huge screen. Even little ones get caught up in the activity. The noise level is such that any noise your kids make will be absorbed.

Choose from delicious hot fresh turkey, roast beef, ham, pastrami, and more. Sandwiches are $4; full meals (which include salad, vegetable, and bread) are $7. Typical breakfast fare is priced equally appealingly at $4.25 to $4.75. For children, they'll give you smaller portions for half price.

There are highchairs but no boosters, and the staff will warm baby bottles or baby food in the kitchen. Open for breakfast from 7 to 11 a.m.; lunch and dinner, from 11 a.m. to 2 a.m. No credit cards or reservations accepted. There are family sing-alongs every night at the piano bar (but children are only allowed in areas where food is served).

NORTH BEACH: Famed for beatniks, coffeehouses, and strip joints, North Beach also offers a tantalizing array of restaurants everywhere you turn. If standard sit-down meals aren't your style, let the kids enjoy one of the many cafés or gelato places during your stroll through the area. But beware—parking is among the worst in the city, especially on Friday and Saturday nights.

You may want to avoid the area anyway on Friday and Saturday nights. Not only is the parking next to impossible, but on weekend nights, even the action on the sidewalks may be difficult to take with kids in tow. The barkers in front of the cabarets and shows on Broadway may make you—and the kids—uncomfortable.

We start with **Mara's Bakery,** 503 Columbus Ave. (tel. 415/397-9435), not really a restaurant but possibly one of the best places in North Beach for Italian pastry and cookies. Some say you rarely see these kind of pastries outside Italy. The tempting goodies are so plentiful that our 10-year-old took 20 minutes trying to pick which pastry he wanted. There are only three tables, so plan to take the sweets out (you might wander to nearby Washington Square to eat your treats). Espresso, tea, and coffee are also served. Open daily from 7 a.m. to 10:30 p.m.

Expensive

North Beach Restaurant, 1512 Stockton St. (tel. 415/392-1700), serves award-winning northern Italian cuisine—and serves it up to loads of families. They make their own pasta every day, hang and cure their own prosicutto hams, cut and prepare the veal in their own kitchen, and vow to serve the finest food they can. Choose from almost 30 different fish entrees (for example, petrale stuffed with shrimp and crab, abalone, or crab puff au gratin), 20 different veal entrees (veal piccata, veal with marsala wine, veal cutlets parmigiana, veal portafoglio with Grand Marnier sauce), as well as pasta, lamb, chicken, and steak. Full dinners come with antipasto, salad or soup, pasta, and fresh vegetable. Lunches range in price from $6.25 to $17.75; dinners, from $8.50 to $25.75 (à la carte prices, from $8.50 to $19.75).

While there is no children's menu, kids can choose from a large part of the menu and the chef will create a half-order at half price. Owner Lorenzo Petroni says that orders are so large that many parents just share with the children. Highchairs and boosters are available, and your server will gladly get the kids specialty drinks from the full bar. Bottles and baby food will be warmed.

Open daily for lunch and dinner from 11:30 a.m. to 11:45 p.m. All major credit cards accepted. Valet parking with $3 gratuity.

Moderate

Capp's Corner, 1600 Powell St., at Green Street (tel. 415/989-2589), is one of those authentic North Beach family restaurants that people associate with

San Francisco. Opened over 20 years ago, the walls are lined with photos of politicians, celebrities, and sports figures who have visited. Pictures of the pennant-winning San Francisco Giants cover the walls. And the colors of the Italian flag line the windows.

The tables are set up for traditional family-style dining. Entrees range from roast beef and leg of lamb to veal in marsala sauce and eggplant parmigiana. They serve clams, mussels, and homemade sausage. All entrees come with soup and salad, pasta, dessert, and coffee. Lunch costs $5.50 to $7; dinner runs $9 to $13. Children's portions are available.

Highchairs and boosters are available, and they'll warm bottles and baby food. Open daily except Monday. Lunch is served Tuesday through Friday from 11:30 a.m. to 2:30 p.m.; dinner is Tuesday through Thursday from 4:30 to 10:30 p.m., on Friday and Saturday till 11 p.m., and on Sunday from 4 to 10:30 p.m. Reservations are recommended. Most major credit cards are accepted. There is a parking lot across the street.

North Beach Pizza, 1499 Grant Ave., at Union Street (tel. 415/433-2444), is known for some of the best pizza in all San Francisco. This is a warm family place where waitresses laugh and joke with kid-customers. Small and cozy, with traditional red-checked cloths, candles in wine bottles, and garlic ropes hanging along the walls, this restaurant serves up over 20 kinds of pizza—from the tame to the exotic. Some of our favorite combinations are clams with garlic and cheese, and the Coit Tower special, which has mushrooms, sausage, salami, and pepperoni. There are vegetarian and seafood pizzas, as well as a wide selection of pastas, submarine sandwiches, and hot entrees. Reasonably priced full-course dinners ($7 to $11) of veal, poultry, seafood, or barbecued ribs include vegetables, spaghetti, soup or salad, and bread and butter.

Highchairs and boosters are available, but there's no children's menu. The staff will gladly split meals in the kitchen or bring an extra plate for the little ones. Ask for crackers for the kids to munch on while waiting for dinner. One drawback is that no reservations are accepted and you may have to wait if you come during the prime dinner hours.

Hours are Sunday through Thursday from 11 a.m. to 1 a.m., on Friday and Saturday to 3 a.m. Most major credit cards are accepted. Street parking. Also delivers pizzas (in moisture-controlled ovens) to hotels, and bills itself as the city's fastest delivery service. A second branch, called **North Beach Pizza, Too,** is at 1310 Grant Ave., at Vallejo Street (tel. 415/433-2444).

The Gold Spike, 527 Columbus Ave., between Union and Green Streets (tel. 415/986-9747), has been serving huge six-course family-style meals since 1920. Although the place is small, the walls are filled with business cards, postcards, pictures, signs—it's almost like being in a fantastic old junk store. The kids love to inspect the old treasures everywhere.

Dinners include antipasto, minestrone soup, salad, pasta, dessert, and a choice of entree for $12. À la carte and side orders are also available. Children can choose from many of the same items as adults. Portions and prices are adjusted.

No highchairs here, but boosters are available. Weekends tend to be busy, and because they don't take reservations there's often a long wait. The staff tries to be helpful with kids, but warns that Friday and Saturday nights are difficult because of the crowds. Open for dinner only, every day but Wednesday: weekdays from 5 to 10 p.m., on Friday and Saturday until 10:30 p.m.

New Pisa Restaurant, 550 Green St. (tel. 415/362-4726 or 415/362-5188), is an institution in North Beach. Opened in 1921 by the Benedette family, who came to San Francisco from Torre del Lago (a town near Pisa, Italy), the restaurant has been serving family-style American and Italian food ever since. Prices have changed since 1921, however. Back then, lunch was 25¢ and dinner was 35¢! Today, lunch is $7 and dinner runs $11; children's meals are $4.75.

The choice of entrees is straightforward—roast beef, roast veal, roast pork, breast of lamb, veal sauté, chicken cacciatore. All meals include soup, salad, pasta, dessert, and coffee.

There are highchairs and boosters here, and they'll warm baby bottles and baby food in the kitchen. But reservations are taken for large parties only, and no credit cards are accepted. If you have to wait for a table, the kids can amuse themselves with the baseball exhibit in the waiting area. Open daily except Wednesday from 11:30 a.m. to 3 p.m. for lunch and 3 to 11 p.m. for dinner. There is a parking lot at 1641 Powell St., and the restaurant will give you a two-hour validation.

If you're not taking young kids, the famed **Washington Square Bar & Grill,** 1707 Powell St., North Beach (tel. 415/982-2823), is a fun place to watch local and visiting celebrities. It has a bustling, comfortable, almost clubby ambience (especially for journalists and visiting literary figures) where almost everyone is a regular. People talk back and forth from table to table, and everyone seems to know everyone else, but they make you feel like a local yourself.

Opened in 1973, it was the first bar and grill in the Bay Area. The food is good, and while there aren't any special services for children, the staff love kids and will use telephone books and cushions to fashion makeshift booster seats. They'll gladly split adult portions in the kitchen for children, serve quarter-size pasta dishes, and warm baby bottles or baby food (if you do decide to bring your little one). They'll even concoct special children's drinks as well as the standard non-alcoholic drinks.

There is jazz at night, at which time "The Washbag" acquires a more romantic tone. The place is really best for older kids and teens. The modern Italian cuisine ranges from pasta, veal, and chicken to a good choice of seafood. There are hamburgers and daily specials too. The restaurant is famous for its special egg dishes—known as Joe's Specials (with mushrooms or chopped beef). Prices range from $5.50 to $8.

Open weekdays from 11:30 a.m. to 3 p.m. for lunch, 3 to 5 p.m. for light snacks, and 5:30 to 11 p.m. for dinner; on Friday and Saturday until 11:30 p.m.; and for Sunday brunch from 10 a.m. to 3 p.m. Reservations are recommended. Most major credit cards accepted. Validated parking nearby.

Best Bet for the Money

With a motto like "Rain or shine there's always a line" for **Little Joe's on Broadway,** 523 Broadway (tel. 415/982-7639), you'd expect good food at reasonable prices. And that's what you'll get. You might find that hard to believe when you first walk into the place because it's not much to look at. The restaurant consists of one large room: part of it is a counter area, part a dining room. The dining room has a mural of old San Francisco with the Golden Gate Bridge outlined in tiny white Christmas lights.

The story goes that at the first Joe's location on Columbus, the line got so long it went out the door and around the corner. They then opened a second location next door (called Baby Joe's), but the line continued to grow, so they moved to their present location—a large storefront on Broadway.

Mounds of cooked spaghetti are in a tray waiting to be smothered with the sauce and used for hungry diners. Fresh French bread is served as soon as you sit down. Daily specials include beef stew, caciucco (fish stew), and calamari, and come with a choice of vegetables, spaghetti, rigatoni, or beans. The diverse menu includes sandwiches, omelets, pastas, and entrees such as New York steak, pot roast, lamb chops, and all manner of veal. While there's no children's menu, a side order of Joe's spaghetti marinara is so large that it's a meal itself, and certainly enough for a child. Or your waitress will be happy to bring you an extra plate so that junior can have samples from all the adults. Kids roll up their sleeves for Joe's ravioli, minestrone soup, and spaghetti and meatballs. Prices for entrees range from $4.75 to $11.25.

No highchairs here, but boosters are available. Kids may share their parents' orders at no extra charge. Of course, this family place will also split one adult portion between two kids, as well as warm baby bottles.

The restaurant is open daily for lunch and dinner from 11 a.m. to 10:30 p.m. There is no wait between 2 and 5 p.m. Between 5:30 and 6 p.m. there may be a short line, but then the crowds come. People have been known to stand on line as long as two hours. Call ahead to find out the best time to come. There's a parking lot across the street on Broadway. No credit cards accepted.

You may be confused by the number of restaurants with the name "Joe" in the title. (There's Old Joe's, Original Joe's, Little Joe's, New Joe's.) At first we thought they were all connected, and became very confused when the type of cuisine changed from place to place. We discovered that "Joe" refers to an open kitchen with an open flame and food made to order. The restaurants usually aren't related, so when you get a recommendation to a restaurant with "Joe" in the title, be sure to get the exact name and location so you don't end up at a completely different place.

CHINATOWN: We had our most potent lesson about parking in San Francisco when we went to a restaurant in Chinatown. To start off, the valet service at our hotel was extremely slow in delivering our car, making us late for our dinner reservation. When we arrived at the restaurant we couldn't find a parking space, so the kids and Grandma went into the restaurant to let them know we had arrived. After ten minutes of no luck at street parking, we tried the parking lot, only to find that it was full—of course, it was a Saturday night at 8:15 p.m. We continued to try to find street parking. After ten more minutes of frustration, we decided on a drastic measure: return the car to the hotel—and take a cab. So learn a lesson from us. Don't drive in Chinatown.

There are so many restaurants in Chinatown catering to the family trade that you really could try almost any place that catches your fancy. But here are the ones that we like the best.

Moderate

Don't let the lack of décor fool you. The **Canton Tea House and Restaurant,** 1108 Stockton St. (tel. 415/982-1032), is a wonderful place to go for breakfast (dim sum), lunch, and dinner. Delectable, reasonably priced food is served by people who are attentive and helpful.

We told our waiter that Andrew was very hungry, and in an instant he was served wonton soup. We saw other children deep in conversation with one waiter. Our waiter asked Andrew if he liked cashew nuts and picked out several especially for him with his chopsticks before he served the rest of the party.

More than 20 kinds of dim sum are made, ranging from barbecued pork bun to sweet Lotus buns (prices range from $1.25 to $1.75 per plate). This is a fun place for afternoon tea and dim sum, rice, or noodles.

But don't limit your eating to lunch or breakfast. The restaurant also serves dinner, and the entrees are delicious. If your kids like soup, the chicken wonton soup is the one to choose, whatever the time of day—the soup base is tasty and rich (not thick, though), with large chunks of chicken and vegetables. It is served piping hot—perfect for everyone in the party on a chilly day or evening.

Entrees range from $4 to $7. Try the sweet-and-sour prawns for a real treat. The shrimp are presented in a very light batter that remains slightly crunchy in the savory sauce. The cashew chicken had lots of nuts and was unusual because it also included mini-ears of corn and Chinese mushrooms. The vegetable chow mein, chicken chow mein, and mild (not spicy) vegetarian dishes are also good for children with less adventurous tastebuds.

This would be a great place to go for dim sum or for a full Chinese meal after wandering around Chinatown. Highchairs and boosters are available. Open daily from 7 a.m. to 4 p.m. for dim sum and 5 to 9:30 p.m. for dinner (kitchen closes at 9 p.m.). Reservations accepted. No credit cards.

Want Peking-style Mandarin food? Small and cozy, **The Pot Sticker,** 150 Waverly Pl., at Washington Street (tel. 415/397-9985), enjoys serving children (yes, we did say "enjoys"). This lovely place has very good food and a friendly staff who delight in making suggestions about what the kids might like to eat. Although small, the restaurant feels spacious, and while rather subdued, it's not the kind of quiet in which you have to worry about your kids disturbing anyone. The Pot Sticker is so used to serving large groups (primarily families) that the appetizers and soups come with an estimate of the number of servings you'll get per order.

We all loved the hot-and-sour soup, but try the soup of the day, which can be a treat. Pot Sticker dinners, which include soup and pot stickers (Mandarin-style dumplings) or another appetizer, as well as luscious entrees, range from $6.75 to $9 per person. The mid-priced dinner includes lemon chicken, Mongolian beef, and Mandarin pork (for three people). Highchairs and boosters are available, and the kitchen staff will gladly warm baby bottles and baby food.

Open from 11:30 a.m. to 4 p.m. for lunch and 4:30 to 9:45 p.m. for dinner, seven days a week. Some credit cards honored, and reservations are accepted. Parking in a garage on Washington Street.

The **Golden Phoenix,** 728 Washington St. (tel. 415/989-4400), is what Sunday-night-family-Chinese-dinner restaurants should all be like. Bustling, lots of families (from all over the world—see how many languages you can identify among the other diners), fast service, and good food. Even the décor—phoenix wallpaper and hanging red Chinese lanterns with tassles—lend a certain ambience to the place. This restaurant offers Cantonese, Szechuan, and Hunan dishes.

If you like sweet-and-sour, don't miss the fried wonton appetizers which come with a side dish of yummy sauce—the best we've ever gobbled down. Soups are fabulous too, and include a wide variety (sizzling rice at $5.50, hot-and-sour at $5, plus chicken with winter-melon soup at $4.50). The entrees are equally good and cost $5 to $7.75.

Highchairs and boosters are available, and the server will gladly warm bottles and baby food. Children's drinks are available (Shirley Temples, Darth Vadars, etc.). Open from 11:30 a.m. to 10:30 p.m. Monday through Friday, 2:30 to 10:30 p.m. on Saturday and Sunday. Reservations and major credit cards are accepted. *Very Important:* There is a municipal parking lot across the street between Clay and Washington Streets—enter on Kearny Street.

Sun Hung Heung, 744 Washington St. (tel. 415/982-2319), may be the best place for families, especially big families, but don't expect any glamour. This is a place where locals go on a weeknight for a family dinner. The people here are wonderful, especially with young toddlers (whom we saw—gasp—crawling around), whom they keep an eye out for. There is lots of floor space and lots of room, so little ones can move around and bigger kids can go exploring on the three floors of restaurant.

Favorites include parchment-wrapped chicken, beef with asparagus or snowpeas, grilled prawns with bacon, and of course, a wide array of noodles and chow mein. You might want to try the special mun yee mein (fried noodles sautéed with duck broth). Entree prices range from $4.50 to $7.50.

Boosters and highchairs are available, and the staff will warm bottles and baby food and make special children's drinks.

Open six days a week (closed Tuesday) from 11:30 a.m. to 11:30 p.m. There is a parking lot across the street, called the Portsmouth Square Garage, on Kearny Street between Clay and Washington Streets. Reservations only for large parties. Major credit cards are accepted.

JAPANTOWN: For another real taste of the Orient we love Japantown. You can stroll the area and see which restaurants entice you. Here are some of the ones we like best.

Moderate

One of our favorite restaurants in San Francisco is **Iroha,** 1728 Buchanan St., across the way from Japan Center (tel. 415/922-0321). This part of Buchanan Street is a continuation of the Japan Center shopping area. The plaza area is closed to cars, and the cobblestone walkways are filled with Japanese shops and restaurants. You'll see two huge windows displaying the food specialties in the usual plastic renditions. Enter a tiny courtyard that has a hint of a Japanese garden, complete with bamboo, and walk up a flight of wooden stairs. Walk through the little slats of cloth that greet visitors and you'll be in the mood for a Japanese lunch or dinner. Lots of little booths give the suggestion of privacy, and a painting of Mount Fuji and hanging paper lanterns complete the mood.

For a treat that the kids as well as you will love, try the gyoza, little dough pockets filled with minced pork or beef and shredded vegetables. Other specialties include hot noodles, ramen, and yakitori (chicken, pork, or beef chunks basted and grilled on little skewers). Entrees range from $3.50 to $6.50. Dinners —with soup, salad, rice, and pickles—offer a more varied Japanese menu, including tempura, sashimi, and teriyaki, with prices ranging from $8.75 to $12.50. The child's plate is a replica of a U.S. spacecraft and arrives with a combination of deep-fried chicken and sushi ($4.50). But if two kids want to split an adult order, the server will bring an extra plate at no charge. Although the waiters are attentive to children, management will not warm baby bottles or baby food in the kitchen.

Open daily from 11:30 a.m. to 9 p.m. Highchairs and boosters are available. Reservations only for parties over six, but if you come between 2 and 7 p.m., there shouldn't be much of a crowd. All major credit cards accepted.

Specializing in homemade Japanese noodles (udon and soba), **Mifune,** 1737 Post St., in the Kintetsu Building restaurant mall (tel. 415/922-0337), is an extremely popular eatery with families. White Japanese lanterns hang from the ceilings. The interior is red with black latticework, and there are booths. The story goes that the Miwa family has been serving homemade noodles in Japan for over 50 years. Mifune, with locations in both San Francisco and Los Angeles, is their outpost in the United States.

Be sure to spend time looking at the plastic models of food in the window before you enter the restaurant. The display is fun to look at, and great for kids who get a kick out of seeing the realistic-looking samples on display. Mama-san and Papa-san dolls are in the display case, beckoning you inside.

All manner of noodles can be sampled. Hot noodles (served in a seasoned broth) are accompanied by chicken, tempura, shrimp, and even fishcake. Cold noodles are served with different garnishes ranging from Japanese potato to shrimp and vegetable tempura. For those who prefer something other than noodles, there are hearty rice dishes, and after 4 p.m. a choice of tempura or sashimi. Prices range from $3 to $8.50 for noodle and rice dishes, and from $8 to $11.50 for dinners.

For kids under 12, order the "Bullet Train," a replica of the famous superspeed transport filled with noodles or rice topped with shrimp and vegetable tempura for $4.

Open daily from 11:30 a.m. to 9:30 p.m. No reservations. All major credit cards accepted.

Inexpensive

Located across the street from the Peace Plaza, **Sanppo,** 1702 Post St. (tel. 415/346-3486), is a small, simple Japanese restaurant that has good, standard fare at reasonable prices. We love the different donburi here (rice with a sweetened sauce with different toppings—eggs and vegetables, beef and vegetables, chicken, pork cutlet, even lobster tempura). The kids love the tempura and the ramen (Japanese-style noodles in broth).

The restaurant also offers several kinds of sushi and an unusually wide range of entrees for a Japanese restaurant (ranging from sliced beef cooked in a ginger sauce to lemon steak). The prices are reasonable—$5.25 to $7.75.

Highchairs and boosters are available. No children's menu, but owner Fumiko Suzuki will gladly bring an extra plate so your child can share your meal.

Open Tuesday through Saturday from 11:45 a.m. to 10 p.m. and on Sunday from 3 to 10 p.m.; closed Monday. Validated parking for Japan Center parking lot. No credit cards.

CIVIC CENTER AND VAN NESS AVENUE: While these two areas of the city aren't high on our list for tourist attractions, they offer some great restaurants.

Expensive

Ruth's Chris Steak House, 1700 California St., at Van Ness Avenue (tel. 415/673-0557), is another fine eatery that you can enjoy with your older, well-behaved children. Opened 22 years ago in New Orleans by Ruth Fertel, the restaurant is relatively new to California, but it's already known for juicy steaks and chops. The atmosphere is intimate and cozy, yet tables are widely separated and there are several booths. White tablecloths, mirrored walls, fresh flowers, and dim lighting make this a lovely place to enjoy steak and seafood.

The portions are large, which is good because everything is à la carte. Kids can enjoy a hamburger for lunch ($6) or a petite filet for dinner ($14). (There is a charge for splitting food at dinner.) Lunch entrees include chicken teriyaki, fajitas, ribeye, and New York steak ($5.25 to $13). Dinner choices include several kinds of steaks, fresh catch of the day, veal chops, lamb chops, and chicken ($14 to $21).

Booster seats are available, and the bar will make the kids non-alcoholic drinks. Open Monday through Friday for lunch from 11:30 a.m. to 3 p.m., for dinner Sunday through Thursday from 5 to 10 p.m., on Friday and Saturday till 10:30 p.m. Reservations are recommended. Most major credit cards accepted. Valet parking.

Moderate

Two blocks away from the Museum of Modern Art, the Opera House, Davies Symphony Hall, and City Hall, **Bull's,** 25 Van Ness Ave., at Market Street (tel. 415/864-4288), is a place to go if your family likes Texas-style barbecue and southwestern cuisine. Big and bright, the place is permeated with rustic Texas atmosphere, and kids can move around and make noise while parents can still feel comfortable.

Choose from such favorites as deluxe nachos (chips with pit-smoked brisket of beef, black beans, and jalapeños, baked with cheddar and Monterey Jack cheese), the Bull's Barbecue sampler (smoked chicken, smoked links, smoked pork ribs, and smoked brisket of beef), or steak fajitas. Prices range from $5 to $14. Kids will enjoy the half order of nachos and barbecue sampler appetizer ($6). Sassy seats and boosters are available, and the waiters will split adult portions in the kitchen for two kids, as well as warm baby bottles or baby food.

Open daily from 11 a.m. to midnight, but you might want to avoid weekday happy hours (4 to 7:30 p.m.) because they're very loud. Reservations accepted for six or more, but on weekends there's only about a 15-minute wait. Street parking. Some credit cards accepted.

Inexpensive

Don't pass up **Tommy's Joynt,** 1101 Van Ness Ave., at Geary Street (tel. 415/775-4216), just because of appearances. This long-standing, funky tavern is an inexpensive, fast place to have lunch or dinner, and is an institution in San Francisco. As you stand in line waiting to choose between such specialties as buffalo stew (yes, real buffalo meat), chili, hand-carved barbecued beef, pastrami, turkey, or corned beef, the kids will be fascinated by the "décor." All sorts of artifacts, signs, photos, and plates hang on the wall in the large room that is part bar, part eating area. This is a fun, very casual place to go, and is especially popular with preteens, but don't expect a quiet, pristine environment. Go to have a quick, inexpensive lunch in a lively, noisy place. (One note, though: The bathroom is up a narrow, winding flight of stairs—not the best for young kids, toddlers, or infants.)

Prices range from $3 for sandwiches and $3.25 for chili to $4.50 for dinner plates that include ham, turkey, pastrami, and the like.

For beer-loving parents, Tommy's has over 150 different kinds of beer and the bar will prepare special kids' drinks from Shirley Temples to Luke Skywalkers.

Boosters are available. Management will split adult portions for children, and will warm baby bottles and baby food. Open daily from 11 a.m. to 2 a.m. Parking in an adjacent lot and on the street. No credit cards or reservations, and they're usually busy, but the wait is only a few minutes in this cafeteria-style place.

If you're with teenagers, a meal at the **Hard Rock Café,** 1699 Van Ness Ave. (tel. 415/885-1699), is likely to be a must with at least one of them. The Hard Rock (like its sister restaurants worldwide) is a loud, hard-driving restaurant that serves up rock music (continuous tapes of blues, surf music, golden oldies, and rock 'n' roll) with its standard American fare. Don't expect to carry on a conversation once you're inside, but sit back and enjoy watching your teens do the "people-watch." Don't forget—you're really coming here for the atmosphere (yes, there really is a Cadillac suspended from the wall) and to satisfy the curiosity of your kids. Most teenagers have heard of the Hard Rock at least once and will love to go back home saying that they've been here. (They can even buy Hard Rock Café T-shirts.)

The menu includes such goodies as burgers ($5 to $6), chicken and ribs ($7 to $9), salads ($5 to $7), and steak or swordfish ($12). Boosters, but no highchairs here. Reservations for lunch only Monday through Friday or for parties of nine or more (they add a 15% gratuity for these large groups). For dinner and peak times on weekends you can expect to wait at least a half hour, so come prepared or come before the rush. Most major credit cards accepted. Open daily from 11:30 a.m. to 11:30 p.m. Street parking.

THE RICHMOND DISTRICT / CLEMENT STREET: Clement Street, part of the Richmond District, is a panoply of shops, restaurants, and markets (see the description at the beginning of this chapter). It's a wonderful place to park the car, mosey around, and enjoy a meal or snacks. Street parking here is easier than in some other parts of the city, although not that easy. One public lot is at Clement Street and Eighth Avenue—metered parking. Head there first. You might be lucky enough to get a spot.

Moderate

Yet Wah, 1829 Clement St. (tel. 415/387-8056), is the kind of conventional Mandarin Chinese restaurant that children love. In fact, it's so popular that it has grown from a small, single operation to several locations around the area.

This location is large—with lots of room for kids to move around, and to have highchairs at the table without causing problems. The staff is very experienced with children (and large families), and make it easy for parents.

Choose from such standards as chicken in plum sauce, sesame chicken, egg foo yung, and other specialties like Mongolian lamb, almond press duck, and a wide variety of fish and shellfish (prawns cooked 17 different ways). For children —and parents as well—there are many kinds of chow mein and noodles. Entrees range in price from $3.25 to over $10.

Shirley Temples are served with little umbrellas, a treat for all the kids, and the friendly service is terrific. Highchairs and boosters are available.

Open daily from 11:30 a.m. to 11 p.m. Most major credit cards accepted. Reservations taken on weekends for parties of more than five, otherwise not needed. Other locations in San Francisco: 2140 Clement St. (tel. 415/387-8040) and Pier 39 (tel. 415/434-4430).

Inexpensive

Where do the locals go when they want pizza? **Giorgio's Pizzeria,** 151 Clement St., at Fourth Avenue (tel. 415/688-1266). In fact, some locals claim that you'll see *only* families here—possibly because the staff is very experienced with kids and the pizza is terrific. Giorgio's features 18 scrumptious different pizzas (large size, $11.25 to $15.25), calzone, and pastas (average price, $6.50). If your kids don't eat pizza (is there a child who doesn't?), the staff will split adult pasta portions and of course bring extra plates. They'll also warm baby bottles and baby food.

Highchairs and boosters are available. No reservations accepted, and on typically busy weekend hours between 6 and 8 p.m., you should expect to wait about 20 minutes. Open Monday through Thursday from 11:30 a.m. to 11:30 p.m., on Friday and Saturday till 12:30 a.m., and on Sunday till 11 p.m. No credit cards.

When you're finished with your meal and you want a treat, go to the **Toy Boat,** Clement Street and Fifth Avenue (tel. 415/751-7505), a really fun place for desserts. Toys decorate the entire place. There are robots, pandas, dinosaurs, and dolls—Barbies, Pee Wee Herman, "Sesame Street" characters. This place has great floats (colas and root beer as well as others), smoothies and sundaes (hot fudge, peanut butter), natural ice creams, cakes, and espressos. And in the morning, you can grab a scone or muffin.

Open weekdays from 7:30 a.m. to midnight, weekends from 9:30 a.m. to midnight. No credit cards.

Why would you go all the way to 24th Avenue and Clement Street for a restaurant? **Bill's Place,** 2315 Clement St. (tel. 415/221-5262), has fabulous hamburgers (a third of a pound of freshly ground choice chuck) and thick milkshakes—so good that many San Franciscans believe that this is the best hamburger place in town. (They like to remind you that they're geared for families and that they've been owned by the same family for 27 years.)

Unpretentious, with an open grill at which two cooks race to make sure those burgers keep pace with the customers, this place is a treat—and is very popular, so expect a brief wait if you come during peak hours. While you're waiting —or while you're eating—be sure not to miss the collection of presidential china that lines the wall.

The service is fast and very casual and friendly. Kids are everywhere. For hearty souls who like to eat outdoors even in the Richmond District (which is cooler and foggier than other parts of the city), there is a lovely garden patio. Bring sweaters.

Burgers range from $3.25 for a plain hamburger to $4.75 for "Celebrity" burgers (with fries), to $3.75 for a Herb Caen burger (with Jack cheese), to $4.75 for a Red Skelton burger (made to look like a clown face). There are lots of great sandwiches (grilled cheese for $2.75) and hot dogs (starting at $2), and a child's burger (called a Pearl Burger) that is half the adult size and is served with fries for $2.50. Highchairs and boosters are available.

Open daily from 11 a.m. to 9 p.m. (except Easter, Christmas, and Thanksgiving). No reservations or credit cards accepted. A second branch is located near the San Francisco Zoo at 56 Lakeshore in the GET Shopping Mall at Sloat Boulevard and 34th Avenue (tel. 415/566-1146), open daily from 11 a.m. to 9 p.m. (except Easter, Christmas, and Thanksgiving).

Barbecued rib and chicken lovers will enjoy **Firehouse Bar-B-Que,** 501 Clement St., at Sixth Avenue (tel. 415/221-RIBS), a tiny hole-in-the-wall (only five or six tables) in the busy section of Clement Street, acclaimed as one of the best lunch places in San Francisco for barbecued ribs. Choose your sauce—one-alarm (spicy), two-alarm (hot), or three-alarm (very hot).

No waitresses—you stand in line to get the food, making this a wonderful take-out place for picnic fixings to enjoy in nearby Golden Gate Park. Choose from baby back ribs, beef back ribs, pork spareribs, chicken, and other meat combinations. Plates come with roll or corn muffin and choice of coleslaw, baked beans, potato salad, or corn on the cob. Dinner prices are about $13; lunch runs about $7. Chicken with fixings comes either whole or half for $8.50 and $5 respectively. Children's orders are half price.

Fire-chief hats for kids are for sale ($3.50), and everyone gets a cute paper bib. No highchairs, but boosters are available.

Open Monday through Friday from 11:30 a.m. to 10:30 p.m., on Saturday from noon to 11 p.m., and on Sunday from noon to 9 p.m. Most major credit cards are accepted.

You might be surprised that kids would like authentic Vietnamese food, but at **Mai's Vietnamese Restaurant,** 316 Clement St., between Fourth and Fifth Avenues (tel. 415/221-3046), you'll see large families digging into soft-shell crab, Imperial rolls (similar to eggrolls), and coconut chicken. This little storefront isn't much to look at, but it has wonderful food. The kids love the Vietnamese rolls, which are like Imperial rolls but aren't fried. Hanoi soup is a tempting mixture of sliced beef and noodles in a broth flavored with cilantro and lemon.

Prices range from $4 (for Imperial rolls or Hanoi soup for two) to $4.75 (for coconut chicken and lemon-grass–barbecued beef.)

Mai's has highchairs and boosters. No children's menu is necessary because everyone shares entrees. They'll warm baby bottles or baby food, and will make special drinks for kids. Reservations are accepted—and advisable during the crowded weekend times from 1 to 3 p.m. and 7 to 10 p.m. Open daily from 11 a.m. to 10 p.m. Most major credit cards honored.

There's another branch at 1838 Union St., Cow Hollow (tel. 415/921-2861).

The family-owned **Java Restaurant,** 417 Clement St. (tel. 415/752-1541), is very helpful to any brood of kids you might bring in—infants to teens. Walking into the restaurant is like stepping into the Far East. Although it's very small, there's a definite ambience that makes you feel you're far from your day-to-day routine. Java has good, inexpensive Chinese and Indonesian food. Some of it will be too spicy for children, but the staff will help you pick out appropriate selections.

This is a great lunch place, especially if you're looking for someplace special that's quiet and comfortable, with fast service, in a neighborhood full of attractions—fun bookstores, toy store, movie theaters, and comic book store—but where dinners are good too. When you step inside, even with the window facing out onto Clement, you'll feel like you've walked into a little Indonesian enclave (albeit a simple one). The restaurant is relatively small, with no place for kids to wander around, but it's comfortable. There are all kinds of rice and vegetable dishes available. How about bon dai (noodles with chicken in a curry coconut sauce) or satay ajam (chicken on a bamboo skewer)? Prices range from $2.50 to $5.50 per dish. There is a rijsttafel (rice table) that features 12 main dishes and four appetizers; the cost is $8.50 per person.

Highchairs and boosters are available, and they'll bring as many extra plates as needed. Naturally, they'll gladly warm baby bottles and baby food. Open Wednesday through Monday from 11:30 a.m. to 11 p.m. No reservations. Major credit cards accepted.

FISHERMAN'S WHARF AND PIER 39: The Wharf area has an assortment of restaurants to choose from, as well as a number of small cafés and open-air stands that serve walk-away seafood cocktails. We've selected a few of the full-service restaurants we like.

Upper Bracket

Located in the heart of the original Fisherman's Wharf, overlooking the fishing fleet, **Tarantino's,** 206 Jefferson St. (tel. 415/775-5600), has been a Wharf landmark for 42 years. Manager Gary Burns, who has kids of his own, says, "Fisherman's Wharf is a family destination. We want to take care of kids." White linen cloths on tables and candles at night provide ambience. While Mom and Dad are enjoying the splendid view, servers take care of the children with little oyster crackers and sourdough French bread. As further proof, the restaurant provides child-size portions as well as an interesting children's menu. (From your table, you'll be able to see the harbor lights at night, the Golden Gate Bridge, and in the distance, Sausalito.)

For lunch or dinner, the darlings can choose from fish and chips, seafood plate, linguine, and tortellini, as well as a hamburger for $3.75 to $7. The bar will serve up Shirley Temples, virgin strawberry daiquiris, and whatever else you can think of.

The adult daytime menu (available from 11 a.m. to 3 p.m.) consists of pasta (such as seafood fettuccine Tarantino—scallops, shrimp, and baby clams in a sauce of garlic, herbs, cream, and parmesan cheese), seafood (including calamari, baby salmon, and oysters), soups, salads, and sandwiches. Lunch is priced from $6 to $11 and includes clam chowder and bread and butter.

For dinner, you might try a swordfish steak ($15) or filet mignon with potato and vegetables ($17). There are salads, sandwiches, sautés, and specials as well, ranging from $6.50 to $15.

Highchairs and boosters are available. Open from 11 a.m. to 11 p.m. daily. Reservations are accepted, and suggested during the busy dinner hours of 7 to 9:30 p.m. Two-hour free validated parking is available at the lot on Jefferson and Taylor Streets. Major credit cards accepted.

If you've ever been to San Francisco before, you're probably already familiar with **Lolli's Castagnola,** 286 Jefferson St. (tel. 415/776-5015 or 415/775-2446), a landmark on Fisherman's Wharf since 1916. Located on the water at Pier 45 overlooking the fishing fleet, this restaurant serves breakfast, lunch, and dinner in a simple setting with a view of the Wharf. Kids get balloons. "Our waiters take such good care of children here that they'll do just about anything," says owner Mary Lolli. During most of the fall, winter, and spring, kids can watch the sea lions that have come to feed in the bay; often there will be ten or more. Sometimes you can watch fishermen docking their boats and unloading their catch. Simple décor, white tablecloths, and floor-to-ceiling windows—you'll feel like you're sitting on the water. Things are generally fast-paced here, with tables turning over as many as three times during dinner. You set your own pace, though—your waiter will accommodate.

Standard breakfasts range from $4 to $9.75. A few pasta, meat, and poultry entrees are also offered. Luncheon specials are available from 11 a.m. to 6 p.m., but items from the entree menu may be chosen for lunch or dinner. Dinners range from $7 to $25 (lobster). The enormous seafood menu is great and the variety of shellfish and calamari specials is delightful.

Kids can choose from the old standbys on the children's menu—grilled cheese and tuna sandwiches—or order spaghetti or filet of sole. Many of these selections are served with fries and most range from $3 to $6.

Moderate

Lolli's Castagnola Upper Deck (located upstairs in Lolli's Castagnola restaurant) is a moderately priced self-service light-lunch alternative with soups, seafood salads, sandwiches, and beverage service. The huge room with big windows is bright and overlooks the water. The patio overlooks the Wharf, a good place for Mom and Dad to have a bite while the kids watch the fishing boats unload (any time between 11 a.m. and 4 p.m., depending on conditions). The Upper Deck is open from 11 a.m. to 5 p.m. daily.

At Lolli's Castagnola, highchairs and boosters are available. Reservations are advised, especially in the summer when you can wait up to an hour if you don't reserve ahead. (If you arrive without a reservation, walk in, give your name, and wander the Wharf while you wait.) Open daily for breakfast, lunch, and dinner from 9 a.m. to 11 p.m. Validated parking is available all day at a lot located at the corner of Jefferson and Taylor Streets; valet parking is offered from 10 a.m. to 4 p.m. only. All major credit cards accepted.

In addition to these, you'll find seaside dining at **Alioto's –#8,** 8 Fisherman's Wharf (tel. 415/673-0183), for seafood; **Pompeii's Grotto,** 340 Jefferson St. (tel. 415/776-9265), for seafood; **Scoma's,** Pier 47 (tel. 415/771-4383), for Italian-style seafood; and **A. Sabella's,** 2766 Taylor St. (tel. 415/771-6775), for seafood. At Pier 39, you'll find **Swiss Louis** (tel. 415/421-2913), with Italian food; the **Eagle Café** (tel. 415/433-3689), with American food; and **Neptune's Palace** (tel. 415/434-2260), with seafood. Also located here is a branch of **Yet Wah's** (tel. 415/434-4430), with more than 200 items on the menu.

THE CANNERY:
For a great view and a good children's menu, **Charley Brown's,** 2801 Leavenworth St. (tel. 415/776-3838), is a tempting choice. Window tables look out at Golden Gate Bridge, and we were lucky enough to be there when a ship passed by to dock for the night (6 p.m.). Andrew spent the entire time watching the passing scene out the window—endlessly fascinated—first looking in the distance, then looking down on the streets that lead east to the Wharf.

The adult food here is good (it's known for prime rib), but the place really rates high for the children's plates, which include extremely generous portions of hamburger with thick-cut fries, sliced tomatoes, soup or salad, beverage, and dessert ($5). Kids can also choose from roast beef, flame-broiled white-meat chicken, and "Popeye-style" green noodles in a cream sauce. Adults can choose from several fish entrees (all fresh), prime-rib cuts, steaks, pastas, and shellfish. Entrees include soup or salad, freshly baked sourdough bread, vegetable, and rice pilaf or baked potato ($13 to $23—lobster and prime rib).

Boosters and highchairs are available. Two-hour validated parking can be obtained at the Anchorage parking lot, located at Jefferson and Leavenworth Streets. Open for lunch Monday through Saturday from 11:30 a.m. to 3 p.m.; and for dinner Monday through Thursday from 4:30 to 10 p.m., on Friday and Saturday till 11 p.m., and on Sunday from 4 to 10 p.m. Sunday brunch is served from 11:30 a.m. to 2:30 p.m. Reservations are accepted. Most major credit cards are honored.

Other choice eateries in the Cannery include the **Chart House** (tel. 415/474-3476), for American cuisine; **Three Cheers Café** (tel. 415/673-1668); and **Las Margaritas** (tel. 415/776-6996), for Mexican food.

GHIRARDELLI SQUARE: We love Ghirardelli Square because there are so many dining places to choose from. **Compadres Mexican Bar and Grill,** located on the second floor of the Mustard Building, 900 North Point St. (tel. 415/885-2266), is a lively cantina with good food, a beautiful view, and very friendly, accommodating service. We thoroughly enjoyed our food—Andrew had one of the large chicken tacos ($5.50, with beans, rice, and salad). Watch out for the fresh corn tortilla shell—it tends to crumble (we wrapped it with a napkin). Elizabeth downed a quesadilla ($4). We all enjoyed the delicious guacamole with chips and our Mexican dinners (ranging in price from $6.25 for a beef enchilada to $11 for char-broiled marinated chicken). Sandwiches, burgers, and ribs are offered as well. Try a fresh-fruit smoothie for a treat.

It was one of those nights—baby cranky and needing to be entertained—and this place was terrific. The boisterous cantina atmosphere inside (we dined on the enclosed patio) was perfect—the adults didn't have to worry about the noise the children created. Watching passersby was a treat, and when all the kids got restless (although service was fast), we simply picked them up and went for a walk on the terrace.

Compadres has one fabulous attraction for kids: two live macaws (parrots) sit at the entrance of the restaurant and charm all who pass by. Also of interest to youngsters are Chiclets gum after dinner and the balloons given out on weekends.

Boosters and highchairs are available. While there isn't a children's menu, ask your server for suggestions. He or she will be happy to help you. Open Monday through Thursday from 11 a.m. to 10 p.m., on Friday from 11 a.m. to 11 p.m., and on Saturday and Sunday from 10 a.m. (for brunch) to 11 p.m. Reservations are accepted. Most major credit cards honored. Parking in Ghirardelli lot (beneath Ghirardelli Square).

The Magic Pan is the chain crêperie branch located at 900 North Point St. at Ghirardelli Square (on the third floor of the Mustard Building) (tel. 415/474-6733). Sconces on the wall, hanging chandeliers, and candlelight are the features here. Lots of kids come to dine, but the children's menu is rather sophisticated. For $4 youngsters can choose from pasta, a Monte Cristo sandwich, or a crispy cheese dog (hot dog and cheese wrapped in a crêpe and deep-fried). We got an order of the chicken strips for an appetizer ($5). The fried crêpes with parmesan cheese is another excellent appetizer. Kids also love the special children's dessert crêpes at $2.25—chocolate mousse, strawberries royale, and ice-cream sundae.

Above all, though, the service is very friendly, and children love to stand and watch the chef make crêpes on the open-air stove in the middle of the restaurant. About a dozen frying pans with rounded bottoms rotate on this turning stove. The chef dips the outside bottom of the pan into the crêpe batter and cooks the crêpe upside down. When it's done, he simply flips it off the bottom of the pan onto the stack of crêpes. Kids are fascinated—but need to be careful of the heat (they're protected from the flame by a glass shield, but it's hot at the stove).

Menu items include spinach-and-shrimp salad ($7) and chicken-pecan salad ($6.75). Lunch includes sandwiches as well as crêpes—try ratatouille ($6), chicken divan ($6.75), or spinach soufflé ($6), all served with salad or soup. Quiche, pasta, stir-fries, chicken, and seafood dishes are also available. Dinner items are more diverse than lunch (although many are the same). Choose from a wide variety of beef, chicken, seafood, and pasta dishes, as well as crêpe specialties (two crêpes come with the dinner, which ranges in price from $7.50 to $11 and includes salad or soup).

Highchairs and boosters are available. Open Monday through Thursday from 10:30 a.m. to 10 p.m., on Friday until 11 p.m., on Saturday from 10 a.m. to 11 p.m., and on Sunday from 10 a.m. to 9 p.m. Major credit cards honored. Reservations are accepted.

Another branch is located at 341 Sutter St. (tel. 415/788-7397).

In addition, at Ghirardelli Square you'll find these fine restaurants: **The Mandarin** (tel. 415/673-8812), for Chinese cuisine; **Paprika's Fono** (tel. 415/441-1223), for Hungarian cuisine; and **Maxwell's Plum** (tel. 415/441-4140), for continental cuisine. You might want to get a babysitter so you can enjoy a night out on the town.

And for families, there's also **Boudin Bakery** (tel. 415/928-7404), for great San Francisco sourdough bread and sandwiches; **Pacific Café** (tel. 415/775-1173), for seafood; **Ghirardelli's Gelateria** (tel. 415/474-1414), for gelato and espresso; and **Vicolo Pizzeria** (tel. 415/776-1331), for deep-dish pizza.

UNION STREET (COW HOLLOW): This is a great area to wander through, with lots of boutiques and little courtyards. You'll find many different places to eat here as well.

Moderate

If you're looking for a good breakfast or lunch, consider **Doidge's Kitchen,** 2217 Union St. (tel. 415/921-2149). This little storefront of about 20 tables and a counter area facing an open kitchen is so popular that on the weekends they turn away as many people as they serve.

This really isn't a place for babies (they don't have highchairs and it's a little cramped), but boosters are available and it's a good place for slightly older children. The food is excellent, and the service is fast.

The waiters are chatty and love to talk with you about what you're doing and tourist attractions you might find interesting. It's a good place to have breakfast if you're staying on Lombard Street or if you're at the Wharf and planning a day of sightseeing elsewhere. You might try it as a starting place for a walk down Union Street (in the Cow Hollow area).

Adults will love the elaborate breakfast menu, with prices ranging from a low of $4.25 for French toast to $8.25 for a omelet stuffed with avocado, ham or bacon, cheese, and tomato. As if the omelets themselves weren't filling enough, you get toast and a choice of potatoes, salad, tomatoes, cottage cheese, even fruit or steamed veggies (extra charge) to accompany your meal. Lunches include homemade soups, salads, and a wide choice of sandwiches (averaging $5). Kids generally request side orders.

Boosters are available. Reservations are a must on weekends and are accepted at all times. (Even if you're lucky enough to get seated without a reservation, you'd wait 45 minutes.) Open Monday through Friday from 8 a.m. to 2 p.m. and on Saturday and Sunday from 8 a.m. to 3 p.m. Major credit cards accepted.

How's this for a family restaurant? **Margaritaville Restaurant and Bar,** 1787 Union St. (tel. 415/441-1183), has family night (Tuesday), during which time children under 12 dine *free*.

This is a lively, fun Mexican restaurant whose motto is "Where celebration is a tradition." It's a great favorite of kids. Dine in south-of-the-border décor amid hanging plants and servers in tropical-style skirts and shirts. Let the kids enjoy the large aquarium filled with tropical fish—it beguiled little Elizabeth while the food was being prepared.

Fajitas, burritos, enchiladas, and tacos range in price from $7 to $10, with platillos (small plates) for light appetites at about $5 and à la carte orders around $2. Combination plates may be the way to go ($6.25 to $9). Seafood specials are a little more.

The extensive children's menu was a treat to our eyes-bigger-than-appetites crew of little Mexican food lovers. All dishes come with rice or beans (hamburger comes with fries). Kids have a choice of soft taco, burrito, corn or cheese quesadilla, or burger. Andrew had his first virgin Margarita here.

Hours are 11 a.m. to 2 a.m. daily. Boosters and highchairs are available. In addition to the extensive children's menu, they'll split an adult portion for two kids. Reservations are recommended on weekends. Major credit cards accepted.

Many of you are already familiar with the northern Italian food created at **Prego,** 2000 Union St., at Buchanan Street (tel. 415/563-3305), through sister restaurants in Los Angeles, and the San Francisco version is another good one. A huge bar greets you in this spare, contemporary-style restaurant with wooden floors, stark décor, white tablecloths, and linen napkins.

We love the calzone (stuffed pizza), and always have the crusty, hot item when we come here. Pizza in general is good at Prego, and ranges from the tame (tomato and cheese) to the exotic (lamb sausage, tomato sauce, basil, garlic, feta cheese, and mint), with prices from $6.75 to $10.25. Other items include pollo all'aglio e rosmarino (boneless double chicken breasts in garlic and rosemary) for $10, and pappardelle alla carbonara (flat noodles, pancetta, bacon, green peas, cream, parmesan) for $9. There is fresh fish daily for $12.50.

Highchairs and boosters are available. There's no children's menu, but the servers will help you split adult portions. They'll be glad to warm bottles and baby food, and will cheerfully bring breadsticks to the table for ravenous little ones. You can request paper and pencil from these helpful people.

They serve from 11:30 a.m. to midnight daily, except Christmas and Thanksgiving. Reservations are accepted for lunch, and for six or more only at dinner. The wait can be long (up to an hour) during the prime dinner hours on Friday and Saturday (7:30 to 9:30 p.m.), but early dining isn't usually a problem. Most major credit cards accepted.

Inexpensive

We like bakeries, and **La Nouvelle Pâtisserie,** 2184 Union St. (tel. 415/931-7655), is a good one. It has eight tables, a variety of coffee selections (and hot cocoa for the kids), and is a good place to stop for energy renewal while wandering in the Union Street area. There are mouthwatering displays of tarts, pastries, muffins, croissants, and chocolates. Plan to stop in for a quick treat (no boosters or highchairs here, however). Open Monday through Thursday from 6:30 a.m. to 7:30 p.m., on Friday and Saturday to 11 p.m., and on Sunday from 8 a.m. to 7 p.m.

There's another branch at 900 North Point St., Ghirardelli Square (tel. 415/776-5533).

What's Cooking, 1830 Union St., between Laguna and Octavia Streets (tel. 415/921-4540), is a homey, informal coffeeshop-type restaurant with only 17 tables that allows for a quick in-and-out meal. You can choose from old-fashioned breakfast specialties, such as link sausage and eggs (with home fries and sourdough toast) for $5.50, and poached eggs (with English muffin and fries) for $5.50, and a large selection of omelets from $6 to $7.25. For lunch, why not try the home-style chicken with homemade biscuits or a salad. Prices at lunch range from $4.75 to $7. Dinners feature barbecued ribs or chicken (with the fixings) from $10 to $15.

Boosters and highchairs are available, and while there's no children's menu, talk to your server, who will bring your kids something they'll enjoy. Open Tuesday through Saturday from 7:30 a.m. to 11 p.m., on Sunday and Monday until 4:30 p.m. Most major credit cards accepted. Street parking.

MARINA DISTRICT: One of the distinct neighborhoods in San Francisco, the often-sun-drenched Marina fronts Marina Green. A lovely area for a stroll, it also offers a few great restaurants.

Expensive

Scott's Seafood Grill and Bar, 2400 Lombard St. (tel. 415/563-8988), may not be the best place for young kids, but it's a winner with older children or those with sophisticated enough palates that they can choose from the almost strictly seafood menu.

There are no highchairs, nor is there a children's menu, and the place does not cater to young ones, but the line out the door will tell you that there's great fresh seafood here. Scott's Caesar salad is good for starters, and our resident expert on fresh oysters on the half shell ($8) swears to their appeal. For parents (and other adults), the cioppino with fresh local crab ($16) is excellent, as is the fettuccine with shucked Willapa Bay oysters in a spicy Cajun beer-butter sauce ($11). For less adventurous appetites, the Hawaiian albacore tuna ($16) or local snapper ($10.50) or petrale sole doré ($14) might be best. When we go, someone always orders (and shares) the seafood sauté ($15). New York strip steak and filet mignon ($15 to $17) are available, as are hamburgers ($6.25) and cheeseburgers ($6.75).

Open Sunday through Thursday from 11:30 a.m. to 10:30 p.m., on Friday and Saturday to 11 p.m. Most major credit cards are honored. The most difficult thing about Scott's with a child is the wait for a table during the prime dinner hours. No reservations are accepted, and we suggest that you go early to avoid the crowds.

There is a second branch at Three Embarcadero Center (tel. 415/981-0622).

Greens at Fort Mason, Building A, Fort Mason (tel. 415/771-6222), may be one of the busiest restaurants in town. The food is so good and the place so well known that it operates at capacity almost every night. Owned by the San Francisco Zen Center, Greens may change your opinion about vegetarian dining. (The San Francisco Zen Center also owns the famous Tassajara Zen Center in Carmel, which is known for its food and Tassajara cookbooks.)

Not only is the food good (much of which is organically grown at Greens Gulch), but the view is spectacular. The restaurant is housed in an old World War II army barracks. There is a full wall of windows that overlooks the marina filled with sailboats and the Golden Gate Bridge. The restaurant is open and airy, and the wooden tables (many of them redwood burl) and high ceilings make you feel as if you're in a California forest.

The gourmet vegetarian cuisine is quite varied. You can get pizza with sautéed spinach and feta cheese or with eggplant and provolone, or with fettuccine and vegetables. There are brochettes (tofu takes the place of meat) with marinated vegetables and a wide array of delicious salads. One favorite is the Gujrati dahl (mushrooms, carrots, zucchini, and other vegetables stewed with tomatoes, ginger, chilies, and curry served on rice). Prices range from $6.50 to $10.50.

On Friday and Saturday nights there is a fixed-price dinner for $27 per person. This luscious combination of vegetarian delights will probably not appeal to your kids, no matter what their age. But if you can, attempt it without them. There is also a fabulous Sunday brunch which appeals to everyone.

Highchairs and boosters are available, as are toys, crayons, and coloring books! There is no children's menu, but they'll gladly split portions. They're quite accommodating folk.

Open for lunch Tuesday through Saturday from 11:30 a.m. to 2:15 p.m., for à la carte dinners Tuesday through Thursday from 6 to 9:30 p.m., and for fixed-price dinners on Friday and Saturday from 6 to 9:30 p.m. Sunday brunch is served from 10 a.m. to 2 p.m. Reservations are highly recommended; make them up to a few months ahead if you really have your heart set on going at a special time. There is a parking lot. They accept major credit cards.

Inexpensive

If you remember the movie *American Graffiti*, you'll feel right at home in **Mel's Drive-in**, 2165 Lombard St., at Fillmore Street (tel. 415/921-2867). Even if you don't remember the movie, you'll love this place. It isn't a trendy

1980s re-creation of a 1950s drive-in—this is an original. Waiters and waitresses wear white shirts and black bow ties and soda-jerk-style hats. There are giant black-and-white blowups of the early days on the walls and loud music (although not too loud) coming from the jukeboxes. "Watch the juice" is the warning on the menus. Dine to Dion's "The Wanderer" and Neil Sedaka's "Calendar Girl."

You'll know you're there by the black-and-white checkerboard tile building with neon lights. Groups of kids with one or two adults wander in and wait for tables. There are boosters, but no highchairs and very small booths, but don't let that stop you from bringing your toddlers and little babies. During the day you'll see all manner of kids crawling on their parents while the folks dig into their delicious one-third-pound burgers, chili, salads, or American specials (such as chicken pot pie, meatloaf, fish and chips, New York steak, fried egg sandwich, or tuna melt). Prices range from $4.50 to about $8.50 (for seafood specials). The hot dogs are terrific, and our 7-year-old wanted seconds of "Samantha's Lunch" (a kid's hot dog for $2.75).

Then there are the fountain items—milkshakes, malts, sundaes, and flavored Cokes—which everyone loves. Desserts and other beverages are also available.

Mel's is also open for breakfast, and offers the usual (and unusual) omelets, pancakes, French toast, and eggs. Prices range from $3.25 for buttermilk pancakes to $6 for an elaborate omelet.

Open Sunday through Thursday from 6 a.m. to 1 a.m., on Friday and Saturday till 3 a.m. You can also call ahead for orders to go. No credit cards or reservations accepted. At peak hours you might wait 15 minutes. A parking lot is adjacent; if it's full, try to find street parking.

There's another branch at 3355 Geary St., next to the Coronet Theater (tel. 415/387-2244).

You'll be surprised by **Original Joe's No. 2,** 2001 Chestnut St., at Fillmore Street (tel. 415/346-3233). It's not much to look at and you could entirely pass it by from the street if you didn't look for the little flashing neon sign (in handwriting/script). Opened in 1938, this Italian restaurant has been serving lunch and dinner to the locals since that time.

The waitresses bring fresh French bread and butter to the table as soon as you sit down. There is a huge variety of food, from Italian meatloaf to corned beef and cabbage to pastas and veal entrees. The lunch menu is so extensive that it runs the gamut from special omelets to sandwiches and burgers (ranging from $3.25 to $8.75, most in the $5 to $6 range). The dinner menu includes pasta and other specialties such as veal, sweetbreads, and prime rib, roast lamb, pork chops, and New York steak (ranging from $7 to $16).

Many portions are so large that children can share the adult's meal. You can request the kitchen to split an adult entree for two or three kids. Boosters are available, but no highchairs.

Open daily from 11:30 a.m. to 1 a.m., except Christmas and Thanksgiving. Reservations are accepted for parties over four. There's street parking and a city parking lot on Lombard Street between Fillmore and Webster Streets. Major credit cards accepted.

GOLDEN GATE PARK / OCEAN BEACH: Sitting off by itself, perched
on the cliff overlooking Seal Rock, is the Cliff House restaurant, the only San Francisco restaurant overlooking the ocean. This tourist attraction is also popular among the locals, since the view is amazing on clear days. These are really two restaurants in one location, the **Cliff House Seafood and Beverage Company** (tel. 415/386-3330) and **Upstairs at the Cliff House** (tel. 415/387-5847)— both at 1090 Point Lobos Ave.

This is one attraction that many first-time visitors to San Francisco want to see. There is also a giftshop, a hot dog stand, and an arcade, called the Musée Mechanique, which has amusements from the turn of the century as well as modern video games. Kids and adults love the place. From this landmark you can see another landmark—the Golden Gate Bridge. (For more about the Cliff House, see the "What to See and Do" section, below.)

The Seafood and Beverage Company (located downstairs) is a large area, dimly lit with nice atmosphere, where you can sit with your food and drinks and watch the waves and seals. While the menu is very limited, it is fast-food style and consequently service is very quick. Kids can munch on sourdough rolls and fruit if they don't like any of the seafood offerings. Adults will enjoy Manhattan clam chowder ($3 to $4.75); chef and Cobb salads ($9.75 to $14), or steaks, veal scaloppine, and the like (from $11 to $14.50).

Open Sunday through Thursday from 11 a.m. to 10:30 p.m., on Friday and Saturday from 11 a.m. to 11 p.m. They have boosters and accept most major credit cards.

Upstairs at the Cliff House is a lovely restaurant with huge picture windows so guests can enjoy the view. Although it's somewhat pricey, you'll see dozens of families here at any given time—little ones watching for seals, older ones looking at the waves breaking on the rocks. Expect leisurely dining and a long wait for tables on weekends (between 45 minutes and 1½ hours).

The varied menu offers such luncheon fare as soup, chili, and hot and cold sandwiches. There is an astonishing array of omelets, 45 in all, as well as daily specials. Prices range from $5.50 to $8.50. Dinner entrees (which are accompanied by potatoes and fresh vegetable) include chicken, veal, steaks, and seafood, and cost $10 to $16.50. Highchairs and boosters are available. There is no children's menu.

Open for breakfast and lunch daily from 9 a.m. to 5 p.m. Dinner is served Sunday through Thursday from 5 to 10:30 p.m. and on Friday and Saturday to 11 p.m. Most major credit cards are honored. Street parking available.

Located near the Panhandle of Golden Gate Park in the Haight-Ashbury area, **Hog Heaven,** 770 Stanyan St. (tel. 415/668-2038), offers a huge range of barbecued food plus soups, salads, and unusual desserts (such as pecan or black-bottom pie). The fairly large restaurant is a place to get comfortable and enjoy your barbecue meal.

All barbecue platters come with beans, cornbread, and choice of coleslaw or potato salad. Choose from beef and pork ribs, chicken, sausage, brisket, and other goodies (or don't choose at all and order a sampler plate). Prices range from $5.50 to $12. Children may choose from smaller versions of the rib platters (about $5) or may get a kid's burger (about $4). Any main dish can be split (add $1 per person).

Highchairs and boosters are available. Open on Monday and Tuesday from 5 to 9 p.m., and Wednesday through Sunday from 11 a.m. to 10 p.m. Some credit cards accepted.

RESTAURANTS BY CUISINE:
You may find that you want to use the restaurant guide by cuisine instead of by location. The following list is alphabetical by type of food. Where applicable, we include locations other than the main one we previewed.

American
Bill's Place, 2315 Clement St., Richmond District (tel. 415/221-5262). Another branch near the San Francisco Zoo (tel. 415/566-1146).

Bull's, 25 Van Ness Ave., Van Ness (tel. 415/864-4288).

Charley Brown's, 2801 Leavenworth St., The Cannery (tel. 415/776-3838).

Doidge's Kitchen, 2217 Union St., Cow Hollow (tel. 415/921-2149).

The Dutch Kitchen, located in the Westin St. Francis Hotel, 335 Powell St., Union Square (tel. 415/397-7000).

Firehouse Bar-B-Que, 501 Clement St., at Sixth Avenue (tel. 415/221-RIBS).

Hard Rock Café, 1699 Van Ness Ave., Van Ness (tel. 415/885-1699).

Hog Heaven, 770 Stanyan St., in Haight-Ashbury near Golden Gate Park (tel. 415/668-2038).

Lefty O' Doul's, 333 Geary St., Union Square (tel. 415/982-8900).

Lori's Diner, 336 Mason St., near Geary Street, Union Square (tel. 415/392-8646).

Mama's of San Francisco, 398 Geary St., near Mason Street, Union Square (tel. 415/788-1004). Another branch at Washington Square (tel. 415/362-6421).

Mel's Drive-in, 2165 Lombard St., Marina District (tel. 415/921-2867). Another branch at 3355 Geary St. (tel. 415/387-2244).

New Pisa Restaurant, 550 Green St., North Beach (tel. 415/362-4726 or 415/362-5188).

Original Joe's No. 2, 2001 Chestnut St., at Fillmore Street (tel. 415/346-3233).

Ruth's Chris Steak House, 1700 California St., Van Ness (tel. 415/673-0557).

Salamagundi, 442 Geary St., near Mason Street, Union Square (tel. 415/441-0894). Other branches at Two Embarcadero Center (tel. 415/982-5603) and the Civic Center, 39 Grove St. (tel. 415/431-7337).

Sears Fine Food, 439 Powell St., Union Square (tel. 415/986-1160).

Tommy's Joynt, 1101 Van Ness Ave., at Geary Street, Van Ness (tel. 415/775-4216).

What's Cooking, 1830 Union St., Cow Hollow (tel. 415/921-4540).

Chinese

Canton Tea House & Restaurant, 1108 Stockton St., Chinatown (tel. 415/982-1032).

The Golden Phoenix, 728 Washington St., Chinatown (tel. 415/989-4400).

The Pot Sticker, 150 Waverly Pl., at Washington Street, Chinatown (tel. 415/861-6868).

Sun Hung Heung, 744 Washington St., Chinatown (tel. 415/982-2319).

Yet Wah, 1829 Clement St., Richmond District (tel. 415/387-8056). Other locations at 2140 Clement St. (tel. 415/387-8040) and at Pier 39 (tel. 415/434-4430).

Continental

The French Room, at the Four Seasons Clift Hotel, 495 Geary St., Union Square (tel. 415/775-4700).

Italian

Capp's Corner, 1600 Powell St., North Beach (tel. 415/989-2589).

Giorgio's Pizzeria, 151 Clement St., at Fourth Avenue (tel. 415/688-1266).

The Gold Spike, 527 Columbus Ave., North Beach (tel. 415/986-9747).

The **Iron Horse Restaurant,** 19 Maiden Lane, Union Square (tel. 415/362-8133).

Little Joe's on Broadway, 523 Broadway, North Beach (tel. 415/982-7639).

Mama's of San Francisco, 398 Geary St., near Mason Street, Union Square (tel. 415/788-1004).

New Pisa Restaurant, 550 Green St., North Beach (tel. 415/362-4726 or 415/362-5188).

North Beach Restaurant, 1512 Stockton St., North Beach (tel. 415/392-1700 or 415/392-1587).

North Beach Pizza, 1499 Grant Ave., at Union Street, North Beach (tel. 415/433-2444).

Prego, 2000 Union St., Cow Hollow (tel. 415/563-3305).

Washington Square Bar & Grill, 1707 Powell St., North Beach (tel. 415/982-2823).

Japanese

Iroha, 1728 Buchanan St., across from Japan Center (tel. 415/922-0321).

Mifune, 1737 Post St., Japantown (tel. 415/922-0337).

Sanppo, 1702 Post St., Japantown (tel. 415/346-3486).

Mexican

Compadres Mexican Bar and Grill, 900 North Point St., Ghirardelli Square (tel. 415/885-2266).

Margaritaville Restaurant and Bar, 1787 Union St., Cow Hollow (tel. 415/441-1183).

Seafood

The Cliff House Seafood and Beverage Company (tel. 415/386-3330), and **Upstairs at the Cliff House** (tel. 415/387-5847), both at 1090 Point Lobos Ave.

Lolli's Castagnola, 286 Jefferson St., Fisherman's Wharf (tel. 415/776-5015 or 415/775-2446).

Scott's Seafood Grill and Bar, 2400 Lombard St., Marina District (tel. 415/563-8988). Another branch at Three Embarcadero Center (tel. 415/981-0622).

Tarantino's, 206 Jefferson St., Fisherman's Wharf (tel. 415/775-5600).

Other Types of Cuisine

Greens at Fort Mason, Building A, Fort Mason (tel. 415/771-7955). Gourmet vegetarian food.

Java Restaurant, 417 Clement St., Richmond District (tel. 415/752-1541). Chinese and Indonesian food.

The Magic Pan, 900 North Point St., at Ghirardelli Square (tel. 415/474-6733). Crêpes. Another branch at 341 Sutter St., Union Square (tel. 415/788-7397).

Mai's Vietnamese Restaurant, 316 Clement St., Richmond District (tel. 415/221-3046). Other branch on Union Street.

The Tonga Room, in the Fairmont Hotel, on Nob Hill (tel. 415/772-5280). Polynesian food.

6. WHAT TO DO AND SEE

Many people think of San Francisco as an adult paradise—which it is—but children love it too. This exciting city offers more than simple sightseeing. Its international flavor and its historical buildings permeate your daily adventures, making even the mundane a lively—often educational—experience.

Just getting from one place to another can be exhilarating. In fact that's what we start with—a one-of-a-kind form of transportation.

CABLE CARS: San Francisco is synonymous with cable cars. Proclaimed a national historic landmark, these are the only vehicles of their kind in the world. These delightful, clattering, almost musical open-air cars run up and down the steep San Francisco terrain at speeds of up to 9½ miles per hour, creating roller-coaster fun out of going from one point to another. Kids love these motorless cars that have been gracing San Francisco streets since 1873. The bracing wind in your face, the close fit when cable cars pass going in opposite directions, the conductors so reminiscent of old America—it's all part of the thrill. At one time there were over 600 cars traveling 100 miles of track; today fewer than 40 cars ride the remaining 12 miles of track, offering passengers grand vistas of the city and the bay.

The **Powell-Hyde Line** offers what some people think is the most thrilling —and scenic—ride. It runs from Powell and Market Streets through Union Square to Victorian Park near Ghirardelli Square. During the course of its ride to the Wharf, it passes Lombard Street (the crookedest street in the world), where you can see the towers of downtown beyond. This car goes down the steepest grade of all, presenting spectacular views of Alcatraz, Angel Island, and Marin County. The **Powell-Mason Line** also starts at Powell and Market Streets, but it goes to the other end of the Wharf, near Pier 39. On its run, you'll see part of North Beach, Coit Tower, and glimpses of the bay. The **California Street Line** starts at Market and Drumm Streets (near the Hyatt Regency San Francisco) and ends at Van Ness Avenue. You ride through the towering canyons of the financial district and then through Chinatown and Nob Hill, where you'll see the Mark Hopkins and Fairmont Hotels and beautiful Grace Cathedral.

Once we were "lucky" enough to have the cables go out on us. Imagine what it's like to back down one of those steep hills. What a thrill! Great America and Magic Mountain could do no better.

Here are some tips on riding cable cars with kids. Cable cars can be crowded, so travel as light as you can. We looked pretty funny catching a ride with a huge diaper bag, a collapsible stroller, a large purse, and two children in tow. With that much of an entourage it's difficult to get off and on except at the turnarounds. People are polite, but it's more difficult to find adequate seating or standing space if you're carrying armloads of stuff. Also, remember that you'll be buying souvenirs, which will take up room. Remember to hang onto the kids around those curves, and be sure they don't lean out while standing on the running boards.

Rides cost $2 for adults, $1 for children 5 to 17, and 15¢ for seniors. The cable-car system operates from 6 a.m. to 1 a.m. Call 415/673-MUNI for more information. You can purchase an all-day MUNI pass (see the "Getting Around" section, above).

If your kids are especially fascinated with cable cars, they'll enjoy the **San Francisco Cable Car Museum,** located in the Cable Car Barn and Powerhouse at 1201 Mason St., near Washington Street (tel. 415/474-1887). This is the only operating street-cable powerhouse in the world, and here you can view the machinery that powers the cables and makes the cars run. Don't miss seeing the collection of early cable cars, including the first one, developed by Andrew Hallidie. To get to the museum—you guessed it—take any of the cable cars, all of which pass within three blocks. (The Powell-Mason and Powell-Hyde Lines stop one block away, and the California Street Line leaves you three blocks away. Buses 1, 30, and 83 also stop nearby. The museum is open daily: from 10 a.m. to 5 p.m. November through March, to 6 p.m. the rest of the year (closed Thanksgiving, Christmas, and New Year's Days). Admission is free. Stroller-accessible.

CHINATOWN: Heralding its presence, the Gateway to Chinatown (on Grant Avenue at Bush Street) is a two-level structure crowned with a dragon and guard dogs that tells you you're entering a city within a city. San Francisco boasts the largest Chinese settlement outside Asia, and once you see Chinatown, you can believe it. In fact, figures put the Chinese population at around 120,000. In recent years North Beach and the Richmond District have become similar enclaves. The Chinese settled this area just after the Gold Rush of 1849, but the

"Great City of the Golden Hill" was almost completely destroyed in the earthquake and fire of 1906. Rebuilt entirely in the Chinese style, it's a neighborhood where you'll see pagoda-style roofs, Chinese-style filigreed balconies, and lots of bright-red paint.

This bustling section of town is one of the most popular tourist destinations in San Francisco. And no wonder . . . it's like stepping into another world of sights, sounds, and smells. The exotic shops, grocery stores, fruit markets, herb stands, fish markets, souvenir vendors, tea rooms, and streams of people make you feel as if you're part of a parade that's spilling out onto the street. Kids love it here. Have them look for the dragons on the street lamps.

You can get to Chinatown via the California Street cable car or bus 1, 15, 30, 41, or 83.

The **Chinese Culture Foundation,** at 750 Kearny St., on the third floor of the Holiday Inn (tel. 415/986-1822), offers educational and cultural programs, including lectures, art exhibits, films, and festivals. The organization's main objectives are to promote the Chinese cultural heritage and provide an understanding of the Chinese to the surrounding English-speaking community. Changing exhibits are presented year round, but you should call for schedules. Ask if such children's favorites as the Shanghai Puppeteers or the Shanghai Children's Music and Dance Corps will be performing during your visit. The center is open Tuesday through Saturday from 10 a.m. to 4 p.m. Admission is free.

You might also want to stop at the **Chinese Historical Society of America,** 17 Adler Pl., off Grant Avenue near Broadway (tel. 415/391-1188), where you'll see the important role Chinese immigrants played in the Gold Rush and railroad eras. Open Wednesday through Sunday from noon to 4 p.m. Admission is free, but a donation is appreciated.

Strolling Around Chinatown

The best way to see this city within a city is to take a walk or two here. (In fact, the first rule is to leave your car at the hotel and take public transportation or taxis to this area. If you're stuck with the car, two parking lots are available, but they are likely to be filled.)

Walk down Grant Avenue or Stockton Street at a leisurely pace. Sample the authentic Chinese markets. Look into some of the herb shops. Be sure your stroll includes the **Bank of Canton** at the corner of Grant Avenue and Washington Street. Designed like a pagoda, it is a cultural treat for kids—even if it's not the real thing. Take your time and perhaps stop for a dim sum breakfast or Chinese lunch.

Walking tours of the area are very popular.

Culinary Walks

Definitely for older children—those with an avid interest in food (or in cultural delights)—these tours include markets, food stores, sweet shops, a fortune cookie factory, and a Chinese herb store. Afterward you might plan to stop for a dim sum lunch.

Two outfits offer these tours. **Shirley Fong-Torres** (tel. 415/355-9657) delights in introducing Chinatown to youngsters and adults alike. She offers 2- and 3½-hour tours. Reservations are necessary. The **Chinese Culture Center** also sponsors culinary walks. Reservations are required at least one week ahead. If you have a group of six or more, you can schedule a tour Tuesday through Saturday. Otherwise, you can call to see if you can join an already-scheduled Wednesday tour. The price is $18 for adults, $9 for children under 12 (tel. 415/986-1822.)

Heritage Walks

This guided walking tour is a wonderful way to experience Chinatown's cultural, historical, and social achievements. Visit a newspaper, a fortune cookie

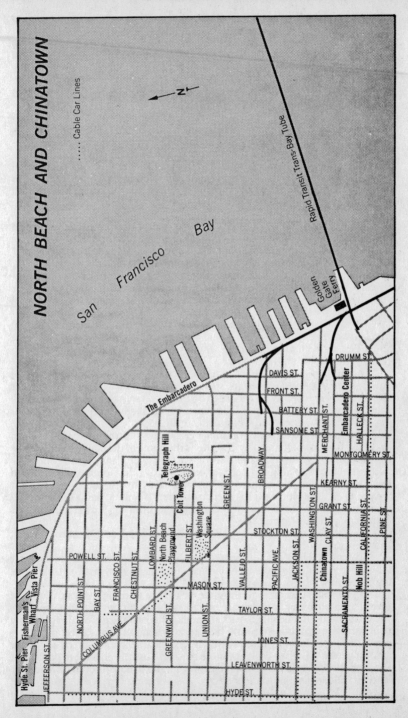

NORTH BEACH AND CHINATOWN

factory, a Chinese temple, the historical society, and other places you request. If you have a group, you can schedule a tour for Tuesday through Friday. For you and your family only, tours are held on Saturday at 2 p.m. and reservations are required. The cost is $9 for adults, $2 for children under 18. There is also a **Chinese New Year Walk** given during this special season. Call early for details: the charge is $6 for adults and $3 for children.

All walks begin at the **Chinese Culture Center,** 705 Kearny St., on the third floor of the Holiday Inn (tel. 415/986-1822).

Chinese New Year (which occurs every year sometime between mid-January and late-February) is a week in which Chinatown comes alive with folk dancing, pageants, and the Miss Chinatown USA Beauty Contest. There are Chinatown festival walks, exhibits, and displays, all culminating in a spectacular finale called the Golden Dragon Parade. The Chinese Culture Foundation sponsors special activities. Usually 450,000 spectators line the parade route. For information about tickets to the pageant—and the exact dates each year—call 415/982-3000 or 415/986-1822.

THE NORTHERN WATERFRONT:
No matter how often we go to San Francisco (and it can never be often enough!), we head to this area as soon as we can. Comprised of **Ghirardelli Square, Aquatic Park,** the **Hyde Street Pier** (and its historic ships), **The Cannery,** and **Fisherman's Wharf** all the way to **Pier 39,** this is a children's playland and well-known tourist mecca. In fact, we find ourselves in the general area several times during the same trip either because we don't have enough time to do everything in one day, or because we want a meal down by the Wharf.

We think of this area as having three sections—eastern (Pier 39), central (the heart of Fisherman's Wharf), and western (which takes you to the Hyde Street Pier and Ghirardelli Square). You'll want to purchase a map of the area available through MUNI (tel. 415/673-MUNI).

One good way to see the area is to start at one end and work your way to the other. Wherever you start, plan to spend all day. If you have little kids, break it into two shorter trips. If you choose to do that, you can start at Pier 39 and work your way to Fisherman's Wharf. The next time, start at the Wharf and work your way west to the Cannery and Ghirardelli Square.

Don't bother to eat lunch or dinner elsewhere—there's more than enough to choose from here. Remember that this is the home of the famous San Francisco walk-around seafood cocktail. And leave your diet plans at home too. The sweets and breads you'll find here are out of this world. To get to Pier 39 and Fisherman's Wharf, take a Powell-Mason cable car to the last stop, Taylor and Bay Streets. Walk three blocks north to Jefferson Street (for the Wharf), or for Pier 39 walk two blocks north to Beach Street and go east until you see the colorful flags beckoning you to the pier.

You can also take the no. 15, 19, 30, 32, 39, 42, 47, or 49 bus from almost anywhere in town.

To get to Ghirardelli Square and the Cannery, take the Powell-Hyde cable car to Victoria Square. You'll be right there. You can also get there on the following buses: nos. 19, 30, 32, 39, 42, 47, and 49.

If you choose to drive to the area, we're here to dispel a myth. There are several all-day parking lots that are not as costly as you might think, especially with validations. But be sure to park and walk. This isn't the place to keep moving your car. Wear walking shoes and be sure to bring a stroller. (Street parking is scarce and expensive. However, at Ghirardelli Square there are several affordable lots.) If you're willing to walk one more block, it's usually possible to park in the residential neighborhood up the hill from Ghirardelli Square, even on Saturday. There is validated parking at Pier 39.

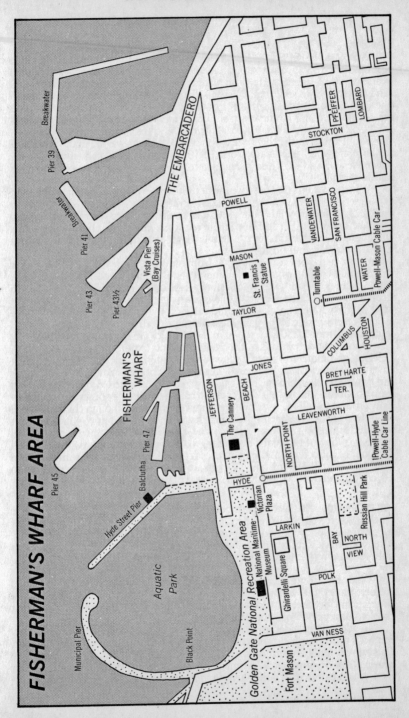

FISHERMAN'S WHARF AREA

Municipal Pier

Pier 45

Breakwater

Pier 39

Breakwater

Pier 41

Pier 43

Pier 43½

Vista Pier (Bay Cruises)

THE EMBARCADERO

PFEIFFER

LOMBARD

STOCKTON

POWELL

VANDEWATER

SAN FRANCISCO

WATER

MASON

St. Francis Statue

Turntable

Powell-Mason Cable Car

TAYLOR

COLUMBUS

HOUSTON

FISHERMAN'S WHARF

JONES

BRET HARTE

TER.

Pier 47

BEACH

JEFFERSON

The Cannery

LEAVENWORTH

NORTH POINT

Powell-Hyde Cable Car Line

Balclutha

Hyde Street Pier

HYDE

Victorian Plaza

LARKIN

BAY

Russian Hill Park

Golden Gate National Recreation Area

National Maritime Museum

Ghirardelli Square

NORTH

VIEW

Aquatic Park

POLK

Black Point

VAN NESS

Fort Mason

We usually like to start our northern waterfront tour at Pier 39.

Pier 39

Pier 39 (tel. 415/981-PIER) is a festive and inviting two-tiered marketplace of more than 135 specialty shops, video arcades, and restaurants—and special treats for kids. Named the favorite place in San Francisco in a survey of 45,000 San Francisco schoolchildren, Pier 39 is like getting a taste of all San Francisco in one spot. Located at the northernmost point of the San Francisco peninsula, you can see all the major landmarks from here: the two bridges, Alcatraz, Angel Island, Coit Tower, the TransAmerica Pyramid, and the skyline.

You'll know you're there when you see the banners waving in the breeze. At the entrance you'll see **Waterfront Park,** a fabulous little park stretching between Piers 35 and 41. There's sand, play equipment, and large wooden benches for lounging.

Whether your little ones love the double-decker carousel, or enjoy the street performers—mimes, dancers, musicians, and jugglers—who entertain daily, or they're older and are wild about video games, this is a place where you'll want to spend several hours. In addition, there are some innovative shops that parents will adore, and the exquisite panoramic views of both the East Bay and Marin County will take your breath away.

Constructed of weathered wood from old piers, Pier 39 is a 1,043-foot pier with a 350-berth marina that is home of the Blue and Gold Bay Cruise Fleet. While there is stroller (and wheelchair) access to almost everything, pushing a stroller on the wooden-planked walkways may get a little frustrating. You might want to tuck along a Snuggly or child carrier for your ease. Several elevators are located on either side of the pier. Most shops are open from 11 a.m. to 7:30 p.m.; restaurants, from 11:30 a.m. to 9 p.m. Most major credit cards are accepted.

One of the attractions is the **San Francisco Experience,** (tel. 415/982-7394), a 25-minute multimedia show (35 computerized projectors are used) that covers the history of San Francisco. Learn about the city's Barbary Coast origins and how the cable cars came into existence. Experience the 1906 earthquake and learn about the '60s and the flower children. The huge 40-foot screen wraps partially around a wall, really bringing the images to you. Although children over 5 shouldn't have any problems, here are a few things to tell your young kids about the three-dimensional effects. During the Chinese New Year scenes, a dragon will pop out of one of the walls; during the Barbary Coast scenes, two bodies will drop out of the ceiling; and during the earthquake, the seats will rumble. Open from 10 a.m. to 8:30 p.m. daily. Tickets are $5 for adults, $2.50 for children 6 to 16; children under 6 are free. Show times are every half hour.

FOR OLDER KIDS AND TEENS. For the uninhibited in your crowd, head for **Music Tracks,** where your favorite 13-year-olds can sing and record their favorite hit songs. You simply walk into the sound booth and sing along with the lead singer. After your track is recorded, technicians knock out the lead singer's voice so it's only you singing with the backup group. You get to bring home a cassette recording.

We don't know if there is a magnetic field that draws children over 6 to video arcades, but even if you can't find **Funtasia,** your children will. This place is a large, clean video arcade with wide aisles and lots of room between games so that children don't elbow each other as they're playing.

In addition to video games, the kids will love the roller-coaster simulator. But hold onto your hats (and your stomachs) when you go on the **Mindscaper.** This movie weds advanced cinematic technology with ride technology. The movie is not 35 mm, but a 70-mm film, so the image is larger and much clearer than a normal movie. It's shown at a rapid rate—in fact, it's shown at the maximum rate that your nervous system can absorb. We saw two movies—one for a roller coaster, and another like a Grand Prix. You forget that you're in a seat and believe you're on a roller coaster. The seat moves and jerks around so that the sensations seem real. (This is not recommended for pregnant women, people with heart conditions or bad backs, or those prone to dizziness. We think it's best for kids over 8.)

FOR YOUNGER KIDS. Especially good for little children is the double-decker **carousel**, where the music isn't too loud and the carousel isn't too big. Don't miss the topiaries of Mickey Mouse and Donald Duck. Kids also love **Puppets on the Pier** (tel. 415/781-1255). This shop brings the puppets out in the open to show kids how they work. You'll see groups of children intently watching the puppeteers as their little dolls dance.

SHOPS AND RESTAURANTS. Some of the unique shops we love are **Left-Hand World** (tel. 415/433-3547), where we buy gifts for those hard-to-shop-for left-handers; **Cartoon Junction** (tel. 415/392-2220), for all kinds of stuff from all kinds of cartoon characters (our favorite is the Betty Boop collection); **Palace of Magic** (tel. 415/434-3122), for magic gifts of all kinds; and **Geppetto's Toy Store** and **Barbary Coast Dolls** (tel. 415/822-7272), with a wide selection of the best. Another favorite for cute, packable gift items and souvenirs is **Magnet P.I.** (tel. 415/989-2361), for the largest selection of fanciful magnets we've ever seen. Even if you have no intention of buying a magnet, go into the shop to see the display. Finally, for wonderfully full evenings back at the hotel when you want the television off and the kids entertained, try **The Puzzle People** (tel. 415/421-5090) for a very large assortment of unusual puzzles.

There is a wide variety of restaurants and fast-food places to choose from. (See the "Where to Eat" section, above, for details.) Restaurants here are generally open from 11:30 a.m. until 9 p.m. For lighter, walkaway food, don't miss **Chowders** (tel. 415/391-4737). We love the clam chowder in the scooped-out sourdough bread. It's delicious. For a quick snack, there's always **Mrs. Field's Chocolate Chippery** too.

Fisherman's Wharf

World-famous Fisherman's Wharf is a panorama of sights, smells, and sounds, from souvenir vendors who sell T-shirts, cable-car renditions, posters, and books to sidewalk seafood stands with their bubbling cauldrons of crab and inviting sourdough bread. This is where you'll see fishermen working on their vessels alongside mimes, jugglers, and street performers plying their trades. You'll see gulls snatching at pieces of food, plus pelicans and an occasional sea lion.

We love the general hubbub, although during the weekends and busy summer days it gets a bit much to navigate a stroller through the crowds. (We use a carrier.)

Alcatraz

Only 1½ miles from Fisherman's Wharf, a trip to ominous Alcatraz Island (tel. 415/546-2805 for tour information)—known as "The Rock"—seems like you're days away from friendly civilization. Once a notorious prison that housed the likes of Al Capone, "Machine Gun Kelly," and "Doc" Barker, a trip to the prison island makes you feel as if they cleared the place of inmates just moments before your arrival.

You can explore Alcatraz with the self-guided tour (about 1½ miles), which takes you through the buildings, cellhouse, and grounds. There is a slide presentation that gives you more background about the grim prison. You can also rent an audiotape program that brings the tour to life (the charge is $7.50 for adults and $5.25 for children 5 to 11). National Park Service rangers offer free outdoor walking tours of Alcatraz; the tours leave from outside the cellhouse at regular intervals during the day.

The trip involves stairs and some steep climbs. Be sure to wear walking shoes and bring warm sweaters. (Ask your personal physician for advice in advance if any member of your group has a heart or respiratory condition.) The National Park Service offers some cautions when you're on the Rock. Be sure to follow them. The round trip, including the tour, takes about 2½ hours.

The **Red and White Fleet** (tel. 415/546-2896, or toll free 800/445-8880 in California) offers transportation to the island from Pier 41. Departures during the summer, from the end of May to October, are daily at 8:15 a.m. and then every 30 minutes from 9:15 a.m. to 4:15 p.m. From October through May, weekday departures are every 45 minutes between 9:30 a.m. and 2:45 p.m.; departures on weekends and holidays are every half hour from 9:45 a.m. to 2:45 p.m. Tickets cost $5 ($7 with recorded tape) for adults, $3 or $4.50 for children 5 to 11. Reservations are recommended. (During the summer when these walking tours are sold out they also offer a "no-walking" cruise around Alcatraz Island narrated by a former Alcatraz guard.)

U.S.S. *Pampanito*

This World War II submarine (tel. 415/929-0202), is part of the Historic Ships Collection of the National Maritime Museum. Docked at Pier 45, this is a special treat for children who are interested in ships, torpedoes, and maritime war duty. Most 8- and 9-year-old boys are enchanted with the idea of living under water in those tiny quarters for a period of time.

For a small fee ($4 for adults, $2 for children 12 to 18, $1 for children under 12 and seniors; children under 6, free), you get an audio tour. Walk the deck and go below on this submarine, taking a step back in time to World War II.

Be careful of toddlers and babies too old to carry in a Snuggly. The steps from the deck that go into the main part of the sub are steep ladders, and the doors from room to room are like windows, forcing you to bend down while lifting each leg. There is no way to take a stroller, and it's tough to carry a baby. Open Sunday through Thursday from 9 a.m. to 6 p.m. (until 9 p.m. during the summer months) and on Friday and Saturday from 9 a.m. to 9 p.m.

Not only is the submarine fun, but on clear days this location affords great views of Alcatraz Island, Sausalito, and the East Bay. Try looking at Alcatraz through the powerful telescopes at the foot of the pier.

You may be lucky enough to be at the pier when a working ship is temporarily docked there as well. They often hold "open house" on Saturday and Sunday.

Bay Cruises

There are other kinds of boats in the area too.

On Pier 39, you'll find the **Blue and Gold Fleet** (tel. 415/781-7877). They offer 1¼-hour bay cruises that take you under both the San Francisco–Oakland Bay Bridge and the Golden Gate Bridge, and come within yards of Alcatraz Island. Other points of interest along the way are Sausalito, Tiburon, and Angel Island.

Departures are on the hour, but call to verify since schedules vary throughout the year. Tickets cost $12 for adults, $6 for seniors and children 5 to 18, free for children under 5.

If you have older children, they might enjoy the two-hour Historical Bay Cruise on the catamaran *Gold Rush*. You'll cruise under three bridges, past Alcatraz and Angel Islands, all the way to Marin and the East Bay. Departure times vary, so call ahead. Tickets cost $16 for adults, $8 for seniors and children 5 to 18, free for children under 5. Charters are also available.

Piers 41 and 43½ are home to the **Red and White Fleet** (tel. 415/546-2896, or toll free 800/445-8880 in California). San Francisco Bay cruises depart daily from Pier 41. This 1- to 1½-hour narrated cruise goes past Alcatraz and Angel Islands and under the Golden Gate Bridge. Tickets are $8 for adults, $6 for seniors and children 12 to 18, $5 for children 5 to 11; under 5, free. Call for schedule information.

This company also offers ferry service to Sausalito, Tiburon, and Angel Island from Pier 43½, and to Alcatraz and Marine World Africa USA (a 55-minute cruise on a high-speed catamaran) from Pier 41. Schedules vary depending on the time of year; call for specific information. If you're planning to take bicycles to Angel Island, be sure there is room for them on the ferry since space is limited.

Other Treats in the Area

You might take a horse-drawn carriage ride around the area, offered by **Carriage Charter,** located at Pier 41 (tel. 415/398-0857). A ride around Fisherman's Wharf is $12 to $15 for three to five people and takes about 10 minutes; a ride up to the Cannery is $18 to $23 for three to five people and takes about 15 minutes; and a ride through the Wharf and Ghirardelli Square area costs $25 to $32 for three to five people and lasts about 25 minutes. There is a one-hour tour ($60 to $75) for three to five people that includes the Wharf, Ghirardelli Square, and the Cannery, and goes to the Hyatt Regency. The first ride is at about 1 p.m.; the last is at 10 p.m. on weeknights and midnight on weekends. Reservations are accepted but not necessary.

Our kids' favorite among the amusement areas (and we mean amusement) is **Ripley's Believe It or Not! Museum,** located at 175 Jefferson St. at Fisherman's Wharf (tel. 415/771-6188). Not only did they like it, but because they couldn't believe many of the 2,000-plus exhibits, they begged us to return. Not surprisingly, our 7-year-old was entranced by the child who grew a beard at the age of 4 and died of "old age" when he was 7! (That was food for thought for many hours.) The two-headed animals were also a real treat.

The adults in the group, on the other hand, were taken by the miniatures—the smallest violin ever made, the tiniest gold tea set, and itsy-bitsy roller skates that actually work. (Don't go there with a smirk . . . people take this place seriously. There's even an official guidebook with a short biography of the founder, Robert LeRoy Ripley.)

Open Sunday through Thursday from 10 a.m. to 10 p.m. and on Friday and Saturday until midnight. Admission is $6.25 for adults, $5 for kids 13 to 17 and seniors, $3.25 for children 5 to 12; under 5, free.

The **Wax Museum at Fisherman's Wharf,** 145 Jefferson St. (tel. 415/885-4975), fascinated and frightened our youngsters. The 270 wax figures are well organized—sports figures, political celebrities, and movie stars together—on four floors. Some of them appear startlingly real.

For sensitive children under 9, we would avoid the Chamber of Horrors, or at least warn them that it's coming. This room was the basis for several evenings of night frights. (At the fork, don't go downstairs to the Horrors; instead, go up to the left to the Gallery of Stars.)

Open daily in summer from 9 a.m. to midnight; in winter, from 10 a.m. to 11 p.m. (on Friday and Saturday from 9 a.m. to midnight). Admission is $8 for adults, $6 for seniors, $4 for children 6 to 12; under 6, free. Stroller access.

Lazer Maze, 107 Jefferson St., between Mason and Taylor Streets (tel. 415/885-4836), is a walk-in video game with four chambers. In each chamber there are robots that light up. With the purchase of a ticket, the customer gets a lazer gun and wanders through the maze, trying to zap the robots between the eyes. There is no minimum age here, but your kids have to be able to handle the gun and know what's going on. (The operators say that they get children as young as 6 years old.) Each game is about three to four minutes long. Admission is $2.50 if you are a member ($5 for membership, which includes two free plays and discounted future plays), $3 flat fee for each play for nonmembers. The Lazer Maze is open the same hours as the Wax Museum: in summer, daily from 9 a.m. to midnight; in winter, from 9 a.m. to 11 p.m. Sunday through Thursday, to midnight on Friday and Saturday.

Of particular interest to kids over 9 is the **Guinness Museum of World Records,** 235 Jefferson St. (tel. 415/771-9890), which makes visual the astounding phenomena in the *Guinness Book of World Records.* See the shoes worn by the world's smallest woman and the world's tallest man. While Andrew (age 7) was a bit young, he enjoyed the ESP machine, where two people face each other with a partition between them; one person chooses a symbol and the other person has to show his powers of ESP by guessing the correct one. There is stroller access. In summer it's open daily from 9 a.m. to midnight; the rest of the year, Sunday through Thursday from 10 a.m. to 10 p.m., on Friday and Saturday till midnight. Admission is $6 for adults, $4.75 for students and seniors, $2.75 for children 5 to 12; under 5, free.

Be sure not to miss the area filled with commercial and charter fishing boats between Lolli's Castagnola and Tarantino's restaurants. Walk out to the **Finger Pier** for a better look. If you're lucky, you'll see pelicans, sea lions, lots of gulls, and at the right time of day, fishermen unloading their catch.

Nearby is the **Dog House Video Arcade,** 2693 Taylor St., between Beach and North Point Street (tel. 415/928-3083). So named because it sells hot dogs and different snacks, this is one of the few arcades in the area. Open daily from 10 a.m. to 2 a.m.

The Cannery

While many people think of the Cannery, 2801 Leavenworth St., at the foot of Columbus Avenue (tel. 415/771-3112), as an architecturally award-winning place to shop, we think of this old Del Monte Fruit Cannery as a place that houses the Toy Museum. We enjoy the street performers in the lovely courtyard while we partake in al fresco dining.

This brick landmark withstood the earthquake and fire of 1906, and has been transformed to a three-level complex of shops and restaurants.

Don't miss the hands-on **San Francisco International Toy Museum,** located on the second floor of the Cannery (tel. 415/441-TOYS). Kids of all ages (but especially those age 10 and under) will enjoy it. While the museum itself is small, the play area is wonderful. Your kids will love the tons of toys available for play—construction toys, boats, dolls and dollhouses, trucks, computer toys. We found it a nice place to relax among the scattered toys and playing children. The museum is open Tuesday through Saturday from 10 a.m. to 5 p.m. and on Sunday from 11 p.m. to 5 p.m.; closed Monday. General admission is $2; $1 for seniors and children of all ages. Proceeds from the museum and giftshop go to child abuse prevention services and to UNICEF. At the time of this writing, there were plans to provide drop-in child care for $5 per hour so parents could spend a few hours shopping while the kids play.

One of our favorite shops in the Cannery is **Play,** on the second level (tel. 415/775-5483). Huge kites of yellow, orange, red, blue, and green decorate the ceiling, cascading down some of the walls. But the main reason we love this store is the large selection of suitcase toys, ones we can buy and easily pack away for the next trip.

After Play, head downstairs to the first level and peek into **Aerial** (tel. 415/474-1566). While this store isn't really for kids, you (and your teens) will love the eclectic, one-of-a-kind items available here. Especially fun are the environmental videos that feature relaxing music to go with clouds, rain forests, and other New Age settings. This store has such things as roller blades (state-of-the-art roller skates that are a cross between ice skates and roller skates).

Next there's **Confetti La Chocolatier** (tel. 415/474-7377), not to be missed by the chocoholics in your crowd. You'll find milk-chocolate crayons, hand-dipped candied fruit, handmade Swiss chocolates, and chocolate-covered truffles, among other goodies.

And for a dessert experience, seek out **Café Zero/Celsius,** located on the street level (tel. 415/474-9199), where the kids can enjoy exotic ice-cream and sorbet treats while adults luxuriate with Italian coffee drinks.

Stroller access is tricky. We located elevators outside near Café Zero and indoors near the Chelsea Shop.

Now, for a little treasure. Across from the Cannery is the **American Carousel Museum,** 633 Beach St., next to the Hyde Street cable-car turnaround (tel. 415/928-0550). As you walk up the stairs to the patio and enter the museum, you're transported to another time—the golden age of carousels. It's 1880 to 1920, when carousel horses and other animals were deemed works of art, when the Wurlitzer organ music played on Sunday in amusement parks, and fairs traveled across the country.

This museum houses one of the world's finest collections of hand-carved antique wooden carousel animals, a bejeweled menagerie of horses, pigs, elephants, tigers, giraffes. If you're lucky, craftsmen will be restoring the animals when you are there.

Run by the Freels Foundation, the place has a feeling of reverence for the majesty of the artwork you see. Volunteers are only too happy to show you whatever you want to see, and to talk with you about the displays. This is a small museum and it can be toured in about a half hour. Even toddler Elizabeth loved it.

Open daily from 10 a.m. to 6 p.m. (in winter till 5 p.m.). Admission is $2 for adults, $1 for seniors and youths from 12 to 17; under 12, free. Public parking available under the museum.

Hyde Street Pier

Don't miss the Hyde Street Pier (tel. 415/929-0202 or 415/556-6435), a high point of this area. Part of the **National Maritime Museum,** this is a wonderful place to spend an hour or so. Home of the Historic Ships Collection, there are currently six merchant ships docked at the pier—three of which can be boarded. If it's warm, you can enjoy the sun and the view of Angel Island, Marin, the Golden Gate Bridge, and other sights. If it's a foggy, cool day, you'll feel like you're a part of the seagoing community.

The *Eureka* is a sidewheel ferry built in 1890. Curious young explorers love to run through this place. If you're lucky enough to be there on a day when there aren't many visitors, the deck is quiet and very calming. Children can go into the wheelhouse and pretend they're captains on what was once the largest passenger ferry in the world. There are tours of the engine room daily at 3 p.m., but check ahead because times vary. And below, on the garage level, is an exceptional exhibit of restored classic cars—a 1924 Dodge Express wagon, a 1931 Model A Ford for the U.S. Mail, and the like.

The *Balclutha* is a square-rigged Cape Horn sailing ship that is done in the traditional black and gray colors. Launched in 1886, this impressive ship has three main masts and several decks. Kids love to see the crew's quarters, the captain's cabin, the charthouse, and the holds where the cargo was stored.

There are other historic ships docked here too. The *C. A. Thayer* is a vessel (one of only two surviving from a group of 900) that carried lumber from the Pacific Northwest to California. Each day at 2 and 4 p.m. there is a film about the schooner. The *Hercules* is an oceangoing tugboat that once towed ships through the Straits of Magellan. *Eppleton Hall* is a 1914 side-wheeled tugboat reminiscent of ships used during the California Gold Rush. The **Alma** is a tiny two-masted flat-bottomed schooner built in 1891.

The **Maritime Book Store** is devoted to books, maps, posters, cards, and gifts on sailing and marine life. We loved the boats-in-a-bottle kits. This is a place that local kids enjoy after school. There's also a small-boat shop on the pier that gives boatbuilding classes.

The pier is open daily from 10 a.m. to 6 p.m. in summer, to 5 p.m. in winter. Currently, admission is $2 for everyone over 16; under 16, free.

Across from the pier is **Aquatic Park,** where our kids love to romp on the grass, an area we also love because of the bayside scenery. The lagoon offers a sand beach and swimming too. (Rest rooms are located in the park.)

The National Maritime Museum

Located in a white art deco building at the foot of Polk Street, across from Ghirardelli Square, is the National Maritime Museum (tel. 415/556-8177). Considered very fine by serious nautical enthusiasts, the collection includes a changing exhibition of photographs, ship models and other seafaring memorabilia, a small rowboat, and whaling artifacts. Call for information about all kinds of interesting events—there are work parties on the historic ships, Christmas at Sea festivities, and special children's programs. Open Wednesday through Sunday from 10 a.m. to 5 p.m. Admission is free.

Ghirardelli Square

That famous red-brick chocolate factory with the 15-foot-high illuminated sign has greeted millions of tourists and delighted the kid in all of us. In fact, we never miss a trip to Ghirardelli's when we're in San Francisco. Sometimes we make it part of a half-day trek from the Wharf to the Cannery to the square, then a cable-car ride back to the hotel. Other times, we make it a quick stop via auto for an Emperor Norton at the Ghirardelli Chocolate Manufactory. Either way, this is one of our enduring favorites.

Bordered by Beach, Larkin, Polk, and North Point Streets, Ghirardelli Square, 900 North Point St. (tel. 415/775-5500), is a great place to end a walk from the Wharf. Plan to have dinner here so you can watch the sun set over the Golden Gate Bridge. By day, you can see Alcatraz Island, Sausalito, and the East Bay.

Ghirardelli Square, named for Italian merchant and chocolate maker Domingo Ghirardelli, was built between 1900 and 1916. For the last 20 years the square (which consists of 14 buildings and eight levels) has undergone extensive restoration. Today it twinkles with a fresh open-air quality that continues to beckon tourists.

In addition to numerous clothing and accessory stores (from **Ann Taylor** and **Benetton** to **Original Furs by Max**), there are craft and art galleries, gift stores, and import shops. We love to stroll in the children's shops—**Arlequin for Children** (West Plaza), **Jeffrey's Toys** (plaza level), and the **Kite Shop** (Beach Street). Don't miss **Bears To Go** (fountain plaza)—"A honeypot of bearaphernalia"—and **Sweet Zoo** (first floor, Woolen Mill Building), which features lots of stuffed animals.

When you get hungry, there are any number of good restaurants to choose from (see the "Where to Eat" section, above, for details). Then there's the **Ghirardelli Chocolate Manufactory,** on the plaza level of the Clock Tower Building (tel. 415/771-4903), worth the trip in itself. It's the ultimate ice-cream shop, and you can get sodas, ice-cream sundaes, and Ghirardelli chocolate of all kinds there—even smaller, one-scoop sundaes for children. If you are going to be in San Francisco for a birthday, call ahead and ask the manager about their special party program.

If you stop here for a treat, be prepared to wait in line at peak times in the busy season. You have to fill out your order and present it to the cashier before you enter the restaurant. When it's ready, your number will be called.

Our kids love to watch the goings-on at the small chocolate manufactory at the back of the store while they wait for their treats. Adults will enjoy browsing in the giftshop. How about a long-stemmed chocolate rose or a milk-chocolate teddy bear?

Open Sunday through Thursday from 10 a.m. to 11 p.m., on Friday and Saturday till midnight. Booster seats are available.

A Warning: This delightfully constructed set of buildings is tricky to navigate with a stroller unless you know where you're going. If you have stroller, don't attempt the stairs from Beach Street. Enter at Larkin or North Point Street and ask at the information desk (fountain level) for directions to ramps and elevator access.

In addition to strolling, browsing, and snacking, Ghirardelli Square boasts some of the city's great restaurants. See the "Where to Eat" section (above) for details, or get a copy of the free *Shop, Dine, Enjoy . . . Ghirardelli Square* guide at the information booth in the courtyard.

If you come by car, use the underground lot with validated free parking. If you come or go by cable car, get on or off at the Hyde Street turnaround at **Victoria Park,** also a lovely place to sit and watch the world go by.

THE EXPLORATORIUM: Don't miss this children's delight. Located at 3601 Lyon St., at Marina Boulevard, in the Palace of Fine Arts, the Exploratorium (tel. 415/563-7337 for information, or 415/563-3200 for a recorded message) is like nothing else you've ever seen. Also called the "Playful Museum," this innovative, hands-on museum was designed so that everyone would gain an understanding of nature and science. There are over 500 exhibit pieces for children to fiddle with and explore. If you walk into the massive 86,000-square-foot structure, you and your kids will be immediately drawn into ingenious exhibits that will help you learn about light, color, sound, motion, language, touch, and electricity. Throughout the museum, exhibit "explainers" work with children to encourage their explorations.

Younger kids will especially enjoy the following exhibits: the Balancing Ball (a traffic cone standing up with a column of air blowing through, and a beach ball that levitates from the air, which kids chase after), the Shadow Box (a walk-in box where a strobe light catches kids' shadows on a phosphorescent wall), the Distorted Room (with a slanted floor that has no right angles; when someone outside looks into the room, people inside look like dwarves or giants), and the Duck Into Kaleidoscope (where children duck under partitions and then see an infinite number of reflections in the three mirrors set up).

Older kids will enjoy: Light Strokes (a converted Macintosh computer that offers a sensitive, sophisticated finger-painting experience), and "Everyone Is You and Me" (a two-way mirror that both reflects and can be seen through, so that by adjusting knobs, two kids can superimpose their images one on the other).

Tactile Dome is another great exhibit—kids crawl through this darkened area using their sense of touch to experience another dimension. You must make a reservation (tel. 415/563-7272 between 2 and 4 p.m.) and pay an extra fee to enjoy this experience, recommended for children over 7.

Yes, we have our favorite exhibits too. Andrew couldn't get enough of the Momentum Machine, where he—and five other school-agers—pushed off on a scooter-like structure that kept him spinning as long as he balanced evenly. Then we discovered "Viewing the Golden Gate," an interactive video disk where, by moving a rotary control ball, you "fly" over the Golden Gate Bridge. Children (and, we confess, adults too) read radar and see the corresponding environment at the same time. While moving the steering wheel you see the blips on the radar screen, and if you look over that small air-traffic-controller-like screen, you can see a larger screen of the scenery you'd be flying over. This was such a big hit that it was difficult to get kids to take turns. Once on, they wanted to stay.

If you know ahead when you'll be there, call for information on special workshops and field trips (tel. 415/563-7337). The museum is completely stroller-accessible. From July 4 to Labor Day, it's open on Wednesday from 11 a.m. to 9:30 p.m., on Thursday and Friday from 11 a.m. to 5 p.m., and on Saturday and Sunday from 10 a.m. to 5 p.m.; in winter it's open on Wednesday from 1 to 9:30 p.m., on Thursday and Friday from 1 to 5 p.m., and on Saturday and Sunday from 10 a.m. to 5 p.m.; closed Monday and Tuesday all year.

Admission is $5 for adults (includes a six-month pass), $2.50 for seniors (a lifetime pass), and $1 for children 6 to 17 years (a six-month pass); children under 6 and members are free.

As if the Exploratorium isn't enough, the view of the **Palace of Fine Arts** is worth the trip by itself. This ornate Greco-Roman fantasy composition rises out of a lagoon, and is the last remaining structure from the 1915 Panama-Pacific Exposition. You can bring a picnic lunch and enjoy the lagoon and lawn area.

The Exploratorium is near the Golden Gate Bridge. Free parking is available. It is a short bus ride from Fisherman's Wharf on the no. 30 bus. Buses 28, 41, 43, and 45 stop within walking distance.

GOLDEN GATE PARK: With park headquarters at McLaren Lodge (tel. 415/558-4268 or 415/558-3706), this is one of the places that makes San Francisco special, and a must-see for anyone visiting the city. There are so many faces to the park, so many things to see and do—fabulous museums, a planetarium and aquarium, a buffalo-grazing paddock, a lake with boats, an antique carousel, great playground equipment, and of course the famous authentic Japanese Tea Garden—that it's hard to know where to start.

Plan to spend lots of time here. We usually try to get to the park at least once, sometimes twice, each trip. Allow at least a half day—a few hours for the planetarium or aquarium, some time to meander, and some time at the playground or Stow Lake. If you want to hike, roller skate, or bike ride, you can do that too.

If you've never been to Golden Gate Park, you're in for a wondrous treat. If you have already been there, you know some of the joys of this park—the largest man-made park in the world—that stretches from the ocean three miles inland. You can go back repeatedly for new adventures.

If you want to get an overview of the park, you can drive west on John F. Kennedy Drive toward the ocean. At the Great Highway, take a left, and another left onto Martin Luther King Drive, which will bring you back into the park heading east. The **Music Concourse** is considered the heart of the park. On Sunday (weather permitting) you can hear everything from opera to Irish folk bands.

You may be surprised to learn (as we were) that Golden Gate Park wasn't always the beautifully wooded haven it is today. In fact when the land was purchased in 1868 it was considered a vast wasteland of sand dunes, a white elephant that the city would later regret. Undaunted by public opinion, William Hammond Hall, the first park engineer, laid out the basic plan of the park. In 1887 John McLaren, who later became affectionately known as "Uncle John," was appointed park superintendent. McLaren consulted with botanists around the world to find plants that were suited for the area and set out to create one of the most beautiful parks in the world. Today Golden Gate Park is a 1,017-acre wonderland of trees, meadows, lakes, and gardens.

Stretching from the ocean (be sure to drive there just to see the Dutch windmill welcoming visitors to San Francisco) to 3 miles inland, and 1½ miles wide, Golden Gate Park is a recreation area par excellence for families. It's more a matter of finding out what you want to do here . . . because there's so much you can do.

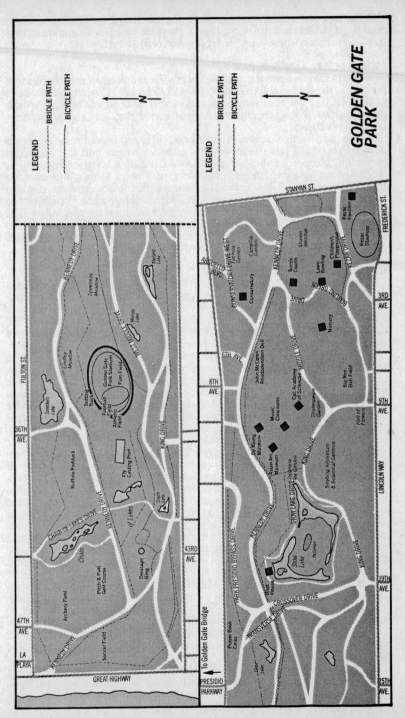

GOLDEN GATE PARK

The area that most families consider the hub is near the **De Young Compound** (also called the Music Concourse). There are lots of picnic areas here, museums too. This is where you'll find roller skaters and bicyclists.

Japanese Tea Garden

One of the most popular, and possibly the most unique, of the attractions of the park is the Japanese Tea Garden (tel. 415/752-1171), located at the Band Concourse Area. The handsome, delicate Oriental garden is a delightful step into a world halfway around the globe. Pathways meander through Japanese greenery, koi-filled ponds, and bonsai.

Kids particularly love the arched moon bridge and the elaborate five-tiered dark-red pagoda. The hand-carved red gateway entrance and the wonderful bronze Buddha intrigue them. If you're in the city during March and early April, you'll find the Japanese cherry trees blossoming. There is a lovely little teahouse in which kimono-clad women serve Japanese tea and cookies. Stroller access is to the left of the main gate entrance on Tea Garden Drive (marked "Exit"), but be prepared to carry little children, as certain areas are not open to strollers. The garden is open daily from 9 a.m. to 5:30 p.m. Admission is $2 for adults, $1 for children 6 to 12 and seniors. There's free admission on the first Wednesday of each month and on major holidays.

California Academy of Sciences

Located on the Music Concourse (tel. 415/221-5100), the California Academy of Sciences is one of the finest natural science museums in the country. The complex bills itself as the "lively museum of adventure," and includes the Steinhart Aquarium, the Fish Roundabout, the Morrison Planetarium, the SafeQuake Ride, and the Discovery Room. It's a place where every member of the family will find something to delight and interest him.

There is stroller-access throughout the exhibits, and an elevator can be taken to the cafeteria (salad bar, sandwich bar, hot dogs, and other snacks), on the lower floor. The complex is open daily from 10 a.m. to 5 p.m. (from July 4 through Labor Day, until 7 p.m.). Admission is $4 for adults, $2 for seniors and youths 12 to 17, $1 for children 6 to 11; those under 6, free. There is free admission for all on the first Wednesday of the month. *Note:* Some of the attractions have separate admission charges and different hours of operation.

The **Steinhart Aquarium** (tel. 415/750-7145) gives kids the chance to see what it feels like to be surrounded by fish. Be sure to walk up to the top of the Fish Roundabout and take a few moments to sit down (even if it's on the floor). You'll hear oohs and ahs as other people catch their first views of the circular fish tank around you. Our kids love to choose one fish and follow it on its journey around the huge round tank. There's always lots of laughter as we all try to keep track of the fish. (Of course, we lose it and have to start over again and again!) On your way up to the Roundabout, don't miss the California tidepool, where the kids can handle starfish, anemones, and other sea creatures. The docent will explain whatever the children want to know, and is sure to keep the kids gentle with the sea life. (If you can take available-light photos, this is the place to capture priceless expressions on the kids' faces.)

Morrison Planetarium (tel. 415/750-7127, or 415/750-7141 for recorded information) is well known for its high-quality shows and is northern California's largest planetarium. School-age children and those older love to spend the hour gazing up at the "night sky," learning about the celestial bodies. Our only qualifier (which applies to all planetarium shows) is that children under 6 find the shows very long, and the darkness seems to scare many of them. The planetarium staff agrees.

Shows range from *Skywatch* to *Mars!* to *Exploring the Skies of the Season*, and are presented Monday through Friday at 2 p.m., on Saturday and Sunday at noon and 1, 2, 3, and 4 p.m. From July 4 through early September there are extra shows (call for information). Admission is $2 for adults, $1 for seniors and children 6 to 17.

Morrison also has a **Laserium** (tel. 415/750-7138), which offers a fabulous, colorful lightshow that plays in sync with the planetarium's state-of-the-art sound system. Music can be classical or rock, and is a treat for all but the littlest ones in the crowd. (In fact, the Laserium staff says that the shows are not recommended for infants and children under 6.) Shows are presented on Thursday at 8 p.m.; on Friday at 7:30, 9, and 10:30 p.m.; on Saturday at 5, 7:30, 9, and 10:30 p.m.; and on Sunday at 5, 7:30, and 9 p.m. From July 1 through Labor Day there are also shows Wednesday through Friday at 5 p.m. Tickets are available at Ticketron or at the Academy a half hour before showtime. Admission is $5.50 for adults and $3.50 for seniors and children 6 to 12 (the rate is $1 less at the 5 p.m. show).

You'll want to see the **Discovery Room,** a small, quiet area (designed for children kindergarten to sixth grade) with lots to see and touch. "Please Touch!" are the words you'll hear. Children are invited to handle such things as shark jaws, dinosaur bones, and birds' nests. This is where your 6-year-old might want to sort through a box of shells, where your 8-year-old can match sounds with the things that make the sounds. Even though your toddler won't be able to participate fully, this is a good place to calm him down if he's overstimulated. The Discovery Room is open—free—Tuesday through Friday from 1 to 4 p.m., and on Saturday and Sunday from 11 a.m. to 3:30 p.m. The room is staffed by volunteers, so call ahead for exact hours.

The **SafeQuake Ride** is part of a large exhibit on earthquakes. Elbow your way through the large crowd of kids that stand around waiting to participate in this exhibit. Here you stand on a platform and watch a video about earthquakes. At the same time, the platform is programmed to simulate the vibrations of quakes of different strengths. This is a great favorite of the 8- through 11-year-old set.

When the kids need a break from indoor activities, there is a courtyard with a fountain and statues. On warm days, you'll see lots of families sunning themselves, and children throwing pennies in the fountain. The preschoolers enjoy climbing on the statues and all the kids enjoy running in the plaza area.

The M. H. De Young Memorial Museum

The De Young Museum collection (tel. 415/750-3659) is the most comprehensive in the city, with artwork from ancient Egypt, Greece, and Rome all the way to 20th-century America. It features sculpture, decorative arts, tapestries, and oils from the old European masters.

This is where you can take the kids to sample Rembrandt, Reubens, El Greco, and Goya. There are also Saturday workshops for children 7 to 12, called "Doing and Viewing Art." The children visit a different museum gallery each week, and then participate in an artistic experience in which they create their own art. These occur every Saturday at 10:30 a.m. and no reservations are necessary.

The museum is open Wednesday through Sunday from 10 a.m. to 5 p.m. Admission is $4 for adults, $2 for seniors and children 12 to 18; children 12 and under, free. Admission is free to all on the first Wednesday of each month.

Located adjacent to the De Young Museum is the **Asian Art Museum** (tel. 415/751-2500), an internationally acclaimed collection with over 10,000 objets d'art from Asia. There are films and storytelling for children. Call for information.

Stow Lake

This is a delightful little retreat—a place where you can rent boats or hike. Stow Lake comes complete with an island. You can see the **Chinese Pavilion** (until recently visitors were allowed inside, but the pavilion has fallen into disrepair and is no longer open). Wander to the top of the hill to the reservoir that feeds **Huntington Falls,** a lovely man-made waterfall with hand-sculpted rocks. There is stroller-access all around the lake (although it can get muddy) and to the top of the falls. Plan to spend about an hour if you're going to walk around the lake and up to the top. You can picnic, but carry out what you bring in. Electric motor-boats can be rented by the hour ($9 to $10.50), as can rowboats ($7.50 to $8.50), and pedal boats ($7.50). A deposit is required for all rentals. The boat-house is open Tuesday through Sunday from 9 a.m. to 4 p.m.

You can picnic anywhere around this area or on the top of the hill. There is a nearby playground that is very good for toddlers. It has a couple of small slides and swings, designed for little ones.

Nearby **Spreckels Lake** is the delight of hobbyists, who bring out their remote-controlled "toy" sailboats and powerboats on weekends. Our little 2-year-old squealed when she saw the buffalo feeding nearby at the **Buffalo Paddock.**

Carousel

This magnificent merry-go-round has a wonderful menagerie of animals. Recently restored at a cost of $800,000, it is one of the last complete Hershell-Spillman carousels still operating. A ride costs $1 for adults, 25¢ for children over three feet tall; children under three feet are free. Open daily June through September from 10 a.m. to 5 p.m.; October through May, Wednesday to Sunday from 10 a.m. to 4 p.m.

The nearby **Children's Playground** can rightfully be called a young one's exercise complex. Several huge slides, tires for swinging, and huge wooden climbing structures beckon kids from all over the city . . . and all over the world. Outside the playground are lots of meadows for picnicking. And for the babies, there is a tiny elephant slide and low swings. This is where the **Petting Zoo** is located.

If You Have Time

You might want to visit the glass-paneled **Conservatory of Flowers** (tel. 415/558-3973), a tropical garden of rare plants located on Main Drive near Arguello Boulevard. Open daily, April to November from 9 a.m. to 6 p.m. and November to April from 9 a.m. to 5 p.m. Admission is $2 for adults, $1 for seniors and children over 6; under 6, free.

You can also visit **Shakespeare's Garden,** in which all the flowers mentioned in Shakespeare's plays have a home, and the **Strybing Arboretum and Botanical Gardens,** on South Drive at Ninth Avenue, where plants from all over the world reside. Open weekdays from 8 a.m. to 4:30 p.m. and weekends from 10 a.m. to 5 p.m. Admission is free.

Note: Weather permitting, there are also open-air performances of Shakespeare, etc., in the park. Check with the park office (tel. 415/558-4268) for details.

The **Polo Field** is a weekend haven for rugby and soccer matches. There's a track and a paved bicycle path for serious bicyclists. Polo matches can even be seen during the summer (call the park for information). **Jogging trails** and **nature trails** are located throughout the park.

In addition to the roadway, one of the best ways to see the park is to take the scenic well-marked **bike trail.** You can start at Fell and Stanyan Streets, and wind your way down John F. Kennedy Drive, across Speedway Meadow, past the polo field to Martin Luther King Drive. The path takes you all the way to the Great Highway. (This is a good way to see the windmill.) Each Sunday John F. Kennedy Drive is closed to automobiles. This is a great area to bicycle and roller skate.

For bicycle rentals near the park, go to **Lincoln Cyclery,** 772 Stanyan St. (tel.

415/221-2415), which rents three-speed bikes at $2 per hour and ten-speed bikes at $3 per hour. They also rent children's bicycles for $2 per hour. They'll rent you a bike with a toddler carrier only if you have your own helmet. Open on Monday and Wednesday through Saturday from 9 a.m. to 5 p.m., and on Sunday from 11:30 a.m. to 5 p.m.; closed Tuesday.

There are free guided **walking tours** (tel. 415/221-1311) of specific areas of the park on weekends from May through October. See the "Family Walks" section, below, for information.

There are a few concessionaires in the park, but not many. Pack a picnic lunch or plan to eat at one of the few eateries in the De Young compound. Or try one of the restaurants that borders the park. There is a McDonald's on Stanyan Street at Haight Street. (We also recommend Hog Heaven; see the "Where to Eat" section, above.)

How to Get There

Parking in the park is a problem. Park authorities suggest that the best place to park for the Academy of Sciences, the children's playground, the Music Concourse, and Japanese Tea Garden is outside the park between 7th and 11th Avenues along Fulton Street. Then walk into the park, following the directions to the Music Concourse. On Sunday, John F. Kennedy Drive is closed as far as Crossover Drive, about a mile.

You can go by bus to the park. From Market Street, take the no. 5 Fulton or the no. 21 Hayes, which runs along the north side of the park; the no. 71 Noriega runs along the south side of the park on Lincoln Avenue; or the no. 7 Haight goes to the east end of the park, from which you'll have to walk a block or two. The only bus that stops in the park itself is the no. 44 O'Shaughnessy, which stops in the Music Concourse. We always call MUNI (tel. 415/673-MUNI) for specific bus information before we go.

THE SAN FRANCISCO ZOO: If you have kids, you've probably seen more zoos than you care to count. But when you enter the San Francisco Zoo (tel. 415/661-2023, or 415/661-7777 for recorded information), you're likely to realize (as we did) that this one is really for children. Located on 125 acres of land at Sloat Boulevard and 45th Avenue, the zoo actually has places for people to roam around and enjoy themselves. A large bank of children's swings greet you as you enter the 45th Avenue entrance. Our children took off to play on the equipment, and were so content to amuse themselves that animal viewing took a back seat.

This zoo boasts over 1,000 animals and birds, and is considered one of the best in the country. But, you say, "A zoo is a zoo." Ah, that's where you're wrong. One little innovation is the Zoo Key. You purchase a key for $1. At exhibits throughout the zoo, there are boxes with locks. The keys slip into the locks, and with a turn, you hear an audio explanation of the animals. Children are delighted with this key, and scramble to be the one to "unlock" the information.

The **Children's Zoo** is a four-acre park within a park that lets your boys and girls get close to little animals. The Barnyard is the place to pet and feed the domestic barnyard animals (it's worth going in just to watch the toddlers chase the chickens and see the 4- and 5-year-olds feed the sheep and goats—get your camera ready!). But beware of the goats—some of them can get kind of pushy if you have food.

Our little ones love the insect zoo, and talk about it for days afterward. There is also a Baby Nursery, nature trail, and duck pond.

There is a wooden carousel near the entrance to the Children's Zoo. The restored hand-carved horses, giraffes, ostriches, and cats are works of art.

Among the major exhibits is the **Doelger Primate Discovery Center,** considered one of the most sophisticated zoological exhibits ever built. This naturalistic setting provides the animals with outdoor atriums, lush meadows, and a nocturnal gallery. This translates into monkeys coming within touching distance behind glass walls. You see kids nose to nose with the primates. At one point, Andrew Elizabeth, and other young children were entertained by (and were entertaining to) a group of monkeys, interacting as if they were in a dance together. This is not only a delight, but it makes the animals more real—and the term "endangered species" becomes more ominous. Included in this area is the **Phoebe Hearst Discovery Hall** of 23 interactive exhibits, where visitors explore the fascinating world of the primates.

The cute little koala bears of Australia have a home at **Koala Crossing,** one of only three United States zoos to have koalas. The exhibit is patterned after an Australian outback station. There are videotapes and graphics that help both parents and kids learn more about these likeable characters.

One of the world's largest natural gorilla exhibits, **Gorilla World,** is a large stretch of outdoor area for the huge animals to roam and play in. Other exhibits include **Penguin Island, Wolf Woods, Musk Ox Meadow,** and the **Lion House** (the 2 p.m. feedings—daily except Monday—are a *big* attraction; the trainers get all the big cats "talking" before they're fed).

The zoo is dedicated to breeding several endangered species—gorillas, orangutans, black rhinos, snow leopards, musk oxen, Megellanic penguins, and many rare insects.

A free informal walking tour of the zoo leaves from Koala Crossing at 12:30 and 2:30 p.m. on weekends. The *Zebra Zephyr* train takes visitors on 20-minute excursions daily (except in winter when it runs only on weekends). The train tours cost $2 for adults and $1 for children. Be sure to bring clothing that can be layered—the weather can turn very chilly.

The zoo is open daily from 10 a.m. to 5 p.m. Admission is $5 for adults, $2 for seniors and children 12 to 15, and free for children under 12 when accompanied by an adult. The children's zoo is open daily from 11 a.m. to 4 p.m. Admission is $1 for everyone over age 2 (children 2 and under are free). To get to the zoo, you can take the no. 10 bus or the L Taraval streetcar from Market Street.

JAPANTOWN: Like stepping into the Far East, Japantown's core is the Japan Center, a five-acre complex of restaurants, shops, and hotels. **Peace Plaza,** with its five-tiered pagoda, is a lovely spot to stop for a few minutes. Many exhibitions and festivals take place in this open-air arena.

We love Japantown on rainy days because of the huge indoor malls bordered by Post, Geary, Fillmore, and Laguna Streets. We wander around the **Japan Center** (tel. 415/922-6776) and looking at Japanese arts, going into the **Kinokuniya bookstore** (tel. 415/567-7625), with a huge selection of Japanese books, or sampling the gift stores while we wait for a movie at the **Kabuki 8 Theaters,** 1881 Post St. (tel. 415/931-9800). If your family likes to bowl, there's **Japantown Bowl,** 1790 Post St., at Webster Street (tel. 415/921-6200), a two-story bowling alley with 40 lanes, shoe rental, video games, coffeeshop, and two bars. During the day games cost $1.85 for adults and $1.60 for children under 18; at night (from 6 p.m. to midnight), games are $2.50.

GOLDEN GATE NATIONAL RECREATION AREA (GGNRA): Not to be confused with Golden Gate Park, GGNRA is an enormous urban coastal preserve—a U.S. National Park—of over 114 square miles that stretches from San Mateo County (in the south) through parts of the city's waterfront (including the Hyde Street Pier and the National Maritime Museum), across the Golden Gate Bridge and north to include parts of Marin County.

Think of the entrance to San Francisco Harbor at the Golden Gate Bridge. This is part of GGNRA, and is probably the one park landmark most people know best.

Headquartered at Fort Mason (tel. 415/556-0560), this most popular of the U.S. National Parks attracts upward of 20 million visitors a year (more than twice the combined total of the Grand Canyon, Yosemite, and Cape Cod). Within its boundaries are abundant adventures for families. It offers 100 miles of trails, ranger-conducted walks, and historical tours, all within 30 minutes of downtown San Francisco. (Because it spans San Francisco and Marin Counties, many of the park's attractions are covered in Chapter III, "The Bay Area and Vicinity." The following are the sights in San Francisco itself.

Fort Mason Center

The headquarters of the GGNRA (tel. 415/556-0560) is located here. This is where you'll want to pick up maps and other information about the GGNRA. (Public transportation is easiest if you take MUNI bus no. 22, 28, or 30. If you drive, parking is available.) Open weekdays from 7:30 a.m. to 5 p.m.

Anchored at Pier 3 in Fort Mason is the last unchanged ship of the fleet of 2,751 Liberty ships built for World War II. The *Jeremiah O'Brien* (tel. 415/441-3101) took only six to eight weeks to build so that it was operational during World War II. Children (and adults) are stunned by the magnitude of the vessel. You can go through the engine room and the crew's quarters, and see the captain's cabin. It's open daily from 9 a.m. to 4 p.m. Admission is $2 adults, $1 for seniors and children.

Fort Mason also offers beautiful picnic facilities and is a favored spot of hikers, joggers, and bicyclists. It is a link in the Golden Gate Promenade. You'll find Green's Restaurant here (see the "Where to Eat" section, above, for details).

Golden Gate Promenade

This spectacular 3½-mile walk is a footpath along the shoreline that takes you from Aquatic Park to Fort Point at the foot of the Golden Gate Bridge. The promenade passes Marina Green (great for kite flying), the yacht harbor, and Fort Mason, offering lovely views through the trees. You can start at Aquatic Park or Fort Point. There is parking at Fort Point, and the walk toward the city provides very dramatic views.

Fort Point (tel. 415/556-1693) is an old brick fort built during the Civil War. It now houses a museum (open daily from 10 a.m. to 5 p.m.), an old jail cell, and the old army barracks.

The best thing about Fort Point are the views of the Golden Gate Bridge and San Francisco. Be sure to go all the way out to the fort itself. If you're driving, get out of the car—even if it's cold and blustery—because it gives you fantastic views of the city and the Bay Bridge as it crosses over to the East Bay.

Cliff House and Seal Rocks

Located above Ocean Beach, the **Cliff House**, 1090 Point Lobos (tel. 415/556-8642), has some of the best views of the Golden Gate National Recreation Area. Cliff House was originally built in 1896 by one-time San Francisco mayor Adolph Sutro, a few years after he had built the Sutro Baths. The baths (which burned down in the 1960s) was a swimming/bathing complex that could accommodate 24,000 people in either saltwater or freshwater pools. The first Cliff House also burned down, but much earlier—in 1907. This is the third structure to be built on this site. The present one (opened in 1909) houses several restaurants (see the "Where to Eat" section, above, for details), a small musical museum, rest rooms, and a gift shop.

One of the more interesting aspects of the Cliff House is its proximity to the **Sutro Baths** ruins. Before you enter the building, look to the north and you'll see the empty shells that used to be the famous Sutro Baths. While it may be a little obscure for children to find interesting, parents can envision what it must have been like. If you can get your kids to stand still long enough, you can watch the waves rush in and out of the ruins until the motion becomes almost mesmerizing.

Cliff House is the place to view the **Seal Rocks.** This group of rocks in the ocean is home to sea lions and many birds. It's a great place to bring binoculars and watch the scenery.

To get to the Cliff House, you can take MUNI metro no. 18, 38, or 38L.

Ocean Beach is a four-mile shoreline that gives you a real flavor of a San Francisco beach. You may get lots of fog, and you'll almost always get lots of wind. Although it looks lovely, the water is dangerous.

. . . AND MORE SIGHTS: We never have enough time in the Bay Area, so we return again and again. Most often, we like to return to many of the same places. But sometimes we look for new sights. Here are some suggestions.

The **Randall (Children's) Museum,** 199 Museum Way, near Buena Vista Park (tel. 415/863-1399), has ravens, hawks, raccoons, opossum, lizards, and lots of snakes that the kids can interact with. There is a working seismograph and a mineral exhibit that the children can handle. The history of San Francisco is presented in photographs and artifacts, and there's a film series geared toward kids. One of the highlights, though, is the dinosaur exhibit. (During the summer there are nature movies and Walt Disney movies for a small additional charge.) The museum also offers special workshops. Call ahead for one-day workshops.

Open in summer Monday through Friday from 10 a.m. to 5 p.m.; during the school year, hours are Tuesday through Saturday from 10 a.m. to 5 p.m. Admission is free.

Located in the Wells Fargo Bank, 420 Montgomery St., at California Street the **Wells Fargo History Museum** (tel. 415/396-2619) is a large 6,000-square-foot space devoted to the Old West and the Gold Rush. Youngsters love to climb on the authentic Wells Fargo Overland Stage Coach—and pretend they're back in the Old West. They can work with the telegraph and learn how to drive a team of horses. This is a fun exhibit with lots of pictures and items kids love. Open Monday through Friday from 9 a.m. to 5 p.m. (closed bank holidays). Admission is free.

The **Old Mint** is located at 88 5th St., at Mission Street (tel. 415/974-0788). The museum focuses on the turn of the century, the Gold Rush, and the San Francisco earthquake. The building, built in 1870, survived the earthquake and fire, and there is a dramatic documentary film about why it survived. You'll find restored rooms and exciting displays as well as galleries with exhibits of gold bullion and gold coins. The vaults are used like exhibit space, one of which has $5 million in gold bars stacked on top of each other. There's also a miner's cabin. Kids enjoy seeing the gold. Ours gasped to see so much money in one place. The museum is open from 10 a.m. to 4 p.m. Monday through Friday; closed weekends and holidays. Admission is free.

The **Fire Department Museum,** 655 Presidio Ave., at Bush Street (tel. 415/861-8000, ext. 365), is for kids who are really into fire engines. They can see old uniforms, hand-pumps, and even fire engines (the firehouse is next door). Good for children 6 and up. Stroller-accessible. Open Thursday through Sunday from 1 to 4 p.m. Admission is free. Call ahead as hours may vary.

Perched on a hill in Lincoln Park is the **California Palace of the Legion of Honor,** 34th Avenue and Clement Street (tel. 415/221-4811). It houses an all-French collection with works from painters of the 16th through the 20th century, including such masters as Degas, Manet, Monet, and Renoir. Fans of the sculptor Rodin will delight in the extensive collection of his work here—*The Thinker,* for instance. A trip to the park is worthwhile in itself, rewarding you with a fantastic view.

The museum is open Wednesday through Sunday from 10 a.m. to 5 p.m. Admission is $4 for adults; $2 for children 12 to 17 and seniors; children under

12 are free. The first Wednesday of each month and Saturday mornings from 10 a.m. to noon are free for everyone.

The **San Francisco Museum of Modern Art,** located in the Civic Center in the War Memorial Veterans Building at Van Ness Avenue and McAllister Street (tel. 415/863-8800 for recorded information), has rotating exhibits of 20th-century art. While this is low on the list of activities with young children, older ones may find the collection interesting. We saw many teens (decked out in the artiest fashions) wandering around and enjoying the exhibits, which include Matisse, Klee, Motherwell, and Pollock. The museum has a terrific book and giftshop with a great section for children. It's open on Tuesday, Wednesday, and Friday from 10 a.m. to 5 p.m., until 9 p.m. on Thursday. On Saturday and Sunday it's open from 11 a.m. to 5 p.m. Closed Monday and major holidays. Admission is $3.50 for adults; $1.50 for seniors and children 5 to 16; children under 5, free. It's free for everyone on Tuesday.

PERFORMING ARTS: San Francisco offers some treats to families interested in the performing arts. If your family is culturally minded, you can take part in some of the fabulous theater and dance available here. The **San Francisco Ballet** performs at the Opera House, Van Ness Avenue and Grove Street (tel. 415/621-3838). Regarded as one of the country's finest ballet companies (and the country's oldest), the regular season runs from January to May, with such classic performances as *Romeo and Juliet, La Fille Mal Gardée,* and *Swan Lake.* Matinees are on Saturday and Sunday at 2 p.m. The price of tickets ranges from $7 to $49. During the holiday season there are about 30 performances of the *Nutcracker.*

The **American Conservatory Theatre** (also known as A.C.T.), 415 Geary St. (tel. 415/673-6440), is a Tony Award–winning repertory company that presents top theatrical productions. The season runs from September through May, and productions range from the classics (Shakespeare and Shaw) to modern dramatists (Coward and Shepard). Matinees are on Wednesday and Saturday at 2 p.m. The family summer show season presents Broadway-style musicals. There are matinees on Wednesday and Saturday at 2 p.m. During the months of November and December, *A Christmas Carol* is presented. There are more matinees for the Dickens classic. (The Four Seasons Clift Hotel, located next to the theater, has a children's Christmas tea in conjunction with the Sunday matinee performances; call 415/775-4700 for details.)

The **Curran Theater,** at 445 Geary St. (tel. 415/474-3800); the **Golden Gate Theater,** at 25 Taylor St. (tel. 415/474-3800); and the **Orpheum,** at 1192 Market St., at Hyde Street (tel. 415/474-3800), are three other theaters that run Broadway productions and individual musical acts, such as *Cats, H.M.S. Pinafore,* and the likes of Linda Ronstadt. Matinees are held on Wednesday, Saturday, and Sunday. Prices vary dramatically. Call for information.

Beach Blanket Babylon, at Club Fugazi, 678 Green St., near Columbus Avenue (tel. 415/421-4222), is a 90-minute fantasy-filled mini-extravaganza. Now in its 15th year, this upbeat colorful show is San Francisco's longest-running legitimate musical revue. Minors are welcome at Sunday matinees at 3 p.m. A good entertainment for kids over 13. Prices range from $13 to $21 per ticket. Reservations are advised.

And for comedy, there's **Cobb's Comedy Club,** at the Cannery (tel. 415/474-9199), a place we love to come with our teens and preteens. Don't worry, minors are welcome with a legal guardian, and the comedy here is rarely off-color, although you should call ahead to see what the program includes. Tell them you're bringing your teenager and ask them if they think the act is appropriate. The cover charge is $6 to $8; there's a two-drink minimum.

Children also love the **Young Performers Theater,** at 2121 Market St. (tel. 415/346-5550). Professional adult actors and children who come from the theater's conservatory program perform six main stage shows throughout the year.

In the past they've done such variety as *Mother Goose, Inc.* (a young people's version of *The Tempest*), *Peter and the Wolf,* and an adapted version of Chaucer called *Chaucer in a Mud Pit.* Performances take place at Fort Mason. Prices are $6 for adults, $4 for children under 13.

SPORTING EVENTS: San Francisco is home to several national sports teams. The **San Francisco Giants** baseball team plays at Candlestick Park, located eight miles south of San Francisco (tel. 415/467-8000 or 415/392-7469). The **San Francisco 49ers** football team also plays its home games in Candlestick Park (tel. 415/365-3420 or 415/468-2249). Across the bay, Oakland is the home of the **Oakland A's** baseball team; they play at the Oakland Coliseum (tel. 415/638-0500). The **Golden State Warriors** basketball team plays at the Oakland Coliseum (tel. 415/638-6000).

SPECIAL ACTIVITIES: In a city with so much to do, we love to combine activities so we can do more.

Family Walks

Walking anywhere in the city is a treat, but we especially love the following walks. A walk across the **Golden Gate Bridge** is an outing you'll never forget. On the 1.7-mile bridge you'll be able to see the area around Fisherman's Wharf and the skyline, as well as Angel Island and Alcatraz. Looking north, you can see Marin County and much of the Golden Gate National Recreation Area. Looking back to the city, you'll get incredibly beautiful vistas at the north edge of the bridge.

There are vista points on both sides of the bridge. The one on the Marin side is where you take the spectacular photos of the bridge with the city in the background. There are also barbecue tables and drinking fountains here.

If you're going to walk on the Golden Gate Bridge, bundle up because it's always windy and often very cold. In fact, you should be sure to bring layers of clothing—the best way to keep warm. We love to take this walk on overcast, drizzly days because it seems more scenic. Even on dismal days, you see fathers and mothers holding their children's hands as they walk across the pedestrianway. This is a good time to bring your slickers, if you have them, because the rain and wind make an umbrella useless.

Another of our favorite places to walk is **Clement Street** in the Richmond District. Clement Street is known for the many shops, restaurants, and diverse cultural influences that characterize it. From Arguello Boulevard (the north or lower end of Clement Street) all the way to 15th Avenue, you will find some of the best toy stores, new and used-book stores, antique shops, produce markets, and restaurants in San Francisco.

In just the first ten blocks (Arguello Boulevard to Tenth Avenue) on Clement Street, there are Chinese, Indonesian, Vietnamese, Thai, Persian, Italian, and French restaurants. This neighborhood is very family oriented—you'll see children on the streets, in the stores, and in most restaurants throughout early evening.

The parking situation is bad, but traffic is not downtown-like heavy and fast. A midwesterner should be at home here—and might want to come out to the Richmond District on a Saturday in order to get one day away from the downtown congestion.

Golden Gate Park is an easy six blocks east of Clement Street. Anyone who is hungry or still restless after a day there should come here. Beware of the daytime weather, though. Even when it's warm and sunny elsewhere, it can be cooler and foggy here. (At night, everywhere in San Francisco is chilly.)

Two of our favorite stores are here. The **California Comic Book Company,** 606 Clement St. (tel. 415/387-4118), is a high point of the walk. The shop is devoted to new and vintage comic books, fantasy games, role-playing games, and science-fiction books. We always leave at least a half hour here for browsing. In fact, this is the place we determine *ahead of time* how much money the kids can spend. The store is open Monday through Thursday from 11 a.m. to 6:30 p.m., on Friday until 9 p.m., on Saturday from 10 a.m. to 7 p.m., and on Sunday from noon to 6 p.m.

Then there's **Green Apple Books,** 506 Clement St., at Sixth Avenue (tel. 415/387-2272), one of those places we like as much as the kids do. It's a book lover's dream that welcomes browsers—and readers—into the stacks of new and used books. There's a terrific children's section too. Plan to stay a while. Open Sunday through Thursday from 10 a.m. to 10 p.m., on Friday and Saturday till midnight.

If for some reason you don't have a meal while you're on Clement Street, at least don't miss the treats at the **Toy Boat** (see the "Where to Eat" section, above, for details).

WALKING TOURS. The **Friends of Recreation and Parks** in Golden Gate Park (tel. 415/221-1311) lead free guided walking tours on Saturday and Sunday at 11 a.m., 2 p.m., and 3 p.m., May through October. These walks include the Strawberry Hill Tour (Huntington Falls, Stow Lake, the Chinese Pavilion, and a walk up to the top of Strawberry Hill); the East End Tour (Conservatory Valley, Children's Playground, Hippie Hill, the Rhododendron Garden, and the Music Concourse); the Japanese Tea Garden Tour (inside the main Japanese Tea Garden gate, it covers the history and design of the Japanese Tea Garden); and Special Interest Tours (such as bicycle tours, statue tours, etc.). Call for specific information.

City Guides (tel. 415/558-3981) offers a wide variety of guided walking tours. Tours include the Gold Rush City Tour, City Hall Tour, Fire Department Museum, North Beach Walk, Japantown, the Presidio, Coit Tower, and various mansions and Victorian homes in the city.

Swimming Beaches

Although the area is surrounded by an enticing seashore, San Francisco has only two swimming beaches that we recommend. **Aquatic Park,** located at the foot of Polk Street (tel. 415/556-2904), offers lagoon swimming and fishing. There are rest rooms and showers, and lifeguards are on duty from mid-April to mid-October. **China Beach,** located near Seacliff (tel. 415/556-7894), is a small sandy area that has lifeguards during the summer. Showers and rest rooms are also available. Open from 7 a.m. to dusk.

Skyrooms

Brunch is a good time to enjoy some of the famous skyrooms that are a little too pricey for dinner, while drinking in fabulous views at the same time. Children are allowed in the skyrooms as long as food is served there, so don't be shy. If you don't want to go for brunch, you and the kids can go for an early-evening non-alcoholic cocktail hour too. Here are some of the skyrooms we like.

Victor's, in the Westin St. Francis Hotel, Powell Street at Geary Street (tel. 415/956-7777), serves a Sunday champagne brunch from 10 a.m. to 2:30 p.m.

Henri's, in the San Francisco Hilton & Tower, 333 O'Farrell St. (tel. 415/771-1400), serves a Sunday brunch from 11 a.m. to 2:30 p.m.

The **Crown Room,** in the Fairmont Hotel, 950 Mason St. (tel. 415/772-5131), has a Sunday brunch from 10:30 a.m. to 3 p.m.

Top of the Mark, in the Mark Hopkins Inter-Continental Hotel, California Street at Mason Street (tel. 415/392-3434), serves a Sunday buffet brunch from 11 a.m. to 3 p.m.

Equinox, in the Hyatt Regency Hotel, Five Embarcadero Center (tel. 415/

788-1234), doesn't serve a brunch (only lunch, dinner, and cocktails), but the revolving platform offers a wondrous 360° view.

And Something Really Special

Another fun special activity is a **Hornblower Yacht Cruise Brunch** at Pier 33, on the Embarcadero (tel. 415/434-0300), a two-hour cruise on San Francisco Bay with a champagne brunch, live music, and glorious views from every table.

The sights and natural beauty of the bay are really enhanced by the casual, leisurely atmosphere of the activities on board. The ship is a three-level yacht, with outside decks and indoor dining rooms (and bar) on each. The Pilot House is at the top. Each dining room has its own staff, live music, and buffet tables. And brunch is a gourmet affair, served the entire trip. There's something for everybody: green salads, pasta salads, eggs Benedict, loads of fresh fruit slices, and beautiful tiny custard tarts with fresh strawberries on top. Our 10-year-old couldn't stay away from the five or six different kinds of pastries and cakes and the all-you-can-eat idea.

The captain and crew are friendly, knowledgeable, and caring. A trip upstairs to the pilot house (where the boat is steered) reveals lots of kids waiting patiently for their turn to navigate the ship's course. A crew member reminded us of possibly the only kid-type hazard aboard—slippery steel stairs and decks. Wear rubber-soled shoes, not patent leather!

The weekend brunch cruise sails on Saturday and Sunday from 11 a.m. to 1 p.m., at a cost of $29 (on Saturday) or $31 (on Sunday) for adults; children under 12 are half price. Reservations are required. Dinner and luncheon cruises also available.

Shopping

Yes, we consider shopping for books and toys an essential activity! And there are many places to get great toys while the kids have a good time looking.

Embarcadero Center is a five-block shopping-center complex that has over 175 retail shops, restaurants, and galleries. The Hyatt Regency is part of the complex. What we love most about this place is the huge open-air plaza. Birds flock there; skateboarders congregate. Here is the famous Vaillancourt Fountain, a strange-looking concrete jumble that fascinates children and parents alike. It's a wonderful place to romp and spend time. There are often midday performances or concerts. We make a few hours of it by also walking into the Hyatt Regency and wandering through the spectacular 17-story atrium lobby.

F.A.O. Schwarz Fifth Avenue, 180 Post St., on Union Square (tel. 415/391-0100), is a branch of the famous New York toy store. This large shop has a great array of toys, hobby supplies, and games. It's open Monday through Saturday from 9:30 a.m. to 6 p.m. and on Sunday from noon to 5 p.m.

Don't miss **Heffalump,** 1694 Union St., at Gough Street (tel. 415/928-4300), which claims to have the best rocking horses in the West. It also has an impressive array of European dolls, wooden puzzles and games, and lovely children's books. Validated parking (and you'll need it in the Cow Hollow area). Open Monday through Saturday from 10 a.m. to 6 p.m. and on Sunday from 11 a.m. to 5 p.m.

Another delightful place is **Quinby's,** 3411 California St., in the Laurel Village Shopping Center (tel. 415/546-7800). It features one of the largest selections of children's books and educational materials in the Bay Area. Calling itself a place "for the curious child," Quinby's specializes in books and products designed to make family travel easier, items like magnetic toys and cassette tapes for the plane, train, or car journey, as well as other products for newborns to children aged 14. Kids are encouraged to spend time trying out some of the toys and books while parents mosey through the store.

Quinby's also has book signings and performances for children about twice

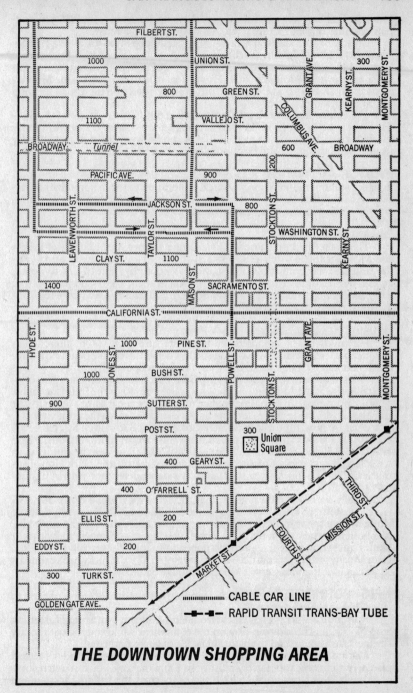

THE DOWNTOWN SHOPPING AREA

a month. Call for their schedule of special events. It's open from 9:30 a.m. to 6 p.m. Monday through Saturday and noon to 5 p.m. on Sunday.

Do you like sea shells? Then you must see **Andre Imports,** at 693 Post St. (tel. 415/673-9087), which sells shells from around the world. Prices range from 10¢ to $200. There are coral, minerals, insects, and butterflies as well. A fun shop to browse—great for kids. Hours are 10 a.m. to 3:30 p.m. Monday through Friday and 10 a.m. to 3 p.m. on Saturday. Knock on the door if the shop appears to be closed.

The **California Comic Book Company** is at 606 Clement St. (tel. 415/387-4118); see the "Family Walks" section, above, for details. It's open Monday through Thursday from 11 a.m. to 6:30 p.m., on Friday until 9 p.m., on Saturday from 10 a.m. to 7 p.m., and on Sunday from noon to 6 p.m.

INDOOR ACTIVITIES: Rain or fog got you down? There are plenty of indoor activities in the San Francisco area. In addition to the major indoor attractions (California Academy of Science, the De Young and Asian Art Museums, and the Exploratorium), you can spend some time in these places:

Libraries

The **Main Children's Room,** Civic Center Library, at the corner of Larkin and McAllister Streets (tel. 415/558-3510), is open on Monday, Thursday, Friday, and Saturday from 10 a.m. to 6 p.m., on Wednesday from 10 a.m. to 9 p.m., and on Sunday from 1 to 5 p.m. The **Marina Branch,** 1890 Chestnut St. (tel. 415/346-9336), and the **Richmond Branch,** 351 Ninth Ave. (tel. 415/752-1240), also have children's reading rooms. Call for hours.

Unusual Hotel Lobbies

For children who are interested in architecture (or if you're interested in heightening their awareness), you can spend a delightful couple of hours in three outstanding hotel lobbies, and enjoy this unusual indoor activity.

We start off with the **Hyatt Regency San Francisco,** Five Embarcadero Center (tel. 415/788-1234), and let the kids wander through the futuristic lobby. This is a place they can enjoy even if they're active because it's like a little city. Be sure they go for a ride in the elevators up to the top and catch the great view.

Next we head for the **Westin St. Francis Hotel,** 335 Powell St. (tel. 415/397-7000). Or if you have quiet children, we also love the **Mark Hopkins,** 1 Nob Hill (tel. 415/392-3434, or toll free 800/327-0200), where the children can see splendid examples of ornate, stately décor (of course, the Mark Hopkins is much smaller and intimate) with blazing crystal chandeliers and palatial furnishings.

Finally, we head for the understated elegance of the **Four Seasons Clift,** 495 Geary St. (tel. 415/775-4700, or toll free 800/268-6282), by which time the children have spent most of their energy and are ready to sit for a little while. Most often, we take tea in the small lobby, nibbling on cucumber sandwiches or scones and people-watching—always pretending that we're actually in London. Occasionally we sit in the art deco Redwood Room. If we're lucky, we've timed it so we can have high tea (served Monday through Saturday).

NEIGHBORHOOD PARKS: San Francisco has hundreds of acres of parks to enjoy. Here are just a few we like.

Huntington Park is a few blocks from Union Square—in a beautiful setting atop Nob Hill. The kids can play on the equipment while you look at the city skyline, lavish hotels, and the beautiful façade of Grace Cathedral.

Marina Green has acres for running and Frisbee throwing. And it's a good place to watch some top-notch windsurfers. From the park, you can watch flocks of seagulls swooping down and see the boats cross the bay to Larkspur and

Sausalito. It's certainly beautiful, even if a bit overcast and gray. At those times you can watch birds lighting on white-capped water. When it's very windy, the surf splashes up on the parking lot and kite acrobatics decorate the sky.

Alta Plaza is a gorgeous, quiet little park at Clay and Scott Streets. Pathways lead up to the top of a steep hill, giving a crisscross effect. You get fabulous views of the bay and Marin County as you come over the hill on Scott. This is a great park to walk through.

ANNUAL EVENTS AND FESTIVALS: You might say that every day there is a special event or festival in San Francisco. The city is alive with street performers, vendors, and all manner of ethnic pride celebrations. Here are some of the highlights of the year.

Chinese New Year Celebration (January or February). There are all kinds of festivities, culminating with the Golden Dragon Parade. (Call 415/982-3000 for details.)

Cherry Blossom Festival (April) in Japantown. This annual event includes Japanese performers and a wonderful parade.

Cinco de Mayo Parade and Celebration (May) in the Mission District. There are two days of cultural activities and entertainment. The fiesta queen is crowned.

Renaissance Pleasure Faire (August) in Novato.

Fleet Week (October). This festival honors the U.S. Navy. There are aerial performances and a parade of naval vessels through the Golden Gate.

For information on any of these events, you can write for a copy of *The San Francisco Book*. Send $1 to the San Francisco Visitor Information Center, P.O. Box 6977, San Francisco, CA 94101. Or you can call 415/391-2000 for a recorded description of current events.

ACTIVITIES BY AGE GROUP: The following listings suggest activities divided into specific age brackets. Refer back to the individual descriptions for details and any age restrictions.

Teens and Preteens
Alcatraz Island
American Conservatory Theatre
Bay Cruises
Beach Blanket Babylon
Cable Car Museum
California Palace of the Legion of Honor
The Cannery
Chinatown (including the Chinese Culture Center, Chinese Historical Society, the Chinese New Year festivities, Culinary Walks, and Heritage Walks)
Cobb's Comedy Club
Curran Theatre
Exploratorium
Fire Department Museum
Fisherman's Wharf
Ghirardelli Square
Golden Gate National Recreation Area (including the Cliff House, Fort Point, and the World War II ship *Jeremiah O'Brien*)
Golden Gate Park (including the Asian Art Museum, California Academy of Sciences, Conservatory of Flowers, De Young Museum, the Discovery Room, Japanese Tea Garden, Morrison Planetarium and Laserium, SafeQuake Ride, Spreckles Lake, Steinhardt Aquarium, Stow Lake, and Strybing Arboretum)
Golden Gate Theatre
Guinness Museum of World Records

Lazer Maze
National Maritime Museum
The Old Mint
Pier 39 (including Funtasia, the Mindscaper, Music Tracks, and the San Francisco Experience)
Ripley's Believe It or Not! Museum
San Francisco Ballet
San Francisco Museum of Modern Art
U.S.S. *Pampanito*
Wax Museum
Wells Fargo History Museum

School-Age Kids

Alcatraz Island
American Carousel Museum
Aquatic Park
Bay Cruises
Cable Car Museum
The Cannery (including the San Francisco International Toy Museum)
Chinatown (including the Chinese Culture Center, Chinese Historical Society, Chinese New Year festivities, Culinary Walks, and Heritage Walks)
Curran Theatre
Exploratorium
Fire Department Museum
Fisherman's Wharf
Ghirardelli Square (including the Chocolate Manufactory)
Golden Gate National Recreation Area (including the Cliff House, Fort Point, and the World War II ship *Jeremiah O'Brien*)
Golden Gate Park (including the California Academy of Sciences, Children's Playground, the Discovery Room, Japanese Tea Garden, Morrison Planetarium and Laserium, the SafeQuake Ride, Spreckles Lake, Steinhardt Aquarium, and Stow Lake)
Guinness Museum of World Records
Lazer Maze
National Maritime Museum
The Old Mint
Pier 39 (including Funtasia, the Mindscaper, Music Tracks, and the San Francisco Experience)
Randall (Children's) Museum
Ripley's Believe It or Not! Museum
San Francisco Ballet
San Francisco Zoo (including the Children's Zoo)
U.S.S. *Pampanito*
Wax Museum
Wells Fargo Museum
Young Performers Theatre

Preschoolers

American Carousel Museum
Aquatic Park
The Cannery (including the San Francisco International Toy Museum)
Chinatown
Fire Department Museum
Fisherman's Wharf
Ghirardelli Square (including the Chocolate Manufactory)
Golden Gate Park (including the California Academy of Sciences, the

Children's Playground, the Discovery Room, Steinhardt Aquarium, and Stow Lake)

National Maritime Museum
Pier 39 (including the Carousel and Puppets on the Pier)
Randall (Children's) Museum
San Francisco Zoo (including the Children's Zoo)
Wells Fargo History Museum
Young Performers Theatre

IN CASE OF EMERGENCY: Just in case of trouble, here are a few resources you might need to know about.

Police, Fire, Ambulance

For the police, fire department, or medical emergencies, call **911.**

The **ambulance service** can be reached at 415/931-3900; the **Poison Control Center,** at 415/476-6600.

Hospitals

The **Medical Center at the University of California,** 505 Parnassus Ave., at Third Avenue (tel. 415/476-1000 or 415/476-1037), for 24-hour emergency care; **San Francisco General Hospital,** 1001 Potrero Ave. (tel. 415/821-8200), for 24-hour emergency service and trauma facilities; **St. Francis Memorial Hospital,** 900 Hyde St., on Nob Hill (tel. 415/775-4321), for 24-hour emergency service; **Mount Zion Hospital and Medical Center,** 1600 Divisadero St. (tel. 415/885-7520), for 24-hour emergency service; and **Pacific Presbyterian Medical Center,** 2300 Sacramento St., at Buchanan Street (tel. 415/923-3333), for 24-hour emergency service.

24-Hour Pharmacies

The following pharmacies are open 24 hours daily: **Walgreen's Drugstore,** 500 Geary St., Union Square (tel. 415/673-8411 or 415/673-8413); and **Walgreen's Drugstore,** 3201 Divisadero St., near the Lombard, Marina, and Fisherman's Wharf area (tel. 415/931-6415).

CHAPTER III

THE BAY AREA AND VICINITY

□ □ □

With San Francisco as its core, the Bay Area towns that radiate from it are as diverse as the cosmopolitan city itself. Within 30 minutes of San Francisco you can choose from a rainbow of activities.

To the east is the college town of Berkeley, home of the world-renowned University of California. Well worth a day trip, this colorful community reflects the youthful intellectual life at its center. It has some wonderful family outings as well. Neighboring Oakland is the largest city in the East Bay, and is a major industrial port.

To the north, Marin County offers exquisite oceanfronted scenery, charming villages, and majestic woods. Unparalleled views of San Francisco and the bay await you. Known for some of the most expensive real estate in the country, the Marin communities have a completely different atmosphere from those in the East Bay.

1. BERKELEY

The city of Berkeley grew up around the University of California. While the town is an old, established community, it has an intellectual, innovative core that is youthful and forward-looking. In fact, some people say that if everything happens first in California, it gets its start in Berkeley. Think of hippies and the Free Speech Movement, and you automatically think of Berkeley. When bare feet, long hair, and women in "men's jobs" were creating controversy in other places, people here were blasé.

Even today a day in Berkeley is like spending time in a small, almost foreign enclave where much of the population is under 30, and vestiges of the counter-culture movement of the 1960s are still evident. Street vendors selling candles and jewelry line Telegraph Avenue. Musicians play on street corners and at lower Sproul Plaza. Political activism is still evident in the rallies and speeches given at

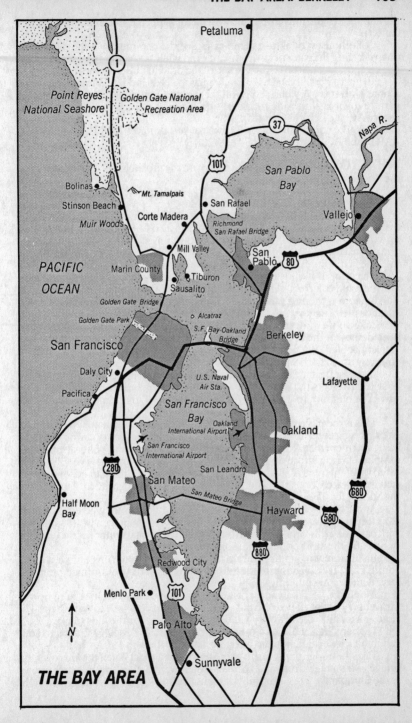

Petaluma

Point Reyes
National Seashore

Golden Gate National
Recreation Area

Napa R.

37

San Pablo
Bay

101

Bolinas

Mt. Tamalpais

Stinson Beach

San Rafael

Vallejo

Corte Madera

Muir Woods

Richmond
San Rafael Bridge

PACIFIC

Mill Valley

San
Pablo

OCEAN

Marin County

80

Tiburon

Sausalito

Golden Gate Bridge

Alcatraz

Berkeley

Golden Gate Park

S.F. Bay-Oakland
Bridge

San Francisco

Daly City

U.S. Naval
Air Sta.

Lafayette

Pacifica

San Francisco
Bay

Oakland
International Airport

Oakland

San Francisco
International Airport

280

San Leandro

San Mateo

San Mateo Bridge

680

Half Moon
Bay

Hayward

580

880

Redwood City

101

Menlo Park

N

Palo Alto

Sunnyvale

THE BAY AREA

the entrance to the university. And you might happen upon an impromptu jazz concert.

Coffeehouses, bookstores, and cafés dot the community around the campus, reflecting the student environment. And while you shouldn't miss the glorious campus, save a little time for some of the other family activities.

To get to Berkeley, take the San Francisco–Oakland Bay Bridge to I-80 east. Exit at University Avenue and go all the way to Oxford Avenue. Locals refer to parts of town as Northside and Southside. This refers to north and south of University Avenue near the campus.

If you're coming from San Francisco, you can take BART (tel. 415/788-BART) and AC Transit (tel. 415/839-2882).

WHAT TO DO AND SEE: Let's start with the probable reason you've crossed the bridge.

The University of California at Berkeley

Nestled at the foot of the Berkeley hills at Bancroft and Telegraph Avenues, the University of California at Berkeley (tel. 415/642-6000) is one of the finest universities in the world. With an enrollment of over 30,000 students, it is also one of the largest. The University of California charter was signed in 1868, and this, the first campus of the U.C. system, opened in 1873.

The campus itself is beautiful, filled with distinguished-looking buildings, redwood and oak trees, a delightful creek, and views of the San Francisco Bay. A walking tour is the best way to see it. We'll start our tour on Southside. (There is street or meter parking, and some parking lots are available.)

Take a little while to wander along Telegraph Avenue. Some people refer to it as a sideshow at the circus complete with hippie-looking characters, vendors, and "street people." Whatever your impressions, it is certainly unusual. Then make your way north to the intersection of Telegraph and Bancroft Avenues.

Just past the entrance is **Sproul Plaza,** the most famous area of campus. To your left (west) is the **Student Union,** home of many demonstrations in years past. The building to your right (east) is **Sproul Hall,** the administration building.

This is the place where the Free Speech Movement began in 1964. Even today this is a center for political and social activities. Rallies occur on a regular basis, and more than 20 tables are set up by organizations and political groups on campus, offering information and conversation. On any given day you'll see such diversity of interests as the Indian Students Group, the Christian Fellowship Society, the Peace Corps, the Young Republicans, the Jewish Student Union, even the Society for Creative Anachronisms.

At the foot of Sproul Steps is **Ludwig Fountain,** a place where kids dangle their feet in the water on hot days. If you look north, you'll see a white stone gate with baroque grillwork. This is **Sather Gate,** a traditional symbol of the university, and still the most popular meeting spot on campus.

Just before you get to Sather Gate, there's a path that runs east-west along Sproul Hall. Take that toward the hills (heading east). As you continue, you'll see several interesting buildings.

Along the left, redwoods, oaks, and pines grace your walk. You're now at **Strawberry Creek.** There's a trail along the creek if you wish to walk there. The large, grassy hill called **Faculty Glade** is a great place for the kids to play. You'll see **Stephens Hall,** a Tudor Gothic, built in 1923. The **Faculty Club** is to your east, built by world-famous architect Bernard Maybeck in 1903.

Take the bridge to the north over Strawberry Creek (watch the kids over this bridge—it's a high drop) and keep walking toward Sather Tower, better known as the **Campanile.** This is the most famous landmark of the university. Modeled after St. Mark's Campanile in Venice, it was built in 1914. For 25¢ you get a great ride to the top, where a heart-stopping view greets you. Kids love to ride to the top of the bell tower, and you can see San Francisco, the Golden Gate Bridge, and Marin County. The bells chime every half hour and play songs every hour. The four clock faces can be seen everywhere in town.

The campanile is open daily from 10 a.m. to 4:15 p.m. (closed university holidays).

If you look to the west, you'll see the oldest building on campus, **South Hall.** Built in 1873, it is, in fact, the oldest building in the entire University of California system.

Keep walking north to University Drive. Turn right (east). Soon you'll come to the Mining Circle. There is a lily pond and a grassy area. On the north is the **Hearst Mining Building,** built in 1907 in the Italian Renaissance style. Inside are pictures of the California Gold Rush.

Go back to University Drive and walk down to the large white building on your left (south). There are large, sweeping marble stairs to the entrance. This is the **Main Library,** built in 1911, and you'll want to walk inside. You can see the rounding of the marble steps from the thousands of students moving in and out of this entrance. The Berkeley campus has over seven million books—and this library houses many of them.

Take the stairs up to the circulation and reference room. Look up. This has to be the most beautiful room on campus. Three-story windows flank the entire north wall, and four-story arched windows adorn the west and east walls. The card catalog, made of oak, looks like it spans a football field.

Leave the library through the same sweeping steps. The street in front of you is University Drive. Take it west, over the bridge, and keep walking until you find yourself at West Circle. From here, walk south past the **Life Science Building.** You'll find yourself in the eucalyptus grove as well as at the south fork of Strawberry Creek. Kids love this area.

Go over the creek again and there will be a fork in the walk area. Veer to your left and you should see the **Alumni House** on your right. Keep walking and you'll be at Lower Sproul Plaza, back where you started.

Lawrence Hall of Science (tel. 415/642-5132) is a hands-on science center located in the hills above the university on Centennial Drive south of Grizzly Peak Boulevard. Part of the University of California, it is dedicated to educating children (and adults) about science, and serves as a resource for public schools.

Kids of all ages are intrigued by the many unusual, imaginative exhibits. For example, there is an exhibit that shows how lasers are used. Kids can control the laser beam and create their own light shows. Another popular exhibit is about holograms, with information about how they are made. Visitors from out-of-state are fascinated by the earthquake exhibit, which maps out the earthquake faults and includes a working seismic recorder. Other displays offer colorful computer-activated games on many different scientific topics.

There is an ongoing schedule of temporary participatory exhibits, including a popular animated life-size dinosaur exhibit that has *Triceratops* babies and a huge *Tyrannosaurus rex.*

The hall presents special events during the summer and on weekends and holidays. There are biology labs where children can touch frogs, chinchillas, rabbits, tarantulas, and other animals. The Wizard's Lab has physics gadgets and gizmos so children can learn more about magnetism, electricity, motion. There are daily planetarium shows during the summer and on weekends and holidays. The Discovery Corner sells science kits, games, and books that are difficult to find elsewhere. The shop also has science-oriented cassette tapes.

Lawrence Hall is open weekdays from 10 a.m. to 4:30 p.m. (on Thursday to 9 p.m.), and on Saturday and Sunday from 10 a.m. to 5 p.m. Admission is $3.50

for adults, $2.50 for seniors and children 7 and older, $1.50 for children under 7. There is complete stroller access. Labs are available on a drop-in basis. Call for information about one-hour workshops and planetarium shows.

At the head of Strawberry Canyon is the **University of California Botanical Gardens.** This 30-acre garden was started in 1926, and serves as a laboratory as well as a garden. It contains more than 8,000 species, totaling more than 50,000 plants, including 5,000 rare rhododendrons, 2,000 cacti and succulents, and a vast rose garden. Open daily from 9 a.m. to 5 p.m. Guided tours are offered on the weekend. For more information about these docent-led tours, call 415/642-3343 or 415/642-0849. There is no admission charge.

Charles Lee Tilden Regional Park

Located in the rolling hills behind Berkeley, 2,078-acre Charles Lee Tilden Regional Park is a favorite with local East Bay families, and the lucky visitors who know about it. Known for good hiking trails (beware of poison ivy, though), lake swimming, a golf course, equestrian trails, pony rides, a Hershell Spillman merry-go-round (with antique hand-carved animals), a botanic garden, several playgrounds, and a nature area with a petting farm. Tilden also has an Environmental Education Center, which offers naturalist-led programs.

Tilden's **Lake Anza** (tel. 415/531-9300) offers beach sunbathing and swimming from May through October. There is a shallow area that is roped off for children, which offers great swimming even for toddlers. Lifeguards are on duty in summer from 11 a.m. to 6 p.m. The admission fee is $2 for adults, $1 for children 6 through 17 and seniors, 50¢ for children 2 to 5.

One of our favorite areas is the **Nature Area.** This is where **Little Farm** is located. Kids can see cows, pigs, goats, donkeys, and a stunning variety of bunnies. Monthly programs have children come to the early-morning barnyard feed where they can milk goats, churn butter, and just get out there with the animals. **Jewel Lake** is a small area that has a self-guiding trail, perfect for little ones, and the **Environmental Education Center** holds at least one interpretive program each Saturday and Sunday. Naturalists will often bring out animals (a big favorite are the snakes) for the children to see and learn about. Hikes and wildflower walks are frequently offered. Most of the events are free. For program information, call 415/525-2233.

The **pony rides** are within walking distance from the Nature Area and the **merry-go-round** is about five minutes away by car. The pony rides are open from 11 a.m. to 5 p.m. daily during spring and summer vacation. Rides are $1. Call 415/527-0421 for more information. The merry-go-round operates from 10 a.m. to 5 p.m. weekends and holidays all year, and daily during spring and summer vacation. The charge is 50¢ per ride.

Little Train is another favorite. This miniature version of a steam train is located at the southern end of the park. It operates from 11 a.m. to 6 p.m. weekends and holidays all year, as well as weekdays during spring and summer vacation. A ride costs $1.

For park information and directions to Tilden, call 415/843-2137.

For a Treat

For an incredible children's bookstore, **Mr. Mopps' Children's Books and Toys,** 1405 Martin Luther King Jr. Way (tel. 415/525-9633), is a delight for parents who want to inspire their children to read. The huge bookstore has books for infants to 12th-graders, arranged in a room away from the toys. Open from 9:30 a.m. to 5:30 p.m. Monday through Saturday; closed Sunday.

If you're looking for a good little toy store, **Sweet Dreams Toy Store,** at 2921 College Ave., and **Sweet Dreams Candy Shop,** at 2901 College Ave. (tel. 415/548-TOYS), have large, colorful stuffed animals and rows and rows of delicious candies. The stores don't have a lot of traditional toys: they're more like a kid's heaven with tiny trinkets and barrels of trendy little goodies. You'll find Betty Boop paraphernalia and other knickknacks. Open Monday through Saturday from 10 a.m. to 6 p.m., and on Sunday from noon to 5 p.m.

WHERE TO STAY: Some people who come to the Bay Area prefer to stay in Berkeley, where the pace is slower and there is more open space than in San Francisco. The 20-minute ride (without traffic) on the San Francisco–Oakland Bay Bridge into the city makes sightseeing in San Francisco very convenient. Generally, the rates in the East Bay are a bit lower too. The accommodations we offer here are all conveniently located. There are many budget-priced motels located on University Avenue, but we suggest that you personally inspect them before booking a room.

A Grand Resort Hotel

The only resort in the San Francisco Bay area is located at the foot of the Oakland-Berkeley hills. The **Claremont Resort Hotel and Tennis Club,** 41 Tunnel Rd., Berkeley (tel. 415/843-3000; for reservations, write to P.O. Box 23363, Oakland, CA 94623), is a classically beautiful Victorian hotel that has hosted the likes of Cornelius Vanderbilt and Eleanor Roosevelt. The imposing white structure with its lavish grounds and facilities has quite a colorful history.

In the 1870s a former farmer made wealthy by the California Gold Rush bought 40 acres of land on which he built a mansion (known as the Castle) and elaborate gardens for his wife. When his wife died he sold the property, which eventually burned to the ground, leaving only the stables and barn (which you can see to this day—as the locker rooms for the swimming pool).

The property changed hands and was sold to a group of entrepreneurs, whose vision included development of a line on the electric rail system that would end at a grand hotel. Although construction was started, severe financial problems beset the partners. Local gossip says that the three owners decided that the winner of a checkers (or dominoes) match would take possession of the hotel! One owner emerged, and was finally able to finish the hotel just before the 1915 Panama-Pacific International Exposition held in San Francisco.

The hotel has seen several owners—and changes—since that time. In 1971 it underwent a $20-million renovation, and in 1982 guest room renovation was completed. In 1988 complete spa facilities were added.

This full-service hotel offers room service from 6 a.m. to midnight. There are several snackbars and restaurants with children's selections, ten tennis courts, a gorgeous outdoor Olympic-size swimming pool with a children's area, a Jacuzzi, exercise par-course, and complete spa facilities. Nightly turndown service is offered, with fruit instead of chocolates. The concierge will arrange babysitting.

The rooms are tastefully appointed, and decorated in blues and rich browns. All rooms are spacious, and have hill views, televisions with SpectraVision, and individual coffee makers. Suites have refrigerators; you can request one for other rooms.

Rooms rent for $130 to $200 single and $150 to $220 double. Suites range from $235 to $535. Children under 18 stay free in their parents' room. Cribs are free, but rollaways cost $10 per night.

Other Choices

The **Hotel Durant** is a Berkeley tradition. Located at 2600 Durant Ave., Berkeley, CA 94704 (tel. 415/845-8981), one block from the University of California campus, the Durant has been hosting visitors to the area for over 60 years. The European-style hotel has a small, quiet lobby with sofas and love seats, and is a good place to stay if your children don't need a lot of room to run around. It is *the* accommodation on the south side of campus.

The stately Durant offers complimentary continental breakfast, valet and laundry service, valet parking ($3 per day), and airport service (for an additional fee). The hotel provides babysitting service with high school students.

Henry's restaurant and pub are similar to a San Francisco fern bar. There are Tiffany-style lamps, cluster tables, and lots of polished wood and brass. This is where the free continental breakfast is served (from 7 to 9:30 a.m.). Henry's has highchairs and booster seats, and is best for kids during the breakfast period. As the day wears on, college students frequent the eatery and bar, making it smoky and noisy—and there is no children's menu.

The Hotel Durant has 140 rooms, each of which has color television, free HBO, and AM/FM radio. No air conditioning. Many of the rooms have a view of the University of California campus or the bay.

Rooms cost $68 to $70 single and $76 to $84 double. Suites range from $100 to $180. Children under 12 stay free in their parents' room; children 12 and over and additional adults pay $10 each per night. No charge for cribs.

Gramma's Bed and Breakfast Inn, 2740 Telegraph Ave., Berkeley, CA 94705 (tel. 415/549-2145), is a lovely alternative to a regular hotel, and many of the rooms are suitable for families. The inn consists of two restored mansions totaling 29 rooms. Decorated with antiques, and loaded with country charm, each room has its own bath or shower and television. Many have fireplaces.

As the name indicates, breakfast is included in the room price, as is evening wine and cheese or cookies and milk. There is a huge grassy lawn in the front, and a large redwood deck in the back where kids can play.

Rooms range in price from $71 to $130—the more expensive rooms can handle families. The price (including tax—which is unusual) is for double occupancy. If your child needs a futon, there's a $10 additional charge per night. The management will try to accommodate you in the most economical way, so tell the clerk what you need.

WHERE TO EAT:
For a small town, Berkeley has a surprisingly wide array of excellent eateries. In fact, North Berkeley is known in some northern California circles as the "Gourmet Ghetto." Crowned by Chez Panisse, whose owner, Alice Waters, is credited with having started California cuisine, Berkeley's eateries run the gamut. Even the poorest student in Berkeley talks lovingly about some of the specialty food stores—the Cheese Board, Cocolat, and Peet's Coffee—all within a block of Chez Panisse.

Upper Bracket
Internationally acclaimed, **Chez Panisse Café and Restaurant,** 1517 Shattuck Ave., between Cedar and Vine (tel. 415/548-5049 or 415/548-5525), is the place where California cuisine got its start in 1971. In fact, many famous chefs have worked here with Alice Waters and then gone on to open their own successful restaurants. The award-winning restaurant emphasizes freshness and creativity in its nouvelle cuisine.

Naturally, we don't take our kids to the prix-fixe dinner (at $50), which might consist of caviar; pigeon sausage with cabbage, bacon, and mustard; roasted red onion and garlic soup; grilled rack of veal with green beans and sautéed potatoes; garden salad; and baked figs. Instead, we enjoy the same kitchen (with lighter fare) at the upstairs café.

Alice Waters opened the café in 1980 because she wanted a place where her friends, family, and neighbors could eat light in a casual setting. Often you'll see Alice with daughter Fanny in the café. The pizza comes from the brick oven, and the pizza maker will show the kids how he does it, and will even create a pizza in the child's initials. You can also get pasta, salads, and fish. The "tamest" item is the pizza with tomato sauce and sausage ($11.50), but our kids will share our grilled swordfish ($14) and calzone with goat cheese, mozzarella, prosciutto, and garlic ($11). If you went only according to the menu, you'd think your kids would have to have refined taste, but we always tell our server to hold some of the items that seem too "gourmet." To our delight, the food is consistently excellent.

Booster seats are available. They give crayons to the kids for them to use on the white paper table coverings.

The café's lunch hours are 11:30 a.m. to 3 p.m. Monday through Friday, to 4:30 on Saturday; dinner hours are 5 to 11:30 p.m. Monday through Saturday. And Tuesday through Saturday dinner is served in the downstairs restaurant, with four seatings: at 6, 6:30, 8:30, and 9:15 p.m. (people make reservations months in advance). The café takes reservations for lunch only. Most major credit cards are accepted. Street parking.

Moderate

Perhaps one of the most popular restaurants in town, **Christopher's Café,** 1843 Solano Ave. (tel. 415/526-9444), is a lively, noisy place to eat. Its simple white linens, wood-and-brass wine bar, and mirrors give it a clean look. The service is fast, and bread is on the table as soon as you're seated.

Good choices for kids are the pastas (they'll serve half orders), shoestring potatoes, burgers, and steaks (which they'll split in the kitchen). The lunch menu includes a poultry salad of the day, fresh fish of the day, and fresh pasta of the day, as well as other selections. (Prices range from $4.75 to $7.25.) Dinner offerings are unusual and diverse. For example, fresh salmon is served with a mango beurre blanc; grilled chicken breast is marinated in chile, cumin, dark beer, cilantro, and orange juice. There is other, more standard fare as well, and Christopher's makes the best Caesar salad in town. Prices range from $5.50 (for hamburger) to $14. If you like blackened fish, this is a good place to try it.

No highchairs, but booster seats are available. Open for lunch Monday through Friday from 11:30 a.m. to 2:15 p.m.; for dinner, Monday through Thursday from 5:30 to 9:30 p.m., on Friday and Saturday till 10:15 p.m., and on Sunday till 9:15 p.m. Reservations are recommended. They accept some major credit cards. Street parking.

Larry Blake's has been a tradition in Berkeley since 1940. Located at 2367 Telegraph Ave., off Durant Avenue (tel. 415/848-0886), one block south of the university campus, Larry Blake's has been a student gathering spot for many years. It is a lively place where children fit right in.

Specializing in barbecued chicken and ribs, there are other American-style selections as well: grilled cheese, turkey, ham or roast beef sandwiches, and fried chicken. Daily dinner specials include fresh fish, pasta, and prime rib. Lunch prices are $4 to $7. Dinner runs $7 to $15.

Weekend brunch is off the menu, and includes such favorites as steak and eggs, eggs Benedict, and strawberry pancakes. Prices (including champagne, plus potatoes or fruit, and toast) range from $4 to $8.

Highchairs and boosters are available. They don't have a children's menu, but will gladly split portions in the kitchen without charge, or scramble an egg for dinner (if the restaurant isn't packed). They're always willing to make a fruit platter or mash bananas.

Larry Blake's has a downstairs cellar with local entertainment. Kids are allowed down there if accompanied by an adult.

Open Monday through Saturday from 7 a.m. to midnight, and on Sunday from 10 a.m. to 10 p.m. All major credit cards accepted. Street parking is difficult to find.

Inexpensive

If you want to see your kids wolf down a whole order of French toast, the **Homemade Café,** 2454 Dwight Ave. (tel. 415/845-1940), is where it's likely to happen. The place is nothing fancy and somewhat crowded, but the best breakfasts in town are said to be served here. Since it's bursting with locals—and their kids—the restaurant staff knows how to handle youngsters, and the food is served quickly.

Besides the great French toast, you might like try the homemade cornedbeef hash or the lox and eggs scrambled with onions. Creative sandwiches are also a specialty. (How about guacamole, cheese, lettuce, and tomato?) Prices for breakfast and lunch start at $2 and go as high as $5.25.

There are highchairs and boosters, but no children's menu (which didn't bother us at these prices). The servers will gladly split adult portions and warm bottles or baby food. Open Monday through Friday from 7 a.m. to 2 p.m. and on Saturday and Sunday from 8 a.m. to 3 p.m. No reservations or credit cards accepted.

And you wouldn't want to leave town without having tasted one of the great muffins or pies from **Fatapples**, 1346 Martin Luther King Jr. Way (tel. 415/526-2260). Simple dishes made from scratch, using quality ingredients, is the way they do things here. While they're known for their baked goods, the burgers, fries, and soups are also excellent. And the coffee is excellent too. Prices range from $3.75 for breakfast to about $4.50 for lunch and dinner items.

Highchairs and boosters are available, but there is no children's menu. They'll gladly split portions in the kitchen, and the servers will try to bring you whatever you think the kids might like.

Open Monday through Friday from 6 a.m. to 11 p.m. and on Saturday and Sunday from 7 a.m. to 11 p.m. No reservations or credit cards accepted. Street parking.

Chester's is another café that specializes in terrific breakfasts and lunches. Located at 1508B Walnut St. in the Walnut Square shopping area (tel. 415/849-9995), this casual eatery with wooden benches and chairs offers both indoor and outdoor service. The owners actively promote children coming to the café by presenting a nice children's menu ($2.50 to $3), little contests for the kids, and friendly servers who will actually bring fruit and crackers for little ones. If you prefer to have the children split an adult order, there's no charge if you do it at the table ($1 extra if you request it done in the kitchen). They'll also warm baby bottles and baby food.

Egg specialties, omelets, burgers (seven kinds), sandwiches, and salads round out the adult menu, with prices ranging from $3.25 to $6.

Highchairs and boosters are available. Open daily from 8 a.m. to 10 p.m. Street parking. No reservations or credit cards accepted.

IN CASE OF EMERGENCY: If a medical emergency arises during your stay in Berkeley, there's an emergency room at **Alta Bates Hospital,** 3001 Colby Ave. (tel. 415/540-0337, or 415/540-1303 for the emergency room).

---

2. OAKLAND

The city of Oakland, with some 350,000 people, is the largest city in the East Bay. It is a culturally and ethnically diverse city, and qualifies as the quintessential melting pot. In fact, in a recent survey, Oakland was rated the most integrated city in the country.

Known as a major world port, Oakland's waterfront is 19 miles long, and has 28 deep-water berths. The city has dozens of parks, quaint Victorian neighborhoods, and a variety of museums.

To get the full story about what to do and where to go, you'll want to contact the **Oakland Convention and Visitors Bureau,** 1000 Broadway, Suite 200,

Oakland, CA 94607 (tel. 415/839-9000). For information on upcoming events, telephone **"The Great Time Line"** (tel. 415/839-9008) for a recorded message.

WHAT TO SEE AND DO: The city is quite diverse, with outdoor activities ranking high on the list of things to do. Let's start with the heart of the city.

Lake Merritt
At the center of Oakland is the lovely 155-acre saltwater lake (tel. 415/ 444-3807). Originally a swampy area, it was transformed in 1870 by the then-mayor, Samuel Merritt. The area is a haven for joggers, walkers, and picnickers, as well as boaters. If your family likes to be on the water, you can rent sailboats, canoes, and paddleboats. If you like to watch birds or feed the ducks, you can do that too.

Lakeside Park (tel. 415/273-3494) is considered one of the most beautiful city parks around. Bordering the lake, it not only offers the above-mentioned diversions, but it also has free musical entertainment on summer weekends. If you love horticultural displays, you can see a wide variety at the **Garden Center.**

Located in Lakeside Park is the fun-for-smallfry **Children's Fairyland.** Great for toddlers and young schoolchildren, it's located at Park View Terrace and Grand Avenue (tel. 415/452-2259). Fairyland is a world of make-believe and fantasy that has over 60 three-dimensional nursery-rhyme sets. There are farm animals, a sea lion exhibit, a merry-go-round (just right for little kids), and the Jolly Roger train ride. Kids can roam around, climb on and in the storybook attractions. The Puppet Theater is well known and has daily shows at 11 a.m., 2 p.m., and 4 p.m.

We were delighted to find that the proprietors of Fairyland are ever-careful about the children. Adults are not allowed inside if they don't have children with them.

Open daily in summer from 10 a.m. to 5:30 p.m. and during the winter and holidays from 10 a.m. to 4:30 p.m.; closed Thanksgiving, Christmas, and New Year's Days. Admission is $2.50 for adults, $1.75 for children 12 and under. Completely stroller-accessible.

The Oakland Museum
Unique in its focus, the Oakland Museum, 1000 Oak St. (tel. 415/273-3401, or 415/834-2413 for recorded information), is a regional museum showcasing the art, natural sciences, and history of the state of California. Sometimes referred to as the "California Smithsonian," it is a microcosm of California. There is one gallery devoted strictly to California art, from the earliest explorers to today. The Cowell Hall of California History is the largest collection of artifacts relating to California. There are objects from the Gold Rush and 1906 earthquake, back to the Spanish-American colonization and further. Another gallery is devoted to California ecology.

The museum holds Sunday-afternoon family programs on natural history and cultural anthropology. Recent programs have included "Meet a Reptile" and "California Indian Life." Programs use art and stories to bring history to life.

There is a restaurant and snackbar, a collector's gallery, and a museum store. Open Wednesday through Saturday from 10 a.m. to 5 p.m. and on Sunday from noon to 7 p.m.; closed Monday, Tuesday, and legal holidays. Free admission.

Jack London Square and Jack London Village
Jack London was only one of the literary figures who lived in Oakland. Others have included Bret Harte and Robert Louis Stevenson. Located on the waterfront at the Embarcadero where Broadway and Jackson Street end, this pic-

turesque area has dozens of restaurants and shops. The village is a nice place to window-shop with the kids and find a good place to eat.

To get to Jack London Square from San Francisco, take the San Francisco–Oakland Bay Bridge to I-880 south. Exit at Broadway and take a right on Broadway to the Embarcadero (tel. 415/893-7956).

When you're there, you can see **Jack London's Log Cabin.** This tiny cabin with a sod roof is where London spent an entire winter.

Or you might be interested in a walking tour of the historic area. Free guided tours of the area are offered by the **Oakland Tours Program** (tel. 415/273-3234) from May through October (call for further details). There are also tours of the Estuary and outer harbor conducted by the Red and White Fleet. The tour takes 1¼ hours and goes through the Port of Oakland. Call 415/839-7493 for reservations.

Knowland Park and Oakland Zoo

Knowland Park, located at 98th Avenue and I-580 (tel. 415/632-9525), is 525 acres of rolling green hills that has picnic and barbecue facilities, and is home to the **Oakland Zoo.** The zoo sits on 100 acres, and has more than 330 birds, reptiles, and mammals.

The children's petting zoo, miniature train, and skyride are the main attractions. The park is open daily from 9 a.m. to sunset; closed Christmas Day. The Oakland Zoo is open daily from 10 a.m. to 4 p.m. Admission is $2.50 for adults, $1 for children.

Sports

A big draw in Oakland is the **Oakland Athletics,** who play baseball at the Oakland Coliseum (tel. 415/638-0500) during the season (April through September). The **Golden State Warriors** play basketball at the Coliseum (tel. 415/638-6000) during their season (October through April). The Coliseum is located at Nimitz Freeway and Hegenberger Road.

IF YOU'RE LOOKING FOR SOMETHING TO EAT: With a large selection of restaurants, Jack London Square is probably the best place to find something good to eat.

One of the places we like is **Shenanigans,** 30 Jack London Square (tel. 415/839-8333). Located on the water, this attractive rustic restaurant has stained-glass windows and antiques, and serves such standard fare as sandwiches, burgers, and fresh fish for lunch, and chicken, prime rib, and seafood for dinner. Lunch prices range from $4 to $9; dinner prices are $10 to $18. There is no children's menu, but they'll gladly make up a grilled-cheese or tuna sandwich, and the burgers can be split in the kitchen.

Highchairs and boosters are available, and the servers will warm bottles and baby food. Open for lunch Monday through Saturday from 11 a.m. to 3 p.m. Dinner hours are Sunday through Thursday from 5 to 10 p.m., on Friday and Saturday until 11 p.m. Sunday brunch is served from 10 a.m. to 3 p.m. Reservations are recommended on the weekend. There is ample validated parking, and most major credit cards are accepted.

Scott's Seafood Grill and Bar has a branch here on the waterfront at 73 Jack London Square (tel. 415/444-3456). You'll find the same fine food here as at the restaurant in San Francisco, but this Scott's is also open for lunch. Its wide range of seafood dinner entrees are priced from $12 to $18. Lunch costs a little less. Children tend to prefer the pastas and burgers.

This location has booster seats and will take reservations (in fact, they're recommended). Open Monday through Thursday from 11 a.m. to 10 p.m., on Friday and Saturday till 11 p.m., and on Sunday till 9 p.m. Some major credit cards are accepted, and there's lots of parking.

IN AN EMERGENCY: If a medical emergency arises while you're visiting Oakland, you should contact one of the following local emergency rooms: **Kaiser Permanente,** 3451 Piedmont Ave. (tel. 415/596-1120 or 415/596-7600 for the emergency room); or **Merritt Hospital,** Hawthorne and Webster Avenues (tel. 415/655-4000, or 415/420-6116 for the emergency room).

---

3. ANGEL ISLAND

Angel Island State Park (tel. 415/435-1915) is like a jewel of 740 thickly forested acres sitting in the middle of San Francisco Bay. It offers good hiking trails, bicycle paths, and wonderful picnic spots. On warm summer days the coves are lovely spots to sit with the kids and do some serious work on elaborate sandcastles.

The treat begins even before you set foot on the island. Take the **Red and White Fleet** from Fisherman's Wharf, Pier 41 (tel. 415/546-2896 or toll free 800/445-8880 in Calif.) for a short cruise. (Call ahead as schedules vary.) Round-trip fares are $7 for adults and $4 for children 5 to 11. The bracing air usually prevents seasickness, but be sure to bring windbreakers even when it's warm. If you plan to bicycle, you can rent bicycles and take them with you on the ferry. But you should call the ferry service ahead of time because bicycle space is limited.

The island has 17 miles of paved trails for easy walking, even if you lug a stroller with you—which may be the best way to go if you have a preschooler who tires easily.

The museum at **Ayala Cove** offers browsers information about the natural history of the island. There is also a 20-minute video shown on the hour on the weekends, April through October.

If you want to venture out of Ayala Cove, **China Cove** has an old Immigration Station where tours are given on weekends from 11 a.m. to 4 p.m. At **East Garrison** there is a large army fort that was in operation from the Spanish-American War through World War II. There are docent tours of the grounds upon request from 11 a.m. to 4 p.m. April through October. At **West Garrison** you'll find Camp Reynolds, a Civil War camp that you can tour. It's a little bit of history for the kids while they're enjoying themselves in the outdoors. Our kids love the cannon firings, which take place at 1 and 2 p.m. on weekends, April through October.

Walking the island is possible with children. Most kids (even those under 5) can walk the easy one-mile to West Garrison to the cannon firings without any trouble. Park officials suggest that you bring a wagon (or stroller) for little tykes, if you want to see more. Older children will love bicycling through the island, and if you decide to take bikes, the hills are slight enough so that toddler carriers won't present a problem.

The one main road around the island is five miles and is completely suitable for walking or bicycling. This main road is the best for young children. This is where you'll see kids with little red wagons or furiously pedaling tricycles.

The snackbar is open daily during the summer, and on weekends from 10 a.m. to 4 p.m. or sunset. But we always take a picnic lunch because the selection of food is very limited.

4. TIBURON

If you want to know why people love living in the Bay Area, grab the kids and go to Tiburon. This tiny village is surrounded by picturesque Richardson Bay. Any way you get there, you'll discover incredible sights. You'll see Mount Tamalpais emerge on the Marin side, all three bridges across the bay (the Golden Gate, the Bay Bridge, and the San Rafael), and spectacular views of San Francisco,

Alcatraz, and Angel Island. Much smaller and less crowded than Sausalito, Tiburon plays host to families who come to enjoy a meal at bayside, and to bike-ride or wander in one of the most spectacular settings on the bay.

Possibly the most pleasant way to get to Tiburon is to cross the bay on a **Red and White Fleet** ferry (tel. 415/546-2896 or toll free 800/445-8800 in Calif.). Boats leave from Pier 41 at Fisherman's Wharf several times a day for the 15-minute ride. The crossing costs $8 round trip for adults, $4 for children 5 to 11; free for under-5s. If you're driving, take the Tiburon exit off U.S. 101. If you prefer to go by bus, **Golden Gate Transit** (tel. 415/332-6600) offers service from downtown San Francisco. Many families make a full day of it by spending part of the time in Tiburon and then taking the ferry to Angel Island (tel. 415/435-2131) for the remainder of the day.

Before you start, you might want to contact the **Tiburon Peninsula Chamber of Commerce,** 96 Main St., Tiburon, CA 94920 (tel. 415/435-5633). They'll send you free brochures about the downtown shopping area and maps that show various activities in the peninsula region.

WHAT TO SEE AND DO: Plan to spend a few hours in the Tiburon area so you can enjoy the beautiful surroundings and get a flavor of the town.

Wandering Around

Tiburon was once the hub of the Bay Area, with heavy ferry and railroad traffic; people used it as a main link in their trip to San Francisco. Today the best way to enjoy the quaint village is to walk the main streets and the area called Ark Row. Many of the alluring-looking shops are housed in what used to be summer cottages and old arks (houseboats) built in the 1800s.

One of the shops our kids like best is **Main Things,** at 32 Main St. (tel. 415/435-1033). This store has toys, cards, stuffed animals, and T-shirts. On Ark Row you'll find several other interesting stores. Probably the best for kids is **Ark Row Smart Toys,** 80 Main St. (tel. 415/435-1002), which has a large collection of dollhouse furniture.

Blackie's Pasture

Just before you enter town, you'll come across a lovely large green pasture. We often stop here since it's a great place for a picnic. We used to wonder at its name, and we learned that Blackie was a horse born in Kansas in 1926. He began his career as a rodeo horse, then worked in Yosemite and at the San Francisco Presidio. He came to Tiberon in 1938 and grazed in this pasture until his death in 1966. When he died, he was buried in the pasture he loved so well. You can see his grave here, marked by the white cross. He's a legend in Tiburon.

National Audubon Society's Richardson Bay Audubon Center

Located at 376 Greenwood Beach Rd. (tel. 415/388-2524), this sanctuary for thousands of waterfowl is sometimes called a "window on the bay." It has several different habitats that reflect the bay's environment. The center sometimes offers children's programs about the environment. Here you'll find the **Book Nest** bookstore, one of the largest natural-history bookstores in the state.

Walks and Bike Paths

Tiburon is a place to explore on foot or by bike. One of our favorite bike paths runs all along Richardson Bay. (Unfortunately, hordes of bicyclists, joggers, and walkers agree.) Known as the best bike path in Marin County, it passes the Audubon Society's bird reserve and historic Lyford House. You'll also ride by beautiful McKegney Green, which faces Sausalito across Richardson Bay, and offers wonderful picnicking. You might want to pack that lunch before you hop on the bicycles.

You can start at Tiburon Boulevard. Take Tiburon Boulevard to Blackie's Pasture for the entrance to the Tiburon Bike Path. The path leads into town, and is level for about five miles. Once you get into the village, you'll see one of the most spectacular views of San Francisco there is. The city jumps out at you, making you think you could touch it.

WHERE TO EAT: Alfresco dining is *the* thing in Tiburon—weather permitting. The following are but a few of the choice places to eat.

Our favorite restaurant in Tiburon—and a great place for kids—is **Sam's Anchor Café,** 27 Main St. (tel. 415/435-4527). The view is special, the service is good, and the food is tasty. The deck is the place to eat during the day. You get a spectacular view of San Francisco, the Golden Gate Bridge, and Angel Island. Although the deck sways, you do get used to it. The friendly sea gulls are entertaining for the kids, but don't let the kids feed them or they'll pull food off your plate before you know it.

The café has its own bit of folk history. It was built in 1920 during Prohibition. Ever-clever entrepreneurs are said to have built a trap door under the building so boats could pull up under the pilings and pass liquor. Amusing as the story is, today's café is a wholesome place, offering savory food. And the deck where they smuggled liquor is where you'll prefer to dine.

If you are outside, watch the little ones. There are railings all around the deck, but the restaurant does sit over the water. Servers keep an ever-watchful eye after the kids—and they say they've *never* had one go overboard. But be careful just the same!

This very casual restaurant offers two indoor rooms in addition to the outdoor deck. The bar, which is located in front, has a large television and serves free popcorn.

Known for their delectable swordfish and salmon, they also have daily seafood specials. Cioppino, steamed clams, and sautéed or deep-fried local oysters are other treats. The burgers here are very good. Other fare includes sandwiches (the Dungeness crab on a toasted English muffin is yummy), omelets, chicken, and steak. Prices range from $5.50 to $13. The children's "color-in" menu (which includes a Samburger, spaghetti, fish and chips, and a hot dog—for $2.75 to $4.25) comes with crayons.

Highchairs and boosters are available, and the management will do whatever it can to accommodate children. Reservations are not accepted, so in the summer you can expect to wait for up to one hour. We usually put our name on the waiting list and then wander around Tiburon.

The restaurant's hours are a little unusual. It is open Monday through Friday at 11 a.m. for lunch; in summer (Daylight Savings Time) Monday through Thursday it stays open till 10:30 p.m. and on Friday till 11 p.m. On Saturday it's open from 10 a.m. to 11 p.m., and on Sunday from 9:30 a.m. to 10:30 p.m. During Standard Time the restaurant closes a half hour earlier. To be safe, call ahead. Parking on Main Street. Most major credit cards accepted.

Another local favorite, though more expensive, is **Guaymas,** 5 Main St. (tel. 415/435-6300). This open, airy, traditional Mexican restaurant boasts the best unimpeded view of San Francisco and Angel Island in Tiburon. This colorful restaurant has floor-to-ceiling glass windows, a cement floor, and brightly tinted inside walls of pink, yellow, and turquoise. Even the serving dishes have a Mexican motif. The restaurant is adorned by traditional Mexican paper lace placemats hanging from the ceiling.

Guaymas is a seaport in Mexico, and the staff pride themselves on serving mouthwatering traditional cuisine from that locale. All the food is made from scratch. The open kitchen affords you the chance to watch the chefs cook and the local women make fresh tortillas.

Mexican delicacies are abundant here, and the kitchen has a special flare. Have you ever tried chicken with chocolate, chiles, fruit, and spices? There are giant shrimp marinated in lime and cilantro; also butterflied baby chicken with tomatillo-jalapeño chile sauce. We find that good choices for the kids include tamales, guacamole and chips, and banana-wrapped red snapper. Prices range from $7 to $14.50.

They have highchairs and boosters, but no kids' menu. They'll split adult portions in the kitchen, and will bring chips and tortillas to the table as soon as you are seated.

Guaymas is open Monday through Friday from 11:30 a.m. to 10 p.m., on Saturday from 11:30 a.m. to 11 p.m., and on Sunday from 10:30 a.m. to 10 p.m. They accept most major credit cards and recommend reservations; without them, the wait can be extremely long, especially during peak times. Parking is available.

5. SAUSALITO

Located only eight miles north of San Francisco (2¾ miles from the Golden Gate Bridge), this picturesque village is built into a steep hillside and is surrounded by the bay. Known as an artists' colony, Sausalito has about 7,500 residents. This is a place most first-time visitors to the Bay Area want to see. We find there's enough to do in town to keep the kids busy for a few hours. Then we hightail it to some of the other nearby attractions.

To get to Sausalito from San Francisco, you can drive (take Calif. 1 to the Sausalito exit and follow the signs) or you can take the children's favorite, the ferry. If you go by ferry, choose the 30-minute ride on the **Golden Gate Transit ferry** (tel. 415/332-6600 or 415/453-2100), which leaves from the San Francisco Ferry Building; one-way fare is $3.50. Or ride the **Red and White Fleet** (tel. 415/546-2815 or toll free 800/445-8800 in Calif.), which leaves from Pier 41 at Fisherman's Wharf; one-way fares are $4 for adults and $2 for children. Numerous tour buses include Sausalito in their tours, including **Greyhound** (tel. 415/433-1500). **Golden Gate Buses** (tel. 415/332-6600) also come here. Some people who come by ferry use taxi service to get to places outside Sausalito. You can reach **local taxi** service in Sausalito by calling 415/332-2200.

Before you leave San Francisco on your Sausalito outing, you might want to first get information from the **Redwood Empire Association Visitor's Information Center,** at One Market Plaza / Spear Street Tower, Suite 1001, in San Francisco (tel. 415/543-8334). It's open Monday through Friday from 9 a.m. to 4:30 p.m.

WHAT TO SEE AND DO: Sausalito is just a little over two square miles, and is a place to wander, watch the boats, and do some shopping. Sausalito's main street is **Bridgeway**—sometimes referred to as Old Town—a long line of shops, restaurants, and sailing masts. All the attractions on Bridgeway are conveniently located.

Near the entrance to town is the **San Francisco Bay Delta Model,** 2100 Bridgeway (tel. 415/332-3871). This working scale model of the entire delta area is actually a scientific tool that scientists and engineers use to analyze and solve problems affecting the region. We recommend it for kids 8 and up. Think of it as you would a model airplane. Instead it's a model of currents, tides, and rivers—and visually helps you begin to understand the estuary where Pacific Ocean salt water mixes with fresh water.

You'll see a layout of a 17-mile ocean, several bays, and the delta, two football fields in length. It looks like someone took a map and cut out the bay. When it's in operation, there is water inside and you get an idea of how tides go back and forth.

This is a testing facility, so it's sometimes closed. It's generally open Tuesday through Saturday from 9 a.m. to 4 p.m., except from June through September when it's also open on Saturday and Sunday from 10 a.m. to 4 p.m. Call ahead. No admission charge.

Meet at the bay model for a tour of the steam schooner *Wapama* (part of the National Maritime Museum). Built in 1915, this is the last wooden steam vessel of the approximately 225 that were built. Guided tours are conducted on Saturday and Sunday at 3 p.m. No charge.

Shopping

Located in the center of town is the **Village Fair,** a group of 40 shops featuring everything from candles to crafts. We like **The House That Jack Built,** on the second floor (tel. 415/332-4502), a store devoted to dollhouses—wallpaper, furniture, everything. Outside the Village Fair, you'll find other pleasant shops. Meander through **High as a Kite,** upstairs at 691 Bridgeway (tel. 415/332-6355) for some fun. You'll see all colors, styles, and sizes of kites, from the most basic to the most elaborate. And there's **Games People Play** at 695 Bridgeway (tel. 415/332-4151), which has lots of preschool items as well as imported toys for children (and their parents). **Charlotte's Web,** 1207 Bridgeway (tel. 415/332-2244), offers a distinctive collection of literature for children and young adults. Open Monday, Tuesday morning, and Thursday through Saturday from 9 a.m. to 6 p.m., and on Sunday from 12:30 p.m. to 6 p.m.; closed Tuesday afternoon and all day Wednesday.

And Other Places to See Nearby

In the cliffs just west of Sausalito are the **Marin Headlands** (tel. 415/331-1540), part of Golden Gate National Recreation Area. Some of the cliffs are sandstone, and provide a dramatic setting with the ocean below. It's spectacular scenery. The **Marin Headlands Visitor Center** (located in Fort Cronkhite) is open from 8:30 a.m. to 4:30 daily. A fine little one-mile trail is located behind the Visitor Center. **Lagoon Loop** is a fairly level walk that gives you a good idea of the scope of the headlands. From the top of the trail you can see the ocean, and all along the way there are quiet areas where you can hear the birds. This is an area where one of the park's bobcats hangs out, so you might be "lucky" enough to see him.

The Visitor Center offers guided family walks during which children learn about the wildlife and habitat of the region. Special art programs for children are also offered at times. Call for information.

The **California Marine Mammal Center,** Marin Headlands (tel. 415/331-7325), is dedicated to rescuing and treating orphaned and injured sea mammals. When recovered, the animals are released back to the wild. Children will enjoy a visit to the center, where they can see recovering seals, sea lions, and otters, and talk with animal caretakers, who will gladly share their expertise and love of the animals with the kids.

Educational materials instruct children about all the kinds of sea mammals on the West Coast. During the weekends docents give tours of the area. For special educational programs, call 415/331-0161. Open daily from 10 a.m. to 4 p.m. Admission is free.

WHERE TO EAT: While restaurants in Sausalito are quite pricey because they cater to tourists, they are numerous.

A little off the beaten tourist path is **Café Trieste,** 1000 Bridgeway (tel. 415/332-7770), a good alternative for a quick, fairly reasonably priced bite to eat if you don't need a highchair or booster. This little cafeteria-style bistro is one place you could keep your child in a stroller. Frequented by locals, Café Trieste has a changing assortment of sandwiches, pizza, muffins, and delicious specialty coffees, caffè latte, and teas. Open daily from 7 a.m. to midnight.

We also like **Flynn's Landing,** 303 Johnson St., just off Bridgeway (tel. 415/332-0131). This restaurant reflects the nautical ambience of Sausalito. The natural-wood flooring and paneled walls offer a casual atmosphere, while colorful sea flags, white tablecloths, and blue napkins add to the authentic flare of seaside dining. Your server will bring the kids crackers, and offer paper and crayons (if there are some on hand). The menu has a wide variety of seafood, pasta, soups, salads, and sandwiches—something for everyone. While there is no children's menu, they'll be glad to split orders in the kitchen (and of course, warm bottles and baby food). Our children have no trouble choosing from the menu, which includes half-pound burgers and club sandwiches. Items range from $5.50 to $13.

Reservations are accepted, and you may expect a 20-minute wait at peak hours. Highchairs and boosters are available. Flynn's is open Monday through Thursday from 11:30 a.m. to 10:30 p.m., till 11 p.m. on Friday and Saturday, and till 10 p.m. on Sunday. Metered street parking is available. Most major credit cards are accepted.

Really a family-style place, **Zack's By the Bay,** at Bridgeway and Turney (tel. 415/332-9779), is a very large, casual serve-yourself affair. Located just off Bridgeway on the waterfront, Zack's caters to large, informal groups who want to take their time and who don't mind helping themselves. There is a good side dining area and a fun patio where you and your family can enjoy the sun. The menu is handwritten on a chalkboard, so there's no fussing with a waitress. The menu includes an array of burgers ($4.75), grilled sandwiches (including grilled cheese), and deli sandwiches (ranging from $3.50 to $4.75). Standard breakfasts begin at about $4.

At night there is often a band and dancing. Boosters and sassy seats are available, and because it's a serve-yourself grill, you can split portions.

Winter hours are Wednesday through Friday from 11 a.m. to 2 a.m. and from 10 a.m. on Saturday and Sunday. In summer, Zack's is open weekdays from 11 a.m. to 2 a.m., on weekends from 10 a.m. Parking on the street. No credit cards accepted.

For a more formal dining event, we like **Scoma's,** 588 Bridgeway (tel. 415/332-9551). One of five Scoma's restaurants (others at Fisherman's Wharf, Larkspur, Palm Springs, and Rancho Mirage), this attractive bayside branch restaurant has one of the most beautiful views in Sausalito. Overlooking the water, Scoma's has a relaxed atmosphere but a sophisticated seafood menu. A medium-size dining room and comfortable yet intimate seating arrangements encourage leisurely dining. The appeal of the white-walled entrance with blooming flowers in wooden boxes is evident to all passersby. All this attention tends to gather a crowd, so be prepared to wait for about 15 minutes for a table (no reservations accepted). You can drop by, leave your name, and continue your seaside stroll for a few minutes.

Booster seats are available. While there is no children's menu, they'll gladly serve your kids grilled-cheese sandwiches or mild pasta dishes, and they'll split portions in the kitchen. Their special children's drinks have come into the 1980s as "Darth Vaders" take their place alongside the ever-popular "Shirley Temples" and "Roy Rogerses." Prices range from $7 to $15.25.

Open for lunch Friday through Monday from 11:30 a.m. to 3 p.m. and for dinner from 5:30 to 10:30 p.m. (on Sunday till 9:30 p.m.). On Tuesday, Wednesday, and Thursday hours are 5:30 to 10:30 p.m. Street parking available. Most major credit cards accepted.

Another alternative is **Yet Wah,** 300 Turney, off Bridgeway (tel. 415/331-3300). Part of the Yet Wah chain, this spacious Mandarin restaurant is a treat for large, hungry families. The two-story structure has plenty of room for even the most active bunch, and they claim that there's rarely a wait longer than 15 minutes. You'll be served promptly and efficiently by waiters dressed in short, "proper" red jackets who are ready to answer any dining questions.

If the view of the docks doesn't keep your youngsters occupied, the video games on the first floor will. Black marble floors and Oriental prints add to the authentic feel and the plentiful windows allow everyone to enjoy the nautical scenery outdoors. Entrees range from $6.25 to $9. Open Monday through Saturday from 11:30 a.m. to 11 p.m. and on Sunday from 11:30 a.m. to 10 p.m. Highchairs and boosters available. Parking in rear. Most major credit cards accepted.

If you want to pack something to eat as you stroll along or sit and people-watch, **Marin Fruit Company,** 605 Bridgeway (tel. 415/332-3700), has a complete line of picnic items in addition to fresh fruit and vegetables. You can buy disposable diapers here too.

6. MUIR WOODS

Less than 20 miles from San Francisco (via U.S. 101 and Calif. 1), **Muir Woods National Monument** feels like a million miles from civilization (except for the hordes of other sightseers). To get to the woods, you drive on winding two-lane roads through the coastal hills that take you through groves of eucalyptus and California black oak. You feel as if you've gone a long way.

There's something about the huge grove of giant redwoods *(Sequoia semper virens)* — this monument to nature — that is at once exhilarating and calming to the kids. The towering redwoods that have stood for hundreds of years, the fern thickets, and the moss that covers the barks of some of the trees are simply beautiful . . . and the forest is peaceful. Our kids love to run along the paved pathway, but they, too, seem to revere these natural giants.

The tallest trees here are in **Bohemian Grove.** Some stand 250 feet tall. The widest is 13½ feet. Most of the main trails are level and paved, easy for strollers and young children.

A wonderful feature in Muir Woods is the Junior Ranger program. It is designed to heighten children's enjoyment and skills of observation. Kids are encouraged to pick up a Junior Ranger Pack at the Visitor Center. The pack comes equipped with cards that correspond to a map and activities to be done in certain areas of the park. Included also are bug boxes, a dip net, a magnifying lens, a clipboard, and a trash bag. The cards present many different ideas for the kids to try. It's a wonderfully involving way for the children to be introduced to nature.

Muir Woods National Monument has a snack counter, a giftshop, a bookstore, and a Visitor Center. No picnicking or camping is allowed. Bring warm clothing, as the forest is cool. Open daily from 8 a.m. to sunset. Admission is free.

SIDE TRIPS FROM THE BAY AREA

□ □ □

Day and weekend jaunts from the greater San Francisco area are rich with excitement and diversity. Within an hour of San Francisco, there are two theme parks, a water park, lovely swimming beaches, and treats from before the turn of the century. As if that's not enough, Napa and Sonoma Counties offer lush scenery, winery tours, and other natural wonders.

1. GREAT AMERICA

Located 45 minutes south of San Francisco in Santa Clara (on U.S. 101 at the Great America Pkwy. exit), Great America (tel. 408/988-1800), possibly best known for its classic wooden roller coaster, the Grizzly, is a 100-acre theme park that caters to children of all ages. Teens and preteens who love wild rides, thrilling roller coasters, and action are going to love this park. So will the junior set.

Designed around the general theme of North America's past, there are **six theme areas,** each with rides, shows, shops, and restaurants—Carousel Plaza, Hometown Square, County Fair, Yukon Territory, Yankee Harbor, and Orleans Place. The park has a total of 31 rides. It can be crowded, yet the atmosphere is not frenzied. People are friendly and helpful.

According to a spokesperson for the park, they try to be particularly sensitive to the needs of small children and offer many attractions and services geared to kids under 12. In fact, she says that a primary goal of Great America is to help parents enjoy their day at the park too.

RIDES AND ATTRACTIONS: The double-decker **Hanna-Barbera Carousel,** denoting Carousel Plaza, is the entrance to "Fort Fun," the action area for little ones. In addition to the carousel are rides such as **Little Dodge Em, Yakki Doodle's Lady Bugs,** and **Boo-Boo's Ball Bounce.** Favorite Hanna-Barbera cartoon characters roam the area. Our kids went wild over Scooby Doo.

A hit with the little ones is **Smurf Woods.** The **Blue Streak,** located in Smurf Woods, is a mini–roller coaster—a "training" roller coaster for the kids (and the adults who need it) with speeds of only 25 mph. Comparing the Blue Streak to the Grizzly is like comparing a skier's bunny hill to a mogul field! Surprise! Our baby, as well as the older tots, loved Smurf Woods.

The **Grizzly** and the **Revolution** may be the favorite rides of teens who go to the park. The Grizzly, a classic wooden roller coaster—the largest ever built in northern California—speeds up to 50 mph for almost three minutes. Another attraction, the Revolution, is a 360° swinging ship that works like a pendulum: as it goes higher, passengers are suspended upside down—two complete loops are made before the ride is over. The **Demon** and **Tidal Wave** roller coasters, and the free-fall ride, the **Edge,** will keep you and your teens shook up for hours. The newest ride is **Skyhawk,** a flight ride where riders use a control stick to regulate the angle of flight and rotate the cabin. (These, along with **Yankee Clipper, Logger's Run,** and **Whizzer,** are the most popular rides in the park and are busiest between noon and 5 p.m.)

When you tire of the thrill rides, or just want to experience something different, there are a number of shows—musical productions, puppet shows, and the like—that you'll enjoy. Don't miss the **Pictorium Theatre,** which, using the IMAX projection process, gives spectators the feeling they are in the action. While this is fabulous for older kids (our 8- and 10-year-olds wanted to see it three times), inquire about the specific show and seating arrangements if you're taking in little ones. It can be very loud and overwhelming to them.

Another place jammed with young teens is the recording studio, where you can record your voice singing over the soundtrack of a favorite song (extra fee required).

FACILITIES: Stroller rentals are available inside the front gate ($2 plus deposit). In Fort Fun is a **Pampers Infant Care Center** for changing and nursing (carpeted, roomy, with two rocking chairs, and free diapers, tissues, and baby lotion; there's even an attendant on duty). The **Lost Children Center** is a large carpeted place filled with toys and supervised by a caring attendant who watches the kids until lost parents arrive.

Of course, hot dogs, hamburgers, fries, and soft drinks abound around the park, but if you want to sit and have a meal, three of the **restaurants** feature children's menus: Maggie Brown's, the Harbor Inn, and the Klondike Cafe.

There's a large **picnic area** in front of the main gate. This is where we come to enjoy a healthy, less expensive lunch than we would have inside the park. We bring along all our favorite goodies. (Remember to get your hand stamped as you leave the park for your picnic.) We also suggest that you bring lots of liquids for the little ones (unless you want your toddler drinking soft drinks all day)—it can get hot, and only a few places sell milk. Plan to spend lots on drinks and snacks in the park. Bring sun hats, sunscreen, and cool clothing if you're coming here during the summer—otherwise your crew may get sunburned.

HOURS AND PRICES: Open daily during Easter week, Memorial Day weekend, and from late May through early September, from 10 a.m.; closing times vary. Open weekends from March through May and September through mid-October. The park is closed from mid-October through the beginning of March. Dates vary; for specifics, call 408/988-1800; or contact the Santa Clara Chamber of Commerce and Convention and Visitors Bureau, P.O. Box 387, Santa Clara, CA 95052 (tel. 408/296-7111); or write Great America, P.O. Box 1776, Santa Clara, CA 95052. Admission (which includes all rides and attractions) is $18 for adults, $9 for children 3 to 6, $11 for seniors; children under 2 are free.

2. SAN JOSE

Just 50 miles south of San Francisco, in the Silicon Valley, is the thriving city of San Jose. With over 700,000 people (and rapidly growing), it's the fourth-largest city in California. It boasts over 50 wineries, 70 parks, and many other attractions, making it a wonderful day trip with the kids. You might want to contact the **San Jose Convention and Visitors Bureau** at 333 W. San Carlos St., Suite 1000, San Jose, CA 95110 (tel. 408/295-9600, or 408/295-2265 for a recorded message).

WINCHESTER MYSTERY HOUSE: This is usually our first stop. Located at 525 S. Winchester Blvd., between Stevens Creek and I-280 (tel. 408/247-2101), it's the strangest house you'll ever see. It has 160 rooms, 47 fireplaces, 13 bathrooms, 10,000 windows, and countless spiritual symbols throughout the mansion. The story goes that Sarah L. Winchester, heiress to the Winchester rifle estate, was convinced by a spiritualist that the untimely deaths of her husband and baby daughter were caused by the spirits of people killed with Winchester rifles. She was told that she would be killed too, unless she built a home for the spirits. As long as construction continued, she would not die.

Sarah (even today, the tour guides refer to her as if she is still their employer) kept a crew of carpenters working 24 hours a day from 1884 until her death in 1922, ultimately spending over $5 million on the bizarre mansion.

Winchester House is at once strange and splendid—strange because Sarah's dread and fascination with the spirits motivated her to construct ways to foil ghosts who might come to kill her, and splendid because it's filled with fabulous articles of Victorian culture and art (furniture, accessory pieces, etc.). There are several staircases that lead nowhere, a switchback stairway that has seven turns and 44 steps but rises only nine feet, and several doors that open to blank walls. Sarah was obsessed with the occult, and the number 13 comes up again and again —she even had 13 sections to her last will and testament and signed it 13 times!

The **Winchester Historical Museum** is located here too, and features a huge collection of Winchester rifles and antique firearms.

And don't miss the **Victorian Gardens** either.

You may choose a self-guided tour or the Winchester Estate Tour (65 minutes for a guided tour of mansion, plus self-guided tours of the Victorian Gardens and outlying buildings, and the Winchester Historical Museum). The frequency of the tours depends on the season. Open daily (except Christmas): mid-June through Labor Day, from 9:30 a.m. to 5:30 p.m.; in October and from March through May, from 9:30 a.m. to 4 p.m. (weekends and holidays till 4:30 p.m.); from November through February, from 9:30 a.m. to 4 p.m.; and from early to mid-June and in September, from 9:30 a.m. to 4:30 p.m. (weekends and holidays till 5 p.m.). Admission is $10 for adults, $6 for children 6 to 13, free for children 5 and under. You can rent cameras and backpacks (to carry babies).

KELLEY PARK: Next on our list of sights is Kelley Park. At this point in our itinerary, the kids are usually ready to run off energy and rollick in the park. Located on Senter Road between Story and Phelan Avenues (tel. 408/292-8188), this 176-acre family-oriented park complex has large grassy areas, picnic tables, barbecues, games, and activities geared to kids 10 and under. It's easy to spend more than a few hours here. Youngsters love the **Happy Hollow Park and Zoo,** 1300 Senter Rd. (tel. 408/292-8188 or 408/295-8383), a tiny theme park and petting zoo. The park and rides—Danny the Dragon, Mini-Putt-Putt Car Ride, and King Neptune's Carousel—are perfect for younger children and parents alike. Kids can run around here and just *play* with a minimum of supervision. Another treat is the Happy Hollow Puppet Theater Castle, with several shows daily (free), suitable for the entire family. The zoo is small but interesting, and makes viewing the animals easy for the very young, very short, or handicapped. There are some interactive informational displays that add a nice touch. Admission is $1.50 for children up to 14, $2 for adults. Parking is $2 per car on weekends and in summer.

The **Kelley Park Express** miniature train is the mode of transportation we use. The **Japanese Friendship Garden,** located at 1300 Senter Rd., near Keyes (tel. 408/287-2290), is a lovely traditional Japanese stroll garden. It's patterned after Korakuen Park in Okayama. Our kids—and lots of others we watched—enjoyed looking at the rare koi fish, the giant brilliantly colored Japanese goldfish. A nice place to wander, the garden is open daily from 10 a.m. to sunset.

The **San Jose Historical Museum,** located in Kelley Park at 635 Phelan Ave., on Senter Road past the Happy Hollow Park and Zoo (tel. 408/287-2290), is a collection of restored turn-of-the-century buildings. There's an original post office, doctor's and dentist's offices, bank, stables, print shop, candy shop, hotel, and homes.

Older kids will like this museum in general, especially if they're interested in history. Our young ones had a great time at the firehouse (which displays old fire engines and photos of San Jose's biggest fires) and the Trolley Barn (the only building not restored). Here, San Jose's trolleys are being beautifully restored—some are even hand-painted—by volunteers. We climbed on them, sat in them, walked through them. Adults particularly like the post office, set up to represent its original community function—as a gathering place for those waiting for news.

There's lots of space surrounding the museum, just perfect for picnic lunches and time playing on the grass. It's an easy place to take strollers, and diaper changing can be done on the tables outside in the park. Special events abound here. Call ahead to see if there's something going on.

The museum is open Monday through Friday from 10 a.m. to 4:30 p.m. and on Saturday and Sunday from noon to 4:30 p.m. Admission is $2 for adults, $1 for children, and $1.50 for seniors.

RAGING WATERS: Located in Lake Cunningham Regional Park, 2333 S. White Rd., at Capitol Expressway and Tully Road (tel. 408/238-9900), this 14-acre water-theme park has more than 25 waterslides and other aquatic activities.

For little dippers, there's a small slide area and two wading pools, with a large sandy area and picnic areas. For kids a little older but not quite ready for the speed slides (you have to be 42 inches tall for those), the three serpentine slides are good. These are five stories tall with curves and turns, but are slower than the slides for the older kids. Slide Creek is another good attraction—it's an innertube ride. For older kids (10 and up), there are the speed slides, which are 400 feet long and go about 25 miles an hour. There's also the Shotgun—a slide about 50 feet long that gets you going fast enough to fly off a six-foot drop into ten feet of water.

Open daily from Memorial Day through mid-September from 10 a.m. to dusk. Admission is $12 for everyone over age 2 and includes all-day use of rides.

As with all water parks, we advise parents to tell their kids to be extremely careful.

ROSICRUCIAN EGYPTIAN MUSEUM AND PLANETARIUM: This unusual attraction deserves mention. Located in Rosicrucian Park at Park and Naglee Avenues (tel. 408/287-2807), this is the kind of place that will delight some children and bore others. Only you know your kids. Housing the West Coast's largest collection of Egyptian, Assyrian, and Babylonian artifacts, there are mummies, ornate coffins, jewelry, and sculpture. The museum is open Saturday through Monday from noon to 4:45 p.m. and Tuesday through Friday from 9 a.m. to 4:45 p.m. The science museum and planetarium next door will delight children. Check for planetarium show times, as they change; it's open daily from 1 to 4:45 p.m. Admission to the planetarium is $2 for adults, 75¢ for children under 18. Admission to the science museum is free. Admission to the Egyptian Museum is $3 for adults, $1 for children 12 to 17; under-12s are free.

IF YOU WANT LUNCH: For a quick bite, try **Marie Callender's Restaurant,** at 620 Blossom Hill Rd. (tel. 408/578-0643). A cut above the standard coffeeshop fare, this restaurant chain is always a good bet. Highchairs and boosters are available. The kids will enjoy the puzzles and the drawings to color on the children's menu.

This family-style restaurant not only offers great deep-dish pies, burgers, and pasta, but also has some of the best fruit pies around. Open Monday through Thursday from 10 a.m. to 10 p.m., on Friday and Saturday until 11 p.m., and on Sunday from 10 a.m. to 10 p.m. (10 a.m. to 1 p.m. for brunch). Ample parking nearby. Major credit cards accepted.

3. SANTA CRUZ

Santa Cruz is a picture-perfect seaside town hugging the shoreline of Monterey Bay. With good swimming beaches, an old-fashioned boardwalk, and the historical Roaring Camp Steam Railroad, Santa Cruz is a favorite family fun spot. From San Francisco, you can take Calif. 1 right into Santa Cruz. You might want to contact the **Santa Cruz Area Chamber of Commerce,** at 105 Cooper St., Suite 243, Santa Cruz, CA 95060 (tel. 408/423-1111), for information about the area.

THINGS TO SEE AND DO: Santa Cruz is the kind of place to which families return again and again. So once you arrive, the question becomes where to start first.

The Santa Cruz Beach Boardwalk

Dating back to the early 1900s, the Santa Cruz boardwalk is everything a boardwalk should be. At either end are rides for small kids, and in the middle is a wonderful **merry-go-round** (a treat for all ages).

There's an enormous game-filled **arcade** with an assortment of video games, skee-ball, pinball, and "oldies" that date back to the 1920s.

With rides galore (over 20), there's a lot to choose from. Teenagers pass by the tame rides and line up for the **Pirates Revenge** and the **Big Dipper,** or stroll self-consciously in swimsuits and shorts, trying to see and be seen.

While there is lots of boardwalk-style food, it's hard to find juice and milk, so you might want to bring those or any other healthy snacks you desire. Bring sunscreen, as sunburn is a major health hazard here. Rest rooms are huge (located in the middle of the boardwalk), but have no changing counter. Although you can make room for yourself, you'll have to improvise.

Along the boardwalk are benches for crowd-watching and resting. Infants and toddlers can sometimes be overwhelmed by the crowds here, so it's a good idea to bring your stroller. Youngsters might get worn out from having to manage the crowds.

The sandy beach is popular with swimmers, surfers, and sunbathers. Located just off the boardwalk, it has rest rooms, parking, and a lifeguard.

If you want something other than fast food, the **Pacific Garden Mall** is a nice place to stroll. This lovely six-block area near the boardwalk is filled with restaurants, cafés, bookstores, and boutiques. Little ones will enjoy the walk, and there are benches to sit on for that occasional rest. In summer, a free shuttle operates daily from the beach to the mall and back every 20 minutes.

Santa Cruz City Museum

You'll recognize this museum by the statue of a whale in front of it (and probably five little kids climbing on it). Located at 1305 E. Cliff Dr. (tel. 408/429-3773), this little museum has a great Ohlone Indian exhibit and a few wonderful hands-on exhibits, including a tidepool where kids can touch sea creatures. If you haven't been to the Monterey Bay Aquarium, this will be a real treat. It is open Tuesday through Saturday from 10 a.m. to 5 p.m. Admission is 50¢ for adults; children and seniors, free. While the beach across the street is inviting, it can be a bit windy for picnicking. We use the picnic tables and lawns behind the museum instead.

Four blocks away is the **Santa Cruz Yacht Harbor,** a good place to stroll, with fine beaches on either side of the harbor. Beach-loving teenagers will find great shops nearby. The original **O'Neal's Surf Shop** (tel. 408/475-4151) is the place our teens go for bikinis, surfboards, and skateboards (they rarely buy anything, but love to browse).

Roaring Camp and the Big Trees Narrow-Gauge Railroad

This is billed as a way to relive the excitement of the 1880 pioneer days. Located in Felton, six miles north of Santa Cruz via Graham Hill Road (tel. 408/335-4484), on land covered with remarkable redwoods, the authentic **steam logging train** recalls a time when locomotives took giant logs from the forest to the mills to be made into lumber. This is one of our kids' favorite places. It's the site of an original steam/gauge railroad, and the site of Brett Harte's short story "The Pride of Roaring Camp." It has been wonderfully restored. As you cross from the parking lot through a covered bridge, to your right is a pond full of geese. Up to the left is an old schoolhouse. Wander down the dirt road until you come to the station, where you will buy tickets from a man dressed in 1800s garb. Departures are frequent, but if you have to wait, you can sit on a bench in the shade or amble to the general store, which has the required glass jars of peppermint sticks and is filled with memorabilia about trains and the camp. There's a snack shop next door.

The camp also has good bathroom facilities plus a stationary set of train cars that kids adore playing on, plus picnic tables, barbecue pits, and lots of grassy areas where you can plunk down a blanket and enjoy your lunch while lazing in the sun. Sometimes country-and-western musicians perform, and during the summer there are a few volleyball nets set up. What a lovely spot to spend the afternoon!

The glorious ride up the mountain in the open cars takes about an hour and 15 minutes, and goes in and out of sun and cool forest (bring hats and light sweaters—sunscreen too). It's said that these are the steepest railroad grades in North America. You might want to bring along a snack and juice, and be sure your kids use the bathroom *before you board,* as there are no facilities on the train or at the top of the mountain. The conductor narrates the trip with wonderful stories, dropping in jokes and relating history. The train stops at the top, among the elegant grove of redwoods, and everyone gets a chance to stretch. When we have gone with only our older kids, we've actually disembarked and hiked down the mountain. Some people picnic at the top of the mountain and try to catch a later train. However, check with the conductor and the ticket seller before you do that (or be prepared to hike down), since you will only be let back on a train if there are seats available, and during the summer months trains tend to be crowded.

The fare is $10.50 for adults, $7.50 for ages 3 to 15; under 3, free.

There is also a train that runs from the camp to Santa Cruz (round trip takes 2½ hours), the **Santa Cruz, Big Trees & Pacific.** We have some friends who split up, one parent taking the train with the kids, the other one meeting them with the car in town. The fare is $16 for adults, $8.50 for ages 3 to 15; under 3, free.

Another option is the Moonlight Steam Train Party (June through October on Saturday night at 7 p.m.). Call for reservations—a must—and fares. Also from May through October on Saturday and Sunday from noon to 3 p.m., there is a chuckwagon barbecue. Menu items range from quarter-pound burgers (with all the trimmings) to Gold Rush steak (12-ounce top sirloin), and include salad, western-style beans, sourdough roll, beverages, and marshmallows for roasting. Prices range from $8 to $14.

You might be lucky enough to visit on a special-event day. If you do, be prepared to witness a train robbery or participate in an egg hunt or autumn harvest fair. If you'll be in Santa Cruz in May, call ahead to find out when the Roaring Camp Annual Civil War Memorial will be held. This reenactment of Civil War battles and camp life is played out by hundreds of soldiers in Union and Confederate uniforms.

Bike Paths

There is lovely bicycling in this town. The **San Lorenzo River Bike Path** is one good route. It follows the river from Santa Cruz Beach.

Above Santa Cruz Wharf is **West Clift Drive,** where you can rollerskate and bicycle. The path hugs the ocean and goes past Lighthouse Point to Natural Bridges State Beach. On good days there are lots of seals just past the lighthouse. From the wharf up to the top is the only hill—but what a hill! Then it's flat and easy bicycling and rollerskating.

South of the Yacht Harbor is **East Clift Drive,** another spectacular bicycle route. It stretches from the harbor into Capitola, a hilly two-lane road that goes through residential areas and the beaches.

You can rent bikes at **The Spokesman,** 501 Cedar St. (tel. 408/429-6062) for $15 per day. **Clark's Cyclery,** 927 Pacific Ave. (tel. 408/458-9551), is another choice.

A Day at Capitola by the Sea

Picture this: You're sitting on a charming little beach with children romping in the calm ocean or wading in the water of nearby Soquel Creek. The sun is warm, the kids are enjoying themselves, and you are relaxing. Yes, that's a day at Capitola, just a bit south of Santa Cruz.

Here's how we suggest you "do" Capitola.

Start out at **Gayle's Bakery & Rosticceria,** 405 Bay Ave. (tel. 408/462-1127). Gayle studied in France for a number of years as a baker's apprentice before opening her business here. The bakery is full of wonderful French pastries, cookies, cakes, and breads. Four-year-old Janey used to spend a very long time examining the choices before she made up her mind. The Rosticceria, with a huge wood-fired barbecue spit, has everything one would want for a gourmet picnic. Our favorites are the twice-cooked baked potatoes with cheese, roast chicken, salads, and pastas.

Picnic in hand, head down to the beach in Capitola Village. It's a good one for kids (there's a lifeguard here during the summer), and has a changing room, rest rooms, and outdoor showers for rinsing off sand. Soquel Creek runs into the beach.

During the summer you can rent paddleboats (a favorite of all the kids). Remember to bring scraps of bread to feed the ducks from the boat.

If you need a break from the beach, Capitola Village is loaded with boutiques and craft galleries, restaurants, and even coffeehouses.

After you finish lounging and playing at the beach, perhaps you might enjoy a full meal at the **Greenhouse at the Farm,** 5555 Soquel Dr. (tel. 408/476-5613). The food is good here and the staff is wonderful with kids. There's a huge garden in which they grow many of the vegetables they use in the restaurant; there's also a huge flower garden. The giftshop is a favorite of teenage girls—take a look at the soaps and bath accessories from Europe. Our kids especially love the brunch on Sunday, with its all-you-can-eat fresh-fruit bar. Brunch prices range from $6 (French toast) to $9 (omelets). Lunch costs from $5 (turkey croissant and fruit) to $9 (fresh seafood luncheon). Dinners range from $8.50 (vegetable quiche) to $15 (scampi and sirloin). Children under 10 choose from steakburger or barbecued chicken breast ($6 to $7).

Highchairs and boosters are available, and there's room to change diapers in the bathrooms. Open daily for dinner from 5 to 9 p.m.; for lunch Monday through Saturday from 11:30 a.m. to 4 p.m.; and for Sunday brunch from 9 a.m. to 2 p.m. No reservations are accepted, so on Sunday you might have a 15- to 30-minute wait. Most major credit cards are welcome. Plenty of parking.

OTHER PLACES TO EAT IN THE AREA: You might try **Tampico's Kitchen,** 822 Pacific Ave. (tel. 408/423-2240), a family-style Mexican restaurant. You can choose to eat on the restaurant side or on the bar side (which has murals and a bit more noise). They have a fantastic little mariachi band that will play requests or simply serenade you at your table. One of our teenagers blushed bright red when they played "Happy Birthday" to her. Dine on tacos ($3.75), burgers ($4.25), and beef or chicken fajitas ($9). Other entrees range from $4 to $11.

Open daily from 11 a.m. to 10 p.m. Highchairs, boosters, and a children's menu are available. Reservations are accepted, as are most major credit cards. Parking available.

Another nearby eatery is **Zachary's,** 819 Pacific Ave. (tel. 408/427-0646), a fine place to begin the day with a great brunch or breakfast (they're open for lunch too). We love their homemade breads, but for a special treat, be sure not to miss the jalapeño cornbread. And nothing on the menu costs over $5! A basic breakfast of eggs, potatoes, and toast runs $2, and a plain burger just $2.75.

This casual restaurant is bright—full of natural light—and the servers are great with kids. Boosters and highchairs are available but there's no children's menu (although they'll split adult portions for two kids). No reservations are accepted. Ample parking nearby. Some major credit cards honored.

4. MARINE WORLD AFRICA USA

A must-see for families who love animal and marine life, a day at this state-of-the-art oceanarium and wildlife park promises to be an adventure to remember. Picturesque Marine World Africa USA (tel. 707/643-ORCA for a recorded announcement) is situated in the rolling hills of Vallejo, 30 miles northeast of San Francisco and 10 miles south of the Napa Valley. (Take I-80 East and exit at Marine World Parkway or Calif. 37 or U.S. 101 north to Calif. 37 and east to Marine World Parkway.) If you're coming from San Francisco, the **Red and White Fleet** now offers daily service to the park from Pier 41 at Fisherman's Wharf (tel. 415/546-2896 for details).

The 160-acre wildlife park features hundreds of animals—land, sea, and air, exotic and common—with the goal of offering families wonderful entertainment and learning experiences. The philosophy here is that because there are strong bonds of respect and affection between the animals and their trainers, visitors are able to enjoy close interaction with the animals. In themed shows and inventive activities, people and animals are brought together, and visitors learn while they're having fun. The animals roam through the park with their trainers, giving visitors a close look.

We usually try to arrive at opening time. Then we get a show schedule at the Clock Tower and choose those we intend to see (shows run 20 to 30 minutes each). Next we hightail it over to the storage lockers (to the left of the admission gate) to stow extra sweaters, baby food, and everything we don't want to carry around. We always lather sunscreen on the kids at this time, just in case we can't grab a wiggly, excited child later on. We choose a meeting place in case someone gets lost, load our cameras, and get ready. We also remind the kids not to feed the animals. Then we're off.

Everyone loves the **scheduled shows,** including the Killer Whale and Dolphin Show, the Sea Lion Show, the Waterski and Boat Show, the Jungle Theater (with tigers, lions, elephants, and chimps), and the Bird Show. Our family favorite, though, is the **Whale and Dolphin Show,** where the 9,000- and 6,000-pound killer whales swim and leap effortlessly through the water. One word of caution, though. At the marine shows, there is a "wet zone." If you sit in this area during any of the shows, be prepared to be splashed with salt water, which can burn the eyes; during the whale show you'll simply be drenched. Unknowingly, we sat there once and were soaked.

The **Gentle Jungle** is a great area where toddlers can hang out with llamas, goats, prairie dogs, and bunnies. As in many petting barnyards, children can feed the animals food pellets. Pony rides (75¢) are available to children 65 pounds and under.

For **Whale of a Time World Playground** is an innovative active play area for children under 90 pounds. The ball crawls, rope crawls, and net climbs are a treat for preschoolers to preteens. This place is very well supervised by park attendants, and is a favorite place for kids to spend close to an hour.

The small but respectable **Aquarium** is set up to give a view of the Tropics, the Caribbean, and the California coast, and is arranged so comparisons can be made between the different habitats. There are tidepools where kids can touch and pick up their favorite creatures—anemones, hermit crabs, sea stars, and the like. The Discovery Room inside the Aquarium is staffed by assistants who will answer questions and show you how animals adapt to specific environments.

To everyone's delight, animals and their trainers are located throughout the park. Chimps, baby snow leopards, and monkeys wander with their human companions, giving us a chance to watch them close up. Our kids loved the **elephant and camel rides,** and were entranced at **Tiger Cove,** where trainers and cats are always together.

The food at the park is remarkably diverse, so kids should be able to find anything they want—ours sure did! Located close together, at Lakeside Plaza, the various food concessions are great if you have one child who wants a burger and another who wants a deli sandwich. We enjoy lunch overlooking scenic Lake Chabot, but if you prefer, you can use one of the public barbecue grills throughout the park. *A tip:* Eat while one of the shows is going on; it's much less crowded then.

If you know ahead of time when you'll be at the park, you might be able to participate in one of the **family evening programs** (usually from 7 to 9 p.m.; $8 additional fee). There are also **sunrise and moonlight tours** (coinciding with the full moon) that give people a chance to see animals at different times of day. Children's workshops, such as **Afterschool Seafaris** (for school-age children), help children learn what animals eat, what their tracks look like, and what their habitats consist of. Most of these programs are offered in the spring and fall. For more information, call 707/644-4000, ext. 433.

At the Main Gift Shop you can rent strollers that look like seals for $3, regular strollers for $2, and cameras. This is also where the first-aid station is located. There are diaper-changing facilities in each rest room. Marine World Africa USA is open daily in summer from 9:30 a.m. to 6:30 p.m., and the rest of the year on Wednesday through Sunday from 9:30 a.m. to 5:30 p.m., with a special winter holiday schedule. Admission is $16 for adults, $12 for seniors, and $11 for children 4 to 12; children 3 and under, free. Credit cards are accepted.

5. THE NAPA VALLEY

Robert Louis Stevenson called it "The Valley of Plenty." You'll call it beautiful.

Tucked in among the California coastal mountains about an hour northeast of San Francisco, the tranquil Napa Valley awaits, ready to unfold all her gardenlike splendor to families. Each season brings its own delights. Just before spring, yellow mustard plants cover the ground. In summer you see lush green vines, rich dark soil, and verdant green hills. In late August and September grapes cluster on the vines, awaiting harvest. And in autumn the changing colors and dark clouds present a dramatic, sometimes stormy canvas. The countryside is dotted with cattle ranches and is becoming an important breeding ground for thoroughbred horses.

Known simply as "The Wine Country," the 30-mile-long Napa Valley includes the towns of Napa, Yountville, Oakville, St. Helena, Rutherford, and Calistoga. It is a full-day trip or a good one-night stay. Be prepared for your trip to be pricey, though, since this is a place that attracts wine lovers. Realistically, to truly enjoy the area, the older the children the better.

While visiting wineries and wine tasting have become a tradition, there are other, more family-oriented ways to spend time together. On clear mornings, brilliantly colored hot-air balloons grace the sky. Soaring and gliding are other air adventure possibilities. There is golf and tennis, and the area is an exquisite place to picnic. Or maybe you'd like to go horseback riding. Near Calistoga, you can see one of the world's three geysers and visit a petrified forest.

The Napa region is an interesting blend of traditions. The Gold Rush was the initial impetus for building up the area. Enticed from the goldfields into the small towns in Napa Valley when it was too cold in the hills (or when they needed paid work), the miners created a need for services and goods. At the time, cattle ranching and lumbering were the main industries.

In the mid-1880s Napa (among others) was host to the Great Silver Rush. The most famous mine was the Silverado, made immortal by Robert Louis Stevenson's *The Silverado Squatters*. In 1865 a railroad line was completed, linking Napa city with Vallejo to the south, and stagecoaches were already making regular trips as far north as Calistoga.

To this mining area mix, add a dash of early California mission influence. The Spanish settlers brought with them vine cuttings from the nearby missions, where wine was made for sacramental uses. Because of Napa's perfect wine-growing climate, these took hold and the Napa Valley is now known throughout the world for its excellent California wines.

GETTING THERE: Most people visit the wine country by car. We suggest that you do too. From San Francisco, cross the Golden Gate Bridge and continue on U.S. 101 to Calif. 37. Take that to Calif. 29. From the east, take I-80 past Sacramento to the Napa exit. If you're coming from Sonoma, be prepared for a hilly, narrow road.

The Napa Valley southern boundary starts at the city of Napa, which is at the southern tip of Calif. 29 (a two-lane road). The other Napa Valley towns are easily reached going north on Calif. 29 or the Silverado Trail.

Although half a dozen little towns dot the Napa Valley, it's so small we will talk about it as a region. Here's a brief rundown of the time it takes from one place to another: from Napa to Yountville is 9 miles; to St. Helena is 18 miles (about 30 minutes); to Calistoga is 28 miles (about 40 minutes).

Gray Line Tours (tel. 415/896-1515) offers a wine country tour (which originates in San Francisco) that is nine hours long and takes you through Napa and Sonoma, with stops for wine tasting. The tour costs $37.50 for adults, half price for kids 5 to 11, and free for under-5s. Call at least a day in advance for reservations.

Before your trip you might want to do a little research. Maps are available from the **Napa Chamber of Commerce,** 1900 Jefferson St., Napa, CA 94559 (tel. 707/226-7455), and you can get more information about the entire wine-growing region from the **Redwood Empire Association,** One Market Plaza, Spear Street Tower, Suite 1001, San Francisco, CA 94105 (tel. 415/543-8334).

WHAT TO SEE AND DO: The combination of exquisite scenery and interesting sights (especially the wineries) is the main reason people come to the Napa Valley. Let's start with . . .

The Wineries

Of course you can enjoy them even if you have children with you. What it takes, though, is a slightly different perspective. Remember that children aren't going to enjoy the wineries as you do. This won't be a romantic sojourn into transplanted French countryside for them, but it can be fun.

It's likely your kids will appreciate the wineries in an educational light, much as they would if you took them on any other industrial tour. Approach it that way. Winery tours show the wine-making process from grape picking to crushing, fermenting, storing, and bottling. You see different aspects of the process at different times of the year.

Adults will find the history and architecture of the buildings themselves fascinating. Children will enjoy seeing the wine-making process—huge oak barrels, stainless-steel vats, crushers, and bottles with their labels.

There are 118 wineries in the Napa Valley today, and many give tours and have tasting rooms. While wine tasting is not possible for your young ones, the adults in the crowd can still enjoy a trip to the wineries while keeping the kids amused.

Some parents of teenagers take them to nearby Vallejo, so they can spend the day at Marine World Africa USA (see the previous section for details), while the adults enjoy the fruit of the vineyards. If your children are too young for that, however, a solution is to bring a babysitter or choose one adult at each stop to stay with toddlers who are too young to enjoy the tours. Another possibility is to choose self-guiding tours.

But first you have to decide which wineries to stop at. Here are a few we think are the most interesting for children. A word of caution: Don't try to visit too many. People who've tried it say that two wineries is the limit for most children. We've done a few more with older kids, but with several activity breaks in between.

We usually start at one of the wineries in the northern part of the valley. The **Beringer Vineyards,** just north of St. Helena at 2000 Main St. (tel. 707/963-7115), is unique. Built in 1877, the family home, called the Rhine House, is an example of old German architecture and is a California National Landmark. You will be able to view the house as well as take a walking tour of the limestone caves, during which you'll learn some California history. These hand-dug tunnels were carved out of the mountainside by the Chinese laborers, and are currently used to store the barrels of wine for aging. The winery is open daily from 10 a.m. to 5 p.m.

Nearby, the **Christian Brothers Greystone Winery Hospitality Building,** 2555 Main St. (tel. 707/963-0763), is another good choice. Located just north of St. Helena (near the Beringer Vineyards), the magnificent four-story building (which the kids call "the castle") is one of the largest stone buildings in the world. Our kids love Brother Timothy's corkscrew collection. There are over 3,000 corkscrews, some of them unusual animals and figurines.

The guided tours last about 35 minutes and are given from 10 a.m. to 4:30

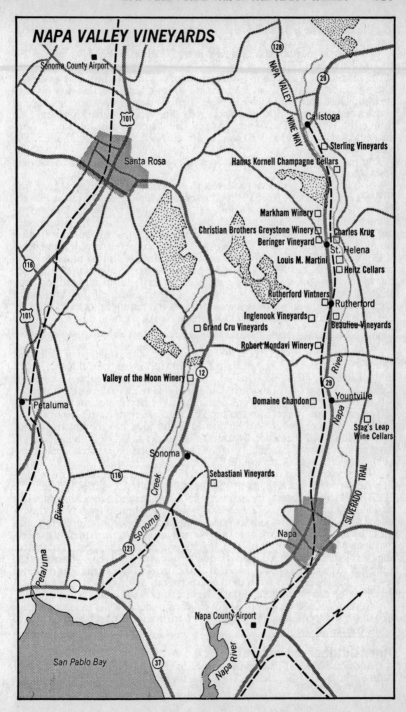

NAPA VALLEY VINEYARDS

Sonoma County Airport

Santa Rosa

Calistoga

Sterling Vineyards

Hanns Kornell Champagne Cellars

Markham Winery

Christian Brothers Greystone Winery

Beringer Vineyard

Charles Krug

St. Helena

Louis M. Martini

Heitz Cellars

Rutherford Vintners

Rutherford

Inglenook Vineyards

Beaulieu Vineyards

Grand Cru Vineyards

Robert Mondavi Winery

Valley of the Moon Winery

Petaluma

Domaine Chandon

Yountville

Stag's Leap Wine Cellars

Sonoma

Sebastiani Vineyards

Napa

Napa County Airport

San Pablo Bay

p.m. daily. During the wine-tasting session, you might want to have one adult take the kids to the giftshop or to play in the grassy area in front of the mansion. Free public tours.

The tour at the **Robert Mondavi Winery,** 7801 St. Helena Hwy. (Calif. 29) in Oakville, north of Yountville (tel. 707/963-9611), gives a complete overview of the wine-making process in a modern, state-of-the-art facility. The guide will take you through all phases of production—from grape to bottle—in a 60-minute tour, which ends with a wine tasting. There is a large lawn with stylized sculptures outside the tasting room where kids can wander while Mom and Dad sample the vintages. The winery is open daily: from 9 a.m. to 5 p.m. April through October, and from 10 a.m. to 4 p.m. November through March. The tour is free.

In July the winery holds an outdoor jazz festival, and at Christmas there are other musical performances.

You'll never forget a visit to **Sterling Vineyards,** 1111 Dunaweal Lane (tel. 707/942-5151, ext. 34 or 35). Farther north than Beringer and Christian Brothers (located two miles south of Calistoga), this is a good family place. Board the four-seater aerial tram (at $5 per person over age 16) for a fun ride up the mountain to the hilltop winery. You'll get a sweeping view of the surrounding mountaintops, valley, and vineyards (the steep climb can be scary for those afraid of heights). The stark-white monastic-style building is also an unusual visual treat. Once there, the tour is guided by signs, not people, allowing you and the kids to move at your own pace. Be prepared to carry your infants and toddlers, however, because there is no stroller access. There is a large giftshop and lots of open places for children to wander. Sales hours and tasting times are 10:30 a.m. to 4:30 p.m. daily. The tour is included in the cost of the tram ride.

Nature's Wonders

Let's start our adventures at the northern end of the valley, near Calistoga. About 45 minutes from Napa City is **Old Faithful Geyser of California,** 1299 Tubbs Lane (tel. 707/942-6463). (It can be reached from either Calif. 29 or Calif. 128.) This is one of the three Old Faithful Geysers in the world (the other two are in Yellowstone and in New Zealand). Every 40 minutes, the geyser spews 350° water about 60 feet into the air. This regular geyser wasn't "regular" the day we were there—much to the dismay of our kids and the surprise of our guide, who hinted that the only reason for this deviation could be impending earthquake activity (the next big earthquake didn't occur for several weeks, however). Strollers can navigate around the area.

The geyser is open daily from 9 a.m. to 5 p.m. in winter, till 6 p.m. in summer. Admission is $2.50 for adults, $1 for children 6 to 12; under-6s, free.

The **Petrified Forest,** located between Calistoga and Santa Rosa, at 4100 Petrified Forest Rd. (tel. 707/942-6667), about 50 minutes from Napa City, is indeed a treat. Giant redwoods, covered with volcanic ash from an eruption years earlier by Mount St. Helena, have been turned into stone, permanently preserving them. Many other kinds of trees, insects, and plantlife have been unearthed. The petrified trees are dug out on the quarter-mile trail. Kids enjoy touching the stone-like redwoods, and will marvel at all the petrified specimens. The museum describes the process of fossilization and petrification, of interest to young and old alike. You can picnic here, and strollers are fine on the trail.

Admission is $3 for adults, $1 for children under 4 to 11, and free for children under 4. Open daily: from 9 a.m. to 6 p.m. in summer, and from 10 a.m. to 5 p.m. the rest of the year.

Other Outdoor Adventures

Another beautiful place, just west of St. Helena, is **Bothe–Napa Valley State Park,** at 3601 St. Helena Hwy. North, four miles from St. Helena (tel.

707/942-4575, or toll free 800/444-7275). This is a great place for picnicking, horseback riding, camping, swimming, and hiking. There is a public swimming pool open from mid-June through Labor Day. Admission is $2 for adults, $1 for children 17 and under. There are 50 developed campsites, and a charge of $3 per vehicle plus $10 per campsite. Make reservations in advance for the busy summer months. (You can reserve campsites through MISTIX: call 619/452-1950, or toll free 800/444-7275 in California.)

GOOD PICNIC SPOTS. In Napa itself, **Skyline Park,** at Fourth and Imola (tel. 707/ 252-0481), is a lovely place to hike, fish, or just have a picnic, with more than 900 acres of wilderness grounds. Open Thursday through Monday from 9 a.m. to 5 p.m., in summer to 8 p.m. Admission charges are $3 per vehicle, $1 for horse trailers, 50¢ each for walk-ins. **Conn Dam–Lake Hennessey** is 15 miles north of Napa off the Silverado Trail. This park offers fishing and picnicking. There is no admission fee. Another good place to picnic is **Crane Park,** on Grayson Avenue off Calif. 29 in St. Helena, with a playground, tables, and barbecue pits, but no admission fee.

BICYCLE RIDING. Although a very popular way to experience the lushness and beauty of the vineyards, parents who bring their children biking need to be wary of the cars—and the drivers who have been wine tasting. That said, the relatively flat, historic **Silverado Trail** is one of the best routes and considered the safest because there are wide shoulders all the way. The trail affords lovely views of the green Mayacamas Mountains.

You can rent bikes at **Bryan's Napa Valley Cyclery,** 4080 Byway East in Napa (tel. 707/255-3377). Bryan's doesn't rent ordinary bicycle seats for toddlers but rather little trailers that go behind the bicycle and will carry children up to 100 pounds. Rates are $4 for the first hour, $2 for each additional hour to a maximum of $12 for a business day. Overnight, or 24 hours, is $17. Open Monday through Saturday from 9 a.m. to 6 p.m. and on Sunday from 10 a.m. to 5 p.m. (in winter, till 4 p.m.). They'll supply maps and even one-way rentals (charge based on where you go), if you want.

HORSEBACK RIDING. This is another adventure we love. **Wild Horse Valley Ranch,** at Wild Horse Valley Road in Napa (tel. 707/224-0727), is the place to go. Guided trail trips cost $25 for a three-hour ride through 3,000 acres of gorgeous countryside. Children must be 8 years old to ride. For groups of ten or more, they offer breakfast and dinner trail rides—$35 for breakfast (eggs, sausage, and pancakes), $40 for lunch or dinner (barbecued chicken with corn on the cob and all the fixings).

Each March, July, and October there are equestrian events—horse trials, including cross-country and stadium jumping—that spectators can watch for free. Wander around and enjoy the show. Bring a picnic lunch or buy one from the foodstands on the grounds. During the spring you can watch the United States Equestrian Team conduct training camps.

HOT-AIR BALLOONING. For the adventurous who want a once-in-a-lifetime experience, hot-air ballooning is something to try. The balloons take off in the early morning when the air is cool and the winds are gentle. The flight over exquisite countryside is an expensive adventure. Some kids do quite well in the balloons and love floating up high. Others find it very frightening to have nothing but the balloon between them and the ground hundreds of feet below. This is one activity in which it's difficult to ask the operator to stop and let the kids out.

If you want to try, here are a few companies to choose from. **Adventures Aloft,** at the Vintage 1870 complex in Yountville (P.O. Box 2500), Yountville, CA 94599 (tel. 707/255-8688), is the oldest outfit in the valley. Be prepared to spend three to four hours. Hot coffee and fresh pastries greet you before you take off. Then you're in the air for about one hour, during which time you'll be aloft above the vineyards. The landings can be really exciting as the pilot searches for an open spot to land (remember that wind drifts take you horizontally—pilots have vertical control). A champagne brunch awaits you upon your return. Reservations are required. They'll even provide loaner cameras if you have forgotten yours. The minimum age is 8. Rates are $145 per person, regardless of age.

Other choices are **Napa Valley Balloons,** P.O. Box 2860, Yountville, CA 94599 (tel. 707/253-2224); **Balloon Aviation of Napa Valley,** 2299 3rd St., Napa, CA 94559 (tel. 707/252-7067); and **Once in a Lifetime,** P.O. Box 795, Calistoga, CA 94515 (tel. 707/942-6541, or toll free 800/722-6665).

Indoor Activities

Housed in an old winery dating to 1871, the **Vintage 1870** shopping complex offers an array of specialty shops to browse through. Vintage 1870 is located in Yountville, a quarter of a mile off Calif. 29 at Washington Street (tel. 707/944-2451). Shops of particular interest are the **Toy Cellar** (tel. 707/944-2144); **The Chocolate Tree** (tel. 707/944-2113), for ice cream and chocolates extraordinaire; and **Hansel and Gretel** (tel. 707/944-2954). While there are lots of places to eat, you might want to try the Vintage Café.

The **Vintage Café,** 6525 Washington St. (tel. 707/944-2614), offers breakfast, lunch, and dinner in a rustic casual atmosphere. Customers place their order at a counter, take a table, and wait for their number to be called.

Known for their deluxe nachos (those savory Mexican appetizers made of tortilla chips topped with melted cheese), the Vintage Café also serves up burgers, grilled-cheese sandwiches, and hot dogs for big and little appetites. Prices range from $3 to $5. The cooks will be glad to make up half sandwiches for kids.

Open weekdays from 10 a.m. to 5 p.m., weekends till 6 p.m. Boosters and highchairs are available. Most major credit cards accepted. No reservations are taken, but there usually isn't a wait except for outdoor dining during the summer. Parking lot.

The **Silverado Museum,** located at 1490 Library Lane in St. Helena (tel. 707/963-3757), is devoted to the life and works of Robert Louis Stevenson. This distinguished museum is the fulfillment of a lifetime dream of Norman Strouse, who started collecting Robert Louis Stevenson memorabilia at the age of 25, when he purchased a John Henry Hash edition of *Silverado Squatters.*

Robert Louis Stevenson spent only two months here, but he has become part of the region's folklore. Already in the advanced stages of tuberculosis, Stevenson found an abandoned bunkhouse near the old Silverado Mine in 1880 and honeymooned there with his bride, Fanny Osbourne. If the tales are true, this is where he began to regain his health. Soon after he returned to Scotland and subsequently wrote *Treasure Island* and *Silverado Squatters.*

More than 130,000 people have visited the museum with its 8,000 objects (including original manuscripts, letters, photographs, and first editions).

The curators suggest reading something by the author to your kids before your arrival. *A Child's Garden of Verse, Treasure Island,* or *Dr. Jekyll and Mr. Hyde* top their list.

Open Tuesday through Sunday from noon to 4 p.m.; closed Monday and holidays. No admission charge.

Annual Events

The **Napa Country Fair** (on the Fourth of July weekend) in Calistoga features livestock exhibits, a carnival, and name entertainment. There is an elaborate fireworks show and parade on the Fourth (call 707/942-5111 for details).

The **Napa Town and Country Fair** (August) in Napa. Over 100,000 people attend this fair which includes a carnival, PRCA rodeo, destruction derby, name entertainment, and fireworks. There's a junior horse show and junior livestock auction.

WHERE TO EAT: Most of the restaurants we've chosen are in Napa City. If they are not, we so indicate. We recommend that you make reservations at all restaurants, especially in season.

One of our favorite places is **Jonesy's Famous Steak House,** 2044 Airport Rd., at the Napa Airport (tel. 707/255-2003), off Calif. 29 as you're driving south toward Vallejo. Don't let the bland décor fool you. Kids love to watch the small planes taking off and we love the good hearty fare they serve.

They boast that steak is their specialty (a juicy, half-pound top sirloin is $8 —probably one of the best deals in town). The aged Kansas steaks are succulent, perfectly cooked, and accompanied by a huge dinner salad that's topped with beets, garbanzo beans, a scoop of cottage cheese, and tossed with homemade bleu cheese dressing.

The servers are friendly and especially fast—no wait for food here. The kitchen is quite an operation to watch, and the owner is only too happy to walk through the place making sure that diners are satisfied.

Salads, sandwiches, broasted chicken, and a small sampling of seafood specialties complete the menu. Prices range from $4.75 to $12.75. The children's menu has steak for $4.25, an ample portion for two small children; also chicken and a hamburger for $3.25. And the real favorite is the block of Jell-o on the kiddie plates. The food and the entertainment make this is a great place for lunch or an early dinner. Be sure to request a window seat.

Boosters and highchairs are available, and the staff will warm baby bottles or baby food in the kitchen. Open Tuesday through Sunday from 11:30 a.m. to 9 p.m. (till 8 p.m. on winter weeknights). Major credit cards are accepted and parking is available nearby.

One of the great little food finds in central Napa is the **Blue Plate Diner,** 811 Coombs St. (tel. 707/226-2583), whose motto is "Good fun, good food, good service." Opened recently by Robin Merwin and Dave Palagi, this upscale diner is a fun place for lunch, dinner, or Sunday brunch. Upbeat and buzzy, locals like it because it's different. The booths have old-fashioned jukeboxes, and there's a large jukebox near the bar. Order your meal as a "45-inch," a "78-inch," or "33⅓-inch" item. Or choose from the list of "Bobby Soxers" (beverages) and "Sock Hoppers" (desserts and coffees).

The diverse menu includes classic diner fare and some California favorites, including nacho skins (with salsa, guacamole, and sour cream), blackened chicken wings, pasta, grilled T-bone veal steak, and braised rabbit. There's classic diner food too—fried chicken, liver and onions, meatloaf, all served with mashed potatoes and gravy. Prices range from $4.50 to $12. Time-honored favorites for kids include hot dogs, peanut butter and jelly sandwiches, burgers, and grilled cheese ($2.50 to $4).

Highchairs and boosters are available. Reservations are accepted, but there's only a 15- to 20-minute wait on Saturday night if you don't have one. Open Monday through Saturday from 11:30 a.m. to midnight, on Sunday from 10 a.m. (for brunch) to 10 p.m. Street parking and a parking lot nearby. Most credit cards are accepted. Take-out orders are available if you want to picnic.

Want to dine in a 110-year-old winery? **The Sherry Oven,** 1711 Main St. (tel. 707/226-3777), is the place. While toddlers and infants aren't encouraged, they are accommodated, and young well-behaved kids as well as older children are treated congenially. Located in the restored, historic Joseph Matthews Winery Complex, built in 1882 (hand-cut stone with exposed-brick walls two feet thick), the somewhat formal upstairs dining room is replete with etched glass and antique chandeliers, and overlooks the working winery. Downstairs is a seafood bar that serves 15 Napa Valley wines by the glass (there's also an extensive wine list).

The food here is special. The Swedish chef combines traditional fare with American and continental recipes to come up with such new dishes as salmon fettuccine (fresh dill fettuccine with smoked salmon and wild mushrooms in a vodka and black pepper cream sauce) and breast of duck roasted in a brandied cherry glaze. All food is fresh (clams, shrimp, crab, oysters), including homemade soups, sausages, and sauces. They not only make their own pasta, they also grow their own lettuce in a small garden and butcher their own meats. Dinner ranges from $10 to $19; lunch costs $6 to $12. Kids like the club sandwich (turkey, bacon, lettuce, and tomato for $6.25) and the Napa Valley burger ($6).

Highchairs and boosters are available. Parking lot nearby. Reservations are accepted, even encouraged in the high season. Open for lunch Monday through Friday from 11:30 a.m. to 2:30 p.m. and on Saturday from 11:30 a.m. to 2:30 p.m. (downstairs only). Outdoor patio seating is available when possible. Sunday brunch is served from 10 a.m. to 2:30 p.m. Open for dinner Sunday through Thursday from 5 to 9 p.m., on Friday and Saturday till 10 p.m. Most major credit cards are accepted.

Picnic Fixings and Light Bites

When you don't want a full-fledged sit-down meal, you might try the following. The **Butter Cream Bakery**, 2297 Jefferson St. (tel. 707/255-6700), is a well-kept secret. Once inside, you're reminded that Napa is a small town. You'll know the building by the pink and white stripes. Inside, the pink-and-white color scheme continues. Located in the bakery, a long counter of 20 seats overlooks the fountain and grill, where you can watch the short-order cook whip up his specialties. Ten booths accommodate parties of two or more. For lunch, burgers are wonderful, but get the hash browns (not fries)—they're great. Lunch prices average $3. The kids will gobble down the dollar-size pancakes, which you can order by the number—one, two, or three. Or you can split a thick malted waffle topped with strawberries and whipped cream ($3.50). Traditional egg breakfasts go for $3.50 to $4.50.

Boosters and highchairs are available. While there is no children's menu, the kids will find plenty to choose from. Open Monday through Saturday from 5:30 a.m. to 5 p.m., on Sunday to 4 p.m. Peak times on weekends are 8:30 a.m. to noon, when you should expect a long wait for a booth (but you could eat at the counter). Lots of street parking. No reservations or credit cards accepted.

At **Nunn's Cheese Barn**, 1427 Main St. (tel. 707/255-0262), you can either order take-out from the deli or eat on the patio. If you want a quick, inexpensive lunch or a delicious picnic-to-go, this is the place to come. No boosters or highchairs are available.

We always order roast beef or turkey sandwiches ($2.75) at Nunn's, buy produce and some cheese, and then picnic at one of the beautiful places in Napa.

Nunn's is open Monday through Saturday from 10 a.m. to 6 p.m. Most credit cards are accepted. Parking nearby.

IF YOU DECIDE TO STAY OVERNIGHT: For those of you who don't worry about the price of doing it up in style, the **Silverado Country Club**, 1600 Atlas Peak Rd., Napa, CA 94558 (tel. 707/257-0200, or toll free 800/532-0500), is a large 1,200-acre resort surrounded by lush foliage, golf courses, and jogging trails. This 280-unit condominium complex has 20 Plexi-paved tennis courts, eight swimming pools, and two 18-hole championship golf courses.

There are children's tennis lessons, bicycle rentals, and acres of grass for playing. Nearby horseback riding is available. A favorite with parents are the video cassette players and tapes that you can rent (the $10 fee includes the player rental and one movie; each additional movie costs $4.50).

Room service is available from 7 a.m. to 10 p.m. and offers several good items for children. Babysitting can be arranged through the concierge, but you might want to make your plans when you reserve your room.

Children are welcome at all three on-premises dining facilities; boosters and highchairs are available. The Royal Oak Room overlooks the gardens. This lovely restaurant with hand-carved tables and open-beam ceilings offers char-broiled steaks and chops. Vintner's Court, a grand salon with chandeliers, serves California cuisine. While boosters and highchairs are available here, this jacket-and-tie-required dining room might be better for the night you have a babysitter. The Silverado Bar & Grill overlooks the North Golf Course and is the most casual dining area. It's open for breakfast and lunch.

All the accommodations have fully equipped kitchens and some (the cottage suites) have fireplaces as well.

Rates are seasonal, but ask for specials, which are cheaper and frequent off-season. Studios rent for $145 to $165, single or double occupancy; and one-bedroom suites cost $175 to $195, single or double occupancy. Two-bedroom suites rent for $310 to $330 for up to four people, and three-bedroom suites are $380 to $465 for up to six people. Children under 12 are free in their parents' room. No charge for cribs. Each additional person in a room is charged $15 per night.

The **Clarion Inn, Napa Valley,** 3425 Solano Ave., Napa, CA 94559 (tel. 707/253-7433, or toll free 800/CLARION), is a great moderately priced hotel located in the heart of Napa Valley. The lobby is warm and welcoming and has the charm of a country inn. The fireplace, inviting chairs, and sofas make the lobby a cozy, relaxing place to be. Under the management of John Brost, the hotel staff is extremely helpful and congenial. They'll recommend restaurants, shopping, and bike trails, and help solve general problems. (We needed to get our infant carseat repaired and Guest Services was very helpful.)

The pool and Jacuzzi area is beautiful. Surrounded by grass, the pool is shallow enough and shaped so that it's easy for kids to navigate. There is a playground with a sandbox and jungle gym. For tennis buffs, there are two lighted tennis courts. Babysitting service requires 24 hours' advance notice. Room service is available from 6:30 a.m. to 10:30 p.m.

The "Family Fun Package" is presented to each child upon arrival—a small packet of goodies that includes crayons and paper. The management is developing a small library of children's games.

The country-style Signature Restaurant, an open, spacious dining area just off the lobby, is open daily and has a complete children's menu.

The 191 oversize rooms continue the country theme. Decorated with oak furniture and brass headboards, they all have remote-control TV and a shower massage, and are equipped with HBO and in-room movies. Many face the grassy courtyard and pool. If you want a refrigerator, request it in advance—there will be a charge of $10 per night. You have a choice of rooms with a king-size, queen-size, or two double beds.

Room rates are seasonal, and range from $62 to $100 per night, single or double. Higher rates are in effect on Friday and Saturday nights. Cribs and roll-aways are free. No charge for children under 17 in the same room with their parents; $6 per night for each person over 17. A few connecting rooms are available.

The **Embassy Suites,** 1075 California Blvd., Napa, CA 94559 (tel. 707/253-9540, or toll free 800/EMBASSY), is another moderately priced alternative. The Mediterranean-style hotel has a spacious lobby. There is a large pond outside with all manner of ducks, swans, and carp, and the courtyard has tables and chairs, inviting guests to sit and relax. The indoor/outdoor swimming pool and Jacuzzi are relaxing retreats. Bicycles are available for use free of charge.

All accommodations are two-room suites, though they're a bit on the small side. Full kitchens with microwaves, wet bars, and a full range of utensils and cookware make it very convenient. Babysitting can be arranged, and room service is available from 11 a.m. to 10 p.m.

The Swan Court restaurant is a three-story atrium-style room that makes you feel like you're outdoors. Open to guests for breakfast.

The suite rates include a full cooked-to-order breakfast (including seconds) in the restaurant and two hours of free cocktails in the courtyard. The winter rates are $89 single and $99 double; summer rates are $109 single and $119 double. Children under 12 stay free in their parents' suite; those over 12 are charged $10 per night. No charge for cribs; rollaways not available.

IN CASE OF EMERGENCY: If a medical emergency occurs during your visit to the Napa Valley, there's an emergency room at **Queen of the Valley Hospital,** 1000 Trancas, Napa (tel. 707/252-4411).

---

6. SONOMA COUNTY

Sonoma County is a combination of beaches, rugged coast, redwoods, quaint towns, and the "big city" of Santa Rosa. It also includes the Valley of the Moon, once home to Jack London, and is California's oldest winery and grape-growing region.

The town of Sonoma, like most early California towns once governed by Mexico, has a plaza that forms the center of the town.

U.S. 101 north from San Francisco leads you to Calif. 37, then to Calif. 121. From there, take Broadway directly to the Plaza.

WHAT TO SEE AND DO: The **Sonoma Valley Visitors Bureau,** 453 1st St., in the Plaza (tel. 707/996-1090), is open weekdays from 9 a.m. to 5 p.m., on Saturday to 4 p.m., and on Sunday to 3 p.m.

On warm summer days you'll see families taking advantage of the Plaza's park. Swings, picnic tables, and a duck pond beckon you, and you can drop by the **Sonoma Cheese Factory,** 2 Spain St. (tel. 707/996-1931), for sandwiches and drinks. Makers of the famous Sonoma Jack cheese, the Cheese Factory is open from 9:30 a.m. to 5:30 p.m. daily.

Historic Sites

You can get a walking tour map of the Plaza area at the Visitors Bureau for $2 and a *Visitors Guide* with key historic sights for $1. There are a number of key historic sites surrounding the Plaza, but we'll just mention those the kids might enjoy.

One ticket is good within the same day at Sonoma Barracks, Vallejo's home, and the Petaluma Adobe (a 20-minute drive from Sonoma). The charge is $1 for adults, 75¢ for children 6 to 17. The mission, barracks, and Vallejo's home are all open daily from 10 a.m. to 5 p.m. All these sites have stroller accessibility, but there are stairs in Vallejo's home. Rest rooms can be found in the Plaza, near the mission.

It was Gen. Mariano Vallejo who was given the responsibility of creating a fort and a town here, and who was put in charge of the mission by the Mexican government. His grand rule ended when American settlers captured the region in 1846. Some of the buildings that Vallejo had built for the town are still standing.

Vallejo's home, called **Lachryma Montis,** was built in 1851. His first home, **Casa Grande,** was built in 1836 and is on Spain Street. At the time it was built it was considered one of the grandest homes in all of California. You'll see only the servants' quarters, as the main wing burned down 30 years after it was built.

The **Toscano Hotel** is next door at 20 E. Spain St. Built to be a general store and library, in 1886 it was converted into a hotel. No longer in use, the rooms are still furnished with original items. Free docent-guided tours are given on Saturday and Sunday from 1 to 4 p.m., and on Monday from 11 a.m. to 1 p.m.

The **Sonoma Barracks,** at the corner of Spain Street and 1st Street East (tel. 707/938-1519), which was built in 1836 by Vallejo, displays Sonoma's Indian, Mexican, and American historical periods.

Across the street is the **Mission San Francisco Solano de Sonoma** (tel. 707/938-1519). This was the last of the 21 missions built in California.

Kitty-corner to the mission is the **Bear Flag Monument,** which marks the revolt that took place in the Plaza between a band of 30 Americans and General Vallejo, who was captured by the raiders in the early-morning hours. The Americans claimed Sonoma as part of the California Republic, and raised the Bear Flag, which later became the official flag of California. A month later an American naval officer claimed the area for the United States, and raised the Stars and Stripes.

Jack London State Park

Any kid (or adult) who has wept through *Call of the Wild,* been mesmerized by *The Sea Wolf* and impressed by the simplicity of *To Build a Fire,* knows the name Jack London. (Take Calif. 12 toward Santa Rosa, left on Madrone Road to Arnold, right to London Ranch Road, and then left into the park.) Just seven miles out of Sonoma in Glen Ellen (tel. 707/938-5216), this is part of London's original 1,400-acre Beauty Ranch. Now over 800 acres, the park includes the ruins of London's house, his grave, his wife Charmian's house, and the cottage in which he wrote much of his later works.

At the entrance is **Happy Walls,** Charmian's house, which is now used as a museum for London's photographs and other mementos. At **Wolf House,** you'll see the remains of the house they planned so carefully, but which burned before they could move in. It is reachable by a half-mile trail, and takes approximately one hour round trip. London's ashes are buried next to the marked graves of two pioneer children, and this hike is a half mile. You might have to carry the toddlers on the way back, as the trail is fairly steep.

There's a rest room near the parking lot (and not another one until Wolf House, half a mile away), and picnic facilities in the area. Beware of a few rattlesnakes and poison oak. The park is open daily from 8 a.m. to sundown; the museum is open daily from 10 a.m. to 5 p.m. There's a $3-per-car entrance fee.

Horseback Riding

You can enjoy 20 miles of horse trails in Jack London State Park. Beginners and experts alike are accommodated by the **Sonoma Cattle Company** (tel. 707/996-8566). The minimum age for riding is 7. Rides are guided and are usually restricted to no more than seven people. These stables also have guided rides through Sugarloaf Ridge State Park, 20 minutes north of Sonoma. Rides in both parks depart at 9 a.m., noon, and 3 p.m. during spring and summer. For fall hours, check ahead. Rates for adults and children are $15 for one hour; $25 for two hours. Reservations are strongly suggested during summer and on weekends. When you call, ask for directions to the stables. There are separate locations for Jack London and Sugarloaf.

Miniature Train Ride

Train Town is located on Broadway, one mile south of the Plaza (tel. 707/938-3912). Little kids especially will love the miniature train ride. The train stops midway on its 1½-mile route so that the passengers can feed the goats and peek through the windows of the miniature buildings. Open weekends through-out the year and daily in summer through Labor Day from 11 a.m. to 5 p.m. The fare is $2.50 for adults, $2 for children 2 to 16 and seniors; those under 2 ride free.

Wineries

There are several famous wineries in the immediate area that offer tours and have picnic areas as well. It's a nice way for you to get a look at the art of making wine and enjoy a picnic with the kids afterward. Be sure to call ahead, as hours change, and sometimes the picnic facilities are not open. There are many more wineries in the neighboring towns. The **Wine Institute,** 165 Post St., San Francisco, CA 94108 (tel. 415/986-0878), can send you a list of California wineries, or else you can contact the Sonoma Valley Visitors Bureau.

Buena Vista Winery–Haraszthy Cellars is located at 18000 Old Winery Rd., one mile east of the Plaza (tel. 707/938-1266). This is California's oldest premium winery and has been declared a historic landmark. There is a self-guided tour and picnic facilities. Open daily (except Thanksgiving, Christmas, and New Year's Day) from 10 a.m. to 5 p.m. No charge.

Haywood Winery is at 18701 Gehricke Rd., not far from the Plaza (tel. 707/996-4298). There is no tour here, but the picnic area overlooks the vine-yards. It's open daily for tasting and retail sales from 11 a.m. to 5 p.m.

Sebastiani Vineyards, 389 4th St. East (tel. 707/938-5532), has guided tours daily from 10:20 a.m. to 4:20 p.m. There is also a picnic area.

WHERE TO STAY: The **Sonoma Valley Inn** is a block from the Plaza, at 550 2nd St. West, Sonoma, CA 95476 (tel. 707/938-9200, or toll free 800/334-KRUG). Built in a turn-of-the-century design, this Best Western inn features rooms with either fireplaces or with kitchenettes and private whirlpools. Rooms have either one king-size or two queen-size beds, and there are some adjoining rooms. There is a heated pool, HBO in the rooms, and complimentary continental breakfast.

Room rates April 1 through October 31 are $85, $95, and $105; the rest of the year, $65, $75, and $85. Children under 12 stay free in the same room as their parents; those over 12 are charged $10 each per night. Cribs and rollaways are free.

WHERE TO EAT: Being in the heart of the wine country, Sonoma is dotted with some pricey, intimate gourmet restaurants. To be on the safe side, call ahead and ask about the menu and atmosphere.

One place you can't go wrong at is **La Casa Restaurant,** 121 E. Spain St. (tel. 707/938-1866 or 707/996-3406), close to the Plaza and right across from the mission. The service is excellent and quick. The wonderful tortilla chips our kids love so much are brought immediately, and parents are warned of hot plates and food that might be too spicy for the tots.

There is a child's combination plate of taco or enchilada with beans and rice ($3). Or management will split a regular entree between kids. À la carte orders are reasonably priced, and house specials cost about $7.25. There's nothing too complicated on the menu. So even if this is your first time ordering California Mexican food, you won't have a problem making a choice.

Highchairs and boosters are available, and they'll gladly warm bottles and baby food.

Open daily from 11:30 a.m. to 10 p.m. for lunch and dinner. Street parking. Major credit cards accepted.

SIDE TRIPS: Located approximately 20 minutes from Sonoma, and within easy reach of San Francisco (39 miles), Santa Rosa (16 miles), and Bodega Bay (26 miles) is Petaluma, a small town of 19th-century buildings and Victorian homes. Once a leading river town that used to ship food downriver to the '49ers (the gold-seekers, not the football team), Petaluma's 20th-century claim to fame is as one of California's leading dairy centers.

Stop here to see the **Petaluma Adobe State Historic Park,** 3325 Adobe Rd., at Casa Grande (tel. 707/762-4871). Originally this was General Vallejo's estate. The kids can run around the headquarters building and see the tools and weaving displays, as well as the huge pots used to feed the people. There's a picnic area on the grounds, and sheep and roosters roam free. Be sure to go around the back of the building to see the other animals in the corral.

Open daily from 10 a.m. to 5 p.m. Guided tours are available by reservation only, on Monday, Wednesday, and Friday (tel. 707/938-1519). If you don't use your ticket from Sonoma, the fee is $1 for adults, 75¢ for children.

Throughout the area, all sorts of farms let you enjoy a look at what they make or grow, including fruits, vegetables, flowers, dairy products, trees, and animals. The **Sonoma Country Farm Trails** map points out locations and gives phone numbers. It is available at the Petaluma Chamber of Commerce, the library, the museum, and at some hotels and businesses, or write Sonoma County Farm Trails, P.O. Box 6043, Santa Rosa, CA 95406.

Some highlights of the Farm Trails are:

Pet-A-Llama Ranch, 5505 Lone Pine Rd., Sebastopol (tel. 707/823-9395 after 4 p.m.). Tours by appointment only. The kids can pet and feed actual llamas here. There are also hand-woven goods for sale and spinning demonstrations. Call for directions. The admission fee is $2 for adults, 50¢ for children.

Winners' Circle Ranch, 5911 Lakeville Hwy., Petaluma (tel. 707/762-1808 or 707/762-0220), will also make an interesting stop. This is the home of the famous miniature horses, a breed that dates back to the 16th century. Besides just seeing these cute little horses graze, you can see mares and their new foals, and there are wagon rides and demonstrations. Be careful, or the kids will want to take one of these horses home! Shows are given at 11 a.m. and 2 p.m. There's a picnic area, snackbar, trophy room, and giftshop. Open Wednesday through Sunday, June through October, from 10:30 a.m. to 4 p.m. No reservations necessary. The entrance fee is $5 for adults, $3 for seniors and children 12 and under. There's a small extra charge for wagon rides.

2 Lazy 2 Farm is located at 7103 Julianna Dr., off Snow Road, in nearby Sebastopol (tel. 707/823-8650). What will interest the children most here is that the Cossey family takes in abused and neglected horses and ponies. They feed them and care for them until they're well, then sell them for the amount of money they spent nursing the animals back to health. What sensitive child wouldn't be affected by this! They also raise horses, sheep, ponies, and goats. Be sure to call to make an appointment. Open daily April through September (closed October to April) from 10 a.m. to 4 p.m. No admission fee.

About an hour north of Sonoma is Dick and Shellie Dilworth's **Stage-A-Picnic,** which meets at the Hope-Merrill House Bed & Breakfast Inn, 21253 Geyserville Ave., Geyserville (north on U.S. 101 to the Geyserville Avenue exit; tel. 707/857-3356 or 707/857-3619). You and the kids will leave Geyserville in a horse-drawn covered stagecoach which dates back to 1872. You will ride through the vineyards, at the most picturesque times of the season, to one major winery and two smaller family-run operations. Then you'll have a picnic in the lush vineyards. Lunch is included in the price of your ride. Many of the wineries visited will serve grape juice to the children. When the Dilworths know kids will be part of the group, they make sure the gourmet lunch will also appeal to the finicky eaters. Parents themselves, the Dilworths always try to make the ride fun for the children.

Tours are conducted May through October on weekends at 10 a.m. and 12:30 p.m. Call for weekday schedules. Fares are $40 for adults and children 7 and up; children under 7 are free.

CHAPTER V

THE NORTH COAST

□ □ □

1. POINT REYES
2. BODEGA BAY
3. MENDOCINO
4. FORT BRAGG

The California coast is known throughout the world for its beauty. The northern portion (especially the drive from San Francisco to the border of Oregon) is unparalleled for its extraordinary scenery—a dramatic, ever-changing landscape. North of San Francisco the view might be bleak and foggy on the ocean side and lush and sunny on the other. Curving roads hug cliffs that lead to sheer drop-offs and the raging ocean below. Just 15 minutes farther on, the road might become a narrow forest lane framed by giant redwoods and filled with the fragrance of pine and wildflowers. There's a different sight around every curve— and are there curves! Parts of the drive are flat and easily negotiated, while others take all your driving skills and concentration. Some areas will make you want to stop and take off your shoes, grab the kids' hands, and walk along a beach or hike a certain trail. Other places will entice you to find a cozy cabin with a fireplace and flannel sheets.

You'll drive through artists' colonies, fishing villages, and historic settlements. One village is even a former outpost of Russian fur traders! You'll hear ocean waves pounding against massive rocks and follow the glorious Russian River's smooth trip from Sonoma County to Mendocino County.

Besides just viewing exquisite scenery, you and your family can do so much together, and you can do it your own way—hike, camp, fish, clam, explore, whale-watch, and just generally enjoy the outdoors.

We will take you on a four-day trip from San Francisco north to Fort Bragg —approximately 450 miles round trip. If you choose to continue farther north, you'll be swept away by the beauty of the northern California giant redwoods, the biggest in the state. If you want to detour inland at various points, you can visit the wine country.

But back to the coastal road. For all of this beauty, you'll probably get one of the most rugged rides you've ever had! The road curves and twists. There are few places to stop between towns, and no rest stops to speak of. Children (and parents) who suffer from motion sickness might want to consider taking U.S. 101. Or perhaps take the coast route partway, then change over to 101 (which, by the way, can also be pretty trying—it frequently changes from freeway to a two-lane, curvy, slow highway).

As unappealing as it might sound, just throw a roll of paper towels and some plastic bags in the car, take a change of clothes out of the suitcase for each child just in case, and put some crackers and even a can of soda in the front seat. Also, eat something earlier, or bring food along in the car. The first 9 miles out of San Francisco seemed like 20 with our hungry daughter in tow. Speaking from experience, these little items would have helped us out on that trip!

Take Calif. 1 (the coastal road) north from San Francisco to **Stinson Beach,** 9 miles from the Golden Gate Bridge. We like to stop here, as it's the first place that offers a good rest stop and somewhere to eat, and it's a good introduction to the coast. The large beach is rugged and bordered by dense foliage. There's a big parking lot and no admission fee. The picnic area near the parking lot is nice, and there's a snackbar right on the beach and clean rest rooms. The beach is open for swimming from May to mid-September. The park is open daily from 9 a.m. to sunset.

First-time surfers might want to try their skill here, as the waves are good and the lifeguards are considered to be some of the best. You can rent wetsuits, flippers, boogie boards, and skimboards from **The Live Water,** 3450 Shoreline Hwy., in the town of Stinson Beach (tel. 415/868-0333).

We find that a 30- or 45-minute break here is perfect before continuing up the coast.

1. POINT REYES

Located approximately 50 miles north of San Francisco, **Point Reyes National Seashore** is 65,000 acres of rugged, windswept beaches, marshland and grassland, estuaries, forests, and ranges. It's land ripe for exploration by car, on foot, or on bicycle. It is a wilderness area filled with things to see, from whales and sea lions to tule elk and bobcats, and it offers trails for hiking, plantlife to admire, tidepools to explore, and paths for horseback riding.

The seashore is a series of surprises. Everywhere you turn the terrain—and weather—seems to change. One minute you're in a park-like setting with gentle grassy hills and a forest nearby. Suddenly you reach a portion of the seashore that is hauntingly bleak, not unlike the marshes of northern England. Then there's sun again, and a bay calm enough for swimming.

ORIENTATION: The best way to learn all you can do here is to begin at the **National Seashore Visitor Center,** located at Bear Valley, just off Calif. 1 at Olema (tel. 415/663-1092). From this point, there are several sites that can be reached on foot. Right near the Visitor Center are picnic tables and rest rooms. The center has maps and a good driving tour, which may be your best bet with toddlers. In general, Point Reyes is a great place for ages 6 and up.

The weather can change from hour to hour and place to place. Heavy fog can roll in without warning. Even though it's sunny in one spot (like Inverness Ridge), this doesn't mean it will be like that throughout the area. So if you decide to hike or swim at one of the beaches, be sure to take water and layers of clothing. Always check with the Visitor Center first for weather and tide information, and ask first which beaches are safe.

Summers can be foggy and windy; very early fall is a good time for a visit. Or come in early February (through July) when the wildflowers bloom. No matter what time of the year you visit, bring jackets in order to be prepared for the unpredictable weather.

WHAT TO DO AND SEE: Directly behind the Visitor Center is the **Morgan Horse Ranch,** open year round. You can learn about the history of the Morgan horse via interpretive talks, and the family can see them grazing in the fields. These horses are bred and trained here and used by rangers throughout the park system.

Nearby is **Kule Loklo,** a replica of a Coast Miwok Indian Village, the tribe thought to have migrated to the area from Siberia nearly 3,000 years ago. There is a self-guiding tour of the village (it takes approximately 20 minutes), on which you'll see mockups of sweathouses, ceremonial areas, grass huts, and other items indigenous to the tribe. There are usually cultural demonstrations on Saturday at 1 p.m. Call ahead.

Hiking

The 140 miles of trails through Point Reyes offer the novice and ardent hiker a choice of terrain and level of difficulty. Trails can be reached from four trailheads. The Visitor Center has trail maps, and the rangers can tell you about the difficulty or ease of a hike. Also check with them for weather conditions.

The **Earthquake Trail,** which begins close to the parking lot of the Visitor Center, is a 0.7-mile hike (a half-hour loop trail) along the San Andreas Fault. It's fascinating (not just for Californians) to see how damage caused by the quake of 1906 created the Point Reyes peninsula. There are interpretive signs along the trail describing earthquakes. The paved trail is no problem for children.

Our troop enjoys the short, self-guiding **Woodpecker Nature Trail** (also 0.70-mile), which takes us into a Douglas fir forest. There are lots of varieties of birds to accompany us on our hike. The kids like to point out the wild mushrooms (be careful—don't let them touch), ferns, and mosses.

Beaches and Ocean Activities

The beaches are rugged, dangerous, and usually unswimmable on the ocean side. The Visitor Center will give you specific information about each beach.

Limantour Beach, on the Drakes Bay side, is fine for swimming and picnicking. There's also great birdwatching nearby.

This is the time to check the kids' history knowledge. Ask them what they know about Sir Francis Drake, since this is the bay historians argue that Drake arrived at in 1579, making him the first English explorer to land on this continent.

Drakes Beach, on Drakes Bay, is a good swimming beach. It's the only spot on the seashore with food service, and it has its own information center.

Several beaches on the Tomales Bay side are also good for swimming and collecting seashells. Although not part of the national seashore, **Tomales Bay State Park** is within easy driving distance and is just north of Inverness.

From December to April, the **lighthouse observation platform** at the tip of Point Reyes is a wonderful place to watch the migration of the California gray whales—if you can make it up the 300 steps. During whale-watching season, a shuttle bus runs from Drakes Beach to the lighthouse every 20 minutes (weekends and holidays only). The lighthouse is also a good place from which to watch the sea lions.

For tidepool viewing, try **McClures Beach.** But be careful of the steep and narrow trail.

Horseback Riding

Another way to see the area is on horseback. **Five Brooks Stables,** on Calif. 1, three miles south of Olema at the Five Brooks Trailhead (tel. 415/663-8287), offers trips of varying lengths. Kids must be a minimum of 12 years old to ride. One trek goes through the deep forest and ends at the ocean for lunch ($50 per person). Be sure to call for reservations, or write Lauri Seeger at P.O. Box 51, Olema, CA 94950.

. . . and More

The kids might also enjoy a look at the **Johnson Oyster Company** on Drakes Estero. It's an authentic old oyster company—still selling them fresh—where children will be fascinated at seeing how these highly valued oysters are grown on wire strings on wooden platforms, and are fed by the nutrients carried in by the tide. There are mounds of empty oyster shells everywhere.

Guided experiences that can be enjoyed by the whole family are offered by **Point Reyes Field Seminars** (tel. 415/663-1200). The tours are limited to eight families of four people each, so call ahead for information and sign up early. Ask to be put on the mailing list—brochures will be sent three times per year.

These are one-day classes, and there are three to five per session, three sessions per year. One class, called "Family Nature Experience," consists of short walks (totaling about three miles) exploring the sounds, sights, and smells of the various plants and animals, led by a well-known naturalist ($32 for a family of four). Another, for infants and parents only, is a five-mile hike along the coast with a stop for lunch and playtime near the beach ($18 for parent and child). The suggested age for children participating in the regular family classes is 4 to 12. Classes last from 10 a.m. to approximately 3:30 p.m.

WHERE TO STAY: Although the seashore is primarily a day-use area, there are several campsites accessible by hiking in. They're not very big, so find out from the Visitor Center what's available way in advance.

If you want to stay overnight in the immediate area but don't want to camp out, there are two tiny inns that definitely welcome families. One is **Jasmine Cottage,** 11561 Calif. 1, Point Reyes Station, CA 94956 (tel. 415/663-1166). Be sure to call for reservations—it's booked far in advance—although Monday through Thursday are usually available.

Owner Karen Gray converted this carriage house into a guest cottage because so many friends who had enjoyed bed-and-breakfast inns were no longer welcome at them with children. Her one cottage sleeps four, and has a queen-size bed and two twins, a wood stove, fully equipped kitchen, private patio, and picnic table. Kids have the run of the pasture in the back, or can play at the school playground across the street. Porta-cribs are available.

Karen will take one-night reservations on the weekends. She is also building a second accommodation above the barn called The Hayloft, equipped with one queen-size bed, two doubles (fold-out couches), one twin, and one porta-crib. The rates are the same. (Check when you call for reservations to be sure it's ready.)

Rates are $95 per night double on weekends, including breakfast; $15 extra for each additional person. Single weekend nights cost $115.

Susan's House, 12201 Sir Francis Drake Blvd. (corner of Balboa and Inverness Park), Point Reyes, CA 94956 (tel. 415/663-1600), is another small accommodation. Susan Deixler rents the bottom of her two-story house, which offers a bedroom with a double bed and a living room with two futons. A porta-crib and a highchair are also available. There's a full kitchen and a private porch. The refrigerator is fully stocked for breakfast. *Note:* The front door is 30 steps up and not wheelchair-accessible.

Summer rates are $95 double for one night, $85 per night for two or more nights; each additional person is charged $10. Off-season (January through March) rates are $85 and $75 respectively.

The **Inns of Point Reyes** (tel. 415/663-1420) is a referral service that can tell you about accommodations in seven area homes and bed-and-breakfast establishments in the general West Marin / Point Reyes area. Call anytime.

WHERE TO EAT: Because the area is so popular with visitors, nearly every restaurant here is suitable for kids. But don't miss enjoying a meal at the **Station House Café,** on Main Street in Point Reyes Station (tel. 415/663-1515). The food is innovative and fresh, and the selections will appeal to even the most finicky eater. There's an extensive breakfast menu that includes omelets, country and city breakfasts, waffles, pancakes, and more, plus a long list of coffees and teas. Lunch and dinner entrees range from salads and seafood to sausages, pasta, sandwiches, and omelets. There are also daily specials. The average lunch or dinner entree is between $5 and $9. Be sure to save room for the locally prepared desserts. There are plenty of selections suitable for young tastes, and the kitchen will split dishes for kids under 6 at no charge.

There are boosters only here, no highchairs. Reservations are accepted for six or more. During the busy season, the best time to come for lunch is between 11:30 a.m. and 12:30 p.m.; for dinner, between 5 and 6 p.m. After 6:30, the wait can be a long one—up to an hour.

Open from 8 a.m. to 9 p.m. Wednesday through Monday (until 10 p.m. on Saturday in summer); closed Tuesday. Street parking available. Credit cards are accepted.

2. BODEGA BAY

Discovered by Spanish explorers in 1775, Bodega Bay continues its life as a commercial fishing village. As small as the town is, it boasts the largest fishing port between San Francisco and Fort Bragg. Charter a fishing boat and cast your line into the deep blue sea. Don't worry if you aren't successful—the fishermen you see docking here will more than likely be bringing their fresh catch to the local restaurants. Sparkling when it's sunny, moody-looking when it's foggy, Bodega Bay was the site where Hitchcock filmed *The Birds.* In addition to fishing opportunities, it signals the beginning of a series of beach parks heading up the coast, and has many beaches of its own for exploring.

The best fall/winter months to visit, weather-wise, are September through October and January through March. August brings heavy fog.

WHAT TO DO AND SEE: The **Bodega Bay Area Chamber of Commerce** will give you information on area activities. The office is located at 555 Coast Hwy. 1, Bodega Bay, CA 94923 (tel. 707/875-3422), and is open daily from 9 a.m. to 5 p.m.

Spud Point Marina is where the kids will see the commercial fishing boats at work. You can't miss it.

The beaches, of course, are the number-one attraction here—great for exploring tidepools as well as collecting shells and driftwood. **Doran Beach County Park** is one choice. You'll see the sign for the beach right off Calif. 1 near the Best Western Bodega Bay Lodge. **Sonoma Coast State Beach** is over 14 miles of uninterrupted shore, accessible from Calif. 1 at various places, beginning just north of Bodega Bay. **Bodega Bay** itself is great for a day's outing.

You can go **clamming** too, which is permitted on the state beaches. If you're not familiar with clam-eating safety, note: "These clams can be eaten safely from November through February. Although they can be eaten year round, the dark parts should be discarded from March through October."

In April, Bodega Bay hosts the annual **Fishermen's Festival.** The blessing of the fleet, boat parades, skeet shooting, bathtub races, and other festivities bring in more than 10,000 people to the three-day event. Make hotel reservations early if you plan to stay over.

What else can you do here? **Hiking,** and **whale-watching** (from Bodega Head) in winter from November to April. Check with the park ranger at Bodega Head on weekends for the status of the migration.

For the hungry, abalone season is April to November (it stops for the month of July). Crabs are plentiful from mid-November through June. Salmon can be had fresh from the middle of May through September. Any of these catches are perfect for a family beach picnic.

Horseback riding is available at the **Sea Horse Stables** (for more information, see the Sea Horse Guest Ranch listing in the "Where to Stay" section).

WHERE TO STAY: For luxury accommodations, try the **Inn at the Tides**, 800 Coast Hwy., Bodega Bay, CA 94923 (tel. 707/875-2751, or toll free 800/541-7788 in California). Set on a hill overlooking the bay, the 88 rooms are situated in 12 lodges, each with a bay view. The bright, spacious rooms are equipped with queen-size sofa beds, refrigerators, in-room movies, remote-control TV, and terrycloth robes. Some have fireplaces, skylights, and vaulted ceilings.

Our kids loved the indoor/outdoor pool. Loaner games (Trivial Pursuit, backgammon, and others) are available to keep everyone entertained on foggy nights. Ask for them at the front desk.

A bountiful complimentary continental buffet breakfast is served in the dining room and includes salads, sweet rolls, croissants, fresh fruit, and hot cocoa. While the dining room is more intimate at dinnertime, room service features many selections suitable for children. Babysitting services can be reserved in advance. There are self-service laundry facilities for guests. Cribs are available at no charge with advance notice.

In summer (April 1 to October 31), rooms rent for $110 to $185; rates are lower the rest of the year. Children under 12 always stay free; those 12 and over are charged $10 each per night.

The **Best Western Bodega Bay Lodge,** Coast Hwy. 1 (Calif. 1), Bodega Bay, CA 94923 (tel. 707/875-3525, or toll free 800/528-1234 or 800/368-2468), is the recipient of the AAA four-diamond award. Set above the dunes of Doran Beach, each of the 78 rooms overlooks Bodega Bay. There's enough grassy area close to the lodge for kids to play safely, or you can rent bikes at the hotel and take them down to the beach paths and backroads. Two huge 500-gallon saltwater aquariums in the lobby will enchant youngsters of all ages.

Complimentary continental breakfast is served, but there is no room service or restaurant on the premises. Amenities include an outdoor pool and whirlpool, and a nine-hole golf course. Babysitting is available with advance notice.

Rooms are nice-sized and comfortable. Deluxe ground-floor rooms have large patios, and some have fireplaces. Loft rooms are available with a queen-size and king-size bed, but no fireplace. There's also a two-room suite with two queen-size beds and a twin-size hideabed.

Standard rooms rent for $99, and deluxe rooms are $129. The two-room suite costs $175, and loft rooms run $93. Rooms with a fireplace and a private whirlpool rent for $175. Children under 12 sleep free in the same room with their parents; those 12 and over are charged $10 per night. Cribs are free, but rollaways cost $10 per night.

For a truly rustic experience, you might want to check in at the **Sea Horse Guest Ranch,** 2660 Calif. 1, Bodega Bay, CA 94923 (tel. 707/875-2721), at the edge of town. Although this 700-acre working ranch is not the Ponderosa, there are horses, chickens, cattle, and sheep for the kids to make friends with. There is playground equipment, and the owner's young kids love having other children to play with.

You can bring your own horses or rent theirs. The owners offer guided trail rides for two to eight people; the charge is $10 per hour per person, with a four-hour minimum in force. There are also pony rides for the little ones, starting at $2.50 per hour.

The nicest rooms are in the Ranch House (the main house). There are three bedrooms with private baths and color TVs; two of the rooms could be used as a suite. The Bunk House, the original ranch house, can sleep up to 12 people, and the rooms are rented individually or you can rent the whole house. It has a large shared living room, a kitchen, eating area, three bedrooms, and two baths. One porta-crib and one playpen are also available for use. A complimentary continental breakfast is served.

Ranch House rooms rent for $65 to $70; Bunk House rooms cost $50 to $65, or the entire Bunk House can be let for $200. Children 12 and over are charged a $10 supplement; those under 12 stay free in their parents' room.

WHERE TO EAT: Like most towns in the area, kids are made to feel comfortable almost anywhere. The **Tides Wharf** restaurant (tel. 707/875-3652) is a good place for your first meal. Located across the street from the Inn at the Tides, and under the same ownership, this is a pleasant, casual seafood restaurant for breakfast, lunch, or dinner. If you request a window table when you make your reservation, the tots will have a good view of the bay and boats. If you don't request a window table in advance, you will encounter a long wait for one.

Breakfast prices are reasonable, and there are plenty of selections. Lunch and dinner choices are somewhat pricey, with adult entrees ranging from $6 to $15 at lunch, and up to $28 at dinner. There's a nice children's lunch and dinner menu, which includes prawns and fish as well as the usual hamburgers, hot dogs, and grilled cheese. Children's entrees range from $2.75 to $7.25 (limited to kids under 12). Highchairs (plastic wrapped!) and booster seats are available. The staff will supply extra plates for splitting orders and is willing to warm baby bottles and baby food, as well as make Shirley Temples. If you ask, they'll bring crackers right away and provide pencils for drawing.

With a reservation, the wait is five minutes (they say); without one, it could be 45 minutes to 1½ hours. Open daily in summer from 6 a.m. to 10 p.m., in winter (end of October through May) from 7 a.m. to 9 p.m. Parking lot. Major credit cards are accepted.

Can't get a window seat at the Tides? Try **Lucas Wharf** restaurant, just south at 595 Calif. 1 (tel. 707/875-3522)—but you'll have to request a view table here too. Seafood is the specialty. Daily specials are written on the board. Ask for children's portions. Quick service is common when children are at the table.

The regular menu has choices for both light and hearty eaters. Adult dishes vary from fresh shucked oysters and fisherman's stew to New York steak and pasta primavera. Prices range from $6.25 to $16.50. There is a split-plate charge of $1.

The staff will gladly warm baby bottles and baby food, and will make special children's drinks. Reservations are accepted for parties of six or more. The length of wait varies with the day and season. For dinner, come by 6 p.m.; lunchtime is usually no problem. Highchairs and boosters are available.

In summer, Lucas Wharf is open Sunday through Thursday from 11 a.m. to 9:30 p.m., on Friday and Saturday till 10 p.m.; in winter it opens at 11:30 a.m. Parking lot. Major credit cards accepted.

3. MENDOCINO

A bit of Cape Cod on the Pacific coast, Mendocino is a small artists' colony and picturesque stop, whether as a destination or a place to stay overnight on the way to the giant redwoods farther north. It was settled in the 1850s and you can still see the original homes of the wealthy lumber barons who made this their town during the great logging boom. Mendocino became a haven for the artists of the '60s and '70s who wanted to "drop out" and move to the country. The entire town has been declared a historic monument, and it retains its weathered, noncommercial personality while still hosting some great artists.

After you've exhausted the charming boutiques and interesting art galleries in town, take the children to the nearby state parks, ride bikes, play at the beach, or walk through the Mendocino Coast Botanical Gardens.

WHAT TO DO AND SEE IN TOWN: Although the town is tiny, there are several things you can participate in as a family depending on what time of year you visit.

Art

The **Mendocino Art Center,** 45200 Little Lake St. (tel. 707/937-5818), features programs and displays geared to heighten public awareness of the arts. In addition to the gallery, which is open daily in summer from 10 a.m. to 5 p.m., in winter till 4 p.m., the center also sponsors a Sunday Afternoon Concert Series, featuring mostly classical music. Children are always welcome. Free.

Festivals

Contact the **Mendocino Area Parks Association** (tel. 707/937-5397) or the **Department of Parks and Recreation** (tel. 707/937-5804) for specific dates and other information on the following festivals: Whale Festival (March), Memorial Day Festival (May), Mendocino Music Festival (July), Oktoberfest & Medieval Fair (October), Mushroom Festival (November).

Children's Events

Historic **Ford House,** at 332 N. Main St., originally the home of one of the co-owners of the first sawmill in Mendocino, also serves as the local Visitor Center. Drop by to look at the house and to get a copy of the "Calendar of Events," which lists children's activities, such as the annual Sand Castle Building Contest held on Labor Day in the Mendocino Headlands State Park; plus art shows, Christmas events, an Easter egg hunt, a July 4th Carnival, and more.

WHAT TO SEE AND DO IN THE AREA: Outdoor activities are abundant in places within driving distance of Mendocino. Whether you stay in Mendocino or Fort Bragg, these activities are easily accessible.

Gardens

The **Mendocino Coast Botanical Gardens,** 18220 North Calif. 1 (tel. 707/964-4352), are six miles north of Mendocino and two miles south of Fort Bragg. There are several thousand types of plants here, including heathers, succulents, ivies, roses, and rhododendrons. It's a peaceful and beautiful place for a walk with the family, and there are picnic areas. The paths are stroller-accessible. Open daily during the season from 9 a.m. to 5 p.m.; off-season, from 10 a.m. to 4 p.m. Call first. Admission is $5 for adults, $3 for children 12 to 17 and seniors, free for children under 12 accompanied by their parents.

Parks and Beaches

The state parks in this area are wonderful and unique. You'll see headlands, canyons, forests, meadows, dunes. And each park usually offers a view of or accessibility to the ocean at some point. There are lots of picnic areas and camping sites. For further information, call 707/937-5804.

Three miles south of Mendocino on Calif. 1 is **Van Damme State Park,** with its 72 campsites, a beach (relatively safe for ocean swimming—no lifeguards), and hiking trails. The big attraction is the **Pygmy Forest Discovery Trail,** where you will see decades-old trees only a few feet tall, stunted due to poor soil conditions.

If you want to see just the trail, drive south on Calif. 1, past the Van Damme State Park entrance to Little River Airport Road. Go east 3½ miles to the intersection of Little River Airport Road and Albion Road. There's a sign noting the entrance to the Pygmy Forest parking lot. You'll find a trail guide at the entrance. Small children may need help through this trail—root systems are exposed atop the ground, making walking difficult. If you plan to visit for the day, the charge is $3 per car.

For reservations at the campgrounds ($10), call MISTIX (tel. toll free 800/ 444-7275).

Nearby **Mendocino Headlands State Park** (which horseshoes around the town of Mendocino), for day use only, is a mecca of activities ranging from fishing and sport diving to surfing and hiking. Via the north end of Hesser Drive, you can reach a public fishing area. Accessible on the south side of Mendocino is Big River Beach, which can be reached by car from Calif. 1, or by hiking down the bluffs. There are lots of chances here for tidepooling, climbing rocks, and just plain beachcombing. Rest rooms available. Free day use.

Russian Gulch State Park is two miles north of Mendocino on the west side of Calif. 1. Families can camp here (there are 28 family campsites, plus hot shower and flush toilet facilities), or just hike one of the many trails. **Falls Loop Trail,** which is 3½ miles long, is partly paved and accessible for bikes. During the summer a ranger will direct you to the trail. Also during summer are ranger-led hikes, bike hikes, and other activities, all of which are posted throughout the park.

North of Mendocino and Caspar is **Jughandle State Reserve,** just north of the north entrance to Caspar on Calif. 1, five miles south of Fort Bragg. If you only have time for one hike, take the **Ecological Staircase Trail,** where changes in the ocean's level over hundreds of thousands of years, along with other geologic activity, created a series of terraces. Near the entrance to the trail are self-guiding brochures. On Saturday rangers lead hikes in the area (two to three hours in duration, over five miles of moderate terrain), weather permitting. Kids should be able to make this hike. (There are chemical toilets in the parking lot, north of Caspar on Calif. 1.)

Canoeing

Canoes are available for rent for riding down the Big River. You can rent by the hour or take overnight trips. **Catch-a-Canoe** is found at Big River Lodge, Coast Hwy. 1 (Calif. 1) and Comptche-Ukiah Road (tel. 707/937-0273), at the mouth of Big River, just below the bridge on the south shore. A trip down the river by canoe is a trip through still-undeveloped wilderness. You can pack a lunch and stop for a picnic at a sandy beach. Rates range from $10 to $14 per hour, depending on the number of people. Overnight rates are $45 to $49.

WHERE TO STAY: Right in the heart of town, **MacCallum House,** 45020 Albion St., Mendocino, CA 95460 (tel. 707/937-0289), is a grand old inn, comfortable and cozy, with a perpetual aura of cheerfulness about it. With roots dating back to 1882, the Victorian mansion has retained its authenticity and charm. You and the kids will be comfortable and will feel like you're staying in someone's private, rambling home. (See the discussion about staying in a bed-and-breakfast inn with children in Chapter I.) In fact, the inn's rate card announces: "Children are welcome."

All accommodations are individually decorated, many with authentic pieces dating from the original owners. Remember, no TVs here!

A complimentary continental breakfast is included in the price. MacCallum House Restaurant (tel. 707/937-5763), well thought of throughout the area, is on the premises. It's open for dinner Tuesday through Sunday. Although children are welcome, prepare for an intimate setting with a menu that offers such adult fare as veal champignon and bouillabaisse. No credit cards accepted here.

There are 20 accommodations at the inn. When you call to reserve, tell them you'll have kids with you and they'll let you know which room will meet your needs. For example, the Watertower is a split-level accommodation with a queen-size bed and a private bath, which has a view of the ocean and it rents for $85 per night. The Greenhouse is a separate cottage with a Franklin fireplace, two double beds, and a private bath, and it costs $95. The Barn Suites are ideal for families, sleeping two to six people, and they let for $125 and $165 respectively; and the Barn Apartment is a full-sized apartment, perfect to rent by the week—it costs $115 per night. Rollaways, futons, or cribs are available for a charge of $10 extra per person. If you're bringing your own sleeping bag, or your child is under 3 years old, there's a $4-per-night charge. A two-night minimum is required on weekends from May through December. A three-night minimum is required on holiday weekends.

Hill House, 10701 Palette Dr., Mendocino, CA 95460 (tel. 707/937-0554), is a sprawling, newly constructed Victorian-style guesthouse with 44 rooms, most with private bath, direct-dial phone, and TV. You'll enter an elegant *Town & Country*–style lobby, complete with sweeping staircase and grand fireplace. This would be a perfect place to spend a New England–style Christmas— roaring fire, traditional Christmas decorations, cold, foggy days and nights. As a matter of fact, this is where the "Murder, She Wrote" cast stays when they film the inside and outside of the hotel for use in the show. But bring only kids who promise to be on their best behavior. One gets the feeling that rowdy children would earn disapproving scowls here.

The staff can recommend babysitters with advance notice. Cribs and rollaways are available, and there are some adjoining rooms.

Double rooms range from $65 to $95. There are four suites, and these rent for $135 per night. Children under 12 sleep free in the same room with their parents; those 12 and over are charged $7.50 per night each.

The **Mendocino Hotel and Garden Cottages,** 45080 Main St., Mendocino, CA 95460 (tel. 707/937-0511, or toll free 800/548-0513), is conveniently located. Reflecting the opulence of the 1800s, the restored Temperence House has 24 elegantly decorated rooms. Families usually stay in the newer garden cottages behind the hotel.

Rates begin at $75 for singles or doubles with private baths, and top out at $160. The special suites are $175 to $250. Children under 12 stay free in the same room with their parents; all those 12 and over pay $20 each per night. There's a three-night minimum stay on holidays and a two-night minimum on weekends. Lower rates are available off-season.

WHERE TO EAT: Whether for light or more substantial meals, **The Sea Gull,** at the corner of Lansing and Ukiah Streets (tel. 707/937-2100), is a good choice. The outside deck is open for lunch and is a good place to sit with kids if it's not too hot. The inside tables and booths are cozy and warm on foggy days.

Adult lunch fare includes everything from sandwiches and salads to chili, and from homemade French toast to omelets. Dinner can be anything from cheeseburgers to cioppino, and prices range from $7 to $15. There is a children's menu at dinner that features cheeseburgers, grilled chicken breast, or filet of red snapper, each item at $6. Adult portions can be split for two kids at no charge, and the staff will warm baby bottles or baby food and make special children's drinks like Shirley Temples. Highchairs and boosters are available.

Open daily for breakfast from 8 a.m. to 11:30 a.m.; for lunch, from 11:30 a.m. to 4 p.m.; and for dinner, from 5 to 9 p.m. Sunday brunch is served from 11:30 a.m. to 2 p.m. Reservations are highly recommended for dinner during the summer and on weekends year round. Street parking. No credit cards accepted.

Stop at the **Mendocino Bakery & Café** on Lansing Street (tel. 707/937-0836) for a morning pastry or afternoon snack. You can also get sandwiches and pizza by the slice at lunch. Be sure to treat the kids to a Cowboy Cookie (chocolate chip, walnut, and oats). Open daily from 8 a.m. to 5:30 p.m.

They're lined up out the door on weekends at the **Mendocino Ice Cream Company,** on Main Street (tel. 707/937-5884)—you can't miss it. Some fans say they have the best black-cherry ice cream anywhere. Open daily in summer from 11 a.m. to 10 p.m. on weekends, till 6 p.m. on weekdays; the rest of the year they close at 5 p.m.

The **Main Street Deli,** on Main Street (tel. 707/937-5031), is the perfect spot to pick up sandwiches and drinks to take to the beach. Open weekdays from 8 a.m. to 6 p.m.; on weekends, from 8:30 a.m. to 6 p.m.

MENDOCINO MISCELLANY: Bike rentals are available at **Mendocino Cyclery,** up the brick path behind the Main Street Deli (tel. 707/937-4744). There is only one infant/toddler carrier and a couple of small bikes, so call ahead to reserve. Ten-speeds and cruisers are available. Rental charge begins at $5 per hour. Reservations and credit cards are accepted.

Bébé Lapin, 551 Ukiah St. (tel. 707/937-0261), features gifts and apparel for children. Open daily from 10 a.m. to 5 p.m. **Mendocino Dry Goods,** 45050 Main St. (tel. 707/937-1226), offers local crafts and some children's items, including baby blankets. Open daily from 10:30 a.m. to 5 p.m. **Local Motive,** 45011 Ukiah St. (tel. 707/937-5683), is a "treasury of international crafts," including toys and stuffed animals. Open daily from 10:30 a.m. to 5 p.m. **The Collector,** on Main Street (tel. 707/937-0888), will entice kids with its wonderful selection of shells and rocks at affordable prices. Open daily from 10:30 a.m. to 5 p.m. Try **Sky's No Limit,** 10450 Lansing St. (tel. 707/937-4633), for kites, toys, and Frisbees. Open from 10 a.m. to 5 p.m.; in summer and on weekends, till 7 p.m.

4. FORT BRAGG

The actual fort was built in 1857 by the army to maintain order for the Mendocino County Indian Reservation. The fort was abandoned in 1864, but in 1885 the first sawmill opened, reinstating the town once more. Now Fort Bragg is home to one of the world's largest redwood sawmills, and to the California Western Railroad.

WHAT TO SEE AND DO: The **Skunk Railroad** is known throughout the West. You'll find the depot between Pine Street and Laurel Avenue off Main Street (tel. 707/964-6371). The "Skunk" line was originally a logging railroad in the late 1800s, hauling lumber inland. After steam service was discontinued in 1925, the trains were powered by gas engines, and picked up their classy name from the perfume of the gas fumes. Now the California Western Railroad operates the two passenger trains called Super Skunks, which are powered by historic diesel logging locomotives. Each has open observation cars.

The shorter trip, which stops in Northspur, a former logging town, runs along Pudding Creek and then follows the Noyo River and the ubiquitous redwoods over tracks 100 years old. The longer trip, which stops in Willits (7½ hours round trip) climbs the rolling hills on the way back to Fort Bragg, reaching 1,700 feet at the summit. Kids who love trains will adore this trip. And you'll all get to travel over bridges, through tunnels, and past breathtaking scenery.

"Know thy child" definitely applies here, as the shortest trip you take can seem forever with a toddler who wants "off."

The Super Skunks run daily from the third Saturday in June through the second Saturday in September. Advance reservations are not a bad idea, as these trains get pretty full during tourist season. Arrive a half hour early to secure your reservation.

The price of a round-trip ticket for the full-day run is $22 for adults, $11 for children 5 to 11; under 5, free. Half-day tickets cost $18 for adults, $10 for children 5 to 11; under 5, free. Check schedules, as trains leave at different times in summer and winter. Parking lot.

Noyo Harbor is Fort Bragg's tiny fishing village. Turn off Calif. 1 on to

North Harbor Drive, and you can't miss it. It's a working harbor with charter boats available for fishing or whale watching. **Noyo Fishing Center,** 32450 N. Harbor Dr. (tel. 707/964-7609), gives you a choice of chartering a party boat, fishing (including tackle), or whale-watching. There are full- and half-day arrangements. Call for prices and schedules.

Since small children (and even the bigger ones) can get restless when the family sightsees all day, you might want to take an "energy break." Perfect for toddlers, **Bainbridge Park,** at Laurel and Whipple Streets, is a tiny public park in a residential area of town, not far off Calif. 1 and near the Skunk Railroad. Turn east on Laurel and go about six blocks. It's open to the public during daylight hours, is stroller-accessible, and has two swings, two slides, a neat "climber," and rest room facilities.

Mackerricher State Park is located about three miles north of Fort Bragg. You'll find seven miles of beaches, campgrounds, and Cleone Lake (the only freshwater lake on the north coast). December through April is a good time to spot the California gray whales, which can be viewed from the bluffs. Seals can be seen from the point.

Nearby is **Ricochet Ridge Ranch,** 24201 N. Calif. 1 (tel. 707/964-PONY), which is equipped to accommodate almost any visitor who wants to ride. There are ponies for the younger children, and riders of all skill levels are welcome, including beginners. Rides are professionally guided into Jackson State Forest or over Fort Bragg's Ten Mile Beach. There are treks that include children, like Kids' Overnight Trail Rides ($45) and Teens' Overnight Trail Rides ($45). There is also a children's riding camp in the summer, which accommodates drop-ins (from 9:30 a.m. to 4:30 p.m.). Kids will spend the day on horse care, a trail ride, and riding in the arena. It's advisable to make advance reservations.

For information on festivals and other seasonal events, be sure to contact the **Fort Bragg–Mendocino Coast Chamber of Commerce,** 332 N. Main St., Fort Bragg, CA 95437 (tel. 707/964-3153).

If you've come in the winter and find yourself in the middle of a rainstorm, you have a few options. Bowl a line at the **Noyo Bowl,** 900 N. Main St. (tel. 707/964-4051), or check out the marquee at the **Fort Bragg Coast Theater,** at South Franklin Street and Madrone (tel. 707/964-4540). Nearby Ukiah offers alternatives: **Daddy's Family Entertainment,** 208 S. State St. (tel. 707/462-6749), gets lots of teens for the video games and pool tables. The **Ukiah Library,** 105 N. Main St. (tel. 707/463-4153), offers children's story hours throughout the year. Ask for the Children's Room when you call for details. The **Ukiah Movie Theater,** 612 S. State St. (tel. 707/462-6788), periodically shows matinees of children's movies. Call for the schedule.

WHERE TO STAY: Most of the bed-and-breakfast establishments in Fort Bragg don't accept children under 12. If you have a teenager, be sure to reserve a room at the homey and spacious **Grey Whale Inn,** 615 Main St., Fort Bragg, CA 95437 (tel. 707/964-0640, or toll free 800/382-7244 in California). This lovely redwood mansion was once the local hospital, and was only converted in 1971. It is now maintained with loving care by owners John and Colette Bailey.

Like most bed-and-breakfast establishments, the inn has neither a pool nor TVs in the rooms, but it does have a recreation room with cards, board games, billiards, and television.

The inn features 14 accommodations with private baths. Particularly comfortable and spacious for families are the two rooms with kitchens. If you want a kitchen, be sure to request one when you make your reservation. The Baileys can find you a babysitter if given advance notice. A breakfast buffet (featuring homemade breakfast breads) is included in the room rate.

Rates run $45 to $90 single and $60 to $125 double. Kitchen units cost

$75 to $120. Additional guests sharing a room are charged $10 per night. Children over 12 only. A minimum two- to three-night stay is required during holiday periods and on weekends from April through October.

The conveniently located **Quality Inn Seabird**, 191 South St., Fort Bragg, CA 95437 (tel. 707/964-4731, or toll free 800/228-5151, 800/345-0022 in California), has large, clean rooms. What it may lack in atmosphere is made up for in the attitude of the particularly friendly and helpful staff.

Some rooms have small patios, while others have balconies. Be sure to ask for a room that does *not* face the Burger King, which can get quite noisy at night. There is an indoor pool and whirlpool, and coin-operated laundry facilities for guest use. One pleasant surprise is the complimentary continental breakfast of orange juice and danish. There's instant coffee in each room. Three rooms have kitchenettes, and all have refrigerators. Connecting rooms are available.

The Home Style Café, next door (tel. 707/964-6106), serves breakfast and lunch at extremely reasonable prices. Boosters and highchairs are available. It's open daily, March through October, from 5 a.m. to 2 p.m.; in winter it's closed Monday. Parking lot. Some credit cards accepted.

Rates vary seasonally: $40 to $65 for standard rooms, $65 to $75 for kitchenette units, $95 to $110 for family suites, and $105 to $125 for two-bedroom suites. Kids under 3 sleep free in the same room as their parents; children 3 and over are charged $6 per night. Cribs are $5 per night; rollaways, $7.50.

WHERE TO EAT: The **Wharf Restaurant** is located at 780 N. Harbor Dr., at Noyo Fishing Village (tel. 707/964-4283). For a pleasant view of the fishing harbor, this large and casual restaurant is a perfect choice. Most of the restaurant's fish selections are caught locally.

There is no children's menu at lunch, but there are many sandwiches to choose from. There is an extensive children's menu at dinner, which includes fish, seafood, and even a petite filet mignon. Children's dinner entrees average $7.75.

Adult fare includes fish and seafood, of course, as well as steaks, prime rib, and salads. Complete lunches range from $5.75 to $8; dinners, $12 to $22. Highchairs and boosters are available.

Open daily (including holidays) for lunch from 11 a.m. to 4 p.m., and for dinner from 4 to 10 p.m. (in summer, to 11 p.m.). Reservations accepted. Parking lot. Some major credit cards accepted.

Next door is the very popular and comfortable **Cap'n Flints** (tel. 707/964-9447). Selections here include fish, seafood, hamburgers, salads, and chowder. Although there is no children's menu, management will serve smaller portions at a reduced price. Speaking of prices, they are extremely reasonable: from $2.25 for a hot dog and fries to $9.75 for grilled salmon. Boosters and highchairs are available.

Open daily (except Thanksgiving and Christmas Days) from 11 a.m. to 9:30 p.m. No reservations accepted. A 45-minute wait for dinner is possible during the summer months. For the shortest wait, come before 6:30 p.m. or after 7:30 p.m. Parking lot. No credit cards accepted.

For Sunday brunch, you'll find the **Redwood Cookhouse,** at Redwood and Main Streets (tel. 707/964-1517), a great deal. There is an all-you-can-eat buffet for $4 that includes rolls, biscuits and gravy, French toast, pancakes, eggs, ham, and more.

Dinner buffets include ham and roast beef, red snapper and fried chicken, with all the accompaniments. There are specials on certain evenings. Adults pay $7.50; children are charged 40¢ per year of their age, up to 15. The prices include drinks and dessert. Boosters and highchairs are available.

Sunday brunch is served from 8 a.m. to 1 p.m. Sunday-night dinner features barbecued ribs and begins at 4 p.m. Tuesday through Saturday, dinner is served from 4:30 to 8:30 p.m. The only time there's a real wait is on Friday night, when you may have to be patient for 10 to 15 minutes until there's a table. Reservations accepted for seven or more. Street parking. Major credit cards honored.

CHAPTER VI

MOUNTAIN AREAS AND NATIONAL PARKS

□ □ □

California's famed mountains are family vacations extraordinaire. You'll be amazed how exciting it is to discover nature together. Prepare yourselves for peak experiences—the first time your children see a giant Sequoia; their first view of Yosemite; squeals when they enter an enormous, dark cave; their first meals cooked over an open fire. Imagine the fun of sharing time together on a houseboat, floating down the river on a raft, watching natural bubbling pools rising from the earth. These are treasured memories you create as a family, made even more pleasurable because telephones and televisions don't get in the way.

You'll discover that you remember more about science and nature than you thought. Your senses will be heightened because you are seeing this aspect of the world through young eyes. And when you're in a national park, there are abundant educational opportunities to share. Wherever you turn you'll discover self-guiding trails that describe the terrain and ecology, visitor centers that offer information to hungry minds, and naturalist-led activities for specific interests.

1. FRESNO: GATEWAY TO YOSEMITE AND SEQUOIA–KINGS CANYON

Before we had children, we used to go to Yosemite National Park for weekend excursions. We'd leave Los Angeles at the crack of dawn, making good time through the San Joaquin Valley listening to rock music and suffering through the early-morning radio farm reports. We'd drive right through Fresno and enjoy a leisurely lunch in Wawona before we'd enter the valley. Or we'd stop in one of the small towns along the way and assemble a delectable array of picnic goodies, which we'd enjoy off the road on the way to the park. There were even times when we'd arrive in the valley at dusk and scrounge for a campsite.

We tried to reenact the same experience with our children—after all, having kids wasn't going to change *our* lives! Needless to say, the attempt nearly ruined our entire vacation. Waking two of them up at the crack of dawn was an insane idea—they were exhausted by 10 a.m. but wouldn't nap. They didn't want to stop for a leisurely lunch—they just wanted to get there. A delectable picnic to them meant fast food devoured in the backseat of the car. Between the whining and bickering, trash all over the car, and Mom's bout with car sickness from having to face backward a good portion of the trip, we were lucky to make it at all. (At least we were intelligent enough to have made reservations in the park in advance!)

We learned our lesson. Now we always stop overnight in Fresno, and of course we stop many times along the way (see the "How to Travel with Kids" section in Chapter I). The next morning after breakfast, we leave for Yosemite (the same applies to excursions to Sequoia or Kings Canyon) full of energy, looking forward to a whole day in the park.

(Those of you coming from San Francisco might want to plan to leave early, make lots of stops, perhaps have a picnic, and make it to the park in one day.)

ORIENTATION: Fresno, the San Joaquin Valley city of almost 300,000, is the gateway to Yosemite National Park and Kings Canyon and Sequoia National Parks.

Located just off Calif. 99, and serviced by Fresno Air Terminal, Fresno offers a surprising variety of accommodations and activities for families. If you contact the **Fresno Visitors Bureau,** located at 690 M St. (tel. 209/233-0836, or toll free 800/543-8488), they'll be glad to answer any questions you might have.

GETTING AROUND: Fresno sprawls, so it's a good idea to get a map of the area. **Blackstone Avenue** (Calif. 41) is the main road leading to Yosemite. **Calif. 180** is the road to Sequoia and Kings Canyon. The numerous hotels in the area make it especially convenient for you to stay overnight before leaving for one of the parks. Some families even make Fresno their base in the summer and take day trips to Yosemite, about two hours away.

Children's activities are found throughout the city, with the prime attraction, Roeding Park, located near Calif. 99 (along with many motels). North Fresno, a newer section of town, is where you'll find shopping malls and many good accommodations.

WHAT TO DO AND SEE: Bordered by Olive and Belmont Avenues, **Roeding Park** (tel. 209/488-1551) is a large tree-filled area with activities for the whole family. It boasts the Fresno Zoo, Storyland, Playland, Lake Washington (where you can rent small boats), fishing ponds, and wide-open spaces wonderful for running or Frisbee throwing. **Fresno Zoo** (tel. 209/488-1549), with its 1,000 animals and large aviary, is open daily from 10 a.m. to 5 p.m. (Don't miss the nursery's newborn animals.) Admission is $3 for adults, $1.25 for children 4 to 14; under-4s, free. **Playland** (tel. 209/486-2124) is an irresistible treat for the under-7 set. They will squeal with delight on the tiny roller coaster, and have as much fun on the pint-sized Ferris wheel as most teenagers do on giant thrill rides. Open from 10 a.m. to 7:30 p.m. daily in summer, on weekends and holidays the rest of the year. Rides are only 20¢. Go to **Storyland** (tel. 209/264-2235) next, where the fairytale characters will come alive for the kids as they visit each of the make-believe homes. There are children's plays, puppet shows, and other events in this tiny land of enchantment. Open daily from 10 a.m. to 5 p.m. May through mid-September, on weekends and holidays the rest of the year; closed December and January. Admission is 75¢.

Blackbeard's Family Fun Center, located at 4055 N. Chestnut, between Dakota and Ashlan (tel. 209/292-4554, or 209/292-9000 for a recorded announcement), is another place that will delight all members of the family—regardless of age. It has six water slides, three 18-hole miniature golf courses (each with a different theme), a video arcade, mini racing cars, a batting range, baby bumper boats, snacks, and a picnic/barbecue area. Fees for the attractions vary. Open daily from 10 a.m. to 11 p.m. (till 1 a.m. on weekends). Teens are particularly enchanted with **Blackbeard's Lighthouse Dance Party,** a dance "club" that serves non-alcoholic drinks, and treats 16- to 20-year-olds to a night out on the town. Open on Friday and Saturday from 9 p.m. to 1 a.m.

The **Discovery Center,** 1944 N. Winery Ave. (tel. 209/251-5533, or 209/251-5531 for a recorded announcement), is billed as *the* science center for the central San Joaquin Valley. Interactive exhibits and hands-on participation make this place delightful for 7-year-olds and seniors alike. Open all year: Tuesday through Friday from noon to 5 p.m. and on Saturday and Sunday from 11 a.m. to 5 p.m.; closed Monday. Friday-evening Star Parties (appropriate for children 7 and older) run from dusk to 10 p.m. Admission is $1.50 for adults, $1 for children 5 to 12 and seniors, 50¢ for children 3 and 4; children under 3, free.

Fresno Metropolitan Museum of Art, History, and Science, 1515 Van Ness Ave. (tel. 209/441-1444), is an important cultural center in Fresno. The "Met," as it's affectionately known, is a fun place to explore. If you're here during the Christmas season, don't miss the spectacular Christmas tree exhibits. Open Tuesday through Friday from 11 a.m. to 5 p.m. and on Saturday and Sunday from noon to 5 p.m. Admission is $2 for adults, $1 for seniors and students, 75¢ for children 3 to 12; kids under 3, free.

. . . and More

Whispering Waters Fishing Lake, 17601 E. Kings Canyon (tel. 209/787-2625), is just outside Fresno on the way to Sequoia–Kings Canyon. This fishing hole is a great family outing and picnicking spot. No licenses are required, and you can rent everything you need to catch "the big one" right there. Open on Saturday and Sunday from 9 a.m. to 6 p.m. Admission is $1.

If you're going to make a day of it, you might try swimming or tubing on the Kings River. **Scott's Canoe Rental,** 17439 E. Kings Canyon, Sanger (tel. 209/787-3450), is a place to rent inner tubes, or begin your trip down the river.

Another way to spend an afternoon is at neighboring **Clovis Lakes Water Park,** 11413 E. Shaw Ave. (tel. 209/299-7824). Kids can rent boogie boards and inner tubes to ride the "Blue Wave," simulated waves for surfing, to experience the thrill of the ocean in this land-locked city. The Children's Activity Area has four small water slides and two small pools. Lifeguards are on duty. Open daily during the summer from 10 a.m. to 10 p.m.; the rest of the year, on weekends from 10 a.m. to dusk. An all-day ticket costs $11, $6 after 5 p.m.; children under 2, free. *Caution:* Water parks require special attention to the kids.

Willow Gardens Nursery and Petting Zoo, 10428 N. Willow Ave., Clovis (tel. 209/299-5402), is a treat for the toddlers in the group. Little Elizabeth got to meet and pet her first goat, sheep, and burro here. Open Monday through Saturday from 8 a.m. to 5 p.m. and on Sunday from 10 a.m. to 5 p.m. No admission fee.

Indoor Activities

Although the weather is usually warm here, valley fog or rain can cut short outdoor excursions. But take heart. You might try the **Fresno Children's Playhouse,** located at 2425 Fresno St. (tel. 209/237-9734), which produces such plays as *Charlotte's Web, Rumpelstiltskin,* and *Robin Hood.* Or visit Fresno's indoor ice-skating rink, **Icelandia,** 2455 N. Marks Ave. (tel. 209/275-1118), open Tuesday through Sunday from 1:30 to 4 p.m., plus on Wednesday, Thursday, and Sunday from 7:30 to 9:30 p.m. Admission is $3.50 for adults, $2.50 for children, plus $1 for skate rentals.

Agricultural Tours and Fruit Picking

The San Joaquin Valley is a world supplier of agricultural products. You'll notice vineyards and orchards throughout the area. Care to partake a little more actively? From April through August you can pick Thompson grapes, strawberries, and melons at **Sam Ando's Farm,** 2501 10th St., in nearby Kingsburg (tel. 209/897-3472). Call before going.

In October, eager ghosts and goblins can choose their own pumpkins and even go for a hayride at **Pumpkin Valley,** 11868 Old Friant Rd. (tel. 209/435-8272), open Monday through Friday from 3 to 6 p.m. and on Saturday and Sunday from 10 a.m. to 7 p.m.

At **Bar 20 Dairy Farm,** 144 E. Belmont Ave., in Fresno (tel. 209/264-6583), kids can see where milk *really* comes from. At **Harris Farms,** I-5 and Calif. 198 in nearby Coalinga (tel. 209/935-0717, ext. 626), you can tour the farm and its 100,000 head of cattle. Here, 18,000 acres are planted with cotton, cantaloupe, tomatoes, lettuce, and a variety of other crops.

For a different kind of taste treat, tour the **Hershey Chocolate Factory,** at 1400 Yosemite Ave. in Oakdale (tel. 209/847-0381), 1½ hours from Fresno. As your mouth waters and your tastebuds come alive, you'll watch the making and packaging of chocolate. If you're patient you'll get a taste at the end of the tour. Tours last a half hour and are given Monday through Friday from 8:15 a.m. to 3 p.m. The whole family is welcome and the tour is mostly stroller-accessible. No reservations are necessary, and no admission fee is charged.

WHERE TO STAY: The Best-Bet-for-the-Money is the **Hill House Vagabond Inn,** located at 1101 N. Parkway Dr., Fresno, CA 93728 (tel. 209/268-6211, or toll free 800/522-1555), just off Calif. 99 and near Roeding Park. Managers Bob and Pam Wallis take great pride in this motel and it shows, making this a great place to stay, and an especially good value. A spacious pool area is attractive for kids, and there's a small play area with swings and a slide. Plenty of parking adjacent to rooms.

Complimentary continental breakfast. Small refrigerators are available ($7 per night). There's no restaurant on the premises, but a 24-hour Denny's Restaurant, which is inexpensive to moderately priced, is next door.

Rooms here are nice sized, clean, and bright. No-smoking rooms are available. Standard doubles range in price from $36 to $44, but the best bets are the family suites (there are only three available, so request them well in advance). The largest, for $62, is a two-room unit with three queen-size beds—and there's still room for a crib or rollaway. The smaller units cost $56 and $45. There is no charge for cribs and rollaways, and kids sleep for free in their parents' room. Extra adults pay $6 per night.

Our recommendation for a first-class all-suite hotel is the **Piccadilly Inn Hotel,** 2305 W. Shaw Ave., Fresno, CA 93711 (tel. 209/226-3850, or toll free 800/468-3587, 800/468-3522 in California), in North Fresno. There are three of these four-star Piccadilly suite hotels in Fresno, but most families come to this location. This elegant European-style resort hotel has a beautiful fenced-in pool and spa area, with beverage service, and plenty of grassy areas where kids can play. The resort is spread out on 7½ acres and has 200 elegantly furnished rooms—some even have working fireplaces. Room service delivers from 6 a.m. to 10 p.m., and fresh-perked coffee is available in each room.

Oliver's Restaurant, off the lobby bar, will strike you as formal, yet it caters to children as well as adults for breakfast, lunch, and dinner. Although there is no children's menu, the staff will improvise, and they will warm baby bottles and split orders. The outside patio is not only pleasant for dining, it is perhaps more comfortable for those with a wandering child. Meal prices range from moderate to expensive.

Choose from large doubles, mini-suites, mini-suites with parlor, or full suites. Rates range from $68 to $81 for rooms and $150 to $210 for suites. Children under 12 stay free in their parents' room, and cribs will be provided at no charge. Children 12 and over are charged $8 per night each.

Another first-class hotel conveniently located on the road to Yosemite is the **Sheraton Smuggler's Inn**, 3737 N. Blackstone Ave. (at Dakota), Fresno, CA 93726 (tel. 209/226-2200, or toll free 800/321-0920, 800/742-1911 in California). The pool area at this four-star resort-like hotel will make you want to stay longer. Large and fenced in, it has a Jacuzzi that is high and out of the way of little explorers.

The rooms here are comfortable, bright, and clean. All have queen- or king-size beds, and some have sofas. No-smoking rooms and adjoining rooms are available. There are refrigerators in each of the four suites, and drip coffee makers in every room. All rooms come equipped with hairdryers and an extra telephone in the bathroom. Room service is available from 7 a.m. to 10 p.m. daily, and you can make arrangements at the front desk for box lunches to take to Yosemite.

Rates are $64 single and $70 double. Children under 17 stay free in their parents' room; additional guests 17 and over pay $3 per night. Cribs are free, but rollaways cost $6.

The **Village Inn Best Western** is also on the road to Yosemite at 3110 N. Blackstone Ave., Fresno, CA 93703 (tel. 209/226-2110, or toll free 800/742-1911). This hotel has a small gated pool area and a reasonably priced chain restaurant, Denny's, next door. Each of the 154 large rooms has two queen-size beds, and no-smoking rooms are available. Unfortunately, there are no suites or adjoining rooms. Continental breakfast is served in the room, as well as fresh-brewed coffee.

Singles cost $40 to $44 and doubles are $44 to $48. Children under 12 stay free in their parents' room; additional guests are charged $2 to $4 per night each. Cribs are available for a $6 charge; rollaways cost $10.

Another alternative is the **San Joaquin,** located at 1309 W. Shaw Ave., Fresno, CA 93711 (tel. 209/225-1309), North Fresno's other all-suite hotel. Although the steel-gray furnishings and the quiet atmosphere convey a luxurious adult hotel environment, many families stay here, especially in the summer. The pool and Jacuzzi are open 24 hours. There are one-, two-, and three-bedroom suites, each with a living room, some with a full kitchen. Although there is no room service, the front-desk clerk is quite resourceful and can get anything you need.

Room prices include complimentary continental breakfast and complimentary wine and hor d'oeuvres in the evening. Rates run from $56 for a one-bedroom unit (there's room for a crib in the bedroom or living room) to $135 for the three-bedroom suites. But add on the extras: the sleeper sofa costs $10 if used, and cribs and rollaways are $10 per night.

Budget priced and adequate for an overnight stay is the **Best Western Parkside Inn**, at 1415 W. Olive Ave., Fresno, CA 93728 (tel. 209/237-2086, or toll free 800/442-2284). Rooms are large but dark, and some adjoining rooms are available. There are no refrigerators. No-smoking rooms can be requested. There is a heated pool and children's wading pool. The nearby coffeeshop, Tiny's, allows you to charge meals to your room. Prices are moderate.

Singles run $37 to $42; doubles, $42 to $50. Children over 12 and additional adult guests are charged $4 per night. Cribs are free but rollaways cost $6 per night.

WHERE TO EAT: A regular stop for us is the **Iron Horse Restaurant,** at 4944 Blackstone Ave. (tel. 209/222-4252), on the way to Yosemite. We like the food, but even if we didn't, our kids would insist on a stop there to get their fill of train whistles and clanging bells. It's designed like an old-fashioned train depot, complete with ticket booth and waiting room. Small electric trains perched high on small shelves chug through the restaurant commanding attention from children and grown ups alike. When Junior's order is taken and ready, the train whistle blows, a bell clangs, and waiters yell "All aboard." With all that going on, not even the crankiest kid will embarrass you because few others will hear him.

These fun, casual coffeeshops have an extensive and marvelous menu for those 10 and under. Our breakfast favorites are the Casey Jones (pancakes plus an egg and bacon for $2.75) and the Puffing Billy (a two-egg Spanish omelet with hash browns and a biscuit for $3). At lunch there are great burgers and sandwiches. Adult fare is reasonably priced too.

All locations have highchairs and boosters. They don't take reservations, so at prime times you may have a wait of approximately 15 minutes. Other branches are located at 1820 N. First (tel. 209/233-6443) and 4244 E. Kings Canyon, on the way to Kings Canyon (tel. 209/251-2323). All locations are open daily from 6 a.m. to 2 p.m. Each restaurant has a parking lot. Credit cards are accepted.

If you don't feel like eating at the rather sophisticated Oliver's at the Piccadilly Inn, there is a nice coffeeshop across the street, **Knock Three Times,** 2257 W. Shaw Ave. (tel. 209/222-5481). The children's menu features everything from peanut butter and jelly sandwiches ($2.75) to filet of sole with tartar sauce and soup or salad ($4). In the dining room, kids under 3 eat free at the Prime Rib Buffet. There's also a salad, dessert, and soup bar. The Breakfast Bar features morning goodies (all you can eat for $5) and dessert. They have booster seats and highchairs, and will warm bottles or baby food. Convenient parking lot. Open daily from 6 a.m. to 9:30 p.m. in the coffeeshop, from 11 a.m. to 9 p.m. in the dining room. All major credit cards accepted.

The **Old Spaghetti Factory,** at Ventura Avenue and R Street in downtown Fresno (tel. 209/442-1066), is traditionally a fun place. Kids love the child's spaghetti plate for $2.75, and the adult meals are equally inexpensive. Dinners (which include salad, dessert, and beverage) range from $3.50 (spaghetti with tomato sauce) to $6.50 (slices of tenderloin with a side of spaghetti). Boosters and highchairs are available.

Open for dinner only, Monday through Thursday from 5 to 9:30 p.m., on Friday and Saturday until 10:30 p.m., and on Sunday from 4 to 9:30 p.m. No reservations, and the average wait on weekends is 15 minutes. No credit cards accepted.

Wiliker's Bar and Grill, 1713 E. Shaw Ave. (tel. 209/226-1984), is a local favorite of families. And no wonder. Very few places have a kid's menu a full page long (all food items are $2.25 and include fries or fruit and milk or soda) and a beverage and dessert list. A 4-year-old might fall for the chicken nuggets, but there are other standbys, such as peanut butter and jelly, burgers, grilled cheese, and French toast. The real treat, though, is the beverage menu! Kids may have trouble deciding between the Shirley Temple and the child's daiquiri (not that many will know what a daiquiri is—it just sounds good!). Other choices include a grapeberry slush and a pint-sized piña colada. A child with a real sweet tooth will love the chocolate mint surprise ("a peppermint patty in a glass"), flavored Cokes, and smoothies.

The adult menu is extensive also. Dinners include fresh bread, soup or salad, and coffee or cordial of homemade Irish cream. Choose from fish (average dinner is $11), steak ($12.50), chicken ($7.50), salads, pasta, Mexican food, and sandwiches. The adult bar menu is also unusual.

Highchairs and boosters are available. Open Monday through Saturday from 11:30 a.m. to 1 a.m. and on Sunday from 9 a.m. to 1 a.m. Parking lot. All major credit cards accepted.

Picnics

Some people make day trips to the national parks. To meet that need, the following places will pack picnics for you. (Also check with your hotel; many provide the service—if you give one or two days' notice.) Try the **Greenhouse Restaurant**, 1440 E. Shaw Ave. (tel. 209/225-1041); **Grape Tray**, 5091 N. Fresno Ave., in Fresno Shaw Plaza (tel. 209/226-6828); and **Moveable Feast**, 736 W. Bullard (tel. 209/439-3777).

BOOKS AND TOYS: We love to browse in children's bookstores—and the kids enjoy the diversion. We can recommend two in the Fresno area: **Pegasus Books for Young People**, in the Mission Village Shopping Center at the southwest corner of Fresno and Shaw Avenues (tel. 209/221-8524); and **Story Time**, 1440 N. Van Ness Ave. (tel. 209/237-5481).

You may also want to stop at **Arthur's Toy Shop**, 5215 N. Blackstone Ave. (tel. 209/431-0101), or **Mother Bear's Toy Emporium**, 6021 N. Palm Ave. (tel. 209/438-6300).

IN CASE OF EMERGENCY: If you're in need of an emergency room, contact the **St. Agnes Medical Center**, 1303 E. Herndon Ave., at the corner of Millbrook Avenue (tel. 209/449-3205); **Fresno Community Hospital and Medical Center**, located on Divisadero between Fresno and R Streets (tel. 209/442-3998); or **Clovis Community Hospital**, 2755 Herndon Ave. (tel. 209/298-8041).

ACTIVITIES BY AGE GROUP: The following listings suggest activities divided into specific age brackets. Refer back to the individual descriptions for details and any age restrictions.

Teens and Preteens

Agricultural Tours and Fruit Picking
Blackbeard's Fun Center
Blackbeard's Lighthouse Dance Party
Canoe Rentals
Clovis Lakes Water Park
Discovery Center
Fresno Metropolitan Museum of Art
Icelandia

School-age Children

Agricultural Tours and Fruit Picking
Canoe Rentals
Clovis Lakes
Discovery Center
Fresno Children's Playhouse
Fresno Metropolitan Museum of Art
Icelandia
Pumpkin Valley Hayride
Roeding Park (and Zoo, Storyland, Playland)
Whispering Waters Fishing Lake

Preschoolers and Toddlers

Clovis Lakes (children's activity area)
Fresno Children's Playhouse

Pumpkin Valley
Roeding Park (and Zoo, Storyland, Playland)
Willow Gardens Nursery and Petting Zoo

2. YOSEMITE NATIONAL PARK

If you have but one national park to visit with your children, it should be Yosemite. Everyone has heard stories about the crowds of people and about traffic problems in the valley (which is true only in summer, anyway), but all of that fades when you enter the park and behold the first grand vista. This is as close to natural perfection as you're ever going to get.

Known for thundering waterfalls and glacier-carved cliffs rising from the valley floor, Yosemite is also meandering rivers, magnificent meadows, spectacular wildflowers, and abundant wildlife. No matter how much you hear about the park before you go, your expectations will not be too high.

Most people think of Yosemite as a summer vacation spot. But off-season it's a gem. Many of the activities are still open, and there are fewer people to contend with. In spring after the snow starts to melt, the waterfalls are full. The change of color in fall is breathtaking. Skiing at Badger Pass and snow play throughout the area is fun for all family members during the winter months.

Yosemite, in addition to being a paradise of wild terrain, is a family vacation paradise of hiking, rafting, swimming, picnicking, skiing, and ice skating. (See the "How to Travel with Kids" section in Chapter 1 for specific information about preparing your family for an outdoor vacation.)

GETTING THERE: Four scenic driving routes take you into the park. And while most people don't think of it, you can also get there by public transportation via air, train, or bus.

Public Transportation

By air, fly into Fresno Air Terminal, then take a Greyhound bus or rent a car. **By train** from Los Angeles, you first take a bus to Bakersfield, then the train to Merced and a bus to Yosemite. Amtrak (tel. toll free 800/USA-RAIL, 800/872-7245 in California) can arrange the whole package. Amtrak services San Francisco via Oakland by train to Merced.

California Parlor Car Tours (tel. 213/381-3925 in Los Angeles, 415/474-7500 in San Francisco, or toll free 800/227-4250 elsewhere in California) offers two- and three-day excursions from Los Angeles or San Francisco, daily May through October. Fares include lodging. Rates from Los Angeles range from $292 to $338 for adults, $135 to $181 from San Francisco. Kids 5 to 18 are charged half fare; under-5s, free.

By Car

From San Francisco (via Merced), take Calif. 140. From Sacramento (via Manteca, near Stockton), take Calif. 120. From Los Angeles (via Fresno), take Calif. 41. From the east—Reno, Lake Tahoe, Bishop—take U.S. 395 to Calif. 120E, also known as Tioga Pass Road. It's a beautiful drive—the highest mountain pass in the Sierras, but open summers only. Check road conditions with the California Highway Patrol if you're concerned about rain, snow, or road closures, or call 209/372-4605.

The entrance permit costs only $5 per car. If you plan to stay longer than seven days—or combine this trip with visits to Sequoia–Kings Canyon National Parks and Lassen National Park—it might be worth your while to purchase an annual **Golden Eagle Passport:** for $25 you get free entrance to all national parks that charge fees. Or you might want to buy an annual **Yosemite Passport** for $15, which allows you to enter and leave the park at will for the whole year your permit is valid. As you enter the park, you'll be given a copy of *Yosemite Guide*, a free newsletter describing the week's activities.

An Attraction and a Restaurant En Route

If you take Calif. 41, you'll come to a great little stop before you enter the park proper. **Yosemite Mountain–Sugar Pine Railroad,** just four miles before you reach Yosemite Basin (tel. 209/683-7273), is an authentic logger steam train that takes you back in history as you ride through magnificent scenery. Kids love the popular open-air Jenny railcars, quaint "Model A"–powered trains. The giftshop is a mecca for children (and adults) who love train paraphernalia. You'll find a snackbar and clean rest rooms.

The Logger Steam Train operates daily in July and August, and on weekends May through June and September through October; fares are $7 for adults, $3.75 for children 3 to 7. The Jenny railcars operate daily from mid-April to mid-October; fares are $5 for adults, $2.75 for children 3 to 7. Call for hours as they change seasonally.

Next door to the Sugar Pine (you'll have to get back on the highway) is a charming restaurant, particularly nice for breakfast. The **Elkhorn Cookhouse,** in the Narrow Gauge Inn, 48571 Calif. 41, Fish Camp (tel. 209/683-6446), affords a splendid view of the High Sierra. The dining room is an eclectic mix of early-19th-century Victorian and western décor. The food is fresh and the portions abundant. Breakfasts include pancakes, eggs, French toast or waffles, and yummy home-baked biscuits. Prices are reasonable—$3.25 to $7.25 for full breakfasts. Dinner selections aren't quite as varied for young children. Regular entrees such as medallions of beef or scallops au champagne are available in half portions at a 25% discount. But there is Swiss fondue ($11.50 for two), which might entice the kids, and large hamburgers. There is no "extra plate" charge for small children, so you could split your dinner.

Open daily for breakfast from 7:30 to 10:30 a.m.; then closed until dinner, served daily from 5:30 to 9 p.m. (reservations essential). Brunch is offered on Sunday from 7:30 a.m. to 1 p.m. The restaurant is open Easter through October 31, and for Thanksgiving and Christmas. Highchairs and boosters are available. Parking lot. Major credit cards are accepted.

ORIENTATION: Yosemite National Park, on the western slope of the Sierra Nevada range in the central part of the state, attracts more than three million visitors each year, many from abroad. There are 750 miles of trails and 360 miles of primary roads to make the park accessible.

Yosemite Valley is the area that comes to most people's minds when they think of Yosemite. Within this area are Bridalveil Falls, Yosemite Falls, exquisite views of El Capitan and Half Dome, Mirror Lake, beautiful meadows, and the Merced River. There are numerous trails and self-guided walks.

Yosemite Village includes the Village Center store, the Ansel Adams Photography Gallery, the Visitor Center, a small giftshop, and a theater for evening programs, as well as Degnan's Deli and the Loft Restaurant.

Although the valley is the hub of activities, there are many other areas of the park to visit, including Wawona, Tuolumne Meadows, and Tioga Pass, plus Glacier Point and Badger Pass.

Remember: Don't feed the wild animals, no matter how cute and tame they appear. Not only will they suffer in winter when there's no one to feed them, but you never know just how tame an animal is—after all, these are *wild* animals.

Getting Around the Valley

Once you've arrived in the valley, there's no need to drive. A free **shuttle bus** (complete with overhead windows so you are never far from the sight of the

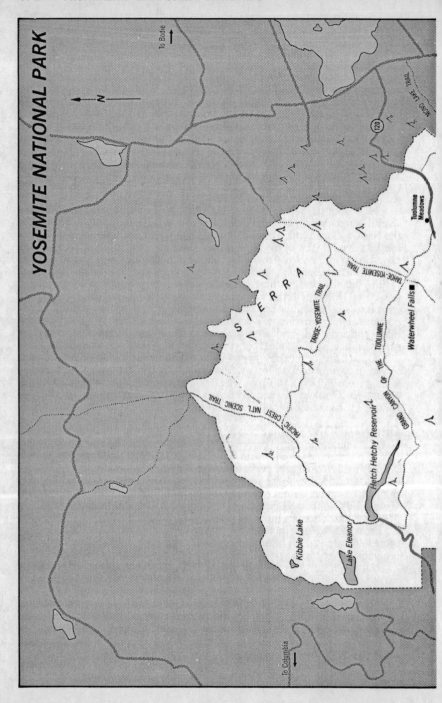

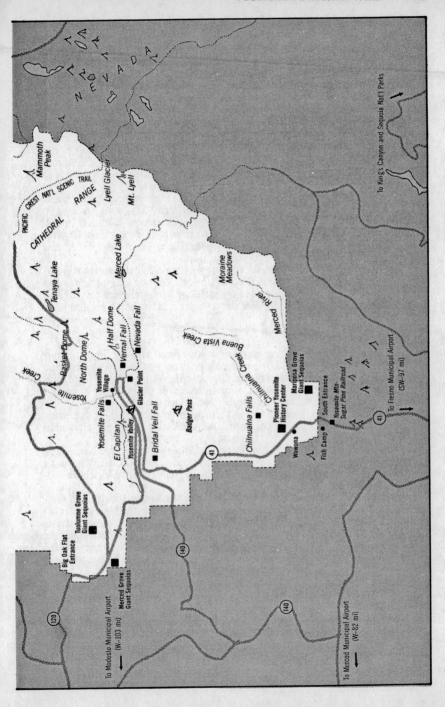

towering mountains) will take you to any of the hotels, and most of the major trailheads and other valley attractions. Shuttle bus hours are 8 a.m. to 9 p.m., longer in summer.

Bus tours also operate every day. There is a two-hour guided tour of the valley, a four-hour tour of Glacier Point, a half-day guided tour of the Mariposa Grove of Big Trees, a full-day Grand Tour, and a two-hour Moonlight Tour. Some of these tours are seasonal. Fees start at $11. For information and tickets, contact the Tour/Activities desks at Yosemite Lodge, The Ahwahnee, Curry Village, and the booth next to the Village Store, or call 209/372-1240.

WHAT TO DO AND HOW TO DO IT IN YOSEMITE VALLEY: Sometimes the beauty and size of the park overwhelm visitors and they don't know where to begin. Although the park is the size of Rhode Island, 80% of the visitors don't venture out of the seven square miles of Yosemite Valley. Here's the way to get around that:

When you receive the *Yosemite Guide* at the park entrance, keep it and read it. It gives the lowdown on all that's going on in the area and is your first step in planning what you want to do during your stay. After you've settled in and browsed through the *Guide,* you might want to go to one of the Visitor Centers (located in Yosemite Village, Mariposa Grove, Glacier Point, and Tuolumne Meadows). They have a lot of specific information.

Ask the park rangers for suggestions. Just tell them what you want to do and the ages of your children, and they'll come up with loads of ideas. They're also great about giving you the skill level of the various hiking trails and current trail and weather conditions. The people at the tour desks in the hotels are also helpful.

Valley Hiking

The key to enjoyable hiking is to know your limits and the limits of your children, and to come prepared. Many an enjoyable day has been spoiled because of blistered feet and too much walking. Check at the Visitor Center for details about your hike. Layer your clothes, wear comfortable shoes, bring water and sunscreen (and hats for the little ones), and don't push too hard.

In addition to the many trails you can hike yourselves, there are many ranger-guided walking tours throughout Yosemite Valley. These are detailed in the *Yosemite Guide.*

In general, all the hikes in the valley are good for children. If you have a little one with you who is likely to insist on being carried ten minutes after you start a hike, you'll be glad to know about the lead-and-ride ponies (see "Horseback Riding" for details).

Don't miss the self-guiding tour of the **Yosemite Indian Village and Garden** located just behind the Visitor Center. This short, easy stroll was perfect for our toddler's first hiking adventure and introduced the rest of us to the Yosemite Miwok Indians. Signs and displays show you how the Native Americans used the natural environment to create homes and food. Kids can walk into the wooden tepees. During the summer, Native Americans demonstrate basket-weaving, cooking techniques, and ceremonial functions—children love it.

Lower Yosemite Fall is also a great walk with young ones. Only half a mile long, it's easy and beautiful, and it gives the kids the feeling they are actually hiking.

Mirror Lake is approximately a two-hour walk that starts at the Mirror Lake shuttle-bus stop. You might want to check with the rangers if you're in the park during the summer. The lake is in the process of becoming a meadow. As the water evaporates in summer, Mirror Lake becomes Mirror Meadows. It's easy walking.

Bridalveil Fall is reached from the Bridalveil Fall parking area. It, too, is an easy half-mile walk. Even if you don't intend to hike, visit the parking lot anyway. It's an experience to look straight up and see the water rushing (or trickling, if it's summer) down the side of this enormous mountain.

Happy Isles Family Nature Center is the trailhead for many of the park's popular hikes. You can get there by shuttle bus during the busy months of May through October. The center is especially suited for families with young children. Special programs for kids even as young as 5 are ongoing from mid-June to Labor Day. There are puppet shows, wildlife programs, and a diorama. Different movies are presented for all ages, but with the tots in mind. This is also a great starting point for a hike to Vernal Falls.

The **Mist Trail** is a beautiful hike that will take you to Vernal Falls and Nevada Falls. It's a leisurely half-day hike, but is *not* for the under-8 set. Parents should use caution with children of any age as there are slippery areas. It's well worth the trip with good hikers.

For more trails, check with the rangers at the Visitor Center. They'll tell you how steep a trail becomes and the average length of time it takes to hike it with children.

Horseback Riding

Yosemite has the largest public riding stable in the world. There are 400 head of stock—all of which carry riders. Stables are located in **Yosemite Valley** near Curry Village (open Easter to mid-October), in **Tuolumne Meadows,** at **Wawona,** and at **White Wolf** (open in summer only). All horseback riding (other than lead ponies and burros) is by guided tour.

Older children (7 to 12) will love the guided Burro Picnics (only available in the valley), Monday through Friday from 9:30 a.m. to 3:30 p.m. during summer. The destination is Sentinel Beach. Send along lunches, bathing suits, towels, and anything else your kids might need for a good time. Be sure to include drinks, and put lots of sunscreen on your children before they leave. Pack mules will carry all the belongings. When they arrive at the beach, there is swimming and games. No previous riding experience is necessary, and the burros go slowly. Make reservations (see below) at least a day in advance. The cost is $25 per person.

Lead-and-ride ponies and burros are available for children who weigh less than 100 pounds. Children can enjoy the gentle ride as adults lead them on trails. Availability is on a first-come, first-served basis. In summer there could be a waiting list. Cost is $7 per hour.

For older children and adults, there are two-hour ($20), half-day ($27), and all-day ($45) guided rides to such places as Yosemite Falls, Nevada Falls, even Glacier Point. Make reservations in advance. If you're planning a summer trip, write for your horseback riding-trip reservations ahead of time. Write the stables, c/o Yosemite Park and Curry Co., 5410 E. Home Ave., Fresno, CA 93727.

Yosemite Stables also has four- and six-day saddle trips to the High Sierra. The camps, located about eight miles apart, are equipped with tents and beds and serve breakfast and dinner. Minimum age is 7, children under 12 must have previous riding experience, and children under 18 must be accompanied by an adult. For information, call the High Sierra Reservations Desk (tel. 209/252-3013), or write Yosemite reservations at the address above.

Bicycling

Bicycling is an increasingly popular way to see the area, and a fun way to do it with the children. (Child carriers and helmets are available.) When you bicycle in Yosemite, stay on paved bikeways, shuttle-bus routes, and one-way roads. Bicycles are not allowed on trails or in the meadows. If you're unsure of the area, ask at the bicycle-rental areas located at Yosemite Lodge Bike Stand and Curry Village Bike Stand. Rental hours vary according to season and weather.

If you're bike riding in the fall or during cooler weather, bring mittens for yourself and the kids. The weather can be brisk and uncomfortable for a little kid with exposed hands sitting in the carrier.

Water Sports

Swimming: The hotels have swimming pools for their guests. In addition, the Merced and Tuolumne Rivers, as well as Tenaya Lake (especially in the warm, shallow areas near the shore), are good places to cool down on hot summer days. Usually swimming is good near the campgrounds, but check it out to be sure that you've chosen a safe place. During spring and early summer, rivers and streams run quickly and the temperatures are low, sometimes too low for safety (and certainly for pleasure). One good check is to ask at Curry Village raft rentals. They will only rent river rafts if the water is low enough and warm enough to be safe. If they are renting rafts you can assume it's safe to go swimming; if they're not, don't try it.

One suggested summer outing is to go up to Tuolumne River, bring a picnic, and go on to Tuolumne Meadows Lodge. From there the river is easy to follow. Walk down the river to the shallow pools where the sun warms the granite, making swimming very pleasant.

River Rafting: During June and July there is great rafting on the Merced River. You can rent rafts at Curry Village. All children must wear life jackets. While it's not for the tiniest children, it's safe for kids over 4. The recommended age is 6 and older. Don't expect white-water rafting. This is more like a gentle float down the river.

Fishing: Although fishing in the valley isn't the best—those fish are hard to catch—there are good pools up and down the Merced that offer little spots for kids to try for rainbow, brook, and golden trout. The best place is in the high country in out-of-the-way streams. You'll have to bring your own equipment, though, since there are no rentals in the park. Adults—and kids over 16—need licenses (available at the Mountaineering School in Curry Village or at the Sports Shop in Yosemite Village).

Tubing: If you bring your own inner tubes, the Merced River offers terrific tubing.

Winter Sports

This is a great place for winter sports. There is an outdoor **ice-skating rink** at Camp Curry that is open morning and night and features a warming hut, fire pit, and snackbar. Admission costs $4 for adults, $2.50 for children; skates may be rented for $1.25. It's open mid-November through March, depending on conditions.

Did you know that **Badger Pass Ski Area** (tel. 209/454-2000) is the oldest established ski area in California? Many of us don't think of Yosemite as a winter retreat, but this ski area is particularly good for families. Badger Pass offers cross-country and downhill skiing, and they have family ski packages. Nordic and downhill ski schools teach you and the kids (the little ones have downhill school only; cross-country lessons are for those 7 and older). Skis can be rented right there. Best of all, there is the **Badger Pass Children's Ski Programs.** Pre-ski school (ages 3 through 6) is $6 per hour and includes learning games and snow fun. Rentals—at $4 per day—include skis, boots, and poles. Children 7 and older take lessons according to ability.

For those of you whose children either don't want to ski or who tire easily in the cold outdoors, the **Badger Pass Babysitting Service** ($2.50 per hour) will sit for your 3- to 9-year-olds. Games and activities are provided in this group-care facility.

If you're able to take off during the middle of the week, be sure to call Badger Pass and ask about the Midweek Ski Package, which includes lift tickets, lessons, babysitting, and recreational and social activities in one price. (The room charge is not included in the package.)

If you're not the sports type—or if your family has had enough of the active life for a while—why not take a **Snowcat Tour**? This one-hour tour from Badger Pass ($5.50 per person) takes you through the winter wonderland and offers spectacular views of the High Sierra. Or you might try a two-hour **guided sightseeing tour** that explores the valley's awesome sights. Depending on weather conditions, tours to the Mariposa Grove of Big Trees may also be available. The Valley Floor Tour costs $10; the Mariposa Tour, $20; the Glacier Point Tour (available June to Thanksgiving), $16.50; and the Grand Tour (available June to Thanksgiving) is $25.75. You can check with the Tours/Activity desk at your hotel, or call the Winter Hotline—209/252-2700—for more information.

Mountaineering

For brave souls who like to climb mountains, Yosemite is *the* place. Yosemite offers a Mountaineering School and Guide Service. Occasionally there are classes for children. If your kids are at all interested in rock climbing, be sure they get some professional training or assistance before they go off on their own. Rock climbing can be dangerous here, as in any park. All inquiries should be sent to: Yosemite Mountaineering School, Bruce Brossman, Director, Yosemite National Park, CA 95389. Or call 209/372-1244 (September through May) or 209/372-1355 (June through August).

Special Family Programs

No matter what the season, there are special family programs available through the Visitor Centers. Some can be shared with the whole family; others are ranger-led activities for the kids, independent of Mom and Dad. There might be a high-country family backpack (which is designed for beginners), or full-day hikes in Tuolumne Meadows. You'll quickly discover how special it feels to hike several miles with your family, enjoying the outdoors and sharing new experiences. Minimum ages vary depending on the program; fees vary also.

Junior Ranger Programs are offered in the summer and winter. The interpretive programs are in-depth and cover an aspect of ecology or natural or human history. Children sign up to "work" with a ranger on a naturalist program. After they complete the program they receive a certificate; after two certificates they receive a patch. Winter programs might be a snowshoe walk, cross-country ski tour, or a nature walk. This program, which is divided into groups according to age, also allows kids to earn certificates and patches. For more information, write to the Visitor Center, National Park Service, P.O. Box 577, Yosemite, CA 95389.

Evening Programs

During the summer rangers present nightly evening campfire programs. Topics change and will be posted at the Visitor Center and campgrounds and accommodations. Sometimes you can join a ranger for an early-evening stroll.

What to Do When It Rains or Snows

If it's warm, the two-hour sightseeing tours are a good choice.

Or pack up the family and drive up to Glacier Point. It's really something to watch the weather change, because the clouds get hung up on the rocks and swirl through the valley.

Sometimes the Visitor Centers will have activities. Call or ask at the front desk of your hotel.

Visit the Indian Cultural Center in town.

Walks through the heavily forested areas are nice during the rain. Some areas are so dense you won't even get wet. In the fall the vibrant colors are even prettier when the sky is overcast and dark.

The Wawona Big Trees tour is one thing to do during wet weather. Check on conditions even during the winter, because sometimes tours are available if there's no snow on the ground.

Ice skating and skiing are always ongoing in the winter.

ACTIVITIES AND SIGHTS OUTSIDE THE VALLEY: Glorious as Yosemite Valley is, there are some attractions of interest in the surrounding area.

Glacier Point

Views and vistas are *the* thing in Yosemite. For two magnificent views, don't miss Washburn Point and Glacier Point. It's difficult to describe the grandeur and beauty from these locations. From both, you can look out to the high country and see a succession of snow-capped granite peaks. From Glacier Point, you have an amazing view of the surrounding peaks, and you can look down into the valley. The views of Half Dome are incredible.

Kids will love to look down to the village and see the miniature cars, swimming pools, and other landmark structures. We took Andrew and Elizabeth to the Ahwahnee first, walked through it, and then drove to Glacier Point. Then we pointed out where they'd just been—this time with a bird's-eye view. It gave Andrew a great sense of just how high up he was.

Wawona

Wawona's **Pioneer History Center,** next to the Wawona Hotel, is likely to entice kids of all ages. From mid-June to Labor Day, visitors are greeted by costumed pioneer hosts and hostesses who re-create the days when the cabins were first built in the late 1800s. There is also a working blacksmith's shop and horse-drawn stagecoach rides. On Monday and Tuesday rangers conduct tours from here. The center is open Wednesday through Sunday from 9 a.m. to 1 p.m. and 2 to 5 p.m. For current programs, ask at any Visitor Center.

Not far from Wawona is the **Mariposa Grove of Giant Sequoias** (36 miles south of Yosemite Valley and two miles from the south entrance to the park). Be sure to see Grizzly Giant, the oldest tree in the grove. Tram tour and ranger walks are available. Tour rates are $4 for adults, $2 for children 5 to 12 and seniors. Tour times vary throughout the year, so check with the Visitor Center.

Tuolumne Meadows and Tioga Road

The highest paved road in the Sierra, Tioga Pass is known for its exquisite beauty. Tuolumne is an enormous alpine meadow. These are wonderful places to venture if you're planning to be in the park for a while. Tuolumne Meadows offers abundant places to have a delightful picnic breakfast or lunch, as well as good easy hikes. One of the real assets of Tuolumne is that it's not as crowded and you are closer to the wilderness areas. The **Tuolumne Grove of Giant Sequoias** is located here, and the kids will watch with fascination as small bubbling pools of minerals rise from underground. The Visitor Center offers a "Lunch with a Ranger" program. In summer the park operates a large campground and conducts a full-scale naturalist program here. The Valley Visitor Center has information about all these programs.

WHERE TO STAY: Going to Yosemite in the summer requires a bit of advance planning and persistence. For key summer weekends—if you want a hotel room or cottage with a bath—you need to reserve a year and a day in advance. (They won't take your reservation any earlier.) For tent cabins, plan to reserve six months ahead.

To make reservations at any of these accommodations, call 209/252-4848, a central reservations number. Or send a deposit covering one night's lodging by check or money order to **Yosemite Park and Curry Co. Reservations,** 5410 E. Home Ave., Fresno, CA 93727.

All room rates quoted below are approximate and change according to seasons.

The **Wawona Hotel,** in Wawona, seven miles past the south entrance to the park on Calif. 41 (P.O. Box 2005), Yosemite National Park, CA 95389 (tel. 209/252-4848), is a venerable hotel dating back to the 1800s when travelers to Yosemite used it as a stopover for lodging and food. Looking somewhat like a misplaced southern plantation, the Wawona is surrounded by pines and redwoods and visited by small herds of nearly tame deer. The advantage of staying here, especially in summer, is that it is out of crowded Yosemite Valley, yet near enough to enable you to go back and forth in a reasonable amount of time. It affords you peace and quiet, while still offering gorgeous surroundings.

The large pool, enclosed by a white picket fence, is surrounded by magnificent grounds for children to roam about. Breakfast, lunch, and dinner are served in the restaurant on the premises, but there is no room service. Restaurant selections for kids are limited, but they do exist (southern fried chicken is one possibility, the Wawona burger another). Dinner entrees range from $5 to $20. Golf and tennis are available. For babysitting arrangements, inquire at the front desk.

There are 105 rooms, 50 of which have private baths. The rooms in the Annex building are small, dark, but very clean. Don't expect amenities here. The bathrooms are not modernized and don't have showers. A large family might want to rent two rooms connected by a bathroom. Ask for a corner room in the Annex, as they are a little larger. Also inquire about the Little White House and whether it's available. The rooms look spacious and light.

A double room without a bath is $51.50; a double with bath, $64.50. Children under 3 are free in their parents' room; those 3 and over (and additional adults) are charged $5 per night. Cribs are $3, but rollaways are included in the additional expense of an extra person. Make summer reservations one year in advance. For spring or fall reservations, call three months ahead. The hotel and restaurant are open from approximately early March to November.

The **Ahwahnee Hotel** is one mile east of Yosemite Village on Calif. 140, Yosemite National Park, CA 95389 (tel. 209/252-4848). The British penchant for good taste was the reason for the creation of the Ahwahnee. In the early 1920s a titled Englishwoman came to visit, and at that time the only hotel in the park was called the Sentinel. She declared that the Sentinel was primitive and classless, and her refusal to stay there caused the director of the National Park Service great consternation. Thus when the two main concessionaires in the park were directed to merge, they had to agree to build a modern luxury hotel, and so the Ahwahnee was born.

Whether or not you stay at the Ahwahnee (if you can even get a reservation during summer season), you must see it. The Great Lounge is decorated in the unlikely combination of American Indian and German Gothic. But rare rugs hanging on the walls warm the massive room, and original art is found everywhere.

The view from the huge dining room is picture-postcard-perfect. Breakfast and lunch are served here. At dinner, you might want to put Junior in a special outfit, as guests really do dress for the occasion. Although there is nothing per se on the menu for children, the chef will customize dinners for kids. Ask for peanut-butter sandwiches, hamburgers, or children's portions of what you find appealing on the menu. *(Note:* Ask specifically what the meal includes. Many's the time that a simple hamburger has actually been a ground sirloin steak served with grilled onions and a sauce. Our kids see that and won't touch it. It's safer to know right away that the "burger" comes with a sourdough roll than to have the child cry because there's no bun.) Prices here are not cheap. Lunch ranges from

$7 for a club sandwich to $9.25 for seafood pasta. Dinner for two adults costs about $45, without drinks.

The hotel has a heated pool and a small playground for the kids. There is a giftshop and a sundries shop. Concierge service is available to make all your arrangements, including babysitting.

While each room has its own personality, all cost the same: $144.50 single, $149.50 double. There are 97 rooms in the main hotel and 24 rooms in seven cottages on the hotel grounds. Cottages are ideal for families: they are spacious and comfortable, and have little patios. Some include fireplaces and two pull-out sofas. Separate dressing areas are actually big enough to fit a crib. If you want to stay in the main hotel, explain your needs when you call. Some rooms have two double beds and a balcony, others have a queen-size bed with room for a crib. There are no adjoining rooms in the hotel. The reservationists will attempt to put you in a room appropriate for your needs. As we said earlier, the catch is that you have to make a reservation for summer one year and one day in advance. But there is availability the rest of the year. Cribs are $5 extra per night. Children 3 to 12 are charged $5 per night (no charge for those under 3); children over 12 and additional adults pay $10 per night.

Yosemite Lodge approximately a mile west of Yosemite Village, on Calif. 41 and 140, Yosemite National Park, CA 95389 (tel. 209/252-4848), is like a self-contained little resort. A tour desk in the lobby lets you make arrangements for horseback riding, mountaineering classes, tours, and transportation. This is also where you'll find out about the myriad activities offered in the park. In addition, the lodge has a full-service post office, giftshops, snacks and sundries, a swimming pool (open daily during the summer, weather permitting), showers and changing rooms, an amphitheater (used nightly in the summer for slide presentations, movies, and ranger programs), and a bike-rental stand (open daily from April through October; and the rest of the year, weather permitting). The bike stand has child carriers and helmets. The free shuttle service that serves the valley stops outside the lobby. Babysitting arrangements can be made at the front desk.

The Yosemite Lodge Cafeteria is open daily year round, and serves breakfast, lunch, snacks, and dinner. Although it's a typical cafeteria, you'll be surprised at the wide selection, the quality of the food, and the very reasonable prices (50¢ for a cup of coffee!). The Four Seasons Restaurant is great for families. Serving breakfast (weekends only, after November 8) and dinner during summer and the holiday season, and on weekends off-season, there are appropriate items for kids. The Mountain Room Broiler serves steaks and lobster at dinner and is open most of the year. Prices here are naturally a bit higher. All the dining facilities have no-smoking areas. The Mountain Room Bar has the only public big-screen TV in Yosemite Valley and is operated when there is a major sporting event going on. A refreshment stand near the swimming pool is open daily in the summer.

There are 484 rooms to choose from. The spacious Lodge Rooms may remind you of accommodations at a ski resort. Each two-story building houses eight clean and comfortable modern rooms with balconies or patios. Singles or doubles rent for $75.25. Cottage Room accommodations are similar to standard hotel rooms. Singles or doubles with bath are $58.50; without bath, $37.75. Cabins—really very small sleeping rooms—go for $44.75, single or double, with bath; $33 without bath. Cribs and rollaways are available for a $3 charge. Kids 3 to 12 pay $5 per night; under 3, free.

Curry Village, one mile east of Yosemite Village on Calif. 41 and 140, Yosemite National Park, CA 95389 (tel. 209/252-4848), was formerly called "Camp Sequoia" and once offered tent cabins at $2 a night. That was in 1899. While you can't get them at quite the same rate, Curry still offers tent cabins at reasonable prices. This rustic Yosemite resort has 180 cabins and 426 tent cabins.

There are also a number of standard rooms and loft rooms. The accommodations are quite basic, and the prices are reasonable. Curry Village also has its own tour desk, where you can find out about all the same valley activities and can arrange tours, classes, and horseback riding. There is a giftshop, bike rentals (available mid-April to October daily; has child carriers and helmets), raft rentals (in summer, as conditions permit), a swimming pool (open daily in summer), showers, and changing rooms. Babysitting can be arranged through the front-desk clerk.

The Village also houses an amphitheater, the Mountaineering School (cross-country skiing instruction and equipment rental November to April, rock-climbing instruction and equipment rental April to June and October to November), the Mountain Sport Shop, and the Ice Rink, which opens daily November to March and offers skate rentals and instruction.

Food is plentiful here too. The Cafeteria is open daily mid-April to October for breakfast and lunch. There is also a hamburger stand, ice-cream stand, and snackbar open during that period. Parents often eat outside on the deck while the kids are nearby at one of the stands.

Loft rooms are the best bet here for larger families. There are two double beds downstairs and one double upstairs, with room for a crib, for $58.50. Tent cabins, especially suitable for families with one older child, are soft-sided structures that can't be locked and have one double and one single bed; rates are $24.25 for one or two people, and $4.25 for each additional person. Standard rooms are small and cute, furnished in pine and calico prints, and have two double beds. These rooms would be cramped with a crib. The rate for these rooms is $58.50. The cabins with baths are tiny and rather primitive, but can be joined with a second room; they rent for $44.75. The charge for cribs is $5, and rollaways are available. Each additional extra person is charged $6 per night. If you're planning to be in Yosemite during summer, make reservations one year in advance—except for tent cabins.

Campgrounds
There are eight campgrounds in the valley, totaling 825 campsites; Tioga Road and Big Oak Flat Road have eight campgrounds with 908 sites; Glacier Point and Wawona have two with 210 sites. Sites outside the valley itself are on a first-come, first-served basis. Reservations at the five valley campgrounds with sites for tents and RVs can be made through Ticketron. Advance reservations are taken no more than eight weeks before your stay. In summer especially, it is important to make reservations eight weeks (to the minute) before your planned visit. The valley has one walk-in site, one for groups, and one for backpackers. Both the auto site and the walk-in site are open year round.

Outside the valley, to the south and west, are two auto sites that are open year round. The limit on stays in summer is seven days in the valley, 14 days outside; September 15 through May 31, 30 days in the valley and outside. There is a maximum stay of 30 days per year for any one person.

Rates are $2 per person for walk-ins, and $11 per auto per site, with a maximum of six people per site.

WHERE TO EAT: All hotel dining rooms and cafeterias are open to the general public.

In addition, **The Loft Restaurant** is located near the Village center. It serves typical American fare, lunch and dinner only, at very reasonable prices. Lunch prices range from $3.50 to $5, and selections include cheeseburgers, soup, and salads. There's no children's menu, but you'll find plenty for kids to choose from. The restaurant is open May through October, weekdays from 11:45 a.m. to 2 p.m. and 5:30 to 9 p.m., on Saturday and Sunday until 10 p.m. No reservations accepted. The average wait at lunch is 10 to 15 minutes; at dinner, 20 minutes to an hour. Best time to come for dinner is right when they open, at 5:30 p.m. Highchairs and boosters are available. Major credit cards accepted.

Degnan's Deli, in the same building as the Loft, is the perfect place to pick up food for a picnic. They carry bread, cheeses, cold cuts, wine, soda, etc.

There's also a **market** in the Village center store. No deli food here, but lots of basics.

3. SEQUOIA–KINGS CANYON NATIONAL PARKS

A visit to these two national parks encompasses a full range of climatic zones, from Mediterranean to Arctic. Here is where you'll find some of the most varied terrain in the world. And of course, most people come for a view of the mammoth giant sequoias, the biggest trees on earth. These parks preserve some of the best examples of these trees in the world.

In addition to these big groves of sequoias, Kings Canyon and Sequoia National Parks contain miles of wilderness—canyons, lakes, meadows, and spectacular mountain peaks abound.

GETTING THERE: From the south, take I-5 to Calif. 99N to Fresno. From the north, take I-80 to Calif. 99S to Fresno. Take Calif. 180 from Fresno to the entrance of Kings Canyon and Sequoia National Parks. You can also enter on Calif. 198 via Visalia and Three Rivers, but the road is far more difficult to drive.

ORIENTATION: Some people aren't aware that Sequoia is California's oldest national park, and that Sequoia and Kings Canyon are actually two separate parks. If you enter the parks from Fresno, you'll enter Kings Canyon, which puts you within a few miles of Grant Grove. The parks are open all year. However, during winter months, check with the National Park Service (tel. 209/565-3351 or 209/565-3341) for temporary road closures. Visitor Centers at Grant Grove, Lodgepole, and Ash Mountain are open all year: from 9 a.m. to 5 p.m. in summer, 8 a.m. to 5 p.m. the rest of the year. During the summer, Cedar Grove and Mineral King also offer visitor information. Check at each Visitor Center for guided walks offered.

The General's Highway runs through both parks. It meets Calif. 180 at Grant Grove and Calif. 198 at Ash Mountain. This scenic road takes you to many of the important features of the parks and connects the four major visitor areas— Giant Forest, Mineral King, Grant Grove, and Cedar Grove. The main mode of transportation is the automobile. There are no trams or shuttles, and the areas of interest are far enough apart to necessitate driving.

Entrance permits are $5 per car. At the time you enter the parks, ask for a copy of the *Sequoia Bark* visitors' newspaper.

WARNING: Animal life is abundant. You're likely to see lots of chipmunks, squirrels, marmots, and mule deer. Sequoia and Kings Canyon are *bear country!* These bears are used to people and are not afraid to approach trashcans, coolers, and cars that contain food. *Don't leave food in the car or car trunk.* Many disbelieving tourists have come back to automobiles with broken windows and torn-out backseats. Bears are more afraid of people than people are of them. Usually, if you see a bear, all you have to do is clap your hands and it will run away. But *don't tease the bears with food*—it's very dangerous.

Remember that these are wild animals. Don't encourage your children to get close. But that goes for all wildlife.

WHAT TO SEE AND DO IN KINGS CANYON: The center of activity in

Kings Canyon is **Grant Grove Village.** There you'll find the lodge, a full-service restaurant, a giftshop, and the Visitor Center.

What to See

General Grant Grove and the **Trail for All People** (a short walk, fully accessible to strollers) are a wonderful introduction to the big trees. The General Grant Tree is the second-largest living thing in the world and has been dubbed "The Nation's Christmas Tree." Make a game of it: as you stand there staring up, ask the kids to imagine it bejeweled with lights and ornaments. Our kids love decorating it in their minds.

Big Stump Trail is located near the park entrance (Calif. 180). This short self-guided trail gives you an idea of the numbers of trees that were logged before the park was created to protect them. This is a great opportunity to talk to the children about ecology.

Roaring River Falls is found approximately 2½ miles east of the turnoff for the Cedar Grove Ranger Station. From the parking area, walk about 200 yards to a viewpoint of the roaring falls. The surging river is swift and dangerous.

What to Do

During the summer there are **campfire programs.** Check with the Visitor Center for specific programs and for information on programs offered at other times of the year.

Stables for **horseback riding** are located at Wolverton Pack Station (tel. 209/565-3445), Grant Grove (tel. 209/335-2374), and Cedar Grove (tel. 209/565-3464), and are open June through August. Hour-long, half-day, full-day, and overnight riding is available. As each stable is privately owned, you'll need to call for rates, locations, and reservations.

Bicycling is best in Cedar Grove because of the flat terrain. Bicycles can be rented there. They may not be ridden on hiking trails.

For information on **winter sports,** see "Winter Sports" in the Sequoia section.

WHAT TO SEE AND DO IN SEQUOIA: The place to congregate in Sequoia is **Giant Forest Village.** It consists of a giftshop, market, bar, the Village cafeteria, and a studio that is also a giftshop. Nearby **Lodgepole Village** has a market, giftshop, showers, laundry, and quick-food places (open during summer), as well as a Visitor Center (open year round).

What to See

The **General Sherman Tree** is the largest living thing on earth. Measuring 274 feet tall and weighing about 1,400 tons, it is estimated to be between 2,500 and 3,000 years old (this tree was standing when the pyramids were being built!). It's mind-boggling to see, and even kids are amazed at its size. Ours like to figure out how many people holding hands it would take to encircle it. The **Congress Trail** is a self-guided walk that takes you through this breathtaking forest of giant trees. The trail is easy enough for all children, although you might have to carry the toddlers after a while. Point out to your kids the beautiful ferns that grow all over the forest floor.

Hazelwood Nature Trail is an easy, mile-long trail that takes about an hour to walk and is good for the whole family. You'll find the trailhead across the highway from Giant Forest Lodge. **Round Meadow,** also near the lodge, is a wonderful place for a picnic lunch.

Moro Rock provides spectacular views of the high country, including the Great Continental Divide. Stairs—with hand rails—provide access to the top of the rock. The climb is quite steep, but the view is worth the effort, even if you only get part way up.

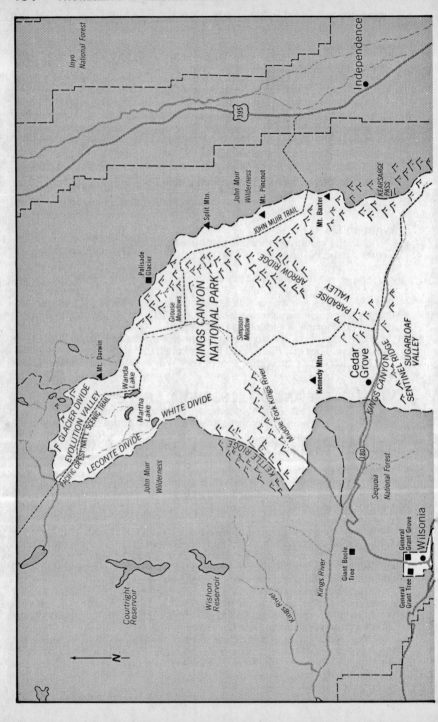

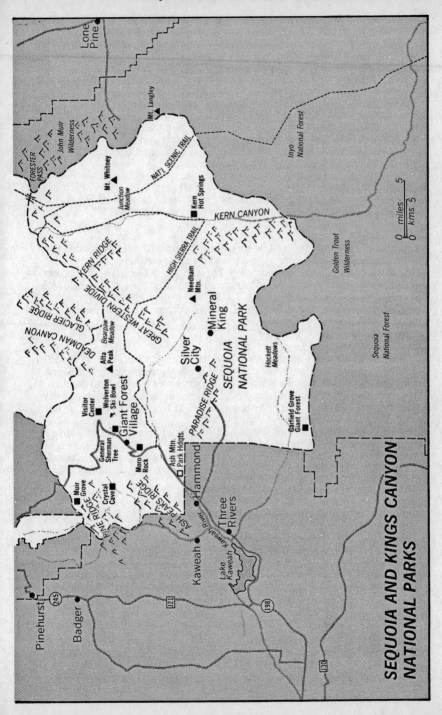

SEQUOIA AND KINGS CANYON
NATIONAL PARKS

On the way to **Crescent Meadow** (a great spot for a picnic and bear-watching), you'll come to **Auto Log**—a natural novelty that's sure to delight youngsters. This fallen tree has been leveled so cars can drive right on it. Our kids scrambled for pictures of *their* car perched right on top of a giant fallen tree. Nearby is **Tunnel Log,** a fallen tree that cars can drive through.

Crystal Cave is a huge cave where children will see fascinating stalagmites and stalactites in various shapes and configurations. Tours are one hour long. Bring warm clothing. *Note:* The entrance to the cave is half a mile downhill—which means a steep uphill on the way back. It's a long but not horribly difficult walk for people in good health, and there are rest stops along the way. In May, June, and September it's open Monday through Friday; during July and August, open daily. Admission is $1.50 for adults, 50¢ for children 6 to 12; under-6s, free. Tours are conducted from 10 a.m. to 3 p.m.

Special Programs

There are evening programs at Giant Forest and Lodgepole. The Visitor Center will have information about specific times and programs.

Water Sports

Try river **fishing** in the middle fork of the Kaweah River or lake fishing at Hume Lake. *(Don't swim in rivers before checking safety conditions.)* State fishing licenses are required for everyone over 16, and are available at all markets throughout the parks. You'll have to bring your own fishing poles, but tackle and bait are for sale at all markets.

Rafting can be arranged through King's River Expeditions, in Fresno (tel. 209/233-4881), for rafting the lower end of Kings River.

Downhill Skiing

Sequoia and Kings Canyon are alive with winter activities. **Wolverton Ski Bowl,** near Giant Forest (tel. 209/565-3435), is open weekends and holidays during the season. You can also rent ski equipment here for adults and children. Wolverton rents only downhill, not cross-country, ski equipment; Giant Forest has cross-country rentals. There's a snow play area at Wolverton, but bring your own snow play equipment.

At Wolverton, a full-day slope pass is $13.50 for adults and $8.50 for kids; a half-day slope pass, $9.50 for adults and $6.50 for kids (a half day starts at 12:30 p.m. and the slopes close at 4:30 p.m.). Full-day equipment rentals (skis, boots, and poles) are $12.50 for adults and $9.50 for children; half-day rentals, $9.50 for adults and $7.50 for children.

Cross-Country Skiing

Contact the following centers for information on cross-country skiing: **Sequoia Ski Touring Center** (tel. 209/565-3461), open from 8 a.m. to 5 p.m. mid-November to mid-April; **Grant Grove Ski Touring** (tel. 209/335-2314), open approximately the same hours and days; and **Wilsonia Lodge** (tel. 209/335-2311). **Montecito-Sequoia** (tel. toll free 800/227-9900) is a family resort located just outside the park.

Rental of cross-country skiing equipment for a full day is $9.50 for adults and $7 for children; for a half day, $7 for adults and $4.50 for kids. You can rent snowshoes at Giant Forest and Grant Grove for $6.

WHERE TO STAY: Rates quoted below are for summer (May through October) and holidays. For reservations in both parks, contact **Sequoia Guest Services,** P.O. Box 789, Three Rivers, CA 93271 (tel. 209/561-3314).

In Kings Canyon, **Grant Grove** offers three types of very basic accommodations. Cabins, two to a unit, run $43; they have private baths and little unenclosed porches. Rustic "housekeeping cabins"—the only cabins you're allowed to cook in—are $26. "Rustic cabins," without private baths, are $24. There's plenty of room for kids to play. A giftshop/mini-mart offers the essentials.

The Grant Grove Restaurant is perfect for breakfast, lunch, or dinner. Breakfast choices are vast, and meals average around $4. Lunches range from $3 to $5, and dinner averages $7. There is a children's menu with prices starting at $1.75.

In Sequoia, **Giant Forest** offers four kinds of accommodations in 245 units. Motel rooms are quite spacious, with two queen-size beds and plenty of room for a crib or rollaway. There are cabins with two double beds, cabins with one double and one single bed, two-room cabins with bed space for seven people, and one cabin with a fireplace. Accommodations run from rustic (no electricity or running water) to comfortable (carpeted, with showers and electricity). Prices range from $35 to $85, single or double. Additional guests are charged $3.50 to $6 per night. Cribs cost $4 additional.

A dining room is open mid-May to mid-October and serves breakfast, lunch, and dinner. There is also a buffet and salad bar at the evening meal. The cafeteria, next door to the giftshop, serves typical cafeteria fare, has plenty of seating, and is open year round.

In addition there are 18 units at **Cedar Grove Lodge** in Kings Canyon (tel. 209/561-3314) and 11 units at **Stony Creek Lodge** in Sequoia.

Campgrounds

For further information on the following campgrounds, contact the **National Park Service** (tel. 209/565-3341).

IN SEQUOIA. Nearby **Lodgepole,** with 260 tent/RV spaces, is the only campground for which reservations can be made. The grounds are open all year, but reservations are taken (through Ticketron outlets) in summer only, no more than eight weeks to the day in advance; it's open in the winter for snow camping. Stays are limited to 14 days in summer, to 30 days the rest of the year. Rates are $6 per site per night.

Two other small campgrounds (with a total of 72 sites) at low elevation are available. One takes tents and RVs; the other, tents only. No reservations, and they're crowded on weekends. Rates: $6 per site per night.

There are three more small (73 sites) drive-in grounds available in remote areas off the main road. Pit toilets only. No reservations. Rates: $4 per site per night.

KINGS CANYON. The **Grant Grove** area has three campgrounds, all in a row, totaling 369 sites for RVs and tents. These are the last grounds to fill up. There are flush toilets. No reservations. Rates: $6 per site per night.

Some 30 miles farther into the canyon off the main road are the most popular campsites, which are situated along the Kings River. There are 314 general sites (one area is for groups only) in these campgrounds. Weekends it gets very full. No reservations. Rates: $6 per site per night.

4. MAMMOTH LAKES

In 1937 Dave McCoy lassoed a Model A Ford truck to a rope tow and a tree, which marked the beginning of Mammoth Mountain's skiing tradition. Some 18 years later the first chair lift was built and more than 2,000 people came to participate. Since then Mammoth has become synonymous with skiing.

Mammoth is the place to be in winter if you like winter sports, crisp alpine fields, fresh air, and plenty of room to explore.

But it's also the place to be in summer, the season that is the area's best-kept secret—and the locals' favorite time of year. When the snow melts, Mammoth becomes a summer playground for families who love to experience such outdoor activities as horseback riding over mountain trails, fishing for fat trout in emerald lakes, hiking through rugged wilderness trails, camping out under the stars, picnicking amid wildflowers, bicycling on any of 300 open roads, sailing, windsurfing, and waterskiing, or playing tennis and golf.

GETTING THERE: From Los Angeles **by car,** take Calif. 14 north to U.S. 395 north through Bishop to Mammoth. The drive takes approximately 5½ hours. The best way to get to Mammoth from San Francisco in the winter is to fly. In the summer, take Tioga Pass Road through Yosemite; it's about a 6-hour drive.

Fly into Mammoth/June Lakes Airport via **Alpha Air** (tel. 213/417-9744) from Los Angeles, Oakland, or San Jose; **Mammoth Air Shuttle** (tel. 619/935-4737) from Burbank or Orange County; or **Sierra Mountain Airways** (tel. 415/569-2898, or toll free 800/247-9299) from Oakland, Burbank, or Long Beach.

Greyhound Bus has service once a day from Los Angeles. From San Francisco, you'll get off in Bishop and will then have to rent a car to Mammoth.

ORIENTATION: Your first activity in Mammoth should be a trip to the **Mammoth Lakes Resort Association,** on Calif. 203; P.O. Box 48T, Mammoth Lakes, CA 93546 (which is the main road that leads to Mammoth Mountain; (tel. 619/934-2712, or toll free 800/367-6572), and gather as much information as you like on all the activities and festivities. They will be glad to answer your questions and offer many suggestions. The office is open to visitors Monday through Saturday from 8 a.m. to 6 p.m.; in winter from 8 a.m. to 5 p.m.; daily in summer.

Another "must stop" is at the **Forest Service Visitor Center,** also on Calif. 203, right outside town (tel. 619/934-2505). You'll find this stop a fascinating way to learn everything about Mammoth Lakes and the surrounding areas. The rangers, who are very knowledgeable and helpful, have a computerized screen that will tell you about activities available. This is also where to get a fishing license or a permit for camping. Open May to July daily from 8 a.m. to 4:30 p.m.; July to mid-September daily from 6 a.m. to 5 p.m.; and mid-September to May weekdays from 8 a.m. to 4:30 p.m.

Other important phone numbers: **Parks and Recreation** (tel. 619/934-8983), **24-hour snow information** (tel. 619/934-6166), and **road conditions** (tel. 619/934-6611).

GETTING AROUND: You really do need a car in Mammoth, especially in the winter. But for daily trips to the slopes, a shuttle service (50¢) runs from numerous stops around town (winter only). Some condominiums and lodges have complimentary van service to the slopes and into town.

WHAT TO SEE AND DO IN WINTER: Two mountains, Mammoth Mountain and June Mountain, give alpine skiers everything they can possibly imagine, including a season that seems to go on forever. From November to June Mammoth Mountain is resplendent with an average of 335 inches of packed powder. But what really makes Mammoth Lakes such a perfect family vacation spot is that it offers more than just fabulous alpine skiing during the winter. There are miles of well-groomed cross-country ski tracks on which to discover the beauty and peacefulness of the surrounding wilderness, winter hot-air ballooning over the glacier-carved peaks, snowmobiling through the woods, old-fashioned sleigh rides, exciting dog sledding, ice skating on a frozen pond, and lots of spots for just plain snow fun.

If you are new at downhill or cross-country skiing, learn the ability signs for the trails immediately—a green circle means an easy trail; a blue square means more difficult; a black diamond means most difficult. These are important signs to remember if you get lost and are looking for a trail back. Do not ignore or underestimate these signs—they are for your safety.

Alpine Skiing

MAMMOTH MOUNTAIN. Mammoth Mountain can accommodate the largest number of skiers in the United States. To find out about the level of a run, facilities at each lodge area, ski instruction, and package rates, contact **Mammoth/June Ski Area,** P.O. Box 24, Mammoth Lakes, CA 93546 (tel. 619/934-2571). The mountain has 150 miles of runs (30% advanced, 40% intermediate, and 30% beginner). There are 32 lifts (including three new quad chairs, six triples, 16 doubles, two T-bars, two pomas, two gondolas, and one Mighty Mite).

There are three areas from which to start your skiing at Mammoth Mountain: The **Main Lodge** is found at Minaret Road and Calif. 203. You can purchase lift tickets, rent or buy equipment, rent a locker, and sign up for the ski school here. There is a cafeteria on premises.

To get to **Warming Hut II,** take Canyon Boulevard off Minaret Road, or take Lakeview Boulevard off Mary Road. You can also get your lift tickets, rent skis, and sign up for ski school here. This section also has a cafeteria.

To get to **Mid-Chalet,** you'll need to take one of seven chair lifts—inquire at the Main Lodge. There's a cafeteria up there, and a sundeck.

In addition to the above facilities, Mammoth Mountain has four ski shops, a race department, lockers, a full-service hotel, motel, and condominiums, and two additional restaurants (at Mammoth Mountain Inn).

Lifts operate midweek from 8:30 a.m. to 4 p.m., on weekends and holidays from 8 a.m. to 4 p.m.

Full-day lift tickets cost $27 for adults, $14 for children 12 and under; 4 and under, free. Half-day tickets are $20 for adults, $10 for children. Seniors 65 and over can ski free. There are discounts available for midweek and multiday packages, and season tickets are available. Sign up for group and private lessons through the ski school. Call for prices.

There are three skiing options for children. They can ski with you (30% of the runs are for beginners), or they can join one of two ski schools, both located at the Main Lodge. The **Children's Ski School** is recommended for kids 5 and older. There's usually only one instructor for each eight to ten children here, so if you have a child who has never been on skis, or who is shy or has a hard time separating from you, you might want to start him in **Funland** instead and let him progress to the ski school after a day or so of getting used to the slopes. Our fearless 5-year-old was intimidated by the older kids in the ski school and by the fact that there was only one instructor for nine children. He was not able to get the attention he needed for his first time on skis. When he was switched to Funland, he blossomed and was able to advance gradually to ski school.

Funland, for children 3 to 5 years old, is in a small, safe, roped-off area. To keep from distracting the kids, yet to check out their adjustment, you can watch from a balcony above the school. The ratio of instructors to children here is better—usually there are not more than four children per instructor.

There are three options for Funland and Ski School. You can enroll the kids for a half day, from 10 a.m. to noon or 1:30 to 3:30 p.m. ($16); for a full day, including lunch, from 10 a.m. to 3:30 p.m. ($38), while you go off to the slopes feeling confident that they're being well supervised; or let them ski the morning session, meet them for lunch, and then bring them back for the afternoon session ($24). Both Funland and the Ski School will even supply hot chocolate. Lift tickets are not necessary for children in Funland or beginning skiers in Children's Ski School. A-level skiers and above in Ski School must purchase lift tickets.

What do you do with infants to 3-year-olds? Child care is available at the **Small World Day Care Center,** located in the Mammoth Mountain Inn, near the Main Lodge. Reservations are essential: call 619/934-2581 and ask for the day-care center. (See the Mammoth Mountain Inn in the "Where to Stay" section for details.)

JUNE MOUNTAIN. Just 25 minutes from Mammoth on U.S. 395 and Route 158 (tel. 619/934-2571). It offers 30 runs, six chair lifts, and one tram. You can buy lift tickets at the Tram Haus in the parking lot. At the top of the tram is June Meadows Chalet, which has a ski school, race department, rental and repair shop, lockers, rest rooms, and a cafeteria. At Lake Haus, at the base of Chair J5, there is a day-care facility. There is also a Children's Ski School (for ages 4 to 12) and a snow playground for the kids. Lift tickets between Mammoth and June Mountains are interchangeable, and the hours of operation are the same.

Cross-Country Skiing

Cross-country skiing is a wonderful family outing, but it is not recommended for children under 7, except for young children who can ride along on a "pulka" pulled by an adult. Our 5-year-old loved the snowy trail and our trek over the open fields, but he was too young to fully maneuver the equipment.

Being such a winter wonderland, Mammoth has lots of trails for this peaceful activity. **Tamarack Cross-Country Ski Center,** on Twin Lakes (tel. 619/934-2442, or toll free 800/237-6879), is a beautiful and tranquil setting for experiencing the pleasures of this sport. From town, take Lake Mary Road to Twin Lakes Road all the way up to the top—about a ten-minute trip. There are 25 miles of meticulously groomed trails here for exploring, with at least ten easy trails. There are some—but not many—rest rooms and telephones along the trails.

On weekends the trails are open from 8 a.m. to 5 p.m.; on weekdays the hours are 8:30 a.m. to 5 p.m.

Trail passes cost $9 for a full day, $6 for a half day; children under 18 ski free. Full-day rentals cost $12 for adults, $6 for children over 6, $4 for those 6 and under. Half-day rentals cost $8 for adults, $5 for children over 6, $2 for those 6 and under. Group and private lessons are available. Make advance reservations for lessons for children 10 and under.

Another wonderful place for cross-country skiing is **Sierra Meadows Ski Touring Center,** Old Mammoth Road, three blocks past Safeway (tel. 619/934-6161), with more than 35 miles of machine-groomed trails, a rental shop, ski school, warming hut, and lunch room. The Meadows occupies a beautiful open field with vistas of snow-capped peaks all around. The friendly and helpful employees will be glad to point out the different mountain ranges to you and explain a little about the history of the area.

Trail passes cost $7 for a full day, $5 for a half day; children under 12 pay $4 for a full day, $2 for a half day. Full-day rentals cost $12 for adults, $8 for children. Half-day rentals are $8 for adults, $5 for children. Private and group lessons are offered daily, and reservations are suggested for private lessons. Trails are open during daylight hours. Office hours for reservations are 8:30 a.m. to 5 p.m. daily.

The **Shady Rest / Inyo Craters Trail** system begins behind the Forest Service Center (tel. 619/934-2505). While not great when it's very cold or icy, it has a nice flat portion beginning at the Shady Rest area that's good for beginners. Trees are marked with trail directions and the level of difficulty. No opening or closing times. No charge.

Dog Sledding

A real treat for kids of all ages is dog sledding, and **Sierra Meadows,** on Old Mammoth Road, three blocks from the Safeway (tel. 619/934-6161 or 619/934-6270), also offers this activity. A charming New Zealander named Paul Marvelly runs this dog-sledding operation, and he is extremely knowledgeable and accommodating. Paul is used to kids, as 60% of his business is families. He takes the time to introduce youngsters to his affectionate huskies and lets the kids make friends with them. Then he leads an interesting guided tour of Mammoth while guests recline in comfort on his specially crafted sleds. Kids love the feeling of wind blowing on their faces as they race through the open fields. All dog sledding is subject to weather and trail conditions, so don't show up without calling first or you may be disappointed.

The cost for a two-mile, 25-minute ride through Sierra Meadows is $25 for adults, $15 for children 12 and under, and all ages are welcome. A one-hour ride through Minaret Vista is $55 per adult and $25 per child 12 and under. A "Wilderness Adventure," such as a picnic, sunset trip, or half-day trip, has a base rate of $175 per hour. Paul runs the sleds daily. Call for hours, which vary.

Hot-Air Ballooning

Hot-air ballooning is often thought of as a spring or summer adventure. But in Mammoth, you can go ballooning all year round. **High Sierra Ballooning,** Shell Center Building in town (tel. 619/934-7188), and 201 S. Warren in Bishop (tel. 619/873-5838), will take you soaring in the skies, with an advance reservation, for a 15-minute, half-hour, or one-hour flight. The view over the east side of the Sierra during one of these sunrise flights is unforgettable. Balloon flights are made daily, wind and weather permitting. The 15-minute flights cost $40 per person, half-hour sojourns cost $65, and one-hour trips top out at $150. Children under 12 pay half price. Children as young as 3 are welcome, but we recommend 5 as the youngest age. Telephone reservations are accepted daily from 1 to 5 p.m.

Ice Skating

There are several lakes—June Lake, Convict Lake, Twin Lakes, and Mammoth Ponds—on which to skate, but beware of thin ice. Contact the **U.S. Forest Service** at 619/934-2505 for the current skating conditions, and don't go out on skates without first establishing the safety of the lake.

Skates can be rented at **Pine Tree Sports** (tel. 619/934-8020); see "Where to Rent Equipment" (below) for details.

Sledding and Tobogganing

Mammoth offers numerous places for sledding and tobogganing. A good place for adult and teen sledders who like a challenge is the **Crestview-Deadman** area, approximately ten miles north of Mammoth, just off U.S. 395 (there are signs). For children, there is a hill on the corner of Sierra Park Road and Meridian Boulevard. There is no particular place to rent sleds, but you could buy a plastic one at the local Safeway market or at one of the many sporting-goods stores. Our little one dragged his sled over to a hill adjacent to our condominium and had a ball going up and down the gentle slope. With very little effort you can find a hill to delight the youngsters.

Sleigh Rides

"Over the meadows and through the woods, to grandmother's house we go. . . ." Is there a more cozy-sounding, nostalgic activity you can think of doing in the snow than taking a sleigh ride? And what a perfect way to go—at night, in the crisp winter air, accompanied by sparkling snowflakes and the shining moon.

Sierra Meadows offers these evening rides at its Ski Tour Center, on Old Mammoth Road, three blocks from Safeway (tel. 619/934-6161 for reservations), and all ages participate in this family activity, even babies (naturally, you should wrap everyone up in very warm gear). You ride through the meadow for a half hour and are then warmed up with hot spiced wine and cider. Choose a 5 p.m. ride without dinner, or a dinner sleigh ride, the first one beginning at 6 p.m. A full-course dinner—accompanied by lively guitar or fiddle music—is served in the lodge after the ride, along with hot spiced cider or wine.

Sleigh rides without dinner cost $15 for adults, $10 for children under 12. Sleigh rides with dinner cost $29.50 for adults, $24.50 for children under 12, $19.50 for children under 6; under-3s are free. Sleigh rides are scheduled on Friday and Saturday nights and on holidays. Special midweek group sleigh-ride dinners can be arranged. Reservations are necessary.

Snowmobiling

One action-filled way to take in the magnificent scenery of Mammoth is to rent a snowmobile and explore the snow-filled forests. (We don't recommend this activity for children under 5.) A guide from **Sierra Meadows**, P.O. Box 2008, Mammoth Lakes, CA 93546 (tel. 619/934-9645 or 619/934-6161), will take you and your family on a one-hour tour through the wilderness. (You may want to write ahead to reserve your snowmobile.) When you arrive, pick up your tickets at the Sierra Meadows Ski Tour Center on Old Mammoth Road, and they'll direct you to the snowmobiles.

You follow your guide in your own snowmobile. The cost is $35 per hour for a single or $55 for a double (your youngster can ride behind you). Two-hour tours are $65 for a single or $95 for a double. Reservations are strongly recommended for weekends and holidays.

Another establishment that rents snowmobiles is **D.J.'s Snowmobile Rentals,** located on U.S. 395 north at Smokey Bear Flat (tel. 619/935-4480), approximately eight minutes from Mammoth. Open Friday through Monday from 10 a.m. to 4 p.m. Also open holidays and midweek with one-day advance notice.

One-rider machines rent for $20 per half hour; two-rider machines, for $30 per half hour. You can choose half-hour trips driving your own machine on loop trails. One-hour guided adventure tours to a ranch on the river are available Friday through Monday. The charge is $35 per hour for one person, $55 per hour for two. On Saturday only, there is a 2½-hour guided lunch tour. Singles pay $70 with lunch, $65 without; doubles pay $95 with lunch, $85 without. (Make reservations for the lunch tours.)

Winter Horseback Riding

Winter horseback riding is something you won't be able to experience in too many places. Imagine all of you riding over rolling hills to enjoy the panorama of the Sierra, the magnificent White Mountains, and Mammoth Mountain. These guided tours are conducted by **Sierra Meadows**, Old Mammoth Road, three blocks past the Safeway (tel. 619/934-2434 or 619/934-6161) on weekends and holidays, or you can make special midweek arrangements. (The address for reservations is P.O. Box 2008, Mammoth Lakes, CA 93546.) Children should be at least 7 or 8 to participate in this adventure. The charge for adults or children is $16 per hour.

WHAT TO SEE AND DO IN SPRING AND SUMMER: In the 1930s
Mammoth was strictly a summer resort frequented by those who wanted to get away from city noise and relax in the tranquil setting of crystal lakes, flowering meadows, and alpine mountains. For those in the know now, Mammoth is at its best during the summer, when family activities abound and days are warm but

never hot. The many lakes surrounding Mammoth make it a haven for water sports. The many alpine fields make hiking a glorious experience. Passes that were closed for the winter linking Mammoth with Yosemite and other park areas reopen in the spring. From April through October the opportunities are endless.

Backpacking and Hiking

An important source for information about these activities is the **U.S. Forest Service,** Mammoth Ranger District, on Calif. 203 (P.O. Box 148), Mammoth Lakes, CA 93546 (tel. 619/934-2505). Not only can the rangers tell you about the various hiking trails and levels of ability, but they can also explain the free interpretive tours and programs they offer during the summer.

Hiking trails in Mammoth are everywhere. Whether you want to pack your family up for a week or for a few hours, you'll find a trail suited to your needs. The landscapes are beautiful everywhere you look, so you won't be disappointed in any hike you choose. If you're at all concerned that you and the little ones may not have the stamina to make it back, make prior arrangements with **Alpine Adventures** (tel. 619/934-7888 or 619/873-5838) for its Trailhead Shuttle Service, which will drop you off or pick you up from various trailheads. For prices, call between 1 and 5 p.m. daily.

The **John Muir and Ansel Adams Wilderness Areas** are magnificent, but they can get congested during the busy summer months. You will need a wilderness permit for overnight use. Half the daily quotas are on a first-come, first-served basis the day you plan to hike, the rest by advance reservation (address above). Pick up permits in person at the Visitor Center. When you stop by, be sure to pick up a copy of "Mammoth Trails," which has maps of the individual hiking trails, as well as levels of ability. This will be your guide to hiking through Mammoth.

Tamarack Lodge Resort, P.O. Box 69, Mammoth Lakes, CA 93546 (tel. 619/934-2442), puts out a short guide to hiking trails in the Tamarack area. It's available to nonguests, and the staff is happy to give you specific information about trails, including those hikes appropriate for young children.

You might be interested in taking a guided hike through the eastern Sierra. That can be arranged through **Alpine Adventures** (tel. 619/934-7888 or 619/873-5838 between 1 and 5 p.m.) for a fee of $40 per hour, adult or child. Children should be at least 10 years old for this adventure.

Devils Postpile National Monument, located 14 miles from the Mammoth Visitor Center via Red's Meadow Road, is a fascinating site to visit. It was created 100,000 years ago by lava flowing from the earth's crust through Mammoth Pass. As a result, the formations consist of basaltic rock standing in columns 40 to 60 feet high. An easy 15-minute hike takes you to these imposing sights, which will fascinate the kids. There are picnic areas and a lovely 1¼-mile hike down to Rainbow Falls (the colors of the falls are best seen midday). From June to September you have to take the shuttle from the Mammoth Mountain Inn. The shuttle departs daily from 7:30 a.m. to 5:30 p.m. The round-trip fare is $3.50 per person; children under 5, free. A family of four can get a group rate of $10.

Another geologic site and an interesting place to hike is **Hot Creek,** three miles south of Mammoth Junction on U.S. 395. A paved trail goes down 250 feet to Hot Creek Geyser, a hot spring that heats a cold mountain stream. Open from sunrise to sunset in the summer, Hot Creek is a sanctuary for many interesting mammals and birds, such as great horned owls, bald eagles, and cliff swallows. This is a great place to explore nature, but don't plan to swim here, as the extreme temperatures of the hot spring make swimming inadvisable.

Mono Basin National Forest Scenic Area, also located on U.S. 395, 20 miles north of Mammoth, is a haven for hundreds of sea gulls. The Lee Vining Ranger Station, Mono Lake Ranger District, is on Calif. 120W, Tioga Pass Road, two miles off U.S. 395 (tel. 619/647-6525). The rangers have plenty of information about this, June Lake, and other parts of the district, as well as coloring books, books on fire prevention for kids, and a book about the area for adults.

These lava-strewn islands of Mono Basin are the result of volcanoes millions of years ago, and the lake is said to have a lunar landscape effect. This is a wonderful area to take the children, as it is flat and easy to walk. A walking trail goes around the lake (you'll only take part of it—it's 30 miles around). If you take Calif. 120E for five miles (off U.S. 395) you'll come to the Tufa Reserve where there is parking and picnic tables. A half-mile self-guiding nature trail begins there. Every day in the summer at 10 a.m. and 1 p.m. at South Tufa there are also ranger-guided walks, perfect for kids from ages 4 to teens. Walks last one to two hours. Call the ranger station for information on where to meet. The station is open daily in summer from 8 a.m. to 5 p.m.; in winter, weekdays only. You can also just start walking west or east from South Tufa and birdwatch and explore the springs and the sand tufa.

Hiking trails in the June Lake area are quite steep. Instead you can take your own driving tour that makes a loop of June Lake. Start 15 miles north of Mammoth on U.S. 395, which begins the southern portion of the loop. It takes you by four of the beautiful mountain lakes—June, Gull, Grant, and Silver—and the village of June Lake. June Lake offers not only beautiful scenery but fishing, hiking, camping, boating, and swimming in an alpine setting. Although the Forest Service offers a driving tour of June Lake, it's too long for children.

Mammoth Lakes Basin, carved out of a glacier, contains 13 mountain lakes. Five of them are accessible by car and offer short hikes. Contact the Forest Service for information on what area is appropriate for your family's hiking abilities.

Bicycling

Mountain bikes have become increasingly popular in Mammoth. The difference between them and a standard bike is that they have 18 gears and can climb hills with greater ease. There are 300 miles of open roads to explore in the Mammoth Ranger District. The **U.S. Forest Service** (tel. 619/934-2505) will be glad to furnish you with information on the best routes to take if you want to ride on your own. If not, there are two companies that provide guided rides.

Mammoth Adventure Tours, operating from the Mammoth Mountain Inn, P.O. Box 353, Mammoth Lakes, CA 93546 (tel. 619/934-2581, ext. 2211), now offers a Mountain Bike Package that makes a wonderful family trip. It includes three nights in a condo at the inn, three breakfasts, two lunches, two full days, and two half days of guided riding. They will choose trails based on your and your children's abilities, riding to the upper lakes, Owens Valley, and many other areas. What a neat way to see the area and spend time together. Bikes are included in the price. Children should be at least 7 years old. Prices are $199 per person, adult or child. The package is offered May through October. This trip can be arranged without accommodations as well. Call for prices.

If your children are at least 10 years old, **Alpine Adventures,** in the Shell Building in Mammoth (tel. 619/934-7188), will arrange guided rides wherever you want to go. Bikes are not included, but they'll recommend rental shops. Rates begin at $40 per hour per person, adult or child. Reservations are necessary. Call between 1 and 5 p.m. daily.

Fishing

The fishing season in Mammoth officially opens in April, when the anglers come out to try their luck. There are rainbow, eastern brook, cutthroat, golden, and brown trout in the local lakes and streams. Fishing is a wonderful activity for the whole family, since even the smallest toddler can participate. **Crowley Lake,**

Lake Mamie, Horseshoe Lake, and the **Twin Lakes** are just a few of the many places to catch some of the best trout around. Anyone over 16 will need a permit to fish which is obtained through the State Department of Fish and Game (tel. 619/872-1171). Fishing gear can be rented at almost any of the local sporting-goods stores in Mammoth.

For the serious fisherman, there are base camps where the whole family will be supplied with everything necessary for a memorable experience. One such place is **McGee Creek,** run by John and Jennifer Ketcham. (From October to May, contact them at Star Rte. 1, Box 100A, Independence, CA 93526; tel. 619/878-2207. From June through October, Rte. 1, Box 162, Mammoth Lakes, CA 93546; tel. 619/935-4324.) They will take you on horseback to selected sites where you can fish to your heart's content, and then they will cook the delectable trout for your dinner. The cost is $90 per person per day (adults or children), with a minimum of four days' stay.

Mountain Adventure Tours, in the Mammoth Mountain Inn, P.O. Box 353, Mammoth Lakes, CA 93546 (tel. 619/934-2581, ext. 2211), can instruct you and the children in fly-fishing as part of their Fly Fishing Package. This package includes three nights in a condo, three breakfasts, two box lunches, and two full and two half days of fly-fishing. The guide will take you to Crowley Lake, Owens River, and any other place he thinks is good that particular day. While children of any age are welcome, you'll have to decide if this trip is right for your youngster, as it is not cheap. The cost is $249 per person and does not include equipment. It's offered from May through October.

Horseback Riding

Sierra Meadows offers horseback riding for the whole family on its splendid grounds on Old Mammoth Road, three blocks from the Safeway (tel. 619/934-6161). Ride to the top of a glorious alpine peak and take in the beautiful sights. Minimum age for riding is 7. The rates (for adults and children alike) are $16 for one hour, $26 for two hours, $35 for a half day, $50 for a full day.

Pack Trips

Pack trips are a unique way of seeing the wilderness area. If you and your family are real horseback riding enthusiasts, you shouldn't miss the chance to explore the mountain trails on horseback and enjoy the camaraderie of eating and singing around an open campfire. Several area companies offer this exciting experience, and some have special parent-child trips regularly scheduled. Most packers provide the horses, food, and other gear, while you provide personal items (sometimes even tents). Contact the packers for brochures which give all trip options as well as lists of necessary gear. Find out which packers make camp at one location and take day trips from there. This is sometimes easier on younger children or first-time packers.

For a complete list of packing stations, contact the **Mammoth Lakes Resort Association,** P.O. Box 123, Mammoth Lakes, CA 93546 (tel. 619/934-2712).

Bob Tanner's Red's Meadow Pack Station is one such station. Contact P.O. Box 395, Mammoth Lakes, CA 93546 (tel. 619/934-2345) in summer or (tel. 619/873-3928) in winter. Bob Tanner has a variety of trips, ranging from three to ten days. His parent-and-child excursion is a five-day trip designed especially for young buckaroos. You travel at a leisurely pace, and the staff offers special assistance to the novices. They supply the horses, food, kitchen, and eating utensils. You supply your own bedroll and tent. Trips are offered in July and August. The price is $395 for adults, $265 for children 14 and under.

Mammoth Lakes Pack Outfit, P.O. Box 61, Mammoth Lakes, CA 93546 (tel. 619/934-6161), also offers an array of packing options. It's run by the Lou

Roeser family, the same people who run Sierra Meadows. They will take you on three- and four-day trips that are great for families. Children should be at least 7 for these trips. The three-day Woods Lake family trip is $295 per person, adult or child.

In addition to its regular pack trips, **McGee Creek Pack Station,** Star Rte. 1, Box 100-A, Independence, CA 93526 (tel. 619/935-4324 in summer, 619/878-2207 in winter), offers Junior Packer Campouts. Sometimes parents will drop their children at camp, then spend their vacation time in Mammoth playing tennis or golf. Beginner camp, Camp I, is for kids age 7 and up, and includes lessons, care of horse and equipment, fishing, and camping, and costs $275 for one week. Camp II is for intermediate riders 10 years and up and is $300 for one week.

Seeing a Ghost Town

For aficionados of the great Old West, **Bodie** (tel. 619/647-6486) is a must-see. It's an easy—and pretty—one-hour drive from Mammoth. Take U.S. 395 north about 60 miles. This "ghost" town, which had a population of 12,000 in 1879, was a gambling, drinking, and "shoot-'em-up" mining town. It reportedly saw around $100 million in gold during its heyday years. Preserved as is when it became a state historic park in 1962, more than 170 buildings remain in various stages of deterioration. Rather than just empty, interesting-looking buildings, some still have their contents intact, including the schoolhouse, in which you'll see books and desks and lessons that were written on the blackboard. Kids have a ball reenacting the days of the Old West here. This is the only Gold Rush–era town to be maintained like this—there are no souvenir shops, no T-shirts for sale, no food stands, not even modern rest rooms. Tours are conducted during the spring and summer by the U.S. Forest Service. The town is open year round (in summer from 9 a.m. to 7 p.m., till 4 p.m. the rest of the year), but it's best to visit in spring or summer because of the weather. A $3-per-person contribution is requested.

Swimming

A summer dip is always great entertainment for the kids. Mammoth has a large public facility designed for the whole family, and it's surrounded by breathtaking natural beauty. **Whitmore Pool,** on Whitmore Road (tel. 619/935-4222 or 619/934-8983), has a kiddie pool, showers, a grassy play area, and a picnic area. The outdoor pool opens in June and closes in September. Pool hours are 7:30 a.m. to 6:45 p.m. weekdays, 9 a.m. to 6:30 p.m. weekends. Admission costs $2 for adults (16 and over), $1 for youths 7 to 15, 50¢ for toddlers 1 to 6; infants, free. Showers are $1. Lessons are also available.

Tennis and Golf

Stop by the **Department of Parks and Recreation,** in the Minaret Shopping Mall, upper level (tel. 619/934-8983), for information on the community center public tennis courts and public golf courses outside of Mammoth Lakes.

Water Sports

If canoeing, sailing, catamaraning, kayaking, waterskiing, windsurfing, or anything else you can imagine doing on water sounds inviting, you'll find it at Mammoth. **Sierra Water Sports** (tel. 619/934-7188 or 619/873-6340) can fix you up with the equipment needed and will give you instruction as well on Crowley Lake. They specialize in teaching waterskiing to children, and will take kids as young as 4. Ski rentals or instruction begins at $40 per hour. You can also sail on Crowley Lake (with a guide) for $40 per hour. Reservations for either of these activities is a must.

Indoor Activities

If it's too cold out or you've just had enough outdoor activities, the **Department of Parks and Recreation** (tel. 619/934-8483) offers classes for the family during winter and summer. A cooking class is offered for children ages 6 to 12 at different times during the year. There are teen dances, film festivals, and even an Easter egg hunt. Call the department for dates and times.

For a step back in time, take the family to the **Mammoth Museum,** on Old Mammoth Road. Interpretative displays demonstrate the past and present of the Mammoth area, including the Gold Rush days. The museum is housed in an authentic log cabin built in the 1930s by Emmett Hayden, a mapmaker for the eastern Sierra. Open May through September, Friday through Sunday from 1 to 3 p.m. Admission is free.

Summer Events

Mammoth offers a wide variety of activities and special events during July and August. Contact the Department of Parks and Recreation for this year's exact dates.

The **Fourth of July** is an exciting time in Mammoth—the locals put on a show that lasts for days. There is a western parade complete with horses, a mule train, stagecoaches, carriage rides, buggies, cowboys, and saloon girls, who enact the days of the Old West.

Sierra Meadows puts on a wonderful rodeo July 4th weekend. It's open to the public, with a barbecue, hayrides, square dancing, team roping, a volleyball tournament, and many other exciting activities for the whole family. If you want your kids to experience the Old West firsthand, this is the time to go.

The **Mammoth Cycling Classic** (tel. 619/934-0651 or 619/934-2571, ext. 3250), the mountain bike world's championship event, is in its sixth year. Dates change every year, so call for this year's information. Bike enthusiasts are welcome to join in on the fun, which includes all levels of riding and is open to the public. Fun Day is set aside for all age riders.

The **Sierra Summer Music Festival** (tel. 619/934-2515) is held in July and August and has workshops for the kids, along with special theater presentations and many concerts.

WHERE TO RENT EQUIPMENT:
There are numerous places to rent ski equipment in Mammoth, including locations at the ski areas themselves, and at some hotels. There are also stores that rent summer-activity equipment, such as bikes and camping or backpacking items. As there are so many types of equipment, half- and full-day rates, multiday discounts, children's discounts, etc., we will not list prices here. Inquire when you call.

Kittredge Sports has two locations: in Mammoth, on Main Street (tel. 619/934-7566); in June Lake, on Boulder Drive (tel. 619/648-7274). Cross-country and downhill ski equipment is for rent. Both locations are open daily from 7 a.m.

Mammoth/June Ski Resort, in the Main Lodge (tel. 619/934-2571, ext. 3311 or ext. 3270), in Warming Hut II (tel. 619/934-2571, ext. 3370), and at June Mountain (tel. 619/648-7733), rents skis, boots, and poles for downhill, as well as cross-country ski equipment. The rental shop opens at 7:30 a.m. weekends, at 8 a.m. weekdays.

Mammoth Sporting Goods has two locations in Mammoth: on Main Street, across from Chevron (tel. 619/934-8474), and in the Sierra Centre Mall on Old Mammoth Road (tel. 619/934-3239). In addition to downhill and cross-country equipment, Mammoth Sporting rents mountain and road bikes, canoes, and fishing and camping gear. Both locations are open daily from 7 a.m.

The Outfitter is on Old Mammoth Road in the Minaret Village Shopping

Mall (tel. 619/934-3308). Here you can rent ski equipment, and you'll get a 20% discount if you show your room key. Open daily from 8 a.m. to 8 p.m. in winter, from 10 a.m. to 6 p.m. in summer.

Pine Tree Sporting Goods is located in Mammoth on Main Street (tel. 619/934-8020), and in June Lake on Boulder Drive (tel. 619/648-7203). The Mammoth location rents skis, ski bibs, and ice skates for adults and children; and mountain bikes, with sizes starting for ages 10 and up. The June Lake location rents sailboards. The Mammoth branch is open in winter on weekdays from 7 a.m. to 7 p.m. (on Friday till 11 p.m.), and on Saturday till 9 p.m. The June Lake branch hours are the same, except they close on Friday at 9 p.m. Spring and summer hours vary, but both shops are open daily.

Village Sports Center, on Main Street at Old Mammoth Road (tel. 619/ 934-8220), will rent junior equipment, clothing, skis, tents, and mountain bikes. Open daily in winter from 7 a.m. to 10 p.m. (till midnight on Friday). Summer hours vary.

WHERE TO STAY: Because Mammoth is a world-class winter resort, you will have an abundance of condominiums and motels to choose from when booking your accommodations. Be sure to ask about midweek and holiday rates, and minimum length of stay when you call or write for reservations. Each establishment has its own policy.

One of the most luxurious condominium rentals in Mammoth is **Snowcreek Resort,** situated on Mammoth Creek in town (write to Snowcreek Property Management, P.O. Box 1647), Mammoth Lakes, CA 93546 (tel. 619/934-3333, or toll free 800/544-6007). Snowcreek offers every kind of convenience for families, including indoor recreational facilities at the Snowcreek Athletic Club on the premises, and child care. During the winter months a courtesy shuttle transports guests to and from the ski area at Mammoth Mountain, a ten-minute ride. In the summer, hiking trails, lakes, and nature walks are close by. The resort is surrounded by picturesque mountains on all sides, and the stream that runs through the complex even provides trout fishing for the youngsters. There are plenty of open spaces for kids to run around and play. In the winter the kids can sled on the nearby hills—the first thing our 5-year-old did when we arrived. The geese, ducks, and dogs that roam the wooded area provide hours of entertainment.

The adjacent Snowcreek Athletic Club (tel. 619/934-8511) offers hours of activities après-ski, when you don't want to ski, and in the summer. Racquetball and tennis, an indoor lap pool and outdoor pool, a full-size gym for team sports, weight rooms, steam, and spas are just some of the facilities you can use. The club issues guest passes for its facilities for $10 per adult and $5 per child. The club also has a day-care center, which charges $1.50 per child per hour, and $2.50 per hour for two children from the same family.

All condominium units have wood-burning fireplaces and are completely furnished with towels, linens, and kitchen appliances. The open lofts and beamed ceilings create a feeling of spaciousness and warmth. There are one-, two-, and three-bedroom town houses with lofts available. A one-bedroom unit can sleep up to five people; three bedrooms can sleep ten. There is no daily maid service; if you stay more than seven days, there is a midweek cleaning. Fresh towels are provided daily.

Rates are $75 to $190 in winter, $60 to $110 in summer. There are some cribs available at no charge; be sure to request them ahead of time. No rollaways. The extra-person charge is $5 or $10 per night, depending on the season. Children 5 and under sleep free in their parents' room. Winter reservations are taken beginning October 1. Make weekend reservations at least one month in advance.

Another lovely condominium complex right next to Warming Hut II at Mammoth Mountain is the **1849 Condominiums,** P.O. Box 835, Mammoth

Lakes, CA 93546 (tel. 619/934-7525, or toll free 800/421-1849). There is an assortment of units here, depending on your needs, ranging from one to four bedrooms.

This complex offers three spas and a pool outdoors, an indoor sauna, showers and exercise equipment, as well as a big-screen TV and table tennis. You can buy your lift tickets and rent skis here. There are no restaurants on the premises, but Mammoth Mountain Inn, with two restaurants, is just up the road.

Most of the units have fireplaces, kitchens, TVs, video recorders, and daybeds. Some units even have bunk beds, sunrooms, and pot-bellied stoves, and are furnished with antiques. The condos come equipped with linens, towels, kitchenware, coffee maker, and toaster. Maid service is provided every third day of your stay, but fresh towels are given daily. For an extra charge, daily maid service is available upon request. There are coin-operated laundry facilities on the premises.

Weekday winter rates start at $120 for a one-bedroom unit (which sleeps two) and go up to $275 for a four-bedroom condo, which sleeps eight. Weekend winter rates are $150 to $300. Summer rates are less than half that (beginning June 1). Inquire about special five-day rates. Cribs and rollaways are available at no charge.

Mammoth Mountain Inn, at 1 Minaret Rd. (P.O. Box 353), Mammoth Lakes, CA 93546 (tel. 619/934-2581, or toll free 800/228-4947), offers the convenience and full service of a hotel within walking distance of the Main Lodge. During the ski season, just walk across the street to the ski lifts; in the summer, the inn offers bus service to many scenic areas. It also provides year-round complimentary shuttle service to the village and airport.

The inn offers standard hotel rooms, suites, and condominiums. There are two restaurants, the Mountainside Grill and the Yodler Restaurant (see the "Where to Eat" section for more information), and the Chili Dog's Arcade snackbar/game room in the basement, which sells sandwiches, hot dogs, pizza bread, chili, sodas, and candy and has a video arcade open from 5 to 10 p.m. daily. Although room service is available for breakfast and dinner, there aren't many selections for young children, and this service is provided only in the Main Building. The inn also has three indoor spas, a game room, giftshop, sport shop, and three cocktail lounges.

As if all this isn't enough, the inn even offers the excellent Small World Care Center, run by Donna Fleming, who can be reached at extension 2246 in the hotel. The day-care program is open seven days a week from 8 a.m. to 5 p.m., and in the winter reservations are recommended three weeks in advance. The center programs are divided by age, beginning with newborns and going up to age 12. Snacks and meals are provided, and they will even take your kids skiing if you sign them up for the program. Half-day rates are $16 for all ages; full-day rates are $30 for newborns, $28 for toddlers, and $26 for all other ages. There is a discount for two or more children from one family. Packages are available for day care / ski school, beginning at $21. Ski rentals cost $6. Summer programs are offered and include hiking, picnicking, and ecological studies.

Because there are so many configurations of rooms at the inn, be sure to explain your needs to the reservationist. All standard rooms come with color television, as do the other units. Condos have kitchenettes and phones, and the two-bedroom units have two bathrooms. There are suites with queen-size beds in the lofts, outdoor decks, and refrigerators.

In winter, hotel rooms (single or double) range from $59 to $90 in midweek, and $72 to $105 on weekends and holidays. Suites run $90 to $99 midweek and $105 to $120 on weekends and holidays. Condominium rates in midweek are $75 for a studio that sleeps two, $120 for one that sleeps four, and $180 for a deluxe accommodation that sleeps up to eight. The weekend and holiday rates are $95 to $200.

Summer rates are $46 to $65 for a hotel room and $65 to $99 for a suite or condominium. Special winter and summer packages are available.

In summer, children 12 and under stay free in their parents' room; in winter, children 2 and under. The extra-person charge is $10. No charge for cribs or rollaways.

The **Tamarack Lodge Resort,** P.O. Box 69, Mammoth Lakes, CA 93546 (tel. 619/934-2442), is a small retreat high up in the mountains surrounded by lakes and beautiful trails. There are 14 rooms in the lodge and 22 newly renovated cabins clustered around it on six wooded acres. The grounds are beautiful and overlook a sparkling alpine lake. In the winter you can rest in front of a blazing fire after a day of cross-country skiing while your children play checkers, cards, or any of the numerous games available in the main room. In the summer, listen to Mozart on the stereo system and put your feet up after a hike through the mountain trails. The Lakefront Restaurant, on the premises, serves fresh homemade goodies for breakfast seven days a week. Lunch is available on weekends, and dinner, nightly from November through April. There is a children's dinner ($6), or you can order smaller portions of grownup entrees.

Five of the lodge rooms have private baths; the others have sinks and mirrors but share toilet and bath facilities. There is a lovely two-bedroom suite on the third floor with living room, dining room, kitchenette, and private bath. The clean cabins all have kitchens and bathrooms, and some have fireplaces.

Winter rates (single or double occupancy) are $50 to $60 for a lodge room with a shared bath, $65 to $75 for a lodge room with a private bath. The upstairs suite is $110 for two to four people, $130 for five or six people. Cabins vary from $75 for a studio cabin, which sleeps two, to $165 for a four-bedroom cabin, which sleeps ten. There are all sorts of configurations in the middle.

In the summer, cabins rent for $70 to $170. There are porta-cribs for a one-time charge of $10. No rollaways. No charge for kids under 2. The extra-person charge is $10 per night. *Note:* There is a no-smoking policy in effect throughout the lodge.

The **Alpenhof Lodge** is a charming little chalet-style lodge on Minaret Road (P.O. Box 1158), Mammoth Lakes, CA 93546 (tel. 619/934-6330 or 619/934-8558), three miles from the main ski area and half a mile from Warming Hut II. This is an excellent choice for moderately priced accommodations. The Alpenhof has a cozy, old-world feeling, and the manager, Anna Lankes, is friendly and helpful. The hotel has a recreation room, inside therapy pool, and outdoor pool (open in summer only). Kids love the forest-like setting that surrounds the hotel. There are even picnic tables and a barbecue.

There is a laundry room for guest use. A babysitter lives on the premises. The charming Matterhorn Restaurant, adjacent to the hotel, is open for breakfast and dinner.

Some units have fireplaces, some have kitchenettes, and all have color TV, HBO, and direct-dial phones. Rooms are clean and charming, and most have lovely views.

Winter midweek rates are $58 to $66 for standard singles or doubles, $70 for a room with a queen-size bed and a fireplace, $100 for a mini-suite. Weekend rates are approximately $10 higher per room. Several ski packages are available in midweek, which include lift tickets and shuttle passes. Summer rates are $45 to $70. There is no charge for cribs or kids under 12 in their parents' room; those 12 and over are charged $7. The fee for rollaways is $7.

The **Best Western Wildwood Inn,** on Calif. 203 (P.O. Box 568), Mammoth Lakes, CA 93546 (tel. 619/934-6855, or toll free 800/528-1234), halfway between town and the Main Lodge, offers a swimming pool in the summer and a Jacuzzi year round. A free in-room continental breakfast is offered, and coffee, tea, and hot chocolate are served all day in the lobby. There is no restaurant on the premises, but the Wildwood is close to lots of restaurants.

The 32 rooms are clean and utilitarian and come with color TV and phone. The rooms with two queen-size beds are quite large, with plenty of room for the kids to play.

Winter midweek rates are $59 for a room with a double bed and $69 with a queen-size and a double; weekend rates are $69 and $84 respectively. Summer rates are greatly reduced (call for new summer rates). There is no charge for children 12 and under in the same room with their parents. Cribs are also free. Rollaways cost $6 per night. There are also ten condo units available, renting for $99 to $120 in winter; lower rates the rest of year.

For the truly budget-minded, Mammoth Lakes offers a **Motel 6** right on the main highway at 473372 Main St. (P.O. Box 1260), Mammoth Lakes, CA 93546 (tel. 619/934-6660). Reservations are essential at this 150-room motel, especially in the winter. Some rooms face the enclosed pool (open in summer only). Local calls are free, and there are free in-room movies. There's no restaurant on the premises, but there are vending machines for soft drinks, soup, coffee, and candy. A ski shuttle to all lifts stops in front of the motel every 15 minutes.

Winter rates are $26 for one person, $32 for two people, and $6 extra for each additional person. No charge for children under 18 staying in their parents' room. Rates go down approximately $5 a day in the summer. Cribs and rollaways are free.

A Bed-and-Breakfast Inn

The **Snow Goose Inn,** on Forest Trail, right off Calif. 203 (P.O. Box 946), Mammoth Lakes, CA 93546 (tel. 619/934-2660, or toll free 800/TRI-RENT), is Mammoth's quaint bed-and-breakfast "home-away-from-home." Unlike some bed-and-breakfast establishments that shy away from renting to children, owner Laurie Johnson has two kids of her own and a closet stocked with games for all ages.

Modeled after a European country inn, the Snow Goose offers 16 rooms, including 4 condo suites. Standard guest rooms sleep two and have private bath, phone, and color TV. There are also some rooms with kitchenettes. One of these sleeps six; the other, four. All condo units include TVs and phones and also have kitchenettes, living rooms, two bedrooms, and fireplaces. A full complimentary breakfast is served daily in the main room, featuring homemade muffins and coffeecake. Wine and cheese is served from 4:30 to 6 p.m., and snacks, coffee, and tea are available all day. There's also a hot tub to relax those sore muscles.

Winter midweek rates are $55 for standard rooms; kitchenette rooms rent for $72, double occupancy. Condo units cost $110 for four people. Weekend rates are $72, $82, and $132, respectively. After June 1, all rates are discounted 20%. Children under 12 are charged $5 for a rollaway or crib; those 12 and over are charged $10 extra.

Camping

This is a great way to experience the open meadows and rustic beauty of Mammoth. There are 19 campgrounds in just the Mammoth Lakes Ranger District, ranging from 5 to 96 sites per campground. We strongly suggest that first you go to the Ranger Station on Calif. 203 to obtain a list of available campsites. Once you have selected a spot, obtain a permit from the self-issue station at the campground entrance. Pay the fee, which will range from $5 to $8 per night per site, and attach your receipt to the numbered post site. Campfires may be built only in designated areas. Campsites are available on a first-come, first-served basis. June and July are the least crowded months; August and holiday weekends are the most crowded.

WHERE TO EAT: The **Mountainside Grill,** located inside Mammoth Mountain Inn, across from the Main Lodge (tel. 619/934-2581), serves breakfast, lunch, and dinner in a typical lodge setting of wooden rafters and high ceilings. Breakfast features lots of choices for adults and kids alike, including omelets ($4 and up), pancakes ($4, $3.50 for short stacks), huevos rancheros ($5.25), "The Demon" (three scrambled eggs with Italian sausage, spinach, mushrooms, onions, and cheese for $5.25), cereals, French toast, and Belgian waffles. The lunch menu includes sandwiches, salads, fresh fish, chicken, and burgers; prices range from $3.50 to $8. At dinner, adults can choose from seafood specialties, pastas, steaks, lamb, fresh fish, and three kinds of chicken. The house specialty, camarones flores, is delicious: jumbo shrimp are wrapped in bacon and served with a jalapeño-hollandaise sauce ($16). Dinners include soup or salad, a fresh vegetable, baked potato or rice, and bread, and cost between $10 and $18. (Leave room for the homemade desserts.)

Although there is no children's menu, special dinners are offered for youngsters. A child's steak dinner costs $10; a chopped-steak dinner, $7. They will supply you with a highchair or booster seat and will split dinner in the kitchen.

Breakfast is served Sunday through Friday from 7 to 11 a.m. and on Saturday from 6:30 to 11 a.m. Lunch is available daily from 11 a.m. to 2 p.m. Dinner hours are Sunday through Friday from 5:30 to 9:30 p.m. and on Saturday from 5 to 9:30 p.m. Reservations are a must on weekends for dinner. Parking lot. All major credit cards accepted.

The **Yodler Restaurant,** adjacent to the main building (tel. 619/934-2581, ext. 2236), serves lunch and dinner only in a casual setting, and it's a real draw for families. This Swiss-style chalet, built in Switzerland and reassembled in 1959 on its present site, has high ceilings, beautiful hand-carved wood designs, and a lovely view of the mountains. Soups, salads, burgers, barbecued ribs, chicken, fish, steak, and pasta are served here. The portions are large and very filling. Lunch and dinner prices range from $4.50 to $11, with lots of choices for kids (but no children's menu). Many families take advantage of the Yodler's take-out service. Call first and your food will be ready when you get there.

Boosters and highchairs are available. The best time to bring kids is between 5 and 5:30 p.m. No reservations accepted.

The restaurant—including take-out service—is open daily from 11 a.m. to 9:30 p.m. On Saturday and Sunday there's a skier's breakfast from 7 to 11 a.m. Parking lot. Major credit cards are accepted.

For a special night out, **Whiskey Creek,** located at the corner of Calif. 203 and Minaret Road, near the town and the slopes (tel. 619/934-2555), is the ultimate in sophisticated family dining. It's said that Whiskey Creek may be the most popular restaurant in town. Inside you'll find big, comfortable booths, polished wood beams, stone fireplaces, dimmed lighting, and a California-chic atmosphere. Children have their choice of teriyaki chicken, hamburger, deep-fried fish, or barbecued ribs, along with freshly baked bread and a choice of risotto, baked potato, or cheese-stuffed potato ($6 to $8).

In the meantime, adults are offered some very interesting menu selections, such as chicken caliente (a lime- and chile-marinated chicken breast on black beans with an avocado-tomatillo salsa and sour cream, for $12.50), or Greek prawns sautéed with leeks, tomatoes, oregano, and garlic ($17). There are also steaks, ribs, other seafood entrees, plus daily specials. All entrees include homemade soup or salad, freshly baked breads, broccoli cheese pie, and a choice of risotto, stuffed potato, or pasta. The house salads are also excellent. Prices range from $10 (for a small sirloin dinner) to $19 (for fresh California halibut served with béarnaise sauce). Be sure to save room for the desserts, which are wonderful. One deep-dish apple pie with vanilla ice cream was more than enough for three of us. There's also chocolate layer cake, a cookie-monster sundae, carrot cake, hot-fudge sundaes, and a mint-chocolate-chip ice-cream pie.

Highchairs and boosters are available. They'll split orders in the kitchen at no charge, and will happily warm baby bottles or baby food. Special non-alcoholic drinks can be ordered.

Open daily from 5 to 10 p.m. Reservations are an absolute must on weekends and are recommended on weekdays. Bring the kids for an early dinner or you could have a long wait in store. Parking in front. Major credit cards accepted.

A great place to take the whole family for breakfast, lunch, or dinner is the **Swiss Café,** on Old Mammoth Road south of Meridian Boulevard, in the center of town (tel. 619/934-6196). This charming chalet-style room with an inviting fireplace is cozy in the winter. Kids love the carved wooden reindeer in the middle of the room, as well as the beautiful view of the mountains from the big windows. In summer, you'll enjoy sitting on the lovely wooden deck outside, where you watch the sun rise or set over the mountains. As soon as you are seated, your children will be brought crayons and a children's menu to color. This will keep them amused while you choose your meal and relax. The service is quick and efficient, and the staff manages to keep kids happy and entertained throughout the meal.

The children's menu features pancakes ($1.50), oatmeal ($1.25), egg with bacon or sausage ($2), or French toast ($1.50), all served with milk or orange juice. For lunch and dinner, the kids can choose from a hamburger or hot dog with fresh fruit ($2.25), fish and chips ($3), a chicken drumstick served with potatoes and vegetables ($2.75), or one of several sandwiches. The regular menu offers lots of selections for breakfast, including omelets, pancakes, French toast, and assorted other goodies. The prices range from $3 to $8. For lunch you might want bratwurst ($6), fish and chips ($5), hot or cold sandwiches ($4 to $4.50), hamburgers or salads ($3.25 to $5). The dinner menu has delicious Swiss-German-style meals such as bratwurst ($7), smoked pork chops ($9), or knackwurst ($7), or American specialties ranging from baked chicken ($5) to a New York steak ($10). Soups, which come with the dinners, are wonderful, as is the fresh-baked bread.

Manager Frank Logan will be happy to accommodate you, and suggests that you make reservations on weekends during the busy meal times. There are highchairs (new and hand-carved) and boosters.

The Swiss Café is open daily except Wednesday from 6:30 a.m. to 9 p.m. Parking lot. Major credit cards are accepted.

Also located in town, in Mammoth Mall on Old Mammoth Road, is **O'Kelly and Dunn Co.** (tel. 619/934-9316). Owner Nancy O'Kelly serves breakfast and lunch in this small country-style café, which resembles a country inn, with lace curtains, fresh flowers, homemade jams, and a small boutique in the front of the restaurant selling beautiful and unusual imported items.

Portions are large, and everything is fresh and appealing. The oatmeal, served with butter, honey, brown sugar, and raisins, is delectable ($2.25) and too much for one person to finish. The omelets and special egg dishes, served with Irish spuds and choice of toast or muffins, are well prepared and delicious. Prices range from $3.50 to $6.50 for a complete breakfast. Although there is no children's menu, the kitchen will prepare scaled-down portions for the little ones. When they see families with young children, the staff are sure to ask how they can best accommodate them.

The grilled-cheese sandwiches and hamburgers are the most popular luncheon choices for kids ($2.50 to $3.75). Adults go for the Cobb salad or open-face beef brisket sandwich. Lunch averages $5.

Reservations are welcomed, especially on weekends and for large groups. Busiest breakfast times are 8 to 10 a.m.; lunch, noon to 1:15 p.m. They will supply highchairs and boosters and will gladly split portions at no charge.

The restaurant is open daily except Tuesday from 6:30 a.m. to 3 p.m. Parking in the shopping center. Major credit cards are accepted.

Another popular breakfast place in town is **The Stove,** on Old Mammoth Road (tel. 619/934-2821). The Stove, named after a big, old-fashioned pot-bellied stove, serves breakfast, lunch, and dinner in a rustic, country-style atmosphere. Breakfast features include pancakes and waffles ($3.25), French toast ($3.50), and many different kinds of omelets ($5 and up). You can purchase muffins, sweet rolls, and coffee from the on-premises bakery while you wait to be seated.

Lunch choices include standard sandwiches (B.L.T., turkey, tuna, etc.), burgers, Mexican selections, fresh fish, or soup and salad ($4.25 to $6). There's no children's menu at breakfast and lunch, but they will serve half orders for little eaters.

At dinner, there is a short children's menu. Entrees include a hamburger, fried chicken, or a grilled-cheese sandwich, and come with French fries and a cookie ($5). For the grownups, there's old-fashioned pot pies or beef stews ($7 and $9) or omelets, salads, sandwiches, burgers, or comforting country dinners like chicken-fried steak, pork chops and country gravy, or grilled liver and onions (all at $8.25).

Sassy seats and boosters are available. Adults portions can be split for two children. Baby food and baby bottles will be warmed by the kitchen staff.

Breakfast is served daily from 6:30 a.m. to 2 p.m.; lunch, from 10 a.m. to 2 p.m.; dinner from 5 to 9 p.m. Expect a long wait if you arrive on a busy weekend. No reservations accepted; no credit cards. Parking lot.

For the best hamburger around, try **Berger's Restaurant,** on Minaret Road (tel. 619/934-6622). This very busy place, located near the slopes, is quite popular with families. The portions are enormous and the service is efficient. The Berger's burger is a quarter pound of char-broiled beef served on a toasted bun with tomato, pickle, lettuce, and special sauce for $3. An order of "chili" fries is enough for four people to split, and consists of French fries loaded with chili. They also offer salads ($5.25), half a chicken with garlic bread and choice of salad or potatoes ($7), beef or pork rib dinners ($9 and $11). Fresh fish at market price, and wonderful hot sandwiches served with French fries starting at $5.50, are also available. Berger's does a big take-out business, with brisket, chicken, soup, chili, and ribs available to go. You can call ahead to order.

They have highchairs and boosters, and will gladly split meals at no charge.

Open daily in winter from 4 to 9:30 p.m.; in summer, from 11 a.m. to 9:30 p.m. Reservations are essential. Plenty of parking. No credit cards accepted.

Another popular place for take-out or dining in is **Angel's Restaurant,** Main Street at Sierra Road (tel. 619/934-RIBS), halfway between town and the ski slopes, next to the Motel 6. Known for its barbecued ribs and chicken, Angel's also serves soups and salads, an assortment of sandwiches ($4.25 and up), hamburgers ($4), and complete dinners after 4 p.m., with such specialties as chicken pot pie, lasagne, Mexican pizza, and chicken Mexicana. Lunch prices average $4.50; dinner, $6.25 to $12.

Kids can order off the children's menu—items such as grilled-cheese sandwiches, hamburgers, ribs, a chicken or beef dinner, all served with French fries. Prices range from $3 to $5.

Angel's has a busy bar area for après-ski lounging, and an early dinner to avoid the crowds is recommended. Take-out is another possibility. Boosters and highchairs are available.

Open Monday through Friday from 11:30 a.m. to 9:30 p.m.; on Saturday and Sunday, open for dinner only, from 5 to 10 p.m. No reservations accepted. Parking lot. Major credit cards welcome.

SHOPPING: For everything you need for kids, visit **Munchkins,** located on Old Mammoth Road (tel. 619/934-7337). You'll find children's clothes, toys, books, ski clothes, stuffed animals, dinosaurs in all sizes and shapes, games, books, baby things, and anything else your child could want. The owner, Susanne Krantz, is very helpful and will be glad to find something for you in the back if you don't see it out front. Open daily except Sunday year round from 10 a.m. to 6 p.m.

EMERGENCY PHONE NUMBERS: The emergency number here is **911.** There is emergency-room service at **Centinelia-Mammoth Hospital,** 85 Sierra Park Rd. (tel. 619/934-3311).

---

5. REDDING: GATEWAY TO LASSEN AND SHASTA-CASCADE

People come to this part of California because they want to get away from crowds and enjoy the out-of-doors. Some have called it the California of the Wild West, with its enormous open spaces, volcanoes, and huge, snow-covered peaks. If elegant accommodations, fine dining, and a fast pace are what you and your family enjoy on vacation, you might prefer elsewhere. But if you want to introduce your kids to an outdoor wonderland of open blue sky, clean azure-blue lakes, and rushing streams, where you can hike with them in dense forests and fish with them in peace and quiet, this is one area you'll love.

Mount Lassen, a dormant volcano that erupted as recently as 1921, rises 10,457 feet and reigns over the national park bearing its name. Mount Shasta, with its five glaciers and majestic stature of over 14,000 feet, towers to the north as you sit on beautiful Shasta Lake. The area is an outdoor-lover's dream.

Be sure to devote your evenings to star watching. Bundle up the kids and watch a blanket of stars cover the vast night sky. We had fun helping ours pick out the Big Dipper and the Milky Way. This, for city adults, is as big a treat as it is for the kids.

Sunrise in the mountains is special too. It's a time to watch and listen. Observe how the dark, shadowy fir trees become outlines against the sky. Then in a matter of minutes the light reveals stately pines with green and brown needles. Listen as the darkness gives way to sunlight, and the sounds of animals and birds start to emerge from the silence.

HOW TO GET THERE: This area requires a bit of time. It's 212 miles northeast of San Francisco, 165 miles north of Sacramento. The Shasta-Cascade area is reached most easily by automobile. However, if you're coming from southern or central California, you might consider flying into Sacramento Metropolitan Airport and getting a rental car. This will shave hours off the trip.

By car from Los Angeles and Sacramento, take I-5 all the way to Redding. From San Francisco, take I-80 to Sacramento; then continue north on I-5 past Red Bluff to Redding. For road conditions and information, call 916/244-1500.

Located just 15 minutes from Shasta Lake and an hour from both Mount Shasta and Lassen National Park, Redding is a good starting point for trips to these northern California wonderlands. It's a good place to stay, buy supplies, and rent equipment. However, if you're going to Lassen National Park, you can also drive from Sacramento straight to Lassen. To do so, take Calif. 36 at Red Bluff all the way to the park entrance.

A Stop Along the Way

Red Bluff itself is an interesting little town with neighborhoods of Victorian-style homes and other areas with great river views. The road from Red Bluff to Redding in summer and early autumn is typical California countryside with black California oaks dotting the brown rolling hills. In spring, it is rich green. Since the trip to Redding is a long one, we were pleased to find a few nice places to stop along the way.

William B. Ide Adobe State Historical Park (tel. 916/527-5927 or 916/225-2065) is a lovely little stop. Located one mile north of Red Bluff on Adobe Road, it's a small park bordered by the Sacramento River, at a spot where the river is very gentle and lazy. We spent a few hours watching the sun play on the slow-moving river. There are lots of places to sit and read a book, or play a game of catch. There are a couple of grassy areas with huge oak trees, as well as the home and barn area of William B. Ide (who was the first, and only, president of California).

There is a picnic area with a few barbecues and several picnic tables. The short, easy walk along the Sacramento River, and the walk to the top of the hill where there are old Indian campgrounds, are worth taking.

The park is open daily from 8 a.m. to sunset. There is a posted warning not to swim in the river because the bottom is uneven and the drop-offs are severe.

Blondie's Diner, 604 Main St., in Red Bluff (tel. 916/529-1668), is a real treat . . . and a real surprise. We happened to drive through Red Bluff on a Sunday afternoon when the town was completely closed up. Our "noses" directed us to Main Street, where we saw some activity in the diner and figured it was the only place open. Not only was it open, it was like a trip back home—a little island of familiarity in a small town—but with small-town hospitality.

This 1950s-style diner is done up in the unusual combination of pink and red, with some green and gray. Waitresses wear Blondie's Diner T-shirts and red aprons. The neon lights all around set a light tone, and pictures of James Dean add to the ambience. There is a jukebox with selections from Ricky Nelson and Elvis Presley to Glenn Miller. Don't miss the Monopoly board in the backroom.

The menu is extensive, and the food terrific. (We were in heaven with the bleu cheese hamburger and huge order of fries.) They offer milkshakes, Coca-Cola floats, and root beer floats. For brunch, wonderful blueberry and banana muffins are included in the price, and during the week, Tuesday through Saturday, they serve hot French bread as soon as you sit down. Prices range from $4.75 to $10.

The place hops during the evening. And some weekdays (and evenings on Thursday, Friday, and Saturday) there is a piano player. Boosters and highchairs are available. The diner is open Tuesday through Thursday from 11 a.m. to 2 p.m. for lunch and 5 to 9 p.m. for dinner, on Friday and Saturday till 10 p.m. Sunday brunch is served from 10 a.m. to 2 p.m.; closed Sunday night and all day Monday. Reservations accepted. Most major credit cards welcome.

If you just want good coffeeshop food (it's hard to find anything open here late and on Sunday), you might try **Perko's Koffee Kup,** located just off I-5 at the Red Bluff exit—take a left and drive to 201 Antelope Blvd. (tel. 916/527-6565) —for standard fare. We found this chain, with over 40 locations in northern California, to be very much to our liking. We enjoyed creating our own omelets. There are also half-pound burgers and char-broiled steaks. Prices for lunch range from $3.50 to $5; full dinners (soup or salad bar, vegetable, and potato) run $5.75 to $7.75. The cute children's menu has favorites like chicken and grilled-cheese sandwiches. Prices average $1.50 to $2.25. Highchairs and boosters are available.

Open daily from 5 a.m. to 11 p.m. Most major credit cards accepted.

GETTING ORIENTED: The town of Redding is located just off I-5, in a beautiful setting where you can see regal, snow-covered Mount Shasta in the distance. Throughout Redding, there are beautiful views of the Sacramento River. It is easy to find your way around town, with Hilltop, Cypress, and Market as the major streets.

You might want to stop first at the **Shasta-Cascade Wonderland Associa-**

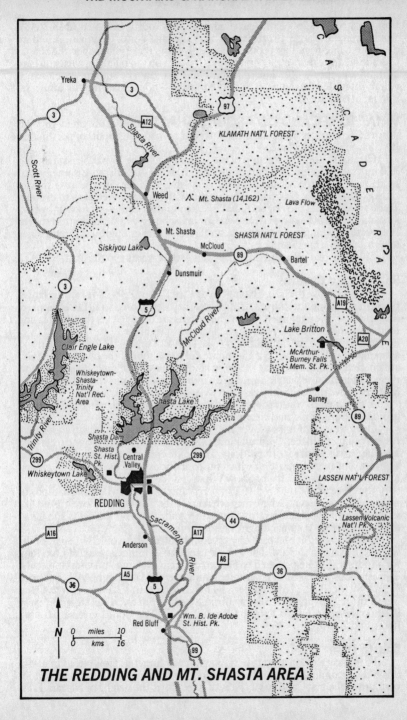

THE REDDING AND MT. SHASTA AREA

tion, located at 1250 Parkview, Redding, CA 96001 (tel. 916/243-2643). You'll never see a larger assortment of brochures and visitor information, and we dare you to find friendlier people. They really try to make your trip to the Shasta-Cascade area one that you'll never forget. In fact, you can tell them what you have in mind and they'll offer lots of helpful information. (Be sure to write them if you're interested in camping or houseboating—houseboats require a reservation far in advance.)

WHAT TO SEE AND DO AROUND SHASTA LAKE: Located 15 miles north of Redding, Shasta Lake is known for its myriad water-sport opportunities. It's a haven for houseboaters.

Created by the construction of the Shasta Dam in the 1940s, Shasta Lake has 370 miles of shoreline and a maximum depth of 515 feet. Because it was created by damming up the Sacramento, Pit, and McCloud Rivers (and two smaller creeks), Shasta Lake is virtually like a hand with several finger-lakes to explore. These smaller areas provide secluded inlets to venture into—on foot or by boat —making Shasta Lake a perfect place for houseboating and other water sports. It's great for fishing and swimming, and it also offers campgrounds in the thick forests surrounding the lake.

There are two other attractions as well—the caverns and the dam.

Shasta Lake Caverns

Located above the lake, **Shasta Caverns** (tel. 916/238-2341) are a relatively recent attraction for tourists. Until 1964 they were closed to all but spelunkers (experienced cave explorers). Today the caverns are open to everyone, displaying their large chambers of brilliant stalactites and stalagmites.

You can get to the caverns by car (take I-5 north to Shasta Caverns Road) and a catamaran will take you on a 15-minute sail to the foot of the caverns. Or if you are boating, you can dock at the ferry landing. From the ferry drop-off point, there is a ten-minute bus ride up a very winding, one-lane dirt road that takes you 800 feet above the lake with very pretty views as you ascend.

A guide takes you through the caverns, carefully explaining the different geological formations, and creating stories for the kids.

Our 7-year-old Andrew loved the Cathedral Room, which has an enormously high ceiling (100 feet), with all kinds of stalactites (those are the ones that look like huge icicles) and rock formations. The guide created a fairy tale about a king, a queen, and an evil wizard in which the formations were the imaginary characters. There were even parts for Snow White and the Seven Dwarfs.

You'll see where the original explorers came through, where the natural entrance to the cave is, and where they often find bats. The kids just love it! And like all good cave tours, there is a time when the guide turns off the lights and it's so dark you can't see your hand in front of your face.

We saw babies in backpack carriers and toddlers who would walk part of the way and be carried the rest. The tour takes about 45 minutes, and isn't too long for a toddler. But be prepared to have to do some walking and climbing stairs. This is a cool retreat on hot summer days when the lake can be 90°. Entrance fees are $9 for adults (13 and older), $4 for children 4 to 12; under 3, free. Open May 1 through September 30 daily from 8 a.m. to 5 p.m.; tours are given every hour on the hour. From October 1 through April 30, tours are given at 10 a.m., noon, and 2 p.m.

Shasta Dam

People say that once you see it, you'll never forget it. Completed in 1945, this is the second-tallest concrete structure ever built in the United States (Hoover Dam is the first), and has a spillway three times the height of Niagara Falls.

Nearby, on a knoll, you can see the entire dam, the power plant, gorgeous Shasta Lake, and the snow-covered volcano, Mount Shasta to the north. Located about 12 miles north of Redding via I-5 (take the Shasta Dam Boulevard exit), this is a nice place for a quick stop as you're on your way to the lake or caverns.

The **Shasta Dam Visitors Building** (tel. 916/275-4463) is open Monday through Friday from 7 a.m. to 4 p.m. There are no tours. It is free.

What to Do on Shasta Lake

There are myriad possibilities on this lake. There are hundreds of coves, dozens of campsites, and all manner of water sports.

HOUSEBOATING. This is one of our favorite things to do. Definitely the aristocracy's form of camping, houseboating has to be one of the best experiences in the world. Where else can you cruise along at a gentle speed on a vibrant blue lake, surrounded by forest-capped, red-brown hills that are under water during the wet months? The houseboat is like a luxury hotel room, but almost nicer because there are separate sleeping areas for adults and kids, and a completely equipped kitchen (even better than ours at home) with a dishwasher, microwave, trash compactor, double refrigerator, and gas barbecue. On the lake, you can travel without ever having to repack your bags and change rooms. The only drawback we found is not having a phone. (If you need contact with the outside world, you'll have to make special arrangements.)

It's heaven to dock in a secluded cove where you won't see anyone for hours. The kids can play on the banks, swim (you should bring extra shoes for walking on the rocky lakebed), fish, or entertain themselves on the boat. The adults can enjoy those activities or do absolutely nothing. A great idea—if you can afford it—is to rent a little powerboat and pull it along. That way you can travel around the lake without having to move the houseboat for short jaunts.

During the summer of dry years, Lake Shasta can be very low. This means that the banks of the lake are graded, almost stair-steps to what is normally the top of the lake. These dirt banks are ideal places for shell collecting. We spent many hours collecting perfectly formed tiny white shells to study and play with. (The low water can also have negative effects, though. For instance, it makes it somewhat more difficult to dock in the designated harbors, because there is much less maneuvering room.)

For more details on houseboating, see the "Traveling with Your Children" section in Chapter I.

There are many marinas that rent houseboats on Shasta Lake, but if you're planning to be there during the high season, be sure to book far in advance. Prices of houseboats fluctuate depending on the time of year. "In-season" is considered mid-June to mid-September; "mid-season" is generally the beginning of May till the June season begins, and again from mid-September through the end of September; "off-season" is generally the beginning of October through April. Some companies also have "pre"- and "post"-season rates that are one week before and one week after the season. All companies require substantial deposits for the houseboats. As with hotel rooms, always be sure to check to see if there are any special discounts and get a complete rundown on all the amenities.

Your best bet is to contact the **Shasta-Cascade Wonderland Association,** located at 1250 Parkview, Redding, CA 96001 (tel. 916/243-2643), for complete information. You'll also want to contact the individual marina with any questions you have before you book the houseboat.

One of our favorite marinas is **Holiday Harbor Resort and Marina,** P.O. Box 112, O'Brien, CA 96070 (tel. 916/238-2383, or toll free 800/251-BOAT, 800/258-BOAT in California). We like Holiday Harbor because it is full service, with a grocery store, restaurant, gift and ski shop, and complete boat-rental shop.

Holiday Harbor even includes pillows with its boats. Most impressive is the large number of staff and orientation people available to make your boarding and unloading as pleasant and as speedy as possible.

Here are some sample rates: in-season, $1,150 (sleeps six) to $1,650 (sleeps ten) per week; "pre"- and "post"-season, $925 to $1,395 per week; mid-season, $145 to $205 per night; and off-season, $105 to $160 per night. (For mid- and off-season, there is a 20% discount for four or more days.)

This is where the Toy Box is located (see below for details). Holiday Harbor also has an RV park.

We also like **Seven Crown Resorts,** which rents houseboats from both Digger Bay Marina and Bridge Bay resort. (For information and reservations, contact them at P.O. Box 1409, Boulder City, NV 89005; tel. 702/294-1770, or toll free 800/752-9669.) We like this outfit because you can rent boats during the high season for three- and four-day excursions as well as for a full week. (With little ones, sometimes the prospect of a week on a houseboat seems like a little too much togetherness for a little too long.) They also offer a linen service. Pillows are provided on each houseboat at no extra charge, and for an additional $10 fee per person (for the entire trip), you can exchange your used linens for clean ones as often as you like. (That's quite a luxury if you're on the boat for several days.)

All boats have fully equipped kitchens, a bathroom with shower or tub, and stereo cassettes. Not all have air conditioning and generators, so check if those are important to you. The peak season is mid-June through mid-September; low season, from mid-September through mid-June.

Bridge Bay is a full-service resort with a lovely restaurant, market, giftshop, swimming pool, and hotel. Several different kinds of houseboats can be rented from this marina. The Cascade 6 sleeps six people and is equipped with air conditioning and generator. Rates vary considerably. During peak season these run $1,580 per week, but you can also rent them for a three-day weekend at $935 and for four days midweek at $1,150. In low season it costs $995 for a full week, or $315 a day. Short, midweek rentals range between those two. The Sierra 10 sleeps ten and also has air conditioning and a generator. During peak season they rent for $1,790 a week. Three- and four-day rentals are $1,055 to $1,305; Low season is $1,130 a week, $360 per day. Three- and four-day rentals are $630 to $815. The other boats that do not have air conditioning and generator cost less.

Digger Bay Marina has a grocery store, marine services, and rents other little boats as well. You can get several kinds of houseboats here, but not the new ones that have air conditioning and generator. They are less expensive than some of the boats at Bridge Bay. For example, the Playmate 10 during peak season rents for $1,385 per week; during low season, $860 per week or $280 per day.

Lakeview Marina Resort, P.O. Box 2272, Redding, CA 96099 (tel. 916/223-3003), is another place to rent from. Lakeview offers different sizes of houseboats, but all have two bathrooms, two refrigerators, microwave, and air cooler. Houseboats range from 53 feet to 56 feet and will sleep from 10 to 14 people. Some boats have "penthouses" on the upper level. Boats are leased only by the week during season. Other times of the year, boats can be rented for three and four days, and there are special holiday packages. Lakeview does not provide pillows.

Since there are so many different combinations, depending on the boat you want and the time you want it, prices vary tremendously. Be sure to write for a current brochure. Here are a few examples: A 56-foot, royal deluxe houseboat that accommodates 14 people starts at $1,855 a week. It costs $190 a day midseason and $160 a day off-season (minimum number of days apply). A 56-foot royale cruiser that sleeps 12 starts at $1,745 a week; it costs $189 a day midseason and $155 a day off-season. You can also rent aluminum fishing boats and patio boats here.

Silverthorn Resort, P.O. Box 4205, Redding, CA 96099 (tel. 916/275-1571, or toll free 800/332-3044), has houseboats that accommodate 10 to 12 passengers, with fully equipped kitchenettes, two bathrooms, two showers, two refrigerators, microwave, two air conditioners, linens, and bedding. Prices for boats range from $1,750 to $1,850 per week in-season, $1,390 in pre- and post-season, $1,050 to $1,125 in mid-season, and $840 to $900 off-season. Mid- and off-season, you can rent houseboats for shorter periods of time. You can also rent fishing, patio, and ski boats here. *(Note:* Even if you don't rent from Silverthorn, be sure to find out if the waterski show will be presented when you're on the lake. It's renowned throughout northern California.)

Located at Packer's Bay Marina, **Holiday Flotels, Inc.,** P.O. Box 336-B, Redding, CA 96099 (tel. 916/221-5666), is another outfit. Houseboats have two bathrooms, two refrigerators, coolers, and a microwave oven. Bring your own linens and pillows. They have some small 44-foot boats that sleep eight people. These rent for $995 per week during the high season. During their low season (from the end of April through early June and mid-September to October), you can get very cheap rates, starting at $110 per night (minimum days required). The larger boats sleep 12 and range from $1,650 to $1,775 per week in high season and $150 to $170 per night in low season. Closed from early October through April.

OTHER WATER SPORTS. Don't miss the "adult toys" here. We had loads of fun at the **Toy Box Fun Rental Center** at Holiday Harbor, P.O. Box 112, O'Brien, CA 96070 (tel. 916/238-2383, or toll free 800/251-BOAT, 800/258-BOAT in California). This rental center bills itself as Shasta Lake's entertainment hot spot. You only have to try a little addictor boat (a tiny two-seater speedboat) once to know what water-sports entertainment is all about. It beats sunning by the water's edge, hands down.

Ever try a full-size speedboat? And how about waterskiing? People here say that if the kids want to learn, and they're comfortable in the water, they can enjoy the sport. The Toy Box has canoes to rent, jet skis (a tremendous hit with teenagers), paddleboats, windsurfers, even fishing poles. One unique feature about the Toy Box is that they'll actually work with you till you know how to use the equipment. Rates vary widely depending on what you want, for how long, and when you want it. Advance reservations are recommended. If you are renting your houseboat from Holiday Harbor they'll give you a 20% "tag-a-long" discount.

If your kids would like to learn how to waterski, **Mike Suyderhoud Water Ski Center** (tel. 916/222-8826) is a good place to do it. Located at Silverthorn Resort, Mike teaches children of all ages. The main criterion is that they feel comfortable in the water and know how to swim. He starts with a special training boom with a solid bar that allows the kids to hold on while they're getting used to the skis. They have enough support so they're pulled without having all the falls. He teaches all skill levels.

Ski lessons cost $25 for a 20-minute session; five lessons are $100, and they can be shared. You can also get instruction by the hour—the rate is $55 for one hour. Rental skis cost extra.

There is a fully stocked pro shop that has waterskis, wet suits, life jackets, and the like. Open daily during the summer from 8 a.m. to 5 p.m. Reservations for rentals advised.

HIKING AROUND THE LAKE. Shasta Lake has several good family trails. They're relatively short and don't climb in elevation. Here are some tips, though. Some of the trails are rocky, so be sure to wear hiking shoes. Also carry sunscreen, bring lots of water to drink, and watch out for poison oak. For information about good trails for your family, you can stop at the **Shasta Lake Ranger District and Visi-**

tor Center, located about ten miles north of Redding on I-5 at 6543 Holiday Rd., Redding, CA 96003 (tel. 916/275-1587).

Here are a few easy walks to get you started.

Waters Gulch Trail is a 3½-mile trail. Even though long, it's an easy, lovely wide trail that winds through oak trees. There are benches halfway up, affording beautiful vistas of the Sacramento arm of the lake. The trailhead is located at Packer's Bay Road, a quarter mile before the boat ramp.

Eastside Trail at Packer's Bay is a short half mile to a good swimming and fishing hole. The trailhead is marked.

Bailey Cove Trail is a 2¾-mile loop that takes off from the Bailey Cove parking lot and winds around an island-type area that has beautiful views of the McCloud arm of the lake. There are some ups and downs, but it is fairly level. There's a picnic area and rest rooms at the start. Kids can swim anywhere along the cove.

OUTDOOR ADVENTURES AROUND MOUNT SHASTA: Mount

Shasta is not only beautiful from a distance, but offers many adventures as well. We suggest that you write or call the **Mount Shasta Ranger District and Visitor Center,** 204 W. Alma, Mount Shasta, CA 96067 (tel. 916/926-4511), for specific hiking information for your family. It's been said that some hearty 9-year-olds have hiked to the top of the mountain, but few of us are ready for a climb that strenuous. The rangers will be able to give you suggestions tailor-made for your family's abilities.

River Rafting and Canoeing

River rafting and canoeing will be some of the most exciting times you share with your kids. The entire Shasta-Cascade area is perfect for rafting because the river terrain varies, offering everything from gentle waters to raging rapids. Once considered an adult sport, river rafting is rapidly gaining in popularity for families. Expect to get wet, do some work, and have lots of fun.

Rivers are classified in terms of difficulty—from I to V. The river classification can change depending on the time of year. Class I is the easiest. Trip lengths vary from an afternoon outing to several days. Many rafting companies run trips on different rivers; all will send you detailed brochures about their trips and the rivers they run.

Of course, the primary safety consideration is how well your children can swim. Most rafting expeditions will not take children under 8, but a few will. If you go with your kids, rafting experts suggest that you be sure the kids will be comfortable; that the trip be designed with children in mind. If you're sure that everyone on the trip knows that kids will be along, you can be assured that there will enough time for the kids to play on the banks and enjoy the trip at a kid's pace. (But don't assume anything—always get details!)

Turtle River Rafting Co., 507 McCloud Ave., Mount Shasta, CA 96067 (tel. 916/926-3223), runs trips for children as young as 4 on very gentle sections of the Klamath River. In addition to their one-, two-, three-, and four-day trips, they design trips especially for families. Some even have storytellers along. They offer a very large selection of special-interest trips. Here are a few examples: A two-day Class II "Kid's Klamath" (river) trip with a storyteller is $90 per child; $125 per adult. A two-day Class III Family Rafting outing on the Trinity or American River (minimum age is 8) with a storyteller is $112 to $118 per child; $140 to $147 per adult. Meals are included, and you can rent inflatable kayaks for personal use for an additional fee. Seasons are spring and summer, depending on the river and the yearly rainfall.

Wilderness Adventures, P.O. Box 938, Redding, CA 96099 (tel. 916/243-3091), is another outfit that takes children. Owned and operated by Dean

Munroe, a professional river guide, Wilderness Adventures runs raft trips on the Scott, Lower Klamath, Sacramento, Trinity, and Upper Klamath Rivers. Several trips welcome children.

The Trinity River and Lower Klamath River are both Class II+ to III rivers, which means that they have long stretches of mellow water, nice beaches, and good places to hike. They're perfect for family rafting. The minimum age for both is 10. There are one- and two-day trips on the Trinity. Prices are $70 for one-day trips, $155 for two-day ones. Trips on the Lower Klamath range from one day to four days. Prices are $70 for one day, $155 for two days, $255 for three days, and $335 for four days.

The trip through the Sacramento Canyon has more than 45 rapids and is a Class III+ trip. There are one- and two-day trips, and the minimum age is 10. Prices are $70 for one-day trips, $155 for two-day trips. The Upper Klamath / Hell's Corner Gorge is the biggest summertime white water on the West Coast, and is considered a Class IV–V trip. Minimum age is 12 for the two-day trips. Prices for a two-day trip to Upper Klamath River / Hell's Corner Gorge range from $205 to $235, depending on the time of year.

If you already know what you're doing, you can also rent your own raft and canoe at **Park Marina Water Sports,** 2515 Park Marina Dr. in Redding (tel. 916/246-8388). The rental rate for a two-passenger raft is $19; for a four-man passenger raft, $29; for a six-passenger, $39. Two-passenger canoes are $29 for one day, $50 for two days. Reservations are required. Open daily from 8:30 a.m. to 6:30 p.m.

Winter Sports

Mount Shasta is a beautiful area with different terrain that offers wonderful downhill and cross-country skiing. The **Mount Shasta Cross Country Area** has three miles of marked (not groomed) trails for beginning, intermediate, and advanced cross-country skiers. To get to the area, take I-5 north to Everitt Memorial Hwy. (past Calif. 89).

The Bunny Flat Trail begins about 12 miles up the highway. This three-quarter-mile trail has gentle, open terrain, and is intended for beginners. The Sand Flat Trail is a level, beautiful, 1¼-mile trail that is designed for beginners. The Overlook Loop Trail is a one-mile trail for intermediate skiers that begins at Sand Flat. The trail heads west, where you get wonderful views.

For more information, call the **Mount Shasta Ranger District** (tel. 916/926-3781).

There are also two snow-play areas, located at Snowman's Hill and Bunny Flat. The season runs from Thanksgiving to Easter, and is most crowded on holidays and weekends.

Mount Shasta Ski Park, 104 Siskiyou Ave., Mount Shasta, CA 96067 (tel. 916/926-5254, or 916/926-6101 for snow conditions), is a family ski area that offers alpine skiing. There is a lodge with food service and a bar, a ski school, retail and rental shops, and a first-aid station. The Pups program is a ski school for children 3 through 7. For one session (1½ hours) the charge is $16; for two sessions, $24. (This is a learn-to-ski package that includes equipment rentals.) Older children attend the regular ski school and are grouped by ability level. For one session (1½ hours) the charge is $14; for two sessions, $19 (not including rentals). Lifts operate daily from 9 a.m. to 4 p.m.; night skiing is available Wednesday through Saturday from 4 to 9 p.m. Children 8 to 12 get reduced fees and children under 8 ski free. Adult full-day lift tickets cost $19; junior (8 to 12) tickets cost $12. Night skiing is $14 for adults, $10 for kids 8 to 12.

OTHER HIGHLIGHTS OF THE AREA: With all of this outdoor paradise, there are still other adventures.

Don't miss this one! An absolutely magnificent day trip is the one to **McArthur-Burney Falls Memorial State Park** (tel. 916/335-2777), located 11 miles northeast of Burney off Calif. 89, in Pit River country. Take Calif. 299 east from Redding to Calif. 89; then go north about five miles.

Burney Falls is a spectacular waterfall located between Mount Shasta and Mount Lassen. Known as one of the wonders of the world, the falls thunders down a 129-foot drop to form emerald pools below, sometimes shrouded with misted rainbows. It's a gorgeous spectacle. The falls remain constant throughout the year, with a temperature of 48°.

The park is forested with Ponderosa pine, as well as a wide variety of firs, cedars, black oaks, and dogwood. It is an unbelievable show of nature's majestic color schemes in the autumn.

The best way to enjoy the show is the self-guiding nature trail. While we prefer to carry Elizabeth, our toddler, we saw a pair of hearty grandparents wheeling a stroller for the first half of the walk. But if you can, go all the way (you'll never be able to use a stroller once you cross the bridge). Bring lots of film, and be sure to get the kids involved in the walk—they'll learn a lot of botany.

During the summer there are naturalist walks and campfire programs conducted by rangers.

Excellent camping facilities are available with 118 campsites, rest rooms, hot and cold water, showers, stoves, tables, and food lockers. A boat ramp is also available at nearby Lake Britton.

Don't miss nearby **Lake Britton** when you're at Burney Falls. We packed a large lunch (with lots of juice and extra water) for our afternoon in the sun. The lake is shallow and just perfect for wading. It has a nice sandy beach.

Our final junket of the day is a stop at **Crystal Lake Fish Hatchery** (tel. 916/335-4111). Located half a mile downstream from McArthur-Burney Falls Memorial State Park, this is an interesting 20- to 30-minute side trip. (To get there from Redding, take Calif. 299 past Burney about five miles toward Alturas. The road sign says Cassel Road. Take a right to the sign that indicates the hatchery.)

We had never seen a hatchery before, and the thousands of fish were a sight to behold! This hatchery has 66 rearing ponds (each is 100 feet long) that have a variety of sizes and kinds of fish—different strains of rainbow trout, brook trout, and eagle lake trout. The sizes vary from catchable trout (about three fish to the pound) to little ones that are as small as 1½ inches. In one year's time the hatchery will raise 1.5 million fish!

The fish-and-wildlife assistant feeds the fish four times a day, and if you time it right, you can watch the fish being fed. Even if you don't get to see a feeding, it's fascinating just to watch the groups of different fish swim in their ponds. If they get startled, they all change direction at once.

The hatchery is open daily from 8 a.m. to 5 p.m.

WHAT TO DO IN REDDING: If you find yourself with some time in Redding proper, there are pleasant ways to pass the time. **Caldwell Park,** on Quartz Hill Road, is located next to the river—a beautiful location with lots of oak trees and small rolling hills. There is a public swimming pool, swings and slides, and a full playground for little kids. Next to the river are picnic tables and barbecues. It is beautiful, especially when the sun is going down. In Caldwell Park is **Redding Museum and Art Center,** 1911 Rio Dr. (tel. 916/225-4155), a good museum of Native American and pre-Columbian artifacts, relics of the Gold Rush, and rotating exhibits of contemporary art. In April, there's a children's lawn festival during which the days of the covered wagons are recalled. The children get to bake bread in wood stoves, do fence painting, and grind cornmeal.

Winter hours are Tuesday through Friday and on Sunday from noon to 5 p.m., and on Saturday from 10 a.m. to 5 p.m. Summer hours are 10 a.m. to 5 p.m. daily except Monday. Closed major holidays. No admission charge.

Also located on the Caldwell Park grounds is the **Carter House Science Museum** (tel. 916/225-4125). There is an animal discovery room with live animals, many of which are native to the northern California area (screech owls, great horned owls, yellow-billed magpies), and some domestic animals (rabbits and guinea pigs) for kids to pet. There is also a greenhouse solarium and another area where they rotate exhibits of natural history of the area. Open Tuesday through Sunday from 10 a.m. to 5 p.m.

The **Sacramento River Trail** is a wonderful place to walk, jog, and bicycle. This recreational trail is on both sides of the river between Deistlehorst Bridge and Keswick Dam, and runs for approximately 2½ miles on each side. To get there, find the intersection of North Market Street and Riverside Drive. Proceed west for almost half a mile (before you cross the Calif. 273 bridge). There is a parking lot. You can also find parking and facilities on the other side of the river.

Waterworks Park, 151 N. Boulder Dr. (tel. 916/246-9550), is one of the cooler ways to spend a hot day in Redding. This water park has three giant water slides, a kiddie water playground, water volleyball, and a white-water inner-tube river ride. Lifeguards and first-aid staff are on duty all the time. Open daily Memorial Day to Labor Day from 10 a.m. to 8 p.m. Admission costs $9.75 for adults, $7.75 for children 3 to 11; children under 3 and seniors over 65 are free. To get there, take the Burney/Alturas exit (Calif. 299 East) off I-5 at North Redding.

Shasta State Historic Park (tel. 916/243-8194). Just 4 miles west of Redding on Calif. 299 stands the remains of the old town of Shasta. Once considered the "Queen" of the Gold Rush towns in the region, it now consists of a small group of restored brick buildings. The museum in the old Courthouse is a good one, with lots of paintings done in the 1800s and displays depicting Shasta County's history back to the beginning of the 1800s. The General Store is restored to its 1880s style with authentically arranged counters that have many antique items and some cleverly designed reproductions. This is a lovely area for picnicking. The park is open daily from 10 a.m. to 5 p.m. (closed Thanksgiving, Christmas, and New Year's Days). Admission is $1 for adults, 50¢ for children 6 to 17.

South Redding Park, located at the corner of South Market Street and Parkview Avenue, is a lovely little park with wonderful children's equipment, baseball and softball fields, and tennis courts.

For another type of entertainment, **Mr. C's Family Billiards** is a fun place too. There are 14 pool tables and a video arcade. Tables rent two ways: either 50¢ a game or $2.20 per hour per person for two people ($1.90 per person per hour for three people). Kids under 12 playing with their parents pay no fee.

Very different from other billiards parlors, and no alcohol is sold here (the hardest drink they sell is Classic Coke). There are signs around proclaiming "No Profanity," and there is a designated smoking area that is not right at the billiard tables. Teens love this place.

Open Sunday through Thursday from 10 a.m. to 10 p.m. and on Friday and Saturday till midnight.

And a Great Little Store . . .

Learning Country, 3286 Bechelli Lane (tel. 916/223-0596), is a delightful educational store. Located in the Shasta View Market shopping area, it's a small store with a nice assortment of workbooks and paperback books, and some unusual toys and discovery items. Science toys and wonderful coloring kits on Native Americans, different species of fish, and animals are also available. There is a table in the middle where children can sit down and work with some of the materials. Open Monday through Friday from 10 a.m. to 5:30 p.m. and on Saturday from 10 a.m. to 4 p.m.

WHERE TO STAY: Accommodations are simple in this neck of the woods. Don't expect luxury if you're up here, but you'll be comfortable and you'll meet some of the nicest people around.

Moderately Priced

The best bet for the money are the rooms at the **Best Western Hilltop Inn,** at 2300 Hilltop Dr., Redding, CA 96002 (tel. 916/221-6100, or toll free 800/ 528-1234)—they are simple but adequate and very comfortable. And the people at the Hilltop Inn couldn't be nicer.

There is a children's swimming pool, and a wading pool for babies. It's a gated area, away from the parking lot. There is also a small grassy area for children's play.

One of the best features of this inn is the complimentary full continental breakfast (served Monday through Saturday), featuring a variety of rolls, sweet rolls and muffins, fruit, orange juice and cranberry juice, granola and raisin bran cereals, as well as coffee, tea, and milk. Though there is no room service, if anyone in your party is feeling under the weather, the staff will very graciously provide a tray so that you may select as complete a breakfast as you wish and take it to your room. Sometimes the older kids will come to the pub by themselves in the morning and have their continental breakfast there. On Sunday only complimentary coffee and rolls are offered in the lobby.

After you're finished with the free continental breakfast, you may choose to buy lunch (and later, dinner) at C. R. Gibbs Alehouse, a traditional English-style pub that has sandwiches, soups, and the like. (See the "Where to Eat" section for details.)

A room features either a king-size, a queen-size, two double, or two queen-size beds, a game table and two high-back armchairs, and a desk. There is a separate vanity area with a large counter, and all rooms have shower/bath combinations. There is free HBO.

Rooms cost $58 to $68 for singles, $68 to $78 for doubles. Request a king- or queen-size bed if you prefer. Adjoining rooms are available, and children under 12 stay free in the same room with their parents. No charge for cribs, but rollaways cost $12 per night.

Also lovely is the **Red Lion Motor Inn,** at 1830 Hilltop Dr., Redding, CA 96002 (tel. 916/221-8700, or toll free 800/547-8010), in a very convenient location. This modern mountain-lodge–looking interior has a two-story lobby done in reds and browns, and features a coffeeshop and restaurant. The help is extremely friendly.

The 195 very pretty rooms are good sized. Most have a table with two chairs, a desk and chair, free HBO, plus complimentary sundries—shampoo, conditioner, and hand lotion. The rooms are quite comfortable, with lots of drawer space; some have balconies. Even though the inn is surrounded by a parking lot and lots of asphalt, the inside rooms overlooking the pool have a view that is wooded and quiet. The area around the pool is lovely, large, with green indoor-outdoor carpeting. Tables, lots of lounge chairs, and many trees complete the inviting picture. In addition to the full-size swimming pool and the Jacuzzi, there is also a wading pool. Pool hours are 10 a.m. to 10 p.m. Kids also love to amble around the putting green (with complimentary clubs and balls).

Other amenities include room service from 6 a.m. to 10 p.m., dry cleaning, and laundry. There is also a reasonably priced coffeeshop and fine-dining restaurant, both of which have highchairs and boosters and will make special menu accommodations for children.

Rates range from $64 to $72 for singles, $78 for two double beds, $72 to $82 for a king-size bed. Suites (large sitting room with bar and refrigerator and king-size bed) cost $225. Children under 18 stay free if they use existing bedding, but cribs cost $5. Each additional person pays $10 per night.

Budget

You'll find many inexpensive places to stay in this area. The **Redding Lodge,** 1135 Market St. (near Calif. 299), Redding, CA 96001 (tel. 916/243-5141), is a step up from a really inexpensive motel. Although it's located downtown, it borders a residential area and there are lots of trees around the parking lot. Nicely kept up by owners Mr. and Mrs. Goldberg, this "mom and pop" operation has many extra little touches.

The rooms feature hairdryers and have real Kleenex instead of some of the sandpapery-type facial tissues. There's fresh-brewed coffee in every room. You have a choice of single-bedded rooms, or deluxe rooms; there are even two no-smoking deluxe rooms. All are quite lovely.

These friendly folks will gladly put in a crib for your child and try to make your stay very pleasant. Although this is a motel, there is a little grassy area in a corner with a gazebo where children can play in pretty surroundings.

Rooms range from $36 to $42. Children under 12 sleep free in their parents' room; additional guests pay $4 per night. Cribs are free.

The **Best Western Ponderosa Inn,** 2220 Pine St., Redding, CA 96001 (tel. 916/241-6300), is a typical two-story motel. In the center is a nice-sized swimming pool and a little wading pool. The motel is located on the south end of downtown, two blocks away from Redding City Park. Lulu's Coffee Shop is on the premises and serves breakfast, lunch, and dinner. There is also a nice lounge.

The units are pleasant. The double-bedded rooms are good sized and have a bathtub. The single-bedded ones are slightly smaller, with showers, but they all have ample drawer space, and all have a table for meals or card playing, two chairs, and instant coffee makers. Adjoining rooms are available.

Rates range from $32 to $50, single or double. Kids under 12 stay free in the same room with their parents. There is a $5 charge for cribs, and additional adults pay $6 per night.

Camping Facilities at Shasta Lake

There are 28 campgrounds at Shasta Lake, which vary from walk-in sites to trailer sites. There are even boat-in campgrounds, and campgrounds where you can choose a site on the shore of Shasta Lake. Most of them are on a first-come, first-served basis. Contact the **Shasta Lake Ranger District,** 6543 Holiday Rd., Redding, CA 96003 (tel. 916/275-1587), for information before you go. There are also several private campgrounds in the area. The **Shasta-Cascade Wonderland Association,** 1250 Parkview, Redding, CA 96001 (tel. 916/243-2643), can send you brochures.

WHERE TO EAT: In such a small city (pop. about 50,000), we were surprised to find so many good restaurants.

Upper Bracket

The restaurant we like is **C. R. Gibbs,** at the Best Western Hilltop Inn, 2300 Hilltop Dr. (tel. 916/221-2335), a dimly lit dinner house great for a leisurely meal with kids who don't have to eat "hurry-up" style. A huge iced shrimp bowl to share among the people in your party, and scrumptious beer muffins, accompany the entrees, which range from chicken in a puff pastry to broiled salmon, blackened redfish, and prime rib. There are pasta dishes, and a salad bar that is priced with and without the shrimp bowl. Prices range from $9 to $15. For kids, they'll make up hamburgers, cheeseburgers, and clam strips, for $5.25, including shrimp bowl and muffin. There are highchairs and boosters available, and the management will gladly warm baby bottles and baby food.

Open daily from 5:30 to 10 p.m. Reservations accepted; most major credit cards welcome. Easy parking.

Moderately Priced

Located at the back of Shasta Center Plaza is **J. D. Bennett,** 1800 Churn Creek Rd. (tel. 916/221-6177). When you walk in, you'll feel like you have been transported to a turn-of-the-century San Francisco–style saloon with Victorian décor, high two-story ceilings, and lots of plants. The place has an outdoorsy feel to it. The staff likes children, and they're pleased to tell you that this is a family-oriented restaurant. You'll know that as soon as you see the children's menu inside a complete little coloring book. Their general attitude is that kids are fun to have along. The children's menu includes a junior burger, hot dog, even a mini-plate of lasagne, as well as other selections. Prices range from $2 to $3 (meals come with either fries, chips, or fruit). They also serve a variety of non-alcoholic "cocktails" for young tastebuds. Of course, there are highchairs and boosters.

The adult choices include croissant sandwiches, a crab melt, fajitas, burgers, salads, pastas, and full entrees (with soup or salad, potatoes and fresh vegetable) and range from $4 to $12.50. There is an extensive brunch menu as well.

Open Monday through Thursday from 11 a.m. to 11 p.m., on Friday and Saturday till midnight, and on Sunday from 10 a.m. (for brunch) to 10 p.m. Easy parking. No reservations. They accept most major credit cards.

Inexpensive

Here's a little gem. **Lim's Café,** 592 N. Market St. (tel. 916/241-9747 or 916/243-2991), will remind you of Sunday Chinese dinners when you were a kid. Nothing fancy, it's decorated in '50s-style black-and-white with black Naugahyde booths in the dining room and Formica tabletops. Little white milk-glass bud vases and a cigarette machine complete the picture. Red Chinese lanterns hang from the ceiling. In the front room there is a counter, and coffeeshop-type tables. The waitresses are all very friendly—ours assured us that kids like the chicken-noodle soup more than the egg-flower soup.

The prices are good. If you order individual entrees, a dinner for four, which is quite adequate, will cost just over $20. Chinese entrees range from $3 to $13 (lobster Cantonese). The full dinners for three (which includes soup, pork chow mein, pork fried rice, fried shrimp, sweet-and-sour pork or sweet-pea chow yuke, eggroll, cookies, and tea) is $16.50 total. They told us that dinner for four will serve five if one is a child.

Lim's is also open for breakfast. Standard breakfast fare is priced from $2.50 to $4.25.

A favorite of locals, this place gets hectic during the weekends, and does not accept reservations. Best to come between 5:30 and 6 p.m. for dinner, and after 1 p.m. for lunch. Highchairs and boosters are available. There is parking in the lot behind the restaurant. Open daily from 7 a.m. to 11 p.m. (on Friday and Saturday until 1 a.m.). Some credit cards accepted.

Set back from the street in the North Market Square Shopping Center is **Le Chimois Delicatessen and Restaurant,** 630 N. Market St. (tel. 916/241-7720). You'll know it by the tables outside. Inside, the owners pride themselves on serving wholesome American food without preservatives—what they like to call "old-fashioned family food." The atmosphere is rustic—round wood tables, lots of plants in ceramic vases, and rough-hewn wood. There is a cheese and deli counter where you can buy goodies for picnics.

Choose from such favorites as French dip, tuna melt, or shrimp salad sandwich; the soup and salad combination; or one of the daily specials. Prices range from $2.75 to $6.50. Kids can have grilled cheese or peanut butter and jelly for

$2. If you ask, they'll bring the kids a chalkboard with colored chalk, and of course, they'll split adult portions in the kitchen and warm baby bottles or baby food.

Open Monday through Saturday from 7 a.m. to 9 p.m. There are boosters and highchairs available. Reservations accepted for parties of five or over, but the service is so fast (some people come on a 30-minute lunch hour) that it probably won't be longer than a 10- to 15-minute wait at most. Parking lot. They accept some major credit cards.

Ferrarese's Ristorante and Deli, 1720 Shasta in central Redding (tel. 916/246-2426), is a great choice for either eat-in or take-out food. The restaurant is inviting, with a country-style interior complete with old-fashioned wall phones, hanging wrought-iron cooking utensils, and dotted Swiss awnings. The food is diverse, with items such as fresh-pressed carrot juice, homemade soups of the day like red potato with dill and Gruyère, or quiche with lightly curried chicken, dill, and Swiss cheese. There is also a large selection of salads, pastas, sandwiches, and the more traditional entrees. (If you like feta cheese, try the creamy feta cheese salad dressing—yummy!) Prices range from $4 to $5 (yes, that's right, a real bargain).

While there is no children's menu, we found it easy to share our meals with the kids because the portions were so large. The kitchen staff will warm baby bottles and baby food for your younger members. Highchairs and boosters are available. Try the outdoor tables if the weather is warm enough.

Open Monday through Friday from 10 a.m. to 6 p.m., on Saturday till 3 p.m.; closed Sunday. Parking lot. Most major credit cards accepted.

6. LASSEN VOLCANIC NATIONAL PARK

Lassen Volcanic National Park is a quiet, lesser-known park of 165 square miles, located in the southern part of the Cascade Range in northern California. While it may not have the same kind of astonishing beauty as its cousin to the south, Yosemite, it has beautiful pine forests, exquisite lakes, and awe-inspiring views of Lassen and other nearby peaks.

Its recent volcanic activity has created interesting geologic formations. It is alive with hydrothermal activity and presents an ever-changing landscape, providing all kinds of opportunities for the kids to learn about geology. Forests give way to twisted manzanita bushes with green leaves and red manzanita berries. In small sections of the park (where a swath of lava once made its way), plantlife stops altogether, and rocks—or rock fields—take over, products of the eruptions that occurred in 1914 and 1915.

We think Lassen is perfect for families because kids can enjoy much of the park's natural wonders without having to be expert hikers or geologists. Lassen Park Road takes you through some of this uncommon scenery, allowing you to see almost all of the interesting geological formations with very little effort. The park road also offers great views of Lassen Peak. If your kids are good car travelers, you can actually drive from one end of the park to the other (from Mineral at the south to Manzanita Lake in the north, or vice versa), enjoy a few, brief nature walks, and still be back to Redding for the evening. And many of the trails in the park are easy enough for novice hikers to enjoy.

The Devastated Areas are fascinating—not for their beauty, but because you see nature in progress. Here, on ground covered with a fine white-gray dust left from the lava flow, there are few pine trees and little saplings. These are evidence of the forest starting to come back.

At turnouts, the National Park Service has provided photographs and descriptions of the mid-May 1915 eruption. The last great eruption sent a cloud of steam five miles into the air.

While the park is open all year, Lassen Park Road is often impassable during the winter. The two seasons that beckon tourists are summer, when hiking, fishing, camping, and backpacking are the outdoor adventures; and winter, when downhill and cross-country skiing are thoroughly enjoyed (mainly in the Lassen Winter Sports area in the southwest).

HOW TO GET THERE: From Redding, take Calif. 44. From Sacramento, take I-5, which goes through Red Bluff, and then continue on Calif. 36.

Visitor Centers are located at the Southwest Information Station (near Mineral) and the northwest entrance (near Manzanita Lake). Be sure to pick up *The Road Guide to Lassen National Park* (less than $2). You can write ahead for information. Contact the superintendent, Lassen Volcanic National Park, P.O. Box 100, Mineral, CA 96063 (tel. 916/595-4444).

WHAT TO SEE AND DO: The park is dominated by summer outdoor lovers —hikers, fishermen, and campers. It is a hiker's paradise.

Lassen Park Road

This road through the park is much more than a way to get around. From the road you can see much of the scenery that makes Lassen special. Road markers with corresponding numbers listed in guidebooks inform you about the geologic activity of the area. The *Road Guide to Lassen National Park* is a thorough guide that gives you a basic understanding of the highlights that can be seen from the park road.

Bumpass Hell Self-guiding Nature Trail

Park rangers describe Bumpass Hell as a window to the middle of the earth. The trail starts at the road, and in a little more than two miles, takes you to the largest active hydrothermal area in the park. You'll see fumaroles (holes in the ground that spew forth hot gases and vapors), mudpots, bubbling hotsprings, and steam vents coming from the earth.

This loop is well marked and completely safe. It's a good trail for children, but there are several dropoffs in places, so be forewarned. Kids should be old enough to either keep on the inside part of the trail by themselves or be small enough to be carried.

The trail changes from heavily forested areas, where you get fabulous views of Lassen Peak, to areas devastated by past volcanic activity. Possibly the most stunning view is the one of Lake Helen, a gorgeous little glacial lake 110 feet deep that is so cold it often has snow patches into the summer. The color of the lake, carved by a glacier, is vibrant sapphire blue. Even if you don't want to take the entire 2¼-mile trail to the thermal area, try to walk as far as the first vista of Lake Helen, which is not too far. You'll be rewarded.

The descent into the hydrothermal area is fairly steep, but very easy. A boardwalk has been constructed so you can get close enough to feel the heat and see the bubbling pots. And the sulfur smell greets you well before your descent. Heed the warnings and don't go off the trail, as the earth's crust is thin in spots and not at all safe to walk on. You can get badly burned.

Be sure to carry water with you! We didn't, and were so thirsty by the time we got to the bottom that it hurt—and there was no drinking water there either. A kind hiker took pity on the kids and offered them her canteen water, but we adults stayed parched and dry until we got back to the trailhead.

Other Sights

Want to see another active hydrothermal area without much effort? **Sulphur Works** (also off Lassen Park Road) is a little loop (less than a half mile) where you can see fumaroles, mud pots, and hot springs. Because of mineral deposits from the geologic activity, the ground is colored in spots—yellow, green, orange. Be sure your children stay on the marked path, since the earth's crust is thin.

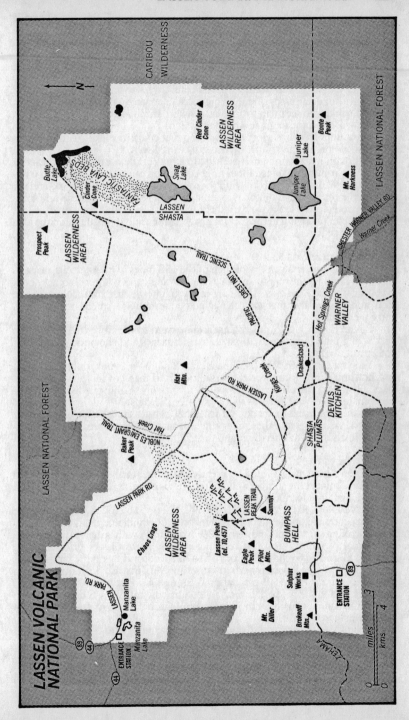

Centrally located in the park, at an altitude of almost 7,000 feet, **Summit Lake** is a beautiful area with two campgrounds, picnic sites, swimming, and good views of the surrounding mountains. Many trails start at Summit Lake. Our kids love to take the easy trail around the lake itself.

Geologically speaking, **Manzanita Lake** is a new one. It formed during the mid-1600s, when rockslides in the area dammed up the nearby creek. We fondly remember this large and beautiful lake because we saw several families of deer grazing within a few yards of our picnic spot. There are so many deer in the park that you're likely to see them too. If you can keep the kids quiet and at a distance, the deer will continue to graze while you watch.

Manzanita Lake has another good loop that circles the lake. With picnic tables, rest rooms, and a parking lot, this is a favored spot.

Although it's a bit of a drive, **Bathtub Lake** (in the northeastern corner of the park, near Butte Lake) is a lot of fun because you can actually swim in it without freezing. This is where you'll find the warmest swimming in the park, and the drive to the Butte Lake trailhead is a scenic one. (This is not on Lassen Park Road; you have to go outside the park and back in again.) Bathtub Lake is an excellent day trip if you're staying in the park. We pack a lunch and swimsuits, and the kids have a great time.

Summer Activities

Lassen is a hiker's paradise. Much of the 150 miles of **hiking trails** are easy. Children can walk the trails because so many of them give you good scenery even if you don't reach the end. There are many trailheads that start right near the road, and a lot of lakes that you can just pull your car up to, spread out a blanket, and have a picnic.

Be careful, though, until you are acclimatized to the altitude. Much of the park is at a high elevation that may cause headaches and shortness of breath if you're not used to it.

Yes, you can go **fishing** (and maybe catch rainbow, brook, or brown trout) and **boating** (only nonpowered boats allowed) in many of the park's beautiful lakes. However, there are no boat rentals in the park. California fishing regulations are in force, which means that adults need a license.

As in other national parks, **educational events** are held throughout the park. Park naturalists lead these free programs that discuss the area's geology, history, animals, Native Americans, and the like.

Winter Activities

Lassen Park Road is closed from early November until early June. The road to Lassen Chalet at the southern end of the park is open, as is the road from Calif. 44 to Manzanita Meadows.

Lassen Park Ski Area (tel. 916/529-1512 or 916/595-3376) is near the southern entrance to the park, and offers both downhill and cross-country skiing. There is a ski school (more than 30 instructors) with special children's instructional programs. You can rent skis, boots, and poles at prices ranging between $7 and $16 (children, from $5 to $13), depending on the kinds of skis and the time of year. Special children's rates apply to lifts also. Lifts operate from 9 a.m. to 4 p.m. (till 4:30 p.m. after Washington's Birthday). There are also midweek/nonholiday specials. For ski conditions, call 916/595-4464. Open during the winter, usually from Thanksgiving through mid-April, depending on conditions.

Childs Meadows Cross-Country Ski Area, Childs Meadows Resort, Calif. 5, Box 3000, Mill Creek, CA 96061 (tel. 916/595-4411), is another area of winter enjoyment. Located 4½ miles from the entrance to Lassen National Park. This is a popular place for cross-country skiing. There are advanced, intermediate, and beginners' courses. Three marked (and groomed) trails are 18 miles, 10 miles, and 4 miles. Lessons are available for all ability levels. Trails are open to the public for $5 per day. Lessons are $5 per hour for groups of three or more. Individual lessons are arranged with instructors. Rentals are available. For skis, boots, and poles, the cost is $10; children's equipment is available. Reservations are required.

There is a lodge and restaurant, service station (with towing), giftshop, and motel.

WHERE TO STAY: Of course, we think the way to enjoy the park is to camp out.

Campgrounds

There are six campgrounds in the park, all on a first-come, first-served basis. These are the ones we like. **Manzanita Lake** has 179 sites and offers swimming, fireplaces, tables, flush toilets, and showers (with electrical outlets in the bath area). Trailers up to 35 feet can camp here. There is a small grocery store. Naturalist programs are also offered.

Summit Lake has 94 sites (divided between the north and south parts of the lake). The campground has swimming, fireplaces, tables, and flush toilets. There are naturalist programs here.

Other campgrounds are **Crags Campground** (45 sites for overflow from Manzanita), **Butte Lake** (98 sites), **Southwest Campground** (21 sites), and **Warner Valley** (15 sites).

Fees range from $4 to $6 per night per site. For information, contact **California Guest Services**, P.O. Box 75, Mineral, CA 96063 (tel. 916/595-3306).

Motels and Other Accommodations

The only accommodation within the park is **Drakesbad Guest Ranch,** Chester, CA 96020 (tel. 916/529-1512), a 100-year-old ranch that is completely off the beaten track. Drakesbad has a trout stream, horseback riding, horse pack trips, hot springs, and a swimming pool. However, most accommodations don't have electricity (you use kerosene lamps), and they are very modest. Some have only half-baths with a sink and toilet. Accommodations are on the American Plan, which includes three meals per day. Children over 12 pay full price; children 2 to 11 are half price when sharing accommodations with their parents; children under 2 are free.

Rates vary depending on the location and type of bathroom. The cost for one adult in a room ranges from $72 to $81; for two adults, $60 to $72. Each additional adult is charged $51 to $54 extra per night.

Or You Can Stay . . .

If you want to stay in a nearby motel or hotel, you have just a few choices. **Lassen Mineral Lodge,** on Calif. 36 (P.O. Box 160), Mineral, CA 96063 (tel. 916/595-4422), just a few minutes from the park's southern border, is one possibility here. Although the rooms are quite modest, in fact almost bare (no television or phone, with a shower only), this lodge has a lovely swimming pool (with a large area that's one to two feet deep) and is nestled in a pretty mountain valley.

The lodge is surrounded by grassy areas, some of which are fenced off and great for young children. The facilities include a reasonably priced restaurant (see below for details), bar (with pool table and video games), giftshop, grocery store, post office, and nearby tennis courts. (We also enjoyed the neighborhood school playground. Just ask a local to tell you where it is.)

Rooms rent for $30 single, $36 to $40 double, $42 triple, $45 quad. Kitchenettes, cribs, and rollaways cost $5 extra per night. For holidays, reserve six weeks in advance.

If you want to rent a three- or four-bedroom chalet in the town of Mineral,

McGovern's Mt. Lassen Vacation Chalets (tel. 415/897-8377) is the place to contact (the mailing address is 563 McClay Rd., Novato, CA 94947). These vacation homes are completely furnished (except for bedding and linens) for summer or winter use, and will sleep 10 to 16 people. In the winter, all wood is furnished.

The chalets are located adjacent to Calif. 36, about 20 minutes from the ski slopes at Lassen. Rates are $175 to $200 for a weekend, $400 for the week. A nonrefundable $50 deposit is necessary when reserving.

A DINING POSSIBILITY: The **Lassen Mineral Lodge Restaurant**, located at the lodge (tel. 916/595-4422), is one of the few restaurants in the Lassen area. If you choose the right dinner (we loved the locally raised Ruby trout), the food is very tasty. You'll lick your fingers from the cinnamon-covered deep-dish apple pie. Full dinners are priced from $7 to $13. Breakfasts and lunches run $4 to $8.

This homey restaurant has a surprisingly extensive wine and beer list, and a wonderful children's menu that includes hamburgers, corn dogs, and barbecued ribs. Children's lunches and dinners include fries and fruit, with prices from $2.50 to $4. Breakfast costs $3 for bacon, eggs, pancakes, and beverage. They have highchairs and boosters, and they'll warm bottles and baby food.

Open daily from Memorial Day to September 15 for breakfast, lunch, and dinner (generally from 8 a.m. to 8 p.m., but check first). The rest of the year hours vary, so call first. Some major credit cards are accepted.

CHAPTER VII

GOLD RUSH COUNTRY

□ □ □

1. SACRAMENTO
2. THE GOLD COUNTRY
3. LAKE TAHOE

Anyone who has ever read about the romance of the Gold Rush era, about towns that sprang up overnight (and just as quickly became ghost towns), riches waiting to be earned, the lusty lives of the '49ers, must make a pilgrimage to California's Gold Country. Here you will find so much of that history—a history not even 200 years old—well preserved. School-age children will be engrossed by the stories they'll hear about miners, child labor, and life in general in the 1800s. History will truly come alive for them.

Sacramento makes a good base from which to explore much of the area, and is a popular stopping-off point for people on their way to Tahoe, Reno, the Gold Rush Country, and the Lassen-Shasta areas. Not only does its history relate to the mad years of the Gold Rush, but it has current significance as the capital of one of the largest states in the Union. Sacramento's best-kept secret is that it is rich with outdoor spring and summer family activities.

Lake Tahoe, while it isn't linked historically to the Gold Rush, lies between the two main roads used by the pioneers, now major highways. Its true significance is as a wonderful year-round family resort area, and an especially great place for skiing.

1. SACRAMENTO

While the Gold Rush was probably Sacramento's most important claim to fame, its history actually began with one John Sutter. Sutter arrived in Sacramento in 1839 to establish a farming community, and ultimately opened it up to the pioneers who flocked there in droves with dreams about discovering the bright-yellow rock. Sacramento—or Sutter's Fort, as it was first called—was in fact the first place in the West to become a town.

But Sacramento has other claims to fame: It was the western terminus for the short-lived Pony Express, for instance. And railroad buffs will tell you that Sacramento was important as the home of the Central Pacific Railway (which, through engineering feats that were considered incredible for that time, was able to climb the steep grades of the Sierras), and as the western terminus for the transcontinental railway. As a matter of fact, the West's very first railroad, the Sacramento Valley Railroad, was based here.

In its efforts to keep time with the 20th century, Sacramento hasn't lost its positive connections to the past. And it hasn't lost its quiet charm either, although it is the capital of one of the country's most powerful states. It remains a city of Victorian houses, blooming camellias (it's called the "Camellia Capital of the World"), and lush trees (over 200,000 in the city of Sacramento). Most of its modernity is found in the suburbs, where you'll also find Cal Expo, home of the California State Fair.

If you are planning a trip to Sacramento, depending on what you like to do and what time of year it is, your average stay will probably be two to three days.

GETTING THERE: By car from Los Angeles, Orange County, or San Diego, take I-5 north all the way. From San Francisco, take I-80. Most major domestic and many international airlines land at Sacramento Metropolitan Airport. Amtrak services Sacramento direct from Los Angeles and Oakland.

ORIENTATION: There are two offices to assist you with questions about what to see and do in Sacramento. The **Sacramento Convention & Visitors Bureau** is located at 1421 K St., Sacramento, CA 95814 (tel. 916/442-5542). The office is open weekdays from 9 a.m. to 5 p.m. The **Old Sacramento Visitor Information Center** is on Front Street, near the Railroad Depot (tel. 916/443-7815), and its hours are Monday through Saturday from 10 a.m. to 5 p.m. The **California Office of Tourism,** is at 1121 L St., Suite 103, Sacramento, CA 95814 (tel. 916/322-1396). It's open to the public for information on the state of California on weekdays from 9 a.m. to 5 p.m.

We've arranged our Sacramento sightseeing, dining, and overnight stays by area: Old Sacramento, Downtown/Capitol, and Cal Expo. You'll find information about the American and Sacramento Rivers in the "Outdoor Activities" section.

GETTING AROUND: Downtown Sacramento is a series of one-way streets, but it's easy to find your way around. Numbered streets go north and south; lettered streets go east and west. Just remember that autos are not allowed on the K Street Mall. A tram runs on that mall from 7th and K to Old Sacramento and back. A trolley runs from 6th and B Streets to Old Sacramento and back every ten minutes Monday through Friday from 11 a.m. to 4 p.m., on Saturday and Sunday from 1 to 4 p.m. There is also a light rail system, and Rapid Transit buses that stop at every historical location (call 916/321-BUSS for route and schedule information).

Major car-rental agencies such as Hertz, Budget, Dollar, and National service the area. Check the *Yellow Pages* for local addresses and phone numbers.

WHAT TO SEE AND DO: We have broken down the list of places to see by geographical location. However, Sacramento is small enough that you'll be able to visit several areas in a day. Old Sacramento is at the edge of downtown, for instance, and the Capitol area is just ten minutes away by car. If you're in good shape, you can even walk from Old Sacramento to the Capitol via the K Street Mall. It's approximately ten blocks.

There is a one-ticket admission price for several of the sights detailed below —the California State Railroad Museum, Sacramento History Center, Crocker Art Museum, Historic Governor's Mansion, Sutter's Fort, and the State Indian Museum. Tickets cost $8.50 for adults, $3.25 for children 6 to 17. Tickets are good for one year and can be purchased at any of the sights mentioned above.

Old Sacramento

Old Sacramento was the original riverboat landing for Sutter's Fort. As the city grew and spread out, Old Sacramento, which by the 1950s had become a

skid-row area, was almost lost to modern freeways. Luckily, some prominent citizens did not want to see the destruction of what was once the pulse of Sacramento, and they were able to convince authorities to save it. It is now a 28-acre historical park. Many of its original buildings have been meticulously renovated, and it is considered one of the best restoration projects in the country.

You will probably want to allow about a day for a look at Old Sacramento. You can make a circle, touring the area on foot. The borders of the park are the Sacramento River and 2nd Street, and I Street and the Capitol Mall. Either come via the pedestrian walkway from the K Street Mall, or park under the freeway at I Street. (A caution to the women in the group: The slated wooden walkways covering the cobblestone streets love to catch hold of high heels—leave them in your hotel and wear sensible walking shoes instead.)

Begin your tour at the **California State Railroad Museum,** 2nd and I Streets (tel. 916/448-4466), the largest railroad museum of its kind in the country. The 21 magnificently restored locomotives and train cars on display within this 100,000-square-foot museum are examples of the massive "iron horses" that helped connect the West to the East, and helped to build California. A brief movie explaining the history of the railroads begins your self-guiding tour. As you move through the museum the mournful sound of the whistle of the steam engine follows you. It's a sound that hasn't been heard since trains changed to diesel.

Kids love being able to enter an authentic 1929 Pullman passenger car, which simulates a moving train, complete with railroad noises. The life-like displays of passengers sleeping in their compartments produces endless conversation for the kids. You'll also be able to enter an actual mail-sorting car, which was retired as recently as the 1970s. It's amazing to see how millions of letters and packages were transported before our postal service was modernized.

You'll also see the first engine of the Central Pacific Railroad, which was used to help build the transcontinental railroad. There's lots of chronological information on nearby displays explaining the history behind the building of the railroad. You—and the kids—will marvel at the huge locomotives, which have been beautifully restored to show off their artistic workmanship. You can also introduce the kids to the history behind the lavishly decorated private railroad cars. The first view of the giant one-million-pound locomotive of the Southern Pacific Railroad is awesome. And these are just some of the locomotives on display.

You can all test your skill at an electronic question-and-answer game that asks which style locomotive belongs to what railroad line. There are re-creations of little passenger waiting rooms and a toy train exhibit displaying original cars.

The museum is open daily from 10 a.m. to 5 p.m., except Thanksgiving, Christmas, and New Year's days. It's stroller accessible except for the two train cars you can enter. The same ticket is good for entrance to the Central Pacific Passenger Depot (see below). Admission for adults is $3; children 6 to 17, $1; under 6, free.

Next door to the train museum, on your way to the History Center, is the **Huntington Hopkins Hardware Store** exhibit, 113 I St. (tel. 916/323-7234 or 916/445-4209). Over 400 hardware items dating from the 19th century are on display here. You can point out to your kids the housewares and tools used by our grandparents. There's even authentic gold-panning paraphernalia on sale for would-be gold diggers. Open Tuesday through Sunday from 10 a.m. to 5 p.m. Admission is free.

Next you'll come to the **Sacramento History Center,** 101 I St. (tel. 916/449-2057). This small center houses four different galleries depicting Sacramento history through displays and video history computers. The exhibits are lively and eclectic. The family can have a peek at all aspects of Sacramento's history from Sutter's day until now. Kids will see a straw-covered tepee and can even pan for gold. There are dresses from various periods in history, dolls, toy trains, a wonderful re-creation of a 1928 kitchen, and a large exhibit of gold ore. Plans are to increase the number of hands-on exhibits so that more children can directly participate. The self-guiding tour takes from 15 minutes to an hour, depending on how long you and the kids spend at each display.

Open daily from 10 a.m. to 5 p.m. Closed Christmas and New Year's Days. Admission costs $2.50 for adults; children 6 to 17, $1; under 6, free.

One look at the **Central Pacific Passenger Depot**, 930 Front St. (tel. 916/445-4209), and you'll think it's the real thing. This is a well-done reconstruction of the depot of 1876, with several exhibits depicting the activities that went on when train travel was so popular. On weekends, from May until Labor Day weekend (excluding the 4th of July weekend), there are steam-train rides that last one hour and leave every hour on the hour. Open daily from 10 a.m. to 5 p.m. The fare is $3 for adults, $2 for children 6 to 17; under 6, free. Admission to the depot is $3 for adults, $1 for children 6 to 17; under 6, free. Free admission if you paid entrance to the California State Railroad Museum.

The **Old Sacramento Schoolhouse Museum** is at Front and L Streets (tel. 916/371-0813). One look at this replicated one-room schoolhouse from the 1800s and your kids will know they never had it so good. It is set up with the little desks of that period and displays the original readers. A guide tells you a bit about the schoolhouse, or for a $2-per-group fee (maximum of four or five people), a costumed 1800s schoolmarm will give a one-hour re-creation of a school lesson complete with slates and *McGuffey's Readers*. Open Monday through Friday from 9:30 a.m. to 4 p.m. and on Saturday and Sunday from noon to 4 p.m. Free admission.

The historical **B. F. Hastings Building** is located at 2nd and J Streets (call first to be sure it's open—tel. 916/323-7234 or 916/445-4209). Once a bank housing the Alta California and California State Telegraph Companies, the California Supreme Court, and the Wells Fargo Bank, it is now a museum. You'll see displays from the Wells Fargo Bank, the reconstructed Supreme Court, and the Pony Express. A plaque on the wall outside gives the destinations for the Pony Express when the building was originally a stage stop. Open Tuesday through Sunday from 10 a.m. to 5 p.m. Wells Fargo is open daily. Free admission.

At this point you're almost back at the Railroad Museum. Before you leave Old Sacramento, you might want to explore two other places, besides the myriad souvenir, candy, and specialty shops. One is **Mike's Puzzle Shop**, 1009 2nd St. (tel. 916/444-0446). The store is full of nothing but—you guessed it—puzzles! There are whimsical and educational puzzles for kids and aficionados alike. Open daily from 10 a.m. to 6 p.m. The other interesting store is **Heidi's Music Boxes, Etc.**, at 116 I St., across from the Railroad Museum (tel. 916/442-2440). This is a treasure trove of music boxes from around the world. There are some interesting choices for the children, and some great gifts to bring home. Open Monday through Saturday from 11 a.m. to 5:30 p.m., on Sunday till 5 p.m.

Downtown and the Capitol Area

You can't miss the **State Capitol** at 10th Street and Capitol Mall, between L and N Streets and 10th and 15th Streets (tel. 916/324-0333), because of its glorious gold dome. Some 50 years after its birth, the Capitol building was in a state of major disrepair—so drastic was its condition that it was almost torn down. Fortunately, the building was gutted, reinforced, and then painstakingly restored to its original glory over a period of six years.

The **California State Capitol Tour** gives you a good look at this elegant monument to government. Docents at the door lead you to the tour desk in the basement, where you'll pick up your tickets. The general tour is most suitable for fourth-graders and up. Kids younger than that often get bored. If there are lots of children on the tour (there's a limit of 30 people), the guide will attempt to draw the children into the discussion. The Senate and Assembly chambers are included in the tour, but usually anyone can view those proceedings without taking the tour. While some children won't be able to appreciate the work that went into the restoration of the grand building, adults will be able to stop and look at the faux marble and the delicate detail work on the ceilings and walls.

The **General Tour** gets filled in the summer months, so be sure to be there a half hour before the tour you want to take. If you don't want a docent-guided tour, you can take a self-guiding one. Brochures are available in the tour office.

Children or teenagers studying government will be most interested in the **Historic Tour,** which goes into detail about individual government offices. This tour includes a look at the original offices of the governor, attorney-general, and others, from the early 1900s. A maximum of ten people are allowed. Young children may become fidgety on this walk. You could manage it with a sleeping infant.

From Memorial Day through Labor Day, the General Tour leaves every hour on the hour from 9 a.m. to 4 p.m. Pick up tickets a half hour before tour time.

There is also a **Park Tour** daily from Memorial Day to Labor Day at 10:30 a.m., or by special arrangement. Each tree in the 40-acre park, which is adjacent to the Capitol building, represents a different part of the world. Signs specify where the vegetation is from. On a pleasant day, this is a nice outdoors tour to take with the family. Free.

The tour office is open daily from 9 a.m. to 5 p.m., except Thanksgiving, Christmas, and New Year's Days. Fall and winter hours are 10 a.m. to 5 p.m. on weekends.

Five minutes by car from the Capitol is the **Historic Governor's Mansion,** at 16th and H Streets (tel. 916/323-3047). This grand Victorian mansion was the home to 13 California governors. Ronald Reagan was the last to live there—Nancy declared it a firetrap. It's a look at what tastes were in vogue at the time of each governor.

Young children will possibly fidget during this one-hour tour. Take infants in carriers or older kids.

Open daily from 10 a.m. to 5 p.m. Tours are given on the hour beginning at 10 a.m.; the last tour is at 4 p.m. The charge is $1 for adults, 50¢ for children aged 6 to 17; kids under 6 are free.

It seems strange to see **Sutter's Fort** in downtown Sacramento, flanked by office buildings and private residences. It's located at 27th and L Streets (tel. 916/445-4209). Dating back to 1839, Sutter's Fort was the first settlement in Sacramento. Each of you gets a listening wand to tour the reconstructed fort. The blacksmith's shop, Sutter's quarters, the tannery, and other shops used by his troops are part of what you see, and the history behind them comes from the listening wand.

Check ahead for Living History Days, at which time volunteers appear in the costumes of 1846 and re-create the daily life of the residents of the fort. There are also Demonstration Days, which feature spinners, weavers, candlemakers, and bakers practicing their crafts.

The fort is open daily from 10 a.m. to 5 p.m. Stroller-accessible. Admission is $1 for adults, 50¢ for children. Fees are doubled on Living History days.

On the same grounds, but accessible by a separate entrance (2618 K St.) is the **State Indian Museum** (tel. 916/445-4209). California Indian artifacts, from prehistoric times to now, are displayed here. Open daily from 10 a.m. to 5 p.m. Admission is $1 for adults, 50¢ for children 6 to 17; under 6, free.

And If You Have Time . . .

Automobile aficionados love to visit the **Towe Ford Museum,** at 2200 Front St. (tel. 916/442-6802). There are more than 150 cars and trucks at this museum, which is dedicated to preserving antique and classic automobiles. Moms, dads, and grandparents can talk about which models they remember, as one model of every Ford car from 1903 to 1953 is displayed here.

Free parking. Stroller-accessible inside. Open daily year round except major holidays from 10 a.m. to 6 p.m. Admission is $4 for adults, $3.50 for seniors, $2 for high school students, and $1 for grade school students; younger children, free.

The **Crocker Art Museum,** 216 O St., at the corner of 3rd and O Streets (tel. 916/449-5423), is housed in a grand Victorian building named after its founder, Judge Edwin Bryant Crocker, who commissioned it to be built in 1869. It is the oldest public art museum in the West. The museum contains collections of early California and European paintings and contemporary art. It makes a nice indoor activity for the family, especially when there are special exhibitions such as "Alice in Wonderland" (held one recent January). Call when you get to Sacramento to find out the current schedule of exhibitions.

Open on Tuesday from 1 to 9 p.m. and Wednesday through Sunday from 10 a.m. to 5 p.m.; closed Monday. You can arrange a guided tour by phone. Stroller-accessible. Admission is $2.50 for adults, $1.50 for seniors, $1 for children 7 to 17; under-7s, free.

The **Blue Diamond Visitor's Center,** at the California Almond Growers Exchange, 17th and C Streets (tel. 916/446-8409), gives you all the chance to tour the world's largest almond-processing plant. Almonds, if you didn't already know, are California's largest export crop. The free tours last approximately 1¼ hours. Fine for children of all ages. These tours are offered Monday through Friday at 9 a.m., 10 a.m., 1 p.m., and 2 p.m. No reservations are necessary.

Music Circus, in a canvas-roofed, open-flap tent put up at 15th and H Streets (tel. 916/441-3163 or 916/443-6722), is a summer-stock theater-in-the-round presenting musicals perfect for the whole family. Past performances—with name stars—have included *Annie, Carousel,* and *Cats.* There are six to eight different plays performed each season. Performances are given on summer evenings (mid-July to early September) at 8:30 p.m. (at 7:30 p.m. on Sunday). Reserved-seat tickets cost $17.50 for adults and $16 for children. Check the local newspapers for information on what plays are being featured. (*Note:* Call in advance, as single tickets are hard to secure.)

Cal Expo Area

Get to the Cal Expo area via Bus. 80 or Calif. 160—they meet right near Cal Expo. The area is about ten minutes by car from downtown Sacramento.

The kids will love **Waterworld USA,** a 14-acre family water park located at Cal Expo, 1600 Exposition Blvd., at I-80 (tel. 916/924-0555). It boasts the only wave pool in northern California, a 25,000-square-foot area called Breaker Beach. The four-foot waves are fine for bodysurfing, and there are lifeguards everywhere. There's a 70-foot-high six-slide complex, paddleboats, one pool for adults and another for children, and a children's area called "Tom Sawyer's Landing," perfect for kids 11 and under.

The park is open daily from Memorial Day weekend to Labor Day weekend from 10:30 a.m. to 6 p.m. The admission price covers all attractions. Adults pay $11; children 48 inches tall and under, $9; children under 3, free.

The **Sacramento Science Center and Junior Museum,** 3615 Auburn Blvd., near I-80 and Watt Avenue (tel. 916/449-8255), is an exciting place for all ages. Set on 12 acres, the center includes a nature trail planted with native California plants and inhabited by local animals. The center itself hosts the most extensive natural science collection in the area. There are hands-on exhibits, permanent and changing displays, and a planetarium. Weekends and certain holidays are an especially good time to visit, as that's when the center offers planetarium shows, live animal presentations, and the Action Lab—where the whole family can participate in special science activities. The center is geared for children 4 and up. The 40-minute planetarium presentation is appropriate for children 6 and up. The center is stroller-accessible.

In summer it's open weekdays from 9:30 a.m. to 5 p.m. and weekends from noon to 5 p.m.; during the school year, daily from noon to 5 p.m.; closed major holidays. Center admission is $2.50 for adults, $1 for children 3 to 15; under-3s, free. The planetarium entry costs an additional $2 for adults, $1 for children.

Not far from Cal Expo is the **Iceland Ice Skating Rink,** at 1430 Del Paso Blvd. (tel. 916/925-3121). Call for public hours, as they change seasonally. Sunday night is family night—at that time a family of four can skate for $8, including skate rental. Admission is $4 per adult, $3 per child. Skate rental is $1 per person.

Surrounding Sacramento

The **Sacramento Zoo** is located in lush William Land Park, at the corner of Sutterville Road and Land Park Drive (tel. 916/449-5885), a quarter mile off the Sutterville exit on I-5. It's only a few minutes from downtown Sacramento in a lovely location. The park itself has a playground and picnic areas. The zoo is open daily (except Christmas Day) from 9 a.m. to 4 p.m. Admission costs $2.50 for adults, $1 for seniors and children 3 to 12; under 3, free.

Across the street from the zoo entrance is **Fairytale Town** (tel. 916/449-5233), which is a trip into fantasyland for the short set. Kids wander through displays ranging from Cinderella's pumpkin coach to the house the wolf tried to blow down in *The Three Little Pigs.* Call for a schedule of puppet shows and other demonstrations held throughout the day. Open daily in summer from 10 a.m. to 5 p.m.; in December and January, on weekends only, from 10 a.m. to 4:30 p.m.; weather permitting.

Admission is $1.50 for adults, 75¢ for children 3 to 12. A discount combination ticket to Fairytale Town and the zoo is available at $3.50 for adults, $1.75 for seniors, $1.50 for children 3 to 12; under-3s, free.

OUTDOOR ACTIVITIES: The American and the Sacramento Rivers beckon thousands of travelers every summer. The two rivers converge at Discovery Park, which is right off I-5 and Calif. 99.

Families enjoy numerous activities in and around the rivers.

Bicycling

The city's exciting and famous bicycle trail is called the **Jedediah Smith Memorial Bicycle Trail** and is located along the **American River Parkway.** (The parkway itself is a beautiful place for a walk.) You can start your ride at Discovery Park and ride all the way to Folsom Lake. It's a great family activity, and you'll see some of the most beautiful parts of Sacramento this way. The trail is a little over 30 miles long, with various cut-offs along the way.

American River Bike Centers has two locations for rentals: 9203 Folsom Blvd. (tel. 916/363-6271), and 6391 Riverside Blvd., in the Nugget Shopping Center (tel. 916/427-6199). At both locations, adult bikes rent for $2.50 per hour, or $12.50 per day. Child carriers are $8 per day; helmets are free with the rental. The Folsom Boulevard location does not have children's bikes; they do suggest reservations on weekends and in the summer (make reservations in person only). Open Monday through Friday from 9 a.m. to 7 p.m., on Saturday till 6 p.m., and on Sunday till 5 p.m.

The Riverside Boulevard location has children's bikes at the same rate as adult bikes. No reservations are necessary. Open Monday through Friday from 10 a.m. to 6 p.m., on Saturday till 5:30 p.m., and on Sunday till 5 p.m.

Fishing

Fishing locations are numerous and the fish are abundant. Contact the **Department of Fish and Game** (tel. 916/355-0978) for information on what type of fish are found where, and what the local rules are about licenses.

Horseback Riding

A way to experience yet another side of Sacramento is on horseback. **Shadow Glen Riding Stables,** 4854 Main Ave. in Fair Oaks, at the intersection of Sunset and Main Avenues (tel. 916/989-1826), offers guided rides in Folsom Lake State Park. Guides lead you along the shore of Lake Natoma, over ridges, down canyons, and up hills where you spot deer, coyotes, wild turkeys, and scores of birds. Children must be at least 6 years old to ride.

The stables are open daily year round from 9 a.m. to dusk. Reservations are necessary. Rides cost $12.50 per hour in the winter, $14.50 in the summer, adult or child.

Houseboating

An excellent way to spend a vacation is on a houseboat (see the Introduction for more details). The Sacramento Delta area offers a pleasant way to experience that adventure in its hundreds of miles of gentle waters.

You can contact **Delta Country Houseboats,** P.O. Box 246, Walnut Grove, CA 95690 (tel. 916/776-1741); **Herman & Helen's Marina,** Venice Island Ferry, Stockton, CA 95209 (tel. 209/951-4634); and **Seven Crown Resorts,** P.O. Box 1409, Boulder City, NV 89005 (tel. toll free 800/752-9669). Or call the **Delta Rental Houseboat Hotline** (tel. 209/477-1840).

You can write for brochures to Houseboats, 6333 Pacific Ave., Suite 152, Stockton, CA 95207.

Parks

Sacramento is a mecca for parks, some of which you can get to off the bike trail or by river raft. Visit or call the **Sacramento County Department of Parks and Recreation,** 3711 Branch Center Rd., Sacramento, CA 95827 (tel. 916/366-2061), for specific information on directions, hours, and activities, and for a map showing riverfront access for the following county parks:

Discovery Park, located at Jibboom Street and Richards Boulevard, the confluence of the Sacramento and American Rivers, has 275 acres. It offers boat launching, picnic areas, and archery ranges. Begin the Jedediah Smith Bike Trail here.

Ancil Hoffman Park is in nearby Carmichael at California Avenue and Tarshes Drive. There's golf, walking trails, a nature center with special programs and exhibits, and a horse arena at this park.

At **Rancho Seco Park,** off Jackson Hwy., all ages enjoy a 165-acre lake with beach, bathhouse, fishing, and boat docks, plus 400 acres of shaded picnic areas, bike trails, and more.

C. M. Goethe Park is off Folsom Boulevard in Rancho Cordova. This wooded park is a great place to picnic, hike, or to access the bike trail.

Gibson Ranch is a small farm-like facility off Elverta Road East to Gibson Road. Kids can watch and feed various farm animals, families can picnic or go horseback riding here, and there's an eight-acre pond stocked with fish. The swimming complex spans 3½ acres and includes sand and lawn areas, showers, and changing areas.

River Rafting

Almost any kind of boat you can imagine is found up and down the American River. But rafting remains the river sport of choice in this area. Although white-water rafting can be energizing, enervating, hard work, exciting, and sometimes dangerous, rafting on the Lower American (Sacramento area) takes you floating leisurely down the river, making it a perfect family activity. The river is rated Class I, meaning that the water is flat, has small waves, and no serious obstacles. (For information on white-water rafting, see the "Other Outdoor Activities" section in the Gold Country.)

With **American River Raft Rentals,** 11257 Bridge St., Rancho Cordova, CA 95670 (tel. 916/635-6400), you can have your raft picked up at one of two take-out points along the river, three or six hours from the starting point. Shuttle buses from those take-out locations run every hour on weekends and three times a day on weekdays (after Memorial Day) to take you back to the starting point. (Shuttle-bus fees are $2.50 per person.) The season runs from mid-April through mid-October, with hours daily from 9 a.m. to 9 p.m. Reservations are recommended for weekends. Rentals include the raft, paddles, and life vests. The minimum age is 4, and they do have life vests for that age group. Rates are for all day: $18 for two people, $24 for four people, $30 for six people. Identification and a deposit are required for the six-person raft.

ANNUAL EVENTS: The **Dixieland International Jazz Festival** (tel. 619/372-5277) is held every Memorial Day weekend. Attracting more than 150,000 people, the festival lets 100 jazz bands loose in locations all over the city. Transportation is usually available at all major hotels (make hotel reservations far in advance). You can purchase one pass for all events. Teens love this festival.

The **California State Fair,** for 2½ weeks ending Labor Day each year, draws over 800,000 people. It's held on the grounds of Cal Expo, 1600 Exposition Blvd. (tel. 916/924-2000 or 916/924-2032). Not only are you able to watch the traditional state fair competitions, but there is also such free entertainment as the Golden Bear Bodybuilding competition, the Maid of California Pageant, and dance and theater companies. There are daily horse shows, thoroughbred horse racing, the P.R.C.A. Rodeo, and motor sports. Children, of course, love the Midway and its children's rides, carnival games, and other attractions. There is even a special Children's Carnival Area for the little tykes. Teens love the amphitheater with its top-name concerts. There are nursing and diaper-changing facilities, and strollers for rent.

Admission to the fair is $5 for adults, $3 for children 5 to 12; under 5, free.

WHERE TO STAY: No matter where you choose to stay, you'll be only 15 minutes away from any sightseeing venue.

Weekends are when you'll find the best hotel rates. Be sure to ask if there is a weekend rate or special when you make your reservation. Also remember that rates are often higher during the Jazz Festival in May. When it comes to making reservations, you're better off calling the hotel directly rather than the toll-free 800 number. Reservations clerks at the hotel know much more about special rates and what's a good room for a family.

Downtown and Capitol Area

The **Clarion Hotel,** across from the Governor's Mansion at 700 16th St., Sacramento, CA 95814 (tel. 916/444-8000, or toll free 800/CLARION), is a business person's hotel during the week, but its convenient location makes it perfect for weekend family travelers. In the deluxe class, the Clarion is most affordable and "family-appropriate" only on the weekends and in the summer. There is a pool, usable summers only.

A bright, attractive restaurant serves breakfast, lunch, and dinner. It has a children's menu featuring burgers, grilled cheese, and other simple selections, at prices ranging around $2. There are booster seats and highchairs. Hors d'oeuvres are served in the open lounge area.

Room service, with selections for kids, is available from 6 a.m. to midnight. There's also in-room pizza, prepared by the hotel chef, at limited times during the day. You'll find the pizza choices listed in a cute little take-out box in your room. It doesn't belong to the guest before you—don't throw it away!

Rooms are large and clean, decorated with comfortable traditional furnishings, all with full-size bathrooms. Each of the 239 rooms and suites (in two buildings) have remote-control TVs and VCRs. You can rent movies for the VCR for $6 per day (as many movies as you can watch within 24 hours at the same rate!), or bring your own. There is a whole floor of no-smoking rooms. The hotel uses a babysitting referral service.

Most families, we're told, rent connecting rooms with two double beds or a king-size bed. If your children are sensitive to noise, we'd advise staying in the second building, or at least requesting a room not facing the courtyard in the main building, as the lounge opens to that courtyard and it can be quite noisy at night.

Singles rent for $88 to $98; doubles, $98 to $108; suites with one or two bedrooms, $125 to $250. The weekend rate is $55 all year round, on a space-available basis. Check weekend rates for the parlors and suites, as well as for the 44 deluxe accommodations on the Governor's Court level. Cribs are free, but roll-aways cost $10 per night. Kids under 18 are free in the same room with their parents; additional guests are charged $10 per night.

The **Best Western Ponderosa,** at 1100 H St., Sacramento, CA 95814 (tel. 916/441-1314, or toll free 800/528-1234), is run practically like someone's home. Owner operated, this comfortable 98-room hotel is immaculate and quite family-friendly.

Complimentary continental breakfast is served either in the lobby or in your room. The pool area is large and clean, and equipped with chaises lounges, plus tables and chairs so you can eat around the pool. In fact, you should request a larger room (with a queen-size bed) near the pool area on the ground floor. Then just open your sliding glass door and have your breakfast outdoors (watch out for toddlers, who are good at opening doors!).

The nice-sized, newly decorated rooms come in mauve and beige or purple, and are furnished with dark-mahogany furniture reminiscent of the '40s. In the deluxe room (with a king-size bed) you could fit a crib and a rollaway. Amenities include Select TV (they will be adding other cable stations), full-length mirrors, and hairdryers in the bathrooms. There are no-smoking floors and connecting rooms.

Many of the families that stay here are repeat customers, attesting to the popularity of this hotel. Tell the reservationist you are bringing your family when you reserve your room, and she will accommodate you as best as possible. The hotel even provides rubber sheets upon request, and extra towels for lots of little hands are no problem. Although there are no refrigerators in the rooms, you can use the one behind the front desk. Babysitting arrangements can usually be made with advance notice. There is airport shuttle service for $5.50.

Rates are $64 to $72 single and $74 to $87 double. Kids under 12 stay free in their parents' room; children 12 and over, and additional adults, pay $8 per night. Cribs are free; rollaways cost $8 per night.

The **Downtown Travelodge,** at 1111 H St., Sacramento, CA 95814 (tel. 916/444-8880, or toll free 800/255-3050), is across the street from the Ponderosa. Rates here are extremely reasonable, but check whether the hotel has been renovated before making your reservation (the job is due to be completed by the fall of 1989).

There is no pool at this Travelodge, which consists of two buildings across the street from each other. When renovation is complete, they are planning to put families in one building, corporate people in the other.

Be sure to request the large rooms. There are rooms with two double beds and connecting rooms. There are also a few suites available. Rooms are big enough to include cribs.

Brewed coffee comes with the room, and a complimentary continental breakfast is served on the patio. A nearby restaurant will deliver pizzas and salads.

Rates are $36 to $46, single or double. Rollaways and cribs are provided at no charge. Kids up to age 17 sleep free in their parents' room.

Days Inn, 200 Jibboom St., Sacramento, CA 95814 (tel. 916/448-8100, or toll free 800/325-2525), is just on the outskirts of downtown, off Calif. 5, ten minutes from the airport, one mile from the Capitol, half a mile from Old Sacramento, and adjacent to Discovery Park, the Sacramento and American Rivers. In addition to offering a great location, this motel allows kids under 12 to eat free in the on-premises Daybreak restaurant—three meals a day, if you choose. There is no room service, but the Daybreak is open 24 hours.

There is a fenced-in, fairly large pool area, free airport transportation, gas pumps outside the lobby doors, a shuttle that can drop you at the Amtrak or bus station (putting you practically in the heart of Old Sacramento or downtown), and in-room movies that can be turned off in the front office. The motel will accommodate special family requests with advance notice.

These are small motel-style rooms with little bathrooms and vanity areas. You might want to request one of the rooms with one double bed and a small couch if you need to put a crib in the room; there are a limited number of these available. There are a few connecting rooms; also no-smoking rooms.

Reserve far in advance if you plan to come during the Jazz Festival. Rates run from $45 to $68, depending on the time of year and how full the hotel is. The average rate is about $50. Ask for current rates when you reserve. No charge for cribs or rollaways (request rollaways when you reserve your room); no charge for kids under 18 staying in their parents' room.

A BED-AND-BREAKFAST. The **Briggs House,** 2209 Capitol Ave., Sacramento, CA 95816 (tel. 916/441-3214), is whimsical and homey at the same time. Light-blue rooms and white lace curtains combine with Oriental rugs and frilly quilts and comforters. There are lots of little belongings all around, not just decorations. You won't be worried about your kids versus the antiques.

A *full* complimentary breakfast is served daily, along with wine, fruit, and nuts in the evening.

There are seven rooms, two of which share a bath. Kids over 8 can stay in the main house. Families with young children stay in the cottage in the back, which is really quite comfortable. The first floor of the cottage is a two-room suite with a little sitting room for the kids to sleep in. (Be careful of the open fireplace!) It includes a queen-size bed, refrigerator, and vintage clawfoot tub. Upstairs, the suite is decorated with cuddly teddy bears. There is a carved oak bed, a sitting room with a sofa bed, a private bath, and a kitchenette with eating space. All rooms are air-conditioned, and there's a Jacuzzi, sauna, and bikes available for guest use.

Babysitting can be arranged with advance notice. Rollaways are available, or bring sleeping bags for the kids. The crib is actually a playpen. There are no TVs; private phones are available by prior arrangement.

Rates are $60 to $95 for main-house rooms, $90 and $95 for cottage rooms. Each extra person is charged $10 per night.

If Briggs House cannot accommodate you, they will help you find lodging at another bed-and-breakfast in town.

Cal Expo Area

On the deluxe end of the scale in this part of town is **Red Lion Inn Sacramento,** at 2001 Point West Way, Sacramento, CA 95815 (tel. 916/924-4903, or toll free 800/547-8010). Situated in a suburban setting, the Red Lion is close to Arden Fair Mall and is within walking distance of two movie theaters and several restaurants. It's also five minutes from Cal Expo and Waterworld USA.

This is a large hotel with 448 rooms and suites (219 of which have two double beds). There are two pools, two restaurants, and a fitness room for adults, plus parking accessible to the rooms. Each wing of the hotel has a sunroom, where kids can bring their games or coloring books for a change of pace or on a rainy day. The front desk will give a referral number for babysitters.

Poolside food service is available at the main pool, which is fenced in and surrounded by artificial turf.

The Coffee Garden coffeeshop and the more formal Maxi's have Early Bird Specials—a convenient and affordable choice for many families. Children are welcome in both restaurants, which have booster seats and highchairs. Room service is available from 6 a.m. to 10 p.m.

Newly decorated rooms are a little larger than average and have space for a crib and a rollaway. They have double vanities, small bathrooms, full-length mirrors, cable TVs, and desks. Upper rooms have balconies (watch your toddlers on these narrow balconies). Hairdryers, curling irons, extra towels, ironing boards, and irons are available for the asking. A room with a king-size bed and a connecting room with two double beds is perfect for a larger family. The hotel offers no-smoking rooms.

Weekday rates for singles are $89 to $110; doubles cost $104 to $125; parlor suites let for $295. The hotel is attempting to attract families with a special weekend rate of $75 per night, but check first—rates are higher at Jazz Festival time. The rollaway charge is pretty steep at $15 per night; cribs cost $8. Kids under 18 sleep free in existing bedding. Older children and extra adults are charged $15 per night.

The **Beverly Garland Hotel** is just around the corner from Cal Expo, at 1780 Tribute Rd., Sacramento, CA 95815 (tel. 916/929-7900, or toll free 800/BEVERLY). Owned by actress Beverly Garland, this is a family-run hotel with 210 rooms. There are two restaurants on the premises—the cheerful Garden Court Café, which is open for breakfast, lunch, and dinner, and Fillmore's, cozy and charming and open for lunch and dinner. Both restaurants have nice selections and booster seats and highchairs. Complete lunches average $7.50; dinners, $14.50. Room service is delivered from 6:30 a.m. to 10 p.m. daily. There's also a fenced-in pool and spa, heated in the winter (unusual for Sacramento), and there are self-service laundry facilities for the guests, or valet service.

Rooms are charmingly decorated with country-style prints and lacy curtains. All the double rooms have either queen-size or king-size beds. While they are good-sized rooms, there's space for either a crib or rollaway, but not both. Each room features remote-control TV, HBO, and double sinks. Upper floors have tiny closed-in balconies. Connecting rooms are available.

The two-story town-house suites are great if you have older kids. One floor features a bedroom with a king-size bed. A *steep* circular staircase leads down to a living room with a pullout queen-size sofa, desk, overstuffed chairs, and a table with four chairs. Some have full bathrooms on the living-room level; others feature wet bars and refrigerators instead of baths.

On weekdays, doubles rent for $72; parlors, $110; and suites, $165. On weekends, doubles are $65. No charge for rollaways and cribs. Kids under 18 sleep free in the same room with their parents; older children and extra adults pay $10 additional.

The **Residence Inn**, at 1530 Howe Ave., Sacramento, CA 95825 (tel. 916/920-9111, or toll free 800/331-3131), features apartment-like accommodations with private entrances, full kitchens, and daily maid service—perfect for longer stays. Guests are treated like family, with special arrangements made for special needs. There is a free shuttle to the airport, a self-service guest laundry, and hotel laundry service.

Deluxe complimentary breakfast is served daily in the club room or you can take it back to your suite (it includes waffles, cereals, danish, fruit, and muffins). There are highchairs available. Five nights a week a complimentary food function offers the chance to get to know other people. One night pizza is served; another, cookies and milk; yet another, hot hors d'oeuvres.

There's a small heated pool, three spas, and barbecues for guest use. Little thoughtful things like *real* Kleenex and bags of popping corn make this a homey place for those making extended stays. There's even a shopping service that will pick up groceries for you.

Studios, which measure 550 square feet, feature one or two queen-size beds, a dressing area, a full-length mirror, a makeup stool, and a nice-sized sitting room area, plus good closet space. Studios will sleep four comfortably. There are also penthouse suites—two-story lofts with two beds, two bathrooms, and two TVs. Most have wood-burning fireplaces as well.

Be sure to request a room away from Howe Street, a noisy thoroughfare; in summer, you may wish to avoid rooms near the three spas for the same reason. Unfortunately there are no grassy areas or patios, which would make the Residence Inn perfect.

Rates decrease with longer stays. Studios start at $78 and go down to $66 (for a stay of 30 days or more). Penthouses start at $98 and decrease to $86. Cribs and rollaways incur a one-time charge of $5. Kids under 12 stay free in their parents' room.

Between Downtown and Cal Expo

The **Radisson Hotel Sacramento,** 500 Leisure Lane, Sacramento, CA 95815 (tel. 916/922-2020, or toll free 800/333-3333), is a full-scale resort hotel with 314 rooms, perfect for the family trade. It is located right off Calif. 160 at Canterbury Road, and is only five or ten minutes from anywhere important. The hotel is open during renovation.

A three-acre lake, surrounded by 132 rooms, offers paddleboats and sailing. The new pool is large, and a section of it is cordoned off for the kids. An 800-seat amphitheater offers summer entertainment—something for everyone. There is a jogging trail, bike paths and bike rentals (children's bikes are available), a par fitness course, and places to stroll. The concierge staff can arrange tours. A large minibus is used to take guests to various attractions in the area and shuttles guests to and from the airport. The manager is sensitive to families and his two children are usually around the grounds looking for playmates.

You can also request hairdryers, down pillows, and irons and ironing boards, and there is one-day valet service. Babysitting may be arranged through the housekeeping department.

The café is open for breakfast, lunch, and dinner, and offers a reasonably priced children's menu. Booster seats and highchairs are available. There is room service from 6 a.m. to 11 p.m.

Standard rooms are of moderate size; those around the lake are a little larger. Beamed ceilings, full-length mirrors, and a dressing area are features of these mauve-and-gray rooms. There's not much space for a crib in the rooms with two double beds. It's better to request a room with a king-size bed and add the crib. One- and two-bedroom suites around the pool sleep up to six, with a sleeper sofa in the living room. If you need larger accommodations, they can connect enough rooms to give you four bedrooms and six baths; if you want a refrigerator, request it in advance.

Rooms rent for $69 to $94, single or double. One- and two-bedroom suites go for $214 to $294 for up to four adults. The charge for porta-cribs and rollaways is $10 per night. Children under 12 sleep free in their parents' room; additional adults pay $10 each per night.

The other find in this neighborhood is the **Ramada Inn,** across the highway from the Woodlake at 1900 Canterbury Rd., Sacramento, CA 95815 (tel. 916/927-3492). This charming motel is a good place to stay in the summer. There's a large grassy area in the middle of the grounds, perfect for playing, and a large fenced-in pool area and spa with lots of cheerful navy and white lounge chairs, and tables and chairs for eating outside.

There is room service from 7 a.m. to 9 p.m. featuring light suppers and meals fine for kids, but it's expensive. From 6 a.m. to 8 a.m. there's a specially priced breakfast in the restaurant next door, Howie's Bar and Grill. They say they don't get many families, even in the summer. Probably best for teens.

The rooms are clean and adorable, furnished with bright navy-and-white checked spreads and navy ruffled skirts around the brass beds. Charming pictures on the wall, lace curtains, live plants, and a welcome bookshelf with real books add to the homeyness of the rooms. Bathrooms and vanities are small but clean. Cable TV and a table and two chairs completes the picture. Request a room with a king-size bed or two double beds, poolside—these accommodations are bigger. No-smoking rooms are available. There are connecting rooms and a mini-suite, with a refrigerator, that adjoins rooms with two double beds.

Rooms rent for $52 to $54 during the week; $40 on weekends. No charge for cribs, but rollaways cost $6. Children under 12 sleep free in their parents' room.

WHERE TO EAT: When in Sacramento, you'll probably find yourself eating either in your hotel, somewhere in Old Sacramento (or nearby), or in North Sacramento near Cal Expo. There are a number of interesting choices in the city. Here are some.

Downtown/Capitol Area

Especially good for breakfast is the **Fox & Goose Public House,** 1001 R St. (tel. 916/443-8825). Housed in an old factory building, this is a roomy and comfortable British restaurant. The staff is particularly pleasant, the coffee great, and the food fresh and natural. The owners pride themselves on not using flavor enhancers or additives. Soups, dressings, and baked goods are prepared from scratch daily, and the potatoes are fresh, never frozen.

There are full English breakfasts, lots of omelets, French toast (short orders available), and homemade granola (without sugar) and muffins. The waffles are thin, crispy, and delicious. Breakfast prices range from $2.25 to $6.25.

Lunch includes lots of traditional pub fare, but there are plenty of selections suitable for the kids, and the servers will split orders ($2.75 to $6.25) in the kitchen.

If you're lucky enough to get there on certain Fridays or weekends for breakfast or lunch when the magician comes, he might choose your child as a participant in his act. Call for dates.

There are highchairs and booster seats, and bottles and baby food will be warmed in the kitchen. You'll find parking right in front, or on the street.

Open weekdays for breakfast and lunch from 7 a.m. to 2 p.m., and on Saturday and Sunday from 9 a.m. to 1 p.m. and 1:30 to 3:30 p.m. Open just two nights a week for dinner, and those nights are "adults only." No credit cards accepted. No reservations taken.

It seems that Italian restaurants are often popular with families who have children of all ages. One modern version of a neighborhood Italian restaurant is **Americo's Trattoria Italiana,** within walking distance of the Capitol building at 2000 Capitol Ave. (tel. 916/442-8119). The emphasis here is on fresh spices and homemade pastas and sauces. Set in a renovated factory building, this cheerful restaurant has lots of windows hung with cute red-checked café curtains. The noise level is just right here for young-uns. Even with a large clientele of young singles and couples, the staff is friendly to kids, and you'll see a lot of families here for dinner.

The bread comes quickly, but the entrees not so quickly, probably due to so much individual preparation of dishes. There is a small children's selection— spaghetti or ravioli and soup or salad for $5. Adult à la carte and complete dinners range from $6.25 to $13. Selections include numerous pasta dishes, veal, chicken, steak, and fish. There are fewer choices for lunch. Items off the à la carte menu can be split for $1 extra; bottles and baby food will be gladly warmed.

Highchairs and booster seats are available. There's street parking and a small parking lot.

Open Tuesday through Friday for lunch from 11:30 a.m. to 2 p.m. Dinner is served weekdays from 5 to 9:30 p.m., on Saturday till 10 p.m., and on Sunday till 9 p.m. Reservations can be made for six or more. All major credit cards accepted.

Yet another Italian restaurant, a member of a family-oriented chain, is the **Old Spaghetti Factory,** 1910 J St. (tel. 916/443-2862). They serve only pasta dishes, with several different choices of noodles and sauces. All come with salad and bread. For kids 10 and under, there's a simple version of the adult fare at $2.75, or they will split adult portions. They'll also warm baby bottles or baby food and will make special children's drinks.

Since they only take reservations for 12 or more, come early. On weekends families start lining up at 4 p.m. and by 5 it is often packed.

Open for lunch Monday through Friday from 11:30 a.m. to 2 p.m.; for dinner, Monday through Thursday from 5 to 9:30 p.m., and on Saturday and Sunday from 4:30 to 10:30 p.m. Parking lot and street parking. No credit cards accepted.

One special way to introduce the whole family to formally served, traditional Japanese food is at **Fuji,** located in an Oriental neighborhood just outside of downtown at 2422 13th St. (tel. 916/446-4135). At this popular and accommodating restaurant, owner Julie Fujitue will try to make dining here comfortable for families, and the staff will bring plain rice and chopsticks right away to occupy the little ones. The bar offers a large selection of special non-alcoholic drinks that are nice, festive touches for kids.

Be sure that the children will at least try tempura or sukiyaki or sesame chicken before you commit, because there aren't any American selections on either the lunch or dinner menu. À la carte dinners run from $4.50 to $9; full dinners range from $9.25 to $15.

They will split portions for children and will serve half orders, and they will gladly warm bottles and baby food in the kitchen. Highchairs and booster seats are available.

Open for lunch Monday through Friday from 11:30 a.m. to 2:30 p.m. Dinner is served daily from 5 to 9:30 p.m. Reservations are recommended. All major credit cards accepted. Small restaurant parking lot and plenty of street parking.

Chinese cuisine usually needs no introduction for kids. For really good Mandarin and Cantonese dishes, take the family to **Royal Hong King Lum,** at 419 J St. (tel. 916/443-1584), within walking distance of the K Street Mall and quite close to Old Sacramento.

You'll recognize most of the dishes here; some will be new adventures, but there's something for everyone. Royal Hong King Lum is a large restaurant with a soothing atmosphere, with views of gardens and courtyards. Since they prepare so many family banquets, they are used to the young trade.

Lunch specials are reasonably priced and include chow mein, Szechuan beef, and chicken salad (from $3.50 to $4.50 for full meals). For the less adventurous, there are also hamburgers and a steak sandwich. Dinner offers lots of choices, including seafood, pork, beef, poultry, and vegetable selections, plus lots of seafood specials and an American menu.

The bar will make non-alcoholic drinks, and bottles and baby food will be warmed in the kitchen. Booster seats and highchairs are available. Families with reservations will be seated promptly.

Open daily from 11 a.m. to 10:30 p.m. Street parking. All major credit cards accepted.

If you crave Mexican food, you will enjoy the good, traditional fare at **Luis's,** 1218 Alhambra Blvd. (tel. 916/451-7852), the restaurant that welcomes everyone from "babies to grandparents." In business since 1965, Luis's serves homemade Mexican food. Everything is prepared fresh, and from scratch, at least once a day. The menu selections will please all tastes, and the offerings are familiar to everyone. Prices average around $6; combination plates, slightly higher.

Niños and niñas 12 and under can have a burrito, a quesadilla, or chicken with gravy and beans, rice, salad, and tortillas for $2.50. Or they can order off the lunch menu all day. The helpful staff will try to make anything within reason for the kids, and will warm bottles and baby food and make special non-alcoholic drinks. There are highchairs and boosters. Reservations accepted for six or more.

Open Sunday through Thursday from 11 a.m. to midnight, on Friday and Saturday till 1 a.m. Parking lot. Major credit cards accepted.

Old Sacramento

There's no lack of places to eat in Old Sacramento. Practically every street you visit has some sort of restaurant.

For a super-casual pizzeria, try **Annabelle's Family Restaurant,** 200 J St. (tel. 916/448-6239). Pizza and pasta are the name of the game here. Two notable specials are an all-you-can-eat Italian buffet for $3, which includes pizza, lasagne, spaghetti, macaroni and cheese, and a salad bar. The Family Dinner Special comes with a large pizza, a trip to the salad bar for everyone, and a pitcher of soft drinks for only $15. Complete dinners average $4.50.

Video machines will keep the kids busy while you wait for the pizza. Boosters and highchairs are available.

Open daily from 11 a.m. to 11 p.m. Parking in the municipal structure nearby. No reservations accepted. Major credit cards welcome.

Fanny Ann's Saloon is an interesting lunch spot for older kids (it's a real saloon, and kids aren't allowed in after 8 p.m.). This is a self-serve restaurant offering bare-bones basic American food: burgers, hot dogs, fried onion rings, gooey sandwiches, nondiet salads. Burgers and sandwiches average $4. Booster seats only.

There's lots to look at, several floors of curios from California history, and free popcorn from an oldtime popcorn machine.

Open Tuesday through Sunday from 11:30 a.m. to midnight. No reservations accepted. No credit cards.

Cal Expo Area

This part of town offers a plethora of restaurants.

California Carlos (formerly Carlos Murphy's) is a wonderful surprise. It's located across the entrance to Cal Expo and Waterworld at 1801 Exposition Blvd. (tel. 916/924-3447). This is a great place to take kids because there's so much for them to look at. At the glassed-in tortillería in the front of the restaurant, they can watch fresh tortillas being made. Huge pulleys on the ceiling lead to rotating bamboo fans. Soft-sculpture figures hang from the ceiling, and all sorts of old signs and orange-crate–type art line the walls—it all combines to make a sort of vintage '70s California look. The cheerful apple-green décor blends with the pleasant atmosphere to make this a fun place to eat.

Many Mexican dishes are served here. You can choose from burritos, chimichangas, and enchiladas, or combinations, carne asada tacos, marinated chicken burritos, or fajitas. On the other side of the menu are barbecued ribs and chicken, shrimp or Chinese chicken stir-fry, lasagne, or steaks and burgers. Prices are reasonable, ranging from $5 to $12. There are three kids' selections at $4 or an à la carte list that includes a mini-chimichanga, enchilada, taco, and more. Leave room for the mini-monster cookie or deep-fried ice cream.

They have boosters and highchairs, will split portions, and will warm bottles and baby food. Some Wednesday nights there's a magician, and sometimes a balloon maker.

Open Monday through Thursday and on Sunday from 11 a.m. to 10 p.m., on Friday and Saturday till 11 p.m. Reservations for large parties only. From 5 to 8 p.m. there's not much of a wait, but on weekend evenings it can be 35 to 40 minutes. Parking lot. All major credit cards and in-state checks accepted.

Tony Roma's, 1441 Howe Ave. (tel. 916/922-8787), is another dependable restaurant. The food is good and the service is fast. The Tony Roma's kids' menu features ribs, chicken, or a burger, with fries and coleslaw, from $3.25 to $5. There are also three interesting drinks made with juice. While the kids are coloring, you can choose from Tony Roma's famous ribs, barbecued chicken or shrimp, grilled selections, and light lunches and sandwiches. Ribs cost $9 to $13; other lunch choices range from $4 to $13. Dinner starts at $5.50 and goes up to $13. If you've never tried the onion rings here, at least order a half loaf. If you're staying within a three-mile radius, they will deliver.

They have highchairs and boosters, will warm bottles and baby food, and make special non-alcoholic drinks.

Open Monday through Thursday from 11 a.m. to 10 p.m., on Friday till midnight, on Saturday from noon to midnight, and on Sunday from noon to 10 p.m. No reservations accepted. Weekdays the wait averages 10 to 15 minutes; on weekends, come before 6:30 p.m. or you'll have a 30- to 45-minute wait. Parking lot. All major credit cards are accepted.

"We get plenty of families, particularly on Sunday," says the manager of **Pasta Fresca,** 1407 Howe Ave. (tel. 916/921-2797). Popular with the locals, all sorts of spaghetti, fettuccine, rigatoni, tortellini, and ravioli, as well as cold pasta salads, are served in this casual restaurant. Lunch and dinner selections range from $3.75 to $6.25. Soup and salad cost extra. Although there is no children's menu, they'll gladly split adult portions. Most kids will love the Pasta Fresca–made gelato, a gourmet Italian ice cream.

Highchairs and booster seats available. Baby bottles and baby food can be warmed.

Open daily from 11:30 a.m. to 2:30 p.m. and 5 to 10 p.m. No lunch on Sunday. Parking lot. Major credit cards and local checks accepted.

You can always trust **The Good Earth,** 2024 Arden Way (tel. 916/920-5544), to have natural, fresh food. It has the same bright atmosphere and comfortable feeling typical of the Good Earth chain members.

The children's menu is fairly extensive here. For the under-12 set, there are selections for breakfast like pancakes or French toast (made out of ten-grain cakes and bread); for lunch, chicken salad, tuna, or cheese sandwiches, a burrito or tostada. Prices range from $2 to $3. Crayons come with the children's menu.

Moms and dads will find all sorts of natural foods to choose from, including vegetarian and chicken dishes, hot and cold sandwiches, and lots of breakfast selections. Anything on the menu can be made vegetarian. Desserts are yummy. Breakfast averages $4; lunch and dinner, $5. Specially made muffins and breads are for sale at the register.

There are highchairs and boosters; they'll warm bottles and baby food, and will split portions. The no-smoking area is a separate room, not just a section.

Open Monday through Thursday from 7 a.m. to 10 p.m., on Friday and Saturday till 11 p.m. On Saturday and Sunday they open at 8 a.m. and close at 10 p.m. Parking lot. Reservations accepted for seven or more. Major credit cards welcome.

ACTIVITIES BY AGE GROUP: The following listings suggest activities divided into specific age brackets. Refer back to the individual descriptions for details.

Teens and Preteens

Blue Diamond Visitor's Center
B. F. Hastings Building
California State Fair
California State Railroad Museum
Central Pacific Passenger Depot
Crocker Art Museum
Dixieland International Jazz Festival
Historic Governor's Mansion
History Center
Huntington Hopkins Hardware Store
Iceland Ice Skating Rink
Music Circus
River Rafting
Sacramento Science Center and Junior Museum
Sacramento Zoo
State Capitol
State Indian Museum
Sutter's Fort
Towe Ford Museum
Waterworld USA

School-Age Children

Blue Diamond Visitor's Center
B. F. Hastings Building
California State Fair
California State Railroad Museum
Central Pacific Passenger Depot
Crocker Art Museum
Historic Governor's Mansion
History Center
Huntington Hopkins Hardware Store
Iceland Ice Skating Rink
Music Circus
Old Sacramento Schoolhouse
River Rafting
Sacramento Science Center and Junior Museum
Sacramento Zoo
State Capitol
State Indian Museum
Sutter's Fort
Waterworld USA

Preschoolers and Toddlers

Blue Diamond Visitor's Center
California State Fair
California State Railroad Museum
Central Pacific Passenger Depot
Crocker Art Museum

Fairytale Town
Iceland Ice Skating Rink
River Rafting
Sacramento Science Center and Junior Museum
Sacramento Zoo
Sutter's Fort
Waterworld USA

EMERGENCY SERVICES: If the need arises, there's a 24-hour emergency room at **Mercy Hospital,** 4001 J St. in downtown Sacramento (tel. 619/453-4424).

Consult the local *Yellow Pages* for a list of pharmacies that are open around-the-clock.

---

2. THE GOLD COUNTRY

A trip through the Gold Country is a journey through history—the history of California's most colorful era, the Gold Rush. The height of gold fever burned only a few years, but it spurred the greatest short-term migration of all time and transformed California from a pastoral backwater into the Eldorado of America. It has been 140 years since the cry "Gold!" first rang out along the American River, and the gold itself has long since run short. But the Golden State's sun-drenched fields and burgeoning cities have continued to beckon immigrants from far and wide.

To fully understand today's California, it's crucial to visit the Gold Country. A weekend spent here can be the equivalent of six weeks in a history classroom. But you needn't spoil the fun by telling the kids it's educational. History so permeates the Gold Country that children pick it up without even knowing they've been "educated," as that famous Gold Country denizen, Mark Twain, might have put it.

Your family can pan for gold along pristine rivers just as the '49ers did. Tour an abandoned hard-rock gold mine—one that's still being worked today. Stroll the main streets of towns that look like Wild West movie sets (and in fact have served as such many times). Stop at historic spots where, after enjoying a tale or two of the long-ago, you can relax with a picnic, a swim, a buggy ride, or a river-rafting trip. Stay at 1850s-vintage hotels, where rooms are named for colorful characters like Black Bart and Lotta Crabtree—and where ghost stories come with every room. Even mealtimes can provide historical insights here. Children may not want to try Hangtown Fry themselves, but you can bet they'll ask how it got its name. And a popular Gold Country snack, Cornish pasties, can speak volumes about many of the miners who migrated here seeking a better life. History has never been so easy to digest.

GETTING THERE: From San Francisco, there are three major routes by car. You can take I-80 through Sacramento to Auburn, gateway to the northern reaches of the Gold Country; you can cut off on U.S. 50 at Sacramento heading for Placerville and the center of the Gold Country; or you can take I-580 (from Oakland) to I-205 and (briefly) I-5 to Manteca, where you catch Calif. 120 and later Calif. 108 to Sonora, gateway to the southern Gold Country. The drive from San Francisco takes approximately three hours.

From Los Angeles, take I-5 or Calif. 99 to Calif. 120, and cut over to Sonora; or take I-5 or Calif. 99 to Sacramento and follow the above directions to Auburn or Placerville. Straight through from Los Angeles will take you approximately eight hours. Los Angeles folks often stop in Fresno overnight, then continue to the Gold Country.

You can also reach the Gold Country from the east via U.S. 50 from South Lake Tahoe; via Calif. 108, Calif. 4, and Calif. 88 heading west from U.S. 395; or via Calif. 120 west from Yosemite.

Warning: Some of these roads, especially those heading west across the Sierra, may be closed for long periods during the winter. Carry chains and call the California Highway Patrol for the latest highway conditions and road closures. Tioga Pass is closed all winter.

The closest airports to the Gold Country—all at least 50 miles away—are Reno International, Sacramento Metropolitan, and Stockton Metropolitan. Greyhound buses travel between San Francisco and Auburn, and from there to Placerville or Grass Valley.

ORIENTATION: While there is not, of course, an age minimum for a Gold Country visit, we think children 6 and over will enjoy it the most. The kids 5 and under don't find it as scintillating an experience, because they are too young to appreciate the historical significance and too young to get much out of the stories. Also, many of the overnight establishments don't accept young children, so you are limited as to where you can stay.

The Gold Country lies in the foothills of the Sierra Nevada mountains about 120 miles east and northeast of San Francisco, 35 miles east of Sacramento, 50 miles northwest of Yosemite, and 60 miles west of South Lake Tahoe, at the closest points to each. The entire Gold Country runs nearly 300 miles north to south along a roughly crescent-shaped curve from the town of Vinton, north of Tahoe, down to the town of Oakhurst south of Yosemite.

One road binds the entire region together like a meandering vein of gold: the aptly named Hwy. 49 (Calif. 49). All along this route, which snakes through colorful town after town, you'll find road signs leading to hamlets with such alluring names as Rough and Ready, Fiddletown, Drytown, Volcano, Red Dog, Jackass Hill, and Chinese Camp. Pursuing some of these will mean moving off the highway for a few miles, but you can always return to Calif. 49, knowing you will be on course.

The most traveled stretch of Calif. 49 is the 130 miles between Nevada City in the north and Sonora in the south. The area around Nevada City (as far south as Auburn) was known as the "Northern Mines," and the area south of Auburn was known as the "Southern Mines." Either makes an outstanding destination in its own right if time doesn't permit a visit to both. We take this trip from north to south, but there's no reason why you can't take it in the opposite direction, especially if you are coming from Los Angeles.

In the cold months (roughly November to April), the Gold Country foothills are often blanketed with snow—though early spring may also bring hot sun. Summer, when most tourists flock here, tends to be very hot and dry. Fall and spring, with their wonderfully colored array of changing leaves and wildflowers, can be the nicest times to visit, and far less crowded than summertime.

Getting Around Calif. 49

It's entirely possible—we know because we've done it—to drive the entire 130 miles from Nevada City to Sonora in one day, even making several stops and keeping children relatively content. But do that only if you're in a hurry, as each destination is worth a visit in itself. But if you can take two days or more for the trip, by all means do so. There are simply too many fascinating towns, scenic stops, and historic points to go whizzing past. Or pick one section of Calif. 49 and spend your time on it. *Note:* The road does get quite curvy for stretches south of Auburn, so keep this in mind if your children tend to get carsick.

WHAT TO SEE AND DO: The **chambers of commerce** in each town have lots of information on what to see and do. But here are some highlights of the best things we've found to do with the children.

Nevada City

"Queen City of the Northern Mines," Nevada City is one of a handful of "don't miss" Gold Country destinations. Built on a series of hills, it is a compact little jewel of a town, graced with gingerbread Victorian architecture and gaslamps lighting the streets at night. Deer Creek, whose waters once yielded as much as a pound of gold flakes a day to any man with a pan and persistence, cuts through the hills.

Write for or pick up a walking tour map from the **Nevada City Chamber of Commerce,** at 132 Main St., Nevada City, CA 95959 (tel. 916/265-2692), open weekdays from 9 a.m. to 5 p.m. and on Saturday from 11 a.m. to 4 p.m. Or pick up your map at the **Brass Shop,** 225 Broad St. (tel. 916/265-6631), open daily from 10 a.m. to 5 p.m., and then set out on a pleasant stroll around the center of town. You'll find California's oldest theater building at 401 Broad St., the **Nevada Theatre,** built in 1865, which still presents plays from late March to early December. Down the street at 211 Broad St. stands the ornate **National Hotel** (tel. 916/265-4551), the oldest continuously operating hotel in the state, dating from 1854. Over on Main Street, check out the 1861-vintage Victorian **Firehouse No. 1 Museum** (tel. 916/265-5468). There are also lots of intriguing shops selling everything from fool's gold and gemstones to antique brassware and rattlesnake key chains.

Walking distances are easy for everyone in the family, but if you'd like to relax on an old-fashioned horse-drawn carriage ride around town, just look for the rigs of the **Nevada City Carriage Company** (tel. 916/265-5348). In the daytime, they're parked in front of the chamber of commerce or the National Hotel; in the evenings, in front of Friar Tuck's Restaurant on Pine Street. You can ride weekends year round, and daily in warm-weather months, from 11 a.m. to 10 p.m. (till midnight on Friday and Saturday). Tours of 12 to 15 minutes cost $10 for one or two people, $12 for three or four people, $15 for five or six people; children 10 and under, free. Longer tours are also available.

If you have a half day or more to spare, consider a visit to the **Malakoff Diggins State Historic Park,** reached by taking Tyler–Foote Road off Calif. 49, 15 miles northeast of Nevada City (tel. 916/265-2740). (Be aware that the last part of the road is unpaved.) The park is the site of what was once the largest hydraulic gold mine in the world, and the views of the ravaged cliffs are eerily beautiful. You can camp, hike, or picnic there. Open daily year round. The day-use fee is $3.

Grass Valley

Four miles south of Nevada City, Grass Valley is also an important stop. Though it's not as picturesque as its neighbor, its main street reeks of history. Pick up a copy of the walking tour brochure at the **Nevada County Chamber of Commerce,** 248 Mill St., Grass Valley, CA 95945 (tel. 916/273-4667), which is open weekdays from 8:30 a.m. to 5 p.m. and on Saturday from 10 a.m. to 5 p.m. Then glance around: 248 Mill is a replica of the one-time home of Lola Montez, the internationally celebrated stage performer who lived here in the 1850s. Nearby, at 238 Mill, is Lotta Crabtree's house, a now undistinguished-looking private residence once owned by Lola Montez's protégé, who became dance hall queen of the Mother Lode.

Heading back toward town, Mill Street and adjoining streets are lined by century-old shops, hotels, and bed-and-breakfast inns. Don't miss the **Holbrooke Hotel,** at 212 W. Main St., which dates from 1862; an old hotel register on display contains the names of Mark Twain and Presidents Grover Cleveland and Benjamin Harrison, among other notables. Like many Gold Country inns and bed-and-breakfast establishments, alas, the Holbrooke allows no guests under the age of 12. (The desk clerk does have a sense of humor, however; when our 9-year-old companion asked if he could stay there, he was told, "Sure—your room will be ready in three years!")

The **Empire Mine State Historic Park,** about two miles outside town at 10791 E. Empire St. (tel. 916/273-8522), was once the largest, deepest, richest hard-rock gold mine in the area. It was in operation 107 years, until 1956, and eventually reached a depth of 11,000 feet. The older kids with us were fascinated to see the narrow entrance of the main shaft, where the miners rode deep underground into a dark and damp world from which they didn't emerge for nine hours while they extracted gold from quartz—working for a few dollars a week. You can also tour the English-style manor house on the grounds, where the mine owner vacationed in summer. The mansion, ironically called a cottage, is surrounded by formal gardens and acres of grassy hills perfect for hiking or letting off some energy. Both self-guided and guided tours are available, depending on time of day and year. Open every day from 10 a.m. to 5 p.m. Adults pay $1; children 6 to 17, 50¢; under 6, free.

Back in Grass Valley, be sure to stop at one of the several Cornish pasty shops in town—try **Marshall's Pasties,** on Mill Street, or **King Richard's Pasties,** at 251 S. Auburn—for a taste of the culinary legacy of the hard-working miners from Cornwall, England, who made up 90% of the Empire's hard-rock mining force. Pasties, the miners' favorite lunch, are turnovers filled with various meats and sell for around $1.50 to $2.

Auburn

Auburn is a thriving, modern town except for one small but very colorful Gold Rush–era section called Old Town, which is located just a hundred feet off the late-20th-century Interstate 80. Pick up a walking-tour map from the **Auburn Chamber of Commerce,** at 512 Auburn Ravine Rd., Auburn, CA 95603 (tel. 916/885-5616), which is open weekdays from 9 a.m. to 5 p.m., or just stroll and browse through the twisted streets of weathered brick and clapboard storefronts. There are 32 shops and a dozen restaurants here—including a small Chinese merchants' area—and the West's oldest operating post office and volunteer firehouse.

The **Placer County Museum,** 1273 High St. (tel. 916/885-9570), is enjoyable for kids over 7. The exhibits are constantly changing, but there are always displays depicting the history of the county and artifacts from mining days.

Open Tuesday through Friday from 10 a.m. to 4 p.m., on Saturday and Sunday to 5 p.m.; closed Monday and holidays. A $1 donation is requested.

Coloma

A half hour south of Auburn along Calif. 49 is Coloma. In this tiny town you'll come upon another essential Gold Country attraction: the **Marshall Gold Discovery State Historic Park,** at Main and Bridge Streets (tel. 916/622-3470), where James W. Marshall uttered his immortal words in January 1848: "Boys, I believe I have found a gold mine." At the time the non–Native American population of California was 14,000. Four years later it had mushroomed to more than 220,000. Most were placer miners—men who stood in the often-icy river waters with pans, slowly sifting out the tiny flakes of gold that had come to rest in tons of sand, gravel, and dirt. Some got rich, but many others died poor; ironically, James Marshall was among the latter.

Marshall made his discovery while building a sawmill on the south fork of the American River on behalf of land baron John Sutter. Today a working replica of Sutter's Mill rests near the riverbank. You can soak up some history, then soak up some sun while picnicking on the grass or at nearby tables. If you need a picnic, try the **Sierra Nevada House Ice Cream Parlor** adjacent to the park. Across the highway is an informative museum and visitor center (open daily from 10 a.m. to 5 p.m.), as well as models of miners' cabins and other exhibits. A brochure describes two trails: one an easy one-third-mile walk to the gold discovery site; the other a more difficult 1½-mile hike to the James Marshall Monument, which is flanked by picnic tables. Kids can complete both hikes. Allow plenty of time to relax and enjoy this lovely spot. Our children got a tremendous kick out of trapping tiny flakes of gold—or were they fool's gold?—along the banks of the river.

Open daily from 8 a.m. to dusk; closed Thanksgiving, Christmas, and New Year's Days. The fee is $3 per car.

Placerville

Nearby Placerville—called Hangtown when it was a rough-and-tumble mining camp known for quickly dispatching gold poachers to their higher reward—is an appropriate place to stop for a Hangtown Fry (eggs, oysters, and bacon). Several cafés in town serve it. You can also find Gold Rush–era buildings —and a hanging dummy—along Main Street.

Amador City and Sutter Creek

South of Placerville lies Amador County, a less celebrated but beautiful region of rolling green hills and small, atmospheric Gold Rush towns. Tiny Amador City and the somewhat larger Sutter Creek are gems. Amador City is one block of Victorian-era antique shops, cafés, and hotels.

Sutter Creek has a beautifully preserved Old West main street jammed with antique shops. But don't overlook the **Bubble Gum Bookstore,** at 48 Main St. (tel. 209/267-5680), whose motto is "Reading really sticks to you." The Bubble Gum has an astonishing selection of books for children from toddler to teen— our kids could have browsed for hours. We picked up some essential children's books for the nights in rooms without TVs! Adults can find a wide array of books on amateur gold prospecting, or Gold Country classics by Bret Harte and Mark Twain. You can also pick up a walking-tour map of Sutter Creek here, detailing all the historic buildings.

Volcano

If you have some extra time, a side trip from Sutter Creek to the lovely little town of Volcano (follow the Sutter Creek–Volcano road) is highly recommended. Once a booming Gold Rush town, Volcano is now isolated and pastoral. Our family was mesmerized by the town cemetery, whose many tombstones poignantly etch the history of hardships and dangers facing the Gold Rush pioneers. And if you're here in the spring (around March and April) don't miss **Daffodil Hill,** a spectacular display of some 300,000 flowers three miles north of Volcano at Ram's Horn Grade and Shake Ridge Road. You can picnic here. Call 209/223-0350 for bloom dates.

Jackson

Heading south again from Sutter Creek, you reach Jackson, a bustling town that combines modern amenities with numerous good examples of Gold Rush architecture in its homes and churches. **Kennedy Tailing Wheels Park,** on Jackson Gate Road, north of town, is worth a visit to see the two startling giant wooden mine wheels that are a favorite of Gold Country photographers. Marking the end of the Gold Rush era, these massive wheels (originally there were four) were built to move the tailings from the gold mines to a separate reservoir so as not to pollute the streams any further. What may be interesting to your children is that the construction of these wheels was based on a brand-new law in 1912 signaling a new interest in environmental protection.

There are picnic tables in this small woodsy park, and a parking lot.

Mokelumne Hill and Angels Camp

Next comes Calaveras County, made famous by Mark Twain's tale of "The Celebrated Jumping Frog." Be sure to drive through the tiny village of **Mokelumne Hill**—incredibly, once one of the biggest, wildest, most important towns in all California (it almost became the state capital!)—on the way to **Angels Camp,** site of the annual spring Calaveras County Fair and Frog Jumping Jubilee. Call 209/736-2561 or the **chamber of commerce,** P.O. Box 111, Angels Camp, CA 95222 (tel. 209/736-4444), for this year's dates. The folks around here have not skimped on the commercial potential of frogs; you can rent a frog for the contest, and a frog motif dominates the town at any time of year.

The **Angels Camp Museum,** at 753 Main St. (tel. 209/736-2963), contains Gold Rush memorabilia. Open daily from 10 a.m. to 3 p.m. Admission is 50¢ for adults, 25¢ for children 12 and under.

A worthwhile detour from Angels Camp, passing through the picturesque town of Murphys, is to the **Calaveras Big Trees State Park,** about 25 miles east along Calif. 4 (tel. 209/795-2334). This is a good spot to gaze in awe at giant sequoias and hike, camp, picnic, swim, or fish. The trees were first seen in 1841, but it wasn't until 1852 that the public learned about them from A. T. Dowd. There's a visitor center, which provides interpretive talks on the sequoias, and hiking trails, which the staff will be happy to point out. The visitor center is open daily during the summer from 10 a.m. to 5 p.m.; the rest of the year, on weekends from 11 a.m. to 3 p.m. The fee is $3 per car, day use.

On the way to the Big Trees, you may want to take the kids to **Moaning Cavern,** located on Parrot's Ferry Road off Calif. 4 (for reservations, write P.O. Box 78, Vallecito, CA 95251; tel. 209/736-2708). You can tour the huge cavern, filled with strangely shaped natural statues and the bones of prehistoric people who fell to their deaths. These 45-minute guided tours are suitable for the whole family. The truly adventurous—ages 12 and up only—can opt for guided tours that include making their own rope descents. There is also a three-hour Adventure Tour (the Boy Scouts love it!) which includes a rope descent. The staff prefers 12-year-olds and up for this one, but many younger kids participate successfully. Open daily from 9 a.m. to 6 p.m. in summer, 10 a.m. to 5 p.m. the rest of the year.

Rates for a family tour are $5 for adults, $2.50 for children 6 to 12; under 6, free. The fee is $13 for the rope-descent tours; the Adventure Tour costs $35, no matter what the age.

A few miles south of Angels Camp in Tuolumne County is **Sonora,** a busy commercial town of interest primarily as a base for exploring nearby attractions.

Columbia

Five miles north of Sonora, on Parrots Ferry Road off Calif. 49, lies Columbia—the "Gem of the Southern Mines" (tel. 209/532-4301) and probably the best-preserved town in the Gold Country. A number of western movies —including *High Noon*—were filmed here. Anyone visiting the Mother Lode with children should make this a top priority. It was made into a state historic park in 1945.

Once a boomtown of 15,000, with 67 saloons, 143 gambling halls, and 185 fandango halls, Columbia is now a living museum of Gold Rush history. Its streets are lined with restored or reconstructed buildings from that era that serve as working shops, restaurants, and hotels. There's a blacksmith, a Wells Fargo depot (where you can take a stagecoach ride and even ride shotgun for an extra fee —as the kids complain about their bottoms, explain that this is how many pioneers traveled across vast stretches of country), a baker, a candy store (try the hand-dipped chocolates), two hotels, a theater, riding stables, a carpentry shop, trading posts, and two saloons where "Ladies and Minors Welcome" signs invite the kids to sidle up to the bar and order a sarsaparilla. People who work in Columbia dress in period costume.

Don't miss the **Matelot Gold Mine Supply Store,** at the corner of Main and Washington Streets (for reservations, write P.O. Box 28, Columbia, CA 95310; tel. 209/532-9693), where you can buy nuggets, pan for gold in sluices, and sign up for tours to the **Hidden Treasure Gold Mine,** the only working hard-rock gold mine open to the public. The guided tours are absolutely enthralling—leading you through 800 feet of tunnel into the heart of a granite mountain, where gold has been blasted from quartz veins since 1879. The 9-year-old with us shuddered to hear that had he lived in Columbia circa 1850, he might have spent his days in this mine holding iron spikes to be pounded by muscular John Henrys—risking serious injury for 10¢ a day and one meal. The 1- to 1½-hour tours run from 9 a.m. to 5 p.m. on weekends and 10 a.m. to 3 p.m. on weekdays in summer; from October through April hours vary. The tours cost $6 for adults, $5 for children 6 to 12 and seniors; children under 6, free. You can combine it with gold-panning lessons for an additional fee. They guarantee you'll find gold!

Jamestown

Jamestown, four miles southwest of Sonora on Calif. 49, is another beautifully preserved Gold Rush town. Here you'll find good hotels, restaurants, and antique shops. Train buffs will love to show off what they know at **Railtown 1897,** in the Sierra Rail Depot on Fifth Avenue (tel. 209/984-3953), where they can explore part of the 26-acre roundhouse on a 50-minute walking tour, which children can handle. The roundhouse is the oldest operating steam roundhouse in the country. Tours are available May through September, daily from 10 a.m. to 5 p.m.; September to May, weekends only from 10 a.m. to 4 p.m. Fee: adults, $2; children 3 to 12, $1.25; under 3, free.

There is also a train ride that kids will like. It's a one-hour round trip from Jamestown to Linespur, running behind either a 1922 or an 1891 engine, which was the one used on "Little House on the Prairie" and other TV shows. The children might get a kick out of knowing that it's the oldest running locomotive in the country. Train rides are available May through September only, on weekends and holidays from 10 a.m. to 5 p.m. The fare is $7.50 for adults, $3.50 for children 3 to 12; children under 3, free.

The kids will be enthralled with the remarkable **Gold Prospecting Expeditions,** 18172 Main St. (tel. 209/984-GOLD), which offers sidewalk gold panning (free if you have your own pan, $1 to rent a pan)—big wooden troughs set up in front of the store filled with sand and gold dust. A couple of the oldtimers wander by and will show you the "right" way to do it. Or the whole family can enjoy a number of gold-prospecting expeditions on nearby rivers. Ask for the special family discount rates: two adults and two children can take a one-hour prospecting trip for $35 ($2 extra for each additional child) or a two-hour trip for $60. You can also choose one- or two-day trips (two adults and two children—$135 for one day, $244 for two days; you can camp for free on the latter). The company supplies all equipment, provides lessons in the art of panning—and virtually promises you'll strike gold.

OTHER OUTDOOR ACTIVITIES: In addition to the possibilities mentioned above in specific localities, the following outdoor activities are also available to you and your family.

Gold Prospecting

For other gold-prospecting opportunities, try **Gold Country Prospecting,** 3119 Turner St. (tel. 916/622-2484), which offers three-hour river gold-panning tours for $35 per adult, $15 per child 7 to 12, and free for those under age 7. They supply the equipment; you bring your own lunch. Call ahead.

Roaring Camp Mining Co. (tel. 209/296-4100) offers four- and five-hour guided tours to this remote old gold camp. The four-hour trip is offered daily; the five-hour tour is on Wednesday only, and dinner is included. Make advance reservations for these tours. For those who wish to stay longer, there are cabins. You can pan for gold, hunt for rocks, fish, hike, swim, and canoe. Roaring Camp is open daily, May 1 through September.

The four-hour tour costs $12 for adults, $10 for children 10 and under. The five-hour tour is $24 for adults, $21 for kids 10 and under. There is a family rate for cabins of $295 per week, plus $70 for each child under 18. Extra adults are charged $110 for the week.

A special RVers Gold Prospecting package is offered by reservation and includes one week with full hookup at nearby Pine Acres and five days of transportation to Roaring Camp. The seven-day rate for singles is $180, doubles are $250, and each additional child or adult is charged $95.

White-Water Rafting

White-water rafting is exceptional along all three forks of the American River, offering varying degrees of difficulty. Some trips are suitable for children, while others may be too dangerous or frightening. The best way to judge is to inquire at individual outfitters, most of which offer both one- and two-day trips, at costs ranging from around $40 to $165 per person.

American River Recreation, 11257 Bridge St., Rancho Cordova, CA 95670 (tel. 916/635-4479), offers difficult white-water rafting on the American and other rivers, as do **Wild Water West, Ltd.,** P.O. Box 4833, Davis, CA 95617 (tel. 916/758-9270); **Wild River Tours,** P.O. Box 568, Columbia, CA 95310 (tel. 209/532-0160, or toll free 800/821-0183); **Mother Lode River Trips,** P.O. Box 456, Coloma, CA 95613 (tel. 916/626-4187, or toll free 800/367-2387); **American River Touring Association,** Star Route 73, Groveland, CA 95321 (tel. 209/962-7873, or toll free 800/323-ARTA); **Whitewater Voyages,** P.O. Box 906, El Sobrante, CA 94903 (tel. 415/222-5994); and **Gold Country River Runners,** P.O. Box 477, Coloma, CA 95613 (tel. 916/626-7326). Call or write for information on trips offered and minimum age requirements.

White-Water Kayaking

Adventurous families may also want to learn white-water kayaking on the American River's South Fork. The **Sierra Kayak School,** Camp Lotus, 5461 Bassi Rd. (P.O. Box 460), Lotus, CA 95651 (tel. 916/626-8006), offers two- to seven-day classes with one-day clinics for $130 to $430 per person. The minimum age is 13, and kids pay the same as adults.

Other Water Sports

For more serene boating, head for the marina at **New Melones Lake,** Angels Camp, P.O. Box 1389, Angels Camp, CA 95222 (tel. 209/785-3300), between Angels Camp and Sonora, recently created by damming the Stanislaus River. You can rent houseboats here, at rates as low as $165 a day for a three-day minimum in the off-season, climbing to $775 for a three-day weekend in summer (late May through mid-September). Or take the family on a pontoon boat for the day (half day, $70; full day, $95). Fishing boats are also for rent (a half day for $28, a full day for $38).

Pinecrest is a gorgeous alpine lake situated in the high mountains about an hour up Calif. 108 from Sonora. You can swim, boat, windsurf, and camp here in the summer, and sled or ski cross-country in the winter. Come for a day trip or stay at the **Pinecrest Lake Resort,** P.O. Box 1216, Pinecrest, CA 95364 (tel. 209/965-3411), a woodsy, full-service facility.

Skiing

And speaking of skiing, you can downhill ski in winter at the family-oriented **Dodge Ridge Ski Area**, P.O. Box 1188, Pinecrest, CA 95364 (tel. 209/965-3474), near Pinecrest. Dodge Ridge offers a SKIwee children's school, special beginner's rates (for those 13 years and up), and child care. Dates of operation vary; call toll free 800/233-SNOW for conditions before heading up.

Another winter facility near Pinecrest on Calif. 108, the **Leland Meadows Sno Bowl**, P.O. Box 1273, Pinecrest, CA 95364 (tel. 209/965-4389), offers cross-country skiing and children's sledding for a $5 entry free (under 5, free); you can bring your own equipment or rent there for reasonable rates.

A Working Farm

Sonka's Apple Ranch, 19200 Cherokee Rd., Tuolumne (tel. 209/928-4689), a working farm, not only offers an array of delectable goodies—pies, tarts, jams, syrups, pickles—but has added a miniature train ride that is just the right size for younger children (our 6-year-old was thrilled). The "Short Line Railroad," as they call it, costs $1 per person and passes farm livestock, an orchard, and rolling countryside on a ten-minute jaunt. You can watch apple picking and cider making here in the early fall.

Open daily year round from 8 a.m. to 5:30 p.m.; the train runs weekends only, from 10 a.m. to 5 p.m.

WHERE TO STAY: If you're coming from San Francisco, you might want to spend your first night in Nevada City, although it's the same distance to Sonora. If you're coming from Los Angeles and want to make your Gold Country trip from north to south, stop for your first night in Fresno (see Chapter VI), which is 220 miles from Los Angeles, and your next night in any one of the Gold Country cities.

Nevada City

An exceptional choice for families in Nevada City is the **Northern Queen Motel**, 400 Railroad Ave., Nevada City, CA 95959 (tel. 916/265-5824), an enormous complex just off the first Nevada City exit coming north into town on Calif. 49. The Northern Queen offers immaculately clean, spacious motel rooms, chalets, and cottages. There's a swimming pool and Jacuzzi open year round, and an excellent restaurant (the Trolley Junction Café) open for breakfast and lunch. Breakfast features delicious waffles, French toast, omelets, and egg dishes for between $3.25 and $4.25; but our 6-year-old was delighted with his side order of a short stack of pancakes with fruit for $1.50. Lunch runs to burgers and sandwiches. This is an exceedingly pleasant motel restaurant, with views of a waterfall and a working water wheel; the dining room is bright and cheery, with lots of greenery. Highchairs and booster seats are available. No room service.

The restaurant's name comes from the Northern Queen Motel trolley, which leaves from the parking lot for daily half-hour tours of Nevada City beginning at 9:30 a.m. (adults pay $2; children under 10, $1). The rest of the day the trolley shuttles back and forth between the motel and downtown, which is about a 15-minute walk away.

All the rooms come with queen-size beds, refrigerators, and supplies of coffee and tea. They also have color TVs and VCRs, with a large selection of movies available in the office. Chalets are set along the creek and are designed with a loft bedroom and one queen-size bed, a kitchen, dining room, wet bar, and living room with a fold-out sofa. Cottages are found in the woods above the Trout Pond. They come with a semiprivate bedroom and queen-size bed, a kitchenette, three-quarter bath, and a living room with a wood-burning stove.

Rates for the standard motel rooms (single or double occupancy) range from $38 to $41. Each additional person over 7 pays $3 per night. Cottages rent for $60 to $90; chalets, for $70 to $90, plus $5 per additional person. Rollaways and cribs are available for $5 per night.

As noted earlier, many of the historic hotels and inns of the Gold Country do not accept children, but one that does welcome families is Nevada City's **National Hotel,** 211 Broad St., Nevada City, CA 95959 (tel. 916/265-4551). Rooms here are decorated with Victorian furnishings reminiscent of the Gold Rush era; our children drooled at the prospect of jumping off the high antique beds (but of course we restrained them). Having been in continuous operation for 130 years—the longest west of the Rockies—the hotel is creaky with age in spots, and some of the rooms share baths. But it also exudes old-fashioned charm and hospitality. Modern amenities include a swimming pool, and there's a cocktail lounge, and an ornate Victorian-décor dining room that serves moderately priced breakfasts and lunches and full-course dinners ranging from $9 to $17.50. The chef will prepare children's portions. Room service is available, but it can be pretty slow.

The spacious rooms are all decorated differently. There are only 43 rooms in the hotel, so be sure to book in advance. Rooms with private baths, and suites have TVs. Most families with two children rent one room with twin beds and no bath, connecting with a room with a double bed and private bath (baths can be entered from two sides). Mini-suites are about 1½ times bigger than a standard room.

Twin- or double-bedded rooms with shared bath cost $39; with private bath, $59; Mini-suites (two with kitchenettes) run $83; full suites, $95. Children under 12 sleep free: Those 12 and over and additional adults pay $6.50 per night. There's no charge for cribs. Rollaways are available for $6.50 a night.

Mokelumne Hill

Another historic inn friendly to families in tiny Mokelumne Hill is the **Hotel Leger,** P.O. Box 50, Mokelumne Hill, CA 95245 (tel. 209/286-1401), located between Jackson and San Andreas on Calif. 49 and Calif. 26 in the central Gold Country. The Leger, founded in 1851, looks a bit shabby from the outside but is very comfortable within. The hotel, not so incidentally, is said to be haunted, and several rooms come with resident ghosts attached: an old lady in no. 2, a young boy in no. 3, and the ghost of hotel founder George Leger himself in no. 7 (Leger was shot just outside the room—"Moke Hill" was a wild town back then!). Our children derive endless fascination from the stories the staff tells. If you want (or don't want!) a particular room, call at least three weeks in advance during summer.

The hotel has a nice dining room with full-course dinners for $7 to $10; children's portions are available. Breakfast starts at $2. There's an outdoor swimming pool and garden, but no guarantees you'll see a ghost.

Each of the 13 rooms is different and fitted with Victorian antiques. No TVs. Parlour suites have sitting rooms and fireplaces. Family suites consist of a room without bath connecting to a room with a private bath.

Rates (single or double occupancy) for standard rooms with shared bath are $34; with private bath, $51. Parlor suites rent for $59; family suites (with two rooms and one bath), for $76. All rates rise about $6 on weekend nights. Rollaways and cribs cost $10 extra.

Sonora

In the southern stretches of the Gold Country, a good choice for families is the **Sonora Inn,** 160 S. Washington St., Sonora, CA 95370 (tel. 209/532-7468, or toll free 800/321-5261 in California). Located in the heart of downtown, the Spanish-style Sonora Inn is historic in its own right—it was founded in 1896—and could use a good facelift, but its modern décor and amenities are perfectly adequate, and prices are reasonable. The attached Sonora Inn Restaurant is an excellent family dining spot (see "Where to Eat"). There's an outdoor pool (closed in winter) and some room service available.

There are both standard hotel rooms and motel rooms across the street. Weekdays, singles range from $34.50 to $43.25; doubles, $41 to $49.75; suites, $64.75. Weekend rates are approximately $10 higher per room. Cribs and roll-aways cost $5 per night. Children 11 and under sleep free; over 11, the charge is $5 per night.

For something a little different in the Sonora area, head for the **Llamahall Guest Ranch,** 18170 Wards Ferry Rd., Sonora, CA 95370 (tel. 209/532-7264) —ask for directions when you make reservations, as it's out in the country and difficult to find. Llamahall is one of the few Gold Country bed-and-breakfast inns that welcome children—and what more appropriate place for children than a llama ranch? Your children can play with the llamas (warn them about their tendency to spit, however) while you relax in the sauna or outdoor hot tub. There are creekside trails, outdoor decks, and a library/music room. No TVs in the rooms, and the ranch has a no-smoking policy.

The two rooms with private entrances, baths, and queen-size beds are $85, double occupancy; $10 per additional person.

Camping
There are more than 1,000 campsites in Tuolumne County alone—too many to list individual specifications. For information on camping in the Stanislaus National Forest, contact the **U.S. Forest Service,** c/o Mary Hale, 19777 Greenly Rd., Sonora, CA 95370 (tel. 209/532-3671), or **Ranger District offices** in Summit (tel. 209/962-3434), Mi-Wok (tel. 209/586-3234), Groveland (tel. 209/962-7825), and Calaveras (tel. 209/795-1381). Camping reservations must be made through a Ticketron outlet.

WHERE TO EAT: You shouldn't have a problem finding a place to eat with the children. Here are a few of the best.

Auburn
Our children first spotted **Awful Annie's,** 160 Sacramento St., Old Town Auburn (tel. 916/888-9857), and with a name like that, we had to try it. Fortunately, it proved the opposite—we enjoyed delicious food on Annie's outdoor deck overlooking the sights of Old Town. (There's also a very nice indoor dining room.) A variety of three-egg omelets cost $6 and include potatoes and toast or bagel; sandwiches with lots of healthy-looking ingredients run $4.25. Portions are huge, but special children's and half-size regular sandwiches are offered for $3.25, and the kitchen will split other orders for children.

They will provide you with highchairs and booster seats. Coloring books and crayons are also available to keep little hands busy.

Open daily except Monday for breakfast from 9 a.m. to 2 p.m., and for lunch daily from 11 a.m. to 4 p.m. No reservations accepted. Parking nearby. Major credit cards welcome.

Sutter Creek
The Chatter Box, 39 Main St. (tel. 209/267-5935), is one of those truly old-fashioned small-town neighborhood soda fountains that are fast disappearing in modern America. Come here for basic breakfasts and lunches and to sit at the rickety tables or on a fountain stool to listen to some of the local characters jaw about their days. Décor is strictly antique kitsch.

We took refuge here on a hot afternoon and relished our milkshakes and ice-cream sodas ($1.75). Breakfasts include pancakes and omelets that come with biscuits "while they last" ($1 to $5). Lunches feature burgers, sandwiches, and fries. Nothing on the menu is over $5. No children's menu, but plenty of selections for all ages.

Highchairs, but no booster seats, are available. The kitchen will split portions for kids, and warm baby bottles.

Open Monday through Saturday from 6 a.m. to 5 p.m. and on Sunday from 8 a.m. to 5 p.m. Reservations are accepted. Street parking, or park in a nearby city lot. No credit cards honored.

Sonora

The **Sonora Inn Restaurant,** 160 S. Washington St. (tel. 209/532-7468), is one of the central gathering spots in Sonora. It offers good family dining with very reasonably priced children's menu items. At breakfast, kids can eat for $1.25 (roundhouse pancakes) to $1.75 (scrambled eggs, sausage or bacon, and two small pancakes); at lunch, items range from a 95¢ corn dog to a hamburger for $2.50; and at dinner, children can choose among fettuccine, sirloin steak, and fried shrimp—all from $3 to $3.50.

Regular menus offer extensive American fare at reasonable prices: breakfasts average $3 to $4; lunch—soups, salads, sandwiches, hot entrees, burgers— average $4.25; and full-course dinners of beef, veal, poultry, seafood, fish, and pasta run $9 to $10.

Highchairs and boosters are provided.

Open daily for breakfast from 7 a.m. to noon; for lunch, from 11 a.m. to 2:30 p.m.; and for dinner, from 5 to 9 p.m. Reservations are accepted. Park in the lot or across the street at the bank. Major credit cards welcome.

Jamestown

If you tire of Gold Rush history and want to temporarily trade it in for another kind of nostalgia, head for **Boomer's American Diner,** on Main Street (tel. 209/984-5000). This place does for the 1950s what the rest of the Gold Country does for the 1850s—and to our kids, at least, both seemed equally foreign. Pictures of Marilyn Monroe, basketball hoops, and old Coca-Cola signs serve as décor, and there are real jukeboxes at each Formica table featuring rock-and-roll classics. The restaurant is brand new, however, and immaculate.

Our kids went for the small pizzas ($5 with pepperoni), which they split for a filling, economical meal. There's also a Baby Boomer Burger—a "slider" with grilled onions—for $1.25, and regular burgers and cheeseburgers go for around $3. Also on the menu are onion rings, chicken wings, blue-plate specials of meatloaf and fried chicken, apple pie, and a selection of flavored Cokes (cherry, chocolate, vanilla, and lemon) for $1.25.

The bathrooms are named after Archie and Betty, Frankie and Annette (our kids didn't get it). Boosters and highchairs are available.

Open daily from 11:30 a.m. to 8 p.m. Reservations accepted but not necessary. Parking in the lot. No credit cards honored.

3. LAKE TAHOE

When Mark Twain first set eyes on Lake Tahoe, then a remote destination in the Sierra Nevada, he called it "the fairest picture the whole earth affords." The view remains of a crystal-clear alpine lake that rests like a shimmering blue gemstone in a bowl of snow-capped peaks and deep-green forests. And with the view have arisen the amenities of a year-round outdoor playground that has few rivals. You can even (almost) count on that most unpredictable of all vacation factors— the weather. Despite its heavy winter snowfalls, Tahoe boasts an average of over 300 days of sunshine every year.

Take advantage of that weather to enjoy superb snow sports in winter and water sports in summer, plus hiking, camping, horseback riding, bicycling, cruising on the lake . . . activities aplenty to please every member of a family every season of the year. Even if your family isn't big on the outdoors, you can always head for the indoor action at the casino-hotels on the Nevada side of the lake: for adults, heavy elbow exercise at the slot machines; for kids, arcade games and other activities.

Gambling aside, Tahoe is very much a family-oriented destination. (Unlike Las Vegas or Reno, it offers the option of avoiding the gambling scene altogether —simply stay on the California side of the lake.) You can find ski lessons for your kids, accommodations and meals in all price ranges, and a wide variety of activities guaranteed to enthrall youngsters from toddler to teen. Our own children never tire of Tahoe—whether it's their annual winter romps in the snow or summertime scrambles over rocky trails that lead to pristine sandy beaches and refreshing splashes in cool waters.

Most visitors flock either to the towns of South Lake Tahoe, California, and neighboring Stateline, Nevada—the lake's largest population center—or to the somewhat quieter, more rustic north shore, ranging from Tahoe City to Incline Village, Nevada. Ski resorts, casinos, and other recreational facilities, plus restaurants and lodgings, abound in and about both areas. (The Tahoe region records up to 100,000 visitors per day on peak weekends.) To really get away from it all, you might consider making your base the west shore, where woodsy campgrounds and cabins nestle against the lake, or along Nevada's eastern shore, which is even less developed.

GETTING THERE: Your route by car will depend partially on whether you are heading for North or South Lake Tahoe, but most roads pass first through Sacramento. From San Francisco, take I-80 to Sacramento, then U.S. 50 to the south shore, or continue on I-80 for the north shore (cut down to the lake via Calif. 89 for Tahoe City or Calif. 267 for King's Beach).

From Los Angeles or other points south, take I-5 to Sacramento, then follow similar directions. Or for a more scenic route, cut off from I-5 at Stockton and take Calif. 88 to South Lake Tahoe, which winds through parts of the Gold Country and the Sierra foothills before heading into the high mountains. You can also reach Tahoe via U.S. 395, which cuts east of Kings Canyon and Yosemite; at Gardnerville, Nevada, turn west on Nev. 207 for the south lake.

A note of warning: Winter driving conditions can be hazardous, and some of these roadways may be closed temporarily during snow and sleet. Always carry chains in winter and call the **California Highway Patrol** (tel. 916/587-3518 in North Tahoe; 916/577-1001 in South Tahoe) or the California Highway Information Network (tel. 916/577-3550 for South Lake Tahoe) for the latest highway conditions and road closures.

Numerous airlines, buses, and trains serve the Tahoe area. **Reno Cannon International Airport,** 50 minutes from North Tahoe, provides regularly scheduled service by 11 commercial airlines. Rental cars or bus service from **LTR Stagelines** (tel. 702/358-9676) are available from the airport. A few airlines also serve **Lake Tahoe Airport,** located two miles from South Lake Tahoe, where rental-car, bus, and limousine service is available. **Greyhound** buses ply the route several times daily from San Francisco and Sacramento. And **Amtrak** serves Tahoe via the Truckee rail station, about 15 miles north of Tahoe City (tel. toll free 800/USA-RAIL, 800/872-7245 in California).

ORIENTATION: Lake Tahoe—situated at 6,200 feet above sea level in the eastern Sierra Nevada—straddles the California-Nevada border about 100 miles northeast of Sacramento, 55 miles southwest of Reno, Nevada, and about 100 miles northwest of Yosemite. At 22 miles long and 12 miles wide, it's the largest alpine lake in the United States and second largest in the world. The water is deep

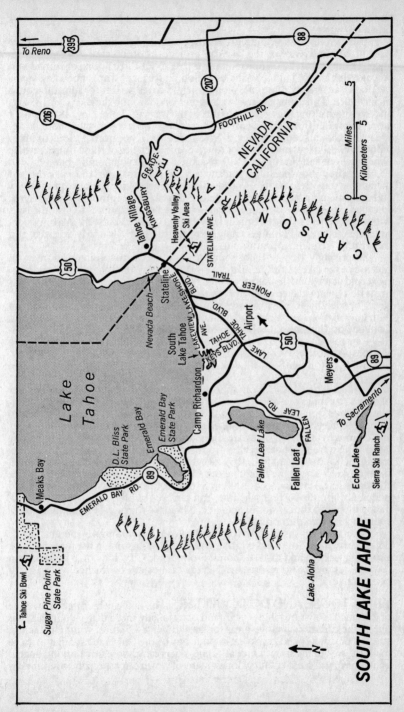

SOUTH LAKE TAHOE

and pure, plunging as far as 1,600 feet down, and said to be cleaner than most urban tap water.

Weather, time, and children's patience permitting, a drive around the entire 72-mile circumference of the lake can provide an unforgettable scenic experience. The drive can be completed nonstop in about three hours, or turned into an enjoyable all-day family outing by including frequent stops at beaches, scenic overlooks, and rocky shorelines along emerald coves perfect for spreading out a picnic lunch. Three separate roadways form a circle around the lake: Calif. 89 zigs and zags high along the mountain rims of the western shore; Nev. 28 runs right along the water from Tahoe City halfway down the lake's eastern shore in Nevada; and U.S. 50 connects Nev. 28 to South Lake Tahoe until it meets up again with Calif. 89 a few miles west of town. Some stretches of these routes involve winding, even hairpin curves, so if carsickness runs in your family, beware.

Keep in mind when planning any trip to Tahoe that the seasons of the year dictate the activities. Winter is devoted primarily to skiing; because of the snow and cold, many attractions are closed during nonsummer months. However, the so-called off-seasons—spring and fall—can be beautiful times to visit the lake, without the crush of wintertime skiers or summertime sightseers. Accommodations are easy to find (and generally cheaper), hiking trails nearly deserted, and the weather frequently magnificent.

Surprisingly, despite Tahoe's high altitude, even many winter days are warm because of the lake's sunny climate. Nights, however, tend to be chilly or downright cold year round, so come prepared to dress for variable temperatures. Layering is best for any day trip, whether to the ski slopes or out on a hiking trail.

The friendly people at the two visitor's bureaus will be happy to provide you with information. For North Lake Tahoe, contact the **Tahoe North Visitors and Convention Bureau**, P.O. Box 5578, Tahoe City, CA 95730 (tel. 916/583-3494, or toll free 800/824-6348). For South Lake Tahoe, it's the **Lake Tahoe Visitors Authority**, P.O. Box 16299, South Lake Tahoe, CA 95706 (tel. 916/544-5050, or toll free 800/822-5922).

GETTING AROUND: From the town of South Lake Tahoe it can be a matter of only a few miles or even a few steps to reach ski resorts, lake cruises, and gambling casinos. You can get around quite well without a car if necessary, thanks to complimentary **shuttle-bus services** operated by several of the big ski resorts and casinos to and from many area lodgings (they know they'll get your money later). There are also boat services from South Lake Tahoe to north lake ski resorts. The **Tahoe Queen** (tel. 916/541-3364), an old-fashioned paddlewheeler, shuttles skiers across the lake in about 2½ hours one way and connects to free shuttle buses on either end; adults pay $16.50 round trip, $8 for children 11 and under. Call for the current schedule. You can even stroll from many South Lake Tahoe motels to the casinos in Stateline, Nevada—the high-rise casinos start literally inches from the border.

Several north-shore ski resorts and casinos are within 45 minutes' to an hour's drive from South Lake Tahoe, and vice versa, assuming the roads are clear along the western and eastern shores. From Tahoe City, the north shore's main town, a number of ski resorts and Nevada casinos can be reached within a half hour's drive or less.

WHAT TO SEE AND DO IN WINTER: Lake Tahoe, which gets an average of 225 inches of snowfall per year (and occasionally more than 700 inches!), is one of the country's premier areas for family skiing. On most winter weekends, streams of cars topped by ski racks pour out of the San Francisco Bay Area to make the trek to the snow. Once at Tahoe, skiers can choose from among dozens of downhill and cross-country slopes, many of which cater specially to families by offering ski schools, babysitting services, and special children's rates for ski lifts and equipment rentals. Don't forget snowmobiling and sleigh rides too. There's plenty of that in Tahoe.

Skiing

Tahoe's ski season runs roughly from mid-November until April or even May, but some resorts may stay open weeks or even months longer than others, depending on snow conditions. For up-to-date information on **snow conditions** at different ski areas, call individual resorts or 415/976-SKIS. Both South Lake Tahoe and North Lake Tahoe also have extremely helpful visitors' bureaus that should be able to advise on resort openings/closings. For South Lake Tahoe, call 916/544-5050; for North Lake Tahoe, 916/583-3494, or toll free, 800/824-8557, 800/822-5959 in California. Many resorts offer lift tickets interchangeable between ski areas for one price. Ask when you purchase your tickets.

A word of caution: Because of Tahoe's frequent winter sunshine, remember to apply sunscreen thoroughly before setting out on the slopes. The high-altitude sun's glare off the snow can be several times more powerful than the rays you get on a summer's day at the beach, and few things short of a broken bone can ruin a ski vacation more quickly than a bad burn.

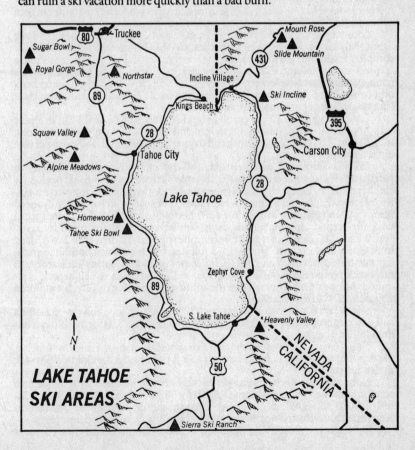

Here are some of the best family-oriented ski resorts:

Sprawling 20 square miles over parts of both California and Nevada, **Heavenly Valley,** P.O. Box AT, South Lake Tahoe, CA 95705 (tel. 916/541-SKII for ski and snow information), is the largest downhill ski resort in the United States, featuring 26 ski lifts and the highest-elevation skiing at Tahoe (10,000 feet).

If your children need lessons, Heavenly's excellent Lil' Angels program at the California Base Lodge (or at Boulder Base on the Nevada side) offers full- or half-day ski schools for children ages 4 to 12, from beginner to experienced. Lessons, lift tickets, lunch, games, and hot chocolate breaks (but not equipment) are included. Reservations are advised (tel. 916/541-1330). The rates: all day, $48; half day, $27.

For nonskiing (but toilet-trained) children between 2 and 4 years old, Heavenly offers all-day and half-day child-care programs at California and Boulder Base, from 1 to 4 p.m. ($20), and from 9 a.m. to 4 p.m. ($35).

Lift tickets cost $35 for adults for a full day, $22 for a half day; children 12 and under are charged $14 for a full and half day. Full equipment packages for adults (skis, boots, poles) cost $15; children pay $9 per day.

Heavenly Valley's California Base is located within minutes of most South Lake Tahoe hotels and motels. (Follow the signs up the hill heading south along Ski Run Boulevard.) The resort also offers ski packages in conjunction with numerous lodgings in the area (ranging from deluxe to moderate) at a wide range of prices. Call 702/588-4584 for reservations and information.

Located off Calif. 267 between Truckee and Kings Beach in North Lake Tahoe, **Northstar,** P.O. Box 129, Truckee, CA 95734 (tel. 916/562-1010), is a complete resort offering a broad range of services for families. Northstar's Village at the foot of Mount Pluto includes lodgings, restaurants (with children's menus), and a recreation center. You will also find a cross-country ski center here; trail passes cost $9 for adults, $4 for children 5 to 12. Lessons (kids must be at least 6) and rental equipment are available.

Children ages 5 to 12 can enroll in StarKids (tel. 916/587-0270), an alpine ski school that includes lessons, lift tickets, and lunch. Open daily from 9:30 a.m. to 3:30 p.m. The charge is $42 for a full day; equipment rental is $7 extra per day. No reservations accepted.

Minor's Camp, a state-licensed, full-day child-care service located in Northstar's Village (tel. 916/587-0278), offers a SkiCubs learn-to-ski option for children 3 to 6. Along with other games and activities, a child can receive a 1½-hour lesson that includes equipment, lunch, and snacks, all for $38. Advanced Minor's Camp children can opt for a 2½-hour lesson for $48. There are special rates for second children in the same family, as well as for multiday stays. Nonskiing child care is also available for toilet-trained children ages 2 to 6, daily from 8 a.m. to 4:30 p.m. The fee for a full day, lunch included, is $30; the half-day rate (if room is available) is $20, lunch not included. During ski season you must make your reservations *at least* two weeks in advance. A $30 deposit is required. Minor's Camp operates in the summer, beginning in July, for children ages 2 to 12. Call for details.

Lift tickets for downhill skiing cost $29 for adults for a full day, $21 for a half day; children 5 to 12 are charged $14 for a full day, $10 for a half day; children under 5 ski free.

Nonskiers can sightsee via the transport gondola or meet friends for lunch at the mid-mountain day lodge. The fare is $5 for adults, $3 for children 5 to 12; under 5, free.

Northstar also offers special ski packages in conjunction with Tahoe area condominiums. For reservations, call 916/587-0200, or toll free 800/824-8516, 800/822-5987 in California. Free ski-shuttle services are available to Northstar from selected north- and south-shore hotels, weather permitting.

Other good children's ski programs include: **Boreal** (Boreal/Soda Springs

Ski Areas), P.O. Box 39, Truckee, CA 95734 (tel. 916/426-3666, or 916/426-FONE for the 24-hour snow line), with a spectacular location just off I-80 at Donner Summit (Castle Peak exit), 30 minutes from Tahoe City. It offers a children's center and ski school called Animal Crackers that features both indoor and outdoor skiing and nonskiing full- and half-day activities.

The ski school, for ages 4 to 12, charges $40 for a full day, $30 for a half day. The nonskiing children's center (ages 2 to 12) costs $32 for all day and $20 for a half day. Lessons, equipment, and lift tickets are included in the ski school, snow games in the children's center, and lunch and snacks in both. Call for registration information. No reservations are accepted—arrive early on weekends to sign up.

Lift tickets cost $22 for adults for a full day, $16 for a half day; children 5 to 12 are charged $12 for a full day, $10 for a half day.

Squaw Valley USA, P.O. Box 2007, Olympic Valley, CA 95730 (tel. 916/583-6985), the past site of the Winter Olympics, boasts a spectacular setting only a few miles north of Tahoe City off Calif. 89. The area bills itself as one of America's least expensive family ski centers. Squaw Valley offers the Ten Little Indians snow school for ages 3 to 5, which includes lessons, equipment, lunch, snack, and all-day care for $40 ($30 for each additional sibling); the half-day rate is $28. There is day care for infants at the same rates. The Junior Ski School (ages 6 to 12) features a four-hour lesson for $27 and a two-hour lesson for $18; all day, including lunch, is $40.

Lift tickets cost $32 for adults for a full day, $22 for a half day. Children under 13 can ski for just $5, and first-time beginners ski for free on weekdays (except holidays), including lift, lesson, and rental.

The Squaw Valley Nordic Center (tel. 916/583-8951) is a complete Nordic ski area and also offers lessons.

Alpine Meadows, P.O. Box 5279, Tahoe City, CA 95730 (tel. 916/583-4232, or 916/583-6914 for the snow phone), located off Calif. 89 a few miles north of Tahoe City in North Tahoe, offers a ski school for 3- to 6-year-olds with varying levels of experience. All day costs $45 ($35 for a second child); a half day is $35.

Lift tickets cost $32 for adults for a full day, $22 for a half day; children 6 to 12 are charged $12 for a full day, $8 for a half day. Group and private lessons are also available daily for all ability levels, ages 6 and up.

Tahoe/Donner, P.O. Box 11049, Truckee, CA 95737 (tel. 916/587-9444), across from Boreal on the north side of I-80 near Donner Summit, calls itself the "complete family winter resort." The Snowflakes Ski School, for children 3 to 6, offers indoor and outdoor instruction and activities. Equipment, lunch, snack, and lift tickets are included in the $42 price for a full day (available weekends and holiday periods only), $24 for a half day. Regular ski lessons are available for children 7 and older, at adult prices.

Lift tickets cost $16 for adults for a full day, $12 for a half day; children 7 to 12 are charged $10 for a full day, $8 for a half day. Children 6 and under ski free when accompanied by an adult. Equipment rentals are discounted for children 12 and under.

Tahoe/Donner also features a cross-country kids' ski school on weekends from 10 a.m. to noon and noon to 2 p.m. (on Sunday, afternoon session only). Rates are $15 for children 3 to 6, $20 for ages 7 to 12, and include lesson, rental, trail pass, and snack. Bring your own equipment and get a $2 discount. For the trail pass only, adults pay $10, $8 for kids 13 to 17, $6 for children 7 to 12; children under 6 ski free.

Speaking of cross-country skiing, don't overlook this rigorous but delightful sport if you haven't tried it. (And once you do, you may never want to return to the expense and bother of downhill lift tickets again.) Cross-country is especially suited to children ages 7 and older because it requires a certain amount of strength and stamina, but much younger children can enjoy a short run.

One of our favorite cross-country spots is **Tahoe Nordic** (tel. 916/583-9858), situated in gorgeous country about 2½ miles east of Tahoe City, just off Calif. 28 six miles west of Kings Beach (turn off on Fabian Way and follow the ski signs to Country Club Road). Tahoe Nordic features 36 miles of scenic machine-groomed trails, some of which are ideal for beginners. A Kiddie Ski School operates on weekends and holidays. Children 3 to 5 are charged $12; those 5 to 10, $16. Lessons are 1½ hours, at 10:30 a.m. and 1 p.m. Trail fees are $9 for adults for a full day, $7 for a half day; children 7 to 11 pay $5.50, and kids 6 and under are free.

SKI RENTALS. You can rent skis at any of the resorts mentioned above, or at numerous other locations around the lake. Try **Rainbow Mountain,** 1133 Ski Run Blvd. in South Lake Tahoe, on the way to Heavenly Valley (tel. 916/541-7686), which rents downhill and cross-country equipment (including clothing) for adults and children. Open daily during ski season from 7:30 a.m. to 9 p.m. **The Ski Renter** has two locations: at 1093 Ski Run Blvd., South Lake Tahoe (tel. 916/544-2100), open daily from 7:30 a.m. to 7:30 p.m.; and at 185 River Rd. in Tahoe City, toward Alpine Meadows and Squaw Valley (tel. 916/583-2548), open daily from 8 a.m. to 6 p.m. **Dave's Ski Shop,** 620 N. Lake Blvd., Tahoe City (tel. 916/583-6415), is open till May: Sunday through Thursday from 7:45 a.m. to 8 p.m. and on Friday and Saturday till midnight.

Other Winter Activities

Even if you aren't a skier, it's well worth a trip accompanying the skiers on the enclosed **Aerial Tramway** (tel. 916/541-1330) at Heavenly Valley's California Base (follow the signs up Ski Run Boulevard in South Lake Tahoe). The tram ascends 1,700 feet up the side of a mountain to a perch 8,200 feet above sea level, where one of the finest panoramic views of the entire lake awaits. It runs every few minutes weekdays from 9 a.m. to 4 p.m., on weekends and holidays from 8:30 a.m. The tramway is closed during the spring and fall off-seasons, but reopens on Memorial Day and runs through the summer daily until 10 p.m. each night. Adults pay $9; children 12 and under, $5.

If you arrive at mealtime, try the **Top of the Tram** restaurant (tel. 916/544-1330), where reasonably priced food comes with a picture-window-perfect view. Our daughter ordered an "appetizer" of nachos (tortilla chips, refried beans, melted cheese, and salsa) that three of us couldn't finish. The lunch menu also includes burgers, sandwiches, and large salads, all in the $5 to $6 range. Lunch is served daily from 11 a.m. to 2:30 p.m. Dinner is also served in summer.

Sleigh Rides

If you'd like to try an old-fashioned horse-drawn sleigh ride along the shores of Lake Tahoe or through mountain meadows, call the **Camp Richardson Corral** on Emerald Bay Road (Calif. 89), a few miles west of South Lake Tahoe (tel. 916/541-3113). A 45-minute ride costs $10 per person for ages 4 and up, and they are offered Friday through Monday and holidays. Call for reservations.

Also on the south shore, try **Borge Sleigh Rides,** next to Caesars Tahoe in Stateline, Nevada (tel. 916/541-2953). A 45-minute ride costs $7 for adults, $4 for children under 12.

On the north shore, you can enjoy sleigh rides at **Northstar-at-Tahoe** (tel. 916/562-1010). The half-hour rides cost $6 for adults and children, and begin at the golf course clubhouse.

Snowmobiling

Snowmobiling tours are available along Tahoe's high-mountain ridges. **Snowmobiling Unlimited,** on Calif. 267 (call for directions; tel. 916/583-

5858), offers small, personalized guided wilderness tours at two locations on the north shore. Prices range from $40 and $60 (for one or two people) for a one-hour ride, $60 and $80 for a 1½-hour ride. Drivers must be a minimum of 16 years old with prior experience. Children under 5 are free. Reservations are required. Hours are 8 a.m. to 5 p.m. daily.

Four miles across the Nevada state border on the south shore, you can try **Zephyr Cove Snowmobile Center,** in Zephyr Cove (call for directions; tel. 702/588-3833), where rates for two-hour tours are $60 for a single rider, $85 for two, adult or child. Drivers must be at least 15 years of age, and tours are not recommended for children 7 and under. Reservations are advised. Tours leave three times daily.

Additional Child Care

The **Magic Pine Tree** day-care centers, with four locations in South Lake Tahoe (tel. 916/577-4848, 916/541-4848, 916/588-7225, or 916/544-8444), offer licensed and insured drop-in child care year round. They'll take children from infancy to 12, and charge $3 per hour. Open weekdays from 7:30 a.m. to 6:30 p.m. Reservations required. Call for details.

WHAT TO DO AND SEE IN SPRING, SUMMER, AND FALL: These
are some of the nicest seasons to visit Tahoe. Fall is possibly the least crowded. Spring might still offer spring skiing, depending on conditions. Summer continues Tahoe's attraction as a great family resort.

Boat Trips

You can cruise the lake on a sightseeing boat at any time of year, but—except for ski-shuttle excursions—the trip is best suited to warm-weather months. You will certainly want to spend some time on the open deck gazing at the spectacular mountain scenery.

The *Tahoe Queen* is an authentic Mississippi paddlewheeler based at Ski Run Marina in South Lake Tahoe (tel. 916/541-3364 for reservations and information). It cruises year round on the lake but operates with a more limited schedule in nonsummer months. We had a delightful family outing on a sunny spring luncheon cruise, which carried us from South Lake Tahoe to beautiful Emerald Bay (where the boat circles the lake's only island) and back in about 2½ hours. The indoor decks feature tables with bar and food service, while the spacious open upper deck provides the best views. There's also a glass-bottom section of the hull (on the lower deck), but as our son pointed out, you can't see much but water.

Fares are cheaper from October to May: the lunch cruise costs $12.50 for adults, $4.50 for children 11 and under. Prices rise an extra dollar or two during summer. Lunch selections average around $3 to $4 and include cheeseburgers, nachos, and hot dogs. Evening cruises (without dinner) cost $16.50 for adults, $7.50 for children. Beverage service includes hot chocolate or Shirley Temples for the kids. We definitely recommend the daytime cruises for children; dinner cruises are more formal affairs and cost $34 for adults, $25 for children.

June to September, cruises leave daily at 11 a.m., 1:30 p.m., and 3:55 p.m., and the evening cruise leaves at 6:30 p.m. October through May there's one lunch and one dinner cruise daily.

Another historic paddlewheeler, the **M.S. *Dixie,*** cruises the lake from its base at Zephyr Cove, Nevada, four miles past Stateline (tel. 702/588-3508). It also offers daytime and evening cruises, with meal service. Adults pay $11 for the Emerald Bay cruise; children 11 and under are charged only $4. Children are not recommended on the M.S. *Dixie's* Sunset Dinner Dance cruise, a different cruise, but they are welcome on the Sunset Cocktail/Dinner cruise. These cruises are offered April through October. A more popular family outing is the

Historic Glenbrook Breakfast cruise, offered June to October; the charge is $14 for adults and $7 for kids 11 and under for this 1¾-hour ride accompanied by a historian, and a buffet breakfast is served. Reservations are suggested for all cruises.

Along the north and west shores, **North Tahoe Cruises** (tel. 916/583-0141), which departs from the Roundhouse in Tahoe City, features sightseeing trips aboard another glass-bottom vessel, the *Sunrunner.* There are daily departures from mid-May through late-October, including breakfast, cocktail, and dinner cruises. Depending on the day and season, one to three cruises depart each day. Daytime cruises cost $9 for adults, $4.50 for children. Breakfast cruises run $11 for adults, $7 for children.

The *Woodwind,* which also sails from Zephyr Cove Pier, four miles north of Stateline, Nevada (tel. 702/588-3000), is a 30-passenger sailboat. It offers four daily cruises between 11:30 a.m. and 4 p.m., May through October. Adults pay $11; children under 12, $5.

Hiking

For information by mail on any of the following state parks, write: **Sierra State Parks,** P.O. Drawer D, Tahoma, CA 95733.

Located on the southwest corner of the lake, **Emerald Bay State Park,** about a 20-minute drive west of South Lake Tahoe along Calif. 89 (tel. 916/541-3030), offers fantastic views, emerald waters, forest trails, rocky ridges, and even a castle. It is perhaps the most beautiful spot in all of Tahoe. Park at the scenic overlook and hike along the rocks toward Eagle Falls for a fabulous panorama; or follow the main trail straight down to the lakeshore, with its small beach, woodsy trails, and authentic Scandinavian Vikingsholm Castle, a 38-room structure built as a private residence in 1929. Guided tours of the castle are available daily June to September from 10 a.m. to 4 p.m.; the cost, 50¢. Families with small children, be prepared—the hike to the lake is jokingly said to be one mile down and five miles back up! But if you're carrying a toddler, it's no joke. Once you get to the lake, you'll find a number of trails to follow.

The **Pope-Baldwin Recreation Area,** managed by the U.S. Forest Service, is off Calif. 89 along the south shore (tel. 916/544-6420). It's ideal for beginning hikers. You'll find a visitor center (open June to September only, daily from 8 a.m. to 6 p.m.), self-guiding nature trails, and the **Tallac Historical Site,** including three stunning 19th-century estate homes, Washoe Indian exhibits, and a museum that is open daily from 11 a.m. to 3 p.m. in summer.

Sugar Pine Point State Park, situated on either side of Calif. 89 on the west shore between Emerald Bay and Tahoe City (tel. 916/525-7982), has scenic hiking trails along both the lake and General Creek. The three-story gabled and turreted Ehrmann Mansion (formerly a private residence and used as a location in *Godfather II*) is only about 100 yards from the parking lot. Or you can hike through cool forests of ponderosa pine and Douglas fir. Hourly tours of the mansion are given daily, mid-June through Labor Day, from 11 a.m. to 4 p.m. Day-use fee, $3.

There are 100 family campsites in Sugar Pine, available by reservation. Call MISTIX (tel. toll free 800/444-7275).

D. L. Bliss State Park is located just north of Emerald Bay (tel. 916/525-7277). You can hike to Emerald Bay from here via the scenic three-mile Rubicon Trail along the lake. It's a pretty level trail, but best suited for children 6 and over. Day-use fee, $3.

Beaches and Picnic Areas

You can swim and picnic in beautiful surroundings at Emerald Bay, Sugar Pine Point, and D. L. Bliss State Parks in California, described above. But the nicest beach at Tahoe, and one of the finest anywhere, is **Sand Harbor** in Nevada's Lake Tahoe State Park on the northeast shore, about 15 minutes past Crystal Bay (tel. 702/831-0494). This place is worth a special trip. It's a fine sandy beach along a horseshoe cove. It has rocky outcroppings that kids love to climb, trails, rest rooms, picnic tables, and a parking lot. The mountain views are splendid. Kids and polar bears may want to swim anytime, but most sane people wait till August. Day-use fee, $2.

Kings Beach Recreation Area, located along the north shore near the Nevada border (tel. 916/546-7248), features a wide sandy beach, rest rooms, waterskiing, boating, and a parking lot. It's not as pretty or isolated as Sand Harbor, but it is a nice facility. Day-use fee, $3.

Pope Beach, Kiva Beach, and **Baldwin Beach** (tel. 916/544-6420 for all day-use fees) are relatively secluded public beaches operated by the U.S. Forest Service off Calif. 89 along the south shore. They offer swimming, parking, rest rooms, and picnic tables.

River Rafting

The children will love rafting during the summer on the peaceful Truckee River, Lake Tahoe's only outlet. You'll float past meadows and forests; don't expect white-water rapids—the pace is ideal for younger children, ages 4 and up.

Two-hour four-mile trips leave from the "Y" intersection in Tahoe City where Calif. 89 and Calif. 29 meet. Try **Truckee River Rafting Center,** 205 River Rd. (right across from the Chevron station), Tahoe City (tel. 916/583-7238), or **Fanny Bridge Raft Rentals** at Fanny Bridge in Tahoe City (tel. 916/583-3021). (If you're wondering how Fanny Bridge got its name, by the way, you won't once you see all the people bending over to have a look at the big trout that swim under the bridge through the river below—a real Tahoe City landmark.)

Each rents equipment at a daily fee of $15 for adults, $10 for children 12 and under. (Truckee offers a $2-per-person discount if you get there before 11 a.m.)

Boat Rentals

For charter boats, sailboats, sailboards, paddleboats, powerboats, kayaks, and the like, call **Tahoe Boat Rentals** (tel. 916/685-3492), **Tahoe Water Adventures** (tel. 916/583-3225), or **High Sierra Boat Rentals** (tel. 916/525-5589); or head for the nearest marina.

Bicycling

Miles of bicycling trails comb the Tahoe area. In the north-lake area, fairly level trails stretch from Tahoe City south along the lake to Sugar Pine Point, and along the Truckee River to the River Ranch Lodge. Along the south shore, you can bike for several miles on a trail alongside Calif. 89 to Baldwin Beach.

For bike rentals, try the **Olympic Bike Shop,** 620 N. Lake Blvd., Tahoe City (tel. 916/583-6415); or **Tahoe Cyclery,** 3552 Lake Tahoe Blvd., South Lake Tahoe (tel. 916/541-2726), for adult-size bicycles only.

Horseback Riding

For horseback riding along meadows and forest trails, try **Sunset Ranch,** a quarter mile west of the South Lake Tahoe Airport on U.S. 50 (tel. 916/541-9001). Open year round, the ranch offers hourly and half-day rates. Beginners and children are welcome (no age minimum). Open daily from 8 a.m. to 6 p.m. No reservations necessary. Adults pay $15 for the first hour, $10 for each additional hour; children 12 and under pay $12 for the first hour, $10 for each additional hour.

Camp Richardson Corral, along Calif. 89 (Emerald Bay Road) on the south shore (call for directions; tel. 916/541-3113), runs guided tours and extended pack trips. Minimum age is 6. The rate is $14 per hour, adults and children. Open daily, June 1 through September 15, from 8 a.m. to 4 p.m. Make reservations one day in advance.

. . . and More

Miniature golf courses include the two **Magic Carpet Golf Courses** at 5167 N. Lake Blvd., Carnelian Bay (tel. 916/546-4279), and at 2455 U.S. 50 in South Lake Tahoe (tel. 916/541-3787). The hours depend on the weather—call for information.

Even if your children have never caught the TV show "Bonanza" in reruns, they may well enjoy the **Ponderosa Ranch** western-themed park, located on Calif. 28 south of Incline Village, Nevada (tel. 702/831-0691), where the long-running series was filmed. Stroll the town where Ben, Hoss, and the gang hung out, with Old West wagons and carriages on display, plus games, horseback rides and hayrides, a petting farm, food, and drink. It's open daily, May through October, from 9:30 a.m. to 5 p.m. Admission is $5 for adults, $4.50 for children 5 to 11; under 5, free.

Kids love the Breakfast Hayride, which is offered daily from Memorial Day weekend to Labor Day weekend. Arrive between 8 a.m. and 9:30 a.m. and partake of an all-you-can-eat breakfast on the upper range. Adults pay $8.50; children 5 to 11, $7.50; kids under 5, $3. The price includes admission, and you can stay all day.

Another way to see Tahoe is from the air. For hot-air ballooning over the lake (we don't recommend this for children under 5), call **High Sierra Balloon Adventures** (tel. 916/583-0573) or **Mountain High Balloons** (tel. 916/583-6292). Scenic flights are a special treat: call **Sierra Tahoe Aviation,** Truckee-Tahoe Airport (tel. 916/587-4433), or **Cal-Vada Aircraft Seaplane Rides,** in Homewood (tel. 916/525-7143).

Donner Memorial State Park, on I-80 in Truckee (tel. 916/587-3841), gives older children a piece of history. It features a museum memorializing the tragic history of the Donner pioneers, many of whom died in the harsh winter of 1846–1847. Admission is $1 for adults, 50¢ for children 6 to 17; under 6, free. Open daily from 10 a.m. to noon and 1 to 4 p.m.; closed Christmas and New Year's Days.

WHERE TO STAY: While you can have your pick of accommodations at Tahoe

much of the year, never arrive in July or August or during winter holiday periods without a reservation. A good way to make your reservation or obtain information is through either the South or North Lake Tahoe visitor's bureaus, both of which have toll-free numbers and provide helpful assistance. For reservations in South Lake Tahoe, contact the **Lake Tahoe Visitors Authority,** P.O. Box 16299, South Lake Tahoe, CA 95706 (tel. 916/544-5050, or toll free 800/822-5922). Or contact the **Tahoe North Visitors and Convention Bureau,** P.O. Box 5578, Tahoe City, CA 95730 (tel. toll free 800/824-8557, 800/822-5959 in California).

Note: Many Tahoe lodgings do not allow you to check in until 3 p.m., so plan accordingly.

South Lake Tahoe

Lakeland Village Beach and Ski Resort, 3535 U.S. 50 (P.O. Box 705002), South Lake Tahoe, CA 95705 (tel. 916/541-7711, or toll free 800/822-5969), is a superb first-class facility right on the lake with 218 modern condominium and town-house units. Stretching over 19 wooded acres, you'll find a thousand feet of private sandy beach, saunas and a hot tub, three pools (including a wading pool for young children), a playground slide on the beach, a game room (in summer), two tennis courts, and canoe and paddleboat rentals. There is daily maid service and complimentary ski and casino shuttles. There is no restaurant or room service, though numerous restaurants are nearby, as well as a 24-hour Safeway grocery store. In the winter, you can rent ski equipment here; in the summer, canoes and paddleboats are for rent.

All units come with fully equipped kitchens, fireplaces, private decks, and cable TVs. One-bedroom condo suites with lofts and 1½ baths can sleep up to five people and cost from $90 to $130 a night, depending on season (spring and fall are cheapest). Roomy two-story town houses with lofts can sleep four to ten people and run from $95 in low season for a one-bedroom/one-bath to $355 in high season for prime four-bedroom/three-bath units on the lakefront. There's no charge for cribs. Special ski packages are available in conjunction with various ski resorts. Call for information.

Of the first-class high-rise casino-hotels in Stateline, Nevada, the best all-around is **Harrah's,** which is perched right on the state line on U.S. 50 (tel. 702/588-6611, or toll free 800/648-3773)—for reservations, write P.O. Box 8, Reno, NV 89449. Harrah's is the only casino in the country with a Mobil five-star, AAA five-diamond rating, and has features that kids could go crazy over: a big indoor pool (with a roped-off shallow section), a video arcade, and an ice-cream parlor. Harrah's children's arcade offers supervision of children aged 6 to 14 for up to five hours for just $2.50, from 9 a.m. to 11:30 p.m. daily. Games, movies, and cartoons are available within a special enclosed facility. The hotel will arrange other babysitting at cost.

For adults, well, pick your game or show of choice. Parents must decide for themselves, however, whether they want to expose their children to a casino atmosphere—it's hard to find the registration desk here for the slot machines and craps tables. *(Note:* It's illegal for children to "loiter"—much less gamble—in the casino areas, though they can, of course, walk through.)

There are *two* full bathrooms in each and every room, and every bathroom is equipped with a telephone and TV! There are no kitchenettes, but all but one of the hotel's several restaurants feature children's menus, and there is 24-hour room service. Parents will be happy to know that the rooms are soundproof. Check with the front desk for babysitters.

Casino-hotels tend to be good values—depending on your self-discipline walking to and from your room. Rates (single or double occupancy): rooms with two double beds range from $95 in the fall low season to $135 in the summer high season; suites run $450 to $850 in the high season. Children under 15 stay free in their parents' room; additional guests pay $20 per night. One rollaway and/or crib to a room at no charge.

Along tightly packed "Motel Row" on U.S. 50 (also called Lake Tahoe Boulevard) in South Lake Tahoe, one of the more distinctive establishments is the **Tahoe Chalet Inn,** 3860 U.S. 50, (P.O. Box 183), South Lake Tahoe, CA 95705 (tel. 916/544-3311 collect, or toll free 800/822-5922, ext. 274, 800/821-2656 in California). An attractive sitting room with fireplace near the reception desk adds a European ambience, and complimentary continental breakfast is served there daily (there is no restaurant, though many are nearby).

There is a heated pool in summer, plus a sauna, a video game room, and an exercise room. Coffee is available around the clock in the lobby. Casinos are just a quarter of a mile away by shuttle bus. All rooms have been recently renovated, and are immaculate and attractively furnished with a European accent.

Rates are reasonable. One-bedded rooms (with a double, queen-, or king-size bed) run $28 to $64, depending on the season; rooms with two double beds, from $42 to $68, depending on the season. Rates rise $6 for some weekend nights. There are also several suites and chalets that sleep up to six for between

$68 and $104 per night. Kitchens can be had for an additional $12 per night. Rates quoted are per room—there's no charge for extra people. There are no roll-aways or cribs, but there is one playpen available.

For a more rustic experience, try **Hansen's Resort,** 1360 Ski Run Blvd. (P.O. Box 316), South Lake Tahoe, CA 95705 (tel. 916/544-3361), nicely situated on two acres of pines on the road to the Heavenly Valley ski resort. Though you'll be just a couple of blocks off U.S. 50, you'll feel miles off the beaten track.

During winter (November to March), Hansen's offers an additional feature that many kids will love: Whiskey's Run Saucer Hill, a thrilling snow ride down banked turns that may inspire some budding Olympians. The charge is $9 per person, adult or child; those aged 18 and under must be accompanied by an adult. Equipment is furnished.

Child care can be arranged through the office, and daily maid service costs extra. There's no restaurant here, but there are plenty along U.S. 50.

Hansen's has both rooms and cabins, but the six cabins are sized better for families. The units are clean and very spacious, but don't expect super-modernity. The cabins include fully equipped kitchen units and cost from $50 in the off-season for a one-bedroom cabin that sleeps four to up to $150 during holiday seasons for a cabin that sleeps eight. Four cabins have fireplaces. No charge for cribs and rollaways. Kids under 15 sleep free; those 15 and over and extra adults pay $5 per night.

Another woodsy spot on the south shore, somewhat cheaper, is the **Lazy S Lodge,** located along Calif. 89 (Emerald Bay Road) about three-quarters of a mile north of the U.S. 50 intersection and a few miles west of downtown South Lake Tahoe (P.O. Box 7676), South Lake Tahoe, CA 95731 (tel. 916/541-0230, or toll free 800/822-5922 from 9 a.m. to 5 p.m.). The Lazy S, which welcomes children, offers both motel-room-type units and cottages, some of which can accommodate up to six people. There is a heated pool in summer, a hot tub, picnic tables, barbecues, games, and green lawns for playing. Parking is adjacent to each cottage. Several restaurants are nearby. Babysitter lists are available.

All the rooms come with coffee and TV, but no telephone. The cottages feature kitchens, dining rooms, and fireplaces. In spring and fall, they run $41 to $61; in summer, $63 to $96. Cottages can sleep two to six people. Motel units with optional fully equipped kitchenettes range from $27 to $42 off-season and sleep up to four; in summer, $42 to $67 (with kitchens, $5 to $8 extra). Winter rates fall somewhere between spring and summer rates, but be sure to check out the lodge's special ski packages. There are also 10% discounts for a week's stay. Cribs (really playpens), rollaways, and highchairs are available at no charge.

Along the West Shore

Along Tahoe's pine-shaded west shore, our recommendation for a first-class resort is **Sunnyside Restaurant and Lodge,** 1850 W. Lake Blvd. (P.O. Box 5969), Tahoe City, CA 95730 (tel. 916/583-7200, or toll free 800/822-2-SKI in California), a marvelous lodge two miles south of Tahoe City, right on the lake probably best suited for families with older children.

Even if you don't stay at the lodge, it's worth a special trip to dig into the spectacular weekend brunch at the attached Sunnyside Restaurant (tel. 916/583-7200). The only thing that can rival the view here—big picture windows look right out on the lake—is the astonishing array of fresh foods on the all-you-can-eat buffet. Fruits, salads, egg dishes, bacon, ham, bagels, cream cheese, lox, fish, roast beef, sweet rolls, juices are some of the items offered—every member of our family was in pig heaven. Brunch is served on Sunday only, from 10 a.m. to 2:30 p.m. Get there early—it fills up fast. Adults pay $11; children 12 and under, $7. It's worth every penny—you won't need lunch.

Recently rebuilt and remodeled with a mahogany-and-rock décor, Sunnyside has 23 immaculate, bright rooms and suites with private decks, some with fireplaces or wet bars. All the rooms have views of the lake. Continental breakfast is included in the rates.

Prices range from $85 to $145, depending on season and room size; add $15 for three or more people. Children under 3 are free. No charge for cribs or rollaways.

North Lake Tahoe

An exceptional lakeside condominium facility in Tahoe City is the **Tahoe Marina Lodge,** on Calif. 28 near the "Y" intersection (P.O. Box 92), Tahoe City, CA 95730 (tel. 916/583-2365). The lodge has its own sandy beach, as well as a heated pool (children under 10 must be accompanied by an adult) and tennis courts. It's within easy walking distance of several restaurants.

The lodge features extremely spacious and beautifully furnished units. There are both one- and two-bedroom condos, all with fully equipped kitchens, fireplaces, TVs, sofa beds, and private decks or patios. The one-bedroom units can accommodate up to four people; the two-bedroom units, up to six people. Linens are furnished, though maid service is extra.

Rates (per unit—not by number of people) for a one-bedroom garden-view unit that can sleep four range from $79 to $133, depending on the season. Two-bedroom lake-view and lakefront units (which can sleep six) run $97 to $175. No rollaways are available; cribs cost $5 per night.

For a good bet on a north-shore casino-hotel, try the **Cal-Neva Lodge,** located at Stateline Point along Nev. 28 in Crystal Bay (P.O. Box 368), Crystal Bay, NV 89402 (tel. 702/832-4000, or toll free 800/225-6382). Most of the lodge is in Nevada—a small, rather quiet corner of it is in California (hence the name Cal-Neva), with the state line painted right through the lobby. Our kids got a kick out of standing with their feet in two separate states in front of the fireplace; and you can even swim from California to Nevada and back in the outdoor heated pool. The Nevada side of the lobby is dominated by a noisy, smoke-filled casino, so bear this in mind when deciding whether or not to stay here with children. For kids, there's a video game arcade just off the front entranceway. And there's a room with displays of Washoe Indian artifacts. The restaurant (rather formal at dinner) overlooks the lake. The room service menu has a children's section.

There's room for a crib or rollaway in the units, which are tastefully decorated with armoires, color TVs, writing desks, and immaculate bathrooms.

Rates for the spacious, bright rooms—all with panoramic views of the lake at lovely Crystal Bay—range from $49 to $99 in low season. There are also special ski packages. Cribs cost $15 per night; rollaways, $15. Children under 5 sleep free; those over 5 and additional adults are charged $5 per night each.

On the California side of the north shore, three miles from the Nevada border, the **Rustic Cottage Resort,** 7449 N. Lake Blvd. (P.O. Box 138), Tahoe Vista, CA 95732 (tel. 916/546-3523), offers quaint pine-shaded cottages. There are two picnic areas on the spacious grounds with plenty of room for kids to roam. Across the highway is a sandy public beach with gorgeous lake views. While there is no restaurant on the premises, Tahoe Vista and nearby Kings Beach and Carnelian Bay are loaded with them.

The cottages are roomy, clean, and well appointed. Most have kitchens, and several also have fireplaces. All cottages feature private baths, although most have showers rather than tubs.

Rates (based on a per-unit charge) range from $35 to $60 for one-bed rooms without kitchens; $30 to $60 for cottages with kitchens (most with one queen-size or double bed), and $45 to $80 for cottages with fireplaces and kitchens (many of which have two doubles and one single or a sofa bed). Rollaways are available at $5 per night, but cribs are not.

A good choice for basic accommodations along the far north shore is the

Sun 'n Sand Lodge, 8308 N. Lake Blvd., Kings Beach, Lake Tahoe, CA 95719 (tel. 916/546-2515). Don't let the name mislead you—this is a motel, but it has its own private sandy beach on the lake, and is situated near Northstar-at-Tahoe and other ski resorts and within a mile of the casinos on the Nevada border.

There are no kitchens, pool, or restaurant at this facility, but there are lots of places to eat in Kings Beach. A complimentary continental breakfast is served on weekends, and the magnificent views are free.

The 26 motel-style rooms run from $30 to $65 for singles or doubles, depending on the number of beds in the room, location of the unit, and time of year. No charge for cribs or rollaways. Each extra person, adult or child (except infants in cribs) pays $5.

Camping

You can camp along the south shore at **Camp Richardson,** on Calif. 89 (tel. 916/541-1801); **Eagle Point,** on Calif. 89 near Emerald Bay (tel. 916/541-3030); **Fallen Leaf Lake,** on Fallen Leaf Lake Road, off Calif. 89 (tel. 916/544-6420); and at **El Dorado,** along U.S. 50, South Lake Tahoe (tel. 916/573-2059).

Along the west shore off Calif. 89 you can camp at **D. L. Bliss State Park** (tel. 916/525-7277); **Sugar Pine Point State Park** (tel. 916/525-7982), open year round; and **Meeks Bay** (tel. 916/544-6420).

Along the north shore, try **Lake Forest Campground,** Calif. 28, Tahoe City (tel. 916/583-3074).

Call for fees and dates; many campgrounds close during winter.

WHERE TO EAT: Possibly because so many San Franciscans vacation here, the Tahoe area offers surprisingly good food, with a number of restaurants actively courting the family trade.

North Lake Tahoe

One of our family's favorite dinner spots is the **Tahoe House,** at 625 W. Lake Blvd. (Calif. 89), about half a mile south of the "Y" in Tahoe City (tel. 916/583-1377). Tahoe House, which specializes in Swiss and California cuisine, is attractively decorated in brick and pine. The atmosphere is pleasant and relaxed, with many families in evidence. Service is friendly and dress is casual. Items on the children's menu are pegged at $6 and include generous portions of fried chicken, fresh spaghetti, and wienerschnitzel (whose name so intrigued our son that he ordered it—and loved it), plus soup or salad.

The regular menu features both Swiss-German and Swiss-Italian specialties, plus several daily seafood specials, priced from around $9.50 to $17, including relishes, soup, salad (try the spinach salad with house dressing), and vegetables. But leave room for the luscious desserts—including lots of Swiss chocolate concoctions—all made on the premises.

The chef will also split adult portions in half for kids, and prepare children's drinks, such as Shirley Temples. Highchairs and booster seats are provided.

Open daily from 4:30 p.m. for dinner. Reservations and credit cards accepted. Convenient parking.

For inexpensive Mexican food on the north shore, try the two locations of **Las Panchitas,** 8345 N. Lake Blvd., Kings Beach, California (tel. 916/546-4539), and 930 Tahoe Blvd., Incline Village, Nevada (tel. 702/831-4048). These are fairly dark and noisy establishments where even the loudest youngster probably won't be heard over the general din of skiers and hikers loading up on burritos, tacos, and fajitas. Children's plates (for the under-12 set) include a choice of cheese enchilada, taco, bean burrito, or hamburger patty served with rice and refried beans, plus ice cream or sherbet, for $4. Adult portions of Mexican combination dinners are pegged at $6 to $7.

Booster seats and highchairs are available. Open weekdays from 11 a.m. to

10 p.m. and weekends from noon to 10 p.m. No reservations accepted. Parking in front. Most credit cards are welcome.

South Lake Tahoe

An elegant spot that welcomes families is the **Hearthside Restaurant,** at the Tahoe Seasons Resort, at the corner of Saddle and Keller, across from Heavenly Valley Ski Resort (tel. 916/541-6700). The dining room is lit by fireplace and candles, and the atmosphere is quiet, but well-behaved children will feel right at home. Full-course adult dinners from the eclectic selection of entrees cost up to $14. Whiskey chicken, saltimbocca, coquilles, and steak are just some of the choices. The "Munchkin Menu," for children 12 and under, includes chicken, burger, spaghetti, or grilled cheese (with potato and vegetable or salad) for $3.

Breakfast is served here also. There's no children's menu, but there are several selections that will appeal to young ones. Breakfast ranges from $2 to $6.

Boosters and highchairs are provided.

The Hearthside is open daily for breakfast from 7 a.m. to noon; for dinner from 5:30 to 9:30 p.m.; for Sunday brunch, from 9 a.m. to 2 p.m. Reservations are accepted. Valet parking. Major credit cards welcome.

Another great family-style place is **Salmar's** (formerly Posh Omelettes), located at 787 Emerald Bay Rd. (Calif. 89), heading west from South Lake Tahoe (tel. 916/541-8400). Owner-chef Sal Cardinale's artistic breakfast creations for kids are not to be missed. Our daughter loved the "Mickey Mouse"—with pancake ears, eggs for eyes, sausage for nose, bacon for mouth, and whipped cream for hair. Our son equally adored the "Tinkerbell"—with sausage for legs, whipped cream for dress, French toast for wings, egg for head, and bacon for halo. It seemed a shame to eat these near-museum pieces, but our kids eagerly dove right in. Portions are huge, and prices cheap (around $2 for the children's breakfasts). Salmar's also boasts perhaps the world's most extensive selection of omelets—2,104 possible combinations!

The dinner menu features Italian dishes that won't gouge the pocketbook —with no dinner higher than $13—and an eight-item children's menu.

As in many Tahoe restaurants, the atmosphere here is casual. Highchairs and booster seats are provided. The outdoor patio is open in warm weather.

Open daily for breakfast from 7 a.m. to 2 p.m. Dinner is served Wednesday through Sunday from 4 to 9 p.m. No reservations accepted. Plenty of parking in front. Major credit cards welcome.

Don't miss **Heidi's,** 3485 U.S. 50, South Lake Tahoe (tel. 916/544-8113), a breakfast spot par excellence. The décor is alpine A-frame; our kids got so into the motif that they immediately decided to read *Heidi,* the book. This place is tailor-made for families. The age-10-and-under children's menu—which doubles as a coloring and puzzle book (crayons are brought to the table)—includes French toast, waffles, pancakes, cereal, and egg dishes ($2 each). The kitchen will also split adult portions for kids—from a menu including 14 types of pancakes, 10 kinds of Belgian waffles, 18 omelet combinations, plus varieties of French toast, breakfast crêpes, pastries, and an array of side dishes. Waffles, crêpes, and pancakes are priced from $4 to $6; omelets, $6 to $7. You can even order a family-style breakfast for four for $32.50. Highchairs and booster seats are available. No-smoking section.

Breakfast starts at 7 a.m. and runs till closing at 9 p.m. Lunch service starts at 11 a.m. No reservations accepted. Parking lot. Major credit cards.

Casino Dining

The high-rise casino-hotels (all near the border in Stateline, Nevada) also offer some good bargains in family dining, though the food in general, we believe, is not quite up to the quality of the above establishments.

Harrah's Forest Buffet, located on the top (18th) floor of the hotel (tel.

702/588-6611) and affording a marvelous scenic view of the south shore, features moderately priced all-you-can-eat buffet breakfasts, lunches, and dinners. Hotel and casino guests get the top pick of tables; arrive early for a window seat.

Adult prices range from $5.25 for breakfast to between $10 and $14 for dinner; children 4 to 10 can eat for between $4.75 at breakfast and $6.75 for dinner; children 3 and under eat free. Boosters and highchairs are provided.

Open for breakfast and lunch daily from 8:30 a.m. to 2:30 p.m.; for dinner, from 5:30 to 11 p.m. No reservations accepted. Major credit cards welcome.

The **Chicken & Rib Barn,** at the High Sierra on U.S. 50 (tel. 702/588-6211), is an informal spot that features decent barbecue dishes at reasonable prices. Family-style combination dinners cost approximately $9 to $10 and include chicken, spareribs, and London broil or sausage, plus cornbread, dessert, and beverage.

Boosters and highchairs are available.

Open for dinner nightly from 5 to 10 p.m. No reservations accepted. Major credit cards welcome.

The **Primavera Room** at Caesars Tahoe, on U.S. 50 (tel. 702/588-3515), located right next to the indoor swimming pool, features Italian food at moderate prices. Highchairs and boosters are available.

Open daily for dinner from 5 to 10 p.m. Brunch is served on Saturday and Sunday from 10 a.m. to 3 p.m. Reservations are accepted. Major credit cards honored.

And if you hit the jackpot at the slots, you may want to splurge on your family at the **Sage Room** at Harvey's Resort, on U.S. 50 (tel. 702/588-2411), which has excellent food and a more formal atmosphere, but isn't cheap. We would not recommend this restaurant for very young children, though service is friendly toward families, and our youngsters appreciated the chance to go upscale a bit. Our son sampled his first filet mignon here. Steaks, seafood, chicken, and veal items run between $14 and $22 but include a good salad, vegetables, and garlic bread. Boosters and highchairs are provided.

Open daily from 8 a.m. to 2 p.m. and 6 to 11 p.m. Reservations are accepted. Major credit cards welcome.

EMERGENCY NUMBERS: In case of a medical emergency, call **Barton Memorial Hospital,** South Lake Tahoe (tel. 916/541-3420), or **Stateline Emergency Clinic,** Stateline, Nevada (tel. 702/588-3561).
The local number for **AAA road service** is 916/541-2430.

THE CENTRAL COAST

□ □ □

Many people think of the Monterey Bay area as romantic—leisurely strolls near Lover's Point overlooking Monterey Bay, a cozy room warmed by a fireplace, or gallery hopping in the quaint village of Carmel. But the Monterey Peninsula has much to offer families too. For example, instead of setting your sights on shopping in Carmel, think about tidepooling in Pacific Grove. Instead of limiting yourself to excursions along the exquisite Seventeen Mile Drive, ride the gilded carousel in Cannery Row or visit the Monterey Bay Aquarium, highlights of any trip to the area.

South of Carmel is the breathtaking Big Sur coast, one of the most beautiful stretches of coastline in the world. Famous in the past as a haven for artists and hippies, Big Sur is now a family's delight, replete with hiking, camping, and outdoor adventures galore.

From San Francisco, take Calif. 1 south. From Los Angeles, you have two choices: you can take U.S. 101 north to Salinas and then take Calif. 68 west to Monterey. Or, if you prefer to drive the coast, take U.S. 101 to San Luis Obispo and then take Calif. 1 north to Monterey.

1. MONTEREY

Situated at the southern end of crescent-shaped Monterey Bay, Monterey is 120 miles south of San Francisco and 320 miles north of Los Angeles.

Rich in historical significance, Monterey is a charming seaside town that still feels very much like a working fishing village. Until recently the canneries were a major part of city life, and even today the wharf bustles with fishing activity.

Monterey was the capital of Alta California long before it was part of the United States. First discovered by Portuguese explorer Juan Rodriguez Cabrillo, who was searching for riches, it wasn't until 1602 that the Spanish began to colonize the area, and on June 3, 1770, it became the capital under Fr. Junipero Serra (who was the head of the California Missions). It remained under Mexican and Spanish rule until 1846, when Commodore John Drake Sloat raised the United States flag over the Custom House. In 1850 California became a state.

You can still see the Spanish and Mexican heritage in the delightful early-California architecture. Many Spanish-style adobe buildings built around patios are still standing. It's an interesting mix with the maritime influence.

HOW TO GET ORIENTED: The main areas of town are located along the waterfront (Cannery Row, Fisherman's Wharf, the Monterey Bay Aquarium) and near downtown (Alvarado Street). A stop at the **Monterey Visitors and Convention Bureau,** 380 Alvarado St. (tel. 408/649-1770), will be very helpful in getting you started. Pick up the walking tour brochure, called *Path of History.* It details all the sights of historical significance. (Since most children have less interest than their parents in this aspect of travel, we have designed a mini-walk with just a few historical sites we think the kids will appreciate, so that you can enjoy them too. Those of you with exceptionally attentive, historically minded kids can use the brochure for additional sites to explore.)

WHAT TO DO AND SEE: The highlights for children in this area are, without question, the Monterey Bay Aquarium, Cannery Row, and Fisherman's Wharf. We head there first. Here's how we make a day of it.

The Monterey Bay Aquarium

The aquarium, located at the west end of Cannery Row at no. 886 (tel. 408/375-3333), is not to be missed and will probably be the high spot of your trip, especially if you have children over 4.

Go ahead, "ooooh and ahhhh" as you enter the tremendous, cavernous building designed to reflect the atmosphere of the huge cannery which used to be here. Looking up, you can't miss the **Marine Mammals Gallery,** a procession of life-size replicas of killer whales, dolphins, seals, and other mammals that hang from the ceiling.

This is the largest aquarium in the country, with more than 6,000 creatures and 100 exhibits, many of them interactive. Don't expect marine life in simple fish tanks though. What makes this aquarium unique is that it gives you an "undersea tour" of Monterey Bay and the rich marine life that inhabits the region. Children may not grasp the superb nature of this place at first. It will help if you inform them beforehand that it is not like Sea World or Marine World. This is marine life in its natural habitat, not a collection of performing animals.

It's a place you'll return to again and again, to experience favorite exhibits and try new ones as the kids get older and their interests expand. You will want to allow different amounts of time for kids of different ages. Little ones may find the experience too educational to be exciting (except the seal feedings), but children 5 and over will love certain exhibits—especially the **Touch Pools,** where they can handle sea stars, anemones, and sea cucumbers under the guidance of patient volunteer instructors who show them what to do. Kids also love the bat ray pool, where they can watch—and pet—the fish. Plan to spend lots of time there. Teens will appreciate most of the exhibits if they don't expect gimmicks.

Don't miss the **Kelp Forest,** a diver's-eye view of a towering forest of California's giant kelp. One of the most impressive exhibits of the aquarium, it is three stories high and can be viewed from different levels. Amazingly, the giant plant can grow up to ten inches a day! Show the kids how the light changes depending on how far it is filtered from the surface. And don't miss the **sea otters.** California's 1,200 sea otters are found mainly along the central coast. This two-story exhibit gives kids a chance to watch these animals at play, in and out of the water. And feeding time for the otters is an event you won't want to miss.

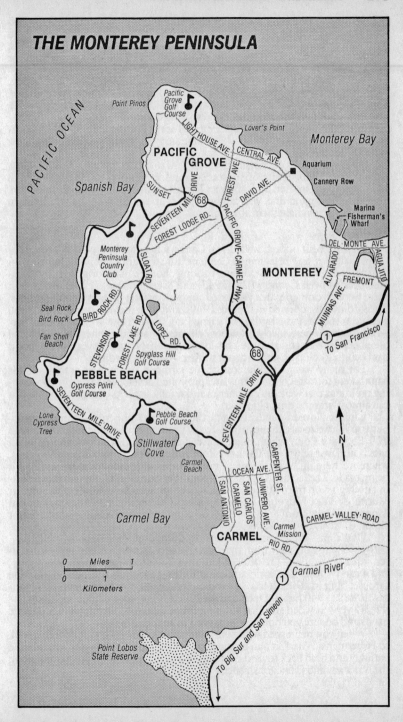

THE MONTEREY PENINSULA

PACIFIC OCEAN

Point Pinos

Pacific Grove Golf Course

Lover's Point

Monterey Bay

PACIFIC GROVE

Spanish Bay

LIGHTHOUSE AVE.

CENTRAL AVE.

Aquarium

Cannery Row

SUNSET

SEVENTEEN MILE DRIVE

FOREST LODGE RD.

FOREST AVE.

DAVID AVE.

Marina
Fisherman's
Wharf

DEL MONTE AVE.

PACIFIC GROVE-CARMEL HWY.

SLOAT RD.

Monterey
Peninsula
Country
Club

MONTEREY

AGUAJITO

ALVARADO

MUNRAS AVE.

FREMONT

Seal Rock
Bird Rock

BIRD ROCK RD.

FOREST LAKE RD.

LOPEZ RD.

To San Francisco

Fan Shell
Beach

STEVENSON

Spyglass Hill
Golf Course

Cypress Point
Golf Course

PEBBLE BEACH

SEVENTEEN MILE DRIVE

Lone
Cypress
Tree

SEVENTEEN MILE DRIVE

Pebble Beach
Golf Course

CARPENTER ST.

Stillwater
Cove

Carmel
Beach

OCEAN AVE.

JUNIPERO AVE.

SAN CARLOS

CARMELO

Carmel Bay

SAN ANTONIO

Carmel
Mission

CARMEL VALLEY ROAD

CARMEL

RIO RD.

Miles 1

0 1
Kilometers

Carmel River

To Big Sur and San Simeon

Point Lobos
State Reserve

N

Monterey Bay Habitats is a spectacular 90-foot-long hourglass-shaped exhibit that re-creates the environment of the bay. It's what you would see if you went scuba-diving in the area—in the order in which you would see it. That is, you see the habitat from the deepest part of the bay to the shallowest, from the reef and the sandy sea floor to the wood pilings of the wharf.

The **Sandy Shore** is an open-air bird sanctuary that re-creates the shoreline. As the waves come in, you can watch the fish that swim just below the surface. You enter this aviary via a revolving door (which helps to confine the birds). Strollers are not allowed through the revolving door.

You might want to get a snack or lunch at the Portola Café/Gift and Bookstore, open from 10 a.m. to 5 p.m. We were surprised at the pleasant café and the varied menu.

The aquarium is open daily from 10 a.m. to 6 p.m., except Christmas Day. Admission is $8 for adults, $6 for students and seniors over 65, $4 for children 3 to 12 years old; children under 3, free. The aquarium is a very popular attraction. To avoid standing in line, you can buy tickets at Ticketron before you arrive in Monterey, or purchase them at your hotel.

Cannery Row

Next on your outing, walk down Cannery Row toward town. A mixture of shops, galleries, and restaurants, Cannery Row was until recently a bustling industrial area filled with sardine-packing houses, immortalized by John Steinbeck's novels *Cannery Row* (1945) and *Sweet Thursday* (1954). At its peak there were 18 canneries that processed almost a quarter million tons of sardines. The sardines disappeared in the late 1940s, and with them went the people who worked at the canneries by day and partied at Cannery Row—in taverns and bars —by night. These lively, raucous characters are the ones who peopled Steinbeck's novels and gave the Row its reputation. Now, after years of neglect, it has become a colorful, inviting spot to visit—sans the sardines.

For many years after the loss of the sardines, the famous author and his haunts kept tourists coming. This later prompted developers to restore the decaying buildings that were once canneries and warehouses. As you look around, you can almost hear the din of long ago.

Children love to wander through the renovated canneries—parents, too— but you'll have to ask about stroller access in some of the buildings. Don't miss **700 Cannery Row,** which houses several delightful places for children of all ages. Our favorite was the **Cannery Row Fudge Factory** (tel. 408/375-7763), where we were in "sugar heaven," tasting free fudge samples as we watched it being made. The factory is open daily from 10 a.m. to 9 p.m., though fudge making itself goes on from 10 a.m. to 5 p.m. The same building houses the **Spirit of Monterey Wax Museum** (tel. 408/375-3770), which tells the story of old Monterey. Open from 8:30 a.m. to 7:30 p.m. Admission is $6 for adults, $3 for children 7 to 17; under 7, free.

Don't miss the **Edgewater Packing Company,** 640 Wave St. (tel. 408/649-1899), up one block from the main Cannery area. Billed as a family fun center, it has an arcade—a favorite of kids over 7—a toy store, an ice-cream shop, and a candy store. The main attraction for us, though, is the fabulous antique carousel built in 1905. It has 34 hand-carved horses, two zebras, and two chariots, as well as 940 lights! Open daily at 11 a.m. One word of caution, though— this is a very crowded area that attracts a lot of teenagers. Be careful to hold little hands and be sure you don't get separated from each other.

When you're finished with your activities at Cannery Row for the day, walk to Fisherman's Wharf. It's an easy walk and takes about 25 minutes. Just take the pathway and head back toward the town of Monterey. This is a pretty walk along the waterway and is fine for strollers.

Fisherman's Wharf

Monterey's Fisherman's Wharf is lined with giftshops, restaurants, and fresh seafood stands in an authentic wharf atmosphere. It is still a working pier (although the commercial fishing fleet is now at the Municipal Pier, Wharf 2—which you can also walk to). It was once a pier for trading schooners to unload their wares when Monterey was the major port on the Pacific. Today, however, the wharf is where you'll find excursions for sport fishing, sightseeing, and whale-watching. **Randy's Fishing Trips,** at 66 Fisherman's Wharf (tel. 408/372-7440), open daily from 5:30 a.m. to 5 p.m., will rent poles, tackle, and anything else you or the kids will need to fish (kids don't need fishing licenses—adults do). They also offer group-charter boats, sightseeing trips to Big Sur, and during the season, bird- and whale-watching excursions. **Princess Monterey Cruises,** at the end of the wharf (tel. 408/372-2628), offers 30-minute sightseeing cruises during the summer. They take you to Carmel Bay, where you can see Carmel from the water—a wonderfully different perspective. Cruises depart Monday through Friday at 11 a.m., 1 p.m., and 3 p.m.; on Saturday and Sunday boats leave on the hour from 9 a.m. to 3 p.m. Adults pay $12; children under 12, $6.

The Wharf is a great place to watch the sea lions. You won't miss them—their loud barks give them away. You can't miss the **Carousel Candy Shop,** either. You'll recognize it by the giant ice-cream cone outside and the clown inside the window. They have specialty candies and very good ice cream. (There's a second location in the Doubletree Plaza.)

Other Sights Around Town

Bordered by Fremont, Del Monte, Camino Aguajito, and Camino El Estero Streets, **Lake El Estero** is a pretty little lake in a pretty park. Your children will love watching the ducks or taking out a paddleboat. (Call 408/375-1484, as hours and rates change frequently.)

Dennis the Menace Park, located at Lake El Estero (tel. 408/646-3866), was designed by cartoonist Hank Ketcham, creator of Dennis the Menace. We've spent many hours here, the kids playing on the steam locomotive, the roller slide, and the spaceship-like structure, while we simply took advantage of the fresh air and beauty of nearby Lake El Estero. Open every day from 10 a.m. to dusk.

Monterey State Historic Park (tel. 408/649-7118) is a group of historically important adobes and other buildings located in Monterey. The buildings, owned by the state, are open to the public for viewing, and many have guided tours. The **Path of History** (mentioned near the beginning of this section) is a delightful walking tour of those buildings as well as many others in the area that are owned by foundations, societies, and individuals. You can pick up a brochure detailing the 45 historic landmarks on the Path at the Visitors Center or the park's offices at 525 Polk St. and begin your tour at any location. If you plan to go to several of the sites in the state park, you can buy an all-day pass ($3.50 for adults, $2 for children 6 to 17). Single-building admissions are $1 for adults and 50¢ for kids.

Our kids, however, are not up to a long walk of historic buildings yet—and we've found this to be true of many children, regardless of age. Here are the highlights of this tour that we recommend. Many people like to start at centrally located **Custom House** (near Fisherman's Wharf), the oldest government building in California, and the place where the United States flag was raised in 1846. The museum is open daily from 10 a.m. to 5 p.m. March through October, till 4 p.m. the rest of the year. Nearby in Custom House Plaza is **Pacific House** (built in 1847), which also houses a museum of American Indian and early-California history (same hours as above).

Colton Hall, at 522 Pacific St., between Madison and Jefferson Streets (open daily from 10 a.m. to 5 p.m.), is where the first Constitutional Congress of California met, the place where the California Constitution was written and the Great Seal designed. This is a delightful place to visit, almost like living history without the people. Tables are set up as if the people who were in the process of creating the constitution were still at work and just got up for a break. Glasses of water, pens and paper, hats on the back of chairs bring history to life. Operating as the first town hall and public school of Monterey, it now houses a historical museum.

Next door is the **Old Monterey Jail**—sure to capture the imagination of little bandits. The **Cooper-Molera Adobe,** near Munras and Polk Streets, is a good example of Monterey colonial architecture. It houses a small maritime museum and sits on two acres of grounds. Open daily except Wednesday. Tours are given at 10 a.m., 11 a.m., noon, 2 p.m., and 3 p.m.—and in summer also at 4 p.m. Another architecturally interesting house nearby is the **Larkin House,** at Jefferson Street and Calle Principal. Built in the New England style, it is considered an architectural treasure. Open daily except Tuesday. Tours are given at 10 a.m., 11 a.m., 1 p.m., 2 p.m., and 3 p.m.—and in summer at 4 p.m. too.

California's First Theater, located at the corner of Scott and Pacific Streets (tel. 408/375-4916), has continually staged productions since the 1840s. During the day you can walk through the empty theater if you'd like, but at night the place comes alive with old-fashioned melodramas. Throughout the year, performances are held on Friday and Saturday nights at 8 p.m. During July and August there are performances Wednesday through Saturday at 8 p.m. The cost is $7 for adults, $6 for seniors (over 60) and teens 13 to 19, $5 for children under 13. Call for program information.

If your children are sea lovers, they may also be interested in the **Allen Knight Maritime Museum,** 550 Calle Principal (tel. 408/375-2553), which has a large collection of models and tools. Kids love the huge Fresnel lens brought up from Point Sur Lighthouse. Another favorite is the old captain's cabin. Open June through September, Tuesday through Friday from 10 a.m. to 4 p.m. and on Saturday and Sunday from 2 to 4 p.m. Winter hours are Tuesday through Friday from 1 to 4 p.m. and on Saturday and Sunday from 2 to 4 p.m.; closed Monday. No charge, but donations are welcome.

An Early-Morning Walk

On those mornings when your little ones are up especially early and you want to let the others sleep, you can treat yourself to a **walk on the Wharf at sunrise.**

We left at about 6:30 a.m., stroller filled and heavy jackets on. Take the path next to the Doubletree Inn (on Alvarado and Del Monte) and through the Doubletree Plaza. The area is quiet and deserted except for an occasional jogger or a hearty bicyclist. The air is chilly, and if you're lucky there will be some mist to add atmosphere. You'll pass the **Pacific House** (see above). Our children enjoyed simply roaming around the large plaza area where the house sits. Next, you'll approach the **Custom House** (see above) and its plaza (with tables for a morning picnic breakfast of muffins and coffee).

As we got closer to the Wharf, we watched the fishermen get ready for the day's work, cups of steaming coffee in their hands. We could hear the barking of the nearby sea lions. It's a special time to be on the Wharf.

If you want a quick cup of coffee or a bite to eat, you might try the **Cove Restaurant,** at 64 Fisherman's Wharf (tel. 408/373-6969). Booster and Sassy seats are available. Open Monday through Friday from 6:30 a.m. to 5 p.m. and on Saturday and Sunday from 6 a.m. to 5 p.m. No credit cards accepted.

As you continue your morning walk, you might go to Wharf 2, where there is a lot more activity.

OTHER ACTIVITIES IN THE MONTEREY BAY AREA: Since the com-

munities of Monterey, Pacific Grove, and Carmel are so close together, there are many activities that you can do in the general area. For example, you can rent bicycles in one town and go for a bike ride in another.

Beaches

Caution! Beaches in Monterey, Pacific Grove, Carmel, and Big Sur may look inviting, but swimming can be quite hazardous. Riptides and cross currents make some areas extremely dangerous, and the water is very cold. Check to see if there are lifeguards on duty, and if so, heed any warning signs. Children have been lost off the rocks in heavy surf, and they can easily be caught in the strong cross currents.

The following beaches may be of interest: **Carmel Beach** (see the "What to Do and See" section in Carmel), **Carmel River State Beach** (see the "What to Do and See" section in Carmel), and **Lover's Point** (see the "What to Do and See" section in Pacific Grove).

Asilomar State Beach (in Pacific Grove) is a wonderful place for exploring dunes and tidepools. You'll find comfortable picnic spots sheltered from the wind, but don't attempt to swim.

Tidepooling

Look for good tidepools along the rocky areas between Point Pinos and Asilomar Beach in Pacific Grove during low tide.

Caution! Remember that the ocean waves can be unpredictable and may surprise you. Always be careful. Remember, too, that the area is slippery.

Here are some tips for tidepooling (courtesy of the Monterey County Visitors and Convention Bureau):

1. Remain with your group—don't go off alone.
2. Don't fool around on the rocks.
3. Walk slowly and carefully, since the rocks are very slippery.
4. Wear tennis shoes.
5. Don't get trapped by the rising tide.
6. Waves can knock you down, so always watch for them.
7. Don't bring glass containers in the tidepool areas.
8. Don't pry animals from the rocks.
9. Return animals to the same area from which you removed them.
10. Return each rock to the exact spot you took it from.
11. Sea animals do not like being stepped on or having fingers poked at them.
12. Leave empty shells on the beach—they may be some animal's future home.
13. Remember that all tidepool life is protected by law.

Bicycling

Bicycling in the area is wonderful. You have a choice of scenery and terrain. You can either stay on designated bike paths or ride in lovely residential areas. One of the most scenic paths is the **Shoreline Bike Path** from Lover's Point (Pacific Grove) to Fisherman's Wharf. This path is also good heading south, where you ride along the shore of the Seventeen Mile Drive (an easy six-mile ride).

Cycles by the Sea (tel. 408/372-1807) is a full-service bicycle-rental company that has free pickup and delivery (in Carmel, Carmel Valley, Monterey, and Pacific Grove), as well as package rates and preplanned tours. They have mountain bikes, beach cruisers, and tandem bikes, plus helmets and locks. They also have children's bikes, and bicycles with training wheels and toddler-carrier seats. Half-day rates are for 4 hours; a full day is 24 hours. For half a day the charge is $15, for adults or children. A full day's rental costs $20 on weekdays, $25 on weekends, but for a two- or three-day rental the rate is $15 per day. These rates include delivery, carrier seats, and helmets. Open sunrise to sunset.

Bay Bikes, 640 Wave St. (tel. 408/646-9090), is located on the Shoreline Bike Path at Cannery Row, one block from the aquarium. They rent mountain bikes, ten-speeds, tandems, cruisers, and children's bikes. They also have quadricycle/surreys that will hold three adults sitting next to each other, with a basket in front that holds two children up to age 6. Helmets are included in the price of the bike. Locks, cables, and little carriers (insulated bags) are also included. Riding from 9 a.m. to 5:30 p.m. (a full day) starts at $12.50, while the hourly rate is $3.50 per hour, with a two-hour minimum. There is a group discount (for five or more) and a discount of 15% if you rent for more than two days. There's a repair stand in front of the shop for people who bring their own bikes. The delivery charge for each bike is $2 (for drop-off or pickup).

Horseback Riding

Group rides are available at the **Pebble Beach Equestrian Center,** on the corner of Portola Road and Alva Lane (tel. 408/624-2756). Escorted trail rides are offered twice daily except Monday, at 10 a.m. and 2 p.m. A one-hour ride through Del Monte Forest costs $25, which takes you on sand dunes and around some of the beautiful golf courses. These rides are by reservation only (no more than six in a group), and children must be at least 10 years old.

Fishing

Your kids can **pier fish** at Monterey Municipal Wharf 2 (tel. 408/646-3950).

Randy's Fishing Trips, 66 Fisherman's Wharf (tel. 408/372-7440), will rent poles and other necessities for your kids to fish off the pier (see above for details).

Chris's Fishing Trips, 48 Fisherman's Wharf (tel. 408/375-5951), offers deep-sea fishing trips. Trips are $19 weekdays and $22 weekends. Children's rate (under 10) is $10 weekdays and $13 weekends. There's no minimum age as long as you're willing to keep track of your own kids. Trips are from 7:30 a.m. to 2:30 p.m. weekdays and 6:30 a.m. to 2:30 p.m. weekends.

Indoor Activities (for Rainy, Foggy Days)

In Monterey, you might enjoy a second visit to the **Monterey Bay Aquarium** (tel. 408/375-3333); see above for details. There's also the **Del Monte Gardens Roller Rink,** 2020 Del Monte Ave. (tel. 408/375-3202). It's open Wednesday through Sunday evenings from 7:30 to 10 p.m., with late sessions on Friday and Saturday nights from 9:30 to 11:30 p.m. Daytime sessions are only on Wednesday from 3 to 5 p.m. and on Saturday and Sunday from 2 to 4 p.m. Fees are $3 for matinee sessions, $3.50 for evening sessions, and $3 for late-night sessions. If you attend the full Friday- and Saturday-night sessions (7:30 to 11:30 p.m.), the cost is $6.

In Pacific Grove, you might try the **Pacific Grove Museum of Natural History** (tel. 408/372-4212); see the "What to Do and See" section in Pacific Grove for details.

Seasonal Events and Festivals

The **Monterey County Fair** (six days in mid-August), in Monterey, is a county fair par excellence. The kids will love the livestock exhibitions and the carnival rides. This event brings you back to the flavor of an old-fashioned county fair. It's held at the Monterey Fairgrounds, 2004 Fairgrounds Rd. (Call 408/372-5863 for details.)

Monarch Butterfly Festival and Parade (October) is a time-honored (and fun) event in Pacific Grove. All the elementary schoolchildren of Pacific Grove welcome the monarch in this colorful parade, which features 900 children in costume.

Whale-Watching (mid-December to March) is the chance to see the yearly migration of whales down the California coast. Randy's Fishing Trips (tel. 408/372-7440) and Sam's Fishing Fleet (tel. 408/372-0577) offer excursions.

And More . . .

Classic Tours (tel. 408/872-3044) and **Seacoast Safaris** (tel. 408/372-1288) offer personalized tours.

WHERE TO STAY: You won't have any trouble finding the kind of accommodation that fits your needs and pocketbook. Here are a few that we like.

The Upper Bracket

One of the great places to stay in Monterey is the **Monterey Sheraton,** 350 Calle Principal, Monterey, CA 93940 (tel. 408/649-4234, or toll free 800/325-3535). One of the tallest structures in Monterey, this ten-story building offers panoramic views of Monterey Bay from many of the rooms. The two-story atrium lobby absorbs much of the tumult and noise from the kids while serving as a comfortable and popular gathering spot. We saw dozens of young-uns, many of whom were rambunctious, and the style of the lobby accommodated them well.

Lovely as the hotel is, what makes the Sheraton exceptional is the service. The staff are warm and attentive, and have a sense of humor, which is always wonderful when you're with your children. From the valets who park your car (secured, underground parking—which means that you cannot get the car yourself, so be sure to take everything you might need first time around, and don't forget the stroller) to the bellmen and staff in the coffeeshop, everyone is friendly. They treat the whole family with respect, and they're only too pleased to talk to you about their own children.

Services and amenities include a full concierge staff, individualized limousine service, daily morning newspapers, 24-hour room service, and nightly turn-down service. (The nightly turn-down service is the closest you'll get to a fairy godmother. Andrew and Elizabeth left toys scattered over the bed when we rushed out to dinner one night. When we returned, the toys were piled neatly on the chaise lounge and the clothes were folded at the foot of the bed!)

The concierge staff is concerned that your stay be pleasant. They will make reservations for you, arrange babysitting, and do all manner of things. There is complimentary limo service that will take you to Carmel, Carmel Valley, and other places that you might want to go, based on availability.

The hotel has an outdoor swimming pool and Jacuzzi that are sheltered from the wind on three sides. The pool is very large and quite inviting when the weather is warm enough. There is also a health club with exercise equipment, weights, and bicycles (but you have to be 18 to use it), a beauty shop and barbershop, and a giftshop.

Continental breakfast is served in the lobby (for an additional charge). The Three Flags Café, a family-style restaurant, is open for breakfast, lunch, and dinner, and has a full menu. When we had breakfast in the coffeeshop and little Elizabeth decided to scream her head off, the waitress was very nice and even offered to hold her! Highchairs and booster seats are available here.

Ferrante's, located on the tenth floor, is an Italian restaurant and bar with a spectacular view. Even if you don't eat there with the kids, take them up there at sunset. There's a cocktail lounge that has live jazz entertainment nightly—the Monterey Bay Club—and a wine shop that features local wines and gourmet foods for snacks and picnics.

The 344 rooms have refrigerators, game tables and chairs, and dressing rooms with vanity areas. They're spacious and airy, and there is plenty of room for kids to play with blocks and puzzles on the floor. You can request a room with two double beds or a king-size bed, and many rooms have a couch or love seat. Connecting rooms are available, and there are a wide variety of suites.

Rates range from $130 to $185, depending on the floor, the view, and the room set-up. Suites vary from $225 to $850. Children under 17 stay free in their parents' room if no additional beds are needed. No charge for cribs (which are some of the nicest around) are free, but rollaways cost $20. Be sure to ask about seasonal, weekend, and family special rates.

Another fine accommodation is the **Monterey Hotel Resort,** at 1000 Aguajito Rd. (near Calif. 1), Monterey, CA 93940 (tel. 408/373-6141, or toll free 800/426-1685, 800/622-2099 in California). This 204-room hotel is open and spacious. The rooms are built around the large outdoor pool, giving it a resort-like atmosphere. There is also a Jacuzzi and sauna, and a putting green that our kids loved puttering around on. The shuffleboard and Ping-Pong kept several 8-year-olds engaged for well over an hour. There are two free tennis courts for guests, underground parking, and in-room movies (for a fee).

Babysitting is arranged by the guests, but the clerk at the front desk will give you referrals. The on-premises restaurant is called Monterey Rose and it has a children's menu.

Rooms rent for $89 to $134 single and $104 to $149 double. Children of all ages accompanied by an adult are free; additional adults pay $15 each per night. Rollaways cost $15 per night, but there's no charge for cribs.

The **Best Western Monterey Beach Hotel,** at 2600 Sand Dunes Dr. (off Calif. 1), Monterey, CA 93940 (tel. 408/394-3321, or toll free 800/242-8627), is on Monterey State Beach, and has been recommended to us by locals. The hotel features a heated pool and Jacuzzi, cable color TV with free in-room movies, and free shuttle service to and from the airport. Babysitting referrals are available from the front desk. There's a full-service restaurant on the premises with a panoramic view of Monterey Bay, and they have a children's menu.

The Monterey Beach has 195 guest rooms, and these rent for $120 to $170 per night, single or double, depending on the season. Suites go for $280. Children under 18 stay free in their parents' room; those over 18 and other adults pay $10 each per night. There is no charge for cribs, but rollaways cost $10. Ask about special packages.

Moderately Priced

If you're looking for moderate and inexpensive motels, you might try driving down "motel row," which is located on Fremont and Munras Avenues. Another option is to check out the recommendations in Pacific Grove (which is adjacent to Monterey). These accommodations are equally close to most sight-seeing attractions as those listed here.

Of the motels in Monterey, **Casa Munras Garden Hotel,** 700 Munras Ave., Monterey, CA 93940 (tel. 408/375-2411, or toll free 800/222-2558, 800/222-2446 in California), is our favorite. Originally built in 1824 as the official residence of the last Spanish ambassador to the state of California, Casa Munras is set on 3½ acres of landscaped, flowering gardens. There is an outdoor heated pool with a large shallow area for children. Babysitting is arranged through a referral service.

Although there isn't any room service, Casa Café and Bar is on the premises. Open from 7 a.m. to 9 p.m. Sunday through Thursday and till 10 p.m. on Friday and Saturday. Boosters and highchairs are available. There isn't a children's menu, but they will give half portions of adult dishes (and cut the price in half). Prices range from $2.50 for French toast, hot cakes, or waffles for breakfast, to $13 for a full prime rib dinner (including soup and salad, garlic bread, and fresh vegetable).

Rooms at Casa Munras are good sized, with plenty of space for a crib and toys for kids. Extra care is shown in the décor—for example, brass beds and comforters are part of the standard room. Rates range from $69 to $149 (for a room with a king-size bed, sofa-sleeper, and fireplace). Children under 12 stay free in their parents' room if extra beds are not needed. No charge for cribs, but rollaways cost $12 per night. Some connecting rooms are available.

The **Best Western Steinbeck Lodge,** at 1300 Munras Ave., Monterey, CA 93940 (tel. 408/373-3203), is a modest little motel of 32 rooms. The quoted rate includes a continental breakfast of danish, juice, and coffee.

Prices range from $45 to $100 single, $54 to $120 double, depending on the season and the kind of room. Rollaways cost $8 additional; cribs, $6.

PLACES TO EAT: The Monterey Bay area towns—Monterey, Pacific Grove, and Carmel—are so small and close to each other that it's easy for you to have breakfast in Pacific Grove, lunch in Carmel, and dinner in Monterey. We list restaurants by their city, but don't forget to check the other areas for ideas before making your choice.

The Upper Bracket

We couldn't believe it when we were told that the famous **Whaling Station Inn,** 763 Wave St., Cannery Row (tel. 408/373-3778), loved kids and catered to families. Nestled one block above Cannery Row, this gem of a restaurant is the perfect place to spend a relaxed evening with or without children. Don't let the candles and elaborate dessert table fool you. While the ambience of this legendary restaurant is quiet and elegant, the service is gracious and helpful to parents. Manager Frank Massaro, waiters, busboys, even the parking valet have an appreciation for a dining experience with children, and even more important, a sense of humor and camaraderie with the parents. "It happens all the time" is the response to a spilled Shirley Temple.

Frank Massaro believes you can have a fine dining experience even when you take your children along. "We don't want the ambience to scare away any family."

Fussy infants are greeted with little goldfish crackers and warm bread. Older children are greeted with a "hello" and a smile. Adults sit down to the artichoke appetizers that come as part of the meal.

The Caesar salad is fabulous—prepared at your table. Our waiter was chatty and efficient, making suggestions about the menu, but never being pushy. While there isn't a children's menu per se, they'll gladly serve you a half portion of the pasta dishes, or split fish or steak dinners between two children. It's hard to imagine anything the staff won't try to do to accommodate your family—three cherries in the Shirley Temple if your child asks, kidding about their own children, and suggestions for places you'll enjoy in the area with your family. So, of course, they have highchairs and boosters here, and they'll warm baby bottles and baby food.

Prices range from $14 for sautéed chicken to $28 for fresh abalone and filet and lobster tail. All à la carte entrees include artichoke for two and fresh, warm bread.

There is a no-smoking policy in the restaurant, although smoking is allowed in the bar. Open Sunday through Thursday from 5 to 9:30 p.m., on Friday and Saturday till 10 p.m. Reservations are recommended for weekends. Major credit cards accepted. Valet parking.

Mark Thomas Outrigger, 700 Cannery Row (tel. 408/372-8543), is a moderately priced seafood and steak restaurant. Set on the water, this is a fine spot in which to enjoy a leisurely meal while watching the seals and pelicans. Ask for a window seat (reservations recommended), and your children are likely to spend their time fascinated by the activity on the water. By day, there is a wealth of boats and fishing vessels. Near sunset, they can watch small fields of floating kelp and the ever-changing colors on the distant shoreline of Seaside and Santa Cruz.

This moderately priced, casual bay restaurant is a relaxing stop for well-behaved children and (well-behaved!) parents. This is the kind of place that you can order a petite filet with béarnaise or an Australian lobster tail while your son or daughter munches on a hamburger. (Adult dinners range from $6 to $30.)

The children's menu caters to a variety of sophisticated palates and includes a kid's shrimp Louie, clam strips, deep-fried calamari, and top sirloin. The kiddie menu also has a drink list that includes non-alcoholic daiquiris (banana, coconut, strawberry, etc.) and piña coladas, along with the more traditional Shirley Temples and Roy Rogerses.

You might want to request seating in the back dining room, which is bright and spacious for obtrusive highchairs and wandering children, rather than in the quiet Polynesian-style main dining room.

Reservations are accepted, but if you have to wait, there's a little beach area next to the restaurant that keeps the kids occupied. (Be careful of the rocks, though.) Highchairs and boosters are available. They will warm bottles and baby food. Parking is available at nearby lots. Open daily from 11:30 a.m. to 10 p.m. Most major credit cards accepted.

The **Captain's Galley,** 711 Cannery Row (tel. 408/649-8676), located in the center of Cannery Row, offers a menu with prices of $5 to $7 for a complete dinner. Your child's dinner includes chowder, salad, pasta, fresh vegetable, and French bread. Food is served family style, with chowder in tureens, salad and vegetables in big bowls. It's the kind of place where kids are comfortable and Mom and Dad can have a fine dining experience.

This seafood restaurant is adjacent to the 700 Cannery Row complex (where the Wax Museum and Fudge Factory are located—see above for details) by an enclosed overpass. It's located on the second floor where the view is great—you can take an elevator at 700 Cannery Row and use the overpass if you have a stroller. There is an Early Bird menu from 3:30 to 6 p.m. featuring such selections as top sirloin or sautéed prawns for $11 and fresh Pacific snapper or teriyaki chicken for $8. Regular menu items range upward from $10 (for barbecued chicken or grilled calamari).

Don't miss the bar where authentic photographs of the old canneries made famous by John Steinbeck's novels line the walls. Kids will love the old fishing boat leaning against the wall. Boosters and highchairs are available. Open daily from 11 a.m. to 10 p.m. Most major credit cards are accepted. Parking in nearby lots.

Moderate to Inexpensive

You may be surprised at how many great places in the Monterey Bay area welcome children.

The **Old Monterey Café,** 489 Alvarado St. (tel. 408/646-1021), is where the locals go for breakfast and lunch. Centrally located, it's a good place to try during a walk downtown (if you're doing part of the Adobe Tour) or after a jaunt in Dennis the Menace Park. The food is fabulous, and the menu varied and unusual. The old-fashioned hash browns are well worth the trip, as are the homemade muffins. For omelet lovers, you can choose from such exotic combinations as avocado, bacon, and onions ($5), or artichoke hearts, bacon, and jack cheese ($6)—and they're all made with four eggs. You can invent your own omelet filling, which might include broccoli, pineapple, or Italian sausage as well as the more usual fixings. Lunch offers the same kind of variety in sandwiches, half-pound burgers, salads, and homemade soups.

There is no children's menu, but they'll serve a child's portion for you, and will gladly warm bottles and baby food. Highchairs and boosters are available. Open daily from 7 a.m. to 3 p.m. No credit cards or reservations are accepted. Street parking.

Another obvious favorite is **Marie Callender's,** 1200 Del Monte Shopping Center (tel. 408/375-9500). For anyone unfamiliar with the Marie Callender's restaurants, these are generally good places to eat. While each one is slightly different (some have children's menus; others don't), you can feel secure that your meal—breakfast, lunch, or dinner—will be a step above coffeeshop fare. Known for their excellent fruit pies (20 to 30 kinds daily) and heartland pot pies, they also serve very good soup and chili, and a surprising variety of entrees. This branch also has good lasagne ($6.50), spaghetti marinara ($5), and quiche ($5.75). The array of pot pies includes such unusual ones as Charlie Chan chicken pot pie, chicken divan pot pie, and Mexican beef pot pie, as well as standard chicken, turkey, and tamale pot pies, all served with salad or soup ($8). Cornbread is one of their specialties.

This location, decorated in a San Francisco saloon motif, like most other Marie Callender's, is a comfortable place to take a child. The noise level is sufficiently loud to muffle the antics of the crankiest child.

The kids' menu offers variety—from hamburgers and fries ($1.75), to half a tuna sandwich ($2.50), to spaghetti ($1.50), to soup ($1.25).

Marie Callender's restaurants tend to be very popular, so you may have to wait for a table at prime time. It's a good idea to go early for dinner or lunch. If you have to wait, there's WaldenKids and Toys, Etcetera nearby. Highchairs and boosters are available. No reservations accepted. Most major credit cards welcome. Parking is available in the shopping center lot.

Deceptively simple from the street, **Gianni's Pizza,** 725 Lighthouse Ave. (tel. 408/649-1500), is an inexpensive, family-owned restaurant that has a cocktail bar, dessert bar, and coffee bar, as well as wonderful Italian food to eat in or take out. The artichoke fritatta (at 40¢ per piece) is a find, and the fresh French bread is delicious.

This is a great place to come after a walk through the aquarium or a few hours at Cannery Row. While there is no children's menu, pizza and pasta are made for sharing, and they'll gladly warm baby bottles and baby food in the kitchen. Pizzas take about 20 minutes to prepare, and at peak hours on Friday, Saturday, and Sunday (from 5:30 to 9 p.m.) you may have to wait 10 minutes to get a table. Boosters and highchairs are available.

Open Monday through Thursday from 4 to 11 p.m., on Friday and Saturday from 11:30 a.m. till midnight, and on Sunday from 11:30 a.m. till 10 p.m. No credit cards accepted. Street parking.

Rosine's Restaurant, 434 Alvarado St. (tel. 408/375-1400). Step into this downtown restaurant (which serves breakfast, lunch, and dinner) and it's like you're entering an early-California outdoor plaza. If there's such a thing as "faux outdoor early California," this is it. The walls are painted to look as if you're sitting in an outdoor plaza, complete with blue shutters painted on the walls that "open" into the restaurant.

There are highchairs and boosters, but no children's menu, plus there's a charge for splitting food. However, at dinner one pasta dish for children is offered. Some of the menu items—such as half sandwich with soup or salad ($3.50) or bagel with cream cheese and soup or salad ($3)—are fine for small appetites. Breakfast is served all day, and a side order of one egg is only 75¢.

For more grownup tastes, there are Reuben, Philly, and calamari sandwiches, as well as full dinners served after 5 p.m. Open Monday through Saturday mornings at 7:30 a.m. and on Sunday at 8 a.m.; closing hours vary. Reservations are not necessary. Street parking. Major credit cards accepted.

> **IN AN EMERGENCY:** The **Community Hospital of the Monterey Peninsula,** 23625 Holman Hwy. (tel. 408/624-5311), has the only 24-hour emergency room in the area. There is also a 24-hour pharmacy.

2. PACIFIC GROVE

Just next door to Monterey is the picturesque town of Pacific Grove. Also known as "Butterfly Town, U.S.A.," because the monarch butterflies return here in droves every year, Pacific Grove is a place you'll remember fondly. The kids especially love to wander around here. A drive down Ocean View Boulevard to Lover's Point will surely be one of the most beautiful excursions you'll take. Or walk through the quaint streets downtown and you'll feel as if you're back at the turn of the century.

WHAT TO SEE AND DO: The best place to start is beautiful **Lover's Point,** near Ocean View Boulevard, a bluff overlooking the crashing water. It offers a spectacular view of the bay, and is not to be missed. There are stairs down to the beach, but swimming is not suggested.

Point Pinos Lighthouse, at the end of Lighthouse Avenue, at Asilomar Boulevard (tel. 408/372-4212), is the oldest continuously working lighthouse on the West Coast. The grownups in our group were more excited about it than the kids (whose great pleasure was counting the number of steps up to the top). If your group has never seen a lighthouse before, take them to this one—the kids will enjoy it in their own way, and you don't need to spend much time there. There is a small museum downstairs. Open on Saturday and Sunday (except holidays) from 1 to 4 p.m. Free.

Pacific Grove Museum of Natural History, located at Forest and Central Avenues (tel. 408/372-4212), is a little museum where you can learn about the monarch butterflies' annual winter return to Pacific Grove. Open Tuesday through Sunday from 10 a.m. to 5 p.m. Admission to the museum is free.

Walkway to Fisherman's Wharf begins at Ocean View Boulevard and 17th Avenue and continues on to Cannery Row and Fisherman's Wharf. It would take a family approximately one hour to walk, and it's a wonderful way to get the flavor of the area.

Touted as "the slowest way between Carmel and Monterey," the **Seventeen Mile Drive** meanders through exquisite coastal scenery. Many people love this route. Others with kids who are poor car travelers aren't so sure. If your kids will cooperate, you'll love it. If you go, begin the drive from the Calif. 1 Gate (Munras Avenue to Calif. 1). Although there are three gates to take you to the drive, this one is the most convenient. At the toll gate, you'll receive a guide that maps out the highlights you'll be passing. During your drive, you'll enter the Del Monte Forest and Pebble Beach (home of the Lone Cypress tree and Seal Rock). Be sure to stop to enjoy the exquisite views. You'll also pass several picnic areas, championship golf courses, and the famous Lodge at Pebble Beach. A stop at Lone Pine or Seal or Bird Rocks will give you a glimpse of thousands of sea birds and lots of seals and sea lions.

You might choose, instead, to bicycle in the area. We suggest the wonderful bike path (which is a continuation of the one that goes to Monterey's Fisherman's Wharf). This one goes in the other direction, continuing on Ocean View Boulevard, and changes to Sunset Boulevard. The path follows the coast, is relatively flat, and is free. (For suggestions about bicycle rentals, see the "Other Activities in the Monterey Bay Area," in Monterey.)

WHERE TO STAY: Pacific Grove has a good selection of mid-priced hostelries.

The **Beachcomber Inn,** 1996 Sunset Dr., Pacific Grove, CA 93950 (tel. 408/373-4769, or toll free 800/445-7745, 800/237-5885 in California), at Asilomar State Beach, is a small inn (26 rooms)—basic but very clean. It's the last property before the beach. If you have very little ones, you'll love the free bikes with child carriers. However, you'll have to rent kids' bikes elsewhere. The rooms are small, but adjoining rooms can be rented. Refrigerators are available upon request. The outdoor swimming pool has a large slide that delights kids.

In winter, rates start at $55 (for a room with a queen- or king-size bed) and go up to $100. In summer, the prices run $65 to $150.

The **Pacific Gardens Inn,** 701 Asilomar Blvd., Pacific Grove, CA 93950 (tel. 408/646-9414, or toll free 800/262-1566), across the street from Asilomar State Park and Beach, is another good choice. Nestled in the trees and lovely gardens, this cozy, rustic motel has 27 units, most of which have fireplaces. We loved the fresh popcorn we could make at night with the popcorn maker that comes with each room.

There are two hot tubs on the property. Kitchen units, adjoining rooms, and refrigerators are available upon request.

Rates include complimentary continental breakfast, and wine and cheese in the evening. Some rooms have fireplaces. Rooms come with one or two queen-size beds or a king-size bed, and range in price from $70 to $98. One- and two-bedroom suites range from $99 to $145. No charge for cribs. Children under 12 stay free in their parents' room if additional beds are not needed; children over 12 are charged $5 each per night.

Bed-and-Breakfast Inns

Yes, even families can partake of the hospitality of a bed-and-breakfast. You just have to know if the inns accept children. The following two accommodations welcome families. (See the Carmel accommodations section for a third bed-and-breakfast inn.) Please, remember that in such close quarters you can usually hear *everything.* Fussy babies and poorly behaved kids don't belong in B&Bs. (Refer to the section in Chapter II for advice on staying with children in bed-and-breakfast accommodations.)

Green Gables Inn, 104 5th St., Pacific Grove, CA 93950 (tel. 408/375-2095, or toll free 800/841-5252), is a Queen Anne–style mansion located on a breathtaking section of the Monterey Bay coastline. You'll be amazed as you first step into the high-ceilinged living room, elegantly decorated with antiques, and face the sea through large, bay-windowed alcoves. The view is spectacular.

Afternoon tea, sherry, and wine are served with hors d'oeuvres in the parlor, and a full breakfast is served in the English-style dining room. Across the street is a trail for jogging or strolling, and a lovely public beach.

The guest accommodations in the main house are furnished with antiques and have shared bathrooms, so they are not advisable for kids. Instead, the Carriage House has five separate accommodations with queen-size beds, fireplaces, sitting rooms, private baths, and color televisions. These are the rooms to request.

The rates for Carriage House rooms are $125 and $135, single or double, including breakfast and afternoon wine, tea, and hors d'oeuvres. Cribs are available at no charge. Children over 4 pay $15 extra per night. Major credit cards accepted.

With older children, you might consider the **Gosby House Inn,** 643 Lighthouse Ave., Pacific Grove, CA 93950 (tel. 408/375-1287, or toll free 800/342-4888), in picturesque downtown Pacific Grove, owned by the same chain as Green Gables. Inspired by European country inns, this bed-and-breakfast has been in operation since 1887, and was placed in the National Register of Historic Places in 1980. It is considered to be an excellent example of authentic Queen Anne architecture, with bay windows and a rounded corner tower reminiscent of a turret. This charming inn is a two-story wooden building painted yellow with white trim.

Formal and traditional, this is a wonderful place for children who are quiet and self-restrained. Girls (and adults too) will delight in the antique doll collection located in the parlor. And the small garden is a perfect place for reading and breakfast.

Some 20 of the 22 rooms have baths, so ask ahead if you insist on one with a tub. (If you're an antique buff, ask for a room with a clawfoot tub.)

Amenities include concierge service, nightly turn-down, and breakfast in bed (on request). You can have the staff fix a picnic basket of fruit and cheese—and wine if you desire (at an extra charge)—so that you won't have to stop at a restaurant. Breakfast and afternoon tea, sherry, and hors d'oeuvres are included in the room price.

Rates range from $85 to $132, single or double. Cribs are available at no extra charge, but children over 4 and additional adults are charged $15 per night (for food). Major credit cards accepted. *Note:* There is a no-smoking policy at the inn.

PLACES TO EAT: Don't be deceived by the fact that these restaurants are in Pacific Grove. They are very close to Monterey and can easily be a choice for a meal from either location.

Moderately Priced Eateries

We love **Tinnery at the Beach,** on Lover's Point in Pacific Grove (tel. 408/646-1040). If you want a spectacular view of Monterey Bay, this is the place to go. The restaurant is situated on the point so as to look out onto the curve of the bay. The contemporary chrome-trimmed interior seems to add to the stunning view outside. Billed as "creative and contemporary dining," there is a good children's menu for breakfast, lunch, and dinner (dinners are $4 with salad, fresh vegetables, fries, beverage, and ice-cream cone). And there are good burgers to be had at lunch.

Adult dinners can be light (such as salads and quiche for $7 to $10), or full continental cuisine meals, including bread, salad, and fresh vegetable (from $9 to $15 for lobster, scallop, and prawn kebab). Highchairs and boosters are available, and they will warm bottles or baby food.

Rather than making reservations, they suggest that you call a half hour before you plan to arrive to put your name on the waiting list; usually there's only a 15-minute wait then. They will, however, take reservations for six or more. If you have to wait, take advantage of the park across the street and walk around Lover's Point. Open daily from 8 a.m. to 2 a.m.—dinner ends at 11 p.m. (full bar until 2 a.m.). Most major credit cards accepted. Street parking.

Inexpensive Places to Eat

Our favorite restaurant in Pacific Grove is **The First Watch,** 125 Ocean View Blvd. (tel. 408/372-1125). The great atmosphere, large portions of good food, and low prices make this a perfect breakfast or lunch place before or after your visit to the Monterey Bay Aquarium. On the border of Monterey and Pacific Grove, it's a short two-block walk along the waterfront from the aquarium to the restaurant (and surrounding shops). It's housed in the old American Tin Cannery building, and the rough cement-and-brick walls and huge two-story windows draw you back into the time when sardine canning was the big industry in Monterey.

Manager K. C. Owsley says that they choose the "right people" to be servers —people with personality who aren't afraid to have fun and help customers enjoy themselves. Rather than flee from crying children, friendly waitresses come by to see if they can raise the children's spirits.

The homey atmosphere (thermos of coffee and pitcher of water at the table) even comes across in the menu, from which children can order gourmet pancakes or luscious French toast by the amount they think they can eat. Unique breakfast items include raisin-walnut pancakes (made from scratch) and fresh vegetable frittatas. Their fresh orange juice may be the best around. Breakfast items range from $2.75 to $6. Salads and sandwiches are served too, with prices from $4 (for a Hawaiian sandwich—pineapple and sliced ham on English muffin) to $5.25 (for a classic Reuben).

Highchairs and boosters are available. Open daily from 7 a.m. to 2:30 p.m. Most major credit cards are accepted, and parking is provided in a lot across the street. Complimentary coffee is served if you have to wait.

You won't find a more beautiful setting than **Fish Wife,** located at 1996½ Sunset Dr., at Asilomar Boulevard (tel. 408/375-7101). This moderately inexpensive restaurant offers consistently good California cuisine and is off the beaten track so you don't have to compete with all the other tourists. If you go for breakfast, brunch, lunch, or an early dinner, you'll have the beauty of Asilomar to enjoy.

More than the setting, this restaurant really cares about food being healthy and nutritious, and offers special dishes to accommodate weight watchers, as well as low-sugar and low-salt dieters. And the kids will love the crayons and paper on the table. Breakfast ranges from $2.75 to $6.50 (children's breakfasts are $2 to $3.50) for such items as yogurt with blueberries, honey, juice, and muffin, or Neptune Omelette (scallops, prawns, and crab with special sauce, "air-fried" potatoes and toast). Lunches can be golden-fried calamari or red snapper sandwiches, omelets, salads, and pastas, with prices from $4 to $6. Dinners include fresh vegetables, French bread, and potatoes, ranging in price from $6.75 to $19. You can choose from soft-shell crabs meunière to New York steak with cracked peppercorns (as well as many of the sandwich, salad, and pasta selections also available at lunch). The child's plate is served with potatoes and fresh vegetables, and costs $4 to $4.50 (for chicken or fish entrees).

They'll gladly warm baby bottles and baby food, and they'll split adult entrees for kids. Highchairs and booster seats are provided. Reservations are accepted. Open every day except Tuesday from 8 a.m. to 10 p.m. Parking nearby. Some major credit cards welcome.

Located in downtown, **Toasties Café,** 702 Lighthouse Ave. (tel. 408/373-7543), is a wonderful home-style American café. "When it comes to kids, we basically do anything you want," says owner Robert Yee. That includes creating items for young palates, warming baby food, and splitting adult portions for children. This homey café boasts great country specialties made from scratch.

The corned-beef hash and Philly steak are favorites, and the pancakes, waffles, and French toast are specialties of the house. Try San Francisco Joe's Omelette (ground beef, onions, spinach, and cheese, with country potatoes, toast, or pancakes, for $5). We had French toast and blueberries (delicious) and Baby Cakes—dollar-size pancakes (25¢ each). They'll even make omelets without egg yolks for people who are watching their cholesterol intake.

Open for breakfast and lunch, Monday through Saturday from 6 a.m. to 3 p.m. and on Sunday from 7 a.m. to 3 p.m. There are highchairs and booster seats, coloring books, and crayons. Some major credit cards are accepted and street parking is available. Although you probably won't have to wait longer than 15 minutes (reservations accepted only for parties of six or more), you can use the time to wander around a few of the quaint streets in Pacific Grove. While you are waiting, or for an after-meal treat, try the little park one small block away on Caledonia and Central Avenues, which has a play area and a basketball net.

Brooks Ranch Family Dining, 401 Lighthouse Ave. (tel. 408/375-5101), is an inexpensive coffeeshop in downtown Pacific Grove that has a children's breakfast menu and children's lunch/dinner menu, and provides highchairs and boosters. During holiday season they offer kids coloring books. But they are always willing to bring crackers to the table and will warm baby bottles and baby food in the kitchen. Prices range from $3.50 to $8.

Open daily from 7 a.m. to 9 p.m. (till 10 p.m. in summer). Some major credit cards accepted. Street parking available.

3. CARMEL AND CARMEL VALLEY

Carmel-by-the-Sea (usually known as Carmel) is known worldwide as a lovers' getaway and an artists' colony. Tiny shops and outdoor cafés (and lots of cars in summer!) give Carmel its European flavor. Nestled among the Monterey cypress and other pines, with grand vistas of washed-white beaches and sapphire-colored ocean, this village is a place you'll long remember. But it is truly a town for romantic getaways, fabulous shopping, and gallery-hopping. There are places for kids to go, things for kids to do, but don't plan extended days in town (although lodging and restaurants that welcome families are abundant).

For information in advance, including a brochure called *Carmel-by-the-Sea* with art gallery listings, contact the **Carmel-by-the-Sea Business Association,** P.O. Box 4444, Carmel, CA 93921 (tel. 408/624-2522). Or stop by when you're in town—it's on the second floor of Vandervoort Court, on San Carlos between Ocean Avenue and 7th Street. The **Monterey Visitors and Convention Bureau,** 380 Alvarado St., Monterey, CA 93940 (tel. 408/649-1770), will also send you material.

WHAT TO DO AND SEE: You might want to start in **Downtown Carmel.** Beautiful stores and boutiques line Ocean Avenue and the surrounding streets. While you may be more interested in art galleries and gift stores, your youngsters will enjoy **Thinker Toys,** on the lower level of Carmel Plaza, near Dolores Street (tel. 408/624-0441). Kids are welcome to play in the store while parents browse through the array of European-made Brio toys, mobiles, model trains, radio-controlled cars, and the like. Open Monday through Saturday from 10 a.m. to 9 p.m., till 6:30 on Sunday.

When the kids get tired of shopping, one of the adults can take them to the lovely pocket park across the street from Carmel Plaza on Ocean Avenue. *One note of caution:* This area can be very crowded at peak tourist times. You may want to consider going on a weekday, or very early in the day if you have young kids.

Carmel Mission (Mission San Carlos Borromeo del Rio Carmel), located at Rio Road and Calif. 1 (tel. 408/624-3600), was the second mission founded by Fr. Junipero Serra in 1770. Set on lovely grounds, its Moorish-style tower and sandstone exterior make it one of the prettiest missions in the state. This was Fray Serra's headquarters as he continued to found missions throughout California. It is the place he chose to be buried. You can walk through and see the spartan rooms in which Fray Serra lived and the cemetery where he's buried. There is also a museum and library with displays of interesting relics of the California mission period. Open Monday through Saturday from 9:30 a.m. to 4:30 p.m., and on Sunday and holidays from 10:30 a.m. Free, but donations are welcome.

Carmel City Beach (at the end of Ocean Avenue) and **Carmel River State Beach** are two of the most magnificent beaches in California. Exotic gnarled cypress and Torrey pines grace the stretches of white sand. Although it can be chilly (and downright cold at times), we've spent hours building sand castles and flying kites at these beaches. Carmel River State Beach is a 106-acre area that also has a lagoon for frolicking and a marshy area that is a bird sanctuary. Picnic tables and rest rooms. To get to it, go south (if you're coming from Monterey) on Calif. 1. Take a right on Rio Road and a left after Carmel Mission. Continue taking left turns until you're there.

Point Lobos State Reserve, three miles south of Carmel on Calif. 1 (tel. 408/624-4909), is referred to as the "Crown Jewel" of the California state park system. It's a spectacular living museum where flocks of pelicans, gulls, and cormorants (as well as 250 other animal species and over 300 plant types) can be seen on the fantastic granite rock formations in the little coves and in the rolling meadows. The ocean is wonderfully wild here, and if you look closely, you'll notice sea otters floating offshore.

Half the reserve is an **underwater refuge,** protecting the rich and varied sea life. You can visit six different areas—the sea lion area, the cypress grove, the pine wood, Bird Island, North Shore Trail, and Whaler's Cove. This is a simply wonderful spot for children over 6, who will love everything about it—from the vividly colored wild mushrooms to the thick, lush ferns.

We always love the **Cypress Grove Trail** (a 30-minute walk starting at Sea Lion Point parking area), which wanders through the stand of Monterey cypress. The ocean views are spectacular. Another favorite of the kids is **Sea Lion Point** (30 minutes, same starting point), an easy trail that takes you to the barking sea lions and past Headland Cove, where you can see sea otters. Bring binoculars, so you can get a better look at the sea lions. There are wooden steps that lead to an overlook of Devil's Cauldron and Sea Lion Point, and if you're lucky enough to be there during the whale migration, you might see enormous blow sprays and the huge flapping tails of a gray whale.

Warning! Poison oak is abundant in the reserve. Have your children stay on trails to avoid it. Show them what it looks like so they don't touch it accidentally. Also, the wild surf and dangerous cliffs make the reserve a place where you want to hold the hands of any young child.

During the summer there are guided nature walks twice a day, and a tidepool walk in early morning when weather and tides permit. The rest of the year, check with the ranger at the entrance, as guided walks are less frequent. On weekends, when weather is clear, you can see cars lined up waiting for admittance. Go early if you want to get in. When the reserve is full, visitors are asked to wait in line and are permitted in one at a time as others leave. Plan to spend at least half a day. Open daily from 9 a.m. to 5 p.m. (in summer, slightly later). The entrance fee is $3 per vehicle, but you can also park outside the reserve and walk in.

The Barnyard shopping complex is located at the entrance to Carmel Valley on Calif. 1, off Carmel Valley Road (tel. 408/624-8886), and has over 55 shops and 11 restaurants. What is most appealing, however, is its setting—flowers, trees, walkways, and terraces create a ranch-like atmosphere. The Barnyard was born years ago with the **Thunderbird Bookshop** (see the "Where to Eat" section for details). When the owners decided to expand, they left the natural feeling of a ranch and built authentic-looking barn structures to house the new shops. You won't want to miss taking the kids to Thunderbird Bookshop. If you have time, your kids will also enjoy **Merlin's** and **Unicorn** toy stores. In addition to the Thunderbird, we enjoy eating at **From Scratch** (tel. 408/625-2448), a casual breakfast-and-lunch place that specializes in frittatas, egg dishes, quiche, soups, and salads (open daily from 7 a.m. to 3 p.m.), and **The Other Place** (tel. 408/625-0340), which has good, inexpensive American and Mexican food (open from 11 a.m. to 9 p.m. daily).

WHERE TO STAY: There are a variety of choices in Carmel.

The Upper Bracket

We like **La Playa Hotel,** Camino Real at 8th Street (P.O. Box 900), Carmel, CA 93921 (tel. 408/624-6476, or toll free 800/582-8900), an elegant, old Mediterranean-style villa that was built in 1904 and grew into a hotel—the only full-service hotel in Carmel. Located two blocks from the beach and four blocks from the central village area of Carmel, each of the 75 rooms has a view of the ocean, garden, residential Carmel, or the red-tiled patio area.

There is a beautiful outdoor swimming pool, exquisite formal gardens, lawn areas for kids to play on, and free parking for guests. Other services include nightly turn-down, concierge desk, golf and tennis, valet parking, same-day laundry (Monday through Friday), and room service from 7 a.m. to 11 p.m., with tasty items available for kids (including burgers and sandwiches; you can ask for peanut butter and jelly or other goodies, and they'll try to accommodate).

Completely refurbished in 1984, the rooms carry out the Mediterranean motif. Decorated in light, airy colors, they have hand-carved furniture, refrigerators, and hairdryers.

The Spyglass Restaurant (tel. 408/624-4010) serves breakfast, lunch, dinner, and Sunday brunch. There is the Spyglass Terrace and the wood-paneled Spyglass Lounge for cocktails. These folks are friendly and will do anything they can to help you and the kids enjoy your stay. Breakfast items average $5 to $12, lunch runs $6 to $15, and dinner prices are in the $14 to $45 range. Sunday brunch costs $14.50 per person. Major credit cards.

Room rates range from $95 to $160, single or double, and suites run $225 to $350. Children under 12 stay free in their parents' room; no charge for cribs. Children 12 and over and additional adults pay $10 per night each.

In the Moderate Range

Located at the entrance to Carmel Valley at Calif. 1 and Rio Road, the **Carmel Mission Inn,** P.O. Box 221550, Carmel, CA 93922 (tel. 408/624-1841, or toll free 800/CHATMAR, 800/348-9090 in California), enjoys the warmer weather and beauty of Carmel Valley. Surrounded by sculptured gardens and winding walkways, the inn has an outdoor heated pool and Jacuzzi that are fenced and gated for safety. Because it's located near the Barnyard shopping area, we found it convenient to wander over there when the kids wanted something to do but wanted to stay close to the hotel.

The Topiary Restaurant and Lounge (tel. 408/624-1841)—so named for the sculptured trees that surround the restaurant and hotel—is open for breakfast, lunch, and dinner and serves American and continental cuisine. For breakfast, try the yummy waffles, omelets, even eggs Benedict, which start at $3. For lunch, you can choose from salads, hot and cold sandwiches, and a buffet that includes prime rib and seafood; items cost $3.75 to $7.50. For dinner there's fish, chicken, prime rib, and steak, with prices from $11 to market price for lobster.

The 165 recently remodeled rooms are spacious and well maintained, and most open onto hallways, not parking areas. Refrigerators are available upon request and there are free in-room movies. Babysitting can be arranged. Room service is available from 7 a.m. to 10 p.m., offering such children's favorites as waffles, grilled cheese, pizza, and peanut butter sandwiches. Poolside food service is available.

Connecting rooms and suites are available. Room rates range from $72 to $119. Suites start at $195. There is no charge for cribs, and children under 17 sleep free if additional beds are not needed. Ask for seasonal and holiday special rates.

A real "find" if you like rustic ranch-style living is **Mission Ranch,** 26270 Dolores St., Carmel, CA 93923 (tel. 408/624-6436), behind the Carmel Mission at the end of Dolores. Originally a working dairy farm, the grounds are spacious and dotted with 100-year-old Monterey cypress trees and even older redwoods. The Ranch looks out onto a meadow, Point Lobos, and the Pacific Ocean. Clint Eastwood recently bought and restored it.

Wonderful for children, it occupies 20 acres (with eight tennis courts) dotted with grazing sheep and huge eucalyptus trees. In fact, the ambience is such that many families come back year after year. It's located between the Old Mission and a school, and the owners are used to having kids move through the property all the time. On weekends and during the summer, children can use the playground equipment at the school next door. If you need a babysitter, the office staff will give you a few names, and then you can make the arrangements yourself.

Mission Ranch (tel. 408/624-3824), the restaurant on the property, began serving meals in 1937. It is a funky old ranchhouse with a sing-along piano bar. Most of the tables look out onto the sheep pastures. A casual, comfortable place where the locals go to eat, it is surrounded by the grassy play area that is the ranch. The restaurant serves American cuisine and specializes in prime rib, but also serves lamb, back ribs, chicken, and fish. Prices for full dinners, which include relishes, bread, soup or salad, vegetables, and potato, are $9.25 to $18.75. The children's dinner costs $7 and includes soup, fries or rice, choice of entree, vegetable, dessert, and milk. Open for dinner every day. Major credit cards accepted.

Several kinds of accommodations are available at this ranch. Meadow- and ocean-view cottages include kitchens/kitchenettes and televisions, but only showers—no baths—and some have living rooms and multiple bedrooms. These are perfect for families and range in price from $70 to $100. There are also motel units, which range from $50 to $66. Finally, there are rooms in the Farmhouse, but these are set up for couples. Children under 16 are discouraged from staying in this area. There is no charge for cribs, but rollaways cost $10 per night. Included in the room price is a continental breakfast of cereal, croissants, fruit, juice, and beverage.

Tucked away in a quiet residential area one block from Carmel Beach, the **Colonial Terrace Inn,** on San Antonio Avenue between 12th and 13th Streets (P.O. Box 1375), Carmel, CA 93921 (tel. 408/624-2741), doesn't even look like a hotel. All rooms look out at manicured gardens or quiet courtyards, and there are grassy play areas for energetic kids.

Each of the 25 rooms is uniquely furnished. Some have fireplaces, some have refrigerators, and others have sitting rooms. Connecting rooms are available, and may be your best buy.

Because each room is different, rates vary widely. Tell the reservationist what you need when you call, and she'll help you. Here are some sample rates: rooms with one queen-size bed, $50; with two double beds, $75; with a queen-size bed and a hideabed, $110; with two queen-size beds, $110; with a queen-size bed and a double bed (with two baths), $145. No charge for cribs. All rates include a complimentary continental breakfast served in the lobby.

Bed-and-Breakfast

If you like the bed-and-breakfast concept, you'll love the **Cobblestone Inn,** at Junipero Avenue and 8th Street (P.O. Box 3185), Carmel, CA 93921 (tel. 408/625-5222, or toll free 800/222-4667). Each of the 24 guest rooms has its own entrance, and is decorated with antiques, a fireplace, telephone, color television, private bath, and fresh flowers. Fresh fruit and a refrigerator are provided in each accommodation, as are bathrobes and complimentary toiletries.

Many rooms open onto a U-shaped courtyard. But remember that this, like other older inns, doesn't have the level of soundproofing that newer hotels might have. Cross the courtyard to the living room with a fireplace, where sherry, wine, tea, and hors d'oeuvres are served every evening. Breakfast is served here too. Guests can dine inside or at tables outside for breakfast in the summer. This is great for kids because they are able to get up from breakfast and run around. The complimentary breakfast and afternoon tea and hors d'oeuvres are included in the price of a room.

Other amenities not often thought of as part of a bed-and-breakfast inn— concierge service, nightly turn-down, complimentary shoeshine, and morning newspaper—are provided here.

A room with a queen-size bed and shower rents for $90 to $105; one with a king-size bed, shower, and wet bar, $125 to $140. A two-room suite with a queen-size bed, shower, and sitting room costs $150, while the suite with the king-size bed and tub/shower combination goes for $170. All rates are for single or double occupancy. Cribs are free. Children over 4 and additional adults are charged $15 each per night.

PLACES TO EAT: Known for good food and restaurants with ambience, Carmel is a sure winner almost anywhere you go. But meals can be pricey.

The Upper Bracket

We love the **Clam Box Restaurant,** on Mission St. between Fifth and Sixth Avenues (tel. 408/624-8597), a lively, fast-moving place that serves excellent seafood and caters to families. The atmosphere is casual and the tables are close together, but it all adds to the geniality of the place. The service is fast—soup, bread, and butter are delivered immediately—and the waitresses are very agreeable. There are not only highchairs and boosters, but our kids were given crayons and coloring books to while away the time. We've heard talk that storybooks and toys often make their appearance as well.

There is a huge selection of seafood, and dinners start with both homemade soup (get the clam chowder if you like chowder) and salad. Dine on tender abalone ($23), broiled filet of salmon ($12.50), and whole Pacific lobster ($21), and enjoy. For the under-8 set there's a choice of filet of sole, old-fashioned ham, or hamburger with fries, plus soup or salad, for $5.50.

With all of this going for it, you'd expect a line—and that's what you'll get if you come after 6 p.m. (waits can be up to an hour long). No reservations are taken, but if you get there before 6 p.m., we've been assured that it is easy to get a table. Open Tuesday through Sunday from 4:30 to 9:30 p.m., this is a great place to go. If you do have to wait, take a leisurely stroll on the nearby streets, and don't miss the park, where your kids can run off any excess energy before they sit down. No credit cards accepted. Street parking.

Most people go to **Hog's Breath Inn** (yes, that's the name of the restaurant), located in central Carmel on San Carlos Street between Fifth and Sixth Avenues (tel. 408/625-1044), because Clint Eastwood owns it and is often seen there. Eastwood and his friend Walter Becker opened this unusual place 15 years ago. Most impressive is its outdoor patio, where you can lunch surrounded by trees, five fireplaces (and warming heaters), wood burl tables, and sculptures of hogs— an experience, indeed.

Even if you're not an Eastwood fan, you'll love the menu. The Dirty Harry burger is a favorite ($5.50, including soup), or there's the Eiger sandwich (roast beef, $6), and Sudden Impact (Polish sausage with jalapeño peppers on a French roll, $5.75). The dinner menu offers Coogan's Bluff (a 12-ounce steak for $18), For a Few Dollars More (you guessed it—this is a 16-ounce steak for $23), and High Plains Rancher (a large cut of prime rib for $23, a smaller one for $18). There are daily specials as well. Anything on the menu is available in a child's portion at a smaller price. Booster seats, but no highchairs, are available.

Be prepared to wait because they do a booming business and don't take reservations. (The lunch wait may be 15 minutes; dinner, from 30 minutes to 1½ hours). We suggest that you go for a drink and people-watching. It's noisy, and the staff welcomes children. So take a rest from a day's wandering, order a hot chocolate for the kids and peppermint tea (or libations from the full bar) for the adults, and enjoy.

Open daily from 11:30 a.m. to 3 p.m. for lunch, from 5 to 11 p.m. for dinner. The bar is open until 2 a.m. Street parking. Most major credit cards accepted.

Moderately Priced

A Carmel landmark, **Thunderbird Bookshop Café,** in the Barnyard, 26400 Carmel Rancho Blvd. (tel. 408/624-9414), is unique. Take your meal surrounded by 40,000 books. You can dine year round in the Solarium Patio that has a retractable glass roof and opens to the children's book section. Wooden tables and a blazing fire in the fire pit make this casual, rustic-style place a real find.

Open daily for lunch from 11 a.m. to 3:30 p.m. (with quiche, sandwiches, and pasta at about $4), and Tuesday through Sunday for dinner from 5:30 to 8 p.m. (with prime rib for $13, pasta primavera for $7.50). Highchairs and boosters are provided, and they'll warm baby bottles (but not baby food) in the kitchen. Reservations are accepted. Parking is available in the Barnyard parking lot, and major credit cards are welcome.

Country charm and excellent food are what you're likely to find at **Katy's Place,** on Mission Street between Fifth and Sixth Avenues (tel. 408/624-0199). They are famous for their eggs Benedict (they have seven different kinds, including crab, salmon, and vegetarian, starting at $6). We luxuriate in the eggs while our kids order dollar-size pancakes (at 35¢ each), all while sitting at the counter and watching the chefs.

You're given juice and coffee as soon as you sit down, and the service is generally very fast. The outside patio is lovely, and a wonderful place to sit on sunny days.

While there is no children's menu, a regular-size breakfast easily feeds two or three children, and the side orders (bacon, cereal, fruit, waffles) will satisfy any picky eater. Portions are enormous. If you like home fries, go off your diet for the home-fried red potatoes here. Open daily from 7 a.m. to 2 p.m. There are Sassy seats and boosters. No credit cards are accepted.

A wonderful find, the **Stickey Wicket English Restaurant and Tea Room,** on Dolores Street south of Ocean Avenue (tel. 408/624-9394), is a warm and welcoming place. We're crazy about traditional high teas, and have often taken even our youngest ones to dine on cucumber sandwiches, clotted cream, and scones. You'll find the experience delightful here.

High tea costs $6. Lunch may be a Cricketer's Favorite (a pub lunch of roast beef, salad, cheddar cheese, pickled onions, French roll, and butter) for $6.50, Leg Before Wicket (British steak sandwich/burger) for $5.50, the Wicketkeeper's Special (fish and chips) for $6.50, or an array of other food. There is more traditional fare for dinner, including beef bourguignon ($12), filet mignon ($13 to $16), and chicken marsala ($12).

Highchairs and boosters are available. There's no children's menu, but they will split dishes in the kitchen, and they're glad to warm baby bottles. Open daily for lunch from 11:30 a.m. to 2:30 p.m., for high tea from 2 to 4:30 p.m., and for dinner from 5 to 11 p.m. We suggest that you make reservations, especially during the summer. Most credit cards accepted. Street parking.

We love **Em Lee's,** between Fifth and Sixth Avenues on Dolores Street (tel. 408/625-6780). The food is great and the service is superb. You'll see owner Ken filling coffee cups and helping the waitresses while Marie cooks (and, boy, does she cook!). Known for her French toast (only served until 11 a.m.), Marie also serves up homemade chili and muffins for lunch, as well as lots of other scrumptious items throughout the day.

Breakfasts and lunches are of ample size, and range in price from $1.75 to $7. For kids there are eggs, bacon, pancakes, and burgers, even though there isn't a children's menu. Sassy seats and boosters are provided, and they'll gladly warm bottles and baby food. Open daily (except Superbowl Sunday) from 6 a.m. to 3 p.m. No reservations taken and you'll have to wait on weekends. Street parking. No credit cards accepted.

Picnic Supplies

Before we're off for the day, we always get a picnic basket full of goodies from the **Mediterranean Market** at the corner of Ocean Avenue and Mission

Street (tel. 408/624-2022). You'll find yummy treats here—and such nice people to help with selections. Open daily from 9 a.m. to 6 p.m.

IN AN EMERGENCY: In a medical emergency, the **Community Hospital of the Monterey Peninsula,** 23625 Holman Hwy. (tel. 408/624-5311), has the only 24-hour emergency room in the area. It also has a 24-hour pharmacy.

---

4. BIG SUR

Without doubt, Big Sur has to be 90 miles of nature's most incredible coastline. To the west, the crashing sea meets steep cliffs that jut out of the sand. Small coves of vibrant aquamarine- and sapphire-colored water greet you on many turns. Huge jagged black rocks that have tumbled into the sea are hosts to gulls and otters. To the east are pine forests and redwoods which create a veil for the wanderer in the woods and provide astonishing backdrops for hiking and camping.

Calif. 1 on the Big Sur coast (also known as Cabrillo Hwy. and the Coast Hwy.) can be some of the most treacherous driving in California. While the road is well maintained, a healthy respect for Calif. 1 is good, and caution is necessary, especially if you're not used to winding roads. Drive defensively, and—although this might sound preachy—never drive it if you have had anything to drink, or if you are fighting sleep. Also check weather conditions, as dense fog or heavy rains can make the highway difficult—if not impossible—to drive.

The drive from Monterey to Big Sur Village takes from 45 minutes to an hour. As you head south past Point Lobos, the coastline gets increasingly rugged. There are plenty of turnouts where you will undoubtedly want to stop and take pictures.

Warning! Because of the makeup of the terrain, it's easy to lose your footing. Little ones must be held by the hand. Exquisite as the vistas are, it's important to wait until you get to a big turnout or vista point where you can park.

Although the beaches are breathtakingly beautiful, don't be fooled. There are few approachable beaches, and swimming is *not* safe along the coast because of riptides and treacherous currents.

WHAT TO DO AND SEE: Probably the one Big Sur landmark that most people recognize is **Bixby Bridge.** This often-photographed bridge, with its huge arch, was built in 1932, and was considered a spectacular engineering feat. The bridge spans Bixby Canyon, where Little Bixby Creek runs. There is a turnout on the north end of the bridge.

Although there's no hiking to recommend for families here, you can drive the South Coast Road, a dirt road that winds through Bixby Canyon across the Little Sur, and comes out at Andrew Molera State Park. You travel through redwoods and high meadows, and the drive affords sensational views of the ocean.

Andrew Molera State Park, about 21 miles south of Carmel (tel. 408/667-2315), is a lovely beach and walk-in campground. Enter the park via a short driveway off Calif. 1 that leads you to the parking lot. You'll have to walk to the park (less than a mile—and it's flat). There is a river, equestrian trails, firepits, pit toilets, and drinking water.

If you like to hike, this is a great place. The Bluffs Trail is an easy two-mile trail that goes along the ocean to the bluff. The Headlands Trail is about a one-mile hike that takes you to the Headlands above the mouth of Big Sur River as it flows into the ocean. You get a beautiful view of the river, the ocean, and the canyon. The Bobcat Trail is about two miles long, taking you through the redwoods along the Big Sur River.

There is no charge for day use of the park.

Molera Trail Rides Big Sur is located here (tel. 408/625-8664). All rides are four hours long and go to the beach. Open daily from March through November. Rides are offered at 9 a.m., 1:30 p.m., and four hours before sunset. These half-day trips cost $50 per rider. Minimum age is 7. There are horses for advanced, intermediate, and beginner riders. Reservations recommended.

As you travel south from Andrew Molera State Park, you enter **Big Sur Village,** the place many consider the heart of Big Sur. This is where you can get something to eat, find a place to stay overnight, and gas up the car. (For details, check the "Places to Stay" and "Where to Eat" sections.)

Even if you're not camping, you'll enjoy a day at **Pfeiffer–Big Sur State Park,** about 26 miles south of Carmel (tel. 408/667-2315). Fabulous hiking and picnicking among the redwoods and thick forests are in store here. There's no beach access in this 820-acre forest, but the Big Sur River runs through the park.

As you enter the park (on the east side of the highway) the rangers in the Information Booth (which operates like a visitor center) will give you detailed maps and let you know if there are any current restrictions on hiking, picnicking, and camping. A Nature Center is located near the Pfeiffer Falls trailhead. The center has displays of natural history and cultural history of the area. Ask about the ranger guided walks.

The most popular hike for families with young kids is the easy half-mile trek that goes up to Pfeiffer Falls. Another one is the Oak Grove Trail (1¼ miles long) which takes off from the Pfeiffer Falls trailhead. The Valley View Trail takes off from the falls and goes up from there. (The climb is 400 feet in a distance of a half mile.) The quarter-mile trail takes you to a high point that gives you a view of the entire Big Sur Valley and Point Sur.

Kids can also fish in the river, and if you time it right, the fish can really bite.

Farther south, **Julia Pfeiffer Burns State Park** (tel. 408/667-2315) is a 1,800-acre wooded day-use park (there is no camping). In addition to telephones, rest rooms, and a picnic area with fire grills, there are several trails, some of them suitable for novice hikers. One easy trail (a third mile long) runs from the parking lot to McWay Cove, where you'll get a wonderful view of McWay Falls as it drops 50 feet into the ocean.

Farther down the coast is the **Coast Gallery** (tel. 408/667-2301), a gift store and art gallery which has a large selection of puppets as well as fine art, wood items, and ceramic pieces. There is a permanent exhibit of watercolors done by author Henry Miller, who once lived in Big Sur. The grounds on which the gallery sits has all sorts of succulents and flowering plants. This is also a good place to buy original gift items. Open daily from 9 a.m. to 5 p.m. in winter, till 6 p.m. in summer.

PLACES TO STAY: If you're lucky enough to get a room, **Big Sur Lodge** on Calif. 1 (P.O. Box 190), Big Sur, CA 93920 (tel. 408/667-2171), is a wonderful place to experience the redwood forest while having some of the comforts of home. Located within Pfeiffer–Big Sur State Park, it is only a short distance from the park entrance, which means that you and your family can enjoy the evening activities (or take sunset hikes) without having to drive anywhere afterwards.

Open year round, the lodge has a grocery store, giftshop, and restaurant. For those who are just looking around, the lodge also has one of the few public rest rooms in Big Sur.

Tucked in among the pines and redwoods, the guest cottages are on a hill surrounded by the mountains and the Big Sur countryside. Surprisingly, there's an outdoor heated swimming pool, but even when it's too cool to swim, the large grassy areas bid children to play Frisbee and tag. Other amenities include a sauna, a laundromat, and a recreation room.

Some rooms have kitchenettes (without cooking equipment), and refrigerators are available upon request. Some units accommodate up to six people, but no cribs are available.

Rates are based on the number of beds and whether or not there's a kitchen or fireplace. Summer rates start at a base of $65 to $85 for two people (one queen-size bed), and winter rates start at $50 to $70. If you want a kitchen or second bedroom, add $10 for each, and if you want a fireplace, add $15. Reservations are a necessity, especially in summer.

Big Sur Lodge Restaurant serves breakfast, lunch, and dinner in a lovely glassed-in little dining room that makes you think you're eating among the pines. With a child's dinner menu that has everything from hamburger with fries ($5.50) to squid rings ($6.50), eggplant parmesan ($8.50), and black-bean tostada ($6), your kids will find something appealing, and you'll be delighted with the place too.

Open from 8 a.m. to 11:30 a.m. for breakfast, from noon to 2 p.m. for lunch, and from 5 to 9 p.m. for dinner. Highchairs and boosters are provided, and some credit cards are accepted.

Camping

You can camp at **Andrew Molera State Park** (see the "What to Do and See" section for details about the area). This is a walk-in campground (50 sites) with a fee of 50¢ per person per night.

There is also wonderful camping at **Pfeiffer–Big Sur State Park,** Big Sur, CA 93920 (tel. 408/667-2315), which offers camping along the Big Sur River with terrain that varies from redwoods to oak groves. There is great hiking. The 218 developed sites (with table and campfire ring) run through the canyon, but no campsite is more than 300 yards away from the river. Flush toilets and showers are nearby. The sites can accommodate trailers up to 27 feet and motorhomes up to 31 feet.

During the summer there are interpretive ranger programs that include guided walks and campfire programs. The fees are $10 per campsite and $3 per extra vehicle. You can reserve through MISTIX (tel. 619/452-1950, or toll free 800/446-7275 in California).

Another place to camp is the privately owned **Ventana campground,** Calif. 1, Big Sur, CA 93920 (tel. 408/667-2331). Located on Calif. 1 just 1½ miles south of Pfeiffer–Big Sur, Ventana has 75 campsites set in among the redwoods. Each site has a fireplace and table, and there are bathrooms with hot showers nearby. The fees are $16 per night per campsite and $3 for electricity. No facilities for RVs or campers. Call in advance for reservations.

WHERE TO EAT: The world-renowned, **Nepenthe,** on Calif. 1, three miles south of Big Sur State Park (tel. 408/667-2345), sits perched high over the pounding sea and looks out onto redwoods and oaks. Magic surrounds the place. The story goes that Orson Wells bought the little house on the property for his then-new bride Rita Hayworth. She kept the place after their divorce and sold it to the family who opened Nepenthe in 1949. Movies have been filmed here, and it remains a favorite spot of some of the celebrities who live in the area. Few restaurants evoke such vivid memories after you return home, whether you have a startlingly beautiful, clear day or a foggy, cold, damp one.

The walk to the restaurant takes you up steps that follow a little fern-lined stream. It's as if you're walking deeper into the forest. You're met at the top with a breathtaking view of Big Sur (if it's not foggy). You'll see the large fire pit that rages every evening that dinner is served outdoors.

Maybe it's the feeling of being quiet and tucked away from the rest of the world, almost as if hiding its inhabitants. Maybe it's the open-air feeling inside the restaurant or the expanse of beauty surrounding you if you sit on the patio or veranda that encircles the restaurant. Quiet and inviting, it is many things to many people. Plan to spend time there.

If you dine on the terrace at night amid the candlelight with the huge fire pit blazing, you'll agree that it's one of the most romantic places on earth. But during the day it's a fabulous place to while away time having a coffee or good lunch with your family.

The patio area is especially inviting for wandering children. Large tables make family seating easy, and the wide-open spaces make it great for accommodating families with young children. Because the place is so famous, the owners are used to children trekking in and out. Crackers are brought to the table right away, or you can walk up to the bar and grab a handful yourself. Ask, and they'll bring your hungry kids carrots to munch on. If the wait is long, you'll enjoy exploring the area around the restaurant or you can visit the famous Phoenix giftshop downstairs. (You'll see it as you drive up.)

For dinner or lunch, try the famous Ambrosiaburger, a delicious ground-steak sandwich on a French roll ($7) or the wonderful French dip ($7). Also available are soup and salad ($6.25), steak sandwich ($13.75), and Holly's (crustless) quiche ($6.75). There is no children's menu, but they will gladly split adult portions into halves or thirds. Boosters and highchairs are provided. No reservations accepted. Major credit cards welcome.

Open daily (except Christmas and Thanksgiving nights and for two weeks in the winter—call ahead if you want to go in December or January to be sure it's open) from 11:30 a.m. to 4:30 p.m. for lunch, and from 5 p.m. to midnight for dinner.

While the Nepenthe is one slice of Big Sur Life, the **River Inn,** south of Big Sur Village (tel. 408/625-5255), is another. The restaurant is very modest, almost rough, but stop for a cup of coffee or a drink for the kids (Mom's homemade biscuits are good too). Go for the outdoor treat as well. Where else can you find a river (the Sur) with a rock sculpture garden? Where else would you see people with table and chairs *in* the river enjoying the morning sun? As you enter, get your food and walk outside to the chairs on one of the two wooden decks or sit on the grass looking out to the river. If it's warm, the kids can play in the shallow water—or they can swim in the inn's swimming pool (no charge). The changing room/bathroom area isn't what you might hope it to be, but it is adequate for changing into swimsuits.

Open for breakfast, lunch, and dinner. Choose from full American breakfast —home fries, trout and eggs, bacon ($4.50 to $7). Lunch is soup, salads, and sandwiches, which range in price from $4.50 to $5.50. Dinners are pasta, fish, or beef, and cost $6 to $8 (including soup or salad, entree, potato, vegetable, and bread). Highchairs and boosters are provided.

Local musicians perform nightly from 7:30 p.m.; there's jazz on Saturday and Sunday. Open daily in summer from 8 a.m. to 9 p.m.; the rest of the year, Tuesday through Friday from 5 to 9 p.m. and on Saturday, Sunday, and Monday from 8 a.m. to 9 p.m. No credit cards accepted. Reservations not needed.

SAN LUIS OBISPO COUNTY

Farther south you'll come to beautiful San Luis Obispo County, a region of green rolling hills dotted with cattle and occasional ranches. Edged by an exquisite, rugged coastline that gives way to high sand dunes, this part of the central coast is the transition from northern California seascape to southern California beaches.

San Luis Obispo County is like an undiscovered jewel for traveling families. The towns of San Luis Obispo and San Simeon offer the historical and cultural riches of the Mission and Hearst Castle, while the beach towns of Pismo, Avila, and Morro Bay have all kinds of outdoor gems. Cambria adds a little artistic flavor to the mix.

The county is small, so you can choose to stay at one end and visit the other, and since it's located midway between San Francisco and Los Angeles, it's a perfect place to spend a few days on a trek from one big city to the other.

From San Francisco, you can choose to take either U.S. 101 South, or the coast route (Calif. 1). If you're coming from the north on Calif. 1 via Big Sur, you'll pass San Simeon, so you might want to tour the castle on your way south, rather than backtrack.

To get to San Luis Obispo County from Los Angeles, just take U.S. 101 North. (You'll have to take Calif. 1 to Morro Bay, Cambria, and San Simeon.)

Greyhound Bus Lines also services this area (tel. 805/543-2121 for information; you can get the toll-free number for your area by dialing 800/555-1212). In addition, **Amtrak** offers daily service on the *Coast Starlight* (tel. 805/541-0505, or toll free 800/USA-RAIL).

Before you start, you might want to contact the friendly folks at the **San Luis Obispo County Visitors and Conference Bureau,** at 1041 Chorro St., Suite E, San Luis Obispo, CA 93401 (tel. 805/541-8000, or toll free 800/643-1414). They have an enormous array of helpful information about the entire county.

5. SAN SIMEON / CAMBRIA

Located in the northern part of San Luis Obispo County, the town of San Simeon straddles Calif. 1 and is divided into two sections: one is near the entrance to Hearst Castle; the other is a few miles south and has lodging and a few restaurants. The main attraction, of course, is Hearst Castle, that palatial structure created by William Randolph Hearst. You may be surprised that it is a trip you can take with children who are over the age of 6 (and infants who will sleep through it).

Cambria is a tiny artists' colony tucked into the rolling hills that snuggle up to the coastline just a few minutes south of San Simeon. After the bustle of city sightseeing, a few hours roaming Cambria Village or wandering in the surrounding hills and on the coast is like taking a deep breath of relaxation. Known by the slogan "Where the pines meet the sea," this is a special family town that is located on Calif. 1.

Because the towns are so close together, you can easily stay in a motel in San Simeon and have your meals in Cambria.

WHAT TO DO AND SEE IN SAN SIMEON: Most people stop in San Simeon because they want to see **Hearst Castle** (really, Hearst–San Simeon State Historical Monument), located off Calif. 1 just north of Cambria (tel. 805/927-4621). The castle is an impressive monument built over the course of 28 years (begun in 1919) by publishing magnate William Randolph Hearst. Our kids are usually excited when we tell them they're going to see a castle, and, indeed, even 6-year-olds can appreciate the wealth that was needed to create this fantastic dwelling. Also known as "La Casa Grande," the castle looks like a Mediterranean-style cathedral with gilt towers, plazas, and incredibly beautiful gardens, and sits on 120 acres known as La Cuesta Encantada, "The Enchanted Hill."

The buildings are only part of the treat. The castle has more than 100 rooms that serve as museum space for the eclectic treasures that Hearst collected during his lifetime. There are priceless antiques, rich tapestries, beautiful Oriental rugs, and all kinds of unusual art objects.

We love to talk with our kids about how it would feel to live in the castle. They always respond that they'd get lost! But the question gets them to look at the art objects a little more closely—if even for a brief period. The kids seem

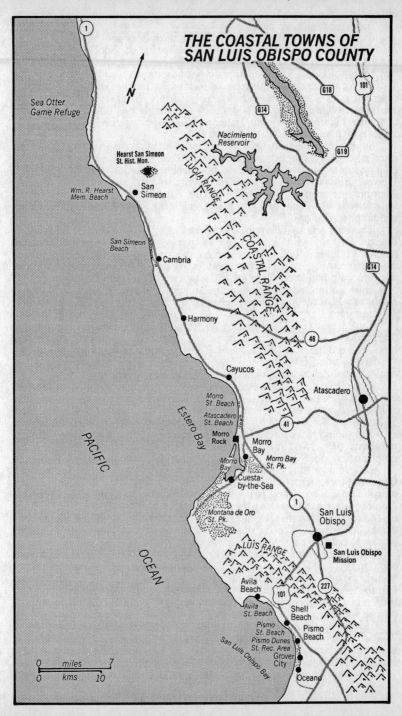

THE COASTAL TOWNS OF SAN LUIS OBISPO COUNTY

Sea Otter
Game Refuge

Hearst San Simeon
St. Hist. Mon.

Wm. R. Hearst
Mem. Beach

San
Simeon

San Simeon
Beach

● Cambria

● Harmony

Nacimiento
Reservoir

SANTA LUCIA RANGE

COASTAL RANGE

● Cayucos

Morro
St. Beach

Atascadero
St. Beach

Morro
Rock

Morro
Bay

Morro
Bay

Morro Bay
St. Pk.

Cuesta-
by-the-Sea

Estero Bay

Montana de Oro
St. Pk.

PACIFIC

OCEAN

Atascadero ●

SAN LUIS RANGE

San Luis
Obispo

San Luis Obispo
Mission

Avila
Beach

Avila
St. Beach

Pismo
St. Beach

Pismo Dunes
St. Rec. Area

San Luis Obispo Bay

Shell
Beach

Pismo
Beach

Grover
City

Oceano

miles
0   7

kms
0   10

impressed by the sheer size and numbers of things they see around them, whether they deem them valuable or not.

Our children's favorite part of the tour is the indoor pool with the 22-karat-gold inlaid tile. The room is dimly lit and the spectacular pool is still and looks like it's filled with liquid glass. They even appreciate the gardens, although they have to stay on the walkways and remain with the group.

We recommend this sightseeing attraction for families with children 6 and older, but even 6- and 7-year-olds need to be fairly sophisticated to really appreciate the surroundings for 1¾ hours. The five-minute bus ride up (then again, down) the hill from the Visitor Center parking to the castle itself adds a few more minutes each way that children must sit still.

Some people find it helpful to carry a few little toys to give the kids as their interest wanes and they become impatient to leave. We saw one little boy contentedly playing with a hand-size plastic robot whenever he lost interest in the tour. However, this really isn't the place for preschoolers, and strollers are not allowed. All tours are considered walking tours. They tell people that they must be able to walk at least a half mile and climb 150 stair steps (there are separate tours for handicapped visitors).

There are several different tours of the castle. Tour 1 is the one you should take on your first visit. It gives you an overview. You'll see one of the guest houses, a beautiful section of the garden, the first floor of the castle (which includes the movie theater—always a shocker for the kids), the Neptune Pool, and the indoor Roman Pool. There are 150 stair steps in this tour.

Tour 2 is limited to a small group, and includes some of Hearst's personal rooms as well as the library and kitchen. You'll also see the two pools. There are 377 stair steps.

Tour 3, also a small-group tour, takes you through the "new wing" of over 30 bedrooms, sitting rooms, and bathrooms, and a video about Mr. Hearst's famous guests during the '20s and '30s. There are 316 stair steps.

Tour 4, another small-group tour, is the garden tour and doesn't go into the castle. It includes the largest guesthouse. There are 306 stair steps.

Open daily except Thanksgiving, Christmas, and New Year's Days. The ticket office is open from 8 a.m. to 4 p.m., and tours are scheduled every hour from 8:20 a.m. to 3 p.m. in winter and more frequently during holidays and summer. Tickets cost $10 for adults, $5 for children 6 to 12; children under 6 are free.

You should make reservations before you leave home. MISTIX is the place to call (tel. 619/452-1950, or toll free 800/444-7275 in California). The office is open daily from 9 a.m. to 6 p.m.

Believe it or not, there are other attractions in San Simeon. **Sebastian's General Store,** across from the castle entrance (tel. 805/927-4217), is an oldtime general store and post office that has a little something for everyone. Don't be surprised if you have the urge to "tie up your horse" out in front. Built in 1852, the store offers a potpourri of knickknacks, toys, kid's books, cold drinks, and snacks. Of course there are lots of Hearst Castle souvenirs. There is a snackbar/outdoor café that is open daily from 8:30 a.m. to 6 p.m.

We also like **Bleschyu Golf Park,** 2285 Fandown, between Hearst Castle and Cambria (tel. 805/927-4221), an 18-hole miniature golf course. A round of miniature golf will cost $3 for adults, $2 for kids 11 and under. The kids will also love the video arcade, and teens will enjoy the pool tables. Open daily from noon to 10 p.m. in summer, weekends from noon to 10 p.m. and weekdays from 3 to 9 p.m. in winter.

If you're in the mood for kite flying, you might pick one up at **Kastle Kites,** 250 San Simeon Ave. in the Plaza del Cavalier (tel. 805/927-5483). Open in winter Sunday through Thursday from 10 a.m. to 6 p.m., till 9 p.m. on Friday and Saturday; in summer, daily from 10 a.m. to 9 p.m.

Now that you've got your kites, choose from one of the local beaches for a place to fly them. **William Randolph Hearst Memorial State Beach** in San Simeon is a day-use area. You can see the castle off on the hill while you enjoy the sandy beach. This is where the **San Simeon Pier** is located. This 700-foot-long wooden pier offers pier fishing and is the starting point for fishing excursions and whale-watching tours. **Virg's Fish'N** (tel. 805/927-4676) will rent you what you need. Open March through October from 5 a.m. to 4 p.m., this is where you can rent pier poles ($3) and other equipment. Virg's offers half-day, full-day, and "long-range" trips for cod fishing. The half-day trips are from 8 a.m. to noon, and cost $16 for adults, $14 for juniors and seniors. Full-day trips are from 6:30 a.m. to 2:30 p.m., and adults pay $27; juniors and seniors pay $23. Long-range trips (on Sunday, Wednesday, and Friday only) last from 6 a.m. to 4 p.m.; the fare for adults is $30, $26 for juniors and seniors. Rod rentals are $5 to $7. Bait is included in the price of a ticket. Call ahead for reservations because some trips don't run every day.

WHAT TO DO AND SEE IN CAMBRIA:

Now to the tiny neighbor just a bit south. **Cambria Village** is actually two little stretches of shops, galleries, and restaurants, called East Village (or "Old Town") and West Village. Main Street connects both parts of the quaint village. Plan to spend part of the day meandering through the village shops. Even though some kids don't enjoy shopping, the surrounding area offers lots of places for them to play, and there are a few shops they'll love.

Two of these shops we think of as highpoints of any trip to the area. **The Soldier Factory,** 789 Main St. (tel. 805/927-3805), is a factory and museum of miniature soldiers from every era, starting from medieval times to World War II. There are little plastic soldiers, tin soldiers, porcelain soldiers; some are displayed in battle with arms raised, others on horseback. Owner Jack Scruby started the factory when he began to cast and paint soldiers himself and became completely engrossed in the hobby. He continued to make soldiers and began selling the miniatures via mail order. Today you can watch them cast soldiers and other miniature figures, such as the Scarecrow from *The Wizard of Oz* and Merlin the Magician from *King Arthur*.

Open daily from 10 a.m. to 5 p.m., except Christmas and Thanksgiving Days.

Nearby is a wonderful little shop, **McKinney's Gems and Mineral Store,** 777 Main St. (tel. 805/927-4742). Not only is there an exciting collection of rocks for the kids to peruse, but the owner loves to talk with children about his collection. There are rocks for sale, some for as little as 50¢. Open daily from 10 a.m. to 5 p.m.

Kids can start their own rock collection at **Moonstone Beach and Shamel Park,** on Moonstone Beach Drive. The beach is beautiful—and great for rock collecting. You can find moonstones, quartz, and petrified wood, but be careful not to swim here—the water is too cold and the undertow too strong for safe swimming. Adjacent Shamel Park has a complete playground, huge grassy area, barbecue pits, and bathrooms with changing areas for sandy children.

By bicycle or on foot, **Santa Rosa Creek Road** makes a great all-family activity. This peaceful rural road winds through a beautiful little farm valley where we enjoy looking at cattle ranches, farms, and orchards. (You can also enjoy the drive in your car.) Start at Santa Rosa Creek Road where it intersects Main Street. While the road is narrow, locals know to watch out for bicyclists. But be advised anyway. As we travel through the pass, we stop at **Linn's Fruit Bin,** five miles east of Main Street (tel. 805/927-8134). In days past we actually picked berries at Linn's, but the Linn family has since changed the place so that now it offers fresh fruit, fresh-baked pies, and beverages instead. Take your goodies and enjoy the shade while the kids play on the homemade rope swing. Open daily in winter from 10 a.m. to 5 p.m.; in summer from 9 a.m. to 6 p.m.

Bicycle Rentals

For those bicycles you might need, **Cambria Bicycle Outfitters,** 1920 Main St. (tel. 805/927-5510), rents a wide selection of mountain bikes. They have baby carriers, but only smaller bikes (for kids around 12), not bicycles for little kids. They have helmets and also rent car racks. Bikes rent for $6 for an hour, $10 for two hours; it's $20 for an 8-hour day, $25 for a 24-hour day. Reservations are advised. Open daily from 10 a.m. to 6 p.m.

WHERE TO STAY: Just a short walk from the ocean, the **Sands Motel,** 9355 Hearst Dr., San Simeon, CA 93452 (tel. 805/927-3243), is a pleasant 32-room place to stay. The motel has a real luxury—an indoor swimming pool that is heated and warm enough to keep even the most finicky child comfortable. The pool has a gate with a high latch so toddlers can't wander off, and a nice three-foot shallow area.

At the beach, the winds are great, and there is plenty of room for flying kites, but the beach isn't good for swimming. This is "rock heaven," so let those little rock collectors go to it.

A free continental breakfast is served each morning in the office. The friendly managers will be glad to warm baby bottles or baby food for you in their little kitchen.

The rooms are average-sized and most have tub/shower combinations. Some rooms have two queen-size beds, and there's still room for a crib or rollaway. In-room amenities include shampoo and hair conditioner, and coffee makers. There is color TV and free HBO.

Rates in season (mid-May to September) range from $42 to $62 single, $53 to $73 double, and $63 to $83 for suites. Cribs and rollaways cost $6 per night. Additional guests pay $6 per night. Rates are lower the rest of the year; check when you make reservations.

Another budget motel close to the castle is the **San Simeon Lodge,** 9520 Castillo Dr., San Simeon, CA 93452 (tel. 805/927-4601). There is a large grassy area where kids can play (but it opens onto the parking lot, so be careful), and an outdoor pool that is heated year round. The fenced-in pool is locked.

The adjacent San Simeon Restaurant is open from 7 a.m. to 2 p.m. and 5 to 9 p.m., and serves three meals a day. It has highchairs and booster seats. Meals range from $4 to $10.

The 63 rooms are clean and simple, and some are large enough to comfortably accommodate families—when you make your reservations, let them know how many are in your group. Some rooms have ocean views, and king- or queen-size beds are available.

Rates in season (May to September) are $48 to $59, single or double; $5 extra for each additional person. Cribs and rollaways cost $5 per night. The rest of the year the rates are $35 to $50, single or double.

WHERE TO EAT: Let's start with the **Brambles Dinner House,** 4005 Burton Dr., two blocks off Main Street in Cambria (tel. 805/927-4716). This is one of the most famous restaurants on the coast. This colorful cottage has an old-world ambience and is adorned with antique plates and a fabulous clock collection. The fireplace and candlelight give the restaurant a quiet, cozy feel. The Brambles was built in 1874 as a family home and was converted to a restaurant in 1965. There are several dining rooms, each with its own mood.

Hot bread is set on the table as soon as you sit down. Known for great prime rib with traditional Yorkshire pudding, steaks, and seafood (there's also chicken and ribs), the delicious dinners are sizable and include soup or salad, baked potato, and peas. Prices range from $10 to $16.

There are not only highchairs and boosters, but "junior chairs" for children in-between. The children's menu is extensive and prices range from $4 to $7, or they'll be glad to split an adult portion for two kids and add $5 for extra salad and potato. With a full bar, they're able to fix all kinds of special drinks for the kids.

Open Monday through Saturday from 5 to 10 p.m. and on Sunday from 4 to 9 p.m. Reservations are advised. Major credit cards accepted. Street parking.

The **Chuck Wagon Restaurant,** at Moonstone Beach Drive and Calif. 1 in Cambria (tel. 805/927-4644), offers an all-you-can-eat buffet for lunch and dinner. You can choose from the complete salad bar, plus fried chicken and gravy, fried fish, vegetables, ham, ribs, or turkey and dressing. Lunch costs $4.50; dinner, $6.50.

Don't expect anything fancy, but the home-style cooking is good, and you can have as much of it as you'd like. Children's prices are about $1.75 (for ages 2 to 5), $2.75 (for ages 6 to 9), $4.50 (for ages 10 and 11). Highchairs and boosters are available.

Open daily from 11 a.m. to 8 p.m. in winter, to 9 p.m. in summer. Call ahead—sometimes they don't open until 11:30 a.m. No reservations or credit cards accepted. Parking lot.

For breakfast, you might try the **Upper Crust Bakery and Tea Room,** 2214 Main St., Cambria (tel. 805/927-8227), for home-baked specialties made from scratch. There are fresh fruited yogurt muffins and carrot and apple bran muffins, croissants, vegetable soup, cream of asparagus soup, and Cornish meat pasties. Prices range from $1 to $2.50 for individual items. European and French roast coffee and teas are served. There are boosters, but no highchairs, in this tiny tea room.

Open Monday, Tuesday, and Thursday through Saturday from 5 a.m. to 5 p.m., on Sunday from 7 a.m. to 3 p.m.; closed Wednesday. No reservations or credit cards accepted. Parking lot.

6. MORRO BAY / SAN LUIS OBISPO / PISMO BEACH

The towns in southern San Luis Obispo County are clustered together in a small area. Surrounding them are wide open spaces. We'll start at Morro Bay, then go to the towns of San Luis Obispo and Pismo Beach.

MORRO BAY: This sleepy little seaside village of fewer than 10,000 residents is the place to go when you want to slow down and relax. Named for Morro Rock (also called "The Gibraltar of the Pacific"), a 576-foot monolith that is one of seven extinct volcanoes in the area, Morro Bay offers lots of outdoor family fun.

There is a long peninsula of sand dunes that separates Morro Bay from the ocean. These dunes, called **Morro Bay Sandspit,** can be as high as 85 feet, providing lots of roaming area.

Morro Bay has been designated a bird sanctuary, and you can see more than 100 kinds of birds in the nearby estuary in Morro Bay State Park. Take your binoculars and watch for egrets, kingfishers, pelicans, and herons. Morro Bay also hosts monarch butterflies. In October the orange-and-black beauties migrate to the area, seeking warmth in the stands of eucalyptus that are throughout the region.

For further information, contact the **Morro Bay Chamber of Commerce,** 895 Napa (P.O. Box 876), Morro Bay, CA 93442 (tel. 805/772-4467). The **San Luis Obispo County Visitors and Conference Bureau,** at 1041 Chorro St., Suite E, San Luis Obispo, CA 93401 (tel. 805/541-8000, or toll free 800/643-1414), is also helpful.

What to See and Do

The **Embarcadero** is the place to get the true flavor of this fishing village. An oceanfront strip, loaded with gift stores, restaurants, and fish markets, this is where you'll get great views of Morro Rock and the sand dunes, and enjoy the sea with its otters, sea gulls, and fresh ocean breezes. You can watch fishermen preparing for the day or unloading their catch.

The **Morro Bay Aquarium,** 595 Embarcadero (tel. 805/772-7647), is a very small place, but one you'll want to stop at with the family. The owners take in injured and abandoned sea otters and seals and nurse them back to health. Working with the Department of Fish and Game, they release the recovered animals back to the sea. You can see the ones they're doctoring as well as 300 other saltwater specimens. Open daily in summer from 9 a.m. to 7 p.m., to 6 p.m. in winter; closed major holidays. The admission fee is $1 for adults, 50¢ for children 5 to 11; free for children under 5.

Many families enjoy a one-hour cruise on the paddlewheeler *Tiger's Folly II,* 1205 Embarcadero, departing from the Harbor Hut restaurant dock (tel. 805/772-2257 or 805/772-2255). The cruise stays within the calm waters of Morro Bay. Tickets cost $6 for adults, $3 for children. Call for the cruise schedule. Note that Sunday brunch cruises depart at 10 a.m. and noon.

A really fun place to go with the kids is the **Giant Chess Board,** located at Morro Bay Boulevard and the Embarcadero (tel. 805/772-1214). These life-size wooden chess pieces were carved by the music director of the high school, and are used to . . . yes, play "life-size" games of chess. It's fun to watch, even if you don't understand the game. Anyone can play, as long as you have a reservation. Make them at the Recreation and Parks Department at 535 Harbor St. Open from 8 a.m. to 5 p.m. The fee is $7.50.

How about a tour of a **Coast Guard cutter?** The boats are docked at the Embarcadero, and the public can tour them on weekends when they're not out on patrol. Call the day you want to tour (tel. 805/772-2167). Kids delight in exploring the Coast Guard patrol boats—the bridge, the search-and-rescue equipment, and the hold. No admission fee.

You can also drive to **Morro Rock.** Take Embarcadero north till it turns toward the Rock. Follow it. You'll pass little Coleman Park on the way, with its smattering of playground equipment. But be sure to get all the way to the Rock. The views looking north are exquisite. With the Rock and breakwater, huge waves file in, one after another, giving you a strong sense of the power of the ocean. You're likely to see surfers and sunbathers as you look north toward Atascadero and Morro Strand State Beaches.

Morro Bay Marina, 699 Embarcadero (tel. 805/772-8085), offers "taxi" service across the bay to the **Morro Bay Sand Dunes.** Taxi service is available daily in summer, and Friday through Monday in the winter. Round-trip fares are $3 for adults, $1.50 for children.

Virg's Fish'N, 1215 Embarcadero (tel. 805/772-1222), offers full-day and half-day sportfishing trips for rock cod. Full-day trips are from 7 a.m. to 3 p.m. and cost $25 for adults and $21 for children (12 and under) and seniors. Rod rental is $5 to $7.

The half-day trips are from 9 a.m. to 1 p.m. and 3:30 to 7 p.m. April through October, or 1:30 to 5 p.m. November to March, and cost $16 for adults and $14 for children and seniors. Rod rental is $3. Bait is included with all rentals.

There are also 2½-hour whale-watching trips between December 26 and mid-March. Dates for trips vary, so call ahead for information and reservations. Boats leave at 11 a.m. and 2 p.m. Rates are $11 for adults, $6 for children and seniors. You can also rent pier poles here at $3 for 24 hours (additional deposit required).

Virg's Fish'N is open daily from 5:30 a.m. to 6 p.m. and later (depending on scheduled trips).

This entire area is a great place for kite flying, and you'll find a terrific selection at **Kites Galore,** at the corner of Embarcadero and Beach Street (tel. 805/772-8322). They are open daily from 9 a.m. to 6 p.m.

STATE PARKS AND BEACHES. Lovely **Morro Bay State Park** is a pretty state park with Monterey pines, eucalyptus, and a large marshy area that is home to more than 250 species of birds. The marsh serves as a bird reserve. In the park on State Park Road is the **Morro Bay Museum of Natural History** (tel. 805/772-2694). Don't miss it, if just to take in the view alone. At White Point, a rocky point that rises above the bay, kids can easily climb the trail to the top to see where the Native Americans used to grind their corn. The museum has displays that explain the natural history of the area—Morro Rock, the lagoon, the large numbers of birds, and the local Chumash Indians. There is a telescope for viewing the shoreline. Call ahead to see if they have any special docent-led family programs scheduled. Open daily from 10 a.m. to 5 p.m. Closed major holidays. Admission is $1 for adults, 50¢ for children 6 to 17; under 6, free.

Montana de Oro State Park (literally "Mountain of Gold") is located along the coast just 11 miles south of Morro Bay. To get to the park, take the Los Osos / Baywood Park exit off Calif. 1. Many people refer to this 7,000-acre area as "petite Big Sur," with its rugged terrain and stony cliffs. Spooner's Cove is a secluded little swimming area of aquamarine-colored water that you and the kids will love. You'll find lots of wonderful hikes in this area that offer splendid views of the coastal bluff or forest streams—and colorful wildflowers in season. Many of the hikes are great with the little ones. Kids will love watching the sea otters at play in the area.

If you have the stamina, one of the great walks in the region starts at the trail called Hazard Reef (which is a short walk through a eucalyptus grove to the beach —where there are tidepools) and continues on to the Morro Bay Sandspit area of high dunes. Don't expect to do a lot because walking in the dunes is hard work, but worth the effort.

The campground here is tucked in among the trees, across from the beach. There are 46 tent or motorhome sites, but no hookups. There are barbecue pits for picnickers.

For more information, contact the rangers c/o Morro Bay State Park, Morro Bay, CA 93442 (tel. 805/772-2560 in summer, 805/772-8812 the rest of the year).

Atascadero State Beach, just north of Morro Rock, is a popular beach because the waves are gentle here and the location is lovely. It's a good place for kids. Rest rooms, showers, and dressing rooms are available.

Morro Strand State Beach is north of Atascadero State Beach. This is a long, sandy beach, with usually gentle waves. Rest rooms and picnic tables are available.

Where to Stay

There are lots of little motels in this nautical town. But if you plan to come during the summer, book your room far ahead—at least a month.

The **Embarcadero Inn,** 456 Embarcadero, Morro Bay, CA 93442 (tel. 805/772-2700, or toll free 800/292-ROCK), is a tastefully decorated motor inn located on the waterfront. The inn is quite comfortable and has nice large rooms that offer lovely views of Morro Rock and the bay it rests in. We enjoyed sunset on the balcony, watching the white-capped water shimmer in the dimming light. There are two Jacuzzis on the premises. All rooms face the bay, and 30 have balconies.

This little 32-room inn has lots of nice touches. Every room has a refrigerator, VCR (cassettes are on loan at the office—or bring your own), and remote-control color TV. There are fireplaces, fresh-perked coffee, and an amenity basket with Neutrogena soap, shampoo, and sunscreen. Some rooms have fireplaces. Free local calls.

The rooms are generously sized, with plenty of space for cribs and rollaways.

Rates vary and are based on room location and number of beds. Single or double, they cost $50 to $105 in winter and $65 to $130 in summer. Suites feature living rooms with wet bars, fireplaces, and refrigerators, and they range in price from $75 to $125. Each additional person (over two in a room) pays $10 per night (except for children under 12). Cribs cost $5; rollaways, $10. Higher rates are in effect during special events.

Another pleasant motel in the heart of Morro Bay is **The Villager,** 1098 Main St., at Beach Street, Morro Bay, CA 93442 (tel. 805/772-1235). The good-size rooms have fireplaces, game tables, and free HBO. There is also a Jacuzzi.

The 22 rooms have amenities you might not expect in a motel—hairdryers, coffee makers in the room, plush towels, and complimentary shampoo. All rooms have showers, no tubs.

The managers are very friendly here. In fact, they put extra towels in a bottom dresser drawer in the two-bedded rooms in case you need more linens.

Rooms come with either one king-size bed, two double beds, or a double bed and a queen-size bed. Connecting rooms are available; ask about special rates. Rates range from $40 to $65 single and $45 to $70 double. Each additional person pays $6 per night (but in winter, children stay free). Cribs and rollaways cost $6. Higher rates are in effect during Poly Royal (April), Poly graduation (June), and the mid-state fair days (August).

The **Sunset Travelodge,** 1080 Market Ave., Morro Bay, CA 93442 (tel. 805/772-1259, or toll free 800/255-3050), is another budget alternative. Within walking distance of the Embarcadero, this 32-room motel has a nice heated pool, a Jacuzzi, and a lovely upstairs glassed-in sundeck. The inviting deck has tables, chairs, and lounges, just perfect for Mom and Dad to use while sunning as the kids play nearby.

All rooms have free HBO, separate vanity areas, and coffee makers. Some have kitchenettes and some have tub/shower combinations (request these when you reserve your room).

Rates range from $38 to $50 single and $43 to $60 double. Each additional person pays $6 (except in winter when children stay free). Suites rent for $56 to $75. Cribs and rollaways cost $6. Higher rates are in effect during special events.

CAMPING. You'll find a lot of good camping in this area. **Morro Bay State Park** has 135 developed campsites with tables and stoves. Rest rooms with showers and laundry tubs are available. Trailers or motorhomes (up to 31 feet) can be accommodated, and there are 20 sites with water and electricity hookups. Sanitation station available.

Atascadero State Beach has 100 developed campsites, but no showers nearby. The sites can accommodate trailers and motorhomes up to 24 feet long.

For information about the above campgrounds, write c/o Morro Bay State Park, Morro Bay, CA 93442 (tel. 805/772-2560), or make your reservations through a MISTIX outlet or call for a registration form (tel. 619/452-1920, or toll free 800/446-7275 in California).

For information about **Montana de Oro State Park,** see the "What to Do and See" section.

Where to Eat

You'll enjoy a meal at **Dorn's, the Original Breakers Café,** 801 Market St. (tel. 805/772-4415). It sits on a hill overlooking the Embarcadero and the bay, and commands a beautiful view. Morro Rock is directly ahead of you.

This seafood restaurant is moderately priced and offers good fresh food for breakfast, lunch, and dinner. It is famous for its buttermilk pancakes, waffles, and omelets at breakfast, and for its delicious fresh fish at lunch and dinner. (The marinated seafood salad is one of the best; it has large chunks of shrimp, crab, calamari, and lobster mixed in among the tossed greens—$10.25). Breakfast is served from 7 a.m. to 2 p.m. and prices range from $2.50 to $9. Lunch is served from 11 a.m. to 4 p.m. and prices range from $3.75 to $9. Dinner is served from 4 to 10 p.m. and prices range from $8 to $21.50.

The child's plate costs $5 for fish and chips, ground sirloin, or chicken. Or order the generous shrimp cocktail appetizer for $4.75.

There are highchairs and booster seats available. The waiter brought fresh fruit for our baby, so she could have something while we were all eating. The service is friendly and fast all around.

Open from 7 a.m. to 10 p.m. You need reservations, but there can still be a wait during peak hours. (It's so beautiful, though, you can just take a walk.) No credit cards accepted. Street parking.

Another choice is the **Galley Restaurant,** 899 Embarcadero (tel. 805/772-2806). This family-owned restaurant serves up a delicious selection of seafood, sandwiches, steaks, and salads. The bay shrimp salad is a favorite, and the fish and chips are crispy but not oily. Lunches range from $4 to $8.75. Dinners include chowder, salad, bread, potatoes or rice, beverage, and dessert, and range from $9.25 to $25. À la carte entrees (including bread and potato or rice) cost $6.25 to $22. The children's dinner special is $4.50 for a choice of fish or ground beef, and the only difference (besides size) from the adult meal is a choice of soup or salad.

Highchairs and boosters are available, and the waiter will bring crackers to the table right away. Open daily for lunch and dinner from 11 a.m. to 8:30 p.m. in winter, till 11 p.m. in summer. Closed from Thanksgiving to December 26. Some credit cards accepted. Street parking.

SAN LUIS OBISPO:

SAN LUIS OBISPO: Nestled in the hills of the Santa Lucia mountain range, San Luis Obispo is a charming, small city (population about 35,000), with an eclectic mixture of early California buildings and small Victorian-style frame houses.

Originally established in 1772 with the founding of San Luis Obispo Mission by Fr. Junipero Serra, it is the cultural and historical center of the county. It has two colleges (California Polytechnic and Cuesta College), a Mozart festival, and a symphony orchestra.

For maps, a calendar of events, and all sorts of information on sights, contact the **San Luis Obispo Chamber of Commerce,** 1039 Chorro St., San Luis Obispo, CA 93401 (tel. 805/543-1323), open seven days a week. The **San Luis Obispo County Visitors and Conference Bureau,** at 1041 Chorro St., Suite E, San Luis Obispo, CA 93401 (tel. 805/541-8000, or toll free 800/643-1414), is also helpful.

What to See and Do

Probably the first place to start your visit is at **Mission San Luis Obispo de Tolosa,** at Chorro and Monterey Streets (tel. 805/543-6850). Founded in 1772 by Fray Serra and José Cavaller, and named for the French saint, Louis, bishop of Toulouse, the mission was the 5th of the 21 missions in the state. It is simple and small, but has a charming little garden that you'll want to spend some time wandering through. Inside, point out to the kids the hand-painted stenciled walls, the simple windows, the huge wood-beamed ceilings, and the wooden pews.

The Mission Museum has artifacts from the local Chumash Indians, and it offers a glimpse into the lifestyles of the Spanish settlers.

Open daily from 9 a.m. to 4 p.m., till 5 p.m. in summer. A donation of $1 (or $2 per family) is requested. Closed major holidays.

Bordering the mission is **Mission Plaza,** at Monterey and Chorro Streets, a tree-filled area with the San Luis Creek running through. This town square offers many shady places to stop for a picnic lunch, just rest, or let the kids run around.

It serves as a gathering area for townsfolk and visitors alike. If you're lucky, you may happen upon a concert in the park. You can walk through Mission Plaza to the downtown shopping area of Higuera Street.

Across from the plaza is the **San Luis Obispo County Historical Museum,** 696 Monterey St. (tel. 805/543-0638), which gives you a look at the county's Native American and Victorian past. There are interesting photographs, and exhibits depicting the life of the local Chumash Indians.

Open Wednesday through Sunday from 10 a.m. to 4 p.m.; closed Monday, Tuesday, and major holidays. No admission charge.

If you want to browse or shop, lots of specialty stores that are located on Higuera Street (one of the streets that border the plaza) back up to San Luis Creek and have entrances creek side. The best shopping is between Chorro and Broad Streets.

Your kids might like one of the **Heritage Walks** of San Luis Obispo. The four walks include different highlights of the town—Downtown, the Historic Core, Old-Town Residential, and an Adobe–Railroad District Walk. You can pick up a map at the above-mentioned Visitor Center and begin your tour at Mission Plaza.

Every Thursday night you can join in the festivities at San Luis Obispo's **Farmer's Market.** Higuera Street is closed to automobiles and several blocks are filled with tables laden with freshly harvested produce to be sold by local farmers. It's more like a fiesta than a market, with local talent performing, and tables set up by neighboring restaurants so you can enjoy a supper—picnic style. People do partake of the ribs, barbecued chicken, hot dogs, and other goodies offered. Even if you're not interested in buying the produce, it's fun to stroll through and enjoy the entertainment and small-town camaraderie. The Farmer's Market starts at 6 p.m.

California Polytechnic State University, affectionately called "Cal Poly," is located in central San Luis Obispo (tel. 805/756-2792). The university is known for agriculture and animal husbandry, as well as for the departments of engineering, architecture, and computer technology. There is a small area in the Animal Science Department where children can pet some of the animals. Open Monday through Friday from 9 a.m. to 5 p.m.

Families can also wander through the campus and look at horses, pigs, and other livestock, but call the information clerk first to find out what is open for viewing when you're planning to be there.

If you're planning to be in the area during the spring (April), check to see if you can attend Poly Royal weekend. This is Cal Poly's open house—more like a carnival—with a Collegiate Rodeo, Tractor Pull, and Poly Royal Parade . . . more than 300 events all told.

Many kids enjoy poking through a little shop at 1033 Chorro St. called **Burris Saddlery** (tel. 805/543-4101). It has saddles, saddlebags, and horse and pack equipment. We love this little store, and our city kids find it hard to believe that it's the real thing. Open Monday through Saturday from 9:30 to 11:45 a.m. and 12:45 to 5:15 p.m.

AVILA BEACH. The tiny area called Avila Beach is a friendly little community, host to Port San Luis Harbor. The beach area is small and the short drive through the oaks and sycamores from U.S. 101 through See Canyon is beautiful. Avila Beach is great for families, with playground equipment at Front and San Francisco Streets. There are picnic tables and lifeguards in the summer. There's fishing from Avila Pier.

The little town of Avila offers ample places to find food and drinks. You might also drive to the jetty and watch the boats being repaired in dry dock, or observe the fishermen at work.

If you're looking for something really unusual, you might stop at **Syca-**

more Mineral Springs, located at 1215 Avila Beach Dr. (tel. 805/595-7302), for a stint in a mineral bath. Children are welcome. Sycamore Springs is really a motel (with 27 units, each with its own balcony and hot tub), but we prefer stopping here for a fun daytime excursion. The big attractions are the 22 private redwood hot tubs (all emptied and scrubbed daily) and the other amenities of a mineral springs (such as facials for Mom and Dad). With the hourly rental of the hot tub comes the use of the facilities, including a heated swimming pool and two volleyball courts. Children 3 to 12 pay $3 per hour and adults are charged $8.50 per hour.

Where to Stay

In San Luis Obispo there are several places to choose from. The **Apple Farm Inn and Restaurant,** 2015 Monterey St., San Luis Obispo, CA 93401 (tel. 805/544-2040, or toll free 800/255-2040 in California), is unique and fun. This brand-new inn (which has already received a four-diamond rating from the Automobile Club of Southern California) is a replica of a 19th-century Victorian inn. The bonus is that while rooms have the traditional accoutrements of the 1800s, such as four-poster beds, fireplaces, and wingback chairs, they also feature modern-day soundproofing and private baths.

Amenities include complimentary wakeup coffee delivered to the room, fresh flowers, VCRs in each room, and complimentary newspapers. Ask about the "Breakfast in Bed" service. There is also a swimming pool and Victorian gardens in which you and the kids can stroll.

The delightful inn, which is near the banks of the Santa Luis Creek, has a Mill House (an authentic reproduction), a picnic area, a gift store, bakery, and restaurant. The Apple Farm Restaurant is wonderful, and serves home-style American breakfasts, lunches, and dinners (for a complete description, see the "Where to Eat" section).

Rooms cost $60 to $120 single and $70 to $130 double, depending on size, view, and special details. Children under 18 stay free when they share their parents' room. Additional adults pay $10 each per night. There is no charge for cribs.

The **Quality Suites,** 1631 Monterey St., San Luis Obispo, CA 93401 (tel. 805/541-5001, or toll free 800/228-5151), is a wonderful moderately priced choice for families.

Built to look like an early California villa, the airy lobby, terracotta tile floors, and large ceiling fans set off the two-story ceilings. There are inviting conversation areas and a little room off the lobby called the Library. But you'll love the landscaped outdoor area best of all. One courtyard has a fenced and gated pool area, complete with a one-foot wading pool and Jacuzzi. Another courtyard features a fountain and grassy area.

Included in the room rates are cooked-to-order breakfasts (served Monday through Friday from 6:30 to 9:30 a.m. and on Saturday and Sunday from 7 to 10:30 a.m.), evening chips, cheese, and non-alcoholic drinks; and free newspapers. This location has a giftshop and sundry store, with microwave items available. Light dinners are served in the breakfast room from 5:30 to 8:30 p.m. for an additional fee. There is a coin-operated laundry for guest use.

The 138 two-room suites have two remote-control televisions, with VCR and AM/FM stereo cassette player, wet bar, refrigerator, honor bar, microwave oven, and two phones. Done in tones of blue with colorful pastel print bedspreads, the living room has a large queen-size sofa sleeper and a dining table. The sleeping room has two double beds or one king-size bed. There is an enormous vanity area in the bedroom. The bathroom includes a tub/shower combination and in-room amenities, such as shampoo, body lotion, and conditioners.

Rates are $69 single and $77 double in winter, $85 single and $93 double in summer. Kids under 18 are free if they use existing beds. Cribs are provided free of charge, but there are no rollaways. Each additional adult is charged $8 in winter, $10 in summer.

Another moderately priced accommodation is **La Cuesta Motor Inn,** 2074 Monterey St., San Luis Obispo, CA 93401 (tel. 805/543-2777, or toll free 800/543-2777 in California). This is a tastefully decorated motor inn with a definite southwestern flair. The lobby has an inviting area for sitting and chatting, a place where you can enjoy the complimentary continental breakfast of danish and coffee or tea. There is afternoon tea-and-cookie service, and a basket of apples sits in the lobby at all times.

The large pool is heated year round and is fenced and gated. There is also a Jacuzzi. Extra touches, such as flowers and paintings in the guest hallways, make this an attractive place.

Rooms are good-sized and new. Some have pretty views of the mountains. All have cable television with HBO, tub-shower combinations, game tables, and chairs. Some rooms even have refrigerators.

Rates are the same for single and double occupancy: $56 on weekdays, $59 on weekends.

And of course there's the ever-famous, ever-astonishing **Madonna Inn,** 100 Madonna Rd., San Luis Obispo, CA 93401 (tel. 805/543-3000, or toll free 800/543-9666 in California). You'll recognize the Madonna Inn as soon as you begin your approach—pink lightposts line the drive up to the multistory gingerbread-style abode. Inside, you'll see pink and red all around you, from the banquettes and napkins to the little cupids.

While this is really more of a couples' hideaway, it is so famous you really must stop by. We're including it as a possible place to stay, but we usually "do" the Madonna Inn as a sightseeing attraction. We stop for a snack or lunch and roam the property. The kids love the wildly colorful coffeeshop (open daily from 7 a.m. to 10 p.m.; breakfast prices range from $4 to $7, and lunch or dinner costs from $6 to $17). Don't let the kids miss the swinging doll in the restaurant lobby. And then, of course, there's the big tourist attraction—the rushing waterfall urinal in the men's bathroom. Yes, that's right. You'll also find a men's and women's giftshop, a gourmet and wine-tasting shop, and beautifully landscaped grounds (that you can admire, not romp through).

If you arrive between noon and 2 p.m., you can go to the front desk and ask which rooms are in the process of being cleaned. You're welcome to poke your head in those unoccupied rooms as long as a housekeeper is inside. It's potluck, but you might be able to see some of the famous rooms. Among the most interesting are the "Cave Man Room," with rock ceiling, walls, floors, and a waterfall in the bathroom, and the "Round Room," which is bright green with a merry-go-round motif. Kids love the "Pony Room"—it has barn-type paneling and is painted red. Pony ornaments decorate the room.

If you choose to stay in this fairyland, expect to pay from $67 (for one person) to $133 (for four people), depending on the room configuration and types of beds. Suites range from $125 to $170, and can accommodate up to eight or nine people. Cribs are free, but rollaways cost $15. No credit cards are accepted at the inn.

Where to Eat

In San Luis Obispo don't miss the **Apple Farm Restaurant,** at 2015 Monterey St. (tel. 805/544-6100). The food is Americana—lots of homemade chicken and dumplings—and absolutely delicious! (Try the hot apple dumplings served with hot cinnamon sauce and ice cream. They make their apple dumplings and apple pies from scratch using local apples.)

The décor of the place is especially endearing. The Apple Farm opened in 1977 as a small restaurant and it continues to expand. The gift store and the main area of the restaurant were originally a Victorian house. The Victorian architecture, the owner believes, is a universal theme that captures the American imagination. He also feels that it ties into the San Luis Obispo community, so you'll see turrets and towers and lots of leaded-glass panels.

There is Tiffany glass, crate-label art of the early 1900s, and patchwork quilts. The apple theme is carried throughout with apple-crate labels decorating the walls and apple souvenirs in the giftshop.

Be sure to see the Quilt Room. It's a dining room where antique quilts line the wall. Another dining room overlooks the outdoor gazebo and waterwheel of the inn.

Owner Bob Davis, who has traveled extensively with his own family, decided to create a restaurant (and the recently opened Apple Farm Inn) that would cater to families. There are highchairs, boosters, and an adorable children's menu. The service is friendly, and the food is great.

The fresh-squeezed orange juice comes with an orange slice on the glass. The preserves are not too sweet, and the blueberry spread has whole pieces of fruit in it. There is a large breakfast menu with prices from $3 to $5.75. Lunches can be a simple soup-and-sandwich combination or meatloaf, roast beef, or turkey sandwiches. Prices range from $4 to $5.50. For dinner you can choose from old-fashioned chicken and dumplings, roast turkey and gravy, or pan-fried trout, as well as other items. All dinners include soup or salad, cornbread, fresh vegetables, and potatoes, and cost from $7.25 to $11.25. Children have similar appetizing treats for $2 to $3.

Instead of formal reservations, you are asked to call and put your name on a waiting list when you're ready to come to the restaurant. At that time, they'll tell you how long the wait will be. In the summer the restaurant is usually busy, but there is normally no more than a 20-minute wait.

There is a patio area as well as a toy store and giftshop. Coffee is served in the waiting area.

Open daily from 7 a.m. to 9 p.m. Major credit cards accepted. Parking lot.

Another fun place is **Hudson's Grill,** at 1005 Monterey St. (tel. 805/541-5999). This American grill has simply fabulous burgers, and rich milkshakes so thick that the kids (and you) can't use the straws.

MTV is piped in via large mounted television screens, but the music isn't too loud. The jukebox and neon lights add a certain '50s touch, but the old Hudson automobile coming out of the wall is classic '40s-era stuff!

The menu includes salads, sandwiches, and Mexican food, along with burgers and malts. Prices are in the $3.25 to $7 range. The kid's coloring book-menu includes burgers, hot dogs, grilled cheese, and junior versions of milkshakes and malts. Prices from $2 to $2.25. Our kids couldn't wait for the bill to arrive, because it comes with a Tootsie Roll pop for each person. There are highchairs and booster seats, and they'll be glad to warm bottles and baby food.

Open daily from 11 a.m. till midnight. No reservations accepted. Most major credit cards welcome. Street parking.

PISMO BEACH: This seaside village is a surfer's paradise and a beach lover's mecca. Located about 11 miles south of San Luis Obispo via U.S. 101, Pismo has lots of surfers and would-be surfers. You'll have a great time here, especially if you have teens. This is also the place to see dunes. You can even drive your car on the beach.

Pismo used to be known for its clams and the clam digging you could do. Sorry to say, because of ecological changes (and people who have overharvested the area) clams are no longer large and plentiful. You can go clam digging, but find out first about regulations (adults need fishing licenses).

Stop by the **Pismo Beach Chamber of Commerce,** 581 Dolliver St. (tel.

805/773-4382), and pick up information about local attractions and clamming instructions for the novice. The office is open weekdays from 9:30 a.m. to 5 p.m. and on Saturday from 10 a.m. to 4 p.m.

What to Do and See

The newly restored 1,200-foot **Pismo Beach Pier** is the center of this village town. The beach stretches for miles both north and south, enticing sunbathers, swimmers, surfers, and Frisbee throwers alike. Kids (and parents) can also fish from the pier. There are public restrooms.

Pismo State Beach is a 20-mile strip of sand dunes, part of which is open to all-terrain-vehicles (often called off-highway vehicles). Some of the areas with hard-packed sand are open to automobiles. A "ride on the sand" will cost you $3 per vehicle. **Pismo Dunes State Vehicular Recreation Area** is the spot if you and your family are aficionados of off-road-vehicle sporting. Or you can enjoy watching the others in their treks up and down the dunes. The recreation area is located at the southern tip of Pismo State Beach.

Another way to enjoy the spectacular scenery is on horseback. The **Livery Stable,** 1207 Silver Spur Pl., in Oceano, about three miles south of Pismo Beach (tel. 805/489-8100), has horses for advanced, intermediate, and beginning riders. You can ride to Pismo Beach. During the summer the stable is open from 8 a.m. to 5 p.m., in winter till 4 p.m. No reservations are taken. Rates are $10 per hour for adults and children, plus a deposit per horse. Children between 2 and 8 must ride on a horse with an adult, and there is no charge for these youngsters.

Playland Arcade, 175 Pomeroy Ave. (tel. 805/773-2978), has something for everyone in the family, from little kiddie rides to air hockey and Skee Ball for the adults. Kids love the mini-basketball and good selection of pinball games. Open Sunday through Thursday from 10 a.m. to 9 p.m., on Friday and Saturday to 11 p.m.

For a simply fabulous sunset view of the coast north and the dunes to the south, you might want to get a snack or cool drink at the **Sea Venture Hotel,** located on the sand at Pismo Beach at 100 Ocean View (tel. 805/773-4994). They have two bars that serve tapas (little bar appetizers). You can munch on fajitas, tempura, fish and chips (from $5 to $7) while you and the kids have a beverage and take advantage of the view. Boosters and highchairs are available. Open from 4 to 10 p.m. (Of course, full dinners are served too.)

You may discover that you need some sand toys or beach paraphernalia. You can get them at **Beach Gear and More,** in the mall at 175 Pomeroy Ave. (tel. 805/773-1999). They sell pails, boogie boards, splash balls, even beach chairs. Open daily from 10 a.m. to 6 p.m.

Where to Stay

There are possibly more motels and inns in Pismo Beach than in any other town in the county.

The **Quality Suites,** 651 Five Cities Dr., Pismo Beach, CA 93449 (tel. 805/773-3773), is our choice here. Located just off U.S. 101 (at 4th Street), this accommodation is quite similar to its sister motor hotel in San Luis Obispo, and is a perfect setting for families.

This all-suite hostelry offers a complimentary made-to-order full breakfast with its rooms, and the rooms are quite lovely (see the description of the Quality Suites hotel in the San Luis Obispo section). In addition to the heated swimming pool, wading pool, and Jacuzzi, this location has a quiet courtyard and a putting green.

Like the other Quality Suites, all 133 two-room accommodations have two remote-control color TVs, two phones, a VCR, AM/FM stereo cassette player, a microwave, a wet bar, and a mini-refrigerator/honor bar.

In summer (mid-June to late September), rates are $59 to $85 single, $69 to

$95 double; the rates are lower the rest of the year. Children under 16 stay free. Those older and additional adults pay $8 each per night. No charge for cribs; no rollaways available.

The **Edgewater Motel Friendship Inn,** 280 Wadsworth Ave., Pismo Beach, CA 93449 (tel. 805/773-4811, or toll free 800/634-5858), is a budget accommodation located on the waterfront. The office has a small adjacent reception room in which free continental breakfast is served from 7 to 10 a.m. There is beach access.

Although the sound of the pounding surf and the sight of white beaches beckon, this motel also has a glassed-in outdoor swimming pool and Jacuzzi. There is a coin-operated laundry available.

The good-sized rooms have refrigerators, cable color TV, game table, and tub-shower combinations. Some have double sinks. Rooms with king-size beds and ocean views have Jacuzzi jets in the bathtub. There are also rooms with queen-size beds and others with one or two double beds. Connecting rooms are available. Cribs and rollaways cost $7 per night.

Rates vary considerably, depending on the room, the number of people, and the time of year. They run from $45 to $75 (for one or two people). Family rooms (with two double beds or two queen-size beds) run $55 to $125—and some have fully equipped kitchens.

CAMPING. As in the Morro Bay area, you'll find good camping here. **Pismo State Beach** has three separate campgrounds. North Beach is developed and has space for 31-foot trailers and campers ($10 fee), Oceano is developed and has space for 18-foot trailers and 31-foot campers ($10 fee), and Oceano (hookup) has spaces for 31-foot trailers and 36-foot campers ($16 fee).

Pismo Dunes Vehicular Recreation Area has 500 primitive sites, with pit toilets.

For more information on these campsites, contact Pismo State Beach, Pier Avenue, Oceano, CA 93445 (tel. 805/489-2684). You can make reservations for state parks at a **MISTIX** outlet or you can call for registration forms (tel. 619/452-1950, or toll free 800/446-7275 in California).

Where to Eat

There is one all-time favorite in Pismo Beach for dinner. It is **F. McLintocks Saloon & Dining House,** 750 Mattie Rd., off U.S. 101 (tel. 805/773-1892), one of the top-ten grossing restaurants in all California. Why? The managers answer that question with "Good food, good prices, and a great show."

This lively down-home place, where your busboy may stand on a chair to pour your water and waiters yell across the large dining room to each other, has a real cowboy atmosphere. They say, "Bring the kids and you'll all have a great time."

But it takes more than ambience to garner customers willing to wait up to two hours. (In fact, they serve 1,200 meals a day in August, and can do 1,000 meals on any hopping Saturday night.)

What people return for is the superb service and the great steaks and seafood. They cut their own meat and age it for 26 days on the premises, then cook it over oakwood. At lunch you can choose from (handmade) burgers, hot sandwiches, steaks, ribs, and seafood. Prices range from $5.50 to $12. Dinners include steaks smothered in sautéed mushrooms or onions (or both), 14 different kinds of steak dinners, and fish and seafood such as halibut, mahi mahi, rainbow trout, and scampi. All dinners include onion rings, fresh spinach or tossed green salad, beans, salsa, garlic bread, ranch fried potatoes, and an after-dinner liqueur or sherbet. Prices for dinner range from $13.25 to $25 (for a 28-ounce T-bone steak!).

This family place has highchairs, boosters, a wide variety of children's drinks, and a nice children's menu of ground steak, fresh fish, steak, or ribs. A complete dinner and dessert (plus a prize from the treasure chest) is $1.50 for kids 5 to 12 and free for kids under 5.

Open Monday through Friday from 11:30 a.m. to 3 p.m. for lunch, and 3 to 10:30 p.m. for dinner. On Saturday, breakfast is served from 8 a.m. to 11:30 a.m.; lunch, from 11:30 a.m. to 2 p.m.; and dinner, from 2 to 10:30 p.m. The Sunday ranch breakfast is served from 9 a.m. to 1:30 p.m., and Sunday dinner, from 2 till 9:30 p.m. With the waits being so long, try to make reservations (which are only taken Sunday through Thursday). The best time is early lunch or 5 p.m. for dinner. In the summer, Friday and Saturday nights are brutal—and no reservations are taken. They accept MasterCard and VISA only. Parking lot.

MORE THINGS TO DO IN THE GENERAL AREA: When you find your-
self trapped in the fog on the coast, you can drive into San Luis Obispo and see if the sun appears. If not and you'd like to try some indoor activities, here are a few suggestions.

Laurel Bowl, 1234 Laurel Lane, San Luis Obispo (tel. 805/543-2711), is open from 9 a.m. to 11:30 p.m. daily except Sunday, when it closes at 10:30 p.m. Prices are $1.80 per game per person, $1 for shoe rentals. Children 12 and under pay only $1.35 per game.

Pismo Bowl, 277 Pomeroy Ave., Pismo Beach (tel. 805/773-2482), is open from noon till midnight (but check for open lanes because they have a lot of leagues). Fees are $1.75 per game per adult, $1.25 for seniors and juniors (12 and under), plus 75¢ for shoes.

Mann Festival Cinemas (tel. 805/481-7553), just south of Pismo Beach, has ten movie theaters.

Picking Fruit and Vegetables

San Luis Obispo County is ripe with agricultural products for the picking. One place to try is **Kaminaka U-Pick Farms,** 945 Pomeroy Rd., about 15 miles south of Pismo Beach (tel. 805/929-1374). This family farm has been in operation for 35 years and has allowed the public to pick crops for 17 years. You can pick strawberries (top-quality, they say), ollalieberries, raspberries, and vegetables—such as carrots, beets, beans, cabbage, tomatoes, and peppers. Fruits and vegetables picked from the fields are usually priced per pound. If you're lucky—and arrange it ahead of time—you can get a tour of the farm by the owners. There's also a complete farm stand if you get tired of picking your own. Open April through August every day but Monday from 8 a.m. to 7 p.m., and from September to the day before Thanksgiving, Thursday through Sunday from 8 a.m. to 5 p.m.; closed December to April.

IF YOU'RE LEAVING FOR POINTS SOUTH: You might want to try a
brief stop if you're traveling all the way to Los Angeles or Santa Barbara. **Pea Soup Andersen's California Highway Center,** at 376 Avenue of the Flags in Buellton (tel. 805/688-5581), is a good place to get out and stretch, and enjoy some of Andersen's great pea soup while you're at it. Pea Soup Andersen's is close to Solvang, and completely embraces the Danish motif. The complex consists of a large giftshop, wine shop and tasting room, gourmet food shop, gas station, and a small toy store (with children's coloring books and the like).

But people come for the soup—it's that good! The Traveler's Special includes all the soup you can eat, bread (yummy Danish onion-cheese or Danish pumpernickel), and a beverage (even a milkshake or house wine) for $4.25—and you can get it to go. Beyond that, there are good salads, sandwiches, burgers, and hot entrees such as pot roast, veal cutlets, calves' liver, or filet of sole. You can order à la carte or a full dinner, which includes all the soup or salad you want, bread and butter, and beverage. Prices range from $3.25 to $13.75.

The children's menu is a small coloring/game book. Kids can choose from a large variety of lunch and dinner items (peanut butter sandwich, soup and a sandwich, macaroni and cheese, or hot dog) and from three breakfast items. All cost $2.25.

In addition to good food, the service is friendly and crackers are put on the table as soon as you sit down. The only problem is the wait. It can be long, especially during mealtimes when everyone on the road decides to stop here. We usually call ahead when we know our approximate arrival time and make a reservation. With a setup expressly for travelers, they have highchairs and boosters, as you'd expect. The women's bathroom has a large vanity area that is good for diaper changing.

Open daily from 7 a.m. to 11 p.m. Parking lot. They accept most major credit cards.

AREA FESTIVALS AND ANNUAL EVENTS: You'll find many local events and festivals all year long in the central coast area. Here are some of the ones we enjoyed.

Poly Royal (April), at California Polytechnic in San Luis Obispo (tel. 805/546-2487), is a campus-wide open house with a carnival, rodeo, and lots of festivities.

La Fiesta de San Luis Obispo (May) takes place at Mission Plaza. This is a lively festival with music, dancing, costumes, and a parade. Call 805/543-1710 for information.

The Renaissance Pleasure Faire (June) takes place at the El Chorro Regional Park in San Luis Obispo (tel. 805/773-2300). This event is a lively affair with participants wearing period costumes, and there's entertainment, food, and crafts hearkening back to the days of old.

The California Mid-State Fair (August) in Paso Robles (tel. 805/238-3565) is an extraordinary state fair, drawing over 400,000 people in two weeks' time. The fair is on the National Rodeo circuit, and has tractor pulls, food exhibits and competitions, and an old-fashioned midway. Kids from all over the county bring their pigs, lambs, and goats to exhibit and sell. Top entertainment has included Bill Cosby, Dolly Parton, Kenny Loggins, and Glen Campbell.

Morro Beach Harbor Festival (October) in Morro Beach (tel. 805/772-4467) is one of the county's highlights. The festival has a carnival, a beach treasure hunt, and a parade of boats. The giant chessboard is used, with people dressed in costumes. A "live" chess match takes place.

Pismo Beach Clam Festival (November) at Pismo Beach pier (tel. 805/773-4382), includes a clam chowder cook-off, carnival, and clam-digging contest.

Morro Bay Lighted Boat Parade (December) in Morro Bay.

Whale Watching (December through mid-March), all along the coast.

IN AN EMERGENCY: Should a medical emergency occur during your stay, the following hospitals in San Luis Obispo have emergency room service: **Sierra Vista Hospital,** 1010 Murray Ave. (tel. 805/546-7600); **French Hospital,** 1911 Johnson Ave. (tel. 805/543-5353); and **General Hospital,** 2180 Johnson Ave. (tel. 805/543-1500).

CHAPTER IX

SANTA BARBARA AND VICINITY

□ □ □

This chapter will introduce you to the Spanish/Mediterranean charm of Santa Barbara, harbor adventures in Oxnard and Ventura, the rural landscape and tranquil hills of Ojai, and the still-distinct Scandinavian heritage of Solvang.

Each town has something different to offer a family in terms of activities, climate, and location. In just a few days you could visit all of them. You might rent a boat in Ventura, loaf on a beach in Santa Barbara, buy souvenirs in Solvang, or just drive down a country road in Ojai.

1. SANTA BARBARA

Santa Barbara is the epitome of a great beach town. It has fantastic, wide beaches and a wonderful, long bike path. It's in a gorgeous setting, with the ocean on one side and the Santa Ynez Mountains on the other. The temperatures are near perfect, and it offers activities for every season. Its Andalusian-like look of red-tile roofs and white Spanish buildings complements the calm, laid-back attitude of its inhabitants. In a nutshell, Santa Barbara is nearly perfect.

Its history goes all the way back to 1542, when the Portuguese explorer Juan Rodriguez Cabrillo discovered the channel. He didn't stay, and so the region was not named until much later—December 4, 1602, to be precise. On that date, St. Barbara's Day, Sebastian Vizcaino, a Spanish conquistador, entered the channel and named it after the saint. By the late 1700s Santa Barbara was a Spanish stronghold. The Europeans followed, ripping down the simple Spanish buildings and in their place putting up a hodgepodge of uninspired post-Victorian buildings. Ironically, it was with the help of an earthquake in 1925 that the city was able to get rid of the nondescript architecture and implement an order that all new structures had to be in the Mediterranean style. What a relief!

GETTING THERE: Just 90 miles north of Los Angeles and 330 miles south of San Francisco, Santa Barbara is reached **by car** via Calif. 1 or U.S. 101. **Santa Barbara Airport** is served by a number of local and national carriers. The Santa Barbara Airbus will whisk you to and from Los Angeles International Airport (tel. 805/964-7759 or 805/964-7374, or toll free 800/423-1618). Major rental-car companies are located at the airport and in town; check the *Yellow Pages* for local addresses and phone numbers. **Amtrak** (tel. toll free 800/USA-RAIL) serves Santa Barbara direct from Los Angeles, San Diego, and San Francisco. There is also the **Greyhound Bus** (tel. toll free 800/237-8211) service linking both major cities with Santa Barbara.

ORIENTATION: There's more to do in Santa Barbara than meets the eye. To get information before your visit, contact the **Santa Barbara Conference and Visitors Bureau,** 222 E. Anapamu St., Santa Barbara, CA 93101 (tel. 805/966-9222). When in town, stop by the **Santa Barbara Visitor Information Center,** at 1 Santa Barbara St., Santa Barbara, CA 93103 (tel. 805/965-3021), to get all the facts you need. The office is open daily from 9 a.m. to 5 p.m.

Outlying Montecito to the south and Hope Ranch to the north are two of the most exclusive residential areas of Santa Barbara. The Visitor Center has mapped out a scenic drive that encompasses these and other points of interest.

State Street is one of the main shopping streets in town, with the hub between Victoria Street and the ocean. State Street is lined with boutiques, cafés and snack shops, bookstores, a balloon store, a toy store, T-shirt shops, and Mexican import shops. On Brinkerhoff Avenue you'll find a large number of antique stores.

State Street and Cabrillo Boulevard is the point at which **Stearns Wharf** (tel. 408/963-0611) begins and the Santa Barbara Trolley stops (you'll find more information in the "What to See and Do" section, below). This is where you'll find the statue of the dolphin. It's a good point to use as a meeting place if the family separates to do different things.

The main streets downtown are one way, running east and west. Santa Barbara is a dream to get around. There are signs to important points of interest. **Cabrillo Boulevard** leads you to most of the important streets; you can find them off U.S. 101 too, but that route gets congested, especially during the summer.

WHAT TO DO AND SEE: Santa Barbara lends itself to doing things leisurely, whether it's a slow ride along the bike path or a visit to the Santa Barbara Mission. This is a place to take your time, never feel rushed, and never feel you have to do "everything."

Bicycling

It seems that everyone in Santa Barbara has a bicycle, and the bicycles here get plenty of use. Just about everywhere you look there are families pedaling those Italian Pedalinas, cute red four-wheel cycles with canvas tops. Junior (up to 50 pounds) sits in the front and Mom and Dad do all the work pedaling. But the Pedalinas aren't just limited to family fun. Teenagers like to rent them too, and go tooling down the beach with their friends.

A 3⅓-mile two-lane bikeway, beginning on Cabrillo Boulevard, is easy to navigate and leads you through the beaches, crossing the boulevard at Milpas Street. Heading east, you'll come to the **Andree Clark Bird Refuge,** at 1400 E. Cabrillo Blvd., a 50-acre preserve of ducks, geese, and other waterfowl, and little islands dotting the lagoon. We like to spend an hour or so walking through the preserve on the footpath. On our way back, we sometimes ride to the Santa Barbara Zoo, but only when we've rented standard bikes rather than the Pedalinas. You can also ride up Stearns Wharf (the Fisherman's Wharf of Santa Barbara), but don't try it with the Pedalinas.

Bicycles are easy to rent in Santa Barbara. Stop at **Cycles-4-Rent,** 101 State St. (park in Rocky's parking lot), one block from the dolphin statue at State Street and Cabrillo Boulevard (tel. 805/966-3804). You can rent beach cruisers and 1-, 3-, 6-, and 18-speed bikes for rates ranging from $4 per hour for the beach cruisers to $7 per hour for the 18-speed. Tandems cost $8 per hour; Pedalinas, $10. Half- and full-day rates are available. There are no child carriers, so take the youngsters on the Pedalinas. Bike locks, seatbelts (for the front of the Pedalina), and child helmets come free. Open daily. No reservations are accepted, but there's hardly ever a wait, even on summer weekends.

Cycles-4-Rent also operates out of Fess Parker's Red Lion Inn at a stand located poolside. Bring ID (driver's license or passport) to expedite your rental.

Beach Rentals is located directly across the street from Stearns Wharf at 8 W. Cabrillo Blvd. (tel. 805/963-2524). Besides ten-speeds, Pedalinas, and tandems, children's bikes, children's helmets, and child carriers for adult bikes are available here. Roller skates (in children's sizes too) and skateboards also may be rented. Bicycles run from $4 per hour for children's bikes to $6 and $8 an hour for the other bikes. Child seats are $4 with a bike rental. Skates and skateboards cost $3 per hour. Delivery can be arranged for a minimum charge, but there are no reservations. Mopeds are available too—call 805/966-6733 for information on those. Beach Rentals is open daily from 7:30 a.m. to 7 p.m. Again, remember to bring ID.

Beaches

If you traveled from Los Angeles, you passed through Carpenteria. Just a few minutes outside Santa Barbara, the beach at **Carpenteria** (tel. 805/684-2811) bills itself as the world's safest, and it's considered a wonderful family beach because of the calm waters and lack of riptides. There are concession stands and rest rooms, and you can camp here. Would-be surfers should get to **Rincon Point,** just south of Carpinteria Beach, famous for having perfect waves, and the best winter waves for surfers. As you continue north through Montecito, you'll come to **East Beach,** our favorite. Here you'll find dozens of volleyball nets and fun playground equipment. At the Cabrillo Bath House at East Beach (you can't miss it), you can rent just about anything you need for a day in the sun, including beach chairs and umbrellas. A parking lot is adjacent, and there's food service and rest rooms. You can't miss **Chase Palm Park** before you get to the pier, with its grassy areas perfect for playing Frisbee and having picnics. Just past the pier is **West Beach,** considered the best spot for windsurfing (parking and rest rooms available); then comes **Leadbetter Beach,** with a parking lot, picnic areas, and rest rooms. The Sea Cove Café, on the beach, is good for an outdoor snack. If you continue farther north, you'll come to **Arroyo Beach,** one of the nicest beaches in the area, with parking, picnic areas, and rest rooms. You can surf here too.

Boating, Fishing, and Cruising

Harbor cruises are less available in Santa Barbara than elsewhere on the coast, but they are possible. **Captain Don's Harbour Cruises** (tel. 805/969-5217) offers a fully narrated tour on the *Harbour Queen*. It's docked at Stearns Wharf next to the Sea Center and offers a one-hour cruise along the waterfront. The boat leaves daily in summer (June through October); weekends and holidays the rest of the year, weather permitting. It sails on the hour, from 11 a.m. to 4 p.m. The fare is $6 for adults, $4 for children 2 to 12; under 2, free.

Sailing is a wonderful activity to pursue in Santa Barbara, and you can partake of it even if you've never sailed before. **Navigators Channel Island Cruise,** 1621 Posilipo Lane (tel. 805/969-2393), which meets at the Breakwater in front of the Yacht Club on Cabrillo Boulevard, will customize your sailing trip. Generally, they recommend either a mid-morning luncheon sail or a mid-afternoon cocktail trip.

The charge is $40 for adults, $20 for children under 12. There's a minimum of two people, a maximum of six, and an overall minimum charge of $100. They sail year round, depending on the weather, and reservations are necessary.

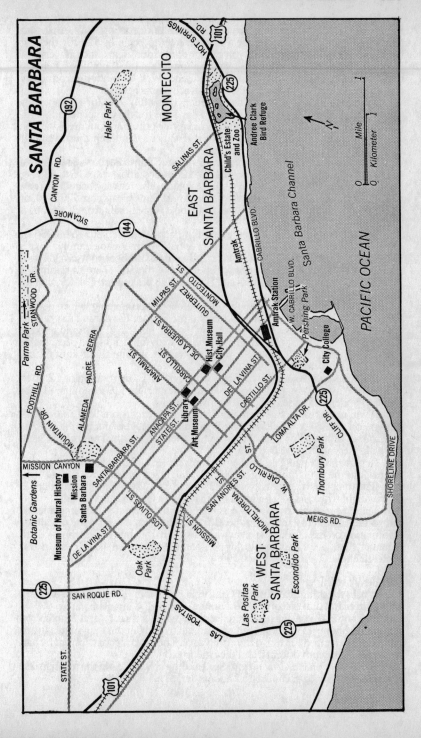

Windsurfing is another popular Santa Barbara sport. You can rent everything you need, or take lessons, from **Windance Windsurfing,** 6 W. Anapamu (tel. 805/962-4774). Rentals for a complete setup begin at $20 for the first hour, $15 per hour after that. Or you can rent individual items, such as wetsuits, kid rigs, masts, etc. Children must weigh a minimum of 50 pounds. There are rental prices by the day, half day, weekend, and week. Two-hour introductory lessons cost $35. Call anytime. Reservations are always necessary.

Sundance Windsurfing, 2026 Cliff Dr. (tel. 805/966-2674), also rents full or partial equipment, starting at $10 per hour for the complete sailboard. Group lessons cost $40 for three hours; one-hour private lessons are $30. The lessons are given at West Beach. Call for reservations. Children must weigh at least 80 pounds and be 10 years or older.

Boat rentals are possible at Breakwater through **Santa Barbara Boat Rental** (tel. 805/962-2826). Rent 21-, 23-, 24-, and 26-foot sailboats for $15 to $25 per hour for a minimum of two or three hours. You can also rent rowboats, or even a rowing scull, for $5 and $10 per hour respectively. Powerboats cost $20, $40, or $75 per hour, depending on the size of the boat. Open daily from 9 a.m. to 6 p.m.

Sea Landing, at Cabrillo Boulevard and Bath Street (tel. 805/963-3564), offers a number of other possibilities appropriate for the whole family. Take a two-hour catamaran cruise, for instance, and even sail the boat yourselves. You'll take off on the *Slingshot,* at one of five times during the day. There's a minimum of three people and a maximum of six. Fees are $15 per person. Call for reservations.

Sea Landing can also set you up on a half day of sportfishing, which is a fun thing to do with children. You'll take off on the 50-foot *Hornet* and stay within view of the coastline. Who knows what you'll catch, but they'll clean and package it for a small fee. There's even a galley on board with soft drinks and beer. Tackle rental is available. When you make your reservation, inquire about adult fishing licenses; children under 12 don't need one.

Summers and weekends, your trip will be from 7 a.m. to noon or 12:30 to 5:30 p.m. Winter hours are 10 a.m. to 3 p.m. The rates are $19 for adults, $15 for children under 12 and seniors. Call for reservations.

If you're seeking yet an even more challenging excursion, Sea Landing will put you on the 55-foot *Seahawk.* You'll join a crew that goes out fishing for bass year round, or for yellowtail, albacore, and halibut in season. The *Seahawk* has a full galley serving food and drinks.

Departures are daily, depending on the weather, and trips last from 7 a.m. to 3 p.m. Join the twilight fishing trip June through September from 5:30 to 9:30 p.m. The three-quarter-day trip costs $28 for adults, $20 for children under 12. The twilight trip costs $19 for adults, $15 for kids. Call for reservations.

Those who scuba-dive will love it around Santa Barbara. Some companies go out to the Channel Islands from here. **Truth Aquatics** is one. Write or call for information on the various packages which can run from one to five days—Truth Aquatics, Inc., Sea Landing Breakwater, Santa Barbara, CA 93109 (tel. 805/962-1127).

Whale-Watching

Whale-watching is a southern California obsession. Join the **Santa Barbara Museum of Natural History,** 2559 Puesta del Sol Rd., Santa Barbara, CA 93105 (tel. 805/682-4711), on its selected excursions in February and March. You can't make phone reservations, but you can call to find out this year's dates and to request a reservation form. Do this in advance. These are special trips, led by naturalists and museum docents, and they fill up early.

You'll leave on the *Condor* from Sea Landing at 9 a.m., and the trip lasts 2½ hours. Adults pay $16; children 12 and under, $12.

The *Condor* also goes out on whale-watching trips not sponsored by the Museum of Natural History (from Sea Landing, Breakwater; tel. 805/963-3564). These trips are available from February to the first of May, daily during the height of the season. There are three departures—at 9 a.m., noon, and 3 p.m. —and the trips last 2½ hours. Adults pay $21; children 12 and under, $15.

Horseback Riding

There aren't too many more beautiful places to go horseback riding than Santa Barbara. Just north of Santa Barbara is **Gene O'Hagan Riding Stables,** 1900 Refugio Rd., Goleta (tel. 805/968-5929), which caters to children. They have very gentle horses that are used to young children, but yours has to be at least 5 (and must have experience). You can take a guided or unguided ride over mountain trails, past streams and waterfalls, and most of the time have breathtaking views of the ocean and even the islands.

Horses go out seven days a week, year round, three times a day, at 10 a.m., noon, and 2 p.m. The 1½-hour rides cost $20 (for adults or children), $5 per hour after that. Reservations are necessary at least a half day before. English and western tack are available.

Santa Barbara Zoo

The Santa Barbara Zoological Gardens, 500 Ninos Dr., off Cabrillo Boulevard (tel. 805/962-5339, or 805/962-6310 for recorded information), is one of those places we return to again and again—not so much to see all the animals, but because we like the atmosphere and because it's such a nice place to let the kids wander and play. In fact, one of the most delightful aspects of the zoo is the intricate (yet small) play area with equipment designed for children aged 2 to 10. We usually picnic on the sprawling grassy area and find it a wonderfully relaxing experience.

The miniature train ride ($1 for adults, 50¢ for children) and children's farmyard are always a huge success, and this children's zoo is a particularly nice one. It is especially popular with the young ones who love to chase after the high-strung goats and the slow-moving sheep.

In the rest of the zoo, they can see wallabies, ant eaters, pumas, toucans, sea lions, monkeys, and many endangered species.

The zoo itself reflects the change in philosophy toward zoo animals. Sitting on 81 landscaped acres, exhibits are designed to incorporate the natural habitat and enhance the outdoor feeling. Instead of chain-link fences and bars, the Santa Barbara Zoo uses moats and other more natural means to keep the animals apart from each other and from the people. We like to visit during the special training demonstrations held during the summer and on weekends. If you're lucky, you'll see them teach the elephants to do their routines. (Call 805/962-5339 for information.)

The zoo has a snackbar and giftshop.

Open daily from 10 a.m. to 5 p.m. (till 7 p.m. in summer). Admission is $4 for adults (over 12), $2 for seniors and children 2 to 12; under 2, it's free.

Mission Santa Barbara

The 10th of the 21 Franciscan missions built in California, this "Queen of the Missions" was founded in 1786. You'll find it at the upper end of Laguna Street at E. Los Olivos (tel. 805/682-4713 or 805/682-4715). Set in a striking locale overlooking the city, the mission is a beautiful structure built of Spanish, Moorish, and neoclassical elements, and its gardens are exceptionally lovely and tranquil. It's the only one of the 21 missions to be in continuous use as a parish church. The little rooms, gardens, chapel, and cemetery don't take long to see. Open daily from 9 a.m. to 5 p.m. You can take a self-guided tour for $1 (children under 16 are free).

Museums

Set in lush Mission Canyon, the **Santa Barbara Museum of Natural History,** 2559 Puesta del Sol Rd. (tel. 805/682-4711), is an interesting place to take the kids. Outside is a fascinating 72-foot touchable blue whale skeleton, a sight that never fails to elicit "oohs" and "aahs" from our group. The museum houses information and displays about the Chumash Indians (the tribe prominent to these parts), a planetarium and observatory with programs every Sunday, and many other permanent and changing exhibits, most of which focus on the Santa Barbara area.

The museum is open Monday through Saturday from 9 a.m. to 5 p.m. and on Sunday and holidays (except Christmas, Thanksgiving, and New Year's Days, and Fiesta) from 10 a.m. to 5 p.m. Admission is by voluntary donation.

The **Santa Barbara Museum of Art** is located in the heart of Santa Barbara at 1130 State St. (tel. 805/963-4364). This small, bright museum hosts a good collection of photographs, dolls, American and European paintings, ancient sculpture, and Oriental art. Take the kids for an hour or two as a nice break in the day.

It's open Tuesday through Saturday from 11 a.m. to 5 p.m. and on Sunday from noon to 5 p.m. On Thursday it stays open until 9 p.m., making it a possible after-dinner attraction. Admission is free.

Santa Barbara Trolley Company

If they've never been on a trolley before, your kids will enjoy a ride on the Santa Barbara Trolley. Catch it at the dolphin statue, State Street and Cabrillo Boulevard (tel. 805/962-0209). Choose one of three tours: the Scenic Coastal Tour takes Cabrillo Boulevard to Montecito and back; the Shopping Tour travels up State Street to the La Cumbre Shopping Center and back; and the Historical Tour goes up State Street to the mission and goes by City Hall, the Courthouse, and Brinkerhoff Avenue. All these narrated tours cost $2 per person, adult or child. The Scenic Tour leaves every hour on the hour; the Shopping Tour, at 10 a.m., noon, 2 p.m., and 4 p.m.; the Historical Tour, at 11 a.m., 1 p.m., 3 p.m., and 5 p.m.

If you want to spend more time seeing the town, buy an all-day pass for $4 and get on and off at whatever stops you want.

Festivals

For five days in early August each year, it's fiesta time in Santa Barbara. **Old Spanish Days in Santa Barbara** is an exciting street celebration created to preserve and perpetuate the city's heritage, which began with its Spanish roots. One of Santa Barbara's important fiestas was the 1820 celebration of the dedication of the Santa Barbara Mission—that's how far back these fiestas go. During the five-day celebration, there are two parades (including the Children's Parade), free performances, and a rodeo. A special marketplace is set up, and dancing goes on in the streets into the night. Everywhere you look there are tortilla stands, piñatas, and women dressed in traditional lace mantillas. Contact the office of Old Spanish Days in Santa Barbara, 1122 N. Milpas, Santa Barbara, CA 93101 (tel. 805/962-8101), for the dates of this year's fiesta. And if you plan to stay over during the fiesta, make reservations as far in advance as possible, as the town gets booked up 100%.

The **Summer Solstice Celebration** takes place annually in June on the Saturday closest to the summer equinox. Consisting of a parade without advertisements, written words, motorized vehicles, or live animals, the parade moves downtown, then turns into a party at Alameda Park with dance, mimes, music, and theater performances.

. . . and More

There's still lots more to do here, some of which has to do with the striking architecture and mission history of the town. Visit the **Santa Barbara County Courthouse,** in the 1100 block of Anacapa Street (tel. 805/962-6464), and ride up the 70-foot clocktower to the observation deck. Kids love to do this. The view from the top is absolutely exquisite. You can get a free guided tour of the unusually beautiful Spanish-Moorish courthouse on Wednesday and Friday at 10:30 a.m. and on Thursday at 2 p.m. Or visit the courthouse weekdays from 8 a.m. to 5 p.m., on Saturday, Sunday, and holidays from 9 a.m. to 5 p.m. Admission is free.

If the kids are game, take them on the **Red Tile Walking Tour,** a 12-block tour of Santa Barbara historical landmarks. A map is available from the Visitor Information Center. Or after dinner, ride up to the parking lot of the Santa Barbara Mission. While the children play near the gurgling fountain, relax and watch the sunset over the city below you.

While you're downtown, stop at **El Paseo,** the grand Spanish-style shopping arcade at 15 E. De la Guerra St. (tel. 805/965-0093). Built around, and in, an actual adobe home dating back to 1827, and owned by a prominent Santa Barbara family, the arcade has import shops, a dining courtyard, and art galleries. It's a good place to walk with the children. Most of the shops are open daily from 10 a.m. on.

Take a hike through the **Santa Barbara Botanic Garden,** 1212 Mission Canyon Rd. (tel. 805/682-4726). There are five miles of easy-to-walk self-guided nature trails to choose from. Lead the children through a wildflower meadow and cactus gardens and to a canyon filled with coastal redwoods. A stream trickles by, and you can cross a dam that dates back to 1807 and was built by Indians under the direction of the Mission padres. In fact, the Mission Creek was once a vital source of water to the Santa Barbara Mission. No picnicking. Open daily from 8 a.m. to dusk. Free admission. You can get a trail map at the Garden Shop, which is open daily from 10 a.m. to 4 p.m.

Drive over to Chapala and Montecito Streets to see what's considered the Northern Hemisphere's largest **Moreton Bay fig tree**. It is said that 10,000 people could stand in the shade of its branches at noon. The kids might find it interesting to know that it was planted as a seedling by a little girl in 1876 and it now has a branch spread of 160 feet.

If you're in town between June and September, take the family to an **outdoor concert** at the Alameda Park Bandstand, near the corner of Micheltorena and Santa Barbara Streets (tel. 805/963-0611, ext. 331). These family-oriented concerts make a lovely way to spend an hour. They are held on Sunday afternoon between 3 and 4 p.m. Free admission.

Stick around for the traditional Sunday **arts and crafts show** on Cabrillo Boulevard, which has been going on since 1966. More than 300 local artists of all media display their wares for sale from 10 a.m. until dusk.

After you've looked around, take a walk up **Stearns Wharf** (tel. 805/963-1979), a three-block extension of State Street, a Santa Barbara landmark built in 1872, once used as a dock from which passengers were ferried to gambling boats. You might get an ice-cream cone at **Hobson's Ice Cream Shop,** or have your palm read. Visit the **Sea Center** to view displays of the marine life of the Santa Barbara Channel. In spite of its being a joint project of the Natural History Museum and the Channel Islands National Marine Sanctuary, very young children (under-5s) will not find this very interesting. The center is open daily June through Labor Day from 11 a.m. to 7 p.m.; in winter, weekdays from noon to 5 p.m. and weekends and holidays from 11 a.m. to 6 p.m. Admission is $1 for adults, 50¢ for children 12 and under. Or stop for fantastically fresh seafood at the **Santa Barbara Shellfish Co.** at the end of the wharf, where there are live shellfish tanks from which to choose crab and lobster. It opens at 10 a.m. Or rent bait and tackle and fish from the pier. Watch the fog roll out from a window at **Moby Dick's,** or stop for a souvenir from one of the many shops on the wharf. (Wharf parking is $2 per hour, or free for two hours with a validation.)

To take some time off on your own to relax or to savor some of Santa Barbara's more intimate restaurants, call **Child's Playtime,** 134 Chapala St. (tel. 805/965-5678). This licensed child-care facility is available to visitors on a last-minute drop-off basis. The staff will take children 2½ to 12 years old on short notice, but they do prefer an advance reservation. And you must make reservations for evening care. In this cute building, just a short walk from the beach and the fig tree, kids will find an outside playground, a stage for plays and puppet shows, arts and crafts, games, and more. Open Monday through Friday from 8:30 a.m. to 10 p.m. and on Saturday and Sunday from 10 a.m. to 10 p.m. A minimum four-hour period is $26; each additional sibling costs $1 per hour extra.

WHERE TO STAY: As distances are not a problem in Santa Barbara, you'll pick your hotel based on cost and amenities. We've given you two or three good choices in each price category.

Deluxe

The **Four Seasons Biltmore,** 1260 Channel Dr., Santa Barbara, CA 93108 (tel. 805/969-2261, or toll free 800/332-3442), is one of the best and certainly one of the most beautiful places in the deluxe category to stay with a family. Built as a private residence in the early 1900s, the Biltmore sits on 21 lush acres, with views of both the ocean and the Santa Ynez Mountains. The hacienda-style main building, the clusters of smaller individual cottages, the extraordinary gardens and walkways, the grand lobby, and Patio dining room are painstakingly maintained. Just walking through the gardens of fuchsias, roses, impatiens, tropical trees, and other plants—which you can tell have been here for years—brings a sense of serenity and is actually a perfect activity with a young child.

The Four Seasons Biltmore has seen its clientele change from an older conservative group to families who take their children of all ages with them on vacations. Consequently, the hotel is now geared more toward that clientele, as is evident by the young energetic staff and the activities and amenities offered to families. On the grounds are tennis courts, shuffleboard, croquet, badminton, and a putting green, which is possibly used more by the kids than by the grown-ups. Bikes are available at no charge, starting with ones sized for 12-year-olds. Child carriers and helmets are available.

In the summer there is a supervised Star Fish program for children 5 through 12. There are four two-week sessions (kids can sign up for one week) featuring Red Cross swimming lessons, day trips, arts and crafts, tidepooling, beach games, and lunch. The programs run from 11 a.m. to 2 p.m. weekdays. The charge is $55 for one week, $100 for two weeks. Also ask about special packages that include rooms and programs.

At the press of a telephone button, you can secure other family amenities. A limited number of strollers are available, so when you reserve your room, let them know you'll need one. When you make your reservation, ask for a child's bathrobe to be included along with your standard terrycloth robe. The concierge will get you baby bottles, blankets, lotion, oil, powder, diapers, and shampoo. They'll also supply highchairs and playpens. Forget the toys? They have tons of toys, ranging from infants' playthings to board games and cards. Naturally, they can arrange babysitting.

In addition to a fenced-in pool on the hotel grounds, guests of the Biltmore can use the facilities at the Coral Casino across the street, which is also a private club. There's an Olympic-size swimming pool (actually one meter longer than Olympic regulations, built that way to ensure that no events are ever held there), a sundeck, spas, and access to the beach. Choose from poolside food service, or take-out from the Raft, which features sandwiches and light meals.

The Patio restaurant at the hotel is a pleasant dining room to share with the children. Set in a glass-enclosed courtyard with a retractable ceiling, the Patio is bright and cheerful. Adults can order salads, full entrees, and a few sandwiches. Some entrees, indicated by an asterisk, are calorie-, sodium-, and cholesterol-controlled. There is a children's menu available from 11 a.m. to 1 a.m., which includes chicken filets, hot dogs, ravioli, and hamburgers, with prices ranging from $3.50 to $4.75. Room service is available 24 hours a day. If the adults want a special night out alone, the elegant La Marina restaurant features nouvelle cuisine and a lovely panoramic view of the ocean.

Rooms at the Biltmore are generous in proportion and feel tropical and cool in the summer, warm and cozy in the winter. A recently completed multi-million-dollar renovation has not ruined the relaxed hacienda feeling. Standard poolside rooms are roomy and come with double or king-size beds (dressed with bed skirts and pillow shams), plantation shutters, ceiling fans, and an armoire containing the remote-control TV with cable and in-room movies. Waiting for every arriving guest is a package of chocolate-chip cookies for munching, a famous Four Seasons trademark. Stocked mini-bars, terrycloth robes, full-length mirrors, hand-held hairdryers, makeup mirrors, and two telephones are additional amenities. Closets are fair-sized, and the bathrooms are average but have marble-topped vanities. Downstairs poolside rooms have small brick patios designed to feel as though you have your own private garden. Upstairs rooms have balconies and cathedral ceilings. None of the rooms has air conditioning; electric blankets and VCRs (and almost any other amenity you can think of) are available. Cottages are popular with large families (but pricey). There are several configurations, and you can get up to a five-bedroom unit. They are bright and adorable, with lots of windows, huge walk-in closets, hideabeds, a full bathroom in the parlor unit, fireplaces, and patios with tables and chairs.

Standard rooms start at $150 (no view, small) and go up to $230 for an ocean view. Cottage rooms without parlor are $225. Junior suites are $280; suites in the main building and cottage suites with a parlor are $435. Large suites go for $475 to $560. (Prices for suites are based on one bedroom and a parlor.) There is no charge for an extra person or for children under 18. Cribs and roll-aways are supplied free.

We almost hesitate to recommend the **San Ysidro Ranch,** 900 San Ysidro Lane (off U.S. 101), Montecito, CA 93108 (tel. 805/969-5046), as a family resort, because it makes such a wonderful romantic retreat. But not only do parents bring their children, but some families hold reunions here. If your children don't need much entertaining, and you want to get away for a relaxing vacation, this is the place to go.

As you drive the winding roads to San Ysidro Lane, all city stress begins to disappear. This residential area of Montecito is glorious—private homes are set behind tall hedges or fences on narrow country-like lanes. The magnificent trees and flowers of Santa Barbara are at their most plentiful, and all you hear is the quiet. Then you pass stables and finally reach the ranch, which is really just 10 minutes off the highway but which seems like 30. There's a small lobby and a lounge, perfect for curling up with a good book or for a game of backgammon. Framed reprints line the walls, with stories about the celebrities who have stayed here, such as Vivien Leigh and Laurence Olivier, whose wedding was held at the ranch practically minutes after they received divorces from their former spouses.

You'll discover that the grounds are for walking and exploring, and the park-like grassy areas are for playing. If you've brought your pet, which you can do, it may never want to leave. Trails leading through the mountains make good walks, or you can go on horseback with a guide. There are gardens everywhere, always blooming with bright purple, red, yellow, and white. Some of the plants are even taller than your toddler! The herb garden used by the chef is in full view, and there's a little lawn-bowling area squared off in front of some older playground equipment (which may be moved elsewhere by the time you read this).

It will be hard to keep your mind on tennis at one of the two courts, as each has a pretty good view of the ocean. Better to take the kids to the heated pool, which has a very small wading area for little children, but a glorious ocean view on a clear day. There's poolside food service, with kid-type selections, so you never have to leave for lunch.

The main dining room, the Stonehouse Restaurant, is open for breakfast, lunch, and dinner and has a patio for outdoor dining on warm days. While children will find something they like at breakfast, lunch and dinner are strictly gourmet (and men must wear jackets to dinner), without entrees for the less sophisticated palate. If you fall into this category, either go out to dinner or order from room service. The room service menu is limited for children, but the chef will prepare special requests for youngsters. There is a snack menu with a hamburger and quesadilla. You can also order a box lunch for a day of hiking and picnicking.

The cottages come in all sorts of configurations. There are only 43, and 11 have private Jacuzzis. All have wood-burning fireplaces and private decks, but some cottages are attached to others, and some are totally private. Color TV with cable and HBO is standard, and you can rent VCRs and use the hotel movies (or bring your own). The cottages are not glitzy; rather, they are quietly elegant in that sort of "old money" way. You might find a brass headboard, country quilt, bright yellow-and-blue dollhouse-style furnishings, track lighting, and electric blankets. One sumptuous cottage has a huge living room with a massive fireplace, a dining area, wet bar, and a large bedroom with a king-size bed. The deck, the length of the cottage, overlooks a small canyon and a bubbling creek. Another cottage is in a stone building. At still another, you have a wonderful ocean view from your deck, and the Jacuzzi is hidden behind high doors. Bathrooms are old-fashioned for the most part, with marble-topped vanities and tub/shower combinations. Makeup lights come in some.

A standard room would be fine for a couple with an infant. There is plenty of room for a crib, which must be arranged for in advance. If you have children who require a bed, you must get a one-bedroom suite, which has a pullout sofa in the living room, as there are no rollaways. Standard rooms without Jacuzzis are $155 to $225—the difference is the view and deck configuration. One-bedroom suites in buildings with other accommodations are $245. Private one-bedroom cottages without Jacuzzis are $269 and $279; with private Jacuzzis, $340 to $490. The extra-person charge, including children, is $15 per night. There is a two-night minimum stay on weekends.

Moderate

Fess Parker's Red Lion Resort, 633 E. Cabrillo Blvd., Santa Barbara, CA 93103 (tel. 805/564-4333, or toll free 800/547-8010), is the newest of the Santa Barbara hotels. You can't miss it as you drive up Cabrillo Boulevard—it's the one painted that gorgeous pink with the huge rotunda in front. Set across the street from the beach and minutes from the zoo and town, the Red Lion is a most convenient place to stay. A nearby Vons market on Milpas, open until 11 p.m., is stocked with everything you might need for the children or for a picnic.

There are no children's programs here, but there is a big heated fenced-in pool and spa open from 7 a.m. to 11 p.m. Poolside barbecues are held on the weekends, and Pedalinas and standard bikes are available for rent poolside. The three night-lighted tennis courts are free (lessons available for a fee). Adults can try out the health club and saunas. Call the concierge to arrange fishing trips, whale-watching, or sailing. When you check in, there'll be a list of recreational activities for the month waiting for you in your room. Babysitting can be arranged.

The place to take the family to eat is Café Los Arcos, the big open-air restaurant in the lobby. Although there's no children's menu, the kids won't have a problem making a choice: there are pancakes, cinnamon-raisin French toast, and Belgian waffles for breakfast, and hamburgers, quesadillas, and pizza at lunch and dinner. It's nice to know that the restaurant is open from 6 a.m. to midnight. Room service is available 24 hours a day.

The standard rooms at the Red Lion are oversize. With two queen-size beds or a king-size one, there is still plenty of room for a crib and for moving around. An armoire holds the remote-control color TV (with cable and HBO) and mini-bar. There are double vanities in every room, and tub/shower combinations. The bathtubs are the tiniest we've ever seen, making it more of a shower-only bathroom. (But what a perfect size for bathing a baby!) If you're on the second or third floor with a toddler, request a stuccoed balcony, not one with wrought-iron fences—too dangerous. There are 360 rooms in this hotel (including 25 suites), so you shouldn't have a problem getting what you request.

Deluxe rooms with two queen-size beds and deluxe rooms with king-size beds are even more spacious and include a small sitting area with love seat and reading chair. The bathrooms in these rooms are huge, and the tub could accommodate two people easily. If you're traveling with a large family, or need the space to spread out, definitely request a deluxe room (the difference in price isn't that great). All rooms are air-conditioned and soundproof, and there is same-day laundry and dry-cleaning service. There are also studio, parlor, and executive suites available.

Rates (single or double occupancy) for standard rooms with two queen-size beds or one king-size bed are $145, $155, and $180, depending on view; deluxe rooms with two queen-size beds or a king-size bed cost $180 and $205; suites run $280 to $550. Children under 18 stay free in the same room with their parents; those 18 and older, and additional adults, pay $15. Rollaways cost $15 per night; cribs, $5. Ask about package plans, which are often available.

The **Sheraton Santa Barbara Hotel & Spa**, 1111 E. Cabrillo Blvd., Santa Barbara, CA 93103 (tel. 805/963-0744, 213/278-8014 in Los Angeles, or toll free 800/325-3535), has also gone through a major facelift and has turned itself into a southwestern guest hotel, decorated in soft desert hues and outfitted with casual wood furniture. If you're traveling with the family, you can't beat the location. It's across from East Beach and the beach's playground equipment, down the street from the beach's great volleyball nets, and within walking distance of the Santa Barbara Zoo.

There's a small fenced-in pool at the hotel, and a health club available to those over 16 that is equipped with a Jacuzzi, weight room, showers, lockers, sauna, and massage room.

Room service is available from 7 a.m. to 9:45 p.m., and there is poolside food service. Zack's is the hotel's restaurant, and it's open from 7 a.m. to 10 p.m. The breakfast menu is extensive, and there's a reasonably priced children's menu at lunch. Mom and Dad get to pick from various American regional cuisine offerings.

Rooms at the Sheraton vary in size. If you need a larger room, indicate this when you make your reservations. Wrought-iron-fenced balconies are not safe for very young children, but some rooms don't have balconies—you might want to request these specially. Doubles come with an armoire housing the TV and mini-bar, and are charming, with their skirted beds and peach and white adobe-like walls. Full-length mirrors and hairdryers are standard, and bathrooms have tub/shower combinations and separate vanities with makeup stools tucked underneath. Suntan lotion is one of the bathroom amenities. Large families should know that there are lots of connecting rooms, as well as several suites of different sizes, including one with a kitchenette.

Room rates in season (July to early September) range from $109 to $184, single or double; the rest of the year, $89 to $169. Suites average $250 to $475. Children under 17 stay free in their parents' room; those 17 and over, and extra adults, pay $10 each per night. Cribs and rollaways are available at no charge.

The Sheraton also owns a 24-unit budget hotel called **Surfside,** a two-minute walk from the Sheraton. Guests there have full use of the main hotel amenities, including room service. Reservations for Surfside are made through the local Sheraton number. Rooms are small, with double beds, TVs, balconies, and small bathrooms. There is no room for a crib. Rates run $74 to $119, depending on the season.

If you plan to be in Santa Barbara for a lengthy stay, ask the Sheraton reservationist about the five apartments that can be rented (minimum stays of one month). These four one-bedroom units and one two-bedroom unit are fully furnished and come with twice-weekly maid service.

For years, families have been heading for the blue-tiled roofs of the **Miramar Hotel,** U.S. 101 at San Ysidro Road (P.O. Box M), Santa Barbara, CA 93102 (tel. 805/969-2203, or toll free 800/322-6983). Take Calif. 1 to the San Ysidro turnoff. The two pools, rooms right on the beach, grassy play areas, and roomy cottages have created its popularity. The rooms haven't been refurbished in years, but the location of the Miramar can't be beat.

In addition to the two pools, in the summer the hotel anchors a raft off the beach for guest use. There's always a lifeguard there, and you can get beach umbrellas and backrests and mats from him or her. You can also rent bikes and play tennis, paddle tennis, table tennis, or shuffleboard.

Your children will love the authentic railcar that sits near the tennis courts and has been turned into a diner. It's a good place for hamburgers, shakes, sandwiches, and salads. Eat there or take your food out to the beach. There's also a full-service dining room (the Terrace), open for breakfast, lunch, and dinner right next to the lobby. Room service is available from 7 a.m. to 1:45 p.m. and from 6 to 9:45 p.m.

You can choose from poolside rooms that have one double bed and one twin bed downstairs or two double beds upstairs. They have color TV and standard cable, a small desk and a dressing area, table and chairs, and tub/shower combinations. There's definitely room for a crib in the downstairs rooms. Oceanfront rooms are big, with two double beds, a rattan desk, and deck chairs on the outside patio. Not only is there room for a crib, but these units can connect with a parlor that sleeps two and has a full kitchen. This could then connect to yet another bedroom, making it a full suite that could sleep ten. Sliding-glass doors look out to the ocean. The two-story oceanfront buildings are fronted by a big old wooden boardwalk that was originally an actual pier.

Cottages come in various configurations. You can get a one-bedroom cottage, with a king-size bed in the bedroom and a living room with a fold-out sofa and a fireplace. A small kitchenette is equipped with an apartment-size refrigerator and stove. This could also connect to two more bedrooms, making it a three-bedroom cottage. Most cottages have small wood decks. Parking is available for one car per cottage.

Light sleepers should note that a train comes through the grounds in the middle of the night. Request a room away from the tracks if you think you'll wake up from it.

Rates for singles or doubles are $65 to $115. One-, two-, and three-bedroom suites are $105 to $245. Children 12 and under stay free in their parents' rooms; those over 12, and additional adults, pay $8 each per night. Cribs cost $8; no rollaways are available. There's a two-night minimum on weekends, three nights on holidays.

The **Sandman at the Beach,** 18 Bath St., Santa Barbara, CA 93101 (tel. 805/963-4418, or toll free 800/433-3097), is a real surprise. From the outside, you're not sure what you'll find because it looks so small. But this little European-style inn contains a collection of different rooms. There's no pool, but the beach is just two blocks away. A very small fenced-in spa sits in the courtyard, surrounded by flower boxes and tropical plants. The charming lobby has a sitting area and a couple of outdoor tables for partaking of the complimentary continental breakfast and evening wine and cheese.

Our favorite room is no. 20, a two-room unit fronting Bath Street. The furniture is modern bamboo, and the living room has a desk, fold-out bed, TV, and two comfortable reading chairs. The bedroom is quite large, with a queen-size bed, a big closet with mirrored doors, and a cute blue-and-beige bathroom with a tub/shower combination. You could fit a crib and two older children in the living room, if you had to. There are two standard double rooms, which are quite roomy and popular with families. One has a queen-size and a double bed and a stall shower, while the other has a double bed and a king-size bed and a bath and shower. Some rooms have fireplaces, and firewood is supplied. Room 39 sleeps six, with a king-size bed and small living area with pullout bed in one room, and a separate bedroom with a double bed. There are lots of windows, a huge closet, and a full kitchen that seats four and has a back-door entrance. Two others have two bedrooms and two bathrooms plus a fireplace. The rooms are not fancy, and there are none of the usual hotel amenities—this is more like a bed-and-breakfast inn—but the rooms are clean and the Sandman is well maintained, with a very friendly attitude. Color TVs and heaters are standard; there's no air conditioning.

Rates vary depending on the season. The standard rooms run $80 in the winter and $90 in the summer, single or double. One-bedroom suites (based on three people) are $85 in the winter, $90 to $95 in the summer; two-bedroom suites are $95 to $120 in the winter, $110 to $125 in the summer. The front room runs $100 to $105. Children 6 and under stay free; those over 6 and additional adults pay $10 each per night. Rollaways and cribs are available at no charge. Weekends are always booked, so call in advance. If you're planning to come on a weekday, ask whether special rates are in effect. Also ask about weekly rates. There's a covered parking area, a car port, and a small lot.

Budget

The **Sandman Inn,** 3714 State St., Santa Barbara, CA 93105 (tel. 805/687-2468, or toll free 800/457-2880 in California), is about 15 minutes from the ocean, and it's within blocks of a big shopping center.

The motel has two fenced-in swimming pools and a spa. There is room service from noon to 9 p.m., and the Cattleman's Restaurant is on the premises—it has boosters and highchairs. There's also a Burger King and other fast-food restaurants right across the street. Room rates include complimentary continental breakfast and complimentary wine and cheese in the afternoon. Besides the standard soda machines, there are also juice machines on the grounds.

One of the nicest rooms, if you need just a crib, is the poolside room with a king-size bed, which is roomy and bright and has two entrances, one to the pool, the other to the parking lot. A small alcove area can hold a crib, and there's a little shaded patio with chairs in front. A nice-size closet, refrigerator, and makeup lights complete the picture. One mini-suite has a tiny living room with a hideabed, a small bedroom, a nice-size bathroom with shower stall, and a little refrigerator. It's fine for a family. Another is a two-room unit with a dressing area, one bedroom with two queen-size beds and the other with one double bed and a tub/shower combination. Color TV with basic cable is standard in all the rooms.

Singles rent for $60 to $74; doubles, $76 to $100. Mini-suites and suites cost $98 to $130. Children under 16 stay free in their parents room; those 16 and over pay $5 per night. Cribs can be had at no charge, but rollaways cost $5. Weekly and monthly rates are available.

The **Motel 6** in Santa Barbara, 443 Corona del Mar, Santa Barbara, CA 93103 (tel. 805/564-1392 or 505/891-6161), has as its claim to fame the distinction of being the first Motel 6 ever built. It's always booked (because of its wonderful location within walking distance of the beach and behind the Sheraton Santa Barbara), so it's necessary to make reservations far in advance. There's a small gated heated pool near the parking lot, and lots of vending machines.

This 25-year-old motel has 52 rooms, 5 of which are no-smoking. Upstairs are some connecting rooms (a single connects with a double) and four corner rooms that are larger than the standard rooms and have partial ocean views. Singles have room for a crib; it would be a tight squeeze in a double—you'd be better off to get connecting rooms. There are color TVs with a movie channel, phones, and little dressing areas. Shower stalls are standard. The rooms are clean and tidy, and the maids even use a room-deodorizing spray after each stay, eliminating most of that "motel smell."

You can't beat these rates anywhere—$33 single and $41 double. Children under 18 sleep free in the same room as their parents; those 18 and over pay $6.

An Alternative

A totally unique stay in Santa Barbara is offered through the **University of California at Santa Barbara Vacation Center,** University of California, Santa Barbara, CA 93106 (tel. 805/961-3123). The only way to participate in this "family camp" is to be a UC alumnus, be part of the UC faculty or staff, or be sponsored by someone in one of these categories—in other words, to know someone who went there or who works there.

For a minimum of one week at a time you'll partake in daily recreational classes, games, excursions, and entertainment programs. Anyone in the family can play tennis (free for group lessons, a charge for private lessons); play golf; go swimming in the heated pool or in the ocean nearby (swimming lessons are free for all ages, including toddlers); enter tennis, volleyball, and chess tournaments; join in dancercize, jogging, sports, and bicycling; get free instruction in the crafts center; and attend seminars led by UCSB professors on timely and interesting topics. There are also shows, tours, wine tasting, and adult mixers.

Child care is comprehensive. Small World takes 2- and 3-year-olds, and there are separate groups for children 4 to 12. There's also a full teen program with an overnight campout and local excursions. Child care runs from 9 a.m. to 9 p.m.

Three meals a day, three entrees per meal, and a full salad bar and fresh fruit at all meals are included in the price. The children get special treats too.

The family stays not in tents but in a fully furnished suite of rooms on campus, consisting of a living room with refrigerator, bath, and two to four bedrooms. And there's daily maid service.

Naturally, the program runs only during the summer, from June to September. Sign up at least two months in advance.

Weekly rates are $395 for adults if you're a UC alum, $425 if you're not. Children 6 to 12 pay $300; those 2 to 5, $275; those 12 months to 23 months, $60; and infants under 12 months, $20. If you can't stay the whole week, they'll give you a special rate.

WHERE TO EAT: For an old-fashioned neighborhood restaurant that's a wonderful place to take the family for dinner, try **Mom's Italian Village,** 421 E. Cota

St. (tel. 805/965-5588)—hardly the kind of restaurant you'd expect in tourist- and beach-conscious Santa Barbara. The place is cavernous and able to seat 250 people in its various dining rooms, yet the attitude is small-town friendly, and you can tell Mom's constantly gets repeat customers, as customers call the bus- boys by name. Children are treated with respect here, and they won't find any problem picking something from the children's menu. As they wait to be served, the children can look around at the full wall murals of Venice scenes, old wrought-iron chandeliers, and lots of separate dining rooms.

The children's menu, for kids 10 and under, consists of spaghetti, ravioli, roast tri-tip (a beef roast, a local favorite), halibut, breaded veal cutlets, ground sirloin with mushroom gravy, and a couple of other spaghetti dishes. Prices range from $4 to $8. For $1 more, kids can have jumbo fried shrimp (and they are jum- bo) with a vegetable and potato. A small minestrone soup costs $2.25.

Adults have a large selection to choose from. There are full dinners of chick- en à la cacciatore, beef spezzatini, veal scaloppine, plus other fish, chicken, and steak dinners, which come with vegetables and potatoes, bread and butter. Pasta dinners, which include a salad and bread and butter, consist of stuffed shells, eight different spaghetti dishes, fettuccine and linguine variations, most- accioli, and ravioli dishes. Many of these entrees are vegetarian. There's also a yummy lasagne and Mom's eggplant parmigiana. Entrees start at $6.50 and go up to $13 for steak and beef dishes. You can get a number of deluxe dinner entrees à la carte.

Highchairs and booster seats are available. Baby bottles and baby food will be warmed in the kitchen, and special children's drinks will be made by the bar- tender. Servers bring bread right away so kids can munch, and the children get suckers on their way out.

Open for lunch Tuesday through Friday from 11:30 a.m. to 2:30 p.m. Din- ner is served Tuesday through Sunday from 5 to 10 p.m. Closed all day Monday. Reservations are accepted for three or more and are strongly suggested during the summer. Street parking. They accept MasterCard and VISA credit cards only.

At **Hola Amigos,** 29 E. Cabrillo Blvd. (tel. 805/963-1968), you can see the ocean and Stearns Wharf from most tables. If a view is important, be sure to re- quest a window table when you make a reservation. Inside are lovely arched win- dows and arches separating the eating areas. Obviously the offerings here are Mexican (pretty mild).

There is a lunch buffet for $6, which consists of chiles rellenos, chimichangas, do-it-yourself tacos, and lots of salad items. Your very young chil- dren could munch on finger food from your plate (there's shredded cheese, broc- coli, and other salad makings) and a warm flour tortilla. Older children won't have any trouble finding something they like, even though there's no separate children's menu. Or order off the regular menu for lunch and dinner. There are quesadillas, taquitos, chicken flautas (all appetizers are the right size for chil- dren—$4 to $4.75), fajitas, carnitas, seafood specialties, burritos, chimichangas, and combination plates. One person can eat here for $5 to $13. They will make half orders of certain items on the menu—ask your server. Don't tell the kids about the special fried ice cream—nieve frita—or they'll drive you crazy all through dinner. Vanilla or chocolate ice cream is rolled in cinnamon and corn flakes, then deep-fried and topped with strawberry or chocolate topping and whipped cream!

An all-you-can-eat Sunday brunch is available featuring Belgian waffles, fresh omelets, chiles rellenos, soft tacos, fajitas, fresh fruit, bananas Foster, and cham- pagne. The buffet costs $13 for adults, $6 for children 7 and under.

Boosters and highchairs are provided. Baby food and baby bottles can be warmed in the kitchen, and special children's drinks can be ordered from the bar. Chips and salsa are brought right away, but beware: the salsa is pretty hot!

Open for lunch Monday through Saturday from 11 a.m. to 2:30 p.m. Din- ner is served Monday through Thursday from 2:30 to 10 p.m., on Friday and

Saturday till 11 p.m., and on Sunday from 2 to 9:30 p.m. Sunday brunch hours are 10 a.m. to 2 p.m. Reservations accepted. Parking lot. Major credit cards honored.

J. K. Frimple's, 1701 State St. (tel. 805/569-1671), is one of those great 24-hour coffeeshops that seems like it's been there forever. Only a few minutes' drive from the beach, J. K. Frimple's is comfortable and casual. There's an incredible giant Moreton Bay fig tree, surrounded by glass, in the center of the restaurant; it's more than 100 years old. An outdoor patio, open in warm weather, sits under the branches of this wonderful tree. The coffeeshop has a full bar.

There's no children's menu here. Breakfast is served anytime. Try a Whimple's, a malted waffle served with apricot or maple syrup. Wheat and honey pancakes, French toast, omelets, egg dishes, and cereal are also on the menu. Breakfast prices start at $2.50 and go to $7.

You can have just about anything for lunch and dinner, from a grilled roast beef, cheddar, and tomato sandwich to liver and onions, baked lasagne, chicken curry, southern fried chicken, steak Guadalajara, salads, and vegetarian dinners. There are daily specials and a fresh fish of the day. Bakery goods are fresh baked (brownies, cinnamon rolls, pies, carrot cake—should we go on?), and there are malts, milkshakes, floats, and hot-fudge sundaes. Lunch costs $2.75 to $6.75; dinner runs $5.75 to $11.

Highchairs and boosters are provided. Baby bottles and food can be warmed in the kitchen, and meals will be split at no charge. Crackers are brought right away.

Open 24 hours. No reservations accepted, but there's hardly ever a wait. Large parking lot. All major credit cards accepted.

Carnaval, 634 State St. (tel. 805/962-9991), is a place your teenagers will love. It's located right on State Street and looks out on the young scene. The minimalist interior and ongoing music will appeal to that age group.

The food is basic hamburgers, sandwiches, and salads, and the prices are reasonable. The menu changes, so call first if you only want hamburgers. Prices for lunch and dinner range from $4 for a half sandwich to $13 for a steak-and-shrimp combo that comes with soup or salad, pasta, vegetables, bread and butter.

If you decide to bring your little ones (we'd suggest at lunch only), they do have boosters and highchairs here.

Open daily for lunch and dinner from 11 a.m. to 9 p.m. Dancing, for those 21 and over, starts at 9 p.m., and there's a $2 cover charge. Reservations are accepted. Street parking. Major credit cards welcome.

Just a couple of blocks from the beach, **The Long Bar,** 111 State St. (tel. 805/564-1215), is a good choice for weekend breakfast and weekday lunch, and fine for an early dinner with young children, and a later dinner with kids nine and up. Big, bright, and airy, there is actually a long bar barely separated from the eating areas. Rock music is heard throughout the restaurant, and there's a big-screen TV and open-style kitchen to keep eyes occupied. The outdoor patio is nice, but butts up against the parking lot.

For breakfast, there's lots of fresh fruit, fresh-squeezed orange juice, French toast, and pancakes ($2.25 to $3.25). Those youngsters in your party might even want a dish of fruit and cream for $2.75. Other breakfast choices run $2.75 to $5.

At lunchtime, you can get a side-order quesadilla for $4.25 or a perfect child's-size one-quarter barbecued chicken for $4. There's also a half chicken ($7), burgers (from $4.75 to $5), fajitas, and tacos asados ($5.75 and $8).

Regional Mexican dishes are served at dinner. For Mom and Dad, there's carnitas lechuga (baked and sautéed pork served on lettuce leaves), carne de res guisada (a Nuevo León regional dish of braised beef sirloin and chile sauce), pescado en papillote (fresh fish baked in a parchment bag, a Baja favorite), and pollo Laredo (boneless breast of chicken stuffed with cheese, bacon, olives, and jalapeños, then mesquite-broiled and topped with cheese sauce). Regional entrees range from $5.50 to $11. Those of you with noncurious tastebuds can order a cheeseburger, seafood pasta, a broiled fish sandwich, or a sirloin steak. The very adventurous can get a Cadillac botana platter, a combination of lots of regional specialties, at $23.50 for two or three people, $37 for four or five people. On this platter, kids could have the chicken taquitos and frijoles borrachos, while you savor the pollo al mesquite and corn chowder. Or for a slightly higher price, do the same thing with the botana del mar, which offers many seafood specialties.

Boosters and highchairs are available. Management will split portions, warm baby bottles and food, and prepare special children's drinks at the bar.

Open Monday through Thursday from 4 to 10:30 p.m., on Friday and Saturday from 9 a.m. to 10:30 p.m., and on Sunday from 8 a.m. to 10 p.m. The hours may change, so call ahead. Reservations are accepted. Parking lot. Major credit cards accepted.

Moby Dick's (tel. 805/965-0549) is Stearns Wharf's answer to the nautical coffeeshop. This casual seaside restaurant, with its rough wood floors, wood beams, and uncomplicated menu, located near the end of Stearns Wharf, affords a great view. Nearly all the tables have some sort of view.

Breakfast, which is served until 11 a.m., offers pigs in a blanket served with applesauce, Belgian waffles, hot cereal with brown sugar, raisins and cream, omelets, eggs, pancakes, and French toast. You can even get yogurt with fresh fruit, honey and wheat granola. Prices start at $1.25 and go to $11 for steak and eggs.

For lunch there are hot and cold sandwiches, salads, fried seafood, and hamburgers. At dinner, you can get full entrees served with soup or salad, baked potato, and rolls. Entrees include sweet-and-sour shrimp; stuffed sole; grilled salmon, halibut, or swordfish; and grilled Maryland crab cakes. Or you can get linguine with clam sauce or with a marinara topping, a New York steak, or fried chicken, as well as fried seafood. The kids can have any of those entrees, if they can finish them, or order from the children's menu for youngsters under 12. That menu includes a four-ounce chopped steak, fried shrimp, or chicken drumsticks, all served with french fries, sliced tomatoes, milk or a soft drink, and sherbet (each entree is $4.25). Lunch prices on the standard menu are $3.25 to $12; dinner entrees, $5.25 to $12.

There are Sassy seats and highchairs.

Open daily from 7 a.m. to 8:30 p.m. Reservations accepted for large parties only. Park on the wharf and get a validation at the cash register. Major credit cards welcome.

In Summerland

The **Big Yellow House,** 108 Pierpont Ave., Summerland (take the Summerland exit off U.S. 101; tel. 805/969-4140), is an excellent choice for breakfast, lunch, or dinner and is only a few minutes from Montecito. The service is efficient and friendly, and the restaurant is occupied by its own ghost whose name is Hector. The house itself, which is more than 100 years old, has an interesting history. Read all about it on the back of the menu. In fact, read the story aloud to the kids. The restaurant is across the highway from the ocean, so there is some view!

Besides the standard French toast and buttermilk pancakes for breakfast, there's also Grandma's fruit stacks—a stack of hot apple, blueberry, strawberry, and banana hotcakes with whipped cream—or blueberry hotcakes with honey and wheat-germ topping. Homemade corned-beef hash, huevos rancheros, and standard egg dishes round out the offerings. Breakfast prices start at $4 and top out at $7.50 for steak and eggs.

If you come for lunch, there's a kid's burger with chips, or a basket of chicken (fried chicken is the specialty here), salads, tempura beef batter fish, standard-size hamburgers, homemade chili, and hot and cold sandwiches. Lunches run $3 to $7.50; kid's plate, $2.25.

Dinner is a great time to come with the family. Adults get broiled tri-tip (a local beef favorite), famous fried chicken, pork chops, chicken breast, prime rib, fish, seafood, pot roast, or a vegetarian platter, all accompanied by soup or salad, a vegetable, mashed potatoes and gravy, and a fresh baked corn muffin. You can order any size portion of main entree for your children; the management will determine the price with their scale. Or order the kid's hamburger, which is $2.50 at dinner. Adults can add two pieces of fried chicken to any dinner selection for an additional $2.25. If yours is a very light eater, order those two extra chicken pieces with your entree. Kids get a free dessert sherbet cone.

Regular entrees begin at $7 for a half-pound hamburger to $15 for a 16-ounce piece of prime rib. Fresh fish and seafood entrees are priced daily.

There are booster seats available, and the management will warm baby bottles and baby food and make special children's drinks.

Open Sunday through Thursday from 7:30 a.m. to 9 p.m., on Friday and Saturday till 10 p.m. Reservations are welcome. Parking lot. MasterCard and VISA only accepted.

The **Omelette Parlor,** 2294 Lillie Ave., Summerland (tel. 805/969-1019), next door to the Big Yellow House, is an alternative stop. Only breakfast and lunch are served in this turn-of-the-century–style restaurant with wooden benches and booths, stained-glass windows, stenciled wall decorations and hanging plants, and ceiling fans. Portions are very large, and although there's no children's menu, you could easily split an order between two children. The "Serendipity," for instance, comes with three eggs, an English muffin, potatoes, fresh fruit, and four big crispy pieces of bacon for $4.25. Or there's oatmeal, Belgian waffles served with or without a fruit topping ($2.75 or $4), lots of omelets, fruit and cheese, and French toast (either topped with powdered sugar and cinnamon for $2.75 or made out of cinnamon swirl bread for $3.50).

Lunch consists of lots of healthy sandwiches (like apples, raisins, and tuna mixed with honey-mustard dressing and served on raisin bread—$4), salads, and hamburgers (besides the traditional burgers, there's one served with peanut butter, bacon, and Jack cheese!). Burgers run $3.25 to $3.75.

Booster seats are available, but no highchairs. They'll bring extra plates for splitting meals at no charge, and will gladly warm baby food and bottles in the kitchen.

Open daily from 6 a.m. to 3 p.m. Reservations accepted for parties of eight or more only. The wait usually isn't more than 20 minutes on busy mornings. Parking lot and street parking. MasterCard and VISA only.

IN AN EMERGENCY: If a medical emergency should arise during your stay in Santa Barbara, there's a 24-hour emergency room at **St. Francis Hospital,** 601 E. Micheltorena St. (tel. 805/568-5711 or 805/962-7661).

---

2. VENTURA / OXNARD

The Ventura/Oxnard area is within easy driving distance of Los Angeles and Santa Barbara. From Los Angeles, take the Ventura Freeway (U.S. 101) north to the Rose exit going west. Go right on Gonzalez, and take that all the way to Harbor Boulevard. Make a right to Ventura, a left to Oxnard. Some people make Oxnard or Ventura their base; others just visit for the day. Ventura and Oxnard are only about 10 or 15 minutes apart on Harbor Boulevard.

VENTURA: Located just off the coast of Ventura is one of the area's main attractions. The Channel Islands are a group of eight islands off the California coast, five of which comprise **Channel Islands National Park.** You'll want to start out at the Visitor Center, which is at the end of Spinnaker Drive (no. 1901) in Ventura, CA 93001 (tel. 805/644-8262). Not only will you get information on the islands, plus maps and brochures, but the children will also enjoy the little museum of marine life that includes an indoor tidepool and displays of Chumash Indian artifacts. A 25-minute film about the islands is shown and some children will enjoy this. It's a lovely place to just sit by the ocean and watch the harbor boats.

Next door to the Visitor Center is **Island Packers,** 1867 Spinnaker Dr., Ventura, CA 93001 (tel. 805/642-1393 for reservations or 805/642-7688 for information), the official park concessionaire. This is where you'll get information and make reservations to tour the islands. Island Packers runs boats to Anacapa and Santa Barbara islands regularly during spring and summer and at scheduled times the rest of the year. They take small groups to the islands on basic, open boats to capture the feel of the environment. You will not be embarking on plush cruise boats. There are rest rooms on board but no food service. There's a deli/snack shop near the embarkation point.

The islands are virtually unsullied by development—their natural state has been and is being maintained. These rugged islands are wonderful fun for boys and girls who love to explore. Come prepared. Wear layered clothing for warmth, and shoes with good gripping soles for walking. If you intend to hike, be prepared to carry young children. Tell the kids they will be seeing some very precious sea and land mammals, plants, endangered brown pelicans, and exquisite wildflowers. Because the islands are so undisturbed, the sea life is abundant. The kids are fascinated by the teeming life in the tidepools. Interesting rock formations, giant sea caves, and steep cliffs vary at the different islands, and some can be seen as the boat gets closer to the islands. Happily, there are no souvenir shops on the islands and no stores. On some of the islands there's not even fresh water, so you will have to fill your own canteens ahead of time.

Anacapa is the island closest to the mainland. It's the one you will most likely visit the first time, as it has the shortest crossing and the easiest landing. But it does have it's drawbacks. The cruise to Anacapa takes 1½ hours. In winter the water conditions vary—be prepared for rough landings. While you can explore it with very young children, there are very sheer cliffs and no guardrails to protect those who run off on their own. When you land on the east side, you must walk up 154 steps to reach the top, where there's a tiny visitor center and the beginning of a 1½-mile self-guiding trail. The landing cove is 20 to 30 feet deep and calm enough for summer swimming. From November through May, Island Packers docks on the west side at Frenchy's Cove, which is noted for its fine tidepools. You're given time to explore the sea life, and are then taken on a narrated cruise around the rugged coastline, where you'll also be treated to views of sea lions, seals, and birds. From June through October, special swim and snorkel days are designated for just relaxing on the small beach. There's no fresh water on the island, and very little protection from the sun. Remember to bring your own water, food, and sunscreen.

To see the wildflowers, you should visit in the spring, from January to April, but the weather is not predictable then. For calmer weather, visit from June through August (which is also the heaviest tourist time).

For specific information about **Santa Barbara, Santa Rosa,** and **San Miguel islands,** contact the Channel Islands National Park Service (information below).

Island Packers also offers half-day nonlanding tours to Anacapa, and cruises to Santa Barbara Island, from Memorial Day through Labor Day (3 hours one way); Santa Rosa Island, May through September (3- to 3½-hour crossings— landings can be rough); San Miguel Island, January, April, and June through October (long and rough crossing); and whale-watching cruises, December through March (half- and full-day excursions).

Camping on Anacapa (year round) and Santa Barbara (Memorial Day through Labor Day) is restricted to 30 people on each island. Reservations and permits are necessary. Call or write the National Park Service, Channel Islands National Park, 1901 Spinnaker Dr., Ventura, CA 93001 (tel. 805/644-8262).

Rates for the full-day excursion to Anacapa are $28 for adults, $14 for children 12 and under. The round-trip fare to camp on the island is $38 for adults, $19 for children. Half-day, cruise-only excursions cost $16 for adults, $9.50 for children.

The fare to Santa Barbara Island is $40 for adults, $27 for children. Camping costs $60 for adults, $45 for children. To Santa Rosa and San Miguel islands, adults are charged $60; children, $50.

Reservations are necessary most times of the year, but especially on weekends. In summer season, reserve two to four weeks in advance by phone. One boat carries a maximum of 45 people, the other two, only 29 each. The stay on the islands is 2½ to 3½ hours.

Once you're back on the mainland, you will want to visit **Ventura Harbor Village,** at 1559 Spinnaker Dr., off Harbor Boulevard, in Ventura Harbor (tel. 805/644-0169), a quaint village of shops selling souvenirs and gifts. Of particular interest to the kids are the shells, kites, and nautical items. Adjacent to the Ventura Yacht Club and overlooking the harbor, it's a charming spot for an afternoon stroll. There are lots of restaurants, including many places to eat outdoors. Keep your eyes open for the **Carousel Market,** which has an indoor carousel surrounded by shops selling cotton candy, popcorn, hot dogs, and souvenirs. Look for boat rentals and a bike path on the street side along Spinnaker. The Village gets crowded on weekends, and parking, even in the lot, can try your patience. Stores are open daily from 10 a.m. to 6 p.m. Restaurant hours vary, so check ahead.

Forty-minute cruises of Ventura Harbor are available every hour on the hour on the **Harbor Queen** or the **Bay Queen,** which are docked at 1567 Spinnaker Dr. in Ventura Harbor Village adjacent to the Coastal Cone Co. (tel. 805/642-7753). Tours depart in the winter on Saturday and Sunday from noon to 5 p.m.; in summer, Tuesday through Sunday at same hours. Fares are $4 for adults, $3 for children under 12; under 2 free.

While you're there, you might want to rent one of the four-seater pedalboats. Rentals cost $10 an hour, with a $20 deposit necessary. A 15-foot runabout rents for $25 per hour, with a deposit of $250 or a major credit card up front.

Places to Eat

Although there are numerous fast-food restaurants in the vicinity, two sit-down restaurants deserve mention.

La Marina Cantina, 1567 Spinnaker Dr., in Ventura Harbor Village (tel. 805/658-7067), has an outdoor patio and a view of the harbor. This place can't be beat. And the prices are reasonable too. Lunch choices include machaca, flautas, camarones, or combination plates of enchiladas, chiles rellenos, tamales, and tacos. There are also tostadas and egg dishes, as well as à la carte selections and appetizers. Prices range from $2.50 to $6.75. Dinner entrees include delicious fajitas, carne tampiqueña, several shrimp dishes, seafood enchiladas, and fresh fish, and all come with soup or salad ($7.50 to $10.50). Children can choose the child's burrito or quesadilla ($1.50 or $1.75), something off the à la carte menu, or a meal-size appetizer.

There are booster seats only here. Management will gladly split orders, warm baby food and bottles, and make special children's drinks.

La Marina Cantina is open weekdays from 11 a.m. to 10 p.m. and on Saturday and Sunday from 9 a.m. to 11 p.m. No reservations accepted. Plenty of parking. Major credit cards honored.

Christy's, 1559 Spinnaker Dr., in Ventura Harbor Village (tel. 805/642-3116), is another good choice. Open for breakfast and lunch, Christy's serves eggs, omelets, sandwiches, salads, and burgers (prices average $4). There's no harbor view or children's menu, but the food is good. They keep a stock of children's books to entertain the kids.

Boosters and highchairs are available.

Open daily from 7 a.m. to 3 p.m. Park in the village lot. Credit cards accepted.

The primary connection between Ventura and Oxnard is Harbor Boulevard, a four-mile stretch with a well-marked bike trail on each side of the road. Off this route is the entrance to **McGrath State Park and Beach.** The beach is a ten-minute walk from the parking lot. Pretty and peaceful, and equipped with barbecue pits and picnic tables, McGrath is a day-use park and has a campground. The public beach makes a great morning or afternoon stop. There's also a nature trail and other hiking areas in the park.

Day use is $4 per car; overnight, $12; walk-in camping, $2. Make campsite reservations (174 developed sites) through **MISTIX** (tel. toll free 800/446-'ARK).

OXNARD: Oxnard's **Channel Islands Harbor** is its main waterfront recreation area. There are seven miles of uncrowded beaches just north of the harbor, and slips for more than 2,500 pleasure boats. Sportfishing boats and boat rentals are plentiful at South Victoria Avenue, Channel Islands Landing. The small visitor center can give you maps and special event information. It's located at 3600 S. Harbor Blvd., in the Marine Emporium, Suite 215, Channel Islands Harbor, Oxnard, CA 93035 (tel. 805/985-4852).

When you spot the mock lighthouse, you will have found **Fisherman's Wharf,** a small New England–style shopping area at the corner of Channel Islands Boulevard and Victoria Avenue. The children can watch the boats unload their catch of the day nearby. While many of the shops cater to tourists, you might want to stop by **Shell World** (tel. 805/985-3030), which has a wonderful selection of both inexpensive and very rare and costly shells. Another interesting establishment is the **Brandon King Seafood Market and Restaurant,** at the end of the block of stores (tel. 805/984-5826). The menu is on the wall, and you can introduce the kids to a wide assortment of seafood at the counter to take home or to eat on the large outdoor courtyard set with tables. Select from such fare as fish and chips, shrimp and chips, all sorts of fish (including shark), chicken, sandwiches, and lots of side orders. Kids love to look at the live lobster and crab bins outside. Cups of cooked shrimp cost $2.50; lobster cocktails, $3.50; sandwiches, $4 to $7. Nothing is more than $9. Open Sunday through Thursday from 10 a.m. to 8 p.m., on Friday and Saturday till 9 p.m.

Another nearby themed shopping center is **Harbor Landing,** located on South Harbor Boulevard. In addition to its retail shops, the enclosed Spanish-style courtyard is surrounded by a number of quick-service restaurants offering fish, barbecue dishes, frozen yogurt, and pizza. In good weather you can sit outdoors overlooking the harbor.

If you plan to be in the area in the spring (early May), be sure to allow time for the annual **Strawberry Festival,** a two-day event that attracts more than 50,000 people. Everything revolves around that tasty fruit, including strawberry shortcake-eating contests and the judging of the outstanding strawberry blonde (there's one of these contests for 5- to 12-year-olds too). There are bands, dances, arts and crafts displays, and tons of strawberry products for sale. Contact the **Ox-**

nard Convention and Visitors Bureau, 325 Esplanade Dr., Oxnard, CA 93030 (tel. 805/485-8833), for this year's exact dates.

Places to Eat

While there are many quick-food establishments scattered throughout the area, you might want to stop for more substantial fare. Or you may want to visit this area just for brunch and a view of the harbor. Here are several selections.

The Whale's Tale, 3950 Bluefish Circle, Channel Island Harbor, Oxnard (tel. 805/985-2511), is an excellent restaurant with a superb view of the marina. The choices here are mainly seafood and beef, and there's a great salad bar set up in a replica of a fishing boat. The portions are large and the food is good. Young travelers will be kept busy while you wait for your food with the crayons and mini-coloring books provided by the restaurant. (If the kids return the crayons, they get a balloon and candy.)

Children can order from their own menu, which features lemon chicken, a junior top sirloin steak and fries, a hamburger, or fish and chips. Meals include a trip to the salad boat or a cup of clam chowder. Prices range from $4.50 to $8.

Adults have loads of choices for lunch and dinner. Besides the salad boat, generous salads include the seafood Cobb, New Orleans fried chicken salad, and the Whale Boat (a seafood salad). There are basic ham-and-cheese sandwiches, crab melts, almond chicken pita, crab and bacon double-deckers, and a marina salad sandwich, among others. For a full lunch (including spinach salad, sliced tomatoes, or green salad), you might pick calamari steak, pork loin roast, red snapper Monterey, or Cajun seafood chili. Lunch prices range from $4 to $9. Dinner has more seafood selections, including baked sole, Gold Coast cioppino, beer-batter-fried shrimp, and scallop sauté. There's also lobster tail, prime rib, rack of lamb, chicken piccata, a filet and a top sirloin, or a pastry basket of fresh vegetables (with hollandaise sauce). Dinners are substantially higher, starting at $11 and going to $26.

Upstairs in The Whale's Tale is a shellfish bar for light eating. Another great view awaits you there. You can easily make a lunch or dinner out of selections such as iced and hot shellfish, sandwiches, salads, burgers, and daily specials. Prices here range from $4.75 to $13.

Boosters and highchairs are provided. Management will gladly split orders for kids, warm baby bottles and baby food, and make special children's drinks.

The Whale's Tale and shellfish bar are open for lunch Monday through Saturday from 11:15 a.m. to 3 p.m. and on Sunday from 10:30 a.m. to 2:30 p.m. Dinner is served Monday through Friday from 5 to 10:30 p.m., on Saturday till midnight, and on Sunday from 4 to 10:30 p.m. Reservations are accepted. Parking nearby. Major credit cards welcome.

Captain Jack's Landing, upstairs at 4151 S. Victoria Ave. (tel. 805/985-5200), has a nautical décor and a wonderful view. It's sure to have something to please most tastes, even though it does not have a children's menu. For lunch, you might interest your young crew in fish and chips or "Pinocchio's Pride" (an open-face sandwich with beef, ham, and shrimp, served with fries). For dinner, bring the older kids, as the selections are more sophisticated and the prices quite high. Veal Oscar is one choice, along with lots of seafood and fresh fish, pasta, steaks, sweetbreads, ribs, and nightly specials. Lunch prices range from $5 to $7. Dinner prices start at $8 and top out at $30 (for chateaubriand for two).

Boosters and highchairs are available. Portions can be split between two children for a $2.50 charge; baby bottles and baby food will be warmed in the kitchen, and special children's drinks can be made. Tuesday through Saturday evenings, there's adult music. Kids can play the video games.

Open for lunch Monday through Saturday from 11:30 a.m. to 3 p.m. Sunday brunch is served from 10:30 a.m. to 3 p.m. Dinner is offered Sunday through Thursday from 5 to 10 p.m.; on Friday and Saturday they serve until 11 p.m.

Reservations are accepted at dinner for parties of six or more; reservations are accepted for everyone at brunch. Parking nearby. Major credit cards welcome.

The best bet for a moderately priced lunch or dinner is **Tugs**, 3600 S. Harbor Blvd., Channel Islands Harbor in the Marine Emporium (tel. 805/985-TUGS). It doesn't have a children's menu, but most children will be satisfied with the selections. Besides, it's comfortably casual, and the view of the harbor is great. The names of the selections are all nautical terms, and some kids will love to know what they mean. For breakfast, they can have pancakes, waffles, or French toast, while you can choose corned-beef hash and eggs, omelets, or steak and eggs. Breakfast runs $2.50 to $6.50. Lunch includes chowders, salads, seafood entrees, sandwiches, burgers, and fruit, cheese, and bread boards ($2.50 to $7.50). There's an interesting afternoon menu served from 3 to 5 p.m. that's perfect for early eaters. It includes a fishburger or hamburger, salads, and appetizers such as nachos grandes, eggrolls, mozzarella marinara, sautéed mushrooms, and clam strips ($2.50 to $6.75). Dinner adds steak, prime rib, and chicken to the seafood entrees, burgers, and chowders ($5 to $15). At Sunday brunch you can have a fruit plate with yogurt and homemade banana bread, a tostada, pancakes, waffles, French toast, omelets, or seafood crêpes ($4 to $7.50).

Highchairs and boosters are provided. The servers will split any entree for two children, and will warm baby bottles and baby food in the kitchen.

Open Sunday through Thursday from 9 a.m. to 9 p.m. and on Friday and Saturday from 8 a.m. to 10:30 p.m. No reservations accepted—the wait's not too long, and the view keeps most children occupied. Parking nearby. Major credit cards honored.

Places to Stay

Many Los Angelenos choose Oxnard as a weekend family retreat. The **Embassy Suites Mandalay Beach Resort**, 2101 Mandalay Beach Rd., Oxnard, CA 93035 (tel. 805/984-2500, or toll free 800/582-3000 in California), is the deluxe hotel of choice. This all-suite hotel is located on the beach, but it also has a very large freeform pool and two huge whirlpools set in secluded areas. Lush foliage, waterfalls, and streams give the Spanish-style buildings a tropical feel. And the lobby, with its three-story-high ceiling, makes a pleasant place to wander with restless toddlers.

Hotel activities include volleyball, smashball, tennis, and Frisbee on the hotel grounds. Single, tandem, and mountain bikes can be rented every day but Monday at the poolside equipment-rental office. They even have children's bikes and adult bikes with child carriers and helmets. On Saturday and busy holiday weekends, a clown entertains the children—and adults—during the complimentary cocktail hour. On the beach during weekends, everybody gets involved in kite-flying contests. Contact the concierge about babysitting.

The Opus One Restaurant is open for lunch and dinner. This is the elegant hotel restaurant, but it does have a limited children's menu. There are boosters and highchairs available for young diners. Complimentary full breakfasts are served in the Surf Room, and complimentary cocktails are provided in the afternoon. There is also room service from 7 a.m. to 11 p.m., with selections the kids will like. You can order smaller portions at half price. A snackbar is open weekends at the pool.

Each suite comes with two full bathrooms, a living room with a queen-size hideabed, two color TVs, multiline phones, a small dining area, a kitchenette with a compact microwave, a small refrigerator, and place settings for four. The marble bathrooms are nice-sized, the showers are separate, and generous bathroom amenities are included. First-floor patio rooms, equipped with table and chairs, open to the courtyard, the beach, or a grassy area. Second-floor rooms have patios with open-slatted balconies, great for relaxing on but best for over-toddler-aged kids. Upper-floor terraces are large enough to play on and are safe for curious toddlers and infants. The first two levels are furnished with king-size beds; the upper floor, with two queen-size beds.

Rates range from $125 to $180 single, $135 to $190 double. Two-bedroom presidential suites rent for $425 to $500. Children under 12 stay free; those 12 and over and additional adult guests pay $10 each per night. Cribs are available at no charge; they have no rollaways.

The **Casa Sirena Resort,** located at 3605 Peninsula Rd., Channel Islands Harbor, Oxnard, CA 93035 (tel. 805/985-6311), is a more moderately priced establishment. This motel-style resort is comfortable and a good place for families who don't want to spend lots of money but still want to be near the water and have things for the kids to do. There's a pool (room service is available poolside) and two whirlpools, a game room with a pool table and video machines, a fully equipped exercise room, tennis courts, a putting green, and bicycle rentals. A beautiful city park in the middle of the resort overlooks the harbor and makes a great area for children to play, with slides, a merry-go-round, and other playground equipment built into a giant sandbox. Five minutes away are clean public beaches.

The resort's restaurant, the Lobster Trap, is open for breakfast, lunch, and dinner. There's no children's menu, but they will accommodate little appetites with small portions at smaller prices. Room service is also available from 6:30 a.m. to 9:30 p.m.

The rooms here come with double or king-size beds; some have gas fireplaces, and all have small refrigerators, coffee makers, and separate vanities and dressing areas. There are lots of adjoining rooms. Family suites are perfect for two adults and two children, with room for a crib. There's a separate bedroom, and the living room has a hideabed. The kitchen comes with a stove, refrigerator, and sink. The bright family suites overlook the marina, with triple-window sliding doors leading out to a balcony with high railings. Larger suites are also available.

Rooms at Casa Sirena rent for $64 to $76 single and $76 to $88 double. Family suites with kitchen cost $105; one- and two-bedroom suites, $125 and $195. Children under 18 stay free in their parents' room; those 18 and over, and additional adults, pay $12 each per night. Cribs and rollaways are available at no charge. Ask about package plans.

3. THE OJAI VALLEY

Ojai (pronounced "*O*-high") was named by the Chumash Indians many, many years ago. It means "the nest," which is really quite appropriate, since the town's quiet, pastoral character and its valley setting really do make it seem like a comfortable retreat.

Ojai is the place to spend the day bicycle riding, hiking, or taking leisurely drives on picture-perfect backcountry roads. It's a town of art galleries, artists' studios, antique stores, and alternative-living centers.

It's a day trip from Los Angeles, or part of a day from Santa Barbara or Oxnard. The 85-mile drive from Los Angeles is an easy one. The exit off U.S. 101 is about ten minutes outside Oxnard. The two-lane highway to Ojai passes through little picturesque towns. Or incorporate a visit with one to Ventura and Oxnard, 14 miles away. Santa Barbara is 20 miles north.

You can't miss the Spanish mission-style architecture of the **Arcade,** the main shopping area in town. Stop by the **Ojai Valley Chamber of Commerce,** 338 E. Ojai Ave. (Calif. 150), Ojai, CA 93023 (tel. 805/646-8126), for a free copy of *The Visitor's Guide to the Ojai Valley.* The chamber has detailed lists of bike and hiking trails and campgrounds as well. The office is open weekdays from 9:30 a.m. to 4:30 p.m.

WHAT TO DO AND SEE: There's nice **shopping** in and around the Arcade.

Libbey Park is across from the center of the Arcade on Ojai Avenue. This is where you'll want to picnic if you've come just for the afternoon. It's a charming park with lots of oak trees, a nice picnic area, and a children's playground. It's also the site of many of Ojai's cultural events, which you might want to enjoy during your visit.

Bicycling is one of the most popular activities in town. There are a number of roads for pedaling, including the paved bike trail that begins at Fox Street and continues for about five miles. The tree-filled neighborhoods and groves of eucalyptus trees make a perfect setting for a family ride. If you don't have bikes, join the rest of the people who use this as a walking trail. You can also take an easy ride through orange and avocado groves by taking Ojai Avenue east and making an easy loop around the east side of town. This is a very popular route for biking because of the flat, paved road and the surrounding perfume of oranges. Camp Comfort Park, two miles south of town, is a good place to stop for a picnic during a ride. Take Creek Road from the foot of south Montgomery Street.

Rent a bike from **The Bicycle Doctor,** 212 Fox St., two blocks from the Arcade (tel. 805/646-7554), who has two bikes for kids 6 or older, but no child carriers and no helmets. Open every day except Wednesday from 10 a.m. to 6 p.m. Adult and children's bikes rent for $5 per hour, or $15 per day.

Besides the Los Padres National Forest (see the Solvang section), there are other places for day hikes in the area. One is **Matilija Lake,** about six miles from Ojai. Take Calif. 33 north toward Taft to Country Campground No. 1. Take the quarter-mile hike to the lake from the old road at the end of the campground. There are plenty of rest stops along the way, which also make great places to picnic. A little spring follows the oaktree-lined road.

Plan to spend the entire day at **Lake Casitas Recreation Area,** 11311 Santa Ana Rd., Ventura (tel. 805/649-2233), just five miles from Ojai. Take Calif. 33 west to Calif. 150. Turn right and go four miles to the entrance. Set on 6,200 acres in the Ojai Valley, Lake Casitas is used as a domestic water supply. There is no swimming or waterskiing allowed, but you can fish, hike, and picnic here.

Fishing licenses, bait, and equipment rental are available at the **Boat, Bait & Tackle Shop,** where you can also rent boats. Janey loved being the captain of the little motorboat, although she fell asleep on the calm, peaceful lake. There are rowboats, a ten-passenger patio deck boat, and motorboats of varying sizes and horsepower, suitable for fishing or just a leisurely ride around the lake. Rentals are by the hour, five hours, or the day. *Note:* Cash only accepted for boat rentals. You can reserve a boat ahead of time by mailing in a full-day deposit. Contact **Casitas Boat Rentals,** 11311 Santa Ana Rd., Ventura, CA 93001 (tel. 805/649-2043), for current rates and deposit information.

There are more than 400 campsites available on a first-come, first-served basis. The fee is $8 per vehicle per night. Coin-operated showers and rest rooms are plentiful, and you'll find a park store, a snackbar, a first-aid station, pay phones, and fish-cleaning sinks on the grounds.

If you aren't camping out, come just for a picnic or a hike. There are lots of picnic tables, easy hiking, and several areas with playground equipment. □

The recreation area is open year round. Day use is $2.50 per vehicle.

WHERE TO EAT: If you're not picnicking or camping and want a bite to eat while in town, there are a couple of places you might try.

Around the corner from the Arcade is a cute, casual place for a quick bite and a soda or sundae. **Soda Bar & Grill,** 219 E. Matilija St. (tel. 805/646-7632), has a jukebox in the center of the room and a few video games to keep everyone occupied. Sit at the counter or in one of the '50s-style booths. "Mitey Bites" are perfect for little appetites—it's a little hamburger with "everything" for 75¢—or buy them by the bag. There are quarter-pound burgers, sandwiches, hot dogs, croissant sandwiches, chicken and chips, and salads ($2 to $4.50). Save room for banana splits, sundaes (each comes in a mini-size as well), shakes, floats, pies, or fudge brownies.

Highchairs and booster seats are provided. Bottles and baby food can be warmed in the kitchen.

Open Monday through Thursday from 11 a.m. to 9 p.m., on Friday and Saturday till 10 p.m., and on Sunday till 7 p.m. No reservations accepted. Park on the street or in the lot behind the Arcade. Cash only; no credit cards honored.

Another quick-stop restaurant—which is also a great place for take-out picnic food—is **Jovone's Deli,** in the Arcade (tel. 805/646-0207), a favorite with locals. No children's menu here, but there are enough choices for everyone. At breakfast there's a huge selection of omelets ($4 to $5) as well as full breakfasts. For the toddlers, you can get a side order of pancakes for 60¢. There's also an eclectic mix of bagels to eat here or to go—ever tried a chocolate-chip bagel?— and with scallion- or honey-walnut-raisin-flavored cream cheese!

At lunch there are hot and cold sandwiches (in large or small sizes), hamburgers, and Mexican food. You can also order small or large salads, pizza bagels, hot dogs, or grilled cheese sandwiches. Prices range from $1.25 to $4.

Open weekdays from 6 a.m. to 8 p.m., on Saturday from 7 a.m. to 8 p.m., and on Sunday from 7 a.m. to 5 p.m. Booster seats only here. Park in the Arcade lot. Major credit cards accepted.

4. SOLVANG

Windmills and copper-covered roofs, aebleskiver and graavlaks, the alluring smell of fresh-baked goods and the taste of rich, yummy ice cream—sometimes it's hard to believe Solvang is in California. But it is. Solvang is an authentic Danish town north of Santa Barbara, about 132 miles north of Los Angeles.

Solvang makes a nice day trip from Los Angeles, or a morning visit from Santa Barbara. From Los Angeles, take U.S. 101 to Calif. 154, which is the scenic route over San Marcos Pass. Or go through Santa Barbara on U.S. 101 to Buellton. That will take you to Calif. 246, which runs right through Solvang. Taking U.S. 101 all the way, Solvang will be about 45 miles north of Santa Barbara, about 35 miles taking San Marcos Pass.

While southern California is known as the land of make-believe, Solvang isn't. The architecture here is authentic. Danish settlers founded Solvang in 1911 in order to establish a Danish colony, and it has been populated mostly by Scandinavians ever since. Holidays are celebrated with all the Danish traditions intact. In fact, Christmas is one of the best times to visit, as the city is decorated to perfection.

Solvang is perfect for walking around. Just park your car and explore the nearby shops and bakeries. Stop by the **Solvang Visitors Bureau,** at 1571 Mission Dr., Solvang, CA 93463 (tel. 805/688-6144), and get a copy of *Velkommen til Solvang,* which tells you what's going on in town. The office is open every day from 9 a.m. to 5 p.m.

The town's center is Alisal Road and Copenhagen Drive. The principal shopping street is Copenhagen Drive, from 4th Street to 1st Street. Most shops close by 5 p.m., and there aren't too many restaurants that serve dinner, so keep that in mind when you make your plans for the day.

WHAT TO DO AND SEE: The kids will love to make a stop at **Hans Christian Andersen Square,** where they can drive the remote-control toy boats that are floating in the square's pond. The cost is 50¢.

Located right in **Rasmussen's Cone Factory,** 435 1st St. (tel. 805/688-0891), are remote-control toy cars. For 50¢ the kids can take a turn "driving" the cars for three minutes. All ages will get a kick out of these. When they've finished their turn, treat them to a yummy Rasmussen's ice-cream cone.

If you find yourselves on Alisal Road, stop by the **Great Danish Ice Cream Co.**, 441 Alisal Rd. (tel. 805/688-8811). Janey didn't want to leave the big window where she was able to watch the huge waffle cones first being made, then dipped in sinful chocolate. For other Danish treats, you'll find bakeries everywhere, including Copenhagen Square, Mission Drive and Copenhagen Drive.

On your walking tour you might want to stop for gifts. **Rasmussen's**, 1697 Copenhagen Dr. (tel. 805/688-6636), is Solvang's oldest and largest Danish products department store and carries a great selection of gifts.

The **Rock'n Horse**, at 1683A Copenhagen Dr. (tel. 805/688-6918), offers a nice line of imported dolls, wooden toys, and some traditional toys. **Nathalie's Doll House**, 463-B Alisal Rd. (tel. 805/688-6533), also carries dolls and imported toys.

If the children tire of shopping, pick up a snack at a local bakery and take them to **Hans Christian Andersen Park,** three blocks north of Mission Drive. This 60-acre park has picnic areas and a children's playground. Open daily from 9 a.m. to dusk.

If you're going to visit in April, check with the visitors bureau for the dates of the annual **Fairy Tale Festival** held in honor of the birth of Hans Christian Andersen. Jugglers, musicians, storytellers, magicians, clowns, and other entertainers perform on street corners.

If you're going to be here on the third Saturday in September, you'll want to take in the **Danish Days Festival**. The townsfolk dress up in Danish costumes, and there's a parade and other festivities.

Seven miles southwest of Solvang on Alisal Road is **Nojoqui Falls County Park,** where you can picnic beside a creek. An easy trail leads to the falls, which are best seen from December through February. The park is open daily from 8 a.m. to dusk.

Another way to see the area is in the basket of a hot-air balloon. **Solvang Ballooning Co.**, 475 1st St., Solvang, CA 93463 (tel. 805/688-7878), will fly you over the Santa Ynez Valley, Los Olivos, Solvang, or Buellton (it depends on wind conditions). No minimum age, but we suggest that you do not take children under 5. Make your reservations three weeks in advance for a weekend ride, or one week in advance for weekdays. Weekdays are a good deal for families: adults pay $125; children 12 and under, 50¢ per pound. On weekends children are charged the same as adults.

If you have more time to spend, you might want to plan a day of hiking in **Los Padres National Forest,** Upper Oso Recreation Area, about 40 minutes from Solvang (tel. 805/683-6711). Take San Marcos Pass (Calif. 154) east out of Solvang and turn right toward Santa Barbara. Go past Lake Cachuma up the hill about six miles to Paradise Road. Go east (left) for about three miles to where the recreation area starts. Six more miles puts you at the trailhead, where there's a fairly easy 1½-mile trail. Stop by the ranger station first for a map and more information.

Lake Cachuma, 15 miles southeast of Solvang (see directions above; tel. 805/688-4658), is a recreational paradise for day-users and campers. There are 600 campsites available year round on a first-come, first-served basis. Some have full hookups, some partial. Besides boating (and rentals), fishing, horseback riding (rentals), and bicycling (rentals), there are evening family programs in the summer, free nature hikes, and two-hour pontoon boat rides (adults pay $7; children under 12, $4). For reservations, call 805/688-4040. There are also monthly program themes and special events, such as "Kids and Dads Fishing Day," "Say Hello to Smokey Bear," and special Easter week activities. Call 805/688-4658 for specific dates. Entry to the lake area is $3 per car.

WHERE TO EAT: When you get to the windmill, you will have found the **Danish Inn Restaurant,** 1547 Mission Dr. (tel. 805/688-4813), known for its gourmet entrees made by award-winning chefs. Although the selections are probably best for kids with well-developed taste buds, it's worth a visit to sample the authentic Danish dishes. The dining room is lovely and comfortable for children, with characteristic Scandinavian decorations.

At lunch, you can sample the Danish open-face sandwiches ($5.50 to $6.50) or the extensive smörgåsbord (adults pay $8; children under 12, $4.50). The kids might want the hamburger or roast beef sandwich instead. Dinner selections include fish and seafood, steaks and chops, veal and chicken, or Danish specialties. The smörgåsbord is also available at dinner. Entrees run $11 to $19.75. The smörgåsbord costs $9.50 for adults, $6.50 for children under 12.

They will provide you with highchairs and booster seats and will split adult portions and warm baby bottles and food.

Open daily for breakfast at 7 a.m., and for lunch from 11:30 a.m. on. Dinner is served from 5 to 10 p.m. Reservations are accepted. Street parking. Major credit cards honored.

The **Belgian Café**, 475 1st St. (tel. 805/688-6316), set in a nice little square surrounded by fine shops, serves up wonderful Belgian waffles, a huge variety of gourmet crêpes, and fresh homemade soups, sandwiches, and salads. You can enjoy them in the comfortable European-style café indoors, or on the inviting outdoor patio. While there is no separate children's menu, the entree selections should accommodate all tastes. There are no items over $8, and most are between $3.50 and $4.75.

Highchairs and boosters are available. Bottles and baby food can be warmed in the kitchen.

Open for breakfast and lunch Monday through Thursday from 7:30 a.m. to 4 p.m., and Friday through Sunday till 5 p.m. Reservations are accepted. Street parking. Major credit cards honored.

Paula's Pancake House, 1531 Mission Dr. (tel. 805/688-2867), is the best spot in town for breakfast. You can sit on the cheerful flower-filled patio or in the bright and airy dining room, which is decorated with Scandinavian adornments. Service is friendly and helpful. Besides eggs and omelets, there are waffles, French toast, buttermilk pancakes—and Paula's famous Danish pancakes, large and thin, with powdered sugar, fruit toppings or fruit fillings, and whipped cream (well worth a try). There is no children's menu, but there are plenty of selections the kids will love. If one of your children is a real light eater, they will make a smaller portion. Breakfast prices range from $2.75 for waffles and pancakes to $7 for steak and eggs. Breakfast is served all day, and there is a lunch menu starting at 11 a.m. which features salads, soups, sandwiches, and hamburgers ($1.50 to $7).

Highchairs and boosters are available. Orders can be split and baby food and bottles can be warmed in the kitchen.

Open daily from 5 a.m. to 2:30 p.m. Reservations are accepted on weekdays only. Weekend lines can mean a one-hour wait, so call ahead to put your name on a waiting list. Parking in front and back. All major credit cards welcome.

Hans Christian Andersen Restaurant, 435 1st St., in the center of Hans Christian Andersen Square (tel. 805/688-8427), with its big, high-ceilinged room indoors and its large outdoor veranda that overlooks a pond with a little waterfall, is also a good choice for lunch. The children's menu (for kids 10 and under) offers a hamburger, a Danish sausage on a stick, grilled cheese (all with fries), or peanut butter and jelly. Prices range from $1 to $1.75. Drinks and dessert are extra. There are Danish lunches, hot and cold sandwiches, a salad bar, and Danish open-face sandwiches for the adults ($3.25 to $7).

Boosters and highchairs are provided. Baby food and bottles can be warmed in the kitchen.

Open daily: in winter, from 11 a.m. to 3:30 p.m.; in May, till 5:30 p.m.; from June to September, till 8 p.m. Always call ahead if you are planning to come after 5 p.m., as the hours change based on the traffic and season. No reservations accepted. Parking in back. Major credit cards honored.

The Little Mermaid, 1546 Mission Dr., at the corner of Mission and 4th (tel. 805/688-6141), makes a good stop for breakfast, lunch, or dinner. This charming Scandinavian restaurant is bright and casual, with lots of windows and an inviting atmosphere. For breakfast, kids will like the traditional Danish pancake balls with powdered sugar (aebleskiver) or French toast. Breakfast prices are very reasonable, ranging from $1.75 to $5.75. At lunch and dinner there are hot entrees and open-face Danish sandwiches, from $4.50 up.

The children's menu, for kids 12 and under, includes peanut butter and jelly sandwiches, fried chicken, or a meatball plate ($2.75 to $3). Ice cream and a beverage are included in the price. Highchairs and boosters are available.

Open daily from 7 a.m. to 8:30 p.m. No reservations, except for large parties. The average weekend dinner wait is about 15 minutes. Parking on the side. Major credit cards honored.

WHERE TO STAY: Two miles south of Solvang lies **Alisal Ranch,** 1054 Alisal Rd., Solvang, CA 93463 (tel. 805/688-6411), a 10,000-acre dude ranch/resort set within sight of the San Ysidro Mountains. No need to worry about dusty cabins and rustic ranch living here. This guest ranch offers a peaceful place to get away with the family and enjoy the outdoors, complete with all the modern amenities.

Basic activities are golf, tennis, horseback riding, fishing, sailing, and swimming. Children need to be at least 7 to ride horses, but they will put younger children on gentle horses and walk them around the corral. There are guided morning and afternoon two-hour rides, and Saturday breakfast rides. Private lessons are available.

A 90-acre man-made lake is stocked with trout and bass. Poles, reels, and bait can be rented, as can rowboats, sabot sailboats, and windsurfing equipment. The large pool and Jacuzzi are surrounded by huge grassy areas on which the kids—and adults—come up with impromptu games. There's also a wide-screen TV and pool and Ping-Pong tables nearby.

And now for the kids. There are seasonal programs geared to children of many ages, some of which are led by counselors. Junior golf school and horseback riding are for kids 7 and up. Arts and crafts programs and lake activities are for any age. There are lakeside dinners for the 6- to 15-year-olds twice a week, adobe breakfast rides (children 6 and under go on the accompanying haywagon joined by a parent), and lakeside barbecues for the whole family. Directed nightly activities include Bingo, movies, and talent shows. You can also teach the kids horseshoes, badminton, croquet, and volleyball. Babysitters are available upon request.

The Alisal is on the Modified American Plan (MAP), meaning that breakfast and dinner are included in the price of your room. (Dads and grownup guys, pack a sport coat, as a jacket is required at dinner.) Lunch is available in the restaurant in the winter. Summer and holiday weekends, order lunch at the snackbar adjacent to the pool.

Bungalows are comfortable and immaculate, with wood-burning fireplaces. But note that none of the rooms has a TV or telephone. You'll find coffee in your bungalow. Refrigerators are available in some rooms, so request ahead. Perfect family accommodations are the two-room lofts, which sleep three or four people and have a king-size bed, two studio beds, and 1½ baths. For large families, there's a three-bedroom bungalow with a youth room. It has one king-size bed, four twin beds, one youth bed, two baths, a front porch, a wet bar, and a portable refrigerator.

Studios start at $170 single and $195 double. Two-room suites are $245 double; the three-bedroom bungalows start at $390 for four people and go up to $590 for six people for the suite mentioned above. Each additional person over 2 years old is charged $50 per night. Cribs are available for $20 per night. (Remember that these rates include breakfast and dinner.) The all-inclusive price for a family with two adults and two children averages $345 to $390 per night. There's a two-night minimum stay, three nights on holidays. Reserve six months in advance. Recreational activities cost extra (greens fees are $24; trail rides, $30). If you have preschoolers, inquire about the winter weekday packages that include unlimited horseback riding, tennis, golf, and fishing.

CHAPTER X

LOS ANGELES

□ □ □

The single most popular tourist destination in the United States, Los Angeles attracts nearly 50 million visitors a year. It's no surprise to native and transplanted Angelenos that visitors flock to this tourist mecca. The glamour, the weather, and the vast number of things to do bring travelers back again and again.

People once joked about the "sleepy little town," founded in 1769 by Gaspar de Portolá's expedition party but not colonized until 1781 by a Spanish party sent from Mexico and named "El Pueblo del Río de Nuestra Señora la Reina de los Angeles" (the Town of the River of Our Lady, Queen of the Angels). But today, as the second-largest city in the country and leader of the Pacific Rim, Los Angeles is no joke. In fact, many consider the "Queen of the Angels" to be in the beginning of its Golden Age.

This "sleepy little town" comprises 464 square miles (the county is over 4,000 square miles), boasts almost $3\frac{1}{2}$ million residents (there are more than $8\frac{1}{2}$ million in Los Angeles County), has some 525 miles of freeway, and copes with over 6 million registered vehicles!

So what does all this mean to you when you're traveling with your family? While Los Angeles has become a leader in business, it still has its "laid-back" attitude. This city of youth-lovers and fun-seekers is an outdoor culture where people place importance on sports and leisure activities. Children fit right in. And there's more to do than you could ever fit into one or two or even three vacations. In the Greater Los Angeles area you can swim and surf off miles of beaches, see movies being shot right on the streets, visit major movie studios, tour renowned museums (including two just for children), attend concerts, watch professional sports, stroll through the spacious shopping malls, and spend days at theme parks.

And much to the delight of your kids, almost every hotel, even motels, will have a swimming pool. Eating out won't be a problem, as there are numerous restaurants perfect for the whole family.

And of course, the climate is wonderful. People talk about smog, and it's a consideration on a bad day (especially if you want to do something very active).

But most people don't talk about the pleasure, the ease of a reliably pleasant 70° to 85° day with low humidity. Angelenos take it for granted. Rain throws them into a tizzy. Spoiled by delightful, predictable weather, even night and morning low clouds (so common in the late spring and early summer) are met with grumbles by natives. There are few activities that must be canceled or postponed because of weather. Sun worshippers should know, though, that May and June bring hazy, foggy mornings, and it's not until afternoon that the sun breaks through. L.A.'s real summer is July through September.

1. GETTING THERE

BY CAR: To get to Los Angeles from San Francisco, take I-580 to I-5 south through the San Joaquin Valley. You can also take the Coast Route (Calif. 1, the Pacific Coast Highway) and U.S. 101 from parts north. From Sacramento and San Joaquin Valley towns, just get onto I-5 south and follow the signs. If you're coming from San Diego, take either I-5 or I-405 north.

A Stop Along the Way

If you travel I-5 through the San Joaquin Valley, you're taking the fast route, but it's truly boring and doesn't have many good places to stop. We find that the kids need a break every few hours. We stop at least twice: once at **Harris Ranch** (tel. 209/935-0717, or toll free 800/942-2333), which is midway between Los Angeles and San Francisco on I-5 (see the San Francisco chapter for details), and once near the town of Buttonwillow (about 110 miles north of Los Angeles at the juncture of I-5 and Calif. 58). (See Chapter II for details.)

If you're taking U.S. 101, you might want to try **Pea Soup Andersen's California Highway Center,** at 376 Avenue of the Flags in Buellton (tel. 805/688-5581) (see Chapter VIII, "The Central Coast," for details). We stop again in Santa Barbara.

BY TRAIN: The train is an exciting way to travel. **Amtrak,** with its terminal at 800 N. Alameda in Los Angeles (tel. 213/624-0171, or toll free 800/USA-RAIL), is the way to go. Amtrak's *Coast Starlight,* originating in Los Angeles, runs the length of California, Oregon, and Washington. The *San Diegan* and the *San Joaquin* travel throughout the state.

If you're coming from out of state, check Chapter I, "Getting There," for details.

BY BUS: The major transcontinental bus line that services Los Angeles is **Greyhound/Trailways Bus Lines,** with its main terminal at 208 E. 6th St. (tel. 213/620-1200, or toll free 800/237-8211 in California).

BY AIR: Los Angeles is a major air transportation hub for the West Coast, with several area airports and many airlines providing scheduled service.

The Airports

The major airport servicing Los Angeles is **Los Angeles International Airport (LAX)** (tel. 213/646-5252). However, depending on your travel plans, you may prefer to fly into the other smaller airports servicing the area. **Burbank-Glendale-Pasadena Airport** (tel. 818/840-8847), **Long Beach Municipal Airport** (tel. 213/421-8293), and **Ontario International Airport** (tel. 714/983-8282) are possibilities that are often more convenient than LAX. If you're planning to start your trip in Orange County, you might consider landing at **John Wayne Airport** in Anaheim (tel. 714/834-2400).

Airlines

Some of the airlines that fly into Los Angeles International Airport include: AeroMéxico (tel. toll free 800/237-6639), Air Cal (tel. toll free 800/424-7225), Air Canada (tel. toll free 800/422-6232), Air France (tel. toll free 800/237-2747), Air Jamaica (tel. toll free 800/523-5585), Air New Zealand (tel. toll free 800/262-1234), Alaska Airlines (tel. toll free 800/426-0333), Alitalia (tel. toll free 800/223-5730), American Airlines (tel. toll free 800/433-7300), America West (tel. toll free 800/247-5692), Braniff Airways (tel. toll free 800/272-6433), British Airways (tel. toll free 800/247-9297), Canadian Airlines International (tel. toll free 800/426-7000), Cathay Pacific Airways (tel. toll free 800/233-2742), China Airlines (tel. toll free 800/227-5118), Continental Airlines (tel. toll free 800/435-0040), Delta Airlines (tel. toll free 800/221-1212), El Al Israel (tel. toll free 800/223-6700), Finnair (tel. toll free 800/223-5700), Hawaiian Airlines (tel. toll free 800/367-5320), Japan Air Lines (tel. toll free 800/525-3663), KLM (tel. toll free 800/777-5553), Korean Airlines (tel. toll free 800/531-2626), Lufthansa (tel. toll free 800/645-3880), Mexicana Airlines (tel. toll free 800/531-7921), Northwest (tel. toll free 800/225-2525), Pan American (tel. toll free 800/221-1111), Philippine Airlines (tel. toll free 800/435-9725), Piedmont Airlines (tel. toll free 800/251-5720), Qantas Airlines (tel. toll free 800/227-4500), Scandinavian Airlines System (SAS) (tel. toll free 800/221-2350), Singapore Airlines (tel. toll free 800/742-3333), Sky West (tel. toll free 800/453-9417), Southwest Airlines (tel. toll free 800/531-5601), TWA (tel. toll free 800/221-2000), United Airlines and United Express (tel. toll free 800/241-6522), USAir (tel. toll free 800/428-4322), and UTA French Airlines (tel. toll free 800/237-2623).

There are also charters that fly into LAX.

Ground Transportation to the City

It's a given that Los Angeles is a huge city. Therefore your choice of ground transportation depends on the airport you use and your destination. Taxi service can be very expensive, so be sure you know how much the tab will run before you tell the driver to go ahead. You can get a taxi at the airport. The average taxi fare between LAX and downtown Los Angeles is about $30. From LAX to Beverly Hills is about $25. Confirm the cost first, however. Should you want to call a taxi, you might try **United Independent Cab Co.** (tel. 213/558-8294), **Beverly Hills Cab Co.** (tel. 213/273-6611), or **Yellow Cab Co.** (tel. 213/413-7890).

The **Super Shuttle** (tel. 213/338-1111, 714/973-1100, or 818/244-2700) is a door-to-door van service that is fairly economical, depending on where you're going and where you're coming from. Children 2 years old or younger ride free. Make your reservations early.

Fun Bus Systems / Airlink Airport Service (tel. toll free 800/962-1975, 800/962-1976 in California) offers regularly scheduled bus service between major airports and downtown L.A., Pasadena, Long Beach, and Orange County hotels. Prices vary.

All major car-rental companies are located in Los Angeles. You might want to try **Avis Rent-A-Car** (tel. 213/645-5600, or toll free 800/331-1212), **Budget Rent-A-Car** (tel. 213/645-4500, or toll free 800/527-0700), **Dollar Rent-A-Car** (tel. 213/645-9333, or toll free 800/421-6868), **Hertz Rent-A-Car** (tel. 213/776-1350, or toll free 800/654-3131), or **Thrifty Rent-A-Car** (tel. 213/645-1880, or toll free 800/367-2277). Most have counters at the airports and offices throughout the Greater Los Angeles area.

Also, check with the hotel where you will be staying. Those near the airport usually have complimentary shuttle service.

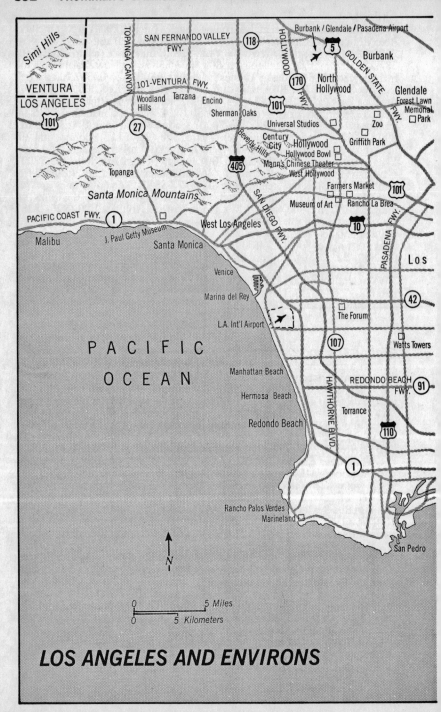

LOS ANGELES AND ENVIRONS

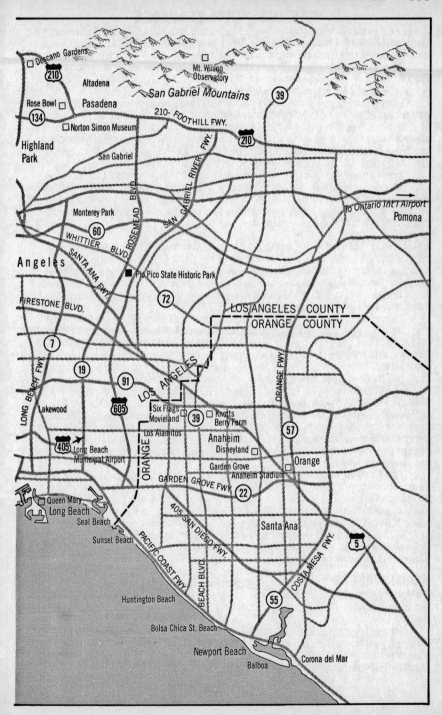

2. GETTING YOUR BEARINGS

Los Angeles lies in a basin. Ringed by mountains, the city grew up between them and the Santa Monica Bay. The Santa Monica Mountains run east to west and divide the city from the San Fernando Valley.

We suggest that you write the **Greater Los Angeles Visitors and Convention Bureau,** 515 S. Figueroa St., 11th Floor, Los Angeles, CA 90071, before you arrive to ask for maps and brochures.

The first thing you'll want to do when you get to town is contact the **Greater Los Angeles Visitors Information Center,** at 695 S. Figueroa St., between Wilshire Boulevard and 7th Street, Los Angeles (tel. 213/689-8822), open daily from 8 a.m. to 5 p.m. There is also another **information center** in Hollywood at the Janes House, Janes House Square, 6541 Hollywood Blvd., near Vine Street (tel. 213/461-4213), open weekdays from 9 a.m. to 5 p.m.

The Visitors and Convention Bureau will help make your visit a memorable experience. And they've had lots of practice. Last year alone, over 48 million guests visited the Greater Los Angeles area. The tourist people know that Los Angeles is a sprawling metropolis that at first impression seems impossible to master. You'll find them very helpful.

PARTS OF TOWN: Yes, Los Angeles has a **downtown.** This is the central part of the city. We include the area surrounding the Civic Center and East Wilshire, as well as Little Tokyo and Chinatown, when we refer to downtown. Most people now think **Hollywood** is a state of mind. But there still is a Hollywood, long known as the world's glamour and film capital, and it's a place everyone seems to need to make a pilgrimage to.

The area loosely bordered by Doheny Drive to the west, La Brea Avenue to the east, Santa Monica Boulevard to the north, and Wilshire Boulevard to the south is called many things. It takes in the **West Hollywood, Mid-Wilshire, Fairfax, and Melrose** areas, and throws together the older European population with artists, designers, and other trend-setters. It's a section of town burgeoning with trendy boutiques, unusual shops, and many ethnic restaurants.

The **Westside,** which includes Beverly Hills, Century City, Westwood, and Brentwood, is alive with shopping, restaurants, and delightful places for the family. Beverly Hills still draws thousands of people to its golden streets, while Century City pulsates with the energy of everyday business combined with professional theater, cinema, and shopping. Westwood is the fun, youthful village of first-run movie theaters, clothing shops for the college set, and good, informal restaurants.

The **Coastal Region** includes Santa Monica, Marina del Rey, and the airport, areas where almost every traveler spends time. Beautiful beaches are everywhere and Marina del Rey and the Santa Monica Pier are fun places to explore with the kids. This is the part of town where the family can get out and roller skate, ride bikes, and simply enjoy what Los Angeles is lucky enough to have.

Universal City and Burbank are part of the **San Fernando Valley.** Although Johnny Carson has traditionally made fun of this part of town, it is where many films are now being produced.

MAIN STREETS: The major east-west streets in "town" are Wilshire, Sunset, Pico, and Olympic Boulevards. Major north-south streets are Lincoln Boulevard, Sepulveda Boulevard, La Cienega Boulevard, La Brea Avenue, and Vermont Avenue.

Santa Monica Boulevard is one of the more confusing streets, at one point running parallel to Wilshire Boulevard, then crossing it in Beverly Hills. There's a short portion of street beginning at Rexford Drive in Beverly Hills and continuing to Sepulveda Boulevard in West Los Angeles; its street signs say "Santa Monica Boulevard," but it's usually referred to as "little" Santa Monica. It's the next street parallel to "big" Santa Monica.

In the San Fernando Valley, Ventura Boulevard is the main east-west thoroughfare.

TELEPHONE AREA CODES: Unlike most other major American metropolitan areas, Los Angeles has two area codes. The entire Los Angeles area used to be 213, and most places other than the San Fernando and San Gabriel Valleys are still 213. The valleys are 818. (Occasionally, you'll even find a 714 number.) If you get the wrong area code, an operator will remind you. Sometimes tourist and leisure activities have two numbers.

3. GETTING AROUND

Okay, so we all know that Los Angeles is synonymous with freeways. If you have a car (and you'd probably be better off with one), you'll want to understand the freeway system. You don't have to be an expert, but if you have a good map (try the Visitors Bureau, the Southern California Automobile Club, or the *Thomas Brothers Map Guide* for suitable copies), you can get anywhere. And don't be shy—you can ask for directions.

DRIVING TIPS: Remember always to wear your seatbelts—this is required by California law. Children 40 pounds and under or 4 years and under must be in an approved car seat. If you're driving to Los Angeles from out of state, be sure to bring one. If you plan to rent a car, ask your rental agency to secure one for you. Before you get behind the wheel, be sure you're familiar with all California driving regulations, as some of them may be different from those in your home state.

Freeway driving can be pleasant, or it can be a harrowing experience. Be sure you allow plenty of time to get to your destination. Know where you're going, and if you get confused, it's a good idea to exit the freeway and stop to read your map so you can get your bearings rather than drive uncertainly on the freeway.

If you can, stay off the freeways between 6 and 9 a.m. and 4 and 7 p.m.— you'll be better off. We often keep water or juice for the kids inside the car (not in the trunk). There have been many times when the freeway has been jammed, making a 10-minute jaunt into a 25-minute ordeal with thirsty, uncomfortable kids.

If you need assistance, the **Automobile Club of Southern California** (tel. 213/741-3111) is extremely helpful to its members with emergency service, travel advice, and other services. AAA members in other states are automatically covered here. Call for information.

For information on **road conditions,** call the California Transportation Department (CALTRANS) (tel. 213/620-3270). Or listen to either of two radio news stations (KFWB-AM at 980 on the dial, or KNX-AM at 1070) for frequent traffic reports that will help you bypass the jams.

BUSES: Los Angeles isn't known for its exceptionally good rapid transit. Don't expect the frequency and choice that many other major cities offer. However, if you need to use public transportation, there are three major rapid-transit companies to call.

The **Southern California Rapid Transit District (RTD)** (tel. 213/626-4455) covers all of Greater Los Angeles, **Culver City Municipal Bus Lines** (tel. 213/559-8310) has service between Culver City and Santa Monica and West L.A., and **Santa Monica Municipal Bus Lines** (tel. 213/451-5444) operates coaches to Westwood, Culver City, Century City, and Marina del Rey. Call for exact route information.

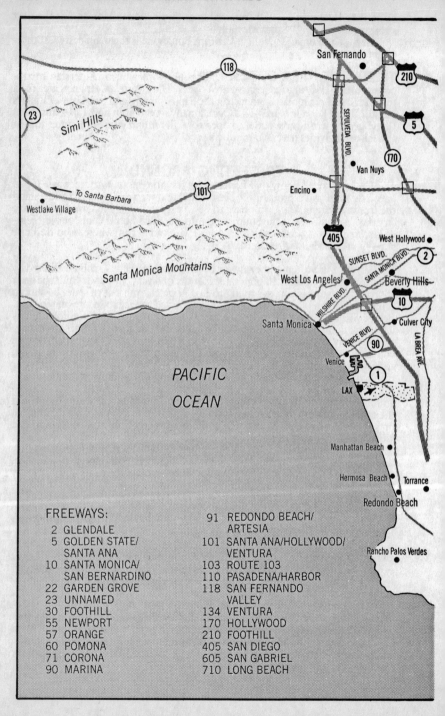

FREEWAYS:

2 GLENDALE	91 REDONDO BEACH/
5 GOLDEN STATE/	ARTESIA
SANTA ANA	101 SANTA ANA/HOLLYWOOD/
10 SANTA MONICA/	VENTURA
SAN BERNARDINO	103 ROUTE 103
22 GARDEN GROVE	110 PASADENA/HARBOR
23 UNNAMED	118 SAN FERNANDO
30 FOOTHILL	VALLEY
55 NEWPORT	134 VENTURA
57 ORANGE	170 HOLLYWOOD
60 POMONA	210 FOOTHILL
71 CORONA	405 SAN DIEGO
90 MARINA	605 SAN GABRIEL
	710 LONG BEACH

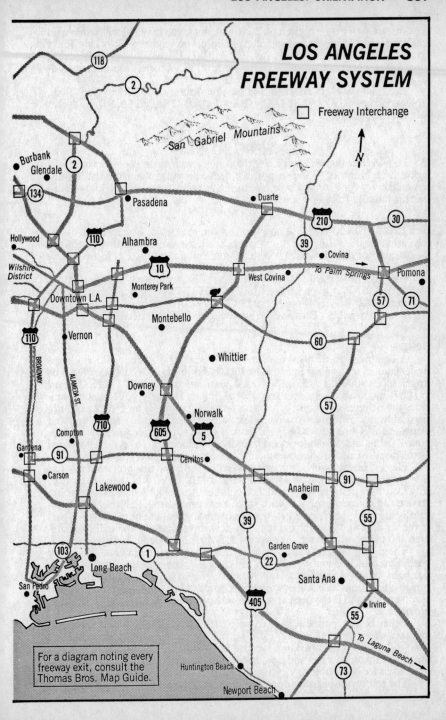

LOS ANGELES FREEWAY SYSTEM

□ Freeway Interchange

N

San Gabriel Mountains

Burbank
Glendale
Pasadena
Duarte
Hollywood
Alhambra
Covina
To Palm Springs
Pomona
Wilshire District
Downtown L.A.
Monterey Park
West Covina
Vernon
Montebello
Whittier
Broadway
Alameda St
Downey
Norwalk
Compton
Gardena
Cerritos
Anaheim
Carson
Lakewood
Garden Grove
Santa Ana
Irvine
Long Beach
San Pedro
Huntington Beach
Newport Beach
Garden Grove
To Laguna Beach

For a diagram noting every
freeway exit, consult the
Thomas Bros. Map Guide.

Tours

We rarely take our children on bus tours, but if you have older children who you believe would enjoy this kind of experience, you might try **Gray Line Tours Co.**, 1207 W. 3rd St., downtown (tel. 213/481-2121), which offers day tours to some of the most popular sightseeing attractions in southern California, including stars' homes. Special rates for children.

You might also try **Starline Sightseeing Tours**, 6845 Hollywood Blvd., Hollywood (tel. 213/463-3131), or **Oskar J's** (tel. 818/785-4039), which also have children's rates.

4. WHERE TO STAY

Los Angeles is such a large city that one of your main considerations will probably be location. Wherever possible, we've provided the name and address of a market for your convenience, and the name and location of a park so you can take the kids out to run off some energy.

BEVERLY HILLS: Needing no introduction, the city of Beverly Hills has its own atmosphere. While you might not actually see movie stars all around you, the glamour of the city makes you think you're about to discover someone any minute.

For those who stay in Beverly Hills and environs, there is a 24-hour Vons Market at 9467 W. Olympic Blvd. (tel. 213/553-5734) and a 24-hour Hughes market at 9040 Beverly Blvd. (tel. 213/273-0977). A fabulous neighborhood playground is Roxbury Park (see "What to See and Do" for details).

Deluxe

A combination of first-class European luxury and American friendliness awaits families at the **Four Seasons Hotel Los Angeles**, 300 S. Doheny Dr., Los Angeles, CA 90048 (tel. 213/273-2222, or toll free 800/332-3442). Opened in 1987, and located adjacent to residential Beverly Hills, the Four Seasons combines the richness of a European manor with the easygoing ambience of southern California. Antiques, marble floors, accent pieces, and fresh flowers and plants indoors give way to lush, manicured gardens and courtyards with Mexican fan palms and jacaranda trees. The indoor-outdoor atmosphere is heightened by the extensive use of windows and French doors. It's a lovely place to be.

Elegant as the hotel is, the staff is so family-oriented that you need not feel worried about your children. The staff is trained to be welcoming and helpful, to anticipate the guests' needs—and that includes those of kids. The 24-hour room service and concierge service (with such attention to detail that they often personally interview babysitters before recommending them to hotel guests) is part of the service. And attitude has much to do with it. Many of the staff have children and talk about what it's like to see life from a 2½-foot perspective.

There is a brochure of children's services and family amenities offered by the hotel. On hand, and without charge, you can get a baby bathtub, disposable bottles, baby shampoo, pacifiers, play pens, and vaporizers. Car seats and strollers are available for guests' use. Older kids are welcome to board games, pool toys, and playing cards, and if the need arises, hot-water bottles and thermometers can be provided.

Other hotel services include complete laundry and valet services, complimentary shoeshine, twice-daily maid service (certainly a gift from someone's fairy godmother), valet parking, exercise facilities, and a wide range of business services. You can rent cars and limousines at the hotel. In addition, courtesy limousine service is available to Century City and Rodeo Drive in Beverly Hills.

The rooftop pool area is open and spacious, designed to make guests feel as if they're part of the surrounding residential neighborhood. The large pool has a nice shallow area for kids. This is a favorite place to have lunch with the little ones.

Of course you'll want to visit area restaurants, but you also have your choice at the hotel. The Café is very informal, and is open for breakfast, lunch, dinner, and late into the night. Prices range from $8 to $18.

The Windows Restaurant is more sophisticated, offering a buffet lunch, afternoon tea, and cocktails. And, the Gardens Restaurant is the fine dining room on the premises. It offers breakfast, lunch, and dinner. The international menu averages about $8 for breakfast and about $12 for lunch. Dinner entrees include such treats as grilled mahi-mahi with celery and warm Thai vinaigrette, marinated grilled shrimp with linguine and fresh basil, Chinese duck with stir-fried vegetables, New York sirloin, rack of lamb, and rack of veal. Prices range from $18 to $27. Alternative menus for those on low-calorie, low-cholesterol, and low-sodium diets are also available.

An extensive children's menu is available at all hotel restaurants. There's a separate one for room service as well. The kids can choose from peanut butter and jelly sandwiches, fresh fruit and yogurt, grilled-cheese sandwiches, chicken fingers, pasta, small sirloin steaks, and more. Prices are $4.50 to $10. Ice-cream floats, cheesecake, hot-fudge sundaes, and brownies are among the other goodies available. (Of course, whenever possible, the servers will bring small portions of adult items if your child prefers that.) And believe it or not, the kids have their own china! There are cereal bowls and little plates with bears and Christmas fantasies. There are even mugs with two handles to make it easier for little hands.

The ultimate kid-pleaser, though, is the Sunday brunch. We've been to lots of them with the kids (Father's Day, Mother's Day, Easter), but this is the only one with a genuine children's buffet table. The table is 2½ feet high, covered with a tablecloth of colorful dinosaurs and robots. The centerpieces are stuffed animals—teddy bears and unicorns—and beach balls. The buffet selection includes such children's favorites as chicken fingers, peanut butter sandwiches, and pizza. There are alphabet cookies and chocolate beyond belief—M&Ms, Hershey's Kisses, brownies. The children's buffet is $14 for children 5 to 11, and no charge for children under 5. (Need we add that highchairs and boosters are available?) Sunday brunch for adults costs $28, with its seafood (oysters, clams, crab legs, smoked tuna, and Nova Scotia salmon), fresh fruit, peppered sirloin, pastry-wrapped veal and loin of lamb, as well as omelets prepared to order by a chef who will indulge any fantasy. Of course, there's fresh fruit, vegetables, and a huge pastry table and other desserts.

The 285 plush rooms are large and beautifully decorated. Each has French doors that lead to a step-out balcony where you have a lovely view of either Beverly Hills or Century City and West Los Angeles. The rooms have remote-control color TVs, refrigerator/mini-bars, multiline phones (at least two in a room), hairdryers, terrycloth robes, and a full line of bathroom amenities. We like the Four Seasons rooms best. They have a parlor area that can be closed off. These have an additional television in the parlor, making them perfect for families.

Regular rooms are $215 to $315 single and $240 to $340 double; suites rent for $430 to $1,700. Ask about specials and weekend rates, which can be much less expensive. The Four Seasons Family Plan means that if two rooms (usually connecting) are used, each is charged at the single occupancy rate. Children stay free. There is no charge for cribs; rollaways are free for kids, $25 per night for additional adults. Valet parking is $12 per night and self-parking is free.

Who hasn't heard of the **Beverly Hills Hotel and Bungalows,** 9641 Sunset Blvd., Beverly Hills, CA 90210 (tel. 213/276-2251), the pink stucco California mission-style legend that embodies early Hollywood? Located in residential Beverly Hills amid other mansions, on 12 acres of fabulously manicured gardens with palm trees and abundant plantlife, the resort-like hotel has 268 guest rooms, including its famous private bungalows.

The legend began in 1912, when developer Burton Green (who named Beverly Hills after his home in Beverly Farms, Massachusetts) opened the doors of the city's first major structure. At that time Beverly Hills wasn't the exclusive area it is today. But in 1920 Mary Pickford and Douglas Fairbanks created their famous country home, Pickfair. Other movie stars followed—Rudolph Valentino, Will Rogers, Charlie Chaplin, to name a few—altering this sleepy little hamlet into a haven for movie industry celebrities. The Beverly Hills Hotel played host to many of the great and famous.

In fact, the acclaimed Polo Lounge got its name because Will Rogers, Darryl Zanuck, and Tommy Hitchcock frequented the restaurant after their polo matches. Even today you might see the likes of Charlton Heston or Michael Douglas enjoying eggs Benedict there. It's still a watering hole for the powerful and popular.

Among the hotel's guest roster has been Prince Philip, the Duke and Duchess of Windsor, Greta Garbo, John Wayne, Henry Fonda, Clark Gable, Carole Lombard, and of course, Marilyn Monroe. Howard Hughes lived in the bungalows for years.

The swimming pool and cabaña club are reminiscent of bygone days as well. Enormous in size, the pool area is surrounded by 22 private cabañas, surely the repository of Hollywood stories—even secrets—we wish we were privy to. You can rent a cabaña ($75 per day) to have complete privacy and a place to rest while out at the pool.

Other amenities offered at the hotel are the men's and women's hair salons, a giftshop, two lighted tennis courts, car rental and limousine service (you can also get a chauffeur), 24-hour room service, concierge, laundry and valet, on-call physician and babysitting services, and a variety of business services.

The hotel has several restaurants, only one of which is really suited for kids. For example, the Polo Lounge is not one we'd recommend for young children. Teens might enjoy star gazing, however. There is indoor and outdoor seating available for breakfast and lunch. Late supper is also served here. The Coterie is an elegant gourmet dinner house. Get a babysitter for this one too.

In addition to poolside service, the place here to take kids to eat is the Fountain Coffee Shop, a small, casual old-fashioned–looking soda fountain. It serves breakfast, lunch, and snacks.

Because the hotel was built at the turn of the century, no two rooms are identical. Guest rooms vary greatly, but all are tastefully decorated, and most are large. The first-floor rooms have enormous private patios with umbrella tables, chaises longues, and chairs. These cannot be beat for children who want to play in the fresh air while Mom and Dad are relaxing inside. Rooms have at least two televisions (one in the bathroom), two or three telephones, and game tables and chairs. Some have love seats; others have sofa beds. Many of the rooms are currently being renovated.

The legendary bungalows are like private little homes, separated from the main building and tucked into the lush foliage of the gardens. Each bungalow has a main suite with its own entrance. To this can be added one, two, even three connected guest bedrooms with baths (all with their own entrances). Each bungalow has a kitchen or kitchenette; most have wet bars and full dining areas. These are bright, cheery places, and make you think you've taken up residence alongside the rich and famous of the neighborhood.

Room rates vary. They start at $225 (for rooms with one bed) and go up to $265, depending on size, view, and furnishings. Each additional person (including children) is charged $20. Suites start at $350. Three- and four-bedroom bungalows go as high as $1,400. The charge for cribs is $20 per stay. Valet parking costs $7.50 per night.

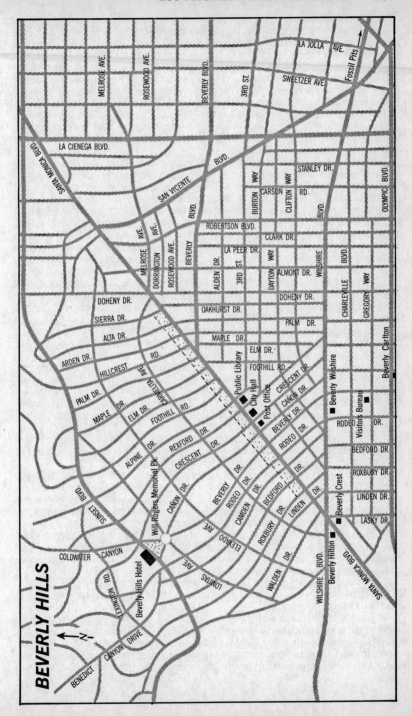

The Upper Bracket

Conrad Hilton opened the famed **Beverly Hilton,** 9876 Wilshire Blvd. (at Santa Monica Boulevard), Beverly Hills, CA 90210 (tel. 213/274-7777, or toll free 800/HILTONS), in 1955 to a throng of guests that included stars and tycoons. But regular folk have always been catered to as well. Today, after a $35-million renovation of its public areas, 592 guest rooms and suites, and restaurants, the Hilton is even more inviting. Its welcome policy for families has been in existence for many years (even before it was fashionable—and profitable), and is still somewhat more generous than many other hostelries. The Family Plan means that there is no charge for children—*regardless of age*—occupying the same room as their parents. And if you take two rooms for the family, you get charged the single rate for each room.

Services abound. The full-time concierge and multilingual staff will help with babysitting arrangements as well as other travel or sightseeing needs. Room service is available from 6:30 a.m. to 2 a.m. In addition, there are car-rental and airline offices, a full-service beauty salon, barbershop, currency exchange, airport shuttle, boutiques, and a complete fitness center with Lifecycles. (Kids under 16 are admitted with a parent.) The Hilton also has a very large giftshop with lots of sundries and an extensive assortment of gifts. You can also arrange for complimentary Lincoln Town Car service that will take you within a two-mile radius (which includes such local sights as Beverly Hills, Century City, and Westwood).

There are two outdoor heated swimming pools. One is Olympic size with a shallow end and an equally large garden area surrounding. The other, which is a circular pool with a fountain in the center, is five feet deep in all spots, but the enclosed patio area surrounding it is perfect for playing children because it's quieter than the area around the larger pool.

In addition, there are three restaurants, a coffeeshop, and two lounges. The romantic L'Escoffier Room serves classic French food, and has a lovely view of the city. Leave the kids with a sitter, though, as this isn't the place for them. Trader Vic's offers Polynesian cuisine, and while a bit on the pricey side, it's a treat for the kids with its festive décor. The Mr. H Restaurant has a tempting array of buffets as well as an à la carte menu for breakfast, lunch, and dinner. This appealing garden-style restaurant sits poolside. Café Beverly is a coffeeshop serving breakfast, lunch, and dinner, and offers a children's menu. Both restaurants and the café have highchairs and boosters.

For evening adult entertainment, there are two cocktail lounges. For something small and special, try the Library—it's like being in someone's home. The other bar, the Red Lion, has the ambience of an English pub.

Guest rooms are located in one of three buildings: the main building, the garden lanai area (rooms around the main pool), and the fountain lanai building (with rooms near the fountain pool). The main building has balconies—some large enough to accommodate lounge chairs—and most rooms have an inviting view, so they are generally priced higher than the other two locations.

Each room has a desk, mini-refrigerator/honor bar, two telephones, and remote-control television with free HBO, ESPN, and CNN. Bathrooms have marble floors and counters, tub/showers, and bathroom amenities. Bathrobes are provided in each room.

Rooms with two double beds may have a balcony and a view of Century City. These have two overstuffed chairs and an end table. The rooms with king-size beds feature love seats.

Garden lanai rooms with two double beds are very large, accommodating a desk and a table and chairs. The rooms downstairs open onto the pool area. The fountain lanai building is a low, four-floor structure adjacent to the fountain pool. Junior suites have two baths, a king-size bed, and a sofa bed. One- and two-bedroom suites have two entrances (one directly into the bedroom) and two baths.

A single-bedded or twin-bedded room ranges from $145 to $215; poolside cabaña rooms are $195 single and $215 double; poolside lanai rooms are $170 single and $190 double. Junior suites cost $195 single to $215 double; one- and two-bedroom suites range from $300 to $600. Children are free regardless of age when occupying same room as their parents. Cribs and rollaways are free. The charge for an extra adult is $20 per night. Parking costs $10 per day.

The Hiltons frequently have specials that can run as low as half the regular rate. When you call for a reservation, be sure to ask if there are any special packages.

Moderate

The **Ramada Hotel Beverly Hills,** 1150 S. Beverly Dr. (at Pico Boulevard), Los Angeles, CA 90035 (tel. 213/553-6561, or toll free 800/2-RAMADA), is close to central Beverly Hills and world-famous Rodeo Drive, and is as good a location as you can get in the city.

The Ramada has an outdoor heated swimming pool (which gets sun all afternoon), complimentary parking, one-day valet service, and a giftshop. Room service is available from 6 a.m. to 10 p.m. For babysitting, the front desk staff will refer you to an agency. Guests may also request privileges at a nearby fitness club (which features a class for children).

Summerfield's, a small, garden-like restaurant, serves breakfast, lunch, and dinner. Prices range from $2.75 (breakfast) to $15 (dinner). You'll find boosters and highchairs, and a children's menu. The ingenious little menu has colorful animals and a game that will keep most youngsters occupied for a few minutes. Kids can choose from spaghetti, chicken, hamburgers, hot dogs, and a turkey sandwich. Prices range from $1.75 to $2.25.

The 260 attractively decorated rooms have either oak or cherrywood furniture, a game table and desk, and a color television in the armoire, with free cable and pay movies. All rooms above the fourth floor have views. All have tub/shower combinations with bathroom amenities.

Room rates are $100 to $110 for singles, $110 to $120 for doubles, $175 for suites (these units have king-size beds, with a living room that has a large couch, a refrigerator, and sink). But weekend rates can be about a third less. For additional people, the charge is $10 per night. Cribs are free; rollaways cost $10. Children under 12 stay free in the same room as their parents. The Family Plan means that adults and their children (up to four people) stay in a room for $100 to $110, depending on location. Free parking.

WESTSIDE REGION: The Westside (Westwood, Brentwood, Century City, and West Los Angeles) includes some of the most beautiful residential areas of the city. Close to Santa Monica beaches and to Beverly Hills, the Westside is pricey, but a favorite of traveling families because of its convenient location. If you're staying in West Los Angeles, the Westward Ho Market, 1515 Westwood Blvd. (tel. 213/477-9850), and Ralph's Market, 12057 Wilshire Blvd. (tel. 213/477-8746), are fairly close to you. If you're looking for a park where the kids can roam, you might try Cheviot Hills Recreation Center (see the "What to Do and See" section for details), or Westwood Park, located just south of Wilshire Boulevard at 1375 Veteran Ave.

Deluxe

Exquisite and gracious, the **Century Plaza Hotel,** 2025 Avenue of the Stars (off Santa Monica Boulevard), Los Angeles, CA 90067 (tel. 213/277-2000, or toll free 800/228-3000), was once considered strictly a businessperson's hotel. This beautiful hotel is now actively courting family and leisure travelers. Located in the heart of Century City, the Century Plaza Hotel is a uniquely attractive, curving 20-story structure set on 14 acres of tropical shrubs, interlaced with reflecting pools and fountains. The setting makes for wonderful walks around the grounds.

In 1961 Twentieth Century–Fox Studios sold off over 200 acres of land. Century City had begun. Celebrated Japanese architect Minoru Yamasaki was commissioned to design a hotel with a resort-like atmosphere that would also fit well with the bustling, connected shopping arcades, numerous restaurants, and nightclubs, while offering space for the city's grand social events. The doors of the Century Plaza opened on June 1, 1966, and in 1984 the $85-million Tower was added.

Since 1966 the Century Plaza has played host to the wealthy and powerful, including President Reagan, who resided in the famed Plaza Suite whenever he was in town. Presidents Ford, Carter, Nixon, and Johnson have also visited. And you're as likely to see a television or movie "shoot" in one of the patio areas as you once were able to spot stars on Hollywood Boulevard.

Plush furnishings, inlaid marble floors, and an exceptional collection of fine art and rare antique pieces grace the colonnaded lobbies and richly decorated public areas. A pianist plays lovely melodies in the grand lobby during the afternoon. Lest you think this is all too grand for your little ones, the hotel staff is accommodating and friendly to children. In fact, when you alert the reservationist that children are in your party, they will get their own little amenity pack upon arrival. It includes such goodies as jacks and a ball, an inflatable beach ball, crayons and coloring books. Little candy lovers might find jars of jelly bellies awaiting them at night in the room.

Regular hotel services include complete concierge staff (they will assist you with babysitting), multilingual staff, twice-daily maid service, complimentary shoeshine, same-day laundry and valet, a large shopping arcade within the hotel (which includes a camera store, convenience shop, travel agency, beauty center, florist, and men's and women's clothing store), and 24-hour room service with children's items on the menu. There is also a complete business center.

You and the kids will want to sample some of the delights in the Century Square Shopping Center and in the underground ABC Entertainment Complex, but you'll also have a choice of five restaurants at the hotel. The Café Plaza is the informal restaurant—reminiscent of a sidewalk café in Paris—and just perfect for families. Prices for breakfast, lunch, and dinner range from $5 to $12. It's open from 6 a.m. to midnight, and the kids will love the freshly baked breads and pastries. We've often purchased a box lunch here to take with us on outings. The Garden Pavilion—also open for breakfast ($3.50 to $11.50), lunch ($6.50 to $12.75), dinner ($14 to $18), and Sunday brunch ($23.75, $19 for kids)—overlooks the peaceful reflecting pools and hotel gardens. The Terrace Restaurant, in the Tower, is open daily for lunch ($8 to $14) and Monday through Saturday for dinner ($12 to $20). This restaurant has huge windows that open onto strikingly beautiful gardens, accentuating a breezy, indoor/outdoor feeling. You may be surprised to learn that these restaurants all have highchairs and boosters, and will provide children's portions.

For fine dining, the Century Plaza has one of the city's acclaimed restaurants, La Chaumière. (Leave the kids with a sitter when you dine here.) The restaurant alone is worth the experience. With the ambience of a European club, amid alderwood paneling, upholstered burled-elm chairs, and five enormous 18th-century French paintings, guests dine on classic French and nouvelle California cuisine. Open for both lunch and dinner, with prices ranging from $15 to $30 and $25 to $45 respectively.

The main building has 750 guest rooms; the Tower has 322 guest rooms. Every room is soundproofed, which we find to be an enormous advantage. We didn't worry about disturbing guests, even when little Elizabeth would waken

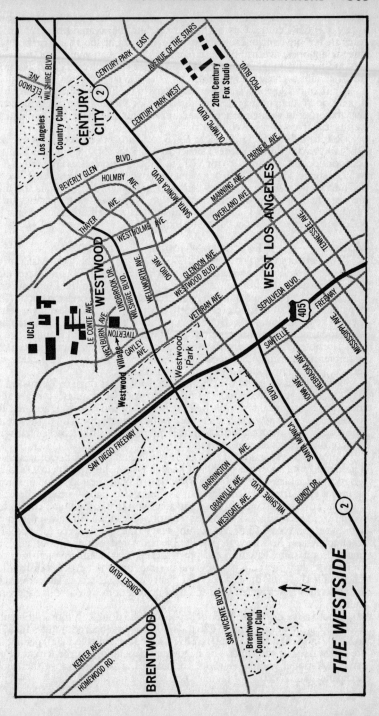

us with her customary 5 a.m. squeals. And each room has a step-out balcony with a view of either Century City or the Westside and the ocean. Other standard features are remote-control cable color TV with 24-hour sports and news, two or three telephones, oversize beds, refrigerator/honor bar, vanity, and individual air conditioning units. You'll also find bathrobes, ice (delivered daily), bathroom toiletries, and oversize bath towels.

With only 14 rooms per floor, the rooms in the Tower are slightly larger and more modern than in the main building. Best of all, they have take-your-breath-away bathrooms with large recessed bathtubs, stall showers, and two sinks, as well as hairdryers and makeup mirrors.

Rates are $150 to $170 single, $175 to $190 with twin or king-size beds. One- and two-bedroom corner suites cost $375 to $500, while one- and two-bedroom penthouse suites go for $700 to $850. Tower rooms range from $195 to $220 single, $225 to $250 for a room with two double beds or a king-size bed, $875 to $3,000 for one- and two-bedroom suites. Children 18 years and under are free when they stay in their parents' room. No fee for cribs; rollaways are free for children, but cost $25 for adults. The charge for an additional person is $25. Valet parking costs $10 per day; self-parking, $6.

Moderate—Best Bet for the Money

The **Century Wilshire Hotel,** 10776 Wilshire Blvd. (between Malcolm and Selby Avenues), Los Angeles, CA 90024 (tel. 213/474-4506, or toll free 800/421-7223 outside California), is a charming small hotel in the European tradition, with only 99 rooms. Thus the staff are able to get to know the guests (some of whom stay for weeks and even months at a time), and take pleasure in helping them. The hotel draws an eclectic mix: staff of consulates who stay at the hotel while looking for homes to rent, traveling businesspeople, and families.

The hotel is decorated with traditional-style furnishings, and exudes a homey ambience, inviting for families. There is a multilingual staff, free parking, valet service, and staff on the premises who love to babysit.

Wonderfully situated on Wilshire Boulevard just outside Westwood Village, the hotel is built around a garden courtyard, where guests can partake of their continental breakfast while basking in the sun and enjoying the lovely little fountain. (Or they may also use the breakfast room that opens on to the garden.) The continental breakfast is not a meager offering, but a full repast of fresh fruit, toast or muffins, cereal, and beverage.

Another lovely feature of the Century Wilshire is the large pool area, also in a garden-like setting with palm and banana trees. There are plenty of chaises longues and tables with umbrellas. The heated pool (heated only fall through spring) is good for lap swimming, but also has a nice shallow area for the kids.

The attractive rooms are clean and airy, with lace curtains and comfortably worn furniture. Some have balconies with poolside views. All have stall showers; some have good old-fashioned bathtubs next to the stall showers. All rooms have color television. Rooms with two double beds are spacious. Junior suites and one-bedroom suites have fully equipped kitchens that will meet your basic needs, even if you stay for an extended period of time (but don't expect a dishwasher). These suites have full dining areas and plenty of storage space. The junior suites are perfect for traveling families, and the one-bedroom suites are like apartment units.

Room rates are $65 to $75 single, $65 to $85 double. Junior suites rent for $80 to $95 (the weekly rate is $475 to $550), and one-bedroom suites cost $125 to $150 (the weekly rate is $750 to $875). Cribs are available at $10 per night, as are rollaways (but the fee can be negotiated depending on the length of your stay). Additional guests per room are charged at $5 each above the double-occupancy rate.

Moderate

Although more expensive than the Century Wilshire, the **Holiday Inn Westwood Plaza Hotel,** 10740 Wilshire Blvd. (at Selby Avenue), Los Angeles, CA 90024 (tel. 213/475-8711, or toll free 800/472-8556, 800/235-7973 in California), is a nice hotel in a fabulous location. Within walking distance of Westwood Village and very close to Beverly Hills, Brentwood, and the San Diego Freeway (I-405), the hotel also provides complimentary transportation within a three-mile radius, which includes Century City, Beverly Hills, U.C.L.A., and Brentwood. The traditional-style hotel has 19 floors and 300 nicely decorated rooms.

Our favorite part of the hotel is the charming ground-level promenade arcade that leads outside to the lovely pool and spa. The promenade—recently remodeled—resembles a quaint seaside village. The area houses a giftshop, video games, and an exercise room. (Children under 14 may use the room when accompanied by an adult.) The pool is heated year round and has a great shallow area for young kids. Food service is available poolside.

Other services provided by the hotel are concierge staff from 8 a.m. to 8 p.m. (they'll help you with babysitters), and room service from 6:30 a.m. to 10 p.m. (but not from 2:30 to 5 p.m.). Café Le Dome serves breakfast, lunch, and dinner from 6:30 a.m. to 10:30 p.m. It has an extensive children's menu with prices ranging from $1.25 to $3.50.

Standard rooms have two double beds with Queen Anne–style furniture, side chairs and a game table, and a desk. You can also choose a room with one queen-size bed and a small couch. Suites come with one or two baths, and depending on the suite, may have a large living room with a couch, desk, and comfortable chairs. Each room has cable color TV with free HBO and CSPA; SpectraVision is available for a fee. There are tub/shower combinations and the usual bathroom amenities.

Rooms cost $105 to $115 single and $115 to $125 double, and suites rent for $150 to $350. Cribs are free; rollaways cost $10. Kids under 18 are free when occupying the same room as their parents. Free parking.

An excellent accommodation for the price—and a favorite of our family's —is the **Del Capri Hotel,** 10587 Wilshire Blvd. (near Westwood Boulevard), Los Angeles, CA 90024 (tel. 213/474-3511, or toll free 800/44-HOTEL), with 81 units. Another garden-style hotel, this is an agreeable place to spend several days. It has a very small office/lobby, a lovely pool area, complimentary continental breakfast in the room, a shuttle service that will take you to the surrounding area, and free parking. Add to this the smartly decorated, newly refurbished rooms and excellent prices, and you've got a great deal.

The nicely landscaped swimming pool area has its share of palm trees, yuccas, and ferns. There are lounge chairs, and a separate patio area where we usually sit and let the young ones play nearby.

One of the staff members says it's their aim to take the 30-year-old hotel out of the '60s and into the '90s. Indeed, the newly furnished rooms are sleek and unusual, with lacquered furniture, cylindrical side tables and coffee tables, and colors such as tan, light rose, and mint green. Each room has a combination whirlpool tub/shower, cable color television with a free movie channel, and game tables with chairs. You can request a refrigerator.

Over half the rooms have small but complete kitchens. These kitchenette suites are like compact one-bedroom apartments with a sofa bed in the parlor. There's plenty of room, so you can enjoy yourself. Both the parlor and bedroom have televisions. You can request kitchenette suites with different bed configurations, so let the reservationist know how many children you'll have with you and their ages when you make your plans. There are even some suites that connect with another bedroom.

Sorry, you'll have to arrange your own babysitting, but cribs are free. Roll-aways are $10 per night. Children under 12 stay free in their parents' room if additional beds are not needed. Other adults are charged $10 each per night.

Rates are $74 to $79 single, $84 to $89 double. Kitchenette suites rent for $94 to $104 single, $104 to $114 double.

Located in the heart of Westwood Village is the **Royal Palace Westwood Hotel,** 1052 Tiverton Ave., Los Angeles, CA 90024 (tel. 213/208-6677), a small motor inn with 35 rooms. Expect a very simple place, but one with advantages. You're paying for an ideal location that is within walking distance of more than 80 restaurants, 20 first-run movie theaters, and shops and department stores, as well as U.C.L.A. You're also on one of the few convenient major bus routes that will take you to the beach, Century City, and Beverly Hills.

There is a small office area, an elevator, and limited free parking (a rarity in Westwood). They do not handle babysitting.

Each room has a small but complete kitchenette with an eating area. The standard rooms with one queen-size bed are on the small side if you have to bring in a crib. If you can afford it, go for a room with two queen-size beds, since these rooms are much larger (they will accommodate a crib) and don't cost that much more. The suites feature a queen-size sofa bed with a very small bedroom in which a king-size bed and dresser just fit. The closet space is very large. The suites also have a complete kitchen and nice bathroom.

Rates are $59 single and $65 double in a room with a queen-size bed and kitchen, $65 single and $71 double in a room with two queen-size beds and kitchen. A mini-suite (with a king-size bed and a single bed, or a queen-size bed and queen-size sofa bed) with a kitchen rents for $70 single and $76 double; a one-bedroom suite (with a king-size bed and a queen-size sofa bed) costs $80 single and $86 double. Cribs and rollaways are $6 per night. Children under 12 stay free in their parents' room. Additional adults over double occupancy are charged $6 per night each.

The **Brentwood Motor Inn,** 199 N. Church Lane, Los Angeles, CA 90049 (tel. 213/476-6255), is an all-suite hotel that has full kitchenettes (with dishwashers), a heated pool, an indoor spa and sauna (complete with bathrooms and showers), free parking, car-rental service, one-day dry cleaning, coin-operated laundry facilities, and free continental breakfast. Although its location is wonderfully convenient (just north of Sunset Boulevard at I-405), it is literally just off the freeway (indeed, it's next to it), and you hear the freeway noise. At the time of this writing, construction is under way to build a Plexiglas sound wall around the rooms to block off more of the noise—so that once you're in the rooms, the sound is muffled. In fact, with a 95% occupancy rate, many people obviously find this no drawback at all. Ironically, because of its position near the freeway, it was built into the hills, so the back side of the rooms look out to a wooded area, which also offers a tree-lined trail for walking.

This motor inn was completely redecorated in 1988 in stylish pastel tones. The "double queen suites" are very large rooms with two queen-size beds, two highback chairs, an eating table, and a small but complete kitchen. The "king suites" (or "town-house suites") are split-level units that are much like apartments. In addition to the kitchen, there is a king-size bed upstairs (with a television and phone), and a full-size sofa bed downstairs in the living room area. The living room also has a television, telephone, and four comfortable chairs. The bathrooms are good size.

Suites with two queen-size beds and a kitchen rent for $74 single, $80 double. Town-house suites (with a king-size bed, sofa bed, and kitchen) are $78 single and $86 double. There is no charge for children under 12 in their parents' room. Cribs are free; rollaways cost $8 per night, as do additional people 12 years old and over.

Budget

If you're looking for a less expensive place to stay, the **TraveLodge Los Angeles West,** at 10740 Santa Monica Blvd., Los Angeles, CA 90025 (tel. 213/474-4576, or toll free 800/255-3050), is a clean little two-story motel unit of 53 rooms about one mile from Westwood Boulevard. It looks onto the lovely Los Angeles Mormon Temple with its imposing statue and vast lawn. Amenities include free parking, a small heated pool (gated and locked), and refrigerators in all rooms.

The rooms are comfortable if somewhat worn, but certainly what you'd expect from a budget motel in pricey West Los Angeles. Rooms have game tables, color TVs, instant coffee makers, radios, and showers. Some have tub/shower combinations (ask if you prefer those).

Rooms with a queen-size bed cost $57 single and $61 double, rooms with a king-size bed are $60 single and $66 double, rooms with two twin beds run $66 double, rooms with a queen-size bed and two twin beds rent for $68 to $72, and rooms with two queen-size beds are $71 to $79. The Family Plan means that one or two children under 17 are free in their parents' room if additional beds are not needed. Cribs are free; rollaways cost $6. Connecting rooms are available.

THE COASTAL REGION:

If you're looking for cool climate and beautiful surroundings, the beach areas are for you. Santa Monica and Marina Del Rey have many more family accommodations than you might think. If you're in need of a market, you'll find a Vons Market at 1311 Wilshire Blvd. (tel. 213/394-1414) in Santa Monica and a Vons Market at 4365 Glencoe Ave. (tel. 213/821-7208) in Marina Del Rey.

If you're looking for a park in Santa Monica, don't miss Douglas Park (see the "What to See and Do" section for details). In Marina Del Rey, you can let the kids roam at Burton Chace Park, which is at the west end of Mindanao Way.

The Upper Bracket

Ah, to be so close to the city and yet feel far away . . . that is the **Marina Del Rey Hotel,** 13534 Bali Way (at Admiralty Way), Marina Del Rey, CA 90292 (tel. 213/301-1000, or toll free 800/882-4000, 800/8-MARINA in California), the only hotel in the marina that's right on the water. As you drive to the end of Bali Way, you're encircled by masts of sailboats and yachts. At the end sits the three-story white stucco building with royal-blue awnings and a rather grand entryway. It's set on the main canal of the Marina Del Rey harbor. The grounds are beautifully planted with bougainvillea. The hotel has views from almost every room. It sits on a private road for the boat owners who rent slips, which keeps the access to the hotel limited.

You can sit by the swimming pool (that has a large shallow area and lots of room to play), surrounded by water and boats, and watch the boats move in and out of their slips. It's a gorgeous sight, and the atmosphere is like a resort.

Other hotel amenities include room service from 6 a.m. to 11 p.m., a giftshop, laundry and valet service, free parking, and car-rental service. In fact, you can even have the Marina cruise line pick you up at the hotel. Babysitting can be arranged through the front desk. There is also a small putting green. The hotel offers free shuttle service to and from the airport and to other points within the marina. Ice machines are located on each floor. You can also request refrigerators, irons, and hairdryers (all at no extra charge).

There are two restaurants and a lounge to serve you. The Dockside Café is a completely glassed-in room facing the water that serves a wide variety of breakfast, lunch, and dinner items, with prices ranging from $4 to $7.50. The Crystal Seahorse is a small waterfront terrace restaurant that offers dinner every night. Prices range from $14.50 to $19. Both restaurants have highchairs and boosters.

The small three-story atrium lobby gives the upper floors a sense of openness and continuity. There is a seating area on each floor that serves as a mini-lobby. It has couches, tables, and a patio.

All 160 rooms have cable color television (including free Select TV) with remote control, pay movies (with locks so children cannot use movie channels without your consent), and AM/FM radios. Most rooms have balconies with chairs and a table so you can enjoy the sea breeze; many have spectacular views. The rooms themselves have nice bathrooms done in marble, tub/shower combinations, separate vanity areas, and closets with floor-to-ceiling mirrors. Of course, bathroom amenities are included.

Rooms are good-sized and comfortably done, but a bit tired. Those with two double beds have enough space for the kids and their toys; the room with a king-size bed has adequate space for a crib or rollaway. Suites are available and can connect to rooms with two double beds.

Singles cost $120 to $165; doubles, $140 to $185; and suites, $350 to $400. There is no charge for children under 12 if additional beds are not needed in their parents' room. Cribs are free; rollaways cost $10. Free parking.

The **Miramar Sheraton Hotel,** 101 Wilshire Blvd. (at 2nd Street), Santa Monica, CA 90401 (tel. 213/394-3731), sits on the bluff across the street from Palisades Park. Close to the Santa Monica Pier and all the Santa Monica beaches, this garden hotel has a perfect location.

The hotel's rich history began over 100 years ago, when United States Sen. John P. Jones built a private mansion on the spot and called it Miramar (literally, "view of the sea"). Jones, a prosperous politician, struck it rich in the silver mines. Looking for a place to build a railroad and harbor so he could carry his silver to be minted in San Francisco, he chose Santa Monica Bay as the port for his endeavor. With his partner, Col. Robert Baker, he founded the city of Santa Monica.

Jones bought the land on which the Miramar sits for $1, and completed building in 1889. Political figures and other luminaries have come and gone, including Susan B. Anthony, Mark Twain, Greta Garbo, Susan Hayward, Eleanor Roosevelt, and John and Jacqueline Kennedy, all drawn to the ocean view and the hotel's lovely tropical gardens. In fact, the story goes that Betty Grable was discovered at the hotel bar. The hotel grounds, swimming pool, and bungalows have also served as the location for television shows and movies.

Hotel amenities include concierge service, 24-hour room service, complimentary newspaper, laundry and valet service, nightly turn-down, limousine and car rentals, hair salons for men and women, boutiques and giftshops, a solar-heated outdoor swimming pool, and three restaurants.

The Café is open from 6:30 a.m. to midnight, offering casual breakfast, lunch, and dinner dining. The kid's menu offers breakfast for $1 to $1.75, and lunch and dinner entrees run $1 to $2.25. The little menu includes games and mazes to keep the kids occupied.

The Garden Room is a delightful poolside eatery open for lunch on weekdays from 11:30 a.m. to 2 p.m. The International Room offers elegant dining from 6 to 10 p.m., and the Stateroom Lounge is open for cocktails and entertainment nightly except Sunday, serving complimentary hors d'oeuvres during the week from 5 to 8 p.m. Children may enjoy the hors d'oeuvres if accompanied by a parent.

Of the 305 guest rooms, 60 are suites. You can choose from two different towers or the small garden bungalows for your family's accommodations.

The hotel's Ocean Tower rooms are newly renovated, and come in two styles—traditional with dark woods and elaborate moldings, and light pastels with rattan, bleached-wood furniture, and polished brass fixtures. You can choose from rooms with a king-size bed or with two double beds. Each room has an honor bar/refrigerator, game table, color television, and bathroom amenities. Most have tub/shower combinations, but request one specifically if it's important to you. Some rooms have remote-control television.

Poolside Lanai rooms are $125 single and $140 double, Palisades rooms cost $130 single and $145 double, Ocean Tower rooms run $155 single and $170 double, and Palisades suites (one-bedroom suites) rent for $160 single and $175 double. Ocean Tower suites start at $275. Children 18 and under stay free in their parents' room if additional beds are not necessary. Additional adults pay $15 per night. Cribs are free. Parking is $4 per day.

Moderate

One of our favorite hotels is the **Marina International Hotel and Villas,** 4200 Admiralty Way (at Palawan Way), Marina Del Rey, CA 90292 (tel. 213/301-2000, or toll free 800/882-4000). This smallish hostelry of 135 rooms set in a pleasant garden setting is just perfect for families. Believe it or not, while it's pricey, it's probably the best value in the moderate price range if you want something near the water.

There is a main building and garden bungalows that give you a choice of the kind of accommodation you'd like for your family. Furthermore, it's across the street from a sandy beach with gentle, lapping water instead of waves. You also have your choice of dining experiences here, with loads of restaurants nearby.

The two-story lobby resembles a large cheery sitting room or enclosed patio. There's a huge skylight and plants that continue the outdoor effect. There are small conversation groups with tables and chairs at which you and the kids can enjoy the happy-hour appetizers served in the adjacent bar.

The hotel offers free parking, and shuttle service to and from the airport and neighboring restaurants in the Marina. Other hotel amenities include 24-hour room service and poolside service, vending and ice machines on each floor, and a very pretty pool area that has a large shallow area and is tucked away so that you don't have to worry about the children. Above the pool is a nice area for sitting. There is a laundromat and shopping center within easy walking distance. Babysitting can be arranged through the front desk.

The Crystal Fountain Restaurant is open for breakfast, lunch, and dinner. They have highchairs and boosters, but no children's menu. Prices range from $3.25 to $7.25 for breakfast, $6 to $7.50 for lunch, and $7.50 to $16 for dinner. This upbeat, purely "Marina del Rey"–style hotel invites guests (including kids) to their Friday "Meet Me Under the Clock" event, which features free appetizers, a disc jockey, and dancing. Periodically the restaurant has a "Magical Sunday Brunch" with a magician, a mime, or harpist to entertain all. The typical buffet brunch runs $15 for adults and $8 for children aged 5 to 12. Kids under 5 eat for free.

Completely redecorated in 1988, the very large rooms are done in a sunny Southwest motif in light sand and turquoise colors that add to the life and verve of the place. They're bright, with large white shutters filtering the light and alternately providing privacy. All rooms have balconies and come complete with free remote-control cable television, including Select TV, and pay movies (the channels are locked so parents can keep kids from watching X-rated movies). There are game tables and chairs, desks, and AM/FM clock radios. Bathrooms have marble floors; most come with tub/shower combinations (but specify your needs because some bungalows have showers only). There are complete amenity baskets.

Bungalows are set up in a charming, flower-filled courtyard where there is ample space for kids to wander. The ones on the ground floor have balconies that are cordoned off by planters so that even toddlers won't wander off. Our kids usually spend time sitting outside playing jacks and pick-up-sticks on the cobblestone ground. Bungalows are split-level rooms with a loft, cathedral ceilings, and large windows. There are huge walk-in closets, two televisions, two telephones, a double bed, and a sofa bed.

Rates are $95 to $155 for singles, $115 to $175 for doubles (two doubles or one queen-size or king-size bed). Bungalows and suites (in the main building) range from $135 to $265. Junior suites (with a queen-size bed and a sofa bed that pulls out to a double bed) are $135 double occupancy. Children under 16 stay for free when sharing a room with their parents if additional beds are not needed. Cribs are free; there is no charge for rollaways for children under 16, but there's a $15-per-night charge for additional adults. Connecting rooms are available. Free parking. Always ask if there are any special discount packages available, which can be as much as 30% lower.

Pacific Shore Hotel, 1819 Ocean Ave. (at Pico Boulevard), Santa Monica, CA 90401 (tel. 213/451-8711, or toll free 800/241-3848), is a pleasant eight-story, 168-room hotel with a breezy, seaside-like atmosphere. Its big attraction, though, is its proximity to the beach, which is across the street. It has an unimpeded view of the ocean so that even second-floor ocean-view rooms have a great vista. (Even if you have a city view, you'll be pleased.)

Very much a family-oriented place, the hotel has a guest laundry, same-day valet service, free parking, complimentary continental breakfast of coffee and doughnuts, a beauty salon, and a giftshop. Babysitting is handled through a referral agency. If you need a refrigerator, request one when you make your reservation (the charge is $10 per night). Room service (which includes a children's menu) is available from 7 a.m. to 10 p.m.

The swimming pool and spa area is quite spacious, and the shallow end of the pool can be cordoned off to keep little swimmers out of the deep end.

A Baker's Square restaurant is adjacent to the hotel. If you're unfamiliar with this chain, they are nice coffeeshops with prices for lunch and dinner ranging from $4.25 to $7.25. A complete children's menu has entrees for about $1.75. In essence, you're paying coffeeshop prices, *not* hotel restaurant prices.

The rooms are decorated in light California pastels and accented with rattan furniture. They all have cable color televisions, in-room movies (for a fee), AM/FM radios, game tables, small desks, tub/shower combinations, and bathroom toiletries. The best family rooms are those with two double beds, but there are also rooms with king-size beds. Connecting rooms can have a king-size bed and two double beds. In fact, you can connect three rooms with two doubles on either side and a king in the middle.

Rates range from $106 to $116 single, $117 to $127 double. Children 12 and under stay for free when sharing a parent's room. Cribs are free; rollaways are $8 per night, and an extra person is charged $10 per night. Free parking.

Also within walking distance from the beach (Venice Beach, that is) is the **BayView Plaza Holiday Inn,** 530 Pico Blvd. (at 6th Street), Santa Monica, CA 90405 (tel. 213/399-9344, or toll free 800/HOLIDAY). The attractive four-story atrium-style lobby is done in contemporary Santa Fe style. Large enough to feel spacious and allow you to let your kids walk around, it's small enough that you don't have to worry about them getting lost.

This full-service hotel has two swimming pools (one has a good shallow area) and two Jacuzzis, a fitness room, giftshop, beauty salon, and complimentary valet parking. Other amenities include room service from 6 a.m. to 10:30 p.m. and help with babysitting through the front desk staff. The piano bar is open nightly, with complimentary hors d'oeuvre service from 5 p.m.

The BayView Café serves breakfast, lunch, and dinner, offering such American standards as hotcakes, burgers, and seafood. Breakfast costs $4.25 to $8, lunch is $6 to $10, and dinner runs $7.75 to $18.25. Even if you don't have a meal there, grab the kids and bring them for a do-it-yourself sundae (one, two, or three scoops are $3, $4, and $5, respectively). The Café has highchairs and boosters but no children's menu.

The hotel has over 300 attractive rooms (four even have their own outdoor Jacuzzis). The rooms are standard size, and most of them have balconies. Each has cable color TV with remote control (pay movies available), bathroom amenities, and a nice view (even if it isn't of the ocean). Some rooms also have sofa beds; some have two bathroom sinks and vanities. Most rooms have a tub/shower combination, but be sure to specify your needs if this is important to you.

Room rates depend on location and view. Singles range from $75 (small rooms) to $115; doubles, from $75 to $125. Suites rent for $250. Cribs are free; rollaways cost $10. Children 18 and under are free in the same room with an adult. Free parking.

If you don't really care that much about the ambience of the hotel and simply want a nice room, you might try the **Jamaica Bay Inn,** 4175 Admiralty Way (near Palawan Way), Marina del Rey, CA 90292 (tel. 213/823-5333), a small motel right on the beach. The motel has a coffeeshop (with highchairs and boosters), a bar, and a nice swimming pool and patio area (although it is completely accessible to the lobby and little tykes can wander off). There is a small, pleasant grassy area.

Room service is available from 6 a.m. to 11 p.m. through the coffeeshop, which keeps the same hours. (The menu runs from $3 to $8 for breakfast and lunch, and $6.25 to $10.50 for dinner.) But don't expect style.

The inn fronts the harbor and a palm-tree-studded beach, giving the second-floor bayside rooms extraordinary views. Second-story rooms are the choice ones here (even if you have the less expensive city views). Ceilings are high and the rooms are away from the hubbub of the downstairs walk-through lobby.

The rooms are spacious and bright, and have color TV, king- or queen-size beds, air conditioning, and a balcony or patio. "King deluxe" rooms have a game table and chairs, wet bar, refrigerator, and microwave oven, as well as a queen-size sofa bed and a king-size bed. "Queen" rooms have two queen-size beds and lots of extra space in which children can play.

Rates are based on double occupancy: king rooms range from $90 to $110 (with either city or bayside views); double queen rooms rent for $110 to $120; and king deluxe rooms cost $110 to $130. Children under 12 stay for free when sharing their parents' room and using existing bedding. Cribs are free. Rollaways cost $10.

Budget

An excellent choice for the money is the well-kept **Comfort Inn,** 2815 Santa Monica Blvd., Santa Monica, CA 90404 (tel. 213/828-5517, or toll free 800/228-5150). Although it isn't within walking distance of the beach (it's actually about ten minutes away), this is a good West Los Angeles / Santa Monica location, just minutes (by car) from Westwood, Brentwood, and Santa Monica. You can't beat it for value.

The swimming pool is quite large, with a good-size shallow area. You can lay around the pool using the lounge chairs provided, or sit on the outdoor patios on the first and second floors. There's plenty of room for kids to wander or play quiet games on these patios, and tables are provided so you can enjoy the outdoors. The staff is friendly, and is used to families. Indeed, so successful is this little motor inn that a large percentage of their business is repeat customers.

The 81 rooms are tidy and surprisingly good sized. All have tub/shower combinations, individual air conditioning, instant coffee makers, oversize closets, game tables, and color TV. Some are a little dark, but you can request a room on the third floor, which is generally brighter.

Rooms with two double beds are especially large and have plenty of room for a crib. The rooms with king-size beds also feature a small love seat.

Rates are $59 to $69 single and $69 to $79 double. Children 17 and under stay free when sharing the same room as their parents. Cribs and rollaways are $5 per night. Adjoining rooms (usually two doubles connect to a king) are available. Free parking.

THE AIRPORT AREA: Most people who stay near Los Angeles International Airport stay here because they want the convenience. If you need a market in this area, your best bet is to ask someone at the front desk.

The Upper Bracket

The **Los Angeles Airport Hilton & Towers,** 5711 W. Century Blvd., Los Angeles, CA 90045 (tel. 213/410-4000, or toll free 800/HILTONS), the largest airport hotel in the world, has more than 1,200 rooms to choose from. This is our pick of the hotels near the airport. (Complimentary airport shuttles run 24 hours a day.)

Don't be put off by the formal-looking lobby with its contemporary fountain and baby grand piano. Children are welcome at this hotel. The Hilton features a large outdoor pool surrounded by four spas and a self-service eating area. There are also three garden terraces at which room service is available and where children can entertain themselves. Mom and Dad can work out, play racquetball, or get a massage at the Family Fitness Center, which also provides child care—or contact the concierge staff, which can arrange babysitting through an outside agency. A very small video arcade on the same level as the health club is a sometimes welcome diversion.

Naturally a 1,200-room hotel is big, and therefore provides lots of places to walk around and things to look at for energetic youngsters. You can walk through the Galleria, for instance, which is part of the Centroplex complex of shops and restaurants adjacent to the hotel.

There are several restaurants at the Hilton, but the best one for families is Café L.A. on the lobby level, open 18 hours a day every day. Breakfast starts at 6 a.m. While there's no children's menu, they offer smaller portions at half the price for kids under 12. Sandwiches and hamburgers cost $5 to $6.75. Entree prices run $7.50 to $18. Or order from room service 24 hours a day. If you still need other choices, there's food service in the Galleria next door, Monday through Saturday.

The clean, nicely lighted rooms come with remote-control TV and free cable. Refrigerators are available for $5 per night. Rooms with king-size beds can fit a rollaway and a crib, while rooms with two double beds could take one or the other. Features include mirrored closet doors, sleek and clean bathrooms with tub/shower combinations, a big lighted mirror, and rattan furniture. A parlor is a good choice for large families. It's quite roomy and has a sofa bed, refrigerator and wet bar, table, chairs, and desk. It can connect to one or two sleeping rooms, affording you extra space in the daytime.

Rates vary depending on the location of the room. Higher-priced units are closer to the elevators—something to consider if you'll have lots to carry every day. A room with one bed costs $110 to $140 single. A room with two double beds or one king-size bed runs $125 to $155 double. Tower rooms are $140 single and $155 double. Suites are priced from $240 to $500. Children sleep free in their parents' room regardless of age. An extra adult is charged $15 per night. Cribs and rollaways are complimentary.

Ask about special weekend packages—when rooms are $59, children sleep free, and continental breakfast is included. Hiltons usually also have special summer rates, so inquire when you call for your reservation. Self-parking is $5 per day, with in-and-out privileges. Valet parking is also available, at $7 per day.

At the **Viscount Hotel,** 9750 Airport Blvd., Los Angeles, CA 90045 (tel. 213/645-4600), you'll find 570 clean rooms and suites. The outdoor Olympic-size pool has a big deck area, but it's not fenced in and there aren't any grassy areas for playing. As with most airport hotels, a complimentary shuttle to and from the airport is available 24 hours a day.

The Palm Grill serves breakfast ($5.50 to $10), lunch (nothing over $7.50), and dinner ($8.75 to $18) beginning at 5 a.m., and has boosters and highchairs.

Getting cribs into any of the rooms is a tight squeeze, except for parlors and suites. Rooms with two double beds, which can adjoin with a parlor room, are great for small families who also need a crib. The parlor has a pullout bed and a nice living area. Or rent connecting rooms. The rooms with a king-size bed feature a sofa bed, as does the junior suite, which is one large room and a king-size bed. There are desks in all rooms, as well as remote-control TV and lots of extra towels. Refrigerators are available upon request for $10 per day. Request hairdryers and irons from housekeeping. The front desk maintains a list of babysitters.

Singles with two double beds or a king-size bed go for $85 to $105; doubles run $95 to $115. Parlors cost $90; junior suites, $150; and one-bedroom suites, $190. Children 17 and under sleep free in their parents' room. An extra adult is charged $10 per night. Rollaways are available for $15 extra; cribs are free. Free parking.

At the **Days Inn Hotel / Los Angeles Airport,** 5101 Century Blvd., Los Angeles, CA 90304 (tel. 213/419-1234), kids 12 and under sleep *and eat* free. Not surprisingly, the Days Inn is attractive to lots of families.

At the fenced-in outdoor pool, you can arrange to have food delivered from the restaurant. The Days Inn Restaurant is open for breakfast, lunch, and dinner. This is where the kids eat free, beginning at 6 a.m. At breakfast there are eggs, pancakes, and French toast; lunch features sandwiches and burgers; dinner offers full entrees, like honey-fried chicken and butterfly shrimp.

The rooms with two double beds, fine for a family of three or four, have tiny outside decks, separate vanities, and chairs and a table. Color TV with cable is in all rooms. A crib or rollaway would fit in a single, but would be crowded in a room with two double beds.

Singles are $69; doubles, $75. There are no suites or adjoining rooms. Kids 12 and under sleep free; an extra adult pays $10. There is a $6 charge for cribs and rollaways. Ask about special weekend rates. Free parking.

The prices at the **Quality Inn** at Los Angeles Airport, 5249 W. Century Blvd., Los Angeles, CA 90045 (tel. 213/645-2200), are excellent. And while the rooms aren't huge, a family of three or four could stay comfortably. The hotel sits in front of the Holiday Inn on busy Century Boulevard, but it's also near major freeways and close to Marina Del Rey.

A large pool—not fenced in—provides relief on a hot day. Babysitting can be arranged through an agency.

Of the two restaurants in the hotel, Brandi's serves dinner only, and has reasonably priced sandwiches on its menu. Tivoli Garden is open all day, and room service comes from this restaurant. Pancakes and eggs, a burger, and pizza are found on that menu. If all else fails, there's a McDonald's next door.

Single rooms, with one double bed, have room for a crib. The rooms with two double beds are what we recommend for a small family, and there are adjoining rooms for larger families. Or for longer stays, suites have one king-size bed and a pullout sofa. Cable TV and direct-dial telephones are included.

Singles with one bed cost $58; doubles with two beds are $66; suites rent for $75. Kids under 16 sleep free. The charge for an extra person in any room is $8. Cribs are complimentary; rollaways cost $6. Parking is $3 per day, with in-and-out privileges. Inquire about special weekend rates.

HOLLYWOOD: This area draws scores of travelers because of its romantic history. While we would not advise taking an evening stroll in the area, it is well patrolled and safe for sightseeing during the day. Universal City is just over the hill from Hollywood, and is a city unto itself. People stay there to be close to the studios and the freeway. Ask the staff at the front desk for the names and addresses of markets in the area.

The Upper Bracket

The **Hollywood Roosevelt,** 7000 Hollywood Blvd., Hollywood, CA 90028 (tel. 213/466-7000), epitomizes Tinsel Town when it was in its heyday. This deluxe hotel, which was the site of the first Academy Awards presentation, was renovated in 1984 and carefully restored to its original glory. While the area isn't great for walking around at night, the hotel is located at the beginning of Hollywood Boulevard and within easy access of a major freeway, downtown, and Beverly Hills.

The two-story lobby with its hand-painted ceilings and Spanish wrought-iron grillwork remains. It's a large lobby with lots of seating for good people-watching. Be sure to take a walk by the Olympic-size pool to see the David Hockney painting on the bottom. There's plenty of room for lounging and eating outdoors, but only a tiny grassy area for wandering toddlers. Poolside food service is available. For those who can't rest, an exercise room is adjacent. The concierge can arrange babysitting. Neither the Stargazer Café nor Theodore's has children's menus. The Stargazer, though, has enough choices to keep most kids satisfied for breakfast and lunch and the prices are quite reasonable. Room service, however, is limited in what will appeal to young appetites.

The rooms have art deco touches, and many are newly renovated. Others date from the '50s. Standard accommodations have room for a rollaway or crib, or rooms can be connected with a parlor between them. Request either two double beds or a king-size bed. Cabaña rooms open to the outside gardens (keep this in mind if you're traveling with young wanderers). Remote-control TVs and SpectraVision are standard. Standard, deluxe, and premium rooms differ in terms of size and location. Suites have great deco furniture; nine of them are three-room suites, and there is a two-story Celebrity Suite, which rents for $1,500 a night.

Rates in standard rooms are $100 single and $120 double. Deluxe rooms cost $110 single, $130 double. Premium rooms let for $125 single, $145 double. Suites range from $160 to $350 and up. Children under 12 sleep free; for those 12 and over, the charge is $20. Cribs are complimentary; rollaways, $15. Valet parking is $7 per night, with in-and-out privileges.

Located in the heart of Hollywood, the **Holiday Inn Hollywood,** 1755 N. Highland Ave., Hollywood, CA 90028 (tel. 213/462-7181), is appropriate for families who want to stay in a moderately priced hotel centrally located to many southland attractions. You'll recognize the hotel by its revolving top floor. This is not an area we recommend that you wander in at night. The hotel offers a small fenced-in outdoor pool area. Babysitting can be arranged with an outside agency through the housekeeping department.

The Show Biz Restaurant is the place to take the family for breakfast, (beginning at 6 a.m.), lunch buffets (both under $7), and evening dinner (with reasonably priced hamburgers and sandwiches). There are no children's menus, but there are a variety of selections at lunch and dinner that will appeal to those who don't opt for the buffet. Windows on Hollywood is a more formal restaurant on the revolving top floor. Only sophisticated tastebuds need attend. Room service is available 24 hours, with appropriate items for the kids.

The modern rooms are simple and compact. All come with two double beds or one king-size bed, and there is room for a crib or rollaway. Rooms with king-size beds are furnished with either sofa beds or small couches. Remote-control TV and in-room movies are standard features. In-room safes ($4 per day), hairdryers, and extra phones are available upon request. There are adjoining rooms suitable for large families. Or rent one bedroom and a mini-suite, which has a bedroom and a seating area.

Single occupancy costs $85; double occupancy is $97. Mini-suites rent for $126. Children under 18 sleep free in their parents' room; those 18 and over are charged $12. Cribs are free; rollaways cost $12. If you are traveling in the summer, ask about special rates. Parking is free, and there's room for motor homes in the lot.

UNIVERSAL CITY: The **Sheraton Universal,** 333 Universal Terrace Pkwy., Universal City, CA 91608 (tel. 818/980-1212, or toll free 800/325-3535), is located on the lot of Universal Studios, perched high above the San Fernando Valley floor. Many of the rooms literally overlook the famous studio, and others have views of the Hollywood Hills. If you want to be close to Hollywood, downtown Los Angeles, and Burbank, you can't beat this location.

The hotel's 471 rooms are in a 20-story tower and in the two-story poolside lanai buildings. The enchanting outdoor pool area is surrounded by clusters of tall palm trees and umbrellas, offering shade to outdoor diners and a wonderful area for sun worshipers. The pool has a large shallow area and lots of space to laze the day away if you and the kids are so inclined.

Hotel amenities include concierge service, 24-hour room service, laundry and valet (Monday through Saturday), a giftshop, an exercise room, and complimentary shuttle service to Universal Studios Tours.

In addition to being within walking distance of Fung Lum's, Tony Roma's and Victoria Station (see the "Where to Eat" section for details), the hotel's restaurant, The Californias, serves breakfast, lunch, and dinner. Breakfast prices range from $2.50 to $10.75, lunch is $7.25 to $11, and dinners average around $15 to $16. Kids can ask for a hot dog ($2.50) or hamburger ($3).

The hotel is in the final phases of a $10-million renovation. Rooms are spanking new, light and bright, set off with pastels and light wood furniture. You can choose from king-size beds (with a comfortable overstuffed chaise longue), two double beds, and parlor suites that have king-size beds with full-size sectional couches. Deluxe suites have a sleeping room that closes off and a parlor.

All rooms have a fancy phone system with "call waiting," a direct-dial to hotel services (such as the housekeeping department and the concierge), and phone jacks that allow you to move the phone around the room. Remote-control television comes with free HBO and video checkout, and pay SpectraVision. All bathrooms have tub/shower combinations as well as the usual toiletry amenities.

Rooms are $119 to $130 single and $140 to $160 double. Suites cost $175 and up. Connecting rooms are available. Cribs are free; rollaways cost $15. Children 17 and under are free if they share their parents' room and additional beds are not needed. Parking is $7.50 per day.

WEST HOLLYWOOD: This area can be trendy and exciting, if somewhat on the expensive side. Many families prefer this part of town because of its location, near Hollywood, Beverly Hills, and the mid-Wilshire District. You'll find a 24-hour Hughes market at 9040 Beverly Blvd. (tel. 213/278-1351) and a 24-hour Pavilion Place (with a pharmacy, open until 9 p.m.) at Santa Monica Boulevard and Robertson Boulevard (tel. 213/273-0977). The West Hollywood Park, with some children's equipment and a big sandbox, is between Melrose Avenue and Santa Monica Boulevard, and Robertson and San Vicente Boulevards.

The Upper Bracket

Set in a quiet residential neighborhood, **Le Parc Hotel,** 733 N. West Knoll Dr., West Hollywood, CA 90069 (tel. 213/855-8888, or toll free 800/424-4443), is convenient to Beverly Hills, downtown, and many local attractions. This all-suite hotel (actually a converted apartment building) hides a small outdoor pool, sundeck, spa, and tennis court on the roof. The restaurant, Café Le Parc, is open only to guests. Breakfast here is no problem, even though there is no children's menu—the standard choices will appeal to most children. Lunch, with a French menu, also offers the ever-faithful cheeseburger. Dinner at Le Parc is for the sophisticated—and rich—only. There are no boosters or highchairs here. A plus, though, is that you'll find all sorts of snacks—pretzels, Famous Amos cookies, and soft drinks—in the cocktail cabinet in your generous-size kitchenette (which you must request). Management will supply appliances, cookware, and dishes at your request also—room service will do the dishes. Every suite has a full-size refrigerator as well. In the evening, complimentary cocktails and hors d'oeuvres are served in the restaurant.

The warm comfortable rooms come with gas fireplaces, two phone lines, and nice-size closets. In the standard executive suites, and the slightly larger deluxe suites, the bedrooms are a step up from the living area, separated by a curtain, and there is a hideabed in the living room.

While there is enough room for a crib, adding a rollaway would be difficult. The deluxe suites have two remote-control TVs; the standard suites, one. All have cable TVs and videocassette players, and movies are available at the front desk. One-bedroom suites have completely private bedrooms.

Rates are based on single occupancy: an executive suite rents for $140; a deluxe suite, $150; and a one-bedroom corner suite, $160. Each additional person is charged $25, but children under 12 sleep free in their parents' room. Cribs and rollaways are available at no charge. Babysitting can be arranged through an agency. Parking is free.

You may wonder why we are going to recommend yet another all-suite hotel, one in the same general neighborhood and owned by the same people. The advantages of **Le Dufy,** 1000 Westmount Dr., West Hollywood, CA 90069 (tel. 213/657-7400), like its sister hotel, are that it is centrally located in a quiet residential area, is a fairly small hotel, and offers apartment-like accommodations that are very comfortable, especially for longer stays.

Le Dufy's pool, spa, and garden are also found on the rooftop and provide good views. A restaurant is being completed at this writing, and there is room service. Babysitting can be arranged through an agency. Those staying longer than a few days will appreciate the coin-operated laundry facilities.

The contemporary apricot and lavender suites, all converted apartments, are furnished with king-size beds, pullout sofas in the living room, gas fireplaces, remote-control cable TVs, and private balconies. There's a small eating area and a long, narrow living room. In the junior suites, the bedroom is semiprivate, divided by a curtain; in the one-bedroom suites, it is completely private. Kitchenettes are standard, but request dishes and pots and pans ahead of time. Hairdryers and full-length mirrors are provided, along with every woman's dream for a hotel amenity—a makeup mirror and makeup lights.

Rates for a junior suite are $115 single and $140 double. A one-bedroom suite rents for $155 single and $180 double. Children under 12 sleep free in their parents' room; there is a $25-per-night charge for children 12 and over. Cribs and rollaways are complimentary. Parking is free.

MID-WILSHIRE / MIRACLE MILE AREA:

You'll find good value for your money in this part of town. Located south of Hollywood, east of Beverly Hills, and bordering on chic West Hollywood, this area is full of attractions. If you choose to stay in the vicinity, you can find a 24-hour Von's Market at 6350 W. 3rd St., at Fairfax Avenue (tel. 213/930-1023). Pan Pacific Park, located between Beverly Boulevard and West 3rd Street, is a big park with a children's play area on the bottom level, and one for very young children above, at the Gardner Avenue entrance.

Moderate

The location of the **Beverly Plaza**, 8384 W. 3rd St., Los Angeles, CA 90048 (tel. 213/658-6600, or toll free 800/62-HOTEL, 800/33-HOTEL in California), makes it a good choice for travelers. It is within walking distance of the huge Beverly Center shopping mall, 5 minutes' driving distance from Beverly Hills, 15 minutes from Century City, 25 minutes to the beach, and 20 minutes from downtown. Complimentary van service (by appointment) shuttles you to and from anywhere within a five-mile radius.

You won't find many recreational facilities in this small European-style hotel, but don't let that stop you from staying here. Families are definitely welcome. There is a tiny pool perfect for young children (it's three feet deep) set on a very small patio on the second floor. The pool area is furnished with lounge chairs and umbrella tables, and poolside food service is provided. The hotel also has a beauty salon and a manicurist for emergency treatment, as well as a small health club and sauna.

Rembrandt's is the hotel restaurant and it serves breakfast, lunch, and dinner. We're told that lots of families dine here, but other than chicken in a basket (at $7) and a hamburger ($5.50), there isn't much on the menu for unsophisticated tastes. But there are lots of excellent small neighborhood restaurants in the area, several within walking distance of the hotel. Room service is available 24 hours a day. Again the selections for lunch and dinner for youngsters are limited; breakfast is no problem.

Light, pleasant hallways with wainscotted walls lead to comfortable-sized rooms. There are 97 rooms here, 50 of which are designated no-smoking. Double rooms with two queen-size beds can be rented with connecting units. You'll find space for a crib in a standard room, but a rollaway would be tight. The décor is French provincial, with rooms featuring writing desks plus a small table and two chairs. Remote-control TVs (with cable) and mini-bars are hidden behind cabinets and armoires. All rooms either have VCRs or one can be requested at the front desk. There are movies for rent in the lobby (with children's selections). The mini-suites are quite roomy and are equipped with a king-size bed and double-size hideabed in addition to the standard furnishings. All rooms have hairdryers and phones in the bathrooms. Tub/shower combinations are featured in the small bathrooms, and closet doors double as full-length mirrors. Terrycloth robes are provided for guest use.

Standard rooms (with two double beds) rent for $98 single and $108 double; superior rooms (with a queen-size bed and a couch) cost $112 single and $122 double; and deluxe rooms (with a king-size bed and a couch) run $136 single, $146 double. Children under 12 sleep free in their parents' room; those 12 and over are charged $10. Cribs and rollaways are complimentary. A special weekend rate of $79, single or double occupancy, is offered year round on a space-available basis. Parking costs $2 overnight, with in-and-out privileges.

Guests who want to stay at the **Best Western Farmer's Daughter Motel**, 115 S. Fairfax Ave., Los Angeles, CA 90036 (tel. 213/937-3930, or toll free 800/528-1234), had better make their reservations far in advance. Because of its location and rates, the motel is sold out almost nightly. It's across the street from the Farmers Market and CBS, and within walking distance of restaurants and a first-run movie theater. Two tour-bus companies stop at the motel, and reservations can be made at the front desk.

There's a very small pool on the premises, fenced-in and surrounded by a few chaises longues, chairs, and umbrella tables. Overlooking the pool on the second floor is a small outdoor patio furnished with an umbrella table, chairs, and a chaise. It's perfect for a rest and a snack with the kids. The motel has plenty of ice (free), soda, candy, and other food vending machines. Parking is plentiful and convenient to the rooms.

The 66 mint-green-and-white rooms are small but clean. The furnishings differ in many rooms, but the setup is the same. Units come with either one queen-size bed, two doubles, or two queen-size beds. In the main building, attractive painted concrete bricks keep the noise out. Color TV, refrigerator, instant coffee maker, an air conditioning unit, and a wall heater are standard. There are also built-in headboards, a round table and two chairs, tub/shower combinations, separate vanities, and small closets. There are only a couple of adjoining rooms. Although they claim to fit a rollaway in the rooms, it's a tight squeeze. Large families should consider taking two rooms.

From January through mid-June and September through December, the rate is $52 single or double occupancy. From Mid-June through August it is $65. Additional persons (including children) are charged $3 each per night. No cribs; rollaways are provided at no charge. Free parking.

The proximity of the **Beverly Laurel Motor Hotel,** 8018 Beverly Blvd., Los Angeles, CA 90048 (tel. 213/651-2441), to the CBS Studios makes it attractive to families and game-show contestants alike. This family-run motel has 52 rooms, most of which overlook the pool/courtyard area. The fenced-in pool is large, and there are plentiful chaises and chairs.

The Beverly Laurel is within walking distance of many small restaurants, and there is one on the premises, but it is not owned by the motel. You can, however, get room service from them, but you may not charge it to your room. Call before you visit, because the restaurant has limited hours. There is a coin-operated laundry one block away, and a health-food store across the street.

Rooms here are clean but worn. Corner rooms with kitchenettes are large and great for families. The kitchen is separated from the room by a breakfast bar with stools, and there's a small table and two chairs in the kitchen itself. Dishes and small pots are provided, but bring your own coffeepot. A small stove, refrigerator, and sink are included. The room itself has two double beds and room for a crib or rollaway. If you need even more room, these accommodations connect to standard-size rooms. Each room features a full-length mirror, a separate vanity, tub/shower combination, two closets, and a color TV. Watch out for the floor heater if you have crawlers or toddlers with you. There is also a separate air-conditioning unit.

Standard rooms with two double beds would be crowded with a crib or rollaway. These units, which can sleep three to four people, come with small refrigerators and color TVs. A makeup table and chair are in the separate vanity/dressing area, which also has a set of built-in drawers. Most of the standard rooms have large shower stalls. If you need a tub, be sure to request one in advance.

Babysitting can be arranged. Parking is free in the underground lot or in the ground-level open garages. Tour buses stop here.

Rates are $51 single, $57 double. Kitchenette rooms cost $10 extra. Additional guests, including children, are charged $3 each per night. Cribs and rollaways cost $3.

DOWNTOWN: Downtown Los Angeles offers elegant accommodations. Ask at the front desk for recommendations if you need to find a market nearby for diapers, formula, or snacks.

Deluxe

The **Westin Bonaventure,** 404 S. Figueroa St. (between 4th and 5th Streets), Los Angeles, CA 90011 (tel. 213/624-1000, or toll free 800/228-3000), is known for its round mirrored towers, huge lobby, and exterior glass elevators, visible to the eye almost anywhere in the downtown area. But remember that staying at the Bonaventure is like staying in a small city. There are nearly 1,500 guest rooms, 20 restaurants and five lounges, and more than 30 retail shops. There's always something to look at and someplace to wander.

The shopping gallery hosts jewelry stores, art galleries, book and card shops, and clothing stores, including a T-shirt shop on the fourth level. The lobby itself is a six-level atrium with six reflection pools. There's a large fenced-in outdoor pool, but there are no grassy play areas. For guests who miss their exercise, there is a fitness center accessible via a skybridge.

The Sidewalk Café in the Lobby Court is perfect for families. Being in the lobby, it has lots of things for active children to look at. Kids get a *Kiddie Kapers* newsletter that gives them all sorts of trivia about the hotel and Los Angeles in general, and challenges them with connect-the-dots, jokes, and a crossword puzzle. On the back is their separate menu, which includes Tony Tiger and toast for breakfast, a Bruin basket for lunch (hamburger, fries, and a salad), and a Tommy Lasorda special for dinner (ravioli, roll, and a salad). Oreo cookies and ice cream are available for dessert. These meals range from $3 to $4.50, including beverage. The breakfast buffet is $8.75 for adults and $4.75 for children. If the kids tire of this restaurant, there are dozens more on Level 4, including delis, falafel shops, and Chinese and health-food restaurants. The 35th-floor Top of Five Restaurant, where every table has a view, features a Sunday champagne brunch for which children up to 12 are charged $1 for each year of their age and adults pay $20. Among the other eateries at the Bonaventure are Beaudry's (gourmet dining), on the lobby level, and Inagiku (Japanese cuisine), on the sixth level—both of which are more appropriate for children over 12—and the Bagel Nosh, on Level 4.

Room service is available 24 hours a day, with a separate children's menu for lunch and dinner. The hotel will also pack a picnic lunch for the beach or park, or you can get take-out sandwiches from the numerous restaurants in the gallery.

All the rooms at the Bonaventure have floor-to-ceiling windows and large mirrors over the beds to make the rooms seem even bigger. A table and two chairs, reading chair with hassock, and remote-control cable TV with in-room movies are all standard. Bathrooms are generously sized and have tub/shower combinations. Private in-room bars are stocked with drinks and snacks. Connecting rooms and no-smoking rooms can be requested. You have your choice of rooms with twin, queen-size, or king-size beds.

The hotel prides itself on the fact that no room is more than seven doors from an elevator—an important fact when you're dragging teddy bears, infant seats, 16 Tonka trucks, and the kids.

Rates are based on location and view, and range from $120 to $160 single, $145 to $185 double. Children 12 and younger sleep free in the same room with their parents; those over 12 are charged $25 per night. Rollaways cost $25; cribs are provided at no charge. Parking costs $15 per night, with in-and-out privileges.

If you're coming on a weekend or holiday, ask about the "Westin Weekend" special. You get a 50% discount on any room or suite in the hotel, and on parking, on any Friday, Saturday, Sunday, or holiday. Some families prefer the "Weekend Under Glass" package: a room, free parking, and $50 in food and beverage credits (good anywhere in the hotel) is yours for $129 per room, double occupancy, or $199 per suite. This also applies to weekends and holidays.

The **Hyatt Regency Los Angeles,** 711 S. Hope St. (at 7th Street), Los Angeles, CA 90017 (tel. 213/683-1234, or toll free 800/228-9000), does not offer family programs and does not have a pool. But the rooms here are quite lovely and the hotel is centrally located. It's connected to the Broadway Plaza Shopping Center, a welcome treat for parents always in search of interesting adventures for their tots. The shopping center is open daily. Hold on tight to your teenagers when you exit the lobby, as Judy's boutique across from the entrance is quite "the thing," carrying the latest in styles for that age group.

The hotel's health club is geared toward adults, and the sundeck adjacent to it is very limited in size. The spa is extremely small and is better suited to aching muscles than to rambunctious children. Babysitting can be arranged.

The Sun Porch restaurant, on the lobby level, is definitely appropriate for families. Designed to look like a Paris street, it's open for breakfast, lunch, and dinner, and boosters and highchairs are provided. Although it doesn't say so on the menu, if you have your server tell the chef you have a child with you, he will prepare half portions at half price. Room service is available from 6:30 a.m. to midnight, and children's portions will be provided if you ask.

The contemporary rooms at the Hyatt are quite comfortable, roomy, and clean. Each has a small seating area in an alcove, divided from the bed by a low built-in dresser/console. The alcove, which looks out floor-to-ceiling windows, has a small settee, table and two chairs, and even a live plant or two. Bathrooms are of average size, but come with a couple of extra-plush towels and built-in hairdryers. Tub/bath combinations are the rule. Full-length mirrors appear on the closet doors. Color TV with cable and in-room movies are standard. VCRs can be rented along with video movies.

A big surprise for a downtown hotel is that the windows open! But they open at the bottom only, and although they don't open all the way, you should be careful with very small, curious, crawling infants.

Rooms with king-size beds have space for a crib, but a rollaway would be tight. Most families, we're told, rent either the corner rooms with king-size beds —which are a half again as big as a regular king-bedded room and come with a refrigerator—or rooms with two queen-size beds. There are connecting rooms available for even larger families. Suites are lovely and feature a bedroom and sitting alcove, plus a living room and dining room, wet bar, refrigerator, stereo, and half-bath. Some suites seat six in the dining rooms. Bathrooms in the suites are carpeted and have wonderful lighting.

Standard rooms rent for $124 single, $144 double. Corner rooms with king-size beds go for $164; suites range from $350 to $550. Children under 18 stay free in their parents' room, but rollaways cost $20, and cribs, $10. Children 18 and over, and additional adults, are charged $20 each per night. Be sure to ask about special weekend and holiday rates. Parking in the 2,800-space lot is $10 per night, with unlimited in-and-out privileges.

Elegance still prevails at the **Biltmore**, 506 S. Grand Ave. (between 5th and 6th Streets), Los Angeles, CA 90071 (tel. 213/624-1011, or toll free 800/421-8000, 800/252-0175 in California). Built in the 1920s, the Biltmore was a showpiece of the grand style, with lavish ceilings and Italian wall paintings. Expanded in 1928, and modernized in 1976, the hotel went through a recent multi-million-dollar restoration to preserve the incredible beauty of its original design. Now while its 700 rooms are somewhat contemporary, the rest of the hotel hasn't lost its elegant Spanish-Italian Renaissance design.

We would suggest that you take school-age children, rather than toddlers, here as the restaurant facilities are limited for young tastes, and the indoor pool area is basically for adults only. A great thing about the hotel is that it provides complimentary shuttle service to downtown Los Angeles, stopping at various points in the area. And it is within walking distance of the Museum of Contemporary Art and the Music Center. Dodger Stadium is just a few minutes away by car.

Parents can engage a babysitter through the concierge staff, and then indulge themselves at the full-service health club. Private massage can be arranged.

The Biltmore has two restaurants (one of which is the award-winning Bernard's), three bars, and a pastry shop. The Court Café is the place to take the family, and it begins service at 6:30 a.m. and is open until 11 p.m. Highchairs are provided. Your kids shouldn't have any trouble choosing something to eat here —all the usual American favorites are featured. Basically the same menu is available through room service, which is open 24 hours.

Rooms come in 26 different configurations and are furnished in contemporary colors with French provincial furniture. A Jim Dine engraving decorates every room. Everything is fresh and clean, lighting is custom-designed, and shuttered windows add an unusual touch. Standard rooms and rooms with king-size beds come with a comfortable reading chair, desk, and armoire. Bathrooms have full-length mirrors and separate vanities, tub/shower combinations with extra-deep tubs, and elegant pedestal sinks.

Gold Room accommodations—similar to a separate concierge floor—include butler service, mini-bars, complimentary continental breakfast, and late checkout. Parlors, which can connect with a Gold Room, have big sitting and dining areas, a sofa and love seats, a small refrigerator, and a liquor cabinet. Gold junior suites, larger than regular suites, come with two remote-control TVs, king-size beds, and other amenities.

Rates in standard rooms range from $120 to $150 single, from $140 to $170 double. Gold Rooms rent for $170 single and $190 double. Junior suites are available at $185 to $205; suites cost $325 and up. Children under 18 sleep free in the same room with their parents. Extra adults are charged $20 each per night. Rollaways and cribs are available at no charge. Inquire about the special weekend rates. Parking is $15 per night, with in-and-out privileges.

Moderate

For a modestly priced hotel in downtown Los Angeles, the **Holiday Inn,** 750 Garland Ave. (at Figueroa and 7th Streets), Los Angeles, CA 90017 (tel. 213/628-5242), is a good choice. It's unpretentious, but well kept, offering 204 rooms and suites.

The outdoor pool does not have poolside food service, but the nearby Garland Restaurant is available for take-out orders. Complimentary hors d'oeuvres and cocktails are served poolside in the evening.

The Garland overlooks the pool and is open for all three meals. It has an extremely varied menu, featuring everything from Mexican entrees to Oriental stir-fry. Kids under 11 can eat for $1—for breakfast they can have an egg and bacon or pancakes; at lunch and dinner there's grilled cheese and fries, a piece of chicken, or a hamburger. Boosters and highchairs are provided. Room service is available.

Standard rooms and rooms with king-size beds can accommodate a crib, but a rollaway might be a squeeze. Instead, consider renting a connecting room if your family is large. The clean and comfortable rooms are furnished with reading chairs and a small table and chairs, and have individual heaters and air conditioners. The front desk can refer you to outside babysitters.

Rates January through August range from $64 to $70 single and $72 to $78 double. From August through November rates increase $2 per room; in December, $4 more. Children under 18 sleep free in the same room with their parents. Extra adults are charged $7 per night. Rollaways cost $4, but cribs are provided free of charge. Free parking.

5. WHERE TO EAT

Los Angeles restaurants have become world renowned for the quality of their chefs. While you probably won't be taking your family to the more elegant of these, you won't have a problem finding good, accommodating places to feed your brood.

BEVERLY HILLS: There are lots of eateries in Beverly Hills perfect for the family. And many of them are surprisingly affordable.

Expensive

Benihana of Tokyo, 38 N. La Cienega Blvd., just north of Wilshire Boulevard (tel. 213/655-7311), is a place where the kids will enjoy the show as much as the food. The building itself is authentic, with wood beams and mammoth stones that were once part of a Japanese castle. A koi pond and arched bridge will intrigue the kids as well.

We know families who take their children here for special birthdays, graduations, and the like. Featuring teppanyaki/hibachi-style cooking, chefs prepare and serve the food in front of you—and prepare it with style. Everything is done with a flourish. Kids are caught up in the dramatic way the chefs cook and juggle the food.

All food is cooked at your table. For lunch, there is hibachi chicken (with fresh mushrooms, onions, and bean sprouts) and four kinds of steak to choose from. The Benihana Special is a combination of the chicken and New York steak with fresh vegetables. All luncheons include salad, shrimp, rice, and tea. Prices range from $7.25 to $10.50.

For dinner, you have a slightly larger selection. In addition to hibachi chicken, sukiyaki steak, hibachi steak, filet mignon, and steak teriyaki, you can have lobster or scallops. Again, all entrees include a shrimp appetizer, soup, salad, rice, and tea. Prices range from $11.75 to $22.50.

Benihana is used to accommodating families. It has highchairs and boosters, makes Shirley Temple cocktails, and accepts reservations. While there isn't a children's menu, kids can split meals.

Open for lunch Monday through Friday from 11:30 a.m. to 2 p.m., and for dinner Monday through Saturday from 5:30 to 10 p.m. and on Sunday from 4:30 to 10 p.m. Valet parking is available. Most major credit cards are accepted.

There's another branch at 14160 Panay Way, in Marina Del Rey (tel. 213/821-0888).

If you're a family of prime rib lovers and your children are able to enjoy a leisurely dining experience, **Lawry's the Prime Rib,** located in the heart of Beverly Hills' Restaurant Row at 55 N. La Cienega Blvd., half a block north of Wilshire Boulevard (tel. 213/652-2827), is a treat you don't want to miss. Walking into Lawry's is like entering a Georgian manor house. Decorated on a grand scale with plush carpets, traditional English paintings, and candelabra-style chandeliers, the restaurant is divided into two dining areas. Huge silver serving carts are brought to your table so that chefs can carve your meat to your specifications. This means that the aisles are very wide.

We usually request one of the booths, which are ornately upholstered and well padded, offering privacy from neighboring diners and allowing us greater peace of mind when the kids get a tad noisier than we wish. Tables are comfortable too, complete with padded high-back chairs.

Lawry's secret to success is that it serves only one entree: prime rib. For 50 years Lawry's has served standing rib roasts that have been dry-aged for two to three weeks. You can choose between "English" and "Lawry" cut or "California" cut (for light eaters) and "Diamond Jim Brady" cut (extra thick with a bone) for $16 to $22. With each dinner comes the house salad, mashed potatoes, traditional Yorkshire pudding, and creamed horseradish. The children's portion ($9.50, which also includes a beverage and dessert) is almost the same as the "California" cut adult portion.

We have only one caution about bringing youngsters here. You must be prepared for a leisurely meal. A 2-year-old may do fine for an hour, but even the best-natured toddler may get restless or even troublesome when it extends beyond that.

There are no highchairs here, but booster seats are available. There is a full bar that offers non-alcoholic drinks as well as standard cocktails.

Lawry's is open Monday through Saturday from 5 to 11 p.m. and on Sunday from 3 to 10 p.m. Reservations are strongly advised, and most major credit cards are accepted. Valet parking is available.

The Mandarin, 430 N. Camden Dr. (tel. 213/272-0267), is the place to introduce well-behaved children to gourmet Chinese dining. This is a pretty, slightly contemporary restaurant with linen tablecloths and arched room-dividers. There are a couple of semiprivate areas that are perfect for large families, but remember that the noise level here is subdued. Those of you who have visited the Mandarin before are sure to be pleased with its transformation since reopening after a major fire.

Your children might taste their first sizzling-rice soup here, or their first almond chicken. You can order small sizes of almost anything from the 125-item menu. And prices for these small orders are reasonable—$6 to $10 at lunch. Prices are steeper for full entrees, so experiment only with willing children. Entrees average around $15—remember that you can share several dishes at a table; seafood dishes are higher priced.

The restaurant has boosters but no highchairs. They regret that they can't warm baby bottles or baby food—they have no microwave.

Open for lunch Monday through Saturday from 11:30 a.m. to 5 p.m., and for dinner Monday through Saturday from 5 to 11 p.m., on Sunday till 10:30 p.m. Reservations are accepted. There's valet parking or a city lot offering free parking for the first two hours. Major credit cards are accepted.

Want a fun place to take the kids? **RJ's, the Rib Joint,** 252 N. Beverly Dr., between Dayton Way and Wilshire Boulevard (tel. 213/274-RIBS), is one of those spots that you remember as much for the experience as for the food—although the food is very good and the portions are very generous.

Everything at RJ's is done on a grand scale. The exposed-brick saloon-style main dining room opens to an enormous bar with a floor-to-ceiling display of bottles (over 500 brands), where customers may wait for tables while they munch on peanuts in the shell. Lots of wood tables and booths line the room, and the walls are decorated with black-and-white celebrity photos and large back-lit stained-glass hangings.

This is where you'll find RJ's famous Green Grocery salad bar, a truly extraordinary assortment of salad fixings, presented among a symphony of fresh fruits and vegetables. The last time they counted, there were over 60 items, including such yummy treats for kids as fruit compote, dates, grated coconut, and fresh fruit, as well as more unusual goodies for adults—hearts of palm, artichoke hearts, and sliced avocado. There are soups to choose from too. The salad bar can easily make a meal in itself ($9). Otherwise you can choose one of the full meals, which includes the salad bar as well. Portions are large and most people walk out of the restaurant with a whimsical aluminum-foil creation that holds their leftovers. Known for hickory-wood smoked ribs, R.J.'s offers pork back ribs and beef ribs or a combination. If you prefer something else, there are three kinds of chicken (hickory-smoked, tarragon, and fresh garlic), steaks (you might want to try the one smothered in chili), and fresh seafood (including scampi and live Maine lobster). Dinner prices range from $9 to $24.

We were especially impressed with the friendly servers—and the large number of them. Even during the more crowded dinner hours, smiles were given all around, and the staff never seemed harassed—"We'll do everything for kids but change their diapers."

Children are treated to smaller portions off the menu for $8 (including the Green Grocery), and they can munch these salad bar items before the main course arrives so you won't have whining youngsters on your hands. Highchairs, Sassy seats, and boosters are available, and the immense bar makes one think that bartenders here can make any non-alcoholic creation your children can come up with.

RJ's is open Monday through Saturday from 11:30 a.m. to 11 p.m. Sunday brunch is served from 10:30 a.m. to 3 p.m., and dinner from 4 to 11 p.m. Reservations are advised. If you don't want to wait (for either a table or in a line at the Green Grocery), try to come early—between 5 and 7 p.m.

Valet parking is available, or if you prefer, there is a Beverly Hills municipal lot just a few doors south, which offers free parking for two hours. Most major credit cards are accepted.

Moderate

The Cheesecake Factory, 364 N. Beverly Dr., in Beverly Hills (tel. 213/278-7270), and 4141 Via Marina, in Marina Del Rey (tel. 213/306-3344), has lots of selections, but, sadly, no children's menu. Take kids aged 6 and up here. All will enjoy the extensive dessert menu.

The Beverly Hills location is small and a bit noisy, but there's lots of action and interesting conversation going on around you with this mostly Beverly Hills crowd. The Marina Del Rey location is much larger and features a patio overlooking the marina.

The extensive menu offers American, Chinese, Mexican, and Italian specialties. Entrees include chicken fajitas, breast of chicken made six ways, moo shu pork and chicken, coconut-beer-batter–fried shrimp, and 12 different pasta dishes. There are sandwiches, omelets, a huge variety of salads, and light lunches as well. Some dishes are salt-free and some are designated acceptable to the American Heart Association.

The price range is vast—from $5 for a hamburger to $15 for Louisiana blackened steak. Bring the little ones for Sunday brunch, though. They'll get a small order of French toast, a cup of fruit, one egg, and two strips of bacon for $4. The rest of you can have eggs, omelets, stuffed French toast, or bagel and lox ($6.50 to $11).

And then there's dessert. If you can choose among the 40 different cheesecake concoctions, you're better than we are! If you can't make up your mind, try the fudge cake, mud pie, banana split, or one of the other tempting, fattening, and wonderful desserts.

Both locations have booster seats and highchairs, and will split orders and warm bottles and baby food.

The Beverly Hills branch is open weekdays from 11 a.m. to 11 p.m., on Saturday to 12:30 a.m., and on Sunday to 10 p.m. No reservations are accepted, and the wait can be 20 to 45 minutes during peak hours. There's street parking or parking in the city lot nearby (two hours free). Major credit cards are honored.

The Marina Del Rey location is open Monday through Thursday from 11:30 a.m. to 11:30 p.m., on Friday and Saturday from 11 a.m. to 12:30 a.m., and on Sunday from 11 a.m. to 11 p.m. No reservations are accepted; expect the same wait. Valet parking. Major credit cards welcome.

Nate'n Al Delicatessen, 414 N. Beverly Dr. (tel. 213/274-0120), is an atypical East Coast deli restaurant. No one yells and screams at the counter, and the corned beef is a little dry. But Mom and Dad will love it because the rest of the food is good and the people-watching is even better. While most families come here on the weekends, you'll sometimes find a local grandpa or mom or dad here with junior before school. You'll also see some of the "old guard" Hollywood types on weekday mornings.

You—and the kids—have to be able to wait on weekends to get in, as they don't take reservations. Get your name on the waiting list, smile nicely at the hostess (who will probably get a bagel to assuage your toddler's hunger), and then take a walk for 20 to 30 minutes—it's a great area for strolling. Once you sit down you will be able to get crackers or a bagel right away for the kids. Service is quick and friendly.

There's no children's menu, but they're willing to split most items. Lots of youngsters go straight for the chicken soup. Cottage cheese and potato pancakes are popular items too. You can get peanut butter or grilled-cheese sandwiches and hot dogs and hamburgers here as well.

Adults can choose typical deli items, including cream cheese and lox, blintzes, and pastrami and roast beef sandwiches. Prices range from $3.25 to

$11. Breakfast is served all day. There are specials for dinner, but take the kids here for breakfast or lunch. Pound cake lovers should save room for the marble pound cake.

Highchairs and boosters are available. The kitchen will split orders and warm baby food and bottles. There's also counter service for take-out items—order there or call ahead.

Nate'n Al's is open Sunday through Friday from 7:30 a.m. to 8:45 p.m., on Saturday till 9:30 p.m. There is street parking, or park in the city lot a half block north (free for two hours—no validation necessary). No reservations accepted. Diners Club and cash only.

Larry Parker's Beverly Hills Diner, 206 S. Beverly Dr. (tel. 213/274-5655), is a Beverly Hills institution. Do you ever have trouble making a decision? You will at Larry Parker's. With a 20-page menu (yes, that's right!), you can get almost anything you want to eat. This diner epitomizes the fun and diversity of Los Angeles. Mom may order lox, eggs, onions, and a bagel ($7); Dad may select a meatloaf sandwich ($5) or a stuffed croissant ($7); Gramps might choose one of the 15 burgers; Gram may eat soft tacos or Szechuan shrimp, and Uncle David may go for one of the vegetarian entrees. And the list of salads (over 30 of them) is truly amazing. The children's menu includes macaroni and cheese and "pisquetti"—spaghetti ($3 to $3.50).

Yet the food is only part of the experience. This is a small restaurant that was built in 1947. Not your flash-in-the-pan trendy diner, this 24-hour restaurant claims to have served over four million people. People come for the food, yes, but they also come for the fun. Helium balloons (with hanging strings) bob on the ceiling, a jukebox plays constantly (and each table has its own selection box as well), neon signs and old pictures line the walls, and old-fashioned pink bubblegum comes with the check.

Read the signs: "If you really were a good customer, you'd order more!" "Dancing in the aisles only." "Help keep Beverly Hills clean. Wipe your feet before you leave." With this sense of humor here, you know that you're not going to feel inhibited with your kids.

Highchairs and boosters are available, and they'll warm bottles and baby food, and chat with you to keep you occupied while the kids are climbing all over you. They may charge $2 extra for splitting orders, though, and they don't take reservations. One Hollywood-style amenity is the free limousine service (for five or more) provided from 11 a.m. to 3 p.m. Another only–in–Los Angeles trademark are the telephones at each table.

Free parking at a nearby municipal lot for two hours or metered street parking available. Most major credit cards accepted.

Inexpensive

Good old **Dolores Restaurant,** now at 8925 W. Olympic Blvd. (tel. 213/657-7455), was once a great drive-in (and one of the last) on La Cienega Boulevard. Now it's basically a coffeeshop, with orangish drapes and crisscrossed windows, but the food is still good drive-in fare—cheap and just a little greasy. Kids like it.

At breakfast time there are egg dishes, including Italian sausage and eggs, the original San Francisco omelet (onions sautéed in olive oil, plus ground beef, fresh spinach, and three eggs, served pancake style and topped with romano cheese!), "regular" omelets, pancakes, French toast, and Belgian waffles. Meals average $4.

At lunch you'll find the wonderfully sloppy Jumbo Jim double-decker hamburger, eggplant patty, several award-winning chili dishes, Caesar burgers, and a couple of barbecue-style sandwiches. Be sure to order the Suzy Q potatoes—one order to share will do it. Lunches cost $3 to $5.

For dinner there's fried shrimp, baked fettuccine, eggplant Palermo, and fresh spinach en casserole, to name but a few entrees. You can even get a half a chef's salad. Dinner prices run $4 to $6.

Desserts are yummy—hot deep-dish apple pie, hot-fudge sundaes, Boston cream cake . . . and more.

There are boosters and highchairs available. They'll split portions and warm bottles and baby food in the kitchen.

Open 24 hours. No reservations. Parking lot adjacent. Cash only.

The American short order is alive and well at **Ed Debevic's Short Orders/ Deluxe,** 134 N. La Cienega Blvd., on Restaurant Row (tel. 213/659-1952). You don't really come here for the food, you come for the theatrics and for a trip back to the 1950s. It's a great place to go with the children if you can take the noise level (and the sometimes slow service), which, in fact, is perfect with noisy children. The vinyl booths are nostalgic, the many signs on the walls will keep the kids busy, and the really low menu prices will keep you happy. But, so you shouldn't think you're *really* back at the Homesick Diner in Talooca, Illinois, in 1952 (after which this is modeled), there's that Beverly Hills touch—valet parking.

The hamburgers are what many people come for, and there are seven different kinds of those ($3.50 to $4). But there are also sandwiches (including 1950s meatloaf sandwiches), plus chili, eggs, hot dogs, a few salads, and side orders of cheese fries, and fries with gravy or chili. Of course, a diner wouldn't be complete without such deluxe plates as chicken fried steak, chicken pot pie, and home-made pot roast ($4 to $5). Naturally there are also blue-plate specials, which change daily.

You can have the world's smallest hot-fudge sundae for 35¢ (who can resist?) or, if you dare, Bea's chocolate puddin' pie, Linda C's fudge brownies, or banana cream pie, to name just a few of the decadent dessert selections.

Boosters and highchairs are available. Baby bottles and food can be warmed. Also, an unbelievable find in a restaurant bathroom—a sign telling you to turn on the switch if the bathroom isn't clean!

Open weekdays from 11:30 a.m. to midnight, on weekends until 1 a.m. Reservations are accepted only for weekday lunch. Valet parking. Major credit cards accepted.

There's another (the original) Ed Debevic's in Torrance, at 23705 S. Hawthorne Blvd. (tel. 213/378-5454).

WESTSIDE: The Westside area is one of the fashionable, trendy parts of town, certainly an area you'll visit frequently because of the large number of restaurants and visitor attractions. Including Century City, Westwood, Brentwood, Rancho Park, and West Los Angeles, this area can also be pricey.

Expensive

For lovers of authentic Japanese food, **Yamato's,** in the Century Plaza Hotel, 2025 Avenue of the Stars (tel. 213/277-1840), will delight your senses— eyes, ears, nose, and palate. This exquisitely fashioned restaurant exudes the quiet aura of Japan, rich with dark woods, Japanese scrolls, and beautiful objets d'art. A place to take sophisticated older children who will enjoy the experience and fit into the hushed atmosphere, we love Yamato's for their private Japanese-style rooms (which you can have for a party of two or more). The rooms are complete with sliding shoji screens to partition you off from the other diners, while you sit on tatami mats on the floor. (They'll give you backrests.) There is also an area for traditional Western-style dining, with lovely, large tables, and an area for teppan grill cooking. A sushi bar caters to the most exotic tastes.

Preteens and teens will likely enjoy the menu, which is full of tempting entrees. Luncheon items include sukiyaki, yakitori (skewers of chicken grilled with fresh vegetables), and a combination plate with tempura, top sirloin teriyaki, and chicken teriyaki. Lunches range from $6 to $12.50. There are also salads and pastas for those who refuse to get into the spirit.

Dinners include soup, vegetables, rice, and tea. Choose from traditional items such as tonkatsu (pork loin slices dipped in breadcrumbs), combination tempura and yakitori platters, or favorites such as crab legs, New York steak, or steak-and-lobster combinations. We always love the meals impeccably prepared at the table. Our favorite is shabu shabu—finely sliced beef, cooked with vegetables and served in a delicious broth. Dinners cost $11 to $30.

There are no highchairs or boosters, nor is there a children's menu, so keep this for a treat for your older boys and girls.

Open for lunch Monday through Friday from 11:30 a.m. to 2:30 p.m. Dinner is served Monday through Saturday from 5 to 11 p.m., and on Sunday and holidays from 4:30 to 10:30 p.m. Reservations are advised, especially if you want a private room. Valet and lot parking are available. Most major credit cards are accepted.

Moderate

Anna's Italian Restaurant, 10929 Pico Blvd. (tel. 213/474-0102), is like walking into a little Italian villa with red-checked tablecloths, big red-leather booths, and old chandeliers on the walls. It's a favorite with neighborhood families (as well as those who come from miles away), so there's always a lot of activity here. This is not your romantic candlelit Italian restaurant, so bring the kids and relax.

We've actually taken a sleeping infant here and kept him in the stroller while we enjoyed our dinner. The waiters weren't crazy about having to serve around the stroller, but they were gracious and accommodating. Our 2-year-old put them through their paces.

If you like marinara salad, this is the place to order it. Anna's version has large chunks of seafood tucked into the well-dressed greens. But, then, everything here is very good.

The lunch menu offers pizza, pasta, salads, sandwiches, omelets, veal, and fish for $5 to $10, as well as weekday specials that include soup or salad at $5. Anna's dinners come with soup or salad, spaghetti, and vegetable. Choose from steaks, poultry, seafood, and 11 styles of veal. There are also pizzas, pasta dishes, and large salads. The dinner specials (Monday through Thursday) cost $10. Dinner items range in price from $5.50 (pizza) to $16.

Highchairs and boosters are available, but there is no children's menu here. We usually share our food with the little ones, or order pizza to split for older kids. The folks at Anna's will warm bottles and baby food, bring warm sourdough bread to the table, and make special children's drinks.

Open Monday through Thursday from 11:30 a.m. to 11 p.m., on Friday from 11:30 a.m. to midnight, on Saturday from 4 p.m. to midnight, and on Sunday from 4 to 11 p.m. Reservations are advised if you don't want to wait. Street parking is available during lunch hours; valet parking is available during dinner. Most major credit cards are accepted.

How about a place that serves two million eggs a year? Or almost two tons of coffee a month? Not only is the food fresh, but the cuisine at **Junior's Deli,** 2379 Westwood Blvd., West L.A. (tel. 213/475-5771), is delicious and the waitresses are fantastic with the kids. All their fish is flown in from New York (whitefish, Nova Scotia lox, smoked salmon, and cod) and the brie comes from France. It's a gourmet deli.

We admit it—we're regulars there. And why not? Just a mention (in passing) to the hostess that it's little Elizabeth's birthday, and much to our surprise, a singing trio presents her with a cupcake and best wishes. And for everyday needs, they have the usual highchairs (and Sassy seats) and boosters, a very good kid's menu (grilled cheese, peanut butter and jelly, hot dog, pancakes, etc., for under

$2), and they'll gladly let you split and share adult portions. Maybe the greatest draw for the kids (and for the sugar-loving adults in our family) is the cinnamon-bread French toast. The bread is baked with thick rings of cinnamon and sugar so that when it's dipped in the egg and grilled, it melts into a sinful goody ($5 for a regular order, $4 for a petite).

This is a real family place. In fact, owner Marvin Saul (who was always called "Junior" when he was a boy) says he developed the children's menu in response to his regular customers who said they couldn't bring their children because it became too costly to feed three kids from the regular menu. He asked other customers what they'd like to see on the menu and then created it.

Serving breakfast, lunch, and dinner, everyone in the family will enjoy something on the 300-plus-item menu. There's old-fashioned "like Grandma used to make" roast brisket of beef ($9, including soup or salad), knockwurst with beans or sauerkraut ($8), and chicken-in-the-pot ($11). Not to ignore the health-conscious, there are low-cholesterol items, such as roast turkey drumstick ($7.25, with kasha and coleslaw) and fresh steamed vegetables ($5).

Of course, there are the deli standbys—corned beef, roast beef, and pastrami sandwiches. Burgers, salads, cold fish platters, soups, and dairy dishes (for a treat, try the bananas and strawberries in sour cream) round out the menu. Breakfast items (including three-egg omelets, matzoh brei, kippers, and eggs) are served all day long. Breakfast prices range from $2.25 to $9.25 (for steak and eggs). Lunches and brunches range from $4 to $15 (for a sturgeon platter, with two bagels). Dinner can start anywhere and cost up to $10.

Open daily from 6 a.m. to 11 p.m. Unfortunately, they don't take reservations for parties of fewer than six, which means that you'll have to wait for at least 15 minutes during the more popular times. We always try to arrive before 9:30 a.m. for Saturday or Sunday breakfast. It's crowded at dinner just as it gets dark, so plan accordingly. Once seated, the turnover is fast. There's a parking lot adjacent and limited street parking. Some major credit cards are accepted.

Lotus West, 10974 W. Pico Blvd. (tel. 213/475-9597), is one of the places our kids ask to return to again and again. This pleasant neighborhood eatery has white linen cloths and a more subdued atmosphere than the typical Chinese-style restaurant. On any Sunday night you'll see a host of families enjoying the Mandarin, Shanghai, and Szechuan cuisine. It's no wonder. Owner Jimmy Hu is a pro with families, and will even give you suggestions about how to handle wailing toddlers. (When everything fails, he simply smiles and tells you about his children.)

We're particularly fond of the lemon chicken (which has a wonderfully tangy flavor and large slices of chicken), and the kids are crazy for the beef with broccoli and the eggroll.

You might be interested in some of the more unusual dishes, such as walnut beef, hot spiced sliced fish, or spicy chicken chunks with pine nuts. Entree prices range from $6 to $16.

In such a family-loving place, you'll certainly find highchairs and booster seats (and lots of chopsticks to replace the ones that fall on the floor). The staff will do just about anything to keep your family happy.

Open weekdays and Saturday for lunch from 11:30 a.m. to 3 p.m., and weekdays for dinner from 5 to 10 p.m. Saturday dinner is served from 5 to 10:30 p.m. Open Sunday from noon to 3 p.m. for lunch, and again from 5 to 10 p.m. for dinner. Reservations are accepted. There is an adjacent parking lot. They accept most major credit cards.

Mario's Italian Restaurant, 1001 Broxton Ave., Westwood (tel. 213/208-7077), is an institution in Westwood Village. Located at the corner of Broxton and Gayley Avenues in the center of Westwood, Mario's has seen over two decades of students, professors, tourists, and families come through "the Village."

Traditional red-and-white-checked tablecloths and a festive atmosphere greet you. This family place has highchairs and booster seats, and while they don't have a children's menu, they gladly do half orders of pasta. Children love the small pizzas and the hamburger entree as well.

Mom and Dad might want to try the house specialty, shrimp alla Anna Maria (with linguine, white clam sauce, and vegetable) for $21, or filetto di tacchino mazzarino (breast of turkey with slices of ham and swiss cheese in tomato and béchamel sauce) for $13.25. Of course, there's always veal—here they serve nine kinds. Dinners include minestrone soup or salad, pasta, and vegetable; pasta entrees include soup or salad and bread. Prices range from $10 to $22.50 (for lobster tails). Pizzas start at $6.75. Lunches are priced from $5.75 to $12.50.

Open Monday through Thursday from 11:30 a.m. to 11:30 p.m., on Friday till 12:30 a.m., on Saturday from 4 to 12:30 a.m., and on Sunday from 4 to 11:30 p.m. Reservations are accepted. Parking is at a premium, but there is a pay parking lot nearby. They accept most major credit cards.

If you like California-style "healthy" food, the **Old World Restaurant,** 1019 Westwood Blvd. (tel. 213/208-4033), is one to try. While no additives or preservatives are allowed in the food, health-food haters will find many items they'll enjoy. For example, this restaurant serves up thick hamburgers and steaks. Our kids love the rich split-pea soup (even for breakfast) that is accompanied by thick-sliced whole-wheat bread ($2.75 for a bowl). The Belgian waffles are another adored entree. Salads come in huge wooden bowls, and burgers are equally large. You can choose from salads and cold plates, meat and meatless sandwiches, burgers and old-world specialties. Breakfasts cost $3.75 to $9, lunches are $5 to $10, and dinners top out at $16.75 for New York steak (with soup or salad, vegetables, rice or potato, and whole-wheat roll).

There are highchairs and boosters, but no children's menu. Talk with your server about half orders for the kids. We also usually ask the server to bring the kids crushed ice because they love it and not many restaurants serve it. The ice occupies our littlest one's attention for at least 20 minutes.

Of the three old-world locations, our favorite with the kids is the Westwood branch. It has two small rooms with windows overlooking Westwood Boulevard, offering lots of viewing possibilities for the kids. When those tables are taken, there are large booths that serve almost equally well.

Open daily from 8 a.m. to midnight. There are parking lots nearby. Most credit cards are accepted.

Other branches are located at 216 N. Beverly Dr. in Beverly Hills (tel. 213/274-7695) and 8782 Sunset Blvd. in West Hollywood (tel. 213/652-2520).

Inexpensive

Some of our family's favorite pizza comes from **Earth, Wind & Flour,** 1776 Westwood Blvd., at Santa Monica Boulevard, in Westwood (tel. 213/470-2499). The menu is simple, the service is fast, and the food is good. In addition to wonderful Boston-style pizza (at $5.50 to $16.75), they'll tempt you with pasta (seven different sauces and five different pasta types), chicken, salads, and a sampling of sandwiches and burgers.

Very casual, this is a place with sawdust on the floors and a rustic cabin-like interior of rough-wood walls and lots of hanging plants. Great for a Sunday quick bite.

Prices range from $3.50 to $16.75 (for a large pizza with five toppings). A family of four can easily have dinner for under $20. Highchairs and boosters are available. Open Monday through Thursday from 11:30 a.m. to 11 p.m., on Friday and Saturday till midnight, and on Sunday from 4 to 11 p.m. No reservations accepted. There's an adjacent parking lot. Some major credit cards are honored.

If you're not yet familiar with **Flakey Jake's,** 2347 S. Sepulveda Blvd., near Pico Boulevard, in West L.A. (tel. 213/477-0405), you're in for an experience. The food is good, and there's plenty of it. You'll find a video game room for the kids. But don't expect to carry on a prolonged conversation with the people you're dining with because the noise level is intense.

Not surprisingly, this hamburger place tops the list of our children's favorites. (In fact, we've been known to use a dinner at Flakey Jake's as a bribe for clean rooms or good report cards.)

Fast food style, you place your order, get your beverages, and grab a table. Actually, Flakey Jake's serves more than just burgers. Among the other treats are hot dogs, chicken (fried, teriyaki, and grilled lemon), fish, entree-size baked potatoes, even a few salads. When your name is called, you proceed to a smörgåsbord setup with salad fixings and condiments for your sandwiches and entrees. It's a real treat if you love your burgers or potatoes loaded with goodies like dill pickle chips, Russian dressing, salsa, or melted cheese!

Flakey Jake's has its own bakery and its own butcher shop, where it makes all the bread and grinds all the meat used for the sandwiches. Customers can also buy items to take home. Prices are good too. A Jake Junior (hamburger or hot dog, fries, and a beverage with free refills) costs $2.50. On Sunday that price drops to $1.25 and includes a cookie as well. Adult prices hover at $4—a little less for a burger, a little more for chicken breast. One nice touch is the luncheon Lite Bite (served all the time), which includes an entree, salad, drink, and fries from $3.25 to $4.50. All beverage refills are free.

We've taken our kids from highchair through booster seat to video-game set in this eatery. Flakey Jake's is open Monday through Thursday from 11 a.m. to 11 p.m., on Friday and Saturday till midnight, and on Sunday till 10 p.m. No reservations accepted. Parking lot. Some credit cards accepted.

Call or check the *Yellow Pages* for other locations throughout southern California.

Your preteens will especially enjoy **Heaven,** 10250 Santa Monica Blvd., in the Century City Shopping Center (tel. 213/557-0387), but you can take children of any age to this cute, lively diner-style restaurant. You'll have to tear them away from the kitschy toys and masks and T-shirts in the front of the store before you can get them to the back, where you'll find the restaurant. Sometimes we buy a couple of wind-up toys for our youngest children to take to the table and a package of magic tricks for the oldest. If we don't have time for lunch, we often stop for an ice-cream treat after some serious shopping in the mall.

In the back of the store, you'll find the vinyl booths and the black and white floor tiles that have come to represent '50s diners, plus a counter and more contemporary tables and chairs. Rock 'n' roll oldies take you on a "blast to the past," and one or two waitresses have been seen dancing in the aisle with a toddler who just can't ignore the beat of the music.

Burgers and double-burgers are the specialties here, but you can also get salads, hot dogs and sausages, and a variety of sandwiches. Order a Gumby and Pokey Combo—a hamburger and a split hot dog grilled with melted cheese, special sauce, and all the fixings—for $4.75; top it with chili for $5.25. The french fries are great—hot and salty—and one portion is enough for two or three people. From the fountain, choose from eight flavors of milkshakes and malts (including peanut butter); cherry, chocolate, vanilla, or lemon Cokes; plus phosphates, floats, and ice-cream sodas and sundaes. Nothing on the menu is priced over $6, and most items cost $2.50 to $4.50.

Booster seats only—no highchairs.

Open Sunday through Thursday from 11:30 a.m. to 9 p.m., and on Friday and Saturday till 11 p.m. No reservations accepted. Park in the mall lot between Bullock's and The Broadway. Credit cards are honored.

There are other Heaven branches at 2222 Wilshire Blvd., at 23rd Street, in Santa Monica (tel. 213/829-7829 and 213/829-1649), and at 17644 Ventura Blvd., near White Oak, in Encino in the San Fernando Valley (tel. 818/986-0772).

Islands, 10948 W. Pico Blvd., West L.A. (tel. 213/474-1144), is a fun and lively eatery that boasts gourmet hamburgers, soft tacos, chicken sandwiches, and great salads. This restaurant is a favorite of the kids—and one we love too, because we can all find something here we enjoy. It's really a bit of southern California "camp," capitalizing on every southern Californian's dream that they'd rather be lazing on an island, riding the surf. Islands comes complete with tropical atmosphere—ceramic parrots hang overhead, servers wear island clothes, and photographs of surfers riding the great waves line the walls.

The food is good, with many unusual burger combinations (try the "Maui," which has guacamole, lettuce, tomato, swiss, and bacon; or the "Makaha," with chili, cheese, and sautéed onions). We also like the variety of chicken-breast sandwiches and salads (five kinds of each). And everybody just has to have at least one side order of Islands fries. The portions are large and can easily be split between two children, but little surfers aged 12 and under may choose from the "Gremmie menu," which features a small burger or hot dog for $2. Adult items range in price from $3.75 to $6.

We prefer the backroom at Islands, which is quieter and has less traffic. Highchairs and boosters are available, and the servers will gladly warm baby bottles and baby food in the kitchen. There is a full bar, so Shirley Temples can be had for the asking.

Open daily at 11:30 a.m. for lunch, and open for dinner and snacks as well, Monday through Thursday until 11 p.m., on Friday and Saturday until 11:30 p.m., and on Sunday until 10 p.m. Reservations are not accepted, which means that at peak lunchtime hours you might have to wait at least 15 minutes for seating. For dinner it's best to come before 7 p.m. (6:30 p.m. on Sunday) if you want to avoid a 20- to 25-minute wait. Once you're seated, though, you'll be served quickly, which we like.

There is limited street parking before 6 p.m. and valet parking afterward. Most major credit cards are accepted.

There's another branch at 404 Washington St., in Marina del Rey (tel. 213/822-3939).

THE COASTAL REGION (SANTA MONICA AND MARINA DEL REY):
The Coastal Region offers good dining possibilities, oftentimes with a view of the Pacific. These restaurants tend to be more casual than in many other parts of the city.

Expensive
Belle-Vue French Restaurant, 101 Santa Monica Blvd., Santa Monica (tel. 213/393-2843), has served generations of diners, and is now serving the grandchildren of those who once ate there as children. It's family owned and run by the Pilloni family, who say that "Although the Belle-Vue is casual dining, it is considered an excellent preparation for children to learn to dine in fine restaurants."

Dark woods, white tablecloths, and flowers on the table are a nice introduction to fine dining. French bread is brought immediately, and you'll be asked if you need anything else for the children, such as crackers or a cup of shaved ice.

There is no children's menu at the Belle-Vue, but the staff and owners are so accommodating that your youngsters won't have a problem finding something good to eat. At lunch there are grilled-cheese, plus swiss cheese and bacon, and lettuce-and-tomato sandwiches for $4.75 and $5.25, and a sirloin steak sandwich with french fries for $10. Kids love the spaghetti and meat sauce ($5.25). Soup lovers can have the creamy tomato soup, and there are egg dishes also on the lunch menu. Bigger eaters can order the chicken à la king in a pastry shell (remember having that when you were a child?) or broiled chicken or fried shrimp —all cost $6.50 to $9. Adults can enjoy all of the above, plus large salads, fresh fish selections, French pot roast à la mode, mixed grill, and broiled pork chops.

These and more entrees are served with soup or salad, a potato, and vegetables, and are reasonably priced from $6.50 to $8. À la carte specials are more costly and include frogs' legs provençal, scallops, gulf shrimp Créole, and lobster. These range in price from $12.50 to $15.50.

Dinner features many of the same selections, plus Dover sole, poached salmon, Lake Superior whitefish, rack of lamb, and a combination of half a lobster with tournedos of beef. Dinner entrees, including an appetizer and salad, cost $13.75 to $17 ($2 less if ordered à la carte).

Children are well accommodated at dinner too. They will enjoy the spaghetti and meat sauce, $5.25 (ask your server—it's not on the dinner menu). Sandwiches are not on the dinner menu either, but they'll gladly make one up for the child in your party. Or kids can split an adult entree.

Boosters and highchairs are available. Baby bottles and baby food can be warmed in the kitchen.

Open Monday through Thursday from 11:30 a.m. to 9:30 p.m., on Friday and Saturday till 10 p.m., and on Sunday from 12:30 to 9:30 p.m. Reservations accepted. There's a parking lot north on Ocean Avenue, or street parking. Major credit cards accepted.

Moderate

"Enough of this light California cuisine," you say? Then make a stop at **Aunt Kizzy's Back Porch,** 4371 Glencoe Ave. (in the Villa Marina Shopping Center), Marina del Rey (tel. 213/578-1005), for some real down-home cookin'. It's not very big, and certainly not fancy. The emphasis here is on food—good southern food, based on recipes handed down from friends and relatives. Daily lunch specials (which come with two fresh vegetables, rice and gravy, or cornbread dressing and gravy), might be smothered pork chops on Monday, smothered liver and onions on Tuesday, meatloaf on Wednesday, chicken and dumplings on Thursday. Get the picture? Fried chicken is a daily special. Lunch specials cost $6. At dinner, you might sample chicken Créole, catfish and hushpuppies, smothered steak, or red beans and rice and hot links. These come with vegetables too—but not your basic broccoli. You'll get black-eyed peas, creamy red beans, fresh collard greens, and more. Dinner runs $6 to $11. Be sure to order the fresh-squeezed lemonade served in a Mason jar (bring your own wine or beer). As you'd expect, the desserts are homemade and rich—sweet potato pie, pineapple-coconut cake, and sweet peach cobbler.

Kids can have the macaroni and cheese, or a child's portion of anything on the regular menu for $6. There's a $3 charge for splitting an order.

One good way to sample lots of this filling food is at Sunday brunch, served buffet style. There are salads; breakfast items such as grits, scrambled eggs, and grilled country potatoes with onions; baked or fried chicken; barbecued beef ribs; smothered pork chops; and lots of their good vegetables. Most children will love the buttery, sugary candied yams they serve at an additional price. Brunch also includes dessert and beverage, and costs $11 (half price for kids).

Boosters and highchairs are provided.

Open for lunch Monday through Saturday from 11 a.m. to 4 p.m. and for Sunday brunch from 11 a.m. to 3 p.m. Dinner is served Sunday through Thursday from 4 to 10 p.m., on Friday and Saturday till 11 p.m. No reservations or credit cards accepted. Parking is easy in the shopping center lot, except on weekends when it fills up with moviegoers, shoppers, and diners.

Café Casino, 1299 Ocean Ave., Santa Monica (tel. 213/394-3717), is an American extension of Casino de France, one of the largest food distributors in Western Europe. This location is a perfect place to stop on a Sunday morning before an outing to the Santa Monica Pier or a trek to Malibu. It sits across from Palisades Park. We've spent many a marvelous morning sipping our first cups of coffee while the kids watched the joggers and seagulls. The large whitewashed patio area outdoors is a perfect spot. It's shielded from the wind by glass, and has heat lamps, should the need arise. It is also a lovely setting for an early dinner at sunset.

Serving French and continental cuisine, this gourmet cafeteria offers delicious food, while allowing you to get in and out in a short time. The only hangup is the long line (at times) waiting to file past the gratin provençale, quiche, and croissants. Average breakfasts run between $3 and $4. Lunch costs around $6, and dinners come in at about $9 or $10. While there isn't a children's menu, the side orders are so varied that you shouldn't have trouble pleasing the kids. For breakfast, there's cereal and such traditional items as sausage, French toast, and delectable fresh fruit (papaya and melons), as well as the more sophisticated eggs Benedict. For lunch, there is cheese, bread, and more fresh fruit sitting alongside the salade niçoise, croissant sandwiches, and salmon basquaise (provençal-style sauce). For dinner, the kids can have soup or share your roast beef, snapper, or beef bourguignon.

Highchairs and boosters are available, but one of the best things about this restaurant is the marble table tops that have a recessed center for the cafeteria trays. We put the food (and later, the little toys or paper and pencils) inside the indented area and find that it miraculously contains spilled milk and other messes.

Open Sunday through Thursday from 7 a.m. to 10 p.m. and on Friday and Saturday from 7 a.m. to 11 p.m. Validated parking lot in the building. Some major credit cards accepted.

There are other Café Casino branches, including one at 1145 Gayley Ave., in Westwood Village (tel. 213/208-1010).

If your kids like seafood, the **Famous Fish Enterprise Fish Company,** at 174 Kinney St., a block west of Main Street, south of Ocean Park Boulevard and north of Rose Avenue, in Santa Monica (tel. 213/392-8366), is a great place to go. The staff at this casual, airy restaurant with high wood ceiling, wood floors, and tasteful nautical decorations is perfectly comfortable with children. There are two glassed-in kitchen areas where you can take the kids to watch the cooks. There's also a small plant-filled patio on the side of the restaurant.

Although there's no children's menu, they do serve a child's portion of shrimp at dinner for $8, which includes a potato or rice, and coleslaw or a salad. The lunch menu offers items from the oyster bar, lots of seafood salads, and a few sandwiches. Mesquite-broiled fresh fish and chicken teriyaki, calamari, and a good ole hamburger are other tempting choices. At dinner you can get much of the same, plus lobster, scampi, cioppino, seafood fettuccine, a Pritikin plate, and a light eater's plate, consisting of choice pieces of fish. There are plenty of desserts here (or take a stroll down Main Street after dinner and have your treat at one of the ice-cream shops).

Lunch prices average $7.50; dinner costs about $12.75.

Boosters and highchairs are available. The servers will split orders for children, warm baby bottles and food, and make special children's drinks.

Open for lunch Monday through Friday from 11:30 a.m. to 4 p.m., on Saturday and Sunday to 3 p.m. Dinner is served Monday through Thursday from 4 to 10 p.m., on Friday till 11 p.m., on Saturday from 3 to 11 p.m., and on Sunday from 3 to 10 p.m. Reservations accepted only for parties of six or more. Park on the street or get validated parking for two hours in a lot two blocks south. Major credit cards are accepted.

Fromin's Restaurant, 1832 Wilshire Blvd., Santa Monica (tel. 213/829-5443), is one of those kosher-style delis that's perfect on a Sunday morning when you're craving bagels and cream cheese. For some reason, there's less of a crowd at breakfast than at lunch or dinner, so that's when we come here most often.

While there isn't a children's menu (the manager says that they're thinking about offering one, so ask when you come in), the portions are good-size, and they'll be happy to split orders. They'll bring the kids a bagel on request (or pickles in the afternoon and evening). For omelet lovers, there are 30-plus different varieties to choose from (ham and cheese, bologna, pastrami, Reuben, bananas, and sour cream), and if that doesn't suffice, they'll let you create your own extravaganza from 17 different ingredients. (Omelets start at $5.)

There are also traditional breakfast offerings, deli platters with lox, whitefish and bagels, soups, 14 different salads, burgers, and a huge assortment of sandwiches—choose from typical deli fare (salami, sardine, cold roast beef) to triple-decker and hot creations. Prices range from $4.75 to $9.

At night you can order à la carte or a complete dinner (with soup or salad; potato, coleslaw, or vegetable; and bread and butter; plus dessert and beverage). Choose from such entrees as sweet-and-sour rolled cabbage, corned beef and cabbage, chicken in a pot, fish, or boiled beef. Dinners range from $9.50 to $11; à la carte entrees run $7.25 to $9.

Highchairs and boosters are available, and if you're bringing tiny ones, your server will be glad to warm baby bottles or baby food.

Open Monday through Thursday from 6:30 a.m. to 11 p.m., on Friday till midnight, on Saturday from 7 a.m. to midnight, and on Sunday from 7 a.m. to 10 p.m. Best times to come are before noon on weekdays and between 5 and 6 p.m. weekdays and weekends. Parking lot. Some major credit cards accepted.

There's another branch at 17615 Ventura Blvd. in Encino (tel. 818/990-6346).

Hamburger Henry, 3001 Wilshire Blvd., half a mile west of Bundy Avenue, in Santa Monica (tel. 213/828-3000), is the first restaurant we discovered that featured a special children's price for the salad bar (children pay $3.75 anytime; adults pay $5 at lunch, $6 at dinner). And were we delighted! With over 40 items (including potato salad, carrot salad, macaroni salad, and tuna salad), plus fruit, soup, and a tostada bar, families gather here. We were first drawn to Hamburger Henry for the unusual—and delicious—hamburger creations. Ever try an applenut burger? How about an avocado burger? And you can even get turkey burgers for non–beef eaters. You can get good old-fashioned burgers as well, plus sandwiches, salads, soups, and entrees. Lunch and dinner items range from $3.75 to $9.75.

The array of Belgian waffles and omelets is equally inviting. Prices for these range from $3.75 to $8.25. Children can choose from a burger, peanut butter sandwich, grilled-cheese sandwich, or scrambled eggs (all with fries, milk, and fresh fruit) for $2.75.

Highchairs and boosters are available, as are Shirley Temple cocktails. Your server will gladly warm baby bottles or baby food, and will help you split adult portions between kids. If the kids are especially hungry, you can request crackers or a piece of fresh fruit before the entrees arrive.

Open daily from 7 a.m. to 1 a.m. Saturday brunch is served from 10 a.m. to 3 p.m.; Sunday brunch, from 9 a.m. to 3 p.m.

Reservations are accepted, there is free parking, and some major credit cards are welcome.

Grab your little pitchers—baseball pitchers, that is—and head for **Tommy Lasorda's Ribs & Pasta Restaurant,** 14130 Marquesas Way, Marina del Rey (tel. 213/827-5330), for dinner or Saturday or Sunday brunch. There's no doubt who owns this place. Pictures of the L.A. Dodgers and the skipper himself are plastered on the walls. The kids will love the baseball decorations, pennants, and the popcorn machine. There are three dining areas, two of which overlook the bar.

There's no children's menu, but most kids order either the linguine and meatballs or a half rack of barbecued baby back ribs. If you ask nicely, they'll even make the children a hamburger, although it's not on the menu. Or there's always Tommy's favorite New York–style pizza.

Mom and Dad can order barbecued chicken and ribs, linguine with garlic shrimp, cheese ravioli, seafood pizza, chicken parmigiana, or many other yummy and generously portioned dishes. Prices range from $6.25 for cheeseless pizza to $15 for a 14-ounce New York sirloin steak. Be sure to try the mouthwatering mud pie served for two, or the New York cheesecake. Sunday brunch features a special menu and includes the ribs and pasta as well as Belgian waffles and an omelet bar.

There are highchairs and boosters here, and the servers will gladly split orders. Baby food and bottles can be warmed in the kitchen.

Open Monday through Thursday from 4:30 to 10 p.m., on Friday and Saturday till 11 p.m., and on Sunday for brunch from 11:30 a.m. to 3 p.m. and for dinner from 4 to 10 p.m. Reservations are accepted; expect a 30-minute wait on weekend nights without one. Valet or self-parking. Major credit cards accepted.

If the kids like fish, the **Pelican's Catch,** 1715 Pacific Ave., Venice Beach (tel. 213/392-3933), is a fine choice in the moderate price range—and it's near the beach. The place is casual—and nautical.

You can eat indoors or dine outside on the patio. The menu is varied and runs the gamut from Mexican specials (such as snapper Vera Cruz, with salsa and jack cheese, at $13; or chicken tostada at $8) to burgers, salads, and sandwiches (starting at $5). There is a selection of chowders and appetizers too. Each day the chalkboard announces the fresh catch. All luncheon entrees include fresh vegetable or coleslaw, rice or shoestring potatoes, and bread and butter. You can choose from cioppino, blackened jumbo shrimp, deep-fried scallops, and the like. Luncheons top out at $15 (except for lobster, which is at market price), but there are specials for $5.

The dinner menu is equally varied, and offers steamed shellfish and charbroiled steaks. The complete dinner includes a choice of chowder or salad, vegetable, and choice of rice or potatoes, plus bread and butter, and costs $11 to $17.

The extraordinarily diverse brunch menu features eggs and omelets as well, with prices ranging from $5.25 to $15.

Highchairs and boosters are available. Although there isn't a children's menu, they'll gladly split adult portions. Also, the servers will warm bottles and baby food, and have the bartender whip up non-alcoholic drinks.

Open Monday through Thursday from 11:30 a.m. to 10 p.m., on Friday and Saturday till 11 p.m., and on Sunday from 11 a.m. to 9 p.m. Sunday brunch is served from 11 a.m. to 4 p.m. Parking lot. Most major credit cards accepted.

There are other branches as well. Café Pelican is at 2720 Main St., in Venice Beach (tel. 213/392-5711).

Most people will agree that southern California is one of the best places to eat Mexican food. Fortunately, Mexican restaurants generally welcome children. **Tampico Tilly's,** 1025 Wilshire Blvd., in Santa Monica (tel. 213/451-1769), is one of those restaurants. The Wilshire branch is inviting, and makes you think you've entered a home south of the border, with high ceilings, tile floors, and lace curtains. Both tables and booths are available, and there are several dining areas from which you can choose. (The library in the back is particularly quaint, but when we're with the kids we choose the main room because there is lots of activity here.) Our kids virtually dive into the bowl of tortilla chips that comes to the table as soon as you sit down.

The menu is especially diverse, offering an enormous assortment of great, tame Mexican food. We love the Monterey salad—with crabmeat, shrimp, and avocado (which doesn't even seem Mexican at all) and the crab enchilada tomatillo (crab rolled in a corn tortilla with tomatillo sauce). As in all good Mexican restaurants, there are scads of other delightful dishes, including tostadas, burritos, tacos, fajitas, and enchiladas. They even offer eight Mexican omelets. Prices range from $4.50 to $9.75.

For dinner, you can enjoy many of the same entrees as at lunch, but with larger portions that include soup or salad, rice, and beans. You may also choose from several steak dishes and other main courses. Prices range from $5.75 to $11.50. For children under 12 there's a kid's menu with four items (taco, cheese enchilada, hamburger, and grilled-cheese sandwich) from $3.50 to $4.

Highchairs and boosters are available, and they'll warm baby bottles and baby food in the kitchen. There's a full bar (that has music and dancing at night).

Open daily from 11:30 a.m. to 10 p.m. (the bar is open later). There is valet parking. Most major credit cards are accepted.

There's another branch at the Santa Monica Place Shopping Center, third level (tel. 213/393-1404).

Inexpensive

Even many locals are not familiar with the **Brentwood Country Mart,** at 26th Street and San Vicente Boulevard in Santa Monica (tel. 213/395-6714). But once you find out about it, you'll return again and again. It attracts people of all ages—neighborhood preteens out for lunch with friends, grandparents with their toddler charges, and whole families. A mini-marketplace of shops (the kids will enjoy browsing through Brentwood Toys and the nearby Candy Alley) and eateries, the Country Mart is housed in a red barn structure that surrounds an open-air plaza complete with outdoor firepit.

Not only is it a delightful place to take the family for lunch and shopping, but the ride down San Vicente (going either east or west) is lovely. Here unusual Coral trees (with their odd-shaped branches) line the wide boulevard strip where joggers make their daily treks down to Palisades Park. As you drive along San Vicente, you'll see some of Brentwood's most impressive homes.

The Country Mart has a wide variety of gourmet fast-food restaurants from which you can choose deli or chicken or fruit-and-yogurt creations. Our favorite is **Reddi Chick,** whose succulent rôtisserie chicken is a winner with everyone. The chicken wing basket (six wings for $3.25) is a wing-lover's dream, and the teriyaki steak sandwich costs only $4.25. If you want to shop for your own picnic, there is a full market where you can buy great produce.

Don't miss the small side patio where two kiddie rides keep preschoolers entertained long enough for adults to enjoy a leisurely lunch. (It's generally less crowded than the central patio too.) After lunch, don't miss a walk through Comparte's, a fabulous gourmet candy store featuring stuffed dried fruits, hand-dipped chocolates, and even low-calorie, salt-free goodies.

Stores and restaurants are generally open from 9 a.m. to 6 p.m., but call before you go because hours can vary.

Now if it's back to the '50s and '60s you want, come home to what almost became an extinct art form—the American diner. **Edie's Diner,** at 4211 Admiralty Way, Marina Del Rey (tel. 213/823-5339), has lots of windows and a small outside patio overlooking the boats. Inside, the black-and-white-tile floor, stainless-steel mixers, red cushioned booths, and long, low counter will put you back in another era. You can impress your wide-eyed children as you find you can suddenly remember all the words to "Itsy-Bitsy, Teeny-Weeny, Yellow Polka Dot Bikini" and can sing along with practically every song on the table-attached jukeboxes.

When you get down to the real job of eating, you'll certainly be able to find something on the four-page menu, such as Edie's special waffles or hot dogs for $4; blue-plate specials (before *our* time) of southern fried chicken, vegetable, mashed potatoes and gravy, soup, and roll and butter for $5.75; meatloaf with gravy for $5.25; chicken or beef pot pie, vegetables, potatoes and gravy, soup, and roll and butter for $6.50; plus chili burgers, regular hamburgers (in the $4 range), and sandwiches (priced reasonably). For very small appetites, there is a mini-burger or two pieces of chicken for $2, and a child's portion of ice cream or fries. Of course you'll find sodas, malts, and milkshakes here too.

Highchairs are available, booster seats are not. Management is willing to warm bottles and baby food.

Insomniacs and parents of children who don't sleep will be happy to learn that Edie's is open 24 hours daily, *except* from midnight Monday to 6 a.m. Tuesday. No reservations except for very large parties. The wait averages 20 minutes. Valet and self-parking in restaurant lot. Major credit cards are accepted.

The small quaint **Ocean Park Omelette Parlor,** 2732 Main St., Santa Monica (tel. 213/399-7892), is a satisfying choice for breakfast or lunch. It serves good old-fashioned breakfasts (Annie May's homemade gravy and biscuits, for example), salads, and sandwiches, as well as an array of omelets—almost everyone will find something to enjoy. It's hard to find better prices. Three-egg omelets cost $4.25 (including potatoes and English muffin), and salads are in the $3 to $4.25 range. Sandwiches are a great bargain at about $3.75.

Sorry, no highchairs or reservations, but booster seats are available. Dining can be enjoyed on the outdoor patio.

Open daily from 6 a.m. to 3 p.m. You can park on the street or in the metered parking lot behind the restaurant. Some major credit cards are accepted.

Known for its great baked goods, **Pioneer Boulangerie,** 2012 S. Main St., Santa Monica (tel. 213/399-7771), is a French-Basque–style eatery with a wonderful assortment of eating possibilities under one roof. This miniature villa has a cafeteria with two patios (one is enclosed), a bakery, a wine shop, a gourmet food and candy shop, a bistro where you can watch the bakers kneading dough and working their magic, and a full-service restaurant (moderately priced) serving French/Basque food.

The soups and chowders are creative: lamb and orzo soup, string bean and cabbage soup, corn chowder, clam chowder, chili and bean soup, veal and noodle soup, cream of carrot soup, and split pea with ham. And the stews—sirloin tips and noodles, shepherds' lamb stew, veal and peppers, beef burgundy—are equally unusual.

The menu in the cafeteria and bistro features continental, seafood, Italian, and French themes, depending on the day. You'll also find special pastas, sweet-and-sour pork kebab, carnitas, rice and beans, lasagne, and Cajun chicken.

The restaurant is lovely, with French provincial furnishings—dark woods, stenciled walls, booths partitioned with etched glass. Hanging plants and greenery add the finishing touches to this enchanting eatery. Featuring Basque poulet, London broil, luncheon omelets, croissant sandwiches, linguine, and more, luncheons include soup and either potato salad or coleslaw, and range in price from $5.50 to $9. The dinner menu is equally eclectic—with scampi, salmon filet, chicken Oskar, baked stuffed pork chops, veal madeira, Basque tenderloin tips, and even Cajun surf and turf. Dinners (which include soup or salad, potato or rice, vegetables, and sourdough bread) range in price from $7 (for Cobb salad) to $20 (for surf and turf).

Highchairs and boosters are available. There's no children's menu, but that presents no real problem because of the diverse side orders and baked goods.

The patio is open daily from 7 a.m. to 10 p.m. The restaurant is open weekdays for lunch from 11 a.m. to 3 p.m. and for dinner from 4:30 to 10 p.m.; on Saturday and Sunday from 10 a.m. to 4 p.m. for brunch and from 4:30 to 10 p.m. for dinner. They'll accept reservations for the dining room only. There's a parking lot adjacent (enter on Bicknell Street). Most major credit cards are accepted.

THE AIRPORT/WESTCHESTER AREA: We define this area as the small confines around Los Angeles International Airport, bordered roughly on the east by Sepulveda Boulevard, and running from Culver Boulevard in the north to Century Boulevard in the south. These restaurants are particularly good when you're going to or from LAX.

We take the kids to **Reuben's Steaks and Seafood,** 6531 S. Sepulveda Blvd., just off I-405 (tel. 213/776-1300), when we want to enjoy good chops and fish, yet we don't want to worry about the kids' behavior possibly ruining an expensive meal. Moderately priced, yet very pleasant, this location is perfect if you're on your way to or from Los Angeles International Airport.

Casually decorated, with an English flair, complete with hunting prints and polished brass, the restaurant has a large family clientele, and thus offers such family amenities as highchairs, boosters, and a children's menu. The staff likes kids and tries to accommodate them, gladly warming baby bottles and baby food upon request. Crackers and bread are brought for hungry youngsters. The children's menu includes burgers, a grilled-cheese sandwich, fried shrimp, fish, and prime rib. All are served with soup or salad, fries, milk, and ice cream, at prices from $3 to $6.

While the kids enjoy their meals, adults can select from a varied menu as well. For lunch, there's fresh seafood as well as sandwiches and salads. Prices range from $6 to $9. Dinners also include several fresh selections, as well as a shrimp sampler, scallops, lobster, and combinations of steak or prime rib with lobster or scampi. Dinners come with soup or salad and bread, potato, or rice, and range in price from $13 to $23 (prime rib and lobster).

Open Monday through Friday for lunch from 11:30 a.m. to 4 p.m. Dinner is served daily: Monday through Thursday from 4 to 10:30 p.m. and on Friday and Saturday from 4:30 to 11:30 p.m. On Sunday it's open from 10:30 a.m. to 10:30 p.m. (brunch is served from 10 a.m. to 2 p.m.). Reservations are advised but not required. Major credit cards are accepted. Parking lot adjacent.

There are several other branches. One we especially like is located at 3620 Cahuenga Blvd. West, in Universal City (tel. 818/980-8132).

Dinah's Family Restaurant, 6521 S. Sepulveda Blvd., near Centinela, Westchester (tel. 213/645-0456), is a basic all-American home-style coffeeshop. With families accounting for over half its business, Dinah's has Sassy seats, boosters, and a children's menu (with spaghetti, fried chicken, and fish and chips for about $2.75). They will warm baby bottles and baby food on request.

The restaurant is known for its large selection of pancakes (be sure to try their specialty, the apple pancakes) and for its original-recipe fried chicken. And the prices are hard to beat. Breakfasts start at $2 (for buttermilk pancakes) and go to $6.75 (for steak and eggs). Lunch and dinner items are equally inexpensive. Salads, sandwiches, and burgers range from $2.50 to $5.50. Then there's the fried chicken. A complete dinner with soup or salad, whipped potatoes and gravy, vegetables, dessert, and beverage is $7. If you want a little less food, it costs less. You can also get spaghetti, fish, beef Stroganoff, chicken fried steak, and the like. Weekdays there are all-you-can-eat specials available.

Open daily from 6 a.m. to 11 p.m. No reservations accepted. Between 4 and 6 p.m. is the best time to come for quick service, but expect a 15-minute wait for weekend breakfasts. Plenty of parking. No credit cards accepted.

HOLLYWOOD, MID-WILSHIRE, WEST HOLLYWOOD: These areas are rich with neighborhood-style restaurants. New eateries are always opening.

Expensive

Antonio's, at 7472 Melrose Ave., in West Hollywood (tel. 213/655-0480), is a special-occasion restaurant. The prices here are higher than in ordinary Mexican restaurants, but you are getting award-winning Mexican food typical of the cuisine of Mexico City. This is a good place for sophisticated tastes, but that doesn't mean hot food; on the whole, the cuisine here is not spicy. Outside, the action on Melrose Avenue is festival-like; inside, the restaurant is subdued and nicely decorated.

There's no children's menu, but tots have no trouble finding something to suit them. At lunch, there are tacos and taquitos, enchiladas, and tostadas, ranging from $4.75 to $5.75; at dinner, the prices for those dishes go up to $8.50 to $9.75. There are one or two different lunch specials each day, and these delicious dishes are made from Mexico City–style recipes. Specials cost $8. At dinner there are four or five of these specials, such as pollo Yucateco on Monday (there are 40 ingredients in the sauce), ropa vieja on Wednesday (beef, peppers, raisins, and tomatoes), and pollo en pipian on Sunday (the sauce is made with pumpkin and sunflower seeds, red chiles, and herbs and spices), plus fajitas and chicken mole served every day. These dinner entrees run $8.50 to $16.

Boosters and highchairs are provided. The best times to bring the kids are during lunch or between 5 and 6:30 p.m. for dinner.

Open for lunch Tuesday through Sunday from 11 a.m. to 3 p.m., and for dinner from 5 to 11 p.m. Reservations are accepted. Valet or street parking available. Major credit cards accepted.

There's another branch at 1323 Montana Ave., in Santa Monica (tel. 213/451-2504).

Scandia, 9040 Sunset Blvd., at Doheny Drive, in West Hollywood (tel. 213/278-3555 or 213/272-9521), is one of Los Angeles's oldest and best-known restaurants, and also one of the most elegant ones. Winner of the Travel/Holiday award for 28 years, Scandia is known for its fine Scandinavian cuisine. In this lovely restaurant, where men are required to wear jackets, you can have a special holiday meal or celebrate a significant event.

Take children here? Yes, the best-behaved and the older ones, although the chef will prepare puréed carrots or potatoes for the little ones. For older children, he'll prepare a special children's plate of chopped sirloin or veal sausage and fries.

While the kids may not be ready for the gravad laks, you probably will be. Or sample Danish sole, biff Lindstrom, or Viking Sword (a large brochette of broiled breast of turkey, small chateaubriand, smoked pork chop, tomatoes, and mushrooms, served on a flaming sword). There are also steaks and chops as well as other dinner specials. Old-fashioned baked Alaska is featured on the dessert menu. The average entree costs $19.

There are boosters but no highchairs, and the staff will even warm bottles and baby food. Special drinks for the children can be ordered from the bar.

Open for lunch Tuesday through Saturday from 11:30 a.m. to 3 p.m., and for dinner weekdays from 6 to 11 p.m., on Saturday till midnight. On Sunday, brunch is served from 11 a.m. to 3 p.m., and dinner, from 5 to 11 p.m. Reservations are suggested. (On weekends, it's best to arrive before 8 p.m. with children; when you make your reservation, let them know you're bringing a young child.) Valet parking available. All major credit cards accepted.

Prices at **Genghis Cohen,** 740 N. Fairfax Ave., Hollywood (tel. 213/653-0640), are a bit steep, but the food is worth it. Just half a block north of trendy Melrose Avenue, Genghis Cohen gets its share of music studio people, Melrose wanderers, and the Westside chic. The dining room is small and the tables are pretty close together, but the service is prompt and helpful.

There's no children's menu, but most dishes are suitable for sharing. If you like duck, try the half a crispy duck. Or sample the candied garlic shrimp, cracker-jack shrimp, spicy garlic lamb, or orange-peel chicken. Or you can order Szechuan ribs, Beijing barbecued chicken, or the three-flavor mu shu (which they call their famous Oriental fajitas!). They will make your Szechuan choices as hot as you want, and they don't use MSG in anything. Entrees range from $6.50 to $15.

Highchairs, boosters, and Shirley Temples are available.

Open for lunch Monday through Friday from noon to 3 p.m.; and for dinner Monday through Saturday from 5 to 11:30 p.m., on Sunday till 10 p.m. There's a small parking lot or try for street parking. Reservations are accepted, as are most major credit cards.

Moderate

The venerable **Brown Derby,** 1628 N. Vine St., at the corner of Hollywood Boulevard, in Hollywood (tel. 213/469-5151), has a long history. The first Brown Derby was opened on Wilshire Boulevard in 1926, and has since been demolished. The Hollywood Brown Derby opened in 1929, an ominous year to open, and when it was found not to be earthquake-safe, the new one was opened just a few hundred feet away and the more casual Brown Derby Café was added. The original fixtures, the red-leather banquettes and other furniture, and the caricatures that made it so famous were divided between this location and the one in Pasadena.

The Brown Derby Café is, in fact, more appropriate for younger children than the main dining room. While it doesn't have a children's menu, the Café serves hamburgers, sandwiches, barbecued dishes (reasonably priced and served with baked beans, corn on the cob, or coleslaw), pasta, salads, and such entrees as liver and onions, seafood crêpes, and steak and shrimp. Prices range from $4 to $8.

The main dining room is open for lunch and dinner, serving a more expensive menu, and has an extensive list of salads and appetizers. The continental menu includes Catalina sand dabs, mignonettes of beef tenderloin, lamb chops, poached salmon, and pasta and egg dishes. Prices here start at $7.50 for sandwiches and go to $18.50 for full entrees.

The Café has booster seats only, no highchairs. They will split orders for a $2 charge, and bottles and baby food will be warmed. Special children's drinks are available. The chef in the main dining room will prepare half orders at half price for children 12 and under.

The Café is open daily from 11:30 a.m. to 6:30 p.m. No reservations accepted—the wait is only about ten minutes at peak hours. The main dining room is open for lunch daily from 11:30 a.m. to 2:30 p.m., and for dinner from 5:30 to 10:30 p.m. Reservations are accepted here. Valet parking or free self-parking in the lot half a block south of the restaurant. All major credit cards are accepted.

Other Brown Derby locations: the formal Brown Derby, decorated with the original items, opened in 1986 at 911 E. Colorado Blvd., Pasadena (tel. 818/796-7139). The more casual Brown Derby Bar & Grill is located at 921 E. Colorado Blvd., Pasadena (tel. 818/796-3670).

The story of **El Cholo,** 1121 S. Western Ave., between Olympic and Pico Boulevards (tel. 213/734-2773), goes back to 1927 when it opened across the street from its present location with six booths and a counter. Somehow it survived the Depression, and in 1931 it moved into a bungalow at its current address. The front room and bedrooms became dining rooms. What you see was the actual house, now decorated in the style of a Spanish hacienda. The various dining rooms are named after employees who stayed with El Cholo more than 30 years.

The bar is separate from the dining rooms and has inviting stuffed chairs and couches perfect for waiting for your table. There are also tabletop video games and a big-screen TV. The lively dining rooms are comfortable for children, and on Monday and Tuesday you can listen to the mariachis serenade your whole family.

El Cholo has won a Restaurant Writers of Southern California award and is famous for its margaritas and green-corn tamales. In addition to the usual Mexican appetizer selections, you can get five crab taquitos or five mini-tostadas ($5 per order). Entrees include fajitas (try the house specialty, shrimp fajitas); combination plates with enchiladas, tamales, tacos, and chile rellenos; the special Sonora-style enchilada, first served there in 1927 (topped with olives and a fried egg); green-corn tamales (served June through September only); tostadas; a taco tray for two; and chimichangas. Prices range from $5.50 to $10.25.

There is no written children's menu. But if your child is under 12, tell your server you want the children's-priced items. They'll make a taco or cheese enchilada with rice, beans, or french fries; a cheese and bean burrito; or a hamburger patty with beans, rice, or french fries. Each of these selections is priced at $4. Small sodas cost 75¢ and non-alcoholic children's drinks are $2.

There are highchairs and boosters. Servers will split adult portions for children at no charge, and will warm baby food and bottles. Special children's drinks are available.

Open Monday through Thursday from 11 a.m. to 10 p.m., on Friday and Saturday till 11 p.m., and on Sunday till 9 p.m. Reservations are recommended; on weekends the wait can be up to an hour without them, 40 minutes on weeknights. There's a parking lot across the street, or park at the meters. Major credit cards are accepted.

If you can stand the noise level, you must visit the **Hard Rock Café,** 8600 Beverly Blvd., in Beverly Center, West Hollywood (tel. 213/276-7605). And if you can't, send your teenagers here anyway. It's one of L.A.'s most popular casual restaurants, and teens love it. The green Cadillac plunging through the roof makes the Hard Rock easy to spot.

Inside you'll be bombarded by loud rock music and rock 'n' roll décor everywhere. (This isn't a place to take very young children who are noise-sensitive.) The big barn-like room seems to hold hundreds of people. Once you get a table (and the wait can be long on weekends and at prime times), everyone's tastes will be satisfied. But you'll be doing so much looking around, as the restaurant draws such an eclectic crowd, that it'll be hard to concentrate on the menu. There are plenty of meal-size salads ($6) and five different hamburgers on fresh whole-wheat buns ($5.50 to $6.75). The lime-grilled chicken is good ($8.50), but the watermelon-basted baby back ribs are better ($10). There is also fresh fish and sandwiches, served with salad and fries. Be sure to make room for the desserts—homemade apple pie with ice cream or melted cheese, chocolate devil's food cake, strawberry shortcake, a banana split, or a homemade brownie.

Highchairs are available.

Open daily from 11:30 a.m. to midnight. No reservations accepted. Parking is available at the Beverly Center or you can opt for valet parking. Most major credit cards are accepted.

Chinese restaurants make great family eating experiences, and **Hunan Taste,** 6031 W. San Vicente Blvd., at the crossroads of Fairfax Avenue and Olympic and San Vicente Boulevards, in the mid-Wilshire District (tel. 213/936-5621), is no exception. This friendly neighborhood restaurant, where you see lots of the same faces over and over again, is perfect for a Sunday-night—or any night—dinner. Unlike some Chinese restaurants that never quite got decorated, Hunan Taste is bright and cheerful, with linen-covered tables set far apart and a comfortable, casual atmosphere. Our 4-year-old, who practically grew up on the wonton soup served here, convinced the staff of the need to bring crispy noodles to the table as soon as a child is seated.

Owner and chef Tommy Yan (a veteran of three well-known L.A. Chinese restaurants) is remembered for his velvet shrimp Peking style and his hot-and-sour soup, but kids seem to like almost everything served here. Some are more partial to the three-ingredients dish, others to almond chicken. As the restaurant name suggests, the dishes here are prepared Hunan style, so be sure to specify if you want milder versions of spicy dishes. Your waiter will be happy to suggest combinations of orders for the best sharing opportunities. Make one of your choices a house special. A few good choices are General Tso's chicken ($8.25), Mongolian-style lamb ($8.25), and velvet shrimp ($9.25). Ask about the weekly specials. Dinner entrees average $8.

We've made Hunan a lunch stop before the Los Angeles County Museum of Art and Page Museum—you may want to try it on your way downtown from the Westside. Such lunch specials as beef with broccoli, cashew chicken, hot braised shrimp, and other Hunan-style dishes come with soup, appetizer, and fried rice, and cost $4 to $5. Or you can order off the regular menu.

Boosters and highchairs are available, and the staff will gladly warm baby bottles and baby food. Shirley Temples (with extra cherries) are cheerfully provided. If you're staying in the area, you might consider ordering take-out.

Open Sunday through Thursday from 11:30 a.m. to 10 p.m., on Friday and Saturday till 10:30 p.m. Reservations accepted. Parking lot. Major credit cards welcome.

Inexpensive

Canter's, at 419 N. Fairfax Ave., near CBS and the Farmer's Market (tel. 213/651-2030), is a find—because it's open 24 hours a day. Eat in the Kibbutz Room, where tables are set far apart and booths are roomy, or in the original dining room at a booth or at the counter. You can also have meats and cheeses, sandwiches, and baked goods wrapped to take back to your hotel or to the beach. Don't take the surly waitresses too seriously—some have been there for years. Ask for a "We love kids" balloon on the way out.

You'll usually find an eclectic crowd—families, and local would-be celebrities, neighborhood residents, and tourists—at Canter's, which is one of Los Angeles's oldest delis.

In addition to oatmeal, egg dishes, Belgian waffles, and matzoh brei, there's Canter's fresh baked goods (a slice of pumpernickel-raisin bread can't be beat). Hot corned beef and pastrami are first on the list of sandwiches, followed by standards—chopped liver, brisket, salami, bologna and cheese sandwiches. There are also hot sandwiches, lots of soups, fish dishes, hot dogs, hamburgers, and steak sandwiches. A plate of lox and cream cheese is the most expensive item on the menu at $9.50. Most selections range around $5.

They will split orders in the kitchen for two children, will warm bottles and baby food, and will make special children's drinks at the bar. Highchairs and boosters are available.

Open 24 hours daily. Reservations accepted. Validated parking in Canter's parking lot, two doors away. Cash only.

Your kids will like eating at **Carneys Express Limited,** 8351 Sunset Blvd., Hollywood (tel. 213/654-8300). They serve what most children love in a place children feel comfortable—an authentic Union Pacific railway car set on train tracks. There are outside tables too, but most youngsters prefer to eat in the train car.

The fare is simple here. There are good old cheeseburgers and double burgers served with chili, hot dogs, tuna melts, chicken sandwiches, and a vegetarian combo—all self-service. Prices start at $1.25 for a simple hot dog, and go up to $3.50 for a half-pound cheeseburger. You'll find ice-cream or orange-juice bars and frozen chocolate-dipped bananas for dessert.

Owner Bill Wolf and his staff like kids and will do just about anything to accommodate families, including warming bottles and baby food. There is only one highchair here, and no booster seats.

Open daily from 11 a.m. to midnight. No reservations. Park in the lot behind the train car. Cash only.

There is also a Carneys at 12601 Ventura Blvd., Studio City (tel. 818/761-8300).

Du-Par's Restaurant, at 3rd Street and Fairfax Avenue in the Farmers Market (tel. 213/933-8446), has been an institution for more than 50 years. While there are five other locations in Los Angeles and the San Fernando Valley, this one seems to be the most popular. You'll sit in booths or at the counter and wonder when they plan to redo the interior. Breakfast is the best time to go. The pancakes are outstanding and the coffee is good and strong. The short order of pancakes is plenty for one child, or split it between two light eaters. You can also choose omelets, French toast (comes in short-order size too), cereals, or eggs. If you're really going to be naughty, pick from the unreal bakery goods, like a fresh, made-on-the-premises butterhorn (crescent) or bear claw, or perhaps a doughnut or two. Prices range from $3.25 to $7 for full breakfasts.

Boosters and highchairs are available. Parking lot. Major credit cards accepted. Open weekdays from 6 a.m. to 1 a.m., Friday and Saturday till 3:30 a.m. No reservations are taken, but the wait isn't more than 10 to 20 minutes, even on Sunday morning.

Lucy's Café El Adobe, 5536 Melrose Ave., Hollywood (tel. 213/462-9421), is a 25-year-old Los Angeles tradition. Thrown into the limelight when customer Jerry Brown was California's governor and was dating Linda Ronstadt, Lucy's is still visited by a big group of recognizable celebrities. But this homey neighborhood restaurant, made up of wooden booths and dark-paneled walls, doesn't need any publicity—it's known for good food. Lucy's is family owned and run. Frank likes his restaurant to be known as a family place, but he expects good behavior from the kids, many of whom are now parents bringing back their own kids.

The food is simple, the margaritas great. You can order the Jerry Brown special—arroz con pollo (chicken and Spanish rice)—or chile Colorado (fresh chopped beef with red chile sauce). Other specialties are ropa vieja (shredded beef in sauce), gallina en mole (breast of chicken in mole sauce), and carne seca con huevo (beef jerky with scrambled eggs). Specialties come with soup, salad, rice, beans, tortillas, and butter, and average around $7. Enchilada dinners come in seven variations and run around $7. There are also tostadas, taco combinations, and steak dinners.

Children can get the "under 12" choices of a taco or enchilada with rice, beans, soup, or salad, or a meat patty with beans or rice, soup or salad, each meal $5.25, or they can order off the à la carte menu—burritos, enchiladas, tacos, tamales.

Only booster seats are available here. Bottles and baby food will be warmed upon request, and special children's drinks can be made.

Open Monday through Saturday from 11:30 a.m. to 11:30 p.m.; closed Sunday. No reservations; the average wait is 10 to 20 minutes. Parking on the side and in back. Some major credit cards accepted.

Walking into the **Old Spaghetti Factory,** 5939 Sunset Blvd., Hollywood (tel. 213/469-7149), is like walking into a turn-of-the-century museum. A mammoth chandelier greets you in the foyer, and stained-glass windows from 1900s Chicago decorate the restaurant, along with one-of-a-kind light fixtures, hand-carved doorways, and antique tables. Children will have a ball looking at all the ornate decorations; all love the 1918 trolley car, which actually ran in Seattle and was lowered into the restaurant because it was too big to get through the door. You can even request a table inside it.

It's pretty obvious what is served here. Lunch and dinner offer many of the same items; just the price is different. In addition to the nine different spaghetti dishes at lunch, you have your choice of fettuccine Alfredo, spinach tortellini with Alfredo sauce, pasta salad, sausage or meatball sandwich, and soup. Prices range from $2.25 to $5. Dinner is spaghetti, fettuccine, and spinach tortellini.

Spaghetti comes with mushroom sauce, or clam sauce, meat sauce, tomato sauce, meatballs, sausage, or browned butter and mizithra cheese. Complete dinners include salad, bread, beverage, and spumoni. An à la carte dish of spaghetti with meat sauce and bread is available for $3.50. Complete dinners cost $3.75 to $6.75. An under-12 dinner for kids consists of spaghetti with meat or tomato sauce for $3.

Boosters and highchairs are provided. Baby food and bottles will be warmed upon request.

Open for lunch Monday through Friday from 11:30 a.m. to 2 p.m., and for dinner Monday through Thursday from 5 to 10 p.m., on Friday and Saturday until 11 p.m., and on Sunday from 4 to 10 p.m. No reservations; during busy times the wait is 15 to 30 minutes, and on weekends it can be 30 to 45 minutes. Come early so as not to wait. Parking lot. No credit cards accepted.

Roscoe's House of Chicken and Waffles, 1514 N. Gower St. (tel. 213/466-7453 or 213/466-9329), is an interesting place to stop if you're in the Hollywood area. The name reflects their specialties, and both are served in many different ways. From delicious chicken smothered with gravy and onions, accompanied by grits and biscuits, to fresh chicken livers, a waffle, potato salad or fries, you'll find large portions at reasonable prices. You can get waffles alone (their special batter, $4.50) or combine them with a southern-style chicken dish ($7.75). There's also a chicken burger and chicken sandwiches ($3.50 to $5). These dishes are served all day.

This small, unassuming restaurant has boosters and highchairs, and will warm bottles and baby food. They'll also split orders for two kids.

Open Sunday through Thursday from 9 a.m. to 11 p.m., on Friday and Saturday till 3 a.m. No reservations (busiest time is 11:30 a.m. to noon). Street parking only. All major credit cards accepted.

UNIVERSAL CITY / BURBANK: Officially part of the San Fernando Valley, Universal City and Burbank are part of the Hollywood state-of-mind. You'll find yourself spending at least one day (and maybe more) in this general area close to Hollywood and downtown Los Angeles.

Make **Fung Lum Restaurant,** 222 Universal Terrace Pkwy. (tel. 818/763-7888), a "must" on your list of interesting restaurants to visit. Set on the side of the hill leading up to Universal Studios, the restaurant looks like an Oriental palace. The palatial look is continued in the interior, which you enter through ornate hand-carved doors. Moongates (arched entryways) lead to exquisite gardens, and inside are embroidered silk decorations and panels inlaid with coral and ivory. But don't let the formality of the décor fool you. This restaurant is a fine place to take the family. The main dining room seats 500 people comfortably.

Cantonese is the primary Chinese cuisine served here, although Hunan and Szechuan selections are also prepared. Since Chinese food is made to share, you won't find a children's menu here. But there are dozens of things that will please the kids, such as chicken chow mein, fried rice, and moo shu chicken. For lunch there is dim sum and an abbreviated version of the large dinner menu. Lunch prices run $4.50 to $8.50 for main courses.

At dinner there are many duck entrees, 11 kinds of soup, a huge list of seafood, and vegetable, chicken, beef, and pork dishes. You could come back over and over again and still not taste everything offered on the menu. Dinner prices range from $6 to $21 (for Maine lobster baked with ginger and scallions). For $30 you can have the celebrated shark's-fin soup with shredded chicken, or whole winter-melon soup, which has to be ordered in advance and serves ten people. Don't wait for fortune cookies here, though. We're told that those are not authentic Chinese desserts, so they won't serve them. Instead there is ice cream, lichee nuts, and Fung Lum pudding.

Sunday brunch features a buffet and nonstop champagne. Adults are charged $11; children, half price.

There are booster seats and highchairs available. The staff will warm baby bottles and baby food, and will prepare special children's drinks at the bar.

Open for lunch Monday through Saturday from 11:30 a.m. to 2:30 p.m., and for dinner Monday through Thursday from 5 to 10 p.m., on Friday and Saturday till 11 p.m., and on Sunday from 3 to 10 p.m. A Sunday brunch is served from 11 a.m. to 3 p.m. Reservations are accepted. Even with a reservation, the wait on Saturday night might be a half hour. Valet parking. Major credit cards accepted.

Victoria Station, 3850 Lankershim Blvd., atop the hill at Universal Studios (tel. 818/760-0714), is located next to the Universal Studios tours. In fact, you can see some of the movie sets from your table. While that intrigues the adults and older kids in our party, the younger ones delight in the fact that they're eating inside a replica of a famous train depot. Victoria Station, as the name suggests, re-creates the ambience of the famous London railroad station. In fact, you can eat inside one of the original Flying Scotsman fleet of British railway cars.

Specializing in carved-to-order prime rib (you can even have it with the bone-in) and continental cuisine, Victoria Station caters to families. "Junior Conductor" dinners for children 12 and under include a peanut butter and jelly sandwich, cheeseburger, barbecued ribs, chicken sticks, and prime rib ($3.50 to $9). All meals come with fries and a beverage. Add $2 for the unlimited salad bar.

For adults, there are barbecued beef ribs or pork ribs, fresh seafood (including Australian lobster tail), and chicken selections. Dinners include salad bar or soup du jour, baked potato or chestnut wild rice, and fresh vegetables. Prices range from $12 to $22. In addition, lunch offerings (which cost $6.50 to $14) include such items as Black Forest ham with swiss cheese and fresh broccoli on a croissant, or shrimp Victoria (large shrimp sautéed with garlic, white wine, and lemon). There are quiche and burgers as well.

For brunch, omelets, quiche, stuffed French toast, and gourmet egg dishes are offered. You can also order prime rib or the fresh catch of the day. Brunch costs $6.50 to $9 and includes a fresh-fruit salad bar, potatoes, breads, and champagne.

Highchairs and boosters are available, as are children's non-alcoholic drinks from the bar. The server will warm baby bottles or baby food, and will gladly bring crackers to the table if your kids are hungry.

Open Monday through Thursday from 11:30 a.m. to 10 p.m., on Friday and Saturday till 11 p.m., and on Sunday for brunch from 10:30 a.m. to 3 p.m. and for dinner from 5 to 10 p.m. Reservations are suggested. Valet parking is available in addition to parking in a nearby lot ($3). Most major credit cards are accepted.

Tony Roma's A Place for Ribs, 100 Universal City Plaza, Universal City (tel. 818/777-3939), is always a good bet for consistent quality, fast service, and a welcoming attitude toward kids.

Probably the most attractive setting of the Tony Roma's in Los Angeles, the one in Universal City has a perfect location next to the Universal Studios entrance. With large picture windows, it offers a lovely view on clear days.

The menu has the usual mouthwatering assortment of barbecued ribs and chicken, and a few other grilled entrees. Dinners include coleslaw and tangy ranch-style beans, baked potato, or fries, and range in price from $6.50 to $12.50. Lunches include the same choices priced from $5 to $13. The terrific little children's menu also doubles as a page to color, and offers chicken-in-a-basket, burger, chicken fingers, and ribs (all with fries and coleslaw) for $3 to $5.

Highchairs and boosters are available. Your server will be glad to let you split adult portions, and will warm baby bottles and baby food in the kitchen.

Open daily for lunch from 11 a.m. to 4 p.m., and for dinner from 4 to midnight. Reservations are not accepted, but most major credit cards are. A large parking lot (the one for Universal Studios) is nearby.

There are other branches at 319 Santa Monica Blvd. in Santa Monica (tel. 213/393-0139) and at 9404 Brighton Way in Beverly Hills (tel. 213/278-1207).

DOWNTOWN: The following restaurants are good choices if you are staying in a downtown hotel or are visiting Olvera Street, the Children's Museum, the Museum of Contemporary Art, or Chinatown and Little Tokyo.

Expensive

Weekend breakfast time is when you'll find the most families with children dining at the **Pacific Dining Car,** 1310 W. 6th St. (tel. 213/483-6000). Although it's open 24 hours a day, don't expect a coffeeshop—the ambience is more luxurious, and the prices are quite high. Weekdays, L.A.'s major powerbrokers spend their breakfasts here making major deals.

Set in an enlarged replica of a real railway dining car, this restaurant has been serving food in this location since 1923. Through the years it became famous for its aged meats. While the coffee is no longer 10¢ and you can't get a sirloin for 65¢ anymore either, it still draws a loyal crowd of diners for breakfast, lunch, dinner, and after-theater supper. The rooms are handsome and the atmosphere subdued. We like to sit in the area near the entrance, the original railway-like car, with windows on one side.

Breakfast features mostly egg dishes such as fresh avocado scramble, Swiss eggs, and omelets. Our kids love the pancakes and the homemade blueberry and bran muffins. You can also get a bowl of yogurt, granola, or Familia muesli. Preserves, marmalade, and apple butter are made on the premises. Breakfast prices start at $4.50 and go to $11.25 for steak and eggs.

Lunch and dinner feature seafood, steaks, and veal. At lunch, steaks range from $18 to $25.75, a hamburger costs $13.75, and the veal chop is tabbed at $24. Dinner selections include loin backribs for $22, shrimp diavolo for $21, and a T-bone steak for $31.50. Chicken dishes and hamburgers are also available. Entrees come with a potato, but vegetables are à la carte.

Booster and Sassy seats are provided. Management is willing to warm baby bottles and baby food in the kitchen, and will prepare special children's drinks at the bar.

Breakfast is served Monday through Friday from 11 p.m. to 11 a.m. On Saturday and Sunday, you can get breakfast until 4 p.m. Lunch is served Monday through Thursday from 11 a.m. to 4 p.m. Afternoon tea may be ordered daily from 3 to 5:30 p.m. And dinner is served 24 hours every day. Reservations are accepted. Valet parking. Some credit cards are accepted.

Moderate

If you're taking the children to the Dorothy Chandler Pavilion, make your dining stop the **Itchey Foot Ristorante,** 803 W. Temple St., at Figueroa Street (tel. 213/680-0007). Itchey Foot is popular with the before- and after-theater crowd and serves Italian and American fare.

The atmosphere here is inviting but is more appropriate for families with children who are over 6 years old. The dining room is divided into lots of wood-paneled dining nooks with a Tiffany-style lamp hanging above each table.

A main attraction here is the backroom theater, which features performances from the Music Center's Mark Taper Forum (usually readings), full shows, and improvisational comedy. Although there are some performances geared for children, they are few, so call first. The other shows, except for the improvisational comedy, are appropriate for teenagers on up.

Polish sausage, Philadelphia steak sandwiches, and hamburgers are good lunch selections. Or you can create your own sandwich from lots of deli ingredients. Four vegetarian specialties are available, plus a number of salads. Italian beef dip, meatball submarine, and steak and peppers are also good sandwich choices. Pizza combinations are plentiful and good. For dinner, add baked lasagne, manicotti, eggplant parmesan, and New York steak. The kids might enjoy spaghetti or ravioli. Appetizers and desserts are abundant as well. Lunch prices run $2.75 to $7.50. A whole pizza costs $9 to $14. Dinner entrees go for $4.50 to $9.50.

Highchairs and booster seats are available. The management is willing to warm bottles and baby food, and make special children's drinks as well. If you're staying downtown, consider having a meal delivered to your hotel (delivery service available from 10 a.m. to 9 p.m.).

Open Monday through Thursday from 11 a.m. to 10 p.m., on Friday till midnight, on Saturday till 9 p.m., and on Sunday from 4 to 8 p.m. Reservations are suggested, especially for before-theater dinners. There's a small parking charge. Major credit cards accepted.

Not too many Los Angeles restaurants can claim more than 64 years of business without having closed their doors once. But **The Original Pantry,** at 877 S. Figueroa St. (tel. 213/972-9279), can. Walking into this place is like entering a time warp circa the 1930s. It's not diner-style, mind you, but there's real linoleum on the floors and Formica on the tables. Waiters in white shirts, aprons, and black bow ties know their business, which is to serve generous portions of real American food.

Locals know that the Pantry's hallmark is the line out the door. Its history has been to take your order while you're in line and have it ready by the time you sit down—and it works. No leisurely lingering over the menu here. While in line, you might want to amuse your children with some fun trivia about the restaurant. For instance, it takes a harvest of more than 20,000 coffee trees to supply the 10½ *tons* of coffee used by the Pantry annually. Or the fact that more than 2,400 eggs are used in the restaurant—every day. On the average, the restaurant buys 46,000 bottles of catsup, 15 tons of sugar, and 2,190 gallons of syrup each year. To make the yummy pancakes served here, the Pantry consumes eight tons of flour, 1,946 gallons of milk, and 2,000 dozen eggs every year.

The menu changes daily, but basically you'll get hearty breakfasts, plus hamburgers, steaks, cutlets, ham, rib roast, pork, lamb, soup, and salads. Prices are quite reasonable—breakfast averages $3.75; lunch, $6; and dinner, $8.

There's no children's menu here, but they'll gladly split orders in the kitchen or warm baby bottles and baby food. Highchairs and booster seats are available.

Next door to the Pantry is its brand-new **Pantry Bake & Sandwich Shoppe,** 875 S. Figueroa St. (tel. 213/627-6825). With the same feel of the 1930s, the Bake Shoppe is dominated by a bakery area located near the entrance where some very tasty and tempting baked goods are made, to be sold at the counter or ordered at the table. The restaurant also has a large quick-service counter area for snacks and fast meals. The main feature of the Bake Shoppe is that it serves a lighter lunch than its neighbor, with such fare as sandwiches; breakfast and dinner items are the same at both places. Hamburgers here run $2.75 to $4; sandwiches cost $2.25 to $5.25.

The Original Pantry is open 24 hours daily (and there's usually always a line). As far as waiting goes, approach this restaurant with a sense of humor—after all, it's an L.A. landmark. The Bake Shoppe is open daily from 6 a.m. to 9 p.m. No reservations at either establishment. Parking across the street. No credit cards accepted at either restaurant, but traveler's checks are welcome with identification.

IN CHINATOWN. In the heart of Chinatown is **Miriwa,** 750 N. Hill St. (tel. 213/

687-3088), known for its excellent Cantonese cuisine. Big windows run the length of the spacious dining room, and Chinese artwork, black lacquered furniture, and bright-orange tablecloths give it a cheery and inviting atmosphere. The lobby, up one flight of stairs, is dominated by live lobster and crab tanks, sure to provide kids with something to look at should you encounter a wait.

This is a good place to introduce children to Chinese food—there are many selections and the waiters here are familiar with serving children, as so many of the customers are Oriental families. Share the Cantonese special, for instance, which costs $8.50 per person. You get appetizers, soup, a main course of beef and snow peas, chicken with black-bean sauce, and Yang Chow fried rice. For three people, add shrimp chop suey; for four people, order sweet-and-sour pork as well. In addition to the seafood, chicken, duck, and pork entrees, there are squab, abalone, clay pot, and shark's-fin dishes. Beef and chop suey selections are also plentiful. Entrees range in price from $6 to $10. A dim sum lunch is served from 1:30 to 4 p.m.

Boosters and highchairs are available, and bottles and baby food will be warmed upon request.

Open daily from 9 a.m. to 3 p.m. and 5 to 9:30 p.m. Reservations are accepted at dinner only. Valet parking. Major credit cards honored.

IN LITTLE TOKYO. Located in the heart of Little Tokyo in Japanese Village Plaza, **Restaurant Plaza,** 356 E. 1st St., on the second floor (tel. 213/628-0697), is a real find when you and the kids want to enjoy authentic Japanese food. This restaurant is actually a combination of several restaurants, each specializing in a different cuisine: sushi, noodles, tempura, teriyaki, bento (traditional Japanese lunch-in-a-box), and nabe (dishes cooked in a pot).

Whenever we eat here, we feel as if we've spent an hour in Tokyo. The dining room, while larger than a traditional Japanese restaurant, exudes an air of the Orient. Maybe it's because Japanese is spoken all around you; maybe it's the paper lanterns hanging from the ceiling or the small indoor gardens.

All food is attractively presented, the way it would be in Japan. Sushi is neatly—and colorfully—arranged on raised rectangular plates. Makunouchi Bento comes in a lacquered luncheon box with rice and pickles. Teriyaki and tempura are artistically presented amid slivered cabbage and colorful orange slices.

The food is delectable and the selections varied. Lunches are priced from $4.75 to $18 (for lobster and crab teriyaki), but average $7. For dinner, you can also have combinations of beef and chicken teriyaki ($9.50), tempura and sashimi ($13), and New York beef teriyaki and sashimi ($14.50). A children's sushi plate for $4.50 is available at lunch or dinner.

Open daily from noon to 9:30 p.m., Restaurant Plaza is perfect for children, with highchairs and booster seats available. Reservations will be honored, and most major credit cards are accepted. Plentiful parking nearby.

Inexpensive

If you're downtown at the Children's Museum, or have had enough Mexican food on Olvera Street, be sure to take the kids to **Philippe's,** 1001 N. Alameda St. (tel. 213/628-3781). Like the Pantry, Philippe's is an L.A. tradition, this one dating back to 1908. The setting is informal, the tables are long and to be shared, and the floors are covered with sawdust. The restaurant draws a clientele that ranges from Westside attorneys, Pasadena accountants, and Los Angeles celebrities to downtown blue-collar workers.

Self-serve is the word here. Pay and order at the counter and choose eggs, French toast, or fresh baked goods for breakfast (25¢ to $4), or the famous Philippe's French-dip sandwiches for lunch or dinner. French dip pork, beef, ham, or lamb sandwiches are scrumptious and reasonably priced at $3 to $3.25. Adults will want to add a cup of Philippe's coffee—still Depression-priced at 10¢—to their order.

Highchairs only here.

Open daily from 6 a.m. to 10 p.m. No reservations. Park in the back or on the street. No credit cards accepted.

RESTAURANTS BY CUISINE: Because we know that children can be such finicky eaters, and because Los Angeles can be overwhelming in the number of its restaurants, we've divided these establishments by cuisine.

American

Brentwood Country Mart, 26th Street and San Vicente Boulevard, Brentwood (tel. 213/395-6714)—fast food.

Brown Derby, 1628 N. Vine St., at the corner of Hollywood Boulevard, Hollywood (tel. 213/469-5151).

Canter's, 419 N. Fairfax Ave., near CBS and the Farmer's Market, Hollywood (tel. 213/651-2030)—kosher-style delicatessen.

Carneys Express Limited, 8351 Sunset Blvd., Hollywood (tel. 213/654-8300). Other branch: 12601 Ventura Blvd., Studio City (tel. 818/761-8300).

The Cheesecake Factory, 364 N. Beverly Dr., off Brighton Way, Beverly Hills (tel. 213/278-7270). Other branch: 4141 Via Marina, Marina Del Rey (tel. 213/306-3344).

Dinah's Family Restaurant, 6521 S. Sepulveda Blvd., near Centinela, Westchester (tel. 213/645-0456).

Dolores Restaurant, 8925 W. Olympic Blvd., Beverly Hills (tel. 213/657-7455).

Du-Par's Restaurant, 3rd Street and Fairfax Avenue, in the Farmer's Market, Hollywood (tel. 213/933-8446).

Ed Debevic's Short Orders/Deluxe, 134 N. La Cienega Blvd., Beverly Hills (tel. 213/659-1952).

Edie's Diner, 4211 Admiralty Way, Marina Del Rey (tel. 213/823-5339).

Flakey Jake's, 2347 S. Sepulveda Blvd., near Pico Boulevard, West L.A. (tel. 213/477-0405).

Fromin's Restaurant, 1832 Wilshire Blvd., Santa Monica (tel. 213/829-5443)—kosher-style delicatessen. Other branch: 17615 Ventura Blvd., Encino (tel. 818/990-6346).

Hamburger Henry, 3001 Wilshire Blvd., Santa Monica (tel. 213/828-3000).

Hard Rock Café, 8600 Beverly Blvd., in Beverly Center, West Hollywood (tel. 213/276-7605).

Heaven, 10250 Santa Monica Blvd., in the Century City Shopping Center (tel. 213/557-0387). Other branches: 2222 Wilshire Blvd., at 23rd Street, Santa Monica (tel. 213/829-7829 and 213/829-1649); 17644 Ventura Blvd., near White Oak, Encino (tel. 818/986-0772).

Islands, 10948 W. Pico Blvd., West L.A. (tel. 213/474-1144). Other branch: 404 Washington St., Marina Del Rey (tel. 213/822-3939).

Junior's Deli, 2379 Westwood Blvd., West L.A. (tel. 213/475-5771)—kosher-style delicatessen.

Larry Parker's Beverly Hills Diner, 206 S. Beverly Dr., Beverly Hills (tel. 213/274-5655).

Tommy Lasorda's Ribs & Pasta Restaurant, 14130 Marquesas Way, Marina Del Rey (tel. 213/827-5330).

Lawry's the Prime Rib, 55 N. La Cienega Blvd., Beverly Hills (tel. 213/652-2827).

Nate'n Al, 414 N. Beverly Dr., Beverly Hills (tel. 213/274-0120)—kosher-style delicatessen.

Ocean Park Omelette Parlor, 2732 Main St., Santa Monica (tel. 213/399-7892).

Old World Restaurant, 1019 Westwood Blvd., West L.A. (tel. 213/208-4033). Other branches: 216 N. Beverly Dr., Beverly Hills (tel. 213/274-7695); 8782 Sunset Blvd., West Hollywood (tel. 213/652-2520).

The Original Pantry, 877 S. Figueroa St., downtown (tel. 213/972-9279), and the **Pantry Bake & Sandwich Shoppe,** 875 S. Figueroa St., downtown (tel. 213/627-6825).

Pacific Dining Car, 1310 W. 6th St., downtown (tel. 213/483-6000).

Philippe's, 1001 N. Alameda St., downtown (tel. 213/628-3781).

Reuben's Steaks and Seafood, 6531 S. Sepulveda Blvd., just off I-405 in Westchester (tel. 213/776-1300). Other branches are found around the city, but one especially good one is at 3620 Cahuenga Blvd. West, Universal City (tel. 818/980-8132).

RJ's the Rib Joint, 252 N. Beverly Dr., between Dayton Way and Wilshire Boulevard, Beverly Hills (tel. 213/274-RIBS).

Roscoe's House of Chicken and Waffles, 1514 N. Gower St., Hollywood (tel. 213/466-7453 or 213/466-9329).

Tony Roma's A Place for Ribs, 100 Universal City Plaza, Universal City (tel. 818/777-3939). Other branches: 319 Santa Monica Blvd., Santa Monica (tel. 213/393-0139); 9404 Brighton Way, Beverly Hills (tel. 213/278-1207).

Chinese

Fung Lum Restaurant, 222 Universal Terrace Pkwy., Universal City (tel. 818/763-7888).

Genghis Cohen, 740 N. Fairfax Ave., Hollywood (tel. 213/653-0640).

Hunan Taste, 6031 W. San Vicente Blvd., at the crossroads of Fairfax Avenue and Olympic and San Vicente Boulevards, in Hollywood (tel. 213/936-5621).

Lotus West, 10974 W. Pico Blvd., Westwood (tel. 213/475-9597).

The Mandarin, 430 N. Camden Dr., Beverly Hills (tel. 213/272-0267).

Miriwa, 750 N. Hill St., Chinatown (tel. 213/687-3088).

Italian

Anna's Italian Restaurant, 10929 W. Pico Blvd., Westwood (tel. 213/474-0102).

Earth, Wind & Flour, 1776 Westwood Blvd., at Santa Monica Boulevard, Westwood (tel. 213/470-2499). Other branches: 2222 Wilshire Blvd., at 23rd Street, Santa Monica (tel. 213/829-7829 and 213/829-1649); 17644 Ventura Blvd., near White Oak, Encino (tel. 818/986-0772).

Itchey Foot Ristorante, 803 W. Temple St., at Figueroa Street, downtown (tel. 213/680-0007).

Mario's Italian Restaurant, 1001 Broxton, Westwood (tel. 213/208-7077).

The Old Spaghetti Factory, 5939 Sunset Blvd., Hollywood (tel. 213/469-7149).

Tommy Lasorda's Ribs & Pasta Restaurant, 14130 Marquesas Way, Marina Del Rey (tel. 213/827-5330).

Japanese

Benihana of Tokyo, 38 N. La Cienega Blvd., Beverly Hills (tel. 213/655-7311).

Restaurant Plaza, 356 E. 1st St. (second floor), Little Tokyo (tel. 213/628-0697).

Yamato's, in the Century Plaza Hotel, 2025 Avenue of the Stars, Century City (tel. 213/277-1840).

Mexican

Antonio's, 7472 Melrose Ave., West Hollywood (tel. 213/655-0480). Other branch: 1323 Montana Ave., Santa Monica (tel. 213/451-2504).

El Cholo, 1121 S. Western Ave., between Olympic and Pico Boulevards, West L.A. (tel. 213/734-2773).

Lucy's El Adobe, 5536 Melrose Ave., Hollywood (tel. 213/462-9421).

Tampico Tilly's, 1025 Wilshire Blvd., Santa Monica (tel. 213/451-1769). Other branch: Santa Monica Place, third level (tel. 213/393-1404).

Seafood

Famous Fish Enterprise Fish Company, 174 Kinney St., Santa Monica (tel. 213/392-8366).

Pelican's Catch, 1715 Pacific Ave., Venice Beach (tel. 213/392-3933). Other branch: **Café Pelican,** 2720 Main St., Santa Monica (tel. 213/392-5711).

Other Types of Cuisine

Aunt Kizzy's Back Porch, 4371 Glencoe Ave., in the Villa Marina Shopping Center, Marina del Rey (213/578-1005)—southern food.

Belle-Vue French Restaurant, 101 Santa Monica Blvd., Santa Monica (tel. 213/393-2843).

Café Casino, 1299 Ocean Ave., Santa Monica (tel. 213/394-3717). Other branch: 1145 Gayley Ave., Westwood Village (tel. 213/208-1010)—French.

Pioneer Boulangerie, 2012 S. Main St., Santa Monica (tel. 213/399-7771)—bistro.

Scandia, 9040 Sunset Blvd., West Hollywood (tel. 213/278-3555 or 213/272-9521)—Scandinavian cuisine.

6. WHAT TO SEE AND DO

Los Angeles is many things to many people. It's a place so well suited to children that you almost don't have to think about where to take them—you just take them. The wide-open spaces and the good weather make it easy and simple to do almost anything with kids.

Because you'll be driving to so many activities, we have clustered them, roughly, according to their location. We will begin with downtown Los Angeles and work our way west to the beaches.

DOWNTOWN: Downtown L.A. is a culturally and historically rich section of the city. Let's start with the oldest section of town.

Old Los Angeles

Even this super-modern metropolis has its historical roots. **El Pueblo de Los Angeles State Historic Park** will give you and the kids a flavor of the Los Angeles of days past. Nothing remains of the original cluster of earth-and-willow huts, circa 1780, that constituted the first incarnation of Los Angeles. However, on the spot of those original huts sits this park, a collection of 27 historic buildings that date from 1818 to 1926. Plan to spend several hours wandering around.

We like to start with the excitement of **Olvera Street,** a colorful Mexican-style marketplace. For kids, this street is definitely the highlight of the tour. In a city with such Hispanic ties, this area gives children a more visual and sensual awareness of the city's roots. Over 85 giftshops and stalls offer authentic Mexican goods, such as sombreros, piñatas, and leather goods. Children especially like to watch the craftsmen—glassblowers, silversmiths, candle makers, and leather makers—forge their wares.

Our kids are always ready to sample the local tasty treats—sugary churros are one such specialty. You probably won't be able to keep your kids away from

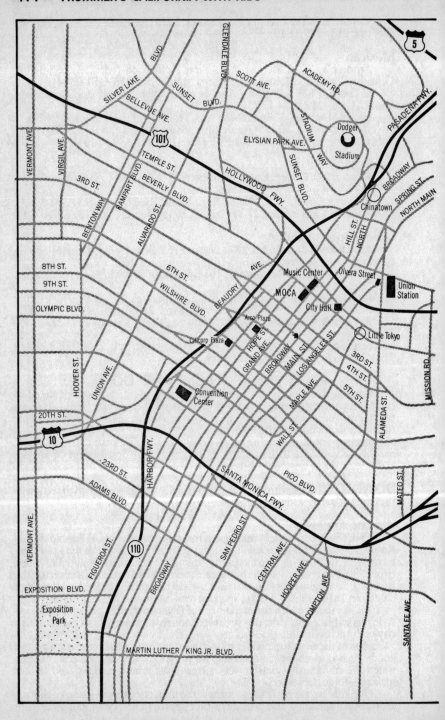

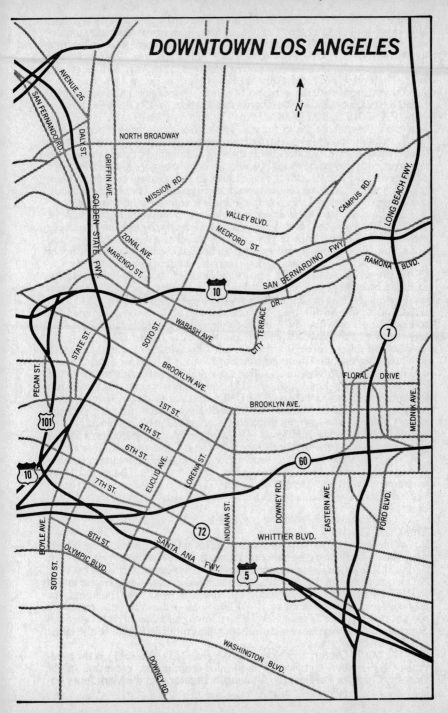

DOWNTOWN LOS ANGELES

the other colorful Mexican candies for sale. If you can bargain with them to have lunch first, you'll find a bounty of choices here, from casual food stalls to sidewalk cafés and full-scale restaurants. The most historic choice is **La Golondrina Restaurant,** housed in the **Pelanconi House.** Built in the mid-19th century as a private residence, it was one of the earliest buildings in Los Angeles made of fired brick. The food served there is very traditional Mexican fare.

Olvera Street is often host to special events, so write ahead for exact dates of events to the **Olvera Street Merchants Association,** W-17 Olvera St., Los Angeles, CA 90012 (tel. 213/687-2525). The Cinco de Mayo (May 1 to 5) and Mexican Independence Day (September 16 to 18) celebrations are especially fun.

Perhaps the most kids-oriented of these events is the Blessing of the Animals in mid-April, in which local residents dress up their animals, parade them down the street, and have them blessed by the local Catholic bishop. Kids of all ages are delighted by the animals, which range from cats in hats, dogs on fancy leashes, cows in bonnets, birds in colorful cages, to even goldfish. The blessing is meant to acknowledge the loyal affection that animals have for their human owners.

At the center of Olvera Street is the historic **Sepulveda House,** built in 1887, which houses the park's Visitor Center. Here, if your kids are historically inclined, an 18-minute film on Los Angeles's past can be viewed at 11 a.m. and noon. You can also buy the walking self-tour brochure for 50¢ and see the rest of the historic park on your own. Also sold here are children's books and gifts.

If you prefer **guided tours,** walk to the Docent Office, 130 Paseo de la Plaza, next to the Old Plaza Firehouse at 501 N. Los Angeles. The tours last 50 minutes, are free, and are conducted Tuesday through Saturday at 10 a.m., 11 a.m., noon, and 1 p.m. At this office, you can also sign up for two-hour guided bus tours of the central city, which are given the first and third Wednesdays of the month at 9:45 a.m. Reservations are required (tel. 213/628-1274).

Beyond Olvera Street it takes a parent's knowledge to determine which sights will interest kids. **Firehouse Number 1,** which displays fire-fighting memorabilia from the 19th century, is often a favorite. The **Ávila Adobe,** the oldest existing residence in Los Angeles, gives kids a sense of what everyday life was like for wealthy California ranchers in the 1840s. And since kids are often intrigued by statues, you might show them the **Felipe de Neve Statue** (the Spanish governor of California who was responsible for founding El Pueblo del Río de Nuestra Señora la Reina de Los Angeles in 1781) and the **Fray Junipero Serra Statue** (the Franciscan padre who founded the first nine of California's 21 missions).

The majority of the park is stroller-accessible. There are a number of bathrooms, most equipped with changing tables. Open daily from 10 a.m. to 10 p.m. in summer, till 10 p.m. the rest of the year. Parking is available on Main Street between Hope and Arcadia Streets for $5 for the full day or $1 for each 20 minutes.

The Civic Center

With young kids in tow, this section of town is best done in a car. This is where Los Angeles city government is centered. The 28-story **City Hall,** 200 N. Spring St., the seat of city government, was for many years mandated by law to be the tallest building in the city, because of earthquake fears. However, that ended in 1957 when architectural techniques improved. (Now the tallest building is the 62-floor First Interstate Building at Wilshire Boulevard and Hope Street. It will soon be bested by the 73-floor New Library Tower, on Hope Street between 5th Street and Grand Avenue, which will open the end of 1989 and be the tallest building on the West Coast.)

The **Music Center,** 135 N. Grand Ave. (tel. 213/972-7211), is the modernistic $35-million complex of performing-arts theaters, consisting of the **Dorothy Chandler Pavilion,** the **Ahmanson Theater,** and the **Mark Taper Fo-**

rum. This is where you'll find the Joffrey Ballet, the Los Angeles Philharmonic, Symphonies for Youth, the Master Chorale, and the Los Angeles Music Center Opera. There are daytime tours available (tel. 213/972-7483), but it's probably best viewed at night when the lights of the complex accent the unusual architecture. At anytime, though, a walk through the plaza and some time spent around the fountains, is pleasant.

Museum of Contemporary Art (MOCA)

If you want to show arts-oriented kids what's really new, come to MOCA. This museum, which opened in 1983, is dedicated to exhibiting only art created from 1940 through the present.

The MOCA collection is housed in two buildings: the **New Museum Building,** at California Plaza, 250 S. Grand Ave. (tel. 213/62-MOCA-2), and the **Temporary Contemporary,** 152 N. Central Ave. (same telephone number). Today, MOCA's permanent collection numbers about 650 paintings, sculptures, prints, photographs, drawings, and mixed-media works.

MOCA wants kids to see and experience the collection. Its new art-education program, currently aimed at fourth-graders, is an ambitious 13-unit program to get kids to respond to and think about art. Unfortunately, only local schoolchildren can participate in the program, but there is a commitment to youngsters appreciating modern art.

This is challenging artwork. In addition, it's a rather adult environment: quiet and subdued. Older kids, infants in carriers, and sophisticated little art connoisseurs tend to do best here.

Regular admission is $4 for adults, $2 for students with ID or seniors over 65; children under 12 go in for free. The museum is open on Tuesday, Wednesday, Saturday, and Sunday from 11 a.m. to 6 p.m., on Thursday and Friday till 8 p.m.; closed on Monday and Thanksgiving, Christmas, and New Year's Days. Parking for the new building is available at the Music Center Garage for $4 per car, and beneath the California Plaza at California Plaza Garage for $12.50 maximum per day, $4 maximum per day after 5 p.m. and on weekends. Parking for the Temporary Contemporary is located near 1st Street and Central Avenue, and costs $1.50 to $3 per day maximum; also at 140 N. San Pedro Pl. for a fee of $4 per car on weekdays and $1.50 on evenings and weekends.

Los Angeles Children's Museum

Located at 310 N. Main St., in the Los Angeles Mall (tel. 213/687-8800 for 24-hour information), this museum is a place that kids always want to visit. The interactive exhibits are fun and educational at the same time. Children love the fact that parents don't have to say "no" to anything—they can participate in everything. Our first-grader enjoyed dressing up in a fireman's costume and playing with giant foam-filled and Velcro-edged blocks, acting as a television anchorman on a videotape of a nightly newscast, and making music on jug-band instruments such as lids, rubberbands, and jugs. Our preschooler got to apply facepaints and drive the once-active city bus, and she was proud of her accomplishments at the drop-in arts and crafts sessions.

Especially educational is the ongoing Ethnic L.A. exhibit, which teaches kids—in an interactive way—about various Los Angeles ethnic cultures. On one visit, the Japanese-American culture was featured, and our first-grader was taught how to make elaborate Japanese paper dolls. Another permanent exhibit, the Louis B. Mayer Performance Space, focuses on the performing arts. Here you might catch a play featuring young King Arthur, or professional brass musicians dissecting the sound and construction of their instruments, or a Kenbu sword dance.

The museum is geared to kids from 2 to 12, but adults will thoroughly enjoy the experience. In summer the museum is open Monday through Friday from 11:30 a.m. to 5 p.m. and on Saturday and Sunday from 10 a.m. to 5 p.m. The rest of the year it's open on Wednesday and Thursday from 2:30 to 5 p.m. and on Saturday and Sunday from 10 a.m. to 5 p.m. Call about special holiday hours. Admission is $4.50; children under 2 are admitted free. Not stroller-accessible. Fast food available downstairs, except Sundays.

Park in the L.A. Mall garage (the entrance is on Los Angeles Street), at 414 Commercial St. (one block south of the museum on Main Street), or at Union Station on Alameda Street (two blocks north). Street parking is available on weekends.

Little Tokyo

A walk through Little Tokyo is like stepping through a portal into the Far East. Los Angeles has traditionally had many Japanese residents. Little Tokyo, located between Alameda and Los Angeles Streets and 1st and 3rd Streets, is a place where Japanese traditions crystallize for your enjoyment. The area is a collection of Japanese shops and restaurants.

A walk around **Japanese Village Plaza,** on 1st and 2nd Streets between San Pedro and Central (tel. 213/620-8861), is a pleasant way to spend an hour. The plaza area features authentic Japanese shops (as well as American ones) in a distinctly Japanese setting. **Mitsuru Toys** and **Pony Toy Go Round Toy Shop** are of special interest to kids. You might want to make a special stop at **Mikawaya Sweet Shop.**

The **New Otani Hotel & Garden,** 120 S. Los Angeles St., at 1st Street (tel. 213/629-1200, or toll free 800/421-8795, 800/252-0197 in California), is the most dazzling building here. The garden walkways are especially beautiful. If you have a chance, go to the rooftop garden for a peaceful few moments.

Of special interest are Nisei Week and Children's Day in Little Tokyo, during which time there are crafts fairs, performances for children, and fun-runs for kids. For specific information about Children's Day, contact the **Japanese-American Cultural and Community Center** (tel. 213/628-2725); for Nisei Week information, call 213/687-7193. For general questions about the area, contact the **Little Tokyo Business Association,** 244 S. San Pedro St., Room 501, Los Angeles, CA 90012 (tel. 213/620-0570).

New Chinatown

This Asian cultural center is neither as modern nor as clean as Little Tokyo, nor as impressive as its San Francisco counterpart. If things Chinese are important to you, however, just remember that it's a congested, small area. The section is bounded by North Broadway, North Hill Street, Bernard Street, and Sunset Boulevard. The centerpiece is **Mandarin Plaza,** 970 N. Broadway. For seasonal festivals and events, contact the **Chinese Chamber of Commerce,** 978 N. Broadway, Suite 206, Los Angeles, CA 90012 (tel. 213/617-0396).

EXPOSITION PARK:
Exposition Park is a culturally and recreationally rich area. The site of the Los Angeles Memorial Coliseum, the Los Angeles Memorial Sports Arena, the Rose Garden, the California Museum of Science and Industry, the Natural History Museum, and the California Afro-American Museum, it is a place you'll want to spend quite a bit of time.

To get to Exposition Park, take the Santa Monica Freeway (I-10) to the Harbor Freeway (I-110) south and follow the exit signs to the museums.

California Museum of Science and Industry

Most people don't know that the California Museum of Science and Industry, 700 State Dr. (tel. 213/744-7400), is the second-largest science/

technology museum compound in the United States. (The largest is the Smithsonian Institution in Washington, D.C.) But you won't be surprised by that fact once you see the complex of buildings. This is a lively place where kids will want to spend time learning and experimenting.

The museum, with its many exhibit halls, gives new meaning to the word "interactive." Here kids and adults can "talk" with the exhibits, go inside them, move them around, even create with them. And there are so many different kinds of exhibits that each family member is sure to find something that strikes a responsive chord.

As you wander through Exposition Park, you'll see an F-104 Starfighter plane suspended on the outside of one structure. This is the **Aerospace Building.** School-age children just love this place because they can almost touch many of the aircraft and satellites suspended in the air. You can see the *Gemini 11* spacecraft and replicas of *Explorer 1, Sputnik 1, Pioneer 1,* and *Pioneer 5* satellites and the Mars lander—*Viking* Spacecraft. In addition to satellites and spacecraft, it has many actual and model airplanes, including the 1911 Wright brothers Model B aircraft and an air force T-38.

Watch the kids at the interactive exhibits. They love them. There's one in which the children maneuver a model rocket, and another where the kids pull levers and push buttons to experience concepts such as "lift" and "thrust."

The Aerospace Building has a wonderful gift store that has many unique items for children and adults interested in astronomy, aircraft, and space paraphernalia.

Don't miss the nearby **Corwin D. Denney Air and Space Garden,** where a full-size DC-8 and a DC-3 are majestically placed for all to view.

The **Science Wing and Industry Hall,** also known as the Ahmanson Building, is the main exhibit building of the compound. You'll know it by the 18-foot bronze propeller stationed in front of the entrance. This was one of the four propellers used by the *Queen Mary.*

Once you're inside, head for the **Earthquake Exhibit,** where a realistic simulation of a large-magnitude earthquake gives you the feel of what a real temblor is like. There are actually three parts to the exhibit, but this one never fails to dramatize the point. You step up several stairs into a model living room complete with television set, bookcases, and the like. The television is tuned to a local broadcast where a popular weatherman is discussing the climate when he (and you) are interrupted by a large tremor. The platform on which you're standing rocks. Simulated newscasts of the destruction are interrupted by power failures and more small jolts. While the exhibit is realistic enough to bring home reality to the adults, children have a lot of fun but are startled when they feel the first shaking. It's best to warn your little children of what's to come.

The two other sections of the exhibit deal with earthquake preparedness and survival information, and geological information explaining earthquakes and how they happen.

While the Earthquake Exhibit may be a bit frightening to the little kids, be sure to take them to the **Agriculture Exhibit.** Set up like a little barnyard, the central exhibit is the hatching chicks. The chicks hatch every day, drawing excited shrieks from little on-lookers. The older kids like the slot machines, where they learn about the risks farmers face every day. A computer screen tells you if you've had a bad year or a bonanza.

Another delight is the **Technology Hall** with its two popular, not-to-be-missed displays, **Mathematica** and the **Automotive Exhibit.** The latter has driver labs and interactive exhibits that older kids are wild about.

The **Kinsey Hall of Health** is unique in that you can actually get a medical self-checkup. Check yourself for breathing, pulse, and heart rate and nutritional habits, and a computer will give you a health profile.

But the highlight of the hall is the neon-lit "Diner," complete with bar stools and "menus" that indicate the protein, fat, and carbohydrate content of foods. The menus are for imaginary restaurants such as "Hamburger Heaven" (hamburgers and apple pie), "Villa Verona" (pizza, meatball submarine sandwiches), "North China" (eggrolls and wonton soup), and "Coliseum" (frozen yogurt and grilled-cheese sandwiches). You are "served" nutritional information by an outrageous waitress, who interacts with you via a touch-screen video terminal.

Don't leave Exposition Park without seeing the **Mitsubishi IMAX Theater.** The IMAX shows live-action movies on a huge screen, which are shot in such a way that you feel you're almost experiencing the real thing. The sound system (developed by Lucasfilm Ltd., which created *Star Wars*) intensifies the experience. It is incredible, and the movies are usually educational to boot. Young children, although welcome, may not do well. The sound effects are quite loud and can be overwhelming to a 3-year-old. For theater information, call 213/744-2014.

The first of its kind, the **Mark Taper Hall of Economics and Finance** explains, in language all of us can understand, the basic rules of economics and finance. There are over 30 exhibits, controlled by computers, in which you can participate. (There are 60 exhibits overall.)

You might be surprised, but this exhibit hall is one of our favorites, and the kids enjoy it thoroughly. (Be sure they're old enough to read and have a concept of money, though.) Dramatic simulations make it entertaining to learn about the laws of supply and demand, inflation, and many other economic concepts. How about trying your hand at making money at an umbrella stand? You're selling them for $3 each. How will a typhoon affect their price? What about sunny weather? What about figuring out inflation on Coconut Island, where an egg might cost $80 billion? It's like a video arcade about the economy.

The Museum of Science and Industry runs children's science workshops throughout the year (although the summer workshops are each a week long). Registration is by mail only, but you can get on the mailing list or find out about openings by calling 213/744-7440. Open daily except New Year's, Thanksgiving, and Christmas, from 10 a.m. to 5 p.m.

(If you don't want to pack a lunch, there is a McDonald's—with an exhibit —next to the main building.)

California Afro-American Museum

Once part of the Museum of Science and Industry, the CAAM is now located in its own modernistic building (with several exhibit halls and a gift store) at 600 State Dr. (tel. 213/744-7432) in Exposition Park.

While the museum is small, it's worth wandering through because it is one of the few museums that focuses on the talents and contributions of Afro-Americans in the fields of the arts, humanities, sciences, sports, etc. The atrium court sculpture garden is a place where children can feel comfortable speaking in normal tones and wandering through the sculptures of Afro-American artists.

Special, hands-on, very involving workshops are available. Call for details. The museum is open daily from 10 a.m. to 5 p.m. Admission is free.

Museum of Natural History

You'll find the Natural History Museum at 900 Exposition Blvd. (tel. 213/744-3466 or 213/744-3414). The museum's permanent collections include a megamouth shark, the second one ever found, and an exhibit entitled "Chaparral: A Story of Life from Fire." You are taught the importance of chaparral through a fascinating multimedia display. Dinosaurs, most every child's favorite thing "ever," are well represented here, as are "younger" North American and African mammals. An American History gallery and an Olympics gallery will appeal to youngsters above toddler age. But don't leave the little ones at home, because one of the best things about the museum is the **Ralph M. Parsons Discovery Center,** a multisensory space for children 2 years old and up.

Finally there is a place where children can touch, examine, smell, and manipulate the things that are so often behind glass in a museum. Once in the Discovery Center, our kids can't wait to check out a "discovery box." Different boxes offer different educational activities, such as challenging a child to identify sounds made with assorted objects with eyes closed, and allowing a youngster to create a turtle from skeletal bones. Our children also love to try on the costumes from around the world, then touch the taxidermied wild animals, which suddenly look so gentle. This is one of the few places that children can actually touch fossils or the teeth of a full-size polar bear. They get to listen to the ocean through sea shells, use a magnifying glass for a better look at butterflies, and make crayon rubbings of fossils which are embedded in a rock-like wall.

The museum is open Tuesday through Sunday from 10 a.m. to 5 p.m. April through September; the rest of the year Saturday and Sunday from 9 a.m. to 6 p.m. The Discovery Center is open Tuesday through Sunday from 11 a.m. to 3 p.m. year round.

Admission to the museum is $4 for adults, $2 for children 12 to 17 and seniors, $1 for children 5 to 12; under 5, free. The first Tuesday of every month admission is free. Admission to the Discovery Center is free with museum admission.

There is an indoor-outdoor cafeteria in the museum open during museum hours. Park on the street or in the lot off Menlo for $1 (quarters only).

GRIFFITH PARK: Griffith Park is 4,100 acres of wooded park area tucked into the Hollywood Hills. The largest park within the boundaries of any U.S. city, it is over three times as large as San Francisco's Golden Gate Park. The terrain is diverse. Dry foothills, shady little valleys, and wooded areas cover the park that ranges in elevation from 384 feet to 1,600 feet above sea level. Like Los Angeles, Griffith Park is huge and sprawling. Indeed, among its abundant recreational facilities it has something for everyone, including the Griffith Observatory, the Laserium, the Los Angeles Zoo, the Greek Theatre, Travel Town, and myriad other delights. Don't even bother to try to see a lot of it in one day, because you can't make a dent in it. There are over 53 miles of hiking trails and bridle paths, four golf courses, and two overnight camps. In fact, the park is so large that many Los Angeles locals who visit the park regularly are surprised to learn that it has a municipal swimming pool.

The park was given to the city of Los Angeles in 1896 by Col. Griffith J. Griffith, and its natural state is largely preserved today. In later years the Greek Theatre and the Griffith Observatory and Planetarium were added.

Griffith Observatory and Planetarium

Located at 2800 E. Observatory Rd. (tel. 213/664-1191 for recorded information, or 213/664-1181 for further information), the observatory and planetarium are a highlight of any trip to Los Angeles. Fascinating and educational at the same time, the **planetarium theater** with its 75-foot domed ceiling re-creates the skies, taking kids and adults on journeys through space. Serious stargazers and awe-struck children alike watch as the enormous domed ceiling is transformed from nothing to astral heavens with thousands of stars. Your narrator takes you on voyages through these stars to different planets and different eras.

This is best for children over 5 (unless yours are exceptional). While children 5 and over delight as the room gets dark (complete with sunset over the mountains) and the "sky" gets jet-black, setting the stage for the evening stars and a lesson in astronomy, younger ones tend to get scared by the darkness. Our 2-year-old couldn't quite decide whether or not she liked it. Elizabeth would be content for a while, and then, when the music rose or the sky changed in a dramatic way, she'd start to cry and one of us would have to stand with her near the exit, where there was more light. There is one performance each Saturday and Sunday at 1:30 p.m. where children under 5 are admitted. These shows are a little shorter and a little more general. We found the major difference to be that young children are in abundance so we didn't have to worry so much about disturbing other people who may be serious about their astronomy education.

The shows generally last one hour, with several different presentations offered during the year.

Planetarium shows are given in summer Monday through Friday at 1:30, 3, and 8 p.m.; and on Saturday and Sunday at 1:30, 3, 4:30, and 8 p.m. In winter shows are given Tuesday through Friday at 3 and 8 p.m.; and on Saturday and Sunday at 1:30, 3, 4:30, and 8 p.m.; closed Monday. Admission is $3 for adults, $2 for children 5 to 15 and seniors; free for children under 5 (only admitted to the 1:30 p.m. children's show or other special shows on Saturday and Sunday).

The **Hall of Science** has displays as well as interactive exhibits about physical science, astronomy, and geology. The Foucault Pendulum is one of the most fascinating exhibits you're likely to see. You watch as the earth's rotation allows the pendulum to knock down little pegs as it swings. There's also a solar telescope, six-foot globes of the earth and moon, and a working seismograph. (Watch the kids jump in an effort to get the needle to register.) There is also a large telescope you can use on clear evenings from sunset to 10 p.m. when the hall is open.

The Hall of Science is open in summer Sunday through Friday from 12:30 to 10 p.m., and on Saturday from 11:30 a.m. In winter it's open Tuesday through Friday from 2 to 10 p.m., on Saturday from 11:30 a.m., and Sunday from 12:30 p.m.; closed Monday. Admittance to the Hall of Science is free.

Don't miss the bookstore, one of the best for astronomical slides, book starfinders, and souvenirs.

The **Laserium Cosmic Light Concert** (tel. 818/997-3624) is presented at the Observatory. This fantastic light-and-music extravaganza is a favorite of teens and adults who like bold, pulsating music. The performer projects laser imagery on the domed planetarium ceiling (five stories high at the top) to accompany and accentuate the musical beat. Two performances are done to rock music; one is done to classical. (If you have a preference, call ahead and ask.) This isn't an event for little ones. In fact, children under 5 aren't admitted.

Shows are given Tuesday through Thursday at 6:30 and 9:15 p.m., on Friday and Saturday at 6:30, 9:15, and 10:30 p.m., and on Sunday at 6:30 p.m. Get there well ahead of time as it's often crowded. Tickets cost $6 for adults, $5 for children 5 to 16.

To get to the Observatory (located at the north end of Vermont Avenue), take either the Hollywood Freeway (U.S. 101) to the Vermont Avenue exit and go north or take the Golden State Freeway (I-5) to the Los Feliz exit and go west to Vermont Avenue and then north.

Hiking

The best way to start is by calling or writing the **Griffith Park Ranger Visitors Center,** 4730 Crystal Springs Dr., Los Angeles, CA 90027 (tel. 213/665-5188), to get information about group nature walks led by naturalists and for hiking maps of the park. Open from 7 a.m. to 5 p.m. daily.

The **Fern Canyon Nature Trail** is a good one for children. Trails start to the northwest of the Visitors Center, but there aren't any trailhead signs. You can hike up about a mile and turn around where you'll see the flora and fauna of the park. Located near the merry-go-round and large grassy areas, this might be a good beginning trail if you're unsure as to how your children will do on a hike.

Rangers also recommend the **Mount Hollywood Trail.** Start at the back of the Observatory parking lot. Take it up to the top of Mount Hollywood (about a mile). There's a constant incline for about a quarter of a mile, but nothing a child can't handle. From the top you can see the Hollywood sign, the Observatory, and the entire L.A. basin. On a clear day you can see the ocean and Catalina Island.

The Rides

Young children love spending the day in Griffith Park enjoying the ponies and riding on the miniature train, the carousel, and the brand-new Simulator, which gives them an opportunity to show how brave they are.

The **Griffith Park & Southern Railroad,** the Simulator, and the pony and wagon rides are located on the east side of Crystal Springs Drive (in the park), near Los Feliz Boulevard (tel. 213/664-6788 for the railroad and Simulator, 213/664-3266 for the pony rides).

The miniature open-air train runs on a 1¼-mile track through an environment that makes junior riders feel like they are actually taking a little trip. It runs year round, weekdays from 10 a.m. to 5 p.m. and weekends from 10 a.m. "till the crowds leave." Adults are charged $1.50; children under 13, $1.25; those under 19 months, free.

The **Simulator** takes you on a 4½-minute ride that imitates a ride on a roller coaster, then an airplane. Children must be over 2 years old, and those under 5 must ride with an adult. Same hours as the train. All tickets cost $1.25.

The **pony rides** provide something for everyone. Little children ride in a circle on ponies tied to a stationary hookup. Older kids can ride around a separate track on their own. All children must be under 100 pounds to ride the ponies. There are also wagon rides, for those kids not yet too keen about horses, that take the children on a short ride around a track. The pony rides are open year round: during the summer, daily from 10 a.m. to 5 p.m.; in winter, the same hours, but closed Monday (except on Monday holidays). Pony and wagon rides are $1 per child. (You'll also find the stationary pony ride in Travel Town).

The **Merry-Go-Round** is far enough away from the miniature train that you'll want to drive to it. Find it just off Griffith Park Drive, near the main concession stand (tel. 213/665-3051). Our young children love to ride this antique carousel over and over again. In summer it runs weekdays from 11 a.m. to 5 p.m., till 7 p.m. on weekends. In winter it's open weekends only, from 11 a.m. till dark. Rides are 75¢ for everyone.

Travel Town, on Zoo Drive, near Griffith Park Drive (tel. 213/662-5874), is a small outdoor museum of transportation vehicles. Some of the most interesting sights are the old Hawaiian narrow-gauge sugar train, the 110-ton Union Pacific steam engine, and 14 other locomotives. Youngsters love to look at the old fire engines. They are also introduced to the yellow streetcars that once ran in Los Angeles. There is a miniature steam engine here that goes around a one-mile track. Travel Town is open weekdays from 10 a.m. to 5 p.m. and on weekends and holidays from 10 a.m. to 6 p.m. Admission to Travel Town is free. Fares for the miniature train ride are $2 for adults, $1.50 for children 2 to 13; under 2, free.

Other Activities

The **Griffith Park Recreation Center** has a **swimming pool** that is open from mid-June through mid-September. Call for hours and fees (tel. 213/665-4372 for pool information, 213/666-2703 for the Recreation Center).

For information about the **tennis courts,** you can call 213/662-7772 for the Riverside Drive courts, 213/664-3521 for the Vermont Avenue courts, and 213/661-5318 for the Griffith Park courts. For reservations, call 213/520-1010.

For information about **golf courses,** call 213/663-2555 for the Wilson/

Harding Starters office, 213/665-2011 for the Roosevelt course, and 213/663-7758 for the Los Feliz course.

Los Angeles Zoo

Actually located within Griffith Park, the Los Angeles Zoo, 5333 Zoo Dr. (tel. 213/666-4650), has over 2,000 different animals and birds, and about 500 different species. Sitting on 113 acres, the zoo is divided "zoogeographically." This means that the animals are divided into the areas (the five continents) in which they live. With a zoo this large (and hilly), it's a good idea first to sit down with the zoo map and chart out what you want to see. During the summer, get an early start because the zoo tends to get hot and smoggy. Plan to spend at least half a day here, probably more with older children.

This is southern California, remember, and the zoo is not to be outdone by all the theme parks and attractions surrounding it. It, too, has special shows. There is the World of Birds, Animals and You, Meet the Elephants, Trainer Tidbits, and the Zoopeteers. It's a good idea to plan around those events when mapping out your day. During the weekends, and daily during summer, you can watch the keepers with their animals—polar and spectacled bears, monkeys and orangutans, elephants, sea lions, and gorillas. It's a treat!

Toddlers especially like the Aquatic section, and school-age boys like Andrew are elated over the Reptile House. But for kids of all ages, don't miss the animal rides. It's an experience your children are sure to remember!

At the time of this writing a 2½-acre children's zoo was under construction and due to be finished in early summer of 1989. The focus is on the wildlife of southern California—the shoreline, the cave, the desert at night, the meadow, the mountain, the hacienda barnyard, and the nursery. There will also be theater for children's entertainment involving animals. There will be many interactive exhibits where children can be eye-to-eye with certain animals. In the nursery, there will be an exhibit that asks the kids to match mother and baby, and an exhibit with artificial eggs that hatch by pressing artificial levers and watch what "hatches."

Open daily except Christmas. Winter hours are 10 a.m. to 5 p.m.; in summer, till 6 p.m. Admission is $4.50 for adults (13 and over), $2.50 for children 2 to 12, $3.50 for seniors, and free for children under 2. Stroller rentals are $1.50.

HOLLYWOOD: Entertainment capital of the world; glitter capital of the

world. Hollywood is a state of mind, where dreams come true. You've probably heard all the clichés, and now you want to see the real thing. Well, the Hollywood of your dreams is no more—it's a bit tacky, a little "under the weather," and certainly not the place for an evening stroll with the family. But everyone who comes to Los Angeles must see Hollywood. So put on your blinders, ignore the shabby parts, and take a daytime stroll down Hollywood Boulevard.

Beginning at Hollywood Boulevard and La Brea Avenue and walking east, you'll come to **Mann's Chinese Theater,** 6925 Hollywood Blvd. (tel. 213/464-8111), where Mary Pickford and Douglas Fairbanks initiated the footprint ceremony in 1927, the year the theater was built by Sid Grauman. From then on, whenever a movie premiered there, the stars embedded their foot- and handprints in the cement. One of the most ornate movie palaces of the time, the building was decorated with rare Chinese artifacts, authentic temple bells, and pagodas. Kids love to try to match their footprints with those of the stars.

One block east is the **Hollywood Wax Museum,** at 6767 Hollywood Blvd. (tel. 213/462-8860). If you don't see a live celebrity on your trip, at least you can see your favorites duplicated in wax. The museum is open on Friday and Saturday from 10 a.m. to 2 a.m., and Sunday through Thursday till midnight. Admission is $7 for adults, $5 for children 6 to 12 and seniors; under 6, free.

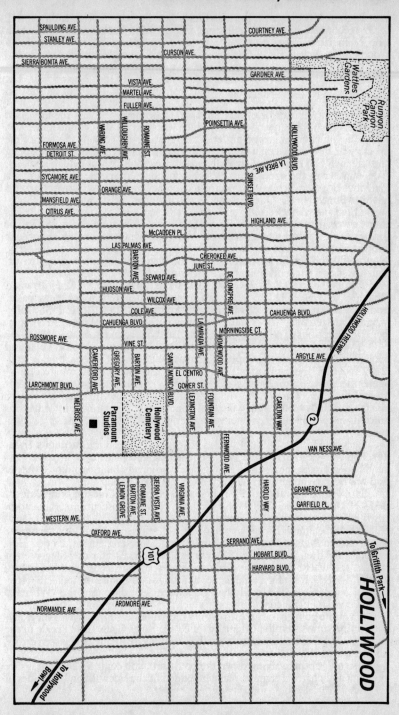

Right across the street, the Max Factor Building, 1666 Highland Ave. (tel. 213/463-6668), houses a retail store and the **Max Factor Museum,** which opened in 1935. What more perfect place for a beauty museum than Hollywood? Stars such as Judy Garland, Claudette Colbert, Rita Hayworth, and Marlene Dietrich attended the museum's opening. Your girls who have just discovered makeup will see how it was used on the stars of the '20s and '30s. The museum is open Monday through Saturday from 10 a.m. to 4 p.m.; admission is free.

Practically next door on the Hollywood Boulevard side is the **Egyptian Theater,** at 6708 Hollywood Blvd., which was built by Sid Grauman in 1922, before he built the Chinese Theater. The Egyptian was actually the first of the spectacular movie palaces, with ornately carved columns and sphinxes flanking the screen. *Robin Hood,* Hollywood's first movie première, was held there.

Walk across the street about half a block and you'll see the arch identifying the **Janes House,** where you'll find an office of the **Los Angeles Convention and Visitors Bureau** in the Queen Anne Victorian home in the rear, at 6541 Hollywood Blvd., Los Angeles, CA 90028 (tel. 213/461-4213). The Janes House was a one-owner private residence from 1903 until its restoration in 1985. The Janeses made it into a schoolhouse for a time, and educated the children of such motion-picture pioneers as Douglas Fairbanks, Jesse Lasky, and Noah Berry. Now you'll find helpful brochures, maps, and even complimentary tickets to various TV shows. Open Monday through Saturday from 9 a.m. to 5 p.m.

Across the street is **Hollywood Toys & Costumes, Inc.,** 6562 Hollywood Blvd. (tel. 213/465-3119), a treasure trove of children's costumes, wigs, masks, and toys. Backtrack one block west to **Larry Edmund's Book Store,** 6658 Hollywood Blvd. (tel. 213/463-3273), where you'll discover one of the most comprehensive collections of movie- and theater-related books and posters.

If you stand at the corner of Hollywood and Vine, just a few blocks east, and look north, you'll spot the **Capitol Records Building,** at 1750 N. Vine St. (tel. 213/462-6252), completed in 1956 in the shape of a stack of 45-rpm records—remember those? In the lobby you'll see displays of gold records (open weekdays from 9 a.m. to 5:30 p.m.). As you're looking up this way, you can't help but see the famous **Hollywood sign,** which has gone through so many transformations since it was put up in 1923 to advertise Hollywoodland, a real estate development.

Back on Hollywood Boulevard, a little east of Vine, is the **Pantages Theater.** Pop your head in, if you can, to see the magnificent art deco interior. Currently a legitimate theater, the Pantages was originally built as a movie theater and was host to the Academy Awards from 1949 to 1959.

Hollywood has also given us **Roscoe's House of Chicken and Waffles,** 1514 N. Gower St. (tel. 213/466-7453), a Hollywood institution serving nothing but those two dishes; **C. C. Brown's,** 7007 Hollywood Blvd. (tel. 213/464-9725), which, although more than 75 years old, still serves the hot-fudge sundae it first created; **Musso and Frank's,** Hollywood's oldest restaurant, at 6667 Hollywood Blvd. (tel. 213/467-7788), where Hollywood's famous writers used to gather, and where important people still stop for a bite to eat; and the **Brown Derby,** 1628 N. Vine St., at the corner of Hollywood Boulevard (tel. 213/469-5151), once frequented by Hollywood's legends of film. (See the "Where to Eat" section for detailed information.)

If you are going to be in town during the winter season, watch for the **Hollywood Christmas Parade,** originally called the Santa Claus Lane Parade in the early 1920s. It has evolved into one of the grandest city parades and is seen on TV all over the world.

As you've been walking down the boulevard, you couldn't help but notice the pink and charcoal terrazzo stars imbedded in the sidewalk on both sides of

Hollywood Boulevard between Sycamore and Gower Streets, and on Vine Street between Sunset and Yucca. Nearly every month since 1961 the Hollywood Chamber of Commerce has honored a movie star on the **Walk of Fame** with a ceremony dedicating his or her star. Call 213/469-8311 for information on the next ceremony.

A short ride in the car will take you to the other sights Hollywood claims as its own. **Paramount Studios,** for instance, is located at 5555 Melrose Ave. This famous studio, in business as Paramount since the 1920s, is still producing movies, making it the longest continuously operating film studio in Los Angeles.

Hollywood also claims the **Barnsdall Art Park,** 4800 Hollywood Blvd. (tel. 213/660-4254), which houses the **Los Angeles Municipal Art Gallery.** If the kids aren't satisfied with those exhibits, walk a few yards away to the **Junior Art Gallery,** where there's always something of interest on display. Both galleries are open Tuesday through Sunday from 12:30 to 5 p.m. Entrance to the Municipal Gallery is $1 for adults, free for children under 13. Admission to the Junior Arts Gallery is free. If you're around on a Sunday (except in June), you're invited to Sunday Open Sunday (tel. 213/485-4474), Barnsdall's Junior Arts Center free family art workshops, where the sessions are open to all age groups (Sunday from 2 to 4 p.m.).

STUDIO TOURS / TV TICKETS: One of the reasons people come to southern California is to see the stars. And one way to do it is by attending an audience-participation TV show. Some shows even allow children. Another way is by taking a studio tour, all of which allow children.

ABC-TV tickets, 4151 Prospect, Hollywood, CA 90027 (tel. 213/557-4396), are available for this network's taped shows by either showing up in person or sending in for tickets with a self-addressed stamped envelope as far in advance as possible. You can pick up tickets one week in advance of a show. The minimum age is 14. Tickets are at no charge.

Tickets for many different network shows and specials are available through **Audiences Unlimited** (tel. 818/506-0043). You can pick up tickets at the Fox Television Center, 5746 Sunset Blvd., Hollywood, on the Van Ness side of the street, off the Hollywood Freeway (U.S. 101) at the Sunset Boulevard exit. Tickets are on a first-come, first-served basis, and are available six days in advance of showtime. The office is open weekdays from 8:30 a.m. to 6:30 p.m.

To order tickets by mail for future shows, send a self-addressed, stamped envelope to Audiences Unlimited, 100 Universal City Plaza, Bldg. 153, Universal City, CA 91608. Expect a two- to three-week response. All tickets are complimentary.

The **Burbank Studios VIP Tour** is a basic behind-the-scenes look at video tapings, television programs, and movies in production. It's located at 4000 Warner Blvd., Burbank, CA 91522 (tel. 818/954-1744). Tours are limited to 15 people, and children under 10 are not permitted. You never know what you're going to see when you sign up, as guides depend on daily production schedules and the whims of various directors. You might see something in production from Warner Bros., Columbia Pictures, or independent production companies. In addition to watching film-making in progress, visitors see where sets are made and visit sound studios where sound effects are created and where music is recorded for shows. No doubt this tour will be interesting for teens infatuated with the production side of the movie industry.

Tours are offered two times a day (sometimes four, depending on how much production is going on), Monday through Friday. There are no tours on weekends or holidays. Tickets are by reservation only. It is best to call one week in advance, but reservations can be arranged up to 60 days ahead. You can also make reservations to eat in the Blue Room (available only to those who take the morning tour), which is the studio commissary. You must make your dining reservations at the time you make the tour reservations. Tickets for the tour are $22 per person, adult or child.

CBS-TV tickets are available at 7800 Beverly Blvd., Los Angeles, CA 90036 (tel. 213/852-4002). You don't need to write for tickets, as they are available on the morning of the show. If you do write for tickets, you must do so eight weeks in advance. Call for show taping schedules. Minimum age is 14. No charge for tickets.

Fox TV tickets can be ordered through Audiences Unlimited, 100 Universal City Plaza, Building 153, Universal City, CA 91608 (tel. 818/506-0067). Enclose a self-addressed stamped envelope for tickets, and expect a two- to three-week response. Tickets are free.

Hollywood **on Location,** 8644 Wilshire Blvd., Beverly Hills (tel. 213/659-9165), offers an interesting way for the entire family to get a look at the stars. You purchase a package which lists what shows, movies, or videotapings are in production that day, where the scenes are being shot, which stars are expected to be there, and what the hours of shooting are. It also includes a detailed map to lead you to the specific locations—down to the details of getting to a scene being shot in an alley. The list is updated daily, and you can look it over (without addresses, of course) before you decide to buy it. Approximately 35 listings are included every day.

We do not recommend this for very young children, as there can be a lot of driving around, lots of waiting for stars to emerge from trailers, and the production people won't like it if junior yells out "I have to go to the bathroom" in the middle of a difficult shot. It's probably best to save this for children 9 years old and up; teens (and preteens) will love you if that day a music video is being shot.

You won't find many people in your way at a shooting, unless it's in the heart of downtown or Beverly Hills. The locals are so used to scenes being shot all over town that they're unaffected by them.

Lists are available Monday through Friday, beginning at 9:30 a.m. Reservations are suggested: pick up the list at the Beverly Hills office. The package costs $29 per carload. No credit cards.

KCET-TV, at 4401 Sunset Blvd., Hollywood, CA 90027 (tel. 213/667-9242), is Los Angeles's public television station. This technical tour lasts 1½ hours, and includes a visit to production areas and a look at lighting, cameras, stages, telecine (where tapes off satellite are stored), and the master control room. Guides tell you about the history of the lot, which is the old Allied Artists studio, but you won't see shows being filmed. This tour requires children to be a minimum of 10 years old. When lots of children are on the tour, guides will speak to their level—they are very used to groups of schoolchildren taking the tour. Write for your reservations one week in advance. There is no charge for the tour, which is offered on Tuesday and Thursday, usually at 10 a.m. Exceptions can be made.

The **NBC Studio Tour** takes place at 3000 W. Alameda Ave., Burbank, CA 91523 (tel. 818/840-3537). There are three ways to visit the NBC Television Studios. One tour is specially designed for children in Grades 1 through 6 and is only available on selected days in the months of May and November. During this two-hour tour, kids will be able to join in a simulated TV production. Your child might even be selected to play a character, hold a cue card, or be an extra. Youngsters are taken through the Sound and Special Effects Center as in the regular tour, but this one is geared to children's questions and answers. All the kids on the tour receive an NBC Peacock jacket patch and a television communication award certificate.

Reservations are necessary. Call or write about this year's tour dates to: Children's Tour, NBC Studio Tours, 3000 W. Alameda Ave., Burbank, CA 91523 (tel. 818/840-3555). Ticket prices are $5.50 for adults, $4.50 for children 5 to

14; under 5, free (no patch or certificate for them). Tickets must be prepaid. Parking is free, and there are picnic areas in Buena Vista Park across from the studio.

Another way to see NBC is to take a studio tour, which is open to all age groups. In this 75-minute guided walking tour, you are taken to a mini-studio built just for the tour with a simulated control booth, a special videotape presentation, and a chance to see yourselves on television. Next you go backstage where, depending on what's going on that day, you might see the wardrobe department, prop and set storage, the set of "The Tonight Show," the KNBC News studio, and a closeup look at the Skypath satellite broadcast system (the setup that transmits programs to NBC affiliates all over the nation). Then you'll go to the Sound and Special Effects Center, where a few members of the group will be chosen to participate in something relating to special effects, and will learn the "secrets" of those special effects. In the sound effects center, you'll learn about the buzzers in the game shows and how audience applause is created.

No reservations are necessary for the tour. It's offered weekdays every half hour from 8:30 a.m. to 4 p.m., on Saturday from 10 a.m. to 4 p.m., and on Sunday from 10 a.m. to 2 p.m.; no tours on major holidays. Pick up tickets at the ticket counter at the Alameda address above. The office is open Monday through Friday from 8 a.m. to 4 p.m. and on Saturday and Sunday from 9:30 a.m. to 4 p.m.

Admission costs $6 for adults, $4 for children 5 to 14; children 4 and under, free.

You can also write for tickets to join the audience of an NBC television show. Age minimums vary by show: the youngest age is 9 for "Punky Brewster"; for "The Tonight Show," the age minimum is 16. At this writing (because you never know when a show will be canceled) the NBC audience shows include "Classic Concentration," "Golden Girls," "Punky Brewster," "Sale of the Century," "Scrabble," "The Tonight Show," "Wheel of Fortune," and various specials. Shows tape at different times, and "Golden Girls" tapes at a different studio. You can write or call for schedules. For information on specials, call 818/464-4300.

Here's how to get tickets for shows: If you live within a 150-mile radius of Burbank, contact: Tickets, NBC Television Network, 3000 W. Alameda Ave., Burbank, CA 91523 (tel. 818/840-3537). Include the name of the show you want, the number of tickets, and the preferred date, if any. Include a self-addressed, stamped envelope. The ticket limit is four for "The Tonight Show." If you're out of the 150-mile radius, you will receive a "Guest Letter" which can be exchanged at the NBC Ticket Counter. Write well in advance for these, as they only hold a certain number of tickets for out-of-towners. Show up early on the day you requested for the best ticket selection. "The Tonight Show" tickets are available only on the day of the show at the Ticket Counter. *Remember:* Holding a ticket does not guarantee admission to a show—it guarantees you a place in line. Be sure to arrive early for seating, as seats are given on a first-come, first-served basis.

Ticket Counter hours: weekdays from 8 a.m. to 5 p.m., on Saturday from 10 a.m. to 4 p.m., and on Sunday from 10 a.m. to 2 p.m. Tickets to all NBC shows are complimentary. If you've got time to spend in L.A. and aren't fussy about what show you see, there are a limited number of tickets made available on the day of a particular show at the NBC Ticket Counter.

The NBC lot also has a retail store that sells licensed merchandise from such shows as "Alf" and "Family Ties," and a café that sells snacks.

Paramount Studios, 860 N. Gower St., Hollywood (tel. 213/468-5575), offers free tickets for tapings of "Family Ties," "Cheers," "Amen," and "Brothers." It's very difficult to get tickets for "Cheers" or "Family Ties," and those tickets can't be sent for. Instead, you must arrive early the same day as the taping

—like 6 a.m. Write for other tickets two weeks in advance, and enclose a self-addressed, stamped envelope. Kids must be 16 or older to attend a taping. The ticket office is open Monday through Friday from 9:30 a.m. to 4 p.m.

Paramount has recently started a tour that covers the historic and current aspects of this celebrated studio. You see the back lot, sound stages, and props from "Happy Days," "Family Ties," and other well-known shows. It's a two-hour tour, best for teens on up, although the minimum age for the tour is 10. When a large number of people sign up, they walk for the two hours; small groups get to ride on a tram. Tours are offered Monday through Friday at 11 a.m. and 2 p.m. Sign up for the tour at the ticket office half an hour to an hour before departure time. Tickets are $10 per person, adult or child.

UNIVERSAL STUDIOS: The world's largest—and busiest—motion-picture and television studio is Universal Studios, at 100 Universal City Plaza, located off the Hollywood Freeway (U.S. 101) at either the Universal Center or Lankershim Boulevard exits (tel. 818/508-9600). Quintessential Hollywood, Universal Studios Tours thrills nearly everyone over the age of 4. Step onto this studio lot and you're stepping into Hollywood-behind-the-scenes.

Like all sightseeing venues, there are certain tricks that make your visit much more pleasant. If this is your first visit, plan to spend at least five to seven hours. We've been to Universal many times, and several of them have been in extremes of weather—very hot, smoggy summer days and bone-chilling (for southern California) windy days. (At night, even in the summer, expect it to be very cool.) So consider what you'll need to make yourself comfortable. In the summer, be sure to bring plenty of sunscreen, sun visors, and little hats for the kids. In the winter, bring warm jackets and layer clothes (it may only be 60°, but the wind on the hill really picks up). Many of the attractions are outdoors, so you'll want to be comfortable.

The **Guided Tram Tour** is a 2½-hour open-air tram excursion through the back lot of Universal. Not only do you get backstage knowledge about the making of movies and television, but visitors are also treated to an array of special-effects creations. The tram travels through the 420-acre back lot that has more than 500 outdoor sets. You'll see façades from *The Sting, Back to the Future,* and "Simon and Simon."

Visitors are treated to an encounter with the enormous 30-foot King Kong (the world's largest animated figure) and Jaws, and also witness the Battle of Galactica (a laser battle), the Collapsing Bridge (from TV's "Bionic Woman"), the parting of the Red Sea, and sound effects from "Miami Vice." This adventurous tour is certainly worth the time, but it's difficult to predict how your youngsters may react to some of the special effects. Enormous King Kong may be frightening to toddlers, although some very young kids love it; others might get scared by Jaws. The spinning Ice Cave is another special effect that alarms some young children. Most children over the age of 5 or 6 delight in almost all of it. There are bathroom breaks. In addition, if partway into the tour you find that your child is having too much trouble, talk with the driver. The tram can be stopped at any time and standby vans will take you back to the central area.

Entertainment Center is the unguided portion of the tour that offers live amphitheater shows. All shows are 15 to 20 minutes in length and are timed so you can see one after another (but on crowded days you may have to line up early, so consider that when you try to schedule viewing the shows).

The Miami Vice Action Spectacular is a live-action show set in an elaborate scene where doubles for Crocket and Stubbs perform amazing stunts amid hi-tech special effects. Set in the Caribbean, the special effects are truly amazing, including aerial, underwater, and pyrotechnic tricks. While our little Elizabeth (age 2) didn't like the noise, the fact that the show is in a large open-air theater diminishes the intensity of the stunts and allows parents with fearful tots to get up and stand on the side so as not to disturb other spectators. We always try to take seats on the aisle, just in case a little one needs to be taken out or comforted.

The Adventures of Conan: A Sword and Sorcery Spectacular is a different story. The special effects are tremendous (in fact, when the show premiered it was acknowledged as the most ambitious and complicated at the studios), costing $4.4 million. This one is really for older children, teens, and adults. We were astonished at some of the beautiful effects created, such as laser-sword play, fireballs, and a fire-breathing dragon, but we saw several kids under 7 leave with their parents because it was too intense. The theater is enclosed, which makes for spectacular effects—waterfall and smoky sorcery—but it's loud and the story is a little difficult for young kids to follow. Watch Conan's dramatic transformation and you'll want to come back again just to see how it happens.

The Star Trek Adventure, a 30-minute show, allows guests to participate in a production of "Star Trek." Using sets, special effects, music, and costumes from the original shows, 29 members of the audience act out a script from a "Star Trek" adventure. They play members of the *Enterprise* crew, Klingons, and other aliens. Taped, edited, and interspersed with new audio material starring Shatner, a seven-minute feature is produced and shown to the audience.

The Western Stunt Show, in an open-air arena, re-creates the Old West. This time, cowboy stunts and gunplay are displayed, demonstrating how actors are able to do what they do on screen. It's a fun show and good for the whole family. Warn the kids about the gunshots, though—they're loud and there are several of them.

Young kids love the **Animal Actors Stage,** where trainers show how they get animals to perform. Older children like the **Screen Test Comedy Theater,** where selected members of the audience "audition." There is one kids' show daily—try to get into that one. Teens love **Soundtraks,** a music-video facility that allows visitors to star in their own music video.

Don't miss **Streets of the World,** actual shooting sets that were used in some of the all-time great movies. See Baker Street (from Sherlock Holmes), the Moulin Rouge, Mel's Diner (from *American Graffiti*) and Faber College (from *Animal House*).

Special live performers include cartoon and science-fiction characters such as Captain Power (of "Captain Power and the Soldiers of the Future") and He-Man and She-Ra (of "Masters of the Universe"). They'll gladly sign autographs for the kids.

Outdoor eating areas abound and offer a choice of Italian, Mexican, and American goodies. If you want regular restaurant fare and would prefer to eat indoors, you can choose from **Tony Roma's** (barbecued ribs, chicken, and sandwiches), **Victoria Station** (prime rib, fish, sandwiches, and salad bar), and **Fung Lum** (Chinese cuisine) (see the "Where to Eat" section for details).

Universal Studios Tour operates daily except Thanksgiving and Christmas. Summer and holiday hours are 9 a.m. to 5 p.m.; the rest of the year, 10 a.m. to 3:30 p.m. on weekdays and 9:30 a.m. to 3:30 p.m. on weekends. Admission is $19 for adults (including children over 11), $14 for children 3 to 11 and seniors; children under 3 are free. A celebrity season pass (unlimited visits for one year) costs $9 over the one-time admission fee. Parking is $3. Your admission price entitles you to see all the shows in the Entertainment Center and to go on the 2½-hour Tram Tour.

MID-WILSHIRE / FAIRFAX / MELROSE AVENUE: These areas, roughly bordered by Wilshire Boulevard to the south, Melrose Avenue to the north, La Cienega Boulevard to the west, and La Brea Avenue to the east, are seeing much of the new boutiques, restaurants, and hotels which have been going

up at breakneck speed. **Mid-Wilshire,** home to the County Museum of Art, the Craft and Folk Art Museum, and the La Brea Tar Pits, was once a very important retail center of town. It is beginning its renaissance. The **Fairfax** area, where you'll find the CBS Studios and the Farmers Market, is also home to much of L.A.'s older Eastern European population. While Fairfax Avenue, between Beverly Boulevard and Melrose Avenue, has been spruced up with new storefronts and a giant mural, it still retains its open-air fish and fruit stands, Hungarian and Israeli restaurants, kosher meat markets, and numerous bakeries. **Melrose Avenue,** an exciting place for a walk with the kids (preteens and teenagers will love this street), has been written up in newspapers all over the country as Los Angeles's trendiest section of town. Non-Equity (99-seat) live-performance theaters, clothing boutiques, casual and chic restaurants, funky stores, and antique shops line the avenue from just east of La Brea, west to La Cienega.

Los Angeles County Museum of Art

Located at 5905 Wilshire Blvd. in the Mid-Wilshire District (tel. 213/857-6000), the Los Angeles County Museum complex, adjacent Hancock Park, and the La Brea Tar Pits / George C. Page Museum make for a day of excitement and culture.

We usually go to one of the museum galleries, have a snack or lunch, let the kids romp in the park (or watch the mimes and musicians), and then spend another hour at the Page.

Let's back up a bit.

Opened in 1965 with three buildings, the Los Angeles County Museum of Art has almost doubled in size. Today it is the largest art museum in the west. The original structure is the **Ahmanson Building,** which houses the permanent art collection that includes American and European paintings and sculpture, decorative arts, costumes and textiles, and Far Eastern, Indian, and Southeast Asian art. The new **Robert O. Anderson Building** is the place for modern and contemporary art. The **Pavilion for Japanese Art** has screens and scrolls as well as paintings. The **Frances and Armand Hammer Building** has special exhibitions. And, the **Times-Mirror Central Court** is a cool, partially covered plaza with a most unusual fountain that the children adore. The new outdoor sculpture garden also is a lovely place to stroll.

If you don't want to bring lunch or go elsewhere, there are two cafés where you can lunch or snack.

Family programs are offered the last Sunday of the month for children 5 to 12 and their parents. There are programs for younger children as well. Call 213/857-6108 for details.

Open Tuesday through Friday from 10 a.m. to 5 p.m., on Saturday and Sunday till 6 p.m.; closed Monday and Thanksgiving, Christmas, and New Year's Days. Admission is $5.50 for adults, $4.50 for students over 12 and seniors, $3 for children.

To get to the museum, take the Santa Monica Freeway (I-10) to Fairfax Avenue. Go north to Wilshire Boulevard and then go right. Or take the Hollywood Freeway (U.S. 101) to the Santa Monica Boulevard exit and go west to Fairfax Avenue. Take a left on Wilshire Boulevard. From Beverly Hills and West L.A., go east on Wilshire. It's just east of Fairfax Avenue. Parking is available at meters on the street or in nearby lots.

George C. Page Museum of La Brea Discoveries

One of our favorite attractions, the **George C. Page Museum,** 5801 Wilshire Blvd. (tel. 213/857-6311 or 213/936-2230), and the **La Brea Tar Pits** has one of the largest deposits of Ice Age mammals and birds in the world. Kids can see displays where optical illusions "change" the skeleton of a mammal into a ferocious saber-toothed tiger, and another skeleton—the "La Brea Woman"—seems to come to life before their eyes. They experience the sticky substance of asphalt by trying to pull large poles out of the matter and see—close up—just how large an Imperial Mammoth was.

Over the last 40,000 years, animals became trapped in what is now called the La Brea Tar Pits. These pits were found by the first people who wandered this part of the world, and again by the first overland explorers in 1769, who saw bubbling pools of asphalt.

But the first American who owned the land, Henry Hancock, didn't think too much about the bones he found when he was quarrying the area. He thought they were just cows and local animals. Later, paleontologists realized these were Ice Age animals. In 1912 George Allen Hancock, Henry's son, gave the Museum of Natural History the rights and jurisdiction over the digging and excavation of the bones. In 1918 he deeded the 23-acre park to the county of Los Angeles.

Some 60 years later George C. Page built the museum so the animals "could have a home," and gave the museum to the county. The Page is a working museum. Visitors stand mesmerized as they watch careful workers behind glass sorting and dusting the delicate bones and fragments.

Even today you'll see ponds of the bubbling material. There is a major dig in the middle of the park, called Pit 91. This excavation is one of the richest, allowing paleontologists to recover hundreds of thousands of specimens over the years since the excavation began. You can watch them work from a viewing station (hours vary). This is the only place like it in North America.

Free one-hour park tours for the general public are given every day, Tuesday through Sunday (weather permitting). Call for times and meeting place. These tours go to the excavation site. There is also a general museum tour on Saturday and Sunday at 11:30 a.m.

Call for special tours (tel. 213/857-6306 after 1 p.m.). Two movies explain various aspects of the museum and archeology. The museum is open Tuesday through Sunday from 10 a.m. to 5 p.m. Admission is $4 for adults, $2 for students and seniors over 62, $1 for children 5 to 12; those 4 and under get in free with their parents. Tours and museum are fine for strollers.

The Craft and Folk Art Museum

The Craft and Folk Art Museum, 5814 Wilshire Blvd. (tel. 213/937-5544 for recorded information), is a very small museum that pays tribute to the ethnic diversity of Los Angeles and southern California. It has rotating exhibits of traditional folk arts and crafts. The museum is located across the street from the Los Angeles County Museum of Art and the George C. Page Museum (La Brea Tar Pits). It's so small that even if the kids aren't particularly interested in the specific exhibit, the colors and textures of the displays and the giftshop will keep them occupied long enough so that you can enjoy the display.

If you're in town during the end of October, call for information about the amazing Festival of Masks sponsored by the museum. The museum also hosts monthly family programs held on Sunday evenings from 5:30 to 7:30 p.m. They may include storytelling, art, or folk music. Craft classes are also available from time to time. Call for information and reservations (tel. 213/934-3082).

Farmers Market

It's hard to believe that 3rd Street and Fairfax Avenue, home to the Los Angeles Farmers Market (tel. 213/933-9211), was once a vacant field on the *edge* of Los Angeles. But that was the case in 1934 when 18 farmers set up their stalls to try to make a living during the Depression.

Today the Farmers Market is made up of more than 150 individually owned businesses. You can take the children here and walk through the various food stalls and stores. Locals love to eat in the open-air dining area, where you can choose from all types of ethnic food for breakfast, lunch, or early dinner from more than 25 kitchens. It's also a good spot just to stop and have a sundae or other afternoon treat. If you go in the morning, don't miss **Bob's Coffee & Donuts,** stall 450 (tel. 213/933-8929), for possibly the best donuts in town. You'll also find **Du-Par's** here for indoor, sit-down dining (see the "Where to Eat" section).

Visitors go crazy over the fresh fruit and vegetables displayed in the stands. This is also a popular place to get gift-wrapped packages of dried fruits and nuts. Many visitors send oranges, grapefruit, and other seasonal fruit back to their homes from here. There's even a good-sized supermarket, **Alexander's,** stall 150 (tel. 213/936-2596), for diapers and other necessary items to take back to the hotel.

Most of the retail stores here are tourist stops. But **David Orgell,** stall 150-38 (tel. 213/936-2426), has some excellent prices on silver and crystal giftware; **Kip's Toyland,** stall 150-2 (tel. 213/939-8334), is a small toy store with some nice selections for those playthings you left at home; there's a **B. Dalton,** stall 1026 (tel. 213/936-7266), for adult and children's books; and the **Paper Shop,** stall 150-5 (tel. 213/935-4938), is a great store for postcards, stationery, and stickers for the kids. No doubt you won't be able to keep the kids away from **"Mickey" Mania,** stall 710 (tel. 213/931-6781), for all sorts of Mickey Mouse–inspired clothes and accessories. Others will like the **Rock 'n' Roll Connection,** stall 140-R (tel. 213/935-8432), which specializes in fan club and concert merchandise. There's also a small post office located around the corner from David Orgell.

In summer the Farmers Market is open Monday through Saturday from 9 a.m. to 7:30 p.m. and on Sunday from 10 a.m. to 6 p.m.; in winter, Monday through Saturday from 9 a.m. to 6:30 p.m. and on Sunday from 10 a.m. to 6 p.m.

The Trolley

If you're looking for something to do for a short time with very young children, take them for a ride on the **Fairfax Trolley** (tel. 213/666-7990). This cute little green-and-orange trolley, with its wooden seats and Grandma and Grandpa passengers, takes you through the Fairfax District, by the Pacific Design Center, Farmers Market, and the Beverly Center. It goes down Melrose Avenue, where you can get off and shop in the fun boutiques, or stop in at the Los Angeles County Art Museum. All these stops depend on which line you take.

The trolley runs about every 15 minutes from 9 a.m. to 5 p.m. Monday through Saturday. No service on Sunday and holidays. Call for pickup points. Fare is 25¢.

BEVERLY HILLS: In the 1880s Beverly Hills was a series of bean fields—lima beans, to be exact. But instead of beans—or underground diamond mines—it was water that made Beverly Hills come alive. Burton E. Green was the man who founded the water company and created the residential community in the early 1900s. The city's growth did not happen all at once, however. Although business tycoons had mansions in the area that now surrounds the Beverly Hills Hotel, few others lived there. It wasn't until the 1920s, when Mary Pickford and Douglas Fairbanks moved in, that Beverly Hills really became a popular place to live for the movie industry crowd.

Today you'll find a Beverly Hills no worse for wear. Household income is one of the highest in the country; property values are astronomical and mansions are common. In fact, the most business licenses given out in Beverly Hills are to gardeners! Even the high school is famous—oil wells under the school grounds pump out nearly $1 million worth of oil annually. The city also has what is possibly the most expensive jogging track in the world, based on land values, located on the parkway that runs parallel to Santa Monica Boulevard. Stars live, work, and dine here, and are regularly seen here.

The Beverly Hills **Golden Triangle** is the business district bordered by Canon Drive, and Santa Monica and Wilshire Boulevards. The streets burst with shops sporting price tags often beyond the reach of the average consumer. But there are also good family restaurants (see the "Where to Eat" section) and stores with reasonable prices. Christmas is a great time to walk the streets of Beverly Hills. You are likely to spot a celebrity running in to his or her favorite store to stock up on presents. You can't help but want to peek into the ever-present limousines to see who might be sitting there. At other times you'll find an almost constant promenade up and down the streets, day or night. In fact, no matter where your family has dinner, Rodeo Drive (pronounced "Ro-*day*-oh") is a great place to walk it off in the evening. Take the kids and join the rest of the crowd, especially on Saturday night, and window-shop and people-watch to your heart's content.

There are other sights to see in Beverly Hills. **Greystone Mansion,** 905 Loma Vista Dr. (tel. 213/550-4864), possibly the most extravagant mansion ever built in Beverly Hills, is open to the public. This 55-room mansion, with an adjacent mini-mansion for the grandchildren, was built by oil magnate Edward Doheny, Sr., in 1928. While the city is restoring the mansion itself, you can stroll through the lush grounds, a part of what was once a 428-acre estate. Open daily from 10 a.m. to 5 p.m. No admission fee.

Although there's no playground equipment, **Will Rogers Memorial Park** (not to be confused with Will Rogers State Historical Park), across the street from the Beverly Hills Hotel, is one of the most beautiful parks in which to push a stroller or relax under the gigantic palm trees. (Also see the "Neighborhood Parks" section below for information on two Beverly Hills parks with playground equipment.)

For more information on Beverly Hills, contact the **Beverly Hills Visitors Bureau,** 239 S. Beverly Dr., Beverly Hills, CA 90212 (tel. 213/271-8174, or toll free 800/345-2210).

WESTWOOD VILLAGE: With its beginnings as a college town, home of U.C.L.A., Westwood Village has become one of the hottest communities in Los Angeles. The area termed Westwood (bordered by Pico Boulevard to the south, Sunset Boulevard to the north, Sepulveda Boulevard to the west, and Beverly Hills to the east), originally called Westwood Hills in 1923, now has over 5,000 shops and services, several hotels, and more than 500 eating establishments. It has within these boundaries four parks (Cheviot Hills Recreation Center, Palms Park, Westwood Park, Stoner Recreation Center), one golf course, and is generally recognized to be the cinema capital of Los Angeles with its dozens of first-run movie theaters. Not surprisingly, Westwood is a favorite of young teenagers and the college crowd.

One way to see Westwood Village is to take the kids in the late afternoon to window-shop or walk on the U.C.L.A. campus, and then have an early dinner. You can do all of this before the Village gets too crowded with evening visitors. Or you might want to take in a matinee.

One caution: The Village is jammed with people—many of them teens—on Friday and Saturday nights. It's alive with activity and a fun place to people-watch, but be careful to hold onto your kids. During these crowded times we never use a stroller but carry our toddlers instead.

This is a particularly popular place for clothing shops and shoe stores for the under-30 set. Don't miss **Aahs!,** 1083 Broxton Ave. (tel. 213/824-1688), a novelty store par excellence; **B. Dalton Bookseller,** 904 Westwood Blvd. (tel. 213/208-7395), is a large, full-service bookstore with a complete line of children's books; and **Tower Records,** 1028 Westwood Blvd. (tel. 213/208-3061), has a large, unusual selection of classical, rock 'n' roll, and jazz records, tapes, and compact discs. **Häagen-Dazs Ice Cream,** 10878 Kinross (tel. 213/208-7405), **Heidi's Frozen Yogurt,** 1001 Gayley Ave. (tel. 213/824-2574), and **Mrs. Field's Cookies,** 907 Westwood Blvd. (tel. 213/208-0096), are great snack places.

U.C.L.A.

The world-famous University of California at Los Angeles (U.C.L.A.), 405 Hilgard Ave. (tel. 213/825-4321), is a beautiful hilly campus set between Westwood Village and Bel Air. The school is large—over 400 acres—with over 30,000 full-time students. If you need information or would like to take a tour, contact the **Community Relations/Visitors Center,** 1417 Ueberroth Bldg., 405 Hilgard Ave., Los Angeles, CA 90024 (tel. 213/206-8147 or 213/825-4574).

If you prefer to simply wander around, a walk on campus during the quieter weekends is delightful and gives the kids an opportunity to rollick in the open grassy areas while you witness an amazing mix of architectural styles.

Don't miss Royce Hall and "the Quad," the spiritual heart of the campus. From there, wander to the **Franklin D. Murphy Sculpture Garden** (north of Royce Hall, near the University Research Library), where green lawns dotted with trees are home to more than 50 sculptures. Originally conceived as a place to bring art to the outdoors where students could enjoy it as they studied, visited, and relaxed, the Sculpture Garden is a welcome retreat for families. You'll see lots of kids playing tag, reading, picnicking with their parents.

If your family likes botanical gardens, you might enjoy a stroll through the **Mildred E. Mathias Botanical Garden** (tel. 213/825-3620), located at the southeastern part of the campus (enter at Le Conte and Hilgard Avenues). This compact garden features 4,000 species (225 families of plants) and specializes in subtropical and tropical plants that aren't grown in other parts of the U.S. except in greenhouses.

Open Monday through Friday from 8 a.m. to 5 p.m. and on Saturday and Sunday from 8 a.m. to 4:30 p.m.; closed university holidays. Admission is free.

SANTA MONICA: Close your eyes and conjure up the images you have when you hear the words "Santa Monica." Palm trees lining the boulevards, miles and miles of ocean, children building sand castles, and almost perfect weather are the fantasies that most people have. Surprisingly, the fantasy is reality.

Hugging the coastline of Santa Monica Bay, the city of Santa Monica is a family wonderland. It has 13 miles of wide, white-sand beaches with endless year-round activities, the historic Santa Monica Pier, beautiful Palisades Park, bike paths, boardwalks for roller skating, and terrific people-watching opportunities. Add to that several wonderful shopping areas, and you have the makings of a sightseer's delight.

You'll probably want to contact the **Santa Monica Convention and Visitors Bureau,** at P.O. Box 5278, Santa Monica, CA 90405 (tel. 213/393-7593). Or you can stop in at the **Santa Monica Visitors Information Center,** 1400 Ocean Ave., in Palisades Park (tel. 213/393-7593).

Santa Monica Pier

The famous Santa Monica Pier, at the end of Colorado Boulevard and Ocean Avenue (tel. 213/458-8964), the oldest pleasure pier on the West Coast, was built in 1908. At that time, it was one of several piers in the area built to house amusement parks and fun zones, probably the most popular one being Lawrence Welk's Aragon Ballroom.

Today, the pier is host to arcades, shops, restaurants, and kiddie rides. **Fun Zone,** at the Santa Monica Pier (tel. 213/458-8900), is a seasonal mini-

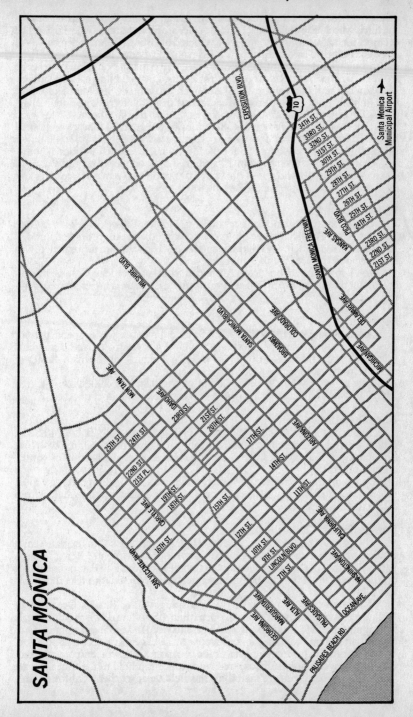

midway of rides for young children. From March to mid-October, you can spot the ferris wheel near the carousel. Kiddie rides are 50¢; the ferris wheel is $1. The cyclone, for 12-year-olds and up, is $1. Open daily from 10 a.m. to 9 p.m.

The beautiful carousel, with its hand-painted wooden horses, is open Tuesday through Sunday in summer from 10 a.m. to 9 p.m., and on winter weekends from 10 a.m. to 5 p.m. Rides cost 50¢ for adults, 25¢ for children 12 and under.

You can rent bikes and roller skates near the pier too. **Sea Mist Skate and Bike Rental,** 1619 Ocean Front Walk, across from the ferris wheel (tel. 213/395-7076), rents kids' and adult bikes at $4 for the first hour, $2 for each additional hour. Tandems rent for $8 for the first hour and $4 for each additional hour. Child carriers rent for $4 and $2 respectively; helmets, $1.50. Roller skates, for kids and adults, are $3 for the first hour, $2 for each additional hour.

Open daily in summer from 10 a.m. to 6 p.m. on weekdays and 9 a.m. to 7 p.m. on weekends; the rest of the year, from noon to 6 p.m. on weekdays and 11 a.m. to 7 p.m. on weekends. Parking lot.

Palisades Park

One of the most famous places in Santa Monica, Palisades Park is a favorite 1-mile stretch. Perched on the bluffs overlooking the ocean, palm-tree-studded Palisades Park is 26 acres of walkways and lawns. The views are unparalleled, and it's a wonderful place for tykes on trikes.

You'll find the park on Ocean Avenue. Its southern border is Colorado Boulevard, but the farther north you go, the prettier it is. There is metered street parking.

Main Street

A walk along Santa Monica's Main Street is a pleasant way to spend an hour or so. Trendy shops, art galleries, one-of-a-kind novelty stores, and restaurants line Main Street from Pico Boulevard to Rose Avenue, but the main cluster of shops is from Ocean Park Avenue to Pier Avenue.

One of our favorite shops is **Colors of the Wind,** at 2900 Main St. (tel. 213/399-8044). It has a wonderful selection of kites and other goodies.

Angel's Attic

This restored Victorian home at 516 Colorado Ave. (tel. 213/394-8331), is now a delightful museum. Especially captivating for those children who love dollhouses, dolls, and miniatures, the museum also has a collection of stuffed animals and toys.

You can buy dollhouses, furniture, and accessories. All proceeds go to an organization that helps autistic children. Open Thursday through Sunday from 12:30 to 4:30 p.m.

Venice Beach Ocean Front Walk

If you take the San Diego Freeway (I-405), north or south, exit at Venice Boulevard. Go west on Venice and you'll run right into Venice Beach. There's parking on the southeast corner of Venice and Pacific for $5 all day, or find a spot on the street (more difficult on summer weekends). Or you can take the Pacific Coast Hwy. (Calif. 1) to Venice Boulevard.

The key words to remember when visiting Venice Beach's Ocean Front Walk are "experience" and "keep an open mind." Strolling down this boardwalk is truly an experience, and one in which parents need to keep an open mind. On a Sunday afternoon you'll see a cornucopia of L.A.'s most eclectic population. Some are scantily clothed; some have blue hair, some yellow; a few come decked-out in chains; one or two are covered with cloth from head to toe. But there are "normal" people here too, including the archetypal southern California man and woman. It's an inexpensive and fun way to spend a Saturday or Sunday afternoon.

You can take children of any age on this walk, but beware of some raunchy language used in some of the street acts. It's also quite crowded on weekends (the best time to come for prime people-watching), so hold onto those little hands.

Begin your walk going north, and the first thing you'll hit is **Muscle Beach,** where men—and women—with giant muscles lift weights and work out in front of dozens of observers. Lots of jugglers, comedians, artists, musicians, and mimes line the walkway, much of which has been designated for bikes, skateboards, and roller skates. You may have never seen the artistic roller skating you'll see here.

There are a couple of **children's playgrounds** on the beach, one a half block north of Ocean Front Walk and Paloma, the other about two blocks north of Venice Boulevard and Ocean Front Walk. We don't recommend Venice Beach as a swimming beach because there are riptides. It is not considered a very safe beach. But for playing and picnicking, the sand is fine.

If you've wanted to find a California souvenir, you should be able to find one on Ocean Front Walk—thousands of T-shirts are for sale, hats of every description, sandals, sunglasses, jewelry, clothes, bathing suits . . . and much more. You'll probably be surprised when you catch a glimpse of the Venice police who are always patrolling the area—in their shorts.

There are lots of fast-food stands serving up hot dogs, sandwiches, ice cream, frozen yogurt, pizza, hamburgers, and popcorn. Rest your weary feet by having lunch on the beach, or stop by one of three sit-down restaurants: **Sidewalk Café,** 1401 Ocean Front Walk, open for breakfast, lunch, or dinner, with an extensive menu with prices ranging from $2.75 to $16; **Figtree Café,** Paloma and Ocean Front Walk, serving sandwiches, salads, and fish for $3 to $15; or **The Beachhouse Market & Deli,** at 1101 Ocean Front Walk, for sandwiches at $2.50 to $6.

Not only can you walk the boardwalk, but you can ride bikes, roller skate, or skateboard your way along. In fact, you can ride all the way from the Venice Beach boardwalk past the Santa Monica Pier. Everything is for rent. **Spokes 'n Stuff,** at the end of Washington Boulevard (tel. 213/306-3332), rents ten-speeds, children's bikes, bikes with baby seats, tandems, mountain bikes, and adult tricycles, as well as roller skates. Rates start at $2.50 per hour for bikes and $3 per hour for skates. They also rent strollers, fins, scooters, and boogie boards, from $2.75 to $5.50 per hour. Prices are better the longer you rent. Open weekdays from 10:30 a.m. to 6 p.m. and weekends from 10 a.m. to 6:30 p.m.

RPM Bicycle Rentals is at 36 Washington St. (tel. 213/399-6331). Their mountain bikes go down to 20 inches. Only one bike with a baby seat is available. They also rent three-, five-, and ten-speeds. Bike rates start at $2 per hour. Open weekdays from 8 a.m. to 6 p.m. and weekends from 9 a.m. to 5 p.m.

Venice Pier Bike Shop, 21 Washington St. (tel. 213/823-1528), has children's bikes for rent as well as 10- and 15-speeds, tandems, bikes with baby seats, and helmets. Rates begin at $2 per hour. Open weekdays from 10 a.m. to 5 p.m. and weekends from 9 a.m. to 6 p.m.

MARINA DEL REY: Just five miles north of Los Angeles International Airport, you'll find Marina Del Rey, a pocket of blue water, sailboats, and yachts. Although just minutes out of the city, the Marina makes you feel as if you've been transported to a European seaside village.

Marina Del Rey is the largest man-made pleasurecraft harbor in the world. Bounded by Lincoln Boulevard, Washington Street, and the Pacific Ocean, the Marina is home to more than 6,000 boats, myriad shops, pricey condos and apartments, movie theaters, singles bars, and a huge array of restaurants.

Here you can rent boats, cruise the marina, sunbathe, swim, fish, windsurf, roller skate, fly kites, walk, and ride your bikes. One of our favorite pastimes is to take breakfast to the **North Jetty** between Via Marina and Pacific Avenue, find a spot, and enjoy our meal while we watch the boats as they pass through the main channel of the Marina. For more information, the Marina has its own Visitor Center. Contact the **Marina Del Rey Visitors Information Center,** 4701 Admiralty Way, Marina Del Rey, CA 90292 (tel. 213/305-9545).

Bike Rentals

One place to try is the **Jamaica Bay Inn Beach Hut,** 4175 Admiralty Way (tel. 213/823-5333). The Beach Hut rents beach cruisers and ten-speeds at $3.50 for the first hour, $10.50 for four hours, $14 for the day (10:30 a.m. to 6:30 p.m.). Mountain bikes are $5.50 for the first hour, $16.50 for four hours, $22 for the day. Tandem bikes are $6 for the first hour, $18 for four hours, and $24 for the day. Children's bicycles are available, as are baby carriers and helmets. Open daily from 10:30 a.m. to 6 p.m.

Robbie's Bike and Skate, at the west end of Washington Street in the county parking lot (tel. 213/306-3332), has beach cruisers, mountain bikes, children's bikes, ten-speeds, and tandems. Rates range from $2.50 to $6.50 per hour, $7.50 to $18.50 for a half-day rental, and $8 to $24 for an all-day rental. Helmets and baby carriers are available. Open weekdays from 10:30 a.m. to 6 p.m. and weekends from 10 a.m. to 6:30 p.m.

For information about the bike path, see the "Bicycling" section.

Boat Rentals

Rent-A-Sail, 13560 Mindanao Way (tel. 213/822-1868), rents sailboats, powerboats, canoes, and catamarans. Rates range from $14 to $28 per hour, depending on the boat. Hours vary.

California Sailing Academy, 14025 Panay Way (tel. 213/821-3433), rents sailboats. Hours vary.

Charter Concepts, 13757 Fiji Way (tel. 213/823-2676), rents sailboats and powerboats.

All companies listed above offer lessons.

Roller-Skate Rentals

Rent skates at **Skatey's,** 102 Washington St. (tel. 213/823-7971). Open weekdays from 10:30 to 6:30 p.m. and weekends from 9 a.m. to 6:30 p.m.

Fishing

For those of you who want to fish, you can try **Marina Del Rey Sportfishing,** 13759 Fiji Way (tel. 213/822-3625). You can also go dock-fishing at Burton Chace Park and Fisherman's Village, 13763 Fiji Way.

Windsurfing

To rent equipment and take windsurfing lessons, try **Wind Surfing West,** 4047 Lincoln Blvd. (tel. 213/821-5501).

And More . . .

If you're just looking for a nice place to let the kids run around, **Burton Chace Park** is a nine-acre waterfront park at the end of Mindanao Way with picnic areas, a fishing dock, and views of the boats.

Admiralty Park is on Admiralty Way between Palawan and Bali Way, near the bird sanctuary.

Serious shopping in the Marina is best at the **Villa Marina Center** at Mindanao and the Marina freeway. Here you'll find 20 restaurants, first-run movie thea-

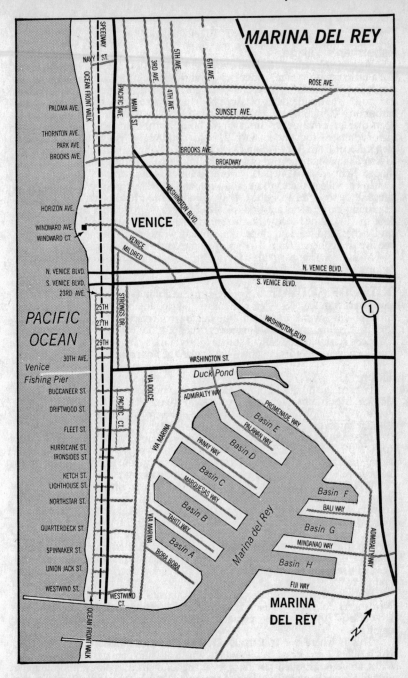

ters, a Von's supermarket, a Savon/Osco drugstore, a video arcade, and other necessities.

Fisherman's Village

Fisherman's Village, located at 13763 Fiji Way (tel. 213/823-5411), looks like a little fishing village, and it is a delightful place to walk and relax with the family for an afternoon. As you stroll along the boardwalk on a sunny weekend day, you'll see hundreds of pleasure boats in all sizes. You, too, can cruise the harbor on a 40-minute tour. **Marina Cruise Line,** located right at the village, has boats that leave daily, every hour on the hour from 11 a.m. to 5 p.m. The fare is $5 for adults, $4 for children 6 to 12, $3 for children 1 to 5. Or you can rent your own sailboat from **Rent-A-Sail** (tel. 213/822-1868). Rental prices range from $14 to $34 per hour, with a two-hour minimum, depending on which boat you choose. Rent-A-Sail is open daily from 10 a.m. to sundown.

In the village there are art, souvenir, and jewelry stores; an import shop; a kite and toy store; and a T-shirt shop all housed in little cottages. Four sit-down restaurants serve Mexican food, pizza and pasta, seafood, and steaks. For outdoor snacks on the boardwalk, there are cookies, ice cream, hamburgers, candy, sandwiches, and fish and chips. On Sunday, weather permitting, you can hear free live jazz concerts from 2 to 5 p.m. in the center of the village.

Most of the shops and restaurants are open daily from 10 a.m. to 10 p.m. Parking is free.

OUTDOOR ACTIVITIES:
You've just read about outdoor activities near the beach areas. Los Angeles offers even more. Take your pick. There's hiking, swimming, boating, windsurfing, surfing, jogging, roller skating, bicycling, walking, horseback riding, and probably scads of other outdoor ventures you'll dream up.

Let's start with the Santa Monica Mountains, a range that offers delightful outdoor adventures for the active—and even the not-so-active—family.

Hiking

For specific hikes and other information, you'll want to contact the **Santa Monica Mountains National Recreation Area Visitor Center,** at 22900 Ventura Blvd., Woodland Hills (tel. 818/888-3770). Their offices are open Monday through Saturday from 8:30 a.m. to 4:30 p.m.

Topanga State Park, located off Topanga Canyon Boulevard at Entrada Road (tel. 213/455-2465 or 818/706-1310), is a wooded area with self-guided nature trails and 35 miles of hiking trails. Open daily from 8 a.m. to 7 p.m. from the beginning of April through October. Fee for parking.

Will Rogers State Historic Park, 14253 Sunset Blvd., between Amalfi Drive and Brooktree Road, about eight miles inland from Calif. 1, the Pacific Coast Hwy. (tel. 213/454-8212), is a wonderful place that's easy to take kids of all ages. Everyone enjoys the self-guided audio tours of Will Rogers's Ranch House, and there are two enormous fields for picnicking and romping. One is a polo ground where polo matches take place Saturday afternoon and Sunday morning. (Call for specific hours.) The trails are relatively easy and offer splendid views of the ocean and city on clear days. The park is open daily from 8 a.m. to 6 p.m. Fee for parking.

Franklin Canyon Ranch is in the hills above Beverly Hills where Beverly Drive meets Coldwater Canyon Drive. Call for directions (tel. 213/858-3834 or 818/888-3770). Here you can enjoy self-guided trails, hiking, picnicking, and jogging.

This is where the **William O. Douglas Outdoor Classroom** is located, which offers a variety of **public walks,** most of which are geared for families. Walks are geared to such varied topics as the food chain, ecology, photography, and wildflower exploration. Two to three times a week they offer **Babes in the**

Woods Walks for children 3 months to 3 years and their parents. And on the weekends, they also offer **Tykes on Hikes** for children 4 to 6 years old and their parents.

On these sensory-oriented nature walks, children smell, touch, look, and listen to nature. Kids sit under the trees and the docent uses puppets to tell stories. The big hit is to feed the ducks. They'll feel soft sycamore leaves, listen to the birds, look for little mosquito fish in the pond and scoop them up to study them. The program also offers **Adventure Quest,** designed for teens. (Teens walk with peers while the family goes on another walk.) There's a **Full-Moon Hike** monthly.

Guided hikes are free but are by reservation only; contact the William O. Douglas Outdoor Classroom, P.O. Box 2488, Beverly Hills, CA 90213 (tel. 213/858-3834).

Coldwater Canyon Park is located at the east side of the intersection between Coldwater Canyon and Mulholland Drive (tel. 213/273-8733 or 818/769-2663). This is where TreePeople Park is found. It is open daily from 9 a.m. to dusk. On Monday, Thursday, and Saturday people can get involved helping the volunteer gardeners. The hours are 10 a.m. to 4 p.m. on Monday and Thursday and 10 a.m. to noon on Saturday. On Sunday at 11 a.m. there's a tour of the park, which includes the nursery, beehive, organic center, and recycling center, as well as a short guided tour of the trails where some of the seedlings are taking hold.

Nursery Walks

A group of volunteers, sponsored by the **Palisades-Malibu Y.M.C.A.** at 821 Via de la Paz, Pacific Palisades (tel. 213/454-4491), leads nature walks for infants and preschoolers and their parents. Attempting to help families develop a love for nature, they offer walks of about two hours' duration and about half a mile in length. About halfway, they take a break.

Using all the senses, they get the tots involved with the surroundings. Activities may include pretending to be Indians, using flowers to make soap, or smelling leaves. The walks are held at Leo Carrillo State Beach, Malibu Lagoon State Beach, Topanga State Park, Will Rogers State Park, Griffith Park, and several others.

Older sisters and brothers are welcome too. Call 213/454-4491 for details about specific walks. Reservations are required—usually two weeks in advance. A donation of $3 is requested.

Swimming Beaches

We'll start at the north and work south. (Check the Greater L.A. Chapter for beaches north and south of these.) Unless indicated otherwise, all parking lots charge a fee, usually $3 to $5. In some cases, you can find street parking as well.

Will Rogers State Beach (tel. 213/394-3266) is a nice clean family beach with two designated surfing areas. It has a few playgrounds—one near lifeguard Tower 8 (near Temescal Canyon), one by Tower 12, one by Tower 10, and one by Tower 14. Located just north of Santa Monica Beach, starting at Chautauqua Boulevard and going for three miles to Topanga Canyon, this lovely beach has parking, rest rooms, showers, snackbar, volleyball courts, and lifeguard stations.

Santa Monica State Beach (tel. 213/394-3266) is the 3.3-mile-long stretch of beach below the bluffs of Palisades Park. This very wide sandy beach has just about all the facilities you could hope for—and the crowds to go with them. Divided by the Santa Monica Pier, it's a tourist-oriented beach with an abundance of parking. (If you want fewer crowds, drive farther north and you'll be rewarded.) Most activity centers around the pier. You might want to stay north of the pier, where the ocean is much safer than the south side. Just south of the pier, you'll find gymnastics equipment and volleyball courts. Both north and south of the pier, you find rest rooms and outdoor showers. There are ample snackbars and concessionaires.

Peninsula Beach (tel. 213/394-3266) is in Marina Del Rey at the end of Washington Street near the breakwater. South of the pier is a very nice part of the beach. Parking is difficult, which keeps the beach less crowded. There are rest rooms and a smattering of little restaurants at the foot of Washington Street. This is more of an adult beach than a kids' beach, but it's lovely.

Neighborhood Parks

With so much land in Los Angeles, neighborhood parks are not too difficult to find. Here are a few we find special.

Douglas Park, 1155 Chelsea Ave., near Wilshire Boulevard and 20th Street in Santa Monica (tel. 213/458-8311), is a charming little park complete with duck pond, wading pool (that doubles as a tricycle demolition racetrack when it's dry), and fabulous wooden play structures. The equipment offers amusement for older kids as well as the younger ones. Picnic facilities, barbecue stands, rest rooms, and tennis courts complete the picture.

Cheviot Hills Recreation Area is a huge well-known park. Located at 2551 Motor Ave. in West Los Angeles (tel. 213/837-5186), the park has playground equipment, basketball courts, baseball diamonds, a pond, a par course (with 18 stations), tennis courts, picnic and barbecue facilities, and a very large municipal swimming pool (tel. 213/836-3365). The recreation center offers a wide variety of activities as well.

One beautiful in-town place to run off some excess energy is at **Roxbury Park** in Beverly Hills, 471 S. Roxbury St., at Roxbury and Olympic Boulevards (tel. 213/550-4864). Besides paths for walking, a softball field, and bocce ball and basketball courts, there are two large play areas for children in the back of the park. Near the equipment are picnic tables and barbecue grills. Come early on weekends for a picnic table, as Beverly Hills residents get first choice by reserving tables by telephone.

The park is open every day from 7 a.m. to 11 p.m. There is ample parking weekdays, and fairly easy parking on nonholiday weekends. Park in the back of the park if you intend to stay by the playground equipment. Rest rooms and soda machines are nearby.

La Cienega Park, 8400 Gregory Way, between Gregory, Olympic, and La Cienega Boulevards, Beverly Hills (tel. 213/550-4864), does not have the new play equipment that Roxbury has, but kids will find plenty with which to amuse themselves. There are also picnic tables and a softball field here, and adequate rest rooms. Parking is at a premium.

Bike Paths

In Santa Monica, the **Pacific Coast Bicentennial Bike Route** runs along Ocean Avenue. Although it's quite scenic, there can be a lot of traffic.

In Marina Del Rey, you can start your bicycle ride at the Bird Sanctuary near the Marina International Hotel, at Palawan and Admiralty Way, for an approximately three-mile ride to Fisherman's Village. There's a county parking lot where you can park for $1. The children will want to stop to see the bunnies and birds that live in the sanctuary, many of which were left there by owners who no longer wanted them. Your ride will take you across Admiralty Way past the huge pleasure boats in drydock on your way to Fisherman's Village. Beware of a couple of unmarked crossings across busy streets. From Fisherman's Village you can ride along the **Ballona Creek Bike Trail,** located at the end of the **South Bay Bike Trail** (see Chapter XI, on Greater Los Angeles, for details). The trail winds along Ballona Creek from Fisherman's Village all the way to Culver City.

And Other Activities . . .

Circle K Horseback Riding, 910 S. Mariposa, Burbank, located at the northeast corner of Griffith Park, just south of Riverside Drive (tel. 818/843-9890), offers guide-led horseback rides through Griffith Park. Your family may have a guide of its own, or you may share with other people. The fees are $11 for the first hour, $9 for each additional; there's a $9 deposit on each horse. The minimum age is 6 years old. Horses are available on a first-come, first-served basis.

Malibu Castle Miniature Golf, 4989 Sepulveda Blvd., in Sherman Oaks (tel. 818/990-8101), is a miniature golf lover's dream. Three attractively designed golf courses with an abundance of fountains, ponds, and greenery delight children. There are also batting cages, a huge video arcade, and two snackbars. The facility is open daily from 10 a.m. to midnight. Adults pay $4.50; kids 12 and under, $3.50.

AMUSEMENT AND WATER PARKS: Outdoor activities are not limited to adventures in nature. L.A. also has its share of hair-raising adventure.

Six Flags Magic Mountain

Ah, but the kids enjoy this place! Located in Valencia (take the Magic Mountain Parkway exit off I-5) about 25 minutes north of Hollywood (tel. 818/367-5965 or 805/255-4111), Magic Mountain's 260 acres offers family fun for every age. Always popular with thrill-seeking teens and preteens who delight in the stupendous roller coasters and water adventures, Magic Mountain has added several attractions to entertain the younger set. There are 100 rides in all, plus live shows, a dance club, petting zoo, and a year-round crafts village.

Magic Mountain is best known for its electrifying roller coaster rides. **Ninja** —the black belt of roller coasters—is the newest. Traveling at speeds of up to 55 mph, on a half-mile route through the surrounding forest, this coaster is suspended from an overhead track. There's nothing underneath riders as they go through steep drops and side-to-side swings of up to 110°. **Colossus** is the gargantuan double-track wooden roller coaster that is invariably rated in the top ten in America. **Revolution** was the world's first coaster with a 360° vertical loop, and has the distinction of being one of the world's largest steel coasters. And for coaster aficionados who want an entirely new experience, there's **Shock Wave,** where riders stand up during the ride (which also includes a 360° vertical loop).

Magic Mountain was one of the first to have water flume rides. **Log Jammer** takes its riders in hollowed-out logs through a winding, twisting voyage that plunges through the water. In **Jet Stream,** riders in speedboats plummet down a 52-foot drop. **Roaring Rapids** is a white-water-rafting adventure.

Younger children enjoy **Bugs Bunny World,** a six-acre area especially designed for little kids. Little squeals of excitement can be heard from **Wile E. Coyote** roller coaster, a scaled-down version of the bigger item. After the young ones have had their share of rides, you'll want to meander to **Foghorn Leghorn Animal Farm and Petting Zoo.** Here, they can see 55 different kinds of animals, including miniature horses, and touch many of them.

When we need a break, we hightail it over to **Spillikin Handcrafter's Junction,** an 1800s-style crafts village where we find some shade and just relax.

Show highlights change from year to year. Try to catch the U.S. High Dive Team stunt show for a real thrill. The Foghorn Leghorn Wild Animal Show is bound to delight kids as young as three. We always like the Dolphin and Sea Lion Show. And don't miss out on the puppet theaters.

Here are some tips for doing the park. Arrive early in the day. If you have very young kids, you might want to bring a stash of juice. Many a time we've been hard-pressed to find a vending machine or snackbar that has anything other than soft drinks and milk. But if your kids are like ours, they will want to try all the goodies and sweets they see, so expect to be reaching in your pockets often. Valencia (like many other spots) can be quite warm on summer days. Be sure to bring sunscreen, hats, and a change of clothes (there are lots of water rides) if you'll be visiting during the summer. Rental strollers and coin lockers are available. You can find diapers at the Pamper Baby Care Center, located near Bugs Bunny World.

Open daily at 10 a.m. from Memorial Day through early September, on weekends and school holidays the rest of the year. Call ahead for specific dates and closing times. General admission (which entitles you to unlimited use of all rides, shows, and attractions) is $20; seniors and children under four feet tall, $10; children under age 3 free. Parking is $4.

Raging Waters

Have you ever been to a water theme park? Get ready, because this is an experience—a day of sun, wet thrills, and throngs of excited, screaming children! Located on 44 acres (within the 2,200-acre Frank G. Bonelli Regional Park in San Dimas), Raging Waters makes you feel as if you've entered a beach town designed for the young and daring. Raging Waters is located at 111 Raging Waters Dr. (tel. 714/592-8181 or 714/592-6453 for recorded information), 30 minutes east of downtown Los Angeles, 20 minutes north of Anaheim, where I-10 and Calif. 210 meet. Exit at Raging Waters Drive.

Large sandy areas (where lotion-covered moms and dads watch swimming youngsters) surround enormous sandy-bottomed swimming holes, where school-age kids and preteens enjoy small water slides, water swings, a lily-pad walk, and rope nets above the water. An area called **Wavecove** is the closest you'll come to bodysurfing in this neck of the woods. Waves as high as three feet give even the meekest among us the chance to experience an ocean-like ride.

But this is not a place for the faint of heart. Teens, preteens, and others who believe they're invincible are the ones who probably enjoy it the most. Billing itself as the largest water theme park west of the Mississippi, Raging Waters has four speed slides, four flume rides, and a water rapids. The **Dropout** is a free-fall experience where adventure seekers descend seven stories in four seconds at speeds of up to 40 mph—straight down. **Rampage** is a ride on a hydro-sled from a tower four stories high. **Raging Rocket** and **Screamer** are slides with eight-story descents that take you up to 25 mph.

The flumes **Demon's Drop, Thunder Run, Tree-Top Twisters,** and **Canyon Chute** have more than 400 feet of curves and dips, ending in a refreshing splash-down pool. **Raging Rivers** is the longest man-made innertube rapids; this quarter-mile waterway has rapids, whirlpools, and waterfalls. For the littlest tots, **Little Dipper** is a grassy area with pools only one foot deep. Not to be outdone, this area has its own fountains and mini-water slides. Children over 8 aren't even allowed in these pools.

A Note of Caution: First, prepare yourself—and your kids—for a place that is very crowded. In other theme parks crowds are more a nuisance factor; in a water park, they may interfere with your child's safety if you and the kids aren't especially alert. In the areas where children use slides into the pools, we always remind our kids not to go down the slide if they see other children swimming into their path. We tell them, too, that they need to watch out when they're in the pools passing near a slide. Younger kids will need your almost-constant attention; older ones will need your guidance, so they don't attempt activities that are beyond their skill level. While there are lifeguards and trained slide operators, we're always super-cautious when there are lots of kids in the water.

For the rapids, flumes, and steep slides, the park has its own rules, which should be strictly adhered to. And at this kind of park, more than almost anywhere else, remember the sunscreen and sunblock, since the kids will be baking in the sun all day.

Dressing rooms and coin-operated lockers are available. Life vests are provided free, and you can rent rafts and innertubes for $5 ($2 is refunded when you return the item). You will find a variety of food—from Mexican to Italian—at the snack stands. There are picnic areas also.

Raging Waters is open from April through the beginning of October, but call ahead for specific dates and times as these vary greatly. (Be sure to get there when the park opens for the smallest crowds.) Admission prices are based on height. General admission (for anyone over 48 inches) is $14 ($9 after 5 p.m.); children (42 to 48 inches) pay $9 ($7 after 5 p.m.). Parking costs $2.

PERFORMING ARTS: No doubt many of you and your teenagers have heard of Los Angeles's outdoor concert venues where some of the world's most popular groups perform. And the Roxy and the Troubador, clubs made popular in the '60s and '70s, are still in full swing with today's newest groups.

Concert Sites

The famed **Greek Theater,** 2700 N. Vermont Ave., Los Angeles (tel. 213/410-1062), is an outdoor amphitheater nestled in the woods of Griffith Park offering a wide range of musical fare. The season runs from late May to early October. Tickets are available through Ticketron (tel. 213/642-4242) and Ticket-Master (tel. 213/480-3232). You can also purchase them at the box office weekdays from 10 a.m. to 6 p.m.

The **Universal Amphitheater** (tel. 818/980-9421) is an indoor theater on the Universal Studios lot, located off the Hollywood Freeway (U.S. 101) in Universal City. Take the Lankershim Boulevard exit and follow the signs. Tickets are available through TicketMaster (tel. 213/480-3232), local May Company stores, and Music Plus stores. The Amphitheater box office is located in the parking lot of the site, above the entrance to the Registry Hotel. It is open daily from 1 to 9 p.m.

Clubs

The **Roxy** is at 9009 Sunset Blvd., West Hollywood, east of Doheny Drive (tel. 213/276-2222 or 213/278-9457). All the shows in this club are appropriate for teenagers, but you might want to call ahead to find out who is playing that night. There's no age minimum, but there is a minimum drinking age in California, which naturally the Roxy adheres to. Tickets are only available at the door before the shows, but call ahead because selected show tickets are available through Ticketron (tel. 213/642-4242).

All ages are also allowed at **Doug Weston's Troubador,** 9081 Santa Monica Blvd., West Hollywood, corner of Santa Monica Boulevard and Doheny Drive (tel. 213/276-6168). Food is available here, and performances are appropriate for teenagers. Call 213/276-1158 Tuesday through Friday between 2 and 6 p.m. for specific show information. All ages can dance to records on Monday nights from 9 p.m. to 2 a.m. Live groups are scheduled the rest of the week. Admission price is $9, including drink minimums.

Music and Theater

The **Music Center,** 135 N. Grand Ave., at 1st Street, downtown (tel. 213/972-7211), is Los Angeles's grand complex of three theaters—the **Dorothy Chandler Pavilion,** the **Ahmanson Theatre,** and the **Mark Taper Forum** (tel. 213/972-7373). The theaters present a mix of the Los Angeles Philharmonic, Broadway theater, experimental theater, ballet, and other live performances. From the Pasadena Freeway (Calif. 110), exit at Hill Avenue to Temple Avenue and make a right, then a left on Grand Avenue. From the Harbor Freeway (I-110), exit at 4th Street to Olive Street, then turn left on Olive, left on 1st Street, and right on Grand Avenue. From the Hollywood Freeway South (U.S. 101), exit at Temple Avenue and make a left, then a right on Grand Avenue.

To get tickets by mail for any of the theaters, write two weeks in advance to the Box Office, 135 N. Grand Ave., Los Angeles, CA 90012. The Dorothy

Chandler Pavilion box office is open Monday through Saturday from 10 a.m. to 6 p.m. The Mark Taper Forum box office is open on Monday from 10 a.m. to 6 p.m., Tuesday through Saturday from 10 a.m. to 8 p.m., and on Sunday from noon to 7:30 p.m. Or you can get tickets through Ticketron (tel. 213/642-4242) or Teletron (tel. 213/410-1062). The Ahmanson Theatre box office is open on Monday from 10 a.m. to 6 p.m., Tuesday through Saturday from 10 a.m. to 8 p.m., and on Sunday from noon to 6 p.m. Or order through Teletron or Ticketron (at the telephone numbers above).

PRO SPORTS: Angelenos are crazy about sports—and about their teams. With league-leading crews like the Lakers and the Dodgers, sporting events rank right up there with fun-in-the-sun and good food.

The **Dodgers** play baseball at Dodger Stadium, 1750 Stadium Way, Los Angeles (tel. 213/224-1400). The season lasts from April through October. Tickets are available by mail from the Dodger Stadium Ticket Office, P.O. Box 51100, Los Angeles, CA 90057. Add $2 for handling and mailing for each order. Prices for tickets: box seats, $7; reserved seats, $6; general admission, $5. Or order through TicketMaster (tel. 213/480-3232) or Ticketron (tel. 213/642-4242). You can also purchase tickets in person at the Dodger Ticket Office, 1750 Stadium Way, open Monday through Saturday from 8:30 a.m. to 5:30 p.m.

The **Los Angeles Raiders** play football at the L.A. Memorial Coliseum, 3911 S. Figueroa St. (tel. 213/747-7111). The football season runs from September through December. For tickets, send a self-addressed, stamped envelope with a money order as early as possible to: Raiders Tickets, 332 Center St., El Segundo, CA 90245 (tel. 213/322-5901). Ticket prices are $25, $18, and $10. You can purchase them in person at the El Segundo office—but for cash only. You can also get tickets through Ticketron (tel. 213/642-4242), TicketMaster (tel. 213/480-3232), and at the Sports Arena, 3939 S. Figueroa St. (tel. 213/748-6136).

The **Los Angeles Kings** play ice hockey at the Forum, 3900 W. Market Blvd., Inglewood. Tickets for the Kings ($7 to $18.50), the **L.A. Strings** tennis team, and the **L.A. Lazers** soccer team are available by mail, one month in advance: Forum Box Office, P.O. Box 10, Inglewood, CA 90306 (tel. 213/419-3182). The **Los Angeles Lakers** also play basketball at the Forum, but it's often impossible to get Lakers tickets. The Forum Box Office is open daily from 10 a.m. to 6 p.m.

The **NBA L.A. Clippers** play basketball at the Sports Arena, 3939 S. Figueroa St. (tel. 213/748-6136). Tickets can be purchased at the gate or through TicketMaster (tel. 213/480-3232).

INDOOR ACTIVITIES: It *never* rains in southern California, but should you experience a little dampness or fog during your stay—or should you prefer an *indoor activity*—here are a few things you can see or do indoors.

The **Southwest Museum,** 234 Museum Dr., at Marmion Way, Highland Park (tel. 213/221-2163 for recorded information, or 213/221-2164), is Los Angeles's oldest museum, moved here from its former location downtown. Devoted to the study of Native American cultures from Alaska to South America, it has one of the finest collections of Indian art in the country.

Children who have studied Native Americans in school love the romance that surrounds the stories they hear. At the museum they get to see many of the things they've read about, such as a real tepee, baskets, pottery and jewelry made by various tribes, and items used for carrying and clothing babies and small children many years ago.

If you plan to be in town a while, check with the museum as to whether any of the special family programs are coming up. Past events have included Navajo storytelling by a real Navajo woman, paper cutting and piñata making during a

Mexican Traditions festival, and a craft workshop on making a simple Native American toy.

Although the Southwest Museum is not near many other attractions and does take some time to get to, it's a special little museum for those people interested in the arts and artifacts of the Americas. It's not too far from Pasadena, and not far from Lawry's California Center. Call for directions.

The museum is open Tuesday through Sunday from 11 a.m. to 5 p.m. Adults pay $3; children 7 to 18 and seniors, $1.50; children 6 and under, free.

Ice Skating

The **Culver City Skating Rink** makes a good place to take a break on sizzling August days. In summer, open Monday through Wednesday from 12:15 to 5 p.m.; on Thursday and Friday from 12:15 to 5 p.m. and 8 to 10:30 p.m.; on Saturday from 9:45 a.m. to 1 p.m., 1:30 to 5 p.m., and 8 to 10:30 p.m.; and on Sunday from 1:30 to 5 p.m. and 8 to 10:30 p.m. The rest of the year, open Monday through Friday from 10 a.m. to 5 p.m.; on Saturday from 9:45 a.m. to 1 p.m. and 1:30 to 5 p.m., and on Sunday from 1:30 to 5 p.m.

Admission costs $3.75 for adults, $3.25 for children 12 and under. Skate rentals cost $1.25 (children's sizes available).

Located in Burbank, **Pickwick Ice Arena,** 1001 Riverside Dr. (tel. 818/846-0032), is a place where the staff believes that any child, any age, can skate. Open Monday through Friday from 1:30 to 5:30 p.m. (on Wednesday also from 8 to 10:30 p.m.), on Saturday from 2:30 to 5 p.m. and 8 to 10:30 p.m., and on Sunday from 2:30 to 5 p.m. Admission costs $4.50 for adults, $4 for juniors (13 to 18), and $3.50 for children to age 12. Skate rentals are $1.50.

Shopping Malls and Children's Stores

The **Beverly Center,** 8500 Beverly Blvd. (tel. 213/854-0070), with 900,000 square feet of retail space, one of Los Angeles's largest fully enclosed shopping complexes, is a good place for shopping, people-watching, or as a change of pace for wound-up little travelers. We can spend a couple of hours just walking from one end of the mall to the other, peeking into stores, visiting the animals in the pet shop, riding the glass-enclosed elevators, and stopping for a piece of pizza and ice cream on the top floor. It's a particularly nice diversion on a hot smoggy day.

Its two flagship stores are The Broadway and Bullock's. Between them are approximately 200 shops and restaurants. On the sixth floor (the first retail floor), look for Sanrio, which specializes in Hello Kitty products; the pet store, with puppies, kittens, and birds on display; the Little Folks Shop, for reasonably priced "in" kids' clothes fitting infants on up; and Brooks Stride Rite Shoes with popularly priced kids' shoes.

The seventh-floor features Intellitoys with its vast array of toys, hobby kits, and interesting "collectibles" for kids; Nanny, with super-expensive little tots designer clothes and shoes; Bébé Boom, for the latest in European children's wear; and Heaven, for unique "stuff" for kids and teens. The Beverly Center has two bookstores, each with small children's book sections. The 13-and-up visitors in your group will love to shop for clothes at Judy's, Express, and The Gap, or Benetton, The Limited, and Laura Ashley.

On the eighth floor is the 14-screen Cineplex movie theater, offering first-run films, fast-food stands, and sit-down restaurants. Starkey's Deli serves pizza by the slice and has a fairly large video arcade in the rear.

On the street level, there's the popular Hard Rock Café, California Pizza Kitchen, and Irvine Ranch Market, the market to the stars and anyone else who can afford its prices.

Strollers are available at the information booth, located on the sixth floor under the escalators near the middle of the center. Parking entrances are on La

Cienega, San Vicente, and Beverly Boulevards. There is free parking for the first three hours. Valet parking is available at the Beverly or La Cienega Boulevard entrance.

The center shops are open Monday through Saturday from 10 a.m. to 9 p.m. and on Sunday from 11 a.m. to 6 p.m. The theaters and restaurants are open after shopping hours.

Century City Shopping Center, 10250 Santa Monica Blvd. (tel. 213/553-5300), is between "Little" Santa Monica Boulevard and Constitution, and Century Park West and the Avenue of the Stars, on what was once the back lot of Twentieth Century–Fox Studios. Since 1964 this center has been a favorite Westside open-air shopping mall. Although it is more than 700,000 square feet and has more than 150 shops, it doesn't feel too large. It has always been a good place to keep energetic kids entertained and a safe place for an evening walk with tireless toddlers. The only negative is the lack of access to elevators for parents with strollers. There is an elevator from the parking lot to The Broadway department store and two in the Marketplace.

There are lots of outdoor places to sit and watch the world go by while chomping on a hot dog from the bright-red cart. Steel shade structures keep the hot sun away.

Toy stores such as Toy's International and Imaginarium are necessary stops. Judy's, Contempo Casuals, Laura Ashley, and The Limited will appeal to the girls in your group. MGA's Guess? clothes are available for boys and girls, as well as young kids and babies. Mom and older daughters will love the fashion jewelry at Glitz. The Broadway and Bullock's are the two major department stores. Heaven is found here, with nifty gift items, costumes, masks, and "toys." (See the "Where to Eat" section for further information about Heaven.)

Besides the outdoor specialty carts selling hot pretzels, popcorn, and hot dogs, there is a section of specialty-food places with outdoor tables.

New to the center, the Marketplace makes a fine place to take the children. In the international food hall, there are lots of vendors specializing in ethnic foods, and there are several sit-down restaurants surrounding them. A 14-theater movie complex shows first-run films.

Parking is plentiful, and there's even that priceless southern California phenomenon, valet parking, near the Little Santa Monica Boulevard entrance. Other parking entrances are on Constellation and Century Park West. Free three-hour parking is available with validation (no purchase necessary). The information booth is near The Broadway. No strollers are available.

Open Monday through Friday from 10 a.m. to 9 p.m., on Saturday till 6 p.m., and on Sunday from 11 a.m. to 6 p.m. Restaurants and theaters are open longer hours.

Santa Monica Place is another good, though smaller mall. Located between Colorado Avenue and Broadway, between 2nd and 4th Streets (tel. 213/394-5451), Santa Monica Place has more than 160 shops and restaurants, including Robinson's (on the west end) and The Broadway (at the east end). The three-story mall is completely covered with a glass skylight, giving it a bright, open feeling, very appropriate for Santa Monica. If you have time, don't miss the Public Ocean View Terrace on the third floor, where you'll see the huge expanse of the Pacific before you.

The highlight of the mall is located on the ground-floor level, where you might find an elaborate sand sculpture of Alice in Wonderland, a Christmas extravaganza, or a wishing pond. This is a great place to let the kids spend some time while you sit and relax.

After that, we start our excursion with a visit to Petland on the third level. Next, we're off to Karl's Toys and Hobbies, and then on to the Music Box Shop, where the kids marvel at the different music boxes. When we're lucky, we get to see Disney music boxes.

The other stores of interest are Brooks–Stride Rite Shoes, Buster Brown Shoes, The Gamekeeper, See's Candy, and The Very Very Beast novelty store. The food court is on the ground floor and gives you a great variety of fast food and other choices. You might also want to try the Panda Inn, a sit-down Mandarin-style restaurant (tel. 213/393-6447), Tre Scalini Trattoria (tel. 213/451-0152), Tampico Tilly's Mexican restaurant (tel. 213/393-1404), or Vie de France (tel. 213/395-6107).

Santa Monica Place is open Monday through Friday from 10 a.m. to 9 p.m., on Saturday till 6 p.m., and on Sunday from 11 a.m. to 6 p.m. There is lots of parking.

The **Westside Pavilion**, 10800 W. Pico Blvd., West Los Angeles (tel. 213/474-6255), is a modernistic mall located between Westwood Boulevard and Overland Avenue. It has one of the best food courts in the city, offering almost anything you could want to eat. With Nordstrom and May Company as the anchor stores (located on either end of the shopping mall), the shops in the Westside Pavilion run the gamut in price.

Our all-time favorite is WaldenKids. This store has an area in which the kids can play on the floor to try out some of the goodies before Mom or Dad purchase them. It has a good selection of educational toys, computer software, and cassette tapes. Although it's a small shop, we've always found it to have a great collection of books.

Other shops of interest are GapKids, Baby Guess, Bergstrom's, Music Box, Records West, Mr. G's Toys, and Ricky's Toys and Hobbies. For older kids and computer buffs, check out the Electronics Boutique. And a treat for everyone is Animal Kingdom on the third level. You'll also find the Samuel Goldwyn Pavilion Cinemas here. There are four theaters, one of which often shows children's films.

Mall hours are Monday through Saturday from 10 a.m. to 9:30 p.m. and on Sunday from noon to 7 p.m. There is a 24-hour Vons Market (tel. 213/470-2284) located below ground level. Free parking. Rooftop parking is good for stroller access.

The **Children's Book and Music Center**, 2500 Santa Monica Blvd., in Santa Monica (tel. 213/829-0215), is one of the best children's bookstores we've ever seen. In fact, they claim to carry the largest collection of children's books and records in the country. You can buy just about any kind of cassette or record for kids, and their selection of books is amazing. Open Monday through Saturday from 9 a.m. to 5:30 p.m.; on Wednesday they stay open till 7 p.m.

Lakeshore Curriculum Materials Store, 888 Venice Blvd., Los Angeles (tel. 213/559-9630), has a fabulous variety of educational books, toys, workbooks, records, and arts and crafts supplies. There are lots of materials you can't find in most children's book or toy stores. Open Monday through Friday from 9 a.m. to 5:30 p.m. and on Saturday till 5 p.m.

Children's Book World, 10580½ W. Pico Blvd., West Los Angeles (tel. 213/559-2665), is a relative newcomer to L.A. It offers an extensive selection of books, educational aids, records, and cassettes for infants up to high schoolers. The staff is very helpful. Open Monday through Friday from 10 a.m. to 5:30 p.m. and on Saturday till 5 p.m.

FESTIVALS AND SEASONAL ACTIVITIES: While Los Angeles doesn't have a parade for every holiday and a festival for every event, it does have its fair share of exciting seasonal activities.

Renaissance Pleasure Faire

Ah, the traditional spring rite that takes place on weekends during mid-April through May, the Renaissance Faire is a taste of Elizabethan England in southern California. The Faire is located at the Old Paramount Ranch in the

Agoura Hills, 40 minutes north of downtown. Take the Ventura Freeway (U.S. 101) to the Chesebro exit. Follow the signs.

Like opening a door to the past, visitors to the Faire often dress in costume and join the over 3,000 Elizabethans (from washerwoman and wench to jousting knight and nobility) in the centuries-old tradition of English rural faire.

The Faire is a *must-see* for children and adults of all ages. Here actors help you believe that you've stepped into Elizabethan England complete with 16th-century marketplace, authentic foods, and crafts. If you're in the mood, you can have quail, shepherd's pye, Cornish pasties, or sausages, not to mention the southern California favorites of falafel and churros. (But you'll not find hamburgers or hot dogs. If your kids are finicky eaters, plan accordingly and pack something for them.)

Adults pay $14.50; seniors and students 11 to 16, $11.50; children 3 to 11, $7.50. You can purchase tickets at the gate, by phone (tel. 213/202-8587), or through TicketMaster (tel. 213/480-3232). For more information, call 213/202-8854.

Los Angeles County Fair

The Los Angeles County Fair goes on from mid-September through the beginning of October. Far from being a rural town fair, most people are surprised to find out that the Los Angeles County Fair is the largest county fair in the world. In 1987 over 1.3 million people attended! Not a tiny event, to be sure.

Since 1922 the event has taken place in Pomona at the Los Angeles County Fair and Exposition Center, 1101 W. McKinley Ave., approximately 30 miles east of Los Angeles, two blocks north of I-10 (exit at Ganesha, White, or Garey Avenue (tel. 714/623-3111). Today the fair is on 487 acres, with an astonishing variety of exhibits. Not only are there livestock and dairy exhibits, but there is fine art, photography, gems and minerals, even wines. Add to this 12 acres of carnival grounds, and you've got a kid's delight in the making.

A Note of Caution: It can be extremely hot and smoggy during the fair. Go early in the day, bring sunscreen, and wear hats and light clothing.

Fair admission costs $7 for adults,; $5.50 for seniors, $4 for children 6 to 12; free for children under 6. Open Monday through Friday at 10 a.m. and on Saturday and Sunday at 9 a.m. Buildings remain open until 10 p.m., except on Friday and Saturday, when they're open until 11 p.m. Call for this year's dates.

Other Annual Events

The **Tournament of Roses Parade** (January 1) in Pasadena (tel. 818/449-ROSE, a 24-hour, year-round hotline for parade and game information), held each New Year's Day.

Kite Flying Festivals (March) on Santa Monica Pier, Santa Monica (tel. 213/458-8900). Also occurs at other times during the year.

Blessing of the Animals (April), on Olvera Street, downtown (tel. 213/625-5045).

Renaissance Pleasure Faire (May—see above for details).

Cinco de Mayo (May 5), on Olvera Street, downtown (tel. 213/625-5045).

Children's Day (in May), in Little Tokyo, downtown (tel. 213/628-2725).

The **Hollywood Bowl** (the season begins in July and runs to September); tickets are usually available (tel. 213/850-2000).

Sports and Arts Festival (August and September) in Santa Monica (tel. 213/458-8311).

Nisei Week, Japanese Festival (August and September) in Little Tokyo, downtown (tel. 213/687-7193). Nisei Week is when Little Tokyo comes alive with carnivals, parades, and crafts.

Los Angeles County Fair (September and October—see above for details).

Marina Del Rey Christmas Boat Parade (December) (tel. 213/822-9344 or 213/821-0555).

Hollywood Christmas Parade (December) (tel. 213/461-4213).

ACTIVITIES BY AGE GROUPS: The following listings suggest activities divided into specific age brackets. Refer back to the individual descriptions for details and any age descriptions. Be sure to also check Chapter XI on Greater Los Angeles for additional activities.

Teens and Preteens

Audience Participation Shows
Barnsdall Art Park
California Afro-American Museum
California Museum of Science and Industry
Chinatown
Circle K Horseback Riding
Craft and Folk Art Museum
Culver City Ice Skating Rink
Doug Weston's Troubador
Farmers Market
Fisherman's Village
George C. Page Museum
Greek Theater
Griffith Park Laserium Cosmic Light Concert
Griffith Park Observatory and Planetarium
Griffith Park Travel Town
Hollywood
Little Tokyo
Los Angeles County Fair
Los Angeles County Museum of Art
Los Angeles Zoo
Malibu Castle Miniature Golf
Museum of Contemporary Art
Museum of Natural History
The Music Center
Olvera Street
Pickwick Ice Arena
Pro Sports
Raging Waters
Renaissance Pleasure Faire
The Roxy
Santa Monica Pier
Six Flags Magic Mountain
Southwest Museum
Studio Tours
U.C.L.A.
Universal Amphitheater
Universal Studios
Venice Beach Ocean Front Walk
Westwood Village

School-Age Children

Angel's Attic
Audience Participation Shows
Barnsdall Art Park
California Afro-American Museum

California Museum of Science and Industry
Chinatown
Circle K Horseback Riding
Craft and Folk Art Museum
Culver City Ice Skating Rink
Fairfax Trolley
Farmers Market
Fisherman's Village
Fun Zone (Santa Monica Pier)
George C. Page Museum
Griffith Park Carousel
Griffith Park Observatory and Planetarium
Griffith Park Travel Town
Hollywood
Little Tokyo
Los Angeles Children's Museum
Los Angeles County Fair
Los Angeles County Museum of Art
Los Angeles Zoo
Malibu Castle Miniature Golf
Museum of Contemporary Art
Museum of Natural History
Olvera Street
Pickwick Ice Arena
Pro Sports
Raging Waters
Ralph M. Parson's Discovery Center (Museum of Natural History)
Renaissance Pleasure Faire
Santa Monica Pier
Six Flags Magic Mountain
Southwest Museum
Studio Tours
U.C.L.A.
Universal Studios
Venice Beach Ocean Front Walk

Preschoolers and Toddlers

Barnsdall Art Park
Culver City Ice Skating Rink
Fairfax Trolley
Farmers Market
Fisherman's Village
Fun Zone (Santa Monica Pier)
George C. Page Museum
Griffith Park Carousel
Griffith Park Miniature Train, Pony Rides, Simulator
Los Angeles Children's Museum
Los Angeles County Fair
Los Angeles Zoo
Museum of Natural History
Olvera Street
Pickwick Ice Arena
Ralph M. Parson's Discovery Center (Museum of Natural History)
Renaissance Pleasure Faire
U.C.L.A.

IN CASE OF EMERGENCY: Should a life-or-death emergency arise during your visit to Los Angeles, call **911** for the police or fire department, or an ambulance. In addition, there are a number of hospitals and pharmacies with extended hours available to you.

HOSPITALS: The following hospitals have 24-hour emergency rooms: **Queen of Angels Medical Center,** 2301 Bellevue Ave., Los Angeles (tel. 213/413-3000, or 213/413-7318 for the emergency room); **Cedars-Sinai Medical Center,** 8700 Beverly Blvd., Los Angeles (tel. 213/855-5000, or 213/855-6517 for the emergency room); and the **Glendale Adventist Medical Center,** 1509 Wilson Terrace, Glendale (tel. 818/409-8000, or 818/409-8202 for the emergency room).

PHARMACIES WITH EXTENDED HOURS: The following Los Angeles pharmacies offer extended-hour services: **Horton & Converse,** 11600 Wilshire Blvd., West L.A. (tel. 213/478-0801), open from 9 a.m. to 2 a.m.; **Horton & Converse,** 9201 Sunset Blvd., West Hollywood (tel. 213/272-0488), open from 9 a.m. to 2 a.m.; **Thrifty Drugs Store,** 300 N. Cañon Dr., Beverly Hills (tel. 213/273-7293), open from 9 a.m. to 10 p.m.; and **Thrifty Drugs Store,** 4633 Santa Monica Blvd., West Hollywood (tel. 213/666-6126), open from 9 a.m. to 9 p.m.
  There is one 24-hour pharmacy in Van Nuys (the San Fernando Valley): **Horton & Converse,** 6625 Van Nuys Blvd. (tel. 818/782-6251).

CHAPTER XI

GREATER LOS ANGELES

□ □ □

1. THE BEACH COMMUNITIES—MALIBU, MANHATTAN, AND REDONDO
2. LONG BEACH AND SAN PEDRO
3. CATALINA
4. PASADENA/GLENDALE

Los Angeles sprawls from the San Gabriel Mountains to the sea, from Malibu south to Long Beach. The communities surrounding L.A. don't have to be in the city proper to be part of the Los Angeles scene. And lucky for us. Greater Los Angeles offers so many family activities to choose from that you'll have trouble deciding what you want to do.

You can spend the day on the island of Catalina, with its tiny town of Avalon and vast wilderness. Or the kids can don some of their Sunday clothes and you can head to Pasadena, the grand dame of the vicinity, and haven of artistic masterpieces.

And if you just want to experience the idyllic southern California lifestyle, there are miles of sandy white beaches on which you and the kids can swim, surf, boogie board—and just soak up the sun. Children can play; teens can people-watch.

We start with a day in L.A.—the beaches, that is.

1. THE BEACH COMMUNITIES—MALIBU, MANHATTAN, AND REDONDO

Malibu is world famous as a haven for movie stars and celebrities. What may not be as widely known are its recreational possibilities for families.

The drive on Pacific Coast Hwy. (Calif. 1) through Malibu is part of the experience. The 27 miles of shoreline front shimmering emerald seas. Eroded cliffs and chaparral-covered rolling hills border the Pacific Coast Hwy. Tile-roofed Spanish-style villas and homes with enormous picture windows line the beach for miles at a stretch. Then, as you get farther up the coast, Malibu becomes more rural. Homes dot the hillsides of the Santa Monica Mountains, and kennels and boarding stables appear. The best beaches are here.

While restaurant prices in this affluent community are higher than many other parts of Los Angeles County, you can picnic on the beach or in the parks, and there are a host of fast-food favorites as well.

Getting your bearings on Pacific Coast Hwy. isn't difficult at all. Just remember that this part of the Santa Monica Bay coastline runs east and west. So when people say they're going "up" the coast to Malibu, here Malibu is actually west of Santa Monica. The coastline starts to curve north near the Los Angeles–Ventura County line. *Note:* During the weekends, and every day in summer, the Pacific Coast Hwy. (PCH, as it is affectionately known) becomes clogged with beach-going traffic. We suggest that you plan this into your time frame, and bring things for the kids to do in the car if you should get hopelessly stuck in traffic (a suggestion you might want to take anytime you hit the freeways in Los Angeles).

Before you start, you might want to contact the **Malibu Chamber of Commerce,** 22235 Pacific Coast Hwy., Malibu, CA 90265 (tel. 213/456-9025 or 213/456-9026).

WHAT TO SEE AND DO IN MALIBU: Here are a few recreational activities for you to enjoy with your family.

J. Paul Getty Museum

Set on a hill overlooking the Malibu shores is the J. Paul Getty Museum, 17985 Pacific Coast Hwy., at Coastline (tel. 213/459-7611). The building that houses the museum is in itself worth the trip. A re-creation of an Italian villa, complete with fountains and ornate pools, the building and the surrounding complex are very impressive.

The Getty has an unusual attitude toward children. Gallery teachers routinely take groups of kindergartners and elementary-school children through the collections, and express delight when children bubble with enthusiasm and questions. As sedate as one might think this museum to be, kids are encouraged (in groups and individually) to look closely. They're even allowed to feel the statue of Aphrodite. (Don't laugh too loudly if you pass a group of children with their hands all over her!) Parents of young children are not admonished if their kids make noise, but instead are invited to take a break with the kids in the lovely gardens.

While second-grade Andrew was completely enchanted by the statues of the mythological gods and the ornate antique furniture, his attention waned after viewing only a few paintings. Even so, he loves to return again and again—each time to soak up just a little bit more of the beauty. Parents who have taken their kids often say it's best to keep the visits very short.

Gallery teachers think that most of the exhibits are good for families, including the Decorative Arts Collection, paintings from the 12th century to the early 20th century, and the Antiquities Collection (artifacts from ancient life). Their attitude is that children are never too young to start appreciating fine art. Children will enjoy the experience if their parents don't expect too much of them.

In the past the Getty has hosted an excellent and extensive series of programs expressly for kids. Each month, small groups of children with their parents would delve into one aspect of art that is presented in the museum. Then they'd create their own work in the same tradition. For example, one workshop was on mythology. The gallery instructor took them through the appropriate collection of art and statues, and when they finished viewing, they were told to talk with their parents and create a myth about their families or their lives. Other workshops might cover portraiture, oil paintings, or tapestries. If you want to participate, you must sign up several months in advance. Call or write for more information about these special family programs.

Because there are limited parking facilities, if you plan to come by car and park, you must make a (free) parking reservation seven to ten days in advance (by mail or by telephone). You cannot park on the streets near the museum either.

Since there is no walk-in traffic permitted, if you don't get a parking permit, you may only enter the museum grounds by bicycle, motorcycle, taxi, or RTD bus (no. 434; get a museum pass from the driver).

The Getty Museum is open Tuesday through Sunday from 10 a.m. to 5 p.m., and there is no admission charge.

Swimming Beaches

Malibu beaches vary from rocky coves and little pocket beaches to long white sandy stretches. We'll start at the western tip of Malibu.

Leo Carrillo State Beach (tel. 818/706-1310) is a 1,600-acre beach and campground that offers a wonderful day in the sun and salt air. In addition to good swimming and surfing, Leo Carrillo has a nature trail, tidepools, even sea caves. The caves remind us of the home of the dragon in the movie *Pete's Dragon.* The waves splash up through the tunnel-like caves, taunting us to get wet. We jump to avoid them, but of course that's all just part of the fun, since we're in bathing suits anyway.

Although exploring the caves is a wondrous experience for most kids, be prepared to carry your younger children. We saw one 4-year-old boy who seemed scared to explore the twisting caves, but enjoyed them when his mother carried him.

The beach has rest rooms, lifeguards, firepits, and a parking lot. (See the "Where to Stay" section for details about the campground.)

Nicholas Canyon County Beach (tel. 213/457-9891) is a delightful, small beach that is hidden from the road by eroded cliffs that rise out of the sand. It's about one mile east of Leo Carrillo (across from the Malibu Riding and Tennis Club) and about five miles west of Zuma. Parking is available above the beach. There are stairs and a ramp down.

Zuma Beach County Park (tel. 213/457-9891) is a large, sandy beach with playground equipment, snackbar, rest rooms, and lifeguards. Lots of parking is available. During spring break and summer vacation, San Fernando Valley children and teens flock to this long, wide stretch of beach for sunbathing, surfing, and ogling.

If you continue to walk southeast from Zuma, you'll come to **Westward Beach** (tel. 213/457-9891). This long, narrow beach has good swimming, boogie boarding, and surfing. Edged by cliffs that give it a secluded feeling, Westward Beach is a good choice for families. Rest rooms and parking are available. Lifeguards are on duty.

Want a beach that's great for little kids as well as teenagers? **Malibu Lagoon State Beach** and the adjacent **Surfrider Beach** (tel. 818/706-1310) are perfect for all ages.

Youngsters watch intently as wet-suited surfers ride in the waves. And until recently, this picturesque beach offered lagoon wading as well. Pollution has taken its toll on that recreational activity, but the lagoon is still home to ducks and birds, and its banks afford wonderful wandering.

Picnic tables, rest rooms, and parking are available. There are lifeguards on duty.

If you know ahead of time that you'll be in the area, why not make reservations for a naturalist-led walk designed especially for tots? **Babes at the Beach** is a sensory nature walk for children 3 months to 6 years and their parents. Sponsored by the William O. Douglas Outdoor Classroom, the group explores the estuary and tidepool habitats. The nature guide points out the various marine animals in the intertidal zone. They actually go out on the rocks and explore the tidepools and look at the starfish, sea urchins, and anemones that live there. (If you're coming in from out of town, be sure to tell the reservationist; he or she will make an extra effort to fit you in.) Free, but reserve months in advance. These walks occur once a month. Call or write for a specific date and time to the William O. Douglas Outdoor Classroom, P.O. Box 2488, Beverly Hills, CA 90213 (tel. 213/858-3834).

If you're interested in the local culture, there is a little-known treasure adjacent to the lagoon that you can tour. **Adamson House and Malibu Lagoon Museum,** 23200 Pacific Coast Hwy. (tel. 213/456-8432), is reminiscent of Hearst Castle on a tiny scale. The home was built for Rhoda Rindge Adamson, daughter of May and Frederick Rindge, who were the last owners of the Malibu land grant. One of the family businesses was the Malibu Tile Company, which produced exquisitely colored ceramic tiles. (In fact, Malibu Pier was built to allow ships to dock to take the tiles to other ports.) The use of the decorative tile throughout the house and gardens is fantastic. There are rare, beautiful fountains, hand-carved doors, and filigreed wrought iron. The small museum gives you a chronology of Malibu's history—from its Chumash Indian origins through its growth as a colony for the rich and famous.

In addition, this is one of the most spectacular views you'll get of the ocean, Malibu Pier, and the lagoon.

Tours are offered Tuesday through Saturday from 10 a.m. to 2 p.m. No admission charge.

Parks in the Santa Monica Mountains

The Santa Monica Mountains, which run east and west along the coast, provide many wonderful places to explore. From deep canyons to beautiful vista points atop the hills, they offer miles of hiking trails and splendid picnicking.

Malibu Creek State Park (tel. 818/706-8809 or 818/706-1310) is located in the mountains halfway between Malibu and the San Fernando Valley about 100 yards south of Mulholland Hwy. on Las Virgenes / Malibu Canyon Road. The park has over 30 miles of hiking trails, canyons, a lake, and waterfalls. The main trail, Crags Road, will take you past the spot where television's "M*A*S*H" was filmed. The trail has one hill—the rest is level—and the round trip is about five miles. Good picnicking. Ask at the Visitor Center about other good trails for your family. The Visitor Center is open weekends only, from noon to 4 p.m. Charge for parking.

Tapia County Park (tel. 805/259-7721) is a smaller park located near Malibu Creek State Park, five miles south of Calif. 101 (Ventura Freeway) on Las Virgenes/Malibu Canyon Road. The park has hiking trails and good picnicking.

The **Peter Strauss Ranch** at Lake Enchanto (tel. 818/888-3770) is actually in Agura, on Mulholland Hwy. (If you're coming from U.S. 101, exit at Kanan Road; go south to Troutdale; and turn left onto Mulholland Hwy. If you're coming from Malibu, go up Kanan Road to Troutdale; take a right to Mulholland Hwy.) There are a few good trails and a nature walk. There are special children's events, including music festivals and ranger-led hikes. Call for information.

Topanga Canyon State Park (tel. 213/455-2465 or 818/706-1310) has a self-guided nature trail in addition to 35 miles of trails. Located off Topanga Canyon Road at Entrada Road, the park is open daily April through October from 8 a.m. to 7 p.m.

For more parks in the Santa Monica Mountains (Will Rogers State Historic Park, Coldwater Canyon Park, and Franklin Canyon Ranch), see the "What to Do and See" section in Chapter X.

Nursery Walks

If you hesitate to take your little ones on nature hikes . . . don't. **Nursery Walks,** sponsored by the Palisades-Malibu YMCA, 821 Via de la Paz, Pacific Palisades, CA 90272 (tel. 213/454-4491), is an organization of volunteers who lead nature walks for infants, toddlers, and preschoolers. Their goal is to develop in families an appreciation and love for the out-of-doors so that as children get older, they have a healthy respect for the environment. The walks are two hours long, and about half a mile in length. About halfway, they take a break.

Leaders get the children to try to use all the senses—they do a lot of looking, listening, and touching. For example, they'll pretend to be Indians so they learn to be quiet and listen to the sounds in the quiet. They'll do such activities as using flowers to make soap, matching rocks to their environment, smelling leaves, and talking about their purposes. During the summer, most of the walks are either along the coast or during the evenings when they're paired with a picnic dinner (each family brings their own).

If you have older kids also, they're welcome. Although the programs are geared for younger kids, leaders attempt to involve the older ones in the activities as well. Call 213/454-4491 to make reservations. It's best to try to make them ten days to two weeks in advance. A donation of $3 is requested.

The nursery walks in this area are conducted at Leo Carrillo, Malibu Lagoon, and Topanga State Park.

WHERE TO STAY IN MALIBU: If you choose to stay overnight, your choices are extremely limited. We suggest that you either take a room in nearby Santa Monica (see the "Where to Stay" section in Chapter X) or camp out.

Just in case you prefer a motel in pricey Malibu, we recommend **Casa Malibu Motel,** 22752 Pacific Coast Hwy. (Calif. 1), Malibu, CA 90265 (tel. 213/456-2219). Opened in the late 1940s, this garden motel is clean and well kept. The tidy little garden with flowering plants opens onto a large patio that looks out to the ocean. There are steps down to a quiet little beach. Showers and sand chairs are available.

The motel gets its share of older families, and openly prefers quiet, well-behaved children or teens.

Since the motel was built in the '40s, each room is shaped differently, and accommodates a different number of people. The beachfront-view rooms have two double beds and decks with lounge chairs. Other rooms have garden views. All rooms have coffee makers and color TVs.

Tell the manager what you want when you reserve your room. For summer, reserve at least four to six months in advance.

The rates are the same, whether single or double occupancy. Oceanfront rooms cost $110; garden rooms, $80 to $100. Rooms with kitchens can be rented for an extra $11 per day (three-day minimum rental). Each additional person beyond double occupancy (including children) is charged $10 per day. Cribs cost $11 additional per night.

Camping

The best camping in the area is at **Leo Carrillo State Beach,** 35000 Pacific Coast Hwy. (Calif. 1) (tel. 818/706-1310 or 805/987-3303). Leo Carrillo has a 134-site campground nestled into the canyon near the beach.

There is a 31-foot limit for RVs or trailers. No hookups, but they do have a dump station. Rest rooms and hot showers are available. The camp convenience store is open from 7 a.m. to 7 p.m. daily in summer. The nightly fee is $12 per campsite (eight people maximum per site).

There are ranger-led nature walks on Sunday, and campfire programs on Saturday nights.

You can reserve your campsite through **MISTIX** (tel. toll free 800/444-PARK), or write Leo Carrillo State Beach, c/o Santa Monica Mtns. District, 2860A Camino Dos Rios, Newbury Park, CA 91320.

WHERE TO EAT IN MALIBU: The **Inn of the Seventh Ray,** 128 Old Topanga Canyon Rd., Topanga (tel. 213/455-1311), is a place uniquely southern California. Located 3½ miles from Pacific Coast Hwy. (take a left on Old Topanga Road) in the canyon between Malibu and the San Fernando Valley, this rustic, unusual gourmet vegetarian-style restaurant is classic 1960s. Soothing classical music plays in the background, servers are "mellow" and relaxed, and the setting is beautiful.

Tucked into the canyon, you can dine outside near the fountains or little creek that runs by, where trees form a light canopy. Children love to frolic near the creek and watch the wildlife. You can also dine inside, where large-windowed rooms bring the outdoors to you.

Even though this is a romantic setting at night, the open-air, generally low-key atmosphere tends to keep young ones relaxed and unobtrusive. We never hesitate to bring our youngsters, who get caught up in stargazing.

Lunches include five different salads, open-face sandwiches, and such entrees as meatless lasagne, cold poached salmon, and Divine Direction (cream cheese with raisins, maple syrup, and nuts piled high on sliced whole-wheat bread). Prices range from $5 to $8.

The dinner menu is unique. The food that has the "highest vibration" is listed at the top; the denser food is at the bottom. Dinner entrees that are at the "top" of the list are a steamed vegetable plate, Queen of Light (millet and acorn squash), chicken rosemary and New York steak are at the list's bottom. Prices range from $10 to $22.

The homemade bread, soups, and other edibles in smaller portions will satisfy your kids, and make you feel you've given them at least one healthy meal. There is a lavish Sunday brunch buffet from 11 a.m. to 3 p.m. for $14. Regular Sunday breakfast costs $5 to $8.

No highchairs here, but booster seats are available. Open for lunch Monday through Friday from 11:30 a.m. to 2:30 p.m. and on Saturday from 10:30 a.m. to 2:30 p.m.; and for dinner Monday through Saturday from 6 to 9:30 p.m. On Sunday, service is from 9:30 a.m. to 3 p.m., but the buffet is served only from 11 a.m. to 3 p.m. No reservations are accepted, so it's best to come early—but plan to spend some time because meals are served at a very leisurely pace.

There is valet and self-parking available. Some major credit cards are accepted.

The ultimate in California casual, **Gladstone's 4-Fish,** 17300 Pacific Coast Hwy. (tel. 213/GL4-FISH), is located on the beach where Sunset Boulevard meets the ocean. A local favorite, Gladstone's has sawdust on the floors, large wooden booths with benches, and leaded-glass panels throughout. Large windows look out at the sandy beach and blue water beyond.

People go for the view, the atmosphere, and the seafood. In fact, on Saturday and Sunday mornings the place is simply brimming over with families who get an early headstart for breakfast and spend the rest of their day at the beach. With all this popularity, the place can get very noisy, and you may have to wait for your table even if you make a reservation. (That shouldn't be a problem, though, because next to the restaurant is a ramp to the little beach where you can stroll while you wait.)

The kitchen says they'll make anything on the menu from 7 a.m. on—including seafood—but we prefer our fish for lunch or dinner. Traditional breakfasts range in price from $5 to $12, and include omelets, eggs, and French toast.

We love the seafood. The six different seafood salads are heavenly, and come as half or whole orders. (If you're in the mood for something unusual, try the papaya-tuna salad served with macadamia nuts and chutney, at $10.) The huge assortment of fish and shellfish will delight seafood lovers. Entrees can be simple (mesquite-broiled fresh sea bass) or more elaborate (fresh salmon steamed in parchment with tomatoes, onions, mushrooms, and scallions). The steamed clams are brought to the table in a cute little metal bucket. Of course, there are shrimp, clams, oysters, mussels, crab, and lobster too. Prices range from $8 to market-price lobster. Steaks and burgers are also available. Dinners include chowder or salad, bread, and potato or vegetable.

The restaurant is open daily from 7 a.m. to 11 p.m. (till midnight on Friday and Saturday). There are booster seats, but no highchairs. No reservations accepted. Valet parking. Most major credit cards welcome.

If you're interested in Mexican food, **Carlos and Pepe's,** at 22706 W. Pacific Coast Hwy. (tel. 213/456-3105), graciously welcomes children. This south-of-the-border lookalike has terracotta floors, man-made palm trees, and parrots all around. But the real kid pleaser is the aquarium filled with tropical fish.

Every seat has an ocean view, and the restaurant is adjacent to a path to the beach. In fact, some parents take a table by the windows overlooking the sand, and let the older kids play outside while they have their meal.

With typical Mexican fare, there's no problem finding goodies for the kids. We do it with à la carte orders of tacos, enchiladas, and quesadillas. (À la carte prices range from $2.75 to $5.75.) Hamburgers and omelets are also served here. Our kids gobble down the chips and mild salsa that are served as soon as you're seated, and pretend to be very sophisticated when drinking the non-alcoholic margaritas in huge glasses with straws. Adult Mexican entrees and dinners range from $4.25 to $14.75, and there are seafood items that are higher (crab legs at $25).

There are no highchairs, but booster seats are available. The server will take care of splitting portions, and will also warm bottles or baby food. No reservations are accepted, so expect to wait. You should come before 6 p.m. if you don't want to linger for 1 to 1½ hours in the waiting area. As with Gladstone's, you can always wander around on the beach if you have a short wait. There is valet parking. Most major credit cards are honored.

If you're looking for more standard, moderately priced American food, the **Malibu Omelette Parlor,** 22969 Pacific Coast Hwy. (tel. 213/456-6106), is a good place to try. As you open the saloon-style doors, it's like stepping into a Victorian-style greenhouse. Wood floors, carved posts, and celebrity photographs on the wall complete the eclectic interior.

After 4 p.m., each table is covered with long sheets of white paper. Crayons are provided for would-be artists. (Some of the artwork lines the walls too.)

Lunch and dinner items include eggs, omelets, and creative sandwiches and salads. Prices range from $3 to $5. For dinner there is seafood, chowder, oyster stew, fish and chips, fajitas—chicken or shrimp—and teriyaki chicken. Prices range from $7 to about $10.

No highchairs here, but booster seats are available. No reservations accepted; on weekends the wait is about 20 minutes to an hour. Avoid the wait on weekends and eat before 9 a.m. or after 2 p.m. Some major credit cards welcome. Parking lot.

WHAT TO SEE AND DO IN MANHATTAN BEACH AND REDONDO BEACH:
If Malibu is a rustic retreat for the rich and famous, the South Bay beach towns of Manhattan and Redondo are the suburban havens for the upwardly mobile. Charming beachfront cottages, multilevel condominiums, and high-priced apartments line the beaches. On busy weekends the beaches teem with vital, active families carrying ice coolers, Frisbees, and exotic sand toys. Bicyclists pedal their way along the shorefront bike path (recognized as one of the best in southern California), and well-built singles roller skate or lounge on the beach, eyeing each other and checking out the action.

You, too, can play volleyball, roller skate, bicycle, surf, and swim in these sandy sanctuaries. And while the beaches may be more crowded than those in Malibu, they are less crowded than those of their northern neighbor, Santa Monica. (Parking is tough, though.)

Redondo Beach is probably the best-known town in the area. It boasts a colorful history. In 1890 well-known entrepreneur Henry Huntington opened the Hotel Redondo on a bluff overlooking the Pacific. In 1907, during a vacation in Hawaii, Huntington saw a young Polynesian man ride the ocean waves using planks of wood. Huntington invited the young man, George Freeth, to do surfing exhibitions at his new Hotel Redondo as a way to advertise the property. In 1909 a plunge was built, and Freeth trained lifeguards to protect the thousands of weekly bathers. Freeth is called the "father of surfing," is acclaimed as the first American lifeguard, and even won congressional medals for his rescues. His notoriety began in the port of Redondo Beach.

For information about these South Bay cities, contact the **Manhattan Beach Chamber of Commerce,** P.O. Box 3007, Manhattan Beach, CA 90266 (tel. 213/545-5313); and the **Redondo Beach Chamber of Commerce,** 1215 N. Catalina Ave., Redondo Beach, CA 90277 (tel. 213/376-6913).

Beaches

One of the first features you'll notice about South Bay beaches are their width. Some are incredibly wide stretches of sand (and unbearably hot on bare feet after the sand has baked in the sun).

Manhattan State Beach is a large beach with a playground, rest rooms, outdoor showers, and volleyball courts. Parking is difficult here, but if you come early, you can get a spot. The South Bay Bicycle Trail runs along the edge of the sand. The adjacent 900-foot **Manhattan Beach Pier** is a lovely place to take a stroll. Located at the foot of Manhattan Beach Boulevard, it marks the area where you can find food and sundries. (Call 213/545-3500 for information.)

The **Seaside Lagoon** (tel. 213/372-1171, ext. 291) is located in Redondo Beach at the southwest corner of Harbor Drive and Portofino Way. This large heated saltwater lagoon has a wading area and diving boards, making it a wonderful swimming area for children of all ages. It has lifeguards. There is a sandy beach, playground equipment, volleyball courts, rest rooms with hot showers, and a snackbar. Open daily from Memorial Day weekend to early September from 10 a.m. to 5:45 p.m. Adults pay $1.50 on weekdays and $1.75 on weekends; children pay $1 on weekdays and $1.25 on weekends.

Redondo State Beach is a very wide beach located below the bluffs. It has lifeguards, rest rooms, and parking. The South Bay Bicycle Trail follows the coast here.

If you're going to be in the area during the last weekend in July, check out the **International Surf Festival.** Your teens will love the lifeguard competitions, and your younger kids will love the sandcastle-design contests. For information, call 213/545-4502.

If you want to rent boogie boards or wet suits, **Dive 'n Surf,** 504 N. Broadway, next to the Sheraton in Redondo Beach (tel. 213/372-8423), is one place to go. Boogie boards rent for $5 per day, wet suits cost $12.50 per day, and short wet suits are $8 per day. All items are half price each additional day.

Bike Path

The **South Bay Bicycle Trail** is part of a longer trail that extends north and south. This bike path is over 19 miles long, if you take it all the way from California Street in Santa Monica to Torrance Beach. This is probably the most popular bike path in the Los Angeles area, which means that it's best to do it early or late in the day to avoid the crowds. It's even better if you can do it off-season. In fact, we prefer the bike path during the spring, fall, and winter because the air is crisp, making it more comfortable to ride long distances. We also find that the kids do better when there aren't so many other riders stacked up.

The wide path (with markers indicating the direction of traffic) follows the beach, making for enjoyable watching as well as easy riding. We usually start at Fisherman's Village in Marina Del Rey (see the "What to Do and See" section in

Chapter X for details) and head south. If you choose to do that and go all the way south, you can ride 12 miles from this point. You can also drive to any parking area near the beach and pick up the bike path there. There are rest rooms and telephones all along the way.

Along the way, you might choose to stop at **Manhattan Beach Pier, Hermosa Beach Pier,** or Redondo's **King Harbor.**

Bicycle Rentals

To rent bicycles, you can try the **Hermosa Cyclery,** 20 13th St., Hermosa Beach (one block north of Hermosa Pier) (tel. 213/376-2720). They rent children's bicycles for $2.50 per hour or $10 per day; adult bikes are $4 per hour or $15 per day. Carriers and helmets are free with bike rental. They also rent rollerskates for $3 per hour or $12 per day.

Open daily from 8 a.m. to 8 p.m. No reservations accepted but in the summer and on weekends it's best to get there before 10 a.m.

Fun Bunns Beach Rentals, 1144 Highland Ave., Manhattan Beach (tel. 213/379-4898), is three blocks from the beach. It rents adult and children's bikes, toddler carriers, and rollerskates (from ladies' size 4). Helmets, knee guards, and wrist guards are available. Rates are $4 to $5 per hour per bike. Tandem bikes cost $7 per hour; skates, $3.50 per hour. Open daily from 10 a.m. to dusk.

King Harbor and Redondo Beach Pier

King Harbor and Redondo Beach Municipal Pier, at the foot of Torrance Boulevard (tel. 213/372-1171, ext. 274), offer restaurants, fast-food places, shopping, pier fishing, fish markets, and a fun zone, all within view of sailboats and yachts. The International Boardwalk, located just north of the pier, has shops and casual restaurants. Open 365 days a year. The **Redondo Fun Factory** (tel. 213/379-8510) has video games, pinball machines, and Skee-Ball. Open Monday through Thursday from 2 to 10 p.m.; on Friday from 2 p.m. to midnight; on Saturday from 11 a.m. to midnight; and on Sunday from 11 a.m. to 10 p.m.

Redondo Sport Fishing Pier, located at 233 Harbor Dr. (tel. 213/372-2111), offers sport fishing and pier fishing. They have a barge that is good for children because there is less motion. You can go out for an hour at a time. The barge is open daily from 6 a.m. to 4:30 p.m. and 6 p.m. to midnight. Adults pay $14 and children are charged $7 for eight-hour shifts. There are half-day and full-day fishing trips. The half-day trips are 4½ hours; adults pay $16 and children (under 12) pay $11. Full-day trips leave at midnight and return at 6 p.m.; adults pay $40 and children pay $30, including bait, bunk, and parking. Pier poles for rent at $5.50. Live bait is available. The pier is open 24 hours a day.

Whale-watching cruises start at the end of December and go through April.

2. LONG BEACH AND SAN PEDRO

Just 30 miles south of Los Angeles on the San Diego Freeway (I-405) or the Pacific Coast Hwy. (Calif. 1) is Long Beach, home of the *Queen Mary* and the *Spruce Goose,* and home to what was once the richest oil strike in North America. When you arrive in town, notice the high-rise "condos" offshore. At night they look like pretty islands, lit with colorful lights and surrounded by palm trees and fountains. They are really decorated oil-rig operations.

Long Beach recently celebrated its centennial with all sorts of festivities. And downtown Long Beach is experiencing a renaissance that denizens hope will make it an appealing destination to all of you who are planning trips to southern California. A huge shopping center is being added to the *Spruce Goose / Queen Mary* complex; downtown's Pine Avenue is becoming the trendy place to be for merchants and restaurateurs; the Greater Los Angeles World Trade Center was recently completed downtown; and Long Beach Harbor has become one of the most important shipping ports for the Pacific Rim trade.

While it might not be your overnight destination point, it's a short trip from Los Angeles if you have extra time. There are all sorts of activities that take place annually, some of which might be going on during your trip to southern California and may be fun for the whole family. The staff at the Convention Council will be happy to tell you what's appropriate and appealing for kids. For information on any of the festivities that go on in the area, call or visit the **Long Beach Area Convention and Visitors Council,** 180 E. Ocean Blvd., Plaza Level, Long Beach, CA 90802 (tel. 213/436-3645). Open Monday through Friday from 8:30 a.m. to 5 p.m.

Without question, the *Queen Mary* and the *Spruce Goose* are the two most popular sightseeing attractions in Long Beach. Both are located at Long Beach Harbor, at the end of the Long Beach Freeway (I-710) (tel. 213/435-3511).

The **Queen Mary** was the biggest, best, and fastest of its time. The ship was truly the most elegant sailing vessel on the sea and carried some of the world's most important people back and forth across the Atlantic. It also played a significant role in World War II, and it could outrun German torpedoes. Take the kids on the Shipwalk, a self-guided tour of the upper and lower decks, the sundeck, and the sports deck. It also includes the wheelhouse, World War II displays, an audio-visual presentation of the story of the vessel, and other exhibits. The Captain's Tour is a personalized small-group tour for $5 extra. It lasts 90 minutes and takes you behind the scenes to areas usually off-limits.

Besides housing a 390-room hotel created from converted staterooms, the *Queen Mary* has four restaurants and two bars.

The **Spruce Goose** was Howard Hughes's 400,000-pound contribution to the war effort, built to transport American troops out of the range of German U-boats. It flew only once, in 1947, and was then placed in a specially built hangar. From special platforms you can see into the flight deck and cargo bay. Many displays and audio-visual presentations surround the plane, which is now housed in the world's largest geodesic aluminum dome.

Also housed in the dome is a made-for-kids audio-visual presentation called *Time Voyager.* This special-effects show is a multisensory series of out-of-this-world experiences.

There is also a multi-image presentation projected onto the side of the *Spruce Goose* called "Ships of Flight."

Londontowne Village, a themed center of boutiques and snackbars, is also part of the *Spruce Goose / Queen Mary* complex.

The complex is open daily, including holidays: July 4 to Labor Day, from 9 a.m. to 9 p.m. (box office closes at 8 p.m.); the rest of the year, from 10 a.m. to 6 p.m. (box office closes at 4 p.m.).

There's one admission price for all attractions: $15 for adults and children over 11, $12 for seniors, $9 for children 5 to 11; under 5, free.

Shoreline Village, 407 Shoreline Village Dr., at the end of the Long Beach Freeway (I-710) and Pine Avenue (tel. 213/590-8427), makes an interesting stop when you're in the area. Set on seven acres, this turn-of-the-century themed shopping center features restaurants, seaside cafés, shops, and an early-1900s carousel.

Long Beach has a very active water-sports life. In addition to five miles of pure southern California beaches to enjoy, **Alamitos Bay** offers seven miles of beaches. **Marine Stadium,** at Marina Park, 5255 Appian Way (tel. 213/594-0951), is the place for waterskiing. Right next door is a "tame" beach, frequented by parents and little kids, called **Mother's Beach.** And **Marina Park** is also the place to rent pedalboats and kayaks. The Department of Parks and Recreation offers sailing instruction and boat rentals at the **Long Beach Sailing Center** at

Alamitos Bay, 5437 E. Ocean Blvd. (tel. 213/439-5427 in summer, 213/429-4220 in winter). Take windsurfing lessons at the **Long Beach Windsurf Center,** 4100 E. Ocean Blvd. (tel. 213/433-1014).

Or go whale-watching from December to April. **Queen's Wharf,** 555 Pico Ave. (tel. 213/432-8993), operates 65- and 85-foot vessels for up to 128 passengers. They sail daily, December 26 through April 1. Adults pay $9; juniors 14 and under and seniors pay $6.50. You can also arrange sport-fishing trips for quarter-, half-, and full-day runs, and children are welcome. Reservations are recommended for both whale-watching and fishing.

Or you can watch from aboard a sailboat or powerboat with **Spirit Cruises,** Berth 75, Ports of Call, in nearby San Pedro (tel. 213/831-1073). Weekday and weekend cruises are guaranteed—if you don't see a whale, you can take another cruise for free. Cruises are scheduled daily during this period. Adults are charged $12.50; kids 12 and under, $9.50. Call for reservations and departure times.

Try fishing off *Annie's Barge,* a 150-foot fishing vessel moored at the west end of Seal Beach Pier, Seal Beach (tel. 213/598-8677).

Long Beach is also a popular departure point for cruises to Catalina. (See the "Catalina" section, below, for departure information.)

Visit the **Long Beach Naval Station** for a tour of the ships in dock. Call 213/547-7234 or 213/547-7727 for tickets and details.

History buffs might be interested in seeing **Rancho Los Alamitos,** 6400 Bixby Hill Rd. (tel. 213/431-3541), which is the oldest adobe structure of its kind in California. Tours are available. In June, the city sponsors California Ranch Day at the structure. There are live animals, and kids get to participate in "hands-on" ranching and farming demonstrations. Call for this year's June date. Nominal fee.

If you plan to be in the area for a while, be sure to contact the **Long Beach Convention and Entertainment Center,** 300 E. Ocean Blvd. (tel. 213/432-2233 or 213/436-3660), to find out what's on the schedule. Everything from the *Nutcracker* performed by children and "Sesame Street Live" goes on there. There are backstage tours daily except Sunday by reservation (tel. 213/436-3661).

WHAT TO SEE AND DO IN SAN PEDRO: Pack up the kids for a journey to the seaside area of San Pedro. San Pedro Bay is home to one of the world's largest man-made harbors—Los Angeles Harbor. But San Pedro offers more than cargo and freighters; it has two enchanting areas that you'll want to explore.

Cabrillo Marine Museum

Children and their parents will delight in an excursion to the Cabrillo Marine Museum. "Excursion" is the way you should look at it, since San Pedro is off the beaten track. But it's a marvelous place to spend at least half the day. Located within a stone's throw of the ocean, the Cabrillo Marine Museum (and Aquarium), 3720 Stephen White Dr. (tel. 213/548-7562), provides children of all ages a glimpse of the marine life of southern California. There are 34 seawater aquariums that are home to hundreds of marine species and plantlife. The elaborate displays—kelp forests, rocky shores, and sandy habitats—are arranged especially for children, and can be viewed from all sides. Skilled docents explain the exhibits at the children's level. The high point of our trip was the touching pool, where the children got to hold anemones, sea stars, and sea cucumbers.

You might want to avoid the tours since they rush you through the exhibits. There are a variety of children's programs, ranging from one-day workshops to week-long sessions. In the past they've had such fascinating family workshops as "Treasures in a Tidepool" and "ABCs of Aquarium Keeping." Call for information and reservations.

There is no admission charge. Open Tuesday through Friday from noon to

5 p.m. and on Saturday and Sunday from 10 a.m. to 5 p.m.; closed Monday, and Thanksgiving and Christmas Days. To get to Cabrillo Marine Museum, take the Harbor Freeway south and exit at Gaffey Street in San Pedro.

But don't leave yet. Across the parking lot from the museum is a grassy area and a wonderful beach. **Cabrillo Beach** (tel. 213/372-2166) has very gentle waves—because it's inside the breakwater that protects the harbor. It offers perfect swimming for children, yet has enough action to let them dodge the low-breaking waves. You'll also want to check the tide tables and try to be there during low tide so you can wander through the tidepools on the rocks. *Careful, though, it's slippery.*

Ports O'Call Village and the Whaler's Wharf

Located at Berth 77 on the main channel of Los Angeles Harbor, Ports O'Call Village (tel. 213/831-0287), and the Whaler's Wharf offer a pleasant few hours. Cobblestone streets and waterfront dining make you feel as if you've suddenly landed in an old New England seaport town. There are three villages, each with its own flavor. One has huge fresh fish markets and open-air barbecues where you can have the fish cooked to order. Many people buy drinks and enjoy the delectable fish on the open-air decks.

Altogether the villages have 15 restaurants (which include a wide variety of fast-food and light-snacks places), 75 shops, and boathouses for harbor cruises and whale-watching trips. Our favorite stop is **Candy Town** (tel. 213/514-2669). This emporium offers everything from imported chocolates to sweet dinosaur eggs.

Strolling throughout the villages are dancers, musicians, and clowns. But the real treat is watching the traffic in the harbor. We saw tugboats and huge freighters, cruise ships, and sailboats. Kids squeal when they see a pelican, and hungry seagulls are part of the fun. Open daily from 11 a.m. to 9 p.m. in summer, till 7 p.m. the rest of the year. There is plenty of free parking. To get to Ports O'Call, take the Harbor Freeway (I-110) south to Harbor Boulevard. Exit in San Pedro, and turn right on Harbor Boulevard, then turn left at 6th Street and follow the signs.

If you really want to get a sense of the harbor, take the **L.A. Harbor Cruise** (tel. 213/831-0996). This one-hour sojourn goes all around the harbor, passing the Vincent Thomas Bridge, Todd Shipyards, and Angel's Gate Lighthouse. Television lovers will enjoy seeing the home of "The Love Boat." Our 7-year-old especially liked the supertankers and freighters that we passed. In fact, the adults enjoyed it even more than the kids. School-age children do well for about half the trip, and after that it's a bit of a struggle to keep them entertained. We brought snacks and little trinkets for them to play with.

The double-decker boat is open-air upstairs and glass-enclosed downstairs. Tours depart at noon and 1, 2, 3, and 4 p.m. But call ahead for schedule information before making your plans. Fares are $5 for adults, $2.50 for children 2 to 12; under-2s, free.

3. CATALINA

"Twenty-six miles across the sea. . . ." Actually, it's 22 miles across the sea to Santa Catalina Island, the island of romance.

First discovered by Juan Cabrillo in 1542, it wasn't until 1892 that the island was purchased and turned into the Santa Catalina Island Company for the purpose of becoming a pleasure resort.

The island has been the home to the Catalina Indians and to sea otters, both of which were wiped out by the Russians and their accompanying tribes of fierce Aleut and Kodiak Indians. It was also the home to pirates, cattle- and sheepherders, fur traders, and miners.

The year 1919 marked the beginning of its prime development phase, when

William Wrigley, Jr., bought controlling interest in the company. He was instrumental in preserving the island's wilderness. The Santa Catalina Island Conservancy was organized in the early '70s to preserve and protect the wilderness areas —over 42,000 acres.

It was the Wrigleys who really made the island a popular vacation spot. Although a great place to spend a romantic weekend, Catalina is not just for twosomes. The activities are numerous, and there's something for almost everyone in the family. But you don't have to stay overnight. You can enjoy Catalina as a day trip from Los Angeles.

GETTING THERE: There are several ways to get to Catalina Island.

By Boat

From Los Angeles, you have your choice of Catalina Cruises or Catalina Express. Liquid Dramamine would be in order for these trips, as well as extra plastic bags and a change of clothes—even for a day trip. Rough waters can obviously cause seasickness, in which case those extra clothes and bags come in handy.

Catalina Express, which leaves only from Berth 95, Los Angeles Harbor, in San Pedro (tel. 213/519-1212, 213/510-1212 on the island, or toll free 800/257-2227 in California), offers a 90-minute trip on a small boat, one with stabilizers for a more comfortable trip. This is the boat service we recommend. It has airline-style seats inside and cabin-attendant service and refreshments. The open upper deck is great on a sunny day or mild evening. Boats travel to Catalina and back year round. In winter there are four to six departures daily; in summer, as many as ten. Call for specific times. Reservations are required. Round-trip fares are $27.75 for adults, $20.50 for children 2 to 11; under 2, $1.50.

Catalina Cruises boasts a 700-passenger triple-deck vessel. It leaves from Long Beach and San Pedro (Berth 95) and offers daily departures. The trips are two hours one way. There's a snackbar and cocktails. Reservations are a must, especially during summer. When you call, ask for directions to the piers. In Los Angeles, call 213/775-6111; in the Long Beach / South Bay area, call 213/514-3838; in Orange County, call 714/527-7111. Round-trip fares October through April are $20.25 for adults, $11 for children 2 through 11, $1.25 for under-2s; May through September, $24 for adults, $12.75 for children 2 through 11, $1.25 for under-2s.

From Orange County, you can leave from the Balboa Pavilion in Newport Beach. Operated by **Catalina Passenger Service** (tel. 714/673-5245), the catamaran *Catalina Flyer* holds 500 passengers and has three decks, snack service, and two full bars. The trip takes 1¼ hours, and there is one round trip scheduled per day, from the end of March through November. Off-season, it leaves once a day, Thursday through Sunday (except in December, when departures are only December 26 through New Year's Day). Round-trip fares are $28 for adults, $15 for children 2 to 12; under 2, $1.50.

By Air

A ride on a jet helicopter is certainly faster, though more expensive. You can reserve a seat with **Helitrans** (tel. 213/548-1314, or toll free 800/262-1472), which leaves from Berth 95 in San Pedro every hour on the hour on Friday and weekends. Weekdays, it departs three times a day. Each jet helicopter seats six, and the trip takes 15 minutes. Round-trip fares are $86 for adults and children.

Island Express (tel. 213/491-5550) is another jet helicopter service that leaves from San Pedro and Long Beach (from a helipad near the *Queen Mary*). Call for reservations and directions to the helipad. Fares are the same as Helitrans, and you get free parking and a courtesy van in Avalon.

San Diego Seaplanes (tel. 619/483-8336) will transport you to Avalon from San Diego, Orange County, Long Beach, Torrance, and Los Angeles. Call for reservations and rates from each city.

ORIENTATION: Welcome to Avalon, Santa Catalina Island's main and only town. You are now on an island 21 miles long and 8 miles wide. Avalon boasts 267 days of sunshine, and an average high temperature of 76° and an average low of 58.4° June through October. Mid-October and mid-April are its wet months. Summers rarely get above 80°; winters, rarely below 50°.

In summer, Avalon's population of a little over 2,000 swells to 6,000 weekdays, and sometimes up to 10,000 people on the weekends.

Avalon itself is only about one square mile in size. The interior of the island is wild, beautiful, and pristine—and off-limits to private vehicles, and hikers and campers without permits. Protected by the Catalina Conservancy, whose job it is to preserve it for posterity, it is accessible by tour bus or permit.

Before you leave, you can get maps, brochures, and information on island activities from the **Catalina Chamber of Commerce,** P.O. Box 217, Avalon, CA 90704 (tel. 213/510-1520). For a very useful 48-page booklet about the area, send $1 to cover the cost of postage and handling.

Or after you arrive, stop by the **Visitors' Information Center,** located in the center of town (see "What to See and Do," below, for more information).

Two Harbors, on the other side of the island at the Isthmus, is a remote, peaceful location for camping, hiking, and water activities. Its **Visitor Services** is in Two Harbors (tel. 213/510-2800).

You'll find that addresses aren't used much here. Instead, directions are given according to certain landmarks and piers. The natives are friendly and are glad to point you in the right direction.

GETTING AROUND: Most hotels have complimentary taxis to take you to and from the boat dock, airport, or heliport. Autos are not allowed on the island except by special permit held by residents. Reasonably priced taxis are always available. Bikes can be rented (see the Brown's Bikes entry under "Land Activities" later in this chapter), and many families with one or two kids are seen in gasoline-powered golf-cart-type vehicles rented from **Cartopia Cart Rentals,** located at 615 Crescent Ave. (tel. 213/510-2493). Drivers 21 years old and up can rent these four-passenger vehicles for $20 per hour (rentals by the hour only) all year round. Open daily during the season from 8 a.m. to 5 p.m., and off-season from 9 a.m. to 4 p.m. for hourly and daily rentals.

Last but not least, Avalon is an easy place to get around on foot. If you only plan to spend the day, you don't need to rent anything.

WHAT TO DO AND SEE: There's much more to see and do in Catalina with kids than you might expect.

After you leave the pier, your first stop should be the **Visitors' Information Center,** located on Crescent Avenue across from the Green Pleasure Pier (tel. 213/510-2000, or toll free 800/4-AVALON). You'll find information on land and water tours here, and you can purchase tickets for different tours at one time. The office is open from 8 a.m. to 5 p.m. daily, year round.

Tours leave a minimum of two times a day—some depart 10 or 12 times a day on weekends. You can make reservations in advance.

The Visitors' Information Center suggests a half-day outing combining the Glass-Bottom Boat Tour, the Avalon Scenic Tour, and the Coastal Cruise to Seal Rocks. You need to decide whether your children can handle all that in a half day. We spread it out over two days with our toddler. Children over 5 could certainly handle all the water tours in one day, but it would be too much to do in just half a day. Inquire about special prices for combination tours.

Land Tours

The Visitors' Center staff will direct you to the bus terminal (for the land tours), which is a short walk past the center. You can leave your strollers at the terminal. Soft drinks and sandwiches are available here, but you can't take the snacks on the buses. There are also rest room facilities nearby.

The **Avalon Scenic Tour** shows you some of the highlights of Avalon. This scenic 50-minute tour is taken in an open-air tram-style bus, and is fine for a sleeping infant or a child who can sit still for an hour. But there are no stops during the tour. The fare is $4 for adults, $3.50 for seniors, $2.50 for children 5 to 11; under 5, free.

Children over 7 will enjoy the **Skyline Drive Tour** because they can catch a glimpse of the buffalo and other animals that roam the 42,000 acres of the Conservancy. A guide narrates the tour, explaining what rare plants and trees you are seeing, as well as outlining the history of the island. The road to the top is pretty scary (kids love it!). We all held our breaths looking down over the sheer cliffs while the driver negotiated the one-car-width turns with her huge bus. There was cheering after each successful maneuver. About 40 minutes into the tour there's a stop at the Airport-in-the-Sky, Catalina's commercial and private airport. This tour will have taken you ten miles into the Conservancy, which is only accessible by tour or hiking. The fare is $8.50 for adults, $7.50 for seniors, $5.50 for children 5 to 11; under 5, free.

If you have the time and the kids can sit on a bus for a while, consider taking the **Inland Motor Tour.** As cars aren't allowed in the backcountry, this half-day tour is a good way to see the remote wilderness and herds of buffalo. In addition to a stop at the Airport-in-the-Sky, you'll visit El Rancho Escondido, where you'll be treated to a performance by the Arabian horses that are raised here. There are several bathroom stops. The tour costs $15 for adults, $12.75 for seniors, $8 for children 5 to 11; under 5, free.

Water Tours

Water tours leave from the Green Pleasure Pier directly across from the Visitors' Center. There are rest room facilities and food stands here. Strollers can't be taken on the boats.

The **Coastal Cruise to Seal Rocks** is a one-hour boat trip that cruises close to shore. From May through September the sea lions return to the area, and the vessel is able to reach their sunning area. We watched one come right up to the boat. The cruise also passes the Amphibian and Helicopter Terminal, where the children are likely to see a seaplane take off or land. This tour is fine for toddlers and children, but teens might find it a bit boring. Be sure to use the rest room facilities on the dock before boarding, as there are no facilities on board. Fares are $4 for adults, $3.50 for seniors, $2.50 for children 5 to 11; under 5, free.

The **Glass-Bottom Boat Trip** is a 35-minute ride, just perfect for short attention spans! The waters of Catalina are so clear that you'll have no trouble spotting the various sea creatures. A guide explains what you're seeing and points out special animal and plant life. Fares are $4.25 for adults (evening trips cost $5.25), $3.50 for seniors ($4.50 in the evening), $2.50 for children 5 to 11; under 5, free.

The **Flying Fish Boat Tour** draws quite a few families. Running from mid-May through September, this 55-minute evening tour can be fascinating. The boat shines a 40-million-candlepower searchlight on the water, attracting the flying fish to sail through the air. Be sure to dress warm. By September it gets chilly in the evenings, and the water spray makes it even colder on this open boat. No bathroom facilities on board. Fares are $5.25 for adults, $4.50 for seniors, $2.50 for children 5 to 11; under 5, free.

Water Activities

Beach lovers have only two choices on the Avalon side of the island. While hordes of tourists enjoy the beach on either side of the Green Pleasure Pier on summer weekends, we prefer the **Descanso Beach Club,** on the other side of the casino (tel. 213/510-2780). You can bicycle there pretty easily. You will spend your day at a private beach where you will be provided with a towel and a beach chair, and have showers and changing rooms available. Rafts, snorkels, and boogie boards can be rented, and you can play volleyball, darts, table tennis, and horseshoes. There are also family cookouts nightly during the summer. Descanso provides the condiments, baked potato, salad bar, and rolls; you bring the entree and grill it in their barbecue pit (make reservations). There is also a sidewalk café and an open-air bar.

Admission to the beach is $4 for adults, $2 for children under 12. Cookout prices are $6 for adults, $3.50 for children.

Brave souls who want to stay at the beach by the Green Pleasure Pier have various beach-supply rentals available to the right of the pier. Sand chairs, umbrellas, mats, tubes, floats, and even beach towels can be rented, summers only, from 9 a.m.

Many kids will love the idea of renting your own boat. Visit **Joe's Rent-A-Boat,** on the Green Pleasure Pier (tel. 213/510-0455). Rowboats, pedalboats, 16-foot-runabouts, and 15-hp sportsters are available. Paddleboards, which are also available, are a favorite with the teens.

Joe's doesn't take reservations, but the wait is usually no more than half an hour on a busy summer weekend. Open from the weekend before Easter Sunday to the end of the school vacation, daily from 6 a.m. to 8 p.m.; closed the rest of the year.

Hourly rates are $3 for paddleboards, $5 for rowboats, $18 for runabouts, $20 for a sportster, and $10 for pedalboats.

Water biking, windsurfing, and scuba-diving equipment is available at **The Float,** at Hamilton Cove (take the shoreboat from the end of the Green Pleasure Pier to The Float; tel. 213/510-1811). Kids have to be a minimum of 16 years old for the Yamaha water bikes, any age for windsurfing, and a minimum of 12 years old for scuba-diving, which is done right off the float.

Open daily from 8 a.m. to 6 p.m. April through October; the rest of the year, open for diving only. Experienced divers can rent just the equipment for $50 for the day. With a guide, experienced divers pay $30 per hour (including equipment). Those with no experience pay $85 per hour (including equipment and guide). Water bikes rent for $30 per half hour, $50 per hour. Windsurfing costs $10 per hour.

If you're interested in diving in Catalina's beautiful waters, there are two places to call: **Argo Diving Service** (tel. 213/510-2208) and **Island Charters** (tel. 213/510-0600, or toll free 800/262-DIVE). **Catalina Diver's Supply** (tel. 213/510-0330) rents equipment.

Are you ready for this? Parasailing. It's not as scary as it looks. Naturally you wouldn't send your 4-year-old up. Maybe not even your 10-year-old. But after you've done it once, you may consider sending your teenager parasailing. If so, contact **Island Cruzers,** 107 Pebbly Beach Rd. (tel. 213/510-1777). The boats take six people per hour, every hour. The parasailing itself lasts eight to ten minutes, and the charge is $35 per hour for adults and children alike. There's no age minimum, but children must be at least 60 pounds to go up.

Land Activities

After you've gotten your bearings, or checked in at your hotel, you may want to visit **Brown's Bikes,** right under the Holly Hill House (tel. 213/510-0986). You can rent bikes by the hour or the day, and there are lockers for those bulky things you brought along. A limited number of child carriers and helmets are available. Be sure to take the bike map provided. It tells you where you can and can't ride, and it indicates slight hills and very steep grades. Reservations are accepted for mountain bikes only. There's not much of a wait for regular bikes, even on summer weekends. Brown's is open daily in summer from 9 a.m. to 5 p.m., and in winter from 10 a.m. to 4 p.m.

Hourly rates are $4 for one-speeds, $5 for five-speeds, $8 for tandems, $8 for mountain bikes, $10 for five-speed tandems, and $4 for children's bikes; strollers are $7 per day.

You might want to take the time to play miniature golf at **Golf Gardens** (tel. 213/510-1200), one block from the beach in the Island Plaza. This is an 18-hole golf course, perfect for the whole family. Open daily from Easter to mid-June, daily and evenings from mid-June to mid-September, and daily mid-September through October. Open winter weekends and holidays when the weather permits. Times vary, so call first or drop by and check the sign out front.

Adults pay $4 per game; children under 4 feet accompanied by an adult pay $2.

Hiking in Catalina is best for families in good condition, or as part of your camping experience. In the interior of the island, routes follow existing roads and Jeep trails. From Avalon into the interior, the trail gains 1,450 feet of elevation in less than three miles. From Two Harbors, it climbs only 800 feet in two miles, but the route is longer.

It's best to contact the **Los Angeles County Department of Parks and Recreation** in Avalon (tel. 213/510-0688) or the **Catalina Cove and Camp Agency** in Two Harbors (tel. 213/510-0303) before you plan to hike on the island. The Los Angeles agency is located in the Island Plaza in Avalon, and is open Monday through Friday from 9 a.m. to 1 p.m. and 2 to 4 p.m. The Two Harbors office is open daily from 8:30 a.m. to 4:30 p.m. Permits are required for hiking. Ask the park staffs about the accessibility of certain trails for children.

If you decide to hike, be aware that temperatures change drastically during certain times of the year—it may be extremely hot in the interior, but only 60° at the beach. Bring layers of clothing and sunscreen—and don't forget to bring water.

Another way to see the island is on horseback. **Catalina Stables,** on Avalon Canyon Road, six blocks from the ocean (tel. 213/510-0478), offers 1½-hour guided rides into the mountains behind the golf course. You'll cover five miles of beautiful Catalina scenery. If your children are between 8 and 12, be prepared to have them interviewed by the owner. Although they don't need prior riding experience, they must be strong enough to handle the horses (these are well-trained gentle horses, but the five-mile ride covers some difficult terrain). There's also a maximum weight limit of approximately 200 pounds, and you must wear closed-toe shoes—no sandals. The group limit is eight, and no one under 8 years old can ride. Reservations must be made in person and can be made only on the day you plan to ride. The stables are open daily in the summer from 10 a.m. to 3 p.m. In winter they are closed Thursday. Rates are $16 per person (adult or child) for the 1½-hour ride.

If you have lots of time, the **Wrigley Memorial and Botanical Gardens** (tel. 213/510-2288) is a nice walk for the family. Located at the head of Avalon Canyon, you can even walk there from the center of town via Avalon Canyon Road—it's a 1.7-mile walk uphill. Once you're there, you'll be able to walk through 37 acres of plants native to Catalina, mostly cacti, succulents, and flowering shrubs. This is a memorial to William Wrigley, Jr., who worked so hard to protect Catalina Island. The actual memorial is built of material indigenous to Catalina. There is bus service from Island Plaza on the Catalina Avenue side. Admission is 50¢; children under 12 are free. Open year round. Call first on holidays.

. . . and More

Located on the other side of the island, **Two Harbors** is a secluded noncommercial area. Catalina Express from San Pedro (tel. 213/519-1212) and Catalina Cruises from Long Beach (tel. 213/514-3838) can take you directly to Two Harbors. Catalina Safari Bus will take you there from Avalon (tel. 213/510-2800), or they will transport you to one of two campsites (see the "Camping" entry in the "Where to Stay" section). Round-trip fares to and from Avalon are $25 for adults, $18.50 for children 2 to 11. The same phone number will give you information on Catalina Safari Tours. You can choose between snorkeling trips by boat from Two Harbors or naturalist-led hikes and short walks. This is a great way to introduce kids to the natural side of the island.

Once you've arrived in Two Harbors, you'll find nearly empty beaches. You can snorkel, dive, hike, and even camp. There's a general store open daily from 8 a.m. to 5 p.m., and a snackbar open from 8 a.m. to 3 p.m.

This side of the island is a place to relax—there are no sights to speak of, except those natural sights you'll see either snorkeling or hiking.

WHERE TO STAY: One of the newest hotels on the island is the **Seaport Village Inn,** at 119 Maiden Lane (P.O. Box 2411), Avalon, CA 90704 (tel. 213/510-0344 or 619/571-0663, or toll free 800/222-8254), about five minutes from town on foot, close to the casino and Descanso Beach. Unfortunately not all the rooms here have a view, but there are several kinds of accommodations to choose from.

There is a Jacuzzi and a sundeck, but no pool. There are barbecue grills that can be used by guests. Rooms have TVs and queen-size beds, and some units have air conditioning. There are also suites with fully equipped kitchens. A suite can be connected with an additional bedroom, accommodating up to seven people. Rooms are modern, clean, and fairly roomy.

Rates in season (May to September) and holidays run $74 to $133, single or double, and suites and kitchen units run $144 to $184. Off-season rates are lower. They have playpens for infants to sleep in. Cribs and rollaways cost $15 per night. Children and additional adults are charged $15 each per night. Ask about package plans.

The **Pavilion Lodge,** at 513 Crescent Ave. (P.O. Box 737), Avalon, CA 90704 (tel. 213/510-1788, or toll free 800/4-AVALON in California), is just steps from the beach. In the middle of the hotel, a large garden court with lawn chairs makes an inviting spot to relax while watching the kids play. And two resident youngsters are always looking for playmates.

Rooms are pleasant and some are connecting; all have refrigerators. There is no restaurant on the premises, but the hotel is within easy walking distance of many eateries. Babysitting can be arranged through the front desk.

In season (mid-June through mid-September) rates run $89 to $120, single or double occupancy; off-season rates are lower. There's a two-day minimum on summer weekends. Kids always sleep free. No charge for cribs, but rollaways cost $10. Each additional adult is charged $10.

Built in 1926, the **Zane Grey Pueblo Hotel,** located off Chimes Tower Road (P.O. Box 216), Avalon, CA 90704 (tel. 213/510-0966), was originally the home of that famous author of western novels. He called it The Pueblo. Built of mortar mixed with goat's milk and furnished with teak beams brought from Tahiti on one of Grey's fishing trips, the hotel is truly the laid-back of the laid-back. Overlooking the ocean and the hills, there are 18 rooms (each named after a Grey novel) and a large living room with a fireplace, TV, and piano for use by the guests.

The atmosphere is casual and cozy (we weren't even sure if the doors to the room locked!). The staff is most helpful, and the maids will introduce your children to the "house" cats—once they locate them. The pool has a large shallow area so the kids can play. Coffee and tea are available all day, and complimentary bread and rolls are waiting poolside at 8:30 a.m. every day. If you want to bring along snacks or baby food, a communal refrigerator near the pool is available. Taxis are available to town, or you can walk—it's about a 10- to 15-minute journey that most toddlers can manage.

Rooms are rustic and sparse, and don't have TVs or phones. But each has a mountain or an ocean view. There is only one crib and one rollaway available, but some rooms have sofa beds. If you need a crib, request it far in advance.

In summer, rooms cost $75 to $105, single or double; each extra person (including children) pays $10. Off-season rates are considerably lower.

Camping

There are five campgrounds on the island. The first three are in Avalon, and the others are in Two Harbors. For reservations in Avalon, contact the **Los Angeles County Department of Parks and Recreation** (tel. 213/510-0688). **Bird Park** is the closest to town. It has 75 campsites, water, toilets, cold showers, and picnic tables. Sites are $5 per person per night. **Black Jack** is approximately 2½ miles from the airport and is at a 1,500-foot elevation. Some 75 campers can stay here, and there are toilets, water, and picnic tables. **Little Harbor** is on the opposite side of the island on the site of a former Indian camp. You can get to the beach easily from here. There are 150 sites, with toilets, picnic tables, and cold showers. Reservations are $5 per night per person, 50¢ for children under 14.

Contact the **Cove & Camp Agency** (tel. 213/510-0303) for reservations in the two Two Harbors campsites. **Little Fisherman's Cove** is a quarter mile from Two Harbors' pier and accommodates 250 campers. Sites have barbecue pits, picnic tables, water, and rinse-off showers. **Parson's Landing,** seven miles west of Two Harbors, is more primitive and accessible only by foot or boat. It has room for 150 campers. There are pit toilets and a water tank. Stoves and lanterns can be rented in Two Harbors.

WHERE TO EAT: While there aren't many restaurants in town with children's menus, your crew won't go hungry. Start off with breakfast at the **Pancake Cottage,** 118 Catalina St. (tel. 213/510-0726), just a block from the beach and the Visitors' Information office. Breakfast is served all day here, so it doesn't matter what time you get the group going in the morning. Bring them in hungry—the portions are big. Choices in pancakes range from banana, apple, blueberry, and strawberry to chocolate chip, macadamia nut, or pecan. There are also waffles, French toast, eggs, and over 100 omelet combinations. Prices range from $3.25 to $8, for a full breakfast with eggs, meat, potatoes, pancakes, juice, and coffee.

If you still have room, you can come back for lunch. Prices are reasonable: from $3 for a bowl of chili to $6 for one of three salads.

They will split adult portions for two kids. Highchairs and boosters are provided. No reservations accepted.

Open daily in summer from 7 a.m. to 2 p.m.; in winter, Friday through Monday only. No credit cards accepted.

If you want to sit outside and have your breakfast, visit **The Busy Bee,** at 306 Crescent Ave. (tel. 312/510-1983), directly across from the National Bank of Catalina. Kids can occupy themselves watching the harbor and feeding the pushy seagulls that congregate beneath the dock. The atmosphere is nautical and casual. Breakfast selections include eggs, lots of omelets, buttermilk pancakes, and Belgian waffles, and prices start at $4 and go up to $7.50. For lunch there are Mexican entrees, a large selection of salads and hamburgers, hot sandwiches, and health foods. Prices at lunch average $6.50. The dinner menu is quite limited— steak, barbecued chicken, corned beef and cabbage, pasta—and prices range from $7 to $9. There are lots of dessert selections, including Häagen Dazs ice cream, cakes, and pies.

Highchairs and booster seats are provided. No reservations accepted.

The Busy Bee is open in summer from 8 a.m. to 10 p.m. weekdays, to 11 p.m. on weekends. Winter hours are 8 a.m. to 9 p.m. daily. Major credit cards welcome.

The Channel House, on Front Street (tel. 213/510-1617), is a big, friendly place, perfectly located right on the main street. It is open for breakfast, lunch, and dinner, and you can sit in either the garden-like open-air room in front, or in the warm, comfortable inside room. When the outside heater just wasn't enough during dinner, they graciously accommodated us in the inside dining room, even though we had already begun our meal.

The breakfast menu has a nice selection of Belgian waffles, pancakes (strawberry, apple, blueberry, regular), French toast, eggs, and omelets. Pancakes and waffles cost $4; omelets, around $5.50. At lunch there are hamburgers, fish and chips, fried shrimp, salads, and sandwiches, at prices ranging from $5 to $7. Dinner prices are high, especially for children—there's no children's menu. But Janey and I shared the steak and shrimp ($15), and it was enough for both of us. Other choices include ribs, steak prepared many ways, and a large list of seafood entrees. Meals range from $10 to $19.

Highchairs and booster seats are available. Adult portions can be split, baby bottles and baby food can be warmed in the kitchen, and special children's drinks can be made. No reservations—just a waiting list.

Open daily for breakfast and lunch from 8 a.m. to 2:30 p.m.; for dinner, from 5 to 9:30 p.m. In winter, breakfast is served on weekends only. Major credit cards welcome.

For elegant dining in a lovely setting, be sure to visit **Ristorante Villa Portofino,** at 111 Crescent Ave., just down the street from the Channel House (tel. 213/510-0508). Your choices here are all northern Italian specialties, and include many pasta selections, fish and seafood, veal, beef, and chicken. Adult entrees begin at $11 for a tasty spaghetti alla bolognese and go up to $19 for stuffed veal chops.

Children have their own menu, which includes spaghetti, chicken breast, fried shrimp, or petite filet mignon. Served with rice and a vegetable, these entrees start at $4 and go up to $7.

Highchairs and booster seats are available (but the restaurant doesn't get many really young children). Reservations are a must, especially in summer.

Open all year for dinner only. Weeknights, the hours are 5 to 9 p.m.; on weekends, till 10 p.m. Major credit cards accepted.

Can't make a decision? Try **Mi Casita,** at 111 Clarissa Ave. (tel. 213/510-1772). There is a children's menu for the under-12 group, which includes a hamburger and fries ($4.25), along with the Mexican selections, such as a taco, enchilada, tamale, or flauta (priced from $4 to $4.25).

The grownups can try burritos, enchiladas, tacos (including a special fish taco), flautas, Mexican pizza, combinations, and dinner specialties. Lunch prices average $4. Dinner specialties cost $8.75 to $10.50, but you can also order off the à la carte menu.

There are highchairs and booster seats available. Baby food and bottles can be warmed in the kitchen, and special children's drinks can be ordered from the bar. No reservations accepted—the average wait is 15 minutes.

Open from April to the end of October: on weekdays from 11:30 a.m. to 9:30 p.m. and on weekends from 10 a.m. to 10 p.m. Major credit cards welcome.

MISCELLANEOUS: Have a picnic at **Bird Park Picnic Grounds.** You can actually make a reservation for a private table by contacting the Visitors' Information Center (tel. 213/510-2000, or toll free 800/4-AVALON). There are shelters, tables, and grills.

Make a stop at **Fred & Sally's Market,** 117 Catalina Ave. (tel. 213/510-1199), to put your picnic together. Don't forget to pick up your dessert across the street at the **Avalon Bake Shop** (tel. 213/510-0361), which opens at 5:30 a.m.

If you need toys for the trip back, or if you've forgotten the important sand toys, visit the **Toy Attic,** 119 Clarissa Ave. (tel. 213/510-1869). You'll find toys for all ages, and some books and plenty of beach toys and balls. Open daily in the summer from 10 a.m. to 5 p.m.; in winter, on Friday and Saturday from 10 a.m. to 5 p.m. and on Sunday till 3 p.m.

If you have extra time before the boat leaves, there's a tiny park, with swings and climbers, between the Cartopia stand and the Catherine Hotel.

IN AN EMERGENCY: In case of a medical emergency during your visit to Catalina, there's 24-hour service at the **Avalon Municipal Hospital,** 100 Falls Canyon Rd. (tel. 213/510-0700).

---

4. PASADENA / GLENDALE

Pasadena is Los Angeles's bulwark of tradition. Originally founded in 1886 as a resort community, called the Indiana Colony, Pasadena was a sunny sanctuary for industrialists and other members of the moneyed classes who came from points east to spend their winters. In fact, the area on South Orange Grove Boulevard near the Rose Bowl used to be called Millionaire's Row because of the many gorgeous mansions there.

In decades past, Los Angeles society was centered exclusively in Pasadena. There's still a lot of wealth in Pasadena, although there are now other such pockets of society in this big metropolis.

In appreciation of the beauty of its once-splendid downtown buildings, Pasadena has restored a ten-block section called Old Pasadena to a facsimile of its original glory. The area is bordered by Pasadena Avenue, Arroyo Parkway, Holly Street / Union Street, and Del Mar Boulevard. The historic buildings are not only interesting for their architecture and interiors, but they now house an eclectic group of restaurants, boutiques, and art galleries. It's a nice place to take a walk after Sunday brunch.

WHAT TO SEE AND DO: Pasadena is well known for its museums, gardens, theater, and music. Two of its most famous attractions are the Huntington Library and the Norton Simon Museum, both of which are known worldwide. But what most people think of when they hear of Pasadena is the Rose Bowl and Parade, officially known as the Tournament of Roses.

The Tournament of Roses

The Tournament of Roses (tel. 818/449-ROSE, a 24-hour, year-round hotline for parade and game information) has been held each New Year's Day since 1890, at which time Pasadena streets are filled with the colors of millions of flowers covering lavishly decorated floats. Each year the parade attracts about 60 floats, 22 bands, and 230 equestrians, and is watched by more than a million curbside spectators and more than 125 million television viewers. In addition to the colorful floats, you see the Rose Queen and her Court (seven beautiful young women chosen from a field of about 1,000 full-time students of the Pasadena Area Community College District), as well as various celebrities riding on the floats. The parade's grand marshals of the past have tended to be celebrities too.

If you're planning to be in Los Angeles at this time, you may want to think about camping out for curbside viewing of the parade. Kids love to do this.

Thousands of people flock to the parade route the night before, secure a good viewing spot, talk it up with other hardy campers, catch a few winks of sleep in a sleeping bag, and then wake up to the New Year's Day excitement. (If New Year's Day falls on a Sunday, the parade and game are held the next day, Monday, January 2.) If a hotel room sounds more comfortable, be sure to make your hotel and grandstand-seat reservations far in advance. Expect a three- to five-night minimum stay, payable in advance, for hotel rooms in Pasadena at this time. Contact the **Pasadena Convention and Visitors Bureau**, 300 E. Green St., Pasadena, CA 91101 (tel. 818/795-9311), or the **Pasadena Chamber of Commerce**, 11 W. Del Mar Blvd., Pasadena, CA 91105 (tel. 818/795-3355), for information on hotels and motels in the area.

The parade starts at 8:20 a.m. and lasts till 10:30 a.m. Grandstand-seat tickets can be purchased for $21 to $35 from the **Sharp Seating Co.**, P.O. Box 68, Pasadena, CA 91102 (tel. 818/795-4171), or at a substantially higher price from Ticketron. Tickets go on sale February 1 for the next year, and the good seats tend to sell out by April. To avoid the driving mayhem, you can take a chartered bus in from Santa Monica Bus Lines (tel. 213/458-1975) or from Gardena Bus Lines (tel. 213/324-1304); call a month in advance for reservations. If you do drive, be sure to park by 6:30 a.m. to get to your seats.

The parade has substantial RV accommodations, available through Sharp Seating (see above). The **Good Sam RV Club** (tel. 818/991-4980) sells packages to RV users.

The Rose Bowl college football game, played after the parade, pits the winner of the Pacific-10 (on the West Coast) against the winner of the Big Ten (in the Midwest) conference, a tradition that was begun in 1902.

Tickets to the game are distributed primarily to loyal fans of the universities involved, but you can participate in a drawing of the sale of 3,500 end-zone seats by mailing a postcard with your name and address to: **Rose Bowl Ticket Drawing**, Pasadena, CA 91184. Postcards must be postmarked between September 15 and October 15 for the November drawing.

If you don't like the crowds but want a closer view of the festivities, you can take the kids for a look at the floats before or after the parade. The **Tournament of Roses Association** publishes a brochure, available in November each year, of locations, hours, and admission charges to the five float-construction sites (the best time to go is two days before the parade up to the time the floats are moved to the formation area). Write or call the association at 391 S. Orange Grove Blvd., Pasadena, CA 91184 (tel. 818/449-4100 or 213/681-3724).

After the parade, the floats are on display in Victory Park, at Paloma Street and Sierra Madre Boulevard. You can see them on parade day from 1:30 to 4 p.m., and the next day from 9 a.m. to 4:30 p.m. If you're not going to the game or parade, you are best off waiting until the next day for viewing. Park on nearby residential streets.

Huntington Library, Art Collections, and Botanical Gardens

There are essentially three major parts to the **Huntington Library**, 1151 Oxford Rd., San Marino (tel. 818/405-2100), each of which is worth a separate visit: the library, the art galleries, and the botanical gardens.

Older kids who know just a bit about art and literature will appreciate the Huntington much more than the little ones, who will get easily bored here. It's a good idea to pick up the short self-guiding tour booklets before embarking on this cultural wonderland.

The Huntington Library is an institution devoted entirely to the study of British and American history and literature. It contains 600,000 reference and rare books, many thousands of photographs, prints, and microfilms, and nearly 2.5 million valuable individual manuscripts. Many of the things your children are already studying in school come alive for them in this wonderful library. Even the 14-year-old who was with us was fascinated by the most reliable manuscript in existence of Chaucer's *Canterbury Tales,* circa 1410; the Gutenberg Bible, one of only three animal-skin copies still in existence in America, circa 1455; and *Shakespeare's Comedies, Histories, and Tragedies* (the First Folio), printed in 1623. In addition, there are documents by Benjamin Franklin, George Washington, Euclid, Milton, Galileo, Thomas Paine, Abraham Lincoln, Robert Frost, James Joyce, W. B. Yeats—even a draft of the U.S. Constitution (1787).

The art collections are prized as well. The **Huntington Art Gallery** is devoted primarily to British art of the 18th and early 19th centuries, and houses a multitude of masterpieces. Kids seem to love Gainsborough's *Blue Boy* and Lawrence's *Pinkie,* which face each other. But there are other notable drawings of children here as well, for the artists of this period showed a tender concern for children. Greuze's *Young Knitter Asleep* is particularly touching. So are the two children posing in such elaborate period dress in *The Young Fortune Teller.* The interesting sibling relationship in Romney's *Beckford Children* is fascinating as well. This gallery also features furniture, decorative objects, and sculpture from the same period.

The Scott Gallery for American Art is much newer, having opened in 1984. Here American paintings from the 1730s to the 1930s are featured, including the work of such artists as Stuart, Copley, Bingham, and Cassatt. Renaissance paintings and 18th-century French sculpture, tapestries, porcelain, and furniture are found in the Arabella Huntington Memorial Collection, housed in the west wing of the main library building.

The **Huntington Botanical Gardens** are equally impressive. They occupy about 130 acres and consist of one wondrous garden after another. There's the Rose Garden, with its 1,100 varieties arranged historically from circa A.D. 1000. And there are various international gardens—the Australian Garden, the Subtropical Garden, the Desert Garden, and the Palm Garden (a must-see because this is, after all, Los Angeles). Our romantic 14-year-old friend still occasionally mentions the 18th-century French stone Temple of Love, in which she saw a statue titled *Love, the Captive of Youth.*

There is restaurant service available from 1 to 4 p.m. The Huntington is stroller-accessible.

The museum and grounds are open Tuesday through Sunday from 1 to 4:30 p.m. Closed on major holidays. Sunday visitors must make reservations in advance. Admission is free, but a donation of $2 per adult is suggested.

The Norton Simon Museum

The Norton Simon Museum is located at Colorado Boulevard and Orange Grove, at the intersection of the Foothill Freeway (I-210) and Ventura Freeway (Calif. 134) (tel. 818/449-6840). Children over 7 will enjoy this museum, and no wonder. There is an abundance of excellent artwork, some contemporary but mostly classical: Matisse, Picasso, Raphael, Rubens, Rembrandt, and others. This may be your child's first opportunity to view such a large collection of rare masterpieces. The sixth-grader in our group liked the sculpture the best, especially the three rooms of Degas miniature *modeles.*

There are 30 galleries and a sculpture garden—about 1,000 works of art altogether. Plan to spend as much time here as your child's concentration will allow. We break up the viewing by spending time in the outdoor sculpture garden, which is a tranquil spot for the kids to roam if they get restless. You may be surprised at how much culture they can soak up just by walking among the sculptures.

There are no eating facilities, but you may leave and return on one admission. Note that there are no changing tables in the bathrooms. The museum is stroller-accessible. Ample parking.

The museum is open Thursday through Sunday from noon to 6 p.m. Admission Thursday through Saturday is $2 for adults, $1.50 for seniors and students with ID. Sunday admission is $4, young or old. Free admission at all times for children under 12 accompanied by an adult.

Other Museums and Attractions

Kidspace, 390 S. El Molino Ave. (tel. 818/449-9143), is a small participatory museum geared to spark the curiosity of children ages 2 to 12. Kids will feel comfortable in this casual museum, which has a number of permanent exhibits as well as special programs throughout the year. Plan to spend a couple of hours here.

The Television Studio and Disc Jockey Booth is a permanent exhibit that gives kids the chance to play at performing in the glamorous broadcast world. Kids feel uninhibited enough to just start dancing to the music coming from the booth. Or they take turns recording their own messages. Human Habitrail allows curious kids to study a live ant colony, and then pretend to be ants in the carpeted Ant Wall (several toddler-aged children got scared in this maze-like unit). Grown-Up Tools gives kids the opportunity to learn about adult occupations by trying on authentic uniforms and using real equipment from various trades and professions—everything from a Dodgers uniform to a real race car. There are clothes for dress-up and mirrors for preening. The little—and big—girls love the face-painting bar.

There's a small giftshop; no food service, but there are picnic tables outside. Street parking.

School-year hours (October through June) are Wednesday from 2 to 5 p.m. and Saturday and Sunday from 11 a.m. to 4 p.m. Summer hours are Tuesday through Friday from 1 to 4 p.m. and Saturday and Sunday from 11 a.m. to 4 p.m. Admission is $2.25 for adults and children; children under 2 free.

The **Pacific Asia Museum,** 46 N. Los Robles Ave. (tel. 818/449-2742), is a gem of a little museum devoted to past and present Asian and Pacific art. Built in 1929 in the Chinese Imperial Palace courtyard style, the museum is listed in the National Register of Historic Places. Let the kids know that the garden they see at the museum is an authentic Oriental courtyard garden, one of only two such gardens in the United States.

Besides the special exhibitions and changing displays from its permanent collection, the museum has a special Student's Gallery designed especially for children, with displays interesting to many age groups. Some of the objects can be handled, and there are hands-on experiences and workshops available at various times.

On the third Saturday of every month the museum sponsors Free-Day, Fun-Days, offering free family programs. There may be dance performances, an origami workshop, a demonstration of the art of fanmaking, or other programs featuring the cultural arts of many different Asian and Pacific countries.

The museum is open Wednesday through Sunday from noon to 5 p.m. Tours are available on Sunday. Adults pay $3; students with ID and seniors, $1.50; children under 12, free.

Descanso Gardens is located at 1418 Descanso Dr., La Canada–Flintridge, at the junction of the Glendale Freeway (Calif. 2) and the Foothill Freeway (I-210) (tel. 818/790-5571). Whether or not you and the family are garden buffs, you'll all be happy you stopped here while in Pasadena. This makes a restful stop in the midst of touring "fast-track" Los Angeles. A picnic (or a stop at a restaurant) and a walk through the gardens will take most of one day.

The gardens' name says it all—rest gardens. Set on 165 acres in the San Rafael Hills northeast of Los Angeles (55 acres are open to the public), Descanso is home to the largest-known camellia forest in the world. Above it towers a 30-acre parasol of California live oaks. There is also a rare lilac grove, a wide selection of azaleas, a History of Roses Garden, and a four-acre garden featuring some of the All American Rose Selection winners since 1940.

There are two ways to experience Descanso. Six miles of garden and hiking trails enable you to see the plants close up and invite you to take your time meandering through the area. A stream flows through the Live Oak Forest, and birds are everywhere. You can hike to the Bird Observation Station to get the best look at the different land and water birds.

Or you can take the 45-minute narrated tram ride through the camellia forest, rose gardens, and California Native Plant Gardens, up into the hills, stopping at the Hospitality House, where there is an art gallery.

Afterward you can visit the Japanese Tea House, set in the tranquility of pools, waterfalls, ornamental stones, and azalea beds. Treat the kids to punch and cookies while you sample Japanese tea or a soft drink. Food service is available at the entrance to the gardens on weekends, or bring a picnic. There are picnic grounds adjacent to the parking lot.

The gardens are open daily from 9 a.m. to 4:30 p.m. Guided tram tours are given Tuesday through Friday at 1, 2, and 3 p.m.; and on Saturday and Sunday at 11 a.m. and 1, 2, and 3 p.m. The charge is $1.50 for adults and children alike.

Descanso Gardens is open daily (except Christmas) from 9 a.m. to 4:30 p.m. Admission is $3 for adults, $1.50 for seniors and students with an ID, 75¢ for children 5 through 12; children under 5, free. Parking is free.

WHERE TO EAT: Originally a warehouse, **Parkway Grill,** 510 S. Arroyo Pkwy. (tel. 818/795-1001), still has bare brick walls and a wood-beamed ceiling that attest to its heritage. While not completely geared to children, the help is very friendly, and the ambience is completely enchanting. There are stained-glass windows, plants, and fresh flowers galore. There is even a fireplace at one end of the dining room.

Serving regional American cuisine, Parkway Grill uses only fresh ingredients of high quality. You might try the blue-corn tortilla tostada ($8) or the antipasti of the day ($8). There is a large assortment of pizzas and pasta, as well as grilled meats and fish. Lunch prices range from $8 to $18; dinner prices, from $10 to $18.50.

They have booster seats and will split adult portions in the kitchen. The helpful servers will warm baby bottles or baby food, and will delight children with all kinds of non-alcoholic drinks.

Open for lunch Monday through Friday from 11:30 a.m. to 2:30 p.m., and for dinner Monday through Thursday from 5:30 to 10 p.m., on Friday and Saturday from 5 to 11 p.m., and on Sunday from 5 to 10 p.m.

Reservations are advised and most major credit cards are accepted. There is parking nearby.

If you want a real taste of southern California, **Lawry's California Center,** 570 W. Avenue 26 in Glendale (tel. 213/225-2491), is one place to go. It's a large, open-air complex reminiscent of a California mission courtyard. You dine outdoors in the garden.

For lunch, two different cafeteria-style food areas tempt you with Mexican specialties, salads, and barbecued meats. Dinner is also al fresco, but a little more elegant dining. Waiters bring your food, so you can enjoy the lighted fountains and the strolling mariachis.

Lawry's is fine for children over 3 and for infants. However, with toddlers, the quarry tile and patio stairs require a parent's constant attention. The self-serve style means that you have to hold onto the kids while ordering at different stations. This is okay if you have one adult to supervise the little kids while another one gets the food.

No highchairs, but booster seats are available. For dinner, there is a children's portion, and the servers will make non-alcoholic margaritas or piña coladas if you wish. Prices for adult food range from $2.25 to $9.

Lawry's is open for lunch daily from 11 a.m. to 3 p.m. Supper is served daily from 3 to 9 p.m. in Los Portales Bar and Patio (tel. 213/224-5889 for reservations).

Dinner is available daily from mid-April through mid-November. (The full dinner menu includes Lawry's famous steaks as well as other entrees.) The restaurant is open from 11 a.m. to 9 p.m. Reservations are accepted (tel. 213/224-6850), as are major credit cards. There is a parking lot on the premises.

There is also a gift and patio shop, and a wine and gourmet shop. During the week you can take a free 45-minute guided tour. The multimedia presentation and a walk through the test kitchens shows you how Lawry's products are made. Tours are given at 11:30 a.m. and 12:30, 1:30, and 2:30 p.m., on a first-come, first-served basis. (Call 213/224-6840 for information.)

Green Street is located in the heart of downtown Pasadena at 146 Shopper's Lane (tel. 818/577-7170). The charming café has white-clothed tables that invite you to dine outdoors. Inside, the large, attractively decorated restaurant is partitioned off so that each area is like a room in itself. Lovely modern artwork covers the walls.

Green Street serves American food for breakfast, lunch, and dinner. The extensive menu offers omelets, eggs, pancakes, and French toast for $4 to $7.75; and sandwiches, burgers, and salads for $4.75 to $6.50. Complete meals include fresh fruit or fries—choose from a variety of steaks, fresh vegetable platter, and chicken. Prices range from $8 to $9.50.

They provide Sassy seats and boosters, and really try to accommodate parents' wishes. Servers will bring crackers to the table and split portions in the kitchen.

The restaurant is open Monday through Thursday from 6 a.m. to 9 p.m., on Friday and Saturday till 10 p.m., and on Sunday from 8 a.m. to 9 p.m. No reservations are accepted. Most credit cards welcome.

Have you ever seen a mile-long salad bar? Well, almost a mile. **The Souplantation,** 201 S. Lake Ave., in the Union Bank building at Cordova and Lake Avenue (tel. 818/577-4797), offers a fresh and extensive salad bar that includes all the fixings—from greens to cold pasta. Try the curried chicken pasta salad or the tuna tarragon. Actually you can sample everything at this all-you-can-eat smörgåsbord. There are over 14 kinds of salad dressings, including such unusual ones as raspberry-walnut vinaigrette and cabernet sauvignon vinaigrette.

Where does the name come from? Souplantation also offers five different soups, plus home-style chili which you can smother with onions and cheddar cheese. The warm cornbread is yummy with the chili, but you can also choose from an assortment of muffins. They have blueberry, honey-bran and nut, peach-poppyseed, and pumpkin-raisin.

If you have room for dessert, you can visit the mini yogurt and fresh-fruit bar where you can create your own ambrosia or top yogurt with granola and carob chips. Price for the soup and salad bar is $6.75; for just the soup or salad it's $6.

On top of all this, the Souplantation welcomes families. They have highchairs and boosters, and while there's no need for a children's menu, they have children's portions at lower prices. And for little ones, you can imagine the samplings of small finger food. If the kids are under 12, the charge is only $3.

The restaurant is open Sunday through Thursday from 11 a.m. to 9 p.m., on Friday and Saturday till 10 p.m. There are no reservations accepted, and you must be prepared for waits of up to 40 minutes at peak lunch and dinner hours. No credit cards are honored. There is validated parking under the building (enter on Cordova).

CHAPTER XII

WEEKEND TRIPS FROM LOS ANGELES

□ □ □

1. PALM SPRINGS AND THE DESERT COMMUNITIES
2. LAKE ARROWHEAD AND BIG BEAR LAKE
3. ANTELOPE VALLEY

Within three hours of downtown Los Angeles sits the highest mountains in southern California and the low desert of Palm Springs. Family travelers will find alpine skiing, mountain hiking, hot-air ballooning, fruit picking, and perfect swimming within the wonderland that surrounds the Los Angeles Basin.

1. PALM SPRINGS AND THE DESERT COMMUNITIES

To sun worshippers, tennis lovers, and golf aficionados, the Palm Springs area needs no introduction. For families who have never visited before, it does.

Palm Springs has been called the "Playground of the Stars" and the "Golf Capital of the World." Although you might still see a star or two, that's not its main attraction anymore. And while Palm Springs is a popular retirement spot, it is also a fun (and relaxing) place to bring the kids. The desert communities offer great weather, plenty of ways to relax for those who seek that, and lots of outdoor activities. Combine those qualities with an abundance of restaurants and a casual atmosphere, and you have the consummate resort.

GETTING THERE: Getting to Palm Springs is easy. It is 107 miles southeast of L.A., about a two-hour drive **by car** via I-10 East (the San Bernadino Freeway). It is about three hours from San Diego, taking I-15 North to I-60 East (the Pomona Freeway) to I-10 East.

The **Palm Springs Municipal Airport** is served by numerous major airlines, including TWA, United, and American, or you can take **Palm Springs Limousine** from Los Angeles (tel. 213/459-1923 or 213/202-8325). The trip takes approximately three hours. Ontario is nearby, and its airport is also served by major airlines.

The nearest **Amtrak** depot is in Indio, 20 miles from Palm Springs (tel. 800/USA-RAIL for schedules and information). **Greyhound Bus** service is available to Palm Springs. Check with your local Greyhound office for connections, or call toll free 800/237-8211.

ORIENTATION: When people refer to "Palm Springs," they usually mean all the desert communities—Palm Springs, Cathedral City, Rancho Mirage, and Palm Desert. Although the towns are set one right after the other along Calif. 111, each has its own identity.

Calif. 111, the main thoroughfare between towns, becomes a big-city nightmare during rush hour. Thus getting from Palm Springs to Palm Desert during prime time can take over a half hour. For alternative routes and detailed maps—and other visitor information services—visit the **Palm Springs Convention and Visitors Bureau,** located at Airport Park Plaza, Suite 315, 255 N. El Cielo Rd., Palm Springs, CA 92262 (tel. 619/327-8411). The office is open weekdays only, from 8:30 a.m. to 5 p.m. Or drop by the **Palm Desert Chamber of Commerce,** 72-990 Calif. 111, at Monterey, in Palm Desert (tel. 619/346-6111). Their hours are 9:30 a.m. to 4:30 p.m. on weekdays and 10 a.m. to 2 p.m. on Saturday.

The climate is the area's greatest draw, and the more than 7,000 swimming pools are proof of that near-perfect weather. This is desert climate, Colorado Desert climate to be exact. Days are mostly warm, sunny, and dry, although the addition of thousands of swimming pools to the area has increased the humidity over what it was ten years ago. Evenings are comfortable, but can get cold in the winter months. The "season" is really October through May. The warmest fall/winter months are October and November, and March and April in the spring, when daytime temperatures average 86°. Summer, which is when family rates are popular, can be unbearably hot, with temperatures reaching 108° in July.

If you plan to visit during the winter, come with warm-weather clothes, but throw in something for unpredictable rains and cold nights. Those of you from the Midwest and East Coast might think we're nuts, but we Californians bring down vests or parkas to Palm Springs during December and January to combat those cold desert nights.

For summer fun, be sure to bring hats and/or visors and lots of sunscreen. If you golf or play tennis, make your plans for the cooler morning hours, or play on night-lighted tennis courts. Bicycling and hiking should be planned for mornings too. The desert sun is not deceiving at all—it burns!

GETTING AROUND: The major car-rental agencies have service desks at the airport, and there are several **taxi companies** in town (check the *Yellow Pages* for listings). Most visitors drive their own car or a rental car when visiting the area. Call **Budget** (tel. toll free 800/527-0700), **Hertz** (tel. toll free 800/654-3131), or **Avis** (tel. toll free 800/331-1212).

A shuttle bus called **Sunline** (tel. 619/343-3451) runs year round through the entire desert from Desert Hot Springs to Indio. The **Sun Special double-decker bus** is mainly for tourists and travels within the downtown Palm Springs area seasonally. The **Sun Trolley** runs within Palm Desert during the season. Call for times and pickup points for all the "Sun" buses.

WHERE TO STAY: The desert cities offer a multitude of hotels and condominiums in a number of price ranges.

Be sure to ask questions before you choose your accommodations: What's the best price I can get? Are two connecting rooms a better deal than a suite? If I come another weekend instead of this weekend, is there a better price? Are you having any specials? Is there a special family rate? In any case, you're better off calling these hotels directly rather than going through the chain's reservation number. The hotel reservationists can meet your family's needs much better, and they are knowledgeable about current packages.

Also check on minimum-stay requirements. Some establishments demand a three- or even four-night minimum on holiday weekends. Be sure to ask.

Hotel and condominium rates are based on three seasons. Winter rates are the highest, shoulder rates in the middle, and summer rates the lowest. To make it less complicated, we will list only winter and summer rates. Also, there are packages galore to choose from, including weekend specials, holiday packages, and summer packages.

Below are the basic cutoff dates for each season. But be sure to double-check at the hotel you choose. Its season cutoff could be a few days before or after the following dates, changing the price of your room substantially.

Summer is May 24 through September 12.

Shoulder is September 13 through December 19.

Winter is December 20 through May 29.

Staying in Palm Springs

Staying in hotel-style condominiums is one convenient way to have the best of both worlds—family-style accommodations with all the services of a full-scale hotel—and your visit doesn't have to be for a month at a time to make it worthwhile.

One such hotel-condominium is the **Oasis Villa Hotel,** at 2345 Cherokee Way, Palm Springs, CA 92264 (tel. 619/328-1499, or toll free 800/247-4664, 800/543-5160 in California). It's located right off Calif. 111, across the street from the Gene Autry Hotel. There's a mini-mart/liquor store across the highway for emergency milk or other supplies, and a 24-hour Vons Market on the highway, five minutes east by car, for grocery shopping.

They call these condos villas, and they are quite luxurious for the price. Each villa has two bedrooms, a private garage, its own patio with furniture and a gas barbecue, and a private washer and dryer. The kitchens are fully equipped with dishwashers, microwaves, dishes, pots, and pans. Some villas have breakfast nooks *and* dining areas. The living rooms are spacious, the décor is bright and light, and the furniture is comfortable. Ground-floor accommodations are the most convenient if you have young children. A section of the complex is reserved for families.

The grounds are set up like a miniature suburban community, gated and with 24-hour security. Some guests bring bikes from home and let the kids ride through the complex. There are also eight pools to keep them occupied, Jacuzzis, night-lighted tennis courts, and two racquetball courts. Equipment can be rented.

For the best value, inquire about the summer packages, at which time villas go for $99 per unit per night (don't forget that you can sleep at least six to a unit) with free passes to the Oasis Water Park (same owners). Winter rates are $199 for a standard two-bedroom 960-square-foot unit, to $299 for a 1,374-square-foot unit, which includes two bedrooms, two baths, and a den with a queen-size sofa. Rates are based on four adults per unit; each extra adult pays $45 per night. Children 12 and under stay free. There are also some special weekend packages available in high season.

For a hotel right in the heart of downtown Palm Springs, you might want to try the newly renovated **Spa Hotel & Mineral Springs,** at 100 N. Indian Ave., Palm Springs, CA 92263 (tel. 619/325-1461, or toll free 800/854-1279, 800/472-4371 in California).

The real reason to stay here is not for your kids—it's for you! The health/beauty spa at the hotel is well known and loved by many repeat customers. Pamper yourself—visit the eucalyptus vapor inhalation room, the steamroom, the cooling room, the solarium, and the gym (which are free to guests); have herbal wraps, loofah rubs, salt glows, massage, aromatherapy, and more (available at an extra charge); and use the suntan machines. There's also the Ilona of Hungary

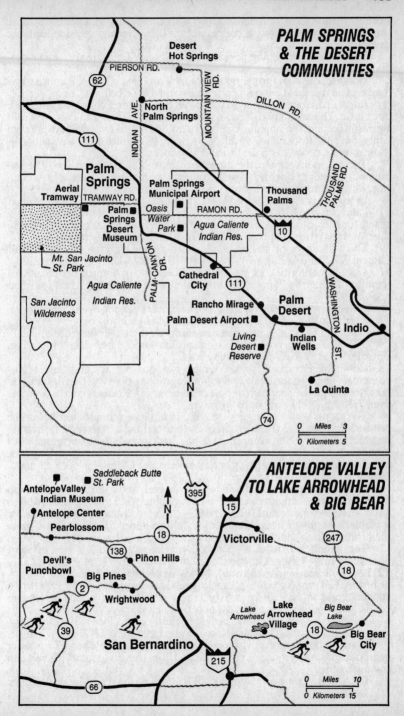

PALM SPRINGS & THE DESERT COMMUNITIES

Desert Hot Springs
PIERSON RD.
62
MOUNTAIN VIEW RD.
North Palm Springs
DILLON RD.
111
INDIAN AVE.
THOUSAND PALMS RD.
Palm Springs
Aerial Tramway
TRAMWAY RD.
Palm Springs Municipal Airport
Thousand Palms
Palm Springs Desert Museum
Oasis Water Park
RAMON RD.
Agua Caliente Indian Res.
10
Mt. San Jacinto St. Park
PALM CANYON DR.
Cathedral City
111
Palm Desert
San Jacinto Wilderness
Agua Caliente Indian Res.
Rancho Mirage
Palm Desert Airport
WASHINGTON ST.
Indio
Living Desert Reserve
Indian Wells
La Quinta
N
74
0 Miles 3
0 Kilometers 5

ANTELOPE VALLEY TO LAKE ARROWHEAD & BIG BEAR

Saddleback Butte St. Park
Antelope Valley Indian Museum
395
15
Antelope Center
247
Pearblossom
N
18
Victorville
138 Piñon Hills
Devil's Punchbowl
Big Pines
18
2
Wrightwood
Lake Arrowhead
Big Bear Lake
39
Lake Arrowhead Village
18
Big Bear City
San Bernardino
215
0 Miles 10
66
0 Kilometers 15

Institute of Skin Care for facials, waxing, and other beauty treatments. If you're smart, you'll arrange with the concierge for a babysitter and spend at least one day at the spa!

The outdoor swimming pool is fine for all ages. There are also several outdoor mineral pools.

Don't let the cool formality of the lobby fool you. Children are welcome here, and no one gets bent out of shape by normal child behavior.

Rooms have been redecorated in restful desert sunset colors, and most are quite large. Those with two queen-size beds have room for both a crib and a rollaway, still keeping the table and chairs intact. Rooms with king-size beds are even larger, but all bathrooms are small. More than 50% of the rooms have patios—those rooms are located on the first and fifth floors.

There is room service; the hours vary depending on the season. The on-premises restaurant does not have a children's menu, and it features "spa" cuisine. But there are many restaurants in the immediate area.

In winter, rates range from $130 to $180, single or double. Suites begin at $190 and run to $230. In summer, rooms cost $55 to $95; suites, $130. No charge for cribs, but rollaways cost $25 per night. Children under 18 sleep free in the same room with their parents. Additional adults pay $25 per night.

The advantages of staying at the **Hotel Seven Springs,** 1269 E. Palm Canyon Dr., Palm Springs, CA 92264 (tel. 619/323-2775, or toll free 800/472-4339 in California), are its location (conveniently located between Palm Springs and Rancho Mirage), nearby restaurants, and the children's wading pool.

This two-story motel-style establishment offers parking close to each room. There are no patios or balconies. A Carrows Restaurant (open 24 hours) and a Jeremiah's (dinner and nightly entertainment) are practically on the premises.

The small, clean pool area is nice and has some grassy space for playing. There is also a small children's wading pool.

Complimentary breakfast is served poolside on weekends, and there is complimentary coffee in the lobby every morning. Some rooms have refrigerators at no extra charge (be sure to request one in advance). Room service is available from 7:30 a.m. to 11 p.m. from Carrows.

The rooms with two queen-size beds do not have room for a crib, but the one-bedded room and the small suites do (one bed and a hideabed). Rooms are small but clean (our only complaint was the "motel smell"). Be sure to request a mountain-view or poolside room—some units face the restaurant parking lots, and since Jeremiah's has nightly entertainment and Carrows is open all night, those locations are apt to be more noisy.

In winter, singles rent for $75 to $85; doubles, $80 to $95; suites, $105 to $185. In summer, singles cost $37 to $47; doubles, $45 to $53; suites, $60 to $105. Holidays may claim higher rates—check in advance. No rollaways are available, but cribs are free. No charge for children under 12 in the same room as their parents. Each additional guest 12 and over pays $10 per night.

The **Vagabond Hotel** is located in a relatively wind-free part of Palm Springs, at 1699 S. Palm Canyon Dr., Palm Springs, CA 92264 (tel. 619/325-7211, or toll free 800/522-1555). Newly renovated, the Vagabond has furnished its 120 rooms in cheerful apple green and dusty rose. Rooms are bright and clean, and big enough for cribs or a rollaway in the vanity area. There are no patios, and windows look out to the pool or walkway.

Rooms have two queen-size beds, table and chairs, clock radios, and tub/shower combinations. The small suite is a good idea for small families. The sitting room has built-in sofas, which can be made into two single beds. The master bedroom with a queen-size bed is partitioned from the sitting room. There's also room for a crib.

Other features are a fenced-in pool and spa area and an indoor/outdoor coffeeshop adjacent to the pool. There are some connecting rooms. Refrigerators are available upon request for $3 per day.

Rates in winter are $64 single and $64 to $68 double. Call for summer rates. Porta-cribs are $3 per day. There's a $6-per-day charge for children. You can get a late checkout for a half-day rate.

For a budget hotel, check out the **TraveLodge,** at 333 E. Palm Canyon Dr., Palm Springs, CA 92264 (tel. 619/327-1211, or toll free 800/255-3050). The hotel is centrally located and features two heated pools, a Jacuzzi, coin-operated laundry facilities, and a small games area.

Rooms are motel style (parking is close to each room), with tiny patios and sliding glass doors. A unit with two double beds still has room for a crib. There is cable TV and instant coffee in each room. Refrigerators are available upon request at $3 per day. Most accommodations have shower stalls, so if you need to bathe a baby in a bathtub, be sure to request such a room in advance.

In winter, rooms run $36 to $62 single and $37 to $80 double; the highest rates are charged on weekends. In summer, rates run $34 to $45. There is no charge for cribs, but rollaways cost $10. Children under 17 stay free in the same room with their parents. Each additional person pays $10 per night. Poolside rooms cost $7.50 extra.

Rancho Mirage

The pace at **Marriott's Rancho Las Palmas Resort,** 41000 Bob Hope Dr., Rancho Mirage, CA 92270 (tel. 619/568-2727, or toll free 800/228-9290), is leisurely, but the service is first class.

The first encounter with this four-star resort is like a step back into old California. First you see gorgeous early California architecture framed in brilliant bougainvillea and surrounded by lush landscaping. You enter a lobby designed in the authentic décor of that era and are met by a gracious hotel staff person. You might not think this resort would be a choice for families—just honeymooners and "old" married folk—but you'll be surprised at what this Marriott has to offer.

Don't expect minute-by-minute entertainment, but do expect some interesting family-style programs. As an example, Halloween weekend ghosts and goblins could choose from pumpkin carving, arts and crafts, and scary movies. Thanksgiving was even more eventful. There was a "Balloon Olympics" carnival in the courtyard with a Ping-Pong throw and ring toss, while air hockey and fooz ball games were being played nearby. In addition, the weekend offered family Bingo, arts and crafts programs, a junior tennis camp, a scavenger hunt, a Tiny Tots cooking class, a kids' cookout and movie, and an ice-cream-eating contest. There was also a Humpty Dumpty walk for ages 1 through 11.

Year-round activities include Friday-night movies for kids 5 and up and a Saturday Children's Camp for the same age group. For some activities you are charged a nominal fee; others are free.

The resort has three swimming pools (with food and beverage service), a golf course, tennis courts (junior tennis is regularly scheduled), a clubhouse (which serves food during season), and lots of green grassy areas. Parents of toddlers, note: when requesting ground-floor accommodations, be sure to avoid the rooms that open up to the little ponds, which are not fenced off.

Babysitting is available through referral. Refrigerators are available upon request at no charge.

There are four restaurants in the hotel, but the Fountain Court is the best choice for families with young children. It offers a children's menu (and crayons) for breakfast, lunch, and dinner at quite reasonable prices. Room-service hours vary with the season.

The rooms here complement the desert surroundings. They are not fancy, but they are certainly deluxe. Double rooms come with small sofas and comfortable reading chairs. There is room for a crib. Patios have a chaise longue and table. All rooms have remote-control TV (you can even check out via TV). Bathrooms are small.

Parlor connectors are a good alternative to connecting rooms for families who are staying more than a weekend. The bedroom has either two double beds or one king-size bed. The parlor is furnished with a Murphy bed or sleeper sofa, a table and four chairs, a lounge chair, a dressing area, and bathroom. By night, you have two bedrooms; by day, a bedroom and a living room. Suites are spacious and elegant.

During high season, rooms are at four-star rates. If these are too steep, come during the summer, when the rates drop substantially but the service doesn't. Rates in winter are $210 to $240, single or double; suites, $445 to $1,275. In summer, rooms run $85 to $115; suites, $210 to $650. There are American Plan (AP) packages, Modified American Plan (MAP) packages, and golf package plans. Check to see if any of these meet your family's needs.

Staying in Palm Desert

When you step into the lobby of **Marriott's Desert Springs Resort & Spa,** 74855 Country Club Dr., Palm Desert, CA 92260 (tel. 619/341-2211, or toll free 800/228-9290), you immediately feel the energy. This is a hotel designed for activity. The sound of waterfalls flowing into the hotel's lagoon greets you first. Look up and you'll see the gigantic eight-story atrium lobby; look down and you'll see an oasis in the middle of the desert—mini-tour boats greet guests at the lagoon dock for a boat tour of the hotel grounds. It will even drop you off at one of the hotel restaurants, the Mikado. Kids love the boats, and the drivers are usually responsive to the hundreds of questions and requests for boat driving.

Not only is the hotel beautiful, but it boasts numerous activities for adults and children alike. A hospitality desk in the lobby offers information on the area, while a separate resort activities desk representative is there to tell you what's going on in-house. Special family programs are planned for Easter, Christmas, Thanksgiving, Memorial Day, and Labor Day. Year round, kids can practice at an outdoor putting green, where they'll be given clubs and balls. The children love the giant lawn chess (or checkers) found outdoors, and they are welcome to play. You can all learn bocce ball or lawn bowling, and can join in on a volleyball game.

Three pools, including one remarkable one surrounded by a man-made sandy beach, offer a variety of places to meet new friends. At one pool, a cafeteria-style snackbar makes it easy to have lunch at the pool without having to change clothes first.

On Friday evenings the hotel hosts a reception for guests who are not with convention groups. It's a time to meet other parents and, if you want, introduce your children to new playmates for the rest of their visit.

There are 12 restaurants, lounges, and snackbars on the premises. The Mikado is a Japanese restaurant that serves teppanyaki tableside style. If you wish, they'll serve kids smaller portions. The Colonnade of Shops is quite impressive and features a children's clothing shop. The Spa is a wonderful place for the adults to spend some time. Inquire, too, about the spa packages—one might be right for you. Since the Desert Springs can arrange for babysitters, you can probably take at least a day for yourself.

There are a variety of rooms to choose from. Rooms with two double beds, by themselves or connecting to a room with a king-size bed, are quite popular for families. And the one-bedroom suites are in high demand. The hotel offers a concierge level, where rooms include special treats, such as complimentary light breakfast, drinks throughout the day, and complimentary hors d'oeuvres. Children are welcome on this floor.

Rooms are furnished in the ubiquitous desert pastels and feature mini-bars, in-house movies that can be turned off at the desk, remote-control TVs, and patios with chairs. Rooms are good-sized, with space for a crib. The large bathrooms are designed in marble and have separate showers. There are lots of personal-care amenities and plush towels.

In winter, standard rooms run $245 to $295, single or double; suites, $450 to $1,400. In summer, the rates are $105 to $125, single or double; and suites run $250 to $500. Concierge-level rooms range from $285 to $325 in the winter, $125 to $150 in the summer.

The busy time for the Desert Springs is summer weekends (for which you should make reservations at least three weeks in advance) and Memorial Day and Labor Day weekends (for which reservations should be made at least one month in advance).

If your love is tennis, or if you want to learn, **Shadow Mountain Resort & Racquet Club,** 45-750 San Luis Rey, Palm Desert, CA 92260 (tel. 619/346-6123 collect, or toll free 800/472-3713 in California), is the place to stay. Not only has it been named one of the top 50 tennis resorts in the country (by *Tennis Magazine*), but Shadow Mountain also offers spacious condominiums at affordable prices, with the comforts of a full-service hotel. There are 16 courts (4 night-lighted), and four swimming pools, one a huge figure-eight near the lobby. Reciprocal golf privileges are arranged at nearby courses.

Accommodations range from bedroom/bath hotel units, kitchenettes, and studios (with a king-size and a pullout bed) to one-, two-, and three-bedroom condos. All condominiums are privately owned, so furnishings and décor vary, but all come fully equipped with kitchenware, linens, and daily maid service. There are some charming ground-floor units with patios that open onto a grassy area complete with shallow creek. Accommodations near the big pool offer Mom and Dad the chance to relax on the balcony or patio as they watch the older kids and teens at the pool. Some villas have cathedral ceilings and huge patio/balconies.

Amenities also include coin-operated laundries for guests, and babysitters are available with advance notice. Besides a poolside snackbar, there is a small restaurant with a children's menu. Entrees for both children and adults are extremely reasonable. Weekend outdoor barbecues for all the guests round out the offerings. This is a friendly residential-style site, where families gather around the big pool, toddlers play on the grassy area, and kids bicycle through the gated/guarded grounds.

Even tennis court fees are included in the nightly rate, although there is a nominal charge for the clinics. There are even tennis clinics for teens.

In winter, rates run $85 (for a hotel unit) to $300 (for a three-bedroom condo), single or double. In summer, they cost $50 to $200. Each additional guest over 16 pays $10 per night. Cribs cost $5 per night; rollaways, $10.

Condominiums in Palm Desert and Palm Springs

The advantages to staying in a condominium or rental home are obvious. For longer stays, the comfort of having separate sleeping quarters, a place to cook, a washer and dryer, a living room, and a private pool (in a rental home) is important to many people. And the rates are usually quite reasonable, especially for long stays. While most of these rentals do not include daily maid service, arrangements can be made for those services separately. There are many folks who visit the area for several weeks or a month at a time, and these accommodations are perfect for them. Some rentals are in country clubs that offer golf and tennis privileges. If you call the following companies and state your family's needs, they'll try to locate the right accommodation for you. There's usually a minimum length of stay, especially for private homes. Rates vary so drastically between accommodations that they will not be listed here. Generally speaking, a two-bedroom condominium in Palm Springs might average $115 per night during high season for a family with two children. Private homes run more.

Sunrise Company Rental Division, 76-300 Country Club Dr., Palm Desert, CA 92260 (tel. 619/345-5695), specializes in renting condominiums located within prestigious country clubs such as Rancho Las Palmas, the Lakes, Monterey, and Palm Valley. All these clubs include tennis and golf facilities as well as pools and spas.

The Rental Connection, 170 E. Palm Canyon Dr., Palm Springs, CA 92264 (tel. 619/320-7336, or toll free 800/468-3776, 800/232-3776 in California, 800/458-3776 in Canada), can provide you with condos or private homes. They'll set you up in one of more than 40 locations throughout Palm Springs. Call with your specific needs.

WHERE TO EAT: Since the Palm Springs area isn't exactly known as the gourmet capital of the world—not that there aren't some very fine eating establishments that cater to adults—you don't need to feel that you are depriving your child of a good meal by going to one of the chain restaurants located throughout the desert communities. Here are some restaurants that either have a big family clientele or have children's menus. And don't forget the restaurants at the hotels we've mentioned. Several have children's menus, and all welcome little diners.

Palm Springs

Although **Billy Reed's,** 1800 N. Palm Canyon Dr. (tel. 619/325-1946), doesn't have a children's menu, it does have a big selection of good food and it's right near the Aerial Tramway. We'd choose this restaurant for breakfast and lunch only. The usual egg, pancake, and cereal breakfast selections are available. All the pastries are made on the premises—be sure to try the cinnamon roll or pecan roll ($2 and $3).

At lunch there are lots of hamburgers, sandwiches, casseroles, and salads. Prices range from $3 to $9. Dinner doesn't offer as many kid-interesting dishes. There is a hamburger steak, pot roast, meatloaf, and shrimp. Think about ordering a dinner entree as a side order for $2 less. Entrees average $13.50. Desserts are sumptuous, and there are lots of choices.

Highchairs and boosters are available. Servers will split adult portions for two kids, and will warm baby bottles. There's a no-smoking section for those who prefer it. There is live entertainment on weekends, and reservations are accepted for eight or more. Call ahead to find out how long the wait is—weekends can be very busy.

Open daily from 7 a.m. to 11 p.m. Parking lot. All major credit cards welcome.

Louise's Pantry, at 124 S. Palm Canyon Dr. (tel. 619/325-5124), is known by everyone in Palm Springs. It's located right on the main strip, and you can't miss it because you'll see a line out the door and halfway down the block. Famous for its home-style cooking, it features chicken pot pie, fried chicken, roast beef, and baked ham, among other favorites. Lunch entrees average around $4, dinners run $8, and each selection comes with soup and salad. Pies, cakes, and sweet rolls are baked on the premises. There's no children's menu, but they'll split orders. They have boosters but no highchairs here.

Louise's Pantry is open daily from 7 a.m. to 10 p.m. The best time to come with restless kids is between 2:30 and 4 p.m. Closed in summer. No credit cards accepted. Street parking.

For breakfast especially, be sure to try **Elmer's Pancake and Steak House,** 1030 E. Palm Canyon Dr. (tel. 619/327-8419). While some folks have said that the quality isn't the same as it used to be, we found the breakfast good and the service fast. There is a children's menu (with little games) that offers varied selections for breakfast ($2.25), lunch ($2), and dinner ($3.25). Adult selections are vast and very moderately priced. There are 25 varieties of pancakes and waffles.

There are highchairs and booster seats. Be aware that they do not take reservations, and during the high season the wait can be pretty long. Elmer's is particularly popular on Sunday mornings. It's open Sunday through Thursday from 7 a.m. to 9 p.m., on Friday and Saturday till 10 p.m. Major credit cards are accepted. Convenient parking lot.

No doubt the preteens and early teens will enjoy the atmosphere at **Fuddrucker's,** 262 S. Palm Canyon Dr. (tel. 619/320-4889). In this big, bright, casual restaurant you can order hamburgers, hot dogs, tacos, malts, and shakes at the self-serve counter, and eat indoors or out. (Meals average $5 with a drink.) For the 12-and-under group, order the Kid's Meal—a smaller burger, Fuddrucker's potatoes, and a drink for $2.50; they'll get a free cookie for dessert. Close your eyes as you walk by the bakery in the front of the restaurant! There are highchairs, but no boosters here.

Open weekdays from 11 a.m. to 10 p.m., on weekends till 11 p.m. Major credit cards honored. Street parking.

Cathedral City

The **Marie Callendar's** chain is known throughout southern California for its fresh pies. But you can also get a good lunch or dinner at most locations. There are two branches in the desert: in Cathedral City, at 69830 Calif. 111 (tel. 619/328-0844); and in Palm Desert, at the Palm Desert Town Center Mall (tel. 619/773-4743). You'll find a comfortable homey atmosphere at nearly every Marie Callendar's location.

For lunch or dinner, adult entrees range from pot pies, chili frittatas, and salads to pasta, chicken, hamburgers, sandwiches, and ribs. The prices average $5 to $10.50.

The children's menu is for kids under 10. They can choose half-sandwiches, pasta, chili, corn dogs, or grilled cheese, and there are barbecued ribs and chicken after 4 p.m. These dishes run $2 to $3.50. If your little one doesn't want pie for dessert, he or she can choose ice cream, cookies, or an apple.

Highchairs and boosters are provided. The servers will split adult portions for two kids, and will warm baby bottles and baby food in the kitchen. Reservations are accepted evenings only.

Open Sunday through Thursday from 11 a.m. to 10 p.m., on Friday and Saturday till 11 p.m. Major credit cards honored. Parking lot.

If your kids are tall enough to play the video games, and you're all in the mood for pizza in a super-casual setting, head for **Nicolino's,** at 35325 Date Palm Dr. (tel. 619/324-0411).

If you eat in, the kids can play the video machines in the next room and the noise of the games won't be right on top of you while you wait for your order. There are the usual Italian entrees for dinner, averaging $9. Pizza comes in three sizes with lots of toppings. Lunch offerings include pasta, sandwiches, and Italian salads. If the kids want pasta, those under 12 can have spaghetti or ravioli with a meatball, garlic bread, and a beverage for $3.50 or $4.

Highchairs and boosters are available. There is a $2.50 charge for splitting entrees. They'll gladly warm baby bottles in the kitchen. Reservations are accepted for groups of eight or more.

Open Monday through Thursday from 11 a.m. to 9 p.m., on Friday and Saturday till 10 p.m.; closed Sunday. Major credit cards honored. Parking lot.

Rancho Mirage

Another good place for breakfast, although it's fine for lunch or brunch too, is **Fromin's,** at 691 Calif. 111 (tel. 619/321-2991). Fromin's is a deli-*cum-*

coffeeshop. With over 200 deli items to choose from, there is no doubt you'll find something for yourselves and the kids. For breakfast, there is a short stack of pancakes for the light eaters at $2.75. They also have cereals, fruit, French toast, and omelets (36 choices, to be exact). There are huge selections of burgers, hot dogs, sandwiches, and salads. Light lunches of petite sandwich and soup ($6) might be perfect for a little tyke. There are also full entrees, fried chicken, Mexican selections, and lots of choices for dessert.

They will split adult portions for two kids and will warm baby bottles. There are Sassy seats and booster seats available, but no highchairs. Eat in the no-smoking section if your little ones are sensitive to smoke. Reservations accepted for eight or more only. If there's a wait, the little kids will get a bagel to assuage their hunger.

Open Easter to mid-November on weekdays from 8 a.m. to 10 p.m., on Friday and Saturday till 11 p.m. From November 15 to Easter, open daily from 7 a.m. to 1 a.m. Major credit cards are welcome. Parking lot.

As long as you're in the area, drop in at **Garcia's,** at 42540 Bob Hope Dr. (tel. 619/340-5531), for some mild Mexican food. Garcia's is large, light, and airy. Adults have a full menu to choose from, which includes lots of Mexican combination plates, interesting house specials, and many à la carte selections, as well as some "Yankee favorites." Prices start at $3 for tacos and go up to $11 for a Mexican-style rib-eye steak.

Kids 12 and under can have a taco, burger, grilled cheese, mini tacos and chimichangas, or a tortilla with melted cheese for $2.50 (including beverage). On the back of the menu the kids can draw a self-portrait, which, if selected by the staff, will be put on a special plaque in the front of the restaurant.

Highchairs and boosters are provided. Adult portions can be split for two kids, and they'll gladly warm baby bottles in the kitchen. Reservations are accepted.

Garcia's is open Monday through Thursday from 11:30 a.m. to 9 p.m., and on Friday, Saturday, and Sunday from 11 a.m. to 11 p.m. Summer hours vary slightly on the weekends. All major credit cards accepted. Parking lot.

Palm Desert

"Children are more than welcome," says Mario Pietro, owner of **Pietro's Italian Restaurant,** 72-221 Calif. 111 (tel. 619/568-0202). You'll find it among a strip of restaurants that includes Reuben's, Mancuso, and the Rusty Pelican. And while Pietro's is a few steps up from your neighborhood Italian restaurant, it's still a comfortable, friendly place to eat for adults as well as for kids. We took Janey there on her first night out on the town. The staff couldn't have been more helpful during our mini-emergency. After biting down on some garlic bread, she screamed out for all the restaurant to hear—it seems she had a cut in her mouth we didn't know about. The waitress promptly brought her ice cream to soothe the pain, and packed the pizza we had just ordered so we could leave quickly.

Adult entrees start at $8, and the average is $12. Veal, seafood, chicken, and pasta selections are vast. Kids can choose from spaghetti, ravioli, or rigatoni for $4, and their meal includes soup or salad and garlic bread. Or you can all order New York–style pizza. They will split adult portions for two kids.

Wednesday and Thursday are great days for pasta lovers. Pietro's features the only pasta bar in the desert. It's "all you can eat," and there are 21 sauces, from a simple marinara to white sherry shrimp sauce. Adults pay $10; the kids, $5.

Highchairs and boosters are available. They'll make Roy Rogers and Shirley Temples, and teens love the virgin margaritas, they report.

Reservations are accepted—and necessary, especially during high season. Open every day of the year except Christmas: on weekdays from 4:30 to 10 p.m., on weekends till 11 p.m. Major credit cards welcome. Valet parking and self-parking in the lot.

The Original Mesquite's is across the highway from the Town Center Mall, at Calif. 74 and El Paseo (tel. 619/340-0999). It's a nice place for lunch because you can sit outside during good weather. Inside you'll find a sort of new-wave '80s look, and a counter with chairs. This is a place for big eaters. The burgers are half-pounders ($6). You can also select from sandwiches, trout, quesadillas, or salads for lunch. Entrees average $6. They get lots of kids at dinnertime, but unless yours like fajitas, chili, mesquite-broiled fish, or steak, there's not much for young children to choose from. Evening entrees (which are full meals) average $17.

Highchairs and boosters are available. They'll split adult portions at no charge, and will warm baby bottles and make special drinks for the kids. Reservations are accepted. Weekends are the busiest time here.

Open in summer from 11:30 a.m. to 10 p.m. daily; breakfast is served on weekends only. In winter they serve Monday through Friday from 11:30 a.m. to 2:30 p.m. and 5:30 to 10 p.m. and on Saturday and Sunday from 11 a.m. to 10 p.m. All major credit cards welcome. Parking lot.

If you can stand the noise level at **TGI Friday's,** at 72-620 El Paseo (tel. 619/568-2280), on a busy day, then definitely take the kids. Selections here include American, Italian, Mexican, and Oriental dishes—something for everyone. Adult entrees, lunch and dinner, range from $5 to $6.

The "Kids' Stuff" menu is a six-page book of selections and drawing games, and comes with crayons. There are the ubiquitous hot dog, hamburger, and grilled cheese, as well as chicken fingers and kids' shrimp. An average entree costs $2.25. At brunch, kids can order French toast, stuffed or plain, or pancakes, etc. The drink and dessert portion of the menu is almost two pages long! No doubt you'll be as thrilled as we were when Junior orders an REO Speedwagon—crumbled Oreo cookies and vanilla ice cream made into a creamy drink. We felt okay when Andrew ordered a Banana King—a drink of strawberries, bananas, orange sherbet, and vanilla ice cream—and we saved the mint chocolate-chocolate-chip malt for ourselves.

Highchairs and boosters are available. They'll split adult portions for two kids, and will warm baby bottles in the kitchen. No reservations accepted. Call to see how long the wait is.

Open daily, year round, from 11:30 a.m. to 2 a.m. All major credit cards honored. Street parking.

If you're going to spend some time at the Town Center Mall in Palm Desert, there are a couple of restaurants you might be interested in.

The Red Onion, 72840 Calif. 111, in the Town Center Mall right next to the Ice Capades (tel. 619/340-0029), is one. This chain can be found throughout southern California. The Mexican food is mild, and the restaurant is big and noisy. Adult selections—à la carte, combinations, and specials—range from $4.75 to $11 at lunch and dinner.

There's a kid's menu for the under-12 set, which comes with stickers. Children's entrees cost $2 and include tacos, enchiladas, hamburgers, and Mexican grilled cheese, all served with rice (or french fries) and fresh fruit. Sunday brunch is very popular, and the selections are vast. Kids pay $3 and can choose from the omelet or fajita bars, or order Belgian waffles, enchiladas, pizza, or pasta. There are also juice and dessert bars.

They will make special drinks for the kids, including virgin margaritas. All adult drinks can be ordered without alcohol. There are booster seats and highchairs available.

The Red Onion is open Monday through Thursday from 11 a.m. to 9 p.m., on Friday and Saturday till 10 p.m. Sunday brunch is served from 10 a.m. to

3 p.m. Reservations are taken—and honored. If it's busy, the wait is usually no more than five to ten minutes. Major credit cards welcome.

Swenson's (also in the mall), 72840 Calif. 111 (tel. 619/340-6229), is especially fun for dessert or for a treat after skating or the movies. It also features children's meals through the day. The Kiddie Korner menu offers an egg or French toast with bacon or sausage ($1.50 to $1.75). At lunch, there's a Cable Car Kid's Meal, which is served in a cable car—choice of hamburger, grilled cheese, peanut butter and jelly, all with fries and a ticket for a free single-dip ice cream cone—for $2.25 (12 and under). Sunday-night dinner might entice the whole family—pan-fried chicken, mashed potatoes and gravy, black-eyed peas, vegetable, soup and salad, biscuits, apple cobbler or apple strudel ice cream. Adults pay $8; children 12 and under, $4.

Boosters and highchairs are available.

Open Sunday through Thursday from 8 a.m. to 10 p.m., on Friday and Saturday till 11 p.m. Major credit cards are welcome.

WHAT TO SEE AND DO: There are things to do in the desert all year round. Just remember that summers can be brutal, and if you choose an activity that takes some physical effort, you're better off doing it in the morning or late afternoon.

Want something to do with the toddlers in the early morning? Drive to the corner of Gerald Ford Drive and Da-Vall Road (Mission Hills Country Club) in Rancho Mirage. There you'll find a large pond filled with ducks and geese. These beautiful birds are spoiled rotten and love to be fed by visitors. To the squealing delight of little children, the birds come right up on the grass and waddle up to the person with the most bread. We've seen families with entire loaves of fresh bread spending an hour with their feathered friends. It's a great diversion for restless kids.

Ballooning

Hot-air ballooning is usually not recommended for children under 5, because very young children are often frightened by the loud noise of the burners used to pump the balloons. Know your child before you decide to spend this kind of money. Ballooning is an exhilarating experience, and one you'll all remember forever. But once you're up there with a group of people, you can't get away from a frightened, screaming child.

The **Great American Balloon Company** flies over the Coachella Valley. Contact them at 4248 Via Marina, Suite 87, Marina Del Rey, CA 90292 (tel. 213/827-5791, or toll free 800/272-3631 in California). Flights take you over date groves, the desert, country clubs—whatever part of the Coachella Valley is having the best weather. Great American flies from September through April. If you can, call two to three days in advance, especially on holiday weekends. You can arrange to be picked up at your hotel. Flights cost $125 per person, adult or child.

Contact the other balloon companies for their rates: **Fantasy Balloon Flights** (tel. 619/568-0997), **Rise & Float Balloon Tours** (tel. 619/341-2686), or **Desert Balloon Charters** (tel. 619/346-8575).

Bicycling

If you're coming by car, you're best off bringing your own bikes, carriers, and helmets to the desert, as most of the bicycle-rental locations don't have child carriers. If you don't need the carrier, there are some small bikes for rent, but no helmets.

Mac's Bike Rentals, 700 E. Palm Canyon Dr., Palm Springs (tel. 619/327-5721), rents by the hour, day, or week. They are open daily in season, and they deliver. Their hours are 10 a.m. to 4 p.m. weekdays and 9 a.m. to 5 p.m. weekends. **Canyon Bicycle Rentals and Tours** is at 210 W. Sunny Dunes Rd., Palm Springs (tel. 619/327-7688). Rentals are by the half day, day, or week. Open Thursday through Tuesday from 9 a.m. to 5 p.m.; closed Wednesday.

Burnett's Bicycle Bar is located at 429 S. Sunrise Way, at Ramon Road, Palm Springs, in the Alpha Beta Center (tel. 619/325-7844). Hours are Thursday through Monday from 8 a.m. to 5 p.m., on Tuesday till noon; closed Wednesday.

There are bike paths all over town, including some within various hotel or condominium properties (for guest use only). *Palm Spring Life's Desert Guide* pullout has a "Bicycle Touring Guide," which outlines paths from 3 to 14½ miles long. The Palm Springs Recreation Department has bike path maps; they're located at 401 S. Pavilion Way, Palm Springs (tel. 619/323-8265).

Parents note: Don't let your kids ride on Calif. 111; the highway is much too busy, and there are many prettier places to ride.

Family Concerts

On Thursday evenings during the summer (beginning the last Thursday in June), there are free **pop and jazz concerts** at Sunrise Plaza, 1901 E. Baristo, one block north of Ramon Road between Sunrise and Farrell (tel. 619/323-8272). These popular concerts begin at 8:30 p.m. and are held outdoors on the lawn.

Hiking

The entrance to the **Indian Canyons** can be found on South Palm Canyon Drive (tel. 619/325-5673). You may not know that the Palm Springs area was originally settled by the Agua Caliente Cahuilla Indians. Much of the land in the area is still owned by Native Americans, and many hotels and homes sit on that land, their owners paying rent on 99-year leases. The Cahuillas created their communities within five canyons, three of which are open to the public, one of which you need a permit to hike in, and the last, Chino, where you'll find the Aerial Tramway. Still part of the Indian reservation, the canyons are maintained by the Agua Caliente Cahuillas.

Palm Canyon is a good place to start. This is where you'll find the Trading Post, which sells hiking maps, snacks, and Native American art and artifacts. There is a footpath near the post that leads down into the canyon. You can hike from this point, or just bring a picnic lunch and sit by the stream. The paths aren't too steep for young children. The native palms, the *Washingtonia filifera,* are in abundance here. In fact this canyon is known to have the most palm trees in the world, and is listed on the National Register of Historic Places.

Hiking in **Andreas Canyon** is for the more adventurous. Not ready for a tough hike? Picnic there instead. There's a foot trail through the canyon and picnic tables along the way. Be sure to check at the Trading Post as to whether the grade is too steep for your kids (or yourself!).

Murray Canyon is less accessible, but if you are determined to see it, you can hike there from Andreas. If you're lucky, the children just might spot a wild pony or some mountain sheep. **Tahquitz Canyon,** just west of Palm Springs, can be entered only by special permit from the Tribal Council Office, 960 E. Tahquitz Way, Palm Springs (tel. 619/325-5673). This canyon is known for magnificent waterfalls.

Admission to the canyons is $3 for adults, 75¢ for children 6 to 12. If you're on horseback, it will cost you $3.50. Open daily September through June from 8:30 a.m. to 5 p.m.

The **Palm Springs Aerial Tramway** is located at Calif. 111 (north) and Tramway Road, in Palm Springs (tel. 619/325-1391). The best thing about the tramway is what you find when you get to the top of Mount San Jacinto. It's too bad that while you're traveling the 18-minute 12,800-foot distance in the 80-passenger cable car, the drivers don't tell you what you're passing. If they did, you would know you're seeing the equivalent of the flora and fauna you'd see if you drove from Sonora, Mexico, to the Arctic Circle. Kids would love to know that.

Be sure to take layers of clothing with you, as the temperature drops greatly at the top. If you aren't prepared, there's a giftshop at the entrance that sells mittens, sweatshirts, hats, and other warm clothing.

Once you get to the top, you'll be in **Mount San Jacinto State Park.** If you never make it to one hiking trail, you'll still enjoy the immediate area outside the tram station. Janey loved her first attempt at "mountain climbing." There's a great hill after you pass the first curve of the concrete hand-railed path. It's an easy climb for older kids, a bit of work for the toddler set. The giant flat-topped boulder is perfect for their first goal. We sat on the top of it for nearly 45 minutes watching the people below, the glorious pine trees, and the sun changing position. Just beyond that boulder is a cave, clean and pretty open. Someone about three feet tall can just about stand up straight in it. There's a narrow crawlspace through the cave to an opening on the other side leading to a trail. It's big enough for an adult, but we wouldn't let the toddlers go through by themselves.

We spent nearly two hours on that one hill, Janey climbing part of the way up alone over and over again. We found all sorts of rocks, big walking sticks, and giant pine cones. Explain to the kids that the natural things they find in a state park cannot be removed. There's even a depository for "found" pine cones right before you leave the park, to remind people not to take them home.

If you do continue down the winding concrete path to the park itself, you enter 54 miles of campgrounds, hiking trails, and a ranger station. A sign at the end of the path illustrates where the three-quarter-mile self-guiding Nature Loop Trail begins and shows you where the ranger station is in nearby Long Valley (walking distance). Check at the station for maps and information on guided nature hikes and summer campfire programs. Camping is permitted in the wilderness with a permit, available at the ranger station. If you don't feel like hoofing it, a guided mule-back Wilderness Trail Ride is available during the hot summer months. The ride is 20 minutes long. Signs at the tram station will lead you to the mules.

During hot desert summers, a visit to the top is a welcome relief. In spring there is an Easter egg hunt for young children. Before Halloween, those under 12 can join in a pumpkin-decorating contest. Winter is also lively in the park. The Moosehead Sled Dog Classic is held the first two weekends in January. The dogs run on a 2½-mile trail easily viewed by visitors from the concrete trail behind the tram station. (See the "Winter Activities" section for ski information.)

Each station (coming and going) has a snackbar, cocktail lounge, giftshop, observation areas, and rest rooms. A Ride 'n' Dine package is available for those who want to have dinner at the top. The round-trip fare and dinner is $18 for adults, $11.50 for children 13 and under. The fare alone is $14 for adults, $9 for children 13 and under.

Cars run at least every 30 minutes. The tramway opens Monday through Friday at 10 a.m., on Saturday and Sunday at 8 a.m. The last tram up is at 7:30 p.m.; the last tram comes down at 9:15 p.m. From May through Labor Day the last car goes up at 9 p.m., and comes down at 10:45 p.m. The tram closes the first two weeks in August for maintenance. Check ahead. During holidays the wait for a tram up can be anywhere from a half hour to two hours. There is ample parking, with shuttle service from outlying lots. Not stroller-accessible.

Horseback Riding

Ranch of the 7th Range, La Quinta (tel. 619/564-1414—if you are calling from Palm Springs or Palm Desert, dial 4 first), is off Calif. 111. Take Calif.

111 east to Jefferson, turn right, and you'll see the PGA Headquarters building —the stables are located directly behind the building.

Horseback riding is one way to really experience the desert the way the pioneers did. Horses and ponies are for rent by the hour, and the staff will allow babies to go double with a parent. (We don't recommend this!) The age minimum for kids alone on a horse is 4, and those horses are experienced with children.

Trail rides cost $15 per person per hour, plus $15 for the guide (this fee split by all the riders). Kids or babies who ride double pay $5. Experienced riders are allowed to go without a guide. It's best to call for reservations.

Smoketree Stables, 2500 Toledo, Palm Springs (tel. 619/327-1372), offers hourly rentals ($15 per hour, adults and children), and all-day pack trips ($63.50 per person with lunch, four people minimum). The stables are open year round.

Indoor Activities

The **Ice Capades Chalet,** Palm Desert Town Center Mall, 72840 Calif. 111, Palm Desert (tel. 619/340-4412), is an anomaly in the middle of the desert. It's great fun all year round, but an especially welcome relief in the summer. Public skating is offered at various times, day and evening. Call for the schedule. For those not staying long enough to get into a class, Director Nalani Philipson offers private lessons at $10 for 15 minutes, $20 for half an hour. Call in advance. Skate rental is available for ages 2½ through adult ($1.50). Tuesday nights are adult-only nights; on Wednesday, skate rental is free. Admission to the large rink is $4.25.

While you're at the mall, you'll see the Red Onion next door to the rink, a ten-screen movie theater next door to the rink entrance, and Swenson's Restaurant next door to the theater. Just upstairs of the rink is the **Yellow Brick Road Family Amusement Center.** Kids who can reach the video machines will enjoy themselves. There's not much there for the toddlers, though. Skip the International Food Mart next door, and go to one of the aforementioned restaurants instead.

There's a toy store in the mall, a children's apparel shop, and numerous bookstores. An index to establishment locations can be found just outside the Ice Capades, as you enter the mall itself.

Museums and Gardens

The **Living Desert Reserve,** 47-900 Portola Ave., in Palm Desert, 1½ miles south of Calif. 111 (tel. 619/346-5694), should not be missed. Although the memory of Janey "petting" her first snake here still causes her mother bad dreams, it isn't every weekend that the reptiles are brought out and described!

Allot one or two hours for this activity, which is perfect for any age. There are animals to see in habitats as close to their original ones as possible. As you walk from setting to setting, you are traveling through botanical gardens made up of eight desert regions. There are fascinating plants, even prehistoric species. The six miles of trails can be walked leisurely with the help of self-guiding booklets. Weekends and holidays are when you, too, can see your first snake up close. Or maybe that day they'll take out a rare animal, or an exotic desert bird.

There's a snack stand and shaded picnic areas. Rest rooms and water fountains are conveniently located. Although there are shaded areas all through the park, you might want to bring extra drinks, a hat for the kids, and even sunscreen, if you're going on a particularly hot day. Stroller-accessible. Plenty of free parking.

Open daily from 9 a.m. to 5 p.m. Closed June 16 through August 31. Adults pay $3.50; children 3 to 15, $1; 2 and under, free.

Moorten Botanical Gardens, 1701 S. Palm Canyon Dr., Palm Springs (tel.

619/327-6555), is a nice place to take the family on a morning walk. There are more than 2,000 varieties of desert plants, including hundreds of kinds of cactus. Open daily from 9 a.m. to 5 p.m. Admission is $1.50.

The **Palm Springs Desert Museum** is at the foot of the mountain, 101 Museum Dr., Palm Springs (tel. 619/325-7186). A visit to this museum is a delightful indoor activity on a hot (or cold) day.

The museum houses fine art and exhibitions of classic western, American, and contemporary California art. Natural-science exhibits and special programs offer something for everyone. Recently, for instance, the museum had a dinosaur exhibit in the natural-science wing, along with special programs leading up to that exhibit, including a family day. Families helped to build a 16-foot stegosaurus and created dinosaur masks and clay sculptures.

Check the museum schedule for events that might be interesting to your family. The museum is open Tuesday through Friday from 10 a.m. to 4 p.m., on Saturday and Sunday till 5 p.m. The museum season is September to June. Closed major holidays. Adults pay $4 admission, children 6 to 17 and students with ID pay $2, and children 5 and under are free. There is free admission the first Tuesday of each month, except for special exhibitions.

Tennis

If your hotel courts are tied up, there are public courts at **DeMuth Park,** 4375 Mesquite Ave. (four night-lighted courts); **Ruth Hardy Park,** 700 Tamarisk Rd. (eight courts); and the **Palm Springs High School,** 2248 Ramon Rd. (five courts). Open to the public for a small fee is the **Palm Springs Tennis Center,** 1300 Baristo Rd. (nine night-lighted courts). Call for more information: 619/320-0020.

The instructors at the **Reed Anderson Tennis School,** located at the Gene Autry Hotel, 4200 E. Palm Canyon Dr., Palm Springs (tel. 619/328-1171, ext. 265), give private instruction to players of any age and conduct tennis clinics for experienced players. Private lessons are $20 per half hour; $40 per hour. Clinics are held from 9 a.m. to noon daily. The charge is $45 for three hours; $195 for 15 hours of instruction (five days). Racquets can be rented.

Water Activities

The **Palm Springs Oasis Water Park,** at 1500 Gene Autry Trail, Palm Springs (tel. 619/325-SURF), is just that—an oasis in the middle of the desert. There is something for every age group here. Starting with the youngest ball of energy in the group, there is "Squirt City"—small slides and giant squirt guns and a large splashy pool. There's also a family slide so Junior can travel down to the 80° water with Mom or Dad on an innertube. A new slide area just for toddlers is in the works.

For the "older" kids, minimum 8 years old, there's surfing on 3½-foot waves. Surf- and body-boards can be rented. There are lifeguards on duty. All together there are seven slides—two are seven stories high, and you travel at speeds of 40 mph.

The rest of the family will enjoy the volleyball courts, hot spas, private cabañas with food service, and day passes to the Oasis Health Club, a private spa and fitness center that offers whirlpool, aerobics, weight room, steam, sauna, and cold plunge.

There are changing rooms, showers, and food concessions. The large parking lot is free, or there is valet parking.

The park is open mid-March to mid-June daily from 11 a.m. to 6 p.m. From mid-June to the beginning of September it's open daily till 8 p.m. For one month (September to October) it is open on Friday from 4 to 8 p.m. and on Saturday and Sunday from 11 a.m. to 8 p.m. During October it is open weekends only, from 11 a.m. to 6 p.m. Closed from October 31 to mid-March.

Admission is $14 for adults, $10 for children 4 to 11; under 4, free. Big families, note: Five or more children with a paying adult are charged just $8 each.

The **Palm Springs Swim Center,** at the corner of Sunrise Way and Ramon Road in the Sunrise Plaza Center, Palm Springs (tel. 619/323-8278), has an outdoor Olympic-size pool open to the public, with lifeguards year round. There are one- and three-meter diving boards, and there is a separate shallow area of the pool roped off for children. Children 6 and under can take private swimming lessons, which cost $41 for five 30-minute classes.

Open daily, year round, from 11 a.m. to 5 p.m. During the hot summers the pool is open for night swimming. Admission for adults (age 13 and up) is $3; children 4 to 12, $2; under 4, free.

If you're willing to make about a 25-mile round trip, you can go fishing at **Whitewater Trout Fishing,** Whitewater exit off I-10 West (tel. 619/325-5570). After Dad (or Mom) has caught "the big one," you can grill and eat it right there. Or the staff will clean and box your catch for no charge.

Open year round, Tuesday through Sunday from 9 a.m. to 5 p.m. The fee is $2 for tackle, bait, bucket, and towel, plus $2.25 for each pound of fish caught.

Winter Activities

Believe it or not, people really do ski in Palm Springs. Cross-country ski lessons are available at the **Palm Springs Nordic Ski Center,** at the top of the tram (tel. 619/327-6002, or 619/325-4227 for snow and ski conditions). When you reach the end of the concrete trail outside the station, you'll see signs leading you to the center.

If you bring your own equipment and don't need lessons, there is no charge to ski in the park. Lessons, for both adults and children (the director suggests a minimum age of 5), last 1 to 1½ hours ($10 per person). Lessons can be taken on weekends at 10 a.m., noon, or 2 p.m. For a weekday lesson, call to make arrangements.

Equipment can be rented. Adults pay $6 per hour or $15 per day; children, $4 per hour or $9 per day. Snowshoes and snowboots can also be rented. There is no need to make reservations for weekend lessons, but the center does close weekdays if business is slow, so call ahead.

Open from mid-November until mid-April: weekdays from 10:30 a.m. to 5 p.m.; and weekends and holidays from 8 a.m. to 5 p.m.

Fairs, Festivals, and Seasonal Activities

Visitors to the area in the middle of February like to take the family to the **Date Festival** in Indio (tel. 619/347-8247 or 619/347-0676). Stay on Calif. 111 east until you get to Indio. Signs will direct you to the festival. For ten days there is special entertainment, displays, camel and ostrich races, a livestock show, art exhibits, contests, a Diaper Derby, and more. Watch the local papers for the schedule of events.

June is **Cherry Festival** time in nearby Beaumont (27 miles west of Palm Springs on I-10—take the Beaumont Avenue exit to the festivities). For information on this year's festival, contact the Beaumont Chamber of Commerce, P.O. Box 291, Beaumont, CA 92223 (tel. 714/845-9541). For five days visitors can see a carnival, attend an old-fashioned pancake breakfast, watch a parade, and attend a horse show. There are also signs directing you to public cherry-picking orchards in Beaumont and nearby Cherry Valley.

For specific information on cherry orchards open to the public for picking (the season usually runs from the end of May to the first of July), stop at the Cherry Festival Association Information Booth at the corner of Cherry Valley Boulevard and Beaumont Avenue (2½ miles north of Beaumont). Or call the president of the Cherry Grower's Association (tel. 714/845-3628). Be sure to tell her you have children in the group, as they are not allowed at certain orchards.

Apple-picking adventures are abundant in the area. This is a fun activity to do as a family. Not only do you all get outdoors, but the children get to eat what they actually pick. Oak Glen is a veritable mecca for apple picking and cider making, as well as just a nice place to visit. To get there, take I-10 west to the Beaumont Avenue exit. Go north six or seven miles to Oak Glen.

There are four orchards open to the public that allow you to pick your own apples, then pay for them by the pound (signs along Oak Glen Road will lead you right to them): **Riley's Log Cabin Farm & Orchard,** for U-pick apples and pears, and U-press cider (tel. 714/797-4061); **Los Rios Rancho,** for apples and cider, bakery, and snacks (tel. 714/797-1005); **Four Oaks Ranch,** for apples, pears, and cider (tel. 714/797-3415 or 714/845-4182); and **Johnny Appleseed Ranch,** for apples (tel. 714/797-4787). The same orchards are not always open each year to the public, so call the Oak Glenn Apple Growers Association first (tel. 714/790-2165), or just take a drive through town and check the signs. If you are coming from a distance, be sure to call first, since each season brings different times for harvest. There are also apple sheds at ranches along Oak Glen Road selling all sorts of apple products.

For those of you *not* escaping the Midwest and East Coast snowstorms, Oak Glen is a place to visit from January to March to introduce the family to snow. Or come mid-April through mid-May to see the gorgeous apple blossoms bloom. In the summer it's a place to escape a day of searing heat in Palm Springs, as the temperatures in Oak Glen are at least 10° to 15° cooler.

Yucaipa hosts a three-day **Apple Fest** in October at Yucaipa Regional Park. From Palm Springs, take the second Yucaipa exit, then turn left at Oak Glen Road to the park. This old-fashioned festival features apples, of course, in all their configurations (cider, pie, butter, etc.), as well as a horseshoe tournament, a chili cook-off, a carnival, and arts and crafts booths. Call the Yucaipa Valley Chamber of Commerce (tel. 714/790-1841) for exact dates.

Teen and Other Activities

Young adults 16 and over will appreciate **The Comedy Haven,** at Delmonico's Fishmarket in the Desert Fashion Plaza on Palm Canyon Drive, Palm Springs (tel. 619/320-7855 or 619/322-6500). Along with dining and dancing, the club showcases live comedy and improvisation shows.

Comedy nights are Wednesday and Sunday. Shows begin at 9 p.m. and last approximately two hours. The cover charge is $7 without dinner, $5 with dinner. After the show, there is disco dancing for the 18-and-over crowd (ID necessary). A "Dance Party" is held on Friday, Saturday, and Sunday evenings beginning at 10:30 p.m.

Lunch (prices starting at $3) is served daily from 11 a.m. to 3 p.m. Early-Bird dinners (beginning at $7) are served from 5 to 7 p.m.; dinner ($7 to $18), from 7 to 10 p.m. nightly, except Monday and Tuesday.

Reservations are suggested. Dress code for "Dance Party." Major credit cards welcome. Parking lot.

A place teens *and* parents can go to together is **Club Cabaret's Stage Door Dinner Theatre,** 1450 N. Indian Ave., Palm Springs (tel. 619/323-2713). This dinner-theater serves Italian food and light entertainment for the whole family. Lunch starts at $5; dinners, at $11. Boosters, yes; highchairs, no. Adult portions can be split (no children's menu available), and baby bottles and baby food can be warmed in the kitchen. However, dinner-theater is not recommended for young children.

Meal and show times: Sunday, lunch at noon, show at 1 p.m.; Thursday through Saturday, late lunch at 2 p.m. and show at 3 p.m., dinner at 6 p.m. and show at 7:30 p.m.; plus a second seating with dinner at 9 p.m. and show at 10 p.m. Cover charge: adults, $7; students and seniors, $6. By reservation only. Most major credit cards accepted. Parking lot.

Shopping Hints
Uncle Don's Toys, 296 N. Palm Canyon Dr., Palm Springs (tel. 619/325-5979), has a nice selection of toys for kids of all ages. In the back there's a great variety of girls' playthings. Open year round, Monday through Saturday from 9:30 a.m. to 6 p.m. and on Sunday from 10 a.m. to 5 p.m.

Hidden away in the Plaza is **Palm Springs Baby Furniture & Toys,** 18-19 The Plaza (tel. 619/325-4457). Remember this establishment if you need to rent carseats, highchairs, strollers, infant seats, cribs and mattresses, playpens, and other children's paraphernalia. They usually rent items by the week, but some can be rented by the day—inquire. Open daily from 8:30 a.m. to 5 p.m.

IN CASE OF EMERGENCY: If a medical emergency should arise during your visit to Palm Springs, there is emergency-room treatment available at **Desert Hospital,** 1150 N. Indian Ave., Palm Springs (tel. 619/323-6511).

2. LAKE ARROWHEAD AND BIG BEAR LAKE
Lake Arrowhead and Big Bear Lake are the two most popular mountain communities in the San Bernardino Mountains. Located about 1½ hours from Los Angeles, and 30 miles from each other, both are considered year-round resorts, and offer winter and summer activities galore. To get to Lake Arrowhead and Big Bear Lake from Los Angeles, take I-10 east to Calif. 215 north. Go 4 miles to the Mountain Resorts turnoff. Continue to Waterman Avenue, which is Calif. 18 (Rim of the World Drive). Turn left and proceed to Lake Arrowhead and Big Bear.

LAKE ARROWHEAD: Lake Arrowhead is actually seven tiny communities surrounding the lake. Its 14-mile shoreline (most of which is privately owned) offers myriad summer delights. You might want to contact the **Lake Arrowhead Communities Chamber of Commerce,** P.O. Box 155, Lake Arrowhead, CA 92352 (tel. 714/337-3715), for further information.

Activities On and Around the Lake
Alpine-style **Lake Arrowhead Village** is the hub of activities in the area. With over 60 shops and restaurants located on the banks of the lake, the village is a good place to spend a little time. It has a swimming beach and marina (open Memorial Day through Labor Day).

Located at Lake Arrowhead Marinas (tel. 714/337-2553), the *Arrowhead Queen* paddlewheeler tours the lake year round. The 50-minute narrated cruises are offered hourly, May through September, on weekdays from 11 a.m. to 4 p.m., on weekends and holidays from 10 a.m. to 5 p.m.; September through April on weekdays from 1 to 2 p.m., on weekends and holidays from noon to 3 p.m. Adults pay $6 (weekdays) or $7 (weekends); children 5 to 12, $3; children under 4, free.

Lake Arrowhead Marinas also rents powerboats and fishing boats for half-day and full-day excursions. Kids will enjoy the bumper boats—a five-minute ride costs $3. Lake Arrowhead Marinas is located on the lake level of Arrowhead Village.

Other Activities
One mile from Arrowhead Village, in the little hamlet of Blue Jay, you and the kids can enjoy hours of ice skating (even on a hot summer day) at **Blue Jay Ice Castle Skating Rink,** 27307 Calif. 189 (tel. 714/336-2111). Ice Castle is a completely covered rink that opens on the sides so that you feel as if you're skating in the forest. Children as young as 2 years old grace the ice—and rent skates here.

Ice hockey matches and private skating lessons are given, so the hours for public skating vary. Call ahead. Admission is $3.50 for adults, $3.25 for juniors (13 to 17), and $3 for children 12 and under. All skates rent for $1.50 a pair.

Another enchanting place is **Santa's Village** (tel. 714/337-2481, 714/336-3661 for recorded information), located just a few miles from Lake Arrowhead in Skyforest. Open summer, fall, and winter (closed March, April, and May), it is especially designed for young children, who enjoy the elves, the miniature rides, and the little petting farm that even includes reindeer. There's an Antique Auto Ride, Cinderella's Pumpkin Coach Ride, and the Magic Train Ride. Of course, since this is Santa's Village, there is a toy shop, a candy store, and a bakery. Open daily mid-June through mid-September and mid-November through December, plus weekends and holidays in January, February, and early June, from 10 a.m. to 5 p.m. Admission is $6.50 for adults, $7.50 for children 3 to 16; children under 2, free.

Snow Valley Ski Area (tel. 714/867-2751) is a 230-acre area that offers both natural and artificially made snow. Located five miles east of Running Springs on Calif. 18 (between Lake Arrowhead and Big Bear Lake, 85 miles from Los Angeles), Snow Valley has 13 chair lifts with 35 runs, a complete rental service, and night skiing five nights a week. The ski school offers half-day and full-day group lessons, and private lessons by the hour. An all-day (3-hour) group lesson is $22; a half-day (1½-hour) group lesson is $16; a one-hour private lesson runs $40.

A beginner's package costs $38 for adults on a weekday, $35 on a weekend; $28 for seniors and children. This includes a ticket for the two beginner's lifts, ski rental, and a 1½-hour lesson. Classes are grouped by ability, not age (the minimum age is 6). For children 4 and 5, there is a snow school that introduces them to skiing at the most basic level. The children should come with rented equipment. This is primarily day-care service, but they do teach the kids to sidestep and snowplow. School is held from 10 a.m. to 3 p.m. and costs $25 per day.

Lift tickets cost $29.50 for adults, $15 for children 12 and under. Night skiing (weekdays from 1 to 9 p.m. and weekends from 1 to 10 p.m.) costs $22 for adults, $13 for children 12 and under.

Open Monday and Tuesday from 8 a.m. to 5 p.m.; on Sunday, Wednesday, and Thursday from 1 to 9 p.m.; and on Friday and Saturday from 1 to 10 p.m.

Snow Valley limits the number of tickets it sells, so you might want to reserve a lift ticket by calling its computerized reservation system (tel. 714/867-5111 or 714/625-6611). You can also reserve through Ticketron. Ask about packages that include lift ticket, lessons, and equipment rentals. For current snow conditions, call 714/867-5151 or 714/625-6511.

There are loads of trails in the area, ranging from easy to difficult. Contact the **Arrowhead Ranger District,** P.O. Box 7, Rimforest, CA 92378 (tel. 714/337-2444), for specific trails for your family. Here are a few easy trails to start with.

The **National Children's Forest** is one small 20-acre area in the San Bernardino National Forest. It was developed so that children—including visually handicapped and those in wheelchairs—could enjoy nature. The origins of the National Children's Forest date back to 1970, when one of the worst fires started in San Bernardino National Forest. After 3,000 firefighters worked for six days, it was finally over, but 53,000 acres had been blackened.

The slopes couldn't be left bare. Thousands of trees were needed to restart the forest and protect the topsoil. In the same year, across the country, five million acres of forest were destroyed. Hunt-Wesson Foods, Inc., began to help the National Forest Service in the huge job of replanting. This started the idea of getting children involved. A National Children's Forest was created to show man's interest in nature and his desire to help. Many children have participated in the replanting of the forest. Three National Children's Forests were chosen, and

San Bernardino was one of them. As in other regions of this national forest, the Ponderosa pine is abundant. You'll also see lovely dogwood trees. To get there from Lake Arrowhead, take Calif. 330 to Calif. 18 east. Pass Deer Lick station. You'll see a road marked IN96; make a right and go three miles. The road is opened in late May.

Trail of the Phoenix starts at the entrance to the Children's Forest. On the half-mile paved nature trail you see pine and oak trees and manzanita bushes. Have the kids watch for animals and birds such as ground squirrels, hawks, and blue jays. During the summer, be on the lookout for rattlesnakes—it's unlikely you'll see them, but they are there. The trail is stroller-accessible.

Outside the Children's Forest, the **Enchanted Loop Trail** is another easy trail that will take about half an hour to walk. This trail is in the Dogwood Campground (not far from the lake) where the Sequoia and Fir loops meet. **Sequoia Trail** is another easy walk. Located half a mile east of Santa's Village (on the north side of Calif. 18), the trail winds through a grove of redwoods.

Where to Stay in Lake Arrowhead

If your budget allows for it, the **Lake Arrowhead Hilton Lodge,** P.O. Box 1699, Lake Arrowhead, CA 92352 (tel. 714/336-1511, or toll free 800/223-3307), offers a variety of family activities in a superb setting. The lodge sits on the edge of the lake, commanding beautiful views of the water and surrounding forests. The large two-story lobby forms a semicircle and is very open and spacious. You feel as if you've stepped into a huge luxurious chalet, with high ceilings, blazing fires, and greenery. Light woods continue the mountain ambience, and a bridge to the second floor rooms gives a sense of enormous height and space.

The special feature of this Hilton is the children's summer program, which offers fully supervised activities for the kids so that you can enjoy the hotel's facilities (health club, tennis courts, pool, and spa) or have fun at the beach or on a boat. For children 3 to 5, there are activities from 9 a.m. to noon Monday through Friday. They'll have short hikes, treasure hunts, and arts and crafts. A snack is included in the fee. Children 5 through 13 can participate in activities from 9 a.m. to 5 p.m. Monday through Saturday. They fish, build sandcastles, go on nature hikes, and ice skate. Lunch and a snack are included in their program. Kids from 5 to 13 can also join an evening program given from 6 to 10 p.m., which features roasting marshmallows and hot dogs at the Hilton's private beach, playing volleyball, and watching movies. The lodge also has concierge service, which will arrange babysitting.

A game room / video arcade (but the children's program uses the room on Friday and Saturday nights) is another feature of the Hilton, and your kids may enjoy playing cards, checkers, horseshoes, shuffleboard, or table tennis.

The Lobby Café has an excellent children's menu that includes such items as pizza, corn dogs, and peanut butter and jelly with marshmallow cream. The waitresses are friendly and helpful. Highchairs and boosters are available. Prices run $1.25 to $3. There are three other restaurants in the lodge, ranging from fine Italian and continental dining to coffeeshop fare. Room service is available from 7 a.m. to 10 p.m.

The rooms at the Hilton are large, some with little balconies with chairs. All have game tables with two chairs, plush towels, and the bathroom amenities you'd expect from a Hilton. One plus is the VCR rental—there are 1,500 titles, and they'll even bring you a pizza to go with the movie, if you so desire.

Rooms have two double beds or a king-size bed. Some come with a couch (not a sofa bed). Rates vary depending on the type of room, the location, and the view. Singles range from $100 to $170; doubles, from $110 to $180. Kitchen units start at $195 (for kitchen, loft, and living room), and one- and two-bedroom suites cost $275 to $645. Children stay free in the same room as their parents. No charge for cribs, but rollaways cost $10. *Note:* When you book your room, be sure to tell the reservationist the number of kids you have and if you'll need a crib. If the crib isn't in your room when you arrive, ask for it immediately. (We spent a few hours with a cranky baby while we waited for the crib so she could take her nap.)

Where to Eat in Lake Arrowhead

When we're in the neighborhood, we like to eat at **Heidi's** (tel. 714/336-1511, ext. 633), a bit of Switzerland in Lake Arrowhead Village. Skirted, red-covered lamps and spacious booths that are divided by glass partitions provide a charming setting for this casual restaurant. Heidi's is actually associated with the Hilton Lodge (although it's not at the Hilton), and kids can choose from the same fine menu at reasonable prices. Pizza, chicken drummettes, corn dogs, and burgers range from $1.25 to $3. Breakfast items for children are adult portions cut in half.

During the weekends, there is a buffet all day that costs $9 for adults, $7 for kids. Breakfast items include eggs, French toast, biscuits and gravy, sausage, and hash browns or German-style potatoes. For lunch or dinner, the buffet offers fish, chicken, stews, a variety of pastas, and an elaborate salad bar. If you choose to eat off the menu, à la carte prices range from $4.75 to $9.50. There is also a daily breakfast bar with yogurt, fruit, granola, and hot cereal for $4.

There are highchairs and booster seats, and your servers will gladly warm bottles and baby food in the kitchen.

Heidi's is open in summer Sunday through Thursday from 7 a.m. to 9 p.m., and on Friday and Saturday till 10 p.m. In winter they are open Sunday through Thursday from 7 a.m. to 8 p.m., and on Friday and Saturday till 9 p.m. They accept most major credit cards. Parking is in the Lake Arrowhead Village parking lot.

BIG BEAR LAKE: The vacation area known as Big Bear centers around Big Bear Lake and the alpine forest surrounding it. At 7,000 feet in elevation, you have a multitude of activities to choose from—winter, spring, summer, and fall. We suggest that you contact the **Big Bear Chamber of Commerce,** 41647 Big Bear Blvd. (P.O. Box 2860), Big Bear, CA 92315 (tel. 714/866-6190), for complete information if you're going to be spending more than a few days.

Winter Activities

It's hard to believe that less than two hours from the Palm Springs desert is one of southern California's major ski areas. **Snow Summit** (tel. 714/866-5766 for the business office or 714/866-4546 for the ski school) is the most popular ski resort in the area. There are ten chair lifts and a complete rental and sport shop, and they offer night skiing. The ski school gives a wide range of group lessons. For adults, there are classes for beginners, clinics, and private and semiprivate lessons. For children 9 to 12, there's a ski school with all-day (four-hour) and half-day (two-hour) classes (priced at $18 and $13 respectively). You can enroll the kids for three consecutive days and get a break on the price. The kiddie ski school is for ages 4 to 8. All-day (six-hour) and half-day (three-hour) classes are $25 and $15 respectively (equipment rental costs extra). Lift tickets are included during classes and can be purchased for a reduced fee after class is over.

Lift tickets cost $27.50 for adults for all day, $27 for a half day (12:30 to 4 p.m.). Children pay $16 for a full-day pass, $11 for the half-day one.

Ask about special packages, as these are the most reasonable. Snow Summit speaks proudly about the short wait in lift lines. They do this by limiting ticket sales. It's recommended that you reserve your lift ticket in advance (tel. 714/866-5841)—there's a fee for this service. Ticketron (tel. 213/216-6666) and

Teletron (tel. 213/410-1062) also reserve tickets. Call 714/866-4621 for snow conditions.

Another good ski area is **Bear Mountain Ski Resort,** P.O. Box 6812, Big Bear Lake, CA 92315 (tel. 714/585-2519, 714/585-2518 for a snow report). Bear Mountain is another of the southern California ski areas that has the capacity to make artificial snow. Eight chair lifts and two surface lifts, a complete ski school, a rental and repair shop, as well as restaurant and snack facilities make this area one of the most popular in the San Bernardino Mountains.

Ski instruction includes the children's Powder Panda's school, for kids 5 to 12 years old (at least 41 inches tall). Offering half- and full-day programs, Powder Panda's is open from 7:30 a.m. to 4:30 p.m. on weekends, 8:30 a.m. to 4:30 p.m. on weekdays. The half-day session is afternoons only. The full-day rate—including lunch—is $40 and the half-day rate is $30. Rentals cost $9.

Lift tickets cost $32 for adults for a full day, $20 for a half day. Junior (12 and under) lift tickets are $17 for a full day, $13 for a half day. Adult group lessons cost $17 for a half-day (two-hour) session; private lessons run $35 per hour. Adult beginner packages include a two-hour group lesson, lift ticket, and equipment rental, and cost $45 on weekends and holidays, $32 on nonholiday weekdays. To make reservations, call 714/585-2518 or Ticketron (tel. 213/216-6666) or Teletron (tel. 213/410-1062 or 714/634-1300). To check snow conditions, call 714/585-2517.

Other Activities

Big Bear offers a wide array of active family entertainment. **Alpine Slide at the Magic Mountain Recreation Area** (tel. 714/866-4626) is a child's delight. Located on Big Bear Boulevard as you enter town, this playland offers year-round recreation. The Alpine Slide whizzes you down the track on a specially constructed sled that has levers to control the speed. There is also a snow-play area that you can innertube down. In addition to video games and a snackbar, Magic Mountain also has a water slide and pony rides.

For the Alpine Slide, adults pay $3 for a single ride, $12 for a five-ride book; juniors (7 to 12 years old) are charged $2.50 for a single ride, $10 for a five-ride book. Children under 6 are free when accompanied by an adult.

An all-day pass on the Water Slide costs $10 for adults, $8 for juniors. A ten-ride ticket book costs $7, or $1 per ride. Children under 5 are free when accompanied by an adult.

Both areas are open daily, mid-June to mid-September, from 10 a.m. to 6 p.m. The Alpine Slide is open year round on weekends and holidays (weather permitting).

Snow-play areas (including use of tube) cost $10 per person for a full day. If you have your own tube, the fee is $8. These areas are open daily during the winter season from 10 a.m. to dusk.

BOATING. This is a treat on Big Bear Lake. Boat rentals are available at **Big Bear Marina,** located at the corner of Pane and Lakeview about a quarter mile west of Big Bear Village (tel. 714/866-3218). You can rent motorboats at $12 per hour, $28 for a half day, and $38 for a full day. Pontoon boats rent for $30 per hour, $75 for a half day, and $115 for a full day. Deposits are required. The marina is open daily from 6 a.m. to 6:30 or 7 p.m.

FISHING. Want to guarantee that the kids will catch fish? The **Alpine Trout Farm,** 440 Catalina Rd., one long block off Calif. 18 (tel. 714/866-4532), is as good as a guarantee. This lake is stocked with trout, so kids can always catch something. Not only are there picnic and barbecue facilities, but all the fixings for cooking your fish are available at a little store. A snackbar is available for drinks and desserts. It costs just $2 for the entire family to fish, but you must pay for what you catch at $4.25 per pound. Fishing equipment rents for $2 per pole. Open daily from March to mid-November. Call for hours during the year.

HIKING. If your family enjoys the outdoors, the San Bernardino Mountains offers lots of different trails to choose from. For specific trails for your family, you might want to contact the **Big Bear Ranger District,** P.O. Box 290, Fawnskin, CA 92333 (tel. 714/866-3437).

We like the **Champion Lodgepole Trail** (less than half a mile long) and the connecting **Bluff Mesa Trail** (also half a mile long). These short family hikes take you through lodgepole and Jeffrey pine trees. In fact, the Champion Lodgepole Trail takes you past one of the largest lodgepoles in the entire state. Another easy trail is the **Pacific Crest National Scenic Trail,** which starts near Calif. 38 at Onyx Summit and ends 39 miles away at Holcomb Creek. You can walk as far as you want and see beautiful vistas along the way.

HORSEBACK RIDING. You can go riding at **Magic Mountain Stables,** next to the Alpine Slide (tel. 714/866-4626). One-hour guided rides through the forests cost $12 per hour. Children must be 6 years old to ride. The stables are open daily from 10:30 a.m. to 5 p.m.

You can also rent horses at **Bolin Stables,** 2025 Garnet St., in Big Bear City, where Big Bear Boulevard dead-ends (tel. 714/585-6503). Horses are rented for $12 per hour, $16 for a double (with a child under 4). If you need a guide, request one. On a busy weekend, it's best to stop by to make a reservation.

MINIATURE GOLF. You'll find this sport at **The Hot Shot,** 42123 Big Bear Blvd. (tel. 714/866-7164). Open Sunday through Friday from noon to 5 p.m. and on Saturday from 9 a.m. to 5 p.m.

SWIMMING. You can go lake swimming at **Meadow Park Swim Beach,** in Meadow Park at the corner of Knight and Park Avenues (tel. 714/866-3652). It's a cordoned-off beach area on Big Bear Lake with lifeguards, snackbar, rest rooms, and parking lot. The beach is open mid-June through Labor Day from 10 a.m. to 5 p.m. Adults pay $2; children 4 to 10, $1.50; under 4, free. Children 10 and under must be accompanied by an adult.

There is an adjacent heated **swimming pool** that is open to the public Memorial Day through Labor Day, on weekdays from 1 to 4 p.m. and on weekends from 1 to 6 p.m. Adults are charged $1.50; children 17 and under, $1.

Annual Events

Old Miner's Days (July and August) are ten days when the Old West visits Big Bear. There are log-rolling and rafting contests, donkey rides and races, and a carnival. The event culminates in a terrific parade.

Big Bear Rodeo (September), with bronco riding and roping competitions, and other rodeo events.

Oktoberfest (October, naturally) is a month-long celebration with German food, dancing, and music.

Where to Stay in Big Bear Lake

Big Bear offers a very unusual service. The **Big Bear Lake Tourist and Visitor Bureau,** 40588 Big Bear Blvd. (P.O. Box 3050), Big Bear Lake, CA 92315 (tel. 714/866-5877 or 714/866-4601), will help you make reservations at cabins, condominiums, bed-and-breakfasts, homes, motels, and hotels. They will try to take your specifications and meet your particular needs. All facilities have been inspected for cleanliness, management, and maintenance by the Tourist and Visitor Bureau and the chamber of commerce. Rentals in this area are an especially enticing way to go—and since these rentals are screened by the tourist people, you're less likely to encounter surprises.

Cozy Hollow Lodge, 40409 Big Bear Blvd. (P.O. Box 1288), Big Bear Lake, CA 92315 (tel. 714/866-9694), is our favorite in the area. This charming rustic retreat is made up of 17 little cabins on wooded acreage off Calif. 18. Owner Mike Allen built the place himself, including the children's play area in the middle of the grounds. The outdoor area has a place to clean fish, have barbecues, and play table tennis or horseshoes.

Each cabin is different. Some are studios or studios with kitchens; others are one- and two-bedroom layouts. They all have rough knotty-pine walls, refrigerators, queen-size beds, color TVs, tub/shower combinations, and fireplaces.

Children under 18 stay free, and there is no charge for cribs. Rates range from $50 per night (for a cabin that accommodates two adults and two children) to $110 per night (for a large two-bedroom cabin that accommodates four adults and four children).

For help finding other kinds of accommodations, try the Big Bear Lake Tourist and Visitor Bureau, mentioned above.

CAMPING. Seven campgrounds are located throughout the Big Bear area. **Big Pine Flats** has 19 sites with water and vault toilets, and charges $7 per site per night. **Cold Brook** has 36 sites with water and flush toilets, and charges $7 per night. **Grout Bay** has 23 sites with water and flush toilets, and is $7 per night. **Hanna Flats** has 88 sites with water and flush toilets, and costs $9 per night. **Holcomb Valley,** with 19 sites, has no water and vault toilets—no charge. **Horse Springs** has 17 sites, no water, and vault toilets—no charge. **Pine Knot** has 52 sites with water and flush toilets, and charges $7 per night.

For more information, contact the **Big Bear Ranger Station,** P.O. Box 290, Fawnskin, CA 92333 (tel. 714/866-3437). For weekend camping, it's advisable to get there by Friday afternoon; for holidays, get there by Thursday afternoon.

Where to Eat in Big Bear Lake

For a real family-style restaurant at amazingly reasonable prices, **Ronardo's European Family Restaurant,** 533 Pine Knot Blvd. (tel. 714/866-7676), is the place to go. Ronardo's offers large portions—family style. First comes the soup du jour with bread and butter. Next, the salad. Then spaghetti and green beans, and finally your entree, accompanied by french fries. To finish the meal, chocolate mints are served. Among the entrees, you can choose from veal parmesan, lasagne, New York and top sirloin steaks, and roast chicken. Prices range from $6 to $9.75. A child's plate costs $4.25. There is a minimum service charge of $3.75 (for children under 12) or $6 (for adults) per person, which includes everything but the entree.

Highchairs and booster seats are available. Ronardo's is open weekdays Monday through Thursday from 4 to 9 p.m., on Friday and Saturday till 10 p.m. Closed Monday and Tuesday during March, April, and May. Reservations are advised. Some credit cards accepted. Parking lot.

Teddy Bear Restaurant, 583 Pine Knot Blvd., in the village (tel. 714/866-5415), is a nice coffeeshop that serves a wide variety of food. For breakfast, there are home-style buttermilk pancakes, Belgian waffles, eggs, and omelets (priced from $1.75 to $6). For lunch and dinner, you can choose from burgers, sandwiches, salads, and a health bar, which has natural-style foods; prices range from $2 to $4. Full dinners of steak, chicken, ham, or fish (served after 5 p.m.) cost $6 to $9. The children's menu consists of fried chicken or shrimp with soup or salad and fries ($3).

Highchairs and booster seats are available. There is parking, and they honor some major credit cards. The restaurant is open every day—from 6 a.m. to midnight Sunday through Wednesday, and 24 hours on Thursday, Friday, and Saturday.

While you're there, stroll over to **Teddy Bear Miniatures and Dolls,** next door (tel. 714/866-2811). This little store is a treasure chest of stuffed animals and miniatures. Open daily from 10 a.m. to 5 p.m.

3. ANTELOPE VALLEY

At the northern tip of Los Angeles County sits 3,400 square miles of wide-open high desert, dotted with Joshua trees and interesting geologic formations, known as Antelope Valley. A day trip here convinces you that California is an enormous state, and reminds you that Los Angeles was once a desert.

The Antelope Valley's claim to fame is its spectacular wildflowers. Each year hundreds of acres are covered with brilliant bursts of color, including California poppies.

If you want to explore the area, take I-5 north to Calif. 14 north. The heart of the valley is the city of **Lancaster.** Believe it or not, Lancaster, and its sister to the south, **Palmdale,** are among the fastest-growing communities in California. Lancaster is a city of almost 50,000, and has many accommodations if you choose to spend the night. For more information about the area, you might want to contact the **Lancaster Chamber of Commerce,** 44943 N. 10th St. West, Lancaster, CA 93534 (tel. 805/948-4518).

The **Antelope Valley California Poppy Reserve,** 15101 W. Lancaster Rd. (tel. 805/724-1180 or 805/942-0662), is open year round for limited day use. The best time to view the orange blaze of colorful poppies is during the spring. Don't let the kids pick the poppies, though, because it's against the law. Open March, April, and part of May from 9 a.m. to 4 p.m. (call for exact hours). Admission is $3 per vehicle. To get to the reserve, take Calif. 14 to Avenue I (in Lancaster). Exit and proceed 14 miles west.

A little-known adventure awaits the kids in Rosamond, just north of Lancaster. The **Exotic Feline Breeding Compound** (tel. 805/256-3793) shelters over 40 exotic cats, including tigers, snow leopards, African and Chinese leopards, bobcats, and cougars. Your children will be able to observe the animals close-up. You can get eye-to-eye with only a chain-link fence between you. All tours are guided by a trained staff member. The compound is open daily except Wednesday from 10 a.m. to 4 p.m. No admission charge. To get to the compound, take Calif. 14 to Rosamond Boulevard. Go west about 4½ miles.

In Lancaster itself, you might be interested in visiting the **Antelope Valley Indian Museum,** at 150th Street East and Avenue M (tel. 805/942-0662). As you approach the building, you won't believe this is a Native American museum. The chalet-style building has seven different roof heights and two gabled turrets, and looks like it belongs in the Alps, not the high desert. Remarkably, it is built into the natural boulders of Paiute Butte. If a walk through this interesting home isn't enough, the collection of Native American artifacts will leave you and the kids with a much better understanding of California Indian history. You can also explore the area on the short nature trail. Closed during the summer, it's open on only the second weekend of each month from October through June, from 11 a.m. to 4 p.m. There is a $3-per-vehicle admission fee.

For outdoor adventurers, there is **Saddleback Butte State Park,** 17 miles east of Lancaster at 170th Street and Avenue J (tel. 805/942-0662). This 2,300-acre reserve boasts the world's largest and oldest Joshua trees. The park offers good hiking and picnicking. During some weekends there are nature walks and campfire programs. Camping is available here on a first-come, first-served basis. Saddleback has 50 sites, with table and stove, pit toilets, and water available, and costs $6 per night.

Located southeast of Palmdale, in Pearblossom, **Devil's Punchbowl,** 28000

Devil's Punchbowl Rd. (tel. 805/944-2743 or 805/944-9151), offers a day's worth of hiking and picnicking amid rare geologic formations. In fact, it is said to be one of the most fantastic formations in southern California. The Punchbowl got its name because it is a smooth cup-like basin set among the boulders. Actually, the Punchbowl is a depression between two earthquake faults: the San Andreas and the San Jacinto. There is a one-mile nature trail that goes into the Punchbowl and through the boulders, open daily from sunrise to sunset. Call for information about weekend family guided walks (summer and spring). Pearblossom is located 15 miles south of Lancaster. Take I-5 to Calif. 14 to Calif. 18 east.

If you're interested in cowboys and television westerns, you might enjoy the **Roy Rogers Museum,** about an hour away at 15650 Seneca Rd. in Victorville (tel. 619/243-4547). We don't know if the adults who remember Roy Rogers and Dale Evans enjoy the museum more than the children do, but it is interesting. Kids like to see Trigger and Trigger, Jr. (They're stuffed, now.) There is a large antique and modern car collection, a wild-game room, and a gun collection.

The museum is open daily from 9 a.m. to 5 p.m. (except Thanksgiving and Christmas Days). Admission is $3 for adults, $2 for children 13 to 17, $1 for children 6 to 12; under 6, free. To get to the museum from the Lancaster area, take Calif. 18 (Pearblossom Hwy.) east to Victorville. Exit left at Kentwood Avenue, then go right at Civic Drive. That takes you to Seneca Road.

You can also come through Victorville from Big Bear Lake. Take Calif. 18 to Victorville. Then take I-15 south to Palmdale Road, turn right on Palmdale Road, then turn right on Kentwood Avenue, and finally turn right on Civic Drive.

CHAPTER XIII

ORANGE COUNTY

□ □ □

1. THEME PARKS—ANAHEIM AND BUENA PARK
2. NEWPORT BEACH AND ENVIRONS
3. LAGUNA BEACH AND SAN JUAN CAPISTRANO

The name Orange County conjures up images of family outings and vacation fun. For most of us, Orange County made it on the map in 1955 when Disneyland opened its gates. At that time orange groves graced the roadsides and the area's famous beach cities were almost unknown.

Today, with a population of over two million, Orange County boasts more than 35 million visitors a year, making it one of the country's premier vacation destinations—and people are not coming just to see Disneyland. They are also interested in Knott's Berry Farm, the Movieland Wax Museum, and the San Juan Capistrano Mission. They travel to see the Los Angeles Rams and the California Angels. They come to play on the beaches and stroll through the tidepools of the fabulous 42-mile coastline that is now being called the Cote d'Orange.

HOW TO GET THERE: Most people come from Los Angeles (via **Los Angeles International Airport),** but a growing number are flying directly into **John Wayne / Orange County Airport,** 19051 Airport Way North, Anaheim (tel. 714/834-2400). From both, there are five major companies that offer ground transportation to and from the airport.

Orange County is also serviced by **Greyhound** (tel. 714/635-5060, or toll free 800/327-8211), and **Amtrak** (tel. toll free 800/USA-RAIL for reservations, or 714/385-1448 for departure and arrival times) makes several stops in the area—the most important in Anaheim and San Juan Capistrano.

Although this is southern California, you can do passably well without a car since most of the hotels offer shuttle service to the major sightseeing attractions. Sightseeing tour buses also operate in the area. **Fun Bus,** 851 E. Cerritos Ave., Anaheim (tel. 714/635-1390), and **Gray Line,** 1441 S. West St., Anaheim (tel. 714/778-2770, or toll free 800/538-5050 outside California), are two very popular ones.

If you find you want a car for a day or two, all the major **rental-car companies** have locations in Orange County; consult the *Yellow Pages* for local numbers.

If you're driving to the area, see the individual sections in this chapter for specific directions.

For the most complete information about the area, you'll want to contact the **Anaheim Area Visitor and Convention Bureau,** 800 W. Katella Ave. (P.O. Box 4270), Anaheim, CA 92803 (tel. 714/999-8999). These folks know a lot about Orange County, and if there's anything they don't know, they'll point you in the right direction.

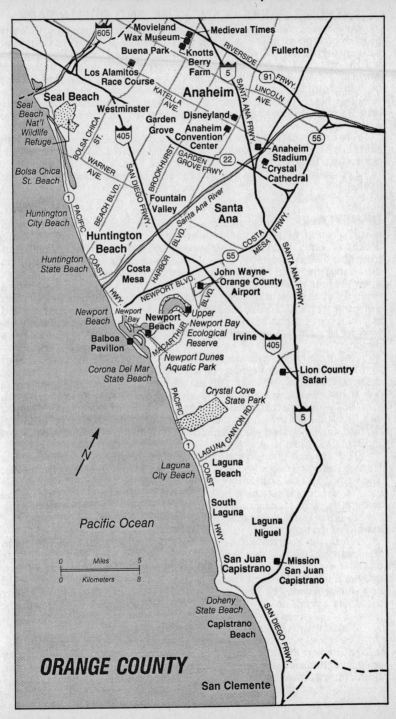

ORANGE COUNTY

1. THEME PARKS—ANAHEIM AND BUENA PARK

Anaheim is the largest city in Orange County, and contrary to many people's perception, it is *not* a suburb of Los Angeles. In fact, if you're talking with a native, be sure you remember that Anaheim is the home of Disneyland—not the other way around! While jokes are often made, no one can laugh at Anaheim's draw of over 900,000 convention delegates a year. And because of Disneyland and the enormous Anaheim Convention Center, it offers services and hotels that will please even the most discriminating family members. Buena Park is its neighbor, and home to several sightseeing attractions as well.

The easiest way to get to Anaheim by car is via I-5. If you're coming from either Los Angeles or San Diego, exit at Harbor Boulevard. To get to Buena Park, exit at Beach Boulevard south.

Let's start our Anaheim tour with the most famous amusement park in the world.

DISNEYLAND: The granddaddy of all the theme parks, Disneyland is still a world of magic and wonderment—even when compared to the dozens of other parks that have sprung up in recent years. Many of us remember Disneyland in its infancy, when orange groves and walnut trees surrounded the park, when you could see the Matterhorn from miles away, when the Jungle Cruise ride was state-of-the-art fun. Disneyland has matured (from 18 attractions to over 60), but it still maintains the Disney hallmarks that make it special. For us, the Disney magic is as much the friendliness and helpfulness of the people who work there as the rides. The streets and walkways are so clean, you never think twice about sitting on the curb to watch a parade.

And of course Disneyland is the place where fantasy is elevated to a classic art form, where the outside world seems less real than the heightened reality inside the park. One family we know tells the tale of visiting Santa Fe, New Mexico, only to have the youngsters exclaim that it looked just like Frontierland. Indeed, a sort of Disneyland reality takes over. For example, Star Tours not only takes you on a fantastic space voyage, but even while you're waiting in line to get a seat on the ride, equipment and videos simulate a space station—complete with aliens and exotic locations.

The "happiest place on earth" is located off I-5, also called the Santa Ana Freeway (take the Harbor Boulevard exit), about 27 miles south of Los Angeles. The story goes that Walt Disney happened upon the idea of a "magical little park" when he was watching his young daughters enjoy themselves at local amusement parks. He originally envisioned a little two-acre park next to the Disney Studios in Burbank, but quickly discovered that his ideas needed more space in which to flourish.

Never the one to do things on a small scale, Disney turned to Stanford University's Research Institute to determine the perfect location. He found it in 1953 and broke ground on July 21, 1954. He risked everything and invested $17 million into a park that everyone else thought would be a dismal failure. But genius and vision prevailed. Only seven weeks after the doors opened in 1955, the one-millionth visitor walked through the gates.

What enchants hundreds of millions of visitors?

Disneyland is where movies come to life, where animation is made real.

Situated on 80 acres (there's another 102 acres just for parking), Disney originated the theme-land concept. Today there are seven theme areas. They radiate out from a central hub at the end of Main Street, U.S.A.

Main Street, U.S.A.

Main Street is the entry to the park. It sets the mood for your excursion into this world of fantasy. In fact, Main Street is like walking through the lens of a camera into a cinematic world.

Modeled on small-town turn-of-the-century America, Main Street has a lot to offer. This is where you rent strollers, grab a storage locker (for that extra change of clothes, sweaters, etc.), and tell the children where to meet if they get separated from you. For parents of infants, the **Baby Center** is an area where you can change diapers (although many rest rooms throughout the park have these facilities), prepare formula, and warm bottles.

There are some intriguing one-of-a-kind shops here. Our favorites are **Main Street Magic Shop** and the **Silhouette Studio.**

Adventureland

The theme here is the exotic regions of Asia, Africa, and the South Pacific. You'll find the **Jungle Cruise** ride, **Swiss Family Treehouse,** and the **Enchanted Tiki Room.** Two tips for families with young children. We have noted that some very young ones are afraid of the mechanical wild animals on the Jungle Cruise, so warn them that they're not real, and prepare them for the gunshots fired by your safari leader. The Enchanted Tiki Room is a great place to calm the kids down if they're wound up. It gives them a chance to sit and rest in a cool spot. However, the show may be a bit long for antsy toddlers.

New Orleans Square

The home of pirates and ghosts, this quaint area is a wonderful place to rest and people-watch. Park favorites **Pirates of the Caribbean** and **Haunted Mansion** (with its 999 ghosts) are located here. **Just a note:** While neither ride is scary for children over 6, younger kids may have a little trouble; there are two lose-your-stomach water slides, and some loud gunshots. The Mansion is one ride we think might best be left for school-agers and older. With ghostly cries and darkened rooms, little ones may find it too frightening.

If you can time it right, a meal at **Blue Bayou Restaurant** is a treat. Where else could you eat by the cool moonlight to the sound of crickets in the middle of a warm southern California day?

Bear Country

The wilderness of the American Northwest is the theme here. Popular with the littlest ones is the **Country Bear Jamboree,** where they can sing along with the animated stuffed animals. Older children enjoy **Davy Crockett's Explorer Canoes.** A new attraction that is due to open in the summer of 1989 is **Splash Mountain,** a water-slide ride based on the movie *Song of the South,* accompanied by a lively rendition of "Zip-a-Dee-Doo-Dah." This thrill ride will have a flume that drops 52 feet, and more than 100 AudioAnimatronic characters, including Br'er Rabbit, Br'er Bear, and Br'er Fox.

Frontierland

Back to the days of the pioneers and the Old West where shoot-'em-ups happened at the town square and riverboats coursed the waters. **Big Thunder Mountain Railroad** is a huge hit with kids over 7. Little ones like **Big Thunder Ranch,** a two-acre replica of an 1880s homestead. There is a petting barnyard here (closes at dusk) and a walk-through model of an antique pioneer log cabin. **Tom Sawyer Island** is the original "run-around play area" for children with lots of energy. It has caves, a rope bridge, and balancing rocks. (And if you're there in the morning, don't miss the Mickey Mouse–shaped pancakes at River Belle Terrace, overlooking New Orleans Square.)

Fantasyland

Ah, Fantasyland. If there ever was a land of fairytales—but one where dreams do come true—it's this one. This is a place where little eyes grow huge as they spot the **Sleeping Beauty Castle** and cross the bridge to Pinnochio, Mr. Toad, and Peter Pan. Larger-than-life Cinderellas, Snow Whites, and Seven Dwarfs greet little ones with big hugs on the Castle drawbridge.

The storybook kingdom has more than 17 attractions. Gentle, non-frightening rides are the **King Arthur Carousel, Dumbo the Flying Elephant, Casey Jr. Circus Train, Motor Boat Cruise, Storybook Land Canal Boats,** and **Fantasyland Autopia. It's a Small World** may well be the favorite of the under-6 set—small boats cruise through a wonderland of singing and dancing dolls who serenade you with the well-known catchy tune with a world brotherhood theme.

Many of the other adventure rides (often in the spooky dark) may be best for children 4 and older, and children under 7 must be accompanied by an adult. **Alice in Wonderland, Peter Pan's Flight, Snow White's Scary Adventures,** and **Mr. Toad's Wild Ride** may frighten very young children. **Pinnochio's Daring Journey** isn't very daring, and children of almost any age love to point out all the characters they recognize.

The one problem with rides in Fantasyland is that they are low capacity, so lines move slowly. If you can't avoid the crowds, it's best to come up with a strategy where one adult wanders with the kids for a time while the other one waits in line.

But Fantasyland is not relegated exclusively to tiny tots. This is also the home of the **Matterhorn Bobsleds,** a thrilling ride through the snow-capped park landmark, the Matterhorn. While older kids and teens love this, don't subject your little tykes to it. Although it is open-air and not darkened, the bobsleds move very quickly, encountering the Abominable Snowman along the way.

And the ultimate teen party has to be **Videopolis** (open from 8 p.m. till closing on Saturday and holidays, and in summer). This futuristic dance area with continuous music has 90 television monitors going at once, two 12- by 16-foot projection screens, and a roving camera. Simultaneously, you might have 30 monitors with a music video, 30 with a Charlie Chaplin silent film, and 30 with dancers from the dance floor.

Tomorrowland

The dynamic, vibrant world of tomorrow is what you'll find here. **Space Mountain, Rocket Jets, Submarine Voyage, Captain EO** (the 3-D movie featuring Michael Jackson), and **Star Tours** are located here. These are among the most popular attractions in the park. *Note:* Although *Captain EO* is one of our all-time favorite attractions, the sound is so loud that it terrified our toddler. Instead, we take the toddlers to **America Sings** and **Skyway to Fantasyland. A** trip on the **Disneyland Monorail** is always a thrill.

You may as well accept it. There will be a very long line for Star Tours (sometimes over 1½ hours). Surprising as it may seem, the long wait is worth it. Here you see what happened when the genius of George Lucas met Disney craftsmen. The result was state-of-the-art ride technology. You'll come away feeling as if you've just been on a journey in space.

Tips on How to "Do" the Park

SOME FACTS. Disneyland's off-season is mid-September through mid-June, except for holiday periods such as Thanksgiving, Christmas, and spring break. Off-season is the best time to come. But, obviously, most people come during the peak times. No matter what season you plan to be there, Saturday is the busiest day. Surprise, surprise—during the summer, Friday and Sunday are less crowded (although not by much). Weekdays are the lightest during the rest of the year.

Peak hours are noon to 5 p.m. A lot of people leave after sunset, and in the summer another large group leaves after the first Electrical Parade and fireworks (about 9 p.m.). If you have older kids who can stay up late, you can do a lot of rides when everyone else is watching the first parade, and catch the second parade at 11 p.m.

For the most popular attractions, such as Star Tours, *Captain EO,* Space Mountain, the Matterhorn, Splash Mountain, Thunder Mountain, Haunted Mansion, and Pirates of the Caribbean, try to do them as early as possible. This goes for many of the low-capacity rides in Fantasyland as well. If you're lucky enough to have more than one day at Disneyland, you might consider doing what many veteran Disneyland visitors do. Get to the park early. When it gets extremely crowded, get your hand stamped and leave the park until late afternoon. You can return in time for dinner—and thinner crowds.

If you're coming in the summer, you can purchase your tickets in advance and arrive at 8 a.m. (when the park opens) to get a headstart on the crowds. If you can't do that, park officials suggest that you get there at 7:30 a.m. because the ticket lines can be long.

As soon as you get your *Souvenir Guide,* take a little time to plan your day so you don't waste time backtracking. And if you've never been to the park before, you can write for the guide ahead of time so you can find out which attractions you want to see most. Address your request to Disneyland Guest Relations, P.O. Box 3232, Anaheim, CA 92803. Or you may want to pick up a copy of *The Unofficial Guide to Disneyland* (1989 edition, published by Prentice Hall Press) at your local bookstore.

LOST CHILDREN. Young strays can be retrieved from the "Lost Children Station," located next to Central First Aid, near Main Street. Or you can go to City Hall, where the staff will contact the "Lost Children Station" for you.

BABY NEEDS. Baby food is available in the Market House on Main Street, which also stocks newborn-size diapers. Baby food is available at the Gerber changing room as well. Diapers are also available at the Emporium on Main Street at the counter where they sell dolls, in Tomorrowland at Star Traders (at the camera counter), and at the Hat Shop in New Orleans Square.

HOURS. The park is open daily, all year. From mid-June through August, it's open from 8 a.m. to 1 a.m. (there are a few nights that it closes earlier). In early June and from late August through Labor Day, the hours vary. From September through May, the park is open weekdays from 10 a.m. to 6 p.m., on Saturday from 9 a.m. to midnight, and on Sunday from 9 a.m. to 9 p.m. There are special hours during holidays. It's best to check hours beforehand (tel. 714/999-4565, or 213/626-8605, ext. 4565).

ADMISSION. Adults pay $23.50 for a one-day pass, $42.25 for a two-day pass, and $56.50 for a three-day pass. Children 3 to 11 are charged $18.50 for a one-day pass, $32.25 for a two-day pass, and $44.50 for a three-day pass. Children under 3 are free.

KNOTT'S BERRY FARM: Don't expect glamour and glitter when you visit Knott's Berry Farm, 8039 Beach Blvd. in Buena Park (tel. 714/220-5200 or 714/827-1776), two miles south of the Santa Ana Freeway on Calif. 39. Knott's is still a pretty down-to-earth theme park, and it can be visited in one day. Knott's has its own charm, mostly because of its small size and the rustic Old West theme that prevails over even the most modern sections.

Knott's began as a real farm, and owner Walter Knott cultivated the first boysenberry here. Mrs. Knott (Cordelia) began selling her boysenberry pies and chicken dinners to make money during the Depression. Her famous dinners and pies are still a roaring success at the **Chicken Dinner Restaurant** in the Marketplace.

But what will the kids find most interesting?

If you have young children, you'll probably want to start with **Camp Snoopy,** where they'll meet up with Lucy, Snoopy, and Charlie Brown. There are over six acres of rides in Camp Snoopy, tailor-made for youngsters. In fact, some of the "toddler-appropriate" rides are extremely short and very gentle. The staff takes longer than necessary to get kids ready for a ride (even with short lines), so be prepared. Beary Tales Playhouse was undoubtedly our 4-year-old's favorite Camp Snoopy activity. She reported that going through the bears' tree house was scary and fun at the same time. In front of some of the bear scenes along the way are narrow semi-enclosed "trails" for the toddlers to crawl through. They are dark and can be claustrophobic. While we were there, several youngsters needed to be pulled out by their parents midway along the trail.

Fiesta Village, next along the road, is where you'll find Montezooma's Revenge. Sure to cause inexplicable excitement in preteens and teens, this roller coaster goes not only in a loop, but backward too! Brave souls can move on to the **Roaring '20s Amusement Land,** home of the Sky Tower, a parachute jump that deposits you 20 stories down at free-fall speed. Not for the faint of heart. The Corkscrew is yet another roller coaster nearby. We prefer to *watch* it take its two 360° loops. It's the world's first upside-down roller coaster.

Calmer experiences can be found in **Ghost Town,** an authentic 1880s Old West Gold Rush town and the original section of the amusement park. Kids love the ride on the authentic stagecoach. Be aware that there are always long lines here. The steam engine fascinates children—and adults—of all ages. Even if they don't take the ride, kids love to stand close to this monstrous iron horse and just see how it's put together.

Kingdom of the Dinosaurs is the newest star in Knott's world. We can honestly say that the "monsters" are extremely realistic and were quite frightening to our 4-year-old (and her mother). Older kids, however, love it. In this age of dinosaur-mania, it's a perfect thrill ride for ages 7 and up. As you exit this ride, you'll come to a huge arcade of games with something for every age group.

Newest to the park is the **Wild Water Wilderness Area,** which features an exhilarating ride down the longest man-made white-water rapids.

Altogether, there are over 165 rides at Knott's, so there will be something to appeal to every age in your group.

BABY NEEDS. Near the exit of Beary Tales in Camp Snoopy, there's a baby station with changing tables and a microwave for heating bottles. There's another one in the Marketplace at the First Aid Station. Stroller rentals are available here.

HOURS. In summer, Knott's is open Sunday through Thursday from 10 a.m. to 11 p.m., on Friday to midnight, and on Saturday to 1 a.m.; in winter, Monday through Friday from 10 a.m. to 6 p.m., on Saturday to 10 p.m., and on Sunday to 7 p.m. The park and Marketplace are open all holidays except Christmas. If you plan to go on another holiday, call first for hours.

ADMISSION. Adults 12 and older pay $19; children (3 to 11), handicapped, and expectant mothers pay $15; seniors 60 and over, $14; children 2 and under are free. Holidays often mean special rates, so call first. Off-season, there's a "Kids

Are Free" promotion, during which time one child is admitted free per paid adult; call for details.

TRANSPORTATION. **The Fun Bus** and **Pacific Coast Sightseeing** offer daily scheduled transportation from most area hotels to Knott's Berry Farm. Contact the front desk at your hotel for pickup and drop-off times and fares.

OTHER THINGS TO SEE AND DO IN THE AREA: Although the kids know Disneyland and Knott's Berry Farm the best, there are other places to visit in Anaheim and Buena Park.

Movieland Wax Museum

Probably one of the best wax museums in the country, Movieland Wax Museum, at 7711 Beach Blvd., just one block north of Knott's Berry Farm (tel. 714/522-1155), is a place that movie buffs shouldn't miss. We wonder just how many of the movie stars children recognize (there are more than 240), but even 6-year-olds appreciate the craft that goes into creating these life-size replicas of celebrities in their most famous roles. The exhibits are staged with realistic props and authentic costumes that re-create famous movie and television scenes.

While your children may not have seen *Dr. Zhivago* or *Gone with the Wind,* they'll surely appreciate the bridge of "Star Trek" Starship *Enterprise* manned by Captain Kirk, Mr. Spock, and the rest of the crew. You can be sure they'll marvel as you join Superman in the walk-through Fortress of Solitude from a scene from the movie. Superman stands in the center of ice crystals while a cool breeze blows to simulate the icy atmosphere. It's a cool, dimly lit alcove where Superman music finishes the mood.

And of course there's Michael Jackson (complete with background vocal) Mr. T, and Sylvester Stallone as *Rocky.* Even though our kids had never seen footage of *The Wizard of Oz* and the Our Gang comedies, they were fascinated by the sets and realism of the wax figures. Kids stand in utter amazement in front of Our Gang's Alfalfa, whose tooth is being pulled. "Doesn't he look real?" they ask each other.

Much to our delight, the Chamber of Horrors is set off by itself and can easily be avoided. In addition to lots of movie-star memorabilia, you can spend time watching old-fashioned moving-picture machines (mutoscopes and biographs). These are a real treat and also give our video-generation kids a chance to see some of the development of the medium.

Allow about one to two hours for the self-guided tour. Open daily from 9 a.m. to 11:30 p.m. in summer, and 10 a.m. to 10:30 p.m. in winter. The box office closes one hour before. It is completely stroller-accessible. Admission is $10 for adults, $8 for seniors, $6 for children 4 to 11, and free for children under 4.

Medieval Times

As kids, many of us daydreamed about castles and kings, knights and chivalry. Perhaps your children do too. Medieval Times, 7662 Beach Blvd., right near the wax museum (tel. 714/521-4740, or toll free 800/826-5358, 800/438-9911 in California), takes you back to 11th-century Europe. You are the guests —the nobility—at the castle of Count of Perelada and his countess, where you partake in a four-course feast and watch the tournament of knights.

Each guest, young and old alike, is given a colored paper crown as he enters the castle. Your colors are the colors of the knight you are to cheer on to victory during the games. Guests enter the Hall of Arms, where there are authentic medieval artifacts and lots of souvenir vendors. (Hold on to your wallets, though, because souvenir vendors and picture-taking minstrels hail you on a regular basis.) One of them will even research your family's coat-of-arms and motto (for an extra fee) and present you with a sketch of it.

The kids really get into the spirit of it, skipping happily through the grand halls wearing their crowns and waving their colored banners in anticipation of the show.

The real production is inside the 1,000-seat main arena, where you and the kids sit at long tables surrounding the open central arena. Serfs and wenches in medieval attire serve you soup, chicken, ribs, and potatoes—all of which you must eat with your fingers as they did in the 11th century (or you'll be thrown in the dungeon). As you eat, the show goes on.

Trumpeters herald the entrance of the knights of the realm, and the show begins. During the two-hour performance, the knights parade on horseback, show how their Arabian stallions were trained, joust, and compete in games on horseback. There is even swordplay.

While you could take children 4 and older here, it requires a considerable attention span to really enjoy it. We think kids between the ages of 6 and 14 most appreciate it.

Shows are given Monday through Thursday at 7:30 p.m., on Friday and Saturday at 6 and 9 p.m., and on Sunday at 1, 4:45, and 7:30 p.m. Admission prices for evening performances are $27 for adults ($29 on Saturday), $19 for children 12 and under (same on Saturday). At the Sunday matinee, adults pay $25; children 12 and under, $17. Major credit cards are accepted. Reservations are required (make them as far in advance as possible, since Medieval Times is a very popular year-round attraction). Parking lot available.

Hobby City

A planned 15-minute visit to **Hobby City,** 1238 S. Beach Blvd., Anaheim (tel. 714/527-2323), turned into a two-hour stay. The kids liked this low-key center with its teeny park in the middle because there was nothing glitzy or showy about it.

Moms and grandmas will likely love the **Doll and Toy Museum** as much as the kids. Behind the doll and toy shop, which is housed in a half-scale model of the White House, is a doll museum filled to the rafters with Barbie and Ken dolls. (Admit it—don't you remember Barbie with a bouffant hairdo?) Barbie's sister, Skipper, is also there, along with ancient and antique dolls, and dolls made out of almost any material you can think of. Over 50 years of collecting went into this display of more than 3,000 dolls and toys, many exhibited at a child's-eye level. It will take you no more than a half hour to go through it.

The store itself sells and repairs antique and modern dolls. The doll accessories and clothes are truly unbelievable. Admission to the museum is $1 for adults; 50¢ for children under 12.

Also at Hobby City is the **Hobby City Choo Choo,** which will appeal to the littlest ones in your group. It's not an exciting ride, but the kids love this tiny, shabby, open-air train, maybe because it's so close to their size, and because they see real things, rather than the make-believe of the amusement parks. There are a couple of picnic tables and a snackbar adjacent to the tracks.

The **Cabbage Patch Adoption Center** is staffed with salespeople dressed like doctors and nurses. There's a small room with an incubator and a doctor's office for preemie Cabbage Patch dolls. Naturally, there are lots of dolls and accessories for sale. Right across the street is the **Bear Tree,** stocked with stuffed animals from around the world, all housed in a replicated tree.

If you're interested in various hobbies, you'll have your pick of shops from stamps and coins, rocks, gems, arts and crafts, and yarn goods to miniatures, aquarium goods, driftwood, and candles. There is also a small restaurant next door to the Doll Museum.

Hobby City is open every day from 10 a.m. to 6 p.m. Parking is plentiful.

Crystal Cathedral

Have you ever seen a building made completely of glass? The unique Crystal Cathedral, 12141 Lewis St. in Garden Grove (tel. 714/971-4000), home of television's Rev. Robert Schuller, is made of 10,000 panes of glass! Free 45-minute walking tours of the grounds, arboretum, and cathedral are conducted daily. The cathedral is open Monday through Saturday from 9 a.m. to 3:30 p.m. and on Sunday from 1:30 to 3:30 p.m. Strollers may be taken on the tours.

Other Activities

The sports fans in your group might enjoy taking in a ballgame while you're vacationing here. The **California Angels** play baseball from April through October at Anaheim Stadium, 2000 S. State College Blvd., Anaheim (tel. 714/634-2000). The **Los Angeles Rams** play football at the stadium from August through December (tel. 714/937-6767).

Would you like to get behind the scenes? Kids who love baseball and football enjoy the **Anaheim Stadium Tour** (tel. 714/999-8990 or 714/937-6761). You'll see the 70,000-seat stadium as you've never seen it before, including the locker rooms and the press boxes. Tours are scheduled daily in summer from 10 a.m. to 3 p.m. (except when there is a day game) and in winter from 11 a.m. to 2 p.m. Adults pay $3; children 6 to 16, $2; under 5, free. Reservations are required.

How about a little activity? **Golf-'N-Stuff Miniature Golf Course** (tel. 714/778-4100) is an 18-hole course and video arcade located across from Disneyland. It opens daily at 10 a.m. and closes at 10 p.m. Sunday through Thursday and at midnight on Friday and Saturday. Admission is $4.25 for adults, $3.25 for children 6 to 12 accompanied by a paying adult, free for children under 6.

Fountain Valley Golf and Recreation Center, 16800 Magnolia St. (tel. 714/842-1011), has bumper-boats, go-karts, and batting cages, as well as two 18-hole miniature golf courses and a game arcade. It opens daily at 9 a.m. Closing times vary, so call when you're planning to go. To play miniature golf, adults pay $4; children 12 and under are charged $3.

Many older kids (and their parents) love **Photon,** 9380 Warner Ave. (tel. 714/968-2749), an electronic amusement battle game. Participants suit up in high-tech electronic battle gear and choose one of two sides. Their objective is to penetrate enemy territory. You score 10 points for each opponent you zap, and lose 10 points each time you're zapped. Games are 6½ minutes long. You must be 4½ feet tall to play. (The majority of those who play are 16 and older, but they do get children as young as 9.)

In summer Photon is open Monday through Thursday from 11 a.m. to midnight, on Friday and Saturday till 1 a.m., and on Sunday till 10 p.m. The rest of the year it's open Monday through Thursday from noon to 11 p.m., on Friday till 1 a.m., on Saturday from 11 a.m. to 1 a.m., and on Sunday from 11 a.m. to 10 p.m. The cost is $12 for first-time players, and $3.50 for each additional game, for adults as well as children. The admission fee includes two 6½-minute sessions plus a token for the upstairs game gallery. To get to Photon, take I-405 to the Warner Avenue exit.

Even in the southern California sun, you can ice skate at **Ice Capades Chalet,** 2701 Harbor Blvd. (tel. 714/979-8880). Children as young as 2 can rent skates here. Afternoon sessions are Monday through Friday from 2 to 5 p.m. and on Saturday and Sunday from 1 to 4 p.m. Evening sessions are on Tuesday, Wednesday, and Thursday from 7:30 to 9:30 p.m., and on Friday and Saturday nights from 8 to 10:30 p.m. Admission costs $5 for adults and children, except for Monday through Friday afternoons when children under 15 pay $4.50. Skate rental is $2.

Evening Entertainment

At night, don't miss **Sgt. Preston's Yukon Saloon** at the Disneyland Hotel (tel. 714/778-6600 or 213/636-3251). This musical review involves kids in the jokes and handclapping. It's a "bawdy saloon" show where the audience is encouraged to get into the act. Much of the music is great for the kids—"Ain't She Sweet" and other oldtime saloon songs fill the hall. Open Tuesday through Sunday. Call for nighttime show times. Finger food is served on Thursday, Friday, and Saturday, and there's no cover charge.

If you're looking for top musical performers, try the **Pacific Amphitheater** in Costa Mesa (tel. 714/634-1300), or the **Irvine Meadows Amphitheater** in Irvine (tel. 714/855-4515). Both have lawn and reserved seating.

The **Orange County Performing Arts Center,** 600 Town Center Dr., in Costa Mesa (tel. 714/556-2121), is a 3,000-seat theater that presents nationally and internationally acclaimed productions. There are children's performances as well. Kids (and their parents) are invited to take tours of the center. They are conducted on Monday, Wednesday, and Friday at 10, 10:30, 11, and 11:30 a.m. Call for further information (tel. 714/556-2787, ext. 833).

WHERE TO STAY:

The Anaheim area abounds with accommodations in all price ranges. You can stay at expensive hotels with complete services or you can find inexpensive motels that are quite adequate. Here are some of the ones we like best.

The Upper Bracket

Let's start with the hotel whose very name produces a smile on the lips and crinkles around the eyes.

Does the **Disneyland Hotel** really need any introduction, though? It's one hotel that you should save your nickels and dimes for so you can experience it once. Known as the official hotel of the Magic Kingdom, the magical aura of Disneyland permeates this family recreation complex. The only stop on the Monorail ride, this hotel is actually located at 1150 W. Cerritos Ave., Anaheim, CA 92802 (tel. 714/778-6600, 213/636-3251 in Los Angeles, or toll free 800/854-6165). With three swimming pools, a small marina, 16 restaurants, free family entertainment, 35 international boutiques, and a full children's program, this 60-acre resort has enough going on that we sometimes find ourselves neglecting other activities in Anaheim and Buena Park.

The complex, which includes three towers, villas, and a convention area, has 1,174 guest rooms and is built around a lovely mini-marina. The marina is called Seaports of the Pacific and it's a child's delight. Here's where you'll find a miniature replica of the *Queen Mary* with tiny remote-control tugboats that scurry around her. There are also two-seater pedalboats.

Nearby a state-of-the art video game center houses 64 games; an adult favorite (much to the chagrin of the children waiting in line) is the off-road raceway with remote-control miniature cars. In addition, there are three swimming pools, ten tennis courts, a white sand beach (on which they hold treasure hunts and sandcastle contests), Ping-Pong, volleyball—and the list goes on and on.

There are also three free family shows. Probably the most unusual is the Dancing Waters Show, in which water, lights, and music create a dazzling effect. These shows are at 9 and 10 p.m. during the summer, and at 8 and 9 p.m. during the rest of the year. The 20-minute Dreyer's Puppet Theatre show is a takeoff of the Adventures of Sgt. Preston. Kids love the Disneyland Hotel mascot—Yukon Klem—who performs along with the eight puppets. During the summer and the Christmas and Easter vacations, the puppet shows take place Tuesday through Sunday at 5, 6, and 7 p.m. During the rest of the year, there are performances on

Friday and Saturday nights. Finally, there is the Polynesian Fantasy, a musical South Seas production that is held at the marina during the summer.

During the summer and holiday season, there are special activities for kids. The Yukon Klem Klub for children between the ages of 4 and 12 is designed to allow parents to have their evenings free while the kids have fun on their own. The program includes supervised dinner, activities, and crafts from 6 to 10 p.m. (parents can actually go out for dinner or back to Disneyland knowing that their children are safe and having fun).

The kids are taken to dinner either at Café Villa Verdi or at the Monorail Café. Then, depending on the weather, they'll play games inside or outside, perform skits, or watch special children's shows. (The Yukon Klem Klub has been so popular that it has been expanded to include conventions—if there is enough demand.) Kids can join Yukon Klem during the summer Wednesday through Saturday; during holidays, the program is available on Friday and Saturday nights. Rates are $16 for the first child, $10 for other family members (this includes dinner and four hours of activities).

And would it be the Disneyland Hotel if you couldn't meet some of the Disney characters? The Character Breakfast (in Café Villa Verde) gives little ones the chance to meet the likes of Mickey Mouse, Minnie Mouse, and Pooh Bear. During the summer and special holidays, the breakfast is offered Monday through Saturday from 7 to 10 a.m. and on Sunday from 7 to 9:30 a.m. At other times, Character Breakfasts are held on Saturday and Sunday. Adults pay $9 and children under 12 pay $5 for the buffet. Reservations are not required.

With 16 restaurants and lounges on the premises, you're sure to find plenty to satisfy your appetite. All restaurants have Mickey highchairs and booster seats. All the lounges except two are geared to children, featuring Shirley Temple and Roy Rogers drinks.

Sgt. Preston's Yukon Saloon and Dancehall is a stage show suitable for the kids (see the "Evening Entertainment" section for details). There are two shows nightly Tuesday through Sunday; call for exact times. Finger food is served on Thursday, Friday, and Saturday, and there is no cover charge. Call for reservations (tel. 714/778-6600 or 213/636-3251).

Other, more ordinary (but still important) hotel amenities include room service (6 a.m. to 2 a.m.) with selections good for kids, laundry and dry cleaning, car rentals, photo processing, video camera rental, and babysitting referrals.

Some rooms have balconies (most have a view of Disneyland, the gardens, or the hotel marina). All rooms have color TV with the Disney channel, plus bath amenities, hairdryers, and a stocked honor bar (which cannot be used as a refrigerator).

Standard rooms are good-sized. Most come with two double beds, though some king-size and queen-size beds are available. Some rooms in the Oriental Court sleep six. Parlor rooms and junior suites vary in size. The suites have refrigerators and wet bars.

Room rates from mid-June through August run $99 to $176 single and $99 to $197 double. From September through January rates are $99 to $158 single and $99 to $179 double. Oriental Court rooms run $168. Suites start at $250. Cribs are free (only one per room), but rollaways cost $14. Refrigerators are $15 the first day and $10 per day thereafter.

The **Anaheim Hilton Hotel and Towers**, 777 Convention Way, Anaheim, CA 92802 (tel. 714/750-4321), is in a perfect location—across the street from the Convention Center, two minutes from Disneyland (complimentary shuttle service), and only 15 minutes from Knott's Berry Farm. This is a huge hotel with 1,600 rooms. The three-story atrium lobby seems tailor-made for children who may need to burn off energy. No one seemed to mind as two new pals chased each other around the reflection pool in the middle of the lobby.

There's a lovely recreation area on the fifth floor with a huge fenced-in pool and four Jacuzzis, open year round. There is food service and showers nearby. Rooftop gardens and sundecks give you many options for a before-dinner walk. A game center houses video games and pool tables.

Most interesting for families is the Hilton's Kids Klub, a program in effect from June through Labor Day. When you check in, your little one gets to go to his own registration desk. He'll get a membership button to this exclusive club, which entitles him to free Disney movies every day in the Kids Klub Disney Theatre, complete with popcorn and punch. He can also check in at the Kids Klub room to enjoy arts and crafts or sports programs and to meet other kids. There are also tours of the hotel, balloon races, raffles, and other special things just for kids. Children must be between 5 and 15.

The hotel features three restaurants, a sushi bar, a nightclub, and two bars. The Café Oasis is especially pleasant for families and is open 24 hours. Breakfasts range in price from $2.75 to $8.75, lunches are $5 to $8.50, and dinners cost $7.75 to $12.50. Hastings serves continental cuisine for lunch (prices start at $7.25) and dinner (with prices from $15.50). Pavia has northern Italian food, with lunches starting at $10 and dinners starting at $15.50. Room service is available until 2 a.m. At breakfast, certain items can be ordered as a child's portion and you'll be charged half price. For lunch and dinner there's a special children's menu. Room service is extremely fast.

Accommodations are comfortable and roomy. Rooms with two double beds have space for a crib or rollaway. Bathrooms are small, with tub/shower combinations. Rooms have remote-control TV and complimentary cable. On the lanai level, rooms open out to the garden; but watch this with the toddlers—there are no screens. Rooms aren't soundproof, so be sure to request that you're not assigned a room over one of the ballrooms. Because the hotel is so big, it can be a long way from your room to the elevators; if your children are at the carrying age, you might want to request a room closer to the elevators.

Singles run $98 to $118; doubles, $114 to $144. Suites range from $250 to $950. Children, no matter what age, sleep free in the same room with their parents. Rollaways and cribs will be provided at no charge. Extra adults pay $16 each per night. Check out the "Disneyland Family Fun" package if you're staying at least two nights. It includes breakfasts, tickets to Disneyland, and, of course, accommodations (two adults and two children for $297).

Quite plush, the **Anaheim Marriott,** 700 W. Convention Way, Anaheim, CA 92802 (tel. 714/750-8000, or toll free 800/228-9290), is located only two blocks from Disneyland. With 1,042 rooms, this large hotel gets many convention guests (it is adjacent to the Convention Center), but is so busy that children's noises and activities get absorbed into the general hubbub.

The highlights of the hotel for families, though, are its complete game room (with more than 20 video and pinball machines) and the two lovely heated swimming pools. The pools have large shallow areas, allowing lots of swimming space for even the tiniest child, although there is room for lap swimming as well. One of the beautifully landscaped pools is partially covered with a skylight-type ceiling that creates an indoor effect while remaining very open and airy—none of that steamy, musty air so often associated with indoor pools. There are also two spas, a fitness center that can be used by children over 14, a giftshop, dry cleaning, and a laundry.

Other amenities include a concierge desk, travel agency, and free shuttle service to and from Disneyland via the Marriott's cute little green-and-white trolley. Room service is available from 6 a.m. to 1 a.m. If you need a refrigerator, ask at the time of booking; it costs $5 extra per night.

Several restaurants offer a wide variety of dining. La Plaza is an early-California–style restaurant that serves breakfast, lunch, and dinner. It has a "Just for Kids" menu that includes standards as well as unusual fare such as beef tostada and prime rib. Prices range from $2 to $3.75. Adult dishes run about

$5.50 for sandwiches, $7 to $16.50 for dinner entrees. The Veranda, another all-day café, overlooks one of the pools. JW's, an elegant restaurant serving continental cuisine, has been voted one of the three best restaurants in Orange County. All have highchairs and boosters.

The guest rooms are decorated in light, airy colors and are standard size. (Tell them you're bringing your family so they'll give you one of the larger rooms.) All rooms have two telephones, cable TV with free HBO, pay movies, and express video checkout. All have tub/shower combinations; most have balconies.

In addition to rooms with king-size and double beds, the hotel has 72 suites. Many of the parlor suites have a Murphy bed, so the room can be used as a living room during the day. Other suites are more traditional, with living rooms that contain a dining table, a love seat, and two chairs. These have wet bars and refrigerators as well.

Room rates vary greatly, but whatever the season, children under 18 stay free in their parents' room. There is no charge for cribs, but rollaways cost $15 per stay. There are so many special packages that you should ask as soon as you get the reservationist on the line. Generally, rooms range from $99 to $138, but some Saturday and Sunday specials include rooms for $85. There is a two-for-breakfast weekend special that costs $69 per night, including breakfast (for two). Suites range from $125 to $700. Another plus—if you get two rooms for your family, each will be charged at the single-occupancy room rate. Ask also about the special Disneyland and Knott's Berry Farm packages.

You'll know this hotel as soon as you see it from the freeway. The **Sheraton-Anaheim Hotel,** 1015 W. Ball Rd., Anaheim, CA 92802 (tel. 714/778-1700, or toll free 800/325-3535), is designed to resemble a medieval castle. Although the lobby is small, the outdoor areas are large, complete with grassy, flower-lined courtyards, a rose garden, a little pond with a bridge, and inviting sitting areas.

While parents are more impressed with the complete concierge service and room service (available from 6 a.m. to 11 p.m.), the kids fancy the video game room. And of course there's a large heated swimming pool. Tennis courts, shuttle service to and from Disneyland, and help with arranging a babysitter are other bonuses.

The hotel has a moderately priced coffeeshop, called the Continental Café, which has a children's menu with prices from $2 to $3.50. Gerber baby foods are available for $1. You can pick up a sandwich, salad, or burger here for about $6. Full meals are also served and start at $6.25. There is also a quick-serve deli. Classy Adrienne's restaurant serves continental cuisine. Entrees start at $11 (there are no children's portions here). Gavin's is a nightclub with a unique oyster bar. Highchairs and boosters are available everywhere. The Spaghetti Station is located across the street (see the "Where to Eat" section for details).

You can request a room that opens out onto the swimming pool, if you desire. Others open onto the grassy areas or indoor hallways. The 500 guest rooms are generously sized and tastefully decorated. In-room amenities include cable color TV, in-room pay movies, honor bar, and a complimentary toiletry basket. Refrigerators are available upon request. You can reserve connecting rooms and suites.

Rooms rent for $65 to $105 single and $80 to $120 double—higher-priced rooms have a view of courtyards. Suites start at $250. Children under 18 stay free in their parents' rooms. There is no charge for cribs, but rollaways cost $10. Ask about the Mickey Mouse package.

Moderately Priced

Located on four acres of grounds, **The Inn at the Park,** 1855 Harbor Blvd., Anaheim, CA 92802 (tel. 714/750-1811), is a large hotel with 500 rooms, 400 of which have two double or two queen-size beds; 44 are suites. This is an attractive hostelry, with a friendly attitude toward kids.

The nicely landscaped pool area has a large patio with lots of chaise longues and a pretty little gazebo for shade. The kids also enjoy the video game room. Other amenities include room service from 7 a.m. to 11 p.m., free shuttle to and from Disneyland, a giftshop with Disney memorabilia, and help with arrangements for babysitting.

For dinner, the Overland Stage Restaurant looks like it was lifted out of Disney's Frontierland, complete with antique prints of the Old West, hanging lanterns, rich velveteen tapestries, and a lovely grandfather clock. The dinner menu consists of steaks, chops, lobster, and prime rib. The inn's moderately priced coffeeshop serves breakfast, lunch, and dinner.

Each room has remote-control TV with free HBO, and in-room movies (for a fee), plus a game table with chairs. Every room has a balcony—with a view of either the gardens or Disneyland. During the summer, we request a room facing Disneyland and enjoy the summer fireworks that don't start until after the toddlers have gone to sleep.

There are a variety of suites to choose from (all with refrigerators and sofa beds), or you can connect three regular guest rooms (and have three baths).

Rooms rent for $74 to $104 single and $84 to $114 double. A mini-suite costs $110 to $125; one- or two-bedroom suites cost $180 to $290. Children under 18 stay free in their parents' room. There is no charge for cribs, but rollaways cost $10 per night.

The **Convention Center Quality Inn Hotel of Anaheim,** 616 Convention Way, Anaheim, CA 92802 (tel. 714/750-3131, or toll free 800/228-5151), is an excellent choice in the moderately priced range. Clean, tastefully decorated, and completely renovated within the last few years, the inn is located only a few blocks from Disneyland.

The heated pool is quite large, and has lots of chaises and chairs for sitting and lounging.

Amenities include room service from 6 a.m. to 10 p.m., shuttle service to Disneyland, and a video game / vending machine area for the kids. Babysitting can be arranged through the front desk.

There are two restaurants—the Tivoli Gardens Café, which serves breakfast, lunch, and dinner, and Captain Greenhorn's Gourmet restaurant. Both have highchairs and boosters, but no children's menus.

There are 284 rooms, all with balconies, some facing Disneyland. Those balconies are large enough to accommodate a few chairs, so you can enjoy Disneyland's summer fireworks from your hotel room if you can't enjoy them from the park. The rooms also have a color television and tub/shower combinations, and at the time you book, you can request a refrigerator, which they'll give you at no extra charge. Two-bedded rooms have just enough space to add a crib. There are family suites available with a king-size bed and a sofa bed. Connecting rooms are also available. Each floor has ice and soft-drink machines.

Rates range from $53 to $83 single and $63 to $93 double, depending on the season and the room. Suites begin at $150. Children 16 and under stay free in their parents' room; those over 16 and additional adults are charged $10 each per night. Cribs are free, but rollaways cost $10 per night.

Located close to Disneyland, **TraveLodge Plaza at the Park,** 1221 S. Harbor Blvd., Anaheim, CA 92805 (tel. 714/758-0900, or toll free 800/255-3050), is an attractive, sprawling hostelry that combines an early-California style with a tropical motif. The inviting lobby has tile floors, salmon-colored walls, and lots of palm trees.

The tropical ambience continues outside to the manicured grounds, which have a large lawn area with palm and banana trees. The pool is quite large and has two shallow ends. There's deck space to walk on, and a grassy area ideal for playing. Babysitting can be arranged through the front desk, and to the delight of the kids, there's a small game room open from 9 a.m. to 11 p.m. Other niceties include a giftshop, valet laundry, and complimentary shuttle service to and from Disneyland and Anaheim's airport and bus terminals. Room service is available from 6:30 a.m. to 10 p.m.

The restaurant on the premises is Poppy's Café, which serves a wide variety of foods from light snacks to full meals. Breakfast prices are $3.50 to $5, lunch costs $4 to $7, and dinner prices ranges from $6 to $14. Highchairs and booster seats are available here.

The smartly decorated rooms are done in shades of gray and blue with salmon-colored accents. Each of the 260 rooms has either king- or queen-size beds, color TV with Cablevision and pay channels, table and chairs, and double-paned windows to drown out freeway noise. Some rooms have a partition separating the couch (which opens to a bed) from the double bed next to it.

Rates in high season (June through mid-December) run $72 to $85 single and $82 to $95 double. In low season prices drop to $65 to $78 single and $75 to $88 double. Children under 18 stay free in their parents' room, and there is no charge for cribs. Children 18 and over and additional adults pay $10 each per night. Poolside rooms cost $3 additional.

Budget-Priced Hotels

In a town with dozens of hotels and motels, you'll find a wide range of budget-priced accommodations.

The best bet for your money is **Raffles Inn & Suites,** 2040 S. Harbor Blvd., Anaheim, CA 92802 (tel. 714/750-6100), a small, well-kept motor inn with prices you can't beat. The 122 rooms are very clean—plain, but nice. Some of them are dark, but all are good-sized.

All rooms have double sinks, tub/shower combinations, and free HBO. A complimentary continental breakfast (coffee, juice, and danish) is served in a charming little parlor room off the swimming pool area. This room is open during the summer and on winter evenings to serve as a sitting room with television and tables for games and other activities. There is free shuttle service to Disneyland, and the front desk will help you arrange babysitting.

There are a variety of rooms to choose from. Family suites can sleep six people. These have large living rooms with sofa sleepers and lots of room, enough even for two rollaways. These suites have master bedrooms with king-size beds, plus sinks and vanity areas. The kitchenettes are outfitted with the basics, and you can request a coffee maker and toaster when you make your reservation.

Mini-suites have small parlor rooms with sofa sleepers and refrigerators. The bedrooms have either king-size, queen-size, or double beds.

Rates for rooms with two queen-size beds range from $45 to $52 single and $45 to $58 double. Mini-suites cost $65 to $78, and family suites range from $78 to $150. Children under 18 sleep free in their parents' room if additional beds are not needed, but cribs cost $5 per night.

Another alternative is **Best Western Stovall's Inn,** 1110 W. Katella Ave., Anaheim, CA 92802 (tel. 714/778-1880). Located near Disneyland, Stovall's is a large, basic motor inn with 290 clean rooms, two swimming pools, two whirlpools, and a small wading pool. Other nice touches include a bathroom at the swimming pool and topiary gardens surrounding much of the property. (Yes, they even have sculpted Disney characters.)

Catering to the traveling family, there is same-day photo processing at the gift store, sightseeing tour and car-rental assistance, and coin-operated laundry machines for guest use. (Valet service is also available.) Another nice feature is the VCR-rental facility. There's free shuttle service to and from Disneyland. You can also arrange to have the shuttle take you to the Spaghetti Station restaurant (see the "Where to Eat" section for details). And the front desk will help you arrange for babysitting.

There's no restaurant on the premises, but Coco's Coffeeshop is next door. This is an inexpensive way to feed the family.

Rooms have double or queen-size beds, and range in price from $68 to $72 in high season and $44 to $48 in low season. Suites run $95 to $137. Children under 18 stay free in their parents' room, and the inn will provide a crib at no charge.

Another good choice for a budget motel is the **Comfort Inn,** 2200 S. Harbor Blvd., Anaheim, CA 92802 (tel. 714/750-5211, or toll free 800/228-5150). This very clean motel offers a few nice touches. There is coffee in the lobby for guests, and a coin-operated washer/dryer is available. The swimming pool has a shallow end that extends over half the area of the pool. Babysitting can be arranged through a service.

Rooms are nicely appointed with large dressing areas, and are attractively decorated with brown carpeting and geometric-patterned bedspreads. All rooms have color TV with cable movies, and table and chairs. King-size, queen-size, and double beds are available.

Rates run $36 to $50 single and $42 to $52 double. Adjoining rooms can be reserved. Children under 12 stay free in their parents' room. There is no charge for cribs, but rollaways cost $5.

The **Harbor Inn TraveLodge,** 2171 S. Harbor Blvd., Anaheim, CA 92802 (tel. 714/750-3100, or toll free 800/222-6081, 800/221-6385 in California), is a basic motel with 128 newly decorated rooms. The fenced-in pool area has a small heated swimming pool and spa, a soft-drink machine, and a bathroom. Free continental breakfast and in-room movies are included in the nightly price. Complimentary shuttle service is offered to Disneyland and the bus depot. The motel has coin-operated laundry facilities, and will rent you a refrigerator for $5 per day.

All rooms have TV, and table and chairs; some have couches. While the bathrooms are on the small side, they have luxurious bath towels. Rooms come with either queen-size or king-size beds. Two-room/two-bath family suites are also available.

Rates range from $36 to $59, depending on the season and the room. Family suites (four beds with two baths and two TVs) run $78 to $118. Children under 17 sleep free in their parents' room. There is no charge for cribs, but rollaways cost $5 per day.

WHERE TO EAT: Your kids may want to spend all their waking hours at the theme parks and fast-food parlors. While Knott's Berry Farm is known for its food and Disneyland has fine fare, the adults in our group sometimes yearn for another choice.

Let's start with **Mr. Stox,** 1105 E. Katella Ave. (tel. 714/634-2994), one well-respected restaurant in Orange County. Leave the mouse ears in the car and get out the Mary Janes for this lovely restaurant that offers very grown-up selections for children. The contemporary California cuisine served here is created with extra attention—they grow their own fresh herbs, for example. The wine list is recognized as one of the best in the country.

Yet the restaurant is so close to Disneyland that the staff handles children of all ages with ease. Of course, they'll make Shirley Temples and Roy Rogerses for young visitors. Booster seats are available.

Selections for children include prime rib, fresh halibut, and mesquite-broiled chicken breast for $9. Adults can choose from a lunch menu that changes daily and includes fresh seafood (swordfish, salmon, and halibut), a large variety of salads, and homemade pastas. Prices range from $6 to $12. At dinner, the emphasis is on fresh seafood and pasta, veal, and rack of lamb, with entrees from $10 to $18.

Open for lunch Monday through Friday from 11 a.m. to 3 p.m. and for dinner Sunday through Thursday from 5 to 10 p.m., on Friday and Saturday till 11 p.m. Most major credit cards accepted. Reservations are advised. Valet parking.

A more eclectic and casual restaurant is **Anthony's Pier 2 / Anthony's Rib Joint,** 1640 S. Harbor Blvd. (tel. 714/774-0322). Located across from Disneyland, this restaurant is plushly decorated with carpeting, brass rails, and ferns, and features a nice seafood and salad bar.

The restaurant has an interesting policy. Children under 12 eat free (except for Sunday brunch) if the adults order a full entree. There is a complete breakfast and lunch buffet ($4) and a small lunch menu. Dinner entrees range from $10 for barbecued chicken to $20 for double-cut prime rib (add $4 if you want the huge salad bar with your entree). Seafood entrees start at $11 and go up to market price for twin one-pound Maine lobsters.

The kid's menu has fried shrimp, barbecued chicken, pizza, and chopped steak with prices from $4 to $5 (but you pay only if the accompanying adult doesn't eat a full meal).

Booster seats and highchairs are available, and the staff will gladly warm bottles and make children's cocktails.

Open daily for brunch and then lunch from 7 a.m. to 2 p.m., and for dinner weekdays from 5 to 10 p.m., on Friday and Saturday till 11 p.m. Sunday brunch costs $5; children pay $2.50. Reservations are advised for dinner, but are not accepted for brunch (expect to wait about 15 to 20 minutes). Most major credit cards honored. Parking lot nearby.

Peppers Restaurant, 12361 Chapman Ave., at Harbor Boulevard, in Plaza Alicante, Garden Grove (tel. 714/740-1333), is a perfect example of an adult restaurant where you can comfortably include the kids. It's lively and fun, charming and sophisticated. Balloons, potted plants, and ceiling fans complement the soft-pink and burgundy décor. A large noisy bar is on the other side of the reception area, out of the way of the diners.

Tortilla chips are brought immediately, and the service is prompt and efficient, even at the busiest hours. The children's menu items include hamburgers, hot dogs, grilled cheese, cheese enchilada, burrito, or taco for $3 (includes a beverage and ice cream).

Mom and Dad get to choose from an array of dishes, including enchiladas, burritos, chimichangas, and such specials as filet mignon, camarones Mérida, fajitas, or Tucson tacos. Dinner prices range from $4.50 to $11. Lunch has many of the same selections, plus tostadas, huevos (eggs), and salads. Prices range from $3.75 to $9. Be sure to leave room for something indecently rich on the dessert menu—deep-fried ice cream, Kahlúa mousse, or white-coffee toffee are just a few suggestions. The "all you can eat" Sunday brunch costs $11 for adults, $6 for kids 10 and under.

The kids love the complimentary shuttle that picks them up from their hotel and takes them back after dinner. Our 4-year-old Janey felt she was riding in her own private coach. If all this isn't enough, Peppers also has a "kids eat free" special. Kids 10 and under who are accompanied by one paying adult order off the kids' menu for lunch or dinner and eat free. There are boosters but no highchairs here. Baby bottles and food will be warmed in the kitchen upon request.

Open for lunch Monday through Saturday from 11 a.m. to 4 p.m. Dinner is served Monday through Thursday from 4 to 10 p.m., on Friday and Saturday till 11 p.m. Sunday brunch hours are 9:30 a.m. to 2:30 p.m. Big parking lot. Major credit cards welcome. Reservations are accepted.

Like a scene from the Old West, the **Spaghetti Station,** 999 W. Ball Rd. (tel. 714/956-3250), greets you outside the door with a sign reading "Welcome Pardner" and a topiary of a stagecoach. Enter the eatery and you step into Fort Spaghetti Station, where several rustic wood-paneled rooms await you. Fort Spaghetti Station claims to have the world's greatest individual Old West gun collection (valued at $1.5 million), and indeed they must. While our kids oooh and aaah over the size of the rifles and Colt pistols, the adults in our crowd reminisce when they see the 1892 Winchester rifle that Steve McQueen used in *Wanted: Dead or Alive.* The collection is fascinating and extensive. Don't let your kids miss the Indian room with the feathered headdress of a Cheyenne chief.

All this and food too?

For lunch, you can choose from many different kinds of spaghetti with several different sauces (all served with salad, bread, and ice cream) for $4 to $6.50, sandwiches and salads for $3 to $8, even steak for $10.50 to $17. For dinner, choose from pastas and steaks (all served with salad, bread, and ice cream). Each of the kids receives a Fort Spaghetti Station fun and coloring book that will keep them busy for the duration of the meal. (There are even coupons to color, cut out, and redeem.) Children will enjoy the spaghetti with tomato or meat sauce for $4.

Highchairs and booster seats are provided. No reservations are accepted, but during the day there's hardly any wait at all. In the evening, be prepared for a 30- to 45-minute wait if you come between 6:30 and 8:30 p.m. on a Friday or Saturday. Best to come before 6, or after 8 p.m.

Summer hours (end of May to September 1) are Monday through Friday from 11 a.m. to 11 p.m., on Saturday from noon, and on Sunday from 2 p.m. Winter hours are Monday through Thursday from 11 a.m. to 10 p.m., on Friday till 11 p.m., on Saturday from noon to 11 p.m., and on Sunday from 2 to 10 p.m. Some major credit cards are accepted. There is a large parking lot.

If the kids are just dying for a good old-fashioned hamburger, **Flakey Jake's,** 101 Katella Ave. (tel. 714/535-1446), is the place to go. This is where you'll find huge hamburgers and grilled-chicken sandwiches for the adults (baked potatoes and taco salads too), and Jake's Junior menus for the kids. Jake's Junior meals (burgers, fish sandwich, and hot dogs) include fries and a beverage with free refills for $2.25. Best of all, the food is as fresh as you'll find anywhere.

If you're not familiar with Flakey Jake's, be forewarned that there is no table service. But the kids love the place, and they occupy themselves during the wait for food in the small video arcade. Highchairs and boosters are provided. No reservations are accepted.

2. NEWPORT BEACH AND ENVIRONS

Of late, the coast from Huntington Beach to San Clemente has been called the American Riviera. That swath of beautiful sandy beach is excellent for swimming, surfing, sunbathing, and boating. In Newport, there are ecological reserves, harbors, and coves waiting to be explored. Newport and its companion, Balboa Island, have been family-resort towns (albeit for the very rich) for many years. Even today, families flock to this sun-drenched area for weeks of relaxation and play.

One of the first things you'll want to do is to contact the **Newport Beach Conference and Visitor's Bureau,** 1470 Jamboree Rd., Newport Beach, CA 92660 (tel. 714/675-7040).

WHAT TO SEE AND DO: The main attractions of the area are the wonderful wide sandy beaches and the harbor with its yachts and sailboats. The other activities of greatest interest for families are concentrated in a small area along the shore.

Balboa Peninsula and Balboa Island

Balboa Peninsula creates a gentle bay where eight small islands sit, old-fashioned auto ferries run, and children play in the warm sand. Homes on the peninsula and on Balboa Island remind you of New England. Indeed, like Cape Cod, since the 1930s Newport Beach (and Balboa in particular) has been a summer-resort town where well-to-do families rent clapboard cottages for a month at a time.

Let's start with **Balboa Pier,** a 919-foot-long structure that is lined with fishermen of all ages. At the foot of the pier you'll find a nice public beach with play equipment, showers, and rest rooms. At the end of the pier is **Ruby's Diner** (see the "Where to Eat" section for details). To get to the pier after you're on Balboa Peninsula, go to Palm Street and turn right to the public parking area.

The boardwalk is a terrific place to skate or bicycle, and enchanting little Main Street offers places to stop and grab a quick snack. You can rent bikes and roller skates at **Ocean Front Wheel Works,** at 105 Main St., just before you get to the pier (tel. 714/723-6510). They rent adult bicycles, bikes with child carriers, children's bikes, and three-wheel bikes (which aren't allowed on the sidewalks). Rentals are $4 for the first hour, $2 for the second, and $1 for the third and additional hours. Adult and child roller skates rent for $3 for the first hour, $2 for the second hour, and $1 for the third hour. Beach items are also available. Chairs, umbrellas, and boogie boards rent for $5 a day. Open weekdays from 10 a.m. to 7 p.m., on weekends from 10 a.m. to 10 p.m. (times vary according to season).

On the harbor side of the peninsula (actually only a few blocks away) is the historic **Balboa Pavilion,** an ornate Victorian structure that today houses a restaurant and giftshop, and is the terminus for harbor excursions, whale-watching trips, and Catalina Island transportation. It is considered the hub of Newport Harbor. This registered historical landmark was built as a bathhouse and originally served as a terminal for the electric Red Car. The pavilion was also the place where many of the Big Band greats played—Benny Goodman and Count Basie among them.

At the pavilion, you can book a cruise on the double-decker **Pavilion Queen,** which has regularly scheduled tours of the harbor. During the summer, tours depart at 11 a.m., noon, and 1, 3, 4, and 5 p.m.; during winter, they leave at noon and 1, 2, and 3 p.m. The 45-minute cruises cost $5 for adults and 50¢ for children; 90-minute cruises are $7 for adults, $1 for children. Call 714/673-5245 for details.

Davey's Locker at Balboa Pavilion, 400 Main St. (tel. 714/673-1434), rents fishing gear, offers fishing excursions, and has all-day boat trips that go to Catalina Island. The fishing trips leave at midnight and return at 4 p.m., and cost $40 for adults, $35 for children (includes a bunk). Half-day boat trips go from 6 a.m. to noon or 12:30 to 5 p.m. These fish locally from Huntington Beach to south of Laguna. The rates are $18 for adults, $12 for kids (12 and under). From December through mid-March there are whale-watching cruises. You can rent fishing reels for $5 to $7, and buy a license here as well. Davey's Locker is open daily, from 5 a.m. to 7 p.m.

The **Fun Zone** is a small area along the waterfront near the Balboa Pavilion that is specifically geared to children. Kids of all ages can spend hours here riding the ferris wheel ($1.50 per ride) and the merry-go-round, with its regular-size and miniature horses perfect for very little children ($1 per ride), as well as playing in the three video arcades. Fast-food stands dot the little strip. You can rent pedalboats or pontoons, or take one of the harbor cruises from this area as well.

This is where you catch the **Balboa Island Ferry** (tel. 714/673-1070). (You can also drive onto the island via Jamboree Road, but parking is atrocious on the island, so we suggest that you park at the public lot near Balboa Pier and ferry across without your car.) This short, delightful ride transports only a few vehicles at a time across to Balboa Island, but it's a treat—one the kids will remember. Ferry service runs from 7 a.m. to midnight on weekdays, till 2 a.m. on weekends, and costs 75¢ for a car with one passenger (20¢ extra for each additional passenger), 30¢ for a bicycle, and 20¢ for pedestrians.

Balboa Island is a tiny, picturesque village with homes placed so close together that windowboxes and miniature gardens replace the more usual southern California front and side lawns. Its very size makes it perfect for walking. Marine Avenue is the place to go for gifts, restaurants, and ice-cream shops. You can comfortably see the island in 45 minutes, which will give you the flavor of it while allowing you time to get back to the peninsula and the better beaches.

Newport Beach and Pier

Known as McFadden's Pier, this is where you'll see the one-of-a-kind **Dory Fishing Fleet.** Each morning at about 6 a.m., the Dory Fishing Fleet sets out to sea. Some of the fishermen may go as far as Catalina Island. At about 9 a.m. they return, set up their weighing scales on the boats, and sell their catch on the beach. It's a taste of a dying lifestyle. The boardwalk area is vintage 1940s. The beach is just over five miles long, with volleyball nets, outdoor showers, and rest rooms. Pier fishing is a popular sport. (No state license is required to fish from the pier.)

You can rent a variety of items at **Baldy's Tackle,** 100 McFadden Pl., at the foot of the pier (tel. 714/673-4150). In addition to renting fishing equipment (as the name suggests), Baldy's also rents beach cruisers (with carriers) and children's bikes for $3 per hour, $15 per day (you leave your driver's license as a deposit). Open from 6 a.m. to 8 p.m. in summer and in winter, from 7:30 a.m. to 5:30 p.m. Sunday through Thursday and 6 a.m. to 6 p.m. on Friday and Saturday. Want to fish? Baldy's also rents rod, reel, hooks, and sinkers for $2 per hour or $7.50 for all day.

Upper Newport Bay Ecological Reserve

For some truly wonderful outdoor experiences, you'll enjoy this 700-acre state ecological reserve, home to all kinds of wildlife and birds. Get the kids out here on bicycles or on foot, and savor the quiet, natural setting. Take Backbay Drive to the reserve.

Newport Dunes Aquatic Park

After the morning clouds burn off, Newport Dunes Aquatic Park is a place where kids can build sandcastles to their hearts' content and swim in the calm water. You can rent paddleboats, sailboats, aqua cycles, and kayaks. This family beach and park is located on a 15-acre lagoon—actually at 1131 Back Bay, Newport Beach (tel. 714/644-0510). It's equipped with a playground (merry-go-round, slides, and swings) and with water slides. For your protection there are lifeguards and first-aid stations. The kids love the floating whales that mark the cordoned-off children's swim areas.

There is a grocery store, snackbar, and fire pits for barbecues. For day use, it costs $2 for adults, $1 for children.

You can also camp here. Fees vary for camping, depending on the spot and your length of stay, so call ahead for more information. There are sites for tents, RVs, trailers, and boats. They begin to take reservations for the summer on January 1.

Other Area Beaches and Tidepools

The protected coves of **Corona Del Mar Marine Life Refuge** (tel. 714/640-2156) are teeming with sea life. To get to the tidepools, park your car where Poppy and Ocean Boulevard meet and walk down the asphalt pathway. You can walk on the rocks when the tide is low, and help the kids spot sea urchins and other wonders. Remember to replace everything you pick up—exactly where you took it from. For tide tables, call 714/644-3047. Most bait-and-tackle stores can also tell you when low tide occurs. During the summer there are tours given by park rangers.

According to people in the know, the best beach in the area for families may be **Corona Del Mar State Beach,** better known as **Big Corona,** off Ocean Boulevard and Iris. The large beach is sheltered so that wave action is usually gentler than at other areas. There are barbecue pits, showers, a snackbar, and rest rooms. The beach is open daily from 6 a.m. to 10 p.m.

Adjacent to Huntington Pier, off the Pacific Coast Hwy. (Calif. 1) **Huntington City Beach** (six miles north of Newport) is where the annual International Surf Competition takes place in early September. There are lifeguards, volleyball nets, and concession stands.

Huntington State Beach is just south of there. With three miles of shoreline, lifeguards, snack stands, showers, and rest rooms, it is very popular.

Surfing

Huntington Beach may be the most popular surfing beach around. In fact, some say that Huntington Beach epitomizes the ever-famous California surf scene. However, this popular sport is allowed at most beaches—with certain restrictions during the summer. Call before you go. **Huntington State Beach** (tel. 714/536-3053), **Huntington City Beach** (tel. 714/536-5281), **Newport** (tel. 714/673-3371), **Corona Del Mar** (tel. 714/644-3047), and **Dana Point** (tel. 714/496-5794) are places to try.

Bike Paths

There is a wonderful bike path that extends from the north at Bolsa Chica State Beach south along the shoreline into Newport Beach. You'll see dozens of families piling out of their cars at any of the beach parking areas along the route.

In Newport Beach, you can take the **Backbay Drive** bike path that winds through the Ecological Reserve. This path climbs gradually up the hill, past the Backbay, offering bicyclists the chance to see all kinds of birds.

The Anaheim Area Visitors and Convention Bureau suggests the following bike tour through Newport Beach and Balboa. Start at the Balboa Pier and head south to the "wedge." This picturesque stop is very popular with body surfers, and the kids will love watching them ride in the waves. Double-back toward the Balboa Pavilion and take the Balboa Auto Ferry to Balboa Island. Take any of the streets on the island and you'll ride past close-set, quaint cottages. You might want to stop at Marine for a snack. Then head back via the ferry and ride north to McFadden's Pier (Newport Pier). If you get there before noon, you're likely to see the Dory Fleet selling their fish. The ride is level, with wonderful views throughout the entire trip. Call the Department of Parks and Recreation for further information (tel. 714/644-3151).

In addition to **Ocean Front Wheel Works** and **Baldy's Tackle** (see above), you can rent bikes at **Pedal Pusher Bikes,** 122 23rd St. (tel. 714/675-2570).

Shopping

Newport Beach and nearby Costa Mesa have some wonderful shopping malls. **Fashion Island,** at Newport Center (tel. 714/760-1250), is an exclusive shopping district with 200 shops and services, including Neiman-Marcus, J. W. Robinson's, and Bullock's Wilshire. Open Monday through Friday from 10 a.m. to 9 p.m., on Saturday from 10 a.m. to 6 p.m., and on Sunday from noon to 5 p.m. The Atrium Court features the Irvine Ranch Farmer's Market, a gourmet grocery experience, and other eateries as well.

Located in Costa Mesa, **South Coast Plaza** (tel. 714/241-1700) is one of the most interesting malls in southern California. With such shops as Nordstrom, Laura Ashley, and Ann Taylor, you know the plaza is upscale. In addition to being a beautiful mall with a stained-glass dome, there's a concierge service, valet parking, and a carousel for the kids. Shops you won't want to miss with the kids are F.A.O. Schwarz, Toys International, the Disney Store, and Gamesmanship. Open Monday through Friday from 10 a.m. to 9 p.m., on Saturday from 10 a.m. to 6 p.m., and on Sunday from 11 a.m. to 6 p.m.

A DAY TRIP OUT OF NEWPORT: You can spend all day at **Wild Rivers** water park, located at 8800 Irvine Center Dr. (tel. 714/768-WILD). With over 40 water rides and other attractions, Wild Rivers, a 20-acre water park, is a big hit with the kids. The park has an African theme and boasts southern California's largest man-made earth mountain, which offers 19 water rides. Wild Rivers Mountain offers white-water innertubing, super-speed rides down a slide the size of a football field, and a jet-speed ride through a dark tunnel.

Explorer's Island is designed for families. Some of the rides at Wild Rivers Mountain have been scaled down for children. Our little ones loved Pygmy Pond —less than a foot deep, with swings and slides. We loved the Safari River Expedition, an innertube float.

The newest attraction is Thunder Cove, which has two side-by-side wave-action pools in which you and the kids can bodyboard and surf. Rentals are available.

As with all water parks, utmost caution should be taken by the kids so that accidents are avoided.

The park is open daily from mid-June through the beginning of September from 10 a.m. to 8 p.m. It is open from mid-May to mid-June and mid-September to October on weekends and holidays from 11 a.m. to 5 p.m. Schedules change, so check before you go. Admission is $13.75 for adults (12 and older), $10.75 for children 3 through 11. Children 9 and under must be accompanied by an adult.

To get to Wild Rivers, take I-405 (the San Diego Freeway) to Irvine Center Drive, which is adjacent to the Irvine Meadows Amphitheater.

WHERE TO STAY: As you might imagine, in a city with so much wealth first-class hotels are easy to find; moderate ones are difficult.

The Upper Bracket

The **Newporter Resort**, 1107 Jamboree Rd., Newport, CA 92660 (tel. 714/644-1700, or toll free 800/341-1471, 800/422-4240 in California), is the quintessential southern California luxury resort hotel. Even the sunny rose-colored buildings invite you to share the good life . . . and to our surprise, you can do it with your kids.

The lobby is California-design, bright and airy, with countless doors opening onto the patio, and inviting you to relax in the sun. The 415 guest rooms, suites, and villas sprawl on 26 beautifully landscaped acres.

Facilities include three large swimming pools, which have patio areas for dining and sunning as well as grassy slopes for playing. One pool is especially for children. Concierge service includes an activity director during the summer who oversees such daily activities as Ping-Pong tournaments (separate ones for adults and kids), volleyball, and hula hoop contests. There is a free airport shuttle service to and from Orange County / John Wayne Airport, full concierge service, same-day laundry and valet, an exercise spa, three Jacuzzis, tennis (for a reasonable court fee), shuffleboard, Ping-Pong, bicycle rentals, and a nine-hole par-three golf course. The John Wayne Tennis Club offers nursery service from 9 a.m. to noon. Finally, room service is available from 6 a.m. to 12:30 a.m., and babysitting can be arranged.

Not only is the hotel enchanting, but the location is superb. We love to rent bikes and ride the bike path along Newport's Back Bay where the wildlife sanctuary is located, or cross the street and let the kids enjoy the sand and water sports at Newport Dunes Aquatic Park (see the "What to See and Do" section for details). Ask the concierge for a pamphlet that lists children's activities; you may pick up some other ideas.

There is indoor/outdoor dining at the Jamboree Café. Prices range from $4.75 to $8.75 for breakfast, $6 to $14.50 for lunch, and $6.50 to $25 for dinner. For those parents who have the energy at night to enjoy live entertainment and dancing, there is Duke's Lounge, where cocktails and appetizers are served.

The rooms are large, light, and pretty, much as you'd expect from the rambling villa-type architecture. They look out onto the golf course or pool areas. All rooms have either a king-size bed or two double beds, remote-control cable TV with free HBO and in-room pay movies, and a complimentary deluxe amenity basket. Some of the larger rooms have small sofas and coffee tables; all have game tables and chairs. All rooms feature tub/shower combinations with separate vanity areas and small refrigerator/mini-bars. Connecting rooms are available, as are suites.

Rooms rent for $125 to $145, single or double, the higher rate for the better views. Newporter rooms (with additional amenities) cost $165. Suites run $275 to $395. Children 12 and under stay free in their parents' room. There's no charge for cribs, but rollaways cost $15 per night. Be sure to ask about specials, as these can save you a great deal of money if you qualify for one.

The **Four Seasons Hotel, Newport Beach,** 690 Newport Center Dr., Newport Beach, CA 92660 (tel. 714/759-0808, or toll free 800/332-3442 or 800/268-6282), is a gracious, elegant hotel. The lobby is done in quiet tones of sand, mauve, and brown, with highly polished marble floors, and comfortable upholstered chairs and couches gathered in nice conversation groupings. There are sculptured carpets and elaborate fresh flower arrangements throughout.

But can an ultra-luxurious hotel welcome families?

How's this? Upon arrival, you receive a booklet that details activities at the hotel and in the surrounding area, and rates them for children. During the summer, a shallow section of the snowflake-shaped 3,000-square-foot swimming pool is cordoned off as a children's swimming area, children's pool toys can be borrowed, and the poolside aerobics studio at times is converted to a youngster's gym. Year round, there are Mousercise videos to use, children's games available at the concierge desk, and cookies with milk at bedtime.

At the time you book, the reservationist will ask the ages of your children and if you have any special needs. If you do, the hotel staff will stock baby bottles, specific baby foods and formula, diapers, and any other items you may need. And you'll be delighted to learn that the cribs here come with bumper guards—a feature you won't find often elsewhere. Bikes can be rented, as can kiddie carriers.

The pool area is exquisitely landscaped with lush ferns and impatiens. There are cabañas where you can relax in privacy or have a poolside lunch, and the fitness club can be used by children if an adult accompanies them. The large whirlpool has room for 25 people, and there are two lighted tennis courts for guest use. Other amenities include twice-daily maid service, complimentary overnight shoeshine, a multilingual concierge staff, 24-hour room service (with a kiddie menu), valet and laundry service, valet parking, limousine service, and a giftshop. The complete health club includes aerobics classes, sauna, massage, and weight rooms.

There are two hotel restaurants. The Pavilion serves breakfast, lunch, and dinner, while the casual Cabañas Café offers lunch daily and breakfast on the weekends. As you might expect at this first-class hotel, restaurants can be on the pricey side. Breakfast at the Pavilion starts at $3.50 and goes to $11. Lunch is $6.50 to $16.50, and dinner entrees range from $18 to $24. The Cabañas Café's lunches range in price from $7.75 to $16.50. The Conservatory lounge has a light lunch menu and serves high tea daily. The Cabañas Café has a creative children's menu (with chicken sticks, burgers, peanut butter and banana sandwiches, and chicken alphabet soup), but all dining facilities will find your kids something they'll enjoy eating. Another feature standard to Four Seasons Hotels is their alternative menus—they will prepare low-calorie, low-cholesterol, and low-sodium dishes.

All 296 oversize rooms have balconies with beautiful views. Rooms come equipped with remote-control color TV, bathrobes (they're looking for kid-size robes), hairdryers, lighted makeup mirrors, several telephones, refrigerator/mini-bars, even a small television in the bathroom. Some of the rooms have stall showers in addition to the tub/shower combinations.

A standard room with a king-size bed has an overstuffed chair and ottoman, a large desk, with plenty of room for a crib or rollaway. Most families stay in the Four Seasons rooms. These L-shaped accommodations have two rooms. You enter a good-size sitting or living room that has a table and chairs, couch, chair, coffee table, and television. The bedroom has doors that shut it completely from the living-room area. There is a small deck with chairs and table that overlook the surrounding area. This unit has a very large dressing area, separate bath, and shower rooms.

Room rates for moderate to deluxe rooms range from $150 to $185 for singles and $170 to $205 for doubles. Four Seasons rooms are $205 to $225. One-bedroom suites start at $250; two-bedroom suites start at $400.

Ask for summer and weekend packages, as these can save you considerable money. For example, the "Escape Weekend" (Friday through Sunday) is $185 for Four Seasons rooms. The "Discover the Coast" package (from Sunday through Thursday) costs $120. Some of these packages even include breakfast.

The **Newport Beach Marriott Hotel and Tennis Club,** located across from Fashion Island at 900 Newport Center Dr., Newport Beach, CA 92660 (tel. 714/640-4000, or toll free 800/228-9290), is a fine hotel in which you can feel quite comfortable with your kids—even at those worst moments when they are cranky and out of sorts. The hotel staff exudes a warmth and delight with children, while maintaining an appreciation that not all guests want to have the room next door to such a group.

The recently renovated hotel is built as a series of towers connected by covered passageways centered around a large outdoor pool and lovely atrium courtyard. The atrium court has an enormous fountain two stories high, flanked by colorful flowers and greenery. Guests are welcome to sit in the atrium when private parties are not using it.

The hotel has two swimming pools, two whirlpools, eight lighted tennis courts, a pro shop, a full health club, and a giftshop. The Newport Beach Country Club is a lush 18-hole golf course located next door. Full concierge service is available, and room service offers children's items (and adult fixings too) from 6 a.m. to 1 a.m. Some families do it in style and order a whole pizza to eat while they all watch a family movie on TV. Babysitting can be arranged through the front desk. Two coin-operated washers and dryers are available for guest use, and there is same-day and overnight laundry service as well.

The pool areas are palm-edged gardens, nice places to sit. The main pool is freeform in shape, with a great shallow end for the kids. It has ample lounge chairs as well as tables with umbrellas. The smaller pool is much quieter, almost as if guests are unaware it exists. This is a great place to come with the kids.

The hotel has several restaurants. J. W.'s Sea Grill is casual dining, open daily for breakfast, lunch, and dinner—and a spectacular Sunday brunch. (Even if you don't eat there, take a peek at the ice sculptures during the brunch.) Breakfast and lunch prices start at around $5; dinners range from $5.25 (sandwiches) to $14 (filet mignon). Most selections on the extensive children's menu are around $2.

Nicole's Grill is a fine, elegant restaurant that serves California cuisine for dinner; Nicole's Pub, next door, offers cocktails in posh surroundings. The View Lounge on the north tower's 16th floor offers snacks and dancing for adults. Food service is available at poolside as well. Highchairs and boosters are provided, as are children's menus. And as with any good hotel restaurant, just ask if you don't see what you want on the menu. The staff probably will be able to accommodate you. (Our kids had their first taste of prime rib here.)

Set up on a bluff, many of the 600 rooms have a view of the golf course or ocean. Decorated in California casual, with floral bedspreads, pale walls in peach tones and slate blues, every room has a balcony or patio, free HBO, remote-control color TV, pay movies, tub/shower combinations, and a complimentary basket of toiletries. There is nightly turn-down service—and Ghirardelli chocolate squares will be left on your pillow to beckon sweet dreams.

The rooms in the north tower are quite spacious. Some have a king-size bed and a couch, easy chair, and coffee table. Others have two double beds. All have adequate space to accommodate a crib.

The rates quoted here are the basic ones. Be sure to ask for special packages, as these appear frequently. (For example, there was a "Two for Breakfast" weekend special recently for $69, including two free full-course breakfasts.) Singles and doubles range from $159 to $166; the concierge-level rooms rent for $174 to $184, and the one- and two-bedroom suites range from $500 to $800. Cribs and rollaways are free. Children under 12 usually stay free in their parents' room (but double-check if you get a special rate). Older children and additional adults pay a $15-per-night supplement.

Moderately Priced

Nothing fancy, the **Best Western Bay Shores Inn,** 1800 W. Balboa Blvd., Newport Beach, CA 92663 (tel. 714/675-3463), is in a wonderful location, one block from the bay and a few blocks from the ocean. This plain but well-kept motor inn has 20 rooms, most of them small. The rooms with two double beds are adequate for four, however, and the suites (which have full kitchens, dining rooms, and separate bedrooms) are large enough to sleep six.

This is straight motel style—no pool, no large lobby (just an office)—but a free continental breakfast (brioche or blueberry muffins, fresh fruit, and coffee or tea) is included in the price.

There are some other nice touches here. A number of the rooms have ocean views; all have amenity baskets with shampoo, conditioner, and even dental floss. Each unit has a videocassette player (and there is a rental store two blocks away), hairdryers, and a tub/shower unit. A free newspaper is delivered to the door each day. There is a coin-operated washer/dryer on the premises.

Rates are $79 to $99 single and $99 to $119 double. Some of the units have one king-size bed (a crib will just fit) and others have two double beds. Suites are available for $129 to $189. Children under 12 stay free in their parents' room. Those 12 and over and additional adults pay $7 each per night. Cribs are free, but there are no rollaways. Check for lower rates out of season (October to April).

Home or Apartment Rentals

When you consider the price of rooms in Newport Beach, it's not surprising that many families simply rent homes or apartments for a week at a time or longer. The prices are much more reasonable, and while you don't have maid service, it is an excellent alternative to consider in this pricey neighborhood. These rental agents will match you with an accommodation that fits your needs (and, hopefully, your budget). Some typical rentals are two-bedroom oceanfront properties (ranging from $750 to $3,000 per week) and beach cottages or duplexes (ranging from $500 to $1,400 per week). Most properties are within a few blocks of the beach. If you're planning to be in Newport during the summer, you should begin to make your arrangements at least six months in advance. Be prepared for a refundable cleaning and breakage deposit, and a 9% bed tax.

Three local rental agents are **Playa Realty,** 108 McFadden Pl., Newport Beach, CA 92663 (tel. 714/673-1900); **Mel Fuchs' Pavilion Realty,** 700 E. Balboa Blvd., Balboa, CA 92661 (tel. 714/675-8120); and **Burr White Realtors,** 2901 Newport Blvd., Newport Beach, CA 92663 (tel. 714/675-4630).

Camping   *673 7368*

Camping facilities are available at a number of beaches. **Huntington City Beach** offers RV camping (but no hookups) from mid-September through May. For reservations, contact City of Huntington Beach–Sunset Vista, P.O. Box 190, Huntington Beach, CA 92648 (tel. 714/536-5281).

For details on **Newport Dunes Aquatic Park,** see the "What to See and Do" section.

Doheny State Beach, 25300 Harbor Dr., Dana Point, CA 92629 (tel. 714/496-6171), has over 100 campsites, and you can make reservations through MISTIX (tel. 619/452-1950, or toll free 800/446-7275 in California).

San Clemente State Beach, 3030 Avenida Del Presidente, San Clemente, CA 92672 (tel. 714/492-3156), has sites with hookups for RVs. Make your reservations through MISTIX (at the numbers above).

WHERE TO EAT: You'll find a wide range of restaurants on the Orange coast.

The Upper Bracket

One of our favorite places in Newport is on the harbor. **Villa Nova,** 3131 Pacific Coast Hwy. (tel. 714/642-7880), is a little Italian villa look-alike that even has a bit of honest-to-goodness history. Created to resemble the owner's ancestral home in Venice, complete with a mini-tugboat docked outside, the restaurant was originally established over 50 years ago on the Sunset Strip (in Los Angeles), where it was the watering hole for many a celebrity during the Strip's heyday. In 1967 the family moved it to Newport. Inside, wall murals continue the theme of waterfront Venetian dining.

Owner Jim Dale says that they want to help give youngsters the chance to appreciate fine dining. Indeed they must, because teens who once came to Villa Nova for prom night are now bringing their children! You'll be surprised at some of the selections for kids—scampi and (according to Dale) the kids' favorite, scaloppine doré (veal dipped in egg and lemon butter). Children's plates cost $5.75 to $10.

The extensive adult menu includes many different kinds of pastas (spaghetti, ravioli, fettucine, mostaccioli, manicotti, lasagne, and on and on) plus more than a dozen veal dishes, and chicken, beef, and seafood. Prices range from $8 to $20.

The kids can start on breadsticks (already on the table) while they wait for their Shirley Temples or non-alcoholic piña coladas, which the bartender will gladly make. Highchairs and boosters are available, and of course, baby bottles and baby food can be warmed in the kitchen.

Special extras include birthday cakes, which can be either ordered or brought in; miniature chocolate sundaes, made on request; and window seats that offer a view of the restaurant's mini-tugboat. The best hours for kids are before 9 p.m., and you can tell your server if you want a leisurely or fast-paced meal. Open daily from 5 p.m. to 2 a.m. Valet parking. All major credit cards are accepted.

Another waterfront restaurant is **The Cannery,** 3010 Lafayette Ave. (tel. 714/675-5777). Housed in the historical landmark building that was a fish cannery from 1920 to 1966, the restaurant is adorned with loads of canning artifacts, which at once make the rooms interesting to look at and maintain the flavor of the building's original use. One wall is lined with huge cans; machinery and equipment are all around. Our kids found the old boiler in the center of the restaurant to be the most interesting.

This is a lively place—great for lively kids—and you can also dine on the patio beneath heat lamps. The patio deck sits just above the water at a boat turnaround area, so kids can watch the boats.

The kids don't have their own menu, but choose instead from the adult entrees, which can be split in the kitchen. Kids' favorites are the Doryman (selection of deep-fried shrimp, scallops, and cod in a light batter), pasta dishes, and the small top sirloin. The lobsters are huge (you can ask the waitress if they're big enough to split between two adults), and the abalone is delectable. And interestingly, the swordfish is speared, not caught in the usual way (it did taste delicious!). Dinners come with soup or salad, rice or potato, fresh vegetable, and bread. Prices range from $15 to $35 (for lobster or abalone).

No highchairs here, but boosters are available. Open Monday through Saturday from 11:30 a.m. to 2 a.m. and on Sunday from 9 a.m. to 2 a.m. Happily, this restaurant takes reservations (which are advised, since the wait can be an hour during the season) and accepts all major credit cards.

For a different kind of treat, the Cannery hosts two-hour harbor cruises for dinner and Sunday brunch. The Sunday brunches, which are the best for kids, are held at 10 a.m. and 1:30 p.m., year round. Adults pay $25; children, $22.

For another innovative place to eat on the waterfront, we like the **Reuben E. Lee Showboat,** 151 E. Pacific Coast Hwy. (tel. 714/675-5910). Built in 1963 to re-create a Mississippi riverboat, the *Reuben E. Lee* is 190 feet long, 52 feet wide, and is a floating restaurant that actually moves slightly on the water. This is a genuine treat for kids, who are always excited to experience something unusual —and indeed this is different! It's like walking onto a Louisiana riverboat. Wooden planks surround the showboat so you can view the harbor from all vantage points.

The interior is enchanting too. Done in antebellum southern décor, with hardwood floors, small-print wallpaper, mirrors, and bas-style walls, there is a huge grand staircase that takes diners up to the top deck and dining rooms. To everyone's delight, there is a magician who entertains nightly and during Sunday brunch. (A Dixieland group also plays during brunch.) Better yet, the management says they "do it all" when it comes to kids.

Specializing in seafood and Cajun dishes, the portions are large and very tasty. For lunch, prices range from $7 to $11; for dinner, prices range from $8.25 to $25. Dinners include soup or salad. The children's menu offers four entrees for $6: prime rib, shrimp, grilled cheese, and a cheeseburger; everything but the prime rib is also served at lunch. There are highchairs and boosters available, and loads of non-alcoholic creations can be made for young patrons.

Reservations are accepted, as are all major credit cards. Valet and self-parking are available.

Moderately Priced

Are you looking for a place for barbecue? **Tony Roma's,** 2530 W. Pacific Coast Hwy. (tel. 714/642-9070), has a branch here. The menu is the same as at other locations—tasty barbecued ribs, chicken, and steak (as well as salads and burgers), and is a good alternative to some of the more expensive restaurants in the area. Adult prices range from $4 to $13 at lunch and $5 to $13 at dinner, and all include coleslaw, beans, or potato.

Highchairs and boosters are provided and a children's menu is available. However, the no-reservations policy means that your family could wait a long time. The manager suggests coming between 4:30 and 6:30 p.m. for dinner, if you prefer not to wait. Open for lunch Monday through Saturday from 11 a.m. to 4 p.m., and from noon to 4 p.m. on Sunday; for dinner, Sunday through Thursday from 4 p.m. to midnight and on Friday and Saturday from 4 p.m. to 1 a.m. Valet and self-parking in the restaurant's lot. All major credit cards are accepted. They'll deliver (even to your hotel if it's within their delivery area).

If your children are fish lovers, the **Crab Cooker,** 2200 Newport Blvd. (tel. 714/673-0100), is a small hole-in-the-wall you'll want to check out. The throngs of people waiting on benches outside this seafood grill should be enough to tell you that the food is good, and the prices are probably the best in all of Newport Beach.

A combination plate with shrimp, scallops, and choice cuts of fish broiled on a skewer is $8.50 at lunch and dinner. Charcoal-broiled oysters cost $6.50 at lunch and $8.25 at dinner, and charcoal-broiled lobsters are $13.25 and $17.50. The child's plate (broiled fish on a skewer) can also be ordered by adult "light eaters," and costs $4.50 for a filling meal. All plates come with potatoes or rice and coleslaw or tomatoes.

But don't expect anything fancy. Linoleum floors, heavy-duty paper plates, and plastic silverware is what you'll get here. The main dining room also houses the glassed-in grill area where you can watch chefs cook the seafood. We suggest that you request the dining room in back, which has a much nicer atmosphere (but you may have to wait a bit longer for a table). We usually put our name on the waiting list, buy a small bowl of the tasty clam chowder, and wander the streets enjoying the town.

Highchairs and booster seats are available. Open Sunday through Thursday from 11 a.m. to 9 p.m., on Friday and Saturday till 10 p.m. No credit cards or reservations accepted. Street parking.

Inexpensive

When you're near Balboa Pier, **Ruby's,** at the end of the pier (tel. 714/675-7829), is a great little place to grab breakfast, lunch, or a very early dinner. You can either order from a fast-food-like window outside and eat on the pier or wait for a table inside the restaurant. Either way, plan to spend time watching the fishermen reel in their catches.

Ruby's is novel, fun, and small. It has four long booths and three long tables that can accommodate families. With windows all around, you feel as if you're on the water (and on clear days, you can see Catalina Island). The setting is beautiful. The tables and walls are white Formica; the napkins and food baskets are bright red.

Chili cheeseburgers with fries are great! And the mocha malts just finish off the meal perfectly. If that sounds a bit heavy for you, you might try the grilled cheese or tuna burger or simple Rubyburger. There are also salads, chowder, and chili to choose from. For breakfast, you can have omelets, eggs, and other breakfast specialties. Prices range from $3 to $4.75.

Sassy seats and boosters are provided, but there is no children's menu (although at these prices, kids can split). *Note:* There are *no* rest rooms here—or at this end of the pier—so proceed with caution. Similar to the Crab Cook, paper and plastic are used here.

Open for breakfast every day from 7 to 11:30 a.m.; Sunday through Thursday from 11:30 a.m. to 9 p.m., and on Friday and Saturday until 10 p.m., for lunch and dinner. No reservations or credit cards accepted, and you can expect a long wait for breakfast or dinner on weekends and during the summer if you want to eat inside. Parking lot at the pier entrance.

B.J.'s Chicago Pizzeria, 106 Main St., Balboa Peninsula (tel. 714/675-7560). Less than half a block from Balboa Pier and beach, this lively pizza house is a great place after a day at the beach. Very basic wood tables and booths set the mood for this inexpensive eatery. Medium deep-dish pizzas cost $7 to $12.25. You can also choose from a selection of pastas and sandwiches as well as a large salad bar.

Highchairs and boosters are available, and they'll gladly warm baby bottles and baby food in the kitchen. There is no children's menu, but they will serve a child's pasta dish or a mini-pizza for $1 less.

Off-season, open from 11:30 a.m. to 11 p.m. weekdays, until midnight on Friday and Saturday. In summer, the hours are 11:30 a.m. to midnight weekdays, until 1 a.m. on Friday and Saturday. There can be a long wait during peak hours, but you can order your pizza ahead of time so it will be almost ready when you sit down. No reservations accepted. Some major credit cards honored. There is a public parking lot.

If you like natural foods (but not vegetarian), **Puffins,** 3050 Pacific Coast Hwy. (tel. 714/640-1573), may be just what you're looking for. Located in Corona del Mar, just a few minutes south of Newport and a few minutes from Laguna, this cute little hole-in-the-wall is famous for its pancakes made with whole grains, almonds, bran, and buttermilk. One huge cake would easily feed a child. Kids (and adults who don't want large portions) can order from the "lighter appetite" side of the menu. There is also a children's menu of standard kid-fare for $2.75 to $4.

Omelets, soups, salads, sandwiches, pastas, and eggs à la Puffins are other choices for adults. Prices range from $2.25 to $7.50. Dinners include choice of soup or salad and whole-wheat roll. Choose from beef, fowl, lamb, seafood, and vegetarian dishes. Prices from $8.50 to $15.

Highchairs and boosters are available. They'll gladly warm baby bottles and baby food, but if you split a children's portion between two kids, they'll add a $1 service charge.

Puffins is open Monday through Thursday from 7 a.m. to 10 p.m., on Friday till 11 p.m., on Saturday from 8 a.m. to 11 p.m., and on Sunday from 8 a.m. to 10 p.m. Reservations accepted for dinner only. Most major credit cards are honored. There is an adjacent parking lot.

If you're looking for good standard fare for breakfast or lunch (which can sometimes be difficult to find), we suggest the following two family restaurants in Fashion Island: **The Good Earth,** 210 Newport Center Dr. (tel. 714/640-2411), open Monday through Friday from 7 a.m. to 10 p.m. and on Saturday and Sunday from 8 a.m. to 11 p.m.; and **Coco's,** 151 Newport Center Dr. (tel. 714/644-1571), open daily from 6:30 a.m. to 11 p.m.

3. LAGUNA BEACH AND SAN JUAN CAPISTRANO

While Laguna Beach and San Juan Capistrano are not far from the other Orange Coast towns, they make excellent day trips from Los Angeles, San Diego, and Anaheim.

LAGUNA BEACH: Some people say that Laguna Beach is the most beautiful beach town in southern California. Whether that's true or not, Laguna is unlike other nearby coastal towns. It prides itself on its artistic core, its galleries and art festivals. It is cultured with a distinctive seaside flair. This delightful upscale village is centered where Pacific Coast Hwy. meets Broadway. On one side you have Main Beach; on the other, little streets filled with boutiques, restaurants, and novelty stores radiate eastward toward the hills. And for blocks along Pacific Coast Hwy. you'll find galleries and craft shops.

Summertime is festival time in Laguna. The world-famous Pageant of the Masters, the Festival of Arts, and the Sawdust Festival draw an international crowd. Laguna is essentially not a child's town, but because of the famous art festivals and the beauty of the setting, it's a place adults enjoy—and one that kids can enjoy for a few hours. The coves of Laguna Beach are well-known play areas for families.

For information about Laguna, contact the **Laguna Beach Chamber of Commerce,** at 357 Glenneyre St., underneath the library (P.O. Box 396), Laguna Beach, CA 92652 (tel. 714/494-1018).

Parks and Beaches

Centrally located **Main Beach** is said to be one of the best planned beaches around. Indeed, it is a beach that integrates the town and the sand. Although it gets a bit too crowded for our taste, Main Beach has lots of goodies. There is elaborate wooden play equipment, lawn areas, showers, and volleyball nets. A lifeguard tends the beach area. The park and adjacent beach back up to some of the local shops, making it extremely convenient if you need any supplies or kiddie treats.

Heisler Park (tel. 714/494-1018), north of Main Beach, is a large park perched on a bluff overlooking the ocean. This is a wonderful place for a picnic or barbecue lunch or dinner. There is a large grassy area, picnic tables, rest rooms, and shuffleboard nearby. Take the stairs to get down to the beach. Located off Jasmine or Myrtle Street (which intersect Pacific Coast Hwy.).

These same streets (Jasmine and Myrtle) will take you down to beaches with tidepools. There is **Picnic Cove,** which has a ramp, and **Diver's Cove.** Lucky children may see sea urchins, starfish, mussels, even baby octopus. And you'll find great shells. (But remember that this is a preserve, so leave everything just where you found it.)

Festivals

During the months of July and August, Laguna hosts its annual **Festival of Arts,** a time when recognized artists display their works in the outdoor setting of Irvine Bowl. Spread over six acres are paintings, sculpture, wood crafts, ceramics, and more.

There are special treats for kids too. Scott Land Marionettes has daily shows, and an art workshop for kids is available every afternoon. On Sunday afternoons, dancers enliven the outdoors with performances on the lawn.

Probably the most famous part of the festival is the completely unique **Pageant of the Masters.** This two-hour pageant (which is held in an open-air amphitheater) presents life-size re-creations of famous works of art in which people play the central roles. As the lights come up on a "painting" (or statue or tapestry), actors take their positions and remain posed for several minutes. These are, indeed, "living pictures." The sight is quite amazing, and is popular with older children (10 and above), especially with teens who have even the slightest interest in art.

The pageant is held nightly at 8:30 p.m., but you must buy tickets far in advance. Contact the Festival of Arts, P.O. Box 1659, Laguna Beach, CA 92652 (tel. 714/494-1145). Ticket prices range from $9 to $35.

The **Sawdust Festival** occurs in conjunction with the Festival of Arts (although they are separate groups). Located at 935 Laguna Canyon Rd., down the street from Irvine Bowl, the Sawdust Festival attracts artists and craftspeople who will either talk with you about their work or demonstrate it for you. Kids are intrigued by the glassblowers and the potters throwing pots on their wheels. There's even a children's booth with free materials for budding artists. For information, call 714/494-3030.

If You're Staying for a Meal

We like **The Cottage** restaurant, at 308 N. Pacific Coast Hwy. (tel. 714/494-3023). The Cottage is a turn-of-the-century home that was a residence until

1938, when it became a café (the current restaurant opened in 1964). Beautiful antiques grace the rooms, and there is a fabulous photographic exhibit in the waiting area. The dining areas were once living areas and are wonderfully restored with solid oak and colored leaded glass.

The Cottage serves home-style food for breakfast, lunch, and dinner.

Items on the breakfast menu include such favorites as buckwheat and cranberry-orange pancakes or eggs with ham, sausage, or top sirloin. Prices range from $2 to $8. The junior breakfast (bacon, eggs, and pancakes) costs $2.50. Lunch offers such entrees as lasagne and Swiss steak, and a lighter fare of salads and sandwiches. Prices range from $3.25 to $8. Dinners include a variety of meat dishes (braised sirloin tips, Swiss steak), poultry, and fish, as well as two chef's specials each day, and are priced at $8 to $12. Junior dinners are luncheon-size portions of selected full dinners and run $6 to $9. Dinners include soup or salad, fresh vegetables, and rolls or popovers.

Highchairs and booster seats are available.

The Cottage is open 365 days a year: Monday through Thursday from 7:30 a.m. to 10:30 p.m., and on Friday, Saturday, and Sunday until 11 p.m. They suggest that you make a reservation, as the wait can be long without one. Street parking is available. Some major credit cards are accepted.

MISSION SAN JUAN CAPISTRANO: Glorified in song, romanticized in stories, Mission San Juan Capistrano is known as the "Jewel of the Missions." This gem takes you back over 200 years to the beginnings of California history when Fr. Junipero Serra was making his way up the California coast on his mission quest.

The mission was actually founded twice. The first undertaking, in 1775, came to an abrupt end when news was received of an Indian attack at nearby Mission San Diego. The missionaries buried the chapel bells and headed south. The next year (1776) Fray Serra—called by some "The Father of California"—returned to the site to establish Mission San Juan Capistrano. Later in that century an elaborate church was built. By its completion in 1806 it was considered the most beautiful mission in the California chain. Unfortunately, it was severely damaged in 1812 when an earthquake felled much of it, leaving only Serra Chapel (the only chapel left in which Serra actually presided) intact. The rest is in ruins.

In the long history of Mission San Juan Capistrano, the annual return of the swallows is a relatively new event. For over 50 years the swallows have faithfully returned to Capistrano on St. Joseph's Day, March 19, to stay until mid-October (or so the story goes), when they leave for their home in the south. No one can explain why they choose the mission.

Contrary to what many people believe, the mission was not simply a place in which to convert heathens to Christianity. Missions served as outposts of Spanish civilization, with educational, health, and housing facilities for the natives as well as religious services. As you walk through San Juan Capistrano, you'll see the breadth of its contributions to the early community it spawned.

Children enjoy wandering through the mission. Its elaborate gardens, contained by graceful archways and time-worn stone and brick walls, are a restful, rejuvenating place to spend time. The four mission bells, flanked by ancient walls, ignite the imagination, and carefully constructed displays such as bread ovens and ceramic kilns educate the youngsters. We've seen older children linger in Serra Chapel, intrigued by the detailed altar that came from Barcelona, Spain.

The mission staff is dedicated to helping children appreciate the historical significance of the structure. A "children's touching table" is set up on one of the walkways. Kids are invited to handle Native American and Spanish artifacts—rawhide, tools, even petrified wood.

In addition, the mission museum holds special days for children, called Saturday at the Mission. Children learn about mission life through skits, crafts, and other hands-on activities. They may play Indian games or make headbands. They might bring you their own handmade adobe brick. The workshops are held the first Saturday of every month from 10 a.m. to 1 p.m. Call three weeks in advance for reservations (tel. 714/493-1424). The charge is $1 for children, $2 for adults.

Mission San Juan Capistrano is located approximately 35 minutes south of Anaheim via I-5 (take Ortega Hwy. to Camino Capistrano), and is open from 7:30 a.m. to 5 p.m. daily. The admission charge is $2 for adults, $1 for children under 12. The mission also serves as a perfect stopping point if you're driving between Los Angeles and San Diego.

If You Want a Meal

Another era awaits you and the kids at the **San Juan Capistrano Depot** restaurant (tel. 714/496-8181). This restaurant is located inside the original train depot, built in 1895 (actually a registered historical landmark). The bar is housed in the 1940 freight house, and two refrigerator cars offer a banquet room that seats up to 80. One of the real treats is the 1938 Pullman car cocktail lounge, complete with worn upholstered seats and authentic accoutrements.

Many of the tables in the main dining room are sitting only eight to ten feet from the track, making for perfect entertainment for the kids. They can watch the trains as they come to San Juan Capistrano, the 15th busiest depot in the country. In fact, this restaurant is so unusual (and perfectly located halfway between Los Angeles and San Diego) that many people make a train trip just to have dinner, then turn around and take the train home. (Just call Amtrak—toll free 800/USA-RAIL—to coordinate travel and dining plans.)

We found it to be an adventure to take the train in the morning, spend a few hours at the mission, eat lunch, and take the train back.

The Depot serves continental cuisine, steaks, prime rib, rack of lamb, and seafood (as well as Sunday brunch), and prices range from $5 (burger and barbecued beef) to $8.50 (prime rib) for lunch, $9 to $18 for dinner, and $8.50 for brunch (kid's brunch is $5). There are highchairs and boosters, a children's menu (for lunch, they'll make grilled cheese, $2.75; at dinner, fried chicken is $5.50 and prime rib is $9), and great kiddie drinks, the most popular of which is a Brooke Shields (Perrier and grenadine). There are several other unique distractions, including still-movie machines and an old-fashioned iron-claw game.

Open Monday through Saturday for lunch from 11:30 a.m. to 2:30 p.m., and on Sunday for brunch from 10 a.m. to 2:30 p.m. Dinners are served Sunday through Thursday from 5 to 9 p.m., on Friday and Saturday till 10 p.m. Reservations are accepted, as are most major credit cards. Should you be driving, there is a parking lot.

Festivals and Annual Events

Whale-Watching (January and February) off the coast of Newport (tel. 714/673-5245).

Festival of Whales, at Dana Point (tel. 714/496-2274 or 714/831-3850). There are lectures, films, and activities.

The Glory of Easter (March and April), at the Crystal Cathedral in Garden Grove (tel. 714/971-4000).

Fiesta de las Golondrinas (Return of the Swallows to Capistrano), at Mission San Juan Capistrano (tel. 714/493-1424). There are parades and special programs.

Strawberry Festival (May), in Garden Grove. There are arts, crafts, pie-eating contests, and food booths. Contact P.O. Box 2287, Garden Grove, CA 92642 (tel. 714/638-0981), for information.

Laguna Festival of Arts, Pageant of Masters, and the **Sawdust Festival** (July and August). See the "What to See and Do" section in Laguna for details.

Character Boat Parade, in Newport Beach (tel. 714/644-8211). Festive, decorated boats travel through Newport Harbor.

Annual Surf Championship (September and October), at Huntington Beach (tel. 714/536-5486). Watch top surfers from around the world compete.

Sand Castle Competitions, in Corona del Mar (tel. 714/644-8211). Everyone gets into the act at this delightful, extraordinary event. Kids are welcome to try their hand at creating a master sandcastle.

The Glory of Christmas (November and December), at the Crystal Cathedral in Garden Grove (tel. 714/971-1400).

Parade of Christmas Boats (December), in Newport Harbor (tel. 714/644-8211). This is a fabulous parade of lights. Make reservations early.

Activities by Age in Orange County

For your quick reference, here's a synopsis of what attractions are most suitable and best enjoyed by children of different ages.

Teens and Preteens

Anaheim Stadium Tour
Balboa Island Ferry
Balboa Peninsula and Balboa Island
Balboa Pier
California Angels
Corona del Mar Marine Life Refuge
Crystal Cathedral
Disneyland
Fountain Valley Golf and Recreation Center
Fun Zone
Knott's Berry Farm
Ice Capades Chalet
Irvine Meadows Amphitheater
Laguna Beach
Laguna's Pageant of the Masters, Festival of Arts, and Sawdust Festival
Los Angeles Rams
Medieval Times
Mission San Juan Capistrano
Movieland Wax Museum
Newport Beach and Pier
Orange County Performing Arts Center
Pacific Amphitheater
Photon
Sgt. Preston's Yukon Saloon
Upper Newport Bay Ecological Reserve
Wild Rivers

School-Age Kids

Anaheim Stadium Tour
Balboa Island Ferry
Balboa Peninsula and Balboa Island
Balboa Pier
Cabbage Patch Adoption Center
California Angels
Corona del Mar Marine Life Refuge
Disneyland
Doll and Toy Museum
Fountain Valley Golf and Recreation Center
Fun Zone

Golf-'N-Stuff Miniature Golf Course
Hobby City
Ice Capades Chalet
Irvine Meadows Amphitheater
Knott's Berry Farm
Laguna Beach
Laguna's Sawdust Festival
Medieval Times
Mission San Juan Capistrano
Movieland Wax Museum
Newport Beach and Pier
Newport Dunes Aquatic Park
Orange County Performing Arts Center
Pacific Amphitheater
Sgt. Preston's Yukon Saloon
Upper Newport Bay Ecological Reserve
Wild Rivers

Preschoolers

Balboa Island Ferry
Cabbage Patch Adoption Center
Corona del Mar Marine Life Refuge
Disneyland
Doll and Toy Museum
Fun Zone
Hobby City Choo Choo
Knott's Berry Farm
Newport Dunes Aquatic Park
Upper Newport Bay Ecological Reserve

IN AN EMERGENCY: If an emergency should occur during your visit in Orange County, you will find 24-hour emergency rooms at the following area hospitals:

Anaheim Memorial Hospital, 1111 W. La Palma Ave., near Harbor Boulevard, in Anaheim (tel. 714/774-1450).

Midwood Community Hospital, 7770 Katella Ave. in Stanton, near Anaheim (tel. 714/893-5051).

Hoag Memorial Hospital, 301 Newport Blvd., in Newport Beach (tel. 714/645-8600).

SAN DIEGO AND VICINITY

□ □ □

All those of you who think the San Diego area is Sea World, the zoo, and the Wild Animal Park, hold onto your hats. You are about to embark on a journey that offers you so many possibilities that it will have you coming back time and time again.

San Diego is one of the most perfect family vacation destinations. It consistently has one of the finest climates in the nation—daytime temperatures average 70°, and it rarely rains. From the heart of San Diego, you can be in the desert or the mountains, at the ocean, in flower fields and even in another country in a short period of time. Whether you stay in San Diego, La Jolla, Coronado, or even Tijuana, you'll be within 10 to 30 minutes of any major attraction. And speaking of attractions, there's something for everyone here. Even those attractions geared for children are done so nicely that adults can't help enjoying them too. In addition to the commercial sights, there are gracious historical sites, outdoor activities galore, and some of the most beautiful beaches in the world.

1. GREATER SAN DIEGO

California history began in San Diego with the arrival of Portuguese explorer Juan Rodriguez Cabrillo in 1542. Later Fr. Junipero Serra established the first mission of the historic El Camino Real here. And Old Town is the site of the first European settlement on California land. It wasn't until 1846 that San Diego came under American rule.

GETTING THERE: Driving to San Diego is simple from most major California cities. From Los Angeles **by car,** take I-5 south for the 2½-hour, 125-mile trip. Same from Orange County—it's 1½ hours, 90 miles. From Palm Springs, take Calif. 74 to Calif. 215 south, which turns into I-15 and runs right into town. It's a 3-hour, 139-mile trip.

Amtrak (tel. toll free 800/USA-RAIL for information and reservations) services San Diego from many cities across the nation, as well as from cities in California. It stops at the Santa Fe Depot in downtown San Diego.

Most of the major airlines, and some minor ones, fly into San Diego's **Lindbergh Field** (otherwise known as **San Diego International Airport**), three miles northwest of downtown (tel. 619/231-7361). For information and reservations, call Alaska Airlines (tel. toll free 800/426-0333), American Airlines (tel. 619/232-4051, or toll free 800/433-7300), Continental (tel. 619/232-9155, or toll free 800/525-0280), Delta (tel. 619/235-4344, or toll free 800/221-1212), Northwest (tel. 619/239-0488, or toll free 800/225-2525), Southwest (tel. 619/232-1221), TWA (tel. 619/295-7009, or toll free 800/438-2929), or United (tel. 619/234-7171, or toll free 800/241-6522).

Major car-rental companies can be found at the airport, as well as throughout San Diego—**Avis** (tel. toll free 800/331-1212), **Budget** (tel. toll free 800/527-0700), and **Hertz** (tel. toll free 800/654-3131).

Greyhound services San Diego, and its downtown terminal is at 120 W. Broadway (tel. 619/239-9171).

2. GETTING AROUND

The best way to see San Diego is by car. The city posts unobtrusive signs that point out routes to most of the major attractions, and a convenient group of freeways makes it pretty simple to get around. Most hotels have maps or helpful preprinted directions indicating routes to various attractions from that particular hotel. You can also get maps from the International Visitors Information Center (see the "Getting Your Bearings" section).

Although it's not that easy to get around the San Diego area without a car, it can be done using **public transportation.**

To make your way through the downtown area, you can use city buses or the **San Diego Trolley** (tel. 619/231-8549 for a recorded announcement, and 619/233-3004 for more information on the trolleys and regular city buses). The trolleys leave from the Santa Fe Depot, at Kettner and C Streets, downtown. This line runs from downtown San Diego to the U.S. border, and stops 100 feet from the border crossing. It's a perfect way to get to Tijuana (about 40 minutes) without having to worry about a car. There are 22 stations on this line, so you can use the trolley to get around parts of San Diego. Be sure to take the kids out of the strollers before you attempt to get on; the trolley waits less than half a minute at each stop. Trolleys run daily every 15 minutes in each direction beginning at 5 a.m. The last trolley leaves the border to return to San Diego at 1 a.m. From the Santa Fe stop to the border, the fare is $1.50. Children 6 and under ride free. Be sure to get your ticket from the vending machine at the station before getting on. Depending on where you want to go other than the border, fares range from 50¢ to $1.25. (Call **San Diego Transit** at 619/233-3004 for specific station stops in between, and for information about the other trolley line.)

Day Tripper Transit Passes are good deals for families staying at least three days and planning to use public transportation exclusively. The passes are also good for the San Diego Ferry. Visit or contact the **Transit Store,** 449 Broadway (corner of Fifth Avenue), San Diego, CA 92101 (tel. 619/234-1060). Passes cost $3 for one day. Remember, children 6 and under ride free. If you order your passes by mail, expect a wait of ten days for delivery. Add 50¢ to cover postage and handling, and be sure to include the dates you need them. You can also purchase passes at the San Diego Bay Ferry, 1050 N. Harbor Dr. For other locations, contact the Transit Store.

Not to be confused with the San Diego Trolley, the **Molly Trolley** is a pri-

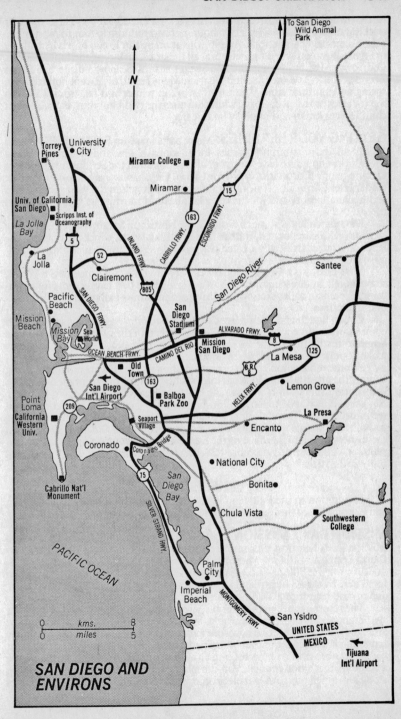

*SAN DIEGO AND
ENVIRONS*

vately owned trolley geared to tourists (tel. 619/233-9177). These open-air trackless trolleys take you on a two-hour narrated round-trip tour to most of the major sightseeing attractions. And it stops at many San Diego hotels. An all-day pass will allow you on/off privileges at all the stops, including the Embarcadero, Old Town, Mission Bay, Harbor and Shelter Islands, Seaport Village, San Diego Zoo, Sea World, and the Gaslamp Quarter. Molly runs daily except holidays—in spring and summer from 9 a.m. to 7 p.m., in winter and fall from 9 a.m. to 5 p.m. Fare for the all-day pass, which includes the two-hour tour, is $6, adult or child (except kids 4 and under, who ride free).

GETTING YOUR BEARINGS: Many parts make up San Diego. There's **La Jolla,** a village of stunning beaches, international shops, and restaurants, and a town lucky enough to have both the Salk Institute and the Scripps Institution of Oceanography. **Coronado,** called the Crown City, has its share of sandy beaches. And its Del Coronado is one of the most famous hotels in the world for both its architectural beauty and for the royal families and movie stars who have stayed there.

Mission Valley is home to Hotel Circle North and South, where many of the city's hostelries are located. **Harbor and Shelter Islands,** which are not really islands, are in fact artificially created playgrounds for boating and fishing enthusiasts. They also have their share of parks and beaches.

Mission Bay is a mecca of aquatic activity. Its 4,600 acres include Sea World, resort hotels, and restaurants. This is also one of the best family spots for swimming, bicycling, roller skating, windsurfing, and almost all other forms of outdoor recreation.

Ocean Beach and **Pacific Beach** are just what their names suggest—beach communities. Now more trendy and upscale than in their former lives—one as home to the hippies of the '60s, the other as a quiet beach community—they make popular tourist beach destinations.

For the most complete tourist information on San Diego and its environs, contact the **International Visitors Information Center** (a part of the San Diego Convention and Visitors Bureau), 11 Horton Plaza (First Avenue and F Street), San Diego, CA 92101 (tel. 619/236-1212, or 619/239-9696 for recorded visitor information). The multilingual staff can provide you with brochures, maps, and other information. The office is open daily from 8:30 a.m. to 5:30 p.m. You can also write the main office of the **San Diego Convention and Visitors Bureau,** at 1200 Third Ave., Suite 824, Dept. 700, San Diego, CA 92101 (tel. 619/232-3101).

3. WHERE TO STAY

In addition to the following hotels, there are accommodations in La Jolla and Coronado; see those sections for suggestions.

MISSION BAY / MISSION BEACH: For years families found their way to Mission Bay's Vacation Village. Purchased by Princess Cruises in 1983, the **San Diego Princess,** 1404 W. Vacation Rd., San Diego, CA 92109 (tel. 619/274-4630, or toll free 800/542-6275), still attracts those same families who were first lured here by the 43 lushly landscaped acres with bayfront rooms, private beach, and myriad recreational facilities on the grounds.

The resort has five outdoor pools, two of which are heated, and an outdoor spa. Eight tennis courts are available, five are night-lighted (instruction can be arranged), and there are two new volleyball courts. A bicycle stand near the lobby rents single, tandem, and four-wheel pedal bikes. The grounds are so large that we spent more than an hour tooling around in our four-wheeler, toddler in the middle. If that's not enough, you can play shuffleboard and Ping-Pong or jog along a mapped-out path. An electronic game room near the giftshop provides young and older children with lots to do. Ask the concierge for a map of the property's botanical gardens and take the kids for a special walk. The Princess's own marina has sailboats, paddleboats, powerboats, and windsurfing equipment for rent. Searching for sea shells on the sandy beach (not another white one!) is a very popular activity.

The Village Café is the place to take the kids. It's a big, bright, airy room, with casual and quick service. (During peak periods when the resort is full of families, service is apt to be slow.) Breakfast, lunch, and dinner are served, and there are plenty of selections for the children. After your meal you can feed the birds from the boardwalk overlooking the lagoon. The Dockside Broiler is a more expensive and adult-oriented eatery, and its specialties are steaks and seafood. If you're here for Christmas, you might want to have your holiday dinner here. The restaurant sets up a great buffet overflowing with food, plus a yummy dessert table; be sure to reserve in advance. Room service is available from 7 a.m. to 10 p.m. daily.

When you make your room reservation, you'll be assigned one of 450 individual-style accommodations. You can have your choice of a bay or lagoon view or a garden setting. All rooms have large dressing areas, a refrigerator, Servibar, and cable TV with in-room movies, and most have a private patio. Air conditioning is standard. There are either two queen-size beds or one king-size bed in the lanai rooms (standard rooms). Some 95 of the units are suites, which are spacious and well suited to large families. Studio suites have a living area with a sofa bed, a table and four chairs for eating, and two separate dressing areas; some have full kitchens. The queen-size bed is not in a separate area, but is slightly apart from the living room. The one-bedroom suites, which can also sleep four, have a private bedroom with a king-size bed.

The concierge will arrange babysitting, if needed. A coin laundry is available on the grounds.

Rates vary depending on location and/or whether the room has a kitchen. Lanai rooms run $120 to $130 single and $125 to $150 double. Studios, based on occupancy by one to four people, rent for $185 to $225. Suites cost $225 to $295. Kitchen units are available for $146 to $295 per night. Children 12 and under sleep free. Those over 12 and extra adults pay $15 each per night. Cribs are free, but rollaways cost $10. Inquire about special holiday and weekend rates.

The **Catamaran Resort Hotel,** 3999 Mission Blvd., San Diego, CA 92109 (tel. 619/488-1087, or toll free 800/821-3619, 800/542-6010 in California), is a South Seas paradise complete with palm trees swaying in the ocean breeze, rolling lawns, and rock-lined ponds. The oversize pool is enclosed with a bamboo-pole fence, and there's a large exercise room nearby for adults. Mission Bay is just a few steps away, and the Pacific Ocean is a short block away. The hotel has its own sailboats, catamarans, pedalboats, and sailboards for rent, and you can take sailing lessons here, too.

The lobby makes a good walk with the children, as they can look at the waterfall, live orchids, and black rock. A cockatoo perches on a branch in the pond and will happily engage in a yelling contest with youngsters. Rich mahogany is abundant, the furniture is caned, and the finishing touch is a catamaran suspended from the ceiling.

The Atoll restaurant serves breakfast, lunch, and dinner. On a warm day, you will especially enjoy lunch on the patio, just yards from the bay. The children's menu, which doubles as a pirate mask, lists a hamburger with fries, Jell-O, and a soft drink for $3.25.

The hotel has been completely relandscaped and remodeled in the last two years. New additions bring the room total to 315, and all accommodations are tastefully decorated in aqua and peach. Each has a private balcony or lanai, and most have a refrigerator.

The high-rise Tower on the bay has 120 rooms, some with stocked kitchenettes and bar stools. A suite in this building has a living area with a sofa bed, a kitchenette, and a bedroom with two double beds.

Rates vary according to room location and season. In the main building, a room with a king-size bed for one or two people, or a room with two double beds for up to four people, rents for $100 to $110 in summer, $90 to $100 in winter. A one-bedroom bayside suite for up to four people is available for $160 to $175 in summer, $140 to $150 in winter.

In the Tower building, a standard Tower room with a king-size bed costs $90 to $120 in summer, $70 to $90 in winter, single or double. A Tower studio with two double beds is $105 to $140 in summer, $85 to $110 in winter, single or double. A one-bedroom Tower suite for up to four people rents for $150 to $195 in summer, $120 to $150 in winter.

Children under 12 stay free in their parents' room. Those 12 and over and additional adults pay $15 each per night. There is no charge for cribs, but roll-aways cost $15. Secured parking is $6 a day. Ask about the popular Saving Safari Holiday, in which your room charge includes tickets to the San Diego Zoo or Sea World, or a sailing lesson.

The **Bahia Resort Hotel,** 998 W. Mission Bay Dr., San Diego, CA 92109 (tel. 619/488-0551, or toll free 800/821-3619, 800/542-6010 in California), is ideally located on a peninsula, with the waters of Mission Bay on one side and the Pacific Ocean on the other. On the land side of the hotel is a large pond, home to a family of seals that will delight you with their antics.

In addition to a private beach (where you can rent sailboats, catamarans, or paddleboats), the hotel has an Olympic-size pool and a helpful pool attendant who doubles as a lifeguard. There's a roped-off shallow area for kids. Poolside snacks and beverages are available.

The Bahia has its very own sternwheeler, the *Bahia Belle,* which offers cock-tails and dancing, and all the water sports you could imagine are close by. The bay and the beach are right there, a perfect place to play with the toddlers. There's also a game room, shuffleboard, and tennis courts. Bike rentals are available in all sizes.

Enjoy your breakfast on the patio of the Bahia Coffee Shop, which opens for the early riser at 6 a.m. and also has a children's menu (orange juice, hotcakes, and milk for $3). There are also lunch and dinner items for the kids on the pi-rate's hat menu, priced from $3 to $3.75. For dinner, there's the more expensive Mercedes Room, which houses the world's oldest Mercedes, built in 1902. This restaurant features continental dining and live nightly entertainment. Or order from room service.

The 325 air-conditioned rooms all come with either a view of the garden, the bay, or the beach. Garden-view rooms have angled front entries giving the appearance of individual front yards. Rooms are spacious and light, and the bath-rooms are large. Bay-view rooms are located in the high-rise. Studios and suites are available in this building, with patios or balconies, and most have kitchens. Spanish-style suites in a separate complex come with a view of the ocean, a large kitchen area, a sofa bed, and a large bedroom with double sinks.

Rates are the same for single or double occupancy and vary according to the view and the season. In summer rooms cost $95 to $120; in winter they run $75 to $100. One-bedroom bayside suites begin at $160 in summer, $130 in winter. Children under 18 stay free in their parents' room; those 18 and over and additional adults pay $15 each per night. Cribs and rollaways cost $15. Some spe-cial rates are available Monday through Thursday. Free parking.

Another good hotel choice is the **Dana Inn,** 1710 W. Mission Bay Dr., San Diego, CA 92109 (tel. 619/222-6440, or toll free 800/445-3339), which also has its own marina, bayside park, paddleboats, bicycle rentals, and tennis courts. And it is right next door to Sea World.

The inn recently had a facelift, and the new marine-blue-and-white exterior is inviting. A large patio surrounds the heated pool and spa. Snacks and drinks are served poolside in the summer. You and the kids can play Ping-Pong and shuffleboard.

Breakfast, lunch, and dinner are served at the Red Hen Country Kitchen. This cozy restaurant is ideal for informal family meals. Stop in for lunch and enjoy a meatloaf sandwich served with french fries or chili for $5.50. A children's menu offers old-fashioned French toast with sausage for $2.25, and also has sandwiches (turkey costs $2.50) as well as dinners (such as fried chicken with french fries and fresh fruit for $4). The restaurant is open from 7 a.m. to 10 p.m. Room service is also available.

For a variety of dining experiences, you can walk to any of seven restaurants across the street from the inn. Some have dancing for teens.

The inn has 196 rooms and suites, many with bayside views. All are comfortably furnished in neutrals and florals. Beds, credenzas, carpets, and drapes are relatively new. Most of the rooms have showers only, so if you prefer a tub, be sure to request one in advance. In-room coffee and color TV are standard. Refrigerators are available on request for a charge of $7.

There are three basic room rates for single or double occupancy, and these are based on view. Rooms with two double beds rent for $69.50, $99.50, or if right on the bay, $129.50. Children under 18 stay free; those 18 and over and additional adults pay $10 each per night. There is no fee for cribs, but rollaways cost $10. During busy summer weeks, a two-night minimum stay may apply, so ask when you reserve. There is a three-night minimum on holidays. Free parking.

SHELTER AND HARBOR ISLANDS: The **Sheraton on Harbor Island,** 1380 and 1590 Harbor Island Dr., San Diego, CA 92101 (tel. 619/291-2900, or toll free 800/325-3535), is a sprawling two-hotel complex and marina in an incomparable setting. Made up of the Sheraton Grand and the Sheraton East, the buildings are connected by a 300-yard marina walkway. Although the hotel is near the airport, you'll have the feeling you are getting away from it all as soon as you cross the bridge to Harbor Island.

The Sheraton makes a wonderful place to stay with the family. There is a beach playground with play equipment and chaises for sunning while you keep an eye on the little ones. Adjacent to the playground is a fitness par course, a challenge for kids and parents alike. You may want to choose the Sheraton East if you are traveling with small children, because the wading and swimming pools, and the playground and grassy areas, are just outside the building. Teenagers, on the other hand, may enjoy the marina walk between the two complexes when they want to play tennis or browse through the giftshop. The complex has three swimming pools, two of which have nearby wading pools (one foot deep) with bobbing inflatable toys. There's also a large video game room for those who have enough of the outdoors. During the summer, the hotel runs a program in which children 12 and under receive full complimentary breakfasts.

The Sheraton's "Summer Program for Kids," for hotel guests ages 4 through 12, runs from mid-June through Labor Day. Activities include art, magic, and cooking classes; T-shirt painting; organized outdoor sports such as swimming, softball, and volleyball; and movies and games. The "camp" program runs on Thursday and Sunday from 10 a.m. to 6 p.m., and on Friday and Saturday from 10 a.m. to 9 p.m. The cost is $10 per day.

You can play tennis on the lighted courts, and even take lessons from the resident pro ($28 an hour). Racquet rentals are $4 per hour. Free tennis clinics are held Monday through Wednesday, and a match-finding service is available in case you are the only one in your family who loves the game.

A paved walkway around the island affords joggers and cyclers a panoramic view. Bicycles rent for $4 an hour, and they are available in all sizes.

While the kids are in "camp," you can join the Sheraton Pro-Fitness Club and use the Nautilus gym or relax with a massage. A professional fitness evaluation is available, and aerobic video classes and aquatic classes are offered in-season. Use of the gym facilities costs $10 a day.

Gift and sundries, toys, and newspapers abound in the lobby shops. The concierge will arrange sightseeing, the Kids Club, and babysitting.

If you are staying at the Sheraton East, the Café Del Sol is a pleasant garden restaurant with wide windows opening onto the bay. Children are welcome here. The breakfast menu includes the standards, and some surprises, such as chicken livers sauté ($7.75) and a petite New York sirloin ($12). The children's menu offers French toast ($1.75), cereal ($1.25), and one egg with bacon or sausage ($2.50). And while they're waiting for the food, the youngsters will be kept busy working the puzzles included on their menus.

Lunch and dinner feature an attractive soup and salad bar ($8.25). The seafood quesadilla, billed as a "Tasty Beginning," is delicious and is filling enough to be your lunch entree ($5.25). For late risers, a dish of eggs, ham, french fries, and toast is served all day ($7.50). Pizza, burgers, salads, and sandwiches can be selected, and for something different, there's a bowl of cold peel-and-eat shrimp with cocktail sauce ($6.75). The children's menu has lunch and dinner items such as hamburgers ($2), peanut butter and jelly sandwiches ($1), and fried chicken ($2.25).

For gourmet dining, there is Sheppard's, the elegant French country restaurant. The atmosphere is that of a wine-country villa, and the cuisine is French and native American. A prix-fixe dinner costs $25, and other entrees start at $19 and go to $27. Definitely for special-occasion dinners for teens and up.

The Sheraton Grand's restaurant is Spencer's. Breakfast, lunch, and dinner are served in this lovely pink-tiled bayside restaurant. Steaks, chops, and seafood are emphasized, and there is an extensive wine list. Children are welcome here, and highchairs and boosters are available, but there is no children's menu. On a sunny day you can eat on the patio and enjoy a lunch of grilled country-style ribs with coleslaw and steak fries ($9). Also offered are salads, such as grilled chicken salad niçoise ($8), and sandwiches, such as the Deli Board Sandwich—roast beef, turkey, salami, corned beef, and Jack cheese ($8.50). If you prefer, you can order your meal from 24-hour room service.

The Sheraton Grand's one building is newly remodeled and features 350 rooms slightly larger than those in the Sheraton East. Although the Grand was designed with the business traveler in mind, families are welcome and feel right at home here too. Butler service is offered on the executive floors. Large suites are also found in the Sheraton Grand, with private sundecks, shuttered windows, and deluxe furnishings. The standard rooms are identical in size and furnishings, and are decorated in French Renaissance, with mauve interiors. Marble-topped dressers and mirrored wardrobe doors lend elegance. All rooms have patios or balconies. The rooms come with two queen-size beds or a king-size bed with a queen-size sofa bed. Cable TV, in-room movies, and a Servibar are standard. Refrigerators are available upon request for a $10 charge.

Although the Sheraton East consists of three buildings, it has a more informal atmosphere, a larger lobby and more amenities just steps from your door. There are 750 rooms and suites, all with patios or balconies. The color scheme is mauve, and every room features original art. You may want to request a ground-floor room in the lanai village area and keep an eye on young children as they play on the lawn.

There are some adjoining rooms. Each floor in the three high-rise buildings has a lobby area with sofas and chairs. Some rooms have mini-TVs and phones in the bathrooms. Oversize towels are standard, as is a cable color TV. Each room is furnished with two double beds or one king-size bed. Bathrooms are spacious and include the usual hotel amenities, such as lotion and shampoo in a cute basket.

Rates at the Sheraton East vary according to the floor (the first 5 floors are the least expensive, and the 9th through 12th floors the most expensive): they run $115 to $165 single and $140 to $180 double. Suites range in price from $250 to $400.

Rates at the Sheraton Grand vary by floor also: $125 to $165 single and $140 to $175 double. The 12th floor has suites ranging in price from $400 to $1,200.

In both hotels, children under 17 stay free in their parents' room; those 17 and over and additional adults each pay $15 per night. There's no charge for cribs; rollaways cost $15. Ask about seasonal specials. Parking is $6 daily.

At **Humphrey's Half Moon Inn,** 2303 Shelter Island Dr., San Diego, CA 92106 (tel. 619/224-3411, or toll free 800/542-7401), you can choose a harbor, marina, or courtyard pool view from your balcony or patio. Fresh flowers decorate the grassy areas around the heated pool and Jacuzzi, where youngsters can romp and grownups can soak up the sun. The service is friendly, and the staff makes you feel at home. Walks along the marina or through the gardens (residence to a family of ducks) are popular. There are free bicycles in all sizes, including ones for children, and a putting green and Ping-Pong tables on the grounds.

The hotel's restaurant, Humphrey's, is well known locally for its outdoor "Concerts by the Bay," held on the lawn from May through September (see the "What to See and Do" section). The restaurant is open for breakfast, lunch, and dinner, and there are a few child-appropriate selections. Prices average $7.50 at lunch, $15.50 at dinner. Boosters and highchairs are provided. Room service is also available.

Accommodations have extra cupboards and drawers for storage. The rooms were renovated in 1988 and are nicely decorated in tan and pink with wood-framed woven-straw headboards and beamed ceilings to carry out the hotel's Polynesian look. Even with two queen-size beds, the rooms have plenty of floor space for a crib or rollaway. The 23 junior suites and 7 executive suites have full kitchens. If you're planning a family reunion, you may want to ask for an executive suite, which has a living room large enough to accommodate up to 50 people for a party. All rooms have in-room coffee, complimentary newspapers, full-length mirrors, color TVs, and free 24-hour in-room movies. Refrigerators are available upon request.

The stairs to the upper floors are steep and the landings have a middle cut-out, so ask for a ground-floor room if you have young children. Babysitting can be arranged.

Rates for standard rooms vary according to location. Singles are $85 to $105; doubles, $105 to $125. Suites with kitchens can be rented for $175 to $250. Children 18 and younger stay free in their parents' room; those over 18 pay $15 per night. No charge for cribs, but rollaways cost $10. Ask about seasonal and package specials. Free parking.

The **Viscount Hotel,** 1960 Harbor Island Dr., San Diego, CA 92101 (tel. 619/291-6700), goes easy on the pocketbook. Located on Harbor Island, near downtown San Diego and the airport, the Viscount offers the panorama of the adjoining marina and the city of San Diego.

The staff loves children, and they have been known to give impromptu tours of behind-the-scenes parts of the hotel, such as the kitchen. They'll even cut up fish for bait so that kids can fish across the street in the San Diego Bay. The nearby Broadway Pier offers boat rentals. Bike rentals are available at the hotel from a private company that will deliver bicycles in all sizes. You are also near the San Diego Ferry embarkation, where for $1 you can catch a ride across the bay to Coronado. The Molly Trolley stops at the hotel for a fun ride to major attractions. Check at the front desk for schedules. The pool is inviting, but not completely fenced in, so keep a close eye on tiny explorers. Babysitting can be arranged by the front desk.

The Palm Grill is the hotel's waterfront restaurant, open for breakfast, lunch, or dinner. Breakfast is buffet style. The lunch and dinner menus are printed each day and include fresh fish specials. Children's fish and chips costs $4, and chocolate ice cream is a treat at only 95¢. Restaurant hours are 7 a.m. to 11 p.m., and room service is also delivered during these hours. The bar has a breathtaking marina view and a wide-screen TV, and children are allowed in when accompanied by an adult.

Each of the 212 rooms has a balcony or patio, and all are exactly the same shape and size (with the exception of a few suites). Rooms are clean and well maintained, with one wall of floor-to-ceiling windows. You have your choice of two queen-size beds or a queen-size bed and a sofa bed. Women will appreciate the separate vanity table and mirror. Rooms come furnished with stocked mini-bars, in-room coffee pots on a burner, and remote-control TV with SpectraVision. Refrigerators are available at no charge upon request.

Rates vary according to view and season. In summer, singles run $109 to $129; doubles, $119 to $139. In winter, singles cost $89 to $109; doubles, $99 to $119. A few suites are available, costing $375 to $475. Creative packaging is the rule here, so be sure to ask about Super Savers and special programs. Children under 12 stay free; those 12 and over and additional adults pay $10 each per night. No charge for cribs, but rollaways cost $10. Free parking.

PACIFIC BEACH: If you want to step from your room onto the beach, try the **Blue Sea Lodge,** 707 Pacific Beach Dr., San Diego, CA 92109 (tel. 619/483-4700, or toll free 800/BLUESEA). Or if you prefer the bay, you're just a block away.

There is no on-premises restaurant, but complimentary continental breakfast is served poolside, and there are at least 12 eateries within a four-block radius. The pool is heated, and there is a whirlpool. Beach access is available from the patio. Babysitting can be arranged.

The blue-and-tan rooms are outfitted with color TVs. Mirrored walls give a feeling of spaciousness, and all beds are queen- or king-size. Every room has either a private balcony or a patio fronting the beach boardwalk. Suites have a sofa bed and modern kitchenette with bar stools, and there is a bedroom, two bathrooms, and two balconies. Two-bedroom suites have three bathrooms. Adjoining rooms have a locked entryway, with separate keys to the rooms. All units have electric fans. Laundry facilities are available. Bathrooms are stocked with plush, deep-blue towels.

Standard rooms have courtyard or side views; deluxe rooms face the ocean. In summer, rooms rent for $100 to $115 single, $110 to $140 double. Suites cost $175 to $260. Room rates are $10 lower from January to mid-June and from September 15 to December 31. Children under 18 stay free in their parents' room. The extra-person charge is $15. Cribs are free, but rollaways cost $15. There's a three-night minimum stay on holidays.

The **Beach Cottages,** 4255 Ocean Blvd., San Diego, CA 92109 (tel. 619/483-7440), has been family owned and operated for 40 years and offers cottages and motel-style accommodations. It's the type of establishment that gives you the feeling you are visiting the home of close friends who go all-out for your comfort. You can play Ping-Pong and shuffleboard, build castles in the sand, take a dip in the ocean, then cook up a barbecue dinner on the patio.

In addition to beach activities, the major San Diego attractions are not far away by car. Within walking distance are shops and restaurants offering everything from fast food to gourmet waterfront dining. On the premises is a giftshop stocked with lots of Mickey Mouse items and fascinating toys. The staff will refer babysitters.

You have a wide choice of accommodations here. The newly remodeled, original 40-year-old cottages are like small detached homes with a kitchen, bedrooms, and a separate living room. A new wing of motel rooms, with microwave ovens and dishwashers, was added in 1988. And there are standard motel-type rooms. One long balcony on each floor of the motel rooms is lined with chaise longues.

Complete kitchens are available in the cottages and in some of the motel sections. Deluxe studios offer a kitchen and adjacent sleeping area. Some families make this their home away from home for a month or two annually.

A motel room with one queen-size bed is $65 in summer, $55 in winter, single or double. A deluxe studio with two queen-size beds and a kitchen is $90 in summer, $65 in winter, for up to four people. A one-bedroom oceanfront cottage is $120 in summer, $80 in winter, for up to four people. A two-bedroom cottage is $140 in summer, $95 in winter, for up to six people. Each extra person costs $7. Cribs and rollaways are $5. Free parking. Because of the popular location of the cottages, you will want to make reservations well in advance.

OLD TOWN: The **Villas Chapultepec,** 4002 Ampudia St., San Diego, CA 92110 (tel. 619/295-6703), offers an alternative form of accommodations, and is especially nice for long visits. These 17 villas, built on a hillside in Old Town overlooking the city and bay, were originally planned as luxury condominiums, and they offer all the comforts of a spacious, modern home. "Privacy" and "quiet" are passwords here, though you are only a block from Old Town's colorful restaurants and shops.

The grounds are terraced, and wood decks built around the lush greenery connect the units. A "hillevator," a glass-enclosed hillside elevator, delivers you to upper-level units. There is a large fenced-in heated pool and a Jacuzzi separated from the pool. Guests have the use of a free tennis and indoor soccer facility only ten minutes away. Babysitting can be arranged.

The two-story villas range in size from 1,600 to 2,000 square feet. All have balconies and decks with breathtaking views of the city. The units are individually decorated (the mauve-and-gray interior design is especially lovely) and feature cathedral ceilings and fireplaces. Kitchens are fully equipped with microwave ovens, Jenn-Air stove tops, dishwashers, trash compactors, small appliances, and utensils. Each unit has its own washer and dryer. Biweekly maid service is included. There are two remote-control color TVs with HBO and cable in every villa, and private phone lines with free local calls are included in the rental price.

The villas come in 14 different layouts. Twelve of them have two bedrooms and 2½ baths and sleep up to six people comfortably. The five deluxe units feature a lawn and fountain, a wet bar, a fireplace in the master bedroom, and a Jacuzzi in the master bath. And the master bathrooms have both a tub and a glassed-in shower. A three-bedroom villa is also available.

Up to six people may stay in a villa for the same price. The 12 standard units rent for $150 per night in summer and on holidays, dropping to $135 per night in low season. The four deluxe two-bedroom units let for $175, and the deluxe three-bedroom unit costs $195, year round. An extra person in any accommodation pays $10 per night. Cribs are available at no charge.

There are special weekly rates in summer: $900 ($2,700 monthly) for the 12 standard units, $1,050 ($3,150 monthly) for the four deluxe two-bedroom units, and $1,110 ($3,510 monthly) for the deluxe three-bedroom unit. Free underground parking.

The **Hacienda Hotel Old Town,** 4041 Harney St., San Diego, CA 92110 (tel. 619/298-4707, or toll free 800/528-1234), combines the charm of the old-world hacienda lifestyle with all the modern amenities. Located in the center of Old Town, this new hotel is fashioned after the rambling old ranches that once occupied this area.

The red-roofed white stucco hotel is made up of 150 suites, each unique in design. It is built on a hill away from busy streets, giving guests privacy and quiet, but is within walking distance of Bazaar del Mundo. There are spacious patio areas on several levels, with tiled fountains and plenty of room to relax and soak up the sun. Walk to Old Town or Heritage Park, or take the Molly Trolley to the sightseeing attractions. Videotapes and board games are available at the front desk if your youngsters become restless.

A buffet breakfast is served in the hotel's El Pueblo Café. For dinner, try the Acapulco Restaurant, located at the top of the hotel's property, with a beautiful vista of San Diego and the bay. The hotel also provides gas barbecue grills near the pool for guest use, and offers room service as well. There are children's menus in both restaurants, and room service offers kids' portions too.

All accommodations here are suites, each with a parlor and sleeping area. The rooms are decorated with Santa Fe–style furnishings, and there are ceiling fans, shutters, and mirrored wardrobe doors. Refrigerators, microwaves, and coffee makers are provided in each suite, as are VCRs with one complimentary videotape of your choice. Each room has double sinks. Some have private balconies; others open onto the courtyard. Every suite has a sofa bed, and bedrooms contain one or two queen-size beds. These suites can sleep three or five people, depending on which layout you choose, and there are a few connecting rooms for larger families.

In winter, accommodations rent for $85 to $95 single and $95 to $105 double. In summer (June through August), rates are slightly higher ($10 per night). Children under 16 stay free in their parents' room, but those 16 and over and additional adults pay $10 each per night. Cribs are free, but rollaways cost $10. Ask about seasonal and promotional packages. There is covered off-street parking.

Built on the site of the Gila House Hotel (one of Old Town's grandest structures from the 1850s), the **Ramada Inn Old Town,** 2435 Jefferson St., San Diego, CA 92110 (tel. 619/260-8500, or toll free 800/272-6232), is a modern version of Old Southwest charm. The exterior has the look of an elegant hacienda, and the lobby and rooms are decorated in adobe and tans with blue accents. The effect is restful and welcoming.

Although the hotel is off the beaten path of Old Town by just a block or two, you can take advantage of Old Town's shops and restaurants. Within a ten-minute drive are Sea World, the San Diego Zoo, downtown, and the beaches.

The fenced-in pool is small but lovely, and there is a Jacuzzi. The Café Ramada provides poolside service and is open for breakfast, lunch, and dinner. Children's selections are plentiful and average around $3. Restaurant hours are 6 a.m. to 11 p.m., and room service is also available during these hours. Babysitting can be arranged by the front desk.

Each of the 152 clean and well-maintained rooms and suites has its own entryway area, giving them a different effect from the usual hotel hallway. You can choose a unit with two queen-size beds, a queen-size bed and a twin sofa bed, or a king-size bed and a double sofa bed, ideal for giving families maximum living space. All rooms are decorated with matching Indian-design bedspreads and drapes. Attractive armoires house the remote-control TV and in-room movies. VCRs are available for rent. Bathrooms have tubs, and there are separate vanities. Some refrigerators are available, and coin-operated laundry facilities can be found on each floor.

Rates are the same for single or double occupancy. Standard rooms rent for $65 to $85 in summer, $55 to $75 in winter. The 14 different styles of suites range in price from $75 to $150. Children under 18 stay free in their parents' room; those 18 and over and additional adults pay $10 each per night. There is no charge for cribs, but rollaways cost $10. Free covered parking. Call the toll-free number for information on the hotel's four-for-one family plan.

HOTEL CIRCLE / MISSION VALLEY: Tucked into a curve of San Diego's

Hotel Circle, the **Seven Seas Lodge,** 411 Hotel Circle South, San Diego, CA 92108 (tel. 619/291-1300, or toll free 800/421-6662), will surprise you with its park-like lawn areas and heated patio pool. The grounds even include a playground with a slide and seesaws, and a video game room. Two Jacuzzis are available (for adults only).

The hotel staff can arrange transportation to and from the airport. Once here, you are just minutes away from the popular attractions of San Diego.

The lodge's cozy coffeeshop opens at 7:30 a.m. and serves breakfast until 2:30 p.m. Lunch and dinner are served from 11 a.m. to 10 p.m. Sandwiches average $4.50; full entrees cost about $6. Room service is delivered from 7 a.m. to 9:30 p.m. For a more formal dinner, try the Pen & Pun Restaurant, open at 5 p.m. daily. Dinners here range from $6 to $17. The children's menu, for kids 12 and under, includes spaghetti, chicken, soup and sandwich, and a junior hamburger, with prices ranging from $2 to $2.50.

Rooms are pleasant and spacious enough for a crib or rollaway. Many of the units open onto the lawn areas, allowing you to relax in your room while you keep an eye on the youngsters playing on the lawn. Dressing areas and vanities are separate from the bathrooms, and all bathrooms have a tub/shower combination. Besides the standard rooms, the lodge has two suites and three waterbeds. Refrigerators are available upon request at no extra charge. Cable TV, in-room movies, courtesy coffee, free local telephone calls, and coin-operated laundry facilities are additional comforts.

In summer rooms rent for $56 single, $64 double. Off-season rates are $2 lower per room. The large suite has a patio and is available for $165. Children under 12 stay free in their parents' room. Those 12 and over and additional adults pay $8 each per night. There is no charge for cribs, but rollaways cost $8. Parking is free in the hotel lot. Ask about the two-night package, which includes tickets to Sea World and the San Diego Zoo.

For those who would rather spend their money on dining and sightseeing than on luxurious accommodations, the **Circle 8,** 543 Hotel Circle South, San Diego, CA 92108 (tel. 619/297-8800, or toll free 800/345-9995), is a good choice. The rooms are clean and attractive, and the motel has a heated fenced-in pool and a heated therapy pool.

The Pam Pam coffeeshop serves breakfast until 2 p.m., and dinner starts at 4 p.m. Sandwiches are the specialty; snacks are also available. The menu includes children's-size sandwiches (grilled cheese or peanut butter and jelly) for $1.50. No room service.

Rooms are furnished with two queen-size beds or one king-size bed. All rooms have mini-refrigerators; some have kitchenettes. All the accommodations have tub/shower combinations, and you can request a room with a separate vanity. One building is newer (and slightly higher in price) and can be requested. Cable TV and HBO, coin-operated laundry facilities, and free local phone calls are standard.

Standard rooms cost $49.50, single or double. In July and August the price goes up $10. Rooms with kitchenettes are $59, $10 higher in July and August. Rates in the new building are slightly higher. Children under 17 stay free in their parents' room; those 17 and over and additional adults pay $10 each per night. Cribs are free, but rollaways cost $10. Weekly and monthly rates are available. Free parking.

You'll find it hard to believe that such comfortable accommodations and amenities can be as low priced as they are at the **Budget Motel of America** in Mission Valley, 641 Camino del Rio South, San Diego, CA 92108 (tel. 619/295-6886, or toll free 800/624-1257).

Complimentary continental breakfast is provided, and lunch and dinner room service is available from the moderately priced TGI Friday's nearby. Three restaurants are close by for lunch and dinner, and a Denny's restaurant is within walking distance.

The Molly Trolley stops here regularly to take guests to Sea World, the San Diego Zoo, and Old Town. Grey Line tours and car rentals can be arranged. There is no pool, but the beaches are about 15 minutes away by car.

The hotel lobby has videotapes available for guest use in the deluxe rooms, complete with complimentary popcorn. Youngsters will also love the array of pinball machines.

A nice feature for those with small children is that all rooms open onto a carpeted walkway rather than directly onto the parking lot.

Rooms are newly redecorated, clean and well maintained, and all have queen-size beds. A special luxury is Eurobath soap in the tub. In fact, the word "budget" applies only to the price. Deluxe rooms come with a choice of two beds, or a bed and a sofa bed, which would give you more floor space and play area for young children. Deluxe accommodations also have VCRs and refrigerators. Some adjoining rooms are available. Standard rooms cost $30 single, $35 to $45 double. Deluxe rooms are $35 single, $39 to $49 double. Children under 12 stay free in their parents' rooms. No charge for cribs or rollaways. There's a three-night minimum stay on holidays. Free parking. Call for special packages and rates.

DOWNTOWN: The **Best Western Columbia,** 555 W. Ash, San Diego, CA 92101 (tel. 619/233-7500, or toll free 800/528-1234, 800/341-1818 in California), is conveniently located at the hub of San Diego's tourist activities and is within walking distance of the San Diego Trolley and the Convention and Performing Arts Center.

Breakfast is served from 6:30 a.m. in the Tatler restaurant. Lunch begins at 11:30 a.m. Sandwiches and salads (both about $5) are served, and entrees include several chicken items ($7) and a vegetarian stir-fry ($6). Dinner is served from 5 p.m. and adds steak and red snapper to the lunch menu. "Children's Corner" items are served at lunch and dinner (a B.L.T. is $4.50; golden fried prawns are $7). Room service is available during regular restaurant hours.

The contemporary rooms have a view of either the harbor or downtown. Rooms typically come with one or two queen-size beds, but a few rooms with king-size beds are available. Ask for the king-bedded rooms if you desire lots of living space. Units are nicely decorated with matching floral bedspreads and drapes. Bathrooms are small but adequate. One side of the hotel looks out onto the bay, the other onto downtown San Diego, and either view can fascinate you for hours. But if you are traveling with a toddler, you may want to ask for the first floor and forgo the upper-floor rooms, which all have balconies. The hotel has a pool.

Summer rates (July to September) are $73 for a single, $83 to $87 for a double. In winter, singles cost $63; doubles, $71 to $75. A room with a harbor view is $6 extra anytime. Children under 12 stay free in their parents' room; those 12 and over are charged $7 per night in summer, $6 in winter. Cribs are $6; no rollaways available. Full-summer, weekly, and monthly rates are available. Free covered parking.

A LITTLE FAR AWAY BUT WORTH IT: For those who enjoy the sporting life, the **Rancho Bernardo Inn,** 17550 Bernardo Oaks Dr., San Diego, CA 92128 (tel. 619/487-1611), is a paradise. The inn is located 30 miles from San Diego near the Wild Animal Park. Set amid rolling green hills on 155 acres of a former California ranch, this golf and tennis retreat offers all you would expect from a contemporary luxury resort in an atmosphere of plush early California. Antique tables, chairs, and chests furnish the spacious lobby, and the rough-hewn beamed ceiling and area rugs add warmth and character.

Famed for its tennis camp and golf courses, the inn also has two swimming pools, a Jacuzzi, volleyball, badminton, and Ping-Pong. The lobby's music room includes a great jigsaw-puzzle table. Children will enjoy the Spanish fountains that decorate the grounds. Take them to the charming wishing well at the end of the lobby walkway.

Family-oriented activities are held at the inn during Christmas holidays, Easter week, and the month of August.

Every December the inn celebrates with a Holiday Festival Program, which includes a Children's Holiday Camp for kids aged 4 to 17. Young guests play miniature golf and tennis, swim, construct kites, go on scavenger hunts, and make ice cream.

Similar programs are held for children of the same age group during Easter week and throughout August. Summer programs add seasonal activities such as cookouts, campfires, and luaus. Sports activities include swimming, soccer, basketball, hockey, softball, and track meets. A Saturday Cartoon Breakfast (breakfast and cartoons) is offered, along with field trips, carnivals, and movies. Youngsters can participate in any or all of the activities. For teenagers, the programs are structured to meet individual interests.

All these children's programs are free to guests, except for optional meals. Activities vary daily and run from 9 a.m. to 9 p.m. When you want to take the kids sightseeing in San Diego, rental cars are available on the premises.

A Tennis College is held at the inn with packages ranging from two to five days, and the rate includes instruction, accommodations, meals, and social activities. The cost varies with the length of your stay and the time of year.

You may choose the Family Tennis College, held in two- and four-day sessions during August, either on Saturday and Sunday or on Monday and Tuesday. The cost is $75 per day for adult and child, and $35 per day for each additional adult or child.

The Golf Holiday Package includes your room, greens fees, dinner on arrival day, breakfast and dinner other days, and breakfast on departure day. Junior golf camps are available for the younger set. Call for dates and details.

Parents will enjoy dining at the gourmet restaurant, El Bizcocho. Here elegant French cuisine is served as patrons take in the panoramic view of the golf course. The wine list features more than 700 selections. The restaurant is open daily for dinner, and on Sunday for brunch. Jackets required for gentlemen.

The less formal Veranda Room is open for breakfast, lunch, and dinner and is suited for families. Seating is indoors or outdoors overlooking the golf course. Mission-style arches and turn-of-the-century furniture set the early-California atmosphere. Toddlers will enjoy sitting on the oversize pillows that serve as booster seats. This is the place for a lazy breakfast on a sunny morning. Wake up with a Sunrise Apple—a spiced apple baked with walnuts and raisins in cream ($3). Then fill up on Swedish pancakes and maple syrup ($4). Or if you're really hungry, there's the Grand Slam—two eggs, potatoes, toast, and a six-ounce filet ($11). For lunch you can enjoy sandwiches such as the Don Diego Hamburger (a burger topped with guacamole and sour cream, for $7), salads such as the Escondido Special (an avocado half stuffed with crab and shrimp, for $9), or fresh scallops provençal ($10.50). Seafood, veal, prime rib, and chicken are served for dinner. Highchairs are available. Ask for children's food items not included with the printed menu. The little ones are sure to enjoy a rich scoop of Häagen-Dazs ice cream for dessert ($2.50). This restaurant also provides 24-hour room service.

A recent addition to the hotel brings the room total to 287. Accommodations come in a variety of shapes and sizes, all with patios or balconies. Pots of plants and colorful flowers will make you feel welcome. Earth tones and heavy wood furniture carry out the early-California theme. The rooms are all spacious enough for a crib or rollaway. Large closets and a wooden vanity are standard.

Upper-floor rooms have beamed ceilings. A room with two queen-size beds will give you a separate vanity. Parlor suites have a sofa bed in the living area and come with two bathrooms and a large closet. Remote-control TV, Servibars, and hairdryers are standard amenities, along with evening turn-down service.

Summer rates for standard rooms are $115 to $135, single or double. October through March, rates range from $145 to $185. Executive suites rent for $140 to $205, one- and two-bedroom suites cost $210 to $445, and the two VIP suites are $600 and up. The rates for suites remain the same year round. Children 12 and under stay free in their parents' room. The extra-person charge is $10. There is no charge for cribs; no rollaways available. Free parking.

CAMPING: Campsites in the area are numerous and the terrain is varied—from mountains to desert to beaches to city. Contact the following places for specific information on campsites:

For Local Camping in County Parks
Write or call the **San Diego County Department of Parks and Recreation,** 5201 Ruffin Rd., Suite P, San Diego, CA 92123 (tel. 619/565-5928 for information, 619/565-3600 for reservations). Reservations are not required but are recommended.

For State Parks
Make reservations through **MISTIX** (tel. toll free 800/446-7275).

For information on specific campsites, contact the **Old Town State Historic Park Visitor Information Center,** 2645 San Diego Ave., San Diego, CA 92110 (tel. 619/237-6770).

For information about beach camping, try the **San Diego Coast Area,** 2680 Carlsbad Blvd., Carlsbad, CA 92008 (tel. 619/729-8947).

For mountain camping information, contact the **Montane Area,** Cuyamaca Rancho State Park, 12551 Calif. 79, Descanso, CA 92016 (tel. 619/765-0755).

For desert camping, the contact is the **Anza-Borrego Desert State Park,** P.O. Box 428, Borrego Springs, CA 92004 (tel. 619/767-5311).

For Camping in the National Forest
Campsites are available on a first-come, first-served basis in the Cleveland National Forest. Contact the **United States Forest Service,** Cleveland National Forest Headquarters, 880 Front St., Room 5-N-14, San Diego, CA 92188 (tel. 619/293-5050); the Palomar Ranger District, 332 S. Juniper, Suite 100, Escondido, CA 92025 (tel. 619/745-2421); or the Descanso Ranger District, 3348 Alpine Blvd., Alpine, CA 92001 (tel. 619/445-6235).

4. WHERE TO EAT
San Diego is full of restaurants that are suitable for families with children of various ages. Don't forget to check the La Jolla dining section also, as those restaurants are only about 15 minutes away from downtown San Diego.

MISSION BAY / MISSION BEACH: The trademark of the **Salmon House,** 1970 Quivira Way, Marina Village (tel. 619/223-2234), is alderwood cooking, a Northwest Indian method of slowly smoking fresh fish over an open alderwood pit. As you savor the moist seafood dishes, you'll also enjoy the superb view of Mission Bay and the adjacent marina.

Youngsters will get a kick out of the giant Northwest Indian totem poles and the large, brightly colored paintings of fish.

Sunday brunch is the local favorite. With the amazing variety of foods offered, each family member is sure to find something to please his or her palate.

Selections include a salad bar, omelets, tacos, crêpes, Italian sausage, smoked salmon, bay shrimp, ham, roast beef, turkey, and ribs, plus pastries and desserts. Brunch costs $13 for adults, $7 for children.

For dinner during the week, try the house specialty of alderwood-broiled salmon (price varies daily) or the seafood brochette (broiled shrimp, scallops, fresh fish, peppers, onions, mushrooms, and tomatoes, for $15). The children's version of the salmon dinner, including salad and french fries, costs $6. Or kids can choose from chicken drumsticks, prime rib, shrimp, or fish and chips for $4 to $7. The children's menu comes with crayons for coloring, and kids are given unlimited refills on soft drinks.

Booster seats and highchairs are provided, and the servers will gladly warm baby bottles and baby food in the kitchen. Special children's drinks can be ordered from the bar.

Salmon House is open for lunch Monday through Saturday from 11:30 a.m. to 3 p.m., and for dinner Monday through Thursday from 4:30 to 10 p.m., and on Friday and Saturday till 11 p.m. Sunday brunch is served from 10 a.m. to 3 p.m. Reservations are accepted. Parking nearby. Major credit cards welcome.

HARBOR ISLAND: Once Coast Guard Beacon No. 9, **Tom Ham's Lighthouse,** 2150 Harbor Island Dr. (tel. 619/291-9100), sits on the picturesque point of Harbor Island with water on three sides. The panoramic view is beautiful after dark, and you may want to time your dinner so that you can watch the sun set over the bay. The children will be pleasantly surprised to discover that the restaurant is also a museum. The whole family will enjoy the framed ship's charts and other seagoing artifacts that decorate the restaurant.

The delicious lunch buffet is served from a large rowboat and includes salads and tasty enchiladas. Seafood entrees include lobster and scampi, and beef is also a specialty. The daily lunch buffet costs $6.50. Be sure to sample the tasty enchiladas, and take generous helpings of the various salads. Or you can order sandwiches, salads, and such house specialties as fried shrimp and salmon. À la carte lunch items run $4.75 to $10.

Dinners are pricey and range from $13.50 for halibut to $29 for twin lobster tails. Several beef and seafood combinations are available, such as medallion of beef and shrimp diablo for $20. Baked potatoes come with most entrees, as does a vinaigrette salad with bay shrimp. Carne asada is another specialty, made with choice cuts of tenderloin of beef. A children's dinner menu is available for kids under 12, with prices from $4.50 to $8 for fried shrimp, prime rib, sirloin steak, or a Mexican dinner of enchiladas and rice.

Booster seats and highchairs are provided. The servers will warm baby bottles and baby food in the kitchen, and Shirley Temples and other children's drinks can be ordered from the bar.

Lunch is served Monday through Friday from 11:15 a.m. to 3:30 p.m. (the buffet closes at 2:30 p.m.); the Sunday buffet hours are 10 a.m. to 2 p.m. Dinner is available Monday through Friday from 5 to 10:30 p.m., on Saturday till 11 p.m., and on Sunday from 4 to 10:30 p.m. No lunch is served on Saturday. Reservations are recommended. Free parking nearby. Major credit cards are honored.

At **The Boathouse,** 2040 Harbor Island Dr. (tel. 619/291-8010), you can relax in the nautical atmosphere and watch the catamarans and yachts sail against the backdrop of the downtown skyline and the Coronado Bay Bridge. There's a view from almost every table. The nautical theme is carried out in the gleaming brass chandeliers and the ship's bell and portholes. You will find the atmosphere elegant yet casual, suitable for either an intimate celebration or a family dinner.

Fresh fish is served daily and includes such selections as char-broiled mahi-mahi in a fresh rosemary, thyme, and macadamia-nut butter ($15), and fresh Alaskan halibut with mint butter ($16). Prime rib and steak ($11 to $15) are other popular choices. The lunch menu features mahi-mahi and sea bass (both $8), and sandwiches such as the half-pound deli burger ($5.50). Fresh fish lunches start at $7.

A children's menu is available at dinner, but you'll have to ask for it. Children 14 and under can choose from chicken, shrimp, fish and chips, and hamburgers (each about $6). We often forget about our diets and order the chocolate-chip cheesecake pie for dessert.

The Boathouse is open for lunch Monday through Saturday from 11:30 a.m. to 2:30 p.m., and for dinner Monday through Thursday from 5:30 to 10:30 p.m., on Friday and Saturday from 5 to 11 p.m., and on Sunday from 5:30 to 11 p.m. Sunday brunch is offered from 10 a.m. to 2:30 p.m. Highchairs and boosters are provided. Reservations are recommended. Free parking. Major credit cards are welcome.

The Boathouse also has branches in Encinitas, La Mesa, and Pacific Beach.

Dining on a floating riverboat may be a treat your family has yet to experience. The **Reuben E. Lee Showboat,** 880 E. Harbor Island Dr. (tel. 619/291-1974), is anchored in the San Diego Bay at the foot of Harbor Island.

This floating restaurant reflects the charm of the old sternwheelers, both inside and out. The sailor-blue-and-gold décor of the top deck conveys the opulence of the days when the wealthy would pamper themselves with a leisurely cruise down the Mississippi on just such a riverboat.

As you might expect, seafood is the specialty here, but they also offer beef dishes. A dinner of crispy fried shrimp comes with green salad, fresh vegetables, and potatoes for $15. A prime rib dinner costs $13.75. For lunch, the shrimp is served with your choice of fresh fruit or french fries for $8.25. Salads and sandwiches are also available at lunch.

The children's menu features Injun Joe's grilled cheese and Huckleberry Finn's fried shrimp, each $4.50. If you bring crayons for them, your young Hucks and Beckys can keep busy coloring the menu while their food is being prepared.

Sunday brunch includes waffles, omelets, pasta, salads, seafood, carved beef, fresh breads, and dessert. Brunch costs $17 for adults, $7 for children.

Boosters and highchairs are provided. The servers will warm baby bottles and baby food in the kitchen, and special children's drinks can be ordered from the bar.

The *Reuben E. Lee* is open Monday through Saturday from 11:30 a.m. On weekdays it stops serving at 10 p.m., on weekends at 11 p.m. Sunday brunch is served from 10 a.m. to 3 p.m. Hours may be extended in the summer. Reservations are recommended. Parking nearby. Major credit cards are accepted.

PACIFIC BEACH: The **Tony Roma's** branch in Pacific Beach, at 4110 Mission Blvd. (tel. 619/272-7427), is a nice large establishment perfect for all age groups. Any day or night, kids automatically get crayons and something to color as soon as they sit down. If you bring them here Friday through Sunday, they'll enjoy the entertainer who creates balloon animals and figures for all the children. Once they get down to business, kids can order off their own menu. Choices include chicken fingers, hamburgers, ribs, or barbecued chicken, each served in a basket with french fries and coleslaw (from $3 to $5). Fun drinks include a Peanut Colada (coconut, pineapple juice, and cream), a Funkey Monkey (cranberry, orange, and pineapple juices with lemon-lime soda), or a Trapeze Freeze (a slush).

Adults can order Tony Roma's great ribs, barbecued chicken, or a burger. There are also nightly specials. Dinner prices range from $5 to $12.

Highchairs and booster seats are provided.

The restaurant is open daily from 11 a.m. to 10:30 p.m. No reservations are accepted. Weekend nights are the busiest, so come early; on weeknights there is usually no wait. There is validated parking in the underground garage. Major credit cards are welcome.

The Spice Rack, 4315 Mission Blvd. (tel. 619/483-7666), is known by locals for its fine food and baked goods. It's a perfect spot for visitors to enjoy a casual breakfast, lunch, or dinner. Children are welcome in this informal, friendly atmosphere. A gazebo ceiling adds charm to the décor, and the location is ideal—a block from the beach. Patio dining is also available.

Yummy breads and pastries are baked from preservative-free ingredients. The continental breakfast basket includes a cinnamon roll, banana bread, and a muffin, along with fresh fruit, for $4. For a heartier breakfast, try the mushroom omelet made with 16 ounces(!) of eggs ($6).

The Sunshine Frosty (ice cream and orange juice) and the Strawberry Shrub (strawberries, ice cream, and milk), each at $3, make great afternoon treats.

Great service and good seafood are the specialties here. Live Maine lobster is a popular dinner selection (market price). Fresh fish Vera Cruz with potatoes or fresh fruit is $8 at lunch and $9.50 at dinner, with a basket of bread and a salad.

The children's menu (for kids under 10) has items such as spaghetti, hamburgers, and chicken, served with fresh fruit or french fries and a beverage for $5.

Boosters and highchairs are provided. Baby bottles and baby food can be warmed in the kitchen, and children's drinks can be ordered from the bar.

The Spice Rack is open daily from 8 a.m. to 9:30 p.m. (or as long as there are customers). No reservations are accepted. Expect a wait, especially on weekends. Free parking. Some credit cards are honored.

For a hearty, inexpensively priced breakfast, try **Café Broken Yolk,** 1851 Garnet St. (tel. 619/270-0045). A step up from a coffeeshop, this cute, bright, casual restaurant draws an eclectic Pacific Beach crowd. The breakfast specialty is omelets, and there are 26 varieties listed, or you can custom-order one made to your taste. Besides traditional choices, there are lots of vegetarian and Mexican omelets. You can split these large portions at no extra charge. You'll also find banana, blueberry, and buttermilk pancakes, plus waffles, biscuits and gravy, quiche, eggs, and many side dishes. Breakfast prices range from $2 to $6.

For lunch, choose from ten different hamburgers, five variations of a grilled-cheese sandwich, or four types of B.L.T.s. There are also other sandwiches and salads. Prices average $4.

Boosters and highchairs are available. The servers will split orders and warm baby food and bottles in the kitchen.

Open daily except Christmas and Thanksgiving from 6 a.m. to 3 p.m. No reservations are accepted, and the usual weekend wait is 10 to 15 minutes. There is parking on the street and in the lot out back. Major credit cards are welcome.

There are other Café Broken Yolk branches at 3350 Sports Arena, Point Loma (tel. 619/226-0442), and at 634 Pearl, in La Jolla (tel. 619/454-2500).

OCEAN BEACH: For a special night out, you might try **Qwiig's Bar & Grill,** 5083 Santa Monica Ave. (tel. 619/222-1101). Across the street from the beach, this is a wonderful place to go to watch the sunset. But tables are hard to get at that time. Because dinners are on the expensive side and there's no children's menu, you might want to bring only older children (although our 4-year-old loved it and felt very grownup in the upholstered chairs, looking out the big windows and being treated to a full shrimp dinner).

Lunch, which comes with soup or salad and rice or french fries, includes a choice of the catch of the day, fish and chips, steak, chicken, a hamburger, or roast beef, barbecued beef, or chicken sandwiches. There are also several salads. Lunch prices range from $6 to $8.

At dinner, when the restaurant gets the most families, your choices include seafood brochette, batter-fried shrimp, cioppino, crab, lobster, fish and chips, sirloin, prime rib, chicken, and such combinations as prime rib and King crab, sirloin and teriyaki chicken, and prime rib or sirloin with lobster—and there's even one hamburger. There are also pasta dishes and a large selection of appetizers and vegetables. Dinner prices range from $7 to $22.

Dishes can be split at no charge, and they will "slice and dice" whatever you want for the kids. Sassy seats and boosters are available. Special kiddie drinks can be created at the bar.

Open for lunch Monday through Friday from 11:30 a.m. to 2:30 p.m. Dinner is served nightly from 5:30 to 10:30 p.m. Sunday brunch hours are 10 a.m. to 2:30 p.m. Although reservations are taken, only three are accepted per half hour. In summer, the wait after 6:30 p.m. can be 1 to 1½ hours. In winter, the best time to come without a reservation is at 5:30 p.m. Underground or street parking. Major credit cards accepted.

EMBARCADERO / SEAPORT VILLAGE: Anthony's Fish Grotto, 1360

N. Harbor Dr. (tel. 619/232-5103), is one of those places where prices are terrific, food is good, and the view is wonderful. But the wait is very long. This is strictly a seafood restaurant, and, surprisingly, it is almost completely filled with families in the earlier hours.

Because it's perched over the water, our kids love to watch the boats, airplanes, and ocean liners (when we're lucky) as they parade past the large glass windows.

Lunch choices off the regular menu include seafood salads, fried shrimp and fried clams, and such sandwiches as grilled crab and cheese, shrimp salad, and tuna and cheese. Lunch prices range from $3.75 to $11 (abalone sandwich). At dinner, some of the selections are Hawaiian tuna, trout, mahi-mahi, and albacore. Those prices start at $6.75 and go to $22 for abalone steak.

The children's menu has a number of choices. There's grilled cheese, fish and chips (one piece), Pacific red snapper, shrimp, a half tuna and cheese sandwich, fried clam strips, and halibut. These selections range from $2.50 to $6.25 and come with salad or coleslaw and french fries.

Highchairs and boosters are provided. Says the management, "We do everything to make it convenient for our customers to come here." They'll bring crackers to the table for little ones, and the children's menu is a dot-to-dot game. They'll split adult portions, warm baby bottles and food, and make special children's drinks.

Open daily except major holidays from 11:30 a.m. to 8:30 p.m. No reservations are accepted. Street parking. Some major credit cards are honored.

Other branches: Anthony's is an institution in the San Diego area. Three of the locations are within yards of each other; the fourth is in La Jolla. **Anthony's Harborside** (which serves chicken and steak as well as fish, and takes reservations) is located at 1355 N. Harbor Dr. (tel. 619/232-6358). **Anthony's Star of the Sea Room** (coat and tie required) is at 1360 N. Harbor Dr. (tel. 619/232-7408). **Anthony's of La Jolla** is at 412 La Jolla Village Dr. (tel. 619/457-5008).

The **San Diego Pier Café**, 885 W. Harbor Dr., Seaport Village (tel. 619/239-3968), attracts lots of families. And no wonder. Situated on its own pier, with wood-planked floors and a great view, it's a comfortable, casual spot for breakfast, lunch, or dinner. Children have their own menu at lunch and dinner, which features fish and chips, chicken and chips, grilled cheese, or cheeseburgers (each $4). It's the same menu at dinner, but the price goes up $1.

Adult selections consist of lots of seafood entrees, such as mixed seafood fry, shrimp brochette, scampi, baked stuffed shrimp, and fried clams. All entrees come with sourdough bread and vegetables and start at $6.75 and go up to $11. Dinner has a lot of the same entrees plus fettuccine and top sirloin. Dinner prices range from $8 to $11.

All breakfasts come with a bowl of fresh fruit and a muffin, so toddlers can nibble on yours. Or there are pancakes, omelets, and waffles, with prices averaging $4.25.

Boosters and highchairs are available.

Open weekdays from 7 a.m. to 9:30 p.m., weekends till 10:30 p.m. No reservations are accepted. In the summer, the wait can be up to 1 or 1½ hours. Come before 7 p.m. to avoid the lines, or put your name on the waiting list and walk around the village. Parking in the village lot. Major credit cards welcome.

OLD TOWN AREA: In Bazaar del Mundo, **Lino's Restaurant,** 2754 Calhoun St. (tel. 619/299-7124), is one of our favorite Italian restaurants. We prefer the outdoor patio (or an indoor table near the patio), where the kids can watch the passersby and the activity of the bazaar. In fact, we'll put in our orders and then take the kids for a look around the little toy store across the way. By the time we get back to our table, the food is almost there, and the kids enjoy the fresh bread while they spend the few extra minutes poring over their newest coloring books or wind-up gadgets.

Family-oriented, the restaurant has children's portions of lasagne and spaghetti from $3 to $4. Pizzas are always a favorite, and range from $8.25 to $10.50. For lunch, adults choose from lasagne, spaghetti, spaghetti and meatballs, pasta primavera, and the like. À la carte prices run $3.50 to $4.25. The full luncheon includes minestrone soup or salad. Dinners include soup or salad as well as bread. In addition to traditional Italian favorites, we like the Triple Special, which has cannelloni, green fettuccine, and lasagne for $8.50. Prices range upward to $13 for veal delicacies.

Highchairs and boosters are available. The bar will whip up children's nonalcoholic drinks, and your server will split adult portions, warm baby bottles or baby food, and bring bread, crackers and soup, or salad before the meal.

Lino's is open daily for lunch from 11 a.m. to 4 p.m., and for dinner from 5 to 10 p.m. From 4 to 5 p.m. they serve from a limited menu of pasta and pizza. Reservations are accepted only for 6, 7:30, and 9 p.m.; otherwise, we were told, reservations are unnecessary, but expect a wait of 15 minutes or so if many diners arrive at once. We found 5 p.m. a good time to come with kids. Parking is easy in a nearby lot. Most major credit cards are accepted.

The **Guadalajara Grill,** 4105 Taylor St. (tel. 619/295-5111), sister of the Tijuana restaurant of the same name, is a newly remodeled eating establishment in Old Town that offers Mexican food with a difference. Recipes are from the southern part of Mexico and require more ingredients and more complicated preparation than dishes from farther north.

Extra care has also been given to the renovation of the building. A hand-painted mural lines one wall, and colorful plates and trays, along with stained-glass windows, liven the neutrals of the tile floors and adobe walls. A patio has recently been completed for outdoor dining. You can begin your meal with an appetizer combo of guacamole, tamale, taco pibil (pork and a red sauce), chalupa, zucchini quesadilla, and cheese quesadilla ($3.75 per person).

A sizzling grill is brought to your table when you order chicken, beef, or shrimp fajitas. The meal includes soup or salad and costs $8 to $9. There's a special Mexican combination plate—tamales filled with chicken and green sauce, quesadilla, chile relleno, burrito, chalupa, rice, and beans—for $8. Complimentary taco chips are served with all meals.

For children, the chef will prepare cheese quesadillas or split adult portions, though no children's menu is available.

Boosters and highchairs are provided. They will warm baby bottles and baby food in the kitchen. Special children's drinks can be ordered from the bar.

Guadalajara Grill is open daily from 11 a.m. to 10:30 p.m. Reservations are accepted. Parking lot nearby. Major credit cards are honored.

Hamburguesa Restaurant & Cantina is a bustling, noisy restaurant in the

Bazaar del Mundo at 4016 Wallace St. (tel. 619/295-0584). Our kids love it. Decorated in typical south-of-the-border décor, there's always something to draw their attention, whether it's their neighbors at tables close by, lots of color and action, or all the decorations. Children 12 and under can have a taco plate with rice and beans, a cheese enchilada, quesadilla, el cheese dog (not hard to figure out—but this one is topped with chili and chopped onions), or a little hamburger (all cost $2.50). And what a relief—for a change, kid-size milk and soft drinks can be ordered for 40¢.

The rest of the family can have all sorts of salads or soups, enchiladas, tacos, burritos, chimichangas, à la carte and combination dinners, house specialties such as chile poblano, and other favorites such as fajitas, carnitas, and carne asada. There are 17 different hamburgers to choose from (thus the name of the restaurant), and lots of baked-potato concoctions. Desserts are more than just flan and include a junior hot-fudge sundae at $1.75. Menu items run $4.25 to $8 (à la carte is less).

The Sunday breakfast extravaganza consists mostly of egg dishes, but French toast is served as well. Adults pay $4.75; children get half portions at $2.50. Boosters and highchairs are available.

Open Monday through Saturday from 11 a.m. to 10 p.m. and on Sunday from 9 a.m. to 10 p.m. Reservations are accepted. Park in the Old Town parking lots. Major credit cards are honored.

El Indio Shop, 3695 India St. (tel. 619/299-0333), is a San Diego institution known for its authentic homemade tortillas. It is located near Old Town, downtown San Diego, and the airport, near the intersection of I–5 and I–8. It's the perfect spot for a quick delicious meal to eat on the premises, to take back to your hotel room, or to enjoy at the beach or park. Until recently the shop only handled take-out orders, but now it has added indoor and outdoor eating areas.

The cheese enchiladas are especially tasty and go well with the crisp flavored tortilla chips. One enchilada is $1.50. Orders such as the chicken burrito plate come with beans, rice, and chips for $3.50.

Breakfast is also served, with items such as huevos rancheros and sweetbreads. There are highchairs here, but no booster seats. The servers will warm baby bottles and baby food in the kitchen.

El Indio opens daily at 8 a.m. Lunch and dinner are served until 9 p.m. No reservations are accepted. Park in the lot or on the street. No credit cards will be honored.

A new El Indio Shop branch has opened in Pacific Beach at 4120 Mission Blvd. (tel. 619/272-8226).

HOTEL CIRCLE / MISSION VALLEY:
Looking like a rustic cabin set amid the pines, the **Hungry Hunter,** 2445 Hotel Circle (tel. 619/291-8074), offers a relaxed ambience accented by brass lanterns, stone planters, and a "hunter's" green color scheme.

Young children will enjoy the resident fireplace moosehead, nicknamed "Bullwinkle." Families are welcome, and the staff has even been known to walk a crying child around the restaurant, allowing Mom and Dad to enjoy their meal.

A complete breakfast menu includes a selection of croissants, omelets, and griddle favorites such as a Belgian waffle topped with fresh fruit, whipped cream, and almonds for $4.

The lunch menu lists salads, sandwiches, and some entrees. Chicken salad is $5, and a French dip sandwich costs the same. Filet mignon is served with salad and fries for $8.

Dinners feature seafood and steak and come with a steaming cup of home-style soup and a lazy Susan–style salad bar served right at your table. Prices for steak are $13 to $16. Tempura shrimp costs $15, and a prime rib and Alaskan King crab combination dinner is pegged at $19.

No children's menu is available at lunch, though the staff will be happy to split orders in the kitchen. There are children's selections at dinner, but they're not on the menu, so be sure to request a verbal rundown from your server. Typical selections are a cheeseburger ($5.50), shrimp ($7), and prime rib ($7).

Booster seats and highchairs with plastic-wrapped trays are provided. The staff will warm baby bottles. There are unlimited free children's drinks, such as Shirley Temples and Roy Rogerses.

Hungry Hunter is open for breakfast Monday through Thursday from 7 to 11 a.m. and on Friday and Saturday from 7:30 a.m. to 2:30 p.m. Lunch is served Monday through Thursday from 11:30 a.m. to 2:30 p.m. Dinner is served Monday through Thursday from 4:30 to 10 p.m., on Friday and Saturday till 11 p.m., and on Sunday from 4 to 10 p.m. Sunday brunch hours are 7:30 a.m. to 2 p.m. Reservations are recommended. Parking lot adjacent. Major credit cards are accepted.

The **Monterey Whaling Company,** located in the Doubletree Hotel in Mission Valley, at 901 Camino del Rio South (tel. 619/543-9000), offers gracious dining in a glass-roofed sunny restaurant decorated in peach and aqua.

The breakfast menu offers Smoothies—a blend of berries, banana, yogurt, honey, and cream ($3)—as well as egg dishes and pancakes. A country-style breakfast for $5.50 includes two eggs; sausage, ham, or bacon; home fries; and toast.

Both lunch and dinner menus are printed daily to indicate the day's selection of fresh fish. A typical entree is mahi-mahi (Hawaiian dolphin) cooked over mesquite ($8.50 for lunch, $11.25 for dinner). Continuing selections include a Monterey omelet filled with bay shrimp, avocado, and Jack cheese and served with shoestring fries for $6, fresh fruit salad for $6.50, and stir-fry cashew chicken for $8.

The Kids' Menu has breakfast, lunch, and dinner items. For breakfast, your youngster can choose from pancakes and sausage ($2.50); bacon, eggs, and toast ($3); cold cereal ($2), and half a waffle with maple syrup ($1.75). The lunch and dinner menu includes soup ($1), a cheese omelet ($3), spaghetti ($4), and hot dogs, grilled cheese, and hamburgers (each about $2.50). For a special treat, you can order ice cream and a chocolate-chip cookie for dessert ($1 each).

Boosters and highchairs are available. They will warm baby bottles and baby food in the kitchen. Special children's drinks can be ordered from the bar.

Breakfast is served daily from 6:30 to 11 a.m.; lunch is from 11 a.m. to 3 p.m., and dinner from 5 to 10 p.m. on weekdays, and till 11 p.m. on Friday and Saturday. Reservations are recommended. Hotel parking. Major credit cards are accepted.

The "Tremors" at the **California Earthquake Café,** 7919 Mission Center Court (tel. 619/297-3603), are the kind that come with crisp corn chips and chunky guacamole. Patrons are told that if the ground starts shaking, they should pay the bill first, then take cover. And that's just the beginning of the fun that's served up here.

The eclectic '50s décor includes Pee-Wee Herman's bike, a large cardboard cow, hula hoops hanging from the ceiling, and graffiti-covered walls. Metal bar stools and diner-style swinging doors add to the '50s look.

On Thursday, Friday, and Saturday evenings, the tables in the center of the floor are pushed back to make room for dancing. From a disc jockey booth in the restaurant, music of the '50s and '60s is played. This is where Mom and Dad can show their teenagers what was "shakin'" when *they* were teens—if they have the nerve!

Several menu items have a Mexican flavor, such as the Mex-blackened chicken with garlic mayo on sourdough. Sandwiches cost $4 to $6. Pasta meals include a green salad and are in the $5 to $8 range. Complete dinners are available from $6 to $11.

There is no children's menu, but many of the items are appropriate for children, such as the "Grilled Cheese on Sourdough—Plain As Can Be," served with curly fries, for $2.75, or the "Very Plain Haute Dog and Fries" for $3.

Booster seats and highchairs are available, and they will warm baby bottles in the kitchen. Children's non-alcoholic cocktails will be whipped up upon request.

Lunch and dinner are served weekdays from 11:30 a.m. to 11 p.m., on Friday and Saturday till 1 a.m., and on Sunday till 10 p.m. Reservations are accepted for parties of six or more; generally there's no wait to seat smaller parties. Free parking lot adjacent, or valet parking. All major credit cards welcome.

The south-of-the-border flavor is apparent from the moment you enter the patio entryway of **La Hacienda,** 875 Hotel Circle South (tel. 619/298-8281). Colorful flowers abound, a wooden burro stands ready to greet you, and the tile floors and heavy whitewashed posts combine to give the interior the look of a Mexican homestead.

The restaurant is located in Hotel Circle amid an abundance of hotels and motels. Much of the clientele is tourist families, and children are always welcome.

Your meal begins with a complimentary quesadilla (cheese melted on a tortilla), great for keeping hungry little appetites satisfied. Entrees come with Spanish rice and frijoles (beans). The "Chimichanga Supreme" is a deep-fried beef or chicken burrito topped with sour cream and guacamole ($7.50 at dinner). You can sample several flavors of Mexico with the "Enchiladas La Bandera," a platter of three enchiladas—chicken, seafood, and cheese. Combination plates, such as the carne asada taco and chile relleno, are also available.

Children 12 and under have their own menu, with a beef or chicken taco for $2.75, fried chicken with vegetables and french fries for $4.50, and a hamburger and french fries for $4.25. Special drinks will be made for the children, such as virgin strawberry daiquiris, Shirley Temples, and Roy Rogerses.

Boosters and highchairs are provided. The servers will warm baby bottles and baby food in the kitchen and will split adult portions for two kids.

La Hacienda serves lunch from 11:30 a.m. to 2 p.m. on weekdays. Dinner is from 5 to 10 p.m. on weekdays and Sunday, and till 11 p.m. on Saturday. No lunch is served on Saturday. Sunday brunch hours are 10 a.m. to 2 p.m. Reservations are accepted. Nearby parking. Major credit cards are welcome.

DOWNTOWN: If you're browsing through Horton Plaza and you want a leisurely sit-down lunch (with kids?!), or you're staying downtown and want a somewhat fancy restaurant, try **Harbor House—Top of the Plaza,** 501 Horton Plaza (tel. 619/233-5923). You'll have three separate dining rooms to choose from, but we personally opt for the French bistro-style room or the outdoor patio in warm weather. Although there's no children's menu, the chef will gladly serve smaller portions for smaller appetites.

At lunch there are lots of appetizers and salads for us older folks, and for the main course there are five different pizza napolitanas, pasta dishes, and sandwiches and hamburgers. Calamari is one of the specialties, and other specials are offered daily. Dinner is much of the same, but adds a number of seafood entrees plus medallions of pork tenderloin and spit-roasted lemon chicken, among other specialties. Lunch prices are $5.25 to $11.50; dinners start at $5.25 and go up to $17.

Boosters and highchairs are available, and they will concoct special children's drinks at the bar.

Open Monday through Thursday from 11 a.m. to 10 p.m., on Friday and Saturday till 11 p.m., and on Sunday till 8 p.m. Reservations are accepted. Free parking in the Horton Plaza lot. Major credit cards are welcome.

Opened in 1944 as a 14-stool lunch counter, **Hob Nob Hill,** 2271 First Ave.

(tel. 619/239-8176), is today a bustling, homey restaurant known for good food and friendly service. It has the distinction of being the oldest restaurant in San Diego doing business in its original location. On a hill overlooking downtown, the restaurant is frequented by a mix of businesspeople, local regulars, and tourists.

The Hob Nob Hill is a winner of several culinary awards, including the Silver Fork and the Southern California Restaurant Writers' Association Family Value Category.

The atmosphere is suited to families, and the owner's recognition of a family's sometimes limited budget is reflected in the prices. There is usually a buzz of conversation to cover up children's noise, and the dark woods and red accents set a pleasant tone. Service is speedy even during the busiest hours.

A roast turkey dinner complete with Caesar salad, sage dressing, and giblet sauce costs about $10. Other dinner selections are chicken and dumplings, beef stew, and pot roast. All are available in a child's portion upon request. A typical breakfast of eggs, bacon, and toast costs $5. Hamburgers, cold and hot sandwiches, and other lunch items average $7. Complete dinners are about $10, and there are nightly specials.

Be sure to sample the items baked fresh daily on the premises. Mouthwatering selections include peach-pecan bundt cake, cinnamon rolls, carrot cake, and coconut cream pie.

Boosters and highchairs are provided. The servers will gladly warm baby bottles and baby food in the kitchen. Hob Nob Hill is open every day except Saturday. Hours are 7 a.m. to 9 p.m. Reservations are accepted. Street parking. Major credit cards are welcome.

5. WHAT TO SEE AND DO

One of the reasons families keep coming back to San Diego over and over again is that there's so much to see and do. Every time their children get a year older, there's always a new way to appreciate an old familiar sight.

SAN DIEGO ZOO: Located in Balboa Park off Park Boulevard, the San Diego Zoo (tel. 619/234-3153 or 619/231-1515) is a must-see for all ages. Included in the vast array of animals in open-air settings here (more than 3,200 animals of 800 species) are a surprising number of rare, exotic, and endangered species. The zoo is also famous for having the largest number of parrots and parrot-like birds ever assembled. Covering 100 acres, the zoo is set in a remarkable botanical garden—be sure to look around at the bountiful plants that have been growing here for some 50 years. Known as one of the finest zoos in the world for its innovative design, the zoo has recently added a three-acre simulated ecosystem called **Tiger River.** This unique exhibit sets up an experience: instead of walking from cage to cage, or from enclosure to enclosure, visitors walk along pathways that lead to groups of animals and plants coexisting as they would in their natural habitat. Predators are separated from their natural prey, but it's done so subtly you hardly know it. As you go through this tropical rain forest, complete with humidity and mist, you feel as if you're actually visiting an exotic natural environment. It's educational for the children (and parents) as well.

The San Diego Zoo also has a well-known **Children's Petting Zoo,** which can be enjoyed by any age, but is geared to 4-year-olds. Our youngest never wants to leave the animals. She gets to pet them, watch eggs being hatched, and view the animal nursery where the little newborns are fed and taken care of. Admission is 50¢; kids under 3, free.

In addition to walking, there are two ways to see this large zoo. A 40-minute narrated **bus tour** covers three miles of the zoo's interior. The open-sided double-decker buses leave every few minutes from the zoo station, to the right of the Flamingo Lagoon, just inside the entrance. This is a good way to see the zoo if you don't have much time to spend. The tour covers a good 80% of the grounds. Be sure your child can sit through 40 minutes on a bus! The bus leaves daily from 9 a.m. to 4 p.m. Adults pay $2.50; children 3 to 15, $2; kids 2 and under, free.

Another way to go, and one that's fun just for itself, is the **Skyfari Aerial Tramway,** which travels over one side of the zoo to the other, 170 feet in the air. You'll find the eastern cable lift at the Reptile House, at the left of the entrance, and the western lift at Horn and Hoof Mesa. The tram runs daily from 10 a.m. The eastern terminal closes at 4 p.m.; the western, at 4:15 p.m. Round-trip fares are $1.50 for adults, $1 for children 3 to 15; 2 and under, free.

There are several free animal shows too. The performances and schedules change, so check at the entrance for current information. There are also daily elephant or camel rides, located past Elephant Mesa. These are free and are held from 11 a.m. to 4 p.m.

Stroller and wheelchair rentals are available near the entrance. You can also purchase disposable diapers there, or buy diapers and baby wipes near the exit in the Jungle Bazaar Gift Shop. Baby-changing facilities are located in the women's rest rooms. There are plenty of food-service stands throughout the zoo.

From July to Labor Day the hours are 9 a.m. to 5 p.m. daily. Between Labor Day and the end of June the zoo closes at 4 p.m. daily. General zoo admission is $8.50 for adults, $2.50 for children 3 to 15; kids 2 and under, free. A combination package includes admission, the double-decker bus tour, a round-trip ride on the Skyfari tram, and admission to the children's zoo; it costs $13 for adults, $6 for kids 3 to 15. Parking is free.

SAN DIEGO WILD ANIMAL PARK:

The animals run free, but the visitors don't, at the San Diego Wild Animal Park (tel. 619/234-6541, 619/480-0100, or 619/747-8702). Take I–15 north to Via Rancho Parkway (45 minutes from downtown San Diego) and follow the signs. Opened in 1972, this 1,800-acre wildlife preserve is home to more than 2,000 wild animals.

You enter the park through **Nairobi Village,** an area that includes shops, restaurants, animal enclosures, and a walk-through aviary. Half a dozen animal shows are performed in various places throughout the park. Children enjoy petting gentle deer and sheep in the **Petting Kraal** (note that the baby animals visit the Kraal from 9 to 11 a.m. daily), viewing the **Animal Care Center,** where baby animals are kept and fed, and riding elephant-back (adults and children over 3, $1.75). **Critter Encounters** give you the opportunity to see rare animals close up and get all sorts of information about them from their trainers.

A narrated five-mile **monorail safari** glides along the periphery of six ecological regions: the plains of Australia, the swamps and highlands of Asia, the South African veldt, the North African mountains, and the East African savanna. For best viewing, sit on the right side of the monorail and bring a pair of binoculars. The animals sleep in the heat of midday (which can get up to 100° in late summer), so plan to go in the morning or early evening.

Infants and toddlers may find the 50-minute ride tiring, but children over the age of 5 will delight in discovering that those gray boulders ("See? Over there, under that tree, near the muddy pond . . .") are really rhinos. They'll also spot wild horses, tigers, lions, cheetahs, giraffes, zebras, impalas, gnus, mountain goats, ostriches, and more.

A special treat, particularly in late spring and early summer, are the many animal babies. The park is proud of its success in breeding endangered species.

All areas are stroller-accessible, and strollers may be rented. Women's rest rooms have diaper-changing facilities. A nursing room is provided in the rest room near the monorail. Forget extra diapers? You can purchase disposables in the giftshop.

From June 19 through Labor Day, the park is open daily from 9 a.m. to 6 p.m.; the rest of the year the park closes at 4 p.m. Admission prices are $13 for adults, $6.25 for children 3 to 15; under 2, free. All tickets include the monorail. Parking costs $1.

SEA WORLD: San Diego's Sea World has so many small experiences to savor that people sometimes forget that there's more to the park than only Shamu. Sea World is located at 1720 S. Shores Rd., Mission Bay (tel. 619/222-6363 in San Diego, 714/826-7213 in Los Angeles, 602/838-0600 in Arizona). To get to the park, exit west off I–5 onto Sea World Drive.

Although we devote only one day to Sea World each time we visit, you could spend two days there (especially with youngsters who tire easily) and still not completely experience everything. That's why people come back to it year after year—either to see their favorite exhibits over again, or to see the ones they missed the last time.

Sea World is a theme park specifically dedicated to the creatures of the sea and the sea itself. And though there are a great many things to do, we will just highlight some of the best.

When you enter the park, to the right you'll see a one-acre map of the United States just made for walking on. Nearby is **Cap'n Kids World,** a two-acre play area for toddlers on up. It's a fun place of nautically themed play elements. Not only did it hold our 4-year-old's attention for more than an hour, but she begged us to come back to it at the end of the day for yet another hour of playing.

Another highlight of the day is the **dolphin-petting pool,** an experience we'll remember forever. Hold onto your little children, lean over the protective wall, and maybe you'll get a dolphin's attention. When they come close enough, toss a fish in their mouths and pet these docile mammals. Not only is petting the dolphins exciting, but it gives the children the chance to see the mammal's sociable nature close up. You can be a sport and purchase a plate of dead fish from a nearby stand to lure them to your group. This is when the fun starts. It becomes you against nature as you see if you can get the smelly fish to the dolphins before the sea gulls swoop down and grab it out of your hand! Once we encountered what must have been the smartest, fastest sea gulls in the world—they managed to steal 80% of our offerings! The children around us were absolutely delighted at this turn of events, and the adults cheered us on, urging us to try again.

The **tidepools** are a most wonderful exhibit, and they educate children without their even knowing it. Park guides explain the wonders you see, including spiny lobsters and sea anemones. We touched our very first starfish here, and were able to gently examine it and feel it before we returned it to its natural-habitat living quarters.

The **Penguin Encounter** is another special exhibit. It's set up so beautifully that you can see nearly all of these comical, overdressed birds as they strut around their 5,000-square-foot re-created Antarctic environment. We were lucky to be there at feeding time, and were fascinated by the interaction between the humans and these now-dependent polar birds.

Naturally, **Shamu** is the big draw here, and even your youngest child will recognize the name and want to go. But, frankly, the show is a disappointment, although now that the trainers are allowed to get back in the water with Shamu and friends, it's a more energizing show. In 1988, hundreds of visitors got to see Baby Shamu's birth during an early-evening show. Children love to see this youngster swim with its mother. Be sure you don't sit in the bottom rows. As a matter of fact, get a seat near the top of the first section so as not to be splashed when the whales perform. There's also a dolphin show and a seal-and-otter show. A graceful pearl diver, an "Ama" girl, dives for pearl-bearing oysters in a special show, which fascinated many children in the group.

The **shark exhibit** is probably more frightening for adults than children. The 8- and 10-year-olds we talked to thought it was a gas. The younger children didn't really understand what they were seeing.

There are many more shows, aquariums, and exhibits, and even three rides. In the summer, when the park remains open until 11 p.m., there are lots of evening special events.

If you want an in-depth look at Sea World, take one of the 90-minute guided tours, which include a behind-the-scenes look at certain park activities. You'll first get a bird's-eye view of the park, and then can go off on your own for the rest of the day. Tours leave every 30 minutes from 9 a.m. to 2 p.m. In addition to regular admission, adults pay $4; children 3 to 11, $3; under 3, free.

Strollers and wheelchairs can be rented right past the entrance. Women's bathrooms have separate diaper-changing facilities. Disposable diapers can be bought at Cap'n Kids World, not far from the entrance. There's one main first-aid station and three satellites (in the summer, nine nurses are on staff full time). Outdoor food stands are everywhere. P.J.'s is the sit-down restaurant near the hydrofoil rides.

Sea World is open daily from 9 a.m. to dusk. In the summer, including July 4, it's open from 9 a.m. to 11 p.m. Other holiday hours vary, so call first. Adults pay $21 admission; children 3 to 11, $15.50; under 3, free. Parking is free, and the lot is huge.

BALBOA PARK: Every city in America should have a Balboa Park. Put a trip to this wonderful 1,400-acre park near the top of your list of places to visit. Known as the cultural hub of the city, it is a park that has something to offer everyone.

Most of the buildings in the park today were built for the Panama-California Exposition of 1915–1916 and the California Pacific International Exposition of 1935–1936. The first thing that will strike you is the beauty of the buildings, then the expansive layout of the park with its bountiful gardens, green lawns, and stately trees. We like to visit off-season when it's not so crowded, but the summer weekend crowds lend a festive air to the surroundings. This is the home of the famous **Old Globe Theater,** where you may find some performances quite suitable for your entire family. Although there are 11 buildings dedicated to the arts and museums, not all of them will appeal to children.

First-time visitors should make their initial stop the **House of Hospitality, Information Center** (tel. 619/239-0512). Take Sixth Avenue to Laurel and turn into the park down El Prado. If you park in the Plaza de Panama lot, you'll find the information center nearby.

Don't plan to do everything in one day, there's just too much. Be sure to leave some time to just wander.

We like to visit the **Museum of Man** (tel. 619/239-2001), which features exhibits describing human and cultural development over the ages. Even though our little one can't appreciate the significance of what she's seeing, she loves to linger in front of the exhibits devoted to Native Americans and their crafts and tools, as well as the other interesting displays. She was fascinated, and a little frightened, by "Lucy," a cast of the oldest human ancestor (only 11 other museums in the world have this cast). Inside the museum is a Kid's Trading Post, open Wednesday through Saturday from 11 a.m. to 2 p.m. Sometimes there are special live exhibits, such as tortilla making—we not only watched this, but were able to sample the resultant product. We also watched as a Native American artist carefully wove brightly colored yarn into a blanket on a loom.

The museum is open daily from 10 a.m. to 4:30 p.m. Admission is $3 for adults, $1 for children 13 to 18, 25¢ for children 6 to 12; under 6, free.

Airplane lovers really appreciate the **Aerospace Museum** and **International Aerospace Hall of Fame,** 2001 Pan American Plaza (tel. 619/234-8291 and 619/232-8322). World War II fighter planes, including those of the enemy, are everywhere—some hang from the ceiling as if they are really flying above you. There are even planes from World War I and exhibits honoring early space exploration. Open daily from 10 a.m. to 4:30 p.m. Adults pay $4 admission; children under 17, $1.

An absolute must-see for school-age children is the **Reuben H. Fleet Space Theater and Science Center,** located right near the huge fountain (tel. 619/238-1168 or 619/238-1233). In the Space Theater, the OMNIMAX films are projected onto a 76-foot dome, which seems to lift you out of your seats and right into outer space. Several different films alternate daily. Youngsters always want to return to the Science Center, where more than 50 hands-on exhibits let them learn about various aspects of science firsthand. There's a concave dish, for instance, called the whisper dish, into which one of you speaks. Across the room is another dish from which one of you hears the first message—but no one else can hear it. Open daily from 9:30 a.m. to 10:30 p.m. General admission is $2 for adults, $1 for children 5 to 15; children under 5, free. Tickets for the OMNIMAX Space Theater cost $5 for adults ($3.50 for seniors over 60), $3 for children 5 to 15; children under 5, free. The price of tickets to the laser show varies, but children under 5 are not admitted at any time.

Most children love natural history museums, and Balboa Park's **Natural History Museum,** located at the east end of El Prado (tel. 619/232-3821), is no exception. Complete with resident dinosaurs, the museum focuses on the geology, plants, and animals of the Southwest. There are hands-on exhibits and films every weekend. The museum is open daily from 10 a.m. to 4:30 p.m. Admission is $4 for adults, $1 for children 6 to 18; under 6, free.

Sports fans get a kick out of the **Hall of Champions** (tel. 619/234-2544), which chronicles the exploits of San Diego's finest athletes, including its surfers. There are videotapes of various important sports events, as well as jerseys, shoes, photos, and other items that will keep fans busy for a long time.

Open Monday through Saturday from 10 a.m. to 4:30 p.m. and on Sunday from noon to 5 p.m. Admission is $2 for adults, 50¢ for children 6 to 17; under 6, free.

We also visit the **Marie Hitchcock Puppet Theater** (tel. 619/466-7128), located in a little building between Plaza de Panama and the Aerospace Museum. Although not the highest form of art, the short shows give young children their very own activity for the day. We've seen children jump into the aisles to participate, and they love to sing along when the puppeteer gives the word. Showtimes are irregular, so call ahead. Admission is $1.50 for adults, $1 for children.

You mustn't forget the **Model Railroad Museum,** in the Casa de Balboa, on the south side of El Prado, west of the fountain and the Reuben H. Fleet Space Theater (tel. 619/696-0199). Look for the two-story semaphore that flags the museum's downstairs entrance. (Pushing a stroller? Take the elevator east of the stairs.)

Friendly, grandfatherly hobbyists wearing blue-and-white-striped caps loom giant-like over miniature mountains and rock-strewn desert gorges. With a sound like rushing water, tiny trains glide past turn-of-the-century stations and villages, cross high trestles, and emerge from mouse-size tunnels.

Visitors view the half dozen exhibits through Plexiglas. The height is convenient to hobbyists, but, unfortunately, small children can't see without being held.

You'll smell sawdust, as some exhibits are still under construction. Older children enjoy figuring out how plywood, chicken wire, and concrete stucco combine to make realistic terrain.

The museum is open Wednesday through Friday from 11 a.m. to 4 p.m. and on Saturday from 11 a.m. to 5 p.m. Admission is $1 for adults; children under 16 are free.

There are even more diversions at this magnificent park. Take the kids for a walk to the **Spreckels Organ Pavilion** between Pan American Plaza and Plaza de Panama. It's a wonderful old outdoor concert area, and on Sunday there are free organ concerts. Or visit the **Lily Pond** at the **Botanical Building** (tel. 619/234-8901). It is surprisingly peaceful even on the busiest days. Watch out, though: your toddlers will want to catch the squirmy goldfish. Some children have never seen lily ponds before, and these are wondrous natural sights to introduce them to. It's open Saturday through Thursday from 10 a.m. to 4:30 p.m.

Walk up to the huge fountain at the **Plaza de Balboa.** Usually there's some sort of street entertainment going on—a mime, perhaps, or the exquisitely scary painted Indians we watched doing their native dances. Even on winter weekends you might see the balloon maker who forms those skittish pieces of plastic into magical animals in front of the adoring eyes of boys and girls who can stand there for as long as an hour waiting for theirs. Then walk over to **Spanish Village** (tel. 619/233-9050) to watch artists at work in one of more than 35 studios. You might see a sculpture being crafted, a pot being thrown, or a piece of jewelry being created, as well as displays by the Mineral and Gem Society and the Enamel Guild. The village is open daily from 11 a.m. to 4 p.m.

If you've made it through Spanish Village, you won't be too far from the **carousel** and the **miniature train** rides adjacent to the zoo entrance. The carousel ride is open daily from 11 a.m. to 5 p.m., and costs 75¢ per ride. The train will take you through five acres of the park. It operates in summer daily from 11 a.m. to 5 p.m. In winter, it operates weekends and holidays, except Christmas and Thanksgiving, during the same hours.

If you didn't notice it yourself, your children will probably have discovered it on their own—it's the huge **Moreton Bay fig tree** located near the Village. The colossal roots and fantastic way in which nature created this setting make this a terrific untouched playground.

THE EMBARCADERO: A hundred years ago, most people who visited San Diego arrived by ship. They came ashore at what is now the Embarcadero on Harbor Drive, just north of Seaport Village, between Market and Hawthorne Streets. Today the area has restaurants, a bayside boardwalk, a three-ship maritime museum, and plenty to explore.

Unless one of the big white *Love Boat* cruise ships is in town, the most prominent ship you'll see is the *Star of India,* a restored 1863 merchant sailing vessel and one of the ships that make up the **Maritime Museum,** located at 1306 N. Harbor Dr. (tel. 619/234-9153). Park your strollers with the ticket taker and turn your tots loose in the 19th century. They'll climb on coiled ropes as thick as boa constrictors, play pirate on the poop deck, and ask you what a chamber pot was used for. In the children's cabin they see toys and a small rocking horse.

Youngsters 7 and older will enjoy the miniature ships in bottles and maritime miscellany on board the 1898 ferryboat *Berkeley,* as well as running across the gangplank to the 1904 luxury yacht *Medea.*

Open daily from 9 a.m. to 8 p.m. A boarding pass good for all three ships costs $5 for adults, $4 for children 13 to 16, $1.25 for children 6 to 12; under 6, free.

If you visit the Embarcadero on a weekend, by all means attend a **navy ship's open house**—perhaps a submarine, aircraft carrier, or destroyer will be in port. Kids love the ladder-like stairways that go through holes in the deck, playing captain on the bridge, and asking questions of the hospitable crew. Visit between 1 and 4 p.m. The treat is free, but there may be up to an hour's wait.

See the city from the bay via one of the harbor tours. The **San Diego Harbor Excursion,** at the foot of Broadway at Harbor Drive (tel. 619/234-4111), runs tours daily, leaving every half hour. There are one- and two-hour excursions that go under the Coronado Bay Bridge on the way to view navy ships. The shorter trip is best for smaller children; it's fine to take strollers aboard. Bring sweaters or windbreakers even if the weather seems warm. The one-hour tour costs $7.75 for adults, $3.75 for children 3 to 11. The two-hour excursion runs $11 for adults, $5.50 for children 3 to 11. Under-3s are free at any time.

The masted ship **Invader** leaves from 1066 N. Harbor Dr. (tel. 619/298-8066 or 619/234-8687, or toll free 800/262-4386 in California) on one- and two-hour trips that sail past the Sixth Fleet and the Coronado Bay Bridge, and through the harbor. Cruises leave daily in summer, Tuesday through Sunday in winter. There are four one-hour cruises per day, and three departures for the two-hour cruises. Adults pay $7.75 for the one-hour tour, $11 for the two-hour tour; children 12 and under pay half price for either tour.

The newest San Diego harbor excursion trip is the **San Diego Bay Ferry** (same address and phone number as the Harbor Excursion, above). The first ferryboat in San Diego sailed in 1886; now you can take the kids and your bikes on a leisurely ride to Coronado. The ferry leaves daily, on the hour, from 10 a.m. to 10 p.m. weekdays, on Friday and Saturday till 11 p.m. It lands at the Old Ferry Landing in Coronado and returns every hour on the half hour, beginning at 10:30 a.m. Get tokens for $1 each way (or an all-day pass for $4) at the San Diego Harbor Excursion's blue ticket booth. In Coronado, pick them up at the Star and Crescent Gift Galley at the Old Ferry Landing. Once you're in Coronado, you won't have any trouble getting around. There are trackless trolleys (50¢), or you can walk or rent a bike.

As you stroll north along the Embarcadero, you'll see high-bowed tuna boats and fishermen mending nets. Listen—the language they're speaking is probably Portuguese.

HISTORIC SIGHTS: Despite San Diego's venerable status as the birthplace of California, the number of historic sights found here isn't overwhelming. The ones that follow will be enjoyed by young and old alike. Most have vast outdoor areas surrounding them, good for strolling, picnicking, or playing.

Old Town / Bazaar del Mundo

Old Town San Diego State Historic Park is the site of San Diego's roots. From the north, take I-5 south to the Old Town exit. From downtown, take I-5 northwest to the Old Town Avenue exit. From Mission Valley, take I-8 west to the Taylor Street exit, follow Taylor south to San Diego Avenue, then turn left. From Harbor Island, take Rosecrans east across Pacific Hwy. right into Old Town.

As the first European settlement in California, it was the hub of San Diego's life from 1821 to 1872. Original buildings from the city's Mexican period still stand, as well as some from its early-California period. The oldest is an adobe building dating from 1827.

Only six square blocks in size, Old Town makes a short but interesting walking tour for the whole family. Stop by the **Visitor Center,** at 2645 San Diego Ave., San Diego, CA 92110 (tel. 619/237-6770), for a map of a self-guided walking tour. You'll see where the first American flag was raised. Your children will enjoy looking at the old one-room Mason Street schoolhouse, and will have a good time poking through the Seeley Stables, where they will find a fascinating collection of stagecoaches and other horse-drawn vehicles and a wonderful collection of western memorabilia. An 18-minute slide show about the history and transportation of Old Town is just short enough to hold kids' attention. It's shown daily, every hour on the hour, from 11 a.m. to 4 p.m., and is free with admission to the stables (adults pay $1; children 6 to 17, 50¢; under 6, free).

There are other historical buildings on and off the tour that you might want to see. It depends on the stamina of your children. But the nice thing about Old Town is that it makes a pleasant place to spend the day. Just walking around the park and enjoying the outdoor scenery will entice you to pop your heads into buildings along your path—not a bad way to sightsee. And there's a free one-hour ranger-guided walking tour that leaves daily at 2 p.m. from Casa Machado y Silvas, across from Old Town Plaza on San Diego Avenue.

You'll find public rest rooms across from the stables on Calhoun Street and behind Casa de Juan Rodriguez at Racine and Laramie Streets. The park is stroller-accessible. Parking in the park itself is quite limited. There are parking lots on the outskirts—there's one between San Diego Avenue and Twiggs Street, and one on Taylor Street near Pacific Hwy.—but you'll have to walk from the lot to your destination.

Bazaar del Mundo, located on Juan Street, is a lively marketplace of shops, food-to-go and sit-down restaurants, most with a Mexican flavor. Set within courtyards and surrounded by lush trees, red-tile roofs, festive gardens, and fountains, it's a fun place to take the family. Our kids love to stop for a sugary-sweet churro (long rolls of dough fried and dipped in sugar) and then accompany us into the little boutiques and art shops. Sometimes there's entertainment going on and we stop for a look. (For information on the sit-down restaurants, see the "Where to Eat" section.)

Several other small retail areas in Old Town beckon curious shoppers. At **Squibob Square,** adjacent to the Visitor Center at San Diego Avenue and Twiggs Street, costumed craftspeople purvey their wares. **Old Town Mercado** has a number of import shops on Congress Street, across from Casa de Machado y Stewart. **Old Town Esplanade** is not only a Mexican marketplace, it's where art shows, craft demonstrations, and strolling musicians gather on weekends. It's located near Conde Street, San Diego Avenue, and Congress Street. If your children have never seen or heard a mariachi band, this is the place to take them—no doubt they'll think the instruments are interesting. Park in the Old Town State Park lot, and walk three blocks.

Serra Museum and Presidio Park

On the top of a hill east of Old Town State Historic Park, overlooking Mission Valley, is the **Serra Museum,** part of lushly landscaped **Presidio Park** (tel. 619/297-3258).

The museum looks so much like a mission that many people assume it is one. Actually, what's left of the original structures—a mission and presidio, or walled city—are under grass-covered mounds on the hillside below the museum.

This is the birthplace of California, the home of the first Spanish settlers, founded in 1769 by Fr. Junipero Serra. Early San Diegans began moving into the area that is now Old Town in the 1820s. The museum and park were completed in 1929.

Museum exhibits of early mission and Native American artifacts will interest older children. Kids of all ages pretend they're soldiers in the Spanish garrison as they climb the tower's steep stairs and peer out narrow windows set in thick walls.

Grassy slopes below the museum are steep enough in places for a good roll (lie on your side, arms over your head, and kick off!). Plan a picnic, walk the trails and enjoy the views.

Museum hours are Tuesday through Saturday from 10 a.m. to 4:30 p.m. and on Sunday from noon to 4:30 p.m.; closed Monday and major holidays. The park is free; museum admission costs $2 for adults, but children under 12 are free.

Mission San Diego de Alcala

California's first mission, founded by Fray Serra on Presidio Hill in 1769, was moved to its present Mission Valley location in 1774. It's located just east of the stadium at 10818 San Diego Mission Rd. (tel. 619/281-8449).

The restored church echoes history in its thick adobe walls, decorated alcoves, and tiled archways. There is a small museum of artifacts, a bell tower, a garden, and a courtyard.

Children 7 and older will enjoy the tote-a-tape tour. For $1, you can rent a portable tape recorder that provides a narrated tour of the mission and details the lifestyle of the early Native American and Franciscan inhabitants.

Because this is a popular place for weddings and funerals, and masses are hourly all day Sunday, the best time to visit is during the week. No snacks or refreshments are available, and because of the many stairs, stroller access is limited.

Open daily from 9 a.m. to 5 p.m. Admission is $1; children under 12 are free.

Cabrillo National Monument / Point Loma Lighthouse

Cabrillo National Monument (tel. 619/557-5450) sits atop the southern tip of Point Loma, a peninsula that forms the west side of San Diego Bay. Take I-8 to the Rosecrans exit. Go west toward the beaches and turn right on Canon Street, then go up Canyon, make a left on Catalina Boulevard, and drive all the way to the end.

The main attraction is also a local landmark: the restored 1887 **Old Point Loma Lighthouse.** Older children can imagine living there 100 years ago. Would they have created ornate picture frames from seashells, like the ones in the lighthouse living room?

Films geared to school-age children are shown in the auditorium near the visitor center. They describe how Spanish explorer Juan Rodriguez Cabrillo discovered San Diego Bay in 1542; another explains the migration of the gray whales, which can be viewed from the point from December through February.

Often-overlooked areas include the bayside trail and the tidepools. Look for the signs or ask directions at the visitor center. These side trips are ideal for children 7 and older; younger children won't enjoy hiking back up the steep trail, and you'll worry about them climbing slippery rocks. Rangers give several tours daily and answer questions about native animals and vegetation. Inquire at the visitor center for current schedules.

The **Visitor Information Center** is located at the east end of the parking lot and is open during peak hours. It and the lighthouse are easily stroller-accessible. Rest rooms have diaper-changing facilities. Vending machines provide snacks, and there is a picnic area.

Summer hours are 9 a.m. to 8 p.m. daily; fall through early spring, it's open from 9 a.m. to 5:15 p.m. daily. Admission is $3 per car.

OUTDOOR ACTIVITIES: There are beaches for every purpose in San Diego and the surrounding areas. What with 70 miles of sand and varied water conditions, the town can afford to specialize. The 53 county parks offer unlimited choices.

Beaches and Parks

The green lawns, wide paved walkways, playgrounds, and sandy beaches of man-made **Mission Bay Park** encompass seven square miles of San Diego Bay. The park entrance can be found at 2688 E. Mission Bay Dr., off I-5 just north of I-8—take the Clairemont Drive exit (tel. 619/276-8200).

Dotted amid the lush landscaping are resort hotels, marinas, sportfishing docks, restaurants, campgrounds, and numerous picnic tables and fire rings. On the south side is Sea World.

Kids enjoy the bay most when they're in it or on it. The best water vehicle for ages 11 and older is the jet ski—a sort of surf-motorcycle. Mastery takes less than 15 minutes. When you fall off, it circles you like an apologetic puppy. But it's not an inexpensive activity: the cost is $30 per hour from **Jet Ski Rentals,** at 1327

Morena Blvd. (tel. 619/276-9200); call a day in advance to reserve one. Open daily from 10 a.m. to 4 p.m.

You can also rent sailboards, sailboats (including Hobie Cats), waterskis, and powerboats from the **Mission Bay SportCenter,** 1010 Santa Clara Pl. (tel. 619/488-1004). They are open weekdays from 10 a.m. to 6 p.m., on Saturday and Sunday till 7 p.m.

On shore, kids 6 and older ride bicycles, skateboards, and roller skates—when they're not fielding Frisbees or chasing breezes with colorful kites. Toddlers and preschoolers spend hours splashing in warm, waveless, shallow water and romping in sand-filled playgrounds.

Parking is plentiful; you can get to the many lots from East Mission Bay Drive, a frontage road that runs between Calif. 5 along the east edge of the bay. The area is crowded only during summer and holiday weekends.

Check with the **Mission Bay Visitor Information Center** (tel. 619/276-8200) for information on park amenities and other San Diego area attractions. The staff can also make hotel reservations, often with a 15% to 50% discount. You'll find the office right at the park entrance. Admission to the park is free.

The shoreline of La Jolla is one of San Diego's loveliest. There are parks, inlets for swimming and diving, and caves to explore. The Côte d'Azur ambience is enhanced by resorts, hotels, winding cliffside streets, and Mediterranean-style homes.

Parking can be a problem, except early in the morning. Expect to do some walking. Leave your car along the south end of Prospect Street, near the La Jolla Museum of Contemporary Art, and walk one block west to the ocean.

Your first stop will be the **Children's Pool Beach,** at the foot of Jenner Street, where you easily could spend the day. This sandy beach, sheltered by a crescent-shaped concrete breakwater, is guarded by a lifeguard in a glass-enclosed tower. Showers and rest rooms are handy. There are rocks to climb and a cave to explore—all ideal for children over 7; younger ones should be watched carefully—the water gets deep quickly and the rocks can be slippery. Be sure to walk along the top of the breakwater. It has a sturdy guard rail, and children of all ages enjoy looking out to sea and watching waves foam, crash, and recede on rocks and tidepools a few feet below. This is considered the most popular family beach, and the scuba-diving and skindiving are considered unparalleled here.

From the Children's Pool, stroll northeast along the coast past the wide green lawns and tall, slender palms of **Ellen Scripps Park** (a good place to picnic). Continue up Coast Boulevard, past the beach at the cove. As you do so, look over the edge of the concrete retaining wall; we watched pelicans cruise the cliffs, squirrels scurry, and a seagull guard a nest that contained two brown-speckled chicks. The ocean below is home to the **San Diego–La Jolla Underwater Park,** a haven for divers and snorkelers.

Your walk up the steep hill will be rewarded by a well-stocked shell shop, **La Jolla Cave and Curio Shop,** in a cottage at 1325 Coast Blvd. Children over 7 will be thrilled to discover stairs that lead to a beach cave—right in the middle of the shop! **Sunny Jim's Cave** is open Monday through Saturday from 10 a.m. to dusk and on Sunday from 11 a.m. to 6 p.m. Admission is $1 for adults, 50¢ for children. The opening in the cliffs at the end of 141 steps frames a view of ocean and coastline. The tunnel is steep, narrow, and dimly lit—but perfectly safe. Small children may be frightened, and the walk back up the stairs may be too much for them, but older children will enjoy the opportunity to pretend they're pirates or explorers.

La Jolla Shores is popular for surfing and scuba-diving. Boating, fishing, and sailing go on just north of the pier. Also on the north side of the pier are tidepools, a wonderful sight to show the children. Lifeguards are always on duty. There are picnic areas and rest rooms aplenty here.

La Jolla's **Windansea Beach** (take La Jolla Boulevard to Nautilus Street) is considered the best place for surfing. Let your surfers out and take a walk along the beach.

Pacific Beach and its boardwalk are popular draws for locals and tourists (take the Grand Avenue exit off I-5 and go west to Mission Boulevard). Families congregate near **Crystal Pier.** And there are roller skates and surfboards for rent near the roller coaster. If you keep following the boardwalk south, you'll eventually reach **South Mission Beach** (but it's not really within walking distance). On the bay side is a nice family beach.

The **Louis A. Stelzer County Park** (tel. 619/694-3049), near Lakeside, 20 miles northeast of San Diego, is a quiet family park with a special mission—to provide mainstream recreational opportunities for needy and disabled children. To get to the park, take Calif. 67 to Maple View Street in Lakeside; go east on Maple View to Ashwood and then to Wildcat Canyon Road, and drive two miles to the park entrance.

Picnic and play areas are shaded by a canopy of ancient oaks, offering relief from summer temperatures that soar into the 90s.

Visitors in wheelchairs appreciate the wide paved paths. Ramps and bridges have handrails. The benches of picnic tables are cut so that wheelchairs can come up close.

This award-winning park has two sets of playground equipment: one for younger children, another for older. Both are made of giant redwood timbers and have slides, swings, and monkey bars. A swinging wood bridge that rattles as they run across it brings squeals of delight from small children.

The park is open Monday through Friday from 9:30 a.m. to 5 p.m.; weekend hours vary depending on the time of year. The admission fee is $1 per car, free for handicapped persons and seniors.

Whale-Watching

A popular California sport, whale-watching usually takes place between December and March, when the whales are on their 10,000-mile journey from Alaska's Bering Sea to the breeding grounds in the warm bays of Baja California, Mexico. It is suggested that you make reservations for a cruise as far in advance as possible with any of the companies listed below. Landlubbers can get a great view of the whales from Cabrillo National Monument (take Chatsworth Street west to Point Loma). On a good day during peak season, you can sometimes spot as many as 60 or 70 of these beautiful grays.

Even if you've escaped winter on the East Coast or Midwest, you'll need to wear layers of clothing on these boat trips, as it can get pretty chilly out at sea at this time of year. Rubber-soled shoes are most appropriate.

San Diego Harbor Excursion, at the foot of Broadway at Harbor Drive (tel. 619/234-4111), offers narrated 2½-hour cruises daily from December 26 through the end of the migratory season (usually March). Refreshments are available on board. Cruises leave at 10 a.m. and 2 p.m. Adults pay $13; children 3 to 11, $6.50; under-3s are free.

At **Fisherman's Landing,** 2838 Garrison St. (tel. 619/222-0391), you can board the 85-foot *Avanti* for 2½-hour whale-watching cruises on a fast 70-foot boat. There's a snackbar on board. Cruises leave from mid-December through mid-March weekdays at 10 a.m. and 1 p.m.; on weekends, there are cruises at 9 a.m., noon, and 2:30 p.m. Adults pay $12; children 13 to 17, $10; 12 and under, $8.

The **San Diego Natural History Museum** offers two-hour whale-watching trips on specific days from December to mid-February. The advantage of these trips is that you have a skilled naturalist as your guide. The museum does not recommend these trips for children under 5.

Tickets can be obtained by mail or by phone with a major credit card. Write or call first to determine this year's dates of departure, then order your tickets from: Whales, Natural History Museum, P.O. Box 1390, San Diego, CA 92112 (tel. 619/232-3821). You can also purchase tickets at the museum, sometimes even on the day of the tour. Adults pay $12; children 12 and under, $10.

Islandia Sportfishing is at 1551 W. Mission Bay Dr., next to the Hyatt Islandia in Mission Bay (tel. 619/222-1164). These boats leave for whale-watching daily at 9 and 11:30 a.m. and 2 p.m. on quick two-hour round-trip excursions. You won't see as much as on the other trips. Adults pay $10; children 12 and under, $7.

Point Loma Sportfishing, 1403 Scott St., Point Loma (tel. 619/223-1627), will take you whale-watching on Saturday and Sunday. Departure times are 9 a.m. and 1 p.m., and trips last approximately three hours. Adult fares are $10; juniors 12 to 17 and seniors pay $8; children under 12 pay $6. No age minimum. Point Loma also has sportfishing boats for private charter and offer half- and three-quarter-day fishing trips.

H & M Landing, 2803 Emerson St., Point Loma (tel. 619/222-1144), will take you whale-watching for a full-day or a three-hour cruise. The full-day cruises sail to the Coronado Islands to see sea lions and sea birds in addition to the whales. The trips are offered January through March, Thursday through Sunday departing at 9 a.m. and returning at 5 p.m. Adults pay $28; children 13 to 17, $22; children 12 and under, $18. The three-hour cruise is offered twice daily from December through March—at 9 a.m. and 1 p.m. Adult fares are $10; children 13 to 17, $8; 12 and under, $6.

Yet another way to go is via a tall ship, the *Invader.* **Waterfront Promotions** (Invader Cruises), 1066 N. Harbor Dr., at the Embarcadero (tel. 619/298-8066 or 619/234-8687, or toll free 800/262-4386 in California), takes you out on the 151-foot schooner for a 3½-hour whale-watching trip. The ship, which holds 250 people, has a galley that serves hot food. It sails twice daily from December through March—at 9:30 a.m. and 2 p.m. Adults pay $15; children under 12, $10.

Boat Rentals / Sailing / Deep-Sea Fishing

Ever sailed a boat before? If you and yours are 15 and older, you can sail with the **San Diego Sailing Club and School,** located at Marina Cortez, 1880 Harbor Island, San Diego, CA 92101 (tel. 619/298-6623). You can learn either through individual lessons or by becoming a member of the club (good for southern Californians). Open daily in summer from 9 a.m. to 5 p.m., till 4:30 p.m. in winter. Group lessons start at $18 per hour on the 21-foot *Victory,* or take private lessons for $10 an hour plus the rental of the boat.

Seahorse Boat Rentals has several locations, but the best one for families is at 1715 Strand Way, Coronado, CA 92118 (tel. 619/437-1514). Located on a calm, sheltered bay, this branch has a large fleet of paddleboats, and the sailing lessons are geared to children. In addition, there are lots of ducks around to feed. Food and snacks are available at the boat-rental shop, and you can picnic nearby at any of the grassy areas.

In addition to lessons, sailboats, fishing boats, ski boats, and speedboats can be rented. Rates begin at $18 an hour for a Hobie 16. Sailing lessons cost $9 per half hour. You can also rent private charter boats for deep-sea fishing. They are open daily from 9 a.m. to 5 p.m.

The other branches are located at 1641 Quivira Rd., Mission Bay, San Diego, CA 92109 (tel. 619/223-1681), which also rents bicycles (open on weekdays from 8 a.m. to 6 p.m. and on weekends from 7 a.m. to 6 p.m.); and 604 Tidelands Ave., Chula Vista, CA 92010 (tel. 619/585-7245), which rents boats only (open in summer on weekdays from 10 a.m. to 5 p.m., on weekends to 6 p.m.; in winter, on weekdays from 11 a.m. to 4:30 p.m. and on weekends from 10 a.m. to 5 p.m.).

Islandia Sportfishing, 1551 W. Mission Bay Dr., San Diego, CA 92109 (tel. 619/222-1164), rents all sorts of sportfishing boats, which can be a fun experience for the whole family. Islandia has a 40-foot diesel sportfisher that accommodates six, for instance, for private charters, or an 85-foot boat available for half-day fishing trips with large groups of people. Prices depend on the boat, the number of hours chartered, and where you want to fish. Call for prices.

The **Harbor Island Sailing Club** (2040 Harbor Island Dr., Suite 118, San Diego, CA 92101 (tel. 619/291-9569, or toll free 800/854-6625), rents—guess what?—sailboats. If you're already a member of a sailing club, check whether you have reciprocal privileges with Harbor Island. Public rentals, with or without a skipper, begin at $24 for two hours on a 14-foot Capri. Reservations must be made in advance for extended charters.

Bicycling

You can pick up a bike trail map at 2905 Juan St., Old Town, or call 619/231-BIKE. Rent bicycles from **Rent A Bike,** at the San Diego Hilton, East Mission Bay Drive, which delivers and picks up free anywhere in San Diego (tel. 619/275-2644, 24 hours a day). You can rent 5-, 10-, and 12-speeds ($6 per hour), tandems ($10 per hour), cruisers ($5 per hour), children's bikes ($4 per hour), and baby seats ($12 with a cruiser). Helmets and baskets are free.

Hamel's Action Sports Center, 704 Ventura Pl. (tel. 619/488-5050), also rents bicycles. Adult bikes are $3 per hour; tandems, $6. No children's bikes are available, but there are child carriers on some of the beach cruisers at no extra charge. Beach cruisers rent for $3 per hour. Helmets for babies are available at no charge. No reservations are necessary; they do not pick up or deliver. Hamel's is open daily in summer from 10 a.m. to 8 p.m.; in winter, from 9 a.m. to 7 p.m.

Horseback Riding

When you have the time to spend and want more than just "a schlepp through the woods on a horse," you'd do well to visit **Holidays on Horseback,** 24928 Viejas Blvd., Descanso, CA 92016 (tel. 619/445-3997). Liz and Earl Hammond offer a multitude of possibilities for getting away to the desert or the mountains. And they are only about 42 miles from San Diego. The Hammonds feel their trips are well suited to families because they provide a complete wilderness experience. And, indeed, these are not ordinary one-hour horse rentals. Guides point out the local flora and how it is used by the mountain and desert people; you'll stop to watch the wildlife and talk about the history of the areas you ride through. They offer guided day trips, two-day, three-day, and all sorts of other rides. Call or write them and tell them your riding experience and what you'd like to do, and they'll figure out which trip is best for you. They take children 8 and up, or younger children who have had riding experience. Prices are the same for kids and adults; they'll give a 10% discount for families of five or more. Prices start at $48 for a 3½-hour ride with buffet lunch on the trail, and go up from there.

SPECTATOR SPORTS: The **San Diego Padres** (baseball) and the **San Diego Chargers** (football) play at Jack Murphy Stadium, 9449 Friars Rd., off Calif. 805, Mission Valley (tel. 619/283-5808).

To get tickets to the Padres' games, write two weeks in advance to: Jack Murphy Stadium Ticket Office, P.O. Box 2000, San Diego, CA 92120 (tel. 619/283-4494). To charge by phone, call TeleSeat at 619/283-7328; or purchase tickets one hour in advance of the game (usually played at 1:05 p.m. and 7:05 p.m.) on the north side of the stadium at Advance Window C.

The best way to get San Diego Chargers tickets is by requesting an order form from the Chargers Ticket Office, P.O. Box 20871, San Diego, CA 92120 (tel. 619/280-2121).

The **Del Mar Race Track,** at the Del Mar Fairgrounds west of Calif. 5, Del

Mar (tel. 619/755-1141 for information, or 619/481-1207 for the ticket office), is open late July through mid-September for Thoroughbred horse racing. It's a beautiful racetrack with a Spanish-style grandstand, first founded by Bing Crosby in 1937. There's satellite wagering on Thoroughbreds and harness horses from other tracks when the Del Mar meet is over. Call 619/755-1141 for current information.

SPECIALTY SHOPPING: San Diego somehow manages to combine its shopping areas and centers with sightseeing possibilities.

Seaport Village

San Diego's wonderful harbors make strolling and watching boats a natural form of recreation. After you've visited the Embarcadero and its harbor sights, make a stop at Seaport Village, West Harbor Drive and Kettner Boulevard (tel. 619/235-4014). Although first and foremost a shopping center, it does have its appeal as a place to visit with the family. Designed to look somewhat like a California fishing village, it's set on 14 acres in three adjacent plazas, each with shops and restaurants. A boardwalk along the oceanfront ties them all together.

There are 85 shops, 13 theme restaurants (you know, one serves Mexican food, one's a deli, another serves ice cream . . .), and four sit-down restaurants. There are crafts shops; clothing boutiques; kite, poster, and souvenir shops; and stores that specialize in jewelry and music boxes. One is devoted to wooden toys and other items for children. The children will be charmed by the circa-1900 carousel, restored to its original glory after being sold piecemeal to museums around the country and then purchased in toto by Seaport Village. A 12-piece brass band plays regularly, and you might see a mime or a juggler or other entertainer—or several entertainers—as you walk through the village. Usually on Sunday at 1 p.m. in the West Plaza, there's a 45-minute program of mime and puppetry called **Kazoo Kids.** The audience participates, and the children each get a kazoo at the end of the show.

The children will also enjoy the **Time-Out Family Amusement Center** (tel. 619/233-5277). It features video games, pinball machines, and other amusements.

Cinderella Carriage stops near the Harbor House Restaurant. For $20 per half hour ($25 in the evenings), you can be transported through parts of San Diego in the old-fashioned elegance of a horse-drawn carriage. Rides are available from 11:30 a.m. to 11 p.m. daily.

The shops and restaurants are open in summer from 10 a.m. to 10 p.m.; in winter, September through May, they are open till 9 p.m. There's free parking in and near the village.

Horton Plaza

Located right in the heart of downtown San Diego, Horton Plaza Shopping Center, between Broadway and G Street, and First and Fourth Avenues (tel. 619/239-8180), is an interesting place to spend some time after you've exhausted all the sightseeing venues in town. Built on the site of San Diego's first park, it is modeled after urban centers found in Europe. Storefronts are varied, and the layout is elaborate. It's not very easy to get around Horton Plaza (and not particularly wonderful with a stroller). It has more than 135 shops and restaurants, with specialty stores such as Horton Toy & Doll, men's and women's clothing shops, four department stores, shoe stores, and sports apparel and equipment stores. There are a number of fast-food spots, including Mrs. Fields Cookies, La Salsa, and Pogo Pizza. Harbor House Restaurant is here (see the "Where to Eat" section for details), as well as Heaven Pop Cuisine, a Marie Callendar's and the Panda Inn.

On the street level, exterior, at First Avenue and F Street (11 Horton Plaza), you will find the **International Visitor Information Center** (tel. 619/236-1212). Open daily (except Thanksgiving and Christmas) from 8:30 a.m. to 5:30 p.m.

Park on G Street at Second and Third Avenues for best results at Horton Plaza. Stores are open Monday through Saturday from 10 a.m. to 9 p.m. and on Sunday from 11 a.m. to 6 p.m.

Gaslamp Quarter

Between Fourth and Sixth Avenues and Broadway and L Street in downtown San Diego are 16 blocks of specialty shops, restaurants, and art galleries called Gaslamp Quarter. The Gaslamp Quarter Foundation is at 410 Island Ave. (tel. 619/233-5227). Baroque revival and Victorian buildings have been restored to their original spirit. Once the site of the town's red-light district, it is now a National Historical District. Walking tours are offered by the council, but the two-hour tours might be too tedious for young children and too boring for older ones. Contact the council for meeting places and times.

FAIRS / FESTIVALS / SEASONAL EVENTS: The **Del Mar Annual Regional Fair** is held for 16 days from late June through early July at the Del Mar Fairgrounds, 20 miles north of San Diego. Take I-5 to the Villa de la Valle exit. Call 619/755-1161 or 619/296-1441 for current dates and schedules of events. Midway rides, carnival games, art shows, agricultural displays, home arts and floral exhibits, and daily grandstand shows with name performers are among the offerings.

Are you with an infant who sleeps through all sorts of music? Or with a teenager who will listen to all sorts of music? Then **Humphrey's Concerts by the Bay** are for you. These outdoor evening concerts overlook Shelter Island Marina at Humphrey's Half Moon Inn, 2303 Shelter Island Dr., and feature pop and jazz stars. Most of us will recognize the performers—Judy Collins and Donovan, the Four Tops, Lou Rawls, Chubby Checker, Kool & the Gang, the Nitty Gritty Dirt Band, and Emmylou Harris are just some of the names. Performances run May through September. Call 619/224-9438 for schedule information. Tickets are available through Ticketmaster (tel. 619/278-8497) or at Humphrey's Restaurant in the hotel (Tuesday through Saturday from 11:30 a.m. to 6 p.m. and on Sunday from 1 to 5 p.m.). There are two shows—at 7 and 9 p.m.—and tickets run $15 to $20, depending on the show.

Throughout the summer there are **Twilight in the Park Concerts** at the Organ Pavilion in Balboa Park (tel. 619/239-0512 until 4 p.m.). Concerts range from jazz to rock to performances by the navy band. The free performances are held June through August on Tuesday, Wednesday, and Thursday evenings from 6:30 to 7:30 p.m.

Each year in September, all of San Diego participates in a weekend celebration to honor Juan Rodriguez Cabrillo's landing in San Diego Harbor. It also marks him as the first European to set foot on what is now the west coast of the United States. Most of the activity is held at the Cabrillo National Monument; the events include an open house, dancing, music, and foods from Portugal, Spain, Mexico, and the U.S. A reenactment of the landing of Cabrillo's ship is portrayed at Shelter Island on Point Loma. Write or call for this year's schedule of events: **Cabrillo Festival, Inc.,** P.O. Box 6366, San Diego, CA 92106 (tel. 619/557-5450).

May signals the **Cinco de Mayo Festival** in Old Town (call Bazaar del Mundo at 619/296-3161 for this year's schedule of events). In December, the Sunday before Christmas, is the **Parade of Lights** on the San Diego Bay, a breathtaking sight of small boats—yachts, fishing boats, other little boats—adorned with Christmas lights, reindeer, Santa Clauses, and other decorations, hooked together and parading from Seaport Village past the Embarcadero to Harbor and

Shelter Islands. Call the Shelter Island Marina Inn for information (tel. 619/222-0561).

. . . and More

If you're still looking for things to do, you can take the kids to the movies on Tuesday, when it's dollar day, or visit the downtown **San Diego Library,** at 820 E St., between 8th and 9th Streets (tel. 619/236-5800), which offers story hours, magic shows, and puppet shows.

Take a 1½-hour drive to the Gold Rush mountain town of **Julian** via Calif. 79 through Descanso Junction, or Calif. 78 outside Ramona. In the winter, there's snow; in the spring, wildflowers. Autumn is harvest time, when apples are plentiful. Julian was built in the 1870s, but its Gold Rush era lasted only ten years. The town kept itself going with its abundant apple orchards. Autumn weekends are crowded with people hunting for apple products. Contact the Julian Chamber of Commerce, P.O. Box 413, Julian, CA 92036 (tel. 619/765-1857), for information on what to do while in town.

Another nice drive is to **Palomar Observatory,** atop Palomar Mountain, 66 miles north of San Diego, via County Road S6, one hour from Escondido (tel. 619/742-2119). Show the kids the country's largest Hale telescope, with an optical range of nearly one billion light-years. In addition to the telescope is an exhibit hall of pictures taken through the Palomar and other telescopes. The telescope and exhibit hall can be visited daily from 9 a.m. to 4 p.m. There is no admission charge.

Take a drive through **North County,** which begins in Del Mar, 20 miles north of downtown San Diego, and extends to the Orange County border. North of Del Mar (home of the Del Mar Thoroughbred Club racetrack) is **Encinitas.** From May through September you'll see ribbons of color throughout the town, as Encinitas is one of the capitals of flower-growing. It, and its neighbor Leucadia, are the world's leading growers of poinsettias. Some of the companies will let you in for a look at the greenhouses. But even driving down the roads you'll see acres of these red, yellow, and white Christmas flowers. Farther north is **Oceanside,** where you'll discover the West Coast's longest municipal pier.

IN AN EMERGENCY: If an emergency should occur during your visit in Orange County, you will find 24-hour emergency rooms at the following area hospitals:

Emergency Rooms
Scripps Memorial Hospital, 9888 Genesee Ave., La Jolla (tel. 619/453-3400).
Coronado Hospital, 250 Prospect Pl., Coronado (tel. 619/435-6251).
University Hospital, University of California Medical Center, 225 W. Dickinson St., San Diego (tel. 619/294-6222).
Mercy Hospital and Medical Center, 4077 Fifth Ave., San Diego (tel. 619/294-8111).

Pharmacies with Extended Hours
University City Pharmacy, 3338 Governor Dr., San Diego (tel. 619/453-4455); open Monday through Friday from 9 a.m. to 9 p.m., on Saturday till 8 p.m., and on Sunday from 10 a.m. to 7 p.m.

---

6. LA JOLLA

Long known as the "Jewel of the Pacific," La Jolla (pronounced "La Hoya") is a perfect place to walk with the family. Whether you choose to walk in the village along Prospect Street and Girard Avenue, or along Coast Boulevard, which parallels the ocean, you'll have lots to look at. The village bursts with boutiques carrying imported clothing, jewelry shops, art galleries, and other specialty shops. Restaurants are everywhere, and there are lots of ice-cream shops to assuage the hunger of "needy" children. A walk above the cliffs is breathtaking. You'll see La Jolla's famous beaches; the magnificent homes you've probably heard about, with their gardens exploding in color; rocky cliffs; and ocean-carved caves.

Even if you don't stay in a hotel here, La Jolla is just 15 minutes from the heart of San Diego. You can plan to spend the day at a beach here, or an afternoon in the village. Or come for an early dinner and a stroll afterward. Parking is not easy on busy summer weekends, so plan on walking. Park wherever you can, and be sure to bring that Snuggly or stroller for your youngsters.

WHERE TO STAY IN LA JOLLA: Walk into the **Embassy Suites Hotel,** 4550 La Jolla Village Dr., San Diego, CA 92122 (tel. 619/453-0400, or toll free 800/EMBASSY), and you enter a 12-story atrium courtyard with plants hanging from balconies and a pond where children can feed turtles and goldfish. The glassed roof gives an open-air feeling, and four glass elevators carry guests through this lush paradise. The pool is indoors, away from cool ocean breezes, and the Jacuzzi is outdoors, surrounded by chaises for sun worshippers. Older children can hang out in the lobby area, where they'll find a billiard table and Pac-Man.

Included in your room price is a complimentary breakfast cooked to order in the lobby restaurant, The Other Place. This restaurant also features a weekly live jazz night and a weekly fashion auction, both at no extra cost to guests. Complimentary cocktails and soft drinks are served each evening, and a deli adjacent to the restaurant is ideal for snacks and quick meals. Room service is available. Babysitting can be arranged through the front desk.

Every room here is a beautifully decorated suite. Most have a bedroom with two double beds or one king-size bed, and all have a living area with a fold-out sofa bed, a kitchen area, and table and chairs. All rooms have two TVs and two telephones. A few larger suites are available, including a two-bedroom/two-bath suite with a larger living area and a formal dining table. All accommodations open onto the courtyard, so you can avoid dark hallways and stairways.

In summer (July to September) regular suites rent for $129 to $179. The remainder of the year, rooms rent for $99. Two-bedroom suites cost $250 double year round. Children under 12 stay free in their parents' room; those 12 and over and additional adults pay $20 each per night. There is no charge for cribs, and no rollaways are available (use the sofa beds).

In the heart of La Jolla's picturesque village, the **Colonial Inn,** 910 Prospect St., La Jolla, CA 92037 (tel. 619/454-2181, or toll free 800/832-5525, 800/826-1278 in California), offers the ambience of a small European hotel. The staff knows you by name and greets you with a smile. The lobby, decorated like a large elegant living room, is done in Williamsburg blue and white, with a silver vase of fresh flowers atop the grand piano and a fire crackling in the fireplace.

Built in 1913, the Colonial Inn is set on a hill over La Jolla's lovely cove and beach. You can walk a block to the beach or take a swim in the hotel's pool. The unusual round pool is ideal for young children, as it is no deeper than four feet anywhere. Snacks and drinks are served on the garden terrace.

Guests can play tennis at nearby privately owned courts at no extra charge.

Putnam's Restaurant and Bar, just off the lobby, serves breakfast, lunch, and dinner and provides room service for guests. Fresh seafood is the specialty here. The atmosphere is formal and subdued (if you have young children, a better bet is to choose a more informal restaurant in the village). For your day at the beach, the restaurant provides a selection of boxed lunches (about $6).

Every one of the 75 guest rooms is unique in design and décor. Some are mini-suites with a separate living area. All will give you the feeling that you're in a grand old home with modern amenities. Rooms have large walk-in closets. Bathrooms are also large and have well-lighted mirrors. Stocked mini-bars, free HBO and cable TV, and a complimentary morning newspaper are standard. Accommodations are furnished with twin beds, two double beds, or two queen-size beds. Some connecting rooms are available. You can choose an ocean view or a village view, and some rooms feature both.

Prices vary according to the view. Year-round rates range from $120 to $140, single or double. Deluxe rooms cost $160 and suites rent for $185 to $205. Children under 6 stay free in their parents' room; those 6 and over and additional adults are charged $12 each per night. Cribs are free and rollaways cost $10 each. Free valet parking.

The main attraction at the **La Jolla Cove Motel,** 981 Coast Blvd., La Jolla, CA 92037 (tel. 619/459-4306, or toll free 800/248-2683), is actually across the street from the motel. Shell Beach, with its large grassy area for picnics, its cove for exploring and beaches for swimming, offers a breathtaking view of the coastline that is spectacular.

The family that built the motel almost 30 years ago still owns and operates it, and pride of ownership is apparent. The comfort and happiness of the guests is important, as is evident in the little touches, such as stocking the solarium with interesting books and games.

The hotel has a large pool and its own small but private grassy park area for family picnics. There's no food service in the hotel, but the village of La Jolla is within walking distance.

These no-frills rooms are clean inside and out. Accommodations are personally decorated in the owners' eclectic taste, each in a different décor. You can choose from standard hotel rooms; suites of one, two, or three bedrooms; and villas of 1,500 square feet in a newer section of the hotel overlooking the pool. Many of the rooms have complete kitchens and large living areas. Kitchens come with oven and stove and are stocked with utensils and dishes. The living area in the studios and suites is generous, but bathrooms are tiny. Not all rooms have tubs, so if you want one be sure to ask in advance.

If you are planning to use a crib or rollaway, you'll probably want a studio or suite rather than a regular room, to avoid feeling cramped. The front-desk staff will work with you to book the room that best suits your family's needs.

Rates are based on single occupancy for hotel rooms (add $10 for every additional adult), double occupancy for suites. Depending on the view, hotel rooms range in price from $55 to $80 in summer. Rates are slightly lower other times of the year. Suites rent for $114 to $240 in the summer. Children under 18 are charged $5 per night; those 18 and over pay the adult charge—$10. No charge for cribs and rollaways. Complimentary covered parking.

Beach lovers will enjoy staying at the **La Jolla Beach TraveLodge,** 412 Playa Del Norte, La Jolla, CA 92037 (tel. 619/454-0716, or toll free 800/255-3050). This newly remodeled motel is only a block from the famous Windansea Beach, where you can swim and surf to your heart's content. A large heated pool in the hotel is suited to play and lap swimming.

Although there is no restaurant in the hotel, four are within a block. Su Casa is right across the street and features Mexican cuisine and fresh seafood (see the "Where to Eat" section).

Rooms are not fancy, but are clean and comfortable and large enough for a crib or rollaway. Some rooms with two double beds have a small kitchenette that can be closed off by a folding door. If you don't want to use the kitchenette, tell the management and the room charge will be $5 less.

Suites are available with a separate living area furnished with fold-out sofas. The motel has no adjoining rooms, so if your family needs to spread out, ask for one of these suites. The suite kitchenettes are stocked with toaster ovens, stoves, refrigerators, and utensils, and there is a kitchen table and chairs.

Prices are by the room rather than by the number of people, and range from $53 to $59. Rooms with kitchenettes start at $69, and suites with a living area are $82. Prices are higher in July and August. There's no charge for cribs or roll-aways. Weekly and monthly rates are available, except in summer. A three-night minimum stay is required on holidays. Parking is free, a big plus in the beach areas of La Jolla.

WHERE TO EAT IN LA JOLLA: The above-mentioned **Su Casa,** 6738 La Jolla Blvd. (tel. 619/454-0369), one block from the beach, is a Mexican restaurant specializing in seafood. The décor here is nautical, with gleaming brass lanterns, and a large aquarium occupying the center of the restaurant. Our kids enjoyed watching the fish while they ate. The deep-blue carpet and napkins and lots of hanging plants add to the inviting atmosphere.

Here you can order the catch of the day or sea bass Veracruz ($14) accompanied by the salad bar and rice and beans or vegetables. Or you may feel more like a burrito mignon, a prime-cut beef filet served with a chile relleno or enchilada, plus rice and beans ($13). Any dish you choose will be satisfying and attractively served. And complimentary tortilla chips come with all entrees.

A children's menu (crayons included) offers a choice of a taco, an enchilada, a hamburger, or two flautas, served with rice, beans, or french fries, all for $4.

Booster seats and highchairs are provided. Your server will gladly warm baby bottles and baby food in the kitchen, and the bartender will make special kiddie drinks.

Su Casa is open weekdays from 11:30 a.m. to 10 p.m. and on Saturday from 11 a.m. to 10:30 p.m. Sunday brunch is served from 10:30 a.m. to 3 p.m., and dinner is from 3 to 10 p.m. Reservations are not accepted, but call right before you come to put your name on a "priority seating" list. Parking lot available (valet parking on weekends). Major credit cards are accepted.

Stop at **The Spot,** 1005 Prospect St. (tel. 619/459-0800), for lunch or dinner during your day of shopping in La Jolla. You can sit back and enjoy the lively décor. Surfboards and skis hang on the walls, copper kettles adorn the used-brick fireplace, and light rock music sets the tone.

Service is fast and friendly, and the menu has a wide variety of foods. A favorite for lunch is the Cobb salad—chunks of roast turkey, bacon, tomato, avocado, and crumbled bleu cheese on a bed of crisp greens—served with the house vinaigrette dressing and a grilled English muffin ($6.50). For dinner, try the full slab of ribs, prepared from an original Chicago recipe more than 25 years old, served with french fries, garlic bread, and coleslaw ($13). Another specialty here is pizza—it's delicious, but be prepared for a 30-minute wait. Sandwiches, soups, omelets, and steaks are also available.

For children, adult portions may be split in the kitchen, or you can order a grilled cheese sandwich.

Boosters and highchairs are available. The servers will gladly warm baby bottles and baby food in the kitchen. Special children's drinks can be ordered from the bar.

Open every day of the year. Lunch is served from 11 a.m. to 4 p.m., and dinner, from 4 p.m. to 1 a.m. Reservations accepted for parties of eight or more. Street parking. Major credit cards are welcome.

The Pump House, 5450 La Jolla Blvd. (tel. 619/459-7870), is a big, bright restaurant serving a tasty breakfast, lunch, and dinner. Even if you're here in the morning, ask for the dinner menu to read about the background of some of the decorations, such as the surfboards and other paraphernalia. Then let the kids choose from the Junior Beachcomber menu. For breakfast they might order a pancake sandwich, sausage and egg, or silver dollar pancakes ($1.50 to $2.50).

Lunch choices include a little Mac meatah (burger), little bacon and cheese, P.B. & J. (guess), junior spinach salad (they must be kidding!), or grilled cheese ($1.50 to $2.75). Dinner selections are junior barbecued ribs, shrimp Victoria, fish, hamburger steak, or teriyaki chicken breast ($4 to $8). Cheesecake is for dessert, and special drinks will be made upon request.

Mom and Dad can order country breakfasts, omelets, pancakes, and even asparagus hollandaise or hand-cut lox with bagel and cream cheese. Don't push away the bakery basket—what's inside is delicious.

At lunch, try burgers, shack salads, sandwiches, and such specialties as fresh seafood or prime rib ($5 to $13). At dinner, the appetizer selections are quite interesting—lumpia eggrolls, char-broiled grape leaves, tempura zucchini, and pot stickers. Entrees—served with salad, vegetable, potato, and sourdough bread—include bacon scallop kebab, swordfish, teriyaki chicken, barbecued beef ribs, steak, and prime rib. Light eaters can also get big salads or burgers. Entrees range from $9 to $13; burgers and salads, $5 to $9.

They have booster seats only. Your server will gladly warm bottles and baby food in the kitchen. Ask and you'll receive crackers at the table right away.

Open daily year round from 7 a.m. to 10 p.m. Reservations are accepted for dinner, or for large parties at any meal. There usually isn't a wait. Large parking lot. Major credit cards are welcome.

El Torito Who-Song and Larry's Cantina, 8910 Via La Jolla Dr. (tel. 619/453-4115), majors in fun. The waitpersons are known for riding tricycles, wearing gorilla masks, and singing "Happy Birthday" to guitar accompaniment. If you need even more entertainment, you can watch as tortillas are made and cooked in the center of the restaurant.

If you find the eight-page menu confusing, turn to the back page for an explanation of the various Mexican food items. A typical Mexican plate, such as a tamale with rice, refried beans, and sweet corn cakes, costs about $7. San Antonio–style fajitas—marinated strips of steak served with tomatoes, salsa, refried beans, guacamole, warm tortillas, and sour cream—are $10.

Children will enjoy their very own menu, which includes a story, mask, balloon, and puzzles. Items are $2.75 each and include a few American offerings, such as a peanut butter and jelly sandwich with fries, as well as traditional Mexican food. You'll find an interesting variation on the hot dog here: it's wrapped with cheese in a lightly fried tortilla.

Boosters and highchairs are provided. The servers will gladly warm baby bottles and baby food in the kitchen. Special children's drinks are available from the bar.

El Torito is open weekdays from 11 a.m. to 10 p.m., on Friday and Saturday till midnight, and on Sunday from 9:30 a.m. to 10 p.m. Reservations are recommended. Large parking lot. Major credit cards are welcome.

WHAT TO SEE AND DO: We've separated La Jolla's sightseeing attractions from those in San Diego only because you might want to spend a couple of days doing things just in this area. Don't forget the beaches—they're wonderful. See the "Beaches and Parks" entry in the San Diego section for information on La Jolla's beaches.

Children's Museum of San Diego

What was intended to be a brief stop on the way out of town turned into a two-hour visit when our 4-year-old found the Children's Museum of San Diego, 8657 Villa La Jolla Dr. (tel. 619/450-0768). Located in the unlikely setting of the lower level of the La Jolla Village Square Shopping Mall, between the May Company and Bullock's department stores, it's a small hands-on museum perfect for ages 2 to 12. It's hard to know what kids will do first. Our Janey went straight for the stage, where would-be thespians can act out whatever they want on a real stage with a real velvet curtain that opens and closes. Helped by props such as dress-up clothes, handbags, shoes, and hats, she and the little girls she met created their own stage production. In the background, little boys exchanged helmets and T-shirts and decided who should join the girls on stage. We found several young children enjoying the giant Leggo set in a separate room, and the broadcasters of the future were "reporting" the news in the KKID newsroom. We waited in a very brief line to play with a computer, and became Janey's patients in an authentic dentist's chair. Other boys and girls couldn't wait to get their hands on paintbrushes to attack a huge sheet of paper just beckoning to them from the wall. Arts and crafts projects go on nearby, and youngsters can take their projects home.

The museum is more than an indoor playground for children. It's an educational experience as well, and one in which children are encouraged to *do* and to *touch*—one in which parents don't have to say no to curious young explorers.

The museum is open Wednesday through Sunday from noon to 5 p.m.; on Saturday it opens at 10 a.m. Admission is $2.75 per person; children under 2 are admitted free. Parking is plentiful in the mall's parking lot.

Scripps Aquarium

The world-renowned **Scripps Institution of Oceanography,** part of the University of California, is at 8602 La Jolla Shores Dr., down the hill from the Torrey Pines Mesa. For detailed directions, call the information recording (tel. 619/534-6933).

The Scripps Aquarium-Museum has 22 tanks that contain colorful and interesting Pacific marine life. Children from toddlers up are mesmerized by living sea creatures just inches away behind glass aquarium walls.

They'll watch delicate seahorses cling to flower-like corals, look at the sucker-lined undersides of octopi, and gaze down the gaping mouths of groupers. The gift and book shop has sea treasures: shells that make great souvenirs at bargain prices.

All ages will enjoy the on-shore tidepool; children 7 and older may imagine what it's like to be an oceanographer while they view exhibits on current research.

Try to schedule your visit to coincide with fish feedings at 1:30 p.m. on Wednesday and Sunday. The fish make the water look as if it's boiling.

The aquarium is open daily from 9 a.m. to 5 p.m., and no admission is charged. Donations are accepted but not required. Parking is limited, particularly on weekends.

La Jolla Museum of Contemporary Art (and environs)

Exhibits at the **La Jolla Museum of Contemporary Art** are colorful, abstract, sometimes tactile—and always unusual. The museum is at 700 Prospect St. (tel. 619/454-3541, or 619/454-0267 for program information). Children over 7 will enjoy the museum's annual **Festival of Animation,** shown in the Sherwood Auditorium during the first part of the year and from time to time during the summer. Youngsters with spending money will want to visit the museum's bookstore, known for creative toys, gifts, and colorful art books.

You can picnic or relax on the grounds of the museum; there are stone sculptures that children can climb on while parents enjoy a view of the ocean and coastline.

Open Tuesday through Sunday from 10 a.m. to 5 p.m. (till 9 p.m. on Wednesday); closed Monday and Thanksgiving, Christmas, and New Year's Day.

Admission is $3 for adults, $1 for students 13 to 18 and seniors, 50¢ for children 5 to 12, and free for children under 5. Call before you visit; the building is undergoing a major structural renovation, and parts of it may be closed until sometime in 1992.

Every room of **John Cole's Bookstore,** 780 Prospect St. (tel. 619/454-

4766), an early–La Jolla beach cottage, overflows with books. You'll find it one block north of the museum, toward downtown. The children's room has a small table and chairs and a view of the sea through lead-paned windows.

If your kids are oozing energy and you need a break, turn them loose at the playground of **La Jolla Park and Recreation Center,** across from the museum on Prospect Street, between Culver and Draper Streets. There's plenty of playground equipment for them to use.

Mingei International Museum of World Folk Art

On the north side of one of San Diego's largest shopping centers, University Towne Centre (inland from La Jolla at 4405 La Jolla Village Dr.), is the Mingei International Museum of World Folk Art (tel. 619/453-5300). Mingei means "arts of the people"; it was coined 50 years ago by a Japanese scholar.

Exhibition items, which range from textiles, folk toys, and weather vanes to pottery and musical instruments, are always colorful and imaginative. Because the museum offers an ideal introduction to art for children, it is a popular destination for school field trips.

Open Tuesday through Saturday from 11 a.m. to 5 p.m. Admission is $2 for adults; children under 12, free. Park near Nordstrom.

7. CORONADO

Coronado's roots go back to 1885, when two midwesterners decided to build "the finest watering spot on the Pacific Coast." Elisha Babcock, Jr., and Hampton L. Story bought the peninsula for a mere $110,000 (big money at that time) and went to work looking for investors. John D. Spreckels, the sugar baron from San Francisco, was a big investor and eventually bought out most of the original people and led the town's development.

Today, like a winding silver-blue ribbon, the Coronado Bay Bridge ties Coronado to San Diego. A slice of beach called the Silver Strand was and still is the land connection between the two, but taking the toll bridge is the easiest way to make the 2.2-mile drive to the peninsula.

Although you'll feel you are on your own small island in Coronado, you are actually only a short drive from San Diego's main attractions. If you're not staying in Coronado, plan to spend a day touring this quaint town with its interesting shops and restaurants. It makes a nice walk with the children. You can stop by, write, or call the **Coronado Chamber of Commerce,** 720 Orange Ave., Coronado, CA 92118 (tel. 619/435-9260), for information on the peninsula. Their office is open weekdays from 9 a.m. to 4 p.m.

It's simple to get around town even if you don't drive. Take the San Diego Ferry over from the Broadway Pier in San Diego for $1 each way. It runs weekdays from 10 a.m. to 10 p.m., on weekends till 11 p.m. From San Diego it leaves every hour on the hour; from Coronado, every hour on the half hour, beginning at 10:30 a.m. Get tokens in San Diego at the San Diego Harbor Excursion's blue ticket booth. In Coronado, pick them up at the Star and Crescent Gift Galley at the Old Ferry Landing.

The **Old Ferry Landing,** 1201 First Ave., at B Street (tel. 619/435-8895), is the newest of the Coronado sightseeing attractions. It's a pleasant place to walk and spend an afternoon. You can fish from the pier, rent a bicycle, browse in specialty shops, and have a bite to eat from a fast-food cart. The shops are open daily from 10 a.m. to 9 p.m.

A trackless **trolley** will take you from Old Ferry Landing down Orange Avenue (the main shopping area, as well as the chamber of commerce, is on Orange) to the Hotel Del Coronado and back.

Bring a bicycle on the ferry from San Diego, or rent bikes at **Hollands Bicycle Shop,** 977 Orange Ave., two blocks from the Del Coronado (tel. 619/435-

3153), and pedal around town. Children's bikes and single-speeds cost $3 per hour; ten-speeds are $5 per hour. No helmets or child carriers are available. Open on Monday from 10 a.m. to 6:30 p.m., Tuesday through Friday from 9 a.m. to 6:30 p.m., on Saturday from 9 a.m. to 5 p.m., and on Sunday from 10 a.m. to 4 p.m.

Bike Coronado, at the Old Ferry Landing (tel. 619/437-4888), has more than 70 bikes for rent. Cruisers and children's bikes cost $4 per hour; tandems, $8; child carriers, $2; carts (attached to the bike for kids too big for child carriers but too small for their own bike), $6. Helmets, locks, and baskets are free. Open daily from 10 a.m. to dark.

Both bike shops have maps of the bike trails. The Silver Strand bike trail is an eight-mile flat route that will take you along the Silver Strand beach.

Summer Sundays, June through September, are delightful in **Spreckels Park,** on Orange Avenue between 6th and 7th Streets (tel. 619/435-9260), which is Coronado's largest park. At 6 p.m., free band concerts entertain families with a different performance each week.

Guided walks of historical streets are available through the **Coronado Historical Association** (tel. 619/435-5993 or 619/435-5892). Tours leave from the Glorietta Bay Inn, across the street from the Hotel Del Coronado. One tour is 1¼ hours and covers an eight-block area. The other may take an hour or more. If your children join you, you'll be able to point out the house where L. Frank Baum, author of *The Wizard of Oz,* spent a lot of time writing his books.

Whether or not you decide to stay overnight in Coronado, you must visit the Hotel Del Coronado. Although there's a self-guided walking tour audiotape you can purchase in the lobby giftshop for $4, children might find the 45-minute walk tedious. Instead, walk around by yourselves—the staff doesn't mind.

It was when the peninsula was made up of acres of sagebrush in the 1880s that construction began on the **Hotel Del Coronado,** 1500 Orange Ave., Coronado, CA 92118 (tel. 619/522-8000), and it opened in February 1888. Thomas Edison himself designed the electrical system and returned to the hotel in 1904 to flip the switch on the West Coast's first electrically lit, live outdoor Christmas tree. The tree still flourishes on the grounds, outside the Crown Room restaurant.

Designated a National Historic Landmark in 1977, the Hotel Del Coronado, under the direction of its sixth set of owners, has recently been renovated to emphasize its Victorian architectural tradition.

Through the first 100 years of the hotel's life, it has housed such notables as Presidents Woodrow Wilson, Franklin D. Roosevelt, Jimmy Carter, and Ronald Reagan. Charles Lindbergh celebrated his historic flight at a hotel dinner in his honor in 1927. It is rumored that the hotel was the site of the first meeting of Wallis Simpson and the Prince of Wales. The hotel served as a backdrop in Marilyn Monroe's classic *Some Like It Hot* in 1958. Astronaut Scott Carpenter was honored here with a rocket-shaped cake. John Wayne, Frank Sinatra, and other Hollywood figures have found the "Del" a quiet getaway.

The hotel originally consisted of 400 rooms. Two buildings of contemporary-style rooms were added in the 1970s, bringing the total to 700. The lobby of the original building is a delightful place to sit and take in the atmosphere. Victorian "lamps" provide soft lighting, and columns of Illinois oak and red velvet chairs add to the luxury. A cage-like elevator takes guests to the upper floors.

At Christmastime the lobby is transformed into a holiday wonderland. Each year the hotel staff decorates a tree that is two stories tall, brought in from the nearby mountains of Julian. A different theme is chosen each year for the decorations. The tree has been hung with hundreds of teddy bears, dolls, and characters from the Land of Oz. The breathtaking finished product is a treat for all ages.

In the lower lobby there is an arcade of specialty shops, including a toy store. Adults will find clothing and jewelry, and everybody will love the candy store, where you can purchase caramel apples or chocolate-dipped strawberries.

The beach is a short walk away. You can swim, picnic, or go for a refreshing stroll down the paved boardwalk. If you prefer warmer water, the hotel has two huge pools, complete with poolside snack service.

Summertime is playtime at the hotel, where you'll find programs for the entire family, as well as just for the kids. Adult and family programs include aquarobics, croquet on the Garden Patio lawn, a daily Power Walk through Coronado at 6:30 a.m., and a daily morning adult lap swim. "Coronado on Wheels" is a popular bicycle spin through town, with a stop for frozen yogurt along the way. The $20 fee includes the bike, yogurt, and a guided tour. Social activities include a complimentary marshmallow roast every Monday and Thursday evening, and an ice-cream social on Wednesday evening for a nominal charge.

Children's activities include a Kids' Summer Jamboree, an evening program with games, door prizes, and a feature movie on Tuesday, Friday, and Saturday from 6 to 9 p.m. The cost is $12.50 for the first child, $7.50 for each additional child in the family, and the program is open to children ages 6 to 14. Poolside video is open to all ages, all day every day, in the arcade.

During the month of August, Del's Fun Camp offers children's games, arts and crafts, educational walks, swimming programs, and sandcastle building. The program runs daily from 1 to 4 p.m. for children ages 6 to 12 (it costs $15 for the first child, $10 for each additional child in the family).

Arrangements can be made for a jog along a prescribed course. Check with the concierge for information. Later in the day, take advantage of the ocean-view tennis courts. The hotel has a pro shop and a tennis pro. Court time and lessons are available at an extra charge. The health club has an exercise room ($8 a visit), lockers and showers, a steamroom, a sauna, and a therapy pool. You can also arrange for a massage (for a fee).

Coronado is ideal for bicycling, with its flat stretches of road and beautiful seaside scenery. Bikes can be rented by the hour at the hotel, and you can choose from single-speeds, ten-speeds, and tandems.

The Coronado golf course, just a few miles from the hotel, is one of the most beautiful in San Diego. Reservations can be made at the hotel for tee-off time.

Dining is truly a pleasure at the hotel. The Crown/Coronet Room, with its crown chandeliers and paneled walls, is an elegant setting for breakfast, lunch, or dinner. Children are welcome here and have their own "Summer Play" menu in season. Selections include the Jammin' Jamboree peanut butter and jelly sandwich ($3.50) and Kid's Corner Crispy Chicken with steak fries and fresh fruit ($5.25). For dessert, the youngsters will delight in the Marshmallow Roast, chocolate-chip ice cream served in a cookie dish with a scoop of marshmallow cream ($2). Booster seats and highchairs are provided.

Gourmet dinners (for adults only) are served in traditional English style in the intimate atmosphere of the famed Prince of Wales Grille, which also has its own wine cellar.

For sandwiches, salads, breakfast items, and late-night snacks, the Del Deli —located in the lower lobby—is open daily from 6 a.m. to 2 a.m. Sandwich prices are quite reasonable. The Ocean Terrace is open seasonally for outdoor lunches and snacks. An indoor bar, elegant in dark wood tones, is adjacent. The Lobby Bar also serves daily from 10 a.m. and features live piano music.

Room service can be ordered around the clock.

If you enjoy Victorian charm, ask for a room in the main building. Each room here is unique in size, shape, and décor. Choose from accommodations with two double beds or king-size beds. All rooms are spacious, and some have large walk-in closets and pedestal sinks. There are two phones and Servibars in each room.

The new complex, built in the 1970s, has traditional first-class accommodations. You can choose from units with two double beds, king- or queen-size beds, and a few rooms with twin beds. Rooms are spacious, and the décor tends to be contemporary. Accommodations are spacious enough for a crib or rollaway, and bathrooms have standard modern fixtures.

Rates in the main building vary according to the view. They range from $135 to $275 for an ocean view, single or double. Oceanfront lanai rooms rent for $250 to $275, and oceanfront suites cost $290 to $475.

Rates in the new complex are also based on view, and start at $155 and go to $235, single or double. Suites cost $400 to $420. A one-bedroom apartment is available for $550, and a two-bedroom apartment costs $750. Children under 5 stay free in their parents' room. Children age 5 to 18 are charged a $15 supplement per night; those over 18 and additional adults pay $25 each per night. No charge for cribs or rollaways. There is a minimum two-night stay on weekends. Parking costs $7 per day.

The newest of the Coronado hotels is **Le Meridien,** 2000 2nd St., Coronado, CA 92118 (tel. 619/435-3000, or toll free 800/543-4300), which opened in summer 1988.

Flamingos bathing in a pond are your introduction to this elegant hotel, which is designed so that wherever you wander on the 16-acre property, you always have a view of water and sky. Twelve man-made lagoons complement the bay, and the walkways between rooms and buildings are open to the stars.

Luxurious as it is, Le Meridien is as suited to families as it is to the adult traveler. The hotel runs organized activities for children age 6 to 12 in the summer from 9 to 11 a.m. and 2 to 4 p.m. Activities, led by students majoring in recreation, are mostly of the outdoor variety and might include swimming, baseball, badminton, smashball, and arts and crafts. There is a nominal charge for participating in the program. Adjacent to the hotel is a new city park and baseball field with plenty of space for running and playing. The wide walkways and beach areas are great playgrounds too. Or take the kids to one of three swimming pools.

The Coronado trolley stops hourly in front of the hotel, and for 50¢ you and the children can spend the day in town.

For adults, the hotel has a full-time activity staff to coordinate sports such as jogging, aquacize, scuba-diving, and snorkeling. Facilities include a European health club and spa, a tanning salon, and six lighted tennis courts. And bring along your golf clubs—an 18-hole course is adjacent to the hotel; the greens fee is $13.

The Lescale Restaurant serves breakfast, lunch, and dinner and is open from 6:30 a.m. to 10 p.m. Prices are steep. Marius serves gourmet food and its atmosphere and prices are more suited to adult dining.

Even the standard rooms are plush. They are decorated in peach and blue and come with one king-size bed or two double beds, a sofa, and tables and chairs. Identical in size and shape, they measure more than 500 square feet. Amenities include a stocked mini-bar, remote-control TV, a radio, hairdryer, shaving/makeup mirror, bathroom scale, and bathroom telephone.

In addition to the standard rooms, there are seven executive suites with kitchenettes. One area of the property houses 28 villas. These condominium-like accommodations are studios or one-bedroom suites with kitchenettes and patios. The villas are named after French impressionist artists such as Gauguin, and are decorated with the art of their respective namesakes. The décor is country French—even the bathrooms have French doors. You'll find extra amenities in the villas, such as Jacuzzis in the tubs.

Families may want to request a studio and an adjoining one-bedroom suite, and spread out in style.

Rates are the same for single or double occupancy and vary according to room location. Standard rooms rent for $140 to $260. Executive suites cost

$360 to $460. A one-bedroom villa rents for $360 to $460, while a two-bedroom villa costs $495 to $595. Studio villas are available for $225 to $370. Children 12 and under stay free in their parents' room; those over 12 and additional adults pay $15 each per night. There is no charge for cribs or rollaways. Parking costs $8 a day.

8. TIJUANA

Tijuana loves to bill itself as the most visited city in Mexico, and indeed it might be. In 1987 more than 25 million people crossed the border there. While in the past most of the reservations made for accommodations in Tijuana and the rest of Baja were for singles or couples, in the last couple of years the tourist bureau has found that many of their requests have been for families.

Before leaving for Tijuana, stop by or call the **Tijuana and Baja Office of Tourism,** 7860 Mission Center Court, Suite 202, San Diego, CA 92108 (tel. 619/299-8518 or 619/298-4105, or toll free 800/225-2786, 800/522-1516 in California). This office also has a Central Reservation System to make your hotel reservations. Just past the border is a tourist information center as well.

The **International Visitors Information Center** at Horton Plaza in San Diego (tel. 619/236-1212) will also supply you with general information on Tijuana attractions.

GETTING THERE: There are three ways to get to Tijuana. You can visit on a tour—but we don't recommend this for children. Or you can **drive over the border** (prepare for long lines returning to the United States, especially in the early evening on weekends). There are signs marked "Centro" that will lead you to downtown Tijuana. You'll find guarded lots near Avenida Revolución, or there is street parking. Or you can park your car on the U.S. side and walk across the border. Taxis wait there all the time to take you into town. Once in town, you can walk to most places, or grab a taxi from where you are.

The other way to get to the border is via the **San Diego Trolley** (tel. 619/233-3004). The big red trolleys depart from the corner of Keltner Boulevard and C Street, across the street from the Amtrak station, every 15 minutes from 5 a.m. to 7 p.m., and every 30 minutes thereafter, with the last trolley returning from the border at 1 a.m. The trip to the border takes 45 minutes, and once at the border you'll need a taxi to get into town.

WHAT TO SEE AND DO: Those of you who visited Tijuana years ago will remember it as kind of tacky and rough—the place where sailors and teenagers came to avoid the drinking-age limit in San Diego. Efforts have been made to spruce up the city. Lucky for us, though, it hasn't lost its Latin flavor and the traditional touches that still make visiting there an adventure.

Tijuana is a place you can safely take the whole family for the day, evening, or overnight. As a whole, the Mexican people love children and they make it comfortable for you to take your kids nearly everywhere with you. Many restaurants in Tijuana will greet your children warmly. We like to go late in the afternoon (the stores stay open late), walk around, visit the Cultural Center, bargain for merchandise in some of the small shops, have a lively dinner, and return to San Diego at 10 p.m. or so.

The **Tijuana Cultural Center,** the city's proudest recent accomplishment, is located at Paseo de los Héroes y Mino Zona Río Tijuana, less than a mile from the border (tel. 706/668-1132). In addition to a museum and exhibit halls, there is an OMNIMAX presentation and a Performing Arts Center. The Space Theater has a 180° screen to wrap you around the presentation. The daily "People of the Sun" show is a dramatic view of such beautiful sights as Copper Canyon, Cancún, and the Mayan and Aztec pyramids. The museum presents a wonderful opportunity for you to introduce your children to the many faces of Mexico. In addition to historical background on the country, exhibits depicting the cultural qualities of the Mexican people—their food, dance, clothes, and other traditions —are nicely displayed. The exhibit halls act as an art museum, often displaying the works of local and internationally acclaimed Mexican artists. If you plan to be there on a Sunday, ask about the Ballet Folklorico performances held in the Performing Arts Theater.

The museum is open weekdays from 11 a.m. to 7 p.m., weekends till 8 p.m. An English version of the OMNIMAX show is featured daily at 2 p.m. Shows in Spanish are shown weekdays beginning at 1 p.m. and weekends beginning at 11 a.m. Adults pay $4.50; children 12 and under, $3.50.

Sports are big draws to Tijuana. You and the older children might enjoy watching **Thoroughbred racing at Agua Caliente Racetrack,** Blvd. Agua Caliente (tel. 619/231-1910, or 817-811 in Tijuana), year round on Saturday and Sunday at 1 p.m. Admission is charged. **Greyhound racing** is scheduled Monday through Wednesday and Friday nights, and admission is free for this event.

Jai alai is a fascinating game that your older kids might enjoy. The only places you can see it in the United States are in Florida and Connecticut. In Tijuana it's played at **Fronton Palacio Jai Alai,** Calle 7 and Avenida Revolución (tel. 619/260-0454, or 851-612 in Tijuana). A Basque game similar to handball or racquetball, jai alai originated in 18th-century Spain. The ball is called the *pelota,* and the basket-like net that catches it is called the *cesta*. It's an extremely fast game (the ball can travel at more than 160 mph) and is played with singles or doubles. Pari-mutuel wagering on the games is offered. The Palacio is open every night except Thursday at 7 p.m. (closed Christmas and New Year's weeks). The first game is at 8 p.m. Admission varies from $2.50 to $5.

Avenida Revolución is the original main shopping thoroughfare, and a part of the city's modernization efforts. Now it sports outdoor cafés and trees and flowers. Most of the stores here carry the finer jewelry, clothing, and artwork of Mexico. These aren't the shops to bargain in. Do that in the souvenir shops on the side streets; in the better boutiques and jewelry stores, they won't accept it. Although the street has been modernized, the ubiquitous photographer and his trusty donkey are still there to snap your souvenir picture. Since Tijuana is a duty-free spot, you'll also want to visit the **Río Tijuana Shopping Plaza,** next to the Cultural Center, to find French perfume, English cashmere, and Baccarat crystal.

If you want to continue farther down the peninsula, you can stop at the **Rosarita Beach Hotel** in Rosarita Beach, about 20 miles south of Tijuana. Built in the '30s, the hotel was once the haunt of movie stars and visiting royalty. Local restaurants offer very reasonably priced fresh lobster lunches. Or continue farther south to **Ensenada,** only 70 miles south of Tijuana. It's an easy and pretty ride on a four-lane toll road. Once you get there, you can walk around town and visit the shops or stroll closer to the water and stop for great food, including fresh lobster, at incredibly low prices. Nearby (you have to drive) is the **Bufadora,** a water spout that shoots spray high into the air when the tide rises. If you're there in May, you may be in time for the international San Diego–Ensenada yacht race.

An easy way to get to Ensenada is by boat via **Ensenada Express,** B Street Pier (next to the Broadway pier) at the Embarcadero (P.O. Box 81823), San Diego, CA 92138 (tel. 619/232-2109, or toll free 800/826-4815, 800/422-5008 in California). You depart San Diego at 9 a.m. and arrive in Ensenada at 12:30 p.m. You'll spend five hours touring, shopping, and eating, and then return to San Diego by 9 p.m. The cruise, on a 100-foot passenger vessel, takes about three hours each way. There is a full galley and bar, and continental breakfast is included in the price of your ticket.

The Ensenada Express leaves daily except Wednesday, year round. Round-trip fares are $59 for adults, $49 for children 12 to 17, $29 for children 3 to 11; under 3, free. On Sunday there's a special family day cruise. Children under 12 sail free when accompanied by two paying adults. Be sure to make reservations at least one week in advance.

WHAT YOU NEED TO KNOW ABOUT TRAVEL TO MEXICO: Although United States citizens do not need a visa or a passport to enter Mexico as long as they remain within 15 miles of the border and stay in Mexico less than 24 hours, U.S. Customs and Immigration officers can be less than accommodating when you try to return. You might find it easier to leave your baggage in San Diego rather than possibly undergo a thorough U.S. Customs inspection upon your return from Mexico. (If you are planning to stay more than 24 hours, or if any of your traveling companions are naturalized citizens or resident aliens, check the current border regulations at a Mexican Consulate or Tourism Office before you enter Mexico. You can get two helpful booklets, "Know Before You Go" and "Travelers' Tips," free of charge from your nearest U.S. Customs Service office.)

Even if all members of your family are U.S. citizens or legal residents of the U.S., because of tightened regulations and for your own peace of mind, we suggest that you bring along birth certificates or other **proof of U.S. citizenship or permanent residence** for each member of your family. (Resident aliens must carry their alien registration cards; naturalized citizens should carry their naturalization certificates.)

If you drive into Tijuana, be sure to have a valid driver's license, and arrange for car insurance prior to crossing the border. **American auto insurance is not valid in Mexico.** If you have a rental car, ask the rental agent whether he has—or can provide you with—insurance for Mexico. Offices for Mexican auto insurance can be found all over San Diego and close to the border. The International Visitors Information Center (tel. 619/236-1212) or the San Diego *Yellow Pages* are sources for these offices.

There are a number of **money-changing services** in San Ysidro, the town right before the border. The value of the peso has been fluctuating on a daily basis, so check the rates on the day you decide to go to Tijuana. The American dollar is accepted almost anywhere in Tijuana, Rosita Beach, and Ensenada.

Each adult can bring back up to $400 worth of **duty-free goods** into the United States, and one quart of liquor.

Most merchants and restaurant employees speak English. But if you should have any sort of problem, here are two agencies you can contact: the **U.S. Consulate** (tel. 817-400 in Tijuana) and the **Office for the Protection of Tourists** (tel. 819-492 in Tijuana, 63718 in Ensenada).

EMERGENCY INFORMATION

□ □ □

No one likes to think about sickness or accidents interrupting vacation plans, but sometimes they do—especially if you travel with kids.

In case of a life-threatening emergency, dial 911 anywhere in California. An ambulance with paramedics (and usually a police squad car) will be dispatched. If they feel that the patient is in bad enough condition to require a hospital, they will take you to the closest medical facility.

For medical emergencies that do not require immediate ambulance transportation—but do require prompt emergency-room treatment—we are providing here a list of hospitals with 24-hour emergency rooms. We have also listed some pharmacies with extended-hour services; you can find out about others from the hotel front desk, the local *Yellow Pages,* or hospital emergency-room staff.

But don't go to emergency rooms for basic medical maintenance. Most hotels have a list of doctors and dentists on call. Or contact the local medical association or dental society for referrals.

Caution: These phone numbers and locations were correct as we go to press, but because you don't want to waste valuable time in an emergency, call first to verify that there have been no changes. In recent years, many hospitals have closed down emergency rooms without much notice. Also, be sure to get directions unless you're familiar with the area.

Berkeley / Oakland
Alta Bates Hospital, 3001 Colby (and Ashby), Berkeley (tel. 415/540-0337, or 415/540-1303 for the emergency room).

Kaiser Permanente, 3451 Piedmont Ave., Oakland (tel. 415/596-1120, or 415/596-1120 or 415/596-7600 for the emergency room).

Merritt Hospital, Hawthorne and Webster Avenues, Oakland (tel. 415/655-4000, or 415/420-6116 for the emergency room).

Catalina
Avalon Municipal Hospital, 100 Falls Canyon Rd., Avalon (tel. 213/510-0700).

Fresno
Fresno Community Hospital and Medical Center, on Divisidero between Fresno and R Streets (tel. 209/442-6000, or 209/442-3998 for the emergency room).

Lake Tahoe

EMERGENCY ROOMS. **Barton Memorial Hospital,** Fourth and South Streets, South Lake Tahoe (tel. 916/541-3420).

Stateline Emergency Clinic, 176 Calif. 50 at Kahle Drive, in Stateline, Nevada (tel. 702/588-3561); open 12 hours a day, from 8 a.m. to 8 p.m.

PHARMACIES. **Payless** discount store, 1020 Tahoe Blvd., South Lake Tahoe (tel. 916/541-2434); open Monday through Friday from 9 a.m. to 9 p.m., on Saturday till 7 p.m., and on Sunday from 10 a.m. to 7 p.m.

Los Angeles and Vicinity

COASTAL REGION. **Daniel Freeman Marina Hospital,** 4650 Lincoln Blvd., Marina Del Rey (tel. 213/823-8911, ext. 442, for the emergency room).
Santa Monica Hospital, 1225 15th St., Santa Monica (tel. 213/319-4000, or 213/319-4765 for the emergency room).
St. John's Hospital and Health Center, 1328 22nd St. at Santa Monica Boulevard, in Santa Monica (tel. 213/829-5511, or 213/829-8213 for the emergency room).

HOLLYWOOD AND DOWNTOWN. **Queen of Angels Hollywood Presbyterian Medical Center,** 1300 N. Vermont Ave., near Fountain Avenue (tel. 213/413-3000, or 213/413-7318 for the emergency room).

WEST LOS ANGELES AND BEVERLY HILLS. **Cedars-Sinai Medical Center,** 8700 Beverly Blvd. (tel. 213/855-5000, or 213/855-6517 for the emergency room).

BURBANK AND THE SAN FERNANDO VALLEY. **Glendale Adventist Medical Center,** 1509 Wilson Terrace, Glendale (tel. 818/409-8000, or 818/409-8202 for the emergency room).

PHARMACIES. **Horton & Converse,** 11600 Wilshire Blvd., West L.A. (tel. 213/478-0801); open from 9 a.m. to 2 a.m. daily.
Horton & Converse, 9201 Sunset Blvd., West Hollywood (tel. 213/272-0488); open from 9 a.m. to 2 a.m. daily.
Kaiser Permanente Pharmacy, 6041 Cadillac Ave., near La Cienega Boulevard and the Santa Monica Freeway (tel. 213/857-2155); open 24 hours daily.
Thrifty Drugs Stores, 300 N. Canon Dr., Beverly Hills (tel. 213/273-7293); open from 9 a.m. to 10 p.m. daily.
Thrifty Drugs Stores, 4633 Santa Monica Blvd., West Hollywood (tel. 213/666-6126); open from 9 a.m. to 9 p.m. daily.
There is one 24-hour pharmacy in Van Nuys (San Fernando Valley): **Horton & Converse,** 6625 Van Nuys Blvd. (tel. 818/782-6251).

Mammoth Lakes
Centinelia-Mammoth Hospital, Sierra Park Road (tel. 619/934-3311).

Monterey County
Community Hospital of the Monterey Peninsula, 23624 Holman Hwy., Monterey (tel. 408/624-5311), has the only 24-hour emergency room in the area.

Napa Valley
Queen of the Valley Hospital, 1000 Trancas, in Napa (tel. 707/252-4411).

Orange County

Anaheim Memorial Hospital, 1111 W. La Palma Ave. near Harbor Boulevard, Anaheim (tel. 714/774-1450).

Midwood Community Hospital, 7770 Katella Ave., near Anaheim (tel. 714/893-5051).

Hoag Memorial Hospital, 301 Newport Blvd., Newport Beach (tel. 714/645-8600).

Palm Springs

Desert Hospital, 1150 N. Indian Ave., Palm Springs (tel. 619/323-6511). The hospital pharmacy is open daily from 8 a.m. to 10 p.m.

Redding Area

Redding Medical Center, 1100 Butte St. (tel. 916/244-5400, or 916/244-5353 for the emergency room).

Sacramento Area

Mercy Hospital, 4001 J St., downtown Sacramento (tel. 619/453-4424).

San Diego

EMERGENCY ROOMS. **Scripps Memorial Hospital,** 9888 Genesee Ave., La Jolla (tel. 619/453-3400).

Coronado Hospital, 250 Prospect Pl., Coronado (tel. 619/435-6251).

University Hospital, University of California Medical Center, 225 W. Dickinson St., San Diego (tel. 619/294-6222).

Mercy Hospital and Medical Center, 4077 Fifth Ave., San Diego (tel. 619/294-8111).

PHARMACIES. **University City Pharmacy,** 3338 Governor Dr., San Diego (tel. 619/453-4455); open Monday through Friday from 9 a.m. to 9 p.m., on Saturday till 8 p.m., and on Sunday from 10 a.m. to 7 p.m.

San Francisco

EMERGENCY ROOMS. The **Medical Center at the University of California,** 500 Parnasus Ave., at Third Avenue (tel. 415/476-1000, or 415/476-1037 for the emergency room).

San Francisco General Hospital, 1001 Potrero Ave. (tel. 415/821-8200, or 415/821-8111 for the emergency room).

St. Francis Memorial Hospital, 900 Hyde St. (tel. 415/775-4321).

Mount Zion Hospital and Medical Center, 1600 Divisadero St. (tel. 415/885-7410, or 415/885-7520 for the emergency room).

Pacific Presbyterian Medical Center, 2300 Sacramento, at Buchanan (tel. 415/923-3333).

PHARMACIES. **Walgreen's Drugstore,** 500 Geary St., Union Square (tel. 415/673-8411 or 415/673-8413); open 24 hours daily.

Walgreen's Drugstore, 3201 Divisidero St., near Lombard, in the Marina and Fisherman's Wharf areas (tel. 415/931-6415); open 24 hours daily.

San Luis Obispo County

Sierra Vista Hospital, 1010 Murray Ave., San Luis Obispo (tel. 805/546-7600).

French Hospital, 1911 Johnson Ave., San Luis Obispo (tel. 805/543-5353).
General Hospital, 2180 Johnson Ave., San Luis Obispo (tel. 805/543-1500).

Santa Barbara
St. Francis Hospital, 601 E. Micheltorena St. (tel. 805/568-5711 or 805/962-7661).

INDEX

NOW!
ARTHUR FROMMER LAUNCHES HIS SECOND TRAVEL REVOLUTION with

The New World of Travel

The hottest news and latest trends in travel today—heretofore the closely guarded secrets of the travel trade—are revealed in this new sourcebook by the dean of American travel. Here, collected in one book that is updated every year, are the most exciting, challenging, and money-saving ideas in travel today.

You'll find out about hundreds of alternative new modes of travel—and the many organizations that sponsor them—that will lead you to vacations that cater to your mind, your spirit, and your sense of thrift.

Learn how to fly for free as an air courier; travel for free as a tour escort; live for free on a hospitality exchange; add earnings as a part-time travel agent; pay less for air tickets, cruises, and hotels; enhance your life through cooperative camping, political tours, and adventure trips; change your life at utopian communities, low-cost spas, and yoga retreats; pursue low-cost studies and language training; travel comfortably while single or over 60; sail on passenger freighters; and vacation in the cheapest places on earth.

And in every yearly edition, Arthur Frommer spotlights the 10 GREATEST TRAVEL VALUES for the coming year. 400 pages, large-format with many, many illustrations. All for $14.95!

ORDER NOW
TURN TO THE LAST PAGE OF THIS BOOK FOR ORDER FORM.

FROMMER BOOKS
PRENTICE HALL TRAVEL
ONE GULF + WESTERN PLAZA
NEW YORK, NY 10023

Date_____

Friends:
Please send me the books checked below:

FROMMER™ GUIDES

(Guides to sightseeing and tourist accommodations and facilities from budget to deluxe, with emphasis on the medium-priced.)

☐ Alaska	$13.95	☐ Japan & Hong Kong	$13.95
☐ Australia	$14.95	☐ Mid-Atlantic States	$13.95
☐ Austria & Hungary	$14.95	☐ New England	$14.95
☐ Belgium, Holland & Luxembourg	$13.95	☐ New York State	$13.95
☐ Bermuda & The Bahamas	$14.95	☐ Northwest	$14.95
☐ Brazil	$14.95	☐ Portugal, Madeira & the Azores	$13.95
☐ Canada	$14.95	☐ Skiing Europe	$14.95
☐ Caribbean	$14.95	☐ Skiing USA—East	$13.95
☐ Cruises (incl. Alask, Carib, Mex, Hawaii, Panama, Canada & US)	$14.95	☐ Skiing USA—West	$13.95
		☐ South Pacific	$13.95
☐ California & Las Vegas	$14.95	☐ Southeast & New Orleans	$14.95
☐ England & Scotland	$14.95	☐ Southeast Asia	$14.95
☐ Egypt	$13.95	☐ Southwest	$14.95
☐ Florida	$14.95	☐ Switzerland & Liechtenstein	$13.95
☐ France	$14.95	☐ Texas	$13.95
☐ Germany	$14.95	☐ USA	$15.95
☐ Italy	$14.95		

FROMMER $-A-DAY® GUIDES

(In-depth guides to sightseeing and low-cost tourist accommodations and facilities.)

☐ Europe on $40 a Day	$15.95	☐ New Zealand on $40 a Day	$12.95
☐ Australia on $30 a Day	$12.95	☐ New York on $50 a Day	$13.95
☐ Eastern Europe on $25 a Day	$13.95	☐ Scandinavia on $60 a Day	$13.95
☐ England on $50 a Day	$13.95	☐ Scotland & Wales on $40 a Day	$12.95
☐ Greece on $30 a Day	$12.95	☐ South America on $35 a Day	$13.95
☐ Hawaii on $60 a Day	$13.95	☐ Spain & Morocco on $40 a Day	$13.95
☐ India on $25 a Day	$12.95	☐ Turkey on $30 a Day	$12.95
☐ Ireland on $35 a Day	$13.95	☐ Washington, D.C., & Historic Va. on	
☐ Israel on $35 a Day	$13.95	$40 a Day	$13.95
☐ Mexico on $25 a Day	$13.95		

FROMMER TOURING GUIDES

(Color illustrated guides that include walking tours, cultural & historic sites, and other vital travel information.)

☐ Australia	$9.95	☐ Paris	$8.95
☐ Egypt	$8.95	☐ Scotland	$9.95
☐ Florence	$8.95	☐ Thailand	$9.95
☐ London	$8.95	☐ Venice	$8.95

TURN PAGE FOR ADDITONAL BOOKS AND ORDER FORM.